SPIRITUAI
AND THE
SECULAR QUEST

World Spirituality

Already published

Christian Spirituality: Origins to the Twelfth Century
Christian Spirituality: High Middle Ages and Reformation
Christian Spirituality: Post-Reformation and Modern
Jewish Spirituality: From the Bible to the Middle Ages
Jewish Spirituality: From the Sixteenth-Century Revival to the Present
Classical Mediterranean Spirituality: Egyptian, Greek, Roman
Hindu Spirituality: Vedas through Vedanta
Islamic Spirituality: Foundations
Islamic Spirituality: Manifestations
Modern Esoteric Spirituality
South and Meso-American Native Spirituality
Buddhist Spirituality: Indian, Southeast Asian, Tibetan, Early Chinese
Spirituality and the Secular Quest

In preparation

Hindu Spirituality: Postclassical Hinduism

Board of Editors and Advisors

EWERT COUSINS, *General Editor*

A. H. ARMSTRONG
Dalhousie University

R. BALASUBRAMANIAN
University of Madras

BETTINA BÄUMER
Alice Boner Foundation, Varanasi

THOMAS BERRY
Fordham University

JOSEPH EPES BROWN
University of Montana

JOHN CARMAN
Harvard University

JOSEPH DAN
Hebrew University

LOUIS DUPRÉ
Yale University

MIRCEA ELIADE
University of Chicago

ANTOINE FAIVRE
Sorbonne

LANGDON GILKEY
University of Chicago

GARY GOSSEN
State University of New York, Albany

ARTHUR GREEN
Reconstructionist Rabbinical College

JAMES HEISIG
Nanzan Institute for Religion and Culture, Nagoya

THORKILD JACOBSEN
Harvard University

STEVEN T. KATZ
Cornell University

JEAN LECLERCQ
Gregorian University

MIGUEL LEÓN-PORTILLA
National University of Mexico

CHARLES LONG
Syracuse University

BERNARD MCGINN
University of Chicago

FARHANG MEHR
Boston University

JOHN MEYENDORFF
Fordham University

BITHIKA MUKERJI
Banaras Hindu University

SEYYED HOSSEIN NASR
George Washington University

JACOB NEEDLEMAN
San Francisco State University

HEIKO OBERMAN
University of Arizona

ALBERT OUTLER
Southern Methodist University

RAIMUNDO PANIKKAR
University of California, Santa Barbara

JAROSLAV PELIKAN
Yale University

JILL RAITT
University of Missouri

DON SALIERS
Emory University

ANNEMARIE SCHIMMEL
Harvard University

KARAN SINGH
New Delhi

VIBHUTI NARAIN SINGH
Varanasi

KRISHNA SIVARAMAN
McMaster University

HUSTON SMITH
Syracuse University

DOUGLAS STEERE
Haverford College

TAKEUCHI YOSHINORI
University of Kyoto

WEI-MING TU
Harvard University

JAN VAN BRAGT
Nanzan Institute for Religion and Culture, Nagoya

FRANK WHALING
University of Edinburgh

SPIRITUALITY AND THE SECULAR QUEST

Edited by
Peter H. Van Ness

SCM PRESS LTD

All rights reserved. No part of this publication
may be reproduced, stored in a retrieval system,
or transmitted, in any form or by any means,
electronic, mechanical, photocopying, recording,
or otherwise, without the prior written permission of the
publisher, SCM Press Ltd.

Copyright © 1996 by The Crossroad Publishing Company, New York

ISBN 0 334 02655 5

First British paperback edition published 1996
by SCM Press Ltd
9–17 St Albans Place London N1 0NX

First Impression 1996

Printed in the United States of America

Contents

Preface to the Series

THE PRESENT VOLUME is part of a series entitled World Spirituality: An Encyclopedic History of the Religious Quest, which seeks to present the spiritual wisdom of the human race in its historical unfolding. Although each of the volumes can be read on its own terms, taken together they provide a comprehensive picture of the spiritual strivings of the human community as a whole — from prehistoric times, through the great religions, to the meeting of traditions at the present.

Drawing upon the highest level of scholarship around the world, the series gathers together and presents in a single collection the richness of the spiritual heritage of the human race. It is designed to reflect the autonomy of each tradition in its historical development, but at the same time to present the entire story of the human spiritual quest. The first five volumes deal with the spiritualities of archaic peoples in Asia, Europe, Africa, Oceania, and North and South America. Most of these have ceased to exist as living traditions, although some perdure among tribal peoples throughout the world. However, the archaic level of spirituality survives within the later traditions as a foundational stratum, preserved in ritual and myth. Individual volumes or combinations of volumes are devoted to the major traditions: Hindu, Buddhist, Taoist, Confucian, Jewish, Christian, and Islamic. Included within the series are the Jain, Sikh, and Zoroastrian traditions. In order to complete the story, the series includes traditions that have not survived but have exercised important influence on living traditions — such as Egyptian, Sumerian, classical Greek and Roman. A volume is devoted to modern esoteric movements and another to modern secular movements.

Having presented the history of the various traditions, the series devotes two volumes to the meeting of spiritualities. The first surveys the

A longer version of this preface may be found in *Christian Spirituality: Origins to the Twelfth Century*, the first published volume in the series.

meeting of spiritualities from the past to the present, exploring common themes that can provide the basis for a positive encounter, for example, symbols, rituals, techniques. Finally, the series closes with a dictionary of world spirituality.

Each volume is edited by a specialist or a team of specialists who have gathered a number of contributors to write articles in their fields of specialization. As in this volume, the articles are not brief entries but substantial studies of an area of spirituality within a given tradition. An effort has been made to choose editors and contributors who have a cultural and religious grounding within the tradition studied and at the same time possess the scholarly objectivity to present the material to a larger forum of readers. For several years some five hundred scholars around the world have been working on the project.

In the planning of the project, no attempt was made to arrive at a common definition of spirituality that would be accepted by all in precisely the same way. The term "spirituality," or an equivalent, is not found in a number of the traditions. Yet from the outset, there was a consensus among the editors about what was in general intended by the term. It was left to each tradition to clarify its own understanding of this meaning and to the editors to express this in the introduction to their volumes. As a working hypothesis, the following description was used to launch the project:

> The series focuses on that inner dimension of the person called by certain traditions "the spirit." This spiritual core is the deepest center of the person. It is here that the person is open to the transcendent dimension; it is here that the person experiences ultimate reality. The series explores the discovery of this core, the dynamics of its development, and its journey to the ultimate goal. It deals with prayer, spiritual direction, the various maps of the spiritual journey, and the methods of advancement in the spiritual ascent.

By presenting the ancient spiritual wisdom in an academic perspective, the series can fulfill a number of needs. It can provide readers with a spiritual inventory of the richness of their own traditions, informing them at the same time of the richness of other traditions. It can give structure and order, meaning and direction to the vast amount of information with which we are often overwhelmed in the computer age. By drawing the material into the focus of world spirituality, it can provide a perspective for understanding one's place in the larger process. For it may well be that the meeting of spiritual paths — the assimilation not only of one's own spiritual heritage but of that of the human community as a whole — is the distinctive spiritual journey of our time.

EWERT COUSINS

Acknowledgments

I WISH TO EXPRESS my thanks to family, friends, and colleagues who have encouraged and assisted me in the preparation of this book, especially Will Phillips, Dana Sue McDermott, Christian Miner, and Frank Oveis. I am grateful to Union Theological Seminary for its support, acknowledging especially Holland Hendrix, James Hayes, and Julie Sawicki. Finally, I thank Ewert Cousins, Michael Leach, and everyone at the Crossroad Publishing Company who helped bring this project to life and to completion.

The insight, cooperation, and patience of the contributors to this volume have been much appreciated.

Introduction: Spirituality and the Secular Quest

THE EDITORS of the World Spirituality series have assumed that because increasing numbers of people profess nonreligious worldviews and values, an encyclopedic history of world spirituality would be incomplete if it did not seriously investigate the relationship between the secular and spiritual aspects of human life. Stated more specifically, we assume the meaningfulness of ascribing a spiritual dimension to some secular beliefs and behaviors. Two considerations have motivated this judgment. The first is simply the empirical observation that there are persons who describe themselves, their beliefs, and their behaviors as spiritual even though they acknowledge no bond of doctrine or community with any historical religion. In research conducted for a cover article on "America's quest for spiritual meaning," *Newsweek* pollsters found that only 60 percent of Americans "think a person needs to believe in God in order to experience the sacred." A large number of Americans apparently believe that the sacred can be experienced without allegiance to a central tenet of biblical religion; in fact, 26 percent of the persons polled said that they obtained a "sense of the sacred during sex."[1]

The second consideration is philosophical. Even though language about spiritual and sacred matters can be very vague — as responses to the *Newsweek* poll illustrate — one terminological distinction is crucial to maintain: being religious is not a necessary condition for being spiritual. This follows from the definition of spirituality provided in the preface to each individual volume in the series. A secular spirituality is neither validated nor invalidated by religious varieties of spirituality. Its status is related to them but separable. This separation is more easily made if what is spiritual is conceived in phenomenological rather than metaphysical or institutional terms. Thus belief in the existence of the biblical God or in the reality of Plato's intelligible realm is not what qualifies a person as spiritual, nor is membership in a religious community the key criterion. Rather being spiritual is an attribute of the way one experiences the world and lives one's life. It is much like what John Dewey called "the religious attitude" and signifies what one attends to and acts upon in daily experience. It is analogous to moral seriousness as a trait of people who act in conscious relation to the sentiments of the community to which they belong, and aesthetic sensitivity as a trait of persons who knowingly relate perceptions of nature and craft to larger frameworks of sensuous experience.[2]

This volume is designed to provide descriptions of a phenomenon one might call *secular spirituality*. Accordingly, part 2 features persons who present themselves as both secular and spiritual and contains accounts of their views relevant to the themes or practices that they believe most fully manifest their spirituality. These featured individuals and groups are not generally academics. They include scientists, environmentalists, artists, and athletes. They are associated with activities like psychotherapy and feminism that have been embraced by both religious and secular persons. Two of the most popular books of recent years have been written by spiritually minded psychotherapists, M. Scott Peck (*The Road Less Travelled*) and Thomas Moore (*Care of the Soul*). Although each writes from some variety of Christian context, the popularity of their books is indebted to their adoption of perspectives that are not explicitly confessional. In *Care of the Soul*, Moore writes: "What I am proposing is not specifically Christian, nor is it tied to any particular religious tradition." He is quick to add, however, that it does imply a recognition of an "absolute need for a spiritual life."[3] Proposals such as Moore's are also included in what is here being described as secular spirituality.

As preparation for such descriptions, contributors to part 1 summarize historical periods and intellectual movements that have served as antecedents for the contemporary voices professing to have found spiritual meaning in secular activities. The origins of secular spirituality, like the origins of secularity itself, are assumed to be located primarily in the theoretical and practical rationalism of ancient Greece and Rome (chapter 1). However, given the current diversity of secular spiritual paths and the eclectic sensibilities of many of their practitioners, attention will also be given to sources of secular spirituality outside European culture. Considered, for example, are influences from the ancient Asian civilizations of India and China and from geographically Western but culturally non-European peoples, like Native American Indians (chapter 2).

In its more popular forms secular spirituality emerged after the passing of a medieval European culture shaped by the Christian church. Hence the Renaissance and especially the Enlightenment constituted crucial early stages in the cultural developments that made it meaningful to posit a spiritual dimension to secular activities (chapter 3). The nineteenth century brought sufficient maturation of democratic institutions in Europe and North America to allow for the promulgation of a wide variety of secular projects by universities and museums, by political parties and labor unions, and by diverse entrepreneurial organizations. Some were closely associated with spiritual sensibilities. This is the case for the emergent tradition of American naturalism (chapter 4). New academic disciplines devoted to the historical study of religion — the progenitors of projects like the present one — also had spiritual meaning for some persons, as did new institutions signaling the changing cultural role of art, for example, Richard Wagner's Bayreuth Festspielhaus. The emergence of academic historical consciousness and the flowering of romantic artistic sensibilities are given special attention in the present volume (chapters 5 and 6).

The ways in which postmodern thinkers have challenged conventional accounts of religion and secularization — of modernity as the overcoming of traditional religions by secular forces — occupy the final section of the volume's historical half. Two forms of the challenge are emphasized. First reviewed is the trend of thought characterized by the intensification of historical criticism of religion to the point that only aesthetic meaning survives the onslaught. Such criticism, at once intense but playful, has been extended beyond religion to all texts and truths, even to those of rigorous science and public discourse. This trend is most directly indebted to the nineteenth-century German philosopher Friedrich Nietzsche and is today commonly associated with the French philosopher Jacques Derrida, who has given it the name 'deconstruction' (chapter 7). Also reviewed in this context will be the postmodern phenomenon of New Age spirituality, in which an extreme eclecticism deracinates spiritual practices and beliefs from their original cultural contexts — be they religious or scientific — and in doing so effectively creates new, secular varieties of spirituality (chapter 8). The New Age is now, and it is a time in which a mix-and-match consumer mentality is brought to the appropriation of diverse spiritual traditions. Its ethos extends to more phenomena than expressly bear this title, a fact to which the heterogeneous spiritual preoccupations of this volume bear ample witness.

Part 2 of this volume is organized under the rubrics "Self," "Society," "Nature," and "Culture." Little more than heuristic significance should be attached to these rubrics and their subgroups. The persons and movements discussed in this part of the volume characteristically resist rigid dichotomies and inflexible principles. Many of them have experienced opprobrium in the way more traditional institutions have categorized them. For instance, most holistic health practitioners have been relegated to a status outside the medical community as that community has been defined by the American Medical Association. Being gay and being spiritual have been held to be mutually incompatible by conservative religious authorities.

The rubrics of the volume's second part are general, but this does not mean that all contributors offer broad surveys of their topics. General perspective and particular detail combine uniquely in the various chapters. The rubrics used are significant in the minimal sense that they depart from some traditional ways of thinking about human spiritual life. The category of "Self" suggests that self-denial is not a major emphasis of many practitioners of secular spirituality. The inclusion of "Nature" and "Society" among the section headings indicates that a *contemptus mundi* will not be a hallmark of persons discussed there. Finally, that a chapter (chapter 15) is entitled "Scientific Inquiry" implies that exclusive polarities of faith and reason, and religion and science, are not constitutive of the approach to spiritual life being addressed.

A tolerance for ambiguity is certainly characteristic of many of the persons who pursue nonreligious paths to spiritual well-being. This embrace of ambiguity, as well as other traits, engenders an ambivalence in some contributors concerning the phenomena they examine and fosters an assortment of divergent views and beliefs. Because of this, readers should not conclude that everything treated in this volume has the recommendation of the editor or all of the contributors. The volumes in the World Spirituality series seek to be encyclopedic in their scope, and so individual volumes are likely to include items that some people will find to be of questionable value.

The divergence of views and perspectives does not, however, compromise the coherence of the two parts of the volume. This coherence can be underscored by giving further specification to the crucial notions of spirituality and secularity and by showing that a secular spirituality is at least conceptually distinguishable from both a religious spirituality and a version of secular life that is not spiritual. In what follows hypotheses about the nature of secular spirituality will not be categorically asserted, nor will they be summarily substantiated; they will simply be given sufficient conceptual precision to serve as a provisional framework for the diverse perspectives included in the volume.

Briefly stated, the spiritual aspect of human existence is hypothesized to have an outer and an inner complexion. Facing outward, human existence is spiritual insofar as one engages reality as a maximally inclusive whole and makes the cosmos an intentional object of thought and feeling. Facing inward, life has a spiritual dimension to the extent that it is apprehended as a project of people's most enduring and vital selves and is structured by experiences of sudden self-transformation and subsequent gradual development. These two formulations should not be rigidly separated. Their integration can be highlighted by expressing them in a more dramatic idiom: "Toti se inserens mundo" (Plunging oneself into the totality of the world).[4] In other words, the spiritual dimension of life is the embodied task of realizing one's truest self in the context of reality apprehended as a cosmic totality. It is the quest for attaining an optimal relationship between what one truly is and everything that is; it is a quest that can be furthered by adopting appropriate spiritual practices and by participating in relevant communal rituals.

The spiritual dimension of human life can be more fully characterized by supplementing the above definition with resources from disciplines collateral to the philosophy of religion (which is my own discipline). Philosophical ethics and phenomenological psychology are two I shall mention. The Scottish-American philosopher Alasdair MacIntyre has provided a theory of virtue that includes a notion of practice quite relevant to discussions of spiritual life. With precision, but little elegance, MacIntyre defines a practice as being "any coherent and complex form of socially established cooperative human activity through which goods internal to that form of activity are realized in the course of trying to achieve those standards of excellence which are appropriate to, and partially definitive of, that form of activity, with the result that human powers to achieve excellence, and human conceptions of the ends and goods involved, are systematically extended."[5] Among the practices cited by MacIntyre are scientific inquiry, musical artistry, and expertise at games like chess. All of these are likewise mentioned in this volume as examples of activities that may be accorded a spiritual significance; that is, they may bear the special meaning of relating their practitioners to the world as a cosmic whole and thereby transforming them in the direction of enhanced vitality. What is deemphasized in this context is the relation of these activities to others that lay claim to human obligation. They are not viewed within the purview of a systematic moral theory.

Clearly MacIntyre is indebted to Aristotle's conception of practical wisdom as good action having itself as its own end (*Nicomachean Ethics* 1140b). When appropriated for the description of spiritual practices, MacIntyre's definition has the felicitous implication that such practices are not deemed good because they earn some otherworldly reward. In this respect the spiritual and the salvific are clearly distinguishable: this distinction is a crucial presupposition for any conception of secular spirituality. Secular spiritual practices are not necessarily competitors with traditional religions that promise salvation. For instance, meditation may be part of a Christian regimen of prayer, and as such it may be theologically construed to be a penitential act occurring within a sacramental system whose ultimate end is the communication of divine grace and eternal life. Meditation as a disciplined practice expressive of a secular spirituality does not share this ultimate end, and so its practitioners will regard the distinctive good of its practice as something more intrinsic, having itself a unique capacity for enhanced vitality and human excellence. Such meditation is spiritually valuable but not salvific. Finally, if a regimen of meditation is undertaken purely for utilitarian reasons, for example, to increase one's job performance or lower one's blood pressure, then, by the definition offered above, it loses its claim to being spiritual or salvific.

Psychological accounts of optimal experience are similarly relevant to the spiritual aspects of human life surveyed in this volume. The psychologist Mihaly Csikszentmihalyi has provided such an account. He identifies optimal experience with a human phenomenon he calls "flow," and, in a book of this same name, he describes eight elements common to profound experiences of human enjoyment. The flow experience, says Csikszentmihalyi, is chiefly constituted by (1) a challenging activity for which skills are needed and for which there are (2) clear goals and ample feedback that make success measurable. To do the activity well (3) great concentration is needed, so much so that (4) a loss of self-consciousness is effected, and (5) one's sense of time is transformed. Also, (6) actions and awareness of those actions become merged, and a paradoxical sense is engendered that (7) control is exercised over one's actions without conscious effort. Finally, Csikszentmihalyi concludes one of his own summary description of flow by noting (8): "An activity that produces such experiences is so gratifying that people are willing to do it for its own sake, with little concern for what they will get out of it, even when it is difficult, or dangerous."[6] This last element is the autotelic quality that Aristotle and MacIntyre highlighted in their respective theories of virtue.[7]

Csikszentmihalyi acknowledges that many activities productive of flow experiences had their origins in religious behaviors and that the values achieved in flow experiences have frequently been accorded a moral significance. He is careful, though, not to make flow experiences accountable to religious or moral criteria. He even allows a soldier's fury in hand-to-hand combat to count as a flow experience! On the basis of his empirical research he does, however, make this pregnant remark: "As contemporary flow activities are secularized, they are unlikely to link the actor to powerful meaning systems."[8] The systems alluded to here are religious traditions, moral systems, and political ideologies. This remark, I believe, is helpful for identifying secular spirituality because it is precisely the intent of persons describing secular behaviors as spiritual that they relate those activities to some larger system of meaning. Secular spirituality reflects an attempt to locate optimal human experience within a nonreligious context of existential and cosmic meaning.

A definition of the spiritual life that includes reference to an enduring self and cosmic totality will be received cautiously by many philosophers. This is so because such notions figure prominently among the ideas that Immanuel Kant treated under the rubric of "transcendental illusion."[9] Kant believed that when these notions are reified in Platonic fashion as the individual soul and transcendent God, they transgress the limits of possible experience and are therefore rationally insupportable. He also said that they are the product of "a natural and unavoidable dialectic of pure reason," such that when conditionally entertained, they are capable of legitimately serving as regulatory ideals.[10] For instance, they can enliven the study of nature and provide transition and support for the comprehension of moral ideas. It is primarily as imaginative ideals of this sort that truest selves and cosmic wholes are enlisted for the identification of the spiritual life. It is especially apt in a project concerned with secular manifestations of spiritual life that spirituality be understood with consideration of Kant's qualification of Platonic idealism.

For the purposes of this volume all religious life may be presumed spiritual; defining the spiritual aspect of life is not offered as a means for determining which religions are most genuinely spiritual. Thus the biblical God who is not directly identifiable with the world, but who is its transcendent creator, may be said in this latter capacity to be that which a Muslim or a Jew encounters as a maximally inclusive reality. Likewise, a Buddhist's belief that there is no self that undergoes suffering may be construed as a truer way of understanding human agency than the commonsense view it challenges. Yet not everything spiritual must be religious; there are ways of understanding the world as a cosmic whole and the self as an enduring agent that are not directly indebted to religion.

This last point pertains to the meaning of secularity. The title of this volume presupposes no particular theory of secularization, nor does it anticipate an uncritical celebration of the "secular quest." Human existence is secular to the extent that it is undertaken according to conceptions of the world and self that are not directly indebted to religion and that, moreover, promote the organization of society in ways that permit its participants to pursue both religious and irreligious paths to fulfillment. A historical judgment is made that scientific beliefs, behaviors, and institutions — mostly originating in Europe but now no longer confined there — have been most successful in challenging religion's traditional role of providing cosmologies and anthropologies. The intellectual achievements and liberal temperaments of figures like Charles Darwin and Albert Einstein exemplify this scientific variety of secularity. Karl Marx certainly deserves mention along with Darwin and Einstein, though his case is more problematic given the questionable scientific status of his theoretical pronouncements and the moral severity of his revolutionary prescriptions. Marx's influence, in any case, was multiform: for instance, it gave a dimension of historical universality and prophetic urgency to the African-American radicalism of W. E. B. Du Bois and to the feminism of Simone de Beauvoir. These latter two figures inaugurated trends in secular thought that many have found rife with spiritual meaning.

While a significant role for science in the constitution of secularity is assumed, no absolute philosophical judgment is made that viable challenges to religion must be scientific. A second tradition of Western secular thought rejects the explanatory projects of scientific and religious personalities alike. The account of the spiritual aspect of human existence given above relies heavily on the relation of wholes and parts and the distinction between truth and illusion. Postmodern advocates of a deconstructionist aestheticism reject the rationalization of the whole/part relation accomplished by mathematicians and logicians; for the sake of the inexhaustible possibilities of artistic creativity they resist all speech about metaphysical totalities. Similarly many persons with this point of view renounce the rationalization of the truth/illusion distinction effected by the experimental methodology of empirical scientists. In fidelity to an unending project of textual interpretation they resist all claims to established truth. Philosophers like Friedrich Nietzsche and Jacques Derrida, previously mentioned, and social theorists like Michel Foucault and Mary Daly are proximate sources for these views among Western intellectuals.[11] They have vehemently criticized all forms of Platonism, but especially its religious forms, and have, at least in some cases, indirectly charted a spiritual path by means of their equally vehement decrial of scientific positivism. It should be noted also that spirituality born of radical skepticism is not an exclusively Western phenomenon. There are arguably more ancient and pervasive antecedents for this type of secularity in the naturalistic and nondoctrinal views of certain Asian sages.

The relation between the theoretical and practical characteristics of secular spirituality is well illustrated by the case of ecological activism. Groups like the Sierra Club and the National Audubon Society work for a more healthy environment through programs of public education and political lobbying. More radical groups like Greenpeace also employ acts of civil disobedience. These practical strategies were inherited from a former generation of political activists who demanded civil rights for African-Americans and American disengagement from the war in Vietnam. Unlike these forebears, ecological activists are united and motivated by not only prescriptive beliefs but also purportedly empirical accounts of the natural world.

One influential articulation of such an ecological vision is J. E. Lovelock's provocative "Gaia hypothesis." (A writer in *Scientific American* says that it "has almost become the official ideology of 'Green' parties in Europe.")[12] The hypothesis claims that "the biosphere is a self-regulating entity with the capacity to keep our planet healthy by controlling the chemical and physical environment."[13] Lovelock's use of the name of an ancient Greek earth goddess involves more that a learned way of naming his theory. He actually posits the existence of a collective living entity in which human beings and all living things participate. He describes Gaia as "a complex entity involving the Earth's biosphere, atmosphere, oceans, and soil: the totality constituting a feedback or cybernetic system which seeks an optimal physical and chemical environment for life on this planet."[14] Under criticism by more traditional biologists, Lovelock has modified his initial claims; however, the precise scientific status of the theory is not crucial here. What is important is how clearly the hypothesis articulates the belief of many ecological activists that it is incumbent upon people to adopt a personal relationship of appreciation and responsibility to the whole natural world. This accent on wholeness is what makes ecological activism pregnant with spiritual meaning. Also, the claim that the natural world is actually Gaia — a living organism — is less important than the insistence that it should be treated as if it were a living being, capable of self-regulation, but still needful of care. In Kantian language, this "as if" characterization suggests that the Gaia hypothesis, though perhaps empirically unfounded, may still be valuable as a regulatory ideal.

Practitioners of holistic medicine advocate a conception of human selfhood complementary to an ecological vision of the natural world. They eschew a view of the body as a mechanical assemblage of parts best nurtured and healed by medical specialists with technical expertise in individual organs or diseases. The holistic alternative sees the human organism as a living system whose parts are interconnected and interdependent. This holistic account of health as a dynamic balance of forces — including mental and physical, and organismic and environmental forces — has ancient precedents in Western medical writings from the *Corpus Hippocraticum* and in Chinese medical texts like the *Nei Ching*. Western religions, unlike the religions of China, have generally adopted anthropologies emphasizing hierarchy and control more than balance and compensation. Hence many advocates of holistic health practices have identified themselves as dissenting from the dominant traditions of both Western biology and theology. Certainly this was true of Andrew Taylor Still, the founder of osteopathy and the inspirer of chiropractic medicine.[15] It is also true of most herbalist practitioners of natural healing. Historically in the West these persons have often been women, specifically women who have been excluded from professional medicine but who have been allocated primary responsibility for food preparation and service.

An organizing tenet of holistic interconnectedness is that a living organism has resources for healing itself, as when its immune system comes to the aid of an organ impaired by infection. It is also held that when complete healing is not possible, an organism can still work to remedy a lost balance, as when damage to one sense organ is partially compensated for by increased acuity in other senses. Holistic medicine especially stresses the power of a vital mind to heal an ailing body. Excessive claims in this regard have drawn harsh criticism from traditional physicians. The genuinely spiritual aspect of holistic medicine is attributable less to its postulation of extraordinary mental powers than to its affirmation that health requires release from a falsely mechanical conception of self. Like Lovelock's Gaia hypothesis, holistic medicine's value as a regulatory ideal is partially independent of its particular empirical claims.

Environmental activism and holistic medicine are just two of the many varieties of secular spirituality that are explored in this volume's second part. The scheme of categorization does not aspire to rigid compartmentalization. Individuals and activities may exemplify more than one of the categories listed. This is the case especially for artists. Consider Walt Whitman's poetry. Whitman's verse eloquently gives voice to the experience of engaging reality as an encompassing whole, and it does so in a way beholden to no religious orthodoxy. Early in the original version of "Song of Myself" he writes:

> Urge and urge and urge,
> Always the procreant urge of the world.
>
> Out of the dimness opposite equals advance.... Always substance and increase,
> Always a knit of identity,... always distinction,... always a breed of life.
>
> To elaborate is no avail.... Learned and unlearned feel that it is so.

> Sure as the most certain sure... plumb in the uprights, well entretied, braced in the beams,
> Stout as a horse, affectionate, haughty, electrical,
> I and this mystery here we stand.[16]

Striking here is the contrast between the abstract generality of the first stanzas and the sensual particularity of the concluding self-description. Whitman's intent is to communicate his exuberant celebration of all of reality. This encounter does not leave him unchanged. Toward the conclusion of this same poem he writes these famous lines:

> Do I contradict myself?
> Very well then... I contradict myself.
> I am large... I contain multitudes.[17]

What others regard as contradictions, as flaws, Whitman proclaims to be fulfillment and freedom. A specific expression of this freedom was the candidly bisexual feelings evident in the first version of *Leaves of Grass.* The world's "procreant urge" is a force of love, and, for Whitman, this love is not constrained by heterosexual strictures. Hence his poetry is both an aesthetic creation and a social vision of a new way of people relating to one another in community—one very much spiritual in the sense defined above, but not strictly religious in the estimate of Whitman's Christian contemporaries.

A second artistic achievement rife with an alternative social vision is African-American blues music. The theologian James Cone has written:

> The blues are "secular spirituals." They are *secular* in the sense that they confine their attention solely to the immediate and affirm the bodily expression of black soul, including its sexual manifestations. They are *spirituals* because they are impelled by the same search for the truth of black experience.[18]

The blues effect a transformed valuation of worldly experience, including human sexuality; they share this power with Whitman's poetry. The blues, says Cone, also give expression to unique elements of black experience. They do so especially in their affirmation of black identity amid a culture that mostly obscures black people's presence; they do this also in their achievement of excellence despite an ambient society that presents African-Americans with many obstacles and few opportunities; and preeminently they do so in their sustenance of the capacity of black people to love even while being the object of much hate. The blues, continues Cone, manifest and effect a "historical transcendence" in which black people overcome worldly restrictions and realize "a being not made with hands."[19] In doing so they deliver protest, enliven hope, and point the way to an alternative way of human beings living together amid their diversity and commonality.

From these several examples it is evident that as a descriptive rubric "secular spirituality" encompasses important traditions like ecological idealism, holistic medicine, and visionary art. It applies to important figures like Hippocrates and Einstein, Nietzsche and Dewey, and Walt Whitman and Bessie Smith. As different as these figures were from one another, they were all willing to speak about a spiritual aspect of life while declining to cast such reflection in the language of any traditional religion. The above-cited instances may suggest that secular spirituality is a marginal and dissenting sensibility. This is not completely true. Institutions that provide courses and workshops in the spiritual options treated in this book have thrived for some time. Esalen Institute in Big Sur, California, has been offering programs on these topics (and others) since 1962, and the Naropa Institute in Boulder, Colorado (begun 1974), and the Omega Institute for Holistic Studies in Rhinebeck, New York (begun 1977), have long offered similar programs.

Even the business community has discovered the allure of secular spirituality. A recent *Business Week* article describes programs at major corporations that respond to the desire of employees to find more meaning in their work; the programs encourage them to engage issues of "values," "mission," "soul," and "spirit."[20] Publishers have spotted a new market: a professor of management edits a newsletter called *Spirit at Work.* Veteran self-help authors have discovered the new spiritual idiom. For instance, Deepak Chopra has authored *The Seven Spiritual Laws of Success,* and Wayne Dyer has written *Your Sacred Self.* Chopra sprinkles his book with quotations from Lao-tzu, Albert Einstein, and the Rig-Veda and offers as his first principle the belief that "when we realize that our true self is one of pure potentiality, we align with the power that manifests everything in the universe." This does sound spiritual, but readers are alerted to a different sensibility when they read that success "is the ability to fulfill your desires with effortless ease." Dyer likewise promises much, but he at least acknowledges the necessity of "denying the demands of your ego if those demands contradict the guidance of your higher self."[21] Tom Chappell's *The Soul of a Business* is a more personally sincere (and a more traditionally religious) attempt at finding spiritual meaning in contemporary work life.[22] These brief citations are sufficient to indicate that the penchant for finding spiritual meaning in secular activities and domains extends also to established institutions and conservative personalities.

The rubric "secular spirituality" also excludes significant options. It excludes expressly religious traditions of spirituality, and so it is different from most of the spiritual paths represented in previous volumes of the World Spirituality series. It also excludes cultural works that aspire to be merely diverting entertainment; much programming on U.S. television fits this description. Likewise omitted are secular views more positivist than Einstein's and more historicist than Nietzsche's. For instance, the physicist Steven Weinberg has said that the more he learns about the world as a cosmic whole, the less meaning it seems to have for the lives of individual human beings.[23] The contemporary philosopher Richard Rorty criticizes Nietzsche for harboring a residual Platonism, because, says Rorty, while rejecting all forms of idealism, Nietzsche nevertheless fled from the radical contingency of life in his search for some variety of personal wholeness.[24] By the definitions just given, Weinberg's and Rorty's views are fully secular but not at all spiritual.

These examples of scientists and philosophers are somewhat unrepresentative of the phenomena surveyed in this volume. As has been the case with preceding volumes, material from diverse sources is included: the book includes the views and practices of persons who are not academics, and it covers aspects of culture other than science and the fine arts. The chapter on spirituality and sports (chapter 19) deals with perhaps the most pervasive leisure activity of contemporary popular culture. The chapter on spirituality and the social justice struggle (chapter 14) deals with a social phenomenon not rooted in the middle classes. Providers of holistic health practices and radical forms of psychotherapy are often regarded as eccentric, if not dangerous, by the professional establishments to which they are related (chapters 9 and 10). Some topics covered are viewed askance even by many religious intellectuals. Much New Age spirituality is dismissed by orthodox theologians as obscurantist retrievals of ancient religious exoticisms (chapter 15). Such strictures are not binding for this volume: its aim is simply to examine the diverse forms of secular activity that have been widely accorded spiritual significance.

Given the inclusion of this volume in a series primarily devoted to the spiritualities of major religious traditions, it is to be expected that many readers of this book will be themselves religious in some sense and not purely secular. Thus an implicit theme of the volume concerns what followers of established religious spiritualities might learn from their relatively more innovative secular counterparts. Different religious traditions respond differently to influences emanating from secular quarters, some traditions being more receptive than others, all receiving such influence in ways peculiar to their intellectual styles and institutional processes. In the most general terms, such influence comes in two varieties. It occurs in one way when a religious tradition appropriates aspects of what is most celebrated and powerful in secular culture. The institutions and theories of natural scientific inquiry certainly have come to have this status, and when religious persons and communities learn from spiritually oriented conceptions of science, they do so on the premise that excellence in religion and science share some root similarity. Thomas Aquinas and subsequent Thomists have been quick to affirm that the various modalities of truth must have a common source, which, for them, is the God who has created the entire world. Hence they have been willing to appropriate elements of classical philosophy. Many contemporary theologians from diverse denominations have learned from the natural philosophy of Alfred North Whitehead in a comparable way.

Yet the secular world may influence religion in a quite different way. Protest and resistance to established institutions and customs can be expressions of secular commitments that warrant comparison with the radical nature of some religious visions. Socialist political movements, especially those of a revolutionary character, have certainly been anathematized by established financial interests, yet in some contexts they have also been forces for revitalizing traditional biblical visions of social justice and traditional Confucian values of cohesive community life. In this second variety of influence, religious persons learn from secular criticisms of social evils and shortcomings, and perhaps they learn most from secular criticisms of religion itself.

These two manners of influence — via secular achievement and secular protest — are not entirely incompatible. For instance, they have a certain dialectical compatibility in some Christians who confess it to be a mark of God's freedom and mercy that the divine presence is revealed in unexpectedly worldly ways. Dietrich Bonhoeffer, the German Lutheran theologian, and Dorothy Day, the Catholic Worker activist, lived according to this perception amid intense twentieth-century travails. Each was deeply critical of aspects of Christianity as an institutional religion, and each was receptive to the possibility of God being present in thoroughly secular persons and practices. In his last prison writings Bonhoeffer called for a Christianity radically open to secular achievements and worldly sufferings, paradoxically positing that a willingness to live without God can make one nearer to God. He did so in part because of his respect for the intellectual achievements of secular scientists and artists but also because he admired nonreligious colleagues who joined him in resisting Nazi tyranny.[25] Day understood her participation in labor movement struggles as a way to resist worker exploitation, restore the dignity of worldly labor, and, at the same time, recover the humbly compassionate lifestyle of the Gospels' portrayals of Jesus of Nazareth.[26]

The examples of Bonhoeffer and Day — and Mohandas Gandhi and others could be added to their company — are suggestive of an important way in which secular spirituality figures in the lives of contemporary men and women. Instead of occurring in a relatively pure form, as the only variety of spirituality that an individual is willing to affirm, it often occurs as a part or moment within a more traditional religious spirituality. In the West this is especially the case for ecumenical Christians and liberal Jews. Elements of feminist and ecological spirituality, for instance, are embraced by many Christians and Jews who know full well that those spiritualities are opposed to aspects of their own religious tradition and are justified by principles chiefly secular in origin. Such secular spiritual projects can serve as shared resources and common reference points for such persons, thereby facilitating mutual understanding and accommodation. Also, secular lifestyles and secular spiritualities are competitors of all historical religions so that through responding to their challenge adherents of traditional religions come to recognize their common concerns for tradition, community, ritual, and morality. Of course, this recognition can take narrowly reactive and defensive forms, but it need not. Indeed, the secular spiritual paths explored in this volume might serve today as means for revitalizing religiously spiritual traditions and also for helping them mediate or bridge some of the historically perceived fissures that separate different religious traditions.

The study of religion and spirituality has increasingly been informed by a commitment to respect the integrity of other cultures and religions. When this respect is interpreted in more than a purely passive way, encouraging conversation with others and even change in oneself, then this undertaking — which some practitioners see as a secular spiritual practice — may also serve as a bridge between different religious traditions. Although there are mandates in many religious traditions for respecting and learning from others, the most systematic and sustained contemporary efforts in this area — such as this very series in world spirituality — are projects of scholarly approaches to religion that are free from parochial religious sponsorship. The self-consciously pluralistic character of many secular forms of spirituality is one of its most notable features and is a feature that makes its inclusion in this encyclopedic series especially appropriate.

In its intrinsic diversity secular spirituality has a considerable potential for spiritual edification. This is true because it often directs attention to what is most accomplished in secular culture. In more critical expressions, it directs attention precisely to those spiritual beliefs and behaviors that are so established that they are seldom consciously examined or practically challenged. By prompting readers to distinguish between what is excellent in the way of spiritual life and what is merely customary, a volume on secular spirituality underscores a shared presupposition of the world's great spiritual traditions: this presupposition predicts that absent a spiritual dimension, human life will not attain excellence and fulfillment of the highest order.

Notes

1. "The Search for the Sacred: America's Quest for Spiritual Meaning," *Newsweek*, 28 November 1994, 56, 61.

2. Dewey distinguishes between the nominative *religion* and the adjectival *religious* while I have offered *spiritual* as a clearer alternative for the latter term; see John Dewey, *A Common Faith* (New Haven: Yale University Press, 1934), 17.

3. Thomas Moore, *Care of the Soul: A Guide for Cultivating Depth and Sacredness in Everyday Life* (New York: HarperCollins, 1992), xv.

4. The Latin quotation is from Seneca (*Letters to Lucilius* 66.6). For the ancient philosophical support for this conception of the spiritual life, see Pierre Hadot, *Philosophy as a Way of Life: Spiritual Exercises from Socrates to Foucault*, ed. Arnold Davidson, trans. Michael Chase (Oxford: Blackwell, 1995), esp. 81–82, 184, 273.

5. Alasdair MacIntyre, *After Virtue: A Study in Moral Theory*, 2d ed. (Notre Dame, Ind.: University of Notre Dame Press, 1984), 187.

6. Mihaly Csikszentmihalyi, *Flow: The Psychology of Optimal Experience* (New York: HarperCollins, 1991), 71.

7. For a direct acknowledgment of kinship with MacIntyre's *After Virtue*, see Csikszentmihalyi, *Flow*, 246 n. 20.

8. Ibid., 77.

9. Immanuel Kant, *Critique of Pure Reason*, trans. Norman Kemp Smith (New York: St. Martin's, 1965), 297ff.

10. Ibid., 300.

11. The *locus classicus* for this radical philosophical tradition is a posthumously published fragment whose English title is "On Truth and Lie in an Extra-Moral Sense"; see *The Portable Nietzsche*, ed. and trans. Walter Kauffman (New York: Penguin, 1982), 42–47.

12. Tim Beardsley, "Gaia: The Smile Remains, but the Lady Vanishes," *Scientific American* 261:6 (December 1989): 35–36.

13. J. E. Lovelock, *Gaia: A New Look at Life on Earth* (Oxford: Oxford University Press, 1987), xii; see also Thomas Berry, "The Gaia Theory: Its Religious Implications," *ARC* 22 (spring 1994): 7–19.

14. Lovelock, *Gaia*, 11.

15. *The Autobiography of Andrew T. Still with a History of the Discovery and Development of the Science of Osteopathy* (Salem, N.H.: Ayer, 1972).

16. Walt Whitman, *Leaves of Grass: The First (1855) Edition*, ed. Malcolm Cowley (New York: Viking, 1961), 26–27 (3).

17. Ibid., 85 (51).

18. James H. Cone, *The Spirituals and the Blues: An Interpretation* (New York: Seabury, 1972), 112.

19. Ibid., 127.

20. "Companies Hit the Road Less Traveled," *Business Week,* 5 June 1995, 82–86; the newsletter *Spirit at Work* is cited in this article.

21. Deepak Chopra, *The Seven Spiritual Laws of Success: A Practical Guide to the Fulfillment of Your Dreams* (San Rafael, Calif.: Amber-Allen; New World Library, 1994), 7, 2; and Wayne W. Dyer, *Your Sacred Self: Making the Decision to Be Free* (New York: HarperCollins, 1995), 315.

22. Tom Chappell, *The Soul of a Business: Managing for Profit and the Common Good* (New York: Bantam, 1993), esp. xiv.

23. Note the concluding reflections in Steven Weinberg, *The First Three Minutes: A Modern View of the Origin of the Universe* (New York: Bantam, 1979), 144.

24. Richard Rorty, *Contingency, Irony, and Solidarity* (Cambridge: Cambridge University Press, 1989), 43.

25. For Bonhoeffer's development of this theme, see Dietrich Bonhoeffer, *Letters and Papers from Prison,* ed. Eberhard Bethge, 3d ed. (New York: Macmillan, 1972), 357–63; for Bonhoeffer's views of his fellow conspirators, see Eberhard Bethge, *Dietrich Bonhoeffer: Man of Vision, Man of Courage,* trans. Eric Mosbacher et al. (New York: Harper and Row, 1977), 760–61.

26. Dorothy Day, *The Long Loneliness: An Autobiography* (New York: Harper and Row, 1981), 204–22.

Part One
PERIODS AND MOVEMENTS

A. Precursors of Secular Spirituality

1

Sources in Ancient Greece and Rome

DAVID E. AUNE

Defining "Secular Spirituality"

SPIRITUALITY MAY BE defined in terms of complementary outer and inner dimensions.[1] The outer or cosmic dimension consists of an awareness of reality as an inclusive whole, while the inner or existential dimension is constituted by the task of the gradual realization of one's enduring self within the setting of this conscious and intentional holistic apprehension of reality. Spirituality and religion have been closely associated throughout the history of Christianity, as they have in such other great religious traditions of the world as Buddhism, Hinduism, and Islam, but they are not indissolubly linked.

The Roman Stoic philosopher Seneca (ca. 4 B.C.E. to 65 C.E.) provides an illustration of how the self can be defined within the context of a holistic perspective on reality. In his lengthy treatise *On Anger*, he argues (following the typically Stoic radical critique of traditional morality) that a person who is truly human must completely eliminate anger (and all other passions) from his or her life. However, this elimination of anger implied the abandonment of a deeply ingrained feature of traditional Greco-Roman morality, that is, the fitting role of anger in taking revenge on one's enemies for wrongs suffered.[2] Seneca's advice is in striking contrast:

> Soon we shall breathe our last. Meanwhile, while we endure, while we are among human beings, let us cultivate humanity. Let us be a cause of fear, of danger, to no one. Let us despise harms, injustices, abuses, and taunts and bear with a large soul our brief inconveniences. While we look back, as they say, and turn around, death is upon us. (*On Anger* 3.43)

Here Seneca's argument turns on the mental contextualization of individual human experience within a universalistic ideal vision of all humanity as the necessary communal setting for ethical living. This perception of the unity of the human race with its ethical implications is in turn an essential aspect of the Stoic view of the cosmos.

From the ancient Greco-Roman perspective, what we refer to as "religion" is primarily restricted to participation in a public or private cult. Yet from a modern Western point of view, that hardly exhausts what is meant by being religious. It is undeniable that various forms of spirituality flourished in intellectual sectors of Greek and Roman culture apart from any vital connection with the public and private cults of the ancient world. While religion and spirituality in the ancient world cannot be identified or equated, neither can they be clinically separated. Most if not all of the ancient authors whose literary legacy permits tentative glimpses into some dimensions of their spirituality participated in one or more of the available variety of public and private cults. In many cases the distinctive features of their spirituality lie in the ways in which they reacted critically to the more conventional religiosity of their contemporaries. Indeed, many of the thinkers whose views will be discussed in this essay were reformers as well as critics of religious practices who did not reject the implicit claims of the cults with which they were familiar so much as propose constructive ways in which such cults should be modified, examples being Xenophanes (ca. 570–470 B.C.E.) and Heraclitus (end sixth, beginning fifth century B.C.E.). In this essay, I will suggest some of the contexts in which an awareness of supramundane or holistic realities could be considered paradigmatic for human life and thought, primarily in the area of personal and social ethics, but also touching other ideologically grounded forms of human behavior such as asceticism and mysticism.

The Foci of This Essay

While there are many ways of approaching the subject of the antecedents of modern secular spirituality in the Greco-Roman world, this essay will focus on just a few. After an initial discussion of the basic features of Greco-Roman religion and of Greek rational thought, I will pursue three particular avenues of inquiry that constitute significant antecedents to various forms of secular spirituality that later emerged in Western civilization. The first antecedent of modern secular spirituality to be considered is the widespread assumption in antiquity that the human being and the cosmos were closely related in a microcosm-macrocosm pattern. The second antecedent has to do with the various views of the human person that formed the basic presuppositions for evaluating the relationship of the human being to the cosmos and to the hierarchical understanding of reality. Finally, the third antecedent involves the view of the function of philosophy shared by all of the major Greek philosophical schools; this view saw philosophy as "the cure of souls" just as medicine is "the cure of bodies." This medical model, derived from the Greek medical writers, emphasized sense perception as the primary source for knowledge of the world, including the plight and solution of the human condition.

Greek Religion and Greek Rational Thought

Greek Religion

While there are certain natural links between spirituality and religion, there are also some critical differences, many of which are perhaps more apparent in an ancient than a modern context. Ancient Greek and Latin had no general terms that correspond to our word *religion,* a fact that suggests that those behaviors and attitudes that we categorize as "religious" were part of a complex sociocultural web of institutions and practices in which categorical and conceptual differentiation had a configuration markedly different from that typical of modern Western societies. The Greek term *eusebeia* (piety) means to behave in the right manner toward the gods, and this behavior primarily involved appropriate sacrificial protocol. The terms *religion* and *religious,* however, though inevitably intrusive, are nonetheless necessary categories for analyzing those institutions in ancient Mediterranean societies that attempted to manipulate supernatural forces for the benefit of human communities. The primary type of institution that sought to mediate between the sacred and profane spheres of existence in the Greco-Roman world was the *cult* — a formalized system of beliefs and rituals, usually centering on a traditional protocol of sacrifice and prayer, performed at specific intervals, utilizing sacred objects, located at sacred places, and supervised by a part-time priesthood.

Despite the great variety of such cults, in general there were two main categories of cults in the Greco-Roman world, public and private. Public cults were comprised of the traditional ensemble of religious rituals supervised by public officials in ancient city-states for the temporal benefit of the polis and its citizens. Through prescribed public prayers, sacrifices, divinatory procedures, feasts, and processions, a harmonious relationship was cultivated with those deities whose cults were officially recognized. Private or domestic cults, on the other hand, were restricted to, and exclusively managed by, a variety of kinship groups including the official subdivisions of the polis: the *phylē* (tribe), the *trittys* (one of three subdivisions of the tribe), and the *phratria* (one of three subdivisions of the *trittys*); the almost entirely aristocratic *genos* (clan); and the *oikos* (extended family, household).[3] Fictive kinship groups, such as *eranoi* or *thiasoi* (clubs or associations), organized for a variety of social, economic, and religious functions, also practiced private religious rituals. The primary concern of the private cults of real kinship groups was limited to the temporal welfare of the tribe, clan, or family. Fictive kinship groups, on the other hand, were *voluntary* organizations, some of which were interested in the spiritual as well as temporal welfare of members. Finally, to the realm of private cults belongs the practice of utilitarian magical rituals by individuals, often imitative of public rituals but on a scale appropriate for the privacy of the practitioner's own home (or the homes of clients). These magical rituals were focused on matters relating to their practitioners' personal welfare and interests, sometimes to the intentional detriment of the welfare and interests of others. It is now generally recognized that the once widespread notion that ancient Greek science and reason supplanted magic and myth, particularly in the wake of the fifth century Athenian "enlightenment," is massively contradicted by evidence from literary, inscriptional, and papyrological sources that apparently (chance finds cannot be considered statistically representative) suggest an increase in the irrational from the fourth century B.C.E. to the second century C.E.[4]

The typology of Greco-Roman cults outlined above differs from modern conceptions of religion primarily in three ways. First, ancient public cults were largely unconcerned with morality and therefore had no investment in developing systems of ethics. Second, ancient cults were largely unconcerned with theology and never developed coherent belief systems that were considered in any way mandatory for participation in the cult. The Greek conceptions of the gods were primarily disseminated through mythology, a carrier of cultural norms and values more comprehensive than that which moderns would associate with the term *religion.* Third, again with some exceptions, Greco-Roman public and private cults, focused as they were on the temporal welfare of various social groups, tended to ignore questions relating to individual immortality. However, it was precisely these three issues (ethics, theology, and the transcendent dimensions of human existence) that were of primary concern to many strands of the Greek philosophical tradition beginning with Pythagoras and continuing through to late antiquity.

Greek Rational Thought

The development of secular spirituality in the West has links to the development of rational thought that began with the Greek natural philosophers from Ionia on the western coast of Anatolia during the sixth century B.C.E.[5] Pre-Socratic thinkers from Anaximander to Democritus were materialists (a problematic term because there was no antithetical conception of the "immaterial") who used the term *physis* to designate the object of their inquiry and were later called *physiologoi* (natural philosophers; see Aristotle *Metaphysics* 986b14, 990a3; *De anima* 426a20). The supposition that these thinkers shared was that *physis* was the reality that underlay appearances and hence was that which is ultimately real. Cosmos and *physis* were closely related, though *physis* was assumed to be more basic than cosmos, and *physis* was also assumed to act in a consistent and predictable manner everywhere in the cosmos. The notion of *physis* presupposed the principle of natural causation, the basis of the scientific method. The *physiologoi* so expanded the concept of nature that it included all that exists, and they applied the term *to pan* (the all) or *ta panta* (all things) to the cosmos, implying that everything that exists is found within it. In this view of the world even the gods were not outside "the all" but within it and part of it. Deity was rationalized by including it within the sphere of *physis.* The assumption that the cosmos produced the gods rather than the gods the cosmos (a notion exactly opposite that of Judeo-Christian tradition) was not an innovation of these *physiologoi* but was a presupposition reflected in those Greek myths that touched on the issue of the origins of the gods and the world, synthesized through the compilation of mythological cosmogonies beginning with Hesiod. The term *theos* (god), or *theion* (divine), was reportedly used by some of the Milesian philosophers to refer to a hypothetical first principle of the cosmos, that is, air for Anaximenes, the "infinite" for Anaximander, and eternal cosmic fire for Heraclitus. However, when the term *theos* is applied to the basic physical element of fire or air, the concept of *theos* has in effect been adapted to a materialistic theory in such a way that there can be no conflict between god and matter, or the supernatural and the natural, because matter in its purest form *is* god. This speculative use of the term *theos* was a distinctive development within Greek philosophical thought, for this god had no cult and was therefore irrelevant for Greek religious practice. While this conception of *theos* had little in common with the popular Greek conception of *theoi* from Homer on, there were persistent attempts to integrate these two very different notions of deity by labeling the one god "Zeus" (thereby allowing this "highest god" to receive divine honors in an existing cult). According to Heraclitus, "The One which is alone wise, is unwilling yet willing to be called 'Zeus' " (Diels-Kranz, frag. B32).[6] This expanded conception of Zeus is expressed in a putative Orphic fragment, though variations of the saying recur in other formulations and literary contexts as well: "Zeus is the beginning, Zeus is the middle, all things are fulfilled by Zeus" (Plato *Laws* 4.715e–716c). The notion of *theos* was therefore abstracted and associated with the orderliness and design of nature, not with unpredictable violations of its order as in traditional Greek mythology. Tension between belief in the One who provided the cosmos with an ultimate and inclusive unity and belief in the traditional pantheon of Greek gods (obviously on a lower ontological level) characterized Greek theistic metaphysics through late antiquity.[7]

Two developments in pre-Socratic philosophy are particularly significant for Greek religion: (1) the pre-Socratics gave naturalistic interpretations of such phenomena as thunder, lightning, and earthquakes, which had previously been attributed to divine intervention; and (2) they critiqued religious practices on the basis of various external criteria, such as the criterion of "decency." Xenophanes, for example, criticized the conception of the gods in Homer and Hesiod, who portrayed them as thieves, adulterers, and liars, using the criterion of decency (Xenophanes, frags. B11–12). He also ridiculed anthropomorphism by claiming that oxen, horses, and lions would depict the gods in their own image and that the Ethiopians depicted their gods as blunt-nosed and black, while the Thracians saw them as having blue eyes and red hair (frags. B15–16). In place of a multiplicity of gods, Xenophanes posited a single deity and, rather than an anthropomorphic conception of deity, defined the one god negatively:

> There is one god, greatest among gods and humans,
> for neither in form or thought is he like mortals.
> (Diels-Kranz, frag. B23)

The vast majority of Greek philosophers were religious in the sense that they participated in both the public and private cults dictated by their social location.[8] Following popular belief, most philosophical traditions (with the exception of the Epicureans) believed in the divinity of the stars (Plato *Republic* 508a; Aristotle *Nicomachean Ethics* 1141a; *Metaphysics* 1026a; *Physics* 196a), though neither the pre-Socratics nor Socrates thought that heavenly bodies were divine (Plato *Apology* 26d). Very few Greek philosophers were atheists, atheists being rare but not unknown in antiquity.[9] Protagoras, however, is famous for his agnosticism: "Concerning the gods, I have no way of knowing whether they exist or do not exist nor what their form is like" (Diels-Kranz, frag. B4).

The Macrocosm-Microcosm Homology

Cosmological Speculation

Beginning with Hesiod, a series of Greek mythographers composed theological cosmogonies, that is, mythological accounts of the origins of the universe and the gods. The first comprehensive naturalistic accounts of the cosmos as an ordered unity (the Greek term *kosmos* means "order" or "ordered whole") were the products of early Greek natural philosophy, which began in the sixth century B.C.E. with the Milesian philosophers Thales, Anaximenes, and Anaximander. They were also concerned with questions of origins such as, What was it from which the world began? and To what will the world eventually return?

Heraclitus departed from the cosmogonic concerns of the earlier pre-Socratics and used the language of past, present, and future to describe an eternal cosmos, one without beginning or end. According to him, the cosmos consists of an eternal cosmological fire, that is, fire in its purest form (*aithēr*), and it is the source of all cosmological changes, transforming from fire to sea to earth and back again: "This ordered whole [*kosmos*] was made by neither gods nor humans, but it always was and is and shall be: an ever-living fire, kindling in measures and going out in measures" (Diels-Kranz, frag. B30).[10] Parmenides, through rigid deductive logic, denied all motion and change in the natural world, by arguing that what exists is (1) ungenerated and indestructible, (2) one and indivisible, and (3) motionless and unchanging.[11] Parmenides also may have argued for a centrifugal universe: that is, the earth is a perfect sphere that remains stationary at the center of the universe (see Plato *Phaedo* 108e–109a), though the first clear reference to a spherical earth and the notion that falling bodies fall toward the center is found in Plato (*Phaedo* 108c–f). The Epicureans, for whatever reason, obstinately stuck to a flat-earth theory (Lucretius *De rerum natura* 1.1060–61).

Models of the Cosmos

The Greek naturalistic models of the universe that emerged from the sixth through the fourth centuries B.C.E. were varied. Modern scholars have proposed several typologies for grouping similar ancient Greek views of the universe. David Furley, for example, proposes that the Greeks had two antithetical pictures of the universe (with subtypes), the "closed world" and the "infinite universe."[12] The closed world picture has three subtypes: (1) the world was created by a god (Plato *Timaeus*); (2) the world had no beginning and will have no end (Aristotle); and (3) the world has a beginning and end, but this is an endlessly repeated cycle in which each successive world is an exact replica of the preceding world (Stoicism). The distinguishing features of the closed world cosmology include: (1) permanence: the various kinds of things that exist in the world do not change; (2) teleology: the world is an organic structure moving toward an end or goal, a structure in which human beings are at the top of a hierarchy of living forms, and each living form has a unique function in the system; the unique function of humans is reason; and (3) the nature of matter: the cosmos is an uninterrupted material continuum, spherical in shape, which fills everything. Motion, an essential characteristic of reality, is therefore problematic, for it must consist of some things moving through other things, that is, the denser and thicker through the lighter and thinner. The problem of continued motion therefore necessitated the hypothesis of a god who could act as prime mover (Aristotle). The difference between the *circular* motion of heavenly bodies and the *rectilinear* motion of earthly objects led some philosophers to propose a radically dualistic model of the universe to account for these differences (Plato followed by Aristotle).

According to Furley, the infinite universe model was espoused by atomists such as Leucippus, Democritus, and Epicurus and has the following characteristics: (1) evolution: the universe changes in the sense of growth and decay; (2) mechanism: the universe consists of inanimate matter; there is no ultimate change in matter itself except for locomotion and no interaction of matter except collision; and (3) the nature of matter: the universe is constructed of extremely small, invisible particles called atoms that move in a void with no center and no boundaries. Continuing motion of particles was presupposed; only changes in motion needed explanation (the "swerve" theory was the basis for free will in Epicureanism). The circular motion of heavenly bodies and the rectilinear motion of entities on earth were explained by the vortex model, evident in the world of human experience in whirlpools and tornadoes.

G. E. R. Lloyd, on the other hand, presents the diverse Greek conceptions of the universe in terms of three models: (1) as a living organism (Plato *Timaeus* 30b; Sextus Empiricus *Adv. math.* 9.104; Diogenes Laertius 7.142ff.), (2) as an artifact (for example, fashioned by a Demiurge), and (3) as a political entity (that is, either kingship, oligarchy, or anarchy).[13] While Lloyd's typology is less satisfactory because less comprehensive than Furley's, it does emphasize important features of Greek cosmological conceptions that characterize both of Furley's models; they are not specified by Furley because he is primarily interested in ancient arguments for and against each cosmic model. These features are the *anthropocentricity* of much Greek cosmological speculation (for example, geocentricity vs.

heliocentricity) and the assumption of *interconnectedness* in the cosmos. While Lloyd's models of the cosmos as a living organism corresponds to Furley's closed world model, his other two models are problematic and do not deal in a positive way with those ancient conceptions that Furley has described with the infinite universe model. Furley's simpler typology, then, is a more adequate presentation of the ancient Greek conceptions of the cosmos.

Individuals and the Cosmos

The three Milesian philosophers Thales, Anaximander, and Anaximenes were materialists who shared an organic or *hylozoistic* view of the world (that is, the view that matter itself has the inherent property of life and growth). For pre-Socratics in general, there was no clear-cut division between the animate and inanimate world. Nevertheless, each held that the cosmos was produced, on an organic model, from original material constituents (which functioned like a seed or seeds), such as moisture or water (Thales), air (Anaximenes), or *to apeiron* (the infinite [Anaximander]). Each of these generative principles was apparently regarded as divine, though clearly distinguishable from the traditional gods of Greek mythology. These comprehensive accounts of the cosmos attempted to determine which things were more basic and more real than others. These theories not only were used to explain the cosmos but also were applied to human beings. Among the later pre-Socratics, Diogenes of Apollonia revived Anaximenes' theory that air was the first principle by arguing that it is the principle of life in humans who live by breathing (Diels-Kranz, frag. B6). Hippon revived Thales's emphasis on water as the basic element in his monistic hypothesis, associating human youth with moisture and old age and death with dryness (Diels-Kranz, frags. A6, A11). Anaxagoras also used his theories of physiology to formulate his views of the cosmos. Similarly, according to Pythagoras, if the world was a living, eternal, and divine creature that lived by breathing in air or breath from the infinite that surrounded it, then there must be a natural kinship between the cosmos and human beings.

The theoretical similarities between the cosmos and the human person were also explicitly rejected by some:

> Certain physicians and philosophers assert that nobody can know medicine who is ignorant what a human being is; he who would treat patients properly must, they say, learn this. But the question they raise is one for philosophy; it is the province of those who, like Empedocles, have written on nature, what a human being is from the beginning, how he came into being at the first, and from what

> elements he was originally constructed. (Ps.-Hippocrates *On Ancient Medicine* 20; LCL trans.)

The author of *On the Nature of Man* is even more explicit in rejecting philosophical proposals that the human being is composed of a single substance:

> The one who is accustomed to hear people discuss the nature of man beyond its relations to medicine will not find the present account of any interest. For I do not say at all that a man is air, or fire, or water, or earth, or anything else that is not an obvious constituent of the human being. (Ps.-Hippocrates *On the Nature of Man* 1)

Variations of the Macrocosm-Microcosm Model

One presupposition of Greek cosmological thought that became increasingly common after the fifth century was the parallel between the human being and the cosmos, first made explicit in medical speculation in the fifth century. This view assumes that human nature could be neither understood nor explained without reference to the larger, more encompassing reality of which it was an integral part. The relationship that is perceived to exist between the individual and the cosmos is frequently characterized by using the terms *microcosm* and *macrocosm. Microcosm* (Greek: *mikros kosmos;* Latin: *mundus parvus* or *mundus minor*) is used for conceptions of human nature that are considered analogous or homologous to a comprehensive external reality that constitutes the "macrocosmos" (*megas kosmos*).[14] The term *mikrokosmos* does not occur in classical or Hellenistic Greek but is a later formation that first appears in Latin transliteration in Isidore of Seville (*De natura rerum* 3.1). The presupposition of the interconnectedness of the cosmos inevitably entails raising questions about the kind and quality of the relationship that is thought to exist between the whole and the part. One aspect of this issue can be illustrated by a problematic passage from Plato's *Protagoras* (311B) in which Socrates and Phaedrus discuss whether the nature of the *psychē* (soul) can be understood "apart from the nature of the whole [*tēs tou holou phuseōs*]." It is clear that for Socrates the *psychē* has a context within which it must be understood, though it is not clear whether "the whole" is the physical body or the cosmos.

The Ionian philosophers, assuming that a consistent *physis* underlay all appearances, proposed basic elements out of which everything in the cosmos developed. Some of these philosophers were monists. Thales apparently thought that the basic element was water, while for Anaximenes it was air. Others proposed more complex theories. Empedocles argued for a four-element theory, earth, air, fire, and water. Accordingly, human beings were also thought to derive from one or another basic element or a combination of basic elements. For Xenophanes, "We are all born of earth and water" (Diels-Kranz, frag. B33), and Empedocles observed that "from all these [elements: earth, air, fire, and water] all things are appropriately fitted together, and by these people think and experience joy and sorrow" (Diels-Kranz, frag. B107). Empedocles thought that because human beings and the cosmos are similarly constituted, perception is possible (Diels-Kranz, frag. B109).

The Ionian philosophers attempted to explain *psychē* (life) and, within the context of their theories of the cosmos, later defined it as that which is self-moving (Plato *Phaedrus* 245c–e; *Timaeus* 37b). Xenophanes, Anaximenes, Anaximander, and Anaxagoras thought that *psychē* was "breath" or "air." Other pre-Socratics proposed that the *psychē* was either "fire" or "fiery" (Parmenides, Heraclitus) or water (Hippon) or a mixture of the hot, cold, dry, and wet (Zeno of Elea), similar to Empedocles' view that the cosmos consisted of four basic elements (fire, air, water, and earth) that mingle and separate under the influence of Love and Strife. The medical theory of Empedocles (who made the stunning proposal that blood is the agent of nutrition) was based on his cosmological theory, for he held that the flesh, blood, bone, and organs of human beings were constituted of the four cosmic elements in varying proportions (frags. A86, B96, 98). The coordination of these oppositions (fire = hot; water = cold; earth = dry; air = moist) became the basis for medical theory from Alcmaeon through the Hippocratic treatise *On the Nature of Man*, through Plato, Aristotle, and the Stoics to Galen (who attributed this theory to Hippocrates), and then into the Middle Ages, where it was dominant until the Enlightenment.[15]

Historians of religion have often recognized the human tendency to understand human life as homologous to the life of the cosmos.[16] Working from a microcosmic perspective, various cultures have considered the human being as a map or model of the universe; based on a macrocosmic perspective, some cultures have considered the universe a paradigm of human existence. In ancient Greek religious and philosophical thought, the human person was often understood as a microcosm of the universe. According to Democritus, speaking from the perspective of his atomic theory: "There is a miniature universe in the individual" (Diels-Kranz, frag. 34).

For ancient religion and philosophy, the human dilemma (evident in such experiences as pain, grief, fear of death, disease, and suffering) was often understood as an encoding of macrocosmic problems in the individual; hence the answer to the human dilemma could be achieved through a proper understanding of the macrocosmos that opened the possibility for the integration of the human microcosmos into the encompassing macrocosm. This is so whether the ultimate quest was for "salvation" mediated by religious cults (understood in both intramundane and extramundane ways) or for *eudaimonia,* meaning "happiness" or "the flourishing life" — a very thin definition that resulted in philosophers expending a great deal of effort explaining just what it is that comprises happiness. The philosophical schools widely assumed that the answer to the human dilemma could be found in the macrocosmos and that *eudaimonia* would result from that knowledge.

The recognition of this widespread perception of the homologous relationship of the human being to the cosmos raises the issue of the anthropocentricity of much Greek cosmological speculation. The famous dictum of Protagoras of Abdera, "The individual is the measure of all matters, of those which are, that they are, and those which are not, that they are not," appears to mean that, in his view, there was no such thing as absolute falsehood or universal truth and that each individual was the sole judge of his own sensations and beliefs (Plato *Theaetetus* 151e–152a; Diels-Kranz, Protagoras, frag. B1). Nevertheless, it is of critical importance to recognize the significance of the basic presupposition: that is, the human person (and all other aspects of reality) is a part of a greater whole and unavoidably exhibits dependence on and takes definition from that greater reality.

However, the kinds of depictions of homologous relationships between the individual and the cosmos with which we are concerned range from primitive scientific attempts to define reality in terms of particular substrata (for example, earth, air, fire, water) to others that are essentially mythological constructs that have no basis in observed reality. Both approaches are fascinating precisely because they begin with the basic assumption of the homologous nature of the human person and the cosmos, though this assumption was conceptualized in a variety of ways. In order to highlight some of the basic patterns in this kind of thought, I propose a typology of two basic patterns, though both occurred in many historical variants, and in some instances the patterns are combined in various ways: (1) *spatial macrocosm:* that is, "salvation" involves an upward movement toward a more perfect reality, accomplished in an anticipatory way through the intellectual contemplation of ultimate realities during one's lifetime and finally by the separation of the soul from the body, enabling the soul to become part of the ultimate reality; and (2) *systemic macrocosm:*

that is, "salvation" involves cognitive and behavioral conformity to a more perfect reality.

Spatial Microcosm Two of the more important presuppositions of the spatial microcosm pattern are that perfection lies in the highest realms of the cosmos and that the properties of the higher world are replicated in the lower world. The individual is therefore composed of two or more separable constituents, and the process of separation is linked with *paideia* (education) in this life and ascension to the perfect realm upon death. For Plato the soul can be considered a "prisoner" within the body (*Phaedo* 82e–83a), and the soul wears the body like clothes that will eventually be discarded (*Phaedo* 87b). The imperfections of the cosmos are mirrored in the imperfections of the individual. In Plato's cosmology, that which is higher is better, while that which is lower is coarser and more inferior. Aristotle distinguished between the sublunary world (defective, perishable) and the superlunary worlds (eternal, imperishable, divine). Plato described the creation of the cosmos in the form of a living creature endowed with both soul and reason (*Timaeus* 30b). Plato rejected the materialistic cosmologies of the pre-Socratics because they failed to argue, as he did, that the worth of theories of cosmology can be decided by appealing to the argument of what is better and more beautiful. Plato's universe, though very different from that of the pre-Socratics, was nevertheless as regular and predictable as theirs. His universe, no less than theirs, had no room for the arbitrary interventions of the traditional Greek gods. According to Plato, the Demiurge fashioned the younger gods and assigned them the task of creating human beings out of the four elements (fire, earth, air, and water) while the Demiurge himself furnished the immortal soul, which contains no physical matter but is self-moving (*Timaeus* 42e–43a). The mortal soul, created by the younger gods, was divided into two parts, following Platonic tripartite psychology, and was placed in the thorax, separated by the neck from the immortal soul in the brain. The immortal soul has contact with the unchanging world of Being, while the mortal soul, through sense perception, has contact with the changing world of Becoming.

The cosmology most appropriate for the spatial microcosm pattern was the new geocentric cosmology that succeeded the storied-universe model and was widely accepted during the Hellenistic period. According to this cosmology, the earth occupies the innermost place in the cosmos and is surrounded by an enormous cosmos consisting of at least seven planetary spheres (that is, five planets with the sun and moon), topped by an eighth sphere of the fixed stars.[17] Since the earth itself occupied the lowest place in the cosmos, the traditional location of the underworld was no longer tenable. The atmosphere between the earth and the moon was thought to be the place where the souls of the dead waited until purified to the point where they could rise to the moon. Gnosticism's anthropology was sometimes bipartite but usually tripartite, consisting of body, soul, and the self.[18] The inner person (for which such terms as *pneuma* and *nous* are used) corresponds on the macrocosmic level to the unknown god: that is, a kinship or affinity exists between the highest god and the inmost core of the person. In most gnostic systems, the knowledge of this correspondence between the innermost person and the highest, unknown god is accessible only through revelation.

Systemic Microcosm Stoics followed the four-element theory of Empedocles in supposing that human beings, like the heavenly bodies, were composed of the four elements (earth, air, fire, and water). Stoics further claimed that the soul (compounded of fire and air) was the active principle, while the body (compounded of earth and water) was the passive principle, a microcosmic correspondence to the active and passive principles in the macrocosm (von Arnim, 1, frags. 85–87).[19] Philo reflects Stoic views when he regards the *nous* of the first human as that which was created in the image of the divine *Nous*: "It [*nous*] is in a fashion a god to him who carries and enshrines it as an object of reverence; for the human mind evidently occupies a position in men precisely answering to that which the great Ruler occupies in all the world" (*De opif. mundi* 69; LCL trans.). The theory of cosmic sympathy, developed as part of a complex philosophical system by the eclectic Stoic philosopher Posidonius, is often considered one of the basic presuppositions of ancient magic and divination in which sympathy (attraction) is understood in the context of the antithetical notion of antipathy (repulsion). One important aspect of this theory is the widespread acceptance of the analogy between macrocosm and microcosm as the primary mythological framework for ancient magical and divinatory practices as expressed in the ancient aphorism of alchemy: that which is above is like to that which is below, and that which is below is like to that which is above. The second- or third-century C.E. astrologer Antiochus of Athens saw a bond between the microcosm of the human person (understood trichotomously) and the macrocosm of the planets: Saturn = body; Moon = spirit; Sun = soul. Yet he did not think that it was the human person alone who was linked to the world above, for the elements of the material world (earth, water, and fire) are correlated with certain metals (lead, silver, and gold, all of which are considered living organisms), forming a complex microcosmic structure. According to the speculations of Zosimos of Panopolis, the first man, whether named "Thouth" (according to the Egyptians) or "Adam" (according to the Hebrews), was such that his body was composed of four elements: earth, water, air, and fire.[20] This means that the human person, which Zosimos believes is constituted of soul and body or mind and flesh, is composed of the basic elements of the cosmos.

Greco-Roman Views of the Person

The concept of the self is one of the central issues of contemporary ethical discussion, and the task of realizing one's "true" self is central for secular spirituality. However, this individualistic conception of the person did not exist during the archaic period in the Greek world or in the Semitic cultures of the ancient Near East as late as the Hellenistic period. The focus in this section will thus be on the various rudimentary conceptions of the human person that emerged from Homer to the early fifth century B.C.E. and then on the ways in which those conceptions were refined and systematized by various Greek thinkers and Greek philosophical traditions. Although traditional Greek views of human nature were usually combinations of inherited conceptions modified by present experience in the world, the distinctive views of human nature proposed by various philosophers and philosophical traditions represent critical reflections on received traditions together with a reasoned attempt to integrate those traditions with conceptions of the cosmos as a whole.

Archaic Greek Conceptions of the Person

The two Homeric epics, the *Iliad* and the *Odyssey*, are the most important early witnesses to ancient Greek conceptions of human nature.[21] The term *psychē* (usually translated "soul") is used in Homer to refer to the "life force," that is, that which must be present for a human being or an animal to be alive. The *psychē* is capable of temporarily leaving the body, particularly in dream experiences, but when the *psychē* leaves the body permanently, death results. The *psychē*, like the body, is a material substance, though extremely fine. This early Greek assumption of a materialistic *psychē* was perpetuated in various ways by the sixth-century Ionian philosophers, by the medical writers, and by the Stoics and Epicureans. After death the *psychē* of a human being departs for Hades (when and if the appropriate rituals are performed), where it continues to lead a shadowy existence less real (and far less desirable) than life on the earth (*Iliad* 22.467; *Odyssey* 11.216ff.).

The gods were thought at times to act directly on people giving them extraordinary courage and abilities (*Iliad* 10.366; 17.451) or causing them to act in irrational and even self-destructive ways (*Iliad* 19.86ff.). It was, of course, this irrational conception of the cosmos that the early *physiologoi* inherited but largely rejected.[22] Because there was no distinction between the physical and the spiritual in archaic Greece, the line between *physis* and *psychē* (the origins of our terms *physiology* and *psychology*) was correspondingly vague. Although the *psychē* itself is not associated with mental or emotional functions in this life, parts of the body (particularly the heart and the diaphragm) are considered to be not only physical organs but also centers for mental and emotional processes as well as sources that provide ideas and induce action. Terms for psychological experience and processes less connected with physical organs include *thumos* (originally derived from a term meaning "smoke," but which then came to mean "spirit," "courage," "anger," or "mind")[23] and *nous* ("spirit," "mind," "understanding," or "reason"); the latter became centrally important as a designation for the intellectual faculty in Greek philosophy.[24] One widespread early post-Homeric view held that the best form of human existence centered in the life of *aretē* (virtue) lived by the *agathos* (good person), that is, the adult male who enjoyed both wealth and social position. Although *aretē* is conventionally translated "virtue," it meant rather the courage of the warrior that produced success in battle (critical for the survival of the city-state), but it was not connected with qualities like justice or self-control. This conception of the person is essentially dyadic since the *aretē* of the good person is defined by the larger social and political unit to which he belongs.

In summary, then, Homeric language describing the person had no focal concept that meant "human nature" or the "human person," and the variety of terms used for mental and emotional states and experiences tended to fragment experience.[25] The Homeric epics had no term for the whole person except for personal pronouns. Although the *psychē* was not the carrier of the personality in life, it was thought to play that role in an extremely attenuated way in Hades. In the remains of seventh- and sixth-century archaic Greek literature, in essential continuity with some Homeric perspectives, the most "real" experience of life was the success of the warrior in battle, while the loss of vitality in old age and the attenuated form of existence in Hades were looked upon as undesirable though inevitable.

The sixth and fifth centuries B.C.E. offer evidence for other views of the *psychē* that were either suppressed or ignored in Homer.[26] One such view was that the *psychē* of the deceased resided with the physical remains of the deceased, where it could receive offerings and prayers from relatives and friends. There were two loosely related dualistic conceptions of the person that emerged by the late sixth century B.C.E. One held that the *psychē* was a center of consciousness, capable of separate existence, which could animate a successive number of physical bodies, that is, metempsychosis or reincarnation. Pindar, for example, claimed to remember three of his previous incarnations (*Olympian Odes* 2.68ff.), while Pythagoras thought that he could remember all of his (Diels-Kranz, frag. A8). The other, reflected in some of the mystery cults (particularly the Eleusinian mysteries), maintained that the *psychē* of the person initiated into a mystery cult would experience a better or more "real" existence in the netherworld.[27] The term *psychē* increasingly came to designate the center and carrier of the personality, and since *psychē* in popular thought was widely assumed to be a material substance, it was understood the same way by philosophers and physicians (Ps.-Hippocrates *Epidemics* 6.5.2).

Variations on the Body-Soul Dichotomy

From the late fifth century, the living human being was thought to be constituted of a *sōma* (body) and a *psychē* (life force, soul), with the *psychē* as the center of the personality. This soul-body dichotomy was conceptualized in Hellenistic philosophical traditions in a variety of ways. The extant dialogues of Plato reflect changing perspectives on the nature of the *psychē* and its relationship to the body. The most obvious change was from his view of the *psychē* as a simple substance in the *Phaedo* to the tripartite division of the *psychē* in the *Republic*. Plato (influenced by Pythagorean and Orphic traditions) regarded the *psychē* as immortal (*Phaedrus* 245c), though this view was not widely shared (*Republic* 608d; *Phaedo* 77b; 84b). Even more controversial was his view that the *psychē* was immaterial or incorporeal (*Phaedo* 85e). Platonism was attacked by both Stoics and Epicureans for the apparently contradictory assumption that the incorporeal could somehow associate with the corporeal to form a single substance, a human person. In the *Phaedo* alone the term *psychē* is used with a striking variety of connotations: (1) the element within us whose good condition constitutes our true well-being; (2) the "true self" or "real person" (115b–116a); (3) the intellect, reason, or thinking faculty (65b–c; 76c); (4) the "rational self" in contrast to emotions and physical desires (94b–d); (5) the "life principle" or "animating agent" (64c; 72a–d; 105c–d); and (6) generic "soul stuff" in contrast to individual souls, just as matter may be contrasted to individual bodies (70c–d; 80c–d). This wide range of meanings of *psychē* in a single composition is extremely problematic, for how can the soul "bring life" to the body (*Phaedo* 105c–d), "rule and be master" of the body (80a; 94b–d), and yet be a "prisoner" within the body (82e–83a)?

Aristotle's views on the relationship between body, soul, and mind are complex and exhibit at least two phases, a "Platonic" phase (in which Aristotle regarded the soul as a separate substance, as in Plato's *Phaedo*) and a final, "hylomorphic" stage in which he regarded the soul as the form or the realization of a natural body (reflected in the *De anima;* cf. Diogenes Laertius 5.33). The *Eudemus* (which actually belongs to the genre of consolation literature) and the *Protrepticus* (an exhortation to pursue the philosophic life), both products of the 350s, are extant only in fragments and represent the earliest stage of Aristotle's views about ethics and psychology. According to the *Eudemus,* the soul is a separate substance (Ross, frag. 8); it existed before entering the body and survives its separation from the body (Ross, frag. 5).[28] This is in tension with Aristotle's later view in the *De anima* that only the *nous* is immortal. The soul-body dualism of the *Eudemus* is linked to ascetic ethics (Ross, frag. 6). The same psychosomatic dualism is also evident in the *Protrepticus* (Düring, frag. B23):[29] "Man is by nature composed of soul and body" (cf. Düring, frags. B59, B107), and the life of the soul is superior to that of the body (Düring, frags. B23, B34, B61). Furthermore, the *psychē* has a rational and an irrational part, and *nous* belongs to the rational part (Düring, frags. B23, B60). In the latest stage of his psychological theory, Aristotle believed that *nous* or the "[productive] intellect" (introduced in *De anima* 430a) is present in the human person but separate from the soul-body complex (*De anima* 408b), and it alone is divine.

In Stoicism, the *psychē* of the person, endowed with *logos* or reason, is a fragment of the divine *logos* in a less pure form. Both the physics and the psychology of the early Stoics are monistic, though the psychology of the Middle Stoa and the Roman Stoa tends to be dualistic. The *logos* of a person is his or her *hēgemonikon* (ruling principle) or principal part of the soul (Sextus Empiricus, *Adv. math.* 7.234). The *logos,* or *pneuma,* permeates a person's entire being but has its seat in the brain or the heart (von Arnim, 2, frags. 836, 837–39, 842). The *pneuma* directs all activities of the mind and body through the faculties of the soul (eight or more faculties were enumerated). Stoicism admits no soul-body dualism, however, for the same force (the *hēgemonikon*) directs both physical and mental processes, and there are no irrational faculties in a person. *Psychē* is essentially distinct from the body but develops its full nature only in conjunction with the birth of the body, with which it is joined. Death is typically understood as a separation of the soul from the body.

While the Old Stoa and Chrysippus maintained the unity of the *psychē,* which they identified with reason, Posidonius rejected that view in favor of the Platonic tripartite distinction between reason, spirit, and passion, though the fundamental distinction is actually bipartite, that is, between the rational and irrational part of the soul (Edelstein-Kidd, frags. 145–46).[30] The irrational part was further divided into the part that seeks pleasure and the part that seeks power (Edelstein-Kidd, frags. 31–35, 142, 148, 152, 157). Posidonius argues that each person has two *daimones* within him or her, a good and a bad (Edelstein-Kidd, 1, 187), and the *daimōn* within is a person's true self.

Despite their many differences, the major Hellenistic philosophical traditions (Platonism, Aristotelianism, Epicureanism, and Stoicism) shared a number of views of the relationship between *psychē* and body: (1) all distinguished the *psychē* from the body; (2) all regarded the *psychē* as the center of intelligence within the human frame; (3) all thought that the *psychē* was localized or at least centered in a particular anatomical part of the human body; (4) all attributed mental and moral qualities to the *psychē,* not the body; (5) all but the early Stoics and Epictetus agreed that the *psychē* had both rational and irrational aspects; (6) all (even Epicureans and Stoics) thought that death could be defined as the separation of the *psychē* from the body; and (7) all but the Epicureans and the Stoic Panaetius (Cicero *Tusc.* 1.79) believed that the *psychē* continued to exist for at least a limited period of time after separation from the body at death. This surprisingly extensive list of common philosophical convictions about the *sōma* and the *psychē,* many of which coincide with popular views widely subscribed to in the Hellenistic and Roman world, clearly indicates how essential *psychē* became as a term for the center of the human personality.

One of the more lasting assumptions of ancient Greek psychology with profound ethical implications was the view that emotions (the irrational) could be separated from both cognition (reason) and motivation (will, volition), with the correlative view that cognition belonged to the "higher" aspects of the personality while the emotions belonged to the "lower." Although Platonists, Epicureans, and Stoics had vastly different conceptions of reality, they did share one major point of agreement in their ethical theories (the later Aristotle and the Peripatetics are exceptions), expressed in the Socratic paradox "Oudeis ekon hamartanei" (No one willingly does wrong), a notion frequently discussed by Plato (*Protagoras* 45d–e; *Timaeus* 86d; *Laws* 731c, 860d).[31] These three philosophical traditions linked moral behavior to human knowledge. According to a widespread ancient tradition, then, people do what is wrong even though they know what is right, and these impulses to action originate either in ignorance (which inhibits rational planning and deliberation) or from irrational emotions such as anger, fear, and hatred. This theory is dramatized in a speech of Medea in Euripides: "But I am overcome by evil. Now I learn what evil deeds I intended to perform; but passion overpowered my wishes, which is the cause of the greatest evil for mortals" (Euripides *Medea* 1077–80). Epictetus also held an exclusively intellectualist explanation of behavior: "Every error involves a contradiction. For since the one in error does not want to err, but to be right, it is clear that he is not doing what he wants" (Arrian *Epict. diss.* 2.27.1). Epictetus, a Stoic, was certainly familiar with the proverbial formulation "No one willingly does wrong," but he assumes in good Stoic fashion that a person who does what he does not want to do is ignorant of what he really wants. Although Plato originally took only rational factors into account when determining human conduct, he later complemented this intellectualist approach to behavior (inherited from Socrates; cf. Xenophon *Memorabilia* 3.9.4) with the recognition of the presence of irrational factors that resulted in psychological conflict.[32] For most Stoics, however, who saw no split between reason and emotion, behavior was based exclusively on the rational faculties (Arrian, *Epict. diss.* 1.28.6–8; citing Medea's speech in Euripides *Medea* 1077–80), though Posidonius was an exception. In the general Greek view, therefore, moral progress was based on education. The traditional bipartition of human nature into intellect and emotion, the rational and the irrational, remained the basic frame of reference for Greek ethical theory.

Philosophy as Therapy for the *Psychē*

The Goals of Philosophy

All the major Greek philosophical schools that were viable during the Hellenistic and Roman periods (Platonism, Aristotelianism, Epicureanism, Stoicism, Skepticism) regarded philosophy as "the art of living" par excellence that provided the necessary answers to the urgent problems of human suffering, including anger and aggression, fear of death, sexuality and love, sickness and misfortune. These human problems, of course, were approached quite differently by the religious traditions and institutions of Greece and Rome. Theism in its various forms was a peripheral issue for most of the central moral questions posed by the Hellenistic philosophical tradition. For the major philosophical traditions the goal of philosophy was *eudaimonia*, that is, happiness or the flourishing life always for the individual and frequently for the social institutions in which the individual was enmeshed. Furthermore, in contrast to popular religion and superstition, the Hellenistic philosophical schools (with the exception of Skepticism), like their predecessors, were committed to discovering truth through the use of reason and argumentation. Although each philosophical school had its own particular form of religious teaching, they all differed from popular religious tradition in using rational argument rather than prayers and sacrifices to facilitate their quest for the good life.

Philosophy as Therapy

Another shared featured of the Greek philosophical traditions, which has important implications for the development of later forms of Western secular spirituality, was the widespread utilization of the medical analogy derived from the assumptions and practices of the Greek medical science tradition.[33] Just as the task of the physician is to heal the body, runs an endlessly repeated commonplace, so the task of the philosopher is to heal the *psychē*. Here the Greek term *psychē* (soul) and its Latin equivalent *animus* refer to the person as a living, rational, and emotional being — that is, the carrier of the true self — and not to an immortal constituent of the human person that survives physical death. In contrast to physical diseases, which have physical causes, however, the diseases of the soul were thought to be caused by false beliefs and opinions engendered by society, that is, false socially taught views on money, competition, status, and the like. The major Hellenistic schools (Epicureans, Stoics, and Skeptics), like Plato but unlike Socrates and Aristotle, were convinced that human social life was corrupt and that socially taught beliefs and values prevented people from achieving *eudaimonia*. The medical analogy suggested a three-step philosophical therapeutic process: (1) diagnosis of the disease (i.e., the identification of those values, beliefs, perceptions, and judgments that prevent people from living a fulfilling life); (2) measurement of its severity in the context of a normative system of health (that is, an intuitive conception of the flourishing human life — frequently derived from observing children and animals or from imaginative conceptions of a Golden Age); and (3) treatment by the method of philosophical dialectic (the Epicureans excepted), which distinguished false from true values, beliefs, and perceptions.[34]

The widespread conviction of the necessity for philosophical therapy was maintained within the context of two critically important presuppositions. The first was that the emotions are directly connected with the reasoning faculty (the core of the *psychē*), so that such emotions as fear, grief, anger, and love are closely linked to belief and can be modified by the modification of a person's beliefs. Also important for understanding philosophy as therapy in the Hellenistic period is the assumption that although one cannot change the world, one can change one's dependence on the world. Epicureans, Stoics, and Skeptics thought that the truly good and virtuous person must be completely independent of economic and material factors, for the achievement of full humanity requires only inner change.[35] This means that the Hellenistic philosophers placed a strong emphasis on education (often described with therapeutic metaphors), and they characteristically assumed the role of radical critics of socially defined phenomena such as religion (especially Epicurus and Lucretius), love, marriage, child-rearing, and existing political institutions. The Stoics, for example, are responsible for the idea that the individual person deserves respect regardless of class, gender, race, or citizenship.[36]

The earliest adaptation of the medical model is found in the fragments of Democritus: "The medical art heals the diseases of the body, but wisdom rids the soul of its sufferings" (Diels-Kranz, frag. B31). The conviction that there is healing power in *logos* (reasoned discourse and argument) became a widespread supposition in classical and Hellenistic Greek culture (Isocrates *Peace* 39) and was bequeathed to the Romans.[37] The important early Stoic philosopher Chrysippus clearly reflects the adoption of the medical model: "It is not true that there exists an art called medicine, concerned with the diseased body, but no corresponding art concerned with the diseased soul" (von Arnim, III, frag. 471). The analogy between scientific medicine and philosophy is echoed and amplified in Roman Stoicism, which emphasized the necessity for students of philosophy to be responsible for their own therapy: "There is, I assure you, a medical art for the soul. It is philosophy, whose aid need not be sought, as in bodily diseases, from outside ourselves. We must endeavor with all our resources and our strength to become capable of doctoring ourselves" (Cicero *Tuscan Disputations* 3.6). The medical analogy for the curative role of philosophy was also used by Epicureans (Porphyry *Ad Marc.* 31) and Skeptics (Sextus Empiricus *Outlines of Pyrrhonism* 3.280).[38]

Greek Medicine and Rationalism

Greek medicine and Greek philosophy were closely related throughout antiquity.[39] Indeed, some philosophers were physicians (for example, possibly: Empedocles and Diogenes of Apollonia; certainly: Sextus Empiricus). Schools of physicians such as the Methodists differentiated themselves from other medical schools of thought on primarily philosophical grounds. The Empiricist school of medicine, however, rejected the dogmatic intrusions of philosophical theory into the more pragmatic practice of medicine (Ps.-Hippocrates *On Ancient Medicine* 1–2). One characteristic that pervades the Hippocratic corpus is the supposition that all diseases have natural causes and that traditional notions of arbitrary supernatural intervention should consequently be rejected. One of the documents belonging to the Hippocratic corpus written at the end of the fifth or the beginning of the fourth century B.C.E., titled *On the Sacred Disease,* argues that epilepsy (the so-called sacred disease) is no more "sacred" than any other disease, but like the others has a particular nature and a specific natural cause (1.2–3). The author argues that the brain is responsible for epilepsy and that a pathological condition of the veins that lead to the brain is the immediate cause of the disease (7.3–7). Each disease, he argues, has a specific cause and cure, and fanciful speculation about supernatural causes is wrong and does not work. He carries on a running polemic against various religious practitioners and healers (*magoi* [magicians] and *kathartai* [purifiers]) who have no idea of the specific physical causes of diseases and who, motivated by greed, prescribe various incantations and ritual purification procedures to treat this and other diseases of the body (1.10–11, 29–32). The central issue that divides the author from those he denounces is the doctrine of the uniformity of nature, that is, the regularity of natural causes and effects. The conception of nature reflected in *On the Sacred Disease* is that every physical phenomenon has a natural causal explanation that, in the case of specific diseases, rules out certain types of supernatural intervention.

Philosophical Therapies

Socrates (469–399 B.C.E.) was committed to reasoned argument as the final arbiter of claims to moral truth (Plato *Cratylus* 45B). He focused on ethical questions, not on the problem of the nature of the cosmos (Aristotle *Metaphysics* 987b; Plato *Apology* 19C; Xenophon *Memorabilia* 1.1.11). Rather than formulate a natural theology, he developed a moral theology (Plato *Republic* 2.379B).[40] He held that the virtues have essences of their own that are independent of the gods and that are as normative for them as they are for us (Plato *Euthyphro* 10A). Socrates' god could not lie, according to Plato (*Apology* 21B), though deceit had been practiced by Greek gods since Homer (*Iliad* 22.299) and by Greek heroes after Odysseus. Socrates, as known from the earlier dialogues of Plato, used the elenchic mode of argumentation (a belief is shown to be inconsistent with its advocate's other beliefs). According to Plato, Aristotle described this as a therapeutic process, for he was centrally concerned with what he considered the most serious of issues: the way people ought to live (*Gorgias* 500b–c; *Apology* 28E, 30A–B; *Charmides* 166c–d).

Gregory Vlastos, who has written one of the more important recent studies on Socrates, contrasts the metaphysical concerns of Plato with the metaphysical disinterest of Socrates:

> One could hardly imagine a world-outlook more foreign to that of Socrates. He [Socrates] is unworldly: he cares little for money, reputation, security, life itself, in fact for anything except virtue and moral knowledge. But he is not otherworldly: the eternal world with which Plato seeks mystical union is unknown to him. For Socrates reality — real knowledge, real virtue, real happiness — is in the world in which he lives.[41]

Vlastos makes an important, though controversial, proposal about what must have been an unstated assumption of the Socratic elenchus:

> Since Socrates does expect to discover truth by this method [*peirastic*, that is, a thesis is refuted only when its negation is derived from the answerer's own beliefs; cf. Aristotle *Soph. el.* 165b], he must be making an exceedingly bold assumption which he never states and, if he had stated it, would have been in no position to defend, namely that side by side with all their false beliefs, his interlocutors always carry truth somewhere or other in their belief system; hence if Socrates pokes around in their belief system he can expect to turn up *true beliefs entailing the negation of each of their false ones.*[42]

For Socrates, then, philosophical dialectic was the primary therapeutic tool for helping people to distinguish true beliefs from the false beliefs that prevented them from living fulfilled lives. Religious beliefs played little or no part in the establishment of truth through the Socratic elenchus.

Although Aristotle agreed with Plato that human knowledge is a knowledge of forms, they disagreed about the nature of these forms. For Plato these forms were transcendent and existed independently of particulars. For Aristotle (in continuity with Socrates) the forms did not exist separately from the particulars of which they are the forms; rather, it is the particulars that primarily exist (Aristotle *Categories* 2a). Therefore, all Aristotelian inquiries, including ethics, were bounded by the appearances that constitute human experience; the search for truth is the search for the most accurate account of the world.[43] Aristotle rejected the autonomy of the individual person, assuming that individuals need parents, spouses, children, and fellow citizens (Aristotle *Nicomachean Ethics* 1097b).[44] Aristotle and his students were concerned about not only their own *eudaimonia* but also that of others. Unlike most Greek thinkers, Aristotle was critical of the medical model used by philosophers. He gave two reasons for this criticism:[45] (1) medical treatment is largely a matter of external intervention, while philosophical argument is necessarily more mutual, with the "patient" playing a role as active as the "physician"; (2) medical therapy is directed toward the health of the individual, while Aristotelian philosophy is directed toward individuals embedded in communities. Aristotle thought that the emotions of the inner life were based on beliefs that were either true or false. Emotions, then, are not always correct and must be brought into harmony with a proper view of what constitutes *eudaimonia*, the flourishing human life.

Epicurus thought that society was corrupt and that the primary causes of human misery were irrational fears and desires (for example, greed and ambition) based ultimately on the fear of death.[46] These irrational desires and fears are the result of ignorance and false beliefs that need correction. Since the senses are completely reliable, all false belief lies in socially transmitted teachings. Like the other major Hellenistic philosophical traditions, the Epicureans believed that people have the natural capacity to lead fulfilled lives but are prevented from doing so because of false opinions. Because of the corrosive influences of society, serious students of Epicurus had to leave their homes and occupations and enter into the Epicurean community, where they remained (Diogenes Laertius 10.17). Epicurus reportedly defined philosophy as "an activity that secures *eudaimonia* by means of arguments and reasons" (Sextus Empiricus *Adv. math.* 11.169), and he defined *eudaimonia* primarily in terms of *ataraxia* (peace of mind). In practice, the Epicureans thought that the dialectical process was inadequate for bringing deeply held beliefs to the surface. They appear to have come very close to discovering the existence of the unconscious, relying heavily on personal narrative as a tool for uncovering deeply buried opinions and beliefs.[47] The models for *eudaimonia* among Epicureans were children, healthy animals, and imaginative conceptions of the Golden Age, positing an opposition between "nature" and "culture." Although Epicurus did not deny the existence of the gods, he held that they are composed of atoms and the void like everything else and are just as subject to change. The gods lack any interest in controlling the world of nature and have no vindictive desire to punish people for imagined impieties. The gods served primarily as models of an ideally tranquil and unperturbed existence (Lucretius *De rerum natura* 2.1093–94). Religious beliefs in general are bad because they entail superstitious and irrational ideas about the gods (such as their vindictiveness) and the *psychē* (such as the fear of punishment after death). For the Epicurean there is joy in the freedom from restless desire, and this can be found only when the false character of beliefs and opinions about the universe are recognized and rejected.

The Stoics, like the Epicureans, were materialistic monists whose doctrine of *oikeiōsis* (acquisition, appropriation) reflected the same optimistic view held by the other Hellenistic philosophical traditions, namely, that people have an innate affinity for their own welfare. A corollary, which formed the basis for Stoic philosophical therapy, was a belief in the dignity and autonomy of reason in all human beings. One tenet of the medical analogy — the tenet that the cure must be individualized to suit the needs of a particular patient — led the Stoics to value personal communication between the teacher and the student over the written treatise.[48] Stoics relied heavily on rational arguments and were committed to the necessity of the student's own active use of his or her critical faculties. Stoicism defined *eudaimonia,* the fulfilled human life, in terms of virtue. The Stoics insisted that the *psychē* had only a single rational part. Rather than attempt to moderate the emotions, like Aristotle, the Stoics argued that the passions must be completely extirpated.

Conclusion

Despite the striking intellectual developments in Greek cosmological speculation that began with the Ionian philosophers in the sixth century B.C.E. and despite the running critique of many of the assumptions of Greek religion and mythology, there is no evidence that this creative speculation had any tangible effect on Greek religious practice.[49] The great diversity exhibited by cults throughout the Greek world, despite the attempt of poets to produce consistent theogonies, stands in contrast to the assumption of the ontological unity of the cosmos proposed by the pre-Socratic philosophers. Although these thinkers were without exception theists, they assumed that *physis* constituted that which underlay all appearances and hence that which was ultimately real. The content of the traditional Greek terms *theos* (god) and *theios* (divine) was radically transformed so that they became simply alternate ways of designating the unity of *physis.*

The microcosm-macrocosm homology in ancient Greek cosmological and anthropological thought is significant as an antecedent to modern secular spirituality primarily because it assumes a very particular form of the unity of the cosmos. All forms of the view that the human person is a microcosm of the cosmos assume that human persons cannot be understood without reference to the encompassing cosmic totality of which people are an integral part. The very fact that some medical writers had to argue that diagnosis should not be dependent on cosmic theory suggests how pervasive such an assumption actually was. Some microcosm-macrocosm theories had theistic features, such as that in which the *nous* (reason, intelligence) of the person was considered "divine," corresponding to the cosmic *Nous.* This use of *divine* had little in common with traditional Greek religious conceptions but was rather a metaphor for that which was ultimately real.

In discussing the Greek views of the person, the second significant antecedent of modern secular spirituality, it became clear that the older conceptions of the person were essentially "materialistic" in that the *psychē* (life principle) and the body were assumed to be material substances. The more sophisticated views of the human person as a body-*psychē* dichotomy — views espoused by Plato, Aristotle, and the Hellenistic philosophical schools — exhibited remarkably close similarities despite evident differences. This anthropology, which located the core of the human personality in the rational faculty, assumed that bad behavior was the result of ignorance, for "No one willingly does wrong." The major obstacle for the realization of *eudaimonia* (the flourishing life) for the person was ignorance, which could be rectified only by the rigors of philosophical training. The exclusive resources for full self-realization lay within the individual person.

Finally, as regards the third and last significant antecedent of modern secular spirituality, we reviewed the Greek notion that the task of the philosopher is to heal the *psychē* on analogy with the physician's task of healing the body. This analogy must be taken quite seriously. Just as physicians assumed that all diseases have natural causes, so for philosophers the diseases of the *psychē* also have natural causes, namely, the false beliefs and opinions absorbed by individuals from the societies in which they were born and raised. Just as physicians routinely ruled out certain types of supernatural causes of disease, so philosophers did not regard supernatural dimensions of reality as the sources for human ignorance and misery.

Notes

1. See the working definition of spirituality formulated by Peter H. Van Ness in the introduction to this volume.

2. Mary Whitlock Blundell, *Helping Friends and Harming Enemies: A Study in Sophocles and Greek Ethics* (Cambridge: Cambridge University Press, 1989).

3. S. C. Humphreys, *Anthropology and the Greeks* (London: Routledge and Kegan Paul, 1978), 193–208.

4. E. R. Dodds, *The Greeks and the Irrational* (Berkeley: University of California Press, 1951).

5. See G. E. R. Lloyd, *Magic, Reason and Experience: Studies in the Origin and Development of Greek Science* (Cambridge: Cambridge University Press, 1979); and idem, *The Revolutions of Wisdom: Studies in the Claims and Practice of Ancient Greek Science* (Berkeley: University of California Press, 1987).

6. Fragments of the pre-Socratic philosophers have been collected and edited by Hermann Diels and Walther Kranz in *Fragmente der Vorsokratiker*, 3 vols. (Zurich and Hildesheim: Weidmann, 1985). In the following discussion, references to specific fragments are listed according to the Diels-Kranz numbering system.

7. J. P. Kenney, "Monotheistic and Polytheistic Elements in Classical Mediterranean Spirituality," in *Classical Mediterranean Spirituality*, ed. A. H. Armstrong (New York: Crossroad, 1986), 269–92.

8. Daniel Babut, *La religion des philosophes grecs* (Vendôme: Presses Universitaires de France, 1974).

9. W. Fahr, *Theous nomizein: Zum Problem der Anfänge des Atheismus bei den Griechen* (Hildesheim: Georg Olm, 1969); A. B. Drachmann, *Atheism in Pagan Antiquity* (Copenhagen, 1922).

10. G. S. Kirk, *Heraclitus, the Cosmic Fragments: A Critical Study with Introduction, Text and Translation* (Cambridge: Cambridge University Press, 1970), 311–19.

11. D. J. Furley, *The Greek Cosmologists,* vol. 1: *The Formation of the Atomic Theory and Its Earliest Critics* (Cambridge: Cambridge University Press, 1987), 36–42.

12. Furley, *Cosmologists,* 1:1–8; see also his "The Cosmological Crisis in Classical Antiquity," in *Cosmic Problems* (Cambridge: Cambridge University Press, 1989), 223–35.

13. G. E. R. Lloyd, "Greek Cosmologies," in *Ancient Cosmologies,* ed. C. Blacker and M. Loewe (London: Allen and Unwin, 1975), 198–224.

14. Walther Kranz, *Kosmos,* Archiv für Begriffsgeschichte 2/1 and 2 (Bonn: Bouvier, 1955–57), 130–31.

15. Owsei Temkin, *Hippocrates in a World of Pagans and Christians* (Baltimore: Johns Hopkins University Press, 1991), 11–13.

16. Mircea Eliade, *The Sacred and the Profane,* trans. Willard R. Trask (New York: Harper and Row, 1959), 165.

17. Martin P. Nilsson, *Greek Piety* (New York: Norton, 1969), 96–103.

18. Kurt Rudolph, *Gnosis: The Nature and History of Gnosticism,* trans. R. McL. Wilson (San Francisco: Harper and Row, 1983), 88–113.

19. The fragments by or about early Stoic philosophers have been collected by Johannes von Arnim in *Stoicorum Veterum Fragmenta,* 4 vols. (Stuttgart: Teubner, 1978). In the following discussion, references to these fragments will give the volume and fragment number in von Arnim.

20. Howard M. Jackson, ed., *Zosimos of Panopolis on the Letter Omega* (Missoula, Mont.: Scholars Press, 1978), 29.

21. A. W. H. Adkins, *From the Many to the One: A Study of Personality and Views of Human Nature in the Context of Ancient Greek Society, Values and Beliefs* (London: Constable, 1970), 13–48.

22. Gregory Vlastos, *Plato's Universe* (Oxford: Clarendon, 1975), 13–17.

23. Hjalmar Frisk, *Griechisches Etymologisches Wörterbuch,* 3 vols. (Heidelberg: Carl Winter, 1960–72), 1:693–94.

24. Ibid., 2:322–23.

25. Adkins, *From the Many,* 23.

26. Ibid., 49–90.

27. Walter Burkert, *Ancient Mystery Cults* (Cambridge, Mass.: Harvard University Press, 1987).

28. Fragments of Aristotle's lost *Eudemus* have been collected by W. D. Ross in *Aristotelis Fragmenta Selecta* (Oxford: Clarendon, 1955).

29. The fragments of Aristotle's lost *Protrepticus* have been collected by Ingemar Düring in *Der Protreptikos des Aristoteles: Einleitung, Text, Übersetzung und Kommentar* (Frankfurt am Main: Klostermann, 1969).

30. The fragments of Posidonius have been collected by L. Edelstein and I. G. Kidd in *Posidonius,* vol. 1: *The Fragments,* 2d ed. (Cambridge: Cambridge University Press, 1989).

31. The problem of the divided mind in Socrates, Plato, Aristotle, and the Stoics is discussed by A. W. Price, *Mental Conflict* (New York: Routledge, 1995).

32. E. R. Dodds, "Plato and the Irrational," in *The Ancient Concept of Progress and Other Essays on Greek Literature and Belief* (Oxford: Clarendon, 1973), 106–25.
33. Martha Nussbaum, *The Therapy of Desire: Theory and Practice in Hellenistic Ethics* (Princeton, N.J.: Princeton University Press, 1994).
34. Ibid., 28–29.
35. Ibid., 10.
36. Ibid., 12.
37. Ibid., 48–77.
38. Hermann Usener, *Epicurea* (Leipzig: Teubner, 1887), 169, frag. 221.
39. Temkin, *Hippocrates,* 8–17; James Longrigg, *Greek Rational Medicine: Philosophy and Medicine from Alcmaeon to the Alexandrians* (New York: Routledge, 1993).
40. Gregory Vlastos, *Socrates: Ironist and Moral Philosopher* (Cambridge: Cambridge University Press, 1991), 162.
41. Ibid., 79.
42. Ibid., 113–14; see also David Furley, "Truth as What Survives the *Elenchos,*" in *Cosmic Problems: Essays on Greek and Roman Philosophy of Nature* (Cambridge: Cambridge University Press, 1989), 38–46.
43. Nussbaum, *Therapy of Desire,* 61.
44. Ibid., 64.
45. Ibid., 69–73.
46. David Konstan, *Some Aspects of Epicurean Psychology* (Leiden: Brill, 1973), 3–34.
47. Nussbaum, *Therapy of Desire,* 133.
48. Ibid., 336–76.
49. Walter Burkert, *Greek Religion* (Cambridge, Mass.: Harvard University Press, 1985), 305.

Bibliography

Adkins, A. W. H. *From the Many to the One: A Study of Personality and Views of Human Nature in the Context of Ancient Greek Society, Values and Belief.* London: Constable, 1970.

Dillon, J. *The Middle Platonists.* Ithaca, N.Y.: Cornell University Press, 1977.

Furley, D. J. *The Greek Cosmologists.* Vol. 1: *The Formation of the Atomic Theory and Its Earliest Critics.* Cambridge: Cambridge University Press, 1987.

Hommel, H. "Mikrokosmos." In *Symbola.* Vol. 1: *Kleine Schriften zur Literatur und Kulturgeschichte der Antike,* edited by B. Gladigow. Hildesheim: Olms, 1976.

Kenney, J. P. "Monotheistic and Polytheistic Elements in Classical Mediterranean Spirituality." In *Classical Mediterranean Spirituality,* edited by A. H. Armstrong. New York: Crossroad, 1986.

———. *Mystical Monotheism: A Study in Ancient Platonic Theology.* Hanover, N.H.: University Press of New England, 1991.

Kenny, A. "Mental Health in Plato's *Republic.*" In *The Anatomy of the Soul.* Oxford: Oxford University Press, 1973.

Lloyd, G. E. R. *Magic, Reason and Experience: Studies in the Origin and Development of Greek Science.* Cambridge: Cambridge University Press, 1979.

Longrigg, James. *Greek Rational Medicine: Philosophy and Medicine from Alcmaeon to the Alexandrians.* New York: Routledge, 1993.

Meijer, P. A. "Philosophers, Intellectuals and Religion in Hellas." In *Faith, Hope and Worship: Aspects of Religious Mentality in the Ancient World,* edited by H. S. Versnel. Leiden: Brill, 1981.

Nussbaum, Martha. *The Therapy of Desire: Theory and Practice in Hellenistic Ethics.* Princeton, N.J.: Princeton University Press, 1994.

Temkin, Owsei. *Hippocrates in a World of Pagans and Christians.* Baltimore: Johns Hopkins University Press, 1991.

Vlastos, G. *Plato's Universe.* Oxford: Clarendon, 1975.

———. *Socrates: Ironist and Moral Philosopher.* Cambridge: Cambridge University Press, 1991.

Wright, M. R. *Cosmology in Antiquity.* New York: Routledge, 1955.

2

Sources Outside of Europe

JUNG HA KIM

"Accidental Tourists"

I DOUBT THAT anyone driving along the major interstate highways from the Bible Belt to Yankee New England expects to experience a dramatic moment of "enlightenment." Myriad automobiles carry bumper stickers with a wide range of messages, a snapshot of public temperament and spiritual yearning: "Jesus is the way"; "Karma, karma, karma"; "Minds are like parachutes: they only function when open"; "Black is beautiful"; "Seek and ye shall find"; "Shop until you drop"; "Think globally, act locally, pray specifically"; "Confucius says, 'Be Happy' "; "Honk if you love Jesus"; "Om. . . ." Tuning into one radio station after another on the road, one finds popular rock groups and rappers vocalizing lyrics that are reminiscent of Sunday school materials and yet are sharply cynical or apocalyptic. All this seems to be quite American. While one station plays a song of the Irish rock quartet U2 ("I went out walking with a Bible and a gun; / the word of God lay heavy on my heart"), another station plays the rap by Snoop Doggy Dogg about the voice that offers the dying body "eternal life forever" after being gunned down in "murder was the case." Neo-Christian lyrics — such as "Would you hold my hand when you see me in heaven?" "Faith lies in the way of sin"; and "When Jesus left Birmingham . . ." — are, perhaps, so familiar to American ears that they are rarely listened to as important windows for viewing American unorthodoxies and for recognizing the parareligious yearnings embedded in these songs.

"Millions of Americans are searching for some clearer understanding of the core principles of religion and how they can be applied to the daily experience of living as well as to humanity's common destiny on this planet," said Bill Moyers, a television producer and commentator, at a weekend-long annual gathering of the Religion Newswriters Association.[1] Hiring a full-time religion correspondent for the first time in the history of network television, Peter Jennings of *ABC World News Tonight* justified his decision in this way: "Religion and spirituality are playing a much larger role in American life than what is generally portrayed [on television news]."[2] Whether one interprets the religious references of the new crop of rock icons and the new spiritual concerns of network television as expressing "religious doubt and the struggle to come to terms with the possibility that there may not be a God" or as "symbols of a thirst for values that transcend the fast-buck ethos of corrupt commercial cultures," it is long overdue for "cultural workers" such as rock singers, rappers, and anchor-persons to take note of the public's quest for spirituality, a quest that is worthy of recognition and analysis.[3] Such cultural workers are prime candidates for playing the role of social critics and secular prophets in the contemporary cultural milieu. For spirituality is far from disappearing on American soil; rather, "it went underground and took expression outside of the religious establishment."[4] Navigating between the "religious" and the "secular," people are creatively and eclectically pursuing their own quest for meaningful spirituality. What is still overdue is closely documenting and critically analyzing a more subtle change that has been taking place in the United States, a nation in which 90 percent of the population claims a religious preference and more than two-thirds of the adult population believes in the existence of angels. That subtle change is the widespread appropriation of elements of non-Western traditions in contemporary American spirituality.[5]

This essay is, then, an attempt to shed some light on the non-Western sources of the contemporary quest for spirituality — it attempts to show how this quest encompasses a highly syncretic and eclectic interweaving of religious traditions of the West and the non-West. An excellent example of this phenomenon is the African-American celebration of Kwanza (alternately, Kwanzaa). The word *Kwanza* is derived from a Swahili phrase meaning "firstfruits," and the celebration it denotes is an African-American adaptation of traditional African harvest celebrations. Kwanza lasts seven days, from 26 December to 1 January, and is characterized by seven principles and symbols. The principles stress the unity of African-Americans as families and communities and as a race. The celebration extends gratitude and commemoration to ancestors in Africa and nurture and commitment to children as the community's future. The symbols reinforce these principles: a unity cup is the symbol for the seventh day, and gifts are given chiefly to children the day before, with the gifts symbolizing aspects of African-American heritage. Clearly the character of the celebration is spiritual. Maintaining ties with ancestors is a prominent theme of many African religions and is likewise prominent in the Kwanza celebration. It is also noteworthy that the seventh, culminating principle is faith. Immediately following Christmas, Kwanza is celebrated by some African-Americans in conjunction with Christmas, as something that complements the Christmas message, and by others as something independent of Christian religion.[6]

A second example points to a more diffuse yet no less influential phenomenon. Many forms of traditional Chinese art have been shaped by Taoist sensibilities. This has given a distinctively spiritual complexion to such arts as poetry and painting, both in the experience of the creative artist and in the experience of the aesthetic observer. In his study *Creativity and Taoism,* Chang Chung-yuan identifies several relevant principles of Taoism, including the yin/yang complementarity as the natural dynamic of the reconciliation of opposites and *tzu jan* as the disposition toward spontaneity and naturalness. Both figure in Hsieh Ho's celebrated canons of painting, informing especially the idea of *ch'i yün,* in which the painter seeks to spontaneously become a vehicle for a cosmic rhythm that achieves manifestation on the painted canvas.[7]

Especially through the influence of Ch'an Buddhism, this Chinese spiritual sensibility and artistic practice influenced other Asian nations, particularly Japan. Daisetz Suzuki's study *Zen and Japanese Culture* explains how Zen Buddhism informs Japanese practices like Haiku poetry, landscape painting, and the tea ceremony. In the twentieth century this influence has reached U.S. shores. Poets as diverse as Allen Ginsberg and W. S. Merwin show strong Buddhist influences. Asian visual art has influenced American painters in varying degrees, as is evident in the work of Georgia O'Keeffe, Ad Reinhardt, and Morris Graves. This Asian spiritual influence extends beyond well-known artists. For some years Julia Cameron and Mark Bryan have led popular workshops cultivating the spiritual dimension of art and recently they published a widely read book entitled *The Artist's Way: A Spiritual Path to Higher Creativity.* From the cover image of cranes flying near Mt. Fuji to quoted epigrams by Lao-tzu and the Buddha, the book gives ample evidence that the spiritual ethos of American artists is much informed by Asian traditions.[8]

Determining what is at stake in such attempts at appropriating non-Western traditions naturally leads to further questions. For example, What does it mean to be spiritual? How do different people experience and express spirituality? How have non-Western traditions and cultural practices been adopted so as to become more American? Are non-Western sources sufficiently homogeneous to be addressed collectively? How does the transplantation of religious and cultural values of the non-West influence the bifurcation of religious and secular identities in the United States? What can one say about the contemporary quest for spirituality in light of recognizing (and advocating) diversity within the United States?

In order to address the foregoing questions, this study brings three topical areas into dialogue with one another: the boundary between spirituality and religion; the privatization of abundant spiritual supplies; and the politics of (re)appropriating the non-West in the United States. These perspectives and constructs are utilized to focus and analyze the rich manifestation of sources that are reappropriated and incorporated in contemporary spirituality in the United States and to stimulate further questions and discussions regarding the political economy of spirituality along the axes of history, culture, and religion.

Although it risks violating what is commonly thought of as coherence and objectivity, locating my autobiographical vantage point is in order. For I believe that the hermeneutical perspective of an academic project is deeply embedded in the author's own life circumstances and is, thus, inevitably political. I defy the general academic perspective that true and pure knowledge is fundamentally nonpolitical. Moreover, by making my own idiosyncrasies and biases explicit, I hope to make this study more accountable to the very subject matter that I seek to analyze and with which I seek to identify.

An Autobiographical Vantage Point

I am a hyphenated American of Asian descent, constantly straddling cultures that are different and at times quite contradictory. Born as the first daughter to North Korean parents in South Korea, I was raised in a Buddhist temple, spent much of my childhood in Japan, followed my parents to the United States as an involuntary immigrant at age twelve, and never stayed in one place longer than five years until age thirty. Thus, I consider myself not only a multicultural but also a multireligious person. I have at various times been a Buddhist, a Confucianist, a Taoist, a shamanist, a Zen Buddhist, a Shintoist, and a Christian.

I attend a local Christian church and participate in its community life, and I also practice sitting meditation (that is, *za-zen*) either at home or at a nearby Zen center whenever possible. I venerate both living and dead ancestors, and I especially commemorate my late grandmother, who raised me, and my late father, who brought me into this land and became the very root of my identity as a hyphenated American. At work, I tend to utilize methodologies and conduct research projects that are community-oriented rather than individually inclined. Although formal educational training in the fields of religion and sociology can explain this tendency to some extent, my conscious efforts not to bring shame to the communities and people with whom I deeply identify and to which I belong may be the primary reason for my choice of methods and projects.[9]

My being a multicultural and multireligious person whose spiritual experiences are ever-fluid and syncretic does not, however, automatically result in greater sympathy for highly eclectic borrowing from other traditions by contemporary Americans questing for spirituality. For I believe that all representations and reappropriations of other cultures serve purposes for particular groups of people, especially groups who have more privileges in the market economy of capitalist society. A main goal in such an economy is to commodify anything and everything that can be marketed, including spiritual sites and styles — from Native Americans' ancestor graveyards to the "exotic" lifestyles of Indian yogis.

The example of peyote is especially instructive. Peyote, or, more specifically, the hallucinogenic drug obtained from this variety of cactus plant, has a long history of religious ceremonial usage by Native Americans in Mexico and the southwestern United States. Late nineteenth-century U.S. Indian policies condemned its usage along with other Native cultural practices, and peyote has generally been defined as an illegal drug by federal policy and statute. In the twentieth century special exemptions have been given to Native American religious usage of peyote — most recently by the American Indian Religious Freedom Act of 1978. Since the 1960s non-Native interest in peyote has disrupted the peyote cult in two ways. First, unauthorized harvesting (and merchandising) of peyote buttons in Mexico and Texas has endangered supplies. More recently, increasing claims of membership by non-Natives in the Native American church, often by persons interested only in the peyote, has created cultural and institutional tensions. One denomination, the Native American Church of North America, has ruled that non-Natives cannot be enrolled in the church.[10]

However brief, the preceding autobiographical discussion provides the hermeneutical lens through which this chapter has been written. I now turn to the relevant issues that were highlighted earlier as important for a scholarly delineation of the various contours of contemporary spirituality in the United States.

The Boundary between Spirituality and Religion

Just what does it mean to be religious? is a question intrinsically related to other questions, such as What does it mean to be spiritual and how do different people experience and express spirituality?[11] Sociologists have generally assumed that every religion and its organizations are composed of largely two systems — belief and ritual — that are based upon a conception of the "sacred."[12] Thus scholars and practitioners (not mutually exclusive categories of people) have historically been inclined to draw boundaries between faith and practice and between religion and spirituality.

Aptly noting that *spirituality* is "a notoriously vague term," Peter H. Van Ness claims that "its scholarly meaning comes from reports of inner experiences offered as personal counterparts to religious doctrines and institutions."[13] Pointing out both different and overlapping aspects of what the words *spiritual* and *religious* mean, he also states that "some instances of spiritual discipline have long and intimate associations with organized religion; others do not."[14] Van Ness has provided a conception of the spiritual dimension of human life in the introduction to this volume. Alternative conceptions are possible. For some people spirituality means one's own "manner of being" religious and "of being a follower" of his or her religion.[15] Some define it more behavioristically as "a set of behavior repertoires which is formal and ceremonial."[16] Others accent discipline, describing spirituality as "the disciplined rehearsal of right attitudes."[17] Still for others, it is "the fullest possible actualization of what [a person] is in his heart, ... wherein the totality of all the dimensions and capacities and contents of his life (soul) are brought to conscious unity in realization."[18] In short, being spiritual does not preclude one's allegiance to a particular institutionalized religion, yet neither does it require such an allegiance.

Calling for a humanistic value system — "the religion of the spirit" — Walter Lippmann contends that a dichotomous categorization of religion and spirituality needs to be reassessed in light of a highly individualized and rapidly changing society:

> In an age when custom is dissolved and authority is broken, the religion of the spirit is not merely a possible way of life. In principle it is the only way which transcends the difficulties.... The religion of the spirit does not depend upon creeds and cosmologies; it has no vested interest in any particular truth. It is concerned not with the organization of matter, but with the quality of human desire.[19]

Resonating with this call for a more humanistic "religion of the spirit," Martin Marty cogently states that critics of religion charge American religion with being "too political, too compromising, too institutionally self-seeking to provide room for spiritual development."[20]

What is more, discerning what spirituality may mean to different people can be met with some suspicion and even hatred from both the right and the left wing of the political spectrum. On the one hand, given the reality of deeply privatized spiritual experimentation in the United States, a resort to spirituality may mean resort to a "false consciousness" that ignores and disguises the systemic causes for social and religious problems as matters of individual mentality and perception. On the other hand, the acknowledgment of parareligious and post-Christian spiritual experimentation as peculiarly "American," and so as entirely legitimate ways of satisfying people's spiritual needs, may push persons who adhere to traditional spirituality to feel the need to defend their own orthodoxies in the name of world religions and their historical establishments.

However one defines spirituality, what appears to be undeniably present in attempts to draw boundaries between religion and spirituality is the duality built into Western conceptualizations. As Pablo Richard cogently demonstrates, Western civilization has been — from its origin in Hellenistic and Greco-Roman civilization — based on a distinction between matter (that is, the body) and spirit (that is, the soul). Reinterpreting Aristotle's dualism of soul and body, Richard contends that the "soul is regarded as the realm of the spiritual and of encounter with God, and the body is regarded as the material realm and the site of sin."[21] This conceptualization of the soul as dominant over the body was, in fact, the underlying framework for the domination of "master over slave, of man over woman, of adult over child, and of the human being over animal and nature."[22] In other words, spiritual life in the West necessitated that people experience alienation from their own bodily experiences, exploitation in human relationships, androcentrism in gender relations, hierarchy in social relationships, and anthropomorphism in attempts to subdue and control the natural world. Thus, to be spiritual in a Western Christian sense entails, for example, observing the Christian Lenten season as a time of self-denial (that is, bodily denial) and sacrifice, and Easter Sunday as a day of remembering how the Spirit-God triumphantly overpowers the human bodily experience of death through resurrection.

Critical of the spirit/body dichotomy underpinning much Christian spirituality, the Hispanic theologian Ada María Isasi-Díaz advocates the term *praxis* to denote a more holistic understanding of spirituality. Warning against equating praxis with practice, she argues that "praxis is both intellectual enterprise as well as action."[23] Much needed attempts to integrate the mutually exclusive dualisms in the West, such as the spirit and the body, man and woman, knowledge and action, master and slave, and humanity and nature, are prevalently taking place in a variety of forms in different social groups. Efforts to take seriously the mundane and bodily experiences of human life are also prevalent in the secular quest for spirituality in contemporary America. For example, in order to advocate women's full and equal access to various levels of organized religious institutions and to foster liturgies and spiritualities that are more reflective of women's bodily experiences, some feminist circles are actively working to provide safe spaces for women both within and without the context of established religions. Reclaiming the preferential option for the poor and the God of the oppressed as the core messages of the Christian good news, "people of colors" and the dispossessed are increasingly denouncing the tendency of the dominant culture to marginalize certain racial-ethnic peoples, and they are challenging the assumptions of the universalized, one-size-fits-all God. James Cone's *A Black Theology of Liberation*, first published in 1970, is a prime example of a theologian radically rethinking the Christian message from such a vantage point, specifically from the experience of the oppressed African-American community.[24]

Pointing to self-evident deterioration of natural resources and the environmental costs of the process of modernization and postmodernization, Native Americans and other environmentally conscious groups are urgently promoting nonanthropocentric and nondualistic perspectives toward the natural world. Native American religious thinkers like Vine Deloria contribute to shaping these new perspectives while at the same time offering distinctive but influential proposals about the nature of God and human spiritual life.[25] The unchurched and postchurched population of the 1960s are now turning to fulfill their quests for spirituality by eclectically borrowing, mending, and quilting various traditions in the multicultural society.

These and other efforts searching for a more holistic and life-embracing spirituality are evident in various spiritual movements, such as: creation spirituality, Goddess spirituality, Twelve Step spirituality, feminist spirituality, self-help spirituality, ecofeminist spirituality, men's spirituality, kenosis spirituality, and image design spirituality. They are also evident in classes and workshops devoted to t'ai chi, transcendental meditation, hatha yoga, therapeutic touch, extrasensory perception, and the reading of tarot cards. Many non-Western sources of spirituality — eclectically and syncretically mixed on American soil — can be found in these contemporary attempts to address and correct Western dichotomies, to affirm the human dimensions of life, and to accommodate rapidly changing everyday realities in a highly pluralistic society.

Numerous scholars and travelers have been fascinated by the diverse nature of "American" national characteristics; Alexis de Tocqueville, Paul Tillich, and Reinhold and H. R. Niebuhr are relevant examples. They have noted that Americans are pragmatic, individualistic, optimistic, utilitarian, and yet deeply religious. For such a future-oriented people to turn away from the organized religions of the West and turn to non-Western sources in their quests for more meaningful spiritual lives, something must have happened. What Lee Yearly calls "spiritual regret" is a partial explanation. Spiritual regret, according to Yearly, "arises from the sense, however implicit, that the traditional ways of dealing with distinctions among religions are deficient, that they fail to meet adequately the specific demands the modern situation produces."[26] Spiritual regret is, then, considered a "virtue" based on the recognition that "extremely varied, legitimate religious ideals exist and that no person can possibly manifest all of them."[27] Needless to say, however, not all non-Western traditions are considered to be equally corrective and/or alternative sources for addressing spiritual regret in the United States. Before discussing the political economy of spirituality along the axes of history, culture, and religion, I now turn to delineating the historical and cultural context in which many non-Western sources have been eclectically adapted in spiritual experiments in the United States.

The Privatization of Abundant Spiritual Supplies

Non-Western sources in general, and Asian traditions in particular, have impacted the spirituality of the United States in various ways. Peter Williams has articulated three areas in which Asian traditions have had an impact on the United States: "ethnic religions"; "export religions"; and "new religions."[28] This threefold designation is based on distinguishable categories of adherents: Asian immigrants and their descendants in "ethnic religions," predominantly Euro-Americans in "export religions," and an eclectic cadre of countercultural, cross-religious, and intellectual practitioners in "new religions." Although Williams's categorizations are predominantly designed for discerning religious groups, they apply also to the spiritual quests of many people in the United States. All three ideal types of groups — and also their typical spiritual experiences — are demonstrative of what Martin Marty calls the "merits of borrowing" from other traditions and cultures.[29] Furthermore, I would argue that the "merits of borrowing" is a peculiarly and categorically American notion. The process of Americanizing non-Western sources entails more than merely transplanting cultural traditions in the United States; in the fuller sense, it means "becoming acculturated, adopting a distinctively American way of living and looking at the world as its own."[30]

For "borrowing" to be perceived as a "merit," however, people must assume at least one thing: an equal access to sufficient supplies. If some can take but others cannot, then borrowing becomes revealed as privilege or exploitation — something other than meritorious. How and why, then, did people resolve what Yearley calls "spiritual regret" by turning to other cultures and traditions as abundant supplies for borrowing? Although the transitions from rural to urban and from a preindustrial to a technological society seem to be the two most salient historical factors that can be pointed to as the original causes of spiritual regret, I would refer to more recent historical phenomena and argue that at least the following two demographic sources have been instrumental in making the cultural milieu of borrowing from the other traditions possible: (1) the emergence of the baby boom generation; and (2) the changing racial-ethnic landscape of the United States.[31]

Baby boomers made up roughly one-third of the nation's population by 1990. Consequently, their values, practices, beliefs, and opinions determine much of the social norms in the United States. Depicting America's religious landscape by focusing on the boomer generation from the 1940s to the 1990s, Wade Clark Roof claims that as Sunday school children of the 1950s arrived at their adolescence in the 1960s, they became unchurched in record number, thereby fundamentally altering the religious landscape in America. By the 1980s, however, some of the unchurched population had turned to evangelical and fundamentalist faiths; some had gravitated to New Age beliefs; and some completely defected from organized religion. As this generation of un-, re-, and postchurched reached midlife in the 1990s, they placed more emphasis on creative and eclectic spiritual projects that are characteristic of the reemergence of spirituality and religious and cultural pluralism on America's spiritual landscape.[32] Assessing the rise of a counterculture during this particular historical era, Steven M. Tipton claims that "the counter-culture's psychedelic wing arose from the postwar generation's experience of affluence not as a promise of panacean security in the future, but as a present fact whose advantages did not add up to happiness or fulfillment."[33]

While the baby boomers have turned away from more traditional spirituality and organized religions and have freely moved in and out and across religious and secular boundaries, people of colors also have actively promoted cultural and religious pluralism by providing cogent criticisms of the cultural hegemony of the dominant group(s) in the contexts of both the religious and secular realms. Mottoes such as "God is Black," "Allah is the One," "Black is beautiful," "God is rice; rice is God," "God is Red," and "En la lucha" are now so widespread that their usage overlaps racial-ethnic boundaries. Illustrating the increasingly diverse landscape of people living in the United States, in 1993 *Time* magazine featured a computerized face of Miss America in the year 2050 on its cover and entitled the multiracial face the "Melting Pot." She is 15 percent Anglo Saxon, 17.5 percent Middle Eastern, 17.5 percent African, 7.5 percent Asian, 35 percent southern European, and 7.5 percent Hispanic. Although these percentages are somewhat skewed from the projected racial-ethnic makeup of the nation's population in the second half of the twentieth-first century, the éclat of portraying how presently dominant Euro-Americans will slip into numerical minority in the United States is an astute argument. Thus, contrary to traditional spirituality's dependence upon homogeneity, the very fact of demographic pluralism will continue to promote more heterodox and syncretic quests for spirituality. The history of Christianity illustrates that the "orthodox rejection of syncretism has to do not with the purity of faith [and praxis], but with who has the right to determine what is to be considered normative and official."[34]

These two distinct demographic factors — baby boomers and people of colors — were instrumental in establishing the broader politico-economic context of the United States wherein individualistic consumerism and "borrowing" of non-Western spiritual sources became possible (though the consequences of such processes have not been equally beneficial to these two categories of people). For substantiating the claim that individualistic consumerism is the underlying politico-economic climate for eclectic borrowing of spirituality from non-Western sources, I rely on Ronald Delattre's dual usage of the word *supply*, the word having both economic and religious meanings in his term *supply-side spirituality*. Delattre claims that among many consistent and important themes in the nation's history is "the assumption that abundance (variously interpreted) rather than scarcity, plenty rather than poverty, is the destiny of Americans (when religiously interpreted) as spiritual children of God."[35] He also claims that this assumption is very distinguishably American. After reiterating an Emersonian conviction that "man is born to be rich, or inevitably grows rich by the use of his faculties; by the union of thought and nature,"[36] Delattre proceeds to argue that "supply-side spirituality" is, then, based on the conviction that abundance rather than lack is natural and that anything less is "an unnatural condition that can be overcome through the right application of a spiritual power, and that such power is at human disposal."[37]

America's entitlement to abundance is evident in various articulations and pursuits of the "American dream" as well as in the obsessive drive to acquire consumer goods even at the cost of accumulating personal and national debts and international trade deficits. Moreover, in searching for more exuberant spiritual styles and meaningful spiritual experiments, people need the availability of abundant supplies both from within and without their own communities. As a means to fulfill the promise of an ever-abundant supply-side spirituality, many non-Western sources of spirituality have been transplanted, reappropriated, and represented as peculiarly American. Consequently, life journeys that can afford to assume abundant supplies of such spiritual sources can take at least two forms. On the one hand, the journeys can lead to a way of life that seems "affirmative, optimistic, expectant, energetic, and confident."[38] On the other hand, by addictively assuming a constant availability of sufficient supply, people can accumulate debts and eventually face bankruptcy.

The Politics of (Re)appropriating the Non-West

I now turn to discussing the politics of (re)appropriating the non-Western sources of spirituality as American. Much of the spiritual experimentation that is based on the "merits of borrowing" in contemporary America can be seen as a ubiquitous effort to transform the Western mentality of, to use Benjamin Disraeli's phrase, "The East is a career"[39] to "The East is a way of life." When Disraeli said that the East is a career, "he meant that to be interested in the East was something bright young Westerners would find to be an all consuming passion," especially in the first half of the twentieth century when the "Orient" was flourishing as an academic field for studying about the Other, and "Orientalism" was flourishing as a "Western style for dominating, restructuring, and having authority over the Orient."[40] After World War II and in conjunction with the increasing liberation of so-called Third World countries from the colonial occupation of Western countries, explicit forms of domination by the superpower(s) in global politics became no longer acceptable or possible. As is suggested by the image and vocabulary of the "global village," interdependence among the world nations necessitated by mutual survival induced the West to apply more subtle ways of representing and (re)appropriating the non-West. Thus, borrowing from non-Western sources of spirituality and adapting them as American can be seen as a new and more subtle form of controlling and possessing the Other — that is, as a neocolonial attempt by the West to dominate its former colonies. For in consumption-driven societies, spirituality is, as with all other consumer goods, easily commodified and marketed. As bell hooks says, new varieties of spirituality are "continually commodified and offered up as new dishes to enhance the white palate—that the Other will be eaten, consumed, and forgotten."[41]

Needless to say, not all forms of (re)appropriation and representation of the Other are necessarily ill-intended, nor do they always result in disservice to a particular source community of people. The very process of borrowing from the Other is not predictably linear. In other words, some of the sources of Eastern spirituality have undergone rather unexpected transformations through the process of Americanization. For instance, deeply gendered and hierarchical practices of Confucian ritual and everyday reality have been filtered and understood through the Western perception as the cosmic complementarity of the yin and yang. Gender-conscious people have turned to the teaching of Confucius as a source of a nondualistic principle of complementarity and as a possible corrective to sexist dualities in the United States. While non-Western sources of spirituality have been (re)appropriated according to borrowers' specific needs and desires, this process has also brought rather unintended and yet profound changes in the ways in which people understand and experience their spirituality in general. For example, a Zen-style sitting meditation has been well adopted as a part of Christian retreat center programs. The stillness and sense of tranquility it provides have become highly sought after by Christians and non-Christians alike. Stated otherwise, even in the process of representation and (re)appropriation of the Other, a fundamentally two-way traffic of Americanizing the non-West and "Orientalizing" the West can be observed (even though this mutual impact may be unintentional).

Regardless of the subtle mutuality between Americanizing non-Western sources of spirituality and "Orientalizing" Western spirituality, appreciating the Other must not be equated with appropriating the Other. This point cannot be overemphasized. From a global perspective, the political and economic realities that enable "white people to roam the world, making contact," are worthy of note.[42] Also rather revealing is the readiness of Americans to interpret their acts of exotic consumption as gestures of acknowledging the Other. Contrary to the commonsense belief that all forms of mutual exchange are mutually beneficial, the very economy of representing and (re)appropriating the Other in the West is based on the unequal configuration of power and varying degrees of economic-cultural privilege. In order to further document the multidimensional contours of the political economy and to muster both the potentially colonizing and the transforming process of Americanizing some of the sources of non-Western spirituality, a few illustrations and a brief discussion follow.

The process of Americanizing ancient sources of Eastern spirituality is exemplified in Gertrude Stein's ability to recast traditional religious images in order to create an alternative spirituality.[43] Her fictive spiritual identity — a "Chinese Christian" — is emblematic of how an assumption of abundant supply in one's searching for meaningful spirituality can explicitly and implicitly bring about transformations of both Western and non-Western spirituality in the name of Americanization. At the outset, Stein's Chinese Christian is rather critical of the androcentric spiritual hegemony that is deeply embedded in institutional religions of the West. At the same time Stein's Chinese Christian exhibits a self-conscious effort "to render Europe's perception of China, the colonizer's view of the colonized."[44] Drawing from images of the "Oriental" as mystical, female-referenced, and always being represented and (re)appropriated by the non-Oriental, the Chinese Christian cultivates the quiet and stillness of contemplation as a spiritual act. Knowledge of Chinese traditions is made to yield a set of activities that one can borrow and perform in order to experience rich spiritual experimentation in the West. This is also rather reminiscent of what Edward Said states about the Oriental expert: "What is required of the Oriental expert is no longer simply 'understanding'; now the Orient must be made to perform, its power must be enlisted on the side of 'our' values, civilizations, interest, goals." He also warns that this in turn will require "a new assertion of control, this time not as the author of a scholarly work on the Orient but as the maker of contemporary history, of the Orient as urgent activity."[45]

The Chinese Christian spirituality does not merely blend Eastern and Western traditions into an alternative spirituality that is female-identified and contemplation-oriented. It also further privatizes spiritual quests by cultivating the desired state of consciousness through personal meditation, indeed, through individually catered lists of how to sit still, empty one's mind, maintain a sense of tranquility, and so forth. Chinese Christian spirituality is, then, made to be ultimately anti-institutional and highly individualistic. In the process of Americanization, therefore, deeply communal rites of conducting sitting meditation in the East have become the highly privatized spiritual discipline of individuals.

To account for some of the fundamentally different understandings of what constitutes spiritual and religious experiences in the West and the East, I refer to N. J. Demerath's observation comparing Japanese and American religious beliefs and behaviors. Demerath points to a national Japanese survey that states that some 70 percent of Japanese describe themselves as "religiously indifferent," while their behavior suggests otherwise. There are credible statistics showing that "as many as 120 percent of Japanese are religious (if one relies on shrines and temple registration) or as few as 10 percent if one looks at regular participation within a given faith community."[46] Based on this data he concludes: "If there is a tendency for Americans to maximize their religiosity, there is an opposite tendency among both the Japanese and Chinese to minimize it."[47] Although Demerath does not explain why these opposite tendencies exist, the notion of an interdependent self (that is, a communal self) in the East seems to be a salient factor. In monistic philosophical traditions of the East, a human being is thought to be by nature interdependent with others. Thus, conducting rituals of ancestor veneration and making pilgrimages to shrines and temple, for example, are matters of the community and not of individuals. Because a premium is placed on collective welfare, people living in the East seem to be rather indifferent to highly individualistic experiences of spirituality and religiosity. It is, hence, rather ironic that some of the deeply community-oriented Asian sources of spirituality have been transplanted and (re)appropriated as highly individual experiences in the spiritual lives of people in the United States. Along with Westernizing ancient Eastern traditions through the process of feminization and exotification, people in the United States have privatized the originally communal experiences of the Asian tradition.

Citing Robert Michaelson's *The American Search for Soul,* Charles S. Prebish contends that "among religious experiments in America, the ones surviving and having long-lasting influence would be those that can, on the one hand, stimulate or elicit the power of spiritually transforming experience and faith and, on the other hand, channel that power into disciplined action."[48] A group of Theravada monks and laity from Sri Lanka (which was then called Ceylon) became prominent in 1893 in the United States; a Hindu ascetic crossed the southwestern desert of the United States on foot in 1912; a Muslim community was established in Cedar Rapids, Iowa, in 1920 — following on these and other events, religions from the East, such as Buddhism, Hinduism, Islam, and Confucianism, have continuously thrived on American soil.[49] These sources of non-Western religions and traditions have survived thus far because they indeed elicited "the power of spiritually transforming experiences and faith" since their appearance in the United States.

Matchmakers of Spiritual Marriages

I have argued in this essay that many non-Western varieties of spirituality have become peculiarly American, in order to meet the needs of people's spiritual quests in the United States. This Americanizing of the Other has been shaped by a number of multifaceted factors, such as the changing of the demographic landscape of America, the phenomenon of "spiritual regret," the assumption of abundant (spiritual) supply, and the commitment to the "merits of borrowing." All of these factors have been instrumental in directing the complex and rapid unfolding of the American saga of eclectic spirituality and will continue to be so.

Since spirituality deals not only with behavioral sets of ritualistic repertoires but also with people's innermost quest for well-being, the challenge of writing this essay was to offer a viewpoint and an analysis that are responsive to the many different spiritual experimenters in America who for themselves and others serve as matchmakers of spiritual marriages.

Notes

1. Quoted in Christopher Herlinger, "News Media Lack Soul, Moyers Says," *The Atlanta Constitution,* 7 May 1994.

2. Michael J. Paquette, "Covering News of the Spirit: Religion Reporter Knows Her Calling," *Atlanta Constitution,* 7 May 1994.

3. Guy Garcia, "Religion and Rock," *Atlanta Constitution,* 8 January 1994.

4. Wade Clark Roof, *A Generation of Seekers: The Spiritual Journeys of the Baby Boom Generation* (New York: HarperCollins, 1993), 242.

5. For the statistics cited, see Nancy Gibbs, "Angels among Us," *Time,* 27 December 1994.

6. On this last point, see Clarice J. Martin, "Celebrations of Afro-American Traditions during the Christmas Season," *Reformed Liturgy and Music* 22 (summer 1988): 139–41; for a more comprehensive treatment, see Maulana Karenga, *The African-American Holiday of Kwanzaa: A Celebration of Family, Community and Culture* (Los Angeles: University of Sankore Press, 1989).

7. Chang Chung-yuan, *Creativity and Taoism: A Study of Chinese Philosophy, Art, and Poetry* (New York: Harper and Row, 1970), esp. 11–13, 210.

8. Daisetz T. Suzuki, *Zen and Japanese Culture* (Princeton, N.J.: Princeton University Press, 1973); and Julia Cameron with Mark Bryan, *The Artist's Way: A Spiritual Path to Higher Creativity* (New York: Putnam's, 1992).

9. Highlighting the difference between "shame" and "guilt," Herbert Fingarette makes the common but mistaken assumption that shame is concerned with "mere appearances rather than moral realities.... Guilt is an attack upon oneself, whereas shame is an attack upon some specific action or outer condition. Shame is a matter of 'face' or embarrassment, of social status. Shame says, 'change your ways; you have lost honor or dignity.' Guilt says, 'change yourself; you are infected'" (Herbert Fingarette, *Confucius—the Secular as Sacred* [New York: Harper and Row, 1972], 30).

10. A 1990 U.S. Supreme Court ruling partially reverses the 1978 statute. For the history of U.S. law on peyote, see Omer C. Stewart, "Peyote and the Law," in *Handbook of American Indian Religious Freedom,* ed. Christopher Vecsey (New York: Crossroad, 1991), 44–62. For evidence regarding the disruption of the peyote cult, see Stewart's book *Peyote Religion: A History* (Norman: University of Oklahoma Press, 1987), esp. 332–36; and David F. Aberle, *The Peyote Religion among Navaho* (Chicago: University of Chicago Press, 1982).

11. N. J. Demerath III, "The Moth and the Flame: Religion and Power in Contemporative Blur," *Sociology of Religion* 55:2 (summer 1994): 108.

12. Emile Durkheim, *The Elementary Forms of Religious Life* (New York: Free Press, 1965).

13. Peter H. Van Ness, *Spirituality, Diversion, and Decadence: The Contemporary Predicament* (Albany: State University of New York Press, 1992), 12.

14. Ibid., 13.

15. Gustavo Gutiérrez, *Las Casas: In Search of the Poor of Jesus Christ,* trans. Robert R. Barr (Maryknoll, N.Y.: Orbis, 1993), 96.

16. John J. Macionis, *Sociology,* 5th ed. (Englewood Cliffs, N.J.: Prentice-Hall, 1995), 488.

17. Suzanne K. Langer, *Philosophy in a New Key,* 3d ed. (Cambridge, Mass.: Harvard University Press, 1957), 153.

18. Arnold B. Come, *Human Spirit and Holy Spirit* (Philadelphia: Temple University Press, 1959), 17.

19. Walter Lippmann, *A Preface to Morals* (Boston: Beacon, 1960), 327–28.

20. Martin E. Marty, "The Spirit's Holy Errand: The Search for a Spiritual Style in Secular America," *Daedalus* 96:1 (winter 1967): 109.

21. Pablo Richard, "Treatise on Politics," in *Spirituality of the Third World: A Cry for Life,* ed. K. C. Abraham and Bernadette Mbuy-Beya (Maryknoll, N.Y.: Orbis, 1994), 105.

22. Ibid.

23. Ada María Isasi-Díaz, *En la lucha/In the Struggle: A Hispanic Women's Liberation Theology* (Minneapolis: Fortress, 1993), 170.

24. James H. Cone, *A Black Theology of Liberation,* 3d ed. (Maryknoll, N.Y.: Orbis, 1995). While participating in a panel with four other women and myself, Satako Yamaguchi used the term *women of colors* rather than *women of color* in order to "make [the] diversity visible." This occurred in a session entitled "The Impact of National Histories on the Women in Religion" at the 1994 meeting of the American Academy of Religion in Chicago. *The dispossessed* is a term borrowed from Jacqueline Jones's *The Dispossessed: America's Underclasses from the Civil War to the Present* (New York:: Basic Books, 1992).

25. Deloria Vine, *God Is Red,* 2d ed. (Golden, Colo.: Fulcrum, 1993).

26. Lee H. Yearly, *New Religious Virtues and the Study of Religion: The University Lecture in Religion 1994* (Tucson: Arizona State University, Department of Religious Studies, 1994), 15 (lecture delivered on 10 February).

27. Ibid., 12.

28. Peter W. Williams, *American Religion: Traditions and Cultures* (New York: Macmillan, 1990), 417.

29. Marty, "The Spirit's Holy Errand," 111.

30. Robert Redfield, *The Little Community and Peasant Society* (Chicago: University of Chicago Press, 1960), 430.

31. Baby boomers are people born between 1946 to 1965. See Roof, *Generation of Seekers;* and Steven M. Tipton, *Getting Saved from the Sixties: Moral Meaning in Convention and Cultural Change* (Berkeley: University of California Press, 1982).

32. Roof, *Generation of Seekers,* 243.

33. Tipton, *Getting Saved,* 27.

34. Ada María Isasi-Díaz and Yolanda Tarango, *Hispanic Women: Prophetic Voice in the Church* (San Francisco: Harper and Row, 1988), 68.

35. Ronald Delattre, "Supply-Side Spirituality: A Case Study in the Cultural Interpretation of Religious Ethics in America," in *Religion and the Life of the Nation: American Recoveries,* ed. Rowland A. Sherrill (Champaign: University of Illinois Press, 1990), 87.

36. Quoted by Delattre from Ralph Waldo Emerson's "Wealth," in *Selected Writings,* ed. Brooks Atkinson (New York: Modern Library, 1990), 140.

37. Delattre, "Supply-Side Spirituality," 93.

38. Ibid., 98

39. Benjamin Disraeli, cited in Edward W. Said, *Orientalism* (New York: Vintage Books, 1979), 5.

40. Said claims that "Orient" and "Orientalism" are "man-made" and are ideas that "have a history and a tradition of thought, imagery, and vocabulary that have given [them] reality and presence in and for the West" (Said, *Orientalism,* 3).

41. bell hooks, *Black Looks: Race and Representation* (Boston: South End, 1992), 39.

42. Ibid., 29.

43. Gertrude Stein, *Everybody's Autobiography* (New York: Cooper Square, 1971), 190.

44. For an excellent study addressing the issues of searching for a woman-centered spirituality and of blending the East and the West, see Linda Watt, "'Can Women Have Wishes?': Gender and Spiritual Narrative in Gertrude Stein's *Lend a Hand or Four Religions,*" *Journal of Feminist Studies in Religion* 10:2 (fall 1994): 49–72.

45. Said, *Orientalism,* 238.

46. Demerath, "The Moth and the Flame," 108.

47. Ibid., 109.

48. Charles S. Prebish, "Asian-American and Euro-American Buddhism: An Increasingly Unfriendly Partnership" (paper presented at the 1994 meetings of the American Academy of Religion, Chicago, 1994), 2. See also Robert S. Michaelson, *The American Search for Soul* (Baton Rouge: Louisiana State University Press, 1975).

49. Allen E. Richardson, *East Comes West: Asian Religions and Cultures in North America* (Cleveland: Pilgrim, 1985), 65, 4, and 151.

Bibliography

Abraham, K. C., and Bernadette Mbuy-Beya, eds. *Spirituality of the Third World: A Cry for Life.* Maryknoll, N.Y.: Orbis, 1994.

Delattre, Ronald A. "Supply-Side Spirituality: A Case Study in the Cultural Interpretation of Religious Ethics in America." In *Religion and the Life of the Nation: American Recoveries,* edited by Rowland A. Sherrill. Champaign: University of Illinois Press, 1990.

Demerath, N. J., III. "The Moth and the Flame: Religion and Power in Contemporative Blur." *Sociology of Religion* 55:2 (summer 1994).

Fingarette, Herbert. *Confucius — the Secular as Sacred.* New York: Harper and Row, 1972.

Marty, Martin E. "The Spirit's Holy Errand: The Search for a Spiritual Style in Secular America." *Daedalus* 96:1 (winter 1967).

Roof, Wade Clark. *A Generation of Seekers: The Spiritual Journeys of the Baby Boom Generation.* New York: HarperCollins, 1993.

Said, Edward W. *Orientalism.* New York: Vintage Books, 1979.

Tipton, Steven M. *Getting Saved from the Sixties: Moral Meaning in Conversion and Cultural Change.* Berkeley: University of California Press, 1982.

Van Ness, Peter H. *Spirituality, Diversion, and Decadence: The Contemporary Predicament.* Albany: State University of New York Press, 1992.

Watts, Linda. "'Can Women Have Wishes?': Gender and Spiritual Narrative in Gertrude Stein's *Lend a Hand or Four Religions.*" *Journal of Feminist Studies in Religion* 10:2 (fall 1994).

Yearly, Lee H. *New Religious Virtues and the Study of Religion: The University Lecture in Religion 1994.* Tucson: Arizona State University, Department of Religious Studies, 1994. Lecture delivered 10 February.

B. Beginnings of Secular Spirituality

3

The European Enlightenment

Mark I. Wallace

Religious Liberalism in the Age of Reason

The European Enlightenment is one of the many historic sources for the varieties of secular spirituality practiced today. Sometimes referred to as the Age of Reason or the Cult of Reason, the Enlightenment promoted a program of new thinking centered on the belief that humankind should be freed to exercise its own reason unfettered by the shackles of religious superstition and political tyranny. "*Sapere Aude!* Have the courage to use your own intelligence! is therefore the motto of the enlightenment."[1] Liberated from the yoke of traditional authority, the enlightened person will be empowered to pursue his or her own moral and rational interests. The new thinking of the Enlightenment has paved the way for our own cultural evolution toward forms of nonsectarian spirituality that promote personal and social transformation. Of course, the Enlightenment was not the only precursor to this development. Other Western traditions have also fed the springs of the contemporary zeitgeist: the classical stress on individual self-cultivation and the ethics of virtue in Greek and Roman philosophy; the valorization of moral idealism and reasoned faith during the Christian era; the promotion of political tolerance and critical thought within Renaissance and late medieval humanism; and the turn to interior experience as a valid source of knowledge within the romantic movement. While these other antecedent traditions have been critically formative of our own time, the Enlightenment is arguably the most important movement in developing the *secular* and *ecumenical* cast of many contemporary spiritual beliefs and practices. The Enlightenment model of toleration and broad-mindedness in matters religious is the primary fountainhead for the diversities of religious liberalism and political pluralism that define important dimensions of late twentieth-century existence.

It is convenient to date the Enlightenment to the period that begins with the Glorious Revolution in Britain (1688) and ends with the French Revolution (1789).[2] Roughly speaking, this marks the time-span of the eighteenth century, an era when relative political stability in Europe helped make possible the pioneering reevaluation of church and society by academics and men and women of letters within the salons and coffeehouses of Europe. The eighteenth century was the era of the *philosophes* and *Aufklärer* — cosmopolitan pundits and intellectuals who used their wit and erudition to promote a new cultural vision that was alternately irreverent and traditional, modern and classical, irenic and polemical, self-critical and dogmatic. In this essay I will examine the new Enlightenment sensibility forged by the *philosophes* and others within the high culture of European intellectual life.[3] I will analyze the basic presuppositions concerning reason, religion, and morality that defined the Enlightenment worldview and conclude with a critical appraisal as to the promise of eighteenth-century thought for our own time.

Philosophical Precursors

René Descartes

The values and ideals of the Enlightenment had their origin in the groundbreaking philosophical innovations of the seventeenth century. In particular, the writings of René Descartes (1596–1650) and John Locke (1632–1704) set the tone for the celebration of reason and the promotion of religious tolerance that defined the work of later Enlightenment thinkers. Descartes's philosophical aim was to establish the certainty of claims in metaphysics and science through a method of radical doubt. In his *Meditations on First Philosophy*, Descartes begins his inquiry by subjecting his most privileged beliefs to systematic doubt in order to establish which beliefs appear dubitable and which appear rationally self-evident. "I will cast aside anything that admits of the slightest doubt, . . . and I will continue always in this track until I shall find something that is certain."[4] The criterion of truth is the clearness and distinctness of ideas that appear incorrigibly certain even in the face of radical doubt. Using the procedure of methodic doubt, Descartes seeks a rational footing for beliefs concerning the existence of God, the reliability of the external world, and the certainty of mathematics.

Descartes's legacy to Enlightenment thinkers such as Voltaire, Jean-

Jacques Rousseau, David Hume, Immanuel Kant, and others is the triumph of autonomous, procedural reason over the authority of the church in establishing the foundations of all knowledge, religious or otherwise. At first glance, it might seem that the Cartesian legacy would lead to the undermining of religious faith insofar as all beliefs must now appear before the bar of reason and be judged on the basis of their innate clarity and distinctness. Yet this is not the case. Descartes's thought does not mark the waning of faith but a paradigm shift in the canons of evidence for faith. After Descartes, it is not enough for faith to have the backing of revelation, miracles, and church authority; rather, faith must now accord with the deliverances of everyday reason and experience or be judged cognitively vacuous. It is the *critical spirit* of Descartes's philosophy — the systematic subjection of all belief to the tribunal of pure, disinterested reason — that becomes the bellwether of the modern age. In defining the spirit of his own time, Kant would later recall the method of Cartesian doubt by labeling the late eighteenth century as the "age of criticism, and to criticism must everything submit. Religion through its sanctity, and law-giving through its majesty, may seek to exempt themselves from it. But they then awaken just suspicion, and cannot claim the sincere respect which reason accords only to that which has been able to sustain the test of free and open examination."[5] Cartesianism gave later European intellectuals the rationale, if not always the tools, for excavating the rational foundations of belief and casting aside, no matter how sacrosanct, whatever could not be critically justified in the process.

John Locke

Locke's influence on the Enlightenment was equal to Descartes's, but for different reasons. He also sought to build a rational base for the edifice of knowledge, but his critique of the foundations of knowledge proposed by other philosophers was more radical and disturbing to traditional assumptions than was Descartes's. At the beginning of his *Essay concerning Human Understanding*, Locke rejects the Cartesian theory of innate ideas and proceeds to argue that all knowledge has its origin in experience. The mind is a tabula rasa that passively receives the bounty of sense impressions that make up experience. The primary source of knowledge is sensible experience of external objects, though Locke maintains that certain mental operations such as perceiving, judging, doubting, and willing can also acquire reliable knowledge. Thus all knowledge is generated by our faculties of either sensation or reflection, that is, the capacity to receive sense impressions, on the one hand, and the capacity to organize and reflect upon the body of ideas that originates in sense experience, on the other.

Locke's thesis that experience, and primarily sense experience, is the source of reliable knowledge is referred to as the beginning of empiricism or sensationalism in Western thought. For Locke, empiricism means that much of what passes for knowledge in common coinage — including many time-honored statements of faith and supernatural beliefs — cannot be called knowledge because such statements and beliefs signify realities far beyond the bounds of sense experience. (We will later see the critical importance of the Lockean notion of boundaries in Kant's attempt to limit knowledge within the bounds of sense.) As with Descartes, then, it may initially appear that Locke's project is hostile to religion just insofar as it casts doubt on the credibility of beliefs that are not available to sensible experience. In fact, however, his argument presses to the conclusion that certain knowledge of God is possible on the basis of rational introspection. Although we have no direct sense experience of God, it is self-evidentially obvious that every being must have its beginning in an original being, God, who generated all beings from eternity. Locke avers that this proposition, while not an innate idea, is intuitively certain and has the force of a mathematical axiom. "[Humankind] knows also that nothing cannot produce a being; therefore something must have existed from eternity. In the next place, man knows, by an intuitive certainty, that bare nothing can no more produce any real being, than it can be equal to two right angles."[6]

Locke's argument that knowledge of the existence of God possesses the same introspective certainty as self-evidential propositions in geometry is less than persuasive, especially given his signal insistence on the primacy of sense experience as the basis of knowledge. Paradoxically, Locke maintains that the claim "God exists" has the status of "intuitive certainty" even though it has no basis in sensible experience. Locke's ascription of incorrigible certainty to the theological claim that there is a God locates such claims very close to the Cartesian realm of innate ideas, his tabula rasa epistemology notwithstanding. Although Locke was confident of the rationality of belief in God, he was dismissive of other theological claims to truth that could not be demonstrated on the basis of either sensation or reflection. He drew a sharp distinction between faith and reason and insisted that "nothing that is contrary to, and inconsistent with, the clear and self-evident dictates of reason, has a right to be urged and assented to as a matter of faith, wherein reason hath nothing to do."[7] Theological propositions that contradict reason are not worthy of belief, even if the churches insist upon their trustworthiness. As were the later eighteenth-century thinkers he inspired, Locke is openly contemptuous of the fanciful assertions and irrational speculations of his scholastic predecessors and many of the clerical theologians of his own era. He inveighs against dogmatic enthusiasts who "have let loose their fancies and natural superstition; and have by them [been] led into so strange opinions, and extravagant practices in religion, that a considerate man cannot but stand amazed at their follies."[8] The exercise of faith for Locke must be disciplined by common sense and a healthy skepticism toward the excesses of religious emotionalism, ritual extravagance, and theological dogmatism.

Locke writes in the aftermath of the destruction wrought by the Thirty Years' War (1618–48) and similar internecine religio-political conflicts in Europe. As a result, he argues for the exercise of toleration in all matters of conscience in order to prevent the forcible imposition of religious uniformity and the suppression of religious dissent. Religious belief is largely a private matter, and the church should be reconceived as a non–state-supported voluntary organization. Neither the church nor the state should use the external authority of the civil magistrate to violate an individual's rights to life and liberty on the basis of his or her personal beliefs. In his famous "Letter concerning Toleration" of 1689, written during the same year as the English Toleration Act in which Protestant dissenters gained the right to exercise freely their religion, Locke writes that "no one should be compelled to the belief of anything by outward force" because "religion consists in the inward and full persuasion of the mind."[9]

The contribution of Locke's philosophy to the development of the Enlightenment is enormous. Like Descartes, he is a staunch defender of the powers of unaided reason to secure reliable knowledge of the world and a dependable, if truncated, body of beliefs concerning things of the spirit. His turn to the testimony of the senses as the basis of knowledge was appropriated and radicalized by other British empiricist philosophers such as George Berkeley and David Hume and became the basis of Kant's critical realism. His disdain for superstition and mystery-mongering paved the way for the rise of the theological liberalism and anticlericalism of the *philosophes.* Furthermore, his championing of commonsense reason in all things, including matters of faith, made possible the popularity of deism in particular, and religious freethinking in general, later in the eighteenth century.

Moreover, Locke's conception of religion as a private and inward activity anticipates the contemporary, nonsectarian understanding of religion as a disciplined journey toward authentic selfhood that is "spiritual" (self-actualizing) if not always "religious" (institutionally based) in orientation. As discussed by Peter Van Ness in the introduction to this volume, many of the newer forms of "secular spirituality" that have emerged in Western culture since the Enlightenment understand religion less in terms of institutional affiliation or propositional beliefs and more in terms of an interior activity that seeks to realize the "true self" of the practitioner. Locke's opposition to religious dogmatism and political totalitarianism is the antecedent of the current quest for spiritual renewal through activities that emphasize personal fulfillment and social responsibility.

The Autonomy of Reason

It has been said that the modern era signals a sea change in the notion of reason within Western thought. Prior to Descartes it was assumed by philosophers that reason gives each person direct access to the visible world of objects and the invisible world of God or Mind. Reason, often referred to as the "agent intellect" by Neoplatonic and medieval thinkers, is like a lamp that is illuminated by the active intellect of God in order to render transparent all reality. Because reason always-already participates in the divine intellect, it is a reliable source of knowledge concerning the nature of the physical world and the proper ends of humankind. We have seen that while Descartes submits this and every other presumption to methodic doubt, he nevertheless returns to the classical model by seeking to demonstrate that we are hardwired, so to speak, with certain inalienable truths the denial of which is intuitively self-contradictory. With Locke's epistemology, however, we enter a new universe of discourse: in spite of Locke's residual conviction about the necessity of God's existence, all claims to truth must now pass the test of empirical demonstration. The Lockean movement gains steam in the eighteenth century and has led many commentators on this period to argue that the Enlightenment drives a permanent wedge between classical, Platonic, "participatory" reason and modern, empiricist, "autonomous" reason.

Both Ernst Cassirer and Peter Gay in their celebrated studies of the Enlightenment argue that the *philosophes'* idea of reason had broken its moorings from the Platonic and Christian notion of reason as participation in the divine Mind. Gay reads the Enlightenment philosophers as embodying a distinctive "*modern* paganism, emancipated from classical thought as much as from Christian dogma."[10] Cassirer writes:

> In the great metaphysical systems of [the seventeenth] century — those of Descartes and Malebranche, of Spinoza and Leibniz — reason is the realm of "eternal verities," of those truths held in common by the human and divine mind.... Every act of reason means participation in the divine nature; it gives access to the intelligible world. The eighteenth century takes reason in a different and more modest sense. It is no longer the sum total of "innate ideas...." Reason is now looked upon

> rather as an acquisition than as a heritage.... It is rather the original intellectual force which guides the discovery and determination of truth.... It dissolves everything merely factual, all simple data of experience, and everything believed on the evidence of revelation, tradition, and authority.[11]

Nevertheless, while this interpretation of the Enlightenment model of experience-based reason is generally sound, in fact the eighteenth-century model has more to do with Neoplatonic participation than might appear at first glance.[12] Notably in the work of the English and American deists, reason has both a *critical* function in adjudicating the evidence of the senses and a *constructive* role in providing a credible foundation for religious belief and moral judgment.

John Toland

In the first half of the eighteenth century, the movement toward a purely rational and ethical religion was furthered by the English deists. Inspired by the Lockean notion that belief incompatible with reason is vacuous, the deists argued that Christianity should be reconceived as a natural religion purified from the many superstitious and doctrinal accretions that have obscured its purely rational essence. Human beings have a natural tendency to discern the truth about God and virtue since they are not inherently depraved and prone to error. The evidence for God in creation is available to the light of natural reason, and the sense of one's duty to others is entailed by the knowledge of God's presence in the world. Using their own natural reason, enlightened persons should come to belief in God and the nature of their moral obligations on the basis of the inherent rationality of such claims — not on the basis of supernatural revelation, church authority, or the evidence of miracles. The enemy of true religion is priestcraft and ritual extremism; the only reliable measure of a religion's worth is the rational coherence of its ethical teachings.

John Toland (1670–1722) wrote his *Christianity Not Mysterious* in order to demonstrate that the gospel message was in perfect harmony with empirical reason. A student of Lockean sensationalism and a thoroughgoing Protestant, Toland writes that the various sectarian doctrines and mysteries of institutional Christianity contradict the reliable evidence of our senses. The Roman Catholic doctrines of transubstantiation (the eucharistic elements of bread and wine are wholly transformed in their inner substance, but not appearance, into the body and blood of Christ) and the virgin birth of Christ (Jesus was conceived miraculously without the agency of a human father) are mythological additions to pure religion that fail the test of rational scrutiny. Toland calls for a ritually purified and intellectually simplified faith in God, divine providence, and the moral efficacy of the Scriptures. He levels special invective against the "Riches, Pomp, and Dignities of the *Clergy*" who seek political control of the church masses through ritual and ceremony that blunt the simplicity and reasonableness of ethical Christianity.[13]

Matthew Tindal

Similar to Toland's rational piety is the work of Matthew Tindal (1656–1733). Tindal wrote *Christianity as Old as Creation* in the full blush of the success of deistic thinking in the early eighteenth century. Tindal's work articulates the main tenets of rational religion at a time when the savants of the Enlightenment agreed that Newton had unlocked the ordered mysteries of the universe. In the famous words of Alexander Pope, "Nature and Nature's Laws lay hid in Night; / God said, Let Newton be! and all was Light." Under the sway of Newtonian mechanics, eighteenth-century thinkers maintained that it is obvious that all of nature, as a law-governed and machinelike realm of harmony and order, is under the wise and benevolent governance of an almighty power. Nature is an open book waiting to be read by any rational inquirer; its elegance, design, and uniformity are obvious to anyone willing to trace the providential hand of God within the intricate orderliness of the natural world. In this clocklike universe unclouded by ambiguity and mystery, God is understood as the supreme ground of natural law and moral reason.

For Tindal, unaided reason finds God's handiwork both within humankind's moral and rational endowments and throughout the perfect order of the universe. He labels this twofold awareness "natural religion":

> By "Natural Religion," I understand the Belief of the Existence of a God, and the Sense and Practice of those Duties which result from the Knowledge we, by our Reason, have of him and his perfections; and of ourselves, and our own Imperfections; and of the relation we stand into him and our Fellow-Creatures.... I suppose you will allow that it is evident by the Light of Nature, that there is a God; or in other words, a Being absolutely perfect, and infinitely happy in himself, who is the Source of all other Beings; and that what Perfections soever the Creature have, they are wholly derived from him.[14]

As we saw with Toland, reason is charged with a natural light that enables it to understand nature's intricate perfection. This natural light also has a moral or practical dimension. The awareness of God's providential oversight of creation is coterminous with the moral knowledge concerning humankind's proper duties and responsibilities. God is an all-wise and all-good being who endows his subjects with a natural capacity to pursue their own best interests in relation to the welfare of others. "It unavoidably follows, nothing can be a part of the divine Law, but what tends to promote the common Interest, and mutual Happiness of his rational Creatures; and every thing that does so, must be a part of it."[15] By following the light of natural reason and regulating our passions and appetites, we discover happiness and well-being in obeying God's laws, which are nature's laws as well.

In the deistic equation, reason and nature are one. According to classical Christian doctrine, natural reason, reason unaided by the knowledge supplied by revelation, is "fallen" because it suffers the corrupting effects of original sin. Without the infusion of supernatural grace, human nature remains captive to its baser instincts and cannot arrive at a saving knowledge of the truth. For Tindal and the other deists, though, reason in its natural state is always-already perfectly transparent upon the truth concerning the existence and character of God and the nature of our ethical duties. Human beings are primordially good not evil: for the deists, the doctrine of the fall of humankind from an original state of grace due to the sin of Adam and Eve is theological nonsense. Moreover, such an idea strips persons of responsibility for their own actions by requiring them to rely on divine intervention for guiding and shaping their lives. God has naturally equipped humankind to live a rational and law-governed existence, and it is our responsibility to realize this natural capacity for good — to realize that we are bearers of God's image through the exercise of sound reason and moral judgment.

The American Federalists and Thomas Jefferson

Although the philosophical influence of deism in England and Europe waned by the mid–eighteenth century, the practical legacy of the movement continued in America beyond the debates it had spawned across the Atlantic. In the fledgling democratic vision of the American colonists, secessionist thinkers like Thomas Jefferson, Benjamin Franklin, and Thomas Paine looked to the writings of the deists as a source for their own programs featuring religious liberty and political change. Paine's pamphleteering on behalf of the Americans' revolutionary struggle is well known. He announces in *The Age of Reason* that "my own mind is my own church."[16] His declarations that true religion consists in the nonsectarian and noncompulsory reverence for the universal God of creation and that all doctrines and creeds must be tested on the basis of their inherent moral value are leitmotifs of Enlightenment spirituality that helped to forge the religious and political sensibilities of the American colonists on the eve of revolution.

Thomas Jefferson (1743–1826) shares in this milieu. He writes as an advocate of religious liberty and representational government; indeed, the distinctly American idea of the separation of church and state has its origin in the Jeffersonian and deistic values of political representation and religious toleration.[17] In the opening of the Declaration of Independence, Jefferson writes that the "laws of nature and nature's God" teach particular "truths to be self-evident" concerning "certain unalienable rights."[18] In the charter documents of the new republic, the God of biblical revelation is deftly supplanted by "nature's God," which to Jefferson stands for the cosmic lawgiver who guarantees a common moral inheritance for all people. "Nature's God" is the deistic architect-creator of the universe rather than the historical, interventionist God of establishment Judaism and Christianity; as a result, it is now the duty of the common citizenry burdened by political tyranny to take matters in its own hands and throw off governments that abuse the body politic. In ancient times God could be trusted to deliver women and men from injustice, but now it is the task of every person endowed with God-given and inalienable rights to pursue freedom and abolish oppression.

After crafting the American revolutionary documents, Jefferson turns to pruning back the Gospel texts to what he deems to be their essential moral essence and publishes his edited version of the New Testament as two volumes entitled *The Philosophy of Jesus* and *The Life and Morals of Jesus.*[19] Love of God and neighbor are the heart of the Christian Scriptures; reports of miracles and threats of damnation for the unrepentant are later editorial additions to the Gospels that do not reflect the original words of Jesus. Jefferson's moral hermeneutic of the Bible is governed by his convictions concerning rational religion. True religion promotes freedom of inquiry and the integrity of conscience: whenever a sacred text, including the biblical text, violates what our reason self-evidentially knows to be true and good, then reason is to be trusted over the authority of the Scriptures.

Deism lost its appeal as a philosophical option later in the eighteenth century, but as an ideological movement against the authority of church and state to stifle the free exercise of reason and common sense it was enormously influential. At the dawn of the nineteenth century, the deistic appeals to "pure reason" and "natural religion" seemed naive and overly optimistic to its critics on both the left and right sides of the theological spectrum; but the deistic legacy of religious toleration and political emancipation — both during the time of the Enlightenment and into our own era — has had, and continues to have, enormous repercussions. As deistic ideas crossed the Atlantic and took root in foreign soil, they particularly came to fruition in the disestablishment of state churches within the United States — and in the American polemic against centralized government, clerical domination, and the suppression of political dissent. Anglo-American deism is one of the precursors to the contemporary emphasis on the rights of free individuals to employ their rational faculties, in whatever way they deem appropriate, in order to craft an authentic and coherent worldview. Today, different forms of secular spirituality continue to privilege the value of critical thinking with respect to the role of religious tradition in the journey toward self-transformation.

In England, Germany, and America, the deists we have studied in this section provide a conflicted model of reason. In some sense these representative thinkers are advocates for nonparticipatory reason — reason exercised under the tutelage of the senses and freed from intolerance and superstition. Together they call for purifying reason of its underpinnings in tradition and authority in an effort to realize its purely natural and moral basis. Even so the philosophers of the Enlightenment did not completely shake off the epistemological assumptions of their classical and medieval forebears. Although reason was no longer a royal road to many of the theological certitudes of the past, it still bore residual traces to is provenance in Greek and later Christian thought. In the deist and American federalist writers, reason is the tribunal of truth that pronounces judgment against all forms of intolerance and superstition. At the same time, reason is understood as being connected to powers greater than ourselves by virtue of its instinctive awareness of the reality of God, the order of the cosmos, and the principles of the good life. In spite of their general allegiance to Lockean empiricism, most Enlightenment thinkers see reason as a broad and generous power for intuiting innate and universal truths that spell out the proper ends of humankind in relation to government, ethics, and religion.[20]

The Question of God

As the Enlightenment is often known for its turn to autonomous reason, it is also regarded as the seedbed of modern atheism; yet just as many eighteenth-century thinkers were only partially removed from the classical idea of participatory reason, so also were most of the *philosophes* generally unwilling to renounce belief in God entirely. The Enlightenment is regarded, and rightly so, as a time of extraordinary latitude in matters religious, a time when men and women of letters openly declared their disgust with clericalism and wore their impiety as a badge signaling their emancipation from the past. Most early modern and modern philosophers, however, possessed at least a vestigial belief in divinity (although a belief often very far removed from Christian orthodoxy). As Carl Becker writes in his study of the Enlightenment:

> If we examine the foundations of their faith, we find that at every turn the *Philosophes* betray their debt to medieval thought without being aware of it. They denounced Christian philosophy, but rather too much, after the manner of those who are but half emancipated from the "superstitions" they scorn. They had put off the fear of God, but maintained a respectful attitude toward the Deity. They ridiculed the idea that the universe had been created in six days, but still believed it to be a beautifully articulated machine designed by the Supreme Being according to a rational plan as an abiding place for mankind.[21]

Although a few important Parisian thinkers were self-avowed atheists — Paul Henri Holbach, Claude Helvétius, and the later Denis Diderot — the general tenor of the Enlightenment, including the second half of the eighteenth century, was not inimical to nonsectarian belief in a deity per se. Rather, as the century wore on it became a time of mounting hostility to most established religious doctrines and institutions, even though some quarter was given to the integrity of a demythologized belief in God that could be pressed into the service of explaining the putative order of the universe. A study of the work of two of the best-known skeptics of this period — Voltaire and Hume — is highly illustrative of the religious temperament of the time within the circles of the *philosophes* and other European intellectuals.

Voltaire

Voltaire (François-Marie Arouet, 1694–1778) was the best known and most celebrated philosophe of the eighteenth century. His famous battle cry against institutional Christianity, "Écrasez l'infâme!" (Crush the infamous thing!), underscores his repulsion toward the hypocrisy and immorality of priestly religion. Voltaire's diatribes against clericalism and superstition stem, however, not from his abandonment of religious faith but from his conviction that what he calls "natural religion" — namely, religion rationally purified of its mythological and immoral supplements — has been compromised by the dogmatism and stupidity of the church hierarchy.

Voltaire's militant spirituality is fundamentally deist. Like Toland and Tindal, he professes belief in an eminently rational and law-governed deity. Such a God does not directly intervene in human affairs but rather guarantees the harmony and design of the universe much like a clock maker ensures the mechanical precision and working order of timepieces through skilled craftsmanship. "I believe in God," writes Voltaire, "not the God of the mystics and theologians, but the God of nature, the great geometrician, the architect of the universe, the prime mover, unalterable, transcendental, everlasting."[22] While Voltaire considers uncompromising atheism to be at odds with his moderated theism, the real enemies of faith are the institutional protectors of ecclesiastical truth based on the Bible and church tradition. For Voltaire and his ilk, "The Church was part of the problem, part of the disease which was infecting any knowledge of god, not part of the solution. The Churches were the soil of atheism."[23] Indeed, Voltaire attempts an "end run" around the flank of establishment religion by arguing that it is he, the celebrated critic, who has a better understanding of true religion than do the guardians of theological orthodoxy! The true blasphemers and desecrators of religion are the theologians and priests who promulgate the monstrous doctrines of transubstantiation and the virgin birth, trade in the remission of sins through selling indulgences, encourage the veneration of artifacts and the practice of exorcism, and mandate obedience to the teachings of the Bible in spite of its horrific barbarism and immorality. Paradoxically, it is organized religion, not skepticism and nonconformity, that provides the fertile ground for apostasy and disbelief.

True to the climate of opinion in his time, Voltaire believed the Bible to be a mishmash of reasoned opinions on matters of faith and practice and a deplorable collection of uncivilized and corrupt teachings and stories. In his *Sermon of the Fifty,* he directs a deistic polemic against the uncritical use of the Scriptures for promoting religious and ethical formation.[24] He is adamant (some might say shrill) in his conviction that the Bible perverts true religion by inculcating among the masses the horrific values of sectarianism, cruelty, war, rebellion, adultery, rape, and injustice. Voltaire deploys a moral hermeneutic of the Bible similar to the method Jefferson employs in his edited versions of the New Testament. For both thinkers the Bible is soaked in blood and violence, burdened with impossible prophecies and miracle stories, and littered with irrational and unethical teachings that are an assault upon common reason and morality. Voltaire concludes the *Sermon* with a prayer expressing his desire for a demystified and universal religion freed from the vulgar beliefs about Jesus proclaimed by sectarian Christianity:

> May this great God who listens to me; this God who surely cannot have been born of a girl, nor died on the gibbet, nor be eaten in a piece of dough, nor have inspired these books, filled with contradictions, madness, and horror; may this God, creator of all the worlds, have pity on that sect of Christians that blasphemes him! May

he lead them back to the holy and natural religion, and spread his blessings over our efforts to have him truly worshipped. *Amen.*[25]

David Hume

Hume is best known for continuing and extending Locke's sensationalism and for articulating the most consistent empiricist philosophy in the West until the rise of logical positivism in Anglo-American analytic circles in the early twentieth century. Unlike Kant, who crafts his own distinctive combination and transformation of rationalist and empiricist themes, Hume jettisons rationalism entirely in favor of a philosophical orientation grounded in sense experience and opposed to all forms of metaphysics. "All of the objects of human reason or enquiry may naturally be divided into two kinds, to wit, *Relations of Ideas,* and *Matters of Fact.*"[26] By the former Hume means propositions in math and geometry that cannot be denied without contradiction; by the latter he intends the variegated sense experiences that make up the common storehouse of our everyday knowledge.

To this point, Hume is reminiscent of Locke, but here the similarities end. Whereas Locke, in spite of his phenomenalist epistemology, clings to certain quasi-innate ideas such as the certainty of God on the basis of universal causality, Hume rejects all such assertions, including Locke's cosmological proof for the existence of God, as stating neither a relation of ideas nor a matter of fact. The Lockean argument that my existence as a contingent being presupposes the existence of an absolutely necessary being greater than myself is a speculative supposition devoid of rational (that is, empirical) credentials. The presumption that contingent existence entails necessary existence is not on the order of a mathematical axiom (relation of ideas) nor based on sensible experience (matter of fact). Hume reads Locke as a halfhearted attempt to develop a comprehensive empirical model of reason still wedded to residual beliefs (such as the belief in God) that cannot be founded on experience.

What makes Hume particularly interesting for the development of nonsectarian spirituality, however, is not simply his negative assessment of traditional justifications for the existence of God but his constructive argument for the rationality of an "ambiguous faith," to paraphrase Hume's position. Hume's case for an ambiguous faith — a humane and purposefully vague form of quasi-religious belief consistent with empirical principles — is developed in his *Dialogues concerning Natural Religion.* Hume's *Dialogues* are modeled after Cicero's *De natura deorum,* and like Cicero's text they take up the question of the nature of God while presupposing, in a broad sense, the existence of the deity. The *Dialogues* consist of three conversation-partners: Demea, a religious rationalist; Cleanthes, a moderate theist; and Philo, a thoroughgoing skeptic. Much of the argument turns on Philo's rebuttal of the argument from design, namely, that the supposed purpose and order of the universe presuppose the necessary existence of an intelligent and benevolent master designer. Philo convincingly maintains that the evidence for design in the world is contradicted by the fact of massive global suffering. The prevalence of evil in the cosmos counts against the traditional belief that God is all-wise and all-good, for if God truly possesses these attributes, why would God then allow the widespread and undeserved suffering and misery that characterize our lives? Philo puts this question to Cleanthes in an oft-quoted restatement of the problem of evil: "Is [God] willing to prevent evil, but not able? then is he impotent. Is he able, but not willing? then is he malevolent. Is he both able and willing? whence then is evil?"[27] Philo then continues that even if we grant the existence of God, we are driven to infer that this God is not unreservedly omnipotent and benevolent on the basis of analogy to the global evil and chaos that define human existence. The inference from commonsense experience leads to the twofold conclusion either that there is *no* God or that there *may* be a God — but a God who is limited, perhaps even malevolent, because this God either cannot or will not correct the faults and ruptures built into the created order itself.

Many of Hume's interpreters conclude that Philo is Hume's mouthpiece and that Philo's/Hume's refutations of the argument from design effectively empties religion of any moral authority or rational content. "For Hume religion has lost all specificity and all authority; it is not more than a dim, meaningless, and unwelcome shadow on the face of reason."[28] The initial problem with this interpretation is that it cannot account for the final words of the text where Pamphilus, the narrator of the dispute who may or may not represent Hume's parting thoughts, states that "upon a serious review of the whole, I cannot but think that Philo's principles are more probable than Demea's, but that those of Cleanthes approach still nearer to the truth."[29] More importantly, the larger problem with the stock interpretation is that it obviates a profound and positive religious sensibility in the *Dialogues* and, indeed, a sensibility that iterates the freethinking spirituality of the Enlightenment in general (as well as an important dimension to contemporary progressive religious life). At the end of the *Dialogues*, Philo concludes that the core affirmation of natural theology — the belief in something like cosmic order and reason — is worthy of cautious rational assent:

> If the whole of natural theology, as some people seem to maintain, resolves itself into one simple, though somewhat ambiguous, at least undefined, proposition, *That the cause or causes of order in the universe probably bear some remote analogy to human intelligence,*... if this really be the case, what can the most inquisitive, contemplative, and religious man do more than give a plain, philosophical assent to the proposition, as often as it occurs, and believe that the arguments on which it is established exceed the objections which lie against it?[30]

Here, in germ, is what appears to be Hume's ambiguous faith stated as a belief in the probability that the origin (or originator) of the universe bears some traces of intelligence analogous to human reason. It is likely, says Hume, though never incorrigibly certain in the manner of Descartes or even Kant, that the physical order of the universe is somewhat akin to the nature of human reason. Beyond this limited statement of probability, however, Hume is not prepared to go. Stripped of metaphysical and even moral content, Hume's position encourages an attitude of vagueness, ambiguity, and humble openness toward the mystery and order within the universe. After his robust dismantling of orthodox theology in the persons of Cleanthes and Philo, Hume concludes the *Dialogues* with an admirable probity about what can and cannot be said about God in the wake of the death of speculative metaphysics. Hume's probability argument for cosmic order articulates a broad-minded theological sensibility that has deep affinities with a variety of secular spiritualities, as well as with the thoughtful theism embodied in the Society of Friends, Unitarianism, progressive black churches, and liberal Protestant, Catholic, and Jewish congregations in general. Hume's tentative, ambiguous faith stands on the threshold of the modern era and portends the rise of both secularism and religious pluralism within Western culture.

The Primacy of Morality

A commonplace assumption in the Enlightenment is that the proper mode of religious expression is the virtuous life. The Enlightenment ideal is to sweep away the cobwebs of religious superstition and tradition and replace them with a purely rational program for moral perfection. In this sense, the Enlightenment puts two questions to the classical deposit of Western religious beliefs: Does the belief in question accord with the plain light of reason? and Does it promote the health and welfare of the human community? Theological beliefs that contradict reason or fail to promote human felicity fail the test of common sense and should be renounced as inimical to the cause of pure religion.

We have seen how various deists and philosophes articulate the primary value of religious belief in moral terms. God is the cosmic lawgiver who guarantees the rationality and coherence of the universe. As a Newtonian megamachine, the universe is an interlocking system of physical and moral order. In this ordered universe, the right understanding of religious truth is not dependent on the aid of supernatural revelation; rather, every rational inquirer can rightly understand the essence of religion by practicing the simple ethic of loving God above all else and loving one's neighbor as oneself. Reason is the primary source for supplying the moral knowledge necessary for realizing the natural and final goal of human beings — to obey God by living a compassionate and humane existence in relation to one's neighbors. To follow, then, the promptings of our moral intuitions is effectively to follow the dictates of the universal lawgiver. As argued by the theorists we will consider in this section, Moses Mendelssohn and Immanuel Kant, the recognition of our duties as divine commands is the essence of authentic spirituality.

Moses Mendelssohn

Mendelssohn (1729–86) is known as the primary inspiration for the early Reform movement within eighteenth-century Judaism. He is credited with redefining Judaism as a rational religion whose special mission in the world is to teach the principles of morality that are universally binding on all persons. An observant Jewish member of the Enlightenment, or Haskalah, Mendelssohn is both like and unlike the other figures we have considered here: he represents a familiar attempt to defend religious faith on the basis of its rational and moral character, but he does so within the confines of a minority religious tradition within a socially and politically Christianized culture.[31]

Mendelssohn's *Jerusalem* is a defense of Judaism for the modern world. It borrows from the deists the notion that reason unaided by revelation has the capacity to achieve a saving knowledge of the truth. As well, it shares the epistemological assumption inspired by Locke and Hume that claims to knowledge are measured by their adequacy to common experience. Mendelssohn further agrees with his enlightened compatriots that claims to religious knowledge concerning what he calls "eternal truths" can only be validated on the basis of reason alone, not by appeals to the authority of religious tradition: "*I recognize no eternal truths other than those that are not merely comprehensible to human reason but can also be demonstrated and verified by human powers.*"[32]

Mendelssohn begins his project with a distinction concerning two types of truth that seems to echo Hume's bipartite division between relations of ideas and matters of fact. Knowledge consists of eternal truths of reason and historical truths of experience. Mathematics and physics, but also the truths of natural morality, comprise the first group, while everyday empirical observation and experience make up the content of the second group. Rational introspection enables the acquisition of eternal truths, while spoken and written language are the media for establishing historical truths. What distinguishes Mendelssohn from Hume, however, is Mendelssohn's argument that truths of reason include the gist of natural theology and not just propositions in mathematics and science. Against the conservative Christian dogma that a saving knowledge of the truth is not possible apart from revelation, and against the empiricist doctrine that no secure knowledge of God and God's designs is possible, Mendelssohn maintains that a comprehensive understanding of the divine will and our corresponding moral obligations is available to the light of natural reason.

Mendelssohn writes that while the evidence of history can assist the apprehension of eternal truths concerning salvation, such truths are still always available to everyone on the basis of rational intuition and through observing the order of creation itself:

> Eternal truths, on the other hand, insofar as they are useful for men's salvation and felicity, are taught by God in a manner more appropriate to the Deity; not by sounds or written characters, which are comprehensible here and there, to this or that individual, but through creation itself, and its internal relations, which are legible and comprehensible to all men.... He awakens the mind, which He has created, and gives it an opportunity to observe the relations of things, to observe itself, and to become convinced of the truths which it is destined to understand here below.[33]

As thought thinks itself, so to speak, and thereby comes to possess universal truths from time immemorial, there is no need for this rational process to be validated by an appeal to special scriptural revelation or the testimony of prophecy and miracles. As we will see again in Kant's thought, revelation and testimony can render more vivid and concrete the deliverances of reason, but the witness of a particular community's special history, even the special history of the Jews, can add no new content to the truths of reason that are universally available at all times to all people. Indeed, an overemphasis on tribal religion can blunt the full effect of reason's apprehension of universal truth. From this perspective, Mendelssohn regards the revelation of the moral law at Sinai to be an *external* confirmation of eternal truths that are *internally* written, so to speak, onto the heart of every person, Jew and Gentile. For Mendelssohn, the essence of Judaism is the Mosaic legislation concerning how the human community can realize ethically its natural *telos* by living in harmony with itself: "According to the concepts of true Judaism, all the inhabitants of the earth are destined to felicity; and the means of attaining it are as widespread as mankind itself, as charitably dispensed as the means of warding off hunger and other natural needs."[34] The essence of Judaism, in sum, is consistent with other religious traditions as well: to enable the practice of caring for self and other apart from the reliance on an external authority to ground the practice of benevolence.

Immanuel Kant

In the second half of the eighteenth century the critical philosophy of Immanuel Kant (1724–1804) comes to the fore. Kant's thought is both a confluence of, and extension beyond, the traditions of Continental rationalism, British empiricism, and the natural religion of the deists. Best known for his philosophical trilogy on the foundations of pure reason, moral reason, and aesthetic judgment, Kant begins his first volume of the series *The Critique of Pure Reason* with this claim: "Though all our knowledge begins with experience, it does not follow that it all arises out of experience. For it may well be that even our empirical knowledge is made up of what we receive through impressions and of what our own faculty of knowledge (sensible impressions serving merely as the occasion) supplies from itself."[35] Kant agrees with Locke and other sensationalists that knowledge begins with experience, but he borrows from the rationalists the notion that our minds consist of a priori categories and concepts – something close to Descartes's innate ideas – that make possible our organization of the manifold of experience into a meaningful whole. Knowledge consists of sense and understanding: the raw material of our sensible experience is synthesized according to a priori (that is, nonempirical) categories of understanding.

Kant's epistemology clearly has a place for the data of experience, but what about nonempirical ideas to which there are no corresponding objects or referents in our sensible experience? Does the idea of God, for example, have a place in Kant's critical project? Kant has sometimes been read as an opponent of religious belief, and his own writings against confessional Christianity give some credence to this interpretation. Heinrich Heine, the notorious German satirist, once remarked to a French audience that "'his' Immanuel Kant was a far, far greater man than 'their' Maximilian Robespierre. For whereas Robespierre had beheaded only a king, Kant had beheaded God."[36] Kant himself writes in a similar vein about his own critical approach to philosophy and religion. He consistently argues against the tendency among institutional Christian apologists to infantilize church members by appealing to the Bible and church tradition as authoritative sources for religious knowledge. In *What Is Enlightenment?* Kant draws an important distinction between the "public" and the "private" mode of adjudicating claims to truth in religion.[37] "Private" appeals to officially sanctioned standards for orthodox belief undermine rational autonomy and moral freedom in matters of faith. Whenever theologians appeal to special criteria of truth for establishing religious faith, rather than the "public" and objective standards of rationality within the academy, they sacrifice the intellectual integrity of faith.

While Kant is highly critical of creedal religion, he is not an opponent of religious faith as such, Heine's witticisms and Kant's own antitheological polemics notwithstanding. Though the intent of his critical philosophy is to delimit the range of knowledge to everyday, sensible experience, Kant clearly recognizes that we possess reliable ideas about supersensible realities that do not correspond to the data of the senses. These "transcendental ideas," as Kant refers to them, supersede the bounds of sense by specifying the conditions that make possible the unity of our experience as such. Reason naturally compels us to postulate certain transcendental ideas — namely, the ideas of God, individual freedom, and the immortality of the soul — on the basis of what we know must be the case even though this knowledge transgresses the boundaries of sense intuition. For Kant, it is primarily our abiding awareness of pure moral obligation, the interior compulsion to perform certain duties for their own sake, that necessarily presupposes these transcendental ideas: our sense of uncoerced moral obligation necessitates the existence of a supreme being (God), who both enables our capacity to choose between right and wrong (freedom) and guarantees our happiness for fulfilling our inherent obligations, a guarantee that will be eventually realized in the life to come (immortality) if not in this life.[38] These ideas of God, freedom, and immortality have a "regulative" rather than "constitutive" function in Kant's project. Such ideas do not extend our theoretical knowledge of the world by allowing for metaphysical assertions on the order of "God actually exists" or "Immorality is a postmortem certainty"; rather, these ideas are practically useful in establishing the necessary grounds for moral action. While it is not possible to *know* these ideas on the basis of sensible experience, it is inevitable and rational for us to *think* these ideas as the necessary conditions for making possible moral experience as we know it — that is, the feeling of happiness and well-being whenever we fulfill our duty.

Although Kant initially delimits the boundaries of knowledge to sensible impressions under the categories of the understanding, he nevertheless maintains that from a practical or moral perspective reason must always violate these boundaries in order to specify the grounds of supersensible moral experience. It is in this sense that Kant writes in the preface to the second edition of his first *Critique* that "I have therefore found it necessary to deny *knowledge*, in order to make room for *faith*."[39] Kant seeks to provide an ethical justification for faith apart from sensible experience, on the one hand, or the claims of rationalist philosophy, on the other. In contemporary parlance, he offers a "moral foundationalist" warrant for faith on the basis of ethical reason rather than by appealing to the data of sense intuition or the axioms of metaphysics.[40] His hope is to steer religious belief between the Scylla of Lockean sensationalism and the Charybdis of Cartesian speculation, to avoid the extremes of positivism and metaphysics by finding a narrow but secure pathway for faith in the realm of ethical duty.

For Kant, the force of the moral law in religious belief rests in its universality. I am pressed upon to obey the biblical command "Thou shalt not lie" not because my obedience is pragmatically useful in the moment but because I would want the precept of my action to be the maxim for everyone else's conduct as well. One then should respond to the interior call of duty as a universal demand on all rational persons and should do so without any regard for external benefits or ulterior motives. "Perform your duty for no motive other than unconditioned esteem for duty itself."[41] As we saw with Mendelssohn, religious Scriptures and traditions at best can help to clarify and confirm the inner demands of moral reason and at worst can work against pure obedience to duty for duty's sake by introducing heteronomous motives and reasons for fulfilling one's ethical obligations. Positive religious traditions provide various "vehicles" for strengthening the response to duty in the form of moral teachings and so forth, but the essence of religion is not in obedience to a tradition but in responding to all "moral duties as divine commands."[42]

In spite of Kant's insistence that "all our knowledge begins with experience," reason is nevertheless construed as inevitably, but legitimately, superseding the empirical limits erected by our knowledge of sensible data. Knowledge, now understood from the perspective of ethical obligation, is extended by reason beyond the bounds of sense experience into the interior realm where we discover what is bindingly self-evident to all persons: the force of the transcendental moral law within. For Kant, our interior sense of duty unencumbered by ecclesiastical authority is the sum and substance of religious life. It appears that on this point he was greatly influenced by Mendelssohn, as well as by the Enlightenment intellectual climate in general.[43] With Mendelssohn, Kant confidently maintains that parochial religious traditions are finally unnecessary for the realization of rational piety because the performance of such piety is its own reward.

Kant's antipathy toward institutional religion, along with his valorization of the moral life as a good in itself, is a harbinger of much of the ethical activism in contemporary culture that has a distinctly spiritual, if not religious, cast. Many practitioners of secular spirituality privilege Kant's ethical idea of doing good for its own sake — even though Kant's "regulative idea" of God as a necessary presupposition for moral experience has lost its intuitive appeal for some people. Various present-day regimens devoted to personal and social transformation provide a fitting coda to Kant's moral philosophy.

Conclusion

The bequest of the Enlightenment to contemporary forms of spiritual expression is enormous. The Enlightenment is a watershed in the history of Western religious thought, establishing the foundations for a pluralistic and nonsectarian vision of faith unburdened by the received wisdom and traditions of the past. In this essay I have examined some of the key elements in this new vision. (1) Religious belief must be proportionate to the evidence of common experience or be found wanting. (2) A purely rational and demythologized spirituality opposes all forms of dogmatism, intolerance, fear-mongering, and theological obscurantism. (3) The universe exists under the wise governance of a benevolent lawgiver and is benignly ordered to serve human well-being. (4) Finally, submission to the cosmic order through sound moral judgment enables the realization of the summum bonum of human existence. Except for a few neopagan philosophers, most Enlightenment theorists — from the deists in England and America to Voltaire, Mendelssohn, Kant, and even, perhaps, David Hume — presuppose that human reason participates in a cosmic order that renders obvious to every rational inquirer the nature of one's practical duties and responsibilities. To carry out one's duty in relation to others is the basis of free religion in the Enlightenment. As Kant puts it, to act morally for the sake of the good itself is to do one's duty as if it were a divine command.

A cursory glance at modern Western thought indicates, however, that some cardinal Enlightenment beliefs and values have not always fared well. In the nineteenth century, the protoexistentialism of Søren Kierkegaard and Friedrich Nietzsche questioned the ordered and predictable worldview of the Enlightenment as a totalizing denial of the unstable and nonrational character of reality. The nature mysticism of New England transcendentalism generated a shift of emphasis away from the mechanistic model of God's relation to the world toward a more organic and holistic construal of the God-world relationship. In our own time, the poststructuralist critique of logocentrism announces a final break with the Enlightenment ideal of pure, universal reason: the realization of the situated and constructed character of knowledge means that all claims to self-evident and transcendent truth are hopelessly illusory.

In spite of its many limitations and pretensions, in spite of its overly optimistic and sometimes pompous tone of argument, the Enlightenment will not go away. It still has a considerable hold on the contemporary consciousness, even though many religious and secular thinkers do not always recognize its purchase on the present. In antireligious terms, the easy dismissal of the Enlightenment (a dismissal fueled in part by the philosophers of the Enlightenment themselves, as well as by its current champions) is that the eighteenth century was a postreligious age and, as such, offers few resources for creating a genuine spirituality in a secular world that has likewise come of age. Part of the burden of my argument here, however, has been to demonstrate the speciousness of this interpretation and to argue that while the Enlightenment was a time that had grown weary of religious dogmatism and fanaticism, it was not an irreligious age.

Indeed, the eighteenth century was an era obsessed with religious questions, and in this respect it is much like our own time. Many persons in contemporary Western culture are seeking transformative and authentic forms of spiritual commitment that are not boxed in by narrow-minded strictures against imaginative reenvisionings of the Jewish and Christian heritage. As well, many of these seekers believe that the essence of true spirituality does not reside in creeds and ceremonies but in the altruistic willingness to do good for its own sake, even though such persons may not attribute their ideals of nonutilitarian virtue to Kant's thought in particular or the Enlightenment in general. The reevaluation of religion in terms of spirituality construes the journey toward authentic and socially committed selfhood as a task to be performed on the basis of one's deepest felt passions and obligations. Becoming a self is a proleptic project of the whole person; for that reason, we can say that such a project always contains a "spiritual," if not always a "religious," dimension.

Today, we are not always aware of our indebtedness to the eighteenth century, but it behooves us to reconsider where precisely its contributions might lie in today's society. What are arguably the most important values of the Enlightenment — the ideals of critical inquiry, political moderation, moral integrity, and religious freedom — now appear again for many critics to be crucial for addressing the troubles of our own time. In much of Western culture, *liberalism* is a bad word; the critical spirit is labeled dangerous and unpatriotic; and religious diversity is considered corrosive of the common beliefs and practices within the civil religion of the body politic. We live in a troubled culture that is awash with defenders of market values, proponents of patriarchal religion, and evangelists for manifest destiny. At this time the ideals of democratic pluralism and the tolerant embrace of difference, in a manner both similar to and different from the Enlightenment project, are again the demands of the moment.

Notes

1. Immanuel Kant, *What Is Enlightenment?* trans. Carl J. Friedrich, in *The Philosophy of Kant: Immanuel Kant's Moral and Political Writings,* ed. Carl J. Friedrich (New York: Random House, 1949), 132.

2. Like all designations for historical movements, the dating for the Enlightenment is somewhat arbitrary. For a defense of the traditional dates, see Peter Gay, *The Enlightenment: An Interpretation,* vol. 1, *The Rise of Modern Paganism* (New York: Knopf, 1967), 16–19.

3. I have confined my analysis to the philosophical currents of the Enlightenment. For a broader look at the historical and institutional changes in the early modern period, see Gerald C. Cragg, *The Church and the Age of Reason 1648–1789* (Harmondsworth, England: Penguin, 1960). For a critical alternative, see Michel Foucault, *Madness and Civilization: A History of Insanity in the Age of Reason,* trans. Richard Howard (New York: Random House, 1965), and idem, *Discipline and Punish: The Birth of the Prison,* trans. Alan Sheridan (New York: Random House, 1979).

4. René Descartes, *Meditations on First Philosophy,* trans. John Veitch, in *The Rationalists* (Garden City, N.Y.: Anchor Books, 1974), 118 (meditation 2).

5. Immanuel Kant, "Preface to First Edition," *Critique of Pure Reason,* trans. Norman Kemp Smith (New York: St. Martin's, 1965), 9n.

6. John Locke, *An Essay concerning Human Understanding,* ed. Alexander Campbell Fraser, in *Great Books of the Western World,* gen. ed. Robert Maynard Hutchins (Chicago: Encyclopedia Britannica, 1952), 35:349–50 (bk. 4, chap. 10, par. 3).

7. Ibid., 384 (bk. 4, chap. 18, par. 10).

8. Ibid. (bk. 4, chap. 18, par. 11).

9. John Locke, "A Letter concerning Toleration," in *Great Books of the Western World,* 35:3.

10. Gay, *The Enlightenment,* 1:xi.

11. Ernst Cassirer, *The Philosophy of the Enlightenment,* trans. Fritz C. Koelln and James P. Pettegrove (Princeton, N.J.: Princeton University Press, 1951), 13.

12. This point is also made by Charles Taylor in his study of modern thought. In contradistinction to Gay's and Cassirer's analyses, Taylor offers a more complicated and nuanced portrait of Enlightenment notions of reason. He notes that while certain eighteenth-century materialist thinkers such as Paul Henri Holbach and Claude Helvétius did define rationality in nontheistic terms, other philosophers, such as Francis Hutcheson, Rousseau, Kant, and even Hume, argued for a notion of participatory reason in harmony with quasi-transcendental notions like "universal law," "the voice of nature," or

"infallible moral sentiments." See Charles Taylor, *Sources of the Self: The Making of the Modern Identity* (Cambridge, Mass.: Harvard University Press, 1989), 321–67.

13. John Toland, *Christianity Not Mysterious,* in *Deism: An Anthology,* ed. Peter Gay (Princeton, N.J.: Nostrand, 1968), 74 (sec. 2, chap. 4).

14. Matthew Tindal, *Christianity as Old as the Creation,* in *Deism: An Anthology,* 102–3.

15. Ibid., 103.

16. Thomas Paine, *The Age of Reason,* in *Deism: An Anthology,* 165.

17. This point is made by Allen W. Wood in his article "The Enlightenment," in *The Encyclopedia of Religion,* ed. Mircea Eliade, 12 vols. (New York: Macmillan, 1985), 4:112.

18. Thomas Jefferson, "The Declaration of Independence," in *Great Books of the Western World,* 43:1.

19. Both collections can be found in *Jefferson's Extracts from the Gospels,* ed. Dickinson W. Adams (Princeton, N.J.: Princeton University Press, 1982). For other American deistic texts and analysis, see Kerry S. Walters, *The American Deists: Voices of Reason and Dissent in the Early Republic* (Lawrence: University Press of Kansas, 1992); and G. Adolf Koch, *Religion of the American Enlightenment* (New York: Crowell, 1968).

20. The deist confidence in the capacity of participatory reason to discern the nature of humankind's proper ends continues to have a wide register in contemporary spirituality, both secular and religious. Instead of understanding reason as a fallen power contaminated by its association with the original sin of Adam, many people in Western culture today, in a fashion apropos of their Enlightenment forerunners, value reason as a capacity for critical engagement with the world in a manner that can promote both personal and social change. For one of the many theological expressions of this view in terms of the ideal of the "thinking-relational" self, the person who uses her or his reason to articulate an integrated and transformative model for relating to God and world, see Rosemary Radford Ruether, *Sexism and God-Talk: Toward a Feminist Theology* (Boston: Beacon, 1983), 93–115.

21. Carl L. Becker, *The Heavenly City of the Eighteenth-Century Philosophers* (New Haven: Yale University Pres, 1932), 30. In opposition to Becker's interpretation of the continuities between the Enlightenment and historic Christianity, Gay argues that the leading European intellectual figures after 1750 were nonbelievers. "In the first half of the century, the leading philosophes had been deists and had used the vocabulary of natural law; in the second half, the leaders were atheists and used the vocabulary of utility" (Gay, *The Enlightenment,* 1:18). Part of the burden of my essay is to question this "atheistic" interpretation of the eighteenth century by Gay and others and to demonstrate how committed most Enlightenment thinkers were to belief in God, although a God now understood as a nonpersonal guarantor of order and removed from direct intervention in human affairs.

22. Quotation is from Cragg, *The Church and the Age of Reason,* 237.

23. Michael J. Buckley, S.J., *At the Origins of Modern Atheism* (New Haven: Yale University Press, 1987), 38–39.

24. See Voltaire, *The Sermon of the Fifty,* in *Deism: An Anthology,* 143–58.

25. Ibid., 158.

26. David Hume, *An Enquiry concerning Human Understanding,* ed. L. A. Selby-Bigge, in *Great Books of the Western World,* 35:458 (sec. 4, pt. 1, par. 20).

27. David Hume, *Dialogues concerning Natural Religion,* ed. Henry D. Aiken (New York: Hafner, 1948), 66.

28. Gay, *The Enlightenment,* 1:417.
29. Hume, *Dialogues concerning Natural Religion,* 95.
30. Ibid., 94.
31. On Mendelssohn's relation to the Enlightenment and Judaism, see Robert M. Seltzer's article "Enlightenment," in *Contemporary Jewish Religious Thought,* ed. Arthur A. Cohen and Paul Mendes-Flohr (New York: Free Press, 1987), 171–75.
32. Moses Mendelssohn, *Jerusalem: Or on Religious Power and Judaism,* trans. Allan Arkush (Hanover, N.H.: University Press of New England, 1983), 89.
33. Ibid., 93–94.
34. Ibid., 94.
35. Kant, *Critique of Pure Reason,* 42.
36. The quotation is from Norburn Greville, "Kant's Philosophy of Religion," *Scottish Journal of Philosophy* 26 (1973): 431–48.
37. See Kant, *What Is Enlightenment?* in *The Philosophy of Kant,* 132–39.
38. Kant, *Critique of Pure Reason,* 635–52.
39. Kant, "Preface to Second Edition," *Critique of Pure Reason,* 29.
40. Foundationalism is the theory that knowledge is a product of noninferential, self-evidential beliefs the denial of which is putatively self-contradictory. For the discussion of Kant's moral foundationalism, see Jeffrey Stout, *Ethics after Babel: The Languages of Morals and Their Discontents* (Boston: Beacon, 1988), 124–44.
41. Immanuel Kant, *Religion within the Limits of Reason Alone,* trans. Theodore M. Greene and Hoyt H. Hudson (New York: Harper and Row, 1960), 148.
42. Ibid., 94–114.
43. Kant wrote Mendelssohn after the publication of *Jerusalem* and lauded him for his defense of the rational basis of Judaism; he later refers to Mendelssohn's position in *Religion within the Limits of Reason Alone,* 154.

Bibliography

Becker, Carl L. *The Heavenly City of the Eighteenth-Century Philosophers.* New Haven: Yale University Press, 1932.

Buckley, Michael J., S.J. *At the Origins of Modern Atheism.* New Haven: Yale University Press, 1987.

Cassirer, Ernst. *The Philosophy of the Enlightenment.* Translated by Fritz C. Koelln and James P. Pettegrove. Princeton, N.J.: Princeton University Press, 1951.

Cragg, Gerald C. *The Church and the Age of Reason 1648–1789.* Harmondsworth, England: Penguin, 1960.

Foucault, Michel. *Madness and Civilization: A History of Insanity in the Age of Reason.* Trans. Richard Howard. New York: Random House, 1965.

Gay, Peter. *The Enlightenment: An Interpretation.* 2 vols. New York: Knopf, 1967, 1969.

Hume, David. *Dialogues concerning Natural Religion.* Edited by Henry D. Aiken. New York: Hafner, 1948.

Kant, Immanuel. *Critique of Pure Reason.* Translated by Norman Kemp Smith. New York: St. Martin's, 1965.

———. *Religion within the Limits of Reason Alone.* Translated by Theodore M. Greene and Hoyt H. Hudson. New York: Harper and Row, 1960.

Mendelssohn, Moses. *Jerusalem: Or on Religious Power and Judaism.* Translated by Allan Arkush. Hanover, N.H.: University Press of New England, 1983.

Taylor, Charles. *Sources of the Self: The Making of the Modern Identity.* Cambridge, Mass.: Harvard University Press, 1989.

Wade, Ira O. *The Structure and Form of the French Enlightenment.* 2 vols. Princeton, N.J.: Princeton University Press, 1977.

Walters, Kerry S. *The American Deists: Voices of Reason and Dissent in the Early Republic.* Lawrence: University Press of Kansas, 1992.

4

The American Experience

NANCY FRANKENBERRY

There is only one world, the natural world, and only one truth about it; but this world has a spiritual life possible in it, which looks not to another world but to the beauty and perfection that this world suggests, approaches, and misses.

— George Santayana, *Realms of Being*

Pragmatic Naturalism, Aesthetic Spirituality, and the American Grain

IT HAS BEEN SAID that the most important problems all turn out to be variations on the ancient metaphysical theme of "the One and the Many." In the American experiment, this theme took on new significance, expressed in the pluralistic ideal of the nation's motto, *E pluribus unum.* It took on spiritual dimensions, as well, in the form of a secular vision of the human quest for individual and communal wholeness. From the time of the Puritans, to the pioneers, to the pragmatists, and now to the postmodernists, Americans have found themselves party to a democratic and spiritual experiment in the evolution of unity from plurality, a covenant in which out of many, a new "one" was to arise. In the overall life of the republic, the experiment has been painfully slow, uncertain, and ambiguous. Like the biblical People of Israel, to whom they were compared as the "New Israel," Americans would only over time begin to acquire an understanding of the meaning of the covenant into which they had entered — its undreamed cost, its unknown demands, and its unfathomed inclusiveness.

Four centuries from its discovery, and after just one hundred years under the constitutional separation of church and state, America was no longer "the nation with the soul of a church" (Alexis de Tocqueville) nor even one that could still construe its "mission into the wilderness" (Perry Miller) under the sacred canopy of Puritanism. By the end of the nineteenth century, American intellectual culture had turned secular in the aftermath of the Civil War and as a result of the inauguration of a developed theory of evolution, the industrializing of society, and the arrival of an immigrant populace that militated against sectarianism. Faced first with Jeffersonian Enlightenment philosophy and later with the rising currents of Jacksonian democracy, the tensions of seventeenth- and eighteenth-century Calvinist theology, brilliantly straddled by Jonathan Edwards, had not long been sustained. The venture of unifying diverse Eastern European groups, together with Irish, German, and Jewish immigrants, as well as according freedom to African-Americans and justice to Native Americans, introduced new strains in the Union. The combined effect of Darwinism and Hegelianism had dissolved the dualism of nature and spirit for many members of the intellectual culture, while the old metaphysical paradoxes and impenetrable rigors of sin and salvation came to elude most ordinary Americans. Even Emersonian self-reliance, only recently regarded as the hallmark of the American character, was metamorphosing into a new pragmatic philosophy that could incorporate Other-reliance, as the "Great God far within" began to appear too transparently narcissistic and romantically overdrawn. It remained only for the Social Gospel of Walter Rauschenbusch to shrug off the metaphysical worldview of the Christian religion and focus explicitly on its moral and social teachings. Between the post–Civil War period and the Great Depression, liberal Protestantism boldly dedogmatized and secularized itself to the point where the dean of the Harvard Divinity School as late as 1946 could affirm the view that "Christianity is a quality of life rather than a fixed system of doctrine."[1]

It is not the purpose of this essay to canvas all the many forms that the secular quest has taken in American culture but rather to consider primarily the philosophical contribution made by one school of thought, which I designate broadly as pragmatic naturalism. My focus is on the period from roughly 1880 to 1930 when an important philosophical vision arose in America and new ideas of self and whole, the one and the many, and God and the world framed a secular spirituality that was distinctively American.

By the designation *pragmatic naturalism* I refer to that nontranscendental worldview that developed around the work of C. S. Peirce (1839–1914), William James (1842–1910), John Dewey (1859–1952), George Santayana (1863–1952), George Herbert Mead (1863–1931), and Alfred North

Whitehead (1862–1947), all of whom delineated a vision of the social self in relation to one or another conception of the whole.[2] For these thinkers, despite their significant differences, the critique of supernaturalism was accompanied by a shift of focus to the transcendent qualities of immanent relationships in this world. No longer pointing vertically to infinite, absolute Being, transcendence came to signify the horizontal process of temporal movement toward an open-ended future state. Under entirely naturalistic auspices these American philosophers developed and refined, frequently with great originality and rigor, a worldview in which the wider spiritual implications of the republic's ideal of *E pluribus unum* found expression. Just as the vision of one nation formed out of many diverse nationalities remains an ideal, not a completed actuality — an unfinished covenant, never a certified achievement — so too the mode of American spirituality depicted here valued possibility, temporality, and contingency in a universe still "in the making." Rejecting the ancient Parmenidean or ontotheological belief in an absolute, unchanging order of being that transcends the temporal world, pragmatic naturalism affirmed a risk-filled cosmos in which becoming has primacy over being. In place of a perfect God, one who creates and preserves the many, it proposed a view in which the many finite and free acts of individuals literally create the one complex cosmic whole, transfiguring or disfiguring the very face of the divine. Inasmuch as its manifestation at any moment marks the emergence of new order out of chaos, the *cosmic whole* is a token-reflexive term, referring with each use to a novel emergent state, one in which the risk of loss and the value of freedom are both genuine. These assumptions about the nature of things defined a perspective not only uniquely suited to the flourishing of democracy but also resolutely secular in its celebration of such qualities as creativity, courage, and freedom and its recognition that ideals, not actualities, are the real referents of conventional religious symbols and creeds.

Although it is not possible here to do justice to the full historical sweep or philosophical expression of pragmatic naturalism, certain characteristic themes and representative figures can be noted. Accordingly, in the first part four distinctive themes are discussed: the theory of aesthetic spirituality; the self as a field of relations; the cosmic whole as the web of life; and natural piety toward the sources of our being. These themes are not necessarily unique to the American experience, but they are distinctively interwoven in both American philosophy and religious thought. In the second part these themes are exemplified in selective profiles of William James, John Dewey, George Santayana, and Alfred North Whitehead.

Characteristics of the American Secular Quest

Aesthetic Spirituality

Defining spirituality provisionally as "the embodied task of realizing one's truest self in the context of reality apprehended as a cosmic totality," we can further specify the meaning of self and cosmic totality according to an aesthetic model.[3] The term *aesthetic spirituality* describes, on a very high level of generality, the structure characteristic of one variety of the secular spiritual quest in the American grain.[4] According to this structure, the self as it relates to the totality undergoes transition from initial unease, insufficiency, or fragmentariness to attainment of a greater, though always incomplete, equilibrium in which unease is momentarily eased, insufficiency salved, and fragmentariness unified. Centered on a continued interrelation between the individual and a larger whole, the process of polar interplay produces a state of self-surpassing transcendence. The mode of transcendence is this-worldly and temporal, as the open future transcends the given present.

If a secular spiritual quest is pursuit of a "blessed rage for order" (Wallace Stevens), it can be argued that aesthetic criteria supply the most inclusive measurement or interpretation of that order. The aesthetics of spirituality are fundamentally determined by the range and intensity of the dimensions of life that an individual can include and sustain in the unity of his or her own integrity. Spiritual life in the secular world consists in the progressive integration of ever more complex feelings, thoughts, and habits by which one reacts to an ever larger portion of the world and relates oneself to the whole of reality. This mode of spirituality, like art, is therefore a matter of maximizing complexity and intensity in some degree of harmony. The more contrast in the harmony, the richer the life. Whereas art, however, is a movement from complexity to simplicity within the limits of a canvas, a musical score, a poem, a novel, or a play, aesthetic spirituality seeks an unrestricted field of value whose harmony involves an ever-enlarging processive synthesis of complexity and intensity. The emergence of right adjustment to life and the growth of greater value require an ability to live with the creative tension engendered between such contrasts as joy and sorrow, good and evil, disjunction and conjunction, greatness and triviality, freedom and necessity, the ideal and the actual, and the one and the many. Also required is the ability to live without insisting that the ambiguities born of these contrasts be completely resolved. The world is just given in all its complexity, while self-integration and growth are achievements of considerable simplification, dependent upon a capacity for harmonizing contrasts that may even border on chaos. Too much elimination procures narrowness without simplicity. Too little yields width without depth. Along the razor's edge between inclusion of discordant elements as effective contrasts and their dismissal as incompatible ingredients, each organic form of life seeks a particular equilibrium. No individual is simply one among many; the many are deeply creative of the internal life of each individual that is constituted by its relations.

Analogously to the republic's ongoing struggle to forge a difficult union out of its manyness, the American secular quest pivots aesthetically around the relational interplay between the one and the many, the individual and the community, and the self and the cosmic whole. Considering the cosmic whole as one pole, we can say that *E pluribus unum* signifies a dynamic dialectic whereby the many actualities of nature become one, and are increased by one, in a moment to moment process. From this perspective the whole is ever unfinished and plural, comprising an inclusive but still incomplete unity. Considering the individual self as the other pole, we can say that *E pluribus unum* signifies the goal of forging more inclusive integrity and harmony of experience out of the many shifting givens of one's world. The characteristic rhythm of aesthetic spirituality, therefore, consists in transcending a given initial state through attainment of a new, and ever provisional, aesthetic unity that momentarily unifies the initial condition of givenness and contributes a new emergent "one" to the "many." Socially and culturally, the American experience has sought unity of purpose, unity of peoplehood, a novel "one" out of a diverse "many." Existentially and psychologically, the personal quest for integrity, harmony, or fulfillment has been thought to involve a similar process of weaving together or uncovering the many disparate strands of one's existence, in order to create or discover a more complex and authentic self. Cosmologically and ontologically, this self-transcendent impulse inherent in life, in matter itself, has been speculatively rendered by American philosophers as itself a process in which the many actualities become one cosmic totality whose manifestation at any one moment will always be superseded, at the next, by another. The secular quest for a renewed and transformed self could be regarded, in this light, as continuous with cosmic reality insofar as it, too, displays a temporal dialectic of processive-relational emergence.

The spiritual quest on this account entailed nothing more and nothing less than a process of increasing the depth, range, harmony, and intensity of felt qualities in relation to some unit of value (self, community, cosmic whole). The distinguishing feature of the spiritual concerned the aim at *increase* in the depth, range, harmony, and vividness of felt qualities. The particular experiences American pragmatic naturalists interpreted as spiritually significant were those that promoted or pertained to the creative transformation of given forms of experience, enabling individuals or communities or occasionally a whole culture to move from narrower, constricted patterns to wider and deeper modes of sympathetic inclusion. Critical, public measurement of such qualitative emergence was a difficult enough matter in the case of a painted canvas, a musical score, a theatrical production, or some other aesthetic object, becoming even more so in the case of an actual life span or historical epoch, yet aesthetic criteria provided a good *general* index of the spiritual life. For aesthetic order comprises the most *inclusive* and at the same time most *concrete* form of order pertinent to *any* interpretation. The aesthetic principles of compatible range, depth, contrast, and intensity of feeling within some harmonious unit served as a constant measure of value always applicable, on this theory, whether the process pertained to selves or to the cosmic whole or to any unit whatsoever. In each case, the type of unity or order emerged from the range and depth of relationships. The greater the range and depth of relations, the greater the contrast and intensity of experience; the greater the compatible contrast, the greater the stature and complexity of the individual unity achieved. The greatest conceivable complexity would occur in the cosmic process of nature's transforming incompatible elements, perhaps even contradictions, into compatible contrasts, yielding the deepest intensity of experience. Pragmatic naturalists who generalized the self's relation to the whole in these terms could conclude to a kind of pantheism (all is god) or to panentheism (all-in-god), but never to supernaturalistic versions of theism.

Aesthetic spirituality presupposed dissolution of dualisms between the natural and the supernatural, the spiritual and the material, ultimate meaning and temporal significance, and the peace that passes understanding and worldly action. Transposed into secular terms, conventional religion's quest for redemption and justification became a matter of personal liberation and/or social transformation; otherworldliness yielded to this-worldly concerns and purposes; and the search for noncontextual absolutes gave way to appreciation of pragmatic relativities. All the powers and principalities, formerly located beyond this world, were now understood as fully available, either actually or possibly, in the many mansions of this one world. There is no other world. Inwardness, or spirituality, therefore, connoted nothing magical, unnatural, or dualistic. Secular spirituality could transpire in the midst of the world, playing an active role in the lives of even those individuals who found themselves alienated from churches or synagogues but still open to what William James called "the More" and John Dewey the "religious quality of experience." Precisely because "the More" or "religious quality" was not tied exclusively to mediation through church, word, sacraments, or prayer, or through temple, Talmud, and text, its spirit bloweth where it will.

The Self as a Field of Relations

No feature is more fundamental to pragmatic naturalism than the doctrine of internal relations, developed principally by James, Dewey, Whitehead, and Mead. In their portrayal of relations as internal, essential, and constitutive, not simply accidental and derivative, these American philosophers articulated the key to a new understanding of the nature of the self as intrinsically social or relational. In contrast to the liberal view that the individual is fulfilled through his or her participation in the lives of others, the theory of the social nature of the self emphasized, more radically, that relations constitute us as being who and what we are. It is not that the self first *is* and then secondarily *has* relations, but that in each moment the self is an emergent from a plenum or field of social relations and is nothing without them. The field is composed of event-processes in changing and overlapping patterns of interdependence, designated *matter* or *mind* according to context. William James's famous 1904 essay "Does 'Consciousness' Exist?" proposed a relational theory of consciousness in place of a division of the self into two ontologically different modes of being — mind and matter. The field metaphor led James to the notion of a "wider self," as he was to call it in *A Pluralistic Universe.* "Every bit of us," according to James, "at every moment is part and parcel of a wider self, it quivers along various radii like the wind-rose on a compass, and the actual in it is continuously one with possibles not yet in our present sight."[5] John Dewey used the field metaphor less frequently but elaborated a similar, biologically based model of the self in terms of organism and environment in continuous transaction. Whitehead's *Process and Reality* (1929) was the most systematic demonstration of the processive-relational nature of the self, viewed as grounded in the temporal and interconnected structure of reality itself. George Herbert Mead's classic work *Mind, Self, and Society* (1934) thematized the dialectic between the spontaneous individual-pole ("I") and the deterministic social-pole ("Me"), cutting a middle position between individualism and collectivism. Arising out of the internalized community or "generalized Other," subjectivity, in Mead's analysis, was first of all intersubjective communication.

The field view of the self undermines stereotypes of American pragmatism as unduly individualistic and displays its affinities not only with postmodern conceptions of the self in recent Western philosophy but also with Buddhist spirituality in the East. Like the Buddhist notion of no-self (*anattā*), realization of which sets one free, the field concept of the self obviates the need for any transempirical agents of unification and dispenses with the category of substances in favor of relational processes. There are no processes that are not relational and no relations that are not processive. Unlike the fully unified self of liberal humanism, transparently self-aware and voluntaristically able to bring about personal changes, relational selfhood is the outcome rather than the presupposition of a complex process of becoming; it is an ongoing achievement, not a given, a conflicted and unfinished project rather than an integrated and unimpeded mode of subjectivity. Aesthetic spirituality, having to do precisely with this struggling and unifying activity of a self-in-transformation, is wholly secular in its orientation to what is naturalistically given, worldly, historical, and contingent. Gone was Puritanism's view of the self as essentially depraved and in need of divine grace. Superseded, too, was the Enlightenment's commitment to the fully autonomous, rational, and independent self.

Deconstructing any perduring substantial self and dissenting also from any notion of the cosmic whole as an absolute, totalizing reality, pragmatic naturalists understood the self's relation to the whole as potentially transformative, calling upon an inwardness that emerged through living the relational life most fully. Greater relationality was required in order to create individuals, societies, and institutions of greater stature, large enough to absorb — without being overcome by — such negative features of modernity as violence, hatred, absurdity, and emptiness, and open enough to transmute complexity into new forms of communitarian experience.

Freedom was an emergent from relationality in this view, rather than the contradictory and more commonplace presupposition that relationality is a function of freedom. The self's fullest well-being and freedom resided in relationality. Its freedom consisted in *how* the self constituted itself as a response to *what* it received from others. We are thus response-able and responsible for how we respond, rather than agents of control and masters of the free play of events in the field. *Spirit* denoted this aspect of freedom, referring to the self-transcending capacity of the self, its potentiality for transformation and growth, for wholeness.

Wholeness and the Web of Life

The ancient paradigm of the transcendent One communicating its unity of existence and creative power to the empirical Many was overturned early in this century by a new evolutionary cosmology in which the many were creative of the one, weblike cosmic and indivisible whole. In the evolving, ever-unfinished universe of ceaseless creative activity assumed by pragmatic naturalists, the fundamental image of nature in terms of interpenetrating fields of forces and organically integrated wholes replaced an earlier picture of self-contained, externally related bits of particles or inert matter. As a result, not only supernaturalisms and transcendentalisms but all subjective idealisms as well became superseded by twentieth-century relativity and field theories in physics. Once mechanistic materialism was no longer the root metaphor of science, idealism was no longer the only recourse for easing the tension between science and religion or for introducing "mind" into "matter." Closely related to the assumption that the being of any natural entity was constituted by its relationships and its participation in ever more inclusive fields, the idea that "the whole is more than the sum of its parts" became central to the development of systems theory, biological ecology, and field analysis. Religiously, this suggested to some American thinkers a speculative vision of the cosmic totality as a complex, unified, individual subject, itself divine. Charles Hartshorne, for example, was to develop Whitehead's philosophy in this emphatically theistic direction throughout the second part of the twentieth century, just as Ralph Waldo Emerson's nineteenth-century transcendental idealism had extolled the virtues of the Oversoul.

Pragmatic naturalists, on the other hand, expressed more caution in depicting the nature of the cosmic whole, preferring to guard against the idealistic tendency to see the human mind writ large in nature itself. The overarching consciousness of "an all-inclusive divine mind," considered essential by the idealist tradition, was generally dispensed with by pragmatists. Nature's unity was "ever not quite," in William James's expression. We do not and cannot experience the whole-as-such, according to this outlook, for the whole never appears as a really existing object. Only in the mode of anticipation or intentionality can cosmic wholeness be apprehended, and only as symbolically mediated. At best, humans experience a certain complex of conditions that can be described as a sense of the whole. On the basis of such experience, it is then possible to construct particular interpretations or imaginative construings. John Herman Randall Jr. summed up the view shared by most pragmatic naturalists: "We never encounter '*the* Universe,' we never act toward, experience, or feel being or existence as 'a whole.' ... There is hence no discoverable 'ultimate context,' no 'ultimate substance.... ' 'The Universe,' or 'Nature,' is not 'a process' — a single process."[6] The unity of nature is derivative from its pluralistic connections.

The view of nature as both pluralistic and continuous ruled out dualisms along with monisms. While nature may be one in certain specified ways, at the same time it was also many, and, contrary to Plato, the many, far from being an appearance or an image of the real, were real themselves. At the same time, while nature exhibited discontinuities in the form of emergent plateaus, its parts were also bound together by common structures of becoming. Nature, though individualized, was not bifurcated. It did not admit of any dualism, whether of spirit-matter, mind-body, value-fact, possibility-actuality, one-many, religion-science, or God-humans. The intricate interrelations in nature's weblike reality could stir the human spirit to deep appreciation of its own creatureliness.

Devotion to the web of life was an affirmation and celebration of the common creaturehood of all beings as attested to in various sciences. Evolutionary theory had found that humankind's roots go back to early primates, backboned fishes, primeval sea worms, and the element-building stars. Biological science had revealed that life extended to an attenuated prelife hidden in the heart of inanimate matter. Human life was now seen as intertwined with the movements of the sun and moon, migrations of animals, and the advance and retreat of polar ice caps. Having no privileged position above or outside this web of life, humans were viewed as creatures of the earth, born of its evolutionary processes, nurtured and sustained by its intricate interchanges, and regenerated within its enveloping environment. This same web also comprised the inescapable matrix of perishing of life and loss of value. Under the philosophical auspices afforded by American pragmatic naturalism, the ancient notion of the web of life as the proper object of natural piety came to have new resonance.

Natural Piety

From Henry Thoreau through Robinson Jeffers and down to Annie Dillard, American naturalists have found in nature's terrible beauty a wild sacredness. Natural piety, the mood of reverence, and the cultivation of cosmic awe were longstanding human responses to the enveloping mystery of life. America's pragmatic naturalists, using philosophical tools, rendered that vision into conceptual models.

In part, American naturalism has been inspired by evolutionary cosmology's revelation of a universe of dimensions unimaginable to the human mind. Today if one imagines an atlas of the galaxy that devotes but a single page to each star system in the Milky Way, so that the sun and all its planets are crammed on one page, that atlas, according to one author, would run to more than ten million volumes of ten thousand pages each. It would take a library the size of Harvard's to house the atlas, and merely to flip through it, at the rate of a page per second, would require over ten thousand years.

Not the product of simple reflection on the sheer vastness of the cosmos alone, natural piety is a complex response of the self to a perception of its relation to and dependence upon an environing whole conceived as the source or purpose of one's being. For George Santayana, piety was loyalty to the sources of one's being and embraced, in ascending order: parents, nation, cultural traditions, species, environment, planet. Spirituality, on the other hand, according to Santayana, directed one toward goals, not sources. Spiritual individuals were disposed to a vision of excellence, loveliness, or preeminent goodness, and they ordered their conduct to realize that vision. For Alfred North Whitehead, religion was "what the individual does with his solitude."[7] Although he called Christian theology "one of the great disasters of the human race," Whitehead could also proclaim that "the end result of all spiritual formation is a kind of world loyalty."[8] For John Dewey:

> Natural piety . . . may rest upon a just sense of nature as the whole of which we are parts, while it also recognizes that we are parts that are marked by intelligence and purpose, having the capacity to strive by their aid to bring conditions into greater consonance with what is humanly desirable. Such piety is an inherent constituent of a just perspective in life.[9]

Viewing the world of nature no longer as the manifestation of inevitable necessity, as in Greek metaphysics, nor as the gratuitous gift of creative love, as in the biblical myth, but as the ungrounded miracle of contingent being, pragmatic naturalists could affirm the ephemeral and transitory quality of values, agreeing with the poet Wallace Stevens that "death is the mother of beauty." In the presumed absence of any "far-off divine event toward which all creation tends" (Tennyson), nature's possibilities, regarded as infinite and inexhaustible, inspired awe and marshaled commitment. No eschatological "time" was envisaged in which all possibilities would be completely exhausted or fully actualized, and the very assumption that temporal process was without absolute beginning or absolute end served to intensify the sense of wonder, of contingency, and of mystery attending the human odyssey.

Natural piety could not be taken as a manifestation of Absolute Being or as a response to divine revelation, and its cultivation could dissipate desire for any such datum. Finding in nature all that one might seek, the human spirit could be at home in the universe. Abandoning the yearning for an absolute of any kind, it was possible to affirm without nostalgia William James's insight that "all 'homes' are in finite experience; finite experience as such is homeless."[10] Consenting to contingency, the self acquired a particular peace that issued from the right balance between attachment and detachment, solidarity and solitude, and self-assertion and self-abnegation. The utter contingency of existence, which was later to inspire the mood of existentialist alienation among several generations of European thinkers, evoked among American pragmatic naturalists a sense of fallibility and revisability, of humility rather than hubris, of equanimity and rapport rather than nausea or rebellion.

The piety of the pragmatic naturalists also differed from Ralph Waldo Emerson's. The difference between an aesthetic spirituality that, on the one hand, directed natural piety toward the creative processes of cosmic nature and one that, on the other hand, viewed nature as included within an all-encompassing Absolute was not unlike the difference between a pluralistic, loosely federated commonwealth and a totality leaning toward monism. In the Emersonian Oversoul, as in later Hartshornian versions of panentheism, pragmatic naturalists were inclined to see the very temptations inherent in totalitarian systems, namely, a tendency to subordinate the parts to the whole, to make freedom instrumental, to value the present mostly in terms of the formation of a vague future, and to find the lasting meaning of all things in their contribution to the perfect whole.

Finally, a disinclination to convert matters of aspiration too solidly into matters of fact characterized the sensibilities of these American philosophers. They thought that traditional theologies and institutional forms of privatized religiosity had tended to treat hypothetical objects of hope too readily as objective powers, confusing ideals with agents and possibilities with actualities. Not only did they introduce a greater degree of differentiation between ideals and actual powers, but they also redefined the types of ideals associated with spiritual aspirations.

Representative Figures

William James (1842–1910)

In the writings of William James, psychologist, philosopher, and lifelong "sick soul," we can trace a spiritual and philosophical odyssey of exceptional interest and originality. Extending from his early psychological studies and reflections on the nature of the self, through his investigations of the varieties of religious experience and presentations of pragmatism as a new humanism, and culminating in his vision of a pluralistic universe, James's pragmatic naturalism was firmly rooted in a sense of human finitude. He opposed the Absolute of the philosophical idealists in every way.

"What boots it to tell me the absolute way is the true way," he asked, "and to exhort me, as Emerson says, to lift my eyes up to its style, and manners of the sky, if the feat is impossible by definition? I am finite once and for all, and all the categories of my sympathy are knit up with the finite world *as such* and with things that have a history."[11] He criticized supernaturalists and theists who posited "a universe in many editions, one real one, the infinite folio, or *edition de luxe*, eternally complete, and then the various finite editions, full of false readings, distorted and mutilated each in its own way."[12] Calling himself "a harmonizer of empiricist ways of thinking with the more religious demands of human beings," James could depict the problem of God not as a problem of the existence or the nonexistence of a being, even a Supreme Being, but rather as a question about the character of the universe, taken as a whole and in its parts. Pragmatist spirituality had more to do with "total reactions" and "cosmic impressions" than with an intentional object or personal deity, and in his pragmatic treatment of God, freedom, and design, James traced the meaning of each of these concepts to something like "the presence of 'promise' in the world." The pragmatic difference between theism and materialism invariably came down to a case of "hope versus no hope." At the heart of James's vision was a world where individual action mattered and there was hope that human ideals could prevail. Belief in free will, a conviction that restored James from his own prolonged identity crisis, entailed that our efforts actually do make a difference in the total texture of life. Feelings of futility and morbidity in the face of life's contingency, therefore, could give way to confidence and commitment.

Known for his interests in trance states, hallucinations, subliminal selves, and psychic research, James actually concluded to very little of any consequence concerning altered states of consciousness. Instead, his genius is to be found in the paradigm shift he helped to bring about in assumptions about the self and the whole. Crucial to his theorizing of both these notions was the doctrine James called radical empiricism. According to radical empiricism, in contrast to British empiricism, the relations that connect experiences must themselves be experienced relations. Instead of taking as primary the experience of reality, as most empiricists did, James focused primarily on the reality of experience. He interpreted both self and environing whole as interconnected aspects of experience, each functioning in certain distinctive ways, but neither carrying substantialist ontological weight. Finding in the flux of experience no substantial self, nor any substantial thing, James first developed the concept of the perceiving self as a field phenomenon in his path-breaking, two-volume *Principles of Psychology* (1890).

James's interest in temperament, a topic often neglected in studies of spirituality, affords a vital entry into the subject of the secular quest. The two types he distinguished — tough-minded and tender-minded in his first lecture on pragmatism, and healthy-minded and sick-souled in lectures 4 to 7 on religious experience — may seem rough and overly dichotomized today. In each case, though, James was describing compelling psychological tendencies toward two extremes and arguing that spiritual ease consisted in their reconciliation. He was also making a case for the relativity of different types of spirituality to different types of need. There was a time for the optimism and self-assertion of the healthy-minded, once-born temperament who is serene and sunny. Too much optimism, however, as in the Mind Cure movement of James's time or New Age and self-help movements in our time, led to complacency or utopianism, just as too much self-assertion turned into self-aggrandizement. Healthy-mindedness broke down in the face of failure and was utterly defunct in dealing with the facts of evil. On the other hand, sick souls like Tolstoy and Bunyan, sensitized to evil, tragedy, and life's thoroughgoing contingency, were vindicated by James for being more inclusive in scope, but no less in need of deliverance from their inner division and dark perceptions. Pessimism and melancholia were signs of spiritual un-ease, rooted in disappointed craving for a wider world of meaning than the self by itself could construct. Regeneration, or self-transcendence, bestowed such crucial psychological characteristics as "a new zest which adds itself like a gift to life, and takes the form either of lyrical enchantment or of appeal to earnestness and heroism"; and "an assurance of safety and a temper of peace, and, in relation to others, a preponderance of loving affections."[13]

Too much willfulness refused any role to resignation in the spiritual life, but James thought that letting go could be just as vital to well-being as holding on. There was a time for strenuous self-creation and a time for receptive self-abnegation, for going with the flow, acquiescing to the rhythms of the web of life in which one was embedded. The sick soul learned that there was "a wider spiritual life with which our superficial consciousness is continuous." The self-as-field phenomenon, described in *The Principles of Psychology* as having a "withness" and a "fringe," grew in *The Varieties of Religious Experience* (1902) to a self in commerce with a "higher part" that is "coterminous and continuous with a More of the same quality, which is operative in the universe."[14] James concluded the latter study with an assessment of the spiritual nature of the self that stressed two things: the needs that bind and the means that deliver. Passing beyond the warring gods and religious formulas that canceled each other out, James discerned "a certain uniform deliverance" consisting of two parts: an uneasiness and its solution. The uneasiness reduced to "a sense that there is *something wrong about us* as we naturally stand," and the solution was "a sense that *we are saved from the wrongness* by making proper connection with the higher powers."[15]

The higher powers were all worldly. Attention to what James called the "More" at the margins of the conscious self could not be construed as though it pointed to an *other* world, but it did point to a *wider* world, a depth of possibility in this one world. The weblike field of conjunctions and relations, filled with connections, was a flux in which every minimal pulse of experience issued in self-transcendence, a constant surpassing of one novel state by the next, possibly more creative or inclusive, state. Temporal experience itself could be said to have spiritual value not because of what it proceeded from or originated in but because of that to which it led. The significant leading-to or terminating-in experiences, in the mode of what James termed "transitive feelings," were those that proceeded in the direction of growth in qualitative meaning, in relational integration, and in shared sympathy, intensity of contrast, and scope of cognized feeling.

James believed that the play of lived experience, with its windows all opening outward to a field of possibilities, made the plural universe always unfinished, freely and contingently still in process of creation. The appropriate response to such an open-ended universe was to greet it knowing "that the next turn in events can at any given moment genuinely be ambiguous, that is, possibly this, but also possibly that."[16] Always to live without certainty, without closure, mixing in as much novelty as previous patterns of lived experience would permit, ready to flow with the stream of experience rather than in resistance to it or in compulsive control of it — this was the wisdom to which Jamesian radical empiricism could lead. We find only provisional and revisable toeholds in the flux, as we perch on the cutting edge between the old and the new, but we live forward.

Do we find a One behind or beyond the Many? In a 1903 notebook entry, James reported with exceptional clarity the line of reasoning that led him to repudiate the orthodox form of theism. He was willing, he said, to assume that a conscious soul is connected with other bodies, even down to the smallest material things that are supposed to exist. He was willing also to believe that there may be larger souls than one's own, whether connected or disconnected with the larger material aggregations. The existence of such larger souls he regarded as a theological question, to be discussed as any other question is discussed, in all the ways that may make a decision seem probable or not. James did not believe, he said,

> picturing the whole as I do, that even if a supreme soul exists, it embraces all the details of the universe in a single absolute act either of thought or of will. In other words I disbelieve in the omniscience of the Deity, and in his omnipotence as well. The facts of struggle seem too deeply characteristic of the whole frame of things for me not to suspect that hindrance and experiment go all the way through.[17]

The facts of struggle and pluralism so impressed James that by the time of *A Pluralistic Universe* (1910) he had concluded to a form of pluralistic pantheism. Monistic pantheism, which James rejected, held that "the divine exists authentically only when the world is experienced all at once in its absolute totality." The pluralistic pantheism of radical empiricism, on the other hand, "allows that the absolute sum-total of things may never be actually experienced or realized in that shape at all, and that a disseminated, distributed, or incompletely unified appearance is the only form that reality may yet have achieved."[18] These reflections mark a crucial culmination of James's religious investigations and shed light on his final understanding of the whole as neither absolutely one nor absolutely many. Rejecting both extreme monism as well as extreme pluralism, James's vision in *A Pluralistic Universe* is of a universe of nature in which powers both human and nonhuman cooperate together. The whole exhibits "concatenated unity" or a multiplicity of irreducibly particular events in the midst of intricate patterns of relatedness. In the end, James found himself "willing to believe that there may ultimately never be all-form at all, that the substance of reality may never get totally collected, that some of it may remain outside of the largest combination of it ever made." Not unlike recent postmodernists who resist totalizing intellectual gestures, James was clear that "ever not quite has to be said of the best attempts anywhere in the universe at attaining all-inclusiveness. The pluralistic world is thus more like a federal republic than like an empire or a kingdom."[19] While conceding that monism, like pluralism, could also stimulate strenuous moods, James noted that "pluralism actually demands them, since it makes the world's salvation depend upon the energizing of its several parts, among which we are." As he had stated in his lectures on pragmatism:

> I offer you the chance of taking part in such a world. Its safety, you see, is unwarranted. It is a real adventure, with real danger, yet it may win through. It is a social scheme of cooperative work genuinely to be done. Will you join the procession? Will you trust yourself and trust the other agents enough to face the risk?[20]

To the end, James himself was haunted by the possibility that "the world *may* be saved, *on condition that its parts shall do their best*. But shipwreck in detail, or even on the whole, is among the open possibilities."[21]

The antiessentialism and nonfoundationalism that were James's chief concerns as early as the 1880s would later gain currency among such late twentieth-century American thinkers as Richard Rorty in philosophy, Jeffrey Stout, Henry Samuel Levinson, and Cornel West in religious criticism, and Frank Lentricchia and Richard Poirier in literary criticism.[22]

John Dewey (1859–1952)

John Dewey grew up in the devout atmosphere of the First Congregational Church of Burlington, Vermont, where he taught Sunday school. When he later underwent something of a spiritual crisis, his religious outlook shifted to new philosophical auspices. In early articles for the *Andover Review* and other theological journals, Dewey refuted materialism and affirmed the compatibility of religion and evolution. Continuing to wrestle with the problem of religion and science, arguably *the* principal problem for American intellectuals during the late nineteenth and early twentieth century, Dewey arrived at a naturalized and secularized understanding of the spiritual quality of experience. He was interested in common, everyday activities and values that had no intrinsic dependence upon particular religious institutions or traditional creeds. Disavowing any dichotomy between God and nature, the supernatural and the natural, he published in 1934 his culminating statement, *A Common Faith.* Here he attempted to show that supernatural principles could now be grasped in and through nature's own processes. Dewey assumed spiritual qualities would survive the death of supernaturalism because they were inherent in human experience. Since the meaning of spirituality did not pertain to a specific type of experience but rather to a quality that may inhere in any experience, it designated nothing sui generis but could refer to qualities that were in principle universally available. Dewey's aim was to uphold distinctive values against what Walter Lippmann would call "the acids of modernity." The spiritual practices that invoked and promoted the values esteemed by Dewey were identical with the democratic life of inclusiveness, openness, and growth. This pragmatist spirituality could be achieved in a variety of ways, according to Dewey. Among them are poetic inspiration, philosophical reflection, and devotion to a noble cause.

According to *A Common Faith,* the spiritual dimension or function was felt as "having the force of bringing about a better, deeper and enduring adjustment to life." This adjustment or harmony of self with environment was attended by a calm resulting less from particular reasons than from life changes that "pertain to our being in its entirety." Because the unification of the self could not be attained in terms of itself, a posture other than sheer will power was important. The self, according to Dewey, was always directed toward something beyond itself, and so its unification depended on the idea of the integration of the shifting scenes of the world into that imaginative totality called the universe.[23]

On the problem of how the self is integrated as a whole, Dewey made three proposals. First, the secular quest points to some complex of conditions that operate to effect a significant adjustment in life, a reorientation that is transformative and integrative in effect. Second, imagination plays a key role in the unification of the self in harmony with its surroundings. The ideal of the whole self and the ideal of the totality of the world are held as imaginative projections, although the work of self-integration, far from being a matter of will power simply projected by the self, is itself dependent upon "an influx from sources beyond conscious deliberation and purpose." Third, insisting that "we are in the presence neither of ideals completely embodied in existence nor yet of ideals that are mere rootless ideals, fantasies, utopias," Dewey proposed that the real object of faith and source of spiritual regeneration was nothing supernatural but rather "the active relation between the ideal and the actual."[24]

Indeed, the meaning of the word *God* consistent with a common faith was one of ideal possibilities unified through imaginative realization and projection. The symbol God, in Dewey's view, stood for that specific unification of all relevant ideal ends, giving normative unity to the whole and "arousing us to desire and actions." As such, the divine was rooted in the natural conditions of history and the material world while transcending any single time and place. Unlike the Hegelian idea of God as the unity of the ideal and the real, Dewey's pragmatic naturalism captured the evolutionary, processive-relational sense of uniting as an ongoing activity. Impressed early in his career with the neo-Hegelian notion of a cosmic organic unity in which the ideal and the real are one, Dewey struggled to slough off the vestiges of idealism, a struggle that was solved by affirming the continuity of the many with each other as many, but not their literal oneness.

Nature was understood as both thwarting and supporting human efforts. Humankind was continuous with and dependent upon an environing world that, however imperfect or riddled with ambiguity, should evoke "heartfelt piety as the source of ideals, of possibilities, of aspirations."[25] Natural piety was a genuine and valuable part of human life in the world, needing more careful cultivation and expression in order to play a positive role in the development of society and culture.

Although no antecedent being could be presumed in whom an integration or unification of all ideal ends was already accomplished, Dewey repeatedly appealed to a "consciousness of the whole" and "the sense of this effortless and unfathomable whole" that is experienced as a natural response of the human organism to its environment.[26] In *Reconstruction in Philosophy* (1920), Dewey described "the miracle of shared life and shared experience" as bound up with a vital feeling of unity with the universe.[27] In *Human Nature and Conduct* (1922), the enveloping world of nature was identified as "the totality of natural events" and described as vague, undefined, and undiscriminated, hardly capable of objective presentation. Present emotionally in appreciations and intimations that yield feelings of freedom and peace, the sense of an enveloping whole could sustain and expand us in feebleness and failure.

Finally, in *Art as Experience*, published in the same year as *A Common Faith*, Dewey amplified the status of wholes and the close relation between the aesthetic and what he called the spiritual in the secular quest. The spiritual represented an intensification and broadening of the aesthetic quality of experience, having to do with what Dewey called "consummatory moments," involving "fulfillments" and "immediately enjoyed meanings." Wholeness was the quality that linked aesthetic experience, ordinary secular experience, and spirituality. Every experience, according to Dewey, possessed a peculiar "dim and vague" quality, of "margins" or "bounding horizon." It was a sense of an "enveloping undefined whole." Any work of art could be described as a whole that elicits and accentuates a sense of "belonging to the larger, all-inclusive whole which is the universe in which we live." The difference between aesthetic and spiritual experiences was one of degree, not of kind. The secular spiritual quest, unlike aesthetic experience, sought an unrestricted field of value whose harmony involved an ever-enlarging synthesis of the widest range and deepest contrasts of relational data.

Is the all-inclusive whole of nature an organic unity, a unitary subject, a single, complex individual? Dewey's final verdict was that the conditions and forces in nature and culture that promote human well-being were plural. There was no inherent unity to the forces and factors that made for good. Organizing and integrating these forces or factors were the work of human imagination and human action. The sense of the whole that animated the spiritual side of life is eloquently expressed in the concluding passage of *A Common Faith:*

> We who now live are parts of a humanity that extends into the remote past, a humanity that has interacted with nature. The things in civilization we most prize are not of ourselves. They exist by grace of the doings and sufferings of the continuous human community in which we are a link. Ours is the responsibility of conserving, transmitting, rectifying and expanding the heritage of values we have

> received that those who come after us may receive it more solid and secure, more widely accessible and more generously shared than we have received it. Here are all the elements for a religious faith that shall not be confined to sect, class, or race.[28]

Finally, the following passage from Dewey's *Experience and Nature* (1925) came as close to a credo, couched in poetic simplicity and suffused with a mystical glow, as anything Dewey wrote:

> Fidelity to the nature to which we belong, as parts however weak, demands that we cherish our desires and ideals till we have converted them into intelligence, revised them in terms of the ways and means which nature makes possible. When we have used our thought to its utmost and have thrown into the moving unbalanced balance of things our puny strength, we know that though the universe slay us still we may trust, for our lot is one with whatever is good in existence. We know that such thought and effort is one condition of the coming into existence of the better. As far as we are concerned it is the only condition, for it alone is in our power. To ask more than this is childish; but to ask less is a recreance no less egotistic, involving no less a cutting of ourselves from the universe than does the expectation that it meet and satisfy our every wish. To ask in good faith as much as this from ourselves is to stir into motion every capacity of imagination, and to exact from action every skill and bravery.[29]

George Santayana (1863–1952)

Heirs of the Enlightenment, both James and Dewey were troubled by the ways in which sectarian religions were responsible for superstition and fanaticism. They each supposed that religious interest in another world canceled out full participation in this world of social and political engagements. George Santayana, the Spanish-born, Boston-educated philosopher who was their passing critic, thought that James and Dewey missed the whole point of religion, which was to offer just such a reprieve, temporarily and intermittently, from this world. Sharply contrasting with the lingering legacy of Protestant moralism, Santayana's secularized Catholic, sacramental sensibility contributed a distinctive texture to pragmatic naturalism in the American grain.

Santayana appreciated the genuinely expressive, poetic, meditative, and festive character of religion in its capacity to present "another world to live in." As a pragmatic naturalist, however, he strongly resisted the literalizing tendency that, in Henry Samuel Levinson's summary, took "fictive gods for material facts, religious literature for revelations of the really real, religious rituals for artful transactions that overturn the conditions of natural life, and religious institutions as politically and socially authoritative."[30] Santayana thought spiritual life, understood on the model of festivity, freed people from their normal routines for refreshment, rituals, and a sense of common humanity. More poetic and less instrumentalist than James or Dewey, Santayana chided other pragmatists for collapsing the realms of law and spirit and duty and beauty in their pursuit of social reform. His alternative was to pursue contemplative disciplines that let people take delight in beauty and catch the joy of finite creaturehood. In *Skepticism and Animal Faith* (1923), he urged skepticism as one such discipline, while promoting a concept of animal faith that insisted on the biological contextuality of human activity and inquiry.

Exercising spiritual disciplines that lend the world an aura of grace called for a certain cultural space, and in *The Life of Reason* Santayana designated religion as the socially marginal and imaginative world in which to do this. In the *Soliloquies*, philosophy was said to perform this role also. Santayana's abiding wisdom, throughout five decades of writing, was that "social order per se does not secure the sense of well-being that comes in the solitary and personal affirmation or avowal of the things that bring joy to fragile human life."[31] Drawing upon the Stoics, Santayana recommended a piety of reverent attachment to the sources of being, consisting of "parents first, then family, ancestors, and country, finally humanity at large and the whole natural cosmos." Still higher and more noble yet was what Santayana called spirituality, or "life in the ideal," involving an "ideal synthesis of all that is good" as well as "devotion to ideal ends." If piety looks to the elemental sources from which humans draw their energies, spirituality is oriented to the end toward which the ideal points in the future. Only the ideal in Santayana's view was worthy of being considered divine.[32]

Santayana could take a starkly realistic view of the universe to which we owe cosmic piety:

> Why should we not look on the universe with piety? Is it not our substance? Are we made of other clay? All our possibilities lie from eternity hidden in its bosom. It is the dispenser of all our joys. We may address it without superstitious terrors; it is not wicked, . . . and since it is the source of all our energies, the home of all our happiness, shall we not cling to it and praise it, seeing that it vegetates so grandly and so sadly . . . ? Where there is such infinite and laborious potency there is room for every hope.[33]

Alfred North Whitehead (1861–1947)

Charles Hartshorne summed up Whitehead's philosophy as an elaboration of the novel intuition that "the many become one and are increased by one."[34] Whitehead himself regarded *Process and Reality* (1929) as an attempt to rescue the thought of James, Dewey, and Bergson from the charge of anti-intellectualism. Shorn of its intricacies, Whitehead's key hypothesis, indebted to James, Dewey, and Bergson, was that reality and the temporal flow of experience are creative of novel events according to a certain rhythm that has three phases. First, an event exercises receptive power in receiving causal influences (the many) from other creative experiences. Second, it exercises the power of self-determination, shaping the way it synthesizes its own experience (becoming one). Third, it exerts creative influence upon subsequent events by sharing some of its unity of feeling (evoking a new one). But what is the "it"? The nature and status of the subject of becoming proved to be the most difficult feature to grasp of this explicitly metaphysical version of pragmatic naturalism. Radically undermining the substance abuse of traditional philosophy, Whitehead gave primacy to processes and relations. The idea that a new subject emerged *from* a rhythmic interplay of the one and the many, rather than presiding *over* the process, challenged American commonsense thinking. Nevertheless, it was an idea with deep spiritual resonance in the long tradition of Buddhism, as it affirmed that "there is no doer who does the deed; no one who reaps the content of the deed as such; . . . the path exists but not the goer." As the poet William Butler Yeats asked, "How can we know the dancer from the dance?"

Whitehead's process metaphysics encompassed not only Eastern modes of thought but also Western scientific theory. Quantum theory had already provided a model of internal relationships at the atomic level of reality analogous to the model of internal relationships that would later become widely presupposed in the feminist, ecology, and holistic health movements. Could that same paradigm apply also to cosmic evolution? According to Whitehead's analysis, it could. Just as we cannot separate particles from the energy field in which they arise or organisms from the environmental niche in which they emerge and on which they depend, the human form of existence is implicated in a vast macrocosmic whole that is characterized, according to Whitehead's descriptive generalization, by the same creative rhythm as its parts.

The concept "from the many, one" therefore provided a succinct paradigm not only for understanding the American social experiment in covenantal relations but also for interpreting the open-ended, novelty-producing process of cosmic evolution. Whitehead's vision was of an evolving universe in which emergent qualities appeared as characteristics of entities at new levels of reality; they were not found in, and could not be predicted on the basis of, the entities at the level of reality from which the new level emerged. Molecular properties were not deducible from atomic properties, and neither were cultural properties deducible from the properties of organisms. If the model applied at the level of cosmic evolution, complex, apparently random situations were capable of spontaneously producing new levels of organization in the totality as a whole that would exhibit properties not found in the earlier level. The whole would literally be more than the sum of its parts.

This is the context for interpreting Whitehead's observation that the spiritual quest "runs through three stages, if it evolves to its final satisfaction. It is the transition from God the void to God the enemy to God the companion."[35] He saw each stage as a possible qualitative manner in which the totality of indefinite extensiveness could be experienced. Negatively, it could appear as a void in which demonic or meaningless qualities rose to dominance and to which despair, anomie, or fanaticism could seem legitimate spiritual responses. In this stage the self lost its sensitivity to the relational matrix of existence. The further transition from the void to the enemy entailed facing the ultimate context of life as an inimical power that exerted a force to be resisted. In this stage the self refused the possibilities inherent in the vital matrix of relationality, rejecting suffering as the cost of relationships, and rebelling against the implacability of the totality by seeking only solitary aims. Unless solitariness utterly failed to become communal and unless out of the many there could only be the same, the enemy that had formerly signaled dissolution could be disclosed to the self as the companion of its growth. A good not of the self's own making entered existence as a grace. In Whitehead's more technical language, it was an experience of "the consequent nature of God" or the "Unity of Adventure" that formed the basis for the intuition of peace. For Whitehead as for the other pragmatic naturalists surveyed here, the companion was neither a superorganism that swallowed up the individual members nor an externally related actuality different in kind from its constituents. The tension between the individual and the community, or the one and the many, constituted a contrast as irreducible for America's philosophical reflection as it was for its cultural experience.

Notes

1. Cited in Willard L. Sperry, *Religion in America* (New York: Macmillan, 1946), 138.

2. Later religious naturalists in the Chicago School (Henry Nelson Wieman, Bernard Meland, and Bernard Loomer), as well as at Yale (Douglas Clyde Macintosh) and Columbia (Frederick J. E. Woodbridge, John Herman Randall Jr.), also contributed to this school of thought. Casting the net more broadly in American culture, one could include such writers as W. E. B. Du Bois and Thorstein Veblen, as well as contemporary philosophers and religious critics such as Cornel West, Jeffrey Stout, Henry Samuel

Levinson, and Giles Gunn, whose work is part of a late twentieth-century resurgence of pragmatism.

3. See the introduction to this volume by Peter H. Van Ness.

4. The term *esthetic spirituality* was used by William A. Clebsch in his classic book *American Religious Thought: A History* (Chicago: University of Chicago Press, 1972) but with a somewhat different meaning than what I describe here.

5. William James, *A Pluralistic Universe* (Cambridge, Mass.: Harvard University Press, 1977), 131.

6. John H. Randall Jr., *Nature and Historical Experience* (New York: Columbia University Press, 1958), 198–99.

7. Alfred North Whitehead, *Religion in the Making* (New York: Macmillan, 1926), 16.

8. *Dialogues with Alfred North Whitehead,* recorded by Lucien Price (Boston: Little, Brown and Co., 1954), 171; Whitehead, *Religion in the Making,* 16.

9. John Dewey, *A Common Faith* (New Haven: Yale University Press, 1934), 25–26.

10. William James, *Pragmatism* (Cambridge, Mass.: Harvard University Press, 1975), 125.

11. James, *Pluralistic Universe,* 27.

12. James, *Pragmatism,* 124.

13. William James, *The Varieties of Religious Experience* (Cambridge, Mass.: Harvard University Press, 1985), 382–83.

14. Ibid., 400.

15. Ibid.

16. William James, *Some Problems in Philosophy* (New York: Greenwood Press, 1968), 140.

17. William James, *Manuscript Essays and Notes* (Cambridge, Mass.: Harvard University Press, 1988), 5.

18. James, *Pluralistic Universe,* 25.

19. Ibid., 145.

20. James, *Pragmatism,* 139.

21. James, *Some Problems in Philosophy,* 73.

22. See, for example, Richard Rorty, *Consequences of Pragmatism* (Minneapolis: University of Minnesota, 1982); Cornel West, *The American Evasion of Philosophy: A Genealogy of Pragmatism* (Madison: University of Wisconsin Press, 1989); Jeffrey Stout, *Ethics after Babel: The Languages of Morals and Their Discontents* (Boston: Beacon, 1988); Frank Lentricchia, *Ariel and the Police: Michel Foucault, William James, Wallace Stevens* (Madison: University of Wisconsin Press, 1988); Richard Poirier, *Poetry and Pragmatism* (Cambridge, Mass.: Harvard University Press, 1992).

23. Dewey, *Common Faith,* 19.

24. Ibid., 19, 51.

25. John Dewey, *The Quest for Certainty: A Study of the Relation of Knowledge and Action* (New York: Putnam, 1960), 244.

26. John Dewey, *The Middle Works of John Dewey, 1899–1924,* ed. Jo Ann Boydston, 15 vols. (Carbondale: Southern Illinois University Press, 1976–1983), 14:227, 180–81.

27. John Dewey, *Reconstruction in Philosophy* (New York: Henry Holt, 1920), 201.

28. Dewey, *Common Faith,* 87.

29. John Dewey, *Experience and Nature,* 2d ed. (Chicago: Open Court, 1929), 340.

30. Henry Samuel Levinson, *Santayana, Pragmatism, and the Spiritual Life* (Chapel Hill: University of North Carolina Press, 1992), 157. Levinson's text is the best book-length study available of Santayana's thought and overall relation to American pragmatism.

31. Ibid., 172.

32. George Santayana, *The Life of Reason: Or, The Phases of Human Progress,* 5 vols. (New York: Scribner's, 1905–6), 3:179, 184, 190, 193–95, 212, 176.

33. Ibid., 191–92.

34. Alfred North Whitehead, *Process and Reality,* corrected ed., ed. Donald W. Sherburne and David Ray Griffin (New York: Free Press, 1978), 21.

35. Whitehead, *Religion in the Making,* 16.

Bibliography

Clebsch, William. *American Religious Thought: A History.* Chicago: University of Chicago Press, 1972.

Dean, William. *American Religious Empiricism.* Albany: State University of New York Press, 1986.

Dewey, John. *A Common Faith.* New Haven: Yale University Press, 1934.

Frankenberry, Nancy. *Religion and Radical Empiricism.* Albany: State University of New York Press, 1987.

Gunn, Giles. *Thinking across the American Grain: Ideology, Intellect, and the New Pragmatism.* Chicago: University of Chicago Press, 1992.

James, William. *A Pluralistic Universe.* Cambridge, Mass.: Harvard University Press, 1977.

———. *The Varieties of Religious Experience.* Cambridge, Mass.: Harvard University Press, 1985.

Levinson, Henry Samuel. *Santayana, Pragmatism, and the Spiritual Life.* Chapel Hill: University of North Carolina Press, 1992.

Mead, George Herbert. *Mind, Self, and Society.* Chicago: University of Chicago Press, 1934.

Santayana, George. *Skepticism and Animal Faith.* New York: Scribner's, 1923.

Stout, Jeffrey. *Ethics after Babel: The Languages of Morals and Their Discontents.* Boston: Beacon, 1989.

West, Cornel. *The American Evasion of Philosophy: A Genealogy of Pragmatism.* Madison: University of Wisconsin Press, 1989.

Whitehead, Alfred North. *Process and Reality.* Corrected edition, edited by Donald W. Sherburne and David Ray Griffin. New York: Free Press, 1978.

———. *Religion in the Making.* New York: Macmillan, 1926.

C. Modernity Reaches Maturity

5

The Emergence of Historical Consciousness

ROBERT CUMMINGS NEVILLE

A Secular Path to Spiritual Depths

AMONG THE CONTEMPORARY FORMS of spirituality is the life of inquiry practiced by some scholars of religion in which they cultivate a peculiar combination of distance from and engagement with the religious matters under study. The academic objectivity sought is a critical engagement that renders scholarship vulnerable to correction where it is off the mark. The discipline involved in this kind of scholarly piety or spiritual cultivation derives from the demands of scholarship in religion. It is distinguishable and even separable from the kinds of piety involved in practicing an organized religion. Some scholars with deep attainments in this spiritual discipline are alienated from and perhaps hostile to organized religion, although others live traditional religious lives while also cultivating the peculiar piety of scholarship.

The distinguishing mark of this scholarly piety is its combination of distance and engagement. On the one hand, scholarship requires critical distance for its objectivity. This was a revolutionary idea originating in ancient Greece and well symbolized by Socrates' daimon, who warned him when to back off.[1] The scholarly implications of critical distance have been drawn out at length in the last two hundred years in the disciplines of the humanities and social sciences. On the other hand, objectivity requires engagement with the material to be studied; not so to engage allows the results of inquiry to be merely the projections of the categories and assumptions in the theories and methods of inquiry. In religion, engagement is particularly problematic because some aspects of religion are accessible only to experience trained through years of what Hindus and Buddhists call yogic practice; in the West it has been said that the important religious truths are accessible only to faith seeking understanding. Therefore, religious scholars must somehow penetrate the tao of religious faith and practice in order to gain access to that from which they can develop critical distance. *Tao,* of course, is the Chinese word for path or way; as in Western languages, the word has associations ranging from simple method, to the path or destiny of an individual's life, to the comprehensive inner essence of the universe. Taoism focuses principally on the cosmic dimension of the Way, which is a religious and spiritual category, and urges that individuals conform their own taos to the Tao. Within Western thought, *daimon* (or *demon*) is a word at one end of a spectrum of meanings for divinity; it can designate a range of beings, from the individual protective divinity (as in Socrates' reference), to gods, to conceptions of the ultimate cosmic God. Across all these meanings, the word *daimon* connotes a personalized judgment that distinguishes standards from performance, and it emphasizes the normative distance between these. I use *tao* to symbolize participation in religious and spiritual life and *daimon* to symbolize questioning that participation while engaging in it.

Scholars now know that two kinds of potential subjectivism bedevil religious understanding. One is the blindness of uncritical participation in some religious path, to which the distancing disciplines of Socratic inquiry are the antidote.[2] The other is the projection of one's methodological, theoretical, and more broadly cultural assumptions onto the religious path being studied, for which engaged participation in that tao is the antidote. Objectivity requires, therefore, the disciplines of both the tao and the daimon together. How this tao-daimon discipline of the academic study of religion constitutes a spiritual discipline of its own for some scholars is the topic of this chapter.[3]

Recent History of the Study of Religions

The study of religions was one of the earliest areas of culture within which historical consciousness arose in the West. In his influential *Theologico-Political Treatise* (1670) Baruch Spinoza sharply distinguished the religion of ancient Israel from the Judaism of his own time. They are distant from one another because of differences in imagination, he argued, and yet the earlier can be known from the perspective of the later because they have logical reason in common. Earlier Renaissance humanists such as Erasmus and the Protestant reformers had brought elementary historical consciousness into religion itself by critiques of the religion of their own time from the perspective of ancient biblical and classical sources.

Historical Consciousness

The nineteenth century was the time of the great flowering of historical consciousness in Europe, North America, India, and China and of its focusing on the understanding of religion. The story is complicated but worth sketching in its bold outlines for the insights this provides into the professional identity of contemporary scholars of religion, which in some cases is also a spiritual identity.

Hegel The sudden popularization of historical consciousness and the development of historically conscious academic disciplines in the nineteenth century were stimulated by two major European philosophers. The first was Hegel (1770–1831), who completed a brilliant and comprehensive philosophical system that was inclusive of metaphysics, logic, epistemology, ethics, political theory, philosophy of culture, philosophy of religion, and philosophy of history, all in historical categories. *Being* itself was interpreted in historical terms or their analogues, and so was logic. Part of the brilliance of Hegel's system was that it attempted to place all other philosophies, including those critical of Hegel's system, in positions of partial understanding within the system. To this day philosophers have difficulty escaping Hegel's implied criticisms of their positions as merely partial. Included within Hegel's system was an interpretation of the world's major religions in their historical development and comparative position. Although Hegel was biased in seeing all religions as partial and preparatory in relation to Christianity (understood in his way) and although knowledge of Asian, African, and Native American religions was scant in European scholarship of his day, Hegel's interpretations were surprisingly insightful. His discussion of "Lamaism," for instance, is a truly profound philosophical understanding of Mahayana Buddhism for a person who knew so little about Buddhism's texts and practices.[4] After Hegel, thinkers such as Marx and Nietzsche undermined the primacy Hegel had given to consciousness in history and developed what has become known as the "hermeneutics of suspicion." Nevertheless, after Hegel no Western scholar, nor any scholar from Asia who had acquired some Western learning, could fail to think of religions historically. Only Islamic scholars have resisted the historical approach to religion until recently.

Kant The other important philosopher for the development of nineteenth-century historical consciousness was Immanuel Kant (1724–1804). His importance lies not in his critical philosophy and ethics, which preceded Hegel's system and were put in place there. Rather his importance lies in the idea of the categoreal scheme or worldview. He had argued in his critical philosophy that we experience the world in terms of categories that the mind brings to experience a priori; what he meant were categories that are universal in all possible experience in which objective truth is possible. But in the nineteenth century that idea was radically relativized so that scholars thought of every culture as being determined by the categories making up its worldview. Different cultures and different religions, because of differences in the categories of their worldviews, experience the world differently.[5] The objective study of religion, then, is neither the defense of one's own religion against criticisms (although that is possible) nor the investigation of deep truths embodied more or less fully in various religions (as Hegel had attempted). The objective study of religions is the investigation of the various worldviews fostered and inhabited by different religions and cultures. Although personal and cultural biases are difficult to guard against, in principle this study of religions is empirical, investigating what various worldviews are and how they work.

Sociology of Religion August Comte (1798–1857) invented sociology as a positivist discipline that is supposed to be value-free, reporting only the positive facts. This derives from the popularization (and misunderstanding) of Kant's categories that human beings bring to experience and to which experience must conform. Peter Berger, a scholar writing in our day, has developed the study of religion through the sociology of knowledge with a far more sophisticated understanding than Comte's of the historical values and biases an investigator brings to the study of a religious worldview. Berger interprets religious cultures as embodying a dialectic of subjective categories about the religious nature of things that are projected into social realities and institutionalized, then to be reappropriated in personal and social experience so as to form what he calls a "sacred canopy" defining the religious dimensions of the world for a religion.[6]

Biblical Studies Meanwhile, the Christian and Jewish religious communities in Europe were encountering the historical consciousness in their studies of the Bible. Some Christian biblical scholars even before the beginning of the nineteenth century began to use historical-critical methods to look at the Bible. *The Life of Jesus Critically Examined*, by David Friedrich Strauss (1808–74), burst upon the German intellectual scene in 1835–36. It cost him his academic position because it asked what could really be known of Jesus if the biblical sources were treated simply as historical documents. For various reasons, many Christian theologians in Germany had come to believe that historical study, rather than appeals to revelation, should be the justification of Christianity. Strauss argued that history justified very little of traditional Christian theology. For different but related reasons having to do with the emancipation of European Jews and other cultural conditions, some Jewish thinkers in the Science of Judaism movement in the 1820s began a reform of their tradition that included looking at its texts and practices through the methods of the historical sciences; Reform Judaism was the outgrowth of this. Within liberal Christianity the historical method in biblical interpretation gave rise to a movement called after, and finished off by, Albert Schweitzer's *The Quest of the Historical Jesus.*[7] The quest by Schweitzer (1875–1965) found fewer than a dozen quotations in the New Testament that can reasonably be attributed to Jesus. Biblical historians found the New Testament worldview itself to be primitive and bizarre from the standpoint of modern science. In response to this Rudolf Bultmann (1884–1976) initiated a new school of interpretation that demythologized the Bible, distinguishing its truths as reinforced by existential philosophy from the mythic or what Spinoza called "imaginative elements."[8] Like Spinoza, Bultmann took the clue to religious truth from his contemporary philosophy and science and therefore was freed to examine the worldview of the Bible with historical curiosity.

Hermeneutics Friedrich Schleiermacher (1768–1834) revived the problems Spinoza had broached about the difficulties of understanding cultures from which we are distant. Schleiermacher was especially aware of the subtle interactions of our own self-consciousness with the consciousness of others, particularly those of the authors of the Bible. For him, hermeneutics is the disciplined strategy of avoiding misunderstanding, and it consists of ways of becoming cognizant of differences and commonalities among worldviews and also of noting how individuals and groups subjectively relate to those worldviews.[9]

Hermeneutical theory developed through the nineteenth and twentieth centuries. Among its major theoreticians with a special impact on religious studies have been Albrecht Ritschl (1822–89),[10] Wilhelm Dilthey (1833–1911),[11] Max Weber (1864–1920),[12] Ernst Troeltsch (1865–1923),[13] Martin Heidegger (1889–1976),[14] Hans-Georg Gadamer (1900–),[15] and Paul Ricoeur (1913–).[16] Now hermeneutics is understood as a complex circle of inquiry. It moves from attempts to understand an ancient or foreign text or culture back to attempts to understand the peculiarities of our own perspective. Then it backs around to distinguishing our perspective from the alien worldview being studied. It moves from attempts to sketch the whole of a worldview to interpretations of local data in terms of the whole, and then to revisions of the vision of the whole in light of local discoveries, on and around without end. In hermeneutics, the scholar attempts to compensate for distortions in the interpretation of what is alien that would come from the interpreter's cultural assumptions, and he or she also tries to identify those assumptions by comparison with the alternate worldview of the other. Although there is no ending or certainty to the hermeneutical circle, it can approach in any instance Schleiermacher's ideal of avoiding or overcoming misinterpretation.

Hermeneutics builds upon but also is a corrective to the positivistic, historicist social science of the nineteenth century. In contrast to simple positivism it understands the intrusive and value-laden character of inquiry itself and seeks to accomplish the needed participation in the religion to be studied by its moves through the hermeneutical circle.

Social-Science Erudition Two further developments decisively influenced the development of religious scholarship toward the objectivity of the tao-daimon contrast during the nineteenth century. One was the practical achievement of the social sciences in gathering masses of data about religions other than those of Western Europe. These studies made possible the great conceptual syntheses of the sociologists Emile Durkheim (1858–1917)[17] and Max Weber (1864–1920)[18] and anthropologists such as Edward Burnett Tylor (1832–1917),[19] Branislaw Malinowski (1884–1942),[20] Ruth Fulton Benedict (1887–1948),[21] and Claude Lévi-Strauss (1908–).[22] In turn these gave rise to the great compendia of religious material by comparative scholars such as G. Van Der Leeuw (1890–1950)[23] and Mircea Eliade (1907–86).[24] The result of this massive collection of empirical studies, sorted according to various theories, is a background awareness of religious diversity that every scholar of religion needs now to take into account.

Translations The other nineteenth-century development was the systematic translation into European languages of the basic texts of non-Western religions. One thinks of Max Müller's editing of the multivolume series Sacred Books of the East and of James Legge's translation of the classic texts of China. Although philologically trained scholars are still at work on critical editions and good translations of texts, it is possible now for scholars working only in English or other European languages to have a sophisticated and responsible knowledge of the religions of Asia for comparative purposes.

Extra-European Developments The great nineteenth-century advances in developing disciplines for studying religions with historical consciousness took place mainly in Europe. Nevertheless, thinkers from both India and East Asia learned from this and instituted at least the beginnings of academic scholarship in the educational traditions of their countries. In India, among the many modernizing movements of that century, the Ramakrishna Mission as led by Swami Vivekananda both made his version of ancient Hinduism popularly known across the world and brought the tools of Western scholarship to India. Sri Aurobindo carried on the reconstruction of ancient Indian religions for the modern world. In China, Korea, and Japan, the nineteenth century saw the first major onslaught of Western imperialism, not the reappropriation of ancient indigenous cultures in the face of earlier imperialism, as in India. The Meiji Restoration in Japan from the late 1860s on brought Western scholarship to that country along with many other things Western. Japanese scholars of religion are now full members of the larger community of religious studies inclusive of North Atlantic scholarly organizations. China resisted Westernization longer than Japan, and when in the 1920s it adopted much of Western culture, it was in a Marxist version that paid little but hostile attention to religion; the attention that was paid in the Marxist universities, however, was Western in its scholarly traditions. Korea welcomed Christian missionaries in the late nineteenth century, and they founded Western-oriented universities. Its relatively enthusiastic embrace of Christianity as a major religion involved as well the embrace of Western modes of scholarship.

Academic Objectivity

As a result of all these movements, and many other conditions besides, the ideals and disciplines of academic scholarship seeking the objectivity of the tao-daimon connection have been established around the world.[25] Perhaps the initial impetus for objectivity in the study of religions came from the general movement in German universities in the nineteenth century to model as much of learning as possible on the natural sciences. The attempts to define objectivity have been complex and controversial. The study of religion now is an academic field comprising many disciplines of the humanities, arts, and social sciences, and it examines religions of all sorts. Its objectivity overall is a procedural one that consists in the vulnerability of its assertions and findings to be corrected. Vulnerability in turn is a function of the different disciplines involved and their interactions.[26]

The academic study of religion has defended its objectivity by sharply separating itself from the activities of professing and proselytizing for some religion. This separation has sometimes expressed itself as hostility to a scholar's practicing religion, although academic objectivity requires only that a scholar separate scholarly inquiry from religious practice and that religious scholarship be tested by the same standards applied to the work of others who are not religious. As a result of the separation of objective academic scholarship in religion from religious practice, it would seem unlikely that research in religion per se would be a candidate for a spiritual path.

Nevertheless, the study of religion has indeed given rise to a dimension of spirituality that stands alongside and supplements those of the world's great religions. A scholar can pursue that path through study while having no other spiritual path or while also participating actively in an organized religious tradition. The next section of this chapter will analyze academic objectivity in religious studies in greater detail so as to make plain the spiritual path of the tao-daimon connection.

Spirituality and a Typology of the Study of Religions

Whereas the previous section rehearsed some of the many historical strands that have contributed to the rich texture of the contemporary academic study of religion, this section will present a typology of the analysis of religions. The typology is only one of several that could be used, each of which has its strengths. The strength of this one is that it displays the contrast between distance and engagement from many angles and in many contexts.

Clifford Geertz's phrase "thick description" is commonly used to characterize an ideal analysis of a religious culture or community. Thick description means combining "knowing about" religious practices and ideas with a participant-observer's understanding of how people existentially relate to those practices and ideas. Thick description reveals not only what religion people have but also *how* they have it. It combines reductive forms of analysis with narrative and other existential forms so that the people whose religion is the subject can recognize themselves in the description.[27] The discussion here will lay out some of the topic areas of thick description.

Religion in Its Spirituality

The general topic, of course, is religion as it is manifested in people being religious or spiritual.[28] This is a narrowly circular definition, however, but appropriate for the point at hand. Religions can be studied demographically, for instance, determining how many people in a given area profess a certain faith; but this is not to study religions in their spirituality. Similarly, religions can be studied for their economic impact, for their influence on world politics, and for their functions within psychopathology. All of these and related studies are interesting but do not as such pick up what is spiritual about religions. No one set of terms can list what is spiritual about religions, and the whole idea is the subject of intense debate. In general, what is spiritual in religions has to do with articulating and relating to fundamental issues of the human condition and place in the cosmos. It has to do also with ultimate sources and characters of obligation; with emotive and self-definitional issues occasioned by glimpses of the limits of one's cultural world as manifested in contrasts between the sacred and the profane; with addressing the fundamental tasks, problems, or flaws in human life; and with calling upon nonordinary resources to address all these issues so as to approach perfection or fulfillment.

Western religions tend to articulate these things in terms of a moral relation people have with one another and God that historically or regularly is ruinously denied and that must be repaired by a combination of divine effort and human response. Many of the religions of India see the human condition to be one of souls, or centers of consciousness, that regularly become confused with or attached to the material world, resulting in a fundamental ignorance of what is real and calling for enlightenment. The religions of China tend to see the human situation as one of a delicate balance of vast natural and social processes. Typically, people become disattuned to this harmony (for reasons about which the Chinese religions differ greatly) and need to be brought back to a harmony that, with proper human participation, is greater than that of nature alone. The academic study of religion that cultivates the tao-daimon contrast of investigation and that can be a spiritual path of its own deals with religions as spiritual in addition to their moral, social, economic, and political elements.

The typology to be used here distinguishes four dimensions of religion, each of which requires investigation with both distance and participation. These are: imaginative structures and practices; assertions about what is spiritually important; cosmic vision; and the personal and social quest for the spiritual path. These are obviously connected and overlap in a variety ways, some of which will be spelled out here.

Imaginative Structures and Practices

Religious imaginative structures and practices include all ideas and symbols, as well as all rituals, music, festivals, domestic religious practices, and public forms of reflection and action, that serve to shape and reinforce people's religious imagination. It is not important here to take up the problem of whether the imaginative elements are true or false (which is the problem for assertions) or whether they are directly effective in accomplishing a goal such as victory over enemies, bringing rain, or giving up addictive habits. The point at hand is rather that imagination shapes the way people take in the world and orient their responses. The religious parts of imagination shape the way people take the human condition, its obligations, flaws, cosmic limits, and ultimate remedies. Certain imaginative elements in religions, such as frequently repeated rituals, postures of prayer, and so forth, are often directly intended to shape individual and community character. For instance, the Christian Eucharist is intended to fix in disciples' souls the conviction and expectation that daily life lived faithfully will be filled with analogues of crucifixion and that this, paradoxically, is the way of resurrected life. Each religion shapes its reflective and social life with meanings that arise from imagination in particular ways.

Imagination is not distinguished from assertion by its pictorial or graphic quality in contrast to more refined intellectual abstractions; abstractions are just as imaginative as brute gestures.[29] The imaginative dimension consists rather in a distinctive function. Religion behaves imaginatively so as to shape social and personal life by the images involved. George Lindbeck picks up this dimension of religion in what he calls the cultural-linguistic method of theology.[30] Philosophical theologians writing in and for a religious community are just as much performing the imaginative shaping function as musicians, liturgists, or cooks at church dinners.

Religious imaginative structures (and structured processes) bear two senses of meaning, which can be distinguished as network meaning and content meaning. Scholarship concerning the imaginative dimension of religions requires the connected work of distancing and participation in at least these two ways.

Network Meaning Network meaning has to do with the syntactic, semantic, and pragmatic ways in which one part of an imaginative structure relates to other parts. A language, for instance, can be viewed in its imaginative dimension, and its network meanings have to do with grammar, vocabulary, and usage. Language is not the only vehicle for the expression of imagination. Imagination in some religions visualizes heaven as up and hell as down; these imaginative forms have become reversed in some modes of recent Christianity, for which the holy is a ground and superficial things are on top. There is an imaginative network logic to time and central space, as explored by Eliade in his discussions of "in that time" and the world tree. Postures for prayer, rhythms for singing, expectations for transformative life stages such as puberty, marriage, childbirth, and so forth, all have imaginative structures with a network logic. There are also imaginative logics to highly reflective elements of religion such as sutra-recitation, commentarial learning, and theological argument and theory.

The distancing part of the scholarly investigation of religious imagination focuses on laying out the logics of network meaning. Many scholarly approaches work at this: the formation of typologies, comparative discriminations, reductive analyses of psychological or social factors, semiotic analyses, logical analysis in the ordinary sense, and various forms of symbolic interpretation. Many religious people are unconscious of the imaginative logic of some of their most important symbols. Christians, for instance, are often surprised to learn that the Eucharist has a layer of cannibalistic logical symbolism, despite the fact they have heard many times the phrase, "This is my body; take and eat." Most of the nineteenth- and early twentieth-century analyses of religions in comparative perspective, including reductive analyses such as Marx's and Freud's, worked by laying out network meanings. The empirical objectivity of network analysis of imaginative structures lies in the ability to see from various angles whether the logic is as the analyst describes.

Content Meaning Content meaning, by contrast, refers to an internal logical structure to any imaginative part as well as the structures connecting that part with others; these are obviously related. The internal logical part, however, is not merely a form of connection but also the real togetherness of the internal components. This is to say, the content meaning is the real experiential content of the imaginative structure. Persons quite possibly can learn the network meanings of their imaginative acts without any of the content, or with very little. They thus can behave and speak correctly, but hollowly.

For instance, a young Confucian can learn the rituals honoring ancestors and perform them correctly without feeling the reverence and piety those rituals are supposed to contain. A Buddhist monk can successfully go begging but without the feelings of humility and selflessness the act of begging is supposed to shape. A new Christian can take Communion in the prescribed manner, and explain to a catechist what it is supposed to mean, without any sense of participation in the life and death of Christ.

The content meaning of an imaginative structure or act consists of other imaginative structures whose own components are imaginative structures, and so on. Any ritual such as the Christian Eucharist contains many levels of meaning compacted together by the ways the imaginative structures work. For any individual, some of those meanings will be truly present as experientially filled content and others only by means of imaginative tokens supplied by network meaning. A person, for instance, might know about and acknowledge the cannibalistic level of meaning in the Eucharist without having the real sense of taking in and taking over the eaten person's power and genius. When the content meanings of an imaginative structure are present only in network forms, they obscure or impede the experiencing of yet other content meanings. One aspect of the Indian practice of cultivating unitary vision, or *samadhi*, is not to blur or confuse things but to be able to enjoy things harmoniously through one another.

Although imagination functions in religion far beyond spiritual practices and rituals, in those areas repetition serves to cultivate the relevant content meanings. Whereas one-pointed meditative focus is difficult to achieve on one's first attempt, long and frequent sessions of quiet sitting help to pull into place the relevant contents and to exclude distractions. Much of spiritual direction, although not all, has to do with testing the imaginative structures of devotional life for the authenticity of their content meanings.

Obviously, for the scholar to study a religion's content meanings it is necessary to participate to the degree necessary to attain to the contents. Given the vast range of different forms and functions of imaginative structures, many kinds of participation are involved. Not all are esoteric or would require "abandoning oneself" to the perspective and feeling-world of the religion, but some do. Where it is impossible to enter the feeling-world, as in the case of lost innocence, participation, and thereby objective scholarship, are truncated.

Distance and Participation in Scholarship of Imagination The spiritual discipline of scholarship with regard to the study of the imaginative structures of religious practices and expressions consists of the cultivation of investigative methods and personal integrity required to balance network meanings and content meanings. For scholars to whom the religion is alien, the temptation is to rely too heavily on network meaning, which of course is the initial entry into the alien imaginative structure. For scholars already participant in the religion and perhaps committed to it, the temptation is to express and affirm the authority of the content meanings without the distancing analysis of the network meanings. With respect to spiritual discipline in the tao-daimon contrast, the balance of network and content meanings in the study of imaginative structures is central.

Assertions

Although appreciation of imaginative structures is presupposed in every scholarly analysis of religions in their spiritual dimension, other dimensions must also be appreciated. The assertoric dimension, for instance, deals with religious assertions about the nature of reality. An assertion is true if reality has the nature or position the assertion attributes to it, taking into account all the qualifications of the various respects in which assertions interpret reality and the various symbolic systems employed for the assertions.

Religious assertions have many forms, from abstract metaphysical and theological propositions explicitly asserted to ways of the world and gods assumed in activities whose explicit purposes are something else. Especially important are what might be called devotional assertions, couched in metaphors that few take literally but that are intended to assert or question the nature of the real. Such assertions (or questions) are supposed to refer to their objects, but the referential path cannot be understood without an elaborate interpretation of what is implied in the imaginative structure. To assert, for instance, that the Buddha-mind is infinite compassion is not to assert that it is a big mind, though it seems to say that. To assert the Christian doctrine of the atonement is to claim to explain how God saves people, not to assert that God is a divine child abuser, although atonement imagery takes that form. Scholarly grasp of religious assertions, particularly devotional and liturgical ones, is highly complicated.

A partial form of inquiry into religious assertions is to describe and interpret what assertions a religion makes or assumes. This can be done by sociological, anthropological, psychological, and historical studies, as well as by the analysis of texts, dialogues with religious spokespersons, and so forth. The analysis of the assertions is not the same as inquiry into whether those assertions are true and in what respects. Only the latter is full-blooded understanding of religious assertions. The former, a descriptive enterprise, is closer to an analysis of the imaginative structure of a religion than it is to an analysis of the truth of its assertions.

Scholarship and the Truth of Religious Assertions From the standpoint of religious practitioners, the concern is with whether their religion's assertions are true. Perhaps only professional religious thinkers are concerned about formulaic theological assertions. Every Buddhist, though, is concerned to identify true nonattachment, true enlightenment, and the truth about compassion; perhaps it is safer to say that every Buddhist is concerned about whether a particular state is true nonattachment, enlightenment, and so on. Christians are concerned about whether God really does save, whether God's love applies to oneself and one's group. Confucians are concerned about whether this or that path is their true destiny. No descriptive statement that this is what Buddhists, Christians, or Confucians believe answers the question of truth, although appeals to community or traditional authority are some ways of answering the question of truth.

Scholarship regarding truth in religious matters pursues the daimon of distancing by asking the question of truth from as many perspectives as possible. The notorious difficulty that many religious people have in focusing questions of truth lies in the fact that religions are so easily confused with authorities, the weight of tradition, habits of practice, and other elements of imaginative structure. That something follows as true within an imaginative structure, as a kind of entailment of the imaginative logic, does not mean it really is true. Insofar as the religions or religious people assert it as true, they mean it as referring to reality. They mean that their imaginative structure makes reference to reality even when it is being used for the cultivation of character in line with the religion's ideals. Therefore, part of the analysis of the truth of assertions is the study of how and whether assertions framed in an imaginative structure relate to reality. This is a matter of distance because the imaginative structure itself must be lifted up and objectified.

Scholarly Participation in Corrective Dialectic The other side of the analysis of the truth of assertions is to get inside the imaginative structure to the content meanings involved and to ask whether those meanings can be used to make true assertions. This is a difficult point because many of the things about which religions make assertions are not objects in the ordinary sense. Reference to them does not mean comparing them to statements or comparing an isomorphism of the objects' structures to things in the representations of them. Rather, deep religious assertions are matters of the heart that have been reinforced or corrected by millennia of engagement with life at its limits. Articulate representations of this heart-knowledge are always far more arbitrary than the heart's evolved lessons. Specific levels of imagination attempt to shape basic imaginative engagement so that tests can be made, but they always say too much. Therefore, it is best to recognize that the proper locus of basic religious assertions is in the long slow process of their correction through history. There are few clear directions. For instance, all religions assert that human beings live under some kind of obligation, to the gods, to purity, to ritual cleanliness, to nature, to other people. Some religions, however, move further to assert that the universe itself, or its ultimate God or principle, is moral: the good shall prosper, and the evil shall be punished. Other religions reject this as empirically false. The analysis of the truth of religious assertions involves participation in the long dialectic of the correction of the assertions.

The American pragmatists learned from Hegel that knowledge never has a beginning point but is always underway, hopefully being corrected rather than corrupted. They put this at the center of their epistemology and treated all knowledge as learning. So, with the scholarly discipline of judging the truth of religious assertions, the scholar must come to find a place within the stream of corrections. All the moves toward distancing, all the typologies, comparisons, and dialogues, need to be embraced as internal to the process of ascertaining religious truths.

Whereas an imaginative structure might be private to a religion, so that to enter it for its content meanings requires entering into the religion, judgment of the truth of religious assertions is essentially public. It transcends any imaginative structure in order to get a hermeneutical grasp of the assertion and the conditions for its truth. Because there is no thought at all without imaginative structures, it is impossible, indeed undesirable, to transcend all of them. The structures are used to triangulate in on one another in the attempt at putting the whole assertion in position to be corrected if it is wrong. Though public, the scholarly study of the truth of religious assertions requires participating in the traditions of habits in which those assertions lie.

Here is one instance in the academic study of religion in which the scholar must indeed have a spiritual discipline. In order to ascertain the truth of the important religious assertions, it is necessary to incorporate religious life, lived with its habits, so that such assertions will encounter reality and so be corrected. The scholar might not be committed to any one imaginative structure and might thus refuse to be identified with any organized religion or tradition. Nevertheless, the scholar fails at scholarly discipline by standing back from the engagement of reality when assertions about that reality's nature are ready to be corrected. Some scholars legitimately refuse the tao-daimon spiritual path at this point by declining to ask the questions of truth about religious assertions. The refusal of the truth questions is explicitly a deliberate setting aside of the most existentially gripping content of religious life. Such scholarship can be only partial with regard to understanding what religions are and do.

Cosmic Vision

Cosmic vision is a dimension of religions that combines both assertions and imaginative structures to provide a sense of the whole of things and of people's places in that whole. The stuff of vision is imaginative structures, and most religions are self-conscious enough to treat their candidate visions as assertions. The function of cosmic vision is not so much to form character and community, or to foster concern for truth, as it is to provide orientation in the world. Myths of creation, time and eternity, cosmic position, reality versus illusion — all provide pivots for cosmic visions that orient life in its most fundamental elements.

The importance of cosmic vision is perhaps best appreciated in our day by noting that in all traditional religions it has been destroyed — or at least deeply shaken — by modernization. Modern science does not genuinely threaten our imaginative structures; indeed, it helps us see how subtle and expressive such structures are. Nor does science threaten many specific assertions of religious truth, especially when these can be hermeneutically reinterpreted in light of our understanding of the workings of symbolism. What science threatens is the sense of how the world hangs together as religions have construed this for the sake of orientation. Traditional visions have a hard time now distinguishing between ultimate things and proximate conditions, affirming obligation in the face of sheer relativism, and expressing what, if anything, is important and valuable for individual and social life. All the traditional cosmic visions are undergoing serious modification by the impacts of modernization and modern science, and it is difficult to predict how those modifications will come out for modern Buddhists, Christians, Confucians, Hindus, Jews, Muslims, and Taoists.

Cosmic Vision and "Other Religions" Perhaps the most pertinent point about a religion's cosmic vision, at least in the modern world, is that it articulates how that religion with its imaginative structure relates to other religions and to the nonreligious secular world. Cosmic vision requires categories that explicitly transcend the core imaginative structure of a religion to embrace its alternatives, while at the same time in some sense remaining faithful to that core. The problem in this respect for academic scholarship is to understand two things. The first is how a religion's cosmic vision represents other religions within its orienting world. The second is to assess how true this representation is, and in what sense of truth.

Orientation As with assertions of truth taken in small scale, cosmic visions can be understood in their comprehensiveness and worth with the means of both distance and participation. Although questions of truth and imaginative structure are involved in understanding cosmic visions, the unique issue regarding this dimension of religion is understanding how and with what validity the vision provides religious orientation. As with questions of truth, it is possible merely to describe what a religion's cosmic visions are and how they orient people, without assessing the validity of the orientation. That is to stand back from understanding what is most vital and interesting in the issues of cosmic vision: How ought people be oriented within the cosmos?

If a scholar presses that last normative question, then as with questions of truth the means to its answer involves a participation in the corrective process of orientation. This is not to say that the scholar needs to adopt any religion's cosmic vision or work out an idiosyncratic cosmic vision. It is to say that academic objectivity requires the scholar to make analytical or speculative hypotheses about cosmic vision vulnerable to correction in experience. When scholars embrace this scholarly discipline directly, it is likely to give rise to extraordinarily sophisticated approaches to cosmic vision, combining the perspectives of many religions and showing facility with vision on many levels. One thinks of the spiritual power in this respect of scholars such as Mircea Eliade, Wilfred Cantwell Smith, Thomas Berry, Huston Smith, and Ninian Smart. Although none of these is particularly alienated from a native organized religion, what is special about their spiritual power derives from their scholarship regarding the cosmic visions of world religions.

Religion as Quest

The process of pursuing the religious life as such, the religious quest, is the fourth dimension to which academic scholars have paid much fruitful attention in their study of religions as spiritual. The pursuit of the tao, as it may be called in light of the usage above, is eminently practical, though shaped by religious imagination, guided by religious assertions, and oriented by cosmic vision. Religious quests or practical religious ways have many forms. Most involve any one of several complicated dialectics of individual versus social life; some are consciously intentional, and others are more like inherited habits of religious living.

The practical side of religious living is guided by some sense of human life as being under obligation. In part, being under obligation defines people as human regardless of the contents of the obligations. The religious problem — ignorance, illusion, sin, disharmony — in some sense results from failing the task of living under obligation (and also failing specific obligations). But different religions define the fundamental obligatedness in various ways. (The term *obligation* reflects the moral orientation of Western theisms, although it has analogues in other traditions.) Four fundamental senses of obligatedness are to be found in most religions.

Righteousness The first, which supplies the metaphors for the others, is righteousness or the obligation to justice. Justice here means an order that is imposed on an otherwise fluid and destructive situation by a god, a people, a king, or some other individual. The point is that righteousness or justice requires the imposition of a form that "gives everyone his or her due" (to quote Plato's phrase). Perhaps the sense of justice arose when a king was needed to depersonalize citizenship and impose order on a society too large to tolerate mere kinship authorities with their blood feuds. Sky gods impose order.

Natural Piety A second fundamental sense of obligatedness is to respect, honor, and defer to the various parts of the world each in its own place with its own value. Such deference is a kind of natural piety, and most religions cultivate it as an essential part of humanity. Sometimes appreciation of things onto which order needs justly to be imposed leads to a conflict between righteousness and natural piety. Late twentieth-century concerns for ecological balance and respect for species thus sometimes have come into conflict with the pursuit of justice for persons whose livelihood threatens the ecology. Deference to nature and natural passions has sometimes been associated with the Earth Mother.

Existential Engagement The third sense of obligatedness is the existential requirement of engaging one's situation. This has been a principal focus of religions that emphasize the distinction between illusion and ignorance, on the one hand, and enlightenment, on the other. Illusion and ignorance are never entirely innocent and have some form of denial, overidentification, or attachment associated with them. Twentieth-century Jewish and Christian theologies have emphasized existentialist concerns about authenticity and faith. The obligation to be true, to be authentically engaged and not self-deceived, is not the same as moral obligation or natural piety. Yet religions take it to be part of the human condition.

The Religious Path The fourth fundamental sense of obligatedness is the individual orientation to the religious path itself. Obligatedness to be religious is inclusive and integrative of all the other fundamental senses of obligatedness. The tao of religious practice has many forms and imaginative structures: finding God; becoming God; becoming enlightened, empty, attuned, individuated, released, freed. It might mean being faithful to a people and its destiny or dying the great death to a culture in order to be empty or reborn. Most religions have multiple representations of the steps of the path and their meaning.

Whereas any of the senses of fundamental obligatedness can be attended to, represented in a religion, and pursued by itself, most religions valorize them all and suggest that if any is missing the religiousness of the religion is compromised. The religious life is something more concrete than morality, natural piety, enlightenment or existential commitment, and even the explicit career of being religious. All of these together add up to religiousness.

Scholarly Participation and Distance in the Religious Quest The scholar of religion in its practical pursuit can attend to any one or all of these fundamental senses of obligatedness or to a part or aspect of one or several. The scholar can look to the imaginative structures, assertions, and visions in any or all of these. Regardless of narrowness or breadth of focus, academic objectivity requires both distance and participation. The distance comes through all the ways practice can be represented through methods of inquiry. The participation comes through taking on the various senses of obligatedness in order to understand specific forms of religiousness. To take them on, of course, is to accept the obligatedness. Scholars who opt for this way to objectivity, as with those who enter into the spiritual discipline of coordinating cosmic visions, are likely to be extraordinarily sophisticated, participating in more than one religion's approaches to obligatedness.

To sum up this section, scholars of religion need to combine distance with participation in order to obtain academic objectivity in at least four dimensions of religious studies. They need distancing disciplines for the analysis of network meaning in imaginative structures and participatory disciplines for the analysis of content meaning. They need logical testing disciplines to get distance on truth claims in religion and participatory techniques to embody religions' deepest claims and engage them where they might be corrected. They need descriptive, distancing, analytical tools to understand the ways cosmic visions orient people, and they need participatory techniques to engage in the creation and correction of orientations. They need distancing disciplines to understand and criticize the nature of the four senses of obligatedness as various religions represent these, and they need participatory disciplines to understand just how and why the obligations are obligatory.

Models of Spirituality among Historically Conscious Scholars

The previous section spelled out at some length a typology for understanding what goes into the study of religions and how disciplines provide both distancing and participatory functions. It was apparent how in each of the major categories a scholar, in the pursuit of academic objectivity, might undertake part of the scholarship as a spiritual discipline. In this section these observations about a scholar's potential spiritual discipline will be integrated, and four models will be presented of how the spirituality of the inquiring role might be related to organized religions' modes of spiritual development.

It would be a mistake to believe that all good scholars of religion are engaged in the secular spirituality of the tao-daimon contrast. Few if any scholars actively study a religion or several religions in all the dimensions mentioned above (or in all the dimensions that might be articulated by other typologies). Most scholars limit their serious research to what one or a very few disciplines can understand about religions' many dimensions, and few scholars have the rare combination of intellectual generosity and speculative wit needed to grasp affinities fully and to embrace studies coming from other approaches than their own. Tensions between descriptive and normative approaches — both of which have been shown above to be necessary for taking religion seriously in its religiousness — are especially high. But even if there were a scholar who studies religions in all their dimensions, with all the appropriate disciplines stretched to the utmost to meet the demands of both distance and participation, that would not necessarily mean that the scholar herself or himself is engaged in the tao-daimon spiritual path.

Qualifications for Scholarship to Be a Secular Spirituality

For the scholar properly to be said to be exercising the tao-daimon spiritual path, the scholarly life would have to be organized self-referentially with the harmonious integrity of the four dimensions of religion. That organization takes place in the scholar's own practical religious pursuits as illustrated in the fourth dimension. Although the scholar would not have to be at all self-conscious about this secular spiritual path — and indeed could be conscious of following a different spiritual path of some organized religion — in practice there would have to be (1) an integration of the imaginative structure of tao-daimon scholarship with (2) assertions the scholar defends as true about religiously important topics and with (3) the scholar's own composite cosmic vision, all (4) as a practical shaping and orientation of the scholar's pursuit of righteousness, natural piety, authentic engagement of reality, and spiritual destiny. These categories for integration are peculiar to the typology used in the previous section and surely allow alternatives. The spiritual matters having to do with authentic engagement correspond roughly to the "outward complexion" of secular spirituality explained by Peter H. Van Ness in the introduction to this volume; spiritual matters having to do with the religious quest and spiritual destiny relate to Van Ness's category of "inner transformation." The spiritual pursuits having to do with righteousness and deference or natural piety extend his classification because they are not exclusive functions of organized religions. The general point is clear about the self-referential integration of the various areas of distance-participation in dealing with religious matters.

The Scholar's Religious Imagination The distinguishing mark of the imaginative structure of the scholar's spirituality, in contrast to the imaginative structures of traditional religions, is that it takes its specific images from the historical development of and debates about the various methodological procedures to attain proper distance and engaged participation for the achievement of academic objectivity. The scholarly imagery would be filled with traditional religious images, but as objectified and hermeneutically understood. Because the field of religious studies is a congeries of disciplines, each at its own stage of internal self-criticism, there is little unity to the religious imagery of the spiritual scholar. The scholar's imagination, then, requires vast erudition to acquire sensitivity to the many issues involved in attaining proper distance and participation so as to make study of this or that problem vulnerable to correction.

The Scholar's Religious Assertions A spiritually disciplined scholar's religiously important assertions, shaped by the imaginative structures reflective of the disciplines of critical inquiry, would have to be informed by critical assessments of the ways religions have made such assertions. Perhaps the scholar's conclusions would not be congruent with any organized religion's assertions; surely they would reflect a level of abstraction involved in comparative judgments. However related to traditional religious assertions, the spiritually disciplined scholar would have assertions about how reality stands with regard to the human condition and ultimate things.

The Scholar's Cosmic Vision The spiritually disciplined scholar's cosmic vision not only would reflect criticisms and reconstructions of traditional religious visions but also would envision how scholarship can relate these visions and the scholar's own vision to the modern world. Perhaps unlike practitioners of traditional religions, the scholar's spiritual discipline does have to envision a place for the scholar's religious practice in a world of modern science where economic development often oppresses and where the cosmic geography is more vast than any traditional religion imagined, even Hua Yen Buddhism with its worlds within worlds. The cosmic vision of the spiritual scholar might be the first place where religions can solve the problem of relating to modernity, and traditional religions can learn from this.

The Scholar's Own Quest The spiritual scholar's own practical pursuit of spiritual practice, shaped by scholarly imagination, guided by scholarly religious assertions, and oriented by a scholarly cosmic vision, must be made specific. The first three dimensions can be notoriously abstract in a scholar's hands, and perhaps some scholars are self-deceived to believe they are being seriously spiritual and religious with only their scholarly imagination, assertions, and vision. The easiest way to be specific and concrete in the practice of religion is to devote oneself to the cultus of an organized religion. The specific practices in a given organized religion might not indeed be reflective of or reflectible in the religious imagination, assertions, and vision of a responsible scholar. From the standpoint of the organized religion, of course, it might be good strategy indeed for coping with the problems of modern culture to reach out to and include the spirituality of good religious scholarship. This likely would entail altering traditional religious practice and incorporating distancing structures as well as processes of reengagement. From the standpoint of spiritual scholarship, however, the scholar would have to ascertain what requirements for righteousness, natural piety, authentic spiritual realism, and the pursuit of spiritual destiny would follow from the scholarship.

Models of Spiritual Scholarship and Organized Religion

Multiple Religious Identity The first model of how spiritual scholarship might relate to the practice of organized religion is that of multiple religious identity. Scholars have long recognized that in some cultures, for instance, precommunist China, individuals and families could compartmentalize and reintegrate their lives so as to practice several religions, each with its imaginative structure, assertions, vision, and practices more or less distinct and intact. Ezekiel took a dim view of this in ancient Israel, but in many modern societies the children of parents who represent different religions are often raised to take part in the cultus of both. Making different religions compatible within one life and social setting — while respecting those religions' differences — is a difficult matter, but it has been resolved many times. In the case of the spiritual scholar, the spirituality of the scholarship itself is one religious identity that can be integrated with full participation in an organized religion; indeed, with multiple religious identity, a scholar can have a rich cultic life in several religious traditions.[31] John Berthrong's *All under Heaven* is an unusually sensitive study of multiple religious identity.[32] This solution to the problem of relating scholarly spiritual discipline to traditional religion recognizes the full weight of participation.

Deconstruction The second model is that of deconstruction, and it recognizes the weight of distancing. Deconstruction privileges deference to and acknowledgment of "the Other." While cultivating respect for any organized religion studied, encountered, or inherited, it fosters self-alienation from the slightest naïveté of participation in any religion. Turned on scholarship itself, deconstruction might acknowledge that it provides a genuine spiritual discipline but would move immediately to deconstruct any rendering, such as in the typology above, of what that might be. Edith Wyschogrod's *Saints and Postmodernism* is a superb study of the issues involved in this model.[33]

Abstraction and Syncretism The third model is appreciative abstraction and syncretism *on secular terms*. Perhaps the majority of North Atlantic scholars with spiritual discipline exemplify this model. While not identifying seriously with any religious tradition except for props and helps, scholars can abstract elements out of one or more religions and reconfigure them to provide for a concrete spirituality congruent with and informed by scholarship. The strength of this model is its integrity with regard to the results of sophisticated scholarship. The weaknesses are its difficulty in developing a concrete cultus or practice beyond scholars talking about spiritual practice and a tendency either to remain in abstraction while deconstructing concrete practice or to leap to multiple religious identities. Peter H. Van Ness's *Spirituality, Diversion, and Decadence: The Contemporary Predicament* is a brilliant argument for this model.[34]

Scholarship as the First Encounter with Religion The final model is that of the scholarly first encounter with religion. Many scholars, both from nations long influenced by Marxism and from North Atlantic modernized countries, have been raised in wholly secular ways, with virtually no religion in their families of origin. They have neither an inherited religion nor one against which to rebel; no religious organizations in their neighborhoods offer serious challenges. When such people enter into scholarship about religion, they significantly encounter religiously important issues for the first time, and then the spiritual disciplines of scholarship can become the most concrete and enriching path for them, with no competitors. Of course, in the participatory elements of their scholarship they might develop deep respect and affinities for one or more traditional religions, but they might not find membership in the traditional community attractive. If they do they can move to the multiple religious-identity model. The concrete practical elements of scholarly spirituality in the first-encounter model might not look at all like those in any traditional organized religion, even suitably abstracted. What public forms the practice of pure scholarly spirituality might take are not yet apparent because this model seems so new, although it is not uncommon among graduate students today in religious studies. Surely their public forms of practice will throw light on the other models.

A further comment is in order here regarding not scholarship but teaching. Because so many undergraduate students come from little or no religious background, often their first introduction to spiritual life comes in classes. Sometimes they are introduced to a specific religious community and commit themselves to it. Sometimes, feeling revolutionary, they commit themselves to New Age spirituality. But many students are introduced to the spiritual dimension as it is manifested in the sacred texts of many religions, even in profound texts of secular culture, such as Camus's novels. They can be explicit in not participating in a religion, or even in a syncretistic New Age sensibility, and still be self-conscious about the development of the spiritual dimension of their lives. We are far from understanding what public forms of spiritual practice are available for these people, or that can be invented. Perhaps in the long run most of these students will return to some reconstructed version of a traditional religion that provides a cultural texture of sensitivity and stability. Some are likely to become scholars with a deep spiritual formation.

Summary

This chapter has described a peculiar secular spirituality of religious scholarship, both historically, from the nineteenth century, and conceptually, from a structural analysis of the field of religious studies based on a typology. Historically conscious scholarship requires methods that produce both critical distance from the subject matter of religion and also a participation or engagement in the subject. Because academic objectivity requires comparison and critical assessment, scholarship in religion cannot be mere faith seeking understanding. Because academic objectivity needs to engage the subject matter directly so as to correct the biases and projections of the methods and theories assumed in study, scholarship in religion cannot be mere detached description. Vulnerability and readiness to correction by the realities of its subject matter as well as the criticisms of the intellectual community give objective scholarship in religion its standing in the academic community. The need for participation in religion can be symbolized as participation in some religious tao, the need for distance as obeying Socrates' daimon. Thus religious scholarship requires methods honoring the tao-daimon combination.

According to the typology of religious elements to be studied by various appropriate disciplines, four dimensions of religion have forms of the tao-daimon contrast: imaginative religious structures, assertions about what religions take to be important spiritual truths, orienting cosmic visions, and the practical pursuit of the religious life. The last dimension has at least four traditionally distinguished aspects: the pursuit of righteousness, of natural piety, of engaged faithfulness or authenticity about reality, and of one's own (or one's group's) spiritual destiny or fulfillment.

Attaining both distance and engagement in these various dimensions requires of scholars various elements of spiritual accomplishment. These can be integrated into a genuine spiritual life for scholars when cultivated so as to flesh out the dimensions of religion mentioned above. Finally, a few common models relating the secular spiritual disciplines of scholarship to organized religions were sketched.

A final comment is in order. The emphasis on critical distance in objectivity may be a peculiar contribution of the West. In scholarship it takes its rise from ancient Greek science and philosophy, as symbolized in Socrates' daimon. Human identity in the Mesopotamian city-states was defined in terms of otherness with respect to the other city-states, and the otherness of one's god was defined in reference to the gods of those other cities. This sense of "us and the others" was taken up in Hebrew religion and the religious cultures derivative from it. For all of the hostility and warfare that self-definition relative to otherness has engendered, it has also engendered an attitude of recognizing and honoring others as Other, not to be reduced to some form of one's own cultural identity nor to be denied status as a culture.

The antidote to the violence to which we-they thinking is prone may well be the participation in the religious and cultural world of the Other, for that participation can correct skewed attitudes about many factors, including differences. Learning through yogic participation and cultivation of experience has been an emphasis of Asian cultures for whom "distancing" has been less important for objectivity. Perhaps the spirituality of the scholar of religion, combining distance and participation, can be a helpful model for the spiritual dimensions of a world society in which many cultures must live in harmony. Religious scholarship will not save the world; however, its tao-daimon disciplines, so hard won for the sake of academic objectivity, might show the way to solving larger issues where the divergences of the spiritual practices of organized religions block the path.

Notes

1. Note, for instance, Plato's *Apology* (40) where Socrates cites his daimon as warning him not to accede to the pressures of the court to rejoin the deme and the state with unthinking solidarity; rather, the daimon says to hold fast to the critical examination of Athenian culture and its religion even if this unacceptable and subversive distance leads to his death. On the question of the "invention" of distancing objectivity and its connection with widespread literacy, see Eric A. Havelock, *Preface to Plato* (Cambridge, Mass.: Harvard University Press, 1963).

2. Plato's *Euthyphro* provides the paradigm case for uncritical participation. On his way to his own trial as recounted in the *Apology*, Socrates encountered the youth Euthy-

phro heading for another courtroom to prosecute his own father for causing, by neglect, the death of a bandit. Euthyphro's motive was the religious one of purifying the stain his father brought on the family, and Socrates attempted in vain to bring Euthyphro to a more balanced view of his father by questioning him about the nature of religious commitment. Euthyphro simply could not gain distance on the religion of the deme. For an unusually insightful discussion of this case as paradigmatic, see Carl G. Vaught, *The Quest for Wholeness* (Albany: State University of New York Press, 1982), chap. 3.

3. For the development of the metaphors of tao and daimon for the attainment of objectivity through distance and participation, see Robert C. Neville, *The Tao and the Daimon* (Albany: State University of New York Press, 1982), esp. chaps. 10–11, and the postscript.

4. G. W. F. Hegel, *Lectures in the Philosophy of Religion*, ed. Peter C. Hodgson, 3 vols. (Berkeley: University of California Press, 1984).

5. Concerning the limitations of the claim to radically different cultural experiences, see Donald Davidson, "On the Very Idea of a Conceptual Scheme," *Proceedings of the American Philosophical Association* 47 (November 1974): 5–20.

6. Peter L. Berger, *The Sacred Canopy: Elements of a Sociological Theory of Religion* (Garden City, N.Y.: Doubleday, 1967).

7. Albert Schweitzer, *The Quest of the Historical Jesus*, trans. W. Montgomery (New York: Macmillan, 1950).

8. Rudolf Bultmann, *Theology of the New Testament*, trans. Kendrick Grobel, 2 vols. (New York: Scribner's, 1955).

9. Friedrich Schleiermacher, *Hermeneutics: The Handwritten Manuscripts*, ed. Heinz Kimmerle, trans. James Duke and Jack Forstman (Missoula, Mont.: Scholars Press, 1977). See also Hans-Georg Gadamer, *Philosophical Hermeneutics*, trans. and ed. David E. Linge (Berkeley: University of California Press, 1976), pt. 1.

10. Albrecht Ritschl, *Critical History of the Christian Doctrine of Justification and Reconciliation*, trans. J. S. Black, H. R. Mackintosh, and A. B. Macauley, 3 vols. (Edinburgh and New York: Edmonston and Douglas, 1872–1900).

11. Wilhelm Dilthey, *Selected Works*, ed. Rudolf A. Makkreel and Frithjof Rody, vol. 1: *Introduction to the Human Sciences* (Princeton, N.J.: Princeton University Press, 1989).

12. *From Max Weber: Essays in Sociology*, trans. H. H. Gerth and C. Wright Mills (New York: Oxford University Press, 1946).

13. Ernst Troeltsch, *Historicism and Its Problems* (Tübingen: Mohr, 1922).

14. Martin Heidegger, *Being and Time*, trans. J. Macquarrie and E. S. Robinson (London: SCM, 1962).

15. Hans-Georg Gadamer, *Truth and Method*, 2d rev. ed., trans. rev. Joel Weinsheimer and Donald G. Marshall (New York: Crossroad, 1989).

16. Paul Ricoeur, *The Conflict of Interpretations: Essays in Hermeneutics* (Evanston, Ill.: Northwestern University Press, 1974). For a masterful review, from a theological standpoint, of the history of hermeneutics, see Ray L. Hart, *Unfinished Man and the Imagination: Toward an Ontology and a Rhetoric of Revelation* (New York: Herder and Herder, 1968).

17. Emile Durkheim, *The Elementary Forms of the Religious Life*, trans. Joseph Ward Swain (London: George Allen and Unwin, 1915).

18. Max Weber, *The Sociology of Religion*, trans. Ephraim Fischoff (Boston: Beacon, 1964; original ed. 1922).

19. Edward Tylor, *Primitive Culture,* 2 vols. (New York: Harper, 1958; original 1872).

20. Branislaw Malinowski, *A Scientific Theory of Culture* (New York: Oxford University Press, 1944).

21. Ruth Benedict, *Patterns of Culture* (New York: Mentor, 1946; original 1934).

22. Claude Lévi-Strauss, *The Savage Mind,* trans. George Weidenfeld (Chicago: University of Chicago Press, 1966).

23. G. Van Der Leeuw, *Religion in Essence and Manifestation,* ed. Hans H. Penner, trans. J. E. Turner, 2 vols. (New York: Harper and Row, 1963).

24. Mircea Eliade, *A History of Religious Ideas,* 3 vols.; vols. 1 and 2 trans. Willard Trask, vol. 3 trans. Alf Hiltebeitel and Diane Apostolos-Cappadona (Chicago: University of Chicago Press, 1978, 1982, 1985). See also John R. Mason, *Reading and Responding to Mircea Eliade's "History of Religious Ideas"* (Lewiston, N.Y.: Mellen, 1993).

25. Many scholars at the newly emerging African universities have been trained in Europe or America. The scholars at Latin American universities have long been connected with the universities of Europe and more recently the United States and Canada. The brief summary in the text of the development of the disciplines of religious studies has slighted these traditions.

26. For a discussion of objectivity and vulnerability to correction, see Robert C. Neville's presidential address to the American Academy of Religion: "Religious Studies and Theological Studies," *Journal of the American Academy of Religion* 61:2 (summer 1993): 185–200.

27. For Clifford Geertz's classic example of thick description, see *Islam Observed: Religious Development in Morocco and Indonesia* (New Haven: Yale University Press, 1968). Wilfred Cantwell Smith has developed the idea that the people being studied should recognize themselves in the scholar's description; see his *Towards a World Theology: Faith and the Comparative History of Religion* (Philadelphia: Westminster, 1981; Maryknoll, N.Y.: Orbis, 1989).

28. Here I follow the introduction to this volume in using the word *religious* to mean the cultural reality of religions and *spiritual* to mean the experiential element of religion that may or may not be expressed through traditional cultural forms. Thus, the spiritual dimension of religion, as opposed to, say, economic aspects, refers to the ways religious forms and practices are vehicles and expressions of spiritual experience. This distinction between the religious and the spiritual is not without its problems, precisely because the spiritual dimension cannot be separated from cultural expression. The question is whether the cultural expressions have to be those usually identified as religious by cultural studies. Two of the purposes of this essay are to explore many of these problems and to offer the answer that the culture of tao-daimon scholarship serves in some instances to embody deep spirituality.

29. The philosophic point underlying this discussion of imagination is that every element of human experience, conscious or not, assertoric or visionary, aesthetic or voluntary, is formed by imagination; the point derives from Kant. Imagination is what transforms the causal impingements of body and world into the shape of experiential elements. See Kant's *Critique of Pure Reason,* especially the A edition's Transcendental Deduction. See also Robert C. Neville, *Reconstruction of Thinking* (Albany: State University of New York Press, 1981), pt. 2.

30. George A. Lindbeck, *The Nature of Doctrine: Religion and Theology in a Post-liberal Age* (Philadelphia: Westminster, 1984). When theological practice is cut off from being

judged by external references, as Lindbeck tends to do, it becomes more nearly limited, if never completely so, to exercising intellect's imaginative character-shaping function.

31. There are many common forms of multiple religious identity in the scholarly world. At one extreme, the chief commitment is to scholarship, and identifying with and participating in organized religion are viewed as hardly more than an exercise in nostalgia or as being "for the sake of the children." At the other extreme, the chief commitment is to the traditional community, and the scholarly spirituality is not even explained to that community. In between are those who attempt to make scholarly spirituality concrete by adapting it to the practicalities of a traditional cultus and those who work within the traditional structures to enlarge them so as to encompass and fully incorporate scholarship with its own spirituality.

32. John Berthrong, *All under Heaven* (Albany: State University of New York Press, 1994).

33. Edith Wyschogrod, *Saints and Postmodernism: Revisioning Moral Philosophy* (Chicago: University of Chicago Press, 1990). See also Mark C. Taylor's many writings, preeminently: *Erring: A Postmodern A/Theology* (Chicago: University of Chicago Press, 1984).

34. Peter H. Van Ness, *Spirituality, Diversion, and Decadence: The Contemporary Predicament* (Albany: State University of New York Press, 1992).

Bibliography

Berger, Peter L. *The Sacred Canopy: Elements of a Sociological Theory of Religion.* Garden City, N.Y.: Doubleday, 1967.

Berthrong, John. *All under Heaven.* Albany: State University of New York Press, 1994.

Eliade, Mircea. *A History of Religious Ideas.* 3 vols; vols. 1 and 2 translated by Willard Trask; vol. 3 translated by Alf Hiltebeitel and Diane Apostolos-Cappadona. Chicago: University of Chicago Press, 1978, 1982, 1985.

Hart, Ray L. *Unfinished Man and the Imagination: Toward an Ontology and a Rhetoric of Revelation.* New York: Herder and Herder, 1968.

Lindbeck, George. *The Nature of Doctrine: Religion and Theology in a Post-liberal Age.* Philadelphia: Westminster, 1984.

Neville, Robert Cummings. *The Tao and the Daimon.* Albany: State University of New York Press, 1982.

Smart, Ninian. *Religion and the Western Mind.* Albany: State University of New York Press, 1987.

Smith, Wilfred Cantwell. *Towards a World Theology: Faith and the Comparative History of Religion.* Philadelphia: Westminster, 1981; Maryknoll, N.Y.: Orbis, 1989.

Van Ness, Peter H. *Spirituality, Diversion, and Decadence: The Contemporary Predicament.* Albany: State University of New York Press, 1992.

Wyschogrod, Edith. *Saints and Postmodernism: Revisioning Moral Philosophy.* Chicago: University of Chicago Press, 1990.

6

The Flowering of the Romantic Spirit

CHARLOTTE DORMANDY

THE THREE ASPECTS of the romantic spirit to be explored in this chapter are distilled in four lines by William Blake (1757–1828):

> To see a World in a grain of sand,
> And a Heaven in a wild flower,
> Hold Infinity in the palm of your hand,
> And Eternity in an hour.[1]

They may be prosaically summarized as follows. At the heart of romanticism lies a conviction that proper attention to the real world allows for the revelation of a profounder reality sustaining alike observed particularities and the particularities of the observer (see the first section below, "Sacramental Symbolism"). The individual, by standing in a right relation to things, may be visited by a sense of sublimity, reassuring or overwhelming (the subject of the second section, "Sublimity"). Although contact with infinite and eternal reality is the apotheosis of consciousness, our most immediate access to it may be through an embrace of our embodied nature. Among its potential firstfruits, therefore, is an enhanced respect for the realm of finitude and the flesh that is revealed as an effective sign of our inhabitancy of another order (see the third section below, "Virtue").

This chapter ranges over a broad chronological field but is not chronologically organized. The peaks of romantic culture do not correspond neatly to the points at which its power to generate religious insights makes itself most manifest. To pretend the existence of a discrete strand of romanticism concerned with religion — let alone with religion specifically falling outside the Christian pale — would be to falsify the interaction under consideration. Jean-Jacques Rousseau (1712–78) was widely recognized by self-styled romantics as the progenitor of their distinctive outlook. Certainly, his "Profession of Faith of a Savoyard Vicar" (1762) is a seminal demonstration of how protoromantic ideas could be infused into Christianity to create what its author called "natural religion." Similarly, Immanuel Kant (1724–1804), himself no romantic figure, must feature in any discussion of the metaphysics of romanticism because of the profound influence of his *Critique of Judgment* (1790).

The point of this chapter's historical closure is necessarily more arbitrary than that of its opening since the romantic impulse is by no means dead. How far romanticism is a useful concept when studying late nineteenth- and twentieth-century thinkers and artists must remain a matter of personal judgment applied to individual cases. The novels of Leo Tolstoy (1828–1910), for example, have been much enriched by critical treatment of them in terms of romantic values. His religious thought, however, was predicated upon a rejection of his identity as an artist and seems to me to have been worked out in characteristically nineteenth-century rather than romantic terms.[2] It also represented a reaction against romantic responses to evolutionism's challenge to metaphysical orthodoxy. The fictional dramatization of man's place in nature offered by Thomas Hardy (1840–1928), on the other hand, definitively contributes to what we recognize as late romantic metaphysics, though it had been the typically Victorian challenges of John Stuart Mill's work *Essays and Reviews* (1860) that had originally unsettled the writer's faith.[3]

Particularly in relation to German culture, wherein it was espoused and rejected with heat and self-consciousness, use of the term *romantic* tends to be strictly circumscribed. In a discussion of romanticism's religious implications, however, we cannot afford to ignore either seminal works of the *Stürmer und Dränger*, at one chronological margin, or, at the other, those operas of Richard Wagner (1813–83) that are conventionally contrasted with his earlier "romantic" ones. Wagner was one of many nineteenth-century artists to explore the potential of medieval romance as a vehicle for modern romanticism. This was a practice brought into the twentieth century by the English author John Cowper Powys (1872–1963), the most recent figure discussed in this chapter, a writer who used not only temporal distance but the stretch of the Atlantic to focus his spiritual vision.

Romanticism celebrates individuality and our power of innovation. Herein lies one reason for not attempting to organize this chapter ideologically. To group the relevant insights, convictions, and experiences under such headings as "atheism," "pantheism," and "humanism" would be to do violence to the deeply personal ways in which they were achieved and held. On the other hand, to discuss each person's faith separately and strictly in its own terms would be to defeat the purpose of the endeavor, which is to outline how romanticism affected and facilitated the growth of non-Christian and even secular formulations of religious experience.

There is, however, a more important reason for treating the subject thematically rather than ideologically, and it is discussed in the chapter's final section. Under the title "Romanticism and Western Religious Culture," I shall reflect on one of the movement's distinctive traits: its simultaneous development by those who dissociated themselves from Christianity and by those who adhered to it. This was not merely an effect of its breadth. In its reaction against rationalism, romanticism was (and is) a profound affirmation of the reality of mystery, and this is an affirmation that definitely transcends dogmatics. One of romanticism's most important legacies to Western religious culture, therefore, may be its creation of a common ground on which ideologically diverse individuals can stand together and meet.

Sacramental Symbolism

The Lutheran doctrine of consubstantiation was echoed in seventeenth-century Anglicanism. Luther's position was defined in contradistinction to the Church of Rome's: the substances, he claimed, of the sacramental bread and wine did not vanish upon their consecration but were united in the elements with the body and blood of Christ. High Anglicanism was a reaction against Protestantism and asserted that the Eucharist's commemorative efficacy depended on its sacramental reality. In the words of a nineteenth-century champion of the Real Presence: "He who is at the right hand of God, manifests Himself in [the] Holy Sacrament as really and fully as if He were visibly there." Coming from opposite angles at the problem of how visible and invisible reality relate, Lutherans and Anglicans thus shared a special respect for the role of the phenomenal in making the spiritual accessible. Concomitantly, the two denominations both stressed the necessity of fusion between the voluntary action of God and the personal receptivity of the communicant. It was not enough to assert the objective presence of Christ in the consecrated elements according to his promise nor the communicant's desire to receive them in his memory. The transfigural conception of the sacrament implied both a present divine will to "convey... His own precious self" "to our hearts and bodies" and a responsive disposition on the part of the recipient: "Though every thing looks as usual to the natural man, ... faith sees in the Holy Communion ... [a] glorious presence."[4]

It was not only in eucharistic doctrine that Lutheranism's and Anglicanism's distinctive sacramentalism developed. It also interacted with biblical hermeneutics, preparing Germany to lead the way in conceiving the possibility of spiritual truth's being unvitiated by its communication through factually questionable histories. Samuel Taylor Coleridge (1772–1834) was one of the first Englishmen to appreciate German "higher criticism." He believed that if people would only read the Bible with a natural openness, its spiritual truth would become evident. This belief transposed the Anglican emphasis on the need for communicants to be in a right condition to the activity of apprehending God through words.[5]

Coleridge was a pioneering mediator not only between German and English culture but also between the realms of religion and art whose fusion was central to romanticism. His classic definition of a symbol rules out that merely semiotic conception upon which depend both the authority of dogmatism and the restrictiveness of mimetic aesthetics. In giving the idea what he regarded as its proper status, moreover, he invested it with the specific power to effect contact between the individual and transcendent reality:

> A Symbol ... is characterized by a translucence of the Special in the Individual or of the General in the Especial or of the Universal in the General. Above all by the translucence of the Eternal through and in the Temporal. It always partakes of the reality which it renders intelligible; and while it enunciates the whole, abides itself as a living part in that Unity, of which it is the representative.[6]

The human faculty that enables us to deal in symbols thus conceived is the imagination. "This world of imagination," wrote Blake, "is the world of Eternity."[7] The classic romantic definition is again Coleridge's:

> The IMAGINATION then, I consider either as primary, or secondary. The primary IMAGINATION I hold to be the living Power and prime Agent of all human Perception, as a repetition in the finite mind of the eternal act of creation in the infinite I AM. The secondary Imagination I consider as an echo of the former, co-existing with the conscious will, yet still as identical with the primary in the kind of its agency, and differing only in *degree*, and in the mode of its operation. It dissolves, diffuses, dissipates, in order to recreate; or where this process is rendered impossible, yet still at all events it struggles to idealize and to unify. It is essentially *vital*, even as all objects (as objects) are essentially fixed and dead.[8]

This paragraph articulates the crucial romantic convictions that the imagination is visionary rather than inventive; that it operates according to transcendent laws rather than the associational ones of experience and thus enacts and affirms the individual's participation in transcendent reality; and that no ecclesiastical authority is required for that perception and creation in a symbolic order that authentically allow contact between the individual and "the infinite I AM."

Perhaps chief among the effects of this perspective on things was the new way in which it inspired people to look at the natural world. It endowed it with symbolic significance. "There is one book which is open to everyone," declares Rousseau's Savoyard vicar, "the book of nature. In this good and great volume I learn to serve and adore its Author."[9] Germans such as Franz von Baader (1765–1841), Novalis (1772–1801), Friedrich von Schelling (1775–1854), and Ludwig Tieck (1773–1853) revived interest in the nature mysticism of Jakob Boehme (1575–1624). In England, painters and poets gave supreme artistic expression to their sense that what they perceived about them was "Seen in the Kingdom of Heaven by Vision through Jesus Christ Our Saviour."[10] John Constable (1776–1837) surely spoke for his companion William Wordsworth (1770–1850) as well as himself when he wrote after a walk in the countryside: "Every tree seems full of blossom of some kind and the surface of the ground seems quite living — every step I take and on whatever object I turn my Eye that sublime expression of the Scripture 'I am the Resurrection and the Life' seems verified to me."[11] J. M. W. Turner (1775–1851) painted yachts that look like angels, and Blake saw not "a round disc of fire somewhat like a Guinea" when the sun rose but "an Innumerable company of the Heavenly host crying 'Holy, Holy, Holy is the Lord God Almighty.' " "I question not my Corporeal or Vegetative eye," he commented, "any more than I would question a window concerning a Sight. I look through it and not with it."[12] As all these quotations attest, romantic pantheism rarely involved denial of a transcendent realm in favor of wholly immanent divinity. Rather, the sense that the phenomenal world was a vehicle of transcendence was what inspired a new intensity of appreciation and exploration of it. Wordsworth pre-eminently let metaphysics take care of itself because to be an "inmate of this active universe," with whose "veins are interfaced / The Gravitation and the filial bond / Of nature," seemed to him manifestation enough of the reality of "one great Mind" behind it.[13] The secularization propagated by romanticism was not a shift to believing invisible reality to be merely an epiphenomenon of matter. Even atheists, agnostics, and humanists — Percy Bysshe Shelley (1792–1822), J. W. von Goethe (1749–1832), and Ludwig Feuerbach (1804–72), respectively, for example — insisted on the reality of metaphysical mystery. Romanticism secularized spirituality, rather, in the highly significant sense that it diverted attention from its interpretation to a celebration of the experience itself.

Two dominant symbols emerged of humanity's spiritual unity: the family and the nation. (The ascendancy of the unity concept itself reflected romantic rejection of the authoritative disposal of souls to eternal suffering or bliss in favor of an extrapolation from the ordinary personal sense of being inveterately connected to other people.) Domestic relations and patriotism became widely recognized as vehicles for the realization of universally and eternally valid truths that render humanity an entity. By the same token, family or national feeling that did not act sacramentally on the individual, that encouraged competitive animus rather than expansiveness, was mistrusted as corrupt — although the concentration of energy it involved was held in awe and honor.

The cult of sensibility, of which Rousseau was the "high priest," spread from France in the mid-eighteenth century; it glorified the experience of emotion, manifest in the shedding of tears for its own sake. By the turn of the century, English novelists as well as poets were looking more soberly at what could and should be learned from the feelings exercised by given relationships and quotidian events. Wordsworth and Coleridge's *Lyrical Ballads* (1775–1817) expose the depths of ordinary relationships and look for insight into duty through an exploration of the feelings invested in them. George Eliot (1819–80) wrote in her first novel (1859):

> These fellow-mortals, every one, must be accepted as they are; you can neither straighten their noses, nor brighten their wit, nor rectify their dispositions; and it is these people — amongst whom your life is passed — that it is needful you should tolerate, pity, and love: It is these more or less ugly, stupid, inconsistent people, whose movements of goodness you should be able to admire — for whom you should cherish all possible hopes, all possible patience.[14]

The authoritative tone of this passage and its direct address to the reader are a reminder of the status the artist had gained through romanticism's faith in the spiritual liquor distillable from all experience apprehended and treated aright. According to Friedrich von Schlegel (1772–1829), artists are to the rest of mankind what human beings are to the rest of creation. They give form and voice to dim, dumb institutions. By the perceptual acuteness of their primary imagination and by the power and integrity with which they dissolve, diffuse, and dissipate what they have perceived so as to recreate it in a purely symbolic order, they make available to the rest of us more intense feelings and more concentrated experience than we could otherwise achieve. Richard Wagner's ideal of a *Gesamtkunstwerk* (total art form) was underpinned by an assumption that the fuller an audience's (controlled) sensual stimulation, the fuller its spiritual benefit. Meanwhile, music was generally regarded by romantics as the highest art because it was felt to preclude the unwanted mediation of thought. In Henriette Feuerbach's words, it is "spirit speaking directly to spirit."[15] The verbal arts have not this luxury, of course, but this did not stop poets being regarded by themselves and others as priests. By the middle of the nineteenth century, the novelists of domestic relations, led by Charles Dickens (1812–70), formed a new branch of the priesthood, omnisciently interweaving insight into their characters and readers to coerce the latter into engaging their feelings to the former and thus enlarging their capacity for sympathy for their fellow mortals in the real world.

As family feeling was supposed to function — sacramentally and expansively — likewise patriotism. Burnett James claims: "Nazism was a direct product of the nineteenth century's Romantic nationalism grown overripe and rotten."[16] It is a simplistic explanation that may nonetheless serve as a reminder of dangers inherent in relying for revelation on the intense experience symbols stimulate without allowing any regulative authority to rational reflection. One danger is that the symbols may be the vehicles of — for want of a better word — evil. Another is that the lack of a definitive formulation of the mystery represented may make the effort of focusing upon it too great to sustain. Sacramental experience may dwindle into a cultic one, transforming the symbol from an icon or vehicle of transcendence into an idol, and the dynamic it effects from an expansive to a combative one. Both the American and French revolutions claimed an essential link between the nationalist fervor upon which they relied and an ideal of universal liberty supported by reference to divine will; yet it took America another century and another war to abolish slavery while French respect for freedom was corrupted first into the self-abuse of the Terror and then into the travesty of Napoleon's "wars of liberation." George Eliot (1819–80) pleaded eloquently at the end of her career that English national pride offered no excuse for the oppression of other nations but should, rather, make the English sympathetic to the desire of Jews to establish themselves in a homeland where their national pride could flourish equally.[17] Her eloquence was exercised against a background of understanding how easily the universalism implicit in righteous nationalism could curdle into defensive aggression. For her fiction had featured several nationalist leaders who are descendants of the equivocal heroes of early romanticism. The figures of Faust — treated by at least seven *Stürmer und Dränger* beside Goethe — and Prometheus embody romanticism's consciousness of the dangers involved in the freedom from authority it claimed. Just as mankind may need the vision of artists, so it may need the titanic energy of heroes, the one to "wash the gum from [its] eyes" and the other to break through oppressive conditions.[18]

Just as the priesthood of artists created the conditions for a rejection of the bond between art and ordinary life, signaled by the coinage of the word *philistinism* and later by the slogan "art for art's sake," so the unboundedness of heroic power could betray those it should have released (including the hero himself). Goethe's Faust gives classic utterance to romantic existentialism by way of undermining Gretchen's simple faith and observance before seducing her: "Feeling is all; / Naming is noise and smoke / Obscuring the glow of Heaven." Asked by Fritz Jacobi's wife about the religious education of her children, Goethe urged her to "see that they do believe in something;... whether they believe in Christ or Götz or Hamlet, it's all one."[19] Let us hope she did not bring them up to believe in Mephistopheles.

Several important strands of romanticism are combined in Wagner's work. Like the English lake poets, he believed the future of art to lie in its power to plumb the depths of common feeling — in his case, that which animated the *Volksgeist* (spirit of the people) of Germany. His manifesto *Opera and Drama* (1851) demands a new kind of poetry not unlike that advocated by Wordsworth in the preface to *Lyrical Ballads* (1800). It must draw on primitive elements of speech that must not be corrupted but given new voice by their articulation through the more refined culture of the artist; and a new kind of melodic structure must be developed to match this "word-tone-speech" whose image is not the architectonic one of a temple but the organic one of a web. This pervasive metaphor of nineteenth-century culture became closely associated with the realistic novel through George Eliot's use of it in *Middlemarch* (1871–72). Applied to Wagner's music, as to domestic fiction, the web metaphor signifies not only the perceived complexity of life's internal relationships, to be mirrored in art, but also the perceived ubiquitous continuity of its significance. We are inextricably involved in a symbolic order that, by virtue of its common weave, is robust but that, by the same token, lacks the defenses against abuse vouchsafed traditionally sanctified icons.

Since the start of his career, Wagner had instinctively turned to supernatural subjects to signal, like Coleridge, his intent to lay bare deep seams of reality, to make the unconscious articulate. Folk sagas seemed to him authentic expressions of a national unconscious; and he took his artistic authority from the biblical critics' interpretation of religion as myth. It was now up to the artist to distil into representative figures and events the deep instincts and yearnings that had previously been reified as holy lore; and the way to reach universal man was through the symbolism of national character.

In the 1840s, two famous symbols had been invoked to express the parlous conditions in which Germans and Frenchmen had felt their respective countries to be. Ferdinand Freiligrath (1810–76) had opened a poem with the words "Deutschland ist Hamlet!" (Germany is Hamlet!) (1844), and Jules Michelet (1798–1874) had declared that Théodore Géricault's *The Raft of the "Medusa"* (1819), depicting shipwrecked men in midocean, represented "la France elle-même" (France herself) (1847). In 1871, Wagner completed *Siegfried* and furnished Germany with a more cheering hero than Hamlet. It is doubtful, though, whether his pretensions to represent universal man were evident in either France or Germany in the aftermath of the Franco-Prussian War.

Sublimity

When John Keats (1795–1821) referred to "the Wordsworthian or egotistical sublime," he was conjuring up an imaginative activity whereby experience of sublimity was achieved and expressed in poetry through the sheer afflatus of the ego.[20] Yet it is Wordsworth who has furnished English-language readers with some of the most powerful accounts of how the ego may be temporarily abolished by its confrontation "with high objects" in "life and nature." Reflecting in *The Prelude* on a boyhood experience of rowing on a lake and encountering a "huge Cliff," the poet praises the "Wisdom and Spirit of the Universe" for schooling him to "recognize / A grandeur in the beatings of the heart" partly by making his pulse race with a "pain and fear" inspired by overwhelming "forms and images" quick with the "breath / And everlasting motion" of the "Soul that [is] the Eternity of thought." His "brain" is evacuated "for many days" of everything properly its own and becomes a conduit through which move "huge and mighty Forms." The twin lessons of the encounter are thus the fragility of the ego and the enormity of humanity's potential experience.[21]

Shelley similarly seeks to evoke in "Mont Blanc" (1816) a power whose effects the "race / Of man flies far in dread" yet that is only realized through "the Human mind's imaginings." "Silence and solitude were vacancy" without "the adverting mind" to perceive that "Power dwells apart in its tranquility, / Remote, serene, and inaccessible." The "secret Strength of things," though intrinsically indifferent and even effectively hostile to humanity, is known to us only through its presence within us, through our capacity to apprehend it.[22]

The significance that the apprehension of the sublime had for the romantic age was theoretically formulated by Kant. It is the keystone of his aesthetic philosophy, which is the apex of his account of human experience. Alone among the fields of judgment, according to Kant, aesthetic perception is both disinterested and particular. It is through the creation and appreciation of art, therefore, that our capacity for freedom from personal interest is grounded in material reality. Our transcendence of determinism is concretely realized in our drive to make and behold objects that harmonize with the universal patterns of the human mind and are justified in their existence purely by that harmony.

The human mind, in Kant's conception, has two basic faculties: understanding and reason. The first is an interaction of the intuitions of sense (time and space) with innate mental categories such as substantiality and causation. The effect of this interaction is experience of the phenomenal world. Beauty, in turn, is perceived when the form of an object corresponds to the rules by which understanding operates but when it does not present itself as an object to be understood. The viewer's sense of purpose is not engaged, yet insofar as the object conforms to the laws of experience, it is inherently, formally, purposive. The viewer is thus open to the pleasure of apprehending purposiveness as such, a pleasure that arises from the fact that it is a reflection of his own capacity for understanding. By the criteria of an object's inherent purposiveness and effective purposelessness, its beauty is judged.

Our faculty for reason may be similarly apprehended objectively in the form of the sublime. Unlike the understanding, reason does not engage directly with sensual input. Rather, it synthesizes the judgments of experience (made by the understanding) to form inferences. (A chief source of intellectual confusion, in Kant's view, is our tendency to misconceive reason as inherent in experience and to treat inferences as if they were the synthetic judgments of understanding.) An aesthetic object that conforms to the laws of nature is perceived as beautiful because of its correspondence with that mental structure of ours — understanding — that renders experience as it is. To provide an image of reason, therefore, an aesthetic object must flout the laws of nature. Its importance, indeed, lies in its objectification of that independence of nature that we own by virtue of the power of rational judgment and that is the basis of freedom. Kant found in Edmund Burke's *A Philosophical Enquiry* (1757) a term for what we experience when confronted aesthetically with an object whose scale and form do violence to the senses by offending against proportion and regularity: it is "a sort of delightful horror" that we call "sublime."[23]

Kant was a Lutheran who argued that God's existence cannot be proved; Shelley was an atheist; and Wordsworth was unconcerned with metaphysics. Their shared interest in apprehension of the sublime had nothing to do with inferences about transcendent reality that might be drawn from it and given dogmatic form. It was, rather, part of the general romantic preoccupation with our power of experience. They all claimed that, in some sense or other, potential experience exceeds the regularities of connection known as "nature" — that it is, in some sense, transcendent to nature; and they all felt that a realization of such potential threatens the natural individual, the ego, in whom it occurs.

Romantic painting provides an image of this dual conviction in the recurring foreground figure seen from the back. In some works, the figure is tiny, enhancing the viewer's sense of the scale of the landscape drawing the attention of both the figure and the viewer. Exemplary works are *The "Chasseur" in the Forest* (1814) by Caspar David Friedrich (1774–1840); *Stonehenge* (1836) by John Constable; and *Chamonix and Mont Blanc* (1848) by L. F. Schnorr von Carolsfeld (1794–1872). Where the figure is larger, though, the viewer's sense of incompatibility between potential experience and personal identity may be more insistent and disturbing. As Hugh Honour points out, "The figures in [Friedrich's] pictures can generally see more than we can": the wanderer above the mists has a better vantage point than the viewer who must stare at his back, and the couple on the sailing ship can focus on a horizon that is only a blur from beyond the picture frame.[24] Their command of experience commands the viewer's respect; yet at the same time, the fact that they are little more than silhouettes, and silhouettes without faces, renders them blank. In their communion with the sublime, they become mere vessels, drained of personality, their particularities sunk in the uniformity of a shadow cast by transcendent brightness.

The tragic possibilities attendant on the power of experience that romanticism was bent on honoring and exploring were most famously embodied in Goethe's *The Sorrows of Young Werther* (1774). The author provides no objective correlative of the sublime passions by which Werther is wracked. They are mainly inspired, of course, by Lotte, but she is not presented as, so to speak, an intrinsically breathtaking vision such as the Alps. Instead, she is presented as an ordinarily charming girl transfigured by Werther's perception. This does not make the story the license to indulge in emotionalism that has often been found in it. Rather, it sets up the conditions in which the destructiveness of profound human susceptibility to experience may be displayed even as a unique claim is made for that susceptibility's power of insight into the heart of things. Albert sees good sense as dependent upon not having one's faculties deranged; Werther sees it as dependent upon not being open to the depths of experience that are naturally liable to overwhelm judgment. Albert argues that suicide is quite unlike great achievements because it springs from a weak refusal to bear suffering; Werther perceives that it may spring from the same immersion in experience as great art and deeds do. He acknowledges that suicide proceeds from an aberrant state of mind; wherefore moral condemnation of it is inappropriate. He further contends that the conditions that give rise to exceptional acts like suicide are not necessarily delusive and that the constructiveness of the acts themselves cannot be taken as an index of the authenticity of the vision of things by which they are inspired.[25]

Werther's own suicide may be seen partly as an indirect effect of the fact that he has not got whatever it takes to make great art yet is subject to the sublime feelings that are its prerequisite and that make mere mimesis, the production of the beautiful, impossible for him. Early on in the novel Werther reflects on his inability to paint God's presence in nature that he senses so vividly; he concludes: "The glory of these visions, their power and magnificence, will be my undoing."[26] They are, of course, and Goethe's account of his hero's gradual disintegration remains a vital testimony to romanticism's awareness of the dangers of the sublime experience to which it pins its faith.

(The) sublime is a term used indifferently, by romantic writers, of something experienced and of an experience's quality. In using the term they wished to evoke substantiveness and objectivity. Sublimity is the substance of what conditions us, the evidence of empiricism transcended. I have emphasized romantic awareness of sublimity's status as a crux, an intimation exacting sacrifice. It sometimes, though, takes less problematic forms, being conceived as either unpunishing or unrewarding. The work of Ralph Waldo Emerson (1803–82) and Thomas Hardy respectively illustrate these possibilities. In them, furthermore, we may see the disparateness of romanticism's possible responses to one of the nineteenth century's leading ideas: that of evolutionism.

Emerson renounced his ministry, he told his flock, above all out of distaste for the sacraments.[27] This may come as a surprise to any reader accustomed to enjoy Emerson for his passionate advocacy of the symbolical nature of all things: "Nature itself is a vast trope, and all particular natures are tropes. As the bird alights on the bough, then plunges into the air again, so the thoughts of God pause but for a moment in any form. All thinking is analogizing, and it is the use of life to learn metonymy."[28] His quarrel with orthodoxy was, as this passage hints, not, in fact, over its use of symbols but over what he saw as its abuse of them: "mysticism," as opposed to "poetry," "nails a symbol to one sense, which was a true sense for a moment, but soon becomes old and false. For all symbols are fluxional." Life has an "onward force." The flux, moreover, is intrinsically progressive: there is no chance, and no anarchy, in the universe. All is system and gradation. "And, striving to be man, the worm / Mounts through all the spires of form." We do not need salvation, only development. There is no fracture between the natural man and his power of transcendent experience or between the beauty of "ever-flowing metamorphosis" and the sublime "devouring unity [that] changes all into that which changes not."[29]

Although Emerson's writings sometimes refer to Kant, the American's "transcendentalism" fundamentally conflates concepts that to the German were crucially distinct: beauty and sublimity; understanding and reason. Kant would have had little objection to the following sentiments: "The world thus exists to the soul to satisfy the desire of beauty. This element I call an ultimate end. No reason can be asked or given why the soul seeks beauty. Beauty, in its largest and profoundest sense, is one expression for the universe." He would not, however, have gone on to deduce the character of divinity from that of nature, as Emerson does: "God is the all-fair. Truth, and goodness, and beauty, are different faces of the same All.[30] Whereas to Kant, reason's defining quality is its independence from nature, to Emerson "the type of Reason" is "the blue sky in which the private earth is buried, the sky with its eternal calm, and full of everlasting orbs." "The laws of moral nature answer to those of matter as face to face in a glass."[31] In this blithe assertion, we see the essentially preromantic, eighteenth-century basis onto which Emerson smoothly grafted the developmental promise of evolutionism. Why not, after all, "contrast... the Church with the Soul" and "in the soul" alone "let... redemption be sought" if we have in nature a gentle and infallible guide to our destined apotheosis?[32]

Hardy laid claim to the "meliorism" (belief in things' probable improvement) that evidently animated Emerson.[33] Most readers, however, have found grimmer convictions dramatized in his novels. Nature's sublimity was, to him, not the hospitable means of our access to transcendence but, in the words of D. H. Lawrence (1885–1930), an "incomprehensible drama, untouched" by human needs:

> This is the wonder of Hardy's novels, and gives them their beauty. The vast unexplored morality of life itself, what we call the immorality of nature, surrounds us in its eternal incomprehensibility and in its midst goes on the little human morality play, with its queer frame of morality and its mechanized movement; seriously, portentously till some one of the protagonists chances to look out of the charmed circle, weary of the stage, to look into the wilderness raging round. Then he is lost, his little drama falls to pieces, it becomes mere repetition, but the stupendous theater outside goes on.[34]

Hardy's characters and his narrative personae frequently refer to superhuman intentionality (generally malignant), but such references are always ironic. When Eustacia Yeobright, for example, blames "some indistinct, colossal Prince of the World, who had framed her situation and ruled her lot," for her failure to answer the door when her mother-in-law appeared, the reader learns more about Eustacia than about the world's organization. Similarly, authorial references to an "Immanent Will that stirs and urges everything" are regularly undercut so as to seem an articulation of humanity's need to believe in teleological guidance rather than a simple affirmation of faith in its reality. In the poem in which that phrase occurs, for example, dubbing the Titanic's collision with an iceberg a "consummation" merely highlights the impossibility of human insight into any possible universal order.[35]

Characteristic phrases of Hardy's such as "the Spinner of the Years," "the President of the Immortals," and "the waggery of fate" are the rhetorical flourishes of a paganism embedded in his plots.[36] There, it operates as a metaphor for a less reassuring aspect of evolutionism than the promise of development: the role of chance in, and therefore the unmanageability of, human destiny. Many forms of paganism (classical and bucolic), as distinct from the monotheistic faiths, are piecemeal. They lay no claim to a unified global management, a consistent providence. They postulate, rather, an innumerable array of supernatural forces, some of which can sometimes be harnessed and others of which, apparently or not, harness us. They undermine faith in omnipotence in favor of, at best, local and brief satisfactions and, at worst, acceptance of chaos. Such was also Darwin's lesson: random mutation, rather than teleological magnetism, governs organic development, and ecological hazard, rather than intrinsic worth, determines survival or extinction. In drawing on his deeply felt knowledge of rural paganism to articulate the bleakness of existence in an ungoverned world, Hardy commands the cusp between domestic realism in the novel and modernism.[37] He insists that the concatenation of forces at any given moment is, from the point of view of human comprehension, absolutely and inaccessibly sublime: to become aware of "its eternal incomprehensibility" is to face, as Clym Yeobright does, the "horror of... existence" in a world in which not only can one not do as one would, but one is balked from suffering for one's misdeeds.[38] The reader is aware of one more element than is Clym in the events preceding his wife's death — an element that has no other role in the novel than to call into question the validity of any casual explanation, psychological or accidental, of the calamity. Eustacia may have despaired and thrown herself into the flood, or she may have fallen in. It so happens, though, that, as she was making across the heath, a peasant neighbor (Susan Nonsuch) — a minor character — was casting a spell on her because of an unfounded belief that Eustacia had bewitched her child. Is Susan's malignant magic the effective cause of Eustacia's death? The mystery is unfathomable and, in being so, is more terrible than any possible resolution of it could be.

Virtue

If romanticism, as suggested earlier, treads a margin between sacramentalism and idolatry in its faith in symbols and if in its hunger for sublimity it invites personal self-destruction, then its commitment to human virtue embraces both a belief in natural goodness and a determinedly amoral loyalty to what we are. It is as well to bear in mind, therefore, not only the ordinary meaning of the word *virtue* but its connotations of sheer physical vitality. The equivocal connection between the two is embodied in the early romantic figure of the titan. It is his power to be governed only by himself that both renders a supremely valuable energy available and makes it dangerous. (Napoleon, of course, brought the archetype to life.) Stretching back in time from this complex figure is the embodiment of predominantly moral virtue: Rousseau's natural man. Stretching forward into our own time is the development of new kinds of morality, often distinguishing themselves from their contexts by claiming not to be moral at all but merely — fiercely — empirical, based on a growing regard for our historical life, its material conditions, and, above all, its psychological determinants.

Rousseau's *Confessions* was posthumously published in 1782. It contained various information — from the bald admission of abandoning his children to the equally frank disclosure of his addictions to masturbation and masochism — that might have been expected to shake his admirers' faith in his essential moral purity. It did not.[39] Throughout the nineteenth century, the book served as refreshing stimulation to readers with whom we associate the sternest moral judgments — Thomas Carlyle (1795–1881), George Eliot, and Tolstoy, for example. For the shift in moral consciousness Rousseau represented was profound, challenging not the possibility of sin but the doctrine that we are born in original sin and into a fallen world. By releasing the individual from the burden of inherited shame, from the oppression of conceiving himself as essentially scandalous and irretrievable by any will or effort of his own, Rousseau has seemed to many readers to trivialize the reality of evil, both in nature and in us. Bertrand Russell, for example, comments on the *Confessions:*

> He enjoyed making himself out a great sinner, and sometimes exaggerated in this respect; but there is abundant external evidence that he was destitute of all the

ordinary virtues. This did not trouble him, because he considered that he always had a warm heart, which, however, never hindered him from base actions towards his best friends.[40]

On the other hand, the insistence that such sin as we do commit is essentially wanton because it is avoidable lays a new responsibility upon the individual. If to do evil be unnatural rather than natural, its only source can be a perversity of which we have no excuse for not being conscious. The following passages from the Savoyard vicar's profession capture both the invitation to moral glibness inherent in Rousseau's philosophy and the challenge to a new seriousness:

There is therefore at the bottom of our hearts an innate principle of justice and virtue, by which, in spite of our maxims, we judge our own actions or those of others to be good or evil; and it is this principle that I call conscience.

Conscience! Conscience! Divine Instinct, immortal voice from heaven; sure guide for a creature ignorant and finite indeed, yet intelligent and free; infallible judge of good and evil, making man like God!

The feeling of conscience affirms and enacts the good that reason recognizes. Morality is thus lodged in the personal nature of the individual. It becomes essentially embodied rather than abstract just as divine will is embodied in the "physical and corporeal action" of created nature.[41]

Frankenstein (1818), by Mary Shelley (1797–1851), gives pointed and enduringly poignant consideration to the newly emphasized connection between embodiment, feeling, and morality. Frankenstein's attention is "peculiarly attracted [to] the structure of the human frame, and, indeed, any animal endued with life." He is thus often given to asking himself: "Whence . . . did the principle of life proceed?" In order to investigate, he "determine[s] henceforth to apply [him]self more particularly to those branches of natural philosophy which relate to physiology," and, through intensive study of the decay of dead bodies, he eventually "succeed[s] in discovering the cause and generation of life." Even more, he becomes "capable of bestowing animation upon lifeless matter." Man is the model for the organization of the creature Frankenstein creates, but he regards it as a "new species." Intoxicated by his power, he imagines its offspring "bless[ing] me as [their] creator and source; many happy and excellent natures would owe their being to me. No father could claim the gratitude of his child so completely as I should deserve theirs." He takes, though, no pains to create the sort of emotional and moral nature capable of, and inclined towards, such emotions. Indeed, his exclusive concern with life as a corporeal matter is signaled by his disregard for his own narrowing mind and for all ties of affection as his work proceeds.[42]

The upshot of this might have been expected to be an evil or at least an amoral creature (the moral "monster" of some of the cruder reworkings of the tale). The tragedy springs from the fact that, given a physical nature modeled on man's, Frankenstein's creature indeed shares an inclination toward goodness rooted in fellow-feeling. This is corrupted by the unanimous rejection of him because his body is grotesque. He is "born" an innocent, as well disposed, as a Rousseauean infant. Shunned in his attempt to express this and develop through it, he turns delinquent. The crux of the tale is Frankenstein's refusal to create him a mate — a wife who would alleviate his loneliness, loving and letting herself be loved by him — and his consequent dedication to vengeance. The story's thrust is thus that beings physically organized on a human model will have a natural disposition toward morality and that the development of this disposition depends upon the giving and receiving of a personal affection rooted in mutual physical attraction and a respect for the bodies that inspire it. Novalis's aphorism, "We touch heaven when we lay our hand on a human body," might serve as epigraph to the tale of a "modern Prometheus" that both castigates overweening ambition and confirms corporeal nature as the essential medium of morality.[43]

The locus of corporeal humanity is history. Both bodies and deeds are kept, as it were, in parenthesis by what M. H. Abrams calls Christianity's "right-angled" conception of history — a conception governed by "key events," such as the creation and the Second Coming, initiated beyond the realm of natural connection.[44] The romantic age saw a diminution of focus on such events (not necessarily entailing loss of belief in them) and a corresponding growth of interest in historical life. A new historiography emerged, integral to which was the sacramental idea of imagination — that faculty whose action renders as felt reality the individual's participation in a transcendent identity. As R. G. Collingwood puts it, "The historical method of the Romantic school" is "imaginatively" to "re-enact the past." "Sympathy becomes an integral element in historical knowledge, the element which enables the historian to get inside the facts he is studying."[45] The possibility of sympathy with the past and the importance of practicing it, in turn, are sustained by a belief in a shared identity with it that, for the sake of the present's fulfillment, must be realized in the present. Through history, A. L. Rowse writes, "The life of the individual breaks its barriers and becomes coterminous with humanity."[46]

To champions and members of "the Romantic school," history is thus an immediate experience of shared identity with the past through an aroused sympathy that needs for its nourishment the fullest sense of the past's particularity. The historiography of the preromantic age may seem, by contrast, a travesty in its apparent carelessness of the depth and extent to which each time and place is characteristically itself. "Would you know the sentiments, inclinations, course of life of the Greeks and Romans?" asked David Hume (1711–76). His suggestion: "Study well the temper and action of the French and the English: you cannot be much mistaken in referring to the former most of the observations you have made in regard to the latter."[47] To the romantic, the past is a sacramental medium that engages the historical imagination to the universal life of mankind, concentration on a given moment conveying both the infinite variety of that life's refractions and, through aroused sympathy, the individual's participation in its living reality. "Romantic historicism," writes Karl Kroeber, is "part of the aesthetics of... sublimity, specifically the sublimity not of space but of time."[48]

While glib and propagandist comparisons were repudiated by romantic historians, comparativism itself played a major role in undermining the "right-angled" perspective on history and deepening the field of historical investigation to incorporate the role of the subconscious. Indeed, an eighteenth-century theory purporting to explain morally troubling parts of the Old Testament gradually mutated into an account of the Gospels that did not assume the reality of the supernatural events to which they testify. Revelation, it was claimed by orthodox theologians, was accommodated to the stage of development of the cultures to which it was made. If some Old Testament values seemed harsh toward the end of the second millennium after Christ, this was because the judgments reflected in them were made to be understood by more primitive minds than the modern one. Also, that the collective mind developed could be seen by comparing societies both historically and geographically.

Given romantic interest in the subconscious, and its expression through attention to the folk culture deemed to embody the spirit of a nation, it was only a matter of time before a serious attempt was made to assimilate the Gospels to other folk myths. Their supernaturalist claims were interpreted as the unself-conscious projections of the deep-seated psychological needs of a relatively primitive culture under stress. That David Friedrich Strauss (1808–74), who made this attempt in 1846, believed he could continue to act in good faith as a minister and professor of theology testifies to an awakening acceptance of the psychology of the subconscious as a component of spiritual, moral, and rational life. (Coleridge's "Rime of the Ancient Mariner" (1798) provides poetic evidence of the same thing in that the mariner's salvation springs from the fact that he "bless'd [the sea-serpents] unaware.")[49] Strauss was proved wrong, however, by authorities and congregations, indicating a resistance to such an acceptance with which we are still familiar.

Strauss's mentor, G. W. F. Hegel (1770–1831), made the greatest philosophical contribution to establishing the importance of our historical life in that he located reason and freedom firmly within it. The post-Hegelian reaction against idealism — the materialism of Feuerbach and the detachment of will from reason by Arthur Schopenhauer (1788–1860) — occurred in the context of an acceptance that history (even if it is only a dream) is the essential locus of human experience.

Feuerbach is best remembered for his influence on Karl Marx (1818–83). The two placed the materialism to which they were both committed in quite different perspectives, however, for, in Owen Chadwick's words, "Feuerbach had no god but was a religious man. Marx, who owed much to Feuerbach's theory, had no god but was not a religious man."[50] Whereas Marx used materialism to expand the range of strictly secular accounts of human experience, Feuerbach, who saw the *Stürmer und Dränger* as his spiritual ancestors, used it to ground a vision whose essential boundary was mystery. His humanism is romantic and spiritual, as opposed to scientific and irreligious, because one of its premises is that apprehended mystery is fundamental to human consciousness. His endeavor was less to reduce than, in Engels's phrase, to "perfect religion."[51] Under the processes by which man's religious history gradually reveals its humanist heart lay, for him, the essential and unique capacity of human consciousness to acknowledge a reality that transcends material conditions.

Man is distinguished from other animals, in Feuerbach's view, by his "consciousness of the infinite"; therefore "religion has its basis in the essential difference between man and the brute." Animal consciousness, indeed, because it is not more than the expressed sense of individual existence, "is no consciousness; consciousness is essentially infinite in its nature"; therefore "consciousness of the infinite is nothing else than the consciousness of the infinity of consciousness." Since "in the consciousness of the infinite, the conscious subject has for his object the infinity of his own nature," and since the sense of individual existence he shares with other animals is not "consciousness in the strict sense," consciousness is an expression of man's unique awareness of "his essential nature" as a member of a species.

These syllogistic arguments are made in the opening chapter of *The Essence of Christianity* (1841), whose thesis is that humanism is the true religion of human beings in the senses both that it is the faith we should practice and that it is the authentic core of whatever other faith we may profess. Feuerbach's humanism, his reading of religious history as a partly immature and partly perverted expression of individuals' sense of themselves as members of a human body, was, thus, based on a definition of human consciousness as the capacity to apprehend a reality that transcends the finite conditions of that apprehension. Human beings are partakers of "a twofold life," and while "cognisance of species" allows for the intellectual achievements that distinguish them collectively from other animals, the individual's power to acknowledge "the infinite" remains the witness to his personal participation in the "essential nature" of his species, which is the affirmation of itself as such.[52]

Feuerbach's greatest claim was that he had initiated a new philosophical principle — that of materialism. Rather than being the metaphysical principle it became in Marx's work, though, in Feuerbach's it is an insistence on the fullness — the material reality and particularity — of the human individual. His "new philosophy," he boasts,

> does not...regard the *pen* as the only fit organ for the revelation of truth, but the eye and the ear, the hand and the foot; it does not identify the *idea* of the fact with the fact itself, so as to reduce real existence to an existence on paper, but it separates the two, and precisely in this separation attains to the *fact itself*; it recognizes as the true thing, not the thing as it is an object of the abstract reason, but as it is an object of the real, complete man, and hence as it is itself a real, complete thing.[53]

This opens the way to a sacramental view of human experience and human relations.[54] It connects Feuerbach closely to high romantics such as Shelley with his "remorseless quest...for a world where Eros is triumphant always, where desire shall not fail, and a confrontation of life by life is always taking place." Shelley was the classic romantic atheist. Feuerbach's humanism is no less romantic and no less "passionately religious."[55]

"Reason, Will, Love," Feuerbach writes, "are not powers which man possesses, for he is nothing without them; they are the constituent elements of his nature, which he neither has nor makes, the animating, determining, governing powers — divine, absolute powers — to which he can oppose no resistance."[56] To Kant, reason was preeminent among these powers. It alone, in his view, is a general faculty of humanity rather than the property of individuals. Feuerbach elevated feeling, which to him was epitomized in sexual love, to the status of supreme vehicle of our essential, transindividual nature.[57] The third power, will, was elevated by Schopenhauer:

> The will, as the thing in itself, is the common stuff of all beings, the universal element of things: consequently we possess it in common with each and every man, indeed with the animals, and even further on down. In the will as such

> we are consequently all similar, in so far as everything and everyone is filled and distended with will.[58]

As the last sentence makes clear, whereas Feuerbach sought to establish humanity's (as opposed to God's) claim to be recognized as the reality that bounds consciousness, Schopenhauer refused to give a special status to our species. Will, in his conception, is neither the property of individuals nor a collective attribute of animals or living things. It is the "life force" that manifests itself in all matter. The world is dreamed by the will, and its most authentic form is physical and unconscious. That one's body and will are one is the idea that, properly understood, Schopenhauer claimed, constitutes the whole of his philosophy. "Everything primary, and consequently everything genuine, in man works as the forces of nature do, *unconsciously*."[59] To understand truly our own nature and our place in the scheme of things, we must, therefore, regard ourselves as manifestations of "the procreant urge of the world," in the phrase of Walt Whitman (1819–91), rather than as creatures distinguished by power, even the power of love.[60]

This idea is given powerful expression in D. H. Lawrence's *Apocalypse* (1931), which asserts "the marvel of being alive in the flesh" and thus "part of the living, incarnate cosmos." "I am part of the sun as my eye is a part of me. That I am part of the earth my feet know perfectly, and my blood is part of the sea."[61]

As with Rousseau's identification of his conscience with God, it is easy to see how Lawrence's identification of his essential nature with the unconscious forces of the world could entail an abdication of moral responsibility. This was far from his intention, however. For the thrust of all his work is an attempt to establish a more authentic ground of morality than that of "mental-consciousness."[62]

Lawrence followed Schopenhauer in his identification of the unconscious and the "Life force": "The true unconscious is the well-head, the fountain of real motivity." (The "Freudian unconscious," by contrast, he held to be "the cellar in which the mind keeps its own bastard spawn," not "repressed passionnal impulse[s]" but "*ideal[s]* which are refused enactment.") He also followed Schopenhauer and the romantic tradition generally in insisting that the life force essentially manifests itself in individuality:

> This causeless created nature of the individual being is the same as the old mystery of the divine nature of the soul. Religion was right and science is wrong.... Cause-and-effect will not explain even the individuality of a single dandelion. There

is no assignable cause, and no logical reason, for individuality. On the contrary, individuality appears in defiance of all scientific law, in defiance even of reason.[63]

Lawrence thus locates essential mystery, that which is "inconceivable" but which we "know... by direct experience," in the individual's own unconscious. It has traveled, so to speak, a long way from its location in a temporally and materially conceived heaven. The traces of this conviction are present in many elements of Lawrence's thought—in his assertion that "There is no god / apart from poppies and the flying fish, / men singing songs, and women brushing their hair in the sun"; in his respect for darkness as an image, not of evil, but of a motive force that it is futile to try to bring under the light of science; and in his dynamic conception of polar confrontation in which the effects of that force are observable.[64]

It is the last item that Lawrence identifies as "a new moral aspect to life":

Save for healthy instinct the moralistic human race would have exterminated itself long ago. And yet man *must* be moral, at the very root moral. The essence of morality is the basic desire to preserve the perfect correspondence between the self and the object, to have no trespass and no breach of integrity, nor yet any refaulture in the vitalistic interchange.

In a later passage he describes this "vitalistic interchange":

No human being can develop save through the polarized connection with other beings. This circuit of polarized unison precedes all mind and all knowing. It is anterior to and ascendant over the human will. And yet the mind and will can both interfere with the dynamic circuit, and idea, like a stone wedged in a delicate machine, can arrest one whole process of psychic interaction and spontaneous growth.[65]

Lawrence's fiction, writes Gāmini Salgādo, supremely charts "psychic ebb and flow within and between characters," and in doing so it "opened out... a whole new territory... which required a radical modification of conventional ideas of character, plot and moral significance." His "real concern [was] not with whether [people are] successful, happy or even 'good' in the ordinary sense of these words, but ultimately with whether [they] honor... or betray... the bond with life, with the deepest springs of being."[66]

Romanticism and Western Religious Culture

I have indicated, in the course of this chapter, what seems to me the main feature of romanticism that contributed to the proliferation of non-

Christian formulations of religious experience characteristic of the period 1760–1930. It is the shift in focus from religion's interpretation in transcendent terms to its exploration and celebration as experience itself. Another trend also characterizes the period, of course, one that tends, from our point of view, to look stronger than romanticism: that of interpreting religious experience in terms that specifically deny any reality to alleged objects, substantively or conceptually, clearly or hazily, perceived beyond the causal nexus. From this scientific and irreligious perspective, romanticism tends to look like a transitional stage between faith and positivism, an expression of religious yearning intensified by doubt: "One might come closest to a definition of their [the romantics'] aspirations by stating that 'longing' (*Sehnen*) was the first and almost the last word of German romanticism."[67] It would be foolish to deny the presence of this element in romanticism; yet what strikes me far more forcibly when confronted with romantic art and thought is the romantics' apparent confidence in the existence of transcendent realities. It is confidence rather than anxiety that allows romantics to engage with mysteries and uncertainties without any irritable reaching after facts and reasons that would account for them. It is the reality of personal spiritual experience that authenticates religious liberalism.

It is not indifferentism, after all, but assurance that enables the Savoyard vicar to continue performing rites in whose special efficacy he no longer believes; he does so with intensified reverence because his inner spiritual freedom enables him the better to appreciate the spiritual paths of others.[68] Similarly, Goethe insists that faith is primarily an active and intransitive affair:

> In religious faith, I used to say, the important thing is *that* one should believe; *what* one believes is of no concern. Faith is a great feeling of security for the present and the future, and this security arises out of our confidence in a grandiose, all-mighty, and inscrutable Being. Everything depends on the steadfastness of this confidence; but the manner in which we think of this Being depends on our other capacities, yes even on our circumstances, and is of absolutely no concern.[69]

At the other chronological margin, John Cowper Powys's strikingly restrained account of the "greatest event in [his] life at Cambridge" contrasts with Lawrence's indisputable power to articulate mysterious experience:

> I observed, growing upon this wall, certain patches of grass and green moss and yellow stone-crop. Something about the look of these small growths, secluded there in a place seldom passed, and more seldom noticed, seized upon me and caught me up into a sort of Seventh Heaven. . . . [In] this extraordinary moment . . . I felt a *beyond sensation* . . . to do with some secret underlying world of rich magic and

strange romance. In fact I actually regarded it as a prophetic idea of the sort of stories that I myself might write.[70]

This last sentence lays him open to those critics who despise the romantic conflation of religion and art and who see, in such distillations of transcendent experience into the promise of personal achievement, merely repulsive egoism; yet insofar as the romantic impulse, as it works within religion, is to convey rather than explain mysterious experience, it is naturally both allied to our powers of expression and tested on our pulses.

Both Protestantism and Roman Catholicism interacted with romanticism in important and characteristic ways. The emphasis on personal and felt experience, typified in the work of Friedrich Schleiermacher (1768–1834) and Søren Kierkegaard (1813–55), may be seen as a natural development of Protestantism under the influence of an increasing interest in our other-than-rational faculties. Throughout the nineteenth century, on the other hand, numbers of Lutherans and Anglicans found in the Church of Rome a means of satisfying the desire for palpable mystery that romantic culture aroused, particularly as it alone could claim identity with the church of the colorful Middle Ages.

Art was an important part of the religious lives and witness of the orthodox of all denominations as well as of the heterodox. The German Nazarenes sought to reanimate the age of faith by depictions of the medieval church; the Oxford Tractarians were sacramental poets as well as priests; and Charlotte Brontë (1816–55) gave classic expression to evangelicalism's intense fusion of respect for spiritual integrity and acknowledgment of personal need. Few who counted themselves members of a church would, one presumes, have subscribed to Schlegel's dictum: "Only he can be an artist who has a religion of his own, an original view of the infinite."[71] Still, the art of the orthodox in many cases was as committed as that of Blake to revealing and exploring the intensely personal nature of religious experience.

For this reason among others, it is not surprising that much religious art of the nineteenth century regularly crossed sectarian boundaries. *The Christian Year* (1827) by John Keble (1792–1866) was popular across the spectrum of English Christians; and the "devout Protestant" Friedrich sold his *Cross in the Mountains,* exhibited in 1808 and apparently intended for the Lutheran king of Sweden, to a Catholic nobleman specifically for use as an altarpiece in his chapel. Hugh Honour writes about the latter:

This is not without significance, if only because it emphasizes the painting's underlying ambiguity. Expressing a new attitude to religion which transcends sectarianism and makes conventional eighteenth-century acceptance or rejection of the

> Christian creeds seem equally shallow, this deeply moving and, at the same time, perplexing work is unlike any earlier or later devotional image. It is so undogmatic that it holds its potency even in the present age of unbelief.[72]

Whether or not one shares this response to the painting, it brings home the fact that through romantic art, an unprecedented traffic of religious experience was made possible between Christians of all kinds and all kinds of spiritual post-Christians. This, in my view, is the chief spiritual legacy of romanticism; that it transcends the divisions within and between the spiritual orthodoxies and heterodoxies of Western religious culture is of its essence.

Notes

1. William Blake, "Auguries of Innocence," in *The Poems of William Blake*, ed. W. H. Stevenson and David V. Erdman (New York: Norton; London: Longman, 1971), 585 (11.1–4).

2. Tolstoy's declaration of faith, "True religion is that relationship, in accordance with reason and knowledge, which man establishes with the infinite world around him, and which binds his life to that infinity and guides his actions," is made in contradistinction to the quintessentially nineteenth-century positivism of Auguste Comte. See Leo Tolstoy, "What Is Religion, of What Does It Consist?" in *A Confession and Other Religious Writings*, trans. Jane Kentish (Harmondsworth, England: Penguin, 1987), 89.

3. *Man(kind)* and *he* in their old-fashioned inclusive usage occur throughout this chapter because they reflect in a way that modern formulations can only distort the peculiar conflation in the romantic mind between the universal, the individual, and the masculine.

4. E. B. Pusey, *Parochial Sermons*, in *The Mind of the Oxford Movement*, ed. Owen Chadwick (London: A and C Black, 1960), 191, 197.

5. Samuel Taylor Coleridge, *Confessions of an Inquiring Spirit* (New York: Chelsea House, 1983).

6. Samuel Taylor Coleridge, "Statesman's Manual," in *Lay Sermons*, ed. R. J. White (London: Routledge and Kegan Paul, 1972), 30.

7. Geoffrey Keynes, ed., *The Complete Writings of William Blake* (London: Oxford University Press, 1957), 605.

8. Samuel Taylor Coleridge, *Biographia Literaria; or Biographical Sketches of My Literary Life and Opinions*, ed. J. Shawcross, 2 vols. (Oxford: Oxford University Press, 1968), 1:202.

9. Jean-Jacques Rousseau, *Emile*, trans. Barbara Foxley (New York: Dutton, n.d.), 270.

10. These words are inscribed beneath Edward Calvert's woodcut *The Ploughman*, published in 1827.

11. John Constable, *Further Documents and Correspondence*, ed. L. Parris, C. Shields, and I. Fleming-Williams (London: Suffolk Records Society, 1975), 56.

12. The painting by Turner is *Campo Santo, Venice*, 1842; the quotes from Blake are from Keynes, *Complete Writings of William Blake*, 617.

13. William Wordsworth, *The Prelude,* 2.241–60, in *The Poems of William Wordsworth,* ed. Thomas Hutchinson (London: Oxford University Press, 1916), 645–46.

14. George Eliot, *Adam Bede* (Harmondsworth, England: Penguin, 1980), 222.

15. The Schlegel reference is to *Kritische Shriften,* ed. W. Rasch (Munich, 1964), 93; for the Feuerbach quotation, see Andre Coeuroq, *Musique et litterateur* (Paris, 1923), 11–48.

16. Burnett James, *Wagner and the Romantic Disaster* (New York: Hippocrene, 1983), 6.

17. George Eliot, "The Modern Hep! Hep! Hep!" in *Impressions of Theophrastus Such* (Edinburgh: Blackwood, 1879).

18. Walt Whitman, "Song of Myself," in *Leaves of Grass,* ed. Malcolm Cowley (Harmondsworth, England: Penguin, 1976), 81.

19. Roy Pascal, *The German Sturm und Drang* (Manchester: Manchester University Press, 1953), 114–15, 109. Sturm und Drang ("storm and stress") is the name given to the first period (1770s) of German romanticism.

20. "John Keats to Richard Woodhouse, 27 October, 1818," in *The Letters of John Keats,* ed. Maurice Buxton Forman (Oxford: Oxford University Press, 1935), 227.

21. William Wordsworth, *The Prelude or Growth of a Poet's Mind,* ed. Ernest de Selincourt and Stephen Gill, 2d ed. (London: Oxford University Press, 1970), 12–13 (1.394–437).

22. Percy Bysshe Shelley, "Mont Blanc," in *Selected Poetry,* ed. Harold Bloom (New York: Signet, 1966), 83–87.

23. For an excellent, brief account of Kant's aesthetic philosophy, see Julian Roberts, *German Philosophy: An Introduction* (Cambridge: Polity, 1990), 55–66; the quotation from Burke is given on p. 62.

24. The pictures referred to are *The Wanderer above the Mists* (ca. 1817–18) and *On the Sailing Ship* (ca. 1818–19); the quotation is from Hugh Honour, *Romanticism* (Harmondsworth, England: Penguin, 1979), 78–79.

25. J. W. von Goethe, *The Sorrows of Young Werther,* trans. Michael Hulse (Harmondsworth, England: Penguin, 1989), 60–64.

26. Ibid., 26–27.

27. See, for example, "The Lord's Supper" in *Ralph Waldo Emerson,* ed. Richard Poirier (Oxford: Oxford University Press, 1990), 416.

28. Ibid., 444–45.

29. Ibid., 536, 405, 2, 446.

30. Ibid., 12.

31. Ibid., 13, 16.

32. Ibid., 64.

33. William Archer, *Real Conversations* (London, 1904), 46–47.

34. D. H. Lawrence, "A Study of Thomas Hardy," in *Phoenix,* quoted by George Woodcock in the introduction to Thomas Hardy's *The Return of the Native* (Harmondsworth, England: Penguin, 1978), 19.

35. Thomas Hardy, "The Convergence of the Twain," in *Thomas Hardy: The Complete Poems,* ed. J. Gibson (London: Macmillan, 1976), 248; the earlier reference is to Hardy's *Return of the Native,* 361.

36. Hardy, "Convergence of the Twain"; idem, *Tess of the d'Urbevilles* (London: Macmillan, 1974), 449; and idem, *Return of the Native,* 227.

37. It is perhaps easier to appreciate this through his short stories than through his novels — "The Withered Arm," for example, or "The Grave by the Handpost."

38. Hardy, *Return of the Native,* 444.

39. Simon Schama, *Citizens: A Chronicle of the French Revolution* (London: Viking, 1989), 160.

40. Bertrand Russell, *History of Western Philosophy,* 2d ed. (London: George Allen and Unwin, 1961), 660.

41. Rousseau, *Emile,* 252–54, 235–39.

42. Mary Shelley, *Frankenstein,* in *Three Gothic Novels* (Harmondsworth, England: Penguin, 1968), 311–17.

43. Honour, *Romanticism,* 298.

44. M. H. Abrams, *Natural Supernaturalism: Tradition and Revolution in Romantic Literature* (New York: Norton, 1971), 36.

45. R. G. Collingwood, *The Idea of History,* ed. T. M. Know (Oxford: Oxford University Press, 1946), 105, 282, 105.

46. A. L. Rowse, *The Use of History,* quoted in Richard A. E. Brooks, "The Development of the Historical Mind," in *The Reinterpretation of Victorian Literature,* ed. Joseph E. Baker (Princeton, N.J.: Princeton University Press, 1950), 131.

47. David Hume, *Inquiry concerning Human Understanding,* quoted by Karl Kroeber in Karl Kroeber and William Walling, eds., *Images of Romanticism: Verbal and Visual Affinities* (New Haven: Yale University Press, 1978), 150.

48. Ibid., 165.

49. Samuel Taylor Coleridge, "The Rime of the Ancient Mariner," in William Wordsworth and Samuel Taylor Coleridge, *Lyrical Ballads,* ed. R. L. Brett and A. R. Jones (London: Methuen, 1965), 21 (1.277).

50. Owen Chadwick, *The Secularization of the European Mind in the Nineteenth Century* (Cambridge: Cambridge University Press, 1975), 69.

51. Quoted in Bernard M. G. Rearson, ed., *Religious Thought in the Nineteenth Century Illustrated from Writers of the Period* (Cambridge: Cambridge University Press, 1966), 82.

52. Ludwig Feuerbach, *The Essence of Christianity,* trans. George Eliot (New York: Harper and Row, 1957), 1–3.

53. Ibid., xxxiii–xxxvi.

54. Ibid., 155–58.

55. Harold Bloom and Lionel Trilling, eds., *Romantic Poetry and Prose* (New York: Oxford University Press, 1973), 400.

56. Feuerbach, *Essence of Christianity,* 3.

57. Ibid., 156.

58. Arthur Schopenhauer, *Essays and Aphorisms,* ed. and trans. R. J. Hollingdale (Harmondsworth, England: Penguin, 1970), 174–75.

59. Schopenhauer, *Essays and Aphorisms,* 175.

60. Whitman, *Leaves of Grass,* 26.

61. D. H. Lawrence, *Apocalypse* (Harmondsworth, England: Penguin, 1974), 125–26.

62. D. H. Lawrence, *Psychoanalysis and the Unconscious* (bound with *Fantasia of the Unconscious*) (Harmondsworth, England: Penguin, 1971), 249.

63. Ibid., 207, 209, 214.

64. D. H. Lawrence, "The Body of God," in *Selected Poems,* ed. Keith Sagar (Harmondsworth, England: Penguin, 1972), 239; for the theme of darkness as motive force, see *The Plumed Serpent* and *Kangeroo.*

65. Lawrence, *Psychoanalysis and the Unconscious,* 227, 246.

66. Gāmini Salgādo, *A Preface to Lawrence* (London: Longman, 1982), 106–7, 111.

67. Robert Hughes, *Nothing If Not Critical* (London: Collins Harvill, 1990), 90; he is quoting Gert Schiff from his New York Metropolitan Museum of Art catalogue *German Masters of the Nineteenth Century*.

68. Rousseau, *Emile*, 272–73.

69. Goethe, *Poetry and Truth*, quoted in Pascal, *German Sturm und Drang*, 109.

70. Quoted in Richard Perceval Graves, *The Brothers Powys* (London: Routledge and Kegan Paul, 1983), 34.

71. Quoted in Hughes, *Nothing If Not Critical*, 90.

72. Honour, *Romanticism*, 26–27.

Bibliography

Abrams, M. H. *Natural Supernaturalism: Tradition and Revolution in Romantic Literature*. New York: Norton, 1971.

Barzun, Jacques. *Berlioz and the Romantic Century*. 2 vols. Boston: Little, Brown and Co., 1950.

Chadwick, Owen. *The Secularization of the European Mind in the Nineteenth Century*. Cambridge: Cambridge University Press, 1975.

Coleridge, Samuel Taylor. *Biographia Literaria; or Biographical Sketches of My Literary Life and Opinions*. 2 vols. Edited by J. Shawcross. Oxford: Oxford University Press, 1968.

———. *Confessions of an Inquiring Spirit*. New York: Chelsea House, 1983.

Feuerbach, Ludwig. *The Essence of Christianity*. Translated by George Eliot. New York: Harper and Row, 1957.

Goethe, J. W. von. *The Sorrows of Young Werther*. Translated by Michael Hulse. Harmondsworth: Penguin, 1989.

Honour, Hugh. *Romanticism*. Harmondsworth: Penguin, 1979.

Kroeber, Karl, and William Walling, eds. *Images of Romanticism: Verbal and Visual Affinities*. New Haven: Yale University Press, 1978.

Pascal, Roy. *The German Sturm und Drang*. Manchester: Manchester University Press, 1953.

Rousseau, Jean-Jacques. *Emile, or On Education*. Translated by Allan Bloom. New York: Basic Books, 1979.

Schama, Simon. *Citizens: A Chronicle of the French Revolution*. London: Viking, 1989.

D. Contemporary Postmodernism

7

Deconstructionist Aestheticism

Charles E. Winquist

THE WORDS *spirit* and *spirituality* are used infrequently in discourses marked by a postmodern deconstructionist sensibility.[1] Traditional and familiar concepts of "spiritual practices" do not have an easily recognizable kinship with the themes and concepts that constitute what might be called a deconstructive practice. Deconstructive practices appear, at least at first, as oppositional to spiritual practices that have been formulated in the Western ontotheological tradition.

In fact, one of the serious problems in accessing what might be meant by a deconstructionist notion of spirituality is that much deconstructionist thinking is a writing against ontotheology while what is traditionally meant by spirituality in Western culture is deeply rooted in what has come to be understood as ontotheology. Ontotheology is a highly overdetermined notion shaped mostly by critics of the Western metaphysical tradition rather than by any practitioners of a discipline that would call itself ontotheology.

The concept was first developed by Immanuel Kant (1724–1804) to describe a type of transcendental theology that believes that it knows the existence of an original being through "mere concepts."[2] God is the highest being and the original being in ontotheology. God is the "mere concept of a highest original ground."[3] Kant appears to have been specifically referring to the notion of God formulated by Anselm (1033/34–1109) and reformulated by Descartes (1596–1650) in the ontological argument for God's existence. This "mere concept," however, has been oppositionally characterized so that it encompasses Western thought from the thinking of being of Parmenides (ca. 515 B.C.E.) to the thinking of being of Heidegger (1889–1976). God, the original being, is identified as the being of all beings and as such is the archetypal, transcendental signified of all thinking. Ontotheology is a theology or philosophy of presence. Thinking seeks wholeness, presence, and unity. It seeks a total presence that is deeply resonant with traditional formulations of spiritual fulfillment.

In contrast, the a/theological formulations of deconstructive thought seem to favor notions of fissure, displacement, drift, or erring rather than seeking a self-transformative knowledge through an intentional relationship with a metaphysical, ontological, cosmic, or natural whole. The desideratum of thinking or experiencing the unity of being as present to consciousness requires a frame of thinking that deconstructive analyses render impossible. If there are to be notions of spiritual practices within a deconstructive, postmodern sensibility, they will occur in a frame other than the ontotheological tradition. Deconstructive thinking will read against the grain of the theological tradition that includes even the twentieth-century theological achievements of great Protestant or Catholic theologians such as Karl Barth, Paul Tillich, Bernard Lonergan, and Karl Rahner. Postmodernity designates not a new time but a new sensibility.

The equation of theological thought with thinking about being is particularly problematic in any deconstructive rethinking of the theological task and what theology can say about the meaning of spirituality. Tillich's nonsymbolic identification of God with being is an absolute concept that is paralleled by Rahner's concept of the preapprehension of being that is further ramified into the realm of the "spirit."[4] Two quotes from Rahner clearly exemplify the problem of spirituality for a sensibility that cannot think in absolute terms. "Every operation of the spirit, whatever it might be, can therefore be understood only as a moment in the movement toward absolute being as towards the one end and goal of the desire of the spirit."[5] And, "Spirit grasps at the incomprehensible, in as much as it presses on beyond the actual object of comprehension to an anticipatory grasp of the absolute."[6]

The problem with this notion of spirituality is the language of "the one end" and "the absolute." The problem is the dissonance between an understanding of God as identical with absolute being and a thinking that has accepted both the death of God and the end of metaphysics. The meaning of *spirituality* is fully implicated in the meaning of the word *God*. To think the possible meaning of a deconstructive spiritual practice is first of all to think the meaning of the word *God*.

At first this seems paradoxical since deconstructive thinking has sometimes been described as the hermeneutic of the death of God or the death of God put into writing.[7] It must be noted, however, that the name of

God is inscribed in a text that is writing the death of God. A postmodern, deconstructive spiritual practice begins and will be elaborated by thinking the meaning of the name of God in thinking the meaning of the death of God.

This is not a simple task. Mark C. Taylor in elaborating the problematic agenda of a/theological thinking — that is, postmodern, deconstructive theological thinking — notes the coimplication of the proclamation of the death of God with the displacement of the self, the closure of the encyclopedic book, and the end of history as a meaningful explanatory concept.[8] Deconstructive thinking has a complex genealogy that includes the whole of the Western ontotheological tradition extending back to Plato, and deconstructive thinkers such as Jacques Derrida and Gilles Deleuze repeat the totality of this tradition "while simultaneously making it tremble, making it insecure in its most assured evidences."[9]

There are, however, some thinkers indexed in the genealogy of deconstructive thinking who are especially important in conceiving what might be meant by a deconstructive spiritual practice. The Kantian epistemic *aporia,* an "impassable passage" marking the separation of the noumenal world of things-in-themselves from the phenomenal world of things-for-us, was both a fissuring of the assurance of the Cartesian cogito and the opening of a space for a hermeneutics of suspicion in the thinking of Nietzsche (1844–1900), Marx (1818–83), and Freud (1856–1939). A further complication was that the totalization of subjectivity developed by Hegel (1770–1831) in the notion of absolute knowledge overcoming or resolving the Kantian dilemma did, at the same time, conceptually bring forward notions of an end to history and a closure of the encyclopedic book. The realization of absolute spirit through absolute knowledge left no place for thinking to go. Consequentially, in the hermeneutics of suspicion, thinking turned on itself. The oppositional reinscription of finite consciousness marked by notions of the metaphoricity of all language, an efficaciously dynamic unconscious, and the ideological distortion through class interests — all of these magnified the Kantian wound Hegel had sought to overcome. It is almost as if Hegel had conspired with Nietzsche to make meaningful the proclamation of the death of God by absolutizing the self of consciousness, the dialectical meaning of history, and the philosophical completeness of the book of knowledge.

In deconstructionist thinking, the works of Nietzsche, Marx, and Freud mean that absolute spirit is neither a credible ground nor a credible telos for the meaning of "spirituality." If the concepts of spirit and spirituality are to have meaning in a postmodern sensibility, they will have to be rethought in a context of finite experience that does not presuppose absolute meaning. Within this context we might tentatively suggest that "spirit is the metonymical trope of consciousness to index what consciousness cannot touch upon, grasp, or witness."[10] Spirit is not simply identified with consciousness but marks a pressured relationship with consciousness that is also other than consciousness although there are conscious effects. Something must be happening, or there is no reason to designate the word *spirit* in distinction from the word *consciousness.*

Nietzsche gives many clues as to what *spirit* means when disentangled from the frames of the ontotheological and Christian traditions. Very simply, when the words *spirit* and *spirituality* are positively valenced, it would appear that we are talking about an aesthetic phenomenon. In *The Gay Science* he writes very straightforwardly that "as an aesthetic phenomenon existence is still *bearable* for us, and art furnishes us with eyes and hands and above all the good conscience to be *able* to turn ourselves into such a phenomenon."[11] Nietzschean spirituality is being able to say yes to reality, including the reality of the proclamation of the death of God. It is the becoming of ourselves when we can say yes to the eternal recurrence of the same. It is when we can say yes to the question of greatest weight — "Do you desire this once more and innumerable times more?"[12]

Deconstructionist aestheticism is an exfoliation of these insights along many diverse lines of differential thinking. Since there is no paradigm governing thought, and even very little thinking, about deconstructionist spirituality, it will be felicitous to follow several lines of thinking to see how such a practice might articulate itself.

Jacques Derrida is the philosopher who has had the most visible impact on deconstructionist theological thinking. Theological readers of Derrida's philosophy have sometimes noted an affinity between the strategic thrust of his thinking and what is known as negative theology and its relationship to a "mystic" knowing. Derrida repeatedly denies that he is a negative theologian, but "to the precise extent that one identifies God with full presence, as the determinate origin or end of being, one's theology will fall within the scope of Derrida's critique."[13] Thus, Derrida is critically implicated in theological thinking and any assessment of a spirituality based on a theology of presence even though he does not think of his work as theological. He has been drawn into, and not always unwillingly, a theological discussion.

The point of intersection between Derrida's philosophy and the diverse claims of the ontotheological tradition is his insistence that no text can be totalized from within or without. The conditions that make possible textual production also rift the totalization of any theological or philosophical text. There is no word, no speaking, and no text that means total presence. The naming of God can only be a trope of denial. It is what we are not, and it is never itself the manifestation of a total presence to consciousness. "To deconstruct a discourse is to show, by reference to its own assumptions, that it depends upon prior differences which prevent the discourse from being totalized."[14] There are "undecidables" in Derrida's thinking that mark every text with traces of an alterity that escape all representation. Theologically there can never be a word of God, a text of God, that is adequate in its representational completeness.

It is these claims that appear to have an affinity with the apophaticism of negative theology. "In 'apophaticism,' ... 'knowledge' of God is gained through successive denials of 'God,' resulting in an anabasis, an ascent to God through the darkness of unknowing."[15] Derrida can be used in the spiritual practices of negative theology. He, however, has repeatedly objected, in vain, to the assimilation of his "traces" or "undecidables" into negative theology.[16] The discussion of negative theology has always been deferred in his writing except as a denial.

Derrida writes about writing even when he writes in an apocalyptic tone. What is undecidable, the nonconcept *différance,* is transcendental or quasi-transcendental rather than transcendent or quasi-divine. "The ineffability that concerns the theologian differs, then, from the ineffability that perplexes the deconstructionist."[17] What perplexes the deconstructionist is the negation, the unsaying, that is a condition for discourse. The deconstructionist denegation of discourse simply does not speak to the possibility of an anabasis through the darkness of unknowing to an apophatic God that is surreal, hyper-real, hyper-essential, or supereminent being.[18] The epistemic undecidability in deconstructionist analyses can neither initiate nor underwrite what is a wholly contingent event or gift within the operations of discourse, the apophasis of God. Instead, it can only speak the name of God as the instantiation of a radical negativity.[19] The discourse of negative theology is subject to the same indeterminacy or undecidability as every other discourse. The not, the nothing, or nothingness of deconstructive resistance is not sanctioned as a holy nothingness.

An implication of this insight is that deconstruction does not legitimate the world-denying asceticisms of negative theology or any other practices that might be described as a *via negativa.* Once again Rahner's understanding of spiritual life falls outside the scope of legitimation of deconstructive discourse. For example, there is a direct and immediate contrast between his description of spiritual life and Mark C. Taylor's notions of erring and mazing grace that might approximate or approach a meaning for postmodern spirituality. Rahner writes:

> "Spiritual life" in grace means that we realize the inner divine life in ourselves; it means waiting for eternity in faith, hope, and love, bearing the darkness of human existence; it means not identifying oneself with this world, living according to the prayer contained in the Didache: "Let this world pass away and let the grace of God come."[20]

In stark contrast, Taylor writes:

> Within the unending play of the divine milieu, "waiting is the final losing game." ... Through unexpected twists and unanticipated turns, erring and aberrance show the death of God, disappearance of self, and end of history to be the realization of *mazing grace*.... Mazing grace opens "a way of totally loving the world."[21]

What is most apparent in this juxtaposition of quotations is a very different ambiance in thinking the meaning of spiritual practices. A somber, world-denying asceticism is contrasted with a carnivalesque affirmation. Ironically, in deconstruction, affirmation comes out of the denegation of ontotheology. This is not a negation of negation. "To de-negate is to un-negate; but un-negation is itself a form of negation. More precisely, denegation is an un-negation that affirms rather than negates negation."[22] There is a lack that is not a loss. There is a primacy of *not* in Derrida's thinking and in Taylor's thinking that continues to impact what we might infer to be a deconstructive spiritual practice. "The question of the not is older — dreadfully older — than theology, philosophy, and art. It is indeed older than thought itself, for it is impossible to think without already having thought not."[23] The always already having thought not is the other of thinking. It is the primordiality of a lack (of thinking) that is not a loss but an absence that negates every absolute origin. "If primal plenitude is never present and absence is 'original,' then lack does not inevitably entail loss or deficiency."[24] The aporetic passage of *différance* give us only a trace of the having thought not. Thinking can only be the unending play of traces.

This play is not, however, simply the celebration of the carnivalesque. Taylor is also a thinker of *nothing*. He resists Hegel when the name *Hegel* is a synecdochic trope for totalizing thinking. "Resistance is always performed indirectly 'in the name of' an an-archic 'before' that must remain unnameable."[25] When we think theologically, "The 'unrepresentable before' is the 'terrifyingly ancient,' which sometimes goes by the pseudonym 'God.'"[26] The "unrepresentable before" cannot be sublated into absolute spirit because it cannot be thought, written, or spoken except as thinking is able to think not.

The space of thinking resistance is not dialectical. It is not lifted up but is instead spread out or disseminated on diverse surfaces. There is, perhaps, an important coincidence between the space of resistance and the space of the carnival, an oxymoronic serious frivolity or frivolous seriousness. Without origin or ground, totalizing thought is incomplete because the play of the trace is unending. Totalization can be no more than a simulacrum of desire that marks itself on unending surfaces. The meaning of the infinite is reconfigured in a kenotic incarnation that is marked on surfaces. Taylor's spiritual practice is a superficial profundity. "Festive play is an unending game in which the extraordinary becomes ordinary and the ordinary becomes extraordinary."[27]

In the above formulation Taylor is close to Nietzsche. Spirituality is the orientation to reality that allows us to play the unending game, and the unending game is the eternal recurrence of the same. We choose it, value it, and say yes so that extraordinary becomes ordinary and the ordinary becomes extraordinary. The game is a constant transvaluation of values and reconfiguration of meanings.

The floating signifiers of the game in their referential play are meaningful, but the meaning is migratory. It is a nomadic economy and spirituality that might be thought of as a driftwork. It is a celebration of life that is also a resistance against the repression of totalizing thinking:

> Shifty vagrants who err endlessly do not feel the need "to deprive the world of its disturbing and enigmatic character. . . ." When it no longer seems necessary to reduce manyness to oneness and to translate the equivocal as univocal, it becomes possible to give up the struggle for mastery and to take eternal "delight" in "The enigmatical/Beauty of each beautiful enigma."[28]

Drawing closer to the beautiful enigma appears to be the spiritual meaning of thinking the *not* in Derrida and Taylor.

This is not the only postmodern reading or interpretation of thinking *not*. Giorgio Agamben assigns a meaning to spirituality that is more closely akin to the temperament and taste of Gilles Deleuze than Derrida or Taylor. Agamben writes: "Non-thingness [spirituality] means losing oneself in things, losing oneself to the point of not being able to conceive of anything but things, and only then, in the experience of the irremediable thingness of the world, bumping into a limit, touching it."[29] This may be the beautiful enigma marked by Taylor and not unlike erring, but the route to this affirmation follows a different line of differentiation and opens other possibilities for thinking the meaning of a postmodern spirituality.

In Deleuze an ongoing critique of the negative is combined with a critique of interiority. Deleuze's deconstructive thinking is less of a direct attack on Hegel than an exfoliation of series of lines of thinking in Hume, Bergson, Nietzsche, Lucretius, Spinoza, and Leibniz that push Hegel aside.

His "logic of sense" is no less radical than Derrida's nonconcept *différance* and is at the same time a political practice that can be likened to a spiritual practice. He is always concerned with assemblages, aggregates, and arrangements for thinking that are of course also arrangements for living. In this sense all thinking is political. The distribution of concepts is a becoming. Self is a becoming. Community is a becoming. Spirituality will have to find its meaning in the understanding of becoming.

Since there has at this point been very little theological assimilation of Deleuze's philosophical writings, thinking the meaning of spirituality in his terms will be a construct resulting from the deconstructive force of his problematization of familiar words in the lexicon of traditional understandings of spirituality — the subject, the body, interiority, sense, and nonsense. He will also introduce new words and concepts that will bear upon the meaning of spirituality, such as the notion of the "singularity."

Deleuze has written that "the genius of a philosophy must first be measured by the new distribution which it imposes on beings and concepts."[30] His work is an empiricism that can also be thought of as a reversal of Platonism in line with Stoicism and Nietzsche. The "new distribution" that he imposes on beings and concepts necessitates a rethinking of spiritual practices because it deracinates so much familiar language of traditional thinking. He thinks neither of lack nor loss. He focuses on the available surfaces of thinking. On the surface there can be a complexity that is metaphorically named as depth. "To reverse Platonism is first and foremost to remove essences and to substitute events in their place, as jets of singularities."[31]

Deleuze insists that we think on the surface because this is the locus of our experience. " 'Depth' is no longer a compliment."[32] Sense, and the locus of the logic of sense, is the "expressed" of the proposition and not contained in its denotation, manifestation, or signification.[33] There is no originative sense. Sense is produced as an effects-series. He writes that "the expressed sense must engender the other dimensions of the proposition [signification, manifestation, and denotation.]"[34] The problem is that "we have impassibility in relation to states of affairs and neutrality in relation to propositions; ... we have the power of genesis in relation to propositions and in relation to states of affairs themselves."[35] The identity and nonidentity of sense with propositions are an *aporia*, one that we cannot get beneath or behind as we acknowledge the transformation of mind into human nature in the very habit of subjectivity. Whatever might be meant by a spiritual practice is bound to the surface if this practice is referred to the secondary agency of subjectivity. Sense is the event of surface effects, and the sense of the spirit is bound to the logic of sense.

There is no simple or pure subject in Deleuze's thought. There is instead a heterological infrastructure to subjectivity so that the subject is derived and always belated in relationship to states of affairs and the logic of sense. There is a conjunction of causalities in the meaning of subjective consciousness. The logic of sense is an effects-series, but there are other effects that also mark the surface and implicate consciousness in what is neither individual nor personal. Deleuze fashions a notion of the singularity and its longitudinal exfoliation to understand what is other than the sense of subjectivity in the constitution of subjectivity:

> What is neither individual nor personal are, on the contrary, emissions of singularities insofar as they occur on an unconscious surface and possess a mobile, immanent principle of auto-unification through a *nomadic distribution*, radically distinct from fixed and sedentary distributions as the conditions of the syntheses of consciousness. Singularities are the true transcendental events, and Ferlinghetti calls them "the fourth person singular."[36]

Singularities transcend the synthesis of the person although they mark the subjectivity of experience. Singularities are themselves aporetic. We cannot get through them or behind them. They are points of intensity, intersections, conjunctions of forces, incorrigibles from which there is an emission of significations or a becoming of a differential play. This is a modest notion of an intellectual, material, or physical state of affairs that is not yet meaningful. It is an attempt to introduce into epistemic reflection an interpretively neutral notion that will pressure the meaning of interpretation. We have experiences of singularities, but we usually do not notice them as singular unless they are anomalous within the frame of current interpretive discourse.

Deleuze says that "singularities are turning points and points of inflection; bottlenecks, knots, foyers, and centers; points of fusion, condensation, and boiling; points of tears and joy, sickness and health, hope and anxiety, 'sensitive' points."[37] Singularities are points of resistance within the interpretive meaning of experience. They are ambivalent since they are not fixed within the frame of their occurrence. The singularity is an event around which thinking recoils. Thinking turns on itself in an experience of inadequacy. The singularity is yet something to be thought, and we don't know until it is thought whether it can be thought in the frame of its occurrence. In the quotation from Deleuze we realize that singularities are those confusions in life that are sometimes fleeting but can also be a complete breakdown of understanding. The question for rethinking thinking is how to attend to these experiences in the framing of interpretation.

Since we are always already within specific discursive practices, singularities will occur within these practices although their status is of a nature that does not always fit the prevailing practice; that is, an event occurs that can be thought of as singular in the sense that it resists explanation in the current interpretive practice. A new thinking, a new speaking, a new writing flows from the singularity. This new thinking can be within the frame of current interpretive practice; but singular events also can be indexed on multiple registers that are not contained within the frame of prevailing interpretive practices. They are always "other," but these alterities can be empiricities that escape interpretation, heterodoxies that conflict with interpretation, or multiplicities that extend beyond the range of interpretation. Singular events can have the intimacy of a new love affair or a broken love affair and also the generality of cosmic events such as the death of God, the end of history, the closure of the book, and the displacement of the subject. Or a singularity can be a simple gesture, a metaphor, a juxtaposition of images.

What we know in the encounter with singularities is that there are unsolved riddles that bear on our senses of self and world. We know that familiar definitions of selfhood are too simple to carry the complexities of experience that are part of our witness to life. In particular, the self as an individual and yet universal subjectivity is too much of a voluntaristic fantasy to be credible even in the vagaries of everyday experience. The dominant frame of appearances is always unstable if we even only moderately attend to what we experience. Any of our constructed notions of the self simply give way when confronted with exigencies and incorrigibilities of body and mind embedded in a complex nexus of material, physical, and intellectual forces and flows. This nexus is the heterological infrastructure of the subjectivity from which the identity of the self is inscribed. This means that the self is constituted in what is other than self. The relationship with this Other may be a primary meaning of spirituality.

A spiritual practice would then be a constant work against repression and nonrecognition. Singularities mark aspects of the heterological infrastructure that were or are the excluded "Other" in interpretive processes of homogenization, abstraction, or universalization. The reception of singularities into experience can be a doubling phenomenon. On the one hand, the singularity destabilizes prevailing interpretive practices. On the other hand, new possibilities and new lines of interpretation issue forth. The question is whether we can intentionally frame a discursive practice that is less resistant to the disclosure of aspects that we have been calling singularities. Ironically, the path to less resistance in postmodern conditions may be a path of resistance to the interpretive hegemony of a pure, universal understanding of subjectivity.

The problem with trying to define or characterize the singularity is that it is not known directly. We know it by its effects. We know it as it is marked on different registers or recorded on different surfaces. What we give up is the unity of apperception that is constituted in the identity of being and thinking. The privilege of consciousness in the assertion of "I think" becomes an effect alongside of other effects, a secondary process. What is gained is that thinking cannot be reduced to pure subjectivity.

Singularities are contingencies within thinking. Sometimes in specific turns they are generated out of thinking although this is usually outside of an intentional structure. However, independent of their originative status they can be indexed as surface effects in the genealogies of specific thought processes. This indexing does not just happen. It is a differential process. The recording surfaces for the inscription of meaning must be interrogated. This is a way that thinking acts upon thinking. Thinking can initiate meaning when it allows its discourse to trouble itself.

The surface is a figuration in discourse to designate where thinking appears or shows itself. Thinking has to come to some expression or we are not yet thinking. The metaphor of a recording surface is an acknowledgment of the necessity of material expression in the constitution of an event. Preparing the surface is part of the thinking that allows us to think singularities, and it is the singularity that needs to be thought. Singularities include the knots and intensities in our lives. They remain "other" unless they can be thought.

It would appear that in the shallowness of secular culture there are singularities that this culture has not been able to think, and that is why we have raised the question of whether we need to think theologically even in a secular culture. Is there anything special on the surfaces or in the mechanics of theological text production that offers differential possibilities for thickening the meaning of secular lives? Has the silencing of theology diminished the capacity for living? This is not a meaningless question when we are seeking a meaning for spirituality in a secular culture.

The question is whether theology as a discursive practice differs in any important way from other discursive practices. In a remarkable quotation from one of the appendices of *The Logic of Sense,* Deleuze says:

> It is our epoch which has discovered theology. One no longer needs to believe in God. We seek rather the "structure," that is, the form which may be filled with beliefs, but the structure has no need to be filled in order to be called "theological." Theology is now the science of nonexisting entities, the manner in which these

> entities — divine or anti-divine, Christ or Antichrist — animate language and make for it this glorious body which is divided into disjunctions.[38]

The animation of language and the making of a glorious disjunctive body are a Deleuzian meaning of a spiritual practice. Spiritual development is an overcoming of a thinking that is repressive in its totalization. It is a consent to finite reality and a thinking of this reality. It is a saying yes to an aesthetic meaning to existence that is at the same time a thinking enfranchisement of the Other in and of language.

These formulations have a not-accidental resonance with Nietzsche's *amor fati*. The frame of this interrogation has been aesthetic, and Nietzsche's choice of the world is a making things beautiful. This is a valuation that is an ethical decision. What we need to understand is that epistemic undecidability heightens the importance of ethical decidability.

Deleuze's notions of the subject and self as being constituted in the heterogeneous objectivity of the world and not having a status that is other, beneath, or behind the objectivity of the world means that the self is not separate from the world, and its own becoming is efficacious within the world. Ethics is understood in terms of recognition and valuation and not duty. There is an important resonance in Deleuze's thinking with the first proposition of Wittgenstein's *Tractatus logico-philosophicus:* "The world is all that is the case."[39] Wittgenstein's proposition is a nonmystifying restatement of the doctrine of eternal recurrence, and it implies that all spiritual, political, and ethical practices must be strategic initiatives in the world. There is an impassibility to the singularity the recognition of which is a "yes" or "no" valuation of the singularity itself.

In the actual practice of thinking and writing, which is as close as we can get to a spiritual practice with Deleuze, he, with coauthor Felix Guattari, develops the strategic notion of a minor literature.[40] A minor use of language resists the homogenizing and totalizing tendencies of any dominant discourse that sometimes elide the singularities that are disjunctive and destabilizing moments in moves toward discursive completeness. A minor intensive use of language is language working against its abstracting and totalizing capacity. Minor literatures teach us to stammer in our own language.[41] A minor literature is made up of texts that are unsafe and are a contagion that makes all texts unsafe.

Deleuze works with both topological and tropological strategies in the making of a minor literature. Many of his philosophical studies are topological in the sense that they are preparing recording surfaces that are complex enough so that singularities can be indexed as surface effects. Thinking must elaborate itself to be cognizant of its own heterogeneous complexity. The topological strategies for complexifying the inscriptive surfaces are preparatory practices.

In contrast, tropological strategies are interventions in discourse. Tropes can fissure the recording surface of any particular discourse and witness to what is other than its representations by elaborating its own incompleteness. Deleuze understands that theology, as a "science of nonexisting entities," is a complex tropology. Theological figurations of extremity disturb the representational economy of a discourse by being within discourse but not always within the expressivity of sense. Discourse is inhabited by a nonidentity, a moment of deterritorialization, an internal silence. The text is an unfinished business, always becoming, and not safe. Deleuze has made room for theology to insinuate itself into the dominant discourse.

Since "the world is all that is the case," a minor intensive theological literature inhabits spaces in the flux of everyday discourses. Theology acts on the ordinariness of a dominant discourse and transforms its experiential meaning. It is Deleuze's understanding that a minor literature opposes the "oppressed quality" of language to its "oppressive quality."[42] Ordinariness too often has been the satisfaction or dissatisfaction of feeling familiar with a world constricted by the oppressive quality of language. This prematurely closed world of ordinariness is not enough. What is missing are the singularities of experience that can fill and delight us. What is missing are the exfoliations of these singularities that thicken experience and give it a sense of importance.

Deleuze's thought can be extrapolated so that a spiritual practice can be understood as a thinking beside itself that opens discourse to the complex heterological infrastructure of the dynamics of becoming. In particular, a theology beside itself is a way of thinking how theology, when it is juxtaposed with other discourses, pressures those discourses by violating their containment and making them incomplete and unsafe. As a spiritual practice, theology is itself a complex metonymical trope. It is a nomadic thinking wandering about the margins and through the interstices of ordinary discourses continually opening them to what is other than themselves.

Singularities need to be recognized and now can be recognized in a nomadic thinking because their elision will not make the discourse safe since it has already been made unsafe by being abutted by the formulations of a theological discourse. Tropologically relativizing a dominant discourse lifts a veil of repression. The textuality of experience is by this process understood as always already unsafe so that there is no further need or purpose to defend thinking from recognizing the singularities of experience. Decisions can be made following the recognitions of singularities in our experience. Ethical decidability within a spiritual practice is a valuation of people, things, events, and forces that come to appear within the discursive frames on the surfaces of experience. Spirituality is a response to the demand to value positively or negatively what has come to appear. The most intense "yes" to the Other in its finite appearance is love. The intense valuation of finitude itself is *amor fati*. The ordinariness of the world is valued so that it is extraordinary. "Love offers finitude in its truth; it is finitude's dazzling presentation."[43] The joy in this presentation is an aesthetic satisfaction.

Spiritual practices have always been about seeking an experience and a thinking that do not disappoint us. They have often been marked by a dissatisfaction with the surfaces of experience. However, deconstructive thinking emphasizes the surface and surface effects and yet in its nomadic wandering or erring can affirm "finitude's dazzling presentation." Deconstructionist aestheticism is a reconfiguration of what has been called "depth" in what is now a horizontal complexity that does not disappoint thinking. Deconstructionist aestheticism only knows the incarnate spirit, the spirit in the world.

Notes

1. A notable exception to this statement is Jacques Derrida's study of Heidegger, *Of Spirit: Heidegger and the Question*, trans. Geoffrey Bennington and Rachel Bowlby (Chicago: University of Chicago Press, 1989).

2. Immanuel Kant, *Critique of Pure Reason*, trans. Norman Kemp Smith. (New York: St. Martin's, 1965), 525.

3. Immanuel Kant, *Lectures on Philosophical Theology*, trans. Allen W. Wood and Gertrude M. Clark (Ithaca, N.Y.: Cornell University Press, 1978), 80.

4. See especially Paul Tillich, *Systematic Theology*, 3 vols. (Chicago: University of Chicago Press, 1951), 3:238–39.

5. Karl Rahner, *Spirit in the World*, trans. William Dych (New York: Herder and Herder, 1968), 283.

6. Karl Rahner, *A Rahner Reader*, ed. Gerald A. McCool (New York: Seabury, 1975), 113.

7. Mark C. Taylor, *Erring: A Postmodern A/theology* (Chicago: University of Chicago Press, 1984), 6; and Carl Raschke, "The Deconstruction of God," in T. J. J. Altizer et al., *Deconstruction and Theology* (New York: Crossroad, 1982), 3.

8. Taylor, *Erring*, 7.

9. Rodolphe Gasché, *The Tain of the Mirror: Derrida and the Philosophy of Reflection* (Cambridge, Mass.: Harvard University Press, 1986), 180.

10. Noelle Vahanian (unpublished manuscript, 1993).

11. Friedrich Nietzsche, *The Gay Science*, trans. Walter Kaufmann (New York: Vintage, 1974), 163–64.

12. Ibid., 274.
13. Kevin Hart, *The Trespass of the Sign: Deconstruction, Theology and Philosophy* (Cambridge: Cambridge University Press, 1989), 14–15.
14. Ibid., 67.
15. Ibid., 175.
16. Mark C. Taylor, *Nots* (Chicago: University of Chicago Press, 1993), 3, 39.
17. Hart, *Trespass of the Sign,* 187.
18. Taylor, *Nots,* 49.
19. See Robert Scharlemann, "The Being of God When God Is Not Being God," in *Deconstruction and Theology.*
20. Rahner, *A Rahner Reader,* 318.
21. Taylor, *Erring,* 155, 168.
22. Taylor, *Nots,* 36.
23. Ibid., 1.
24. Taylor, *Erring,* 155.
25. Taylor, *Nots,* 73.
26. Ibid., 89.
27. Taylor, *Erring,* 169.
28. Ibid., 176–77.
29. Giorgio Agamben, *The Coming Community,* trans. Michael Hardt (Minneapolis: University of Minnesota Press, 1993), 103.
30. Gilles Deleuze, *The Logic of Sense,* trans. Mark Lester with Charles Stivale, ed. Constantin V. Boundas (New York: Columbia University Press, 1990), 6.
31. Ibid., 53.
32. Ibid., 9.
33. Ibid., 12–19.
34. Ibid., 95–96.
35. Ibid., 96.
36. Ibid., 102–3.
37. Ibid., 52.
38. Ibid., 281.
39. Ludwig Wittgenstein, *Tractatus logico-philosophicus,* trans. D. F. Pears and B. F. McGuinness (London: Routledge and Kegan Paul, 1961), 7.
40. Gilles Deleuze and Felix Guattari, *Kafka: Towards a Minor Literature,* trans. Dana Polan (Minneapolis: University of Minnesota Press, 1986).
41. Gilles Deleuze and Claire Parnet, *Dialogues,* trans. Hugh Tomlinson and Barbara Habberjam (New York: Columbia University Press, 1987), 4.
42. Deleuze and Guattari, *Kafka,* 27.
43. Jean-Luc Nancy, *The Inoperative Community,* ed. Peter Connor (Minneapolis: University of Minnesota Press, 1991), 99.

Bibliography

Caputo, John D. *Against Ethics.* Bloomington: Indiana University Press, 1993.
———. *Radical Hermeneutics: Repetition, Deconstruction, and the Hermeneutic Project.* Bloomington: Indiana University Press, 1987.

Deleuze, Gilles. *The Logic of Sense.* Translated by Mark Lester with Charles Stivale. Edited by Constantin V. Boundas. New York: Columbia University Press, 1990.

———. *Difference and Repetition.* Translated by Paul Patton. New York: Columbia University Press, 1994.

Deleuze, Gilles, and Felix Guattari. *Anti-Oedipus: Capitalism and Schizophrenia.* Translated by Robert Hurley, Mark Seem, and Helen R. Lane. New York: Viking, 1977.

———. *A Thousand Plateaus: Capitalism and Schizophrenia.* Translated by Brian Massumi. Minneapolis: University of Minnesota Press, 1987.

Derrida, Jacques. *Of Grammatology.* Translated by Gayatri Spivak. Baltimore: Johns Hopkins University Press, 1974.

———. *Margins of Philosophy.* Translated by Alan Bass. Chicago: University of Chicago Press, 1982.

———. *Positions.* Translated by Alan Bass. Chicago: University of Chicago Press, 1981.

———. *Writing and Difference.* Translated by Alan Bass. Chicago: University of Chicago Press, 1978.

Raschke, Carl A. *The Alchemy of the Word: Language and the End of Theology.* Missoula, Mont.: Scholars Press, 1979.

Scharlemann, Robert P. *Inscriptions and Reflections: Essays in Philosophical Theology.* Charlottesville: University Press of Virginia, 1989.

———. *The Reason of Following: Christology and the Ecstatic I.* Chicago: University of Chicago Press, 1991.

———. *Theology at the End of the Century: A Dialogue on the Postmodern with Thomas J. J. Altizer, Mark C. Taylor, Charles E. Winquist, and Robert P. Scharlemann.* Charlottesville: University Press of Virginia, 1990.

Taylor, Mark C. *Alterity.* Chicago: University of Chicago Press, 1987.

———. *Erring: A Postmodern A/theology.* Chicago: University of Chicago Press, 1984.

———. *Nots.* Chicago: University of Chicago Press, 1993.

———. *Tears.* Albany: State University of New York Press, 1990.

Winquist, Charles E. *Desiring Theology.* Chicago: University of Chicago Press, 1995.

———. *Epiphanies of Darkness: Deconstruction in Theology.* Philadelphia: Fortress, 1986.

8

New Age Spirituality

CARL A. RASCHKE

When Bill Clinton captured the presidency for "his generation" in the fall of 1992, he may have accomplished more than he bargained for. Clinton, like myself, was a baby boomer and a "valley boy" — from the Red River Valley of Oklahoma, Texas, and Arkansas, that is. Like other valley boys — such as President Dwight D. Eisenhower, House Speakers Sam Rayburn and Carl Albert, and Clinton's own 1990s political shadow, Ross Perot — the young Arkansas governor wanted to take power away from the coastal elites, renew American democracy at the grass roots, and make a "new covenant" between the federal government and the average American. The new covenant, as the au courant political icon of the "'60s generation" proclaimed during a speech in the fall of 1991 at Georgetown University, would create a "government that works at a price [the American people] can afford."

"The New Covenant means change," Clinton told his political biographer, David Osborne, who in turn labeled him a "new paradigm politician" — the kind of idealistic and socially responsible nonpolitician the liberal pundits had been prophesying since the Nixon years. In order to grab the election, Clinton made a much noticed, but barely analyzed, strategic political move. Breaking years of precedent, he chose another "Southerner" and generational confederate — the youthful U.S. senator Albert Gore Jr. from Tennessee — as his vice presidential running mate. Gore's name was already familiar to members of the '60s generation. His father, Al Gore Sr., like George McGovern, had been a leading congressional opponent of the Vietnam War.

Unbeknownst to the functionaries of the Eastern media, who tended to see all of America as a cameo of its own Kennedy-era mythology, the young Gore was embarking on a significantly different mission than traditional liberals with their fantasies of a revived Roosevelt coalition and the reindustrialization of the nation could have conceived. He was also championing a variety of causes and themes that would have struck the majority of "valley folks," who voted overwhelmingly for Bill, as outlandish, crazy, and even "California-ish." Just prior to the 1992 election, Gore had gained some notoriety in the press — and the ridicule of Republicans — with the publication of his "environmentally correct" book entitled *Earth in the Balance: Ecology and the Human Spirit.*

The book was about far more than recycling diapers and protecting porpoises from Japanese tuna fishermen. It was about the total "transformation" of both American culture and the "planet." It was the mature manifesto of the more politically committed and socially radical among the '60s generation. It was about what the '60s author Charles Reich in a best-selling book by the same title had called "the greening of America."[1]

In the 1980s "green" signified ecological responsibility. In the 1960s it had meant something much vaster, more inchoate, and spiritual. When Gore wrote that "there is indeed a spiritual crisis in modern civilization that seems to be based on an emptiness at its center and the absence of a large spiritual purpose," he was echoing Reich. The emptiness was already being filled up, said Gore enthusiastically, by "the popularity of New Age doctrines" as well as "cults of all shapes and descriptions."

For valley boys and girls, like Clinton, reared on Baptist sermons and Baptist hayrides while shaped by a surfeit of spiritual concerns from vacation Bible camp to prayer services before the Friday night high school football game, Clinton's "new covenant" smacked of little more than Rotary Club at the federal level. For the coastal elites of the same generation from Santa Monica, California, to Stamford, Connecticut, for whom there was indeed a spiritual crisis (a crisis first manifested when suburban kids of the Eisenhower era raised on the *Mickey Mouse Club* and the *Ed Sullivan Show* began taking LSD and "blowing their minds" in the streets of San Francisco), the "New Age" sounded a lot better. In fact, Gore was the other half of the '60s generation in the White House. Gore's covenant, in reality, was not so much between Washington and the American people as between all "peoples of the planet" and their "relationship to earth," as his book put it.

For Gore, *change* meant global change.

•

Change was the catchword of the 1992 election. It was also the mantra of New Age activists. It is doubtful that most of the American electorate, which seemed hypnotized by the mantra despite George Bush's protestations, could be considered conscious New Agers. The political seduction of the word appeared to reflect a kind of psychological reconditioning of the public toward the same vague and romantic nostrums that New Age rhetoric had been fostering for nearly a decade.

Global change and New Age thinking were out front with *Earth in the Balance* at the Tattered Cover Bookstore in Denver the day of the Clinton inaugural in January 1993. The Tattered Cover is one of the largest and most celebrated bookstores in North America. It is a true repository of the reading tastes of "literate America." It is several stories high and purveys every published paperback and hardcover volume from the collected works of Aristotle to the biographies of serial killers.

On the stairwell leading up to the second floor of the Tattered Cover are L-shaped bookshelves that one of the store clerks described as a special display of "the most popular and best-selling books." Although not all of these books were on the *New York Times* list of best-sellers, their presence on those shelves indicated that they were indeed popular; a hasty and ad hoc survey indicated that at least a third could be classified in some way as New Age. Intermingled with *Rare and Unusual House Plants* and *The Used Car Buying Guide* were such mind-popping titles as *The Masks of Power: Discovering Your Sacred Self; Earth Prayers from around the World; A Guide for Advanced Souls; Sensuous Spirituality: Out from Fundamentalism;* and Robert Bly's *Iron John,* the bible of the men's movement in which accountants from Kansas City high-rises gather around campfires in the Ozarks, don animal skins, beat tom-toms, and release their primal manhood through therapeutically prompted wolf howls.

In *Discovering Your Sacred Self,* Lynn Andrews explains gently how to "feel yourself merging with your power animal." The howl becomes cosmic. Spirit-possession by archetypal carnivores was apparently not as intriguing to the reading public as the Tattered Cover's hot new softcover entitled *Bashar: A Blueprint for Change, a Message from Our Future.* The subtitle could have been extracted from one of Clinton's political speeches, but the contents were revealed by a lower-left caption on the cover — "Material Channeled from an Extraterrestrial." Bashar's wisdom was profound and sounded remarkably like the text of most New Age self-help books that advise people on "natural" and "nonjudgmental" ways of dealing with everything from low self-esteem to obesity to the threat of nuclear extinction. "You experience the reality you are the vibration of," Bashar opined. If you changed your vibration, you changed your reality.

Another popular book about change was *We the Arcturians,* by Dr. Norma Milanovich. Dr. Milanovich, according to the book jacket, had received a channeled message in her Albuquerque home from aliens hailing from the constellation of Arcturus regarding "their purpose for being here." Their admonition to earthlings? The human race must "change its thinking" while "cleaning up the untruths and injustices that have prevailed all over the planet." "This book is about change," the little volume proudly begins.

According to *Up the Creek* — a weekly Denver newspaper — in March of 1992, Milanovich's intergalactic confidants had already been warmly welcomed at the Baca Ranch in the San Luis Valley of Southern Colorado, where devotees had built a pink pyramid in anticipation of their arrival. The Baca, owned by former UN undersecretary Maurice Strong and his New Age seer wife, Hanne, had become famous in the 1980s when spiritual luminaries and diverse diplomats began to visit the place.

The Baca, where actress and New Age promoter Shirley Maclaine had reportedly purchased property to build a "healing center," enjoyed the highest rate of "planetary vibration," according to aficionados, because of a much coveted underground aquifer of potable waters. Strong, who organized and presided over the 1992 "Earth Summit" in Rio de Janeiro where world leaders and UN bureaucrats met to bash George Bush, halt global warming, and confer about transferring a goodly portion of the earth's wealth to the LDCs (lesser developed countries), was later accused by the *New Republic* and the Colorado press of ripping off local residents and selling off the waters of the aquifer as part of a greedy scheme that might just disrupt the area's ecology as well. Strong's chroniclers and defenders pointed out that materialist motives were far outweighed by the spiritual importance of what was happening on that cold, arid, remote, and scrub-wooded patch of property a half-day's drive from Denver. While strolling on the land one day in the recent past, so the legend went, Strong had seen a bush burst into flame. If it was not Jehovah, it might have been the Arcturians.

Strong's astonishing "revelation," which was reported in the press about the time of the Rio Summit, was certainly evidence that the New Age was close to becoming a subject of common sensibility.

•

It is not clear, of course, when the New Age on this continent was supposed to have dawned. Or, if one adopts a so-called premillennialist perspective, the proper question would be just when precisely in the imminent future the New Age might be expected to erupt along the horizon, like a ceremoniously invoked sunrise following the Tartarean darkness of an arctic winter.

An equally compelling question might be: What exactly is meant by the term *New Age?* By the late 1980s, the term had achieved the kind of concomitant fascination and ambiguity with the public and the press that is usually reserved for high-fashion statements on Parisian runways. Then again, the New Age movement, as it came to be known, turned out to be its own kind of cultural fashion statement. News analysts and armchair sociologists have struggled for more than a half-decade now to define the New Age phenomenon, which even in the context of its own rhetoric has eluded definition. Defining the New Age movement is not much more straightforward than capturing on film the Loch Ness monster, but certain legible themes, or common threads, weave into the picture.

The New Age movement — a lush jungle of exotic spirituality, lifestyle preferences, metaphysical preoccupations, and voguish superstitions — is in many respects a codifying of what in the late 1960s and up through most of the 1970s was called "alternative" culture. When the radicalism and bohemianism of the 1960s decanted into the pop psychotherapies and religious cultism of the 1970s, the result came to be called the Human Potential movement. When the human potential gurus stirred into the mixture a fragrant broth of traditional occultism, old-fashioned American transcendentalism, parapsychology, and utopian one-worldism, it was termed New Age.

In truth, New Age was from the beginning, and in large part remains, a colorful and shape-shifting kaleidoscope of fads, fantasies, and follies. It has also engendered its own "celebrity list," big names who have garnered the lion's share of news visibility and popular curiosity, even while such people have tended to be exhibitionists and publicity seekers more than spiritual exemplars. The most well-known New Age luminaries include actress Shirley Maclaine; Judy (J. Z.) Knight, a blonde businesswoman from Roswell, New Mexico, turned New Age prophetess and "channeler"; erstwhile futurist-cum-"planetary citizen" Barbara Marx Hubbard of the Marx toy fortune; singer John Denver; and not-so-high profile but equally influential writers and social experimenters such as David Spangler, Stuart Brand, Fritjof Capra, Peter Cady, and Peter Russell (author of *The Global Brain*).

Because of certain subjects selected out for scrutiny, and frequently ridicule, by the media, New Age in the popular mind refers largely to seemingly disjunctive styles of "craziness" — the use of crystals, the "channeling" of spirit-entities, the use of holistic health remedies, and a fascination with UFOs and astrology. These burlesque manifestations, however, mask a strange and underlying commonality. The unifying strand is a consistent, philosophical rejection of the Western heritage of rationality, social morality, and political ideals of individual liberty and authority. The New Age movement has been a conscious and multifaceted effort to change that heritage into something "other." The "other," of course, remains undeciphered.

I myself have been riding the cyclone that formed into what are today's New Age sensibilities from the outset. Although I cannot claim to have been "present at the creation," I was a wanderer and an observer in the streets of San Francisco when the "summer of love" in 1967 inaugurated what is now the great myth of the '60s counterculture. When I arrived in Colorado in 1972 as a wet-behind-the-ears, Harvard-educated, first-year college professor, my first encounters in the classroom and on the outside were with cadres of unusual religious beliefs and practices — Hare Krishnas, "happy-healthy-and-holy" yoga devotees, white witches, urban Voodoo practitioners, Nichiren Shoshu Buddhists, clairvoyants, and palm-readers.

At the time, none of them claimed to be part of a movement, but they all shared a profound feeling of having fatefully segregated themselves from "mainline America" and, unlike their historical predecessors, of needing to evangelize the middle class and make it change its conventional ways. Some "New Age watchers" would date the arrival of the nation's own domestically manufactured version of the eschaton to 16 August 1987, when, as the Reagan era finally seemed to be waning, tens of thousands of aging '60s counterculturalists from Greenwich Village to Beverly Hills concocted over a weekend their own thirty-somethingish spiritual Woodstock that came to be known as the "harmonic convergence."

In the famous cartoon strip *Doonesbury* it came to be called the "moronic convergence." *Newsweek* magazine, with its wry caption "The End of the World... Again," profiled the event as a kind of inscrutable swarming of seventeen-year locusts, as a medieval type of episodic religious madness in which Aspen socialites saw visions and the fringe-and-leather set from Santa Fe abandoned their wee ones to babysitters to flock to ancient Indian ruins in the Desert Southwest for the express purpose of burying crystals in the earth, holding hands and humming, and peering over mesatops for the sight of alien spaceships from the Pleiades.

The Pied Piper or Peter the Hermit (depending on which historical analogy best fit this curious mobilization) was one José Arguelles, a scholar of art history and Mesoamerican studies from Colorado who had been pondering over obscure and archaic Mayan prophecies about the completion of certain cosmic cycles of time. Arguelles had also been influenced by the poetry and speculations of an American Indian writer named Tony Shearer, who had prophesied about the "return" of the ancient Mexicans' bearded white god Quetzlcoatl, a return that was to occur at about the same time as the completion of the Mayan cosmic cycles. Shearer had seemingly sought to elaborate a pan-southwestern myth of beauty and redemption, much as William Butler Yeats did with Irish folklore. In his book *The Mayan Factor,* Arguelles turned the Quetzlcoatl idea into a fantasy of social revolution, ecological radicalism, sci-fi, and rococo occultism worthy of L. Ron Hubbard.

The result was a feeding frenzy for the news-starved summer media folk, who pounced upon Arguelles's weird view of things and made the New Age outlook appear only a tad more eccentric than, say, snake handlers at a Newport garden party. Moreover, Arguelles played well to the media's most lurid presumptions. He talked about intergalactic beams of ethereal light descending upon this planet in order to inaugurate another centuries-long round of species evolution and to activate the conscious world-service of the 144,000 members of the New Age "elect"—the Quetzlcotillion, as it were. Supposedly, most of them were assembling around campfires in New Mexico's Chaco Canyon, where antediluvian astronauts had communed with paleo-Indians in an effort to plan for and hopefully prevent diverse global catastrophes.

The harmonic convergence of August 1987 allegedly coincided with the close of a "great year" of fifty-two suns in the Mayan calendar. In addition, it corresponded with a high-water point of publicity for the New Age movement, which had been gaining momentum since the previous autumn. In his book, Bashar insisted that the harmonic convergence of 1987 had been scheduled by the Extraterrestrial intelligences precisely forty years after the first flying saucers appeared over Mt. Rainier in the year 1947. The convergence represented the culmination of four decades of accelerating "global linkage" in the consciousness of the human race and was actually a foretaste of the more dramatic "harmonic initiation" to take place thirty years later in the year 2017, when human beings and extraterrestrials would be as close and familiar to each other as Texans and Oklahomans.

In certain respects I myself was inadvertently responsible for much of that publicity. When Robert Lindsey of the *New York Times* wrote a cover story on the "controversy" over New Age in October 1986, not too many Americans, reporters included, had ever heard the expression *New Age.* If Lindsey had not found an "expert" with academic credentials (that is, myself) through the referral of a religious counselor living in Idaho, who knew of my interests, the story might not have come to press.

Because of the *Times* article, I was quoted extensively in all the national media on the question, What is the New Age? Following that, a *Wall Street Journal* reporter looking for a new angle on a well-worn subject called me in June 1987; if she had not done so, she would not have learned about the harmonic convergence, and the story would have remained a minor issue. At the time it had been advertised only in the metaphysical underground and was not scripted as an overnight, mass media brouhaha.

The New Age, however, was not all that new. The phrase had originated earlier in the century within the writings of an eclectic and obscure religious movement known as "theosophy." Alice Bailey, founder of the Arcane School of Christianity, a wing of the theosophical movement (the latter having exerted a significant influence over avant-garde American intellectuals immediately preceding and following World War II), used the phrase promiscuously in her books, which sold routinely for decades in glossed, navy-blue covers from the back shelves of what used to be called "metaphysical bookstores."

For Bailey, the New Age was the "esoteric" equivalent of what traditional Christianity referred to as the kingdom of God. On the whole, Bailey's religious theories were an intricately carved fretwork of ancient Hindu cosmology, Buddhist doctrines, mystical internationalism, socialist politics, and what she herself termed "white magic." There was very little that was conventionally Christian in her "arcane Christianity," except she did believe along with other theosophists that Jesus had been a "master of wisdom" who arrived on this planet to teach the benighted human race about its godlike powers and divine destiny.

The distinctive theosophical principle, which became the very marrow of New Age thinking, was that the "return" of Christ had little to do with the reappearance of the figure from Galilee in the clouds over the earth. Rather, at some dramatic point in the evolution of the species — the "New Age," so to speak — the race would achieve a sort of quantum leap of consciousness in which it would finally become knowledgeable of its superhuman capabilities. Bailey dubbed this exalted self-awareness the "Christ consciousness." In fact, much of the vast social experimentation throughout the 1960s and 1970s with drug-induced "mind expansion," Eastern styles of religious meditation, and so-called humanistic psychology — all of it designed not so much to cure the sickness of the soul as to expand the "infinite potential" of thought and creativity — can be considered an effort to work through what Bailey seemed to be describing. When certain Bailey-inspired promoters sought to repackage motley fashions and themes from the '60s era as New Age rather than as alternative or countercultural, the fit was slightly less than remarkable.

The *Times*, however, did not focus on the historical background to, or the cultural dialectics of, what the press would soon baptize "New Age rage." Like any newspaper it trained its lenses on some highly current shootouts surrounding New Age religion.

•

By and large there were three sequential sparks that ignited the inferno of controversy concerning the New Age between the fall of 1986 and the spring of 1987. The first was a scathing condemnation of the neo-Baileyites by a Christian evangelical writer named Constance Cumbey. The second was the fad of "channeling" (in olden days it was called holding a "seance"; among anthropologists studying archaic rites it could be considered "spirit possession"), which was rapidly gaining public attention because of its popularity with Hollywood celebrities and the weird antics of the channelers. The third was the airing of an ABC television miniseries based on an autobiographical book by actress Shirley Maclaine entitled *Out on a Limb.* The show amounted to nothing more than a running, almost propagandistic, endorsement of New Age concepts and practices. Conservative Christians were outraged that what they considered blatantly occult teachings could be retailed on prime-time, network TV.

As thunder rolled from the right, curiosity mounted in the heartland. Cumbey's book, *The Hidden Dangers of the Rainbow,* had argued that the New Age rhetoric of a total, spiritual "transformation" of the planet masked the aims of the Antichrist. Cumbey's book was not your garden-variety fundamentalist attack with a broad, theological overview and stock warnings about the undeciphered plans of Satan. While naming names within the "movement," it endeavored to link the New Age ideology to such visible demonisms of the twentieth century as the Nazi Third Reich.

The connections Cumbey drew were more than metaphorical, but the evidence as presented to the public by Cumbey, a practicing lawyer, came across as circumstantial. The Cumbeyean reading of contemporary religious culture was dark and boding, yet in the newspapers, and so far as the popular consensus went, the New Agers appeared as one gigantic clown act, as a colorful mime troupe made up of religious eccentrics, aging hippies, and hucksters and merchandisers. The whole kit and caboodle would soon be replaced, the betting went, by another "wave" of organized craziness to pique the interest of talk show hosts and tweak the jowls of middle-aged Baptist pastors.

Neither the religious right nor the jaundiced, liberal media could fathom that the New Age promoters were doing exactly what they said they were doing in countless seminars, self-published and spiral-bound workbooks, and piles of xeroxed, pastel-paper flyers that gathered and scattered like autumn leaves in the entrance halls of urban community centers and along the free distribution racks of health food stores.

What were they doing? They claimed not to be taking over the world by force so much as "transforming" the culture and planet by a combination of stealth and steadfastness. The term *transformation* has always had the same ring and exhaustless connotations for New Agers as *salvation* does for biblical Christians. Transformation is at once an ethic and a metaphysic, an empirical description and a mythic symbol, a quality of the universe and a private state of mind.

The goal of personal life is to go through a series of transformations from middle-class homemaker to psychic celebrity, just as the path of human evolution is from salamander to superman. The earth itself must be transformed too, according to the New Age imperative. Although official chroniclers of the 1980s seem to have missed the point entirely, the way for the global environmental chic and "new world order" sensibility of the 1990s was paved by the kind of New Age harangue during the prior decade that stressed responsibility to "person/planet," as '60s guru Theodore Roszak (who coined the word *counterculture*) put it.

The New Age perspective, which can be found in most of Bailey's writings, was always as much social and political as it was purely religious. According to Bailey, the source of evil was fanatical nationalism, even U.S. nationalism. Civilization needed a new order of "world servers," who would give themselves to the betterment of humankind with the same zeal and transcendent gaze as the first-century followers of Jesus. The ultimate outcome would be a new planetary culture in which ethnic distinctions were accentuated, while national differences were dissolved, in effect, "the rainbow." At the same time, the entirety of the race would be loving and "Christ-conscious" of the divinity inherent in each person.

The transformation of the planet may be a long way off, given the wars, famines, and galloping hoofs of apocalyptic horsemen that have been resounding lately from Asia to Africa. Yet since the early 1980s, at least, a discernible transformation has been underway in the United States that can be traced directly to the New Age influence. Although broad historical causes and connections are quite difficult to establish, the undergrowth of New Age culture beneath the straight-arrow yuppie society of the Reagan years may have had something to do with the sudden reversal of conservative trends in America around 1990 and the defeat of the Republican Party at the polls. When Americans in 1992 told pollsters they wanted "change" without specifying what kind of change they meant, they were perhaps unconsciously giving vent to feelings that had been shaped by New Age–style messages in the pop cultural environment, in particular, the notion that it was far more natural to throw away the familiar and venerated values of the past than the social guardians of the Cold War period had imagined.

The political shift in November 1992, therefore, was far more profound than a frustrated recoil against a stale economy or a willingness to let the "Big Chill kids" finally take the reigns of the federal government. The almost legendary '60s generation had always been excessively different, not just in its sexual behavior and attitudes toward narcotics but in its basic worldview as well. When anti-Vietnam protesters and other political radicals from 1965 onward began to refer to their own country as AmeriKKKa, the beginning of the end for the type of self-assertive American nationalism whose last hurrah was the 1991 Gulf War could be glimpsed.

The same could be said for all the talk about the "death of God" and the turn to a melange of Asian, neopagan, and spiritist cults during a similar period. The old-fashioned idea of a Christian democratic society derived from a uniquely European intellectual tradition, which had inspired American leaders from the Civil War onward, had crashed and burned long before the "multiculturalist" and "politically correct" rebels began bashing white males and "the canon." If the 1960s in its own time had been tabbed by critic Paul Goodman the "New Reformation," the 1980s was the era of the Counter-Reformation, with Reagan playing the part of Charles V and the Christian right sitting in for the Society of Jesus. Just as the Counter-Reformation quickly smashed on the shoals of modernity, so the vaunted "Reagan revolution" fractured against the granite bedrock of a new, made-in-the-'60s America.[2]

In the end it was Gore and his messianic global environmentalism more than Dan Quayle's evangelical Protestant piety that reflected what was au courant in America at the close of the millennium. Even if the New Age was less a utopian cloudland than a metaphor for the slick, generational politics that carried Clinton to the White House in the autumn of 1992, that year was indeed a turning point.

Hanne Strong had predicted to friends several years before that 1992 would mark the fabled aeon's onset. It would be high times for the augurs and luminaries who, back even before the birth of many of their now-adult children, had been foretelling in the wake of the cultural revolution of the 1960s the wholesale "greening" of America.

To be "green" in those days did not signify ecological vigilance; it denoted what Reich saw as a tidal wave of new consciousness. "Consciousness Three," in fact, was his terminology for the stage that would replace the old Puritanically repressive, work-absorbed, and money-driven consciousness of the industrial age. After a brief, neoconservative backlash among '60s intellectuals in the mid-1970s, these particular green dreams began to disturb the fitful sleep of the exhausted Reichians once more. They were the foxfire of the New Age movement.

The revival got underway almost at the instant that Ronald Reagan, class hero of America's beleaguered small-town and suburban working constituencies, took the oath of the presidency. In 1980 a former technical writer named Marilyn Ferguson, who had a Shirley Temple stage presence and an unusual gift of prose oratory, authored a book entitled *The Aquarian Conspiracy.* The book was an immediate commercial success, and for a time Ferguson, who as a rule did not make television appearances, was the Joanie Appleseed of New Age sensitivities. The term *Aquarian,* however, rang of the 1960s, not the 1980s. Entertainers in the 1960s from the Beatles to the cast of the rock musical *Hair* had celebrated the coming of the "Age of Aquarius," which in the old Baileyite literature had been synonymous with the New Age. For reasons that remain unclear, the latter nomenclature was now preferred.

The Aquarian Conspiracy, Ferguson proclaimed, was both ubiquitous and universal. Its goal was nothing less than a total "transformation" of the existing social and moral order, the definitive expression of a '60s avant-garde bent on manifesting some hitherto latent character of consciousness that would mean a qualitative change in the human species itself. For about ten years before and after *The Aquarian Conspiracy* came out, Ferguson had written a bimonthly newsletter called *Brain/Mind Bulletin.* At one level, the newsletter was nothing more than a chatty and, at times, gossipy monitor of trends, discoveries, and key players in the field of neuropsychology. The subject matter was highly appealing to the post-'60s ex-druggies who, despite the overwhelming evidence that LSD could make people kill themselves by attempting to fly out the windows of tall buildings, still yearned for a safe and truly cosmic chemical elixir that might have the authority of science behind it.

By the mid-1980s the pretense of *Brain/Mind Bulletin* to mere science reporting had broken down, and Ferguson was writing about everything from a man who had visions of Jesus after ingesting the new "designer drug" Ecstasy to plumping for the strange cause of Lt. Col. Jim Channon of the U.S. Army's "First Earth Battalion." Channon, a former Green Beret from Vietnam and graduate of the War College, had succeeded in convincing some of the military's top brass that the army of the future could be created out of a cadre of New Age trainees with cultivated psychic abilities. A soldier who could bend a spoon with his mind was just as valuable, Channon believed, as a grunt with a rocket launcher. Channon also advocated some vague sort of planetary police role for his intensely "conscious" and "transformative" warriors, hence, "First Earth." The whole enterprise struck most observers, including army officials, as looney, but Ferguson was persuaded that the proposal had merit and proceeded to make plugs on the lecture circuit.

At one point in his brief blip of notoriety Channon shocked some of his New Age admirers when he was quoted in a Denver newspaper as saying Americans would be "proud" if the military took over the nation. Presumably, that would have been an easy way to usher in the New Age. Neither Channon nor Ferguson was typical of the second New Age wave that would hit a few years later. *The Aquarian Conspiracy* was a serious book aimed at fomenting social revolution. The high tide of New Age fashion that began tumbling across the lifestyle pages of the news media after 1986 was both dilettantish and frivolous.

In that respect the New Age movement of the late 1980s captured the fancy of the news media in a way that Ferguson's curious crusade for a new psycho-politics did not. Because it received extensive publicity, it spread rapidly. By the early 1990s it had gone mainstream. The mainstreaming of the New Age movement between 1986 and 1992 can neither be documented nor quantified in any obvious way. News writers to this day ask the stock question: What percentage of the American population is New Age? The question is akin to asking what precise slice of the American demographic pie is romantically inclined.

First, defining what specifically is meant by *New Age* is almost impossible. Back in the 1980s the New Age promoters deliberately fuzzed the word sufficiently to encompass everything in popular culture from assertiveness training to acupuncture, from Comanche ritual drumming to co-dependency therapy. If a truck driver from Lincoln, Nebraska, develops a passion for cooking with tofu, does that make him New Age?

Second, it is necessary to distinguish between New Age religion and the innumerable varieties of New Age culture. Although in current usage *New Age* has come to be associated with exotic spiritual attitudes and practices, the preponderance of literature from the "movement" deals with social, psychological, and political topics, generally with a slant that not too many years ago was referenced as "neoliberal."[3]

In brief, the mainstreaming of New Age culture can be mapped alongside the coming to power and prominence of the baby boomers during the age of Reagan, whose most loyal political supporters came chiefly, according to different political analyses during the 1980s, from the generations on either side of the great, postwar demographic bulge. New Age culture did not spring full-armored from the corpse of Cold War Republicanism. The New Agers were the great silent, highly educated minority that attained middle age about the time the Berlin Wall fell. The fall of the wall and the demise a few years later of the Cold Warriors who knocked it down can be explained ironically in view of the same historical circumstances. Both events constituted an instinctive rejection by younger masses of the populace of the political and social preoccupations that had prevailed since the 1940s.

•

If the postwar epoch was a second "age of ideology" with the two great "isms" of the twentieth century — socialism and capitalism — embraced in mortal conflict, then the dramatic worldwide events that took place between 1989 and 1992 signaled the dismantling of an entire half-century-old scaffolding. The Western democracies with their market economies had technically "won" the encounter; yet, as happens with the outcomes of most major wars, the victors must contend with a new, third force that has been waiting in the wings the entire time.

In 1945 the third force was Soviet communism; in 1990 it was a slightly mysterious but very real and far-reaching cultural movement that had been gathering energy for about a quarter-century. The phrase *New Age movement* was nothing more than an advertising byword. In many respects it represented an effort to recover for the graying '60s generation the social myth of heroic activism. In Vietnam days all gestures of defiance toward the "system" — from smoking marijuana to burning draft cards, from casual sex to lesbianism, from smuggling guns to urban guerrillas to demonstrations and occupations of university administration buildings — had been enrolled in the rhetoric of the "New Left" activists and were seen as part of something called "the movement."

The New Age movement had been defined with all the symbolic trappings of its political predecessor but was, in fact, more concerned with cultural revolution, the quiet and methodical and relentless redrawing of all values, visions, and verities in American society.[4] The author of *The Aquarian Conspiracy* had said, quite explicitly, that cultural revolution was the aim of the movement. Ferguson was given to hyperbole and overstatement, but the comprehensive character of her assessment was fairly accurate. To average observers, the changes that were going on seemed quirky, even silly. To them, the New Age movement had about as much significance as a bunch of neighborhood vandals surreptitiously assembling during the night and painting mustaches on the poster faces of all the local aspirants to political office.

What they missed was that the same "vandals" who had drawn the mustaches were concomitantly taking over the management of the corner grocery store, joining the police squad, buying up the banks, and moving into the main offices at city hall. Altogether, the New Age movement, which was not nearly as self-reflective and coherent as its publicity flacks had pretended, was succeeding because the educated and intellectually motivated core of the '60s generation, whose implicit ideology had been forged in the riot-torn urban centers, strike-bound campuses, and drug-sex-and-music-saturated apartment living rooms of that earlier period, had finally grown up and matured. It was almost that simple.

This simple truth was lost on most political analysts in the fall of 1992 with President Bush's defeat and the accession of the Clinton administration. It was most likely grasped with rather sardonic and painful hindsight by the man who had tried to strong-arm the agencies of historical change a few years too early. His name was Gary Hart.[5]

Most people remember that Hart had been the spear carrier for the "new Democratic Party" in 1984 and 1988, long before anybody had ever heard about the young governor from Arkansas. Most people also recall the sensational sex scandal in the spring of 1988, just as Hart was poised for what appeared to be an extremely promising run for the White House; it sent the campaign down in flames. Looking backward now, and considering Bush's early problems at the polls in that year with even such a political whiffet as Michael Dukakis, one might intelligently conclude that if Hart had been the Democratic candidate in the 1988 election, what happened in 1992 might have occurred four years earlier, except that the script would not have included the collapse of communism. Hart knew Mikhail Gorbachev well and would have worked for the "convergence" of the latter's "humanistic socialism" with Hart's vision of an "Atari democracy," whereby the technological might of the United States would be marshaled to help rebuild the crumbling economic infrastructure of what Reagan had branded the "evil empire."

What most people forget, however, is that Hart had been invested with a certain aura of global leadership because his political fortunes had been case-hardened in the foundry of the New Left political radicalism of the 1960s. Hart became a politically known quantity in 1972 when he served as George McGovern's campaign manager. McGovern's calamitous defeat by Nixon set the Democratic Party back for twenty years, but it pried open a space for what would later be dubbed "New Age" concepts to take hold in the policy arena.

Hart's campaign theme of "new ideas" in 1984 and "a new democracy" in 1988 more than coincidentally had the sound of New Age ideas or New Age democracy. Hart's now forgotten positions and pronouncements as a senator from Colorado throughout the 1970s and as a national political figure throughout the Reagan presidency mirrored in many ways the notions of Mark Satin, a New Leftie who published a somewhat successful national newsletter during the 1980s. In the 1970s, Satin had published a book entitled *New Age Politics.* The book was an odd and somewhat sophomoric interweaving of countercultural strategies, sentiments, and shibboleths left over from the 1960s. It combined environmentalism with a kind of soft-core Marxism, transnationalism with "grassroots" communitarianism, feminism with ethnic romanticism, and political activism with religious eclecticism. In other words, it was an early, although unfocused and jumbled, blueprint for the creation of a New Age culture.

The genius of New Age theoreticians during the 1980s was to meld into one glistening, global statement what had been antithetical ideologies during the 1960s. In *The Making of a Counterculture,* Roszak had expounded on the two separate subcultures of the counterculture itself — New Left radicals, with their fascination with community organization and guerrilla theater, and turned-on, "tuned-in" disciples of Timothy Leary and the Maharishi Mahesh Yogi, who preferred sacred mushrooms to Molotov cocktails and the calm and passive exploration of "inner space" to the Marxist concern with seizing the apparatus of the state. Roszak had predicted the eventual triumph of the mystics over the militants, and history bore him out.

The Nixon years — and even the Carter interregnum, which was eventually blown away by the rising winds of political conservatism — were not at all auspicious for social revolutionaries. Fear of an increasingly nasty Soviet imperial thrust around the globe made Marxisms of all kinds seem tinny and bogus. The capitulation of leftist politics was epitomized in the bizarre story of Rennie Davis, who, after gaining national notoriety for his defiant championing of "the movement" in Judge Julius Hoffman's courtroom following the arrest and trial of the so-called Chicago Seven for its role in the violent clashes with police at the 1968 Democratic Convention, threw himself as a humble devotee at the feet of the Guru Maharaj Ji. The guru was a very obese, moon-faced, and beardless fourteen-year-old boy from India, who, despite his obsession with young women and Baskin-Robbins ice cream, was proclaimed "perfect master of the universe" by his tens of thousands of youthful, American followers. From time to time the guru hinted on his own accord that he might actually be God.

Hart, of course, was never taken in by such foolery, but his political rise and fall in the state that the *New York Times Magazine* designated in 1988 as the promised land for all New Agers could not be divorced from the excesses and eccentricities of the "religious left." As late as 1987, one year before his now famous date with destiny, Hart was whispered among local political busybodies to be spending most of his time doing "shamanistic dances" with a secret group of "New Age Indians" and their hangers-on.

Best-selling author Gail Sheehy, in her scalding exposé of Hart's alleged antics for a national women's magazine right after the Donna Rice affair, alluded to these liaisons. In the fall of 1987 I was told by a prominent Denver New Age professional, who ran a clothing boutique, that many in "the movement" were eagerly awaiting Hart's becoming president. At that moment, she surmised, all the prophecies might be fulfilled, and the arsenal of Star Wars weaponry might be replaced with Atlantean caverns of healing crystals.

Hart's public politics and verifiable biographical facts about him do not support such an inference; yet political changeovers are shaped less by the private passions and deportment of the nation's leaders, who for obvious reasons tend to be a quite regular lot, than by the idealized expectations of their myriad backers and fellow travelers. The way in which the mountainous and landlocked state of Colorado — the U.S. "little Tibet" — became one gigantic pea patch for New Age enthusiasms in the 1980s, just as the teeming and rootless metroplexes of California midwived the culture of the 1960s, is a story in itself and cannot be fully told here.

By 1992 the politics of Colorado had become less "crazy" and had metamorphosized into a finishing school for various nationally recognized "new Democrats," from Denver congresswoman Pat Schroeder to U.S. Senator Tim Wirth to the state's governor, Roy Romer. At the same time, one of the biggest and fastest growing religious congregations in Denver, the Mile High Church of Religious Science, was proudly wearing the label of "New Age." Despite protestations from conservative parents, New Age meditation sessions using "guided imagery" were common in the public schools.

The New Age was, indeed, drifting into the mainstream, but its long-term effects remained to be measured. The ferocious clashes and controversies of the late 1980s had been symptomatic of the grinding together of two "cultural tectonic plates" — the dominant, Christian/European culture on which the nation was founded and the upsurging multicultural, poly-religious globalism that undergirded New Age ideology. An earthquake was assuredly not far in the offing. The demurrals of New Age advocates in response to their critics notwithstanding, the civilization envisioned by the green dreamers since Bailey pronounced her own occult version of the New World Order was utterly different from anything conceived in the past.

It was decidedly a civilization without clear precincts or boundaries. There were no simple divisions between goodness and badness, between masculine and feminine, between coherence and chaos, between politics and religion, between East and West, between conscious and unconscious, between groups and individuals, or between culture and madness. Phrases such as "one world" and "planetary responsibility," implying a universal ethic, fused without contradiction with such notions as "godself" and "human potential," implying an extreme individualism and narcissism. In fact, both the mandates of radical individuality and a supernational political loyalty were equally affirmed in the New Age catechism. The civilization that seemed to be emerging remained in rough form. The New Age movement shattered the myth of an integral American culture at the same time it set about proselytizing for a single "global community." Whether history will judge it favorably awaits the experience of the next two or three generations.

In the early 1990s the great transition through which the American people were moving appeared to mark what Michael Murphy, founder of California's Esalen Institute, a kind of test laboratory for the experiments of the counterculture as late as the mid-1970s, called "the end of ordinary history." How extra-ordinary this "new age" will in reality turn out to be remains a matter of speculation.

The quest for a "New Age America" was given birth amid the political violence and romantic utopianism experienced by the baby boomers as they crossed the threshold of adulthood in the tempestuous late 1960s and early 1970s. Although the 1960s are long gone, the cultural imprints and collective psychological stains of that era persist, despite all efforts to make them go away.[6] The New Age movement, in one sense, therefore, is a large-scale form of generational psychodrama that seems unintelligible to those both younger and older. It is a dramatic spectacle of the social unconscious, a colossal return of the repressed. It is a massive working out of issues, as the therapists would say, of issues that never were worked out and perhaps can never be worked out.

Yet it is America's burden for the foreseeable future.

Notes

1. On Clinton's relationship to the New Age, see Jolie Solomon, "A Touching Presidency: Bill Clinton Is a Boss for the New Age," *Newsweek*, 22 February 1993, 44.

2. For an interesting discussion of the shift, see "Whose Family? Whose Values? Who Makes the Choices?" *Newsweek,* 6 June 1992, 19–22.

3. For some major works on the New Age and '60s spirituality, see Robert Ellwood, *The Sixties Spiritual Awakening: American Religion Moving from Modern to Postmodern* (New Brunswick, N.J.: Rutgers University Press, 1994); Michael York, *The Emerging Network: A Sociology of the New Age and Neo-pagan Movements* (Lanham, Md.: Rowman and Littlefield, 1995); Gary Zukav, *The Seat of the Soul* (New York: Simon and Schuster, 1989); and, James R. Lewis and J. Gordon Melton, eds., *Perspectives on the New Age* (Albany: State University of New York Press, 1992).

4. For studies on the impact of the '60s, see David Farber, ed., *The Sixties: From Memory to History* (Chapel Hill: University of North Carolina Press, 1994); Myron Magnet, *The Dream and the Nightmare: The Sixties' Legacy to the Underclass* (New York: Morrow, 1993); Edward Morgan, *The 60s Experience: Hard Lessons about Modern America* (Philadelphia: Temple University Press, 1991); Richard Goodwin, *Remembering America: A Voice from the Sixties* (Boston: Little, Brown and Co., 1988).

5. Gary Hart's major writings are: *A New Democracy* (New York: Quill, 1983); and *The Strategies of Zeus* (New York: Morrow, 1987). For books about Hart's political campaign, see William Cohen, *The Double Man* (New York: Morrow, 1985); and Susan Berry Casey, *Hart and Soul: Gary Hart's New Hampshire Odyssey* (Concord, N.H.: NHI, 1986).

6. For a documentary retrospective on the birth of New Age thinking in the "new politics" of the 1960s, see Mitchell Goodman, *The Movement toward a New America* (Philadelphia: Pilgrim, 1970).

Bibliography

Albanese, Catherine. *Nature Religion in America: From the Algonkian Indians to the New Age.* Chicago: University of Chicago Press, 1990.

Bednarowski, Mary Farell. *New Religions and the Theological Imagination in America.* Bloomington: Indiana University Press, 1989.

Ellwood, Robert. *The Sixties Spiritual Awakening: American Religion Moving from Modern to Postmodern.* New Brunswick, N.J.: Rutgers University Press, 1994.

Ferguson, Marilyn. *The Aquarian Conspiracy: Personal and Social Transformation in the 1980s.* Los Angeles: Tarcher, 1990.

Lewis, James R., and J. Gordon Melton, eds. *Perspectives on the New Age.* Albany: State University of New York Press, 1992.

Melton, J. Gordon, with Jerome Clark and Aidan A. Kelly. *New Age Encyclopedia.* Detroit: Gale Research, 1990.

Miller, Timothy, ed. *America's Alternative Religions.* Albany: State University of New York Press, 1995.

York, Michael. *The Emerging Network: A Sociology of the New Age and Neo-pagan Movements.* Lanham, Md.: Rowman and Littlefield, 1995.

Zukav, Gary. *The Seat of the Soul.* New York: Simon and Schuster, 1989.

Part Two

THEMES AND PRACTICES

E. Self

9

Holistic Health Practices

ROBERT C. FULLER

ONE OF THE CENTURY'S foremost theologians, Paul Tillich, was an early philosophical voice in the explication of what this volume identifies as secular forms of spirituality. Tillich urged us to view religion not as a separate component of human existence but rather as the dimension of depth in all human endeavors. His classic definition of religion as "that which concerns us ultimately" implied that what makes a statement religious is not that it relates to a particular being called God but that it asks ultimate questions about the meaning of existence. "Religion," he wrote, "is not a special function of our spiritual life, but it is the dimension of depth in all of its functions."[1]

Tillich's definition of religion as "ultimate concern" sensitizes us to the fact that authentic spirituality is not confined to the life of theological institutions. It is instead the response to what, at the level of its deepest mystery, is the creative reality and ultimate significance of our lives. Spirituality is thus a mode of human thought and feeling that can be found in any human experience that prompts encounter with the ultimate ground of existence. It was with this in mind that Tillich suggested that "religion is the substance of culture, culture is the form of religion."[2] Which is to say that the human quest for the "ultimate" can be found in almost every cultural enterprise. It is precisely this intuition of the ultimate that gives significance or substance to our various human enterprises.

Secularization refers to the historical process whereby institutional religion has become increasingly separated from such cultural realms as law, science, psychology, and medicine. Tillich, however, eloquently alerted us to the fact that although the process of secularization may have separated certain arenas of cultural life from the institutional church, this does not mean that modern culture is devoid of genuine spirituality. As Tillich put it:

> Our period has decided for a secular world. That was a great and much-needed decision. . . . It gave consecration and holiness to our daily life and work. Yet it excluded those deep things for which religion stands: the feeling for the inexhaustible mystery of life, the grip of an ultimate meaning of existence, and the invincible power of an unconditional devotion. These things cannot be excluded.[3]

Indeed, they have not. Modern individuals engage in secular forms of spirituality through a great range of cultural activities. Insofar as these cultural activities involve a dimension of ultimacy within human experience, they are authentic expressions of the spiritual quest. Insofar as they enable persons to transform themselves in ways that enhance their participation in this source of ultimacy, they deserve to be understood as important vehicles of modern spiritual life.[4]

Medicine and the Spiritual Quest

The value of Tillich's definition of religion as the dimension of depth found in any cultural activity is that it alerts us to the enduring element of spirituality even in what are ostensibly secular practices, including medicine. Indeed, at first glance it would appear that in no other arena has Western religion capitulated more to the forces of secularization than in medicine. Prior to the Enlightenment, the church supplied culturally compelling explanations of nonmaterial or spiritual causes of disease (for example, sin or spirit possession) as well as corresponding schemata for therapeutic intervention (for example, confession or exorcism). Medical science as we know it today emerged by repudiating this entire conceptual scheme. Since the Enlightenment, medical orthodoxy has been defined by commitment to the causal role of organic or material factors in the etiology of disease. The impressive advances made by medical science have gradually relegated religious explanations to the far fringes of intellectual and cultural respectability. Western religious institutions have largely yielded to modern culture's separation of spiritual and medical perspectives on the human condition. Religious orthodoxy, like medical orthodoxy, has been content with a clear-cut division of labor whereby the cure of souls and bodies is entrusted to their respective professions. As a consequence, any attempt to reconnect religion with medicine would at first glance appear to be little more than a symptom of culture lag — the persistence of antiquated beliefs that are destined to become obsolete for all but the most culturally backward members of society.

The fact that numerous forms of what is often called "alternative medicine" continue to attract popular followings is thus of particular interest to scholars of religion. Popular fascination with various forms of holistic healing methods would seem to indicate that a sizable number of Americans subscribe to beliefs that belong neither to science nor to the more academic theologies of our day. By contradicting what might be called the "monistic materialism" underlying medical science, practitioners of unorthodox medicine become defenders of a point of view that medical doctors and denominational theologians alike consider irrational or superstitious. Strictly speaking, though, any medical system is logically valid insofar as its methods of treatment are logically entailed by its fundamental premises or assumptions about the nature of disease. We might, for example, recognize at least four different types of explanations that could "logically" be used to describe the cause of disease and, therefore, of healing: physiological, environmental, attitudinal/psychological, and spiritual or supernatural (that is, caused by the activity of entities or forces that are considered to be extrasomatic and extrapsychological). Those propounding spiritual-cause explanations of healing are thus not necessarily less logical than those engaged in medical science. They are, however, subscribing to a metaphysical claim concerning the existence of causal forces not recognized by contemporary scientific theory. It is also clear that, whether they conceptualize this putatively higher spiritual agency in categories of transcendence or of immanence, they are providing their clientele with both experiential and pragmatic grounds for adopting a religiously charged interpretation of reality.

The point here is that various forms of holistic healing do not draw their constituencies simply from the ranks of either those who are educationally disenfranchised from scientific knowledge or the desperately ill who can no longer expect hope from the methods of conventional medicine. Indeed, a study of alternative medical systems reported in the *New England Journal of Medicine* found that the demographic profile of those who most often used these unconventional therapies was that of "nonblack persons from 25 to 49 years of age who had relatively more education and higher incomes."[5] Moreover, persons who use alternative healing systems are more likely to do so for chronic, as opposed to life-threatening, conditions. Finally, most have sought treatment for the same condition from a medical doctor. It would seem, then, that last-minute panic cannot account for the persistence and popularity of alternative healing systems.

A closer examination of the accounts of alternative healing practices indicates that a significant, perhaps even the most significant, reason for their sustained presence in American culture is their ability to articulate a spiritually significant way of viewing the world. Indeed, from a cross-cultural perspective it is clear that one of the most important functions of healing practices has historically been that of facilitating an existential encounter with a sacred reality. In archaic societies, healing rituals involve participants in the reenactment of cosmological dramas: the shaman is not only a healer but also a mystagogue and mediator between the divine and human realms. In the case of Christianity, healing not only was thought to be a sign of Jesus' divine nature but was thereafter institutionalized as a function of Christian proclamation and ministry.[6] With the gradual divorce of physical healing from the church's routine activities, this means of introducing individuals to a higher spiritual reality necessarily shifted to alternative forms of cultural activity.

Of course, not every system of healing that falls outside the American Medical Association's sanctioned activities propounds a spiritual mode of healing. Nutritional and exercise therapies, for example, have no overtly metaphysical dimension and instead seek to strengthen and regulate basic metabolic processes through diet and sundry fitness regimens. Many massage and breathing systems likewise make no claims concerning the presence and activity of extrasomatic energies when explaining their programs for producing deep muscle relaxation and an overall sense of well-being.[7] The fact remains that most alternative healing systems propound alternative worldviews. They are holistic in the sense that they view the world not as the aggregate of separate material parts but rather as the living expression of an underlying spiritual energy (God). The body, because it belongs to the more expansive cosmos, is said to have inner access to the creative powers by which life itself is possible. Alternative healing techniques are predicated upon the belief that under certain conditions extramundane forces enter into, and exert sanative influences upon, the human realm. They are, therefore, substantively spiritual. They seek to induce consciousness of a sudden, felt intrusion of a "More" that is experienced as other than the material world and thereafter replaces all other forms of reality as normative or ultimately meaningful.[8]

The Nineteenth-Century Background

When in 1836 Ralph Waldo Emerson proclaimed that "nature is the symbol of spirit," he became the principal spokesperson for an enduring strand of secular or unchurched American spirituality. For Emerson, nature is itself "the organ through which the universal spirit speaks to the individual, and strives to lead back the individual to it."[9] Emerson and his fellow transcendentalists made institutionalized religion irrelevant to the individual's quest for an intimate relationship with the universe. Emerson could speak of such things as "instreaming divine spirit" and "an influx of Divine Mind into our mind" without using the biblical language of supernatural intervention. Instead he asked us to look into the ineffable depths of our own individual spirit or psyche to find an inner point of contact with the "currents of Universal Being." His suggestion that our own biological and psychological natures possess an inner correspondence to Universal Being hit such a responsive chord in popular American thought that historian Sydney Ahlstrom refers to him as the "theologian of something we may almost term 'the American religion.'"[10] Among other places, this "American religion" has endured in the form of healing systems that explore the point of inner correspondence between the divine and human realms.

Emerson is one of the most lauded and esteemed intellectuals in American history. We must be prepared for the fact that a good many of the practitioners of alternative medical traditions do not enjoy Emerson's highbrow cultural and educational background. They are, rather, carriers of middlebrow culture. Their attuning to this perduring style of secular American spirituality is for this reason all the more instructive. Thus, for example, during the 1840s and 1850s a number of individuals traveled New England giving lecture-demonstrations of what was variously called mesmerism or the science of animal magnetism. In the act of popularizing this European-born medical theory, the American mesmerists gradually modified their beliefs and practices to meet their audiences' metaphysical interests. In so doing they fashioned a system of medical beliefs that became the template from which a good many alternative healing systems were eventually fashioned.

Franz Anton Mesmer (1734–1815), a Viennese physician, claimed to have detected the existence of a superfine substance or fluid that had until then eluded scientific notice.[11] Mesmer referred to this invisible fluid as animal magnetism and postulated that it permeated the physical universe. He explained that animal magnetism constituted the ethereal medium through which forces of every kind — light, heat, magnetism, electricity — passed as they traveled from one physical object to another. Mesmer believed that animal magnetism was evenly distributed throughout the healthy human body. If for any reason an individual's supply of animal magnetism was thrown out of equilibrium, one or more bodily organs would consequently be deprived of sufficient amounts of this vital force and eventually begin to falter. "There is," Mesmer reasoned, "only one illness and one healing." Therefore, because any and all illness can ultimately be traced to a disturbance in the body's supply of animal magnetism, medical science could be reduced to a set of simple procedures aimed at supercharging a patient's nervous system with this mysterious life-giving energy.

Mesmer, at least initially, thought of himself as the champion of Enlightenment science. In his early years he modeled his healing practices after contemporary discoveries in electromagnetism and consequently passed a magnet over his patients' bodies as a means of inducing animal magnetism to flow into their physical systems. His followers, however, were far more enthused over the hypnoticlike trance that many "mesmerized" patients entered and soon extolled the mental and spiritual dimensions of his cures. Indeed, a good many patients fell into a peaceful trance and, upon awakening, pronounced themselves cured. An American mesmerist by the name of George Bush informed his readers that "the state into which a subject is brought by the mesmerizing process is a state in which the spirit predominates for the time being over the body."[12] The possibility of achieving such an intimate correspondence of the physical and spiritual realms struck the metaphysical imaginations of a good many progressive thinkers. Physicians, Universalist ministers, clockmakers, politicians, publishers, and wealthy dilettantes alike were fascinated by mesmerism's potential for disclosing the metaphysical dimensions of the human condition.

Reports of mesmerism's cures abounded. Among the conditions for which cure was claimed were rheumatism, loss of voice, stammering, nervousness, digestive disorders, epilepsy, blindness, insomnia, St. Vitus's dance, and the abuse of coffee, tea, and alcohol. Even more interesting is the fact that the many books, journals, and pamphlets issued to the reading public dwelled comparatively little on the healings themselves. They instead extolled mesmerism's potentials for expanding the scope of science to include the empirical documentation of humanity's higher spiritual nature. More than its actual healing powers, it was mesmerism's capacity to synthesize science and theology that attracted thousands of middle-class seekers. Mesmerism offered its adherents a new way of understanding how the miracles of the Bible had actually been performed and promised to put them in possession of the lawful means whereby they might consciously draw upon a powerful spiritual force to use in their daily lives.

One American mesmerist, Phineas P. Quimby (1802–66), reasoned that our thoughts function something like shunting valves that either connect us with or close us off from animal magnetism (which he variously referred to as "vital force" or "divine spirit").[13] "Disease," he wrote, "is the effect of a wrong direction given to the mind."[14] If we think spiritually and optimistically, we remain inwardly receptive to the spiritual world and thereby maintain physical vigor. If, however, we become embroiled in pessimism, materialism, or fear, we fall out of harmony with higher spiritual influences and fall victim to physical disease. Quimby taught thousands of patients that by making appropriate adjustments in their own thoughts they could establish rapport with the very spiritual power that makes for health and prosperity. One such patient, Mary Baker Eddy (1821–1910), transformed Quimby's teachings into Christian Science. Others, including Warren Felt Evans (1817–89), expanded Quimby's teachings into what became known as the mind-cure (or "new thought") movement.

The mind-cure gospel of learning to "become one with the Infinite" gained tremendous popularity near the turn of the century. William James, who devoted a chapter to the study of mind-cure in *The Varieties of Religious Experience* and who himself benefited greatly from the movement's writings, observed that its approach to mental healing "must now be reckoned with as a genuine religious power." Its conception of turning within to find our point of personal connection with the "More" of our existence spoke to "those for whom the conception of salvation has lost its ancient theological meaning."[15] He predicted that because mind-cure "gives to some of us serenity, moral poise, and happiness, and prevents certain forms of disease as well as science does, or even better in a certain class of persons," it was destined to play a great role in the evolution of twentieth-century popular religion.[16]

From its initial introduction, mesmerism mingled with other currents of the American metaphysical milieu. Many were quick to note the parallels between Mesmer's science of animal magnetism and the teachings of the Swedish mystic Emanuel Swedenborg (1688–1771). Swedenborg's writings provided a more embellished cosmology and ontology for explaining mesmeric healings. According to Swedenborg, the universe is multidimensional; it is composed of several interpenetrating dimensions — physical, spiritual, and angelic, among others. Each of these dimensions is in some imperceptible way connected with every other. Under the right conditions, energies from higher realms can flow into and produce positive effects within lower realms. Mesmerism had simply stumbled upon a technique for establishing this rapport or correspondence and made possible the "psychic influx" that can promote health and harmony in the human realm.

By the end of the century, both spiritualism and theosophy were to integrate fully into the mesmerism-Swedenborgian mix. As early as 1843, a mesmerist placed a young cobbler by the name of Andrew Jackson Davis into an entranced state of consciousness only to have Davis begin receiving messages from departed spirits. Thus was born American spiritualism, or trance channeling, and to this day it has connections with the vocabulary and techniques found in metaphysical healing systems. The founder of theosophy, Madame Blavatsky, was herself a healer and trance channeler and was responsible for introducing into American popular culture a host of new terms derived haphazardly from Hinduism, Buddhism, and the Western occult tradition. It was from theosophy that significant numbers of Americans were introduced to such metaphysical terms as *auras* and *chakras* and to the existence of astral or ethereal bodies. These metaphysical concepts would factor significantly into New Age healing practices in the late twentieth century.

From the start these metaphysical healing systems mingled together so completely that it is almost impossible to make firm distinctions between them. Their adherents approached them with common intellectual agendas and had no real interest in preserving any sharp differences in their backgrounds or theoretical orientations. Americans read unsystematically from these movements' writings and so mingled their terminologies that these originally distinct philosophies often became fused in popular understanding. Even in the 1990s, alternative medicine continues to be its own subculture within middle-class America. The otherwise disparate practitioners of these systems typically know one another and feel comfortable using the terminology of other healing traditions. They frequent the same bookstores and attend the same seminars. Most important, they all seek a metaphysic that addresses what they perceive to be the narrowness of institutional religion and the excessive materialism of modern science.

Chiropractic Medicine

Throughout the nineteenth century, medical doctors created numerous state and local societies to advance the practice of scientific medicine and to promote licensure laws that favored "orthodox" practitioners. It was not, however, until the turn of the century that the American Medical Association rose above these state and local societies to become the dominant professional organization for scientific medicine. For the first time in American history there was a medical system with sufficient lobbying power to control the accreditation of medical schools and determine who could have access to major hospitals. Henceforth, all other healers who have sought a share of the nation's medical market have had their alternative status clearly and repeatedly defined for them by an organized medical establishment. As the twentieth century dawned, the AMA was to find at its fringes a worthy rival — chiropractic medicine.

Daniel David Palmer (1845–1913) began his career as a grocer and fish peddler in What Cheer, Iowa. Without formal education, Palmer nonetheless read widely and seemed particularly drawn to novel ideas. One of these novel ideas was spiritualism, from which he picked up a number of metaphysical terms for describing humanity's connection with spiritual forces and energies. The young Palmer also came across a mesmeric healer who tutored him in magnetic healing. Palmer procured several books on mesmeric healing that were to remain central texts in his personal library for the rest of his life. He soon opened his own magnetic healing practice in Burlington, Iowa, and later moved it to Davenport. Steeped in a wide variety of late nineteenth-century American metaphysical philosophies, Palmer was well on his way to developing his own theory of illness when a janitor by the name of Harvey Lillard stopped by his office. Lillard, who was deaf, told Palmer that his deafness had begun when he had injured his back seventeen years before. Palmer placed Lillard down on the couch and moved his hands up and down Lillard's spine. He felt an unusual lump at one vertebra and applied pressure with his hands. Palmer felt the vertebra move back into place and, lo and behold, Lillard could hear perfectly.

Similar healing successes followed. Palmer reasoned that the vital energy flowing from the brain to the various organs of the body is occasionally blocked by misaligned spinal vertebrae, and he concluded that this blockage was the direct cause of disease. Healing therefore required that misplaced vertebrae be manually forced back into position. He called his new medical philosophy *chiropractic* from the Greek words *cheiro* (hand) and *prakitos* (done or performed). Palmer was, however, far from propounding a material or physiological cause-theory of disease. Quite the contrary. Palmer's chiropractic philosophy was predicated upon an overtly metaphysical conception of causality. According to Palmer, any truly scientific approach to the human system must begin with the principle that physical life is an expression of a divine reality:

> What is that which is present in the living body and absent in the dead? It is not inherent; it is not in the organs which are essential to life. An intelligent force which I saw fit to name *Innate*, usually known as spirit, creates and continues life when vital organs are in a condition to be acted upon by it. That intelligent life-force uses the material of the universe just in proportion as it is in condition to be utilized.[17]

Palmer made the religious underpinnings of his therapeutic system even clearer when he explained that Innate, as it exists within the individual human being, is in fact "a segment of that Intelligence which fills the universe." He wrote, "Innate is a part of the Creator. Innate spirit is a part of Universal Intelligence, individualized and personified."[18] Universal Intelligence, the god of the various world religions, is the fundamental force that has brought the physical universe into existence. The purpose of creation is to enable Universal Intelligence to express itself through the processes of evolution and development. This monistic and emanationist cosmology was not unique to Palmer or to chiropractic; it also appeared in much of the mesmerist, spiritualist, and theosophical literature with which Palmer was familiar. Palmer's claim to originality lies in his interest in discovering the precise physiological routes through which the individualized segment of divine spirit, Innate, directs the life process within the individual. Palmer asserted that Innate generates life impulses through the medium of the brain, which in turn transmits them along nerve pathways to their different peripheral endings. The nervous system, then, is the key to the proper flow of Innate through the body, and thus the correct alignment of vertebrae along the spinal column is critical to physical health. Displacements of the vertebrae, called subluxations by Palmer, pinch the flow of the Innate-generated nerve impulses and sever affected bodily organs from the ultimate source of life. As the Palmer School of Chiropractic Medicine's official publication, *The Chiropractor*, put it, "We are well when Innate Intelligence has unhindered freedom to act thru the physical brain, nerves and tissues. . . . Diseases are caused by a LACK OF CURRENT OF INNATE MENTAL IMPULSES."[19] It follows that chiropractic medicine "is defined as being the science of adjusting, by hand, any or all luxations of the 300 articular joints of the human body, more especially the 52 articulations of the spinal column, for the purpose of freeing any or all impinged nerves, which cause deranged functions."[20]

Palmer's son, B. J. Palmer (1881–1961), expanded upon the potential for chiropractic theory to provide a comprehensive framework for explaining humanity's physical, mental, and spiritual natures. For over fifty years he trained and lectured chiropractic physicians about abandoning scientific materialism in favor of a faith in Universal Intelligence and Innate. Chiropractic medicine had discovered that the higher power preached by the world's religions resides within each human being in the form of Innate. In one fell swoop chiropractic had brushed conventional religion and conventional medicine aside: "Everything that man could ask or pray for he has within. . . . The Chiropractor removes the obstruction, adjusts the cause, and there are going to be effects."[21]

Not all of chiropractic's growing legion of physicians and instructors were attentive to the Palmers' metaphysical musings. They were acutely aware, for example, that the movement's detractors repeatedly singled out the concept of Innate as an untestable, and hence unscientific, theory. The majority of chiropractic physicians have consequently been eager to relegate the Palmers' writings to dusty archives and have instead concentrated on research into the physical causes of musculoskeletal distress. It is hard to escape the conclusion that chiropractic's public acceptance, professional recognition, and access to insurance industry policies have come in direct proportion to its systematic attention to a range of musculoskeletal disorders largely neglected by medical doctors and its simultaneous abandonment of metaphysical speculation. The Palmers' innovative spirituality is downplayed if not wholly ignored by a majority of the forty thousand chiropractic physicians currently practicing in the United States.

What needs to be underscored, however, is that the aura of metaphysical discovery is hardly absent from contemporary chiropractic. At least some of the more than nine million persons who visit chiropractic physicians each year do so precisely because they find in it an openness to Eastern religious concepts, metaphysical perspectives on the human condition, and innovative spiritual practices. As Eugene Linden wrote in a feature on alternative medicine for *Time* magazine, the chiropractic physician he visited for lower-back pain considered it just as important to give him "a line of Eastern philosophy" as a spinal adjustment. Linden recounts that "at first I found Christoph's messianic zeal as off-putting as the detached manner of the doctor at my H.M.O. Then Christoph checked my 'energy centers.'... Deficiencies in my sixth (or was it fifth?) 'chakra' notwithstanding, once Christoph had finished his Procrustean pullings, crackings and pushings, the pain was gone and I felt 20 lbs. lighter."[22]

A good many chiropractors share Christoph's metaphysical inclination. A popular chiropractic book written in the 1960s lured readers and potential patients with glowing descriptions of the higher power energized by chiropractic technique:

> The smartest man in the world is the Man Inside. By the Man Inside I mean that Other Man within each of us that does most of the things we give ourselves credit for doing. You may refer to him as Nature or the Subconscious Self, or think of him as merely a Force of a Natural Law or, if you are religiously inclined, you may use the term God.[23]

In the 1970s, G. F. Riekman, a chiropractic physician and former dean of philosophy at Sherman College of Chiropractic, summarized chiropractic's distinctive approach to healing for a volume entitled *The Holistic Health Handbook*. According to Riekman, chiropractic is a "New Age philosophy, science, and art":

> The chiropractic philosophy is based on the deductive principle that the Universe is perfectly organized, and that we are all extensions of this principle, designed to express life (health) and the universal laws. Since vertebral subluxations (spinal-nerve interference) are the grossest interference with the expression of life, the practice of chiropractic is designed to analyze and correct these subluxations, so

that the organism will be free to evolve and express life to its fullest natural potential.[24]

The Holistic Health Movement

The holistic healing movement that gathered momentum throughout the 1970s is rife with symbols evoking an explicitly spiritual interpretation of the healing process. The basic premise of holistic approaches to healing is relatively straightforward, and, at first glance, it appears to be little more than the rhetoric of a generation of Americans eager to rehumanize their technological society: "Every human being is a unique, wholistic, interdependent relationship of body, mind, emotions, and spirit."[25] This is, however, far from a bland truism. The introduction of the term *spirit* alongside *body, mind,* and *emotions* takes holistic conceptions of healing well beyond psychosomatic models and stakes out a bold metaphysical interpretation of reality. It entails committing oneself to a belief in the interpenetration of physical and nonphysical spheres of causality to a degree that makes holistic healing not only an alternative approach to medicine but an alternative world view.

A helpful introduction to the general principles underlying holistic conceptions of medicine is Herbert Otto and James Knight's edited volume, *Dimensions in Wholistic Healing: New Frontiers in the Treatment of the Whole Person.* This introductory text explains that holistic healing places "reliance on treatment modalities that foster the self-regenerative and self-reparative processes of natural healing."[26] Implicit in this description is confidence in the beneficence of nature and respect for the fundamental dignity and sovereignty of the individual, both core conceptions of alternative American medicine. Distinctive of holistic medicine is its emphasis on the psychological factors that promote regeneration and well-being. The ill, they note, generally have difficulty coping with their condition and are in desperate need of love, care, and understanding. It is therefore imperative that healing personnel give "abundantly of their warmth, empathy and understanding and [furnish] the type of emotional nurturance particularly needed at a time of illness."[27]

Knight and Otto draw attention to the interpersonal environment and its effect upon healing and health. They counsel that a holistic understanding of healing makes optimum use of the "dynamic and therapeutic forces inherent in group interaction." Their medical advice centers on how healers can relate to individuals in ways that enhance the patient's self-image and mobilize natural self-regenerative tendencies. Knight and Otto's conception of healing becomes most differentiated from orthodox medical practice in their insistence that the "larger environment" that humans inhabit includes not only the social realm but a spiritual realm as well. Like most holistic healers, they set forth this claim rather cautiously. Echoing the aesthetic spiritualities of Ralph Waldo Emerson and William James, they describe holistic medicine as predicated upon the recognition that every human being has vast untapped potential, resources, and powers. Significantly, however, these resources and powers are not self-contained within the physical or psychological system. Rather, "everyone is part of a larger system." Holistic healing must utilize the patient's spiritual resources to help "open the pathways or flows and harmonics necessary to unfold the channels of the self within the body and the self within the world, the Universe, and God."[28] Thus what began as holistic medicine's rather mild acknowledgment of the body's self-recuperative abilities slides imperceptibly into a metaphysical doctrine in which the physical system is seen as receptive to the sanative energies flowing into it from without.

Kenneth Pelletier's *Holistic Medicine* is another text representative of the worldview promulgated under the banner of holistic healing. Like nearly all of the movement's spokespersons, Pelletier introduces holistic concepts as an outgrowth of recent research in the field of psychosomatic illness. The discovery that an individual's mental and emotional states can directly affect physiological processes has convinced Pelletier and others that reliance on material factors is inadequate. He writes, "A fundamental philosophical revision is taking place in our paradigm of medicine. Central to this revision is the concept that all stages of disease are psychosomatic in etiology, direction, and the healing process."[29] At first glance, Pelletier appears to be introducing a causal role for psychological and attitudinal factors into the process of physical healing. On closer examination, however, it becomes evident that psychosomatic interaction alone hardly requires the fundamental revision in concepts of causality that he has in mind. Pelletier's "new paradigm" is far less concerned with introducing the concept of the causal role of mind into our medical vocabulary than with championing the supervenient powers of spirit. Pelletier urges us to adopt the Chinese yin/yang philosophy, which asserts that all physiological processes are governed by a spiritual agency that emanates from the divine (Tao). He also endorses the general drift of Fritjof Capra's *The Tao of Physics*. Capra's book is cited by many advocates of holistic healing because it advocates Eastern mystical traditions that deny any sharp distinction between spirit and matter and portray God as a spiritual energy continuously exerting causal influences within the physical universe. Especially revealing in this regard is Pelletier's anecdotal illustration of this new view of healing. He tells how a Zen practitioner healed herself of diabetes and cardiac irregularities by turning within and opening "a tiny hole of light" through which spirit entered and enveloped her whole being with light.[30]

Among the best-known spokespersons for holistic healing have been Norman Cousins and Bernard Siegel. Cousins, former editor of the *Saturday Review,* confronted a serious illness for which medical physicians gave him a rather bleak prognosis. His best-selling book *Anatomy of an Illness* has become a classic indictment of the medical profession's needlessly materialistic vision of the human person.[31] Cousins recounts his own decision to will himself back to health through a deliberate regimen of optimistic and cheerful thinking. His lengthy remission brought a great deal of popular attention to the role of attitudinal factors in both creating and curing disease. Lurking in Cousins's description of the mind's curative powers are highly suggestive references to the little understood "life-force" that drives the mind and body toward perfectibility. In a later text entitled *Human Options,* Cousins elaborated: "The human brain is a mirror to infinity.... No one knows what great leaps of achievement may be within the reach of the species once the full potentiality of the mind is developed. As we create an ever-higher sense of our cosmic consciousness, we become aware of our ever-higher possibilities and challenges."[32] Physician Bernard Siegel has been even more forceful in linking holistic conceptions of healing with a decidedly metaphysical conception of the human condition. Siegel has cancer patients read books on meditation and psychic phenomena so that they can learn practical techniques for tapping into higher healing energies. Describing the "theophysics" he believes will emerge in the scientific world in the near future, Siegel writes, "If you consider God, and you can use this label scientifically as an intelligent, loving light, then that energy is available to all of us. We are part of it, we have a collective unconscious.... If you get people to open to this energy, anything can be healed."[33]

Another example of Americans' involvement with holistically oriented healing movements can be seen in the five thousand nurses who have studied Dolores Krieger's technique of therapeutic touch. Krieger, a nursing instructor at New York University and student of theosophical teachings, developed a healing technique predicated upon the existence of a universal energy underlying all life processes. She believes that Western science does not understand energy in the same context as do the Eastern religious traditions, and she therefore identifies this subtle energy permeating the universe with the Hindu term *prana.* Krieger states that *prana* is the metaphysical agent responsible for all life processes and is thus the ultimate power behind every form of healing regardless of the particular rationale or technique a physician might employ. Every living organism is an open system and has continuous access to *prana.* So long as an individual retains contact with this vital energy he or she remains healthy; illness ensues when some area of the body develops a deficit of *prana.* The act of healing, then, entails the "channeling of this energy flow by the healer for the well-being of the sick individual."[34]

Recapitulating Mesmer's science of animal magnetism in nearly every detail, Krieger has devised a system of practices for nurses to use in their efforts to "channel" *prana* into patients. She explains that before we can transmit *prana* to a patient, we must first become inwardly receptive to the flow of this spiritual energy into our own system. Healers must learn to purify and open up their own internal *chakras,* or spiritual energy centers, through which *prana* enters into the human nervous system. To do this we must acquire a whole new way of life that will facilitate our entry into spiritually receptive states of consciousness. Instruction in therapeutic touch, Krieger says, is an "archetypal journey" that will initiate newcomers into the symbolic realms of human consciousness. It is an "experience in interiority...[that] presents you with a rich lode of circumstances through which you can explore and grapple with the farther reaches of the psyche."[35]

Nor are nurses involved in therapeutic touch alone in their archetypal journeys. Participants in perhaps the most successful example of holistic medicine — Alcoholics Anonymous — are similarly guided to acquire "an overwhelming 'God-consciousness' followed at once by a vast change in feeling and outlook."[36] Alcoholics Anonymous warns against the attempt to rely on self-sufficiency. It maintains that the key to personal regeneration is attainment of the "feeling of being at one with God and man."[37] AA's founder, Bill W., was wary of organized religion. Knowing that many alcoholics are painfully conscious of their inability to live up to the moral absolutes associated with biblical religion, he instead sought to articulate a spiritual approach to personal regeneration that was free of dogmas and fixed traditions. Its "Twelve Step" program is a unique blend of mysticism and pragmatism pieced together from the writings of such religiously oriented psychologists as William James and Carl Jung. Referring to itself as "spiritual rather than religious," AA is a prime carrier of America's secular spiritual heritage as is exemplified in its Emersonian conviction that true self-reliance is possible only once we have experientially connected ourselves with the Other: "The more we become willing to depend upon a higher power, the more independent we actually are."[38] AA's mystical, nonscriptural approach to spiritual regeneration makes its doctrines anathema to most of America's religious establishment. Its denunciation of both material and psychological/attitudinal factors in favor of an overtly metaphysical view of healing makes it anathema to the American medical establishment. Still, its open-minded and eclectic sense of the presence of spiritual forces in the determination of human well-being makes it one of the most powerful mediators of wholeness in America today. (See chapter 11 in this volume, entitled "Twelve Step Programs.")

New Age Crystal Healing

The revival of metaphysical interests during the 1970s, 1980s, and 1990s has generally been called the New Age movement. One thing common to most New Agers is that they prefer to view God in such impersonal terms as a "pure white light" or "divine spirit" rather in the traditional biblical categories of father or king. Some New Age healers believe in what might be called an emanationist cosmology. That is, they believe that this pure white light continuously emanates throughout the universe, infusing a vital force into each of the many dimensions or planes of existence — mineral, vegetable, animal, human or mental, and astral. The divine spirit is understood to enter each individual's consciousness through the astral body (aura), from which it is then diffused into the seven interior centers (or *chakras*) that supply the body with vitality. One summary of New Age medicine explains: "When white light flows harmoniously [from the astral body] into the interior centers (the *chakras*), our condition becomes healthy and more harmonious. When there is some obstruction in the *chakra,* blocks are formed, and these blocks prevent energy from flowing freely, and the body is unable to heal itself."[39]

New Age color healing and crystal healing are examples of medical techniques that derive from this metaphysical vision of the universe. It is thought that divine white light is refracted into its seven constituent colors as it filters through the human aura. Each *chakra* receives one of the seven color rays and in turn transmits this vital force throughout the body. Red, orange, yellow, green, blue, indigo, and violet thus correspond to the seven *chakras* located along the spinal column. Any technique that can aid us in activating the proper flow of divine light through our various *chakras* can thereby be of medical value. Placing colored gems over appropriate *chakras,* deep massage, and meditation are all thought to promote such healing activity.

The most touted of New Age healing techniques has been the use of crystals. Enthusiasts claim that because rock crystal is almost entirely devoid of color, it is an almost perfect capacitor of divine white light. Explanations of exactly how crystals wield their healing powers vary from practitioner to practitioner. Some maintain that the unique properties of crystals make them excellent receptors of metaphysical energies. Others suggest that crystals work by amplifying the patient's own personal energies. This confusion about whether crystals harness the power of personal or extrapersonal energies is possibly due only to semantic difficulties in the New Age lexicon. The vocabulary employed by New Age healers — largely of theosophical and mesmerist parentage — describes humans as existing simultaneously in the physical, ethereal, and astral planes. Crystals supposedly have the ability to harmonize the physical body with the ethereal fields from which healing energies ultimately emanate. Crystal healer Korra Deaver explains:

> Crystals act as transformers and harmonizers of energy. Illness in the physical body is a reflection of disruption or disharmony of energies in the etheric bodies, and healing takes place when harmony is restored to the subtler bodies. The crystal acts as a focus of healing energy and healing intent, and thereby produces the appropriate energy.[40]

The training to become a crystal healer is undertaken with all the reverence and mystery of a shamanistic ritual. Meticulous attention is given to the selection of the particular crystal that will most enhance one's own personal "vibrations." After an appropriate stone has been selected, healers must learn to center themselves inwardly and to purify their psyches of nonspiritual desires and emotions. Breathing exercises, relaxation techniques, meditation, and the repetition of spiritual affirmations are all recommended as techniques for properly centering oneself. Many hold and meditate upon their crystals in a manner similar to the ancient art of using crystal balls for divination. "Crystal gazing," as Deaver describes it, is "the science of inhibiting normal outward consciousness by intense concentration on a polished sphere. When the five senses are thus drastically subdued, the psychic receptors can function without interference."[41] To aid in this process of inner transformation, crystal healers often repeat such affirmations as "I am the Light of God," "I am filled with the Light of the Christ," and "I am a radiant Being of Light temporarily using a physical body."

As crystal healer Katrina Raphael writes: "Crystal healings are designed to allow the recipient to consciously access depths of being previously unavailable, and draw upon personal resources to answer all questions and heal any wound. . . . The person who is receiving the crystal healing has the unique opportunity to contact the very essence of being."[42] Crystal healers caution us to put our ordinary ego aside in order to become a purer channel of divine energy. We must open ourselves fully and suspend our human will so that we can follow the higher guidance that flows directly from the Supreme Soul. Crystal healing, then, is a spiritual path and spiritual discipline in its own right. Hence Korra Deaver downplays the narrow focus upon physical healings and counsels that "even if the breakthrough is only in your own understanding of yourself-as-a-soul, as a Cosmic Being, your efforts will not have been in vain."[43]

Healing and Secular Spirituality

This survey of alternative healing groups barely scratches the surface of contemporary interest in nonmedical systems of healing and health.[44] Practices such as acupuncture, iridology, reflexology, t'ai chi, yoga, Ayurvedic medicine, shiatsu, rolfing, and sundry forms of psychic healing are also prime carriers of secular spirituality. According to *The Holistic Health Handbook,* each of these systems is concerned with "healing the whole person and awakening the spirit within." Despite their differences, each utilizes techniques predicated upon the belief that "we are all affected by the universal Life Energy."[45] Taken together, these groups constitute an impressive expression of secular American spirituality. They are not simply referring to a different set of material factors dismissed as unimportant by the medical establishment. Instead, they are concerned with pushing any conception of healing to the point that it discloses the ultimate meaning or significance of our lives. In doing so they stake out an intellectual territory outside the boundaries of either scientific or religious orthodoxy. Adherents of these groups have found scientific positivism too confining. Scientific rationality has failed to sustain their general optimism toward life or to further their capacity to participate directly in something that can be affirmed as sacred or holy. Biblical religion is even more problematic to them. Most of those attracted to holistic forms of healing are self-styled progressive thinkers and find scriptural religion intellectually obsolete. Their curiosity about exploring the connections between the physical and metaphysical dimensions of the universe runs too far afield from the conceptual constraints of Jewish or Christian theology.

Recent interest in holistic healing practices is a prime example of what historian William McLoughlin calls the "Fourth Great Awakening" in American cultural life.[46] McLoughlin draws our attention to the ways in which social, political, and even environmental events during the 1960s sent millions of Americans searching for more relevant or more functionally useful ways of understanding their world. People caught up in this awakening thought themselves to be witnessing the death of older ways of viewing the universe and the birth of new ones. The earliest hints of these cultural rumblings can be seen in the appearance of the so-called

Beat Generation in the late 1950s. Writers such as Allen Ginsberg, Alan Watts, Gary Snyder, and Jack Kerouac focused attention on the sense of alienation Americans felt from sources of both scientific and religious authority. Their call for a counterculture echoed a widespread dissatisfaction with the narrow-mindedness of biblical religion and the spiritual bankruptcy of scientific positivism. In the late 1960s and 1970s Americans in increasing numbers seriously experimented with Asian philosophies, psychedelic drugs, and sundry transpersonal psychologies, all in an attempt to find for themselves what Emerson once described as "an original relationship to the Universe." While their quest for harmonizing with nature's higher reaches sometimes smacked of narcissism and hedonism, it far more often bespoke a spiritual hunger for wholeness and union with a transcendent Other.

McLoughlin reminds us that during periods of cultural renewal the theological pendulum almost invariably swings away from emphasis upon God's transcendence to notions of divine immanence. In the urgency of "wholeness hunger," the spiritual and physical worlds seem to intermingle, making it possible to locate God as easily in a rock crystal as in a church. A commitment to theological immanence adds excitement to the religious quest. It implies that the only barrier between us and a higher power is self-imposed and removable by a single chiropractic adjustment, the wave of a crystal, or a nurse's therapeutic touch. It is striking how closely these healing groups resemble McLoughlin's description of the theological reorientation emerging in those who, while deeply spiritual, have moved irretrievably outside the denominational traditions. This reorientation, he writes, is still taking shape but will most likely include a new sense of the mystical unity of all humankind and of the vital power of harmony between humankind and nature. The godhead will be defined in less dualistic terms, and its power will be understood less in terms of an absolutist, sin-hating, death-dealing "Almighty Father in Heaven" and more in terms of a life-supporting, nurturing, empathic, easygoing parental (motherly as well as fatherly) image.[47]

Holistic healing groups are prime carriers of this spiritual awakening. It is, in fact, quite possible that many of these groups attract popular followings not so much for their ability to heal as for their ability to communicate a felt sense of participating in some ultimate reality. As the introductory section of *The Holistic Health Handbook* suggests, "Perhaps more important than the techniques is the expansion of consciousness they foster."[48] Newcomers to metaphysical healing systems go through cognitive and experiential transformations very similar to those that Mircea Eliade describes of participants in the initiatory rites of archaic religions. Specifically, newcomers are introduced to doctrines and practices that by their very nature "involve their entire lives" and restructure their consciousness such that they become "a being open to the life of the spirit."[49] The therapeutic context of metaphysical healing heightens the death/rebirth symbolism through which individuals discard a no longer functional identity and discover a professedly higher self. The sensations of heat and tingling vibrations that so often accompany metaphysical healing are also classic features of initiatory rites.[50] Holistic healing practices evoke a sense of wonder and mystery that supplies an experiential context for believing that one has discovered the primal reality on which life is ultimately dependent.

The transformational power of holistic healing systems can be clearly illustrated by the case of professional nurses introduced to therapeutic touch. No longer agents of a pharmaceutical technology, these nurses commonly report perceiving themselves as "channels." Consider, for example, the self-descriptions provided by two of Krieger's students: "A channel, definitely, for the universal power of wholeness. I am certain it is not 'I' who do it"; and "[I] see myself as . . . a vehicle through which energy can go to the patient in whatever way he or she can use it."[51] Given the fact that Krieger was herself introduced to metaphysical healing by well-known spiritualists and theosophists, the fact that her students now understand themselves as channels or vehicles indicates how quickly this alternative spirituality can catch hold of Americans' metaphysical imaginations.

As one of Krieger's students expressed it, "Using Therapeutic Touch has changed and continues to change me . . . [and] requires a certain philosophy, and this change in philosophy permeates one's total existence."[52] The benefits attributed to this change in outlook resemble Abraham Maslow's description of peak experiences: increased independence and self-reliance; the ability to view things in their totality; a more caring (bodhisattva-like) attitude toward others; the sense of being an integral part of the universe; and the abandonment of scientific method as the sole approach to the nature of life. Persons trained in nursing science now avidly read books on yogic meditation, Tibetan mysticism, and the relationship between the "new physics" and Eastern religious traditions.

In his famous essay "The Will to Believe," William James observes how the secular character of our age tends to make religious beliefs appear avoidable, dead, and trivial. Religion, he argues, only becomes a genuine option when it confronts us in ways that make it forced, living, and momentous.[53] To the seriously ill, of course, religious belief is always forced and momentous insofar as we are confronted with our finitude and mortality. Depending on our upbringing and education, religion may or may not be a live option for us as we confront our frailty within the large universe. It is to the credit of these holistic healing systems that they make religious belief and spiritual outlooks on life both live and momentous (though not forced) even for those who have no physical ailments. Adherents of these systems feel themselves revitalized by both their "harmonizing" techniques and their advocacy of an overtly metaphysical conception of the place of humans in the grander scheme of things. Through their doctrines (myths) and therapeutic techniques (rituals), these groups have succeeded at helping individuals identify their relatedness to what Tillich calls the "unconditional power of Being." The existence and continuing popularity of holistically oriented healing systems thus testify to the fact that the impress of secularization has in no way detracted from Americans' capacity to envision their lives as in some way participating in a sacred reality. Indeed, this secular form of spirituality is a grand testimony to the ability of culture to symbolize what, at the deepest level of mystery, is the ultimate source and meaning of our lives.

Notes

1. Paul Tillich, *Theology of Culture* (New York: Oxford University Press, 1959), 5. See also idem, *Systematic Theology*, 3 vols. (Chicago: University of Chicago Press, 1967), 1:15.
2. Tillich, *Theology of Culture*, 42.
3. Paul Tillich, *The Shaking of Foundations* (New York: Pelican, 1962), 181.
4. For a more complete discussion of how both alternative medical systems and American psychology have functioned as carriers of an "unchurched American spirituality," see Robert C. Fuller, *Alternative Medicine and American Religious Life* (New York: Oxford University Press, 1989); and idem, *Americans and the Unconscious* (New York: Oxford University Press, 1986).
5. David Eisenberg et al., "Unconventional Medicine in the United States: Prevalence, Costs, and Patterns of Use," *New England Journal of Medicine* 328, 28 January 1993, 246–52.
6. Gerhard Kittel, *Theological Dictionary of the New Testament* (Grand Rapids: Eerdmans, 1978), 3:194–215; and William Clebsch and Charles Jaekle, *Pastoral Care in Historical Perspective* (New York: Aronson, 1975).
7. Many massage and breathing therapies utilize Eastern notions of a subtle body energy such as *ch'i* or *prana* and thus implicitly invoke worldviews in which the physical realm of life is ontologically dependent on sustaining continuous harmony with, or periodically receiving "influxes" from, an ultimate metaphysical reality such as Brahman, the Tao, the Great Ultimate, the Cosmic Body of the Buddha, and so on. Thus although many adherents of systems such as acupuncture, acupressure, and shiatsu emphasize their known physiological properties, I contend they continue to propagate spiritual-cause explanations of healing.
8. For a discussion of the formal (as opposed to functional) properties of religious consciousness, see Peter Berger, "Some Second Thoughts on Substantive versus Functional

Definitions of Religion," *Journal for the Social Scientific Study of Religion* 13 (June 1974): 125–34; and Giles Gunn, *The Interpretation of Otherness* (New York: Oxford University Press, 1979).

9. Ralph Waldo Emerson, *The Complete Works of Ralph Waldo Emerson,* 12 vols. (New York: AMS, 1968), 1:62.

10. Sydney Ahlstrom, *A Religious History of the American People* (New Haven: Yale University Press, 1972), 608.

11. For discussions of Mesmer's life and work, see Henri Ellenberger, *The Discovery of the Unconscious* (New York: Basic Books, 1970); and Robert C. Fuller, *Mesmerism and the American Cure of Souls* (Philadelphia: University of Pennsylvania Press, 1982).

12. George Bush, *Mesmer and Swedenborg* (New York: John Allen, 1847), 160.

13. For discussions of the life and thought of Phineas P. Quimby and the subsequent development of the mind-cure movement, see Charles Braden, *Spirits in Rebellion* (Dallas: Southern Methodist University Press, 1963); Donald Meyer, *The Positive Thinkers* (New York: Doubleday, 1965); and Gail Thain Parker, *The History of Mind Cure in New England* (Hanover, N.H.: University Press of New England, 1973).

14. Phineas P. Quimby, *The Quimby Manuscripts* (New York: Crowell, 1921), 319.

15. William James, *The Varieties of Religious Experience* (New York: Collier, 1961), 90, 100.

16. Ibid., 110.

17. D. D. Palmer, *The Chiropractor's Adjuster* (Portland, Oreg.: Portland Printing House, 1910), 35.

18. Ibid., 491.

19. *The Chiropractor* 5 (1909): inside front cover.

20. Ibid., 1 (1905): Inside front cover.

21. B. J. Palmer, *Do Chiropractors Pray?* (Davenport, Iowa: Palmer School of Chiropractic, 1911), 27.

22. Eugene Linden, "My Excellent Alternative Adventure," *Time,* 4 November 1991, 76.

23. Thorp McClusky, *Your Health and Chiropractic* (New York: Pyramid Books, 1962), 48.

24. G. F. Riekman, "Chiropractic," in *The Holistic Health Handbook* (Berkeley, Calif.: And/Or Press, 1978), 174.

25. Mary Belknap, Robert Blau, and Rasaline Grossman, eds., *Case Studies and Methods in Humanistic Medicine* (San Francisco: Institute for the Study of Humanistic Medicine, 1975), 18.

26. Herbert A. Otto and James W. Knight, eds., *Dimensions in Wholistic Healing: New Frontiers in the Treatment of the Whole Person* (Chicago: Nelson-Hall, 1979), 3.

27. Ibid., 10.

28. Ibid.

29. Kenneth Pelletier, *Holistic Medicine* (New York: Delacorte, 1979), 93.

30. Ibid., 94.

31. Norman Cousins, *Anatomy of an Illness* (New York: Norton, 1979).

32. Norman Cousins, *Human Options* (New York: Norton, 1981), 167.

33. Bernard Siegel, "Interview with Bernard Siegel," *ReVision* 7 (spring 1984): 92.

34. Delores Krieger, *The Therapeutic Touch* (Englewood Cliffs, N.J.: Prentice-Hall, 1979), 13.

35. Ibid., 77.

36. *Alcoholics Anonymous* (New York: Alcoholics Anonymous, 1955), 569.
37. *Twelve Steps and Twelve Traditions* (New York: Alcoholics Anonymous, 1952), 63.
38. Ibid., 37.
39. Daya Sarai Chocron, *Healing with Crystals and Gemstones* (York Beach, Maine: Weiser, 1983), 4.
40. Korra Deaver, *Rock Crystal: The Magic Stone* (York Beach, Maine: Samuel Weiser, 1985), 40.
41. Ibid., 16.
42. Katrina Raphael, *Crystal Healing: The Therapeutic Application of Crystals and Stones* (New York: Aurora, 1987), 20–21.
43. Deaver, *Rock Crystal,* 7.
44. A good place to begin a more extensive study of alternative religion in the United States is Norman Gevitz, ed., *Other Healers: Unorthodox Medicine in America* (Baltimore: Johns Hopkins University Press, 1988).
45. *Holistic Health Handbook,* 174. See also *A Visual Encyclopedia of Unconventional Medicine* (New York: Crown, 1978); and Leslie Kaslof, ed., *Wholistic Dimensions in Healing* (Garden City, N.Y.: Doubleday, 1978).
46. William McLoughlin, *Revivals, Awakenings, and Reform* (Chicago: University of Chicago Press, 1978).
47. Ibid., 214.
48. *Holistic Health Handbook,* 13.
49. Mircea Eliade, *Rites and Symbols of Initiation* (New York: Harper and Row, 1965), 3.
50. Richard Katz, *Boiling Energy: Community Healing among the Kalahari Kung* (Cambridge, Mass.: Harvard University Press, 1982). This is an excellent study of the role that belief in a subtle energy (which the Kung call *num*) plays in healing individuals and in creating cultural cohesion. Whether called *num, kundalini, ch'i,* animal magnetism, or *prana,* it would seem that belief in the possibility of experiencing a psychic energy capable of enhancing humans' physical well-being is a common feature of initiation into esoteric belief systems.
51. Krieger, *Therapeutic Touch,* 108.
52. Janet Quinn, "Therapeutic Touch: One Nurse's Evolution as a Healer," in *Therapeutic Touch: A Book of Readings,* ed. Marianne Borelli and Patricia Heidt (New York: Springer, 1981), 62. See in the same book: Patricia Heidt, "Scientific Research and Therapeutic Touch"; Marianne Borelli, "Meditation and Therapeutic Touch"; Janet Macrae, "Therapeutic Touch: A Way of Life"; and Honore Fontes, "Self-Healing: Getting in Touch with Self to Promote Healing."
53. William James, "The Will to Believe," in *The Will to Believe* (New York: Dover, 1956), 3.

Bibliography

Albanese, Catherine. *Nature Religion in America.* Chicago: University of Chicago Press, 1990.

Fuller, Robert. *Alternative Medicine and American Religious Life.* New York: Oxford University Press, 1989.

Gevitz, Norman, ed. *Other Healers: Unorthodox Medicine in America.* Baltimore: Johns Hopkins University Press, 1988.

Gottschalk, Stephen. *The Emergence of Christian Science in American Life.* Berkeley: University of California Press, 1973.

Hufford, David. "Contemporary Folk Medicine." In Gevitz, ed., *Other Healers,* 228–64.

Ingles, Brian. *The Case for Unorthodox Medicine.* New York: Putnam's, 1965.

McGuire, Meredith. *Ritual Healing in Suburban America.* New Brunswick, N.J.: Rutgers University Press, 1988.

Nissenbaum, Stephen. *Sex, Diet, and Debility in Jacksonian America.* Westport, Conn.: Greenwood, 1988.

Numbers, Ronald. *Prophetess of Health: A Study of Ellen G. White.* New York: Harper and Row, 1976.

Numbers, Ronald, and Darrel Amundsen, eds. *Caring and Curing: Health and Medicine in the Western Religious Traditions.* New York: Macmillan, 1986.

10

Psychotherapies

LUCY BREGMAN

Born of Medicine, Growing toward Meaning

PSYCHOTHERAPY AS PRACTICED in the twentieth century is a new phenomenon and is in some of its forms a preeminent example of the type of quest to which this volume is dedicated. Psychotherapy as a unique spiritual path is distinct from earlier forms of religious consolation, exhortation, and pastoral care, although its links with these, and partial reassimilation back into these, have been the subjects of intense debate. Psychotherapy as purely secular, disengaged, and distanced from religious traditions flourishes today in many parts of the world, although its European origins and North American flowerings are the focus of this chapter. Instead of an encompassing review of all psychologies and therapies, I examine some underlying motifs that comprise the secular spirituality undergirding many of them.

What makes a psychotherapy — or for that matter, any not-so-obviously religious enterprise — spiritual? To qualify, it must focus on a "spiritual dimension of life." According to the general definition offered in this volume:

> Facing outward, human existence is spiritual insofar as one engages reality as a maximally inclusive whole and makes the cosmos an intentional object of thought and feeling. Facing inward, life . . . is apprehended as a project of people's most enduring and vital selves and is structured by experiences of sudden self-transformation and subsequent gradual development.[1]

We should note how this definition appears itself indebted to the language of therapies, where wording such as "enduring and vital self" is commonplace. In fact, "the inward face of spirituality" is exactly what many psychotherapies claim to advance. Self-transformation is the very raison d'être of such practices. Even the balance between sudden and gradual change is a familiar theme in psychotherapeutic methods and case studies, where some stress dramatic experiences of healing and relief from suffering while others emphasize the need for gradual, plodding "working through" by means of interpretation and insight.

It is the "outward face" of spirituality that seems more hidden, less obviously relevant. Psychotherapies are dedicated to the self and its transformations, but do they make the cosmos an intentional object of thought and feeling? Clearly, many do not, and many try to avoid this explicitly. They wish at all costs to eschew what Carl Jung labeled "metaphysics." However, no matter how energetically these therapists deny that they are in the business of doing metaphysics, they have nevertheless built their visions of the transformed self upon some framework that indeed "engages reality as a maximally inclusive whole." Discerning this framework and showing how it relates to the practice of psychotherapy, we may discover that the two faces of spirituality are finally inseparable.

However, it is the two faces — or double language — of twentieth-century psychotherapy itself that have most perplexed its practitioners, advocates, and critics. Psychotherapy, starting with Freudian psychoanalysis, arose out of medicine; yet from its inception, it dealt all but exclusively with problems of meaning and living. Moreover, these two languages of medicine and meaning are at first so intertwined in theories and in the social settings of therapy that their partial and gradual separation is a complex tale in itself. This tale is still not complete, for the remedicalization of psychiatry has marked the last two decades, while the question of who can receive professional credentials to practice psychotherapy continues to be negotiated. It is *not* my claim that everything medical in psychotherapy automatically represents its secular side, while everything intending meaning consequently promotes its spirituality; rather, to grasp how psychotherapy can work as secular spirituality, one needs to look at these two sides of it and summarize initially what is involved in each.

Psychotherapy was born of medicine, late nineteenth-century medicine. This means it shared the aura of science, aspired to function as a scientific enterprise, and anticipated becoming steadily more scientific as more clinical data accumulated. Freud hoped that one day his metapsychological language about instincts and his topography (id, ego, super-ego) would translate into biological discourse. To be scientific meant to stake one's authority upon the values of reason, empiricism, and testable hypotheses. To practice scientific medicine meant to bask in the glow of these values, even when one practiced medicine by "the talking cure" (as Freud's method was dubbed) rather than by means of lab tests, pills, and injections. Psychotherapists practice diagnosis, deal with symptoms, and write case histories.

At the most primary level, the medical model makes the therapist a doctor and the one he or she treats a patient. These two roles were well established already by the time Freud treated his first neurotic sufferers through free association. The masculine presence of the doctor dominated the passive, generally female patient, whose story was translated into symptoms, diagnosis, and prognosis. Doctor and patient met as individuals, usually in the doctor's special consulting room. The patient paid fees for services; attempts to break out of this middle-class setting and import psychotherapy into a public-clinic model have never been fully successful.

Over the years, breaks from various features of this medical model can be identified. For example, the switch to the language of counselor and client marked a major innovation, not just because the category of persons who could practice psychotherapy broadened but because counseling lost the scientific status of medicine. Then the one-on-one model of treatment so central to Western medicine was dethroned, in favor of methods where groups or couples or whole families became simultaneous participants in therapy. In at least some of these situations, the members of the group are expected to help one another — a hope radically different from that of medicine, where the doctor is considered to have a monopoly on the needed expertise. Then came psychotherapies that eliminated the remaining medical motif of pathology, so that growth and enhanced health rather than cure of illness became the stated goals. The growth and encounter groups that flourished during the late 1960s and 1970s appeared to have completed the break with these three features of medicine in the psychotherapeutic heritage. Finally, self-help literature written from a psychological framework offers guidance and advice, minus the presence of the living therapist altogether.

Nevertheless, today the link with medicine remains. Should psychotherapy be covered by national health insurance? Which forms of psychotherapy, and for which conditions? These questions reveal how deeply psychotherapy is still entangled with medicine. Its fate depends in part upon the financing of medicine, and its credibility is judged in part upon criteria drawn from scientific research, just as at the time of its origins. The point is not whether any forms of psychotherapy have ever met these criteria, or whether they should be judged by them, but that, in fact, American society does still lump psychotherapy along with other therapies, as one aspect of health care. (See the discussion of "recovery therapies" in the chapter of this volume entitled "Twelve Step Programs.")

The language of science and scientific medicine carried with it a residue of antireligious rhetoric, that is, "the warfare between science and religion," that would have set the new enterprise apart from religion even had Sigmund Freud been the most pious of men. (Although, had he been the most pious of men, he would almost certainly not have been able to invent psychoanalysis.) This antagonism is part of a wider hostility against tradition and against the authority wielded by pre-Enlightenment institutions. Release from dependence upon such authority freed the scientist to hope for a better future in this world, upon this earth. This would be a future freed from the superstitions and artificial limits upon human knowledge that religion had imposed. Hopes that science would replace religion (a process referred to as "scientism" by we who no longer believe in it) or would at minimum refound religion upon rational, scientific grounds were part of this ideology.

This release carried inside it another, more hidden, aspect — a sense of loss. To be freed from the past was also to become aware that one had lost it and even to mourn for it. According to Peter Homans, inner awareness of this loss is the key to the origins of psychotherapy. An inward rupture from traditional interiorized patterns of meaning opened the self to new modes of self-understanding. This "analytic access" enlarged awareness and created new possibilities for remapping identity and revisioning the self.[2] This process of mourning and recovery acknowledges, as Jung did, that one no longer lives by any of the great myths of the past. Jung asked himself the question: "But what then is your myth — the myth in which you live?" He could find no direct answer to it.[3] Loss of religion, and estrangement from its ordering of inner life and its cosmic vision, lies at the heart of the psychotherapeutic ideology. With this loss comes the possibility that through psychotherapy one might discover or create a new "myth in which you live," an emergent, highly individualized, nontraditional spirituality. To an extent extremely difficult to measure, the enterprise of psychotherapy itself became the carrier of both mourning and myth, the forging of meanings as response to loss.

This quest sets psychotherapy squarely in the realm of meanings, of beliefs that persons live by, rather than in the realm of medicine or science. Psychotherapy attempts to answer the question posed by Jung, even in the midst of medically framed problems. Psychotherapies have not often used overtly religious language but have offered direct and indirect answers to concerns for meaning, purpose, and human fulfillment. Most frequently, therapists claim that what they actually do is not give answers but provide a special, liberating space where patients, clients, or participants work out their own answers to problems of meaning and learn for themselves how to find personal myths that are worth living.

In this chapter, I will bracket the scientific status of psychotherapies, although I acknowledge that this language remains intrinsic to their appeal. I will also ignore forms of therapy so intentionally restricted in scope, so bound to narrowly delineated problems (for example, hypnotherapy to relieve fear of driving at night), that they could hardly qualify as "myths in which one lives." Even this exclusion is misleading; some patients come seeking symptom relief, only to find that what they truly yearn for is a new myth and a transformed self. Psychotherapy even in its most inclusive and ambitious goals is a unique enterprise, neither exactly medicine nor exactly religion. To label it as a way to reorder profound inner experience or as a nontraditional spiritual path helps capture this in-betweenness and also helps account for its popularity.

Psychotherapy needs to be viewed in its cultural context: as an enterprise that could not have flourished in a traditionally ordered society and that belongs squarely to twentieth-century, urbanized, postindustrial life. Moreover, if one tries to imagine the latter minus all forms of psychotherapy and all theories of personality developed from psychotherapies, one discovers how far-reaching these enterprises have become. They are secular reorderings of inner life and self-understanding, in an era when religious frameworks no longer can be assured of universal acceptance. Even those persons who never have visited a therapist have been touched by psychoanalysis and its many offspring. Psychotherapeutic ideals and language have permeated education, industry, and religion, not to mention the arts and entertainment.[4] Our society minus this presence and influence of psychotherapies is all but unimaginable.

Carl Jung and Psychotherapeutic Spirituality

Virtually all of the above issues, except that of national health insurance coverage, can be found in the thought and work of Swiss psychiatrist Carl G. Jung (1875–1961). Moreover, Jung was explicitly preoccupied with the relations between his own psychotherapy and religion, a subject developed in essays such as "Psychotherapists or the Clergy."[5] Jung rather than Freud provides a paradigm for a "secular spirituality" flourishing within the psychotherapeutic framework. Jung himself was aware that this spirituality both resembles and differs from that of traditional forms of faith. Unfortunately, Jung is also unrepresentative precisely because of his closeness to these questions and his relative distance from the rhetoric of science and medicine. Jung uses analogies from science. He thought of himself as "phenomenological" rather than "metaphysical" and could assure his readers: "This point of view is the same as that of natural science."[6] But relatively few persons have been convinced by his claims, and the appeal of Jung's thought and therapy has not rested on them. Those who come to Jungian therapy are drawn to what analyst June Singer calls "the way of individuation" primarily because of its resonance with their personal experiences.[7]

The facts of Jung's professional biography are well known. He was raised the son of a Swiss Reformed pastor, completed his medical training as a psychiatrist, and took a position at a psychiatric hospital where he encountered a range of severely ill patients. He became interested in Freud's work in about 1907. For only about five years, he and Freud were allies, friends, and joint advocates of the psychoanalytic movement. Their relationship, which itself has been intensely studied and reinterpreted, ended abruptly and unhappily. After 1912, Jung on his own experienced a near-breakdown, from which he emerged with a set of new concepts and views on personal transformation. He founded his own school of psychotherapy (analytical psychology) and from 1918 until his death wrote and worked as a therapist with individual neurotic patients.

The inward facts of his life, or his retelling of his "personal myth," may be found in *Memories, Dreams, Reflections,* an introspective and highly selective spiritual autobiography he dictated to Aniela Jaffe at the end of his life. Although this autobiography has formed a rich source of information about Jung's development of his theories, its accounts of long-past events cannot be taken as ordinary historical memoirs. Rather, Jung uses the term *personal myth* to describe what he tries to communicate in this work.[8] Jung's primary vocational identity was as a psychotherapist, and it is through this identity that his spirituality or personal myth was expressed in his work and many of his writings (an essay about him appears in *Modern Esoteric Spiritualities,* volume 21 of the present series).[9] Like Freud, he saw himself as a doctor and identified with the medical model up to a point. However, having initially selected psychiatry, the least objective and most marginal of medical specialties at the time, he was prepared to jettison many of the presumptions of the medical framework. For Jung, psychiatry was a field "where the collusion of nature and spirit became a reality."[10]

Jung was prepared to see the relationship between doctor and patient as one between two human beings embarked upon a journey for meaning and wholeness. This was, indeed, the language he used, admitting as well that about one-third of his cases suffered "from no clinically definable neurosis, but from the senselessness and emptiness of their lives."[11] The success of psychotherapy thus cannot be defined by symptom relief or any other medically based measurement. The therapist works by offering these patients participation in a process of self-discovery and self-transformation. The name Jung gave this process is *individuation.*[12] Although not all therapy seekers are ready or able to undergo this process, Jung's teleological language is important: therapy has a positive goal. Individuation is more than relief from illness; it is health, a more integrated, fulfilled, and deeper way of being human. Images of wholeness and completeness abound in Jung's descriptions of this goal, in contrast to Freud's notoriously sparse and reluctant references to the positive aims of psychoanalysis.

In Jung's view, the psyche itself is purposeful, spontaneously pushing toward wholeness and the overcoming of oppositions. The psychological theory of individuation as a process of self-transformation combines conflict and fulfillment with consistency models of personality.[13] According to Jung, the psyche is split into two unequal halves or levels: the narrow upper stratum we know as consciousness and below that, the huge, mysterious, lower stratum of the unconscious. In turn, the unconscious is itself divided into a relatively narrow level of personal unconscious — repressed childhood memories and the like — and a remaining underlying objective or collective unconscious, whose contents are universal, primordial, and archetypal. Jung gives us, typically, an image for this deeper, older, and more inclusive psyche in relation to consciousness: "The latter could easily be compared to an island in the ocean. Whereas the island is small and narrow, the ocean is immensely wide and deep and contains a life infinitely surpassing, in kind and degree, anything known on the island."[14]

Put as simply as possible, Jung's theory states that human problems come about when these two parts of the psyche are out of touch and out of balance. Consciousness forgets that its roots lie in the unconscious and, when isolated, becomes sickly and stifling, arrogant and repressive. From this comes the pervasive feelings of senselessness and emptiness from which one-third of Jung's patients suffered. The specific neuroses that the rest manifest were themselves symptoms of this deeper split-off condition within the soul. Although these patients may initially have hoped only for symptom relief — for a return to life as they lived it before they became ill — the real solution for many required a journey into the ocean surrounding the island, an inner exploration that is, for consciousness, a quest for reunion with its lost roots. Using imagery of a mechanical balance, Jung expressed how individuation aims to integrate conscious and unconscious so as to result in a new, expanded totality of who one truly is. This, the self, Jung referred to as a new "midpoint" in the psyche, different from the previous pretentious equation of psyche and rational consciousness.

This inward journey toward wholeness and completeness is accomplished through a series of encounters with dreams, waking fantasies, artistic creations, and other manifestations of the hidden levels of the psyche. Although the therapist acts as guide and interpreter, the psyche is the source of energy and direction for this process. The therapist waits for the patient to come to inner knowledge of the realities of the unconscious psyche; individuation is not an externally programmed but an inwardly spontaneous process. There is no role for indoctrination on the therapist's part, and any suggestion made to the patient will be ignored (Jung believed) unless the patient is in accord with it anyway.[15] Nature, the psyche as transpersonal source of strength and wisdom, is the real agent at work behind the patient's transformation.[16] The presence of another human being, the therapist, is necessary in practice, but in theory Jung's psychology of personal healing does not focus upon the interpersonal situation of therapy itself. That may be due either to the medical model where each patient is dealt with as an isolated atom or to the fact that Jung's own encounter with the unconscious was done without a human therapist to guide him. (At least, this is so according to the account in *Memories, Dreams, Reflections.*)

There is, however, a real sense of encounter throughout Jung's descriptions of individuation as a journey. It is a journey through an inner landscape filled with a variety of personified figures, for whom Jung coined names: the persona, or social mask; the shadow; the anima and animus; the divine child, the mana personality, the wise old man, and the wise old woman; and, finally, the impersonal mandala that symbolizes the archetype of the self. Who are all these figures? They symbolize various aspects of the unconscious, becoming its voices so that the patient can recognize in them powers of nature and spirit beyond the ordinary self. They are other; they are numinous and strange and not (in Jung's theory) to be equated with the personal memories of, say, parental figures from childhood.[17] By personifying them and treating them as if real, the conscious ego is finally doing them justice. By considering them as other, the ego also protects itself against direct identification with them, a danger Jung labels "inflation." For these collective figures are (like the ocean in relation to the island) huge, mysterious, and very definitely not the ego's personal possession. Under their spell, consciousness can drown. The goal is to establish a relationship of balance that avoids either repression or inflation, a relationship where the power of these figures is truly made available to the ego such that a more creative psychic functioning results.

Jung firmly believed that these archetypal figures haunt the world's mythologies and religions, for the unconscious is the primordial storehouse for all humans' numinous images. While in the past these contents were simply projected by the psyche and apprehended as external, now they are recognized as essentially internal, although still not the creation of the conscious ego. Even Jesus Christ may now be known not as an external historical savior figure but as "archetype of the Self," an instance of a general category of symbols for wholeness and the union of opposites.[18] All figures of religion and mythology express an archetypal pattern, and, understood in this way, they become psychically accessible to modern persons. In this view, connections between myth and ritual, myth and doctrine, and myth and particular cultural ideologies are obscured. As a result, Jung's use of the term *myth* has captured the imagination of many persons in search of spiritual moorings apart from these phenomena.

Jung's claim, whatever its value for the study of mythology, has two important consequences for Jungian psychotherapy. First, the therapist, as an interpreter, becomes of necessity an interpreter not just of symptoms but of myths; he or she must learn to link the archetypal contents of patients' dreams with corresponding contents from these other, seemingly remote, sources. Second, even the most secular, antireligious Jungian patient ultimately recognizes that he or she shares archetypal contents with *homo religiosus,* human beings as mythmakers. At this level, there can be no truly secular psyche, and any distinction between religious and secular spiritual paths vanishes. The contents of any and all are identical: the archetypes of the collective unconscious are timeless and universal, changing only in outward appearance. The "way of individuation" points toward the same underlying realities as originally shaped the world's great mythologies and religions.

Why, then, shouldn't the person who suffers from meaninglessness simply consult the clergy, that is, return to a religious tradition where the archetypal contents of the psyche are present and visible, even if not grasped as essentially psychic? If reconnection with this level of unconscious collective imagery is what heals, why doesn't religion offer a surer, more time-tested pathway to healing? Jung's direct treatment of these questions shows how well he was aware that his style of psychotherapy, at least, functioned in close competition with religious spiritualities. He did not defend it solely on the appeal to its links with natural science.

Instead, he argues that psychotherapy does not compete with religion precisely because the persons who choose psychotherapy are already alienated from clergy, theology, and religion. Why has this happened? Because the clergy — and the religious traditions they represent — have themselves become estranged from the true sources of their own spiritual authority and power. Detached from archetypal realities and mistakenly focused on systems of doctrine, religious traditions have nothing to offer suffering human beings.[19] In the famous essay "Psychotherapists or the Clergy" this position serves as a classic manifesto on behalf of psychotherapeutic spirituality. Psychotherapists do not steal parishioners away from churches or undermine religion's authority. They help persons already lost to the church and antagonized by its authority find their way back to some positive relation to those numinous spiritual realities of which religion's representatives had proved themselves unworthy custodians. This is a distinctively Jungian answer since it depends upon Jung's equation of archetypes with religious realities. To encounter the archetype of the self is a new way to relate to the mythic reality of Jesus Christ — as a living interior presence that calls us to live our own lives rather than imitate his.[20] This, Jung believed, is not only a harder but a worthier task than the one religions have taught.

What completes individuation is death — not in the sense that death comes from outside and interrupts it but rather in the sense that this spiritual transformation is what prepares us to die. Jung often wrote that individuation, his unique formulation of psychotherapy's goal, was appropriate for those in "the second half of life," while those younger needed a method closer to Freud's that would free them from childhood conflicts in order for them to build a stable adult identity.[21] We may follow June Singer, a contemporary Jungian, and make this chronological split less literal. Jung aimed for a spirituality that would anticipate the process of surrender that dying requires.[22] Just as the ego consciousness must yield to the emergent new center, the self, so the person approaching death must be prepared to surrender all that has been gained in individuality, in living through to one's deepest roots and possibilities. In this way, Jung's psychotherapy as secular spirituality replaces one of the classical functions of religious faith. Though it offers no deliverance from death, it helps us gain the wisdom to die well.

Jung's psychology, his ideas about archetypes, religion, and so on, have all been subject to intense criticism and debate. I have selected him as a central and foundational figure for a presentation of psychotherapeutic spirituality because almost every therapy that intends to be a spirituality, or even indirectly points in a spiritual direction, either derives from Jung's approach or unwittingly repeats his answers to the questions such a secular spiritual quest raises. Rather than review all of these, I now turn to a motif of this spirituality that Jung himself admitted was central, but for which his psychological theory itself does not account: the attitude of the therapist and the moral ethos of therapy as practice.[23]

Acceptance: The Psychotherapist's Stance

In the same essay in which he castigates clergy for having lost interest in the psychic roots of religious experience, Jung notes how the therapist's stance toward the patient is radically different from that associated with clergy who take an interest in human problems. The therapists' method denies them the use of moral exhortation and preaching to get results, but their distance from codified moral pronouncements is a great advantage. The therapist does not represent an institution that is identified by patients with such a moral code. Therapy is not an amoral situation at all, but it must begin with reality rather than moral dictums: "But if the doctor wishes to help a human being he must be able to accept him as he is. And he can do this in reality only when he has already seen and accepted himself as he is."[24]

This simple principle is Jung's version of a theme that pervades virtually all of the literature on psychotherapy: the stance of the therapist should be one of acceptance. Other terms used are: *empathic, nonjudgmental,* and *displaying unconditional positive regard.* These are not to be equated with approval of particular actions and attitudes. Neither the intrapsychic balance imagery nor the aim of inward fulfillment in Jung's psychological theory really accounts for this vital role of an empathic, trustworthy, and accepting companion. Moreover, theories of psychotherapy very different from Jung's are just as insistent that the therapist must accept the patient and can do so only insofar as the therapist has reached a high level of self-acceptance.

This motif of acceptance has come to function as a kind of hallmark in psychotherapeutic writings and in the wider culture as well. It does not mean that therapists and therapies passively acquiesce to the status quo. Because of its historical link to the medical model, psychotherapy could for decades claim value neutrality — nonendorsement of any particular ethical, social, or political position. This claim no longer appears credible; therapists want their patients or clients to develop in certain ways, to become certain kinds of persons, to grow out of certain behaviors and attitudes. Moreover, virtually all theories of personality used by therapists include certain normative beliefs about human beings, on topics as varied as gender roles, emotions, work, and religion. Because of this, there can be no value-free therapy, nor should there be. True, the therapist is not like the clergy in representing the values of a wider institution, but he or she is under obligation to be honest that some set of values is being conveyed within the practice of therapy. Therapy is itself an enterprise that carries its own ethical meanings.

If *acceptance* is the key term that emerges again and again in any discussion of the psychotherapeutic relationship, what does it include? Acceptance of self and others is possible only through awareness, a stance that willingly and deliberately attends to one's own psychic contents. This requires both courage and honesty. Although Jung insists that the unconscious functions as a treasure house, and not merely as a garbage heap, to acknowledge one's shadow, one's previously rejected qualities that are nevertheless truly there within one's self, is a frightening task that the vast majority of persons manage to avoid throughout their lives. The therapist is one who has faced this task and who has overcome cowardice and laziness as well as the world's scorn for those who take interior, psychic reality seriously. The courage and honesty Jung showed appeared in his willingness to listen and learn from his own shadow. Acceptance began here; when he had accepted the interior unconscious of others, he became prepared to accept the ordinary human Other — his patient who came to him for help. Therapeutic acceptance models for patients what they should learn to love and accept themselves.

Other therapists have written eloquently and poignantly about what it is like to practice psychotherapies. Works such as Theodor Reik's *Listening with the Third Ear*, June Singer's *Boundaries of the Soul*, Irvin Yalom's *Love's Executioner*, and Scott Peck's *The Road Less Traveled* convey to the rest of us not only what psychotherapists do but who they are and how they see themselves and their patients. These best-selling accounts collectively portray a psychotherapeutic spirituality from the perspective of the therapist wherein intense and exhausting listening is the principle activity. Acceptance and empathy are balanced by a commitment to scrutinize not only what one hears but one's own emotional response to it: again and again, therapists portray themselves as dedicated to this difficult-to-maintain ideal. They cannot resort to preaching, and they cannot show repugnance. Either of these traditional moral responses would destroy the fragile relationship with the patient. Nor can they become the latter's lover, parent, or savior; none of these roles is compatible with true therapeutic acceptance, for all exploit the patient's vulnerability for the sake of the therapist's own needs. Almost all public scandals involving psychotherapists center on violations of this ideal. Heightened awareness of therapeutic malpractice paradoxically reveals how seriously this idealized stance is taken by the public in its understanding of psychotherapy. Unfortunately, some of these scandals have reinforced a view of the patient as a passive, helpless victim rather than as an active collaborator in a relationship aimed at wholeness and empowerment.

Psychotherapy from this point of view is an example of what Alasdair

MacIntyre calls a "practice."[25] In any practice, truthfulness, courage, humility, and justice are intrinsic to its success.[26] I have already noted the direct role allocated to honesty and courage in psychotherapy. Humility — the willingness to renounce one's own fantasies of omnipotence and perfection — complements them. What MacIntyre calls justice or fairness means that the rules and standards of the practice must be the same for all, a principle that admittedly fits best with attempts to perfect a physical skill or with the playing of games. (Without this fairness, no honest assessment of one's flaws and failures is possible.) In psychotherapy, although therapists do not share personal information reciprocally with patients, they should be capable of admitting mistakes and misjudgments, dealing with themselves as honestly as possible. Put this way, it appears paradoxical that psychotherapy draws upon character strengths or virtues that the patient or client may barely possess. However, even to begin therapy, rather than continue trying to cope with one's problems single-handedly or run away from them, demands courage, honesty, and humility. Once this moral language is brought fully to awareness, one wonders what separates it from the religious realm of moral perfectionism. Shouldn't therapy be for those who *lack* these virtues and need to develop them, rather than for those who already possess them? Although it is hoped that therapists themselves have these already, how does the patient appropriate them?[27]

Therapeutic acceptance reminds us that the stance of the therapist is not that of the moralist, let alone that of the athletic coach. By accepting the patient as a person, the therapist mitigates the moral demands built into the nature of practice as MacIntyre defines this. Trust, acceptance, and a nonjudgmental stance: these and other expressions convey that even the most cowardly, dishonest, sneaky, and uncooperative patient is still fundamentally somehow valuable, worthy of attention. When the patient begins to share this sense of self-worth, then and only then can transformation occur. Although to engage in any practice, certain virtues must already be present, these same virtues can be taught; in therapy, emphasis falls on the human mutuality and trust that a model such as MacIntyre's already presupposes.

Admittedly, Jung and other therapists after him have walked a tightrope on these questions. Do therapists have a positive ethic beyond acceptance? Obviously, yes, insofar as honesty, courage, and other traits are intrinsic to their practice; and, yes, insofar as their theories convey images of the fulfilled, the good, the successful, and the wise. Equally, psychotherapy discounts certain other traditional virtues. For instance, nowhere are purity, chastity, and righteous indignation therapeutic virtues, nor does reaching perfection appear as a valid therapeutic goal. Most frequently, therapists find their patients already suffer from the disastrous effects of such virtues (or their distorted counterfeits such as prudishness, hypocrisy, and vindictiveness). Whether acceptance is by itself adequate as a comprehensive ethical vision, meant to substitute for all other norms, is another question. Outside the therapy context, its effects may be more ambivalent.

Jung and other therapists convey the moral seriousness of their vocation as healers of the psyche. Individuation, in their eyes, is far more difficult as a human task than are most external achievements rewarded by society. To confront the unconscious honestly; to integrate its contents within one's self without being "inflated" or overwhelmed by them; to pursue wholeness, even while letting go of fantasies of perfection; to attend to interior life amid a society that devalues it: each and every one of these goals was upheld by Jung and his fellow therapists as worth pursuing devotedly. The situation of therapy is one in which these important aims can be cultivated, even if Jung's own theory of personality places responsibility for the ultimate transformation upon the unconscious or nature, which are transpersonal forces outside the ego.

Seen as an intense, two-person relationship aimed at spiritual transformation, the psychotherapeutic situation recently has been compared to and sometimes amalgamated into the traditional religious situation of spiritual direction. Perhaps the resurgence of interest in spiritual direction is the result of psychotherapy and its impact upon religion, at least in North America. As with psychotherapy, the relationship between spiritual director and directee is intense and assumes a high level of motivation on the part of the directee, as well as a distinctive sense of vocation on the part of the director. Parallels and differences between the two types of relationship are explored in Gerald May's *Care of Mind, Care of Spirit.* Mary Wolff-Salin's *No Other Light* examines Jungian therapy in relation to the Carmelite tradition of spiritual direction in the Roman Catholic Church. Although acceptance plays a role in spiritual direction, the fact remains that the latter finds its niche within wider religious institutions and their theological, ethical, and liturgical frameworks. The spiritual director and the directee both share the goal of interiorizing the ultimate ideals and meanings of that religion. Right relation with God, constant awareness of the divine presence in one's life, and reliance upon divine guidance: these explicit goals may leave much room for psychological concerns and for the therapist's stance as discussed here. Such goals, however, frame the activity of spiritual direction in a manner that relativizes therapeutic values. Holiness, purity of heart, and love of God supersede therapeutic acceptance without negating it. I believe that this, and not some innate interior dichotomy between psyche and spirit, is what distinguishes these two practices.[28]

It may not matter to therapy patients that the images in their dreams are the same as those of ancient myths. It matters quite a bit if the therapist's disclaimer that he or she relies upon suggestion can successfully be challenged. The influence of therapy over patients' inner lives, and even the content of their dreams, continues to be a subject of contention. Jerome Frank (first writing in 1961) views all psychotherapy as "persuasion" and finds therapists naive if they deny this. Recent scandals over recovery of repressed memories in the context of therapy have added fuel to this particular charge. Even dreams are subject to such influences, reshaped by the patient/dreamers to meet the expectations of their therapists.[29] Although nature, the collective unconscious, or some other transpersonal force may still be finally responsible for powerful spiritual transformation, the therapist as persuader, as instructor, and active guide should not be minimized. Therapeutic acceptance is not so evenly and uncritically distributed as Jung and others insisted.

A Patient's Story: Therapy as Spiritual Journey

But what of the patients' perspective? Are patients so persuaded by therapists — as Jerome Frank believes — that they automatically and uncritically adopt the viewpoints of their therapists? Do patients, whose identities as psychotherapy patients are hopefully not primary, nevertheless interiorize psychotherapy's spirituality as they are initiated into its practice? In short, what does the practice of psychotherapy feel like from the point of view of people for whom it is presumably designed? Can a look at patients' perspectives also shed light on ways in which the therapy can go wrong and become a destructive spiritual path, a negative experience for both parties?

In *Fight against Fears,* a book that became a best-seller, journalist Lucy Freeman tells the story of her long, psychoanalytically oriented psychotherapy. Published in 1951, this fascinating narrative documents a secular spiritual journey and reveals both the centrality of the therapeutic stance of acceptance, honesty, courage, and humility and the less obvious (at the time, at least) role of persuasion in the process. Lucy Freeman's therapist was a Freudian, not a Jungian, so the content of their sessions focused on her childhood, her feelings toward her family, her repressed sexuality, and even her constipation. Her portrait of herself, her reasons for coming to therapy, and her mistakes made along the way nevertheless share many features with the therapeutic process as Jung describes it. *Fight against Fears* is an illuminating document of how a practice feels to one who learns it and how participation in psychotherapy can become a secular spirituality, almost in spite of the explicit emphases of the therapist.

Ms. Freeman suffered acute physical symptoms, such as sinusitis and difficulty breathing, for which there was no discoverable physical cause. She agreed to see a psychotherapist only as a measure of last resort. She came to the therapist and deliberately minimized his medical status by calling him "John" and not "Doctor," yet she views this, in retrospect, as itself a symptom, since he was clearly a medical expert. The story of their relationship is told in terms of her gradually increasing ability to trust him with her thoughts, feelings, and memories as she experiences his acceptance of her as a person. Again and again, she tested him. Trust began when she admitted to him that she hated her mother and started to cry. Her nasal congestion was immediately relieved: "For the 'truth' he kept urging me to face could simmer out only as faith in him mounted. Because he had relieved pain I started to trust him — as an animal, whose wounds have been cleansed, licks the hand of the healer."[30] Even to speak the truth was itself an act of trust.

Most of Ms. Freeman's therapy was a matter not of dramatic symptom relief but of agonizing confrontation with her own fears, hatreds, and evasions. The point she repeatedly makes is that psychotherapy is not an escape from life's problems, nor is the quality of attention to one's experiences it demands anything like ordinary self-centeredness or selfishness. She had always found herself hateful and unlovable; to face these fears and find that they represented partial truths took great courage. Only after this step could she also see that they were but *partial* truths. Fears made conscious, and faced directly, lost their power over her. Even the humorous chapter titles reveal how grim this slow journey felt: "Meaning of a Tear," "Double-crossed by Dreams," "Murder Starts at Home," and "Death in Small Doses" are a sample. Although at the end she feels freer — "The Fear Ebbs" and "The Answer" are later chapter titles — that answer is itself a poignant plea for the value of trust and acceptance rather than a triumphant claim to have been cured by psychoanalysis.[31]

Nevertheless, the role of the therapist as persuader, as the one who suggests topics and makes interpretations, looms large to any reader of *Fight against Fears.* This is particularly blatant in the therapist's uncritical advocacy of what today look like destructive gender stereotypes. Ms. Freeman's career as a journalist is mercilessly interpreted away as a fight against femininity, and her wit with words is a symptom, not a strength.[32] As an unmarried woman, she is automatically in flight from men, sex, and true womanhood. These and other judgments she receives and appropriates. At this level, there is no doubt that acceptance did not extend to the borders of what were considered legitimate alternative options for women at the time.

Is Ms. Freeman's account an instance of secular spirituality? Significantly, there is very, very little about religion directly, and yet she insists that "analysis gave me what feeling I possess for religion." She writes: " 'Spiritual — it's a lovely word,' I said to John one day. 'Funny, it never meant anything before I came here.' I had been too busy fighting inner devils to give much thought to the reality of spirituality."[33] We learn little about what she means here by *spiritual* or *spirituality.* However, this dimension of her transformation may represent a challenge to Frank's persuasion thesis; the therapist does not suggest this budding interest in spirituality, nor does he directly encourage it. It appears as a spontaneous outgrowth of her slow victory over "inner devils."

In contrast to this, her therapist's own secular, psychotherapeutic faith is directly communicated to her in words that sound familiar given Jung's vision of therapy and its aims: "John's feeling for nature bordered on reverence. When I asked him what he meant by nature, he said, 'Nature is growth or God or whatever you want to call it.' "[34] Nature, growth, or God — like the collective unconscious — is larger than human egos, a wider, more ultimate reality within which human life finds its meanings and fulfillment. If we are out of harmony with this force, we suffer. Nature itself tries to compensate for our imbalances.[35] John's philosophy becomes his patient's, gradually and less blatantly than do his assumptions about gender, but securely nevertheless. What both share is this framework within which they understand her struggles for truth and freedom, their relationship of acceptance and trust, and their hopes for self-transformation. That no explicit need is felt for a clearer definition of this force does not mean that *reverence* is the wrong word for their attitude toward it. Here, in the midst of a psychotherapy much more clearly secular than Jung's, is the outer face of spirituality in which the cosmos becomes "an intentional object of thought and feeling." The inner face of spirituality, the quest to live out of "one's most enduring and vital self," was never in doubt.

Growth, Wholeness, Fulfillment: Encounter Groups and Self-Help

As the social situation of psychotherapy changed from that experienced by both Jung and Lucy Freeman, certain key themes became more prominent while other motifs slipped away. As mentioned earlier, the transformation of psychotherapy involved certain moves away from the medical model, so that individual, long-term, intense therapy by a medical doctor no longer dominated the practice. In the earlier phase of this transition, individual therapy was shortened and opened up to nonmedical practitioners who, as counselors, took clients rather than patients. The other two steps were the substitution of the small group setting for individual therapy and the rise of therapy-like groups for those whose explicit reason for joining was growth, not relief from illness. Recalling how Jung, even back in 1933, found that fully one-third of his patients had no clinical neurosis or symptoms, we may see the roots of the encounter group movement of the 1960s and 1970s already present. The self-selected population drawn to psychotherapy felt free to ignore the medical dimension of its claims by seeking it out as a remedy to nonmedical, existential problems of meaning. Finally, the rise of psychotherapeutic how-to books, the popular literature identified as "self-help" in bookstores, reveals how even the presence of a living human therapist could be dispensed with, as reading a book and following its advice became a possible substitute (in spite of the warning by almost all authors of such works that they are *not* an automatic replacement for therapy in all cases).

These changes have brought some experience of psychotherapy or its derivatives to a much wider population than Jung had ever imagined. At the same time, they challenged and redefined some of the central motifs of what we have called psychotherapeutic spirituality. Not only was the medical model left further behind, but the sense of trust and acceptance was partially relocated. No longer were therapists themselves the object of trust; the group itself took on this role. Again and again, the willingness of group members to share secrets, to support one another, and to break down barriers of isolation surfaces in accounts of therapy groups and their spin-offs. Moreover, a shift occurs in the manner in which the healing energies of nature or the unconscious are transmitted and experienced.

The movement to substitute growth for therapy as the explicit goal of such groups arose out of several sources other than individual psychotherapy, as recorded in Kurt Back's history, *Beyond Words.*[36] Allied with certain therapeutic themes, what became the encounter group flourished in the late 1960s and early 1970s. Although as a movement this proved short-lived, as a new social format for doing a variety of therapies and spiritual practices, it continues to exist in more subdued forms today. One relatively sympathetic contemporary interpreter compared such groups to those of the left wing of the Protestant Reformation.[37] Enthusiastic advocacy and lurid exhibitionistic activities ran rampant. Because many such groups eschewed the task of therapy, it became even more difficult to evaluate the grandiose claims made for them. Questions about who should lead groups, and how, and whether the experience of participation in a group was potentially dangerous for some persons took careful and controlled research to answer.[38] Retrospectively, we may ask why and how such groups could become — as their advocates undoubtedly felt them to be — a secular spiritual path.

The answer lies in the way a group became a "liminal space," to use anthropologist Victor Turner's phrase: a place where ordinary social boundaries and hierarchies are left behind. This is replaced by a sense of freedom and *communitas,* a heightened sense of power, love, and "merging" with other group members.[39] To many, this experience by itself was therapeutic and was worth seeking out, regardless of what their group did or did not accomplish beyond it. The appeal of encounter groups rested upon this sense of *communitas,* which could be established very quickly, unlike the trust that Ms. Freeman wrote of, trust in another, specific, very separate human doctor. It arose almost no matter who the specific participants were; ironically, the individual personalities of members became almost irrelevant and interchangeable.

This group process thus shares with all forms of psychotherapy a sense of being accepted, a sense of trust that one will be heard and valued as a person, even when in other contexts one would be judged and condemned. Kurt Back, the historian of encounter groups, wonders what, if any, personal revelation a group might not be able to tolerate and actually try to reject; he wryly concludes that his own confession of collecting material for a research study approached the limit![40] In this author's unforgettable experience, a group heard and accepted one member's confession of manslaughter committed many years before and never detected or punished. Although theorists of group process explain the regularity of such *communitas* experiences by showing how the group exists as an entity with a life of its own, the psychologies most often invoked by advocates of encounter groups were individualistic, as much so as those of Jung.

Encounter groups held up the explicit goal of growth, a development of one's inner potential, in language directly parallel to that in our definition of the inner face of spirituality. This goal rests on a fulfillment model of the psyche, not a balance model such as that advocated by Lucy Freeman's therapist, although the term *growth* included some sense of integration, of pulling together into a whole what had previously been fragmented. Unlike *balance*, *growth* significantly expressed the positive expectations of participants or would-be participants. The language of growth, development, and potentials, as heard and used within this context, may be one of the classic instances of "glow" words that are, in the final analysis, all but impossible to define.[41] Moreover, as the title of Back's history, *Be-*

yond Words, indicates, the desire for careful definitions and concepts was inimical to the spirit of the movement.

Growth is, however, both a natural process and something one can strive for and intentionally pursue; thus, this language preserved the paradoxical quality that Jung far more carefully noted in his accounts of psychotherapy's goal and the individual process. Growth requires that one face frightening and shameful experiences, whether through dream interpretation or some other method. It will not just simply happen; it can and most often is blocked by the person's own fears and society's repression. Moreover, although the physical growth of organisms provides the model for this metaphor, the use of organic imagery is highly selective; growth, never decay, is the aim of psychic life. Critics of encounter groups noted that in contrast to individuation, which is difficult, private, and takes a long-term effort, the promises of growth that flourished within the group movement made this goal sound quick and easy.

This charge relates to the compressed time frame of these groups, relative to even short-term individual therapy. The dramatic sense of *communitas* could be experienced within the group setting by the end of a long weekend. In fact, the weekend-workshop format became uniquely convenient, permitting the liminality of the group experience without too much disruption of one's ordinary schedule. Perhaps part of the reason for the popularity of this format is that although trust could be established during the abbreviated time frame, the assumption is that none of the participants would ever have to see each other again after the weekend ended. Recall that the goal of encounter groups is defined individualistically, as personal growth. The group itself existed to help individuals grow, and as a group it disbanded on schedule. Whatever changes individuals experienced from their participation were carried with them each on his or her separate pathway through life. This expectation of future separation, and the ethos of extreme individualism and disinclination for follow-up, was well summarized by the widely quoted statement by Fritz Perls ("The Gestalt Prayer"):

> I do my thing and you do your thing.
> I am not in this world to live up to your expectations.
> And you are not in this world to live up to mine.
> You are you and I am I.
> And if by chance we find each other, it's beautiful.
> If not, it can't be helped.[42]

Very often, however, the "you" and the "I" met again at the next encounter group. Weekend workshops attracted regulars, persons for whom repeated participation became a way of life.

This pattern reveals one of the dilemmas of psychotherapeutic spirituality, for in a sense those whose reason to participate in it lies in "the senselessness and emptiness of their lives" desire and require a new way of life. Psychotherapy as medically based activity oriented toward cure for illness and its symptoms cannot by itself promise or provide this. Encounter groups and weekend workshops abandoned the medical framework but intensified the ambiguity precisely insofar as their stated goals seemed to speak far more directly to the implicit yearnings of their participants. The groups themselves were never intended to become a way a life for anyone, but because after the weekend no follow-up or additional meetings were usually held, the participants struggled alone to integrate the group experiences into their previous lives. The intense *communitas* of such groups drew many participants back. Lack of follow-up and a tendency to assume that only positive changes occur were and remain major flaws in this format, whether the short-lived groups are secular or under the framework of a religious tradition. Psychotherapists and pastoral counselors often complain bitterly that they are the ones left to pick up the pieces after bad experiences, while the group leaders are already unavailable and on the road preparing for their next workshop. The "It can't be helped" of Perls's "prayer" becomes a disclaimer of future responsibilities. Perhaps the voluminous self-help literature written by psychotherapists for popular audiences is the final, logical step in the democratization of psychotherapeutic spirituality and in its adaptation to contemporary styles of identity. Perhaps this literature is also a response to the above-mentioned dilemma of a need for practical guidance rather than solely intense *communitas* experiences. Basically, self-help providers offer those who suffer from senseless and empty lives ways to change themselves by revisioning their own possibilities and implementing new patterns of feeling and action. Self-help as a genre is not a contemporary invention (the *Ars Moriendi* literature of the late Middle Ages is an example from the past); yet today it popularizes psychotherapeutic ideas and values. Self-help programs may rely upon Jungian psychological theory or upon any of the fulfillment theories that fueled the growth groups discussed above. In order to accomplish its goal, self-help literature must emphasize the steps readers can take at home to interpret their dreams, face their shadows, integrate their anima or animus, and discover their real selves. This literature employs second-person, inspirational language and thus through its rhetoric substitutes the dialogue between the author's "I" and the reader's "you" for the lived encounter between therapist and patient.

This substitution is very questionable given the massive agreement that acceptance by another human being or group of human beings is a prerequisite for change. How can reading a book ever accomplish this? Do trust and acceptance play no role in self-help? Occasionally, one finds claims that trusting the author's advice is all that counts, but successful self-help literature usually invokes nature or the unconscious or the real self as the true object to be trusted. To accept oneself is to recognize that within one's self lies a power that is ultimately trustworthy. Once again, naming this power accurately is much less important than listening to it with a receptive, reverent attitude.[43] The person of the therapist is not, even Jung agreed, the source of true change, and so it can be removed from the situation as "you become your own therapist" (in the cliché of self-help).

However, the technique-like quality that permeates much self-help literature has seemed the very opposite of the genuine receptivity and reverent sense of mystery that are intrinsically linked with spirituality. When Jung wrote about the unconscious, and Lucy Freeman's therapist spoke with reverence about nature, they cleared a space for powers beyond the human ego to manifest themselves. Their quests were placed within a wider context of acknowledging a whole, a cosmos, whose power was ultimately trustworthy and transcended the self. Surrender by consciousness of its monopolistic claim to psychic life and power requires letting go of one's sense of control. In contrast, the stance of almost all self-help literature is relentlessly activist. Mastering ten steps to making the most of your dreams is not an act of surrender, but of extending ego-control. Although increased control over one's life is obviously a goal of psychotherapy, this goal is to be pursued within a human situation that requires humility as well as honesty and courage, relinquishing one's faith that one can make it unaided. Self-help shifts this balance, persuading readers that they contain within themselves the resources for solving their problems and providing techniques to evoke and apply these resources. Unlike the disciplines of traditional spiritual life (prayer, fasting, and so on), the promise inherent in the self-help genre is that you, yourself, take charge of the whole process. For example, self-help literature on the interpretation of dreams allows that dreams are mysterious, sometimes awesome, but puts the emphasis on rational methods to record and interpret them.[44] Danger arises when this literature promises us we can control our dreams in ten easy steps and so learn to control our lives. These promises are extravagant assurances of quick success, happiness, and power.

Psychotherapy as Secular Spirituality: Questions

Various secular practices may or may not be intrinsically worthwhile on their original terms. It is a separate question whether they are suitable vehicles for the spiritual quest. For instance, one might assume that psychotherapy is a legitimate activity and then ask if its aims are distorted when it becomes the context for spirituality. Such questions have been raised so frequently that we should try to respond to them. Challenges have come both from those who question the actual efficacy of therapies and from those who allow them validity as techniques for handling delimited problems but not as solutions to senseless and empty lives. The first challenge is that, for all their claims to bring healing and growth, psychotherapies have not been able to produce statistical evidence to demonstrate these effects. Instead, they have produced testimonials and conversion narratives of which *Fight against Fears* is a vivid example. Even if some therapies do work for some individuals, there is no guarantee that they work because the psychological theories that support them are true (this is Frank's point). Moreover, psychotherapies such as Jung's and many later ones seem to become ever more inclusive as to the range of patients and conditions they are willing to treat (especially when the goal is altered so as to encompass growth). Creating more need for themselves rather than less, psychotherapies lie so far outside medicine that they should relinquish once and for all their association with it. This line of argument then feeds into the second challenge.

Allowing that the primary function of psychotherapies is not medicine but a new framework for ordering interiority, for interpreting life's meanings and each person's role in the cosmos (in short, allowing that they lay claim to being spiritualities in the sense used in this volume), are they truly adequate even here? To say that something claims to offer deliverance from the senselessness and emptiness of life or hopes to become a new personal myth for persons who lack connection to the great myths of the past does not mean that it will be worthy of this function and live up to this promise. Moreover, even Jung recommended that those who could, should explore their own religious traditions rather than automatically assume that psychotherapy could help them.

To the degree that psychotherapy directly promises that it is spirituality and not medicine, it also becomes particularly vulnerable to critics who find it a new religion, in many ways as obnoxious as the older ones Jung's patients had already rejected. The many schools of therapies exist with their own priests, dogmas, and rites. Early on, their treatment of dissidents and innovators appeared to repeat religion's schism into orthodox and heretical believers. Meanwhile, religious critics judging it from the standpoint of their own traditions often reject it as ersatz, inferior religion — idolatrous "self-worship" pursued by those who would do better to return to Judaism or Christianity.[45] More fundamentally, to the extent that advocates of psychotherapies sound like advocates of a traditional religion, mirroring the rhetoric of religious conviction, they lose persuasive power because psychotherapy is supposed to be different in stance and style from religion even when its tie with the medical model is gone. The Jungian who, in response to the question "Why should we trust the collective unconscious?" replied serenely, "You must just have faith," forfeited a large measure of credibility. If psychotherapy is to work as a secular alternative to traditional religious spiritualities, it must deal more convincingly with this problem.

The oddness of the niche psychotherapies have carved for themselves remains. Since another option would be to develop new, nontraditional, but distinctively religious spiritualities, an argument must be made for the continuing *secular* nature of psychotherapy as the locus of a spiritual quest. It is not enough to point out that many contemporary persons are uninterested or repulsed by religion and that psychological theories fill this vacancy in their lives. Not only does this argument bypass entirely the truth of any of the psychological theories, but it leaves their ultimate philosophical claims unexamined, along with the basis of their authority. Hence the appeal to faith reemerges, at times in embarrassingly naive forms. True, a new framework for one's inner life and aspirations is offered, but the dilemma remains. As central as psychotherapy is in our society, as influential as it has become as a practice, its status and placing are problematic. It is not religion, certainly not medicine — but perhaps in its in-betweenness lies its promise and its appeal.

Notes

1. See the introduction to the present volume.
2. Peter Homans, *The Ability to Mourn: Disillusionment and the Social Origins of Psychoanalysis* (Chicago: University of Chicago Press, 1989), 127.
3. Carl G. Jung, *Memories, Dreams, Reflections,* recorded and ed. Aniela Jaffe (New York: Random House, 1963), 171.
4. Psychotherapy closely identifies with the language labeled "expressive individualism" by Robert Bellah and associates. This discourse has become the "first language" of most middle-class Americans. Because of this, Bellah turned upon psychotherapists as the chief culprits in his critique of this language's inadequacies. See Robert N. Bellah et al., *Habits of the Heart: Individualism and Commitment in American Life* (Berkeley: University of California Press, 1985), 47–48.
5. The essay is in Carl G. Jung, *Modern Man in Search of a Soul,* trans. W. S. Dell and Cary F. Baynes (New York: Harcourt, Brace and Co., 1939).
6. Carl G. Jung, "Psychology and Religion," in *Psychology and Religion: West and East,* vol. 11 of *The Collected Works,* 2d ed. (Princeton, N.J.: Princeton University Press, 1972), 5.

7. June Singer, *Boundaries of the Soul: The Practice of Jung's Psychology* (Garden City, N.Y.: Anchor, 1973), xii.

8. Jung, *Memories, Dreams, Reflections*, 3.

9. Gerhard Wehr, "C. G. Jung in the Context of Christian Esotericism and Cultural History," in *Modern Esoteric Spirituality*, ed. Antoine Faivre and Jacob Needleman, World Spirituality 21 (New York: Crossroad, 1992), 381–99.

10. Jung, *Memories, Dreams, Reflections*, 109.

11. Jung, *Modern Man in Search of a Soul*, 61.

12. Carl G. Jung, "The Relations between the Ego and the Unconscious," in *Two Essays on Analytical Psychology*, vol. 7 of *The Collected Works* (Princeton, N.J.: Princeton University Press, 1969), pt. 2.

13. Salvatore R. Maddi, *Personality Theories: A Comparative Analysis*, rev. ed. (Homewood, Ill.: Dorsey, 1972), 66–84. Maddi, who treats Jung under the "conflict" category, admits this is inadequate. Don S. Browning (*Religious Thought and the Modern Psychologies: Critical Conversation in the Theology of Culture* [Philadelphia: Fortress, 1987], 180) views Jung as an extremely complex version of the fulfillment or self-actualization model. The difficulties these two thinkers have classifying Jung are partly due to Jung's own obscurity. However, it may also be that in America, Jung's conflict and balance (consistency) language became less important than his individuation and fulfillment motifs.

14. Jung, "Psychology and Religion," no. 141.

15. Jung, *Modern Man in Search of a Soul*, 65.

16. Jung, *Two Essays*, no. 392.

17. See, for example, the dream interpretation in ibid., nos. 211ff.

18. Carl G. Jung, *Aion: Researches into the Phenomenology of the Self*, vol. 9 of *The Collected Works*, pt. 2, 2d ed. (Princeton, N.J.: Princeton University Press, 1969).

19. Jung, *Modern Man in Search of a Soul*, 230.

20. Ibid., 236.

21. Ibid., 95–114.

22. Ibid., 109ff.; and Singer, *Boundaries of the Soul*, chap. 14.

23. Jung, *Modern Man in Search of a Soul*, 243.

24. Ibid., 235.

25. Alasdair MacIntyre, *After Virtue*, 2d ed. (Notre Dame, Ind.: University of Notre Dame Press, 1984), 187ff.; see also the introduction to the present volume.

26. Ibid., *After Virtue*, 190–92

27. M. Scott Peck, *The Road Less Traveled: A New Psychology of Love, Traditional Values, and Spiritual Growth* (New York: Simon and Schuster, 1978).

28. Contemporary spiritual direction has been separated from sacramental confession within the Roman Catholic Church, as it was not in the time of, say, Teresa of Ávila. Moreover, some spiritual directors today are private practitioners only loosely connected with any particular religious community. By their own definition, and that of this volume, they are nonetheless spiritual.

29. Jerome D. Frank, *Persuasion and Healing*, rev. ed. (New York: Schocken, 1974), 212.

30. Lucy Freeman, *Fight against Fears* (New York: Crown, 1951), 52.

31. Ibid., 332.

32. Ibid., 216ff.

33. Ibid., 252–53.

34. Ibid., 232.

35. Ibid.

36. Kurt W. Back, *Beyond Words: The Story of Sensitivity Training and the Encounter Movement* (Baltimore: Penguin, 1973).

37. Joseph Havens, "Gestalt, Bioenergetics and Encounter: New Wine without Wineskins," in *Religious Systems and Psychotherapy,* ed. Richard H. Cox (Springfield, Ill.: Thomas, 1973), 268–83.

38. Morton A. Lieberman, Irvin D. Yalom, and Matthew B. Miles, *Encounter Groups: First Facts* (New York: Basic Books, 1973).

39. Victor Turner, *The Ritual Process: Structure and Anti-Structure* (Chicago: Aldine, 1969), 102ff.

40. Back, *Beyond Words,* 139.

41. Peggy Rosenthal, *Words and Values: Some Leading Words and Where They Lead Us* (New York: Oxford University Press, 1984), chap. 5.

42. Quoted and criticized by Havens as "an old American myth, reformulated" (Havens, "Gestalt, Bioenergetics and Encounter," 276).

43. Lucy Bregman, *The Rediscovery of Inner Experience* (Chicago: Nelson-Hall, 1982).

44. Ibid., chap. 2. See also Ann Faraday, *The Dream Game* (New York: Harper and Row, 1974).

45. Paul Vitz, *Psychology as Religion: The Cult of Self-Worship,* (Grand Rapids: Eerdmans, 1977).

Bibliography

Browning, Don S. *Religious Thought and the Modern Psychologies: A Critical Conversation in the Theology of Culture.* Philadelphia: Fortress, 1987.

Faraday, Ann. *The Dream Game.* New York: Harper and Row, 1974.

Havens, Joseph, ed. *Psychology and Religion: A Contemporary Dialogue.* New York: Van Nostrand, 1968.

Homans, Peter. *Jung in Context: Modernity and the Making of a Psychology.* Chicago: University of Chicago Press, 1979.

London, Perry. *The Modes and Morals of Psychotherapy.* New York: Holt, Rinehart and Winston, 1964.

May, Gerald G. *Care of Mind, Care of Spirit: A Psychiatrist Explores Spiritual Direction.* San Francisco: HarperSanFrancisco, 1992.

Reik, Theodore. *Listening with the Third Ear: The Inner Experience of a Psychoanalyst.* New York: Farrar, Straus and Co., 1948.

Rieff, Philip. *Freud: The Mind of the Moralist.* Garden City, N.Y.: Anchor Books, 1961.

Ulanov, Ann, and Barry Ulanov. *Religion and the Unconscious.* Philadelphia: Westminster, 1975.

Wolff-Salin, Mary. *No Other Light: Points of Convergence in Psychology and Spirituality.* New York: Crossroad, 1986.

Yalom, Irvin. *Love's Executioner and Other Tales of Psychotherapy.* New York: Harper, 1989.

11

Twelve Step Programs

ERNEST KURTZ

SOME TIME IN 1990, reported the *New York Times* religion writer Peter Steinfels, a cleric showing his church to a visitor confided: "There is more spirituality in this building on Tuesday evenings in the basement than on Sunday mornings in the sanctuary."[1] What goes on in that and countless other church basements on weekday evenings are meetings of Alcoholics Anonymous (AA) and other "Twelve Step groups." Even though not all such meetings take place in church basements, there is a problem with this modern version of "upstairs-downstairs." As the 1990s unfolded, many challenged the wisdom of the Twelve Step approach. What had won grudging respect as an effective way of making available time-tested spiritual insight came increasingly to be criticized as a form of New Age religion or mocked as a manifestation of psychologizing fads.[2] Where, then, do Twelve Step programs fit in a study of spirituality and the secular quest?

The term *Twelve Step programs* denotes groups of people who seek to put into practice the "Twelve Steps" formulated and introduced by AA between 1935 and 1939. The term also connotes to many the plethora of therapeutic-spiritual hybrids that have more recently sprung up in the wake of the "human potential" or New Age movements. Because some of these present themselves, or are perceived to be, manifestations of Twelve Step insight, we must begin with a distinction. The distinction is between those programs and groups that emphasize putting the Twelve Steps into practice literally and those other programs and groups that focus their language and practice elsewhere, whether the source of that different thrust be esoteric or psychological.

That distinction is rarely so precise in mushy reality. Not even all gatherings listed as meetings of AA, for example, fall into the first category. Practice, not labels, must guide. What actually occurs within any program or group is more important than how that reality is named. The line between the Twelve Step and apparently related approaches may be blurry, but the differences are real. More importantly, because the difference is, at bottom, between, on the one hand, a modern reformulation of classic spiritual insight, and, on the other, a classic denial of traditional spirituality, the real story is *how* the one engendered the other.

There is a help for exploring that story, for distinguishing between genuine Twelve Step programs and other ventures sometimes confused with them. Programs imbued with the spirit of the Twelve Steps are also Twelve Tradition programs, adhering to the Twelve Traditions also originally set forth by AA. In genuine Twelve Step groups, the Twelve Steps shape the spirituality of participants while the Twelve Traditions shape the groups themselves, making them apt vehicles for conveying Twelve Step spirituality. Nongenuine Twelve Step groups lack this dual underpinning. After an exploration of the Twelve Steps, then, I shall examine the significance of the Twelve Traditions.

The Twelve Steps

Any understanding of Twelve Step programs must rest on some knowledge of the Steps as originally set forth by AA. The text of AA's Twelve Steps begins with the word *we,* which remains implicit at the beginning of each Step. The less important reason for the *we* is its implication of community, a facet I shall explore later. More significant to AA's earliest members was the presentation of these Steps not as prescription but as description: "Here are the Steps we took, which are suggested as a program of recovery"; so begins the introduction to the actual listing of the Twelve Steps in the book *Alcoholics Anonymous.* The Steps do not set rules; they relate experience.

Step 1 reads: "We admitted we were powerless over alcohol — that our lives had become unmanageable." In commenting on this Step, AA cofounder Bill Wilson spoke of "absolute humiliation" and "utter defeat": "The principle that we shall find no enduring strength until we first admit complete defeat is the main taproot from which our whole society has sprung and flowered."[3] This understanding recaptured an ancient insight: classic vocabulary speaks of "emptying" (*kenosis*) and of crying "out of the depths." Alcoholics Anonymous finds the beginning of recovery from alcoholism in the process of "hitting bottom." The admission of limitation and, specifically, of the insufficiency of self-control — this is the beginning of Twelve Step spirituality.

Despite the prominence of the word *believe* in Step 2 ("Came to believe that a Power greater than ourselves could restore us to sanity"), the stories told within Twelve Step programs reveal that this Step deals less with faith than with *hope*. The point of Step 2, according to Wilson's expatiation in *Twelve Steps and Twelve Traditions,* is encouragement to open-mindedness to new possibilities. The "sanity" mentioned in Step 2 signifies the openness that makes possible "an optimal relationship between what one truly is and everything that is," an openness to both the inner and the outer dimensions of spirituality. The "Power greater than ourselves" need not be personalized: the point of this Step is the simple acknowledgment that one's self is not God, not the center of the universe, not "everything that is." Psychiatrists studying the Twelve Steps have found here a check on narcissism.[4] Step 2 attests that even if Step 1 seemed an act of despair, its very desperation contains the seed of hope.

The admission of failure plus the perception of hope opens the door to *surrender,* although that classic term is eschewed in the AA texts.[5] "Made a decision to turn our will and our lives over to the care of God *as we understood Him,*" reads Step 3; the boldface phrase is a late addition insisted on by the more secular (in their own terms, the more agnostically inclined) among AA's earliest members. The literature on this Step portrays the alcoholic as "an extreme example of self-will run riot," insisting that "selfishness — self-centeredness — . . . is the root of our troubles." Members of AA caution each other against demanding to be "in the driver's seat." The attempt to control — their own feelings, other people — is what gets alcoholics into trouble. Wariness of claims to control, then, is a hallmark of sobriety, which AA members understand as far more than mere abstinence from alcohol. As a true practice, AA's "sobriety" consists in *living* the Twelve Steps. Such sobriety is a synonym for spirituality, even for what others term sanctity.

The next six Steps may conveniently be examined as three pairs. These concern self-knowledge, dealing with one's failings, and making restitution for harm done. "4. Made a searching and fearless moral inventory of ourselves. 5. Admitted to God, to ourselves and to another human being the exact nature of our wrongs." Some form of the word *honesty* appears three times in the brief paragraph that opens the chapter titled "How It Works" in the book *Alcoholics Anonymous.* Although the modern term *denial* does not appear in AA literature, cautions against "self-deception" and "self-delusion" are frequent. Alcoholics Anonymous's inventory reflects the traditional practice of the *examen,* but the word *inventory* emphasizes surveying the positive as well as the negative, assets as well as liabilities. The *admission*, in addition to its quiet reminder of Step 1, captures some of the values of the practices of confession and reconciliation. "This feeling of being at one with God and man, this emerging from isolation," is how Wilson described this in concluding his explication of Step 5.[6]

Some see in Steps 6 and 7 the very heart of the Twelve Step program. "6. Were entirely ready to have God remove all these defects of character. 7. Humbly asked Him to remove our shortcomings." Both Steps conspicuously divert attention from any particular disability (such as alcoholic drinking) to the living of life. More deeply, both strengthen awareness of the individual's inability to exert control, thus reinforcing the surrender of all claims to be "in the driver's seat." In this spirituality, one seeks less to change oneself than to be open to being changed. Steps 6 and 7 direct attention to one's own role in the difficulties one experiences, without imposing with that recognition the kind of obligation that wilts resolve. Being "entirely ready" and "humbly asking," however, are not quietist abdications, as anyone who tries to practice these Steps will discover.

"8. Made a list of all persons we had harmed, and became willing to make amends to them all. 9. Made direct amends to such people wherever possible, except when to do so would injure them or others." The practice of making amends has a second and less obvious meaning. Face-to-face candor fosters the honesty that is so central to sobriety. Steps 8 and 9 carry Steps 4 and 5 deeper. Here, in a less protected setting, honesty with others invites even greater honesty with oneself. Also, in a deepening of the "inventory" image of those earlier Steps, the insistence on amends conveys the classic spiritual vision of an ordered universe. There exists a "right order," and one who has disturbed it by wrongdoing has the responsibility to set it right.

Members of AA sometimes refer to the final three of the Twelve Steps as "the maintenance Steps." Step 10 sets that tone by recapitulating Steps 4 through 9: "Continued to take personal inventory and when we were wrong promptly admitted it." Twelve Step spirituality is not a once-and-for-all spirituality. Again there comes the reminder that one does not attain sobriety/spirituality in isolation: to "admit" something requires another to admit it to. Those who seek sobriety need others, and those who associate with persons seeking sobriety will discover that they are needed.

Step 11 opens other classic themes: "Sought through prayer and meditation to improve our conscious contact with God *as we understood Him*, praying only for knowledge of His will for us and the power to carry that out." The traditional disciplines of "prayer and meditation" are presented as means "to improve." As the AA "Big Book" says, "We claim spiritual progress rather than spiritual perfection."[7] For those who live the Twelve Steps, "progress" is like Alasdair MacIntyre's conception of a practice, something midway between the pure perfection of being saved and the pure pragmatism of not drinking.[8] The use of the word *improve* assumes a "contact" already present; the specification *conscious* is also important. Both are noted when members discuss this Step. Finally, consistent with the recognition that spirituality involves mystery and miracle rather than magic, the purpose of prayer is presented not as an attempt to control God but as an expression of deference to God's reality.

Almost as well-known as AA's Step 1 is Step 12: "Having had a spiritual awakening as the result of these steps, we tried to carry this message to alcoholics, and to practice these principles in all our affairs." The Step has three noteworthy parts. First, as with Step 11's "conscious contact," "a spiritual awakening" is not promised or encouraged but assumed, and it occurs "as the result of these steps." The word *awakening* was preferred to *experience* because the latter seemed "too religious," but early confusions led to the addition of an appendix entitled "Spiritual Experience" in the second (March 1941) printing of the book *Alcoholics Anonymous.* Presenting spiritual awakening or experience as "the personality change sufficient to bring about recovery from alcoholism," the appendix notes that it "has manifested itself among us in many different forms" but most often in "what the psychologist William James calls the 'educational variety' because they develop slowly over a period of time."[9]

The second part emphasizes "carrying this message"; note the specification of "this" message and the restriction of its constituency "to alcoholics." Derivative programs have had to vary this last phrase, but it is essential to Twelve Step spirituality that the target be limited. To aim — implicitly or explicitly — at the whole human race is to miss the point and therefore the meaning of the Steps themselves. Accepting limitation is as essential to the spirituality of the program as it is to that of the individual, as AA's Traditions 5 and 10 remind us.[10]

Last comes the phrase Bill Wilson intended to use as the title of his book on AA spirituality, a work begun but never completed: "To practice these principles in all our affairs."[11] Note that as with "carrying this message," "practicing these principles" is something that "we *tried* to" do. The wisdom of AA recognizes a successful Twelfth-Step call to be one that results simply in the alcoholic not drinking: someone "powerless over alcohol" does not define success in terms of any ability to control another's drinking. Finally, as if to underline what became clear in Steps 4, 5, 6, 7, 8, and 10, there is the reminder that spirituality cannot be partial. By its nature, what is spiritual cannot be partly so, and thus its practice must be "in *all* our affairs." Nor is this only a traditional understanding, as the introduction to the present volume makes clear. Such embracing inclusivity —

this sense of necessarily dealing with *wholes* — characterizes all expressions of spirituality, religious or secular.

The ideas and practices contained in these Twelve Steps are not new. The Twelve Steps of AA represent — re-present, make present again — insights embedded in the classic spiritual traditions of the "peoples of the Book." Those richer traditions do contain far more: as Wilson loved to remind, "A.A. is but a kindergarten of the spirit." The earliest members of AA rediscovered that thread of ancient wisdom that has been called "the spirituality of imperfection."[12] In introducing the story of how they accomplished this rediscovery and of the significance of their achievement, two facets of the first presentation of the Twelve Steps merit brief attention.

First, the book *Alcoholics Anonymous* presents the Twelve Steps in a chapter titled "How It Works." That "how" is descriptive rather than analytic. What the chapter and the Steps promise, and deliver, is not the kind of technical explanation that allows for precise manipulation and controlled studies but rather a simple description of how AA's earliest members, obsessive-compulsive drinkers all, had been able to live constructively and even happily without drinking alcohol. Second, the Steps do tell *how* rather than "why." They do not explore causality. Instead, Twelve Step spirituality brings a phenomenological approach to reflection on experience. It achieves this not least by remaining descriptive — for example, by encouraging the inventorying of self rather than the blaming of others. The vocabulary of the Steps attends to *one's own* "unmanageability," insanity, wrongs, shortcomings, and defects of character. It calls for a listing of the persons that the alcoholic has harmed, not for a list of those who may have harmed the alcoholic. Close by the Twelve Steps in the AA "Big Book" comes the reminder: "Resentment is the 'number one' offender. It destroys more alcoholics than anything else."[13] Twelve Step spirituality does not perceive alcoholics as victims. Description, not ascription, is the task of the Steps.

The Story of the Twelve Steps

The Twelve Steps were formulated by AA, which came into existence between 1935 and 1939. Although the early members of AA developed these Steps from their own experience, broader forces shaped their interpretation of that experience. The story of that shaping is the story of the Twelve Step program, the story of a spirituality conveyed precisely by the telling of stories.

In telling their own stories, the early members of AA presented its program as deriving from "medicine, religion, and our own experience." Proximately, AA came into being out of what was at the time termed "the Oxford Group." That group's animus as well as its vision of itself seems best conveyed by both its first and its later names: the First Century Christian Fellowship and Moral Re-armament.[14]

The connection between AA and the Oxford Group began when, sometime in 1931, Carl Jung told an alcoholic American that his only hope of cure lay in finding "a religious experience." Jung's patient, a businessman who never affiliated with AA, joined the Oxford Group and eventually carried its (and Jung's) message to an alcoholic friend, who in turn brought that message in late 1934 to his former drinking buddy, William Griffith Wilson.[15]

Wilson resisted the religious elements in his friend's news. Some weeks later, though, during his fourth hospitalized detoxification, Bill experienced the kind of spiritual awakening classically described by William James in *The Varieties of Religious Experience*, a book that the Oxford Group encouraged Wilson and those who followed him to read. In that book and in his physician's confirmation of the change Bill sensed in himself, he found both validation of his recent experience and a theologically styled understanding of "deflation at depth," a phrase that well described the experience of the middle-class alcoholic of that era.

Both at Towns Hospital, where Wilson had been detoxified, and at a mission run by Calvary Episcopal Church, then the virtual headquarters of the Oxford Group, Wilson's early efforts to share his discovery proved fruitless. Then in May 1935, on a business trip to Akron, Ohio, Wilson found himself again obsessed with the desire to drink alcohol, a craving he had not experienced over the preceding five months. Reaching an Oxford Group member via the hotel church directory, Bill was invited to meet an alcoholic surgeon, Dr. Robert Holbrook Smith. When they met the next day, Wilson, somewhat awed at approaching "a man of science," told Smith not of his spiritual "hot flash" nor of his understanding of alcoholism as some kind of malady but of his own experience of drinking and trying to not drink and especially of his own need, now, to talk to another alcoholic so that he would not drink that day.

Dr. Smith, who had been attending the Oxford Group for over two years as "a student of the spiritual" but who had nevertheless continued his alcoholic imbibing, heard in Bill's story both understanding and hope. Some weeks later, traveling to a medical convention in Atlantic City, Smith went on one last binge. Then on 10 June 1935, Dr. Smith had his last drink — a bottle of beer given him by Wilson to steady his hand sufficiently to allow him to perform surgery. Members of AA regard that date on which their second cofounder achieved sobriety as the birthday of their fellowship, the first Twelve Step program.

"The alcoholic squadron" grew slowly within the Oxford Group until 1937, when the New York contingent left those auspices as too demanding, "too religious." In Akron, the connection lasted until 1939, when separation occurred partly because of the discomfort of some Catholic alcoholics who deemed the Oxford Group "too Protestant." During this time, members spoke of their "word-of-mouth, twenty-four-hour program." The Oxford Group used much popular religious literature, but none of it offered special instructions for alcoholics. By early 1938 many of the alcoholics felt the need to set down in writing what they had learned, and the decision was made to produce a book. In the course of drafting that book, eventually titled *Alcoholics Anonymous,* Bill Wilson one afternoon, in an "anything but spiritual mood," set out to scratch down "what we called 'the word-of-mouth program.' Though subject to considerable variation, it all boiled down into a pretty consistent procedure."[16]

Outlining that procedure, Wilson felt "that the program was still not definite enough." Seeking to be "more explicit," to leave "not a single loophole through which the rationalizing alcoholic could wriggle out," he decided that "our six chunks of truth should be broken up into smaller pieces, ... the better to get the distant reader over the barrel, and at the same time ... to broaden and deepen the spiritual implications of our whole presentation." After scribbling for "perhaps half an hour," Bill paused at what seemed a stopping point to number the new steps. "They added up to twelve. Somehow this number seemed significant. Without any special rhyme or reason I connected them with the twelve apostles." Except for a few very minor changes, these are the Twelve Steps that have come down to us.[17]

Spiritual Rather Than Religious

The changes made to Wilson's first draft — replacing the word *God* in Step 2 with "Power greater than ourselves," the addition of "*as we understood Him*" after the word *God* in Steps 3 and 11, and the deletion of the phrase "on our knees" in Step 6 — were forced by those members who found the original version "too religious." The early members of AA liked to present "medicine and religion" as the source of their insights, claiming William James and Carl Jung as quasi-founders of their program, but the most important contribution to AA of both Carl Jung and William James, as well as of the Oxford Group, was their openness to unconventional spirituality. This is expressed within not only AA but virtually all other Twelve Step groups in their presentation of their program as "spiritual rather than religious."[18]

The claim of AA (and derivative programs) to be "spiritual rather than religious" convinces few at first hearing. It is, after all, hardly original: most new religions begin by denying that they are new and/or that they are religions. Twelve Step programs, however, do come by the claim honestly, for they share the main motivation behind the assertion — the attempt to appeal to those alienated by what they think of as "religion."

Most of the earliest targets — and members — of AA had been raised in conventional religion but had abandoned its practice during their drinking years. Feeling condemned by practitioners of religion, they avoided religious settings. Still, many, their sober stories revealed, experienced a kind of shame over not being good enough for those religions. For many, but not all, such individuals, AA's "kindergarten of the spirit" led to recommitment to formal religion.[19]

Later candidates for Twelve Step programs brought different experiences and attitudes. Most came less versed in conventional religion and more alienated from it. For many of these, "spiritual rather than religious" served as a shibboleth permitting initial investigation. Also, for a time in the 1970s and 1980s, the term *spirituality* bore a positive connotation especially among those young people whose experimentation with drugs led them to the Twelve Step ambit.[20] There is another facet to the claim "spiritual rather than religious." Spoken by an individual, it can signal a choice of the private that rejects the communal. One can seek spirituality by oneself, but religion is never a merely personal affair. As the word suggests, religion binds people to other people. At least one aspect of spiritual life can be found in solitude.[21]

This tendency was balanced within AA itself by locating "the root of our troubles" in "self-centeredness" and discovering the importance of "fellowship" to its program. Some have reproached Twelve Step groups for focusing attention inward. The criticism has validity, although it tends to ignore the very real distinction between "self-help" and "mutual aid" — a difference as important as that between professional assistance and self-help. Genuine Twelve Step groups are "self-help" in the sense that professionals as professionals have no role in them. On the other hand, emphasis on unmanageability, admitting fault, making amends, and relying on a "Power greater than ourselves" creates a setting of "mutual aid" rather than one of bootstrapping "self-help." The invitation is to outreach and connection.[22]

How do adherents to Twelve Step programs understand "spiritual rather than religious"? Twelve Step programs do offer a vision classically termed "religious." But expressions of religion historically seem to involve: (1) doctrines that require belief; (2) rules that command or prohibit actions; (3) an institutional authority that formulates the doctrines and enforces the rules; and (4) worship and ritual that express reverence for the professed source of all of the above.

Twelve Step programs require none of these. Must members believe in God? Fifty-plus years of AA experience suggest that the only belief necessary to sobriety is that one's self is not God, an admission that members who term themselves atheist or agnostic readily make. The only rule likely to be heard around AA runs, "Don't drink and go to meetings" — far from imposing commandments for anyone inclined to claim membership. Authority? "Great suffering and great love are A.A.'s disciplinarians; we need no others. . . . We simply leave it to John Barleycorn." Groups do develop routines, in which outsiders may discern something similar to ritual, but one finds no semblance of worship.[23]

The concept of worship raises another point. Many associations, and not least religious societies, reveal a tendency to fall into a kind of self-worship — a conviction that "we" are somehow better than all the heathen "they." For members of AA, the culture still stigmatizes alcoholics enough that anonymity continues to serve the purposes that begot its practice. Early AA members cherished anonymity because it protected them, attracted new recruits, and guarded the fellowship against the vagaries of some members. They soon discovered an even more important value, recognizing anonymity as a "spiritual ten-strike" because it restrained tendencies to grandiosity. Programs and groups that do not take anonymity seriously, that claim to be "Twelve Step" without also being "Twelve Tradition," thus lose what in Tradition 12 is called "the spiritual foundation." One benefit of the backlash against Twelve Step programs may be a revival of that awareness.[24]

Spiritual Rather Than Material: The Experience of Addiction

More important than the "spiritual rather than religious" contrast proclaimed by Twelve Step rhetoric is the spiritual-as-other-than-material distinction lived out in Twelve Step practice. That the first Twelve Step program was AA is no accident. The tradition out of which the Twelve Steps grew saw the greatest threat to "the spiritual" not in "the material" but in the tendency to confuse the material with the spiritual — a confusion reified in the inability to recognize *enough*, the precise condition that, in turn, renders alcoholism such an apt metaphor for that confusion.

Carl Jung's presentation of alcoholism as an instance of *spiritus contra spiritum* — spirits warring against the spiritual — aptly captured that sense.[25] This vision posits the distinction between the spiritual and the material as fundamental: the very word *spiritual* onomatopoeically conveys that it is other-than-material. Like breath or breeze, the spiritual is experienced in its effects but not directly seen. It can never be owned, bought, or sold. This distinction, though, implies no condemnation of the material. The incarnational insight of mainline Western spirituality recognizes material reality as a vehicle for the spiritual, as reality to be rejoiced in, but also to be respected — for it bears a potential for danger not least because of the power of its connection with the spiritual.

The attitude to alcohol held by most members of AA, especially in the context of AA's 1930s origins, affords a useful illustration. Locating alcoholism in the alcoholic rather than in the alcohol, in the human being rather than in the bottle, displeased Prohibitionists even as it mollified the alcoholic beverage industry, but neither was the intention of early AA members. They were rather reflecting the classic spiritual insight that "sin" resided not in creation but in what people did with it. Some members even describe their alcoholism as a kind of *felix culpa,* expressing gratitude even for being alcoholic, because, as they see it, only the depths of their alcoholism made it possible for them to find the heights of serene sobriety.

Materialism has another facet, as the ongoing story of Twelve Step programs attests: there lurks always the danger of another kind of confusion of the spiritual with the material, the peril that an expression of spirituality will itself become commodity — an item of commerce, a vehicle for greed. Early AA was not immune to this tendency. Wilson located the beginning of the fellowship's "group conscience" in members' opposition to what they saw as the danger of his "selling the program" if he accepted a proffered employment opportunity in the hospital where he had been detoxified. Among many such pulls toward entrepreneurial endeavors, AA's early members hammered out what became its traditions of singleness of purpose, noninvolvement in outside enterprises, and self-support. By establishing these traditions, AA avoided the trap of becoming itself a commodity.[26]

But among some groups too glibly labeled "Twelve Step," programs that ignore the Twelve Traditions, matters developed differently. Often shaped by professional therapies for addictions ever more broadly conceived, these in time formed what came to be called the "recovery movement." Although that term may include programs that remain true to Twelve Step insight, most movement groups, as the term suggests, show little respect for or even awareness of the Twelve Traditions. The story of how Twelve Step programs gave rise to such groups affords a modern example of how a secular spirituality, like a religious spirituality, can cease to be spiritual when it becomes a commodity.

The Commodification of the Twelve Steps

Because of AA's centrality in the story of Twelve Step programs, the process by which recovery programs became commodities is best seen within the history of AA. That development may be outlined in three phases: 1935–55; 1956–76; and 1977 to the present. From the time of AA's conception in 1935 through its self-proclaimed "coming of age" in 1955, members sought cultural acceptance, pursuing this goal as a way of reaching more alcoholics. Paths tried but not taken included affiliating with the National Council for Education on Alcoholism and sacrificing anonymity for the sake of promotion. In both cases, grassroots members' reactions shaped what by 1950 became the Traditions of nonaffiliation with outside enterprises and anonymity as a "spiritual foundation." Most AA members found acceptance best attained by emphasizing their program's respectful connections with medicine and religion, professions at the time viewed as altruistic.

Largely because it carefully eschewed being mistaken for either therapy or theology, AA not only attained the cooperation of medical and religious professionals but avoided being co-opted by either group. It achieved this by (largely implicitly) playing the one off against the other. Echoes of a science-versus-religion debate still resonated in the 1940s, and while that led some in each camp — medicine and religion — to write off AA as belonging to the opposition, it enabled AA itself to fend off a too-smothering embrace by either group. Members remained aware of their debts to both.

The year 1955 marked a turning point because not only did AA itself celebrate its "coming of age," but that twentieth-anniversary gathering was honored by a message from U.S. president Dwight Eisenhower, who echoed the praise accorded AA by the American Public Health Association, which had earlier bestowed upon AA its Lasker Award. During its second twenty years, from 1956 to 1976, AA developed organizational stability, smoothly handling what could have been a major hazard to continuity — the death in 1971 of long-lived co-founder Bill Wilson. This period also witnessed a shift from the organization being merely accepted to being positively valued. In a world that sought the personal salvation of peace of mind from advice columnists and religious popularizers, endorsement by such luminaries brought considerable prominence. Alcoholics Anonymous passed the test. The high point of Twelve Step program respectability likely occurred in 1976–77, when presidential spouse Betty Ford and actors Jason Robards and Mary Tyler Moore — though carefully saying nothing about AA affiliation — spoke openly of their alcoholism in a vocabulary that listeners understood reflected the Twelve Step way of life.[27]

The period after 1977 brought the developments that require distinguishing between those programs and groups that focus on living the Twelve Steps and programs and groups that, though they may have adopted some Twelve Step elements, actually oriented their practice elsewhere. One reason for the respect accorded AA by the professions of medicine and religion was the fellowship's acceptance of its own limitations. Claiming to be neither medicine nor religion, AA threatened neither. But the acceptance of its own limitations as a fellowship — an acceptance that aptly paralleled the individual alcoholic's acceptance of the limitation implicit in the admission "I am an alcoholic" — bore ambiguous fruit. On the one hand, it was the reason why other Twelve Step groups formed: AA members claimed no competence in anything other than their own alcoholism. On the other hand, this awareness, to which so many other groups owed their inspiration, did not always attract their imitation.

As the example of AA's first offspring, Al-Anon (a Twelve Step program for spouses and others who love an alcoholic), attested as early as the 1950s, the Twelve Step way of life could be helpfully applied to difficulties other than alcoholism. In that decade and the next, groups of people stigmatized for other obsessive-compulsive behaviors, notably gamblers and overeaters, quietly adopted and adapted for their own conditions the Twelve Steps — and the Twelve Traditions — set forth by AA. Each group applied the program to its own particular disability, recognizing that though the Twelve Steps make available a way of life livable by all, entry into that way of life comes only through the doorway of a specifically experienced powerlessness. In the 1970s, two complicatedly related changes occurred, changes that eventually affected not only AA's offspring and imitators, but also the way people understood the term *Twelve Step program.* The two changes concerned the notions of alcoholism-as-disability and alcohol-as-drug.

Under the umbrella afforded by civil rights legislation, the Hughes Act of 1970 and additional laws passed in 1973 and 1978 sought to aid alcoholics by moving public policy, if not attitudes, toward understanding alcoholism as a disability meriting the same consideration as others. These acts broadened and in some cases mandated opportunities for treatment, and a new industry soon sprang into being. Early AA had made use of "drying out" facilities. Following Dr. Bob Smith's example, members from the beginning sought hospital admission for the medical detoxification of those who needed such care. Over time, halfway houses emerged for the more severely impaired, and a few treatment settings developed (usually carefully nonmedical), staffed and supported by members of AA who undertook these efforts largely for the sake of their own sobriety, as a part of their Twelfth-Step work.

When the new laws broadened funding for treatment, a slow evolution in practice became a mad race for money. What had been largely a labor of love — and in some settings remained so — became in others mainly a way of making money, as wider cultural awareness and legislatively mandated insurance coverage combined to create a fruit ripe for plucking. Critics pointed out that the consistent bane of spirituality, greed, seemed to guide many who now clothed their projects in Twelve Step language. Alcoholics Anonymous applied the pragmatic phrase *whatever works* to staying away from the first drink. Some of the new treatment providers applied the maxim to developing new products and manipulating diagnoses. Before long, some who worked in treatment found themselves queried more often about "the bottom line" than about "quality sobriety." Many of the most effective, those most experienced in spiritual service, moved to other settings or even other fields. Before long also, some funders of care — governments, companies, insurers — began to suspect that they were being defrauded. Reacting against the abuses, some began to view all recovery programs as rip-offs, rejecting anything that smacked of the Twelve Step programs with which they associated this experience.[28]

The second significant 1970s occurrence was the recrudescence of American twentieth-century "reefer madness" — the apparently rampant use of psychoactive chemicals, or, in the common shorthand, drugs. Medical historian David Musto has termed addiction "the American disease." When drugs are mentioned, few think of ethyl alcohol, but, using the concept of "chemical dependency," many in the treatment industry labored to change that understanding to meet the reality that public opinion (and funding sources) showed more concern over drug addiction than over alcohol abuse. Recognition of the relationship between the two had been present in AA since at least 1944, when an alcoholic physician, interned in the federal facility at Lexington, Kentucky, wrote to *The Grapevine* proposing a "Hopheads Corner" within AA, for members also addicted to "other chemicals." This understanding served well for over three decades. Narcotics Anonymous was begun, in Lexington, by AA members reaching out to their fellow drug addicts who were not alcoholics.[29]

The exigencies of treatment — and the realities of funding — changed perceptions as well as practices. Recognizing that treatment did not cure addiction, for what "cure" took place occurred in the ongoing practice that was recovery, some treatment providers began encouraging their ever broader population of clients to attend AA meetings, even if they were not alcoholics. Another new and different population arrived as judges increasingly began to sentence drunk-driving offenders to attendance at AA meetings.

Individual groups in AA's decentralized fellowship reacted variously. Some agreed to sign (preferably initial) court attendance slips, but others refused. Some began meetings with the request that those who had no desire to stop drinking leave or remain silent and/or that those who had problems other than alcohol speak only of their alcohol-related difficulties in this setting. Others held closed (for admitted alcoholics only) and open (to anyone interested) meetings in different rooms in the same building, referring newcomers to the latter. Still other groups divided, some members leaving to found a new group either more public or more private than the setting that had provoked their departure. The General Service Office of AA, drawing on the experience of the groups, developed "guidelines" for "cooperating with court, A.S.A.P. and similar programs"; most legal authorities were happy to work within them.[30] Although similar guidelines were suggested for treatment settings, cooperation proved more difficult in this more complex area. Some professionals who worked with alcoholics and addicts had entered the rapidly expanding field hastily and lacked real knowledge of Twelve Step programs. Sometimes they made inappropriate referrals. To meet that problem, which increased as the multiplication of addictions and treatments swelled the number of recovery movement candidates, other professionals, as well as the victims themselves, formed new groups.

Many of these groups, especially those concerned with what came to be called "process addictions," tried to cling to the Twelve Step style, but their actual practice often moved away from Twelve Step insight. Cut off from the Twelve Traditions, some programs adopted professional ideology, rejecting the telling of stories of "experience, strength, and hope" for the satisfactions of analyzing the past in the categories of therapy. Others seemed to foster visions of self-as-victim, attracting criticism that added strength to the already forming backlash against anything that smacked of "Twelve Step." As more than one observer noted, some of the new groups offered less a Twelve Step program than a ready-made market for pushers of "recovery" paraphernalia.[31]

By the 1990s, the situation seemed hopelessly confused. On the one hand, the term *Twelve Step* came laden with connotations of self-pity, narcissism, and greed. On the other hand, many continued to find in various Twelve Step programs vehicles for a spirituality that even outsiders recognized as real. "If you have decided you want what we have . . . ," runs AA's introduction to the Twelve Steps. One description of spirituality suggests that it is that which, when I see it in another, I want to partake of, and if I get it, my participation in it enhances rather than diminishes that other's own participation and joy in it. Another description, noting the frequent use of the words *insight* and *vision* in speaking of spirituality, suggests that it involves not so much seeing different things as seeing things differently — the ability to recognize in reality more than that which can be owned or coveted.

Both descriptions well fit AA's understanding of sobriety, the Twelve Step mark of spiritual well-being. Such a reality will always be a mystery, a paradox, and not least because it comes in different forms. The very variety of Twelve Step programs and their members, no less than the variety of saints revered by tradition, reminds us that there is no one way to be spiritual. This is perhaps the key insight mediated by the actual experience of the first Twelve Step program, AA.

Twelve Step Spirituality

Twelve Step programs are marked by variety and paradox. They came into being in Akron, Ohio, when a visiting New York hustler sought out a local alcoholic physician. Although Akron remained a hub of AA activity, New York soon became the new fellowship's main center. Differences between the AA groups in Akron and New York appeared early on, as opinions varied about the word *God* in the Steps and the use of the Oxford Group's "four absolutes." The differing emphases were passed on as the young fellowship spread, but they remained largely latent until later decades brought the wider mobility of a more numerous membership and the blossoming of other, gaudier groups that borrowed the Twelve Step mantle. The chief difference between the AA groups, from the beginning, as the examples suggest, concerned how members understood "the spiritual."

Although some observers interpreted this divergence in terms of the stereotypes of urban sophistication versus heartland wholesomeness, members in both regions reflected each view. More accurately, the distinction was between those perhaps best termed the "transcendentally inclined," who viewed the spiritual as somehow *other* and whose vocabulary tended to echo that of traditional theology, and the "immanentists," for whom the spiritual pervades all reality and whose vocabulary — although it did not predominate in the AA in the 1940s and the 1950s — fits far better both ancient mystical traditions and recent cultural fashions.[32]

For the first forty years of Twelve Step programs, both these approaches were evident, each respectful of the other. That balancing of the two visions, which was an important factor in shaping the Twelve Step insight, can be studied in Bill Wilson's *A.A. Grapevine* articles. Whether because of Wilson's death or, more likely, because of the impact of what have been termed the "culture wars," mutual respect and balancing compromise between the transcendent and immanent spiritual approaches, as well as between therapeutic and spiritual emphases, began in the late 1970s to give way to increasing polarization among programs claiming the Twelve Step mantle. These divisions, though, do not overshadow the essence of Twelve Step spirituality, which involves finding a way of living with incongruity, a way to embrace paradox.[33]

The Paradox of Twelve Step Spirituality

The story of Twelve Step programs suggests that a spirituality, to be recognized as genuine in a secular age, must enable the bridging of difference, the embrace of paradox. Twelve Step spirituality began with the then revolutionary discovery that the terms *sober* and *alcoholic* were not mutually exclusive and could indeed refer to the same person. Similarly, so long as they bridged medicine and religion without claiming to be either, so long as they mediated both transcendent and immanent spiritual understandings, Twelve Step programs helped participants to attain some kind of spirituality and were acknowledged as effective even by many who did not participate in them.

When some imitators deviated from that Twelve Step insight to become either a form of therapy or a mode of New Age religion, they lost respect not least because they lost effectiveness. There is nothing wrong — indeed, there is much right — with both therapy and religion accurately labeled, but it abuses both to present either as the other or to recognize insufficiently their distinction from each other. The Twelve Traditions protect the Twelve Steps from such confusion of spirituality or religion with therapy. They do this by implanting an acceptance of limitation, which encourages respect for difference. These complementary attitudes clear a space within which the realities of paradox may be lived. Programs that ignore the Traditions tend to reject paradox; most seem also to slip away from first the vocabulary, and then the practice, of the Twelve Steps.

Twelve Step spirituality began not only in the admission of "powerlessness" and "unmanageability" but in the acceptance and embrace of the paradoxical identity "sober alcoholic." In finding in *paradox* a key to spirituality, Twelve Step programs reclaimed a tradition perhaps too glibly dismissed in an era intolerant of mystery and mistrustful of anything that cannot be explained and controlled. Twelve Step programs offer an arena for, and a way of, living with the paradoxes embodied in one's life. To be a *sober alcoholic* — a term that was originally shocking but that has become overfamiliar and even banal — is to accept that one lives not only with but also *in* paradox.

Twelve Step programs offer a spirituality of paradox. The stories told at meetings evidence that and reveal how these programs inculcate experiences of release, gratitude, humility, tolerance, and forgiveness. Each involves paradox. Release's freedom comes only to those who "let go." The vision that is gratitude — the recognition of how generously one has received — is given only to those who give of themselves. Humility accepts that living humanely, like being a sober alcoholic, involves embracing the reality of paradox rather than claiming or demanding allegiance to absolutes. Tolerance of others' weaknesses flows from confronting one's own flaws. The ability to forgive comes only out of the experience of being forgiven. These experiences, paradoxes all, hallmark and even constitute Twelve Step spirituality.

Living in paradox involves accepting the tragic as well as the joyous. "The chiefest sanctity of a temple is that it is a place to which people go to weep in common," Miguel d'Unamuno wrote. Twelve Step programs provide such temples. An age that views all suffering as merely evil and a culture frustrated by ambiguity and dominated by a technology intolerant of paradox find such temples threatening, as some criticisms of Twelve Step groups make clear. Yet weeping is not moaning — a distinction sometimes ignored. In theological terms, the critics protest the groups' seeming promise of "cheap grace"; in a more secular vocabulary, they charge the programs with engaging in "soft science": the point is the same. Just as bought love ceases to be love, so spirituality that can be sold and science that can be merchandised lose their unique natures. Those who glibly explain mystery and who confuse miracle with magic should be challenged. Such tendencies lurk in all and perhaps especially in those who are spiritual. Twelve Step experience suggests that only those who recognize that they themselves have both wept in tragedy and moaned in self-pity have standing to point out that difference to others.[34]

Twelve Step Spirituality as Metaphor

A spirituality that embraces paradox will be sensitive to metaphor. Twelve Step programs have significantly influenced the metaphors in which twentieth-century people understand deviant behaviors. Examining these metaphors thus illumines both the rise and the apparent decline of Twelve Step programs as vehicles of spirituality.

The medicalization of deviance is a main characteristic of advancing modernity: those who act contrary to social norms come to be thought of as "sick" rather than as "sinners." Twelve Step programs played a two-phased role in this development, not only advancing that change but advancing beyond it.

First, although AA does not teach that alcoholism is a disease, for such teaching would violate AA's Tradition on "outside issues," the experience of many AA members led them, and others, to move from the moral toward a medical model of alcoholism and other addictions. Second, in its presentation of the alcoholic as suffering from physical, mental, emotional, and spiritual disability — and especially in its emphasis on spiritual issues — the Twelve Step approach broadened the medical model in a holistic direction.

Groups untrammeled by AA's Twelve Traditions even more avidly promoted medical explanations of their members' deviant behaviors. In doing so, some abandoned holistic understanding for legal advantage. How we speak shapes how we think, and so the shift from the language of common experience to the vocabulary of professional therapy had larger ramifications. The Twelve Steps made available in modern terms an ancient spiritual tradition — the core Greco-Judeo-Christian insights that shaped Western civilization. Early imitators of AA — Al-Anon, Gamblers Anonymous — hewed close to that tradition, adapting it as necessary but retaining such insights of the classic spirituality as the centrality of the danger of pride, the embrace of imperfection, and a delight in paradox.

The shift from the Twelve Steps to therapy can be seen as early as Charles Dederick's founding of Synanon in 1958. Synanon and other programs for users of illegal drugs usually presented themselves honestly, as something other than Twelve Step programs. They claimed to go beyond the Twelve Step approach; Dederick, for example, opined that comparing AA to Synanon was like comparing a rowboat to an airplane.[35] Some of these non–Twelve Step programs adhere closer to Twelve Step practice than do some newer phenomena that present themselves as Twelve Step programs. Many (but not all) "adult children" and "codependency" associations, for example, run directly contrary to Twelve Step insight. The reliance on a literature produced by quasi-professionals has led to preferring the vocabulary of therapy to the language of spirituality and to analyzing the past in ways more redolent of 1930s psychotherapies than of any recognizable tradition of spirituality.

Twelve Step programs are, of course, not the only kind of spirituality—not even the only kind of recovery spirituality. Openness to paradox does not mean that Twelve Step spirituality lacks a distinctive character. The literature of AA delineates a spirituality conveyed by the telling of stories of "experience, strength and hope"—stories that "disclose in a general way what we used to be like, what happened, and what we are like now." It is on this basis that the Twelve Steps are presented, as the very next sentence of "How It Works" invites: "If you have decided you want what we have and are willing to go to any length to get it — then you are ready to take certain steps." Groups that center their practice on "sharing what things are like and how we feel about that" do not offer the same program. They may provide great therapeutic benefits and even valid spiritual consolation, but the change from "we" to "things" and the shift from deciding and willing to *feeling* are substantial variations.

Individualism and Community

Two final topics deepen insight into the workings of Twelve Step programs and aid in distinguishing Twelve Step spirituality from ersatz imitators. Twelve Step programs both subvert and foster *individualism*. The resulting ambiguous relationship to *community* is resolved by the way members understand their participation in these programs.

The Great Depression of the 1930s marked the nadir of the deepest American faith—confidence in individual autonomy, in the power of each individual to be "the master of my fate, the captain of my soul." The decade that gave rise to industrial unionism understood that acknowledging a need for others need not signal weakness or aberration.

The "we-ness" of the admission of individual powerlessness, the insistence on needing others implicit in Steps 5, 9, 10, and 12, the fellowship of the meetings that even the AA Big Book did not anticipate: these subverted the ideology of radical individualism and the patterns of thinking that sustained it. Personal situations as well as social conditions attested that the old individualistic ideology was no longer tenable. The revolutionary contribution of AA was not medical diagnosis of the "disease" of alcoholism but its insistence that the most important reality in the life of any alcoholic, sobriety, could not be attained alone. One needed an-other, whether that other was understood as other people or as some kind of more remote higher power. If "the root of our troubles" is "self-centeredness," its uprooting begins with the acknowledgment that there *is* a "Power greater than ourselves."

Yet such an understanding, even as it ostensibly subverts individualism, appeals to a specifically Protestant "Higher Power." Contact with that "Power greater" is unmediated: AA is neither a church nor a people. The Twelve Step approach of AA thus undermined individualism in a very individualistic way. An opening to community emerges in the Twelve Traditions, but the Traditions protect community very gingerly. Tradition 1 recognizes its importance by reminding that "our common welfare should come first; personal recovery depends upon A.A. unity." Tradition 3 enshrines AA's powerlessness to restrict its own community by establishing that "the only requirement for A.A. membership is a desire to stop drinking" — an internal reality almost impossible to gainsay.

What about the larger community? Do Twelve Step programs deflect people from responsibility, from working to change conditions that cause suffering? Twelve Step insight does incline toward the strategy of improving reality outside self by first improving the reality of one's self, as opposed to an approach that seeks to improve self by changing outside reality. In a way of life that embraces paradox, this is a matter of both/and, not either-or. The Serenity Prayer, so cherished by AA members, asks: "Grant me the serenity to accept the things I cannot change, the courage to change the things I can, and the wisdom to know the difference." Those who criticize AA for putting too little emphasis on changing social reality assume that basing affiliation on awareness of a shared flaw will discourage social action. Such an assumption ignores history: many movements committed to changing the world have "founded their sense of internal community on an ideology of common sinfulness and weakness."[36]

"An ideology of common sinfulness and weakness" implies something more about the cohesion of community, offering another useful way of distinguishing Twelve Step programs from imitators that have abandoned the vision of those Steps. What is the basis on which an individual takes part? Does one join this group and participate in its program because one needs to or because one "wants to" do so? In the community created by and within Twelve Step programs, one participates not because one wants to but because one *needs to*. Early AA members, for example, saw the choices available to the actively drinking alcoholic to be "abstinence, insanity, or death," and their experience suggested that at least some alcoholics were able to abstain only within the fellowship of AA.

This distinction — between the style of community created by Twelve Step programs composed of those who *need to* belong and the "self-help" mode of "sharing and caring" groups available for those who *want to* join them – returns us to the core of Twelve Step spirituality, the sense of powerlessness. Alcoholics are not the only ones who hit bottom, and so here again we find not some clean-cut either-or but instead a finely shaded spectrum of both/and. Any group that styles itself "Twelve Step" or "self-help" will likely contain some individuals who profess that they are there by choice and others who attest that they are present out of necessity. It nevertheless remains true that the more closely any program adheres to AA's original Steps and Traditions, the more numerous will be those who say they participate not because they want to but because they have to.

Twelve Step programs and their offspring rehearse in capsule form a common process in the history of spiritual insight. There may be no Second Law of Spiritual Thermodynamics that leads inevitably to the entropy of the Sheilaism described in Robert Bellah's *Habits of the Heart*;[37] but at least within the mainstream tradition of which Twelve Step programs are a part, it is a common phenomenon that the sense that one is being drawn to or compelled by some larger reality becomes for later generations the judgment that one chooses and decides for oneself. Programs that remain true to the Twelve Steps and Twelve Traditions seem able to retain a qualification of the individualism inherent in the tradition: awareness that one needs others for one's own very survival substantially limits any sense of absolute individual autonomy.

Final Reflections

Several themes that recur in the story of Twelve Step programs invite thought. One wonders, first, whether it is preferable to be "sick" or to be a "sinner." As R. D. Laing noted concerning the phrase *mental illness*, changing the name of a reality is less likely to change our understanding of that reality than it is to change our understanding of the name. An age acutely sensitive to pain has, ironically, multiplied stigmata.

Second, must the broadening of a spiritual insight lead inevitably to its loss? Oxford Group historian Walter Houston Clark thought that this eventually happened to the Oxford Group, suggesting that AA's departure from that organization's auspices had allowed it to avoid a similar fate. The new program's insistent singleness of purpose in accepting the limitation of dealing only with alcoholics reflected awareness of the danger. As Bill Wilson later summed up: "Most of all, the Oxford Group taught us what *not* to do."[38] Spiritualities always exist in some material context. In time, the core Twelve Step insight of accepting limitation became attenuated not only in imitators but even within the AA fellowship itself, as the very decentralization that preserved it from professionalization became the avenue for its corruption by commodification. Many both within and outside of AA resist this trend, and so this part of the story continues, albeit differently in diverse Twelve Step settings.

Finally, it is fitting in an age of language theory that the uses and misuses of metaphor — and specifically of addiction as metaphor — summarize the story of the spirituality of Twelve Step programs. A tortuous but real trail runs from AA members' recognition of their own experience in Carl Jung's portrayal of alcoholism as a warring of *spiritus contra spiritum* to the vision that sees virtually every activity as some kind of addiction. Twelve Step programs have to do with spirituality because they have to do with addiction. Only when it is recognized that addiction is *more than* a metaphor can addiction *as* a metaphor work. Because those who have experienced actual addiction know its reality, they can translate that metaphor. The traditional spirituality of the Western world, from which the insight of the Twelve Step programs derives, recognized materialism — the fixation on quantity, on *more* — as the ultimate expression of the core sin of self-centeredness. Related to this sin is the claim that one is the center of the universe or God. Perhaps only a culture capable of questioning its own materialism can produce and sustain individuals who find in Twelve Step programs a vehicle of spirituality.

Notes

1. Peter Steinfels, "Clerics Wonder Whether Religion Can Learn Lessons from Recovery Programs for Addicts," *New York Times*, 28 April 1990.

2. Wendy Kaminer, *I'm Dysfunctional, You're Dysfunctional* (Reading, Mass.: Addison-Wesley, 1992); Charles J. Sykes, *A Nation of Victims* (New York: St. Martin's, 1992).

3. Bill Wilson, *Twelve Steps and Twelve Traditions* (New York: A.A. World Services, 1953), 21–22.

4. John E. Mack, "Alcoholism, A.A., and the Governance of the Self," in *Dynamic Approaches to the Understanding and Treatment of Alcoholism*, ed. Norman E. Zinberg and Margaret H. Bean (New York: Free Press, 1981), 128–62; Edward J. Khantzian and John E. Mack, "Alcoholics Anonymous and Contemporary Psychodynamic Theory," in *Recent Developments in Alcoholism*, vol. 7 of *Treatment Research*, ed. Marc Galanter (New York: Plenum, 1989), 67–89.

5. For an analysis of AA in these terms, see the writings of Harry M. Tiebout, especially "Therapeutic Mechanisms of Alcoholics Anonymous," *American Journal of Psychiatry* 100 (1944): 468–73; "The Act of Surrender in the Therapeutic Process," *Quarterly Journal of Studies on Alcohol* 10 (1949): 48–58; "Surrender vs. Compliance in Therapy," *Quarterly Journal of Studies on Alcohol* 14 (1953): 58–68; and "The Ego Factor in Surrender in Alcoholism," *Quarterly Journal of Studies on Alcohol* 15 (1954): 610–21.

6. Wilson, *Twelve Steps and Twelve Traditions*, 63.

7. Members of AA affectionately refer to the book *Alcoholics Anonymous* as the "Big Book." The term originated when those who produced it, hoping to convince Depression-era drunks that the $3.50 book was worth purchasing, asked its printer to "use the heaviest paper he could find," so that the book would be literally weighty. World War II rules on paper use required changing to more economical stock, but the name stuck.

8. Alasdair MacIntyre, *After Virtue* (South Bend, Ind.: Univ. of Notre Dame Press, 1981), chap. 14; also see the introduction to the present volume.

9. *Alcoholics Anonymous* (New York: A.A. World Services, 1976 [1939]), 569.

10. In explaining why AA left the Oxford Group, Wilson states that this acceptance of limitation was the reason AA came into being: "The Oxford Group wanted to save the world. I only wanted to save the drunks" (letter from Wilson to B. McGhee, 30 October 1940). Tradition 5 reads: "Each group has but one primary purpose — to carry its message to the alcoholic who still suffers"; and Tradition 10 reads: "Alcoholics Anonymous has no opinion on outside issues; hence the A.A. name ought never be drawn into public controversy."

11. For the story of this effort, and its traces, see Ernest Kurtz and Katherine Ketcham, *The Spirituality of Imperfection* (New York: Bantam, 1992), 130–31.

12. Ibid.; Kurtz and Ketcham directly explore Twelve Step spirituality. For the wider context, see Simon Tugwell, *Ways of Imperfection* (Springfield, Ill.: Templegate, 1985).

13. *Alcoholics Anonymous,* 64.

14. Walter Houston Clark, *The Oxford Group: Its History and Significance* (New York: Bookman, 1952), 35.

15. Ernest Kurtz, *Not-God: A History of Alcoholics Anonymous* (Center City, Minn.: Hazelden, 1979); this is the most fully documented presentation of AA's history. It should be supplemented with two AA publications, *Alcoholics Anonymous Comes of Age* (New York: A.A. World Services, 1957) and *Pass It On* (New York: A.A. World Services, 1984); see also Bill Pittman, *A.A.: The Way It Began* (Seattle: Glen Abbey, 1988).

16. *Alcoholics Anonymous Comes of Age,* 160–61.

17. For the original version of the Twelve Steps, with a more detailed discussion of the changes, see Kurtz, *Not-God,* 70–71.

18. In 1961 Wilson wrote to Jung telling the Swiss psychiatrist of his role in AA's origins. Jung's reply indicated familiarity with AA and offered a directly spiritual understanding of alcoholism and recovery from it. This correspondence, slightly edited, appears in *The A.A. Grapevine* issues of January 1963 and January 1968 and in *The Language of the Heart* (New York: A.A. Grapevine, 1988), 276–81.

19. The stories in the first and second editions of *Alcoholics Anonymous* attest to this; Wilson himself had an unconventional religious upbringing and never affiliated with any denomination.

20. Aldous Huxley, *Moksha* (Los Angeles: Tarcher, 1977).

21. The problem was stated by St. Basil, who noted that "the defect of the solitary life was that it provided no opportunity to practice the virtues of humility and patience or to perform the practical works of mercy — 'If you live alone, whose feet will you wash?' " (in Clifford Hugh Lawrence, *Medieval Monasticism: Forms of Religious Life in Western Europe in the Middle Ages* [London: Longman, 1989], 10).

22. Most AA members strenuously deny that their program is one of "self-help"; the usual comment runs: "Self-help,... we tried that, and it didn't work; that's why we're a God-help program."

Some recent imitators, wandering from Twelve Step insight, can seem to foster self-centeredness by suggesting that involvements with others are their adherents' problem. The emblem of Co-Dependents Anonymous, Inc., that appears on its literature, "To Thine Own Self Be True," illustrates the point — perhaps especially for those aware of the line's context in *Hamlet.* The other words on the emblem are "Discovery, Recovery, Self, Respect." Compare this with the terms on the AA emblem being imitated: "Recovery, Unity, Service." Further, AA specifies its Third Legacy as "service," and in 1965 it made a commitment to "The Declaration," which pledges: "I Am Responsible."

23. *Alcoholics Anonymous Comes of Age,* 120; Wilson, *Twelve Steps and Twelve Traditions,* 178; also Kurtz, *Not-God,* 108.

The language and practice of some AA groups have led to the formation of "rational recovery" groups and "secular organizations for sobriety"; see James Christopher, *How to Stay Sober: Recovery without Religion* (Buffalo: Prometheus, 1988). Such groups, which do not claim to offer a Twelve Step program, have thus far drawn few members; on atheists and agnostics and the Twelve Steps, see Jon R. Weinberg, *A.A.: An Interpretation for the Nonbeliever* (Center City, Minn.: Hazelden, 1975).

24. Wilson, "Our Anonymity Is Both Inspiration and Safety," *A.A. Grapevine* (March 1946); and "Why Alcoholics Anonymous Is Anonymous," *A.A. Grapevine* (January 1955); both are reprinted in *The Language of the Heart: Bill W.'s Grapevine Writings* (New York: A.A. Grapevine, 1988), 16–20, 209–18.

25. The letter from Jung (Zurich) to Wilson, 30 January 1961, has been frequently reproduced; see, for example, *Language of the Heart,* 280–81.

26. Wilson, *Twelve Steps and Twelve Traditions,* 140–42; the traditions referred to here are 5, 6, and 7: "5. Each group has but one primary purpose — to carry its message to the alcoholic who still suffers. 6. An A.A. group ought never endorse, finance, or lend the A.A. name to any related facility or outside enterprise, lest problems of money, property, and prestige divert us from our primary purpose. 7. Every A.A. group ought to be fully self-supporting, declining outside contributions."

27. Betty Ford, *The Times of My Life* (New York: Harper and Row, 1978).

28. See, for example, Stanton Peele, *The Diseasing of America: Addiction Treatment out of Control* (Lexington, Mass.: Lexington Books, 1989).

29. Letter from "Doc N.," *The Grapevine* 1:3 (August 1944); see also the letter from "Doc M." of Shelby, N.C., in the following issue.

30. There are fifteen sets of such "guidelines," lists and order forms for all AA literature may be obtained from A.A. World Services, Inc., 475 Riverside Drive, New York, NY 10115.

31. The literature is vast; a good beginning would include Tadeusz Gierymski and Terence Williams, "Codependency," *Journal of Psychoactive Drugs* 18:1 (1986): 7–13; William R. Miller, "Adult Cousins of Alcoholics," *Psychology of Addictive Behaviors* 1:1 (1987): 74–76; Edith S. Lisansky Gomberg, "On Terms Used and Abused: The Concept of 'Codependency,'" in *Current Issues in Alcohol/Drug Studies,* ed. Edith S. Lisansky Gomberg (New York: Haworth, 1989), 113–32; Rick A. Myer et al., "Co-dependency: An Examination of Underlying Assumptions," *Journal of Mental Health Counseling* 13:4 (1991) 449–58. Robin Room, "Alcoholics Anonymous as a Social Movement," in *Research on Alcoholics Anonymous: Opportunities and Alternatives,* ed. Barbara S. McCrady and William R. Miller (New Brunswick, N.J.: Rutgers Center for Alcohol Studies, 1993), 167–87; this text specifically delineates conflicts between "the ideology of codependence" and the Twelve Step vision. For the more popular perception, see Alison Humes, "The Cult-

ing of Codependency," *7 Days,* 1 November 1989; and for a literature review, see Carol LeMasters, "Reading Codependency," *Christianity and Crisis,* 18 June 1990, 200–203.

32. The distribution of ideas in early AA can be seen in the stories printed in the first edition of *Alcoholics Anonymous;* on the affinity with traditional mysticism, see Bernard McGinn, *The Foundations of Mysticism* (New York: Crossroad, 1991).

33. Wilson's *A.A. Grapevine* articles have been collected and published in *Language of the Heart.* On recent events, see James Davison Hunter, *Culture Wars: The Struggle to Define America* (New York: Basic Books, 1991); and Robert Wuthnow, *The Restructuring of American Religion* (Princeton, N.J., Princeton University Press, 1988).

34. Miguel d'Unamuno, *The Tragic Sense of Life* (New York: Dover, 1954 [1921]), 17; the final point is illustrated in many *A.A. Grapevine* stories; see, for example, "Ginger," *A.A. Grapevine* 48:9 (February 1992): 50–53.

35. Lewis Yablonsky, *The Tunnel Back: Synanon* (New York: Macmillan, 1965), 49–55.

36. The final quotation is from: Robin Room, "Healing Ourselves and Our Planet" (paper presented at the eighteenth annual Alcohol Epidemiology Symposium of the Kettil Bruun Society for Social and Epidemiological Research on Alcohol, Toronto, 1–5 June 1992); see also: Frank Riessman and Timothy Bay, "The Politics of Self-Help," *Social Policy* 23:2 (1992): 28–38.

37. One of the women the authors interviewed named her private faith (Sheilaism) after herself; it included a belief in God and an intention to love and care for herself and others. See Robert N. Bellah et al., *Habits of the Heart* (Berkeley: University of California Press, 1985), 221, 235.

38. *Alcoholics Anonymous Comes of Age,* 74–75.

Bibliography

Alcoholics Anonymous. New York: A.A. World Services, 1976 [1939].

Bateson, Gregory. "The Cybernetics of 'Self': A Theory of Alcoholism." *Psychiatry* 34:1 (1971): 1–18. Reprinted in Bateson, *Steps to an Ecology of Mind.* New York: Balantine, 1972, 309–37.

Kaminer, Wendy. *I'm Dysfunctional, You're Dysfunctional: The Recovery Movement and Other Self-Help Fashions.* Reading, Mass.: Addison-Wesley, 1992.

Kurtz, Ernest. *Not-God: A History of Alcoholics Anonymous.* Center City, Minn.: Hazelden, 1991.

Kurtz, Ernest, and Katherine Ketcham. *The Spirituality of Imperfection: Modern Wisdom from Classic Stories.* New York: Bantam, 1992.

Room, Robin. "Alcoholics Anonymous as a Social Movement." In *Research on Alcoholics Anonymous: Opportunities and Alternatives,* edited by Barbara S. McCrady and William R. Miller. New Brunswick, N.J.: Rutgers Center for Alcohol Studies, 1993.

Wilson, Bill. *The Language of the Heart: Bill W.'s Grapevine Writings.* New York: A.A. Grapevine, 1988.

———. *Twelve Steps and Twelve Traditions.* New York: A.A. World Services, 1953.

F. Society

12

Feminist Spirituality

LAURA LEVITT

> I wrote a sentence just now and x'd it out. In it I said that women have always understood the struggle against free-floating abstraction even when they were intimidated by abstract ideas. I don't want to write that kind of sentence now, the sentence that begins "women have always. . . ." We started by rejecting the sentences that began "Women have always had an instinct for mothering" or "Women have always and everywhere been in subjugation to men." If we have learned anything in these years of late twentieth-century feminism, it's that "always" blots out what we really need to know: When, where, and under what conditions has the statement been true?
>
> —Adrienne Rich

> So with many other feminists, I want to argue for a doctrine and practice of objectivity that privileges contestation, deconstruction, passionate construction, webbed connections, and hope for the transformation of systems of knowledge and ways of seeing.
>
> —Donna J. Haraway

IN THE MIDDLE of the 1990s, well into the second wave of the U.S. feminist movement, at a time when it has been argued that there is no longer a single American feminist movement but rather many contradictory positions, a chapter on "feminist spirituality" as such is no longer feasible. The kind of "objectivity" required to produce such an overview has itself been called into question by feminist activists and scholars alike. They have argued that it is no longer possible to speak of a single, universal feminist anything. As Adrienne Rich reminds us, such universal claims "[blot] out what we really need to know: When, where, and under what conditions has the statement been true?"[1]

With this in mind, this chapter offers a partial account of feminist spirituality. It builds on the kind of feminist approach that Donna J. Haraway calls for in her essay "Situated Knowledges: The Science Question in

Feminism and the Privilege of Partial Perspective."[2] Using the metaphor of vision to shape her argument, Haraway suggests that all knowledge is partial and mediated: "The 'eyes' made available in modern technological sciences shatter any idea of passive vision; these prosthetic devices show us that all eyes, including our own organic ones, are active perceptual systems, building in translations and specific *ways* of seeing, that is, ways of life."[3] In this way, Haraway makes explicit what is wrong with the notion that one can write from either nowhere or everywhere. She sees these positions as two sides of the same coin. She writes: "Relativism and totalization are both 'god-tricks' promising vision from everywhere and nowhere equally and fully, common myths in rhetorics surrounding Science. But it is precisely in the politics and epistemology of partial perspectives that the possibility of sustained, rational, objective enquiry rests."[4] Assenting to Haraway's epistemological premise, this chapter presents a partial perspective. In so doing, it participates in a kind of transformative feminist practice that opens up "new ways of seeing." This scholarly practice is, as Haraway suggests, intimately tied to a feminist politics.

It also builds on the tradition of feminist identity politics and its commitment to specificity as well as complexity. As feminist literary critic Teresa de Lauretis has argued, within this kind of feminist politics identities are multiple and shifting. They are contingently within a process of consciousness. She writes:

> As the most recent developments in feminist theory confirm beyond a doubt (developments that have been prompted by the writings of women of color, Jewish women, and lesbians, and that can be sustained only by a serious, critical, and self-critical attention to the issues they raise), consciousness is not the result but the term of a process, ... is a particular configuration of subjectivity, of subjective limits, produced at the intersection of meaning with experience.[5]

Feminist identity politics, in other words, comes out of the work of women of color, Jewish women, and lesbians, often through the work of women who claim all or some of these identities simultaneously. According to the work of these women, identity is a process. It is neither fixed nor singular.

With this in mind, feminist identity politics affirms the differences within, among, and between women as crucial to feminist practices. Such a politics demands an appreciation for multiple and even contradictory feminist positions. Thus, in addressing secular-Jewish feminist spirituality, this chapter explores a specific instance of such a politics. It explores the differences within, among and between Jewish women. It argues that within this identity politics, secular-Jewish feminists have created transformative cultural and political practices that can be read as a kind of feminist spirituality.

Building on the dual legacy of feminist identity politics and feminist theory, this chapter enacts a commitment to difference. By engaging in a strategy of close readings, it offers a way of getting at the complexity of such difference. In this respect, it is unlike most other chapters in this volume. It offers complexity within a specific tradition in order to illustrate when, where, and under what conditions it might be possible to speak of a feminist spirituality at all.

Secular-Jewish Feminist Spirituality

To speak about secular-Jewish feminists and notions of spirituality demands entering into a series of overlapping communities of Jews, Jewish feminists (secular and religious), and Yiddish-speaking, Eastern European, secular-Jewish men and women. Although it is commonly assumed that "secular-Jewish feminists" are feminists for whom Judaism no longer matters, feminists who no longer care much about their Jewishness, this is not true. As I will argue, secular-Jewish feminists include a broad spectrum of Jewish women for whom Jewishness means many different and often conflicting things including knowledge, pride, anger, alienation, ritual, food, culture, language(s), and a broad range of political positions and commitments. These various traces of Jewishness also have histories. In the United States, some of the most significant of these legacies are the various secular-Jewish movements that emerged in Eastern Europe in the nineteenth century. I have chosen to focus on this particular set of traditions because the vast majority of American Jews, both religious and secular, come from Eastern European backgrounds and have in some way been influenced by this legacy.

How does this legacy relate to secular-Jewish feminist politics? American Jewish women played a critical role in the second wave of the U.S. feminist movement in the 1960s. They were leaders in organizations like the National Organization for Women (NOW); they helped create feminist journals like *Ms.*; and within the popular imagination, many of their names became synonymous with the feminist movement. These Jewish women included Betty Friedan, Gloria Steinem, and Bella Abzug. Within more radical circles, Adrienne Rich and Andrea Dworkin among others have also become quite well known. The involvement of these women in the second wave of the U.S. feminist movement helped distinguish this wave from its nineteenth-century counterpart. The first wave of U.S. feminism was very much connected to the work of Christian women. Although Jewish women did engage in some of these efforts, they were not its leaders, and, by and large, much of this feminist work was tied to issues of Christian faith.[6] By contrast, as feminist organizing began to reemerge in the 1960s, it was a decidedly secular movement. In this respect Jewish women were not alone. The fact that the vast majority of these Jewish feminists were self-identified as "secular" was not unusual.

The real question here is, What does it mean to be secular and Jewish? For these women Jewishness was defined in both cultural and political terms. This meant that they did not often identify directly as Jews. Although they argued that the "personal is political," these women rarely addressed Jewishness in these terms. Relative to their reading of the larger feminist agenda, their Jewishness was of minor importance. It was simply a given. Jewishness became a salient issue only in the late 1970s and early 1980s in response to growing anti-Semitism within both the international women's movement and local feminist organizing. Confronted with often unexpected hostility, many Jewish women who were engaged in feminist politics found it necessary to claim Jewish positions as feminists. They began to articulate what would become a Jewish-feminist "identity politics." They made Jewishness a personal and political issue.

Part of the significance of this return to Jewishness is that few of these women took on religious identities as Jews. Instead they claimed secular-Jewish positions. In so doing, they helped further challenge Western attempts to construe Jewishness simply as a religious phenomenon. My focus in this chapter will be on a particular strand within this movement, those secular-Jewish feminists who chose explicitly to build on the traditions of *yidishkayt,* secular Yiddish culture. What interests me about these women is their explicit appeals to secular, Eastern European, Jewish culture and politics as a way of understanding their own Jewish-feminist positions. Many of these women became leaders in what I have referred to as Jewish-feminist identity politics. The vast majority of them were secular-Jewish lesbians. It will be my contention that their efforts to reclaim a kind of Jewish-feminist politics, although often explicitly not religious, nevertheless can be understood in terms of a nontheistic, secular spirituality. Furthermore, I will argue that this secular spirituality shares much with the type of Jewish commitment found within the traditions of *yidishkayt.* Like these earlier movements, secular-Jewish, feminist identity politics has been a site of individual and communal transformation. Here the marking of Jewish time through holidays, anniversaries, and communal commemorations has been crucial. Such activities have come to define this secular-Jewish feminist spirituality as a form of political practice.

In what follows I map out some of the contours of this spirituality by looking at a specific text, Irena Klepfisz's "Secular Jewish Identity: *Yidishkayt* in America (1986)." My reading of this text will offer insights into the broader cultural milieu of *yidishkayt.* I use Klepfisz's text because it demonstrates the historical contestation among secular positions within Eastern Europe while also challenging any simple reading of continuity between these traditions and contemporary secular-Jewish practices.

In these ways Klepfisz's text helps challenge specifically religious readings of what it means to be Jewish in America. By recontextualizing these secular traditions within the emancipatory promises of America, I want to make clear that religion was not the only strategy used by Jews to respond to the Enlightenment. Rather, I will show that the experience of Eastern European Jews who were not emancipated, who were not offered citizenship as a religious minority, helps nuance our understanding of the position of Jews in America at the end of the twentieth century since we are, in part, the bearers of this legacy as well.

With this in mind, I argue that secular-Jewish feminist spirituality as a cultural and political practice stands alongside the traditions of Eastern European, secular-Jewish culture. By taking seriously the Jewishness of a secular-Jewish feminist spirituality, we can begin to rethink the desire to equate "assimilation" or being "unaffiliated" with the term *secular.* By viewing this strand of nonreligious Jewish cultural practice as a kind of secular spirituality, I hope to call attention to the complexity and diversity of American Jewish cultural expressions.

To demonstrate these crucial points this chapter is divided into two sections. The first section uses "secular-Jewish identity" to complicate and make critical links between and among the terms *secular Jewishness, Jewish feminisms,* and *spirituality.* The second portion of the chapter offers a reading of a second critical text by Klepfisz, one that enacts a secular-Jewish feminist approach to spirituality that has emerged within secular-Jewish, feminist identity politics. This essay is Irena Klepfisz's "*Yom Hashoah Yom Yerushalayim:* A Meditation." Here again Klepfisz's text is exemplary. It demonstrates how a secular-Jewish feminist spirituality looks in practice.

Secular-Jewish Culture: *Di yidishe svive* (The Yiddish Environment)

In her essay "Secular Jewish Identity: *Yidishkayt* in America (1986)," Irena Klepfisz writes:

> All my life I have defined myself as a secular Jew. It is how I was raised and taught to think about myself in relation to Jewishness. I was taught that there is

> no God. I was taught that capitalism oppresses the working masses and all poor people, that it has to be smashed, and that we are to work towards building a classless society. I was taught that Jews have a right to be anywhere and everywhere, that they are not necessarily destined to return to their ancient homeland. And I was taught that Yiddish is *mame-loshn*, the mother tongue, the language of the Jews, the medium through which Jewish culture and politics are to be transmitted. *Mame-loshn* was a language that gave all the tenets which I'd been taught form and substance. I internalized all this and fought fiercely with anyone who disputed these "facts."[7]

I begin with this striking quotation from Irena Klepfisz because it makes clear some of the major tenets of her particular secular Yiddish tradition. As she explains, first and foremost, this is a Jewish but not a religious tradition. There is no God here, but there is clearly a community of Jews who share a socialist politics. In this community, capitalist oppression cannot be tolerated. Jews are obligated to work toward building a classless society.

"I was taught that Jews have a right to be anywhere and everywhere, that they are not necessarily destined to return to their ancient homeland." In other words, this Jewish tradition was also not Zionist. For these Jews, Zionism represented a rival secular-Jewish position. Between the lines of Klepfisz's text many other rival positions, both political and cultural, can also be discerned.

The insistence on Yiddish as the *mame-loshn* is significant in this regard. Language becomes that medium through which all else flows, a discursive foundation for a political culture. As such, this too is a site of contention that must be fought for: "I... fought fiercely with anyone who disputed these 'facts.'" Here too are traces of an old argument. By speaking of the tenets of this tradition as "facts," Klepfisz reminds us that Yiddish was not the only Jewish language. It had rivals. There were, for example, whole communities of Jews who wanted to reclaim Hebrew as a modern Jewish language. They used Hebrew to ground other contemporary, secular-Jewish political positions. These rivals included both Zionist and cultural nationalists, those who were committed to leaving Eastern Europe for Palestine and those who were not. Still others were committed to constructing modern Jewish positions in the languages of Eastern European cultures, especially Polish and Russian. Although I am focusing on the tradition Klepfisz has presented, I use her words to remind readers that within Eastern Europe there were many secular and religious possibilities. Klepfisz's Jewishness had to be fought for. It was a tradition that struggled against a range of other Jewish options, religious, secular, cultural, and political.

From here Klepfisz goes on to articulate the history of her socialist tradition, locating it clearly within the context of Eastern European Jewish life. Although it is perhaps unusual for contemporary American Jews to think about Jewishness in these terms, this was not the case in Poland even as late as 1940. Klepfisz tells us that her parents were part of the Jewish Labor Bund (Der Algemeyner Yidisher Arbeter Bund), founded in 1897, a socialist revolutionary *bavegung* (movement) "whose primary influence was among the urban Jewish working class in Eastern Europe, particularly Poland and Russia."[8] As she goes on to explain, "*Di bavegung* swept those regions, becoming a kind of religion itself, claiming thousands upon thousands of adherents in less than twenty years."[9]

Her description of this phenomenon is striking because it emphasizes that it operated as a kind of religious movement. She does not see these secular movements as simply revised versions of the "prophetic tradition." Of course there is some truth to this claim of continuity, but, as Klepfisz reminds us, there is a difference: "I was taught that there is no God." In other words, for those involved in the Bund, religion was explicitly rejected. Despite this, the movement did depend on learned Jews who were able to use their knowledge of Jewish texts and Jewish history to enhance their secular movement. It is not, therefore, surprising for Klepfisz that many Bundists came from religious backgrounds or remained knowledgeable of Jewish traditions. Those who became involved with the Bund, like many others involved in creating secular-Jewish cultures in both Hebrew and Yiddish, did so with great intelligence and Jewish knowledge. Along with creating political movements, they also built whole bodies of secular-Jewish literature.

In writing about this Yiddish literature, Klepfisz recalls songs and poetry about Purim, Hanukkah, and Pesakh (Passover) as well as works by Sholem Aleykem, I. L. Perez, Avrom Reisen, Morris Rosenfeld, Itzik Manger, Mordecai Gebirtig, and Halper Leivik.[10] These authors used Jewish holidays as well as rabbinic and biblical themes in their writing even as they rejected notions of God and religious practice.[11]

In recounting the history of the Bund, Klepfisz writes: "Many were from the religious community, and their 'conversion' to socialism and the Bund often meant a painful break with family and tradition."[12] Here "tradition" takes on a very specific set of religious meanings. In other words, not all Jewishness is rejected, as Klepfisz's initial statement reminds us: "All my life I have defined myself as a secular Jew. It is how I was raised to think about myself in relation to Jewishness." However, her personal connection to this religious tradition is still quite strong even if it is expressed in terms of a rejection. Her grandfather was among these formerly religious Jews who had converted to socialism. In retrospect it is striking that this movement not only converted Jews but transformed Jewishness. Like Western European reformers, in response to the Enlightenment, these Jews also took radical steps to reimagine Jewishness. Unlike those in the West who had been granted political emancipation for the price of Jewish containment to the newly privatized realm of religion and faith, however, these Jews faced a very different set of political circumstances. In Eastern Europe, "Jewishness" became a question of political and cultural commitments, be they Zionist, socialist, or communist, and whether inflected in Yiddish, Hebrew, Russian, or Polish. The diversity and richness of these responses are quite difficult for contemporary Jews to grasp because the vast majority of those engaged in many of these communities were murdered in the Holocaust. Their legacies come to us only in fragments, through the voices of those like Klepfisz, who was born in Poland in 1941 and was a child survivor, or through Yiddish, Polish, and Russian Jewish texts that now have few readers.

In writing about a portion of this fragmented legacy, the chronicles of the Lodz and Warsaw ghettoes, Sara Horowitz explains some of the difficulty of accessing the complexity of Eastern European Jewish life during the Shoah specifically. Horowitz writes:

> Who we are as readers also determines which texts become available. The Polish-Jewish culture that informs much of the *Oneg Shabbes* archive feels alien to most Americans and Israelis. When the writing of an assimilated, marginal Jew or else of a Bundist does not match the contemporary political and cultural climate, it rarely finds its way into translation. Indeed, most of *Oneg Shabbes* documents and much of Ringelblum's [the archive's founder] own writing have never appeared in English. . . . We select works that affirm our sense of continuity or at least diminish our sense of discontinuity.[13]

Here Horowitz makes clear that what we know even about the Holocaust has been informed by contemporary desires for Jewish continuity. To find voices of Jews whose positions do not fit neatly into either Zionist or religious readings of Jewishness is disconcerting. The "marginal Jew" and the Bundist are offered as examples, and even between them important differences remain unexpressed. These are some of what makes the work of reimagining the world of *yidishkayt* so difficult. Because it was brutally destroyed in the Holocaust, those of us who remain are, at best, ambivalent about calling attention to those aspects of this other Jewish world that do not fit neatly into our own narratives. Klepfisz makes a somewhat different point in her essay as she addresses the loss of Yiddish as a way of life in America. She reminds us that *yidishkayt* was not confined simply to Eastern Europe. Yiddish presses, newspapers, theaters, and political and social organizations remained a part of the American landscape until the 1960s. Thus, in conjunction with the brutal loss of Yiddish life in Eastern Europe, Yiddish culture in America has also been lost, though these two losses were brought about by vastly different means. Klepfisz struggles with both these losses, yet the focus of her essay is on the loss of Yiddish culture in America. Through a series of narratives she tries to convey this growing sense of loss. One such narrative is about Camp Boiberik, a summer camp for the children of what would become the last generation of American Yiddish speakers. Klepfisz describes a growing linguistic gap between parents and children, or between the children's camp on the one side and the guest facilities for adults on the other. Among the adults, Yiddish was the primary language while the young campers increasingly spoke English. "Though some Yiddish must have been understood by many of the children because they heard it at home, a rich, adult Yiddish would have been incomprehensible to the majority. The white wooden fence that marked the boundaries between the two camps was also a boundary line that delineated two different cultural territories.[14]

In order to bridge this gap, Klepfisz "became involved in writing and directing a musical comedy about the Jews of Khelm." She explains: "I felt proud because I perceived it as a purely Jewish (which in those days was synonymous with Yiddish) product, even though the Khelemites spoke pure English."[15] This production was not well received by the camp director, a staunch Yiddishist. He considered this "less than pure" Yiddish cultural production blasphemous. Although Klepfisz tried to argue, at that time, that language need not be everything, she explains that she still had more to learn about just how important it actually is. Thus in retelling the story she admonishes herself for being young and irreverent about these matters. This story is striking in part because it foretells her later efforts to preserve *yidishkayt.*

In the final section of her essay, where she reflects on *di tsukunft* (the future), Klepfisz writes:

> What I have come to realize is that if I am to maintain a strong relationship to Yiddish culture I cannot afford the luxury of an "all or nothing" attitude. Nor can *di yidishe velt.* Such a purist attitude is destructive, alienating the vast majority of Jews of Eastern European backgrounds, diminishing our ranks, making *di yidishe kultur* available only to a few. This attitude turns Yiddish into a kind of *loshn-koydesh,* a holy language, makes *yidishe kultur* a religion in which only *di groyse gelernte,* great scholars, can practice.[16]

Building on this, she argues for a different kind of Yiddish cultural practice. It cannot be an all or nothing proposition. For Yiddish culture to survive into the next century, the legacies of *yidishkayt* must be translated into contemporary idioms. A tremendous sense of loss as well as a desire for a complicated continuity accompanies this complex proposition. Yiddish cannot be elite or "holy." It cannot be the "property" of a few scholars. Klepfisz argues for an unholy Yiddish, a secular, cultural practice that combines both Yiddish and English. Klepfisz began to enact these moves in her own writing as she incorporated Yiddish into her poetry, something that did not occur until the late 1980s.[17]

With this in mind, Klepfisz points to various efforts to revitalize Yiddish culture in ways that keep the vitality and diversity of its Jewishness alive. These efforts include a broad range of activities and constituencies. One way of assuring that Yiddish will remain vital is encouraging people to speak it. Here Klepfisz writes about the value of even a "passive knowledge." She notes that many people are taking courses in universities, YMCAs and YWCAs, Hillels, and community centers while Yiddish scholarship continues at YIVO (the Institute for Jewish Research in New York). She also mentions the growing interest in klezmer music. In terms of other signs of Yiddish life, she includes projects like the National Yiddish Book Center in Amherst, Massachusetts, which has saved millions of Yiddish books from being destroyed even though, ironically, few engaged in these preservation efforts are themselves able to read these salvaged volumes.[18] Explicitly feminist efforts to preserve Yiddish culture include the publication of new anthologies of Yiddish writings by and about women, republication of stories and poems by Yiddish women writers in both Yiddish and English, and the publication of books and articles about various aspects of the legacy of Yiddish women writers and activists.[19]

Furthermore, Klepfisz's work is a part of a much broader resurgence of Yiddish cultural production, albeit a production with a difference. This Yiddish culture is not the same as that of the past; it is not the American *yidishe svive* in which Klepfisz grew up, nor is it the one in which she might have grown up in Poland.

By focusing on those persons who are the least knowledgeable links in this new tradition and even affirming them, Klepfisz explicitly rejects a logic of purity. Thus, about "passive Yiddishists" she writes: "They represent a totally new phenomenon, Yiddishists without knowledge of Yiddish language but deeply committed to the survival of Yiddish culture. A paradox, but a reality that should not be dismissed or mocked."[20] These Jews are Klepfisz's allies in a "spiritual" endeavor to keep Yiddish culture alive. As she sees it, the survival of the people is linked with the perpetuation of culture. The preservation of Yiddish is, therefore, about survival. She writes: "Not unlike a *lebn geblibene,* a survivor, of an overwhelming catastrophe, it [Yiddish] seems to be saying *knbin nisht vos ikh bin amol geven.* I am not what I once was. *Ober 'khbin nisht gestrobn. Ikh leb.* But I did not die. I live."[21]

For Klepfisz there is also a politics that must be affirmed, a nonelite, socialist, Jewish politics that needs to find new forms of expression. For her this political legacy finds voice in a secular-Jewish feminist politics. This is an identity politics that ironically embraces differences among Jews, that remembers that, even in America, there are other Jews, Jews who do come from Eastern Europe and who never spoke Yiddish. Even as she affirms her own Yiddish legacy, Klepfisz argues for an embrace of Jewish differences. This is identity politics. To make this connection to the past, she writes: "Yiddish was never the exclusive property of *di groyse gelernte.* It was a language of a people of different ideologies, education, commitment, as much the language of gangsters and shopkeepers as that of poets and intellectuals. Never was it a private cult."[22] The memory of differences among and between those within the *yidishe svive* allows Klepfisz to affirm other kinds of differences in a new political and historical climate.

Through the feminist movement Klepfisz has begun to reclaim her Jewishness in these complicated ways. She explains that combining lesbian-feminist activism and a commitment to *yidishkayt* was not always easy. She often felt torn apart and unable to reconcile these different worlds, but feminist identity politics changed this for her. Along with many other secular-Jewish women, Klepfisz found that this kind of politics allowed for complexity and contradictions. Identity need not be a single unified position. For Klepfisz this meant being able to affirm commitments to lesbian-feminist politics and to *yidishkayt.* For others with different histories of assimilation and reclamation, this opened up yet other possibilities. About this aspect of feminist identity politics Elly Bulkin writes:

> I think...of the decisions to celebrate one's identity: for those Native American women, Latinas, and Black women who could "pass" as white; for the Jewish woman whose father changed his name in the Thirties so he could "make it," and raised her, ignorant of her identity, as a Christian; for the Arab-American woman, who, after internalizing her racial oppression, came only in the last few years to identify as a woman of color; for the Jewish-Latina, the Arab-Jewish woman, for any Jewish woman of color who is too often, as one Jamaican-Jewish woman has said, "a token to everybody"; for any woman of color of mixed heritage;...for the Arab-American dyke who is shunned because she is a lesbian by the only other Arab woman in town, the Jewish lesbian whose family sits *shivah* [seven-day mourning period] for her, the "bulldagger" whose Black community rejects her.

> All of the women who are told to choose between or among identities, insist on selecting them all.[23]

This is Klepfisz's position. Identity politics allowed her to share with women often quite different from herself an appreciation for her own complicated identities. Although I have attempted to present a reading of Klepfisz's particular commitments to *yidishkayt,* this is by no means a full reading of her position. It is a partial account. Like many Jewish feminists, Klepfisz has multiple commitments; her identities are "not divided in, but rather at odds with, language." Hers is "an identity made up of heterogeneous and heteronomous representations of gender, race, and class, . . . across languages and cultures."[24]

In these ways the feminist movement and *yidishkayt* are intertwined in Klepfisz's work. Her explicit debt to the lesbian-feminist movement is always already informed by her secular-Jewish position. It is to these imbricated struggles that she dedicates her collection of essays *Dreams of an Insomniac: Jewish Feminist Essays, Speeches and Diatribes:* "*tsu der bavegung* / to the movement and the lesbian/feminists who made this work possible." As I will demonstrate in the final section of this chapter, like many secular-Jewish feminists, Klepfisz uses her Yiddish, secular-Jewish, and lesbian-feminist cultural and political commitments in transformative ways. Together they make her "work possible."

Jewish Feminisms

The complexity among and between second wave American Jewish feminists can be articulated, in some sense, in terms of a rift between secular and religious Jewish women, although this is by no means absolute. I use this schematic as a way of making clear, in the context of this chapter, the critical role of nonreligious Jewish women in the formation of Jewish-feminist identity politics. It is within this cultural and political reclaiming of Jewishness that, as I see it, a kind of secular-Jewish feminist spirituality has emerged. This spirituality shares much with its Yiddish predecessors. In both cases spirituality is decidedly not religious; rather it is manifest in terms of transformative political and cultural practices.

While some Jewish women who were engaged in the second wave of the American feminist movement were primarily involved in activities within organized Jewish communities, others located themselves outside of these Jewish venues. The former, therefore, I will refer to as religious, the later as secular. These secular Jews primarily identified themselves as feminists, generally considering their Jewishness irrelevant to their work as feminist activists and scholars. Many of these Jewish women were leaders in mainstream, liberal, U.S. feminist political organizations as well as in feminist scholarship. Most of these women shared white skin, middle class, and heterosexual privilege with both other members of these organizations and other feminist scholars in the academy. Betty Friedan is a good example of liberal Jewish feminists speaking for liberal U.S. feminism. Other secular-Jewish women were involved both politically and academically in more radical efforts. This group included, primarily and most importantly, lesbian Jewish feminists. Like Klepfisz, many of these women were involved in mainstream as well as socialist feminist movements, utopian feminist communities, and various other radical political organizations and scholarly activities.[25]

This large and disparate group of Jewish feminists shared similar attitudes toward their Jewishness. During the early years of the second wave of U.S. feminism what was important to these women was the broader struggle for the empowerment of all women. Although they disagreed, often radically, with one another on how to achieve this goal, they did agree that Jewishness was not an issue.

The marginality of many of these women's Jewishness to their feminism(s) did not last. As I have already indicated, by the mid 1970s this situation changed dramatically. The catalyst for much of this shift was the passage of a resolution equating Zionism with racism at the first United Nations International Women's Decade Conference in Mexico City in 1975. As Letty Cottin Pogrebin, a founding editor at *Ms.* magazine and a U.S. delegate to the conference, acknowledges:

> If the Declaration of Mexico was the initial "click" that started me on my life as a *Jewish*-feminist, the first trip to Israel was the opening act of commitment, the first step in my journey towards a conscious advocacy of secular-Jewish interests. It helped me start training the muscles of a different kind of Jewish identity — not the one that belonged to God, prayer, and synagogue, nor the sentimental kind associated with nostalgia, Yiddishisms, and chicken soup, but new political contours that were so robust and sinewy they made everything else in my wardrobe too small.... I'd like to claim a more positive impetus for my reawakened Jewish persona — an impressive mentor or persuasive literary arguments — but it was only feral Jew-hating that forced me to reconsider what I was and what I wanted to be.[26]

Unlike Klepfisz's position, Pogrebin's secular-Jewish position was Zionist in orientation. Her first trip to Israel was critically important. For her "Yiddishisms" were associated with nostalgia and a personal, privatized past that was not "political." Building on a Zionist ideological commitment to newness, bodily strength, stature, and vitality, Pogrebin outgrows her old Jewishness.[27] Those clothes no longer fit, and like Zionist thinkers before her, this move to a secular Zionist position comes in response to the Jewish question of anti-Semitism. As we have seen in the guise of Irena Klepfisz and others, Zionism was not the only newly proclaimed, secular-Jewish feminist option. What is important about Pogrebin's statement, however, is its marking of a shift in secular-Jewish feminist politics, the felt need to reclaim an explicitly Jewish position.

Thus, after 1975 many Jewish feminists became increasingly aware of, and articulate about, anti-Semitism, not only in the international women's movements but in various aspects of the American feminist movement. These experiences were galvanized by the second United Nation's International Women's Decade Conference held in 1980 in Copenhagen. As Pogrebin notes, by 1980 the issue was no longer simply the association of Jews with racism in the international community; there was also anti-Semitism in the U.S. women's movement. In order to verify this fact, Pogrebin began a research project in 1980 (after Copenhagen) that would become her critical 1982 essay for *Ms.*, "Anti-Semitism in the Women's Movement."[28] This essay stirred much heated debate in both the women's movement and the organized Jewish community. The essay chronicled anti-Semitic incidents reported by Jewish women on college campuses, in academic scholarship, in women's publishing houses, and at all levels of feminist organizing. Attacks from both the right and the left wings of the movement were included. Not only were Jewish women's support for the State of Israel and Zionism questioned; incidents also included the invocation of much older anti-Semitic tropes about Jews in feminist organizing. Jewish women were criticized for their disproportionate representation in leadership roles, their aggressiveness, their hard work, and their loudness. Furthermore, the essay explained that attempts by Jewish women to speak out against these accusations were often ignored or dismissed. Finally, on another level, the essay explained that many Jewish women had internalized these negative perceptions of themselves as Jews.

Efforts by Jewish women to work against anti-Semitism within the women's movement were spearheaded by Jewish lesbian feminists, who saw the fight against anti-Semitism as integrally connected to the antiracist work that many of them had already been engaged in. They created forums and workshops to work against both anti-Semitism and racism, not only in lesbian-feminist communities but throughout the women's movement. Much of this critical work can be traced in the pages of various (especially lesbian) feminist journals and newspapers. The collection *The Tribe of Dina,* for example, originally published as a special issue of the lesbian publication *Sinister Wisdom,* includes a handbook on anti-Semitism and Jewish identity.[29] Intended specifically for Jewish women, this handbook helps women to confront their own internalized anti-Semitism. The authors argue that anti-Semitism affects Jews by fostering silence, preventing Jewish solidarity, and isolating Jews from other groups. The strategies for resistance they offer respond to each of these problems; the categories involve breaking silence; building Jewish identity, pride, and solidarity; and creating coalitions.[30]

Other lesbian feminists working against anti-Semitism and racism included Elly Bulkin, Minnie Bruce Pratt, and Barbara Smith, who jointly published *Yours in Struggle: Three Feminist Perspectives on Anti-Semitism and Racism.* Bulkin's essay, "Hard Ground: Jewish Identity, Racism and Anti-Semitism," in particular, chronicles much of the work that was done in lesbian-feminist communities to combat anti-Semitism and racism — efforts critical to articulating feminist identity politics as a cultural as well as a political phenomenon.[31] In this way these early efforts to articulate differences between feminists did include Jewish difference.

Despite these powerful efforts to claim "Jewish identities" in response to anti-Semitism, there are still many Jewish women involved in feminist activism and feminist scholarship whose Jewishness remains unarticulated. In many academic fields of feminist inquiry, only a few critical accounts of Jewishness have been offered. Even in cases where feminist scholars have written about issues of race, class, and sexual orientation, discussions of anti-Semitism or their own Jewishness remain rare. Thus, although many feminist anthologies, including Teresa de Lauretis's *Feminist Studies/Critical Studies*, have included the voices of Jewish women, few if any of these women acknowledge, much less discuss, what it has meant for them to be doing feminist work as Jews.[32] Even in their diversity, however, secular-Jewish feminists can be sharply contrasted with those Jewish women who, although affected by the broader women's movement, primarily identified themselves as feminists within organized religious-Jewish communities.

Beginning in the early 1970s, like the mainstream organizations within the larger women's movement in the United States and like their nineteenth-century and early twentieth-century Jewish-feminist counterparts, these women spoke the language of liberalism. They demanded that women be included not only within the liberal social contract but within the Jewish covenantal community as well. They worked to secure for Jewish women the formal right to participate fully in liberal-Jewish communal life. As a result of these efforts, women have become rabbis and cantors in the Reform, Conservative, and Reconstructionist movements, and laywomen are now included in active Jewish worship and communal governance.

These women shared a commitment to defining Jewishness as primarily a religious identity. Within American liberalism, religion was understood to be a site of acceptable difference. They followed the emancipatory patterns established in Western Europe, where becoming citizens meant confining one's Jewish difference to questions of faith. In this way, liberal Jews remodeled themselves in the image of liberal Christians. They created Jewish religious and social-service organizations to mirror those of their Christian counterparts.

Feminists involved in these Jewish communities were also diverse, including lesbian, bisexual, and straight Jewish feminists from a variety of class and Jewish religious backgrounds. Like Christian feminists, these Jewish women brought feminist concerns about the empowerment of women into liberal-Jewish institutions, synagogues, and Jewish communal-service organizations as well as into explicitly Jewish scholarship.

By the 1980s, these Jewish feminists also became increasingly engaged in more radical projects. Instead of simply gaining access to existing institutions and practices, they began asking more fundamental questions.[33] Like their liberal-Christian counterparts, they were interested in transforming, not simply reforming, their liberal religious communities. Through both critical and constructive social and scholarly interventions, some more radical goals were accomplished.

Strikingly, much of this scholarly and religious communal work was done in connection with liberal Christian-feminist scholars and clergy. The work of Jewish-feminist religious scholarship, especially Jewish-feminist theology, was nurtured within the context of the Women's Section of the American Academy of Religion. Jewish-feminist theologian Judith Plaskow, for example, helped found the section. Through it she also helped establish the *Journal of Feminist Studies in Religion*, which she coedited for twenty years. The collections *Womanspirit Rising: A Feminist Reader in Religion* and *Weaving the Vision: New Patterns in Feminist Spirituality*, both of which Plaskow coedited with theologian Carol Christ, have become classics in the field of feminist studies in religion.[34] These efforts have encouraged an appreciation of difference among religious feminists, especially differences among Christian women in terms of class, race, sexuality, and ethnicity. Here a kind of identity politics has helped establish multiple and contradictory Christian and post-Christian positions. This effort is exemplified in African-American Christian women's work in womanist theologies, ethics, and biblical scholarship; in Latina *mujerista* theologies; as well as in theological work by Asian Christian feminists.[35]

As in the case of secular identity politics, much of this work across differences was spearheaded by lesbian feminists working from multiple positions. What is striking are both the similarities and the differences between these primarily Christian and Jewish efforts to deal with issues of difference within and between religious communities; also notable are the kinds of work in identity politics that were done among secular feminists. Here, from the vantage point of this chapter, two things stand out. First, secular-Jewish voices are absent from these discussions. Second, the voices in these discussions, though different, are overwhelming Christian. Although Jewish women, Goddess worshipers and a few Muslim, Hindu, and Buddhist women enter into these "religious" discussions, the vast majority of the women engaged in this kind of scholarship are Christian.

In contrast to much of traditional Jewish scholarship and religious practice, the creative and celebratory work that these feminists have been engaged in has included: the creation of new women's rituals, the revival of old rituals, the creation of new liturgies, and new interpretations of sacred texts. Among these interpretations were the creation of Jewish-feminist midrashim, stories, and poetry and a full range of Jewish-feminist scholarship in all areas of Jewish studies, including Jewish history, literature, religion, language studies, political studies, folklore, music, art, and archeology. All of these efforts have allowed Jewish feminists to reclaim the voices of Jewish women, both past and present, as a means to transforming Jewish communal and religious practices.[36] In these ways they have created a powerful religious-Jewish feminist spirituality. In many of these endeavors, however, they share much in common with their secular counterparts. All of these women, albeit in different ways, have been engaged in the task of reclaiming Jewish traditions, rituals, and practices as well as creating new ones.

After 1975, particularly in response to anti-Semitism, secular- and religious-Jewish feminists were increasingly forced to confront each other, as in Pogrebin's essay. That essay brought together diverse Jewish-feminist voices to talk about anti-Semitism; women from Jewish studies, lesbian-feminist publishing, and the international women's movement were all cited. *Lilith* magazine, a Jewish-feminist publication created in the early 1980s, also tried to bridge some of these rifts. In addition to this, Jewish-feminist texts like the primarily lesbian-Jewish-feminist collections *Nice Jewish Girls* and *The Tribe of Dina,* first published in the early 1980s, each explicitly tried to include a broad range of Jewish-feminist voices. *Nice Jewish Girls,* first published in 1982, for example, included articles by Judith Plaskow and Annette Daum, religious-Jewish feminists who wrote about anti-Semitism in Christian-feminist theologizing. Their inclusion was a powerful statement across the divide between religiously identified and secularly identified Jewish feminists.

These texts also acknowledged other kinds of differences among Jewish feminists. Both *The Tribe of Dina* and *Nice Jewish Girls* included writings by Mizrahi and Arab-Jewish feminists; lesbian and straight Jewish women; Jewish feminists with different class, national, and educational backgrounds; as well as Jewish feminists with diverse positions on the Israeli-Palestinian conflict. More recently these efforts to acknowledge difference among Jewish feminists have been enhanced by the publication of *Bridges: A Journal for Jewish Feminists and Our Friends.* The journal has worked hard to give voice to many painful, and heretofore invisible, differences among contemporary Jewish feminists and "our friends." Its editors have written about not only those differences that I have already mentioned but also physical handicaps, disease, and histories of abuse, as well as issues of class that separate us.

Although I have thus far painted a rather congenial picture, there have been some very important rifts between these two groups of Jewish feminists. One manifestation of this has been resistance within the organized Jewish community to engage the legacy of secular Jewishness more broadly. In this respect, secular-Jewish feminists are a more recent manifestation of an older problem. What is different in this case is that feminists were asked to work against each other.

In the late 1970s and early 1980s, religious-Jewish feminists were increasingly asked to choose between their Jewishness and their feminism.[37] In this context, books like *Nice Jewish Girls* and *The Tribe of Dina* were marginalized or, worse yet, dismissed. In subtle and not so subtle ways, those of us within liberal-Jewish communities were asked to rank our identities, to set up hierarchies in order to make clear that our loyalties were to the Jewish community first and foremost. Jewish feminists who chose differently, especially secular-Jewish women committed to feminist identity politics, were marginalized. These Jewish women — who, when asked to choose between multiple identities, chose them all — were considered untrustworthy as Jews. Moreover, when some of these women combined their feminism(s) with a more critical stance toward the State of Israel, especially after the invasion of Lebanon in 1982, many in the American liberal-Jewish community considered them dangerous.[38] Ironically, these women, who were sanctioned by other Jews for not being Jewish enough, were besieged by criticism within the feminist movement for just the opposite reason: they were too Jewish. These women were forced to defend their Jewishness in light of Israeli policies. In the pages of the gay, lesbian, and feminist presses this group struggled to find ways of affirming their Jewishness. They did this in the face of growing criticism within not only feminist but other leftist circles as well.[39]

Thus as liberal-Jewish publications and organizations stressed the anti-Semitism within feminist politics, using texts like Pogrebin's as cautionary tales, secular-Jewish feminists fought precisely these battles as Jews within the feminist movement. Sadly, the message within liberal-Jewish communities was that feminism may be dangerous for Jews. Their internal critique of feminist anti-Semitism often went unappreciated. Instead of embracing differences between Jews, the liberal-Jewish community demanded loyalty. That community's message was particularly powerful because it used feminists' own accounts of anti-Semitism to argue against feminism. The message was that Judaism must be the first priority; feminism must be a lesser concern. These issues were again very much in keeping with the experiences of many women from marginal or minority communities. Unlike some of these other women, Jewish women found themselves to be both minority women and able "to pass." Since many Jewish women shared white skin privilege with their white Christian and post-Christian counterparts, their alliance with women of color was not always a simple venture. Rather the issue of Jewish difference continues to be fraught with complexities for Jews and non-Jews alike. The complexity of Jewish difference is not easy to assimilate.[40]

Despite these obstacles, many religious-Jewish feminists continued to identify themselves as feminists. My point is not that there were no liberal-Jewish feminists, but that these women were discouraged from identifying too closely with the more radical secular-Jewish voices of those engaged in the work of identity politics. Instead, these women were often asked to embrace Jewish liberalism and its gestures toward equality and to ask no further questions.

In this section I have made a point of discussing the impact of secular-Jewish traditions and especially secular-Jewish, feminist identity politics on an understanding of American Jewish culture. I have done this from within the study of religion in order to resist the tendency to equate Jewishness with religion only. By stressing the politics of communal transformation that both *yidishkayt* and Jewish-feminist identity politics have offered secular Jews, I ask that we rethink the boundaries of what we mean by "Jewishness" and what we mean by "spirituality."

Spirituality

In the introduction to the present volume, Peter H. Van Ness discusses "the spiritual aspect of human existence." The question here, then, is: How and to what extent does that explanation apply to the tradition(s) of Jewish secularism and, more specifically, to secular-Jewish, feminist identity politics? How does Van Ness's understanding relate to the ways in which I have used the term *spirituality* thus far? His description that one "engages reality as a maximally inclusive whole and makes the cosmos an intentional object of thought and feeling" is not very relevant. Although secular-Jewish feminists may not share the philosophical presuppositions of this description, they would agree, in contrast to a more metaphysical position, that the cosmos gains its integrity by becoming the focus of human awareness. They reject the metaphysical position that understands all that happens as intended by God or otherwise predetermined. Such a position is particularly difficult for many religious Jews to hold in the aftermath of the Holocaust. For both religious and secular Jews, agency, as opposed to intentionality, is crucial. The point here is that if all that happens in the universe is part of a grand scheme that makes sense, the Holocaust has to "make sense"; it must be part of the plan. For all but a very few orthodox Jews, such a metaphysical reading is obscene. Rather, it is more compelling to think about these catastrophic events in terms of human agency. These horrors are human horrors. They can be addressed through human agency. They are not to be considered a part of a divine plan.

To see that life has a "spiritual dimension" in the sense that life "is apprehended as a project of one's most enduring and vital self and is structured by experiences of sudden self-transformation and subsequent gradual development" holds more direct promise. In a somewhat modified form, I have appealed to this kind of transformative reading of spirituality in order to make my case. However, in applying Van Ness's definition to a secular-Jewish "worldview," I have challenged his distinction between an "inner" and an "outer" spirituality. This binary does not hold for the kind of spirituality expressed within either *yidishkayt* or feminist identity politics. In each of these cases individual and collective expressions of transformation are intertwined. Neither exists in isolation.

The personal is especially political in feminist identity politics. Although the personal is stressed in such politics, assertions of self are never done in isolation, as Elly Bulkin reminds us. These assertions are offered within an analysis of power relations. In this way, identity politics offers a kind of solidarity across historical and institutional differences of power. Thus, the phrase *inner self-transformation* is not fully accurate for secular Jews if the word *transformation* has both internal and external implications. In other words, what I have offered is not a psychological reading of feminist politics. This transformation cannot be reduced to an isolated individual endeavor. Rather, for secular Jews spiritual transformation is best understood within an analysis of social conditions. Here the "spiritual dimension" is better understood in terms of its material implications.

Finally, I have added "ritual" and the marking of sacred time to my working definition of spirituality. As I will now demonstrate in my reading of Klepfisz's "*Yom Hashoah, Yom Yerushalayim:* A Meditation," the marking of time and the communal celebration and commemoration of critical moments of the past and of the present are essential elements within secular-Jewish practice.

Secular-Jewish Feminist Spirituality in Practice

By focusing on the short version of Klepfisz's essay, which she prepared for *Jewish Women's Call for Peace: A Handbook for Jewish Women on the Israeli/Palestinian Conflict,* a volume that she coedited, I place her text within a broader feminist political movement for peace.[41] Because Klepfisz is an editor of the handbook, her essay speaks directly to the purposes of the volume. It serves "as a focus for debate to gain greater understanding of the issues and obstacles in the way of action" (5). The essay comes in the section of the volume entitled "Facts and Fears." That section is preceded by an opening section entitled "Women's Voices," which includes a range of Jewish positions both within Israel and in North America, and is followed by two final sections devoted to getting organized and finding resources. These final sections together offer concrete suggestions for action.

At issue in Klepfisz's piece are the complicated interconnections between the legacy of the Holocaust, support for the State of Israel, a commitment to the end of Israeli occupation of the West Bank and Gaza, and a commitment to the creation of a Palestinian state. Like the other pieces in "Facts and Fears" and the *Handbook* overall, Klepfisz's essay attempts to "prove that fears *can* be overcome, that dissent and commitment *are not* mutually exclusive." (6). In this way Klepfisz's essay speaks directly to some of the most painful issues facing Jews at the end of the twentieth century. She speaks directly to the dual legacy of the Holocaust and the creation of the State of Israel.

Although earlier versions of Klepfisz's essay highlighted important changes in Jewish-feminist politics — especially sympathy toward the Intifada — as well as Klepfisz's complicated secular-Jewish, lesbian, feminist, Yiddishist, child-survivor, and poet-activist commitments, I have chosen to focus on the short version of Klepfisz's essay because it makes clear how secular-Jewish feminist politics is Jewish. As a crucial part of this activist handbook, it emerges out of both Klepfisz's role in organizing the Jewish Women's Committee to End the Occupation of the West Bank and Gaza (JWCEO), the organization responsible for publishing the *Handbook* and to which its proceeds were donated, as well as her ties to a community of Holocaust survivors. It invites readers, especially Jewish ones, into the problematics of Israeli occupation in relation to the Holocaust. For Klepfisz, such connections are never simple. Instead she helps readers understand that such connections can be made in such a way that peace efforts need not negate one's commitment to a Jewish state. What is most striking in the essay is the way in which it accomplishes this difficult task. This is where ritual and the marking of Jewish time become so important.

By explicitly marking Jewish time, by using rituals of commemoration and mourning, Klepfisz's essay places political action within the realm of Jewish practice. In other words, it presents political activism as a form of feminist spirituality that offers the possibility of both individual and communal transformation.

"*Yom Hashoah, Yom Yerushalayim:* A Meditation" begins by juxtaposing two dates: 26 April 1987, Yom Hashoah, the day that commemorates the Holocaust; and 5 June 1987, Yom Yerushalayim, the twentieth anniversary of the reunification of the city of Jerusalem. For Klepfisz the link between these two dates is visceral. She begins with the Holocaust.

> As a Jewish child-survivor born in Warsaw during the war, mourning the Holocaust reaffirms my belief that Jews need a safe homeland in a world that for centuries has proven hostile; it makes me consider once more the enormity of our loss, its irretrievability, and the moral lessons to be drawn for the present and future. (39)

I begin with this quotation because it makes explicit the complicated stakes involved for Klepfisz and indeed for many Jews in talking about the Six-Day War. Before getting to the reunification of Jerusalem, however, she argues for reading the present and the future through the lens of mourning and loss. For Klepfisz reunification already brings with it the specter of occupation. Although mourning means a commitment to a safe homeland for Jews, even this desire is tempered by moral responsibility.

When Klepfisz turns to 5 June 1987, she writes that this day, which "was designed for celebration," should "cause deep sorrow, for *Yom yerushalayim* veiled a reality that should be mourned — the twentieth anniversary of Israeli military occupation of the West Bank" (39). Despite the desire of many Jews to celebrate, Klepfisz asks us to look again at this anniversary, to reflect on what it has meant for those who have had to live under Israeli occupation. In the face of this reality, she asks us to mourn. This mourning leads Klepfisz into action.

The section that follows is set a year later, on 25 April 1988. It describes what it meant for Klepfisz to stand "outside the offices of the Conference of Presidents of Major Jewish Organizations, 515 Park Avenue in New York," and "protest American Jewish support of Israeli policies in the Occupied Territories" (39). Klepfisz goes on to write about this protest, about her commitment to working in solidarity with Israeli women and their peace vigils and in support of Palestinian resistance. She also explains what it felt like to object publicly to the policies of the Jewish state. She discusses her doubts not so much about the rightness of her position but about what it meant for her to protest publicly. She writes powerfully about those Jews who questioned her actions. She writes about feeling ashamed as a Jew and the newness of these feelings (39).

However, the rage directed at her by other Jews was more jolting than this shame. The anger of these Jews came out of the deep conviction that after the Holocaust no such protest by Jews could ever be justified. The derogatory remarks hurled at Klepfisz and the other protesters were extreme, were couched in the rhetoric of the Holocaust. They were told that they too should have died in Europe, that they were giving Hitler his final victory. Instead of dismissing those who cursed her, Klepfisz writes compassionately about the familiar fear that produced these remarks. She identifies with this fear. She argues that these Jewish protesters and counterprotesters alike share a "strange mixture of shame and fear" that has generated their different positions. In both instances, Jews are being forced to rethink their connections to Israel and its policies in light of the Holocaust. These efforts are difficult and frightening.

The next section of her text, entitled "Israel and the Holocaust," offers a strategy. It is arranged in roughly three subsections. The first reminds readers that Jews are taught never to use Holocaust analogies except when defending Israel. As corollary to this, they also learn that making analogies to the plight of Palestinians is the worst possible scenario. In response to this, Klepfisz asks, "Yet isn't it impossible *not* to make comparisons?" (40). The second subsection argues that it is problematic to compare Israeli policies to Nazi politics. As she reminds us, such moves nullify the Holocaust; they efface the tragedy of Jewish loss. Klepfisz then moves to the question of passivity in response to Nazi atrocities. Here she returns to the issue of Palestinians and asks that Jews not be passive in the face of Israeli acts of injustice. For Klepfisz such passivity and indifference are the worst of evils. They are about collaboration. The third subsection ambivalently describes in concrete terms how such analogies might work in relation to the Israeli occupation. The example she provides is a discussion with her mother. While reading a newspaper article about Israeli soldiers rounding up Palestinian men, she asks her mother: "What does it remind you of?" The image of men asked to lie face down in a field is all too obvious to both Klepfisz and her mother. Thus, she concludes: "Given the images etched on our collective consciousness, how can this *not* remind us of the Holocaust?" (40).

The next section of the essay brings us back to a specific date, 19 April 1988. She has been asked to speak at a ceremony marking the forty-fifth anniversary of the Warsaw Ghetto Uprising. The invitation raises once again the ambivalences of her current position, the difficulties in putting together the Holocaust and Israeli occupation. This time the connection is more direct, and she finds herself making links between uprisings: the Warsaw Ghetto Uprising that took place forty-five years earlier and the Intifada, the Palestinian uprising, that began in December 1987, only five months prior to this commemoration. She states: "I have to find a way to bring up the *Intifada* without offending the survivors and without disrupting the memorial itself. I have to find a way to express my morality, which is rooted in the Holocaust, without evoking the hated analogy" (40–41). The problem she poses clearly has broader implications. She wants to get out of the simple either-or reading of the analogy without denying the power of this anniversary for the survivors that she will be addressing.

In the next section of her essay, she offers an account of the ritual staging of the commemoration. This is the kind of event that Klepfisz had attended since childhood. Its elements are familiar: candle lighting and the mourners Kaddish, the traditional prayer for the dead. For the forty-fifth anniversary there are five hundred to six hundred people present, mostly survivors and the children of survivors. She watches from the stage as six candles are lit by six separate survivors, one candle for each of the six million who died.

In observing those on stage as well as those in the audience, Klepfisz reminds herself that these people "should not be expected to be morally superior"; and yet even as she reminds herself of this, she struggles not to be angry, especially with those who refuse to see the kinds of connections with which she is struggling. With these thoughts in mind she begins her remarks.

The text of her speech ("The Forty-Fifth Anniversary of the Warsaw Ghetto Uprising: April 19, 1988") is boxed off in this version of the essay. It is framed as a separate entity, perhaps a piece to be read alone but even still intimately connected to all that has preceded it. This talk is also about rethinking the legacy of the Holocaust in relation to contemporary practice. Although the talk itself deserves careful analysis, what is crucial about it is the way in which Klepfisz rereads the legacy of the Warsaw Ghetto Uprising — how she connects it to the present and the future.

According to Klepfisz, the uprising was primarily about the loss of ordinary life. She writes: "I have come to believe that ordinariness is the most precious thing we struggle for, what the Jews of the Warsaw Ghetto fought for. Not noble causes or abstract theories. But the right to go on living with a sense of purpose and a sense of self-worth — an ordinary life. It is this loss that we mourn today" (42).

With this in mind, Klepfisz eloquently asks those who have survived and especially their children, those of the next generation, to take seriously this legacy. In answer to the question of how to go about doing this, she writes:

> I have concluded that one way to pay tribute to those we loved who struggled, resisted, and died is to hold on to their vision and their fierce outrage at the destruction of the ordinary life of their people. It is this outrage we need to keep alive in our daily life and apply to all situations whether they involve Jews or non-Jews. It is this outrage we must use to fuel our actions and vision whenever we see signs of the disruptions of common life. (43)

I quote this passage at length because it signifies Klepfisz's move to the present. The examples she uses to spell out her position are all taken from what were recent events in the Occupied Territories. The passage thus continues with the following list of disruptions of common life:

> The hysteria of a mother grieving for a teenager who has been shot; a family stunned in front of a vandalized or demolished home; a family separated, displaced; arbitrary and unjust laws that demand the closing or opening of shops and schools; humiliation of a people whose culture is alien and deemed inferior; a people left homeless, without citizenship; a people living under military rule. (43)

For Klepfisz, outrage over these kinds of actions is a way of paying homage to the legacy of those, like her own father, who fought and died in the Warsaw Ghetto Uprising. April 19 is a day of mourning, and yet we do not mourn in isolation. We do so within history. Thus despite her own desire to mourn quietly, without distractions, forty-five years later, she tells her audience that this is no longer possible: "The present presses in upon us, insists on our attention;... we do not mourn in a vacuum" (44). In response, outrage becomes crucial. For Klepfisz this outrage is in the name of those who died. She thus argues that it is incumbent upon contemporary Jews to become outraged over Israeli policies. She asks them to do so in the name of preserving the rhythms of ordinary life.

She concludes the essay by offering some reactions to her talk. Overall it went well. She is relieved. Many are grateful to her for acknowledging the problem, for providing them with a way of expressing their own complicated feelings. In this sense, the essay offers its readers similar tools. By speaking of the two uprisings together in this way, in terms of outrage at the loss of ordinary life, it allows reluctant Jews to begin to overcome their fears and their shame in order to act politically. In this respect, what is significant about the structure of the essay is its attention to time.

In rereading we may return to the opening sections and ask again what kind of difference these dates make. Here we notice that the talk is separated by a year from both Yom Hashoah and Yom Yerushalayim 1987. This speech commemorates neither of these events. The Warsaw Ghetto Uprising is not the same as Yom Hashoah. It is a separate event; and only after one has finished reading the essay does it become clear that the events of 19 April 1988, commemorating the forty-fifth anniversary, actually precede Klepfisz's involvement in the JWCEO protest. The protest she writes about took place on 25 April 1988.

What might we make of these connections? As I have argued, for Klepfisz, ritual is already political. It never takes place in a vacuum. Given the situation in 1987 and 1988, these rituals carry very specific meanings. They call for situated responses. This is what Klepfisz provides. She asks Jews to use these dates, these commemorations, in order to reconsider their fears and their shame. She asks them to imagine working for peace, to at least reflect and reconsider their positions. In these moments political actions become possible. However, even in this essay, the outcome and the kinds of actions to be taken are never guaranteed. There are multiple possibilities. Klepfisz is well aware of these other positions. They are embodied in the fears and shame of those who rejected her protest.

Toward Some Conclusions

In this chapter I have argued that secular-Jewish feminist politics stands alongside the traditions of secular Yiddish culture. Building on these legacies of Jewish communal memory and practice, this secular movement continues to mark Jewish time and use such occasion to build Jewish cultural and political practices. Given the legacy of Jewish emancipation in the West, where acceptable Jewish difference was scripted in terms of religious faith, such notions of secular-Jewish practice challenge the idea that Jewishness is solely a religious identity. To think about spirituality as a transformative communal and individual practice opens up other possibilities. It allows us to appreciate different Jewish positions.

In the case of secular-Jewish feminist spirituality, as in *de bavegung*, ritual has helped shape the contours of Jewish life within history. Ritual has offered these secular Jews occasions for contemplation as well as political action. By offering a glimpse at this specific feminist community, this chapter has presented an account of when, where, and under what conditions particular practices might be understood as transformative. Through a kind of situated knowledge, it has offered insights into the complexity and richness of a single, yet already complicated, feminist practice. In this partial way, it has offered a vision of contemporary feminist spirituality.

Notes

1. Adrienne Rich, *Blood, Bread, and Poetry: Selected Prose 1979–1985* (New York: Norton, 1986), 214.
2. Donna J. Haraway, "Situated Knowledges: The Science Question in Feminism and the Privilege of Partial Perspective," in *Simians, Cyborgs, and Women: The Reinvention of Nature* (New York: Routledge, 1991), 183–201.
3. Ibid., 190.
4. Ibid., 191.
5. Teresa de Lauretis, "Feminist Studies/Critical Studies: Issues, Terms, Contexts," in *Feminist Studies, Critical Studies*, ed. Teresa de Lauretis (Bloomington: Indiana University Press, 1986), 8.
6. On this point, see many of the nineteenth-century texts in Alice S. Rossi, ed., *The Feminist Papers: From Adams to de Beauvoir* (New York: Columbia University Press, 1973).
7. Irena Klepfisz, "Secular Jewish Identity: *Yidishkayt* in America (1986)," in *Dreams of an Insomniac: Jewish Feminist Essays, Speeches and Diatribes* (Portland, Oreg: Eighth Mountain, 1990), 143.
8. Ibid., 143–44.
9. Ibid.
10. Ibid., 145.
11. For more on the loss of faith among writers in Hebrew, see Alan Mintz, *"Banished from Their Father's Table": Loss of Faith and Hebrew Autobiography* (Bloomington: Indiana University Press, 1989).
12. Klepfisz, "Secular Jewish Identity," 144.
13. Sara Horowitz, "Voices from the Killing Ground," in *Holocaust Remembrance: The Shapes of Memory*, ed. Geoffrey H. Hartman (Cambridge, Mass.: Blackwell, 1994), 44.
14. Klepfisz, "Secular Jewish Identity," 150; also, 154–58.
15. Ibid., 151.
16. Ibid., 159.
17. For examples of these efforts, see Irena Klepfisz, *A Few Words in the Mother Tongue: Poems Selected and New (1971–1990)* (Portland, Oreg: Eighth Mountain, 1990).
18. Klepfisz, "Secular Jewish Identity," 160–61.

19. Frieda Forman et al., eds., *Found Treasures: Stories by Yiddish Women Writers* (Toronto: Second Story, 1994); in that volume see especially Irena Klepfisz, "Queens of Contradiction: A Feminist Introduction to Yiddish Women Writers," 21–62. See also *Shofar: An Interdisciplinary Journal of Jewish Studies* 9:4 (summer 1991); Judith Baskin, ed., *Women of the Word: Jewish Women and Jewish Writing* (Detroit: Wayne State University Press, 1994); *Bridges: A Journal for Jewish Feminists and Our Friends;* in that journal see especially Irena Klepfisz "Feminism, *Yidishkayt,* and the Politics of Memory," *Bridges* 4:1 (1994): 12–47; and Naomi Shepherd, *A Price below Rubies: Jewish Women as Rebels and Radicals* (Cambridge, Mass.: Harvard University Press, 1993).

20. Klepfisz, "Secular Jewish Identity." 161.

21. Ibid., 164.

22. Ibid., 160.

23. Elly Bulkin, Minnie Bruce Pratt, and Barbara Smith, *Yours in Struggle: Three Feminist Approaches to Anti-Semitism and Racism* (New York: Long Haul Press, 1984), 106.

24. Teresa de Lauretis, "Feminist Studies/Critical Studies," 9.

25. Zillah Eisenstein, *The Radical Future of Liberal Feminism* (New York: Longman, 1981), esp. 175–253; Alison Jaggar, "Liberal Feminism and Human Nature," in *Feminist Politics and Human Nature* (Totowa, N.J.: Rowman and Allanheld, 1983), 25–50; and Alice Echoles, *Daring to Be Bad: Radical Feminism in America, 1967–1975* (Minneapolis: University of Minnesota Press, 1989).

26. Letty Cottin Pogrebin, *Deborah, Golda, and Me: Being Female and Jewish in America* (New York: Crown, 1991), 154–55. See also Evelyn Torton Beck, ed., *Nice Jewish Girls: A Lesbian Anthology* (Boston: Beacon, 1989); Melanie Kaye/Kantrowitz and Irena Klepfisz, eds., *The Tribe of Dina: A Jewish Women's Anthology* (Boston: Beacon, 1989); and Susan Weidman Schneider, ed., *Jewish and Female: A Guide and Sourcebook for Today's Jewish Woman* (New York: Simon and Schuster, 1984).

27. On Zionist embodiment and the creation of new Jews, especially new Jewish men, see Michael Berkowitz, *Zionist Culture and Western European Jewry before the First World War* (Cambridge: Cambridge University Press, 1993), esp. 99–118.

28. The essay is also in Pogrebin, *Deborah, Golda, and Me,* 203–34.

29. Melanie Kaye/Kantrowitz and Irena Klepfisz, with Bernice Mennis, "In *Gerang* / In Struggle: A Handbook for Recognizing and Resisting Anti-Semitism and for Building Jewish Identity and Pride," in *Tribe of Dina,* 334–46; originally published in *Sinister Wisdom* 29/30 (1986).

30. *Tribe of Dina,* 334.

31. Bulkin, Pratt, and Smith, *Yours in Struggle,* 89–228.

32. Evelyn Torton Beck, "The Politics of Jewish Invisibility," *NWSA Journal* 1:1 (1988): 93–102; for a critical reading of de Lauretis's text, see Laura Levitt, *Jewish Feminist Identities: Reconfiguring Home* (New York: Routledge, forthcoming), especially chap. 6; and idem, "Rethinking Jewish Feminist Identity/ies: What Difference Can Feminist Theory Make?" in *Postmodern Jewish Hermeneutics,* ed. Steven Kepnes (New York: New York University Press, forthcoming).

33. Judith Plaskow, "The Right Question is Theological," in *On Being a Jewish Feminist: A Reader,* ed. Susannah Heschel (New York: Schocken, 1983), 223–33.

34. Carol Christ and Judith Plaskow, eds., *Womanspirit Rising: A Feminist Reader in Religion* (San Francisco: Harper and Row, 1979); and Judith Plaskow and Carol Christ,

eds., *Weaving the Vision: New Patterns in Feminist Spirituality* (San Francisco: Harper and Row, 1989).

35. Delores Williams, *Sisters in the Wilderness: The Challenge of Womanist God-Talk* (Maryknoll, N.Y.: Orbis, 1993); Katie Cannon, *Black Womanist Ethics* (Atlanta: Scholars Press, 1988); Ada-María Isasi-Díaz, *En la lucha/In the Struggle: A Hispanic Women's Liberation Theology* (Minneapolis: Fortress, 1993); and Kwok Pui-lan, *Chinese Women and Christianity, 1860–1927* (Atlanta: Scholars Press, 1992). Numerous critical articles on these themes can also be found in the pages of the *Journal of Feminist Studies in Religion* as well as in collections like *Weaving the Vision.*

36. For efforts of this sort, see Judith Plaskow, *Standing again at Sinai: Judaism from a Feminist Perspective* (San Francisco: HarperCollins, 1990), esp. 25–74; and Judith Seid, *We Rejoice in Our Heritage: Home Rituals for Secular and Humanistic Jews* (Ann Arbor: Kopinvant Secular Press, 1989).

37. Audre Lorde writes about this difficulty in relation to African-American feminists and the African-American community. See Audre Lorde, "Age, Race, Class, and Sex: Women Redefining Difference," in *Out There: Marginalization and Contemporary Cultures,* ed. Russell Ferguson et al. (Cambridge, Mass.: MIT Press, 1990), 281–87.

38. See Robert I. Friedman, "The Israel Lobby's Blacklist: Exposing AIPAC'S Activities," *Village Voice,* 4 August 1992.

39. See Jenny Bourne's Marxist critique, "Homelands of the Mind: Jewish Feminism and Identity Politics," *Race and Class* 29:1 (summer 1987): 1–24.

40. On this question, see Sara Horowitz, "Jewish Studies as Oppositional; or, Gettin' Mighty Lonely out Here," in *Styles of Cultural Opposition,* ed. Philip Goldstein (Newark: University of Delaware Press, 1994), 152–64.

41. Rital Falbel, Irena Klepfisz, and Donna Nevel, eds., *Jewish Women's Call for Peace: A Handbook for Jewish Women on the Israeli/Palestinian Conflict* (Ithaca, N.Y.: Firebrand, 1990); subsequent page references to this work will be given in the text.

Bibliography

Beck, Evelyn Torton, ed. *Nice Jewish Girls: A Lesbian Anthology.* Boston: Beacon, 1989.

Christ, Carol, and Judith Plaskow, eds. *Womanspirit Rising: A Feminist Reader in Religion.* San Francisco: Harper and Row, 1979.

Falbel, Rital, Irena Klepfisz, and Donna Nevel, eds. *Jewish Women's Call for Peace: A Handbook for Jewish Women on the Israeli/Palestinian Conflict.* Ithaca, N.Y.: Firebrand, 1990.

Kaye/Kantrowitz, Melanie, and Irena Klepfisz, eds. *The Tribe of Dina: A Jewish Women's Anthology.* Boston: Beacon, 1989.

Klepfisz, Irena. *Dreams of an Insomniac: Jewish Feminist Essays, Speeches and Diatribes.* Portland, Oreg: Eighth Mountain, 1990.

Plaskow, Judith, and Carol Christ, eds. *Weaving the Vision: New Patterns in Feminist Spirituality.* San Francisco: Harper and Row, 1989.

Pogrebin, Letty Cottin. *Deborah, Golda, and Me: Being Female and Jewish in America.* New York: Crown, 1991.
Rich, Adrienne. *What Is Found There: Notebooks on Poetry and Politics.* New York: Norton, 1993.
Rossi, Alice S., ed. *The Feminist Papers: From Adams to de Beauvoir.* New York: Columbia University Press, 1973.

13

Gay Spirituality

J. MICHAEL CLARK

BECAUSE BEING A GAY MAN or lesbian entails far more than sexual behavior alone, homosexuality should never be simplistically reduced to genital logistics. Rather, being gay or lesbian constitutes a whole mode of being-in-the-world, an existential standpoint unique to each gay man and lesbian that stands over against established cultural and religious standards for gender roles, sexuality, and intimate human relationships. Were homosexuality only about where certain individuals put their genitals, it would be far less threatening to the dominant culture. Indeed, the threat that nurtures homophobia is not homosexuality per se, but gay identity and affections. This nexus of identity and affectional orientation — in conjunction with its embodiment in sexual expression, its oppression by society, and its prophetic standpoint toward that society — shapes the ways gay men and lesbians see and experience the world and themselves. The all-encompassing, life-shaping, and frequently spiritual perspectives that result deserve careful examination, particularly insofar as they differ markedly from the theological activities associated with the other liberation movements of the last several decades.

The civil rights movement, for example, depended heavily upon the African-American churches and the development of a liberation theology based upon African-American experiences in America. The student and antiwar movements developed alongside death of God theology and a renewed theological interest in social justice issues. Unrest and social change in Latin America have been intimately bound up with liberation theology and Roman Catholicism's unique role in those countries. Finally, the women's movement has produced a host of eloquent spokespersons who stand in a prophetic relationship with the Judeo-Christian tradition. Even though the contemporary gay/lesbian movement, generally dated from the June 1969 riots outside the Stonewall Inn (a gay bar on New

York's Christopher Street), emerged sequentially from the period that in this country produced the civil rights, student/antiwar, and women's movements, until very recently — nearly two decades after the Stonewall event — gay people had not pursued religious or spiritual discourse in ways comparable to that of these other groups.

Gay/Lesbian Exclusion and Institutional Religion

Clues for understanding this discrepancy between gay spiritual inclinations and gay/lesbian involvement in institutional religion — and also, until recently, gay/lesbian participation in the activity of theological reflection — emerge from feminist resources. Mary Daly, for example, has implied that both women and gay people have been so labeled and marginalized that they have been made "foreigners not only to the fortresses of political power, but also to those citadels in which thought processes have been spent out."[1] Even more so than women, openly gay men and lesbians have been attacked by and excluded from the institutionalized Judeo-Christian tradition. Regardless of what the implicit or explicit admissions policies of seminaries and graduate programs in religious studies might be, the fact that the vast majority of both Jewish and Christian denominations continue to blatantly exclude gay men and lesbians from the clergy, the single area in which most graduates of such programs traditionally find employment, has effectively kept us outside serious theological endeavor until very recently. Only the United Church of Christ, the Unitarian Universalists, and Reconstructionist Judaism, among traditional denominations, have unambiguous policies endorsing the ordination of gay men and lesbians.

Oddly enough, even though institutional religious forms have consistently failed to accept or support openly gay/lesbian individuals or their relationships, either professionally, liturgically and pastorally, or doctrinally, gay men and lesbians have nevertheless consistently participated in these institutional forms in considerable number. John Boswell, for example, has described the extent to which gay men were drawn to pre-Thomist (pre–twelfth-century) Roman Catholicism, and other writers have reported that both gay priests and lesbian nuns still constitute a disproportionately large percentage of Catholic clergy, official church doctrine notwithstanding.[2] Apart from the clergy, gay men and lesbians have formed either officially recognized or unofficial support groups within virtually every Christian denomination and have even established their own denomination (the Universal Fellowship of Metropolitan Community Churches [MCC]) and a loose federation of synagogues (the World Congress of Gay and Lesbian Jewish Organizations), many of which are affiliated with either the Reform or Reconstructionist movements.

This seeming plethora of religious involvement notwithstanding, the vast majority of gay men and lesbians — and certainly those of us who are openly gay — actually find ourselves outside either affirmative theological discourse or institutionalized religion. Many of us are, in fact, quite hostile toward a Western religious heritage whose official doctrine and tradition, both Jewish and Christian, are unabashedly homophobic and heterosexist. This constant exclusion from professional ministry, theological scholarship, and spiritual institutions is especially ironic in view of Carl Jung's appraisal that the gay male temperament, in particular, is "endowed with a wealth of religious feelings... and a spiritual receptivity" or in view of more recent work that demonstrates a historical synthesis of spirituality and homosexuality among indigenous, non–Judeo-Christian peoples.[3] Something in our gay/lesbian being as an all-encompassing existential standpoint — something about our particular sensibility or mode of being-in-the-world, however idiosyncratically varied it may be — appears to heighten our spiritual capacities even as we find ourselves excluded from the citadels of theological and spiritual endeavor.

Gay/lesbian responses to this exclusion have taken various forms, the first of which has been an apologetic or assimilationist approach. A great deal of energy has been devoted to scriptural analyses, for example, as if Leviticus and Romans could be compelled to relinquish their homophobic pronouncements.[4] Similar energies have been expended trying to convince the churches and synagogues that they should accept gay men and lesbians as coequal congregants and clergy who are as good in the sight of the divine as heterosexuals. These struggles have sustained the numerous support groups that have created gay/lesbian spaces for traditional rituals and pursued ordination issues, but that, so preoccupied, have not taken up the tasks of developing critical theology or articulating the specific meanings of gay/lesbian spirituality. Moreover, the single denomination that is uniquely based in the gay community (MCC) has adopted an evangelical Christianity that approaches Scripture and the tradition in a nearly literal manner — except those passages and portions of scripture that pertain to homosexuality.

Fortunately, several exceptions to this otherwise dismal summary of work loyally undertaken within the Judeo-Christian tradition are discernible: Carter Heyward has increasingly fused her primarily feminist theology with her standpoint as a lesbian priest. Both John Fortunato and John McNeill have synthesized theological insights and psychology in their gay-affirmative therapeutic work and writing. Since his coming out over a decade ago, activist Episcopalian priest Malcolm Boyd has interwoven his particular gay experience with his poetic, autobiographical, and devotional writing. Finally, openly gay theological writers have addressed the AIDS health crisis, not from an apologetic point of view, but from theological and pastoral care perspectives firmly grounded in identification with the gay community.[5] Given the theological vacuity of much of the apologetic and assimilationist approach to the Judeo-Christian tradition and the AIDS-specific quality of much of the unapologetic work until very recently, another response to the Western theological and spiritual tradition has naturally been utterly antagonistic. While feminist theologian Sheila Collins has written that "many of us [feminists] have become mental or physical dropouts from institutionalized religion, not because we are irreligious, but because our religious impulses are being killed by [traditional Judeo-Christianity],"[6] many gay people have simply decided to dispose of both baby and bath water simultaneously. No small number of gay men at least have totally eliminated the spiritual dimension from their lives, having renounced both gay apologetics and the tradition, opting for a purely secular approach to life instead.

Yet one other approach lies between the extremes of apologetics and abandonment. The "faerie circles" were founded during the 1970s in the San Francisco Bay area by men such as Arthur Evans, Harry Hay, Mark Thompson, and Mitch Walker and later spread throughout the gay male subculture, most recently into the Southeast.[7] Group members have produced a number of books and periodicals and continue to rely upon a rather esoteric mixture of Celtic mythology, Goddess religion, and other forms of mysticism, metaphysics, and natural ethics, which are neither peculiarly Eastern nor Judaic-Christian.[8] The distinguishing characteristics of faerie spirituality are its persistent questioning of all authority and its antihierarchical and anarchistic refusal to obey any sort of rules, whether rules of sex, gender, dress, schedule, authority, or society. The subcultural function of such anarchy is the inculcation of an understanding of freedom. The recently uncloseted gay man may not understand the extent to which he limits himself by ingrained, heterosexist rules, expectations, and behavior. The faeries offer radical freedom as the spiritual alternative to such socialization and delight in pricking the sensibilities of society at large as well. For example, nudity is acceptable at all faerie gatherings on private land, and both coupled and group sex is a primary method used to facilitate liberation from societal oppression.

Obviously missing from this construct is discipline, structure, focus, agenda, and achievement, the absence of which can result in a lack of focus and substance. Consequently, the faeries often play only a brief, albeit extremely influential, role in the lives of those gay men who find them after coming out — the role of unlearning societal programming and of discovering the full range of possibilities that exist outside the closet. Of course, one further result of this anarchistic style and its short-term value for individual gay men is that, for all its seeming vitality and diversity, this spiritual movement has remained marginal to the vast majority of gay people, most recently vacillating between seeking dialogue and unity within itself and infighting among earlier circle founders.[9] Like the other unapologetic efforts, the gay spirituality work of the faerie circles is fragmentary and piecemeal, testifying to the absence of any monolithic understanding of or approach to gay (or lesbian) spirituality. This same absence of any monolithic understanding or approach is equally typical of more recent efforts to begin developing constructive gay theology.

Unsatisfied with the nebulous and sometimes eccentric aspects of faerie approaches to gay spirituality and equally concerned about the disparity between gay/lesbian experience and liberation theological efforts, two groups emerged during the 1980s within the American Academy of Religion to begin doing work comparable to that of other oppressed minorities. The Lesbian/Feminist Issues in Religion Group began presenting formal papers as a program unit in 1986, followed by the emergence of the Gay Men's Issues in Religion Group in 1988. Although working cooperatively in complementarity from the beginning, they first met in joint session in 1992. These two groups have explored a number of issues: the relationship of gay/lesbian being to homophobia in church and society, doctrines of God and theological methodology, world religions and African-American experience ("womanist" theology), denominational issues, AIDS, feminist issues, and gay/lesbian constructed families and gay-lesbian interactions. Albeit in a more formalized fashion and with epistemological frameworks more associated with Judaism and/or Christianity, this more intellectual approach to gayspirit has been motivated by the same questions, concerns, and deep-seated spiritual urgings as have motivated faerie circles.

Although no monolithic theology or spirituality has developed from any of these unapologetic styles, at least two commonalities are discernible. One of these is clearly a shared valuing of diversity; the other is a peculiar secularity. Whether the chaotic, freewheeling spirituality of faerie circles or the formalized discourse of intellectual reflection, gay/lesbian efforts in spirituality and theology do not depend upon institutional religion, either for grounding or for support. Secular in this particular, anti-institutional sense, both gay spirituality and gay theology are concerned far less about religiosity and far more about connecting spirituality with the real-life existence of gay men and lesbians in a homophobic society. In other words, the focus for both gay spirituality and gay liberation theology becomes less about the divine and shifts instead to human responsibility, including responsibility for reuniting sexuality and spirituality and for synthesizing our spiritual impetus with our liberational praxis. An examination of the sometimes overlapping and always diverse resources and leitmotifs before us can enable a more complete understanding of the multidimensionality of gay spirituality as a secular spirituality begetting liberation.

Gay Spiritual Prehistory

Jungian Myth Studies

Mythology is an area to which gayspirit writers, including faeries, have turned in their spiritual quests. Of particular interest has been the myth work of post-Jungian scholars. For example, Rafael López-Pedraza described the homoerotic origins and dynamics of Pan, and faerie Mitch Walker examined the gay spiritual and psychosexual energies of the Double well over a decade ago.[10] Elsewhere, gay-sensitive readings of mythic figures have credited Orpheus with introducing homosexuality to Greece, although it cost him his life, and Zeus and Ganymede with rescuing Eros from Oedipal domination by the Great Mother, enabling the union of Eros and Psyche.[11] Although arguably at odds with Plato's own position, gay men have also read the myth recounted in the *Symposium* as a positive evaluation of and explanation for the existence of gay people (as halves of primordial wholes seeking appropriate wholeness in gay couplings).

In addition to these specific mythical figures, a number of other mythic archetypes resonate with gay male experience: the *Scapegoat*, threatening a society unprepared for alternatives of sexuality and valuation, finds embodiment wherever individuals are victims of anti-gay/lesbian violence. The *Outcast*, excluded from the moral order, finds embodiment among ACT-UP, Queer Nation, and other militant gay liberation groups. The *Hero*, journeying through death and rebirth, transcending social values, and achieving self-accepting wholeness in "coming out," finds varying embodiment in every openly gay or lesbian individual. *Pan*, discovering masturbation and reuniting body and psyche through fantasy (healing), finds embodiment in that erotic self-loving that facilitates love for another. Similarly, the *Anima* (Jung's term for inner female attributes) may be internalized in gay men as wisdom, nurture, insight, sensitivity, and heightened spiritual openness, while it is externalized in the rituals and seductions associated with the gay bar subculture. The active influence of the Anima also makes a gay *Androgyne* possible, balancing the opposites of masculinity and femininity.

In addition to these mythic associations, the post-Jungian dream work of James Hillman, in particular, yields a psycho-mythic understanding of the dynamics of the gay bar that correspond to the archetypes of Hades or the *Underworld*.[12] This correspondence of images (gates of initiation and Dantean chambers, the dissolution and reconstitution of Ego in self-knowledge, ritualized mating and polygamy, among others) enables some gay men to have a waking means for experiencing the chaotic unreason of the Underworld and, thereby, for balancing the expiatory reason of a homophobic day-world. The bar frequenter can thus become a mythical or spiritual *Balancer* of night and day. The Anima/Androgyne archetype(s) and the Underworld imagery together suggest that the archetypally gay man must be a Balancer, living between and connected to the opposites of maternal unconsciousness and self-consciousness, night-world amorality and day-world morality, masculinity and femininity. As Balancer, he must seek integration (or personal wholeness) through a chaos of options and a richness of archetypally complex experience. Thus is homosexuality one mythic mode of being and the mythic realm one avenue of gay spiritual exploration.

The Native American Berdache

Recent studies in Native American ethnology, particularly those focused on the "third-gender" aspects of the berdache figure, suggest that the berdache may be considered a historical example and embodiment of archetypal androgyny, of the balance of genders and gender-related forces.[13] The berdache were physiological males who upon reaching adulthood exchanged traditional male gender roles and apparel for those usually assigned to tribal women. Usually prompted by a spiritual vision and celebrated in rites of cleansing and an exchange of gendered apparel, the berdachehood was a position of honor and blessing. While the berdache usually enacted a passive or receptive homosexual role, his active partners were not considered homosexual. Although contemporary gay men must be careful not to co-opt the historical meanings and roles associated with the berdache and thereby further contribute to the oppression of native peoples rampant in America, a number of the implications of that institution for contemporary gay self-understanding must be cited for their importance to the full range of gay spiritual resources. Most important to this institution was its own mythical underpinning. Native religions traditionally understood the whole spectrum of human variety and human sexuality to be divinely or cosmically ordained or given. They thus evolved rituals for the process of self-realization and for initiation into this role. Following their example, gayspirit writers have encouraged the development of similar rites of passage in order to ease the anxiety of self-discovery in a homophobic society and to mark coming out as a rite of passage that celebrates the gay or lesbian individual's "rebirth," along with cosmic destiny and human variety within the context of one's new community.

Moreover, as did the berdache, contemporary gay men and lesbians, both in resacramentalizing or respiritualizing their individual and corporate lives — and in their influence upon the larger, nongay world — can be seen as seeking the reunion of the cosmic, sexual, and moral polarities. They can embody and exemplify that all things are interdependent, processive, fecund, and dynamic. Such an androgynous gay spirituality could also facilitate liaisons with other marginalized persons, which could in turn heal wounds both relational and environmental. Following the berdache's example, gay people could be at the forefront of a process to reclaim the spiritual dimension for sexuality as well. For gay men in particular, once again spiritualizing sexual, interpersonal relationships could help alleviate the frequently accompanying senses of urgency and emptiness that inevitably permeate the anonymous, purely genital sexual encounters of the sexual subculture and could thus also humanize gay sexuality with a greater depth, intimacy, and tenderness. At last, a sense of community that transcends marginalized, sexual one-dimensionality could be achieved through a heightened awareness of the value of sexual partners and the spiritual power latent in caring acts of sexual love. The communal empowerment for genuine liberation is indeed nurtured through just such (re)sacramentalized sexuality.

Overall, then, berdache spirituality accepted and celebrated cosmic/divine selectivity, honoring the givenness of homosexuality in rites of passage. The berdachehood united the cosmic, sexual, and moral polarities, thereby achieving spiritual power to nurture wholeness and health within native cultures. As sacred Balancers, they also synthesized spiritual empowerment with sexuality, both reflecting and celebrating cosmic fecundity. Rediscovering the berdache could enable gay people to move toward a renewal of spiritual potentialities and toward the development of supportive language and rituals that nurture community and human liberation.

The Gay I-Thou: Passionate Friendship and Subject-Subject Consciousness

Looking outside the Christian tradition for mythical and historical models of the union of spirituality and (homo)sexuality must not lead to overlooking the occasional breakthroughs within that tradition that also celebrated this union. In the twelfth century, for example, St. Aelred built a "theology of passionate friendship" upon his own self-accepting gay experience.[14] He validated his gay-sensitive theology with three models: Jesus' own befriending of persons, specifically the chaste intimacy of Jesus with John the Beloved; God's own intimacy with Jesus; and the coequal and communal quality of the Trinity. While Aelred would certainly be adamantly opposed to the casual interchangeability of bar-based, purely genital sexual relationships (he was, after all, responsible for the vows of the monks in his charge at Rievaulx, even as he simultaneously encouraged their "particular friendships"), he did not oppose sexual relationships as such. His concern was one of priorities. Irresponsible, dehumanizing, or impersonal promiscuity is precluded while a responsible gay orientation is still affirmed. Sexual love should simply facilitate, rather than hinder, communion with the divine in the encounter with another person.

Aelred was also careful to provide guidelines for supportive human friendships. Friendship is intrinsically valuable, ordained by the divine. It requires vulnerability, trust, and emotional risk. It entails a selfless openness to the sufferings and joys, criticism and praise of one's friend. It is built upon equality, discipline, and committed sharing over time. Friends are to be chosen with care and tested with caution. One is expected never to violate the trust, confidentiality, and love of one's friend and always to embody humility and loving forgiveness before one's companion. In short, a friendship or a sexual relationship is sanctified by the model of Jesus and John, while the two friends are ever to remember that their own intimacy and love (and even sexual sharing) are an encounter wherein the divine is also present. For gay St. Aelred, spirituality, the very presence of the divine, cannot be divorced from human relationships and human sexuality. His theology is thus an important grounding for the efforts of gay people to celebrate the (re)union of sexuality and spirituality.

This impetus toward reconciling the dualism of body and spirit has more recently emerged as a pressing concern in contemporary faerie spirituality. Among faerie leaders, Harry Hay has argued that rather than the subject-object mentality that Western culture has long engendered — including its tendencies to alienate persons from one another, to dehumanize sexual partners, and to objectify nature in ecologically unsound ways —

gay men in particular must develop and nurture a subject-subject consciousness. Unwittingly echoing Jewish philosopher Martin Buber, Hay has encouraged gay men to relinquish I-It thinking in favor of I-Thou thinking.[15] One clear implication is that gay men will thereby cease treating their own bodies and the bodies of their sexual partners as disposable, easily interchangeable objects. When our bodies are no longer treated as objects, the reunion of sexuality and spirituality in healing relationships becomes truly possible. Urging this same healing reconciliation of gay men with their bodies and with one another, another faerie leader, Arthur Evans, has adamantly criticized the leather community, particularly those gay men who pursue either a misogynist, excessive masculinity or sadomasochism (S/m) without regard for its negative consequences in their own lives, both spiritually and sexually.[16]

Gay Leathersex Spirituality

In marked contrast to Arthur Evans, other gay male writers and particularly the late Geoff Mains have argued that leathersex, even S/m within certain boundaries, actually helps gay men to reclaim a genuinely gay male masculinity from the batterings of heterosexist culture (as "sissies" and "not-men") and, in so doing, also helps them to reunite passionate and very bodily sexuality with spiritual transcendence.[17] According to Mains, the significance and potential spiritual power of leather (and S/m) lie in its very stigmatization. Leathersex participants live on the margins of an already marginalized people, disdained even by many gay men and lesbians. Coming into leather requires another coming out: a further process of self-discovery and self-acceptance, of confrontation with social taboos, animal instincts, and human power and its abuses. Surprisingly perhaps, Mains even argues that, like faerie, leathersex seeks mystical transcendence through sexual power, relying on voluntary participation and utter equality while balancing human values with animal instincts.

This quest for transcendence via the passions finds acute expression in leathersex. The rites and role-play of leather create a bridge between our rational, hierarchical, proscribed, and delimited enculturation (the Apollonian) and the sexual, psychic, and spiritual side of human nature (the Dionysian). Mains insists that leather culture is tribal, primordially or archetypally balancing the best of animal instincts with human capacities. It enables freedom from repression tempered by humaneness. As such, leathersex reclaims and resanctifies bodiliness; it reconciles body and psyche (emotions, spirituality) at the point of the body's limits (the pain/pleasure threshold) in compassionate, coequal sexual activity. Leathersex is distrustful of power and power seeking, of arrogance and social facades. Mains insists that its libertarian, fundamental equality opposes all forms of injustice and misogyny. Leathersex further depends upon genuine humility, learned by coming to understand one's own and another's limits, and honors emotional warmth by rejecting any lack of restraint. Mutuality, equality, and respect underlie its highly symbolic role play.

Mains implies that ritualized, symbolic, mutually consensual, and voluntary dominance/submission role-play so clarifies and diffuses power-needs as to enable a psychic resistance to power-abuses and injustices in the world. Ritualized sex-play shifts dominance and submission, power and pain, from the unreflective realm of social interactions and enculturated gender roles into a controlled arena, turning roles inside out and shattering the facades of everyday human power-abuses. The consciously chosen and exaggerated roles of leather (and S/m) disconnect participants from day-world reality, enabling deepened self-understanding. Such rituals require developing trust, relinquishing control, and accepting these with respect and honor. Role-play then reverses day-world securities and fears, status or lack of status, therapeutically. Building upon the interdependence of physiological neurochemicals to so raise the pain/pleasure threshold as to convert pain to ecstasy, S/m in particular moves participants toward a psychic or spiritual catharsis that expunges frustrations, tension, self-denigration, and emotional repression, yielding new self-perspective, deeper and more trusting personal bonding, and an energy that, no longer needed for sexual repression, better equips one for day-world challenges.

Importantly, the reflections and challenges of Arthur Evans and others rightly imply that Geoff Mains's writings about leathersex and S/m represent only the most ideal potential for such radical sexuality, a potential not realized often enough: too many men have chosen leather and, more specifically, S/m activities for the wrong reasons. Some "bottoms" become trapped in roles that repeatedly act out the dysfunctional and sometimes physically or sexually abusive relationships they experienced with their real fathers. So trapped, they never find the catharsis that releases them, heals them, and frees them from their painful pasts. Likewise, some "tops" use their roles to exploit their partners, abusing them not by way of making love to them but by way of physically and emotionally battering them. Moreover, no small number of leathermen wear their leather as only a device for attracting sexual partners, as a gimmick in the sexual marketplace. Likewise, too many participants in leather contests relinquish any other meaningful life in pursuit of pageant titles, while leather clubs founded to nurture community get hopelessly mired in politicking and power-games, being more interested in sex than in siblinghood. As a result, all too often the leathersex and S/m subcommunities discourage long-term, committed couplings. Single persons, as well as individuals in open relationships within those subcommunities, shun those in their midst who make monogamous, long-term commitments — mutual and reciprocal commitments in which sexual techniques are necessarily far less important than the overall quality of life together. In other words, the emphasis in far too much of the leather and S/m subcommunities on sexual activities alone has functioned only to sustain an alienation of body and spirit, of genitalia and spirituality, rather than facilitating the passionately, sexually embodied spirituality Mains described.

At the same time, however, Mains's idealism remains an important, prophetic challenge to gay men (and lesbians) involved to whatever degree in the leather and S/m subcommunities. If wearing leather enables us to reclaim and to heal our battered masculinity as gay men while also enabling us to reaffirm nonsexist values and behavior, if leather identity engenders in us the nearly lost qualities of respect and good manners, and if leather siblinghood encourages courageous activity-in-community in the face of marginalization, injustice, and AIDS — then the apparel is well chosen. If our passions for our spouses and partners becomes playfully and masculinely rough — embodied equivalents of good "bear hugs" because we love each other that much — and if our whole-bodied eroticism enables us to explore all of our bodies and to push our embodied limits together with the power and empowerment of our lovemaking, then our sexuality is truly radical, enhancing everything about our lives.

Gay Spirituality and AIDS

Whether pursuing a faerie spirituality influenced by mythic imagery or berdache associations, or pursuing passionate leathersex spirituality or gentler sexual friendships based on models from Christianity (Jesus and John) or Judaism (David and Jonathan), or even pursuing assimilationist quests for scriptural and clerical inclusion — all efforts at gay spirituality have had to wrestle with the in-breaking reality of AIDS. In confronting the AIDS crisis, which struck the gay male community first in the United States, gay spirituality and theology have had to move beyond the many varied sources and leitmotifs thus far developed. Gay spirituality and theology must wrestle not only with human evil or injustice experienced as homophobic oppression and anti-gay/lesbian violence but with so-called natural evil and cosmic tragedy as well. No form or synthesis of gay spirituality can be further developed, for we gay men at least, without confronting the impact of AIDS upon our lives and our communities. Our understandings of the divine and of the cosmos must take into account the problems of suffering and tragedy (theodicy), as well as confronting the interplay of AIDS, homophobia, and AIDS-phobia that has further nurtured human injustice toward us as gay people. One significant point of difference from the sources upon which our gay spirituality and gay theology have drawn thus far will be the activity of synthesizing a theology of tragedy with an ethic of human justice. Confronting AIDS as a community and making spiritual and theological responses to this biological holocaust in our midst together constitute a vitally necessary gay-related contribution to the spirituality and theology of the larger, nongay society.

While gay psychotherapist John Fortunato has argued that gay men and lesbians can turn their experience of gay oppression upside down, not by denial, but through confronting losses, penetrating grief, and embracing their exile or marginality, nongay rabbi Harold Kushner has argued that although tragedies do not happen for any cosmic reason, meaning can be imposed upon them.[18] Penetrating the realities of grief and anger, rather than denying a tragedy, leads toward a deepened spiritual standpoint that is capable of redeeming tragedy and of responding to those who are suffering. The spiritual challenge of the AIDS crisis, then, involves avoiding answers that are too easy. Blaming the cosmos, the divine, sexual partners, or gay being itself (blaming the victim) will not work. AIDS simply happened; viruses are indifferent to socioeconomic status, race, gender, and sexual orientation. Moreover, the harsh reality of AIDS does not invalidate the basic worth of gay being as one of the various forms of human life that the divine elicited, sanctified, and celebrates.

One response to the spiritual and theological dilemmas presented by AIDS has been a synthesis of process philosophy and Kushner's insights. Kushner argues that while traditional theology has tried to insist simultaneously upon God's all-powerfulness, God's all-goodness, and humanity's essential value, the reality of suffering makes these three propositions incompatible together. Applying Kushner's logic to the AIDS crisis implies that if AIDS is not a punishment and if the divine is good, then divine power must be limited. The divine and chaos (the stuff of creation in Genesis) continue in dynamic tension. The divine does all s/he can do to order chaos, while chaos continues to resist that divine creative urge. The AIDS crisis compels people to relinquish not only a conception of the divine as judge and punisher but also any hope in the divine as a miraculous rescuer, a deus ex machina. Instead, the divine can be reconceptualized as a presence in suffering alongside those in pain or on the margins. Neither judge nor rescuer, the divine is a compassionate presence, a cosufferer, and, ultimately, the embodied spiritual empowerment for appropriate response.

More recent interpretations of the relationship of AIDS and gay spirituality have taken various forms. Ronald Long rejects the process effort to maintain a personal God-concept, particularly that of a limited divine who is at best a cosuffering companion. He instead encourages a spirituality of resistance, whereby human resistance to injustice and tragedy yields hope, and that hope in turn empowers concrete actions of justice making and caregiving. Reconceptualizing the divine as resistance and hope (as horizontal, present- and future-oriented energies), rather than as a vertical creator or personal companion, eliminates altogether the implication that the divine is in any way responsible for evil or for AIDS. Reconceptualizing the divine as resistance and hope also entails the ethical demand that persons incarnationally join in radical participation in healing, caregiving, and the full range of liberation-seeking, sociopolitical activities.[19]

Richard Hardy has taken up this incarnational motif, albeit while also affirming an even more traditional understanding of personal divinity than that espoused in process thought. Building upon traditional, contemplative Roman Catholicism, Hardy believes that as gay men work through their grief and frustration with AIDS, they come to embody a Christlike love for their fellow persons, a love embodied in their caregiving for their partners and other persons living with HIV or AIDS.[20] Finally, Susan Henking has begun studying the memoirs of long-term AIDS survivors, realizing that while HIV and AIDS challenge and strengthen the spiritual growth of both those who suffer and those who grieve, the ways in which that finds articulation and expression are as varied as the individuals who have left written reflections.[21]

For the haunting Why? of suffering and death, there is no satisfying or easy answer that so makes sense of it all as to cancel the pain, anguish, and sense of unfairness we experience in our encounter with AIDS. The variety of spiritual and theological responses to this health crisis poignantly reveals this. Anger at this in-breaking of evil and suffering, and grief at the loss of lives, are valid and real responses. No theology or spirituality that seeks to justify suffering by condemning sexual orientation or otherwise blaming the victim, that seeks to explain away the reality of suffering, or that seeks to stifle righteous anger or grief can ever legitimately command gay spiritual respect. Gay men and lesbians, as well as other people also wrestling with AIDS in their own lives or in the lives of their loved ones, have discovered, however, that they can deepen their spiritual capacities by imposing meaning upon the AIDS crisis. They impose such meaning by supporting efforts for medical resolution (as well as sociopolitical resolution), by responding appropriately to those suffering from the various diseases associated with AIDS, and by enhancing the quality of their own continuing lives.

Overall, both the resources and the methodologies for developing gay spirituality and gay theology remain as varied as the spiritual and theological responses that gay people have created in response to AIDS. No monolithic gay spirituality, theology, or caregiving philosophy is possible or ultimately desirable. The gay community, which carries as its banner the rainbow flag symbolizing its extreme diversity, must both celebrate that internal diversity and allow it to enrich the community's various spiritualities. In so doing, those spiritualities must also look beyond AIDS, pursuing lines of thinking and modes of acting that will enrich spiritual growth and liberational activity beyond the present struggle with AIDS in this community.

Beyond AIDS: Sexual Ethics

One important contribution gay spirituality continues to offer nongay society is an adamant insistence that spirituality and sexuality go together, whether in efforts to create a self-identified, androgynous, berdache-like third gender; in subject-subject or S/m sexual friendships; or in confronting the peculiar confluence of sex, death, and societal erotophobia created by the AIDS health crisis. In fact, at its best gay and lesbian sexuality (like all sexuality) is an urging into relationship with another person. Also, through that relationship, it is implicitly and ideally an urging for justice in all relationships, including our relationship with the earth itself. Indeed, our sexuality is a complex nexus of experiences that is at once emotional, psychological, and spiritual, as well as bodily. Sexuality involves befriending people, making love, and expressing love for our special beloveds in ways that move both lover and beloved to encounter the divine; it involves seeking justice not only in the bedroom but throughout our lives. Because our sexuality permeates all of who we are as persons, it should in no case be reduced to merely genital functions.

With this contention, gay sexual ethics encounters men's studies and its analysis of masculine socialization. Gay men are shaped by the same cultural values and misunderstandings about male sexuality that shape nongay men. Men, whether straight or gay, must reconceptualize their sexuality as something that is not external, alienated, and merely functional. They must learn that the erotic — or, more concretely, our sexuality — becomes a meaningless, genitally reduced notion unless we come to understand the erotic as part and parcel of our urges toward mutuality and human(e)ness. To be human is to be in relationship — with ourselves, with other persons, with the earth and the cosmos, and with the divine. Our erotic and sexual drive toward connectedness with all things, and the experienced connectedness we do in fact achieve, together constitute our embodied spirituality as bodyselves-in-relation. Moreover, our fundamental need for connectedness, love, and self-affirming acceptance undergirds our quest for mutuality and, through the realization of that quest, further nourishes our efforts toward the establishment of justice in all relationships, not just our sexually expressed ones. In other words, our sexuality is not so much about where we put our genitals (genital logistics) but is rather something that permeates our lives and that both urges us toward and sustains our relationships — even those that are not genitally consummated. As the power of relation, our sexuality compels liberational, justice-seeking activity in the world. James Nelson summarily reiterates this idea when he says that the divine Eros is "that fundamental energy of the universe that is the passion for connection and hence the hunger for justice and the yearning for life-giving communion."[22]

If our spirituality and our sexuality are indeed one, this oneness also ideally shapes our deepest valuing and acting in the world. In fact, our embodied capacity for compassion and our embodied capacity for justice making are one and the same: compassion in action, which is justice seeking and justice making, is born in and from our erotically or sexually informed drive toward right-relation. The lovemaking and justice making (the right-relationship making) that we begin at home with our spouses should permeate and inform all our relationships and value concerns. The care and tenderness of our specific relationships must inform all our values, all our ways of relating to and seeking justice within the world, lest we remain in conflict with ourselves: one cannot make love and make hate simultaneously.

Beyond AIDS: Environmental Ethics

If we have not distanced ourselves from the activities of our genitals but have instead realized the healing and shaping power of the erotic as something that permeates, shapes, and even creates our drive toward and our energies for sustaining our most intimate relationship(s), how can we not experience that energy carried out of our committed sexual relationships in such a way that it influences all our value-laden interactions with the world, in terms of both our human and nonhuman fellow creatures? As our understanding of erotic spiritual empowerment expands to encompass that energy that not only compels justice making in all our human relationships but also compels justice making in all other relationships as well, we can move to explore how specifically gay and lesbian sexuality and spirituality inform an ecological perspective. We can examine what the specific experiences of being gay and lesbian in a homophobic society (and a society also permeated by AIDS) can bring to ecological discourse.

One very important theme in both gay spirituality and emerging gay theology is the realization that we cannot wait for institutions to sanction our efforts to theologize in liberationally sound ways. Because the earth, our home in the broadest sense, cannot afford to wait for the status quo's championing any more than we can as gay men and lesbians, we must assume and assert our own prophetic authoritativeness. This critical stance suggests that gay men and lesbians can contribute something unique not only to human liberational efforts but to ecological reflection and analysis as well.[23]

In fact, we can construct a gay, spiritual, ecological analysis in contradistinction to usually heterosexually male "deep ecology" and as a further extension of ecofeminism. According to deep ecology, an *anthropo*centric worldview of human self-centeredness or selfishness has led to environmental problems. In contrast, according to ecofeminism, an *andro*centric worldview of masculine privilege and social structures has devalued and exploited both women and nature. A gay ecological spirituality or ecotheology will insist that both these views are incomplete: the predominantly Western, white, heteromasculinist worldview is the problem. Not only are women, nature, and sexuality *de*valued, but heteropatriarchy's hierarchy of values and categories *dis*values diversity. Reductionism exploits and destroys anyone and anything designated as other. What we see is not just a devaluing or lowering of value that leads to domination and exploitation but a disvaluing that strips away all value and that thereby leads to exclusion, to being disposable, to being acceptable for extinction. As a result, we must move beyond the ecofeminist concerns with domination and exploitation to those of disvaluation, exclusion, and expendability in order to synthesize a spirituality that radically celebrates diversity and the equal and intrinsic value of all that is, whether the human, the biospheric, or the geospheric.

In the history of the gay and lesbian communities, never has our own expendability been so evident as in the rising incidence of anti-gay/lesbian violence; it is also particularly evident in the AIDS health crisis. The same value hierarchy that insists that nature is reducible to expendable resources also insists on dichotomizing innocent and not innocent (read: expendable) victims of AIDS. The U.S. government continues to spend money in the pursuit of testing protocols and vaccines, while the politico-medical system still drags its feet in regard to approving treatment protocols and finding a cure. Gay men, IV-drug users, people of color, and Third World countries where AIDS rages among heterosexuals are still considered expendable, and that expendability mitigates the urgency of cure or treatment. Our experience of expendability becomes a paradigmatic metaphor for Western culture's attitudes toward all the earth. Hence, our gay ecotheological spirituality must adamantly oppose any disvaluation and exclusion that leads to dispensing with diversity and disposing of life. Neither gay men and lesbians, nor the biosphere, nor the geosphere, nor any of the great diversity that the divine creates and delights in is expendable.

At the same time, the implications of such a spirituality also entail our own accountability. We must hold ourselves accountable, for example, whenever we gay men and lesbians accede to or cooperate with the forces of oppression, exploitation, and expendability. An ecologically informed spirituality and theology will challenge any gay/lesbian assimilation that mitigates our difference — our diversity — and it will also call our own lives, particularly our actions as consumers, into scrutiny. In addition, we gay men will want to examine our own socialization as men. We will need to discern how we as gay men have been conditioned to accept exploitation, disvaluation, and expendability (worthlessness) in our own lives, even when these cultural values are turned against our lives as gay men or as persons living with HIV/AIDS. If the typical Western masculine socialization process works against a compassionate, caring, nurturing empathy for nature (anyone and anything not a white, heterosexual, human male), gay men who escape that socialization process to whatever degree may be able to demonstrate for all men a male-embodied love and care for nature, as well as for holistic sexuality and relational styles free of gender roles. Potentially, at least, gay men and lesbians together can become the embodied witnesses for a liberating spirituality of ecological healing.

Conclusion

In some respects, gay men and lesbians, as a community, may be behind other groups in wrestling with ecological issues and environmental causes or in wrestling with traditionally conceived spiritual, theological, or ethical concerns. This may well be the case because our energies are so consumed, and necessarily so, in dealing with AIDS and in dealing with homophobia, both as anti-gay/lesbian violence and as other forms of oppression such as professional barriers, outright job discrimination, denial of legal protections or benefits for couples, exclusion from religious institutions... and the list can and does go on. Nevertheless, even with our considerable in-house agenda, which absolutely must not be forsaken, we are still called to remember that liberation in the broadest possible sense ideally means developing a broader, more inclusive vision that sees the connections among all forms of oppression, exploitation, and disvaluation and that thereby facilitates liaisons to confront all of these. Not through co-optation but through cooperation, working together to achieve liberation for all peoples and for the earth itself, will we find our own liberation achieved as well. As gay spirituality and theology move together beyond the present tragedy of AIDS to develop visions of such expanding inclusivity, so will our spirituality remain diverse, dynamic, and evolving, not mystically alienated from the realities of our lives but always fusing theory and praxis in the embodied and secular, this-worldly, here-and-now tasks of liberation.

Notes

1. Mary Daly, *Beyond God the Father: Toward a Philosophy of Women's Liberation* (Boston: Beacon, 1973), 6.

2. John Boswell, *Christianity, Social Tolerance, and Homosexuality: Gay People in Western Europe from the Beginning of the Christian Era to the Fourteenth Century* (Chicago: University of Chicago Press, 1980); Rosemary Curb and Nancy Manahan, eds., *Lesbian Nuns: Breaking Silence* (Tallahassee: Naiad, 1985); George DeStefano, "Gay under the Collar: The Hypocrisy of the Catholic Church," *The Advocate* 439 (1986): 43–48.

3. Carl G. Jung, "Psychological Aspects of the Mother Archetype," in *Four Archetypes*, ed. R. F. C. Hull (Princeton, N.J.: Princeton University Press, 1954), 21; Walter L. Williams, *The Spirit and the Flesh: Sexual Diversity in American Indian Culture* (Boston: Beacon, 1986).

4. L. William Countryman, *Dirt, Greed, and Sex: Sexual Ethics in the New Testament and Their Implications for Today* (Philadelphia: Fortress, 1988); George R. Edwards, *Gay/Lesbian Liberation: A Biblical Perspective* (New York: Pilgrim, 1984); Robin Scroggs, *The New Testament and Homosexuality: Contextual Background for Contemporary Debate* (Philadelphia: Fortress, 1983).

5. Carter Heyward, *Our Passion for Justice: Images of Power, Sexuality, and Liberation* (New York: Pilgrim, 1984); and idem, *Touching Our Strength: The Erotic as Power and the Love of God* (San Francisco: Harper, 1989); John E. Fortunato, *Embracing the Exile: Healing Journeys of Gay Christians* (New York: Seabury, 1983); John J. McNeill, *Taking a Chance on God: Liberating Theology for Gays, Lesbians, Their Lovers, Families, and Friends* (Boston: Beacon, 1988); Malcolm Boyd, *Take Off the Masks* (Philadelphia: New Society, 1984); John E. Fortunato, *AIDS, the Spiritual Dilemma* (San Francisco: Harper, 1987); J. Michael Clark, "AIDS, Death, and God: Gay Liberational Theology and the Problem of Suffering," *Journal of Pastoral Counseling* 21:1 (1986): 40–54; and idem, "Special Considerations in Pastoral Care of Gay Persons-with-AIDS," *Journal of Pastoral Counseling* 22:1 (1987): 32–45.

6. Sheila D. Collins, *A Different Heaven and Earth* (Valley Forge, Pa.: Judson, 1974), 231.

7. The description of faerie circles was graciously provided by Al Cotton, biweekly columnist and staff writer for *Southern Voice* newspaper. Cotton also serves on the Atlanta organizing committee for the Celebrating Gay Spirit Visions weekend held each fall in Highlands, North Carolina.

8. Randy P. Connor, *Blossom of Bone: Reclaiming the Connections between Homoeroticism and the Sacred* (San Francisco: Harper, 1993); Arthur Evans, *Witchcraft and the Gay Counterculture* (Boston: Fag Rag, 1978); Judy Grahn, *Another Mother Tongue: Gay Words, Gay Worlds* (Boston: Beacon, 1984); Mark Thompson, ed., *Gay Spirit: Myth and Meaning* (New York: St. Martin's, 1987); Mitch Walker, *Visionary Love: A Spiritbook of Gay Mythology and Transmutational Faerie* (San Francisco: Treeroots, 1980).

9. Arthur Evans, "Where the Faeries Came From," *White Crane* 14 (September 1992): 4–7, 16; Harry Hay, Mark Thompson, and Arthur Evans, "The Fairy Letters," *White Crane* 15 (December 1992): 6–9.

10. Rafael López-Pedraza, "The Tale of Dryops and the Birth of Pan," *Spring* [an annual of archetypal psychology and Jungian thought] (1976): 176–90; Mitch Walker, "The Double: An Archetypal Configuration," *Spring* (1976): 165–75.

11. Ovid, *Metamorphoses* 10.1–85; Eric Neumann, *Amor and Psyche* (Princeton, N.J.: Princeton University Press, 1971).

12. James Hillman, *The Dream and the Underworld* (New York: Harper and Row, 1979); and Eric Neumann, *The Origins and History of Consciousness* (Princeton, N.J.: Princeton University Press, 1970).

13. Williams, *Spirit and the Flesh;* Will Roscoe, ed., *Living the Spirit: A Gay American Indian Anthology* (New York: St. Martin's, 1988); and idem, *The Zuni Man-Woman* (Albuquerque: University of New Mexico Press, 1991).

14. J. Michael Clark, "Monasticism, Homoeroticism, and St. Aelred," in *Gay Being, Divine Presence: Essays in Gay Spirituality* (Garland, Tex.: Tangelwuld, 1987), 50–54.

15. Mark Thompson, "Harry Hay: A Voice from the Past, a Vision for the Future," in *Gay Spirit,* 182–99.

16. Arthur Evans, *The God of Ecstasy: Sex-Roles and the Madness of Dionysos* (New York: St. Martin's, 1988), 126, 179, 183.

17. Geoff Mains, *Urban Aboriginals: A Celebration of Leathersexuality* (San Francisco: Gay Sunshine, 1984); the ensuing discussion of Mains's work previously appeared in an unabridged form in J. Michael Clark, "Leathersexuality: Radical Gayspirit Potential," in *Theologizing Gay: Fragments of Liberation Activity* (Oak Cliff, Tex.: Minuteman, 1991), 15–19.

18. Fortunato, *Embracing the Exile;* Harold Kushner, *When Bad Things Happen to Good People* (New York: Schocken, 1981), 136–37.

19. Ronald E. Long, "God through Gay Men's Eyes: Gay Theology in the Age of AIDS," in Ronald E. Long and J. Michael Clark, *AIDS, God, and Faith: Continuing the Dialogue on Constructing Gay Theology* (Dallas: Monument, 1992), 1–21, 27–36.

20. Richard P. Hardy, "Persons Living with AIDS: Elements of a Christian Spirituality," *Église et Théologie* 23 (1992): 339–59; and idem, *Knowing the God of Compassion: Spirituality and Persons Living with AIDS* (Ottawa: Novalis, 1993).

21. Susan E. Henking, "The Legacies of AIDS: Memorialization and Meaning in AIDS-Related Memoirs" (paper presented in the Gay Men's Issues in Religion Group, American Academy of Religion, San Francisco, 23 November 1992).

22. James B. Nelson, *Body Theology* (Louisville: Westminster/John Knox Press, 1992), 186.

23. J. Michael Clark, *Beyond Our Ghettos: Gay Theology in Ecological Perspective* (Cleveland: Pilgrim, 1993); much of the ensuing discussion first appeared in unabridged form in this text.

Bibliography

Boswell, John. *Christianity, Social Tolerance, and Homosexuality: Gay People in Western Europe from the Beginning of the Christian Era to the Fourteenth Century.* Chicago: University of Chicago Press, 1980.

———. *Same-Sex Unions in Premodern Europe.* New York: Villard, 1994.

Boyd, Malcolm. *Take Off the Masks.* Philadelphia: New Society, 1984.

Clark, J. Michael. *Gay Being, Divine Presence: Essays in Gay Spirituality.* Garland, Tex.: Tangelwuld, 1987.

Connor, Randy P. *Blossom of Bone: Reclaiming the Connections between Homoeroticism and the Sacred.* San Francisco: Harper, 1993.

Evans, Arthur. *Witchcraft and the Gay Counterculture.* Boston: Fag Rag, 1978.

Fortunato, John E. *AIDS: The Spiritual Dilemma.* San Francisco: Harper, 1987.

Grahn, Judy. *Another Mother Tongue: Gay Words, Gay Worlds.* Boston: Beacon, 1984.

Mains, Geoff. *Urban Aboriginals: A Celebration of Leathersexuality.* San Francisco: Gay Sunshine, 1984.

Nelson, James B. *The Intimate Connection: Male Sexuality, Masculine Spirituality.* Philadelphia: Westminster, 1988.

Thompson, Mark, ed. *Gay Spirit: Myth and Meaning.* New York: St. Martin's, 1987.

Walker, Mitch. *Visionary Love: A Spiritbook of Gay Mythology and Transmutational Faerie.* San Francisco: Treeroots, 1980.

14

Social Justice Struggle

DWIGHT N. HOPKINS

THE FREEDOM to profess and practice religion is widely acknowledged to be a basic human right. That a just society must recognize this right, along with others, is prominently declared in documents such as the Constitution of the United States (Amendment 1) and the UN's Universal Declaration of Human Rights (Articles 2 and 18). Although proclaimed by the signatories to such documents, human rights do not become real except as the result of the struggles of thousands, and indeed millions, of less well-known people. Many such persons have been motivated to struggle for social justice by religious convictions, and an increasing number of people, both religious and secular, acknowledge that working for a just society is an integral part of their spiritual lives. Nonreligious persons who have this spiritual self-conception will be the topic of this chapter.

Regarding his French forebear, Emile Durkheim, the American sociologist Talcott Parsons said that his greatest insight about religion was not so much that "religion is a social phenomenon" but that "society is a religious phenomenon."[1] Modifying this thought in light of the conception of the spiritual dimension of human life sketched in this volume's introduction, one can say that feeling oneself to be a part of a social community can be a way in which people apprehend their world as an inclusive whole. The effort and effect of transforming the society to which one belongs in a holistic direction — toward peace, equality, and genuine democracy — can also transform individuals. It can give them a more vital and creative sense of well-being. This I think is the faith of persons who identify social justice struggle as an integral part of their spiritual lives.

Succeeding generations of immigrants to the United States have faced discrimination and exploitation at the hands of more established residents; by necessity they have had to struggle for equal treatment, political power, and social recognition. For a long time it was almost an article of American civil religion that the experience of overcoming such adversities was actually salutary in the sense that it gave new Americans a penchant for political participation, a pride in economic accomplishment, and, above all, a faith in the "American dream."[2] For many immigrants the journey from poverty and discrimination to middle-class respectability by means of hard work and talent has been real. It was the soul-making process of American civil religion. However, from many points of view this rendering of social justice struggle in America looks quite false. First, many Americans who have attained conventional standards of success are assessing the cost of that achievement. Despite continuing anti-Semitism, many American Jews have achieved productive, prosperous, and even prominent lives; yet they also question whether the price of that success has been a loss of their community's religious and cultural traditions and might be, by intermarriage, the loss of its very identity. (Chapter 12, above, describes how many secular-Jewish women, in particular, attach spiritual value to maintaining Jewish cultural traditions.)

Second, the American story of immigrants struggling for social justice does not apply to persons who suffer injustice for reasons other than the ethnicity, language, and religion that have distinguished new generations of American immigrants. For instance, gay and lesbian Americans suffer discrimination and prejudice for their sexual orientation. (Chapter 13, above, describes how such bias in government, church, and the general populace contributes to a distinctive gay spirituality.) Class prejudice is likewise a social scourge that oppresses persons of diverse backgrounds and identities. Believing that their country gives real, if less than equal, economic opportunity to all its citizens, Americans have been hesitant to acknowledge the reality of class conflict and class oppression. Broad-based socialist parties have not developed in the United States as they have in Europe and elsewhere. This does not mean, however, that socialist and Marxist influences have been absent from American political life. Labor, civil rights, and antiwar movements have all received intellectual and political impetus from Marxism. Given the views about religion of Karl Marx and Friedrich Engels and the policies of most communist governments, Marxist thinkers have not spoken a great deal about spiritual modes of understanding. This has changed in recent years, as is well documented in the recent publication *Marxism and Spirituality: An International Anthology.*[3]

Finally, an immigrant model of social justice struggle in the United States is lacking because it does not address the realities of Native Americans and African-Americans. Native Americans came to the Americas thousands of years before Europeans did, and though they have suffered the decimation of their populations, the loss of their lands, and the persecution of their cultures by succeeding generations of American immigrants and governments, they retain a unique legal standing vis-à-vis the United States. Their struggle for social justice has always been linked to — indeed, empowered by — spiritual self-conceptions that have made them distinct from white Europeans. Vine Deloria ironically suggests this point in the title of the manifesto "Custer Died for Your Sins" and eloquently makes the case in the book by the same title.[4]

Most African-Americans are the descendants of slaves who came to the Western Hemisphere against their will. They were enslaved because in the eyes of American politicians, jurists, and much of the American public, their race made them undeserving of the democratic and egalitarian rights announced in the founding documents of the United States. Scholars like Gayraud Wilmore have well chronicled how the story of black religion since slavery has intertwined with the history of black social justice struggle. One crucial chapter in this story is what Wilmore calls the "dechristianization of black radicalism."[5] The black church was one of the few institutions that slaveholders permitted African-Americans to control, and it played a prominent role in resisting slavery and achieving civil rights. However, certainly since the 1960s, the sources and contexts of black social justice struggle have extended beyond the doors of the black church. Through the influence of Malcolm X and others, Islam has become an alternative religious framework from which to denounce and resist the racism of the U.S. government and people. Secular influences likewise contributed to this evolution of black radicalism away from the black church. Enlightenment liberalism and Marxist radicalism gave independent grounds for condemning race and class prejudice and for struggling on behalf of genuine democracy and equality.

Marxism and black radicalism have been two of the most pervasive contexts in which social justice struggle has occurred in the last two centuries of U.S. history. They occur jointly in the magisterial figure of W. E. B. Du Bois. Hence, this chapter on social justice struggle as a form of secular spirituality will favor particularity over generality and consist of a detailed examination of the life and thought of this influential African-American.

Spirituality in the Struggle for Democracy and Equality

William Edward Burghardt Du Bois (1868–1963) remains the most productive social justice intellectual and activist ever engendered by black America and, perhaps, by all of American society. Born three years after the close of the Civil War and dead one day before the March on

Washington, Du Bois authored and edited roughly three dozen books and wrote over a thousand articles and letters; he presented papers throughout the world and founded and edited various journals; he initiated civil rights organizations and consulted with heads of states; he was given numerous worldwide honorary degrees, and, for an eight-year period, his passport was revoked by the U.S. Justice Department. His scholarly disciplines included history, sociology, political economy, statistics, poetry, and biblical studies. His political positions varied: integrationism, self-help advocacy, temporary separation of blacks from whites, black nationalism, Pan-Africanism, socialism, and communism.[6]

During his illustrious ninety-five-year career, Du Bois anchored his life's achievements in social justice struggle as a form of spiritual behavior. His enduring passion for struggle was manifest in the fight to achieve democracy and equality for women, poor people, Third World countries, and, especially, African-Americans. He believed that democracy would invest the majority with the power to rule and that equality would guarantee to all the same access to rule with power. This focused passion was fired by a social justice and social transformative spirituality.

Although Du Bois often employed Christian terminology and although his faith opinions, at times, overlapped with Christian discourse, his spirituality was primarily a secular quest in the sense that his ultimate conception of the self and the world was not indebted to religion. To be spiritual did not presuppose being an advocate of religious doctrine or a proselytizer for religious institutions. Indeed, his struggle to bring forth the true self of the oppressed (that is, the inner conversion of the despised of humanity from a victimized state to one of increased vitality) in relation to a reconfigured societal makeup (that is, the total permeation of balanced power among people and in all creation) arose from blending the spiritualities of the European Enlightenment, Marxist thought and politics, and the African-American struggle against racism. The mixture of these three dynamics provided the conceptual and historical context for Du Bois's spirituality in the struggle for democracy and equality.

In his studies of the European Enlightenment at Harvard and in Berlin and in his personal encounter with its application in his childhood in Great Barrington, Massachusetts, Du Bois formulated certain ideas about what defined the human person. To be human denoted a rational being who could, through ascertaining and deploying the most advanced intellectual resources of a cultured society, rely upon scientific methodology and research to persuade fellow citizens about issues of the civic good in the public square. The Enlightenment sensibility detested the notion of an outside authoritarian force subjecting "man" to the arbitrary (even potentially benevolent) whims of a "god" or divine providence.

In Enlightenment culture, human beings take the initiative and work for equality and democracy; furthermore, they shun affiliation with dictatorial religious doctrine and reject blind submission to hierarchical authority. The spirit of the Enlightenment challenges the human being to pursue and attain the full vitality of human possibility and progress — to become a free spirit endowed with the natural ability and right to change the entire world. Throughout his personal life, as well as in his career working on behalf of African-American advancement, Du Bois pursued a notion of the self as continuously transformed through education and hard work within the cosmic totality of things material and spiritual.

Similarly, the secular spirituality of Marxism impacted the battle for democracy and equality embedded in Du Bois's spirituality. Although Du Bois did not subscribe to the Hegelian notion of an overarching Spirit in history, he did profess that the spirit of the oppressed would eventually triumph in the victory of the proletariat and that this victory was assured by the dialectical materialism elucidated in Karl Marx's trenchant social analyses. Through his formal studies as well as his visits to the Soviet Union and the People's Republic of China, Du Bois was quite familiar with Marxism. In his estimation, the collective spirituality of the earth's downtrodden was advanced at each nodal point of history. In other words, the leap from the darkness of prehistoric human entrapment to the forces of nature in primitive communalism to the enlightened social arrangements of socialism and communism (governed by a rational subjugation of nature) would result from a scientific application of humanity's highest intellectual energies to the materialist problems of human labor. From Marx, Du Bois's thinking gained a dimension of historical universality and a prophetic urgency. The proletariat serves as the paradigmatic expression of oppressed people's self-realization; this self-realization will occur in the sudden transformation of the socialist revolution and in the subsequent further development of selves and society through productive mastery of the natural world.

The third historical and conceptual context that situated Du Bois's spirituality as a secular quest was the African-American struggle for equality and democracy. As a student of history, political economy, and sociology, among other disciplines, Du Bois maintained a firm and incisive grasp of the African-American sojourn in the United States since slavery. Within the black tradition, he detected a spirit of determination and persistence in what he perceived as an inevitable, though rough, movement toward a day when black Americans would share in the earth's resources on a par with other citizens in a just social environment. Du Bois acknowledged the important role of the black church in this long lineage of black struggle, but he did not restrict the African-American spiritual drive for freedom solely to black religious formations. Neither the doctrinal proclamations nor the ecclesiastical structures (for Du Bois, both were only partial representations of the revolutionary life of Jesus of Nazareth) of black religious communities circumscribed fully the movement toward a truly vital black self resulting from the removal of racist roadblocks in the world.

The goal of the concrete realization of democracy and equality shaped Du Bois's ontology, epistemology, and way of life. He dedicated his total self to the vision of a new heaven and new earth filled with a new humanity. He subordinated all of his intellectual and organizing activities toward this vision, and, in turn, this vision constituted his life. Briefly stated, Du Bois lived and advocated a spirituality of democracy and equality, speaking first to black Americans, but offering a similar, universal gift to all of humanity.

Roots in Great Barrington

Du Bois's spirituality of democracy and equality grew directly out of his formative childhood experiences in Great Barrington, Massachusetts. His nascent spirituality was nurtured both in his formal church activities and in the broader cultural ethos of a small New England town. "My religious development," wrote Du Bois, "has been slow and uncertain. I grew up in a liberal Congregational Sunday School and listened once a week to a sermon on doing good as a reasonable duty. Theology played a minor part and our teachers had to face some searching questions."[7] Underscoring the point of an early life enveloped by organized religious influences, Du Bois further testified that, outside of school, his "chief communication with the people of the town was through the church."[8] The liberal dimension of ecclesial thinking fostered an openness to new ideas and diverse ways of viewing the world spiritually. Indeed, Du Bois, along with other communicants, constantly queried his Sunday school teacher about prescribed doctrine and normative religious truth claims. Likewise, a liberal notion of faith allowed room for a strong emphasis on humanity collaborating with God in covenantal relations whereby human effort signaled a fundamental mark of Christian identity.

"Doing good as a reasonable duty," a theme Du Bois heard expounded in weekly homilies during his childhood, was the essence of his church's theological imperative. The first instruction (that is, "doing good") exhorted the church member to take seriously the practical nature of Christian faith. A believer acted upon the basis of her or his faith so that correct doctrine received its validity and confirmation by religious action and not solely by affirmation of a creed. Methodologically speaking, the emphasis on doing gave priority to the believers' actions in the world of social relations in contrast to their orthodox affirmations as a religious community. Such an approach looked earthward at the human condition and discovered God as the divinity conspiring with humanity in "doing." Similarly, a true spiritual presence could possibly reside wherever, inside or outside the church, believers are "doing."

Furthermore, this "doing" was to promote the "good": that is, its goal was serving others and enriching the health of the broader community. From this aspect of New England Calvinist thought, Du Bois received an accent on collectivity and communality. In a sense, the spiritual formation of individuals depended upon their positive, value-laden efforts toward benefiting humanity. The worth of persons appreciated and depreciated relative to their serviceable activities for the common good.

"Reasonable duty," the second part of the theme Du Bois heard expounded weekly, further hoisted the hortatory dimension of "doing good" onto an ethical and moral plane. To serve the other became not an option but a spiritual obligation of the self. To be a part of the faith community entailed an imperative ritual of regular work for the greater whole. Likewise, from an anthropological vantage point, religion meant rigorous commitment to a continual implementation of faith claims. Lack of duty implied a lessening of the degree to which one realized the definition of being human. Here, too, "duty" complemented and undergirded "doing." One did not carry out and witness to the good solely out of a secular motivation, without spiritual foundation. On the contrary, the habit of giving of oneself for the sake of the community had a profound sacred meaning. Self-transformation was tied to social transformation toward equality and democracy; this was the touchstone of a spirituality of social justice struggle.

Moreover, the stress on "reasonable duty" drew on a way of life or spiritual worldview that invoked a rational understanding of pragmatic religious obligation. Engagement in demanding intellectual analysis and in inquiry from a multiplicity of perspectives would become a hallmark of Du Bois's own thirst for social as well as spiritual clarity. At the same time, the modifier "reasonable" suggested the necessity of utilizing a "scientific" approach — one grounded in the perspective of material reality — to divine-human encounters. Later for Du Bois, this would mean the acceptance of any spirituality greater than human materiality as long as that spirit rested in and enhanced human struggle for democracy and equality on earth.

Du Bois also gained an appreciation for spirituality from secular experiences in his childhood environment. The most prominent remembrance recounted by Du Bois about his early life was a tale regarding self-governance in Great Barrington, specifically democracy in the representation of each citizen's voice in decision making. "In government," writes Du Bois, "Great Barrington was in theory and largely in practice a democracy of the New England type."[9] In another instance, he echoes these sentiments by portraying the local election processes as if they were almost a paradigm of perfection: "The town approached in politics a pure democracy with annual town meetings and elections of well-known and fairly qualified officials."[10]

From the impressionable age of thirteen or fourteen, Du Bois "religiously" attended the annual spring town meetings where funds were allocated and decisions made for the upkeep and benefit of the common good.[11] The openness and active participation of all citizens regardless of class or race created an unalterable imprint on his inquisitive mind at this formative stage in his life. All could come and participate; all could vote and have their individual decisions influence the final collective plans. Decision making was not monopolized by power brokers who said one thing behind closed doors and another thing in public discourse. On the contrary, Du Bois knew each of the persons involved in the debates:

> I can remember as a boy in high school, attending regularly the Town Meeting held annually in my New England home. I understood the workings of local government when I was thirteen or fourteen years of age. I knew about the hard won appropriations for the high school; the sums set aside for roads and bridges; the provision for the poor, and the various officials who carried out this work. Many of these officials I knew personally; all of them I knew by sight; and I knew what their duties were. It was easy for me to conceive and talk about democracy. I saw it and lived it.[12]

Fundamentally, democracy revolved around citizen participation and knowledge. Everyone was to be present at and in the midst of deliberations about the public's future. For Du Bois, this was like a religious attendance. If one person or a particular segment of the populace suffered by being denied access to the communal discussions, then democracy suffered, and, indeed, the group religious imperative to attend was attenuated.

Citizens not only were to show up at public meetings but were expected to be knowledgeable about the entire democratic process. On the one hand, this implied initiative on the part of the individual in securing the most up-to-date facts on diverse opinions, plans, and allocation of resources. On the other hand, it meant that all individuals had the right to acquire the latest information available. In this sense, collective knowledge ensured open access to, informed decisions about, and semiownership of available community assets. This knowledge also included an intimate awareness of elected officials, both their personalities and their specific duties.

The town meetings exposed Du Bois to the equal representation of various citizens' voices and to the obligation to speak at such forums. Citizens were expected to give voice to their opinions in democratic discourse. Resuming his description of Great Barrington's town meetings, Du Bois states: "While wealth spoke and had power, the dirtiest Irish laborer had voice and vote. Democracy modified industry."[13] Here he touches on the absolute equality of voice that ensures the subordination of class distinctions in the public realm. In other words, the owners of wealth had to listen to the language and preferences of the lowliest classes in the community; and, likewise, the poorest segments leveraged their convictions through a voting mechanism that made their opinions and articulations as forceful and worthy as those of the industrialists.

In sum, a committed voice, an informed vote, and an empathizing practice for the totality of the whole were general components of Du Bois's budding spiritual formation garnered from an experiential setting inside and outside of the church.

A Distinct Spirituality

Du Bois fashioned the characteristic textures and contours of his faith in the context of a spirituality of democracy and equality. This entailed a dynamic process of both rejecting the formal and normative doctrines of Christian churches and affirming positively his own spiritual specificity. Du Bois's rupture with the formal church and doctrinaire creeds occurred while he was an undergraduate at Fisk University in Nashville, Tennessee. Like many American colleges during the late nineteenth century, this black university subscribed heavily to the Christian religion. Given this environment, one of Du Bois's classmates accused him of dancing, which denoted, in this educational institution's theology, sin and evil. Such a claim and the ensuing posture of the faculty altered forever Du Bois's attitude toward dominant religious hermeneutics. He writes: "I resented this [accusation] and said so in very plain terms. The teachers intervened and tried to reconcile matters in a way which for years afterward made me resentful and led to my eventual refusal to join a religious organization.... They quoted Paul.... I began again to dance and I have never since had much respect for Paul."[14] What disturbed him were the pettiness and irrationality of the charge. Spirituality, for him, had nothing to do with policing the innocent frivolities of individual choice. Instead of promoting the higher cultural and spiritual vision that could possibly enhance and develop collective well-being, the theological ethos of the school was narrowed to focusing its energy on the demonic or angelic nature of dancing. Du Bois's convictions convinced him that this stance caricatured and circumscribed a proper spiritual way of life.

Moreover, castigating dancing as sin piqued Du Bois's methodological sense of rational inquiry and materialistic investigation. Religious matters, whether spiritual or creedal, lacked credibility for him when they posed rules of faith that failed to demonstrate their veracity through either logic or his own experience. More fundamentally, he could not see how one could classify dancing as an evil when it did not block human efforts to change this world for the better. For him, spiritual concerns, broadly defined, hinged on the ability to work for the greater whole. Later, in response to a query about his attitude toward organized religion (in this instance, the Roman Catholic Church), Du Bois wrote: "I cannot assent to any creed which demands that I accept on faith the elaborate doctrine and dogma of the Catholic Church. As a scientist I am perfectly aware that there are some things in this world we must accept on faith so long as we rigorously test them by the data of experience."[15] His self-perception as a scientist and his penchant for empirical inquiry directly affected his positive spiritual affirmations, especially as they related to the importance of work, democracy, and "a vague Force" (discussed below).

Du Bois did not characterize the nature of a being greater than humanity as an independent divine person or in other terminology standard in Christian discourse. From his perspective, the word *person* in this context incorrectly connotes an autonomous spirit with abilities that might substitute for human efforts toward social transformation. Likewise, if one granted the supernatural existence of a being embodying the attributes of people, then that person could control, direct, and, thereby, obviate independent human struggle and work. Thus Du Bois held at arm's length the notion of a divine person external to human social relations but engaged in human social life. In a letter, he clarifies the precise nature of his spiritual understanding: "If by being 'a believer in God,' you mean a belief in a person of vast power who consciously rules the universe for the good of mankind, I answer No; I cannot disprove this assumption, but I certainly see no proof to sustain such a belief, neither in History nor in my personal experience." As a social scientist, Du Bois would not acknowledge the existence of a controlling and intentional God—the divine perfection of humanity's attributes — because the human record and his immediate experience weighed heavily against such a possibility. However, this theological orientation did not preclude his faith in spirituality. He continues: "If on the other hand you mean by 'God' a vague Force which, in some incomprehensible way, dominates all life and change, then I answer, Yes: I recognize such Force, and if you wish to call it God, I do not object."[16] In other words, Du Bois did not recognize guidance by a divine person acting outside of, above, and on behalf of humanity, but he did recognize a force that, from his vantage point, engendered human initiative in the struggle for democracy and equality. On the one hand, this force could not dominate "all life and change" and was not the exact equivalent of the human community. On the other hand, unlike the traditional conceptions of a divine person or the Christian God, this force was not external to human relationships. The force was inseparably and inextricably intertwined with the human spiritual quest.

Du Bois assented to a vague force instead of to a doctrinaire divine person because of the moral implications and ethical mandate that ensue from such a conviction. He elaborates his proclivity for a spiritual force:

> Most educated modern men no longer believe in religious dogma. If questioned they will usually resort to double-talk before admitting the fact. But who today actually believes that this world is ruled and directed by a benevolent person of great power who, on humble appeal, will change the course of events at our request...? One could hardly exaggerate the moral disaster of this custom.[17]

For some traditional theists, a practical implication of faith in such a divine person was that one simply did nothing but call on that person to come down and perform the work of social transformation. Du Bois stood so strongly against this dogma that no amount of negative superlatives could suffice in condemning this ethically bankrupt notion. Anything or any individual that made people passive in the face of needed societal alterations was anathema to him.

Du Bois emphasized the spiritual reality of a force rather than a divine person primarily because his faith began with whatever fostered the human ability to untangle oppressive communities and rearrange them into liberating social configurations. This was his basic presupposition. "I assumed," he writes, "that human beings could alter and re-direct the course of events so as to better human conditions." Human beings had the power, a combined spiritual, intellectual, and physical power, to influence historical developments and channel them into building a new heaven and new earth. The key element was "the decisive action of human beings" in relation to everything that existed. Most people, particularly those affiliated with organized religion, dismissed Du Bois's unorthodox faith and entrenched themselves further in a "firm belief in unalterable Law." With this move, the inevitable consequence of espousing an external divine person, they changed "Man into an automaton and [made] Ethics unmeaning and Reform a contradiction in terms."[18] In a contrasting manner and in a dynamic fashion, the vague force of Du Bois's faith toiled with and expressed itself through the human spirit and empowered people to change the world by their own decisive action.

Du Bois added another element to the workings of this force: the vital importance of work in constructing a spirituality of democracy and equality. He did not simply view work as a secular endeavor lacking a higher horizon; for him, it involved a noble aim greater than but always grounded in the human project. One could interpret Du Bois's heavy emphasis on work as an affirmation of a form of spiritual discipline since he sought, by this regular exercise of human capability, to obtain an optimal relation between his best self and the larger effort to rearrange power and balance access to power. In contrast to those who resorted to "superstition, obscurantism, and the formal religion of creeds" during periods of great calamity, Du Bois offered another alternative:

> On the other hand, among some people, there comes in time of stress and depression, an increase of determination to plan and work for better conditions. This is not usually called a "spiritual" awakening, but it is apt to be condemned by the ignorant as "radicalism" and an "attack" upon the established order. It is, however, a manifestation of the spirit in the highest sense and something of this I seem to see beginning today.[19]

In this sense, work became a spiritual calling, an awakening like a conversion experience. Something greater than the individual gripped and compelled her or him into action, particularly in historical moments of tragedy, confusion, and national paralysis. Moreover, Du Bois's description of this process offered a subliminal suggestion about the nature of work as prophetic. When a person opened the self and responded to this "spiritual awakening," formal creedal advocates of traditional religion and defenders of the "established order" would press their agendas as the answer and decry all else as dangerous revolutionary activity. Thus, those who assumed the supreme calling of work would be condemned as radicals and forced to the margins. Both the language of radicalism and gestures of marginalization served as characteristic stones cast at a prophet. Work manifested the highest vocational act of the spirit — a prophetic profession toward a common consensus for a better common good.[20]

Work manifested the spirit; but more than that, it signified a divine offering in the human predicament. Du Bois elaborated the parental nature of God's gift of a vocation to human beings: "And what richer legacy can a parent leave to a child than the opportunity to labor at the work he is fitted for, to toil at the toil he loves? The father may give him wealth and the mother love, but the gift of God is work."[21] The parental molding of a child, whether through inherited wealth or love, remained insufficient unless it was solidified with knowledge of productive toil. Hence human character formation, a part of spiritual vocation, approached the realm of complete love, enjoyment, and purpose when the child grasped God's gift of work. Work was a divine instance of immortality bequeathed to children through the legacy of parents.

The gift of God's work, moreover, entailed a dynamic process in which the spirit of toil for better conditions of democracy and equality came to the individual. The more the person accepted this highest calling, the more he or she gained knowledge of and intimacy with God. Work coupled epistemological and existential questions. First, the only way to partake of the unveiling of divine presence was through work: "God is Love and Work is His Revelation," wrote Du Bois in a series of prayers. Laboring for the greater humanity pinpointed the location for divine giving. Consequently, awareness of God's spirit did not entail a cryptic gnosis, an obscure hieroglyphics, or an abstract axiomatics. On the contrary, Du Bois's theory of knowledge was much simpler and more accessible. Therefore, work informed a democratic epistemology of spiritual wisdom. Work denoted both the medium through which God gave a spiritual gift and a conscious knowledge of God's spirit. Simply put, to know was to do. Second, nearness to divine spirit resulted from laboring for those higher goals of democracy and equality: "God, teach us to work. Herein alone do we approach our Creator when we stretch our arms with toil, and strain our eye and ear and brain to catch the thought and do the deed and create the things that make life worth living."[22] Perhaps other rituals or regimens could advance an individual toward God. But for Du Bois, the intensity of the travail, coded in the signifiers *stretch, strain, catch, do,* and *create,* defined God's living proximity.

In addition to knowledge and presence, work comprised a universal dimension; ultimately, busy activity performed by one person or group was for the larger love of all humanity. It was focused effort immersed in total sympathy for the other who suffered both triumphs and tribulations. Communal labor accepted all people regardless of race, class, gender, and citizenship, and in this way relegated discrimination to the status of a historical relic. Du Bois accentuated this broader dimension of labor by first contrasting it with the opposite of the spiritual reality of work: "Hell is the place where people are idle.... Work is the glory of man." He specified its value-laden substance by saying that it is not blind, self-centered activity. "But work is not simply for work's sake." He continued: "Not simply for aimless doing. It must be inspired for one vast ideal and the great ideal of life is love,... that broad and infinite sympathy with the joys and sorrows of your fellowmen... which sees behind the narrowness and prejudice and evil of wavering human life the soul-beauty of infinite possibility and endless development."[23] For Du Bois, this was the larger love that inspired all work and gave it the meaning to be "worth the doing."[24] To catch a glimpse of the beauty of the other's soul meant seeing that person as an equal and aiding that individual in overcoming all obstacles that would prevent her or him from working toward infinite possibilities and endless development. In other words, to love someone was to see the beauty of the soul that realized its end through the complete participation of all peoples in harmonizing both themselves and their environment with the collective good. The removal of obstacles for universal full humanity demanded democracy and equality for all. To express such feelings toward the other and to achieve such an end for the neighbor were the rationales for Du Bois's conscious faith and spiritual sense summarized in this precise and concise credo: "I above all believe in work, systematic and tireless."[25]

Du Bois elaborated and affirmed his own spiritual specificity by clarifying the nature of "the force" and his faith in work. Greater than but grounded in the human spiritual quest for a universal full humanity, "the force" engendered struggle to attain the ultimate human project. Similarly, the sacredness of work, a spiritual awakening, manifested a divine offering that, in turn, summoned humanity to strive for the highest realization of everyone's infinite possibility and endless development. Both "the force" and work pointed to the essential texture and contour of Du Bois's distinct spirituality — the final goal of democracy and equality.

Though ignorance and deliberate ill-will served to stratify and separate humankind, thereby fracturing equal participation in the local and global communities, Du Bois eventually posited massive human poverty as the fundamental impediment to democracy. As its corrective, he advocated reliance on the majority of the people who performed the world's work so that they would gain the reigns of power "to guide and rule the state for the best welfare of the masses." Furthermore, he assumed that "out of the downtrodden mass of people, ability and character, sufficient to do this task effectively, could and would be found." This fervent conviction about grassroots democracy in all spheres of life consumed Du Bois's greatest energies. "I believe this dictum passionately. It was, in fact, the foundation stone of my fight for black folk," he confessed. "It explained me."[26]

Radical democracy — which involved poor and working people universally and completely utilizing their voice and power — reached fruition when national governmental functions mirrored and served the interests of "downtrodden" people. Commitment to democracy and equality required a reorientation of qualified leadership, national wisdom, and the goal of all forms of government. As Du Bois asserted, the "general welfare was the object of democratic action in the state, of allowing the governed a voice in government."[27] Therefore, in general terms, the spirituality empowering Du Bois's being was the struggle to position the bottom of society (indeed, of the world) at the top in commanding positions. Even though disparaged by the dominant elements of society, the really enlightened sector of society, the one embodying national wisdom, arose from those people who did the world's work. With this majority guiding and leading the state and sharing and implementing their knowledge, the teleological purpose of society would shift from individual interests to the general welfare.

Spiritual Embodiments at the Margins

For Du Bois, a spirituality of democracy and equality is embodied in concrete manifestations of human interactions. Spirituality makes active subjects of people trapped in the cracks or relegated to the margins of society. A liberating spirit inhabits these spaces where forgotten people live. Du Bois wrote:

> We recognize there are other and greater fields to conquer; there is the question of political rights for women, for the poor, for the unrepresented laboring millions throughout the world; there is the problem of economic justice in the distribution process.... There is above all the question of peace and the cessation of imperial aggression on weaker peoples.[28]

In a word, Du Bois committed his life to peace and the full humanity of African-Americans, women, the laboring poor, and the people of the Third World. For these communities of subjugated voices, he believed in "that incarnate spirit of justice, that hatred of a lie, that willingness to sacrifice money, reputation, and life itself on the altar of right."[29]

Du Bois's spiritual affirmations were grounded, first of all, in the particularity of black Americans. From this despised group, democracy and equality could spring forth for all of oppressed humanity. Consequently, as early as 1886, he dedicated himself "toward a life that shall be an honor to the Race."[30] This pledge was launched from spiritual moorings with a divine vocational urgency. "Believing this with my utmost soul," Du Bois proclaimed, "I shall fight race prejudice continually." Such a lifelong journey of empowering African-Americans denoted something consecrated, and, therefore, he concluded: "This contribution to the greatest of causes shall be my most sacred obligation."[31] Indeed, the absolute equality and democratic voice of black Americans signaled a "divine right" with implications for all humanity. Whatever hindered, degraded, or discouraged African-Americans weakened and injured the state to such a degree that black people's exclusion from American democracy had a nearly fatal effect upon the nation, especially during its times of "spiritual crisis."[32]

Consistent with his method of embodying spirituality in the dilemma of the nation's marginalized, Du Bois specified a comprehensive realization of equality for black folk. In order to yield universal equality and democracy (that is, with the state symbolizing the total popular well-being), black people had to occupy all levels of society. Black liberation and freedom provided the conditions for the elimination of the most egregious impediments blocking a healthy nation. "By 'Freedom' for Negroes," asserted Du Bois, "I mean and still mean, full economic, political and social equality with American citizens, in thought, expression and action, with no discrimination based on race or color."[33] Concomitantly, this freedom, one offered to all oppressed humanity, realized itself with the procurement of educational opportunities for black Americans. To be on par economically, politically, and socially required a well-informed and literate population.[34]

On the economic level, Du Bois supported a bifurcated strategy. On the one hand, black workers should tirelessly struggle for equality and democracy in terms of both access to jobs and status in trade union organizations — a move toward fostering black-white unity for all American workers. On the other hand, black labor needed to vigorously pursue and confront instances of racial prejudice and white supremacy wherever such discrimination stifled democracy and equality. Thus the fight would involve working for universal labor and against racial barriers among workers.[35]

Similarly, on the social level, Du Bois advocated a two-pronged approach. Ultimately, he saw black Americans' fullest humanity and the nation's healthiest personality coalescing in a future, racially integrated society. However, he was not so naive as to be blind to the possibility of persistent racism, even ongoing antiblack pogroms, which could devastate, if not eliminate, black life. In response to this latter possibility,

Du Bois held on to temporary segregation as an interim breathing space for black Americans' safety and sanity. In answer to a question regarding "how the American Negro would survive if color caste continued for two or three generations," Du Bois advocated a strategy of all-black internal cohesion, oriented toward African-Americans surviving in their own community with equality and democracy among themselves. This would serve as a response to an externally imposed racial caste system, and it was intended to withstand the assaults of white supremacy until it abated and black Americans obtained the right of "future integration into American and world culture."[36]

Regarding politics, Du Bois stood for blacks' full participation in electoral processes, whether that meant voter registration, running for office, or engaging the political machinery in whatever manner. The denial of political participation not only had positioned blacks at the bottom of power politics but also had stifled the best democratic traditions of the American republic. In other words, the antidemocratic exclusion of African-Americans had served to conceal the fact that the nation suffered from the whims of powerful elite alliances. These elite groups played the antiblack racial card to obscure their own monopolization of power. When black folks' chains of subservience were burst, the spirit of democratic politics would be unleashed and, thus, would enliven all other discriminated quarters of society. When the bottom of the bottom (that is, African-Americans) were brought fully into the electoral process, diverse voices would be heard in decision-making processes throughout the land.

Next, Du Bois urged African-Americans to fight for equal rights to education and to struggle to attain a broad knowledge of social relations. Particularly, he linked education to the process of making well-grounded decisions. While not denying the traditional fundamentals of school curriculum (for example, reading, writing, arithmetic), Du Bois emphasized education about the structural social forces relevant to questions about who controls wealth and how governments function. Responses to such questions would enable black Americans to choose their larger aims and ideals. Basically, education produced a knowledgeable populace who could engage in a rational discourse regarding the configuration of a new society. In this sense, education would promote discernment and debate regarding the class, racial, and caste stratifications that affected and partitioned all Americans.

While encouraging an informed analysis of factors affecting the prospects of democracy and equality for all citizens — a teleological endeavor required of all Americans — Du Bois homed in on an additional educational task of African-Americans. The latter should not forget the importance of their own unique contributions to themselves and to their larger society. Put differently, black people should perceive their preparation for a new reality — a new heaven and new earth for all — as compatible with a distinctive African-American identity. Education for a new democracy and new equality meant, simultaneously, maintaining a black cultural identity. "We must accept equality or die," Du Bois wrote to members of his race. Black people must "lay down a line of thought and action which will accomplish two things: The utter disappearance of color discrimination in American life and the preservation of African history and culture as a valuable contribution to modern civilization." "The utter disappearance of color discrimination" referred to the first concern — education for the hoped-for reality to come. The second educational consideration touched on remembering the historical knowledge of struggles: ties with Africa, black music, art, literature, and "our memory of Negro history and of those racial peculiarities which have long been associated with the Negro."[37] Thus an educated black American was conversant with the exigencies of a citizen's voice and choice as well as with the unique black past, black presence, and black participation in American life. Education of this sort was a special type of spiritual transformation of the individual self within the outer boundaries of a greater societal whole.

Du Bois located spiritual embodiment in the African-American people not only because he arose from this group or because he limited his sights simply to black survival and freedom but mainly because he had faith in the liberating possibilities that black folk offered to all humanity. Therefore, the methodological trajectory of his thrust toward democracy and equality continually returned to the benevolent future of all peoples. Marshaling the best impulses of democratic and equal relations and aspirations among blacks prepared them to assume their rightful place within the larger culture and also proffered a proper paradigm for just relations between peoples and nations of all colors. Affirming his deepest convictions, Du Bois stated: "I believe in Liberty for all men: the space to stretch their arms and their souls, the right to breathe and the right to vote, the freedom to choose their friends, enjoy the sunshine, and ride on the railroads, uncursed by color; thinking and dreaming, working as they will in a kingdom of beauty and love."[38]

This ultimate vision of a new spiritual and material being — of soul, body, free will, mind, and space — could become real only with the upliftment and encouragement of the "negro" people, America's decisive stumbling block. Consequently, the color line remained, for Du Bois, the great divide between an ignominious present and a magnificent new creation. Du Bois drew concise and clear lines of demarcation: "Americans in the immediate future should place most stress upon the abolition of the color line. Just so long as the majority of men are treated as inhuman and legitimate objects of commercial exploitation, religious damnation, and social ostracism, just so long will democracy be impossible in the world."[39] No social construct would ever attain its highest manifestation until the least in society (in this instance, victims of exacerbated race relations) assumed a prominent position. Thus black subordination and subservience were an absolute brake on humankind's movement toward its ultimate potential.

African-American democracy and equality, then, have profound implications for the state of the nation. With this conviction, Du Bois focused on the resources inherent in black life that could resolve black internal problematics and, as a result, propel the African-American community, as a heuristic model, onto the national agenda. One empowering, indigenous resource in black life was the lessons learned from African-American people's connection to an African way of life. Specifically, Du Bois cited African "communalism" as an appropriate signifier of what correct class relationships among contemporary black Americans should entail. Communalism, for him, was a total lifestyle of each group member fully accessing every sphere of the community — art, music, drama, economics, education, politics, work, and so on. Communalism meant more than economic arrangements and sorting out scarce resources. Rather it infused a people's collective personality and reason for being; hence, it encompassed the overall spiritual nature of a social entity.

With this reconnection to a cultural Africanism — to its primordial spiritual sources — the black American community could exhibit its social relations as a prescription for the nation. "We have a chance here," wrote Du Bois, "to teach industrial and cultural democracy to a world that bitterly needs it." Again, what was at stake were the future of life and the necessity for the "American Negro" to move "with the modern world into a new heaven and new earth."[40] The spiritual momentum for this movement could arise out of black America.

Race remained the primary focus of Du Bois's vision of spiritual embodiment at the margins. However, as noted previously, he broadened the horizon of the invisible other at the margins to include women, the working poor, and Third World peoples. Such a complex concern underscored Du Bois's belief that all of creation was the deserving object of his thought and feeling regarding democracy and equality. His inner self-transformation and gradual development would be remiss, indeed, incomplete, without an outward laboring for the whole of society.

The nexus between the spiritual and the material struggle for social transformation, as it pertained to women, converged especially in the contested realms of electoral, democratic power representation and equal independent economic compensation. In the early 1920s, Du Bois forcefully addressed the national debate over the proposed enfranchisement of American women. He engaged this controversy by posing the question: What interests did African-Americans have in supporting all women in the latter's plea for the right to vote? Du Bois offered at least three key responses to his query.

First, he argued that "any extension of democracy involves a discussion of the fundamentals of democracy." Here, in the particularity of one segment of American society longing for electoral representation, Du Bois perceived the possibility of fashioning a universal dialogue around the foundational features of the nation's character and way of life. The debate about women voting, therefore, occasioned an opportunity to weave more tightly the justice issues of nondiscriminatory participation for all. The vote controversy opened a space to do more than simply dismiss adversaries' calls for women to remain in the home. It entailed this debate about the role of women, but on a broader scale, it allowed Du Bois to define national discourse regarding the country's values, sensibilities, and mores — spiritual considerations that defined the national identity. "And in all cases," Du Bois continued, "the broader the basis of democracy the surer is the universal appeal for justice to win ultimate hearing and sympathy."[41] Universal democracy yielded universal right-relations (that is, justice) for all.

Second, women's access to the ballot was a human question, in Du Bois's reasoning. At least one-half of humanity suffered from exclusionary mechanisms because of its gender. Political power and attendant privileges were monopolized in the hands of men who spoke, at least through the electoral voice, for the nation as a whole. Because males had posited their interests and cloaked their agendas under a language of universal American interests, one-half of the country's human resources languished in underutilization, if not in a state of stunted underdevelopment. Thus the forced retardation of women's electoral contributions stifled the nation's progress, and, very directly, men too felt the constraints placed on inevitable benefits that would have resulted from a liberated democratic spirit. What affected one-half of humankind affected all; and, for Du Bois, it had special deleterious effects on black people's participatory voice.

Finally, Du Bois fought for women's right to vote because the damning, irrational logic (held not only by white but also by some black male leaders at that time) deployed by those opposed to women's enfranchisement paralleled stances that had been taken against the enfranchisement of blacks. If one could successfully aid all women in the electoral arena, one could support the democratic involvement of blacks at all levels of society. If disenfranchisement on the basis of sex was wrong, Du Bois asserted, so too was disenfranchisement on the basis of race. The same reasons justifying gender inclusion in the democratic process could be employed to expand racial inclusion in all positions and privileges in the public sphere. Du Bois concluded: "The emancipation of woman is, of course, but one phase of the growth of democracy."[42]

In addition, Du Bois believed that increasing economic freedom for women would promote an embodied spirituality of gender equality. He based this assessment on the increased independence that black women gained by vacating the narrow confines of homemaking and by taking various jobs in the broader society. Forced into domestic labor, African-American women had become appendages to the tenuous economic status of black men in America. Such a precarious existence both hampered the survival of women and relegated the black family to greater instability, but this move of women into the labor arena also lifted them and their loved ones to a higher plane of autonomous living and strength. Most importantly, African-American women's "new economic equality in a great laboring class" became a beacon of light for America and the world. It brought into focus the necessity of economic opportunity accompanying electoral voice. Politics enabled one to speak to and advance one's agenda on national policies, and economics were the material basis for equal and independent practices that enforced democratic desires. Offering a rhetorical, but substantive, question regarding black women in the labor force, Du Bois wrote: "What is today the message of these black women to America and to the world? The uplift of women is, next to the problem of the color line and the peace movement, our greatest cause. When, now, two of these movements — woman and color — combine in one, the combination has deep meaning."[43]

In this significant combination Du Bois perceived revolutionary ideals that could alter the face of the American landscape, a terrain strewn with carcasses of exploitative dependencies and oppressive imbalances. Black women as laborers stood at the vortex of three of the greatest social movements in the United States. They manifested the potential of race, class, and gender aspirations and, thus, heralded and intertwined the combined visions of black freedom, working-class battles, and female emancipation.

Du Bois surmised the import of black women's persistent efforts: "This matter of economic independence is, of course, the central fact in the struggle of women for equality."[44]

Indeed, in addition to issues regarding race and women, labor issues were a third key element in Du Bois's understanding of how a spirituality of democracy and equality should take shape in the process of social transformation. The economy, for Du Bois, marked a crucial site of struggle due to the complete monopolization of the earth's resources by a handful of, primarily American and European, corporate and financial elites. Institutional mechanisms of finance, legal and illegal networks of wealth, and structural privileges of property ownership all militated against any talk of a new heaven and new earth for a new humanity. Because a small percentage of the citizens enjoyed a shameful and disproportionate control of wealth, the utterances and struggles of African-Americans and women in other sectors of society were curtailed due to a lack of democratic and equal access to capital ownership, oversight, and distribution.[45] In fact, workers and the poor did not decide industrial activities. Du Bois stated: "On the contrary, the control of industry is largely in the hands of a powerful few, who decide for their own good and regardless of the good of others. . . . Just here it is that modern men demand that Democracy supplant skillfully concealed, but all too evident, Monarchy."[46] The spirit of individualistic profit seeking had gripped the American economy and had given rise to an increased "monarchy" or "oligarchy" of wealth hoarding. Du Bois detested this worldview and the related material practices because they prevented the full flowering of a beneficent and noble spirit of collective ownership of the means of production and distribution. Those who worked in the labor market and those who were unemployed due to capitalist self-interests were the genuine representatives of the values of collective effort and communal vision.

However, the excessively private spirituality had raged so long and sunk so deep in the national culture and psyche that a major initiative of careful planning, astute strategy, and practical campaigning was needed to kindle and reinforce the structural notion of a spirituality of socialized priorities for the public good. In Du Bois's estimation, "The foundation for such a system must be a high ethical ideal."[47] Industry and profits were collective creations and thus belonged also to those at the bottom of society. In brief, the American people had to take over the control of the nation, had to take the reins of both industrial corporations and electoral governments.[48]

Third World countries and the issue of world peace were the final elements of Du Bois's embodiment of spirituality at the margins. The demonic structures of race, gender, and class (on the domestic level) had been exported internationally:

> The Negro problem in America is but a local phase of a world problem.... The tendency of the great nations of the day is territorial, political and economic expansion, but in every case this has brought them in contact with darker peoples.... This is the problem of the Color Line. Force and Fear have hitherto marked the white attitude toward darker races; shall this continue or be replaced by Freedom and Friendship?[49]

Even more pointedly, the confluence of these three evils (that is, race, gender, and class) led to war against weaker countries and death for people of color on a global scale. Drawing on his Christian heritage, Du Bois opted for the spirituality of peace and justice of Jesus when he confessed: "I believe in the Prince of Peace. I believe that War is Murder." Aggression against defenseless nations contradicted this peaceful religion, whose essential nature opted for the "lowly and unfortunate."[50]

Du Bois argued for world peace and for the right of Third World countries to develop via democracy and equality. If global imperialist countries, particularly the United States, would halt their aggression abroad, then a major condition would be satisfied for achieving democracy and equality in Third World nations and for the cessation of externally instigated wars among them. Du Bois advocated a just world peace wherein the majority of the nations, and the majority within those nations, would gain full participation, full freedom and power to voice convictions, and complete authority over resources. This, in turn, would allow them to make their plans and hopes substantive.

The spirit of world peace and Third World development — a movement of "freedom and friendship," for Du Bois — did not entail imitating the major imperialist powers. Moreover, the type of democracy Du Bois advocated stood in radical contrast to the bourgeois democracy represented by a U.S. government that was dominated by corporate elites. Their statements were duplicitous declarations that served as a smoke screen for privileged monopolies. Du Bois defined democracy from below, from the voiceless and faceless masses, from the underdeveloped and bullied Third World nations. Elaborating this point, he asserted: "The democracy which the white world seeks to defend does not exist." To reach the ideal goal, "it must include not simply the lower classes among the whites now excluded from voice in the control of industry." It must also "include the colored peoples of Asia and Africa." If these sectors failed to define, control, and benefit from future processes of inclusion, then,

Du Bois warned, democracy would become a mockery, rife with seeds of internal self-destruction.[51]

Furthermore, just as the color line within the United States had hindered white labor, so too the forced underdevelopment of Third World nations had impeded international white labor. In this regard, Du Bois contrasted the spirit of democracy and equality with a wicked spiritual xenophobia entrapping white workers throughout the world. For instance, Du Bois painted pictures of the spiritual depravity into which white labor had fallen: "The curious, most childish propaganda," which was accepted by whites, made them believe "almost religiously" that they were "a peculiar and chosen people whose one great accomplishment is civilization and that civilization must be protected from the rest of the world by cheating, stealing, lying, and murder." Born and raised in this environment, the average white worker, Du Bois acknowledged, thrived "in such a spiritual world" — an ethos where "color hate easily assume[d] the form of a religion."[52] Faith, however, remained for those open to the reality of mutual interdependency based on an alternative spirituality of democracy and equality. Essentially, the freedom and friendship of the world's peoples of color acted as preconditions for the radical advancement of white labor's pursuits. International class struggle and global racial liberation were two sides of the same coin.

Du Bois stated: "The chief hope lies in the gradual but inevitable spread of the knowledge that the denial of democracy" in the Third World completely blocks the realization of democracy in Europe and the United States. "It is this," continued Du Bois, "that makes the Color Problem and Labor Problem to so great an extent two sides of the same human tangle."[53] Workers in the developed nations had to realize that they could not attain their rightful positions in industry and politics so long as their darker sisters and brothers in underdeveloped regions of the world were denied access to similar positions in their own lands. White workers bore the burden of exorcising their spiritual hatred of the other and replacing it with complete acceptance of a spirit of universal democracy and equality for all humankind. Du Bois's nondoctrinaire spiritual quest for African-American freedom embraced similar concerns of women, the poor of all colors, and the oppressed of the Third World. Therefore, he embodied the best of the pluralistic character of secular spiritualities.

Conclusion

Du Bois was involved in movements for liberation and justice for almost a century. An embryonic, but permanent, conception of a radical spirit of democracy and equality developed in him when he was a young child in Great Barrington, Massachusetts. Formative influences from his early church life imprinted a message of antihierarchy in social relations and the doing of good for one's fellow citizens. At the same time, they encouraged him to question authority and irrational faith claims. Du Bois lived a New England experiment that allowed the dirtiest citizen, the wealthiest owner, and peoples of different races and ages to participate collectively in determining who they were and where they should go. A spirit of communalism held together this small community in their town meetings; and a faith that open discussion and majority rule were the best means of governing an informed citizenry permeated the way of life of Great Barrington. The young, impressionable Du Bois absorbed these localized influences and forever accepted them in his approach to life.

Eventually, Du Bois outgrew organized religion and doctrinal belief. However, this development did not foreshadow an abdication of a spiritual vision. On the contrary, Du Bois synthesized his foundational encounters in Great Barrington with his subsequent awareness of the abject status of women, African-Americans, labor, and Third World peoples. The result was a life lived with spiritual vigor and hope — and with an embodied spirituality found on the margins of U.S. society and also of the world. The quest to surrender all his energies for the sake of the oppressed became, in a sense, a spiritual journey for Du Bois. One could argue that his faith in the ultimate triumph of this new spirituality was marked with all the passion, commitment, and sacrifice exhibited by fervent adherents of denominational religions.

Spirituality, at its root, entailed both a respect for particularity and a defense of universality. That is why Du Bois could propose vehemently, at times, the imperatives of preserving African-American separateness for survival and maintaining the beauty of black culture, even in the projected "new heaven and new earth." While standing for this uniqueness, Du Bois, simultaneously, fought for broader, interracial, cultural and social relationships. Similarly, he persistently offered black specificity as a heuristic and paradigmatic expression of what all humanity should be about. Consequently, his spirituality wedded the best of particularity (while giving intentional attention to its implications for wider discourse) with the best of universality (while maintaining respect for and encouragement of focused voices of contestation).

Furthermore, Du Bois's spirituality of democracy and equality embraced a holistic approach, based on empowering the least of society and the world. Hence the inner self attained its vitality while embracing the outer whole — the nonreligious context of existential and cosmic meaning. The spirit of realizing full humanity for blacks, women, labor, the poor, and the Third World underdeveloped countries was a radical movement of power sharing in all spheres of human social interactions. To this end, Du Bois fought for antihierarchy and antimonopolization in cultural expressions, political decision making, economic ownership, social classifications, and linguistic usages. In regard to each of these areas, Du Bois focused on the bottom strata of every group and community. If a disenfranchised entity or stigmatized soul suffered, then an adverse spiritual presence was gripping humanity and preventing all peoples from attaining maximum potentiality. Holistic spirituality demanded promoting the spread of democracy and equality, and that spreading was the actual flooding of the entire society with an empowered and reconfigured set of human relationships — a bottom-up, decentralized norm. For Du Bois, ultimate spirituality fostered the enhanced vitality of the poor to exercise decisive power. Social justice was spiritual behavior.

Notes

1. Talcott Parsons, *Structure of Social Action* (New York: McGraw-Hill, 1937), 427.

2. Note the chapter entitled "Nativism and Cultural Pluralism in America," in Robert N. Bellah's *The Broken Covenant: American Civil Religion in Time of Trial*, 2d ed. (Chicago: University of Chicago Press, 1992), 87–111.

3. Benjamin Page, *Marxism and Spirituality: An International Anthology* (Westport, Conn.: Bergin and Garvey, 1993), esp. Herbert Aptheker's "The Spiritual in Marxism," 65–84.

4. Vine Deloria Jr., *Custer Died for Your Sins* (New York: Macmillan, 1969).

5. Gayraud S. Wilmore, *Black Religion and Black Radicalism: An Interpretation of the Religious History of Afro-American People*, 2d ed. (Maryknoll, N.Y.: Orbis, 1983), esp. 167–91.

6. Three important biographies on Du Bois are Gerald Horne, *Black and Red: W. E. B. Du Bois and the Afro-American Response to the Cold War* (Albany: State University of New York Press, 1986); Manning Marable, *W. E. B. Du Bois: Black Radical Democrat* (Boston: Twayne, 1986); Arnold Rampersad, *The Art and Imagination of W. E. B. Du Bois* (New York: Schocken, 1990). For a narrative evaluation of Du Bois's works, see Herbert Aptheker, *The Literary Legacy of W. E. B. Du Bois* (White Plains, N.Y.: Kraus, 1989).

7. W. E. B. Du Bois, *The Autobiography of W. E. B. Du Bois* (New York: International Publishers, 1983), 88.

8. W. E. B. Du Bois, "My Character," in *The Seventh Son: The Thought and Writings of W. E. B. Du Bois*, ed. Julius Lester, 3 vols. (New York: Random House, 1971), 2:733.

9. Du Bois, *Autobiography*, 91.

10. W. E. B. Du Bois, *Dusk of Dawn: An Essay toward an Autobiography of a Race Concept* (New York: Harcourt, Brace and Co., 1940), 17.

11. Du Bois, *Autobiography*, 92.

12. W. E. B. Du Bois, "Federal Action Programs and Community Action in the South," in *Writings in Periodical Literature,* ed. Herbert Aptheker, 3 vols. (Millwood, N.Y.: Kraus-Thomson, 1982), 3:127.

13. Ibid.

14. Du Bois, *Autobiography,* 110–11.

15. W. E. B. Du Bois, "Exchange with John R. Timpany: What the Negro Wants and the Catholic Church," in *The Correspondence of W. E. B. Du Bois,* ed. Herbert Aptheker, 3 vols. (Amherst: University of Massachusetts Press, 1978), 3:27. In another situation, Du Bois commented: "I believed too little in Christian dogma to become a minister" (Du Bois, *Autobiography,* 124).

16. W. E. B. Du Bois, "Exchange with E. Pina Morenao: Belief in God," in *Correspondence,* 3:223. In another letter, Du Bois wrote: "I did not rule out the possibility of some God also influencing and directing human action and natural law. However I saw no evidence of such divine guidance" (see *Correspondence,* 3:395–96).

17. Du Bois, *Autobiography,* 43.

18. Du Bois, *Correspondence,* 3:395–96.

19. W. E. B. Du Bois, "Exchange with George Vaughan: Spiritual 'Awakening,'" in *Correspondence,* 1:477–78.

20. Indeed, in other instances, Du Bois named work as God's prophet: "There is no God but Love and Work is His prophet" (See W. E. B. Du Bois, *Prayers for Dark People,* ed. Herbert Aptheker [Amherst: University of Massachusetts Press, 1980], 60).

21. W. E. B. Du Bois, "The Problem of Work," in *Writings in Periodical Literature,* 1:177.

22. Du Bois, *Prayers for Dark People,* 62.

23. Du Bois, "The Joy of Living," in *Writings in Periodical Literature,* 1:219.

24. Ibid.

25. Du Bois, *Autobiography,* 38.

26. Du Bois, *Dusk of Dawn,* 283–85.

27. Ibid. See also Du Bois, *Autobiography,* 228.

28. W. E. B. Du Bois, "Our Program," in *W. E. B. Du Bois: The Crisis Writings,* ed. Daniel Walden (Greenwich, Conn.: Fawcett, 1972), 76–77.

29. Du Bois, *Autobiography,* 250–51.

30. Quoted in Marable, *W. E. B. Du Bois,* 12.

31. Du Bois, "A Philosophy for 1913," in *Crisis Writings,* 60.

32. For the "divine right" reference, see W. E. B. Du Bois, "I Am Resolved," in *Crisis Writings,* 57; for the plight of blacks in relation to the state, see "Georgia Negroes on the Hardwick Bill, 1899," in *A Documentary History of the Negro People in the United States: from the Reconstruction years to the founding of the N.A.A.C.P. in 1910,* ed. Herbert Aptheker (Secaucus, N.J.: Citadel Press, 1972), 2:784–86; and for the reference on the fatal effect, see W. E. B. Du Bois, "The Problem of Problems," in *Writings in Periodical Literature,* 2:114.

33. W. E. B. Du Bois, "My Evolving Program for Negro Freedom," in *What the Negro Wants,* ed. Rayford W. Logan (New York: Agathon, 1969), 65.

34. W. E. B. Du Bois, "Lecture in Baltimore," in *Against Racism: Unpublished Essays, Papers, Addresses, 1887–1961: W. E. B. Du Bois,* ed. Herbert Aptheker (Amherst: University of Massachusetts Press, 1985), 75–77.

35. See Philip S. Foner, *Organized Labor and the Black Worker: 1619–1973* (New York: Praeger, 1974), 80.

36. W. E. B. Du Bois, "Exchange with Clennon King: Segregation and Booker T. Washington," in *Correspondence,* 3:421.

37. W. E. B. Du Bois, "Whither Now and Why," in *The Education of Black People: Ten Critiques, 1906–1960,* ed. Herbert Aptheker (New York: Monthly Review, 1973), 151.

38. W. E. B. Du Bois, *Darkwater: Voices from within the Veil* (New York: AMS, 1969), 4.

39. W. E. B. Du Bois, "What Is Americanism?" in *Writings in Periodical Literature,* 2:95.

40. W. E. B. Du Bois, "The Position of the Negro in the American Social Order," in *Writings In Periodical Literature,* 3:86–87.

41. W. E. B. Du Bois, "Votes for Women," in *Crisis Writings,* 344–47.

42. W. E. B. Du Bois, *The Gift of Black Folk* (New York: Washington Square, 1970), 141.

43. W. E. B. Du Bois, "The Damnation of Women," in *Seventh Son,* 1:523–26.

44. Du Bois, *Gift of Black Folk,* 142.

45. W. E. B. Du Bois, *In Battle for Peace: The Story of My 83rd Birthday* (New York: Masses and Mainstream, 1952), 170.

46. Du Bois, *Darkwater,* 157.

47. Ibid., 102–3.

48. Du Bois, *In Battle for Peace,* 182–86.

49. In Du Bois, *Writings in Periodical Literature,* 1:330.

50. Du Bois, *Darkwater,* 4; and idem, "Will the Church Remove the Color Line?" in *Writings in Periodical Literature,* 2:312.

51. Du Bois, *Dusk of Dawn,* 169–71.

52. W. E. B. Du Bois, "The Negro Mind Reaches Out," in *The New Negro,* ed. Alain Locke (New York: Atheneum, 1969), 407–8.

53. Ibid.

Bibliography

Aptheker, Herbert, ed. *Against Racism: Unpublished Essays, Papers, Addresses, 1887–1961: W. E. B. Du Bois.* Amherst: University of Massachusetts Press, 1985.

Du Bois, W. E. B. *An ABC of Color by W. E. B. Du Bois: Selections Chosen by the Author from Over a Half Century of His Writings.* New York: International Publishers. 1983.

———. *The Autobiography of W. E. B. Du Bois.* New York: International Publishers, 1983.

———. *The Gift of Black Folk.* New York: Washington Square, 1970.

Hopkins, Dwight N. *Shoes That Fit Our Feet: Sources for a Constructive Black Theology.* Maryknoll, N.Y.: Orbis, 1993.

Horne, Gerald. *Black and Red: W. E. B. Du Bois and the Afro-American Response to the Cold War.* Albany: State University of New York Press, 1986.

Marable, Manning. *W. E. B. Du Bois: Black Radical Democrat.* Boston: Twayne, 1986.

Page, Benjamin, ed. *Marxism and Spirituality: An International Anthology.* Westport, Conn.: Bergin and Garvey, 1993.

Paris, Peter. *The Spirituality of African Peoples: The Search for a Common Moral Discourse.* Philadelphia: Fortress, 1995.

Rampersad, Arnold. *The Art and Imagination of W. E. B. Du Bois.* New York: Schocken, 1990.

Wilmore, Gayraud S. *Black Religion and Black Radicalism: An Interpretation of the Religious History of Afro-American People.* 2d ed. Maryknoll, N.Y.: Orbis, 1983.

G. Nature

15

Scientific Inquiry

HOLMES ROLSTON, III

SURVEYING EVOLUTIONARY NATURAL HISTORY, Loren Eiseley, a paleontologist and anthropologist, concluded: "I would say that if 'dead' matter has reared up this curious landscape of fiddling crickets, song sparrows, and wondering men, it must be plain even to the most devoted materialist that the matter of which he speaks contains amazing, if not dreadful, powers, and may not impossibly be . . . but one mask of many worn by the Great Face behind."[1] The "secular" is the present epoch, this age (sometimes rather puzzlingly contrasted with the "sacred" as though anything sacred must be of some other, supernatural realm, not of this present world). Science is our most recent and sophisticated discipline for studying this secular, empirical world. Some claim that science chases out the holy, but this is proving to be a superficial impression.

Science studies the phenomena, the metaphysicians say; and scientists may agree. What of the noumena, the ultimates that underlie the phenomena, that the metaphysicians, theologians included, desire to make known? To that science has no access, and even the metaphysicians have become increasingly wary about ultimate claims, increasingly sensitive to how all our knowledge is relative to our earthbound circumstances in space and time, theory-laden and culture-bound. Absolutes are out of vogue. Meanwhile, though, what if the phenomena prove increasingly phenomenal? What if the secular world proves to be pretty spectacular stuff? What if we lose our confidence in the supernatural, only to find it replaced by increasing confidence that nature is super, superb, mysteriously animated, and inspirited? We might say that nature has actualized its potential. The molecular self-assembling that issues in evolutionary natural history is a sort of self-actualizing. Is it, though, a complete explanation of these phenomena to find that they are natural, until we have asked whether nature is its own self-sufficient explanation? If not, we may find ourselves asking again, as did Eiseley, whether the phenomena of natural history are a response to the brooding winds of the Spirit moving over the face of these earthen waters. The phenomena could be revealing the noumena.

The secular world, this present, empirical scene, may not be miraculous, but what if it is marvelous? What if it is full of events that make us wonder? Then we have two phenomena to be explained: first, the nature that is full of wonder and, second, the wondering persons, these spirits that have resulted from, and now behold, this wonder-full nature. The forces that animate such nature are the subject of scientific study; the persons who do this are scientists, but they have themselves on their hands as animated spirits. They puzzle over what they find, wondering who they are as they find where they are, and this becomes a quest of the spirit, forced by the character of the secular world they engage. They may, or may not, set the classical religions aside; either way the secular quest makes its own demands on spirituality, demands for spirituality. We will wonder about that at levels that are astronomical, microphysical, biomolecular, evolutionary, and ecological.

Astronomical Spirituality

Even a secular science is driven toward cosmology; one wonders about the origins of the cosmos. Through most of our human intellectual history, these questions could only be speculative, metaphysical, but in our century that has changed. Physics has made dramatic discoveries at astronomical and submicroscopic ranges, remote from ordinary, native-range experience, and these are relevant to solving some cosmological questions. The universe (this universe at least) originated twenty billion years ago in a "big bang" and has since been expanding. From the primal burst of energy, elementary particles formed, and afterward hydrogen assembled, the simplest element, which serves as fuel for the stars. Later, in the stellar furnaces the heavier atoms were forged. Some stars subsequently exploded (supernovae). The heavier elements were collected to form, in our case, the solar system and planet Earth.

In the last twenty years physics has discovered that startling interrelationships are required for these creative processes to work. Recent theory interrelates the two levels; astronomical phenomena such as the formation of galaxies, stars, and planets depend critically on the microphysical phenomena. In turn, the midrange scales, where the known complexity mostly lies (in ecosystems or human brains), depend on the interacting microscopic and astronomical ranges. Physics cannot do experiments revising the universe, but it can do thought experiments to see whether another one would be more congenial. Such *if-then* experiments conclude that the universe is mysteriously right for producing life and mind.

If the scale of the universe were much reduced, there would not have been enough time for the various elements to form. If the expansion rate of the universe had been a little faster or slower, then the universe would already have recollapsed or the galaxies and stars would not have formed. No mechanism for life has ever been conceived that does not require elements produced by thermonuclear combustion. The stars are the furnaces in which all but the very lightest elements are forged, exploding as supernovae and dispersing this matter, subsequently regathered to form planets and persons. Humans are composed of fossil star dust! In this historical perspective, astronomical nature is the precondition of the rational self, of the spiritual self.

No universe can provide several billion years of stellar cooking time unless it is several billion light-years across. If we cut the size of the universe from 10^{22} to 10^{11} stars, then that much smaller but still galaxy-sized universe might first seem roomy enough, but it would run through its entire cycle of expansion and recontraction in about one year! If the matter of the universe were not so relatively homogeneous as it is, then large portions of the universe would be so dense that they would already have undergone gravitational collapse; other portions would be so thin that they could not give birth to galaxies and stars. On the other hand, if the matter of the universe were entirely homogeneous, then the chunks of matter that make development possible could not assemble.[2]

If the universe were not expanding, then it would be too hot to support life. If the expansion rate of the universe had been a little faster or slower, then connections would have shifted so that the universe would already have recollapsed or so that galaxies and stars could not have formed. The extent and age of the universe are not obviously an outlandish extravagance. Indeed, this may be the most economical universe in which life and mind, and embodied spirit, can exist — so far as we can cast that question into a testable form in physics. That makes understanding matter a spiritual quest.

Change slightly the strengths of any of the four forces that hold the world together (the strong nuclear force, the weak nuclear force, electromagnetism, gravitation — forces ranging over forty orders of magnitude), change critical particle masses and charges, and the stars would burn too quickly or too slowly, or atoms and molecules, including water, carbon, and oxygen, or amino acids (building blocks of life) would not form or remain stable. John D. Barrow and Joseph Silk, astrophysicists, calculate that "small changes in the electric charge of the electron would block any kind of chemistry."[3] A fractional difference, and there would have been nothing. It would be so easy to miss, for the universe to have evolved in ways incompatible with human life, and yet this universe is a delicate, intricate hit. "Somebody had to tune it very precisely," concludes Marek Demianski, a Polish cosmologist.[4]

How the various physical processes are "fine-tuned to such stunning accuracy is surely one of the great mysteries of cosmology," remarks P. C. W. Davies, a physicist. He adds:

> Had this exceedingly delicate tuning of values been even slightly upset, the subsequent structure of the universe would have been totally different.
>
> Extraordinary physical coincidences and apparently accidental cooperation... offer compelling evidence that something is "going on...." A hidden principle seems to be at work, organizing the universe in a coherent way.[5]

These results have been summarized as the "anthropic principle" (an unfortunately anthropocentric term), which argues that the universe has been "fine-tuned" from the start and in its fundamental construction for the subsequent construction of stars, planets, life, mind, and spirit. There are both theological/supernatural and nontheological/naturalistic ways of interpreting these discoveries, but either way we have a nature that is remarkable, phenomenal phenomena. One feature of these discussions is their calculations, their equations, their measurements. Cosmology is now as much mathematics as it is metaphysics, and many quantitative calculations support these arguments about the origin of the universe and about its fine-tuned construction.

Astrophysicists and microphysicists have joined to discover that, in the explosion that produced our universe, what seem to be widely varied facts really cannot vary widely; indeed, many of them can hardly vary at all and still have the universe develop life, mind, and our wondering spirits. We find a single blast (the big bang) fine-tuned to produce a world that produces us, when any of a thousand other imaginable blasts would have yielded nothing. Considering the first seconds of the big bang, Bernard Lovell, an astronomer, writes:

> It is an astonishing reflection that at this critical early moment in the history of the universe, all of the hydrogen would have turned into helium if the force of attraction between protons — that is, the nuclei of the hydrogen atoms — had been only a few percent stronger.... No galaxies, no stars, no life would have emerged. It would have been a universe forever unknowable by living creatures. A remarkable and intimate relationship between man, the fundamental constants of nature and

> the initial moments of space and time seems to be an inescapable condition of our existence.[6]

Lovell's astonishment, as he wonders about this universe in which he finds himself, is fundamentally, inescapably, a spiritual quest.

B. J. Carr and M. J. Rees, cosmologists, conclude:

> Many interrelations between different scales that at first sight seem surprising are straightforward consequences of simple physical arguments. But several aspects of our Universe — some of which seem to be prerequisites for the evolution of any form of life — depend rather delicately on apparent "coincidences" among the physical constants.... The Universe must be as big and diffuse as it is to last long enough to give rise to life.[7]

Fred Hoyle, an astronomer, reports that his atheism was shaken by his own discovery that, in the stars, carbon just manages to form and then just avoids complete conversion into oxygen. If one level had varied half a percent, life would have been impossible:

> Would you not say to yourself,... "Some supercalculating intellect must have designed the properties of the carbon atom, otherwise the chance of my finding such an atom through the blind forces of nature would be utterly minuscule"? Of course you would.... The carbon atom is a fix.... A common sense interpretation of the facts suggests that a superintellect has monkeyed with the physics.... The numbers one calculates from the facts seem to me so overwhelming as to put this conclusion almost beyond question.[8]

Stephen Hawking, the Einstein of the second half of our century, agrees: "The odds against a universe like ours coming out of something like the Big Bang are enormous. I think there are clearly religious implications."[9]

Mike Corwin, a physicist, concludes:

> This 20-billion-year journey seems at first glance tortuous and convoluted, and our very existence appears to be the merest happenstance. On closer examination, however, we will see that quite the opposite is true — intelligent life seems predestined from the very beginning.... Any significant change in the initial conditions would have ruled out the possibility of life evolving later.... Yet here we are, alive and aware, in a universe with just the right ingredients for our existence.[10]

In this kind of universe, it is proving difficult to be alive and aware without thinking that the universe is quite wonderful, without engaging it as a wondering spirit. Einstein, who launched so much of this in the first half of the century, had put it this way: "I maintain that cosmic religious feeling is the strongest and noblest incitement to scientific research.... You will hardly find one among the profounder sort of scientific minds without a peculiar religious feeling of his own."[11]

Sometimes we marvel that all these interconnections had to occur for the universe to turn out the way it did. Sometimes we marvel that it could have been otherwise but was not so. Sometimes it is not too clear whether these startling interconnections are necessary or contingent, and we do not know how developing theory will revise the necessities and contingencies of these connections. In the end it hardly matters. So far as these connections are improbable, we seem to need a guiding principle in ongoing superintendence; so far as they are necessary, the guiding principle seems to have been there from the start. We may not know whether to call this a guiding hand, a guiding spirit, or what, but something is going on that challenges our religious sensitivity. We seem to be detecting some astronomical bent toward creativity, even toward spirituality, because here we are, human spirits, alive and well in this universe that was fixed up for spirits. Freeman Dyson, an astronomer, expresses his surprise: "Nature has been kinder to us than we had any right to expect. As we look out into the universe and identify the many accidents of physics and astronomy that have worked together to our benefit, it almost seems as if the universe must in some sense have known that we were coming."[12]

Through it all we marvel how cosmology on the grandest scale and atomic theory on the minutest scale are not irrelevant to what is now taking place in human affairs, with even the further hint that there must be some great Cause adequate to this great effect. The point is not that the whole universe is necessary to produce Earth and *Homo sapiens.* That would be myopic pride; and this is an unfortunate suggestion in the term *anthropic principle.* The issue is richness of potential, not anthropocentrism. There is no need to insist that everything else in the universe has some relevance to our being here. Nature, or God, may have overdone the creation in pure exuberance, and why should the parts irrelevant to us trouble us?

These anthropic necessities and contingencies, by tandem turns on their respective upstrokes, integrate into a governing gestalt that detects Something, Someone, some force behind the scenes arranging for the show. The forms that matter and energy take seem strangely suited to their destiny.

Microphysical Spirituality

Already we are finding the microphysics remarkable, for it is coupled with the astrophysics we have just been describing. There is also a deeper dimension to this. We turn next to a mysterious openness, an indeterminacy in this microscopic nature, to nature's energetic possibility. We might almost call this its immateriality. It is difficult to say what makes up a microparticle. In the days of Newtonian physics, everything seemed to be matter in motion in space and time; but now, after Einstein and relativity theory, nature is more energetic process than substantial material. The particles are really microwave clouds that do not have precise position or momentum, before these are demanded by the observer or coagulated by some more comprehensive world events in which they come to participate.

The most fundamental notion of all is not matter or motion, space or time, but energetic and evolutionary process, not being but becoming. There are, absolutely, no things, no substances, but only events in a space-time something, not bodies that move in empty space over time, but a series of moving changes with continuity, forming a relative rather than an absolute identity in an incurably successive world. Matter and motion, space and time, as well as size and shape, color and temperature, wave and particle, light and form — indeed, all the interpenetrating and mutable textures of things in life, mind, culture, history, all this phenomenal animation and spirited inventiveness — are various dimensions of this process.

The most frequent account, based on general relativity, makes each cloudy wave a kind of wrinkle, bubble, or hill in an omnipresent trans-space-time field, which coagulates relative to each disturbance, to each entity. A particle is not some one substance; it is a concavity that travels in a sort of "plasma" rather as (to use a crude analogy) a dent travels over the surface of a partially deflated basketball. Matter is, so to speak, "freeze-dried energy." In the Newtonian view, space and time provided a passive and empty container, there independently of any contents, regardless of the matter-in-motion within it. While in Einstein's view some kind of plenum remains, evidenced grossly as space-time, it is not passive but is the generator and carrier of all the particle play. Matter is a crinkle in the matrix, an energetic warp in the great plasma-ether. The phenomena come and go; the particles do their trips and identity flips, taking on the spatiotemporal aspects they yield to observers. Ultimately, there is only a kind of gauzy foam through which quantized pulses run.

There is certainly no ultimacy in the ultrastructures as now known. We have hit no rock bottom in physics and have few signs that we ever will or can, or would know when we had. We have only an ether from which events bubble up from below and take place at levels ranging from the microphysical to the astrophysical. Particles, waves, matter-in-motion, stars, planets, persons with their bodies, minds, spirits — all are warps in space-time; all rise up out of a mysterious energy pit. The nature we know has grown soft. Down below, there is something hazy that we can reach with our formulas but hardly imagine. There is a subsurface inaccessibility, plasticity, and mysteriousness that allow us more easily to be spiritual about this now than in the hard world of earlier physics. Each of the old themes of materialism — atomic matter in absolute motion, sensory and pictorial substance, total specifiability, mechanics, predictability, finished logical analysis — has an antithesis in recent physics.

It is hard to know what synthesis to make, but certainly a spiritual synthesis is not precluded. Nature is now less material, less absolutely spatiotemporal, more astounding, more open, an energetic, developmental process. John D. Barrow, a theoretical physicist, says that the principal result of recent physics is that "nature has revealed a deep, hidden flexibility, previously unsuspected."[13] If in one sense this nature is still secular, in another sense it is a suitable arena for the operation of a sacred, creative Spirit. The basic scientific motif in physics is dynamism in power, and in nature, as viewed as process that moves from particles to persons, there is nothing inimical to a spiritual account.

C. W. Misner, a theoretical physicist, calls space-time an impressively creative kind of ether. "A vacuum so rich . . . in potentialities cannot properly be called a void; it is really an ether. The entire spacetime fabric . . . from beginning to end" is "a library of unused designs," which are creatively "enacted into existence."[14] It is not until we leave physics and enter biology that we get an appreciation of what stories can be told with this library of motifs. The astrophysics and the microphysics, profound though they are, pale before the spectacular story of what from them is creatively enacted into existence. On Earth, life appears.

Physics at all its levels differs from biology at all its levels. In biology there is information coded with a know-how for the creation and defense of life. For the first fifteen billion years, there was energetic matter in the stars; for several billion years on Earth matter was churned about. The precursors to life were formed, amino acids, sugars, and the like, but these had no life-code as yet. Then one day, signals appear! Where once there was matter, energy, and where these remain, there is information, symbolically encoded, and life. There is a new state of matter, neither liquid nor gaseous nor solid, but vital. Something begins to catch the constructional upstrokes; there is the informed defense of a life program. That puts adventure, freedom, drama, and surprise into the storied evolutionary course. Matter begins to take on more spirited behavior.

Biomolecular Spirituality

The assembly is of materials, complexity out of simplicity, but there comes with it autonomous life out of dead matter, biofunction out of nonfunctional antecedents, and, with sufficient neural organization, subjectivity out of objectivity. Once there was a world with only matter and energy, but later there appeared within it information centers, and later still, incarnate subjects. Molecules, trillions of them, spin around in complicated ways and generate the unified, centrally focused experience of mind. There is already enough to wonder about when we realize that from a submicroscopic plasma-ether all the creativity in the world is emitted, bubbling up from below; but there is a complementary picture. We discover a nature that is plastic enough for an organism to work its program on, for a mind to work its will on, a nature phenomenal enough to sponsor the joys and anxieties of incarnate spirits.

Biology is earthbound, unlike physics. There is astrophysics, but no astrobiology – not yet at least. This earthbound biology develops, like physics, on two levels: the macroscopic and the microscopic. The macroscopic is evolutionary history; the microscopic is molecular biology; and, like physics, these two levels are coupled, only now the coupling introduces some radical innovations. For there is a coding level, that of the DNA and the cybernetic secret of life, and a coping level, the native-range world of trees and tigers, of organisms making their way through their niches in the world. A first question about this tandem coding-coping is addressed to the present: How does life operate now both from the "skin in" (questions of metabolism, anatomy, physiology, cell biology, genetics, biochemistry) and from the "skin out" (questions of ecology, ethology, biogeography). A second, and harder, question about this coding-coping is addressed to the past: How did it all originate (questions of the chemical origins of life, of evolutionary natural history, of the increase of diversity and complexity)?

Biochemistry, molecular biology, and biophysics have been remarkably successful in describing how life takes place. The information in the genetic set reenacts itself in the next generation; the DNA makes the protein that makes the DNA. Bioscience, however, is still struggling to discover how these vital processes came into place. We know how eggs come from chickens and chickens from eggs, but not how the chicken-egg-chicken loop originated in the first place. Knowing the secret of life biochemically may still leave the evolution of life a secret, until we know how the life loops get established. Lurking behind these questions is a deeper one, whether the scientific account still leaves room for a spiritual response to the phenomenon of life.

Addressing first the coding-coping phenomenon that today makes life possible, and continuing from microphysics, we now find it remarkable that physics leaves room in nature for those emergent levels of structure and experience that operate despite the quantum indeterminacies and even because of them. Microphysics, though it knows neither coding nor coping, gives space for the higher phenomena. An organism can coagulate affairs this way and not that way, in accord with its cellular and genetic programs. By means of its interaction patterns, the macromolecular system of the living cell influences the behavior of the atomic systems. The organism is fine-tuned at the molecular level to nurse its way through the quantum states by electron transport, proton pumping, selective ion permeability, DNA encoding, and the like. The organism via its information and biochemistries participates in forming the course of the microevents that constitute its passage through the world.

To some extent we face just the random bubbling up of indeterminacies from the microphysics below, but we find also the drawing forth from an indeterminate substrate of just those determinations that serve the organism. The organism has to flow through the quantum states, but the organism selects the quantum states that achieve for it an informed flow-through. The information within the organism enables it to act as a preference sieve through the quantum states, by interaction sometimes causing quantum events, sometimes catching individual chance events that serve its program; and thereby the organism maintains its life course. There is a kind of downward causation that complements an upward causation, and both feed on the openness, if also the order, in the atomic substructures.

Life makes matter count. It loads the dice. Biological events are superintending physical ones. The organism is "telling nature where to go." Biological nature takes advantage of physical nature. Organisms gain and maintain internal order against the disordering tendencies of external nature. They keep winding up, recomposing themselves, while inanimate things run down, erode, and decompose. Life is a local countercurrent to entropy, an energetic fight uphill in a world that typically moves thermodynamically downhill (despite some negentropic eddies, that is, some events moving counter to the statistical increase of disorder with increasing entropy). To make and maintain themselves, organisms pump out disorder.

Thermodynamics need be nowhere violated, because there is a steady "downhill" flow of energy, as energy is irradiated onto Earth from the Sun and, eventually, reradiated into space. But some of this energy comes to pump a long route uphill. This is something like an old-fashioned hydraulic ram, where the main downstream flow is used to pump a domestic water supply a hundred yards uphill through a pipe to a farmhouse – except of course that the ram-pump is deliberately engineered and the "life-pump" spontaneously assembled itself as an open cybernetic system several thousand times more complex and several billion years long. Not only is energy present, not only have the precursor materials assembled, but some force or forces are present that suck order in superseding steps creatively out of disorder. The energy irradiated over matter is order waiting to happen.

Photons of light flow from the Sun; they impact rocks, which are heated and then, when the Sun ceases, cool. That much happens on both Earth and Moon, without any especially interesting results. On Earth, though, some of these photons also impact leaves, and then there is quite a different story. They are captured by antenna molecules in the chloroplasts (a half-million of them per square millimeter of leaf), relayed to a reaction center molecule where, in Photosystem II, the energy of the photons is used to move electrons up to a high-energy perch (at the PS 680 chlorophyll molecule). The electrons then move down a transport chain, cocking an ADP molecule up to its ATP high-energy form, and are passed to the reaction center of Photosystem I. There, with more photons absorbed, the electrons are moved back up to a second high-energy perch (at the PS 700 molecule). They descend another electron transport chain, this time producing a high-energy NADPH molecule.

The two high-energy molecules (ATP and NADPH) are then used, in the Calvin cycle, to synthesize sugar. This is a complex series of over a dozen reactions that takes carbon dioxide from the atmosphere and shuttles it around in numerous steps to make, first, three-carbon intermediates and then the six-carbon sugar glucose, as well as other products. The sugar can be stored in the plant as starch, as well as sugar. This is the energy that powers essentially all of life in its negentropic climb uphill against thermodynamic breakdown. This is the fuel for natural history.

Sometimes used by the plant itself, sometimes eaten and digested by animals, the starch is reconverted to a glucose sugar. The energy is extracted from glucose in two stages: first, glycolysis, the oldest energy extraction process (a ten-step descent), and, second, the Kreb's cycle (an eight-step cycle), a process later evolved and extracting considerably more energy. This time the energy molecules are NADH and FADH2. These are next oxidized in the electron transport chain of oxidative phosphorylation, a complex ten-stage descent through an energy gradient down a series of cytochrome and other molecules yielding more ATP molecules. These ATP molecules are the fuel that powers protein synthesis, metabolism, locomotion, and reproduction. All this has been going on in one form or another for some two and a half billion years, for the cytochrome molecules are at least that old.

In animal metabolism, one of the structures that ATP is used to synthesize, guided by the genetic coding in DNA, is cholesterol. The molecule that results from glycolysis is called acetyl CoA, a two-carbon molecule, and it can, as we indicated, be sent into the Kreb's cycle and energy extracted from it. The same molecule can also be sent into a construction sequence where, in a complex series of steps that move thermodynamically uphill all the way, it is formed into the twenty-seven-carbon cholesterol molecule, which, in turn, is the precursor of many other steroids of vital physiological function, among them the sex hormones testosterone and estrogen, as well as cortisone. Every step demands energy to increase the order and is fueled by using high-energy phosphate molecules. Every step is made possible by complex enzymes — protein molecules coded by the DNA.

The astronomers and the physicists were already impressed by how the universe is well-organized (despite the entropy of its increasing disorganization over time), but now in biology we get organization based on a radical new principle: accumulating information storage localized in organisms, transmitted over the millennia, spreading around the globe, increasing in diversity and complexity. Superimposed on the background physical organization of the universe, superimposed on the background increase of entropy, there appears more organization than ever before by many hundreds of orders of magnitude. The secret of it all is these coding molecules — the DNA molecules that "know how" to organize matter in these spectacular ways. The result is the difference between the Earth and the Moon.

We have a naturalistic account of all this molecular biological synthesis in increasing detail. There remains yet much to be known. But what then? After the scientific descriptions are done, is that all there is to be said? Photosynthesis and the anabolism of cholesterol have been explained. Have they been explained away? Moses thought that the burning bush, not consumed, was quite a miracle. We hardly believe any more in that sort of supernatural miracle; science has made such stories incredible. But what has it left instead? A self-organizing photosynthesis driving a life synthesis that has burned for millennia, life as a strange fire that outlasts the sticks that feed it. This is, one might say, rather spirited behavior on the part of dead matter, "spirited" in the animated sense, in the root sense of a "breath" or "wind" that energizes this mysterious, vital metabolism.

This is hardly a phenomenon less marvelous even if we no longer want to say that it is miraculous. Indeed, in the original sense of "miracle" — a wondrous event, without regard to the question whether natural or supernatural — photosynthesis and the life it supports are the secular equivalents of the burning bush. The bush that Moses watched was an individual in a species line that had perpetuated itself for millennia, coping by the coding in its DNA, fueled by the Sun, using cytochrome *c* molecules several billion years old, and surviving without being consumed. To go back to the miracle that Moses saw, a bush that burned briefly without being consumed, would be to return to something several orders of magnitude less spectacular.

Thanks to the biochemists, molecular biologists, and geneticists, we know how this works. But is this an account that demystifies what is going on? The account we have is, if you like, a naturalistic account, but, as before, this nature is pretty spectacular stuff. Again, we want even more urgently to ask whether, once we have set out this naturalistic account, the explanations are over. Yes, there is this spinning round of trillions of molecules, organizing themselves into a code for life, and executing this code in a coping individual. But is there anything that suggests that nature is its own self-sufficient explanation? That question becomes even more intense when we recall how, over time, the matter that first took on life eventually took on spirit, and we ourselves are the proof of that. Again, we who are spirits have ourselves on our hands, bodies and hands, minds and spirits, which emerged out of nature.

Evolutionary Spirituality

Before we can answer whether this self-animating nature is its own explanation, we will have to take a backward look, because the past may hold the secret to understanding the present. That is routinely the case with historical explanations, and biology on Earth is indisputably historical. What can we say scientifically first about the molecular origins of life and subsequently about the natural history by which life has continued over the millennia?

The first stage of the chemical evolution that resulted in life is relatively unproblematic: amino acids were constructed by energy radiated over inorganic materials. These collected in ancient seas into a kind of proto-organic soup. The second stage was much more difficult. Many amino acids must be assembled into long polypeptide chains, with no previous templates or enzymes for their hooking up, with no information to steer the process. One worries that, although some partial sequences might have been produced at random, their spontaneous rate of thermodynamic breakdown would have been vastly higher than their construction rate. The historical pathway from abiological materials to coded, self-replicating DNA megamolecules that, in turn, can code for proteins, is as yet nowhere near being known. Still, we believe that there was such a pathway and hope that someday it may be known reasonably well.

The third stage is to fold these long polypeptide chains into complex functional structures. If — but only if — the sequence is right (from the second stage), they are self-folding. In the presence of the electric pressures of water, the polypeptide chains fold and form their various cross-linkages because they have the sorts of chemistries they have. It is as though shaking the pieces tends to lock a puzzle together. In a fourth stage, coincident with this, other molecules form, which, likewise under the electric pressures of water, organize themselves into hollow microspheres, empty prototypes of cells. These spheres come to envelop the newly emerging proteins, further protecting the about-to-be-life chemistries from their degradation by the outside environment and providing a semipermeable membrane over which can pass the necessary nutrient inputs and waste outputs. Thereby life assumes cellular form.

To have life assemble this way, there must be a sort of push-up, lock-up effect by which inorganic energy input, radiated over matter, can spontaneously synthesize negentropic amino acid subunits. These are complex but partial protoprotein sequences, which would be degraded by entropy except that by spiraling and folding they make themselves relatively resistant to degradation. They are metastable, locked uphill by a ratchet effect, so to speak, with such folded chains much upgraded over surrounding environmental entropic levels. Once elevated there, they enjoy a thermodynamic niche that conserves them, at least inside a felicitous microspherical environment.

Still, it is a long way up any developmental slope to reach an organism with self-coordinating parts in a metabolic whole. When we remember the enormous complexity of even the simplest of these biological molecules, involving hundreds of amino acids chain-linked in a precisely suitable sequence and then folded dozens of times, and when we recall how many such molecules of differing function but equal complexity must be assembled to gain an organism, it is striking that something favors dramatic structural climbs that would otherwise be utterly improbable. Something makes the improbable probable. Something presses for matter to undertake this animation, this vitality, this spiritedness.

To some it seems that life is an accident waiting to happen, because it is blueprinted into the chemicals, rather as sodium and chlorine are preset to form salt, only much more startlingly so because of the rich implications for life and because of the openness and information transfer also present in the historical life process. Life is not an accident, whatever place dice throwing plays in its appearance and maturation. It is something arranged for in the nature of things. The dice are loaded.

When these enormously complex molecules appear, predecessors of DNA and RNA, they are conserved, writes Melvin Calvin, a biochemist and Nobel laureate, "not by accident but because of the peculiar chemistries of the various bases and amino acids.... There is a kind of selectivity intrinsic in the structures."[15] Peculiar chemistries indeed! With an intrinsic selectivity that filters and forces the process up-slope, toward ever greater molecular complexity and at length to an informational molecule! Such selection combines with these peculiar chemistries forced toward biochemistries, with the result that the evolution of life, so far from being random, is "a logical consequence" of natural principles.[16] We seem almost to be saying that life is the earthen destiny of these chemicals. "This universe breeds life inevitably," concludes George Wald, an evolutionary biochemist, another Nobel laureate.[17]

We should not overdo this "selectivity intrinsic in the structures," for there is not much in the physics and chemistry of atoms and molecules, prior to their biological assembling, that suggests that they have any tendencies to order themselves up to life. There is nothing in a "thin soup" of disconnected amino acids to predict that they will connect themselves into proteins, nor that they will arrange for DNA molecules in which to code the various discoveries of structures and metabolisms specific to the diverse forms of life. All these events may come naturally, but they are still quite a surprise. Still there is this remarkable story to tell; and, when it happens, though it is no inference, neither does it seem nothing but accident.

So we do posit a primitive planetary environment in which the formation of living things somehow had a high probability, or, in other words, the archaic Earth was a pregnant Earth. Nature here has all these possibilities of animation. Here we may not so much need interference by a supernatural agency, as rather the recognition of a marvelous endowment of matter with a propensity toward life (and, in due course, toward spirit), not in all its lineages but in some of them. Still, we may still need something to superintend the possibilities. Once again, it is not just the necessities, nor the contingencies, but the prolific mixing of the two that impresses us. What is so remarkable is not just the atomic or astronomical physics, found universally, but the middle-range earthen system, found rarely, with its zest for complexity.

Here there is a mixture of inevitability and openness, so that one way or another, given the conditions and constants of physics and chemistry, together with the biased earthen environment, life will somehow both surely and surprisingly appear. After a long study of the possibility of the evolution of biological molecules capable of self-organization, Manfred Eigen, a thermodynamicist and still another Nobel laureate, concludes "that the evolution of life... must be considered an *inevitable* process despite its indeterminate course."[18] Life is destined to come as part of the narrative story, yet the exact routes it will take are open and subject to historical vicissitudes. So what we really get are possibilities for the story, more than any logical necessity or empirically sufficient conditions for the story to take place.

Not only does life get started, it elaborates. The story goes from zero to five million species in five billion years, passing through over a billion species en route. With the passage of time and trials, there come to pass ever more salient constructions of life, enormous distances traveled upward. Michael Polanyi, a philosopher of science, concludes:

> There is a cumulative trend of changes tending towards higher levels of organization, among which the deepening of sentience and the rise of thought are the most conspicuous....From a seed of submicroscopic living particles — and from inanimate beginnings lying beyond these — we see emerging a race of sentient, responsible and creative beings. The spontaneous rise of such incomparably higher forms of being testifies directly to the operations of an orderly innovating principle.[19]

Responsible, creative beings arising from a creative process, arising to wonder where they are and who they are — that is matter ending in a spiritual quest.

John Maynard Smith, one of the leading theoretical biologists today, says, "There is nothing in neo-Darwinism which enables us to predict a long-term increase in complexity." He goes on to suspect that this is not because there is no such long-term increase but rather because Darwinism is inadequate to explain it. We need "to put an arrow on evolutionary time" (that is, to give time an asymmetric direction) but get no help from evolutionary theory. "It is in some sense true that evolution has led from the simple to the complex: procaryotes precede eucaryotes, singled-celled precede many-celled organisms, taxes and kineses precede complex instinctive or learnt acts. I do not think that biology has at present anything very profound to say about this."[20] Biology may also be reluctant to say much about the formation of spirits, our human spirits, which also arise in the course of evolutionary history, but nevertheless, here we are, profound among the phenomena, even in our hesitating struggles to understand who and where we are.

Ernst Mayr, a leading evolutionary biologist, though he dislikes any suggestions of teleology and has little sympathy for orthodox religions, is forced to concede that there is evolutionary progress. Many life-forms do not progress: *higher* is a troublesome word in biology. He writes:

> And yet, who can deny that overall there is an advance from the procaryotes that dominated the living world more than three billion years ago to the eucaryotes with their well organized nucleus and chromosomes as well as cytoplasmic organelles; from the single-celled eucaryotes to metaphytes and metazoans with a strict division of labor among their highly specialized organ systems; within the metazoans from ectotherms that are at the mercy of climate to the warm-blooded endotherms, and within the endotherms from types with a small brain and low social organization to those with a very large central nervous system, highly developed parental care, and the capacity to transmit information from generation to generation?[21]

Edward O. Wilson, a Harvard biologist who has devoted his life to the conservation of these diverse forms of life that arise in evolutionary history, concludes:

> Biological diversity embraces a vast number of conditions that range from the simple to the complex, with the simple appearing first in evolution and the more complex later. Many reversals have occurred along the way, but the overall average across the history of life has moved from the simple and few to the more complex and numerous. During the past billion years, animals as a whole evolved upward in body size, feeding and defensive techniques, brain and behavioral complexity, social organization, and precision of environmental control — in each case farther from the nonliving state than their simpler antecedents did. More precisely, the overall averages of these traits and their upper extremes went up. Progress, then, is a property of the evolution of life as a whole by almost any conceivable intuitive standard, including the acquisition of goals and intentions in the behavior of animals. It makes little sense to judge it irrelevant.... In spite of major and minor temporary setbacks, in spite of the nearly complete turnover of species, genera, and families on repeated occasions, the trend toward biodiversity has been consistently upward.[22]

But here is the rub. Despite the molecular biologists and thermodynamicists, who may judge that life is an accident waiting to happen, when life does happen, it thereafter develops through its narrative stories — so far as evolutionary theory can see — with as much accident as inevitability. For there is really nothing in the theory that says that life must increase in either complexity or diversity. Many forms of life continue, with new species replacing former ones, but without any increase of complexity; some environments grow colder, drier, and simpler; and even the rich environments are subject to many vicissitudes, including periodic catastrophic extinctions. Life develops over the millennia with many misfortunes as well as fortunes.

In fact, the advances are often puzzlingly coupled with the upsets and even the retreats. Often there is a downside before an upside; the upside is life rebounding after setbacks. Upset and rejuvenation are what make really novel speciation possible, by which life can advance. The pattern, at times at least, is that the big changes, including the advances, come after the environmental stresses that result in extinction. Niles Eldredge concludes:

> The particularly compelling aspect of this account is that the factors underlying species extinction — namely, habitat disruption, fragmentation and loss — are the very same as those conventionally cited as causes of speciation. Thus the causes of extinction may also serve as the very wellspring of the evolution of new species.[23]

There is, for instance, a step up of mutation rates under stress. The extinction of dominant species makes room for innovation. Species evolve most rapidly under conditions where environments change most severely.

David M. Raup, the paleontologist who, with Eldredge, has most extensively explored extinctions, also holds that these periodic cutbacks prepare the way for more complex diversity later on. Raup explains:

> Without species extinction, biodiversity would increase until some saturation level was reached, after which speciation would be forced to stop. At saturation, natural selection would continue to operate and improved adaptations would continue to develop. But many of the innovations in evolution, such as new body plans or modes of life, would probably not appear. The result would be a slowing down of evolution and an approach to some sort of steady state condition. According to this view, the principal role of extinction in evolution is to eliminate species and thereby reduce biodiversity so that space — ecological and geographic — is available for innovation.[24]

There is a big shakeup; this is in some sense random; it is, we must say, catastrophic, but the upset is integrated into the creative system. The loss of diversity results in a gain in complexity. Catastrophic extinction "has been the essential ingredient in the history of life that we see in the fossil record." The storied character of natural history is increased. Once "we thought that stable planetary environments would be best for evolution of advanced life," but now we think instead that "planets with enough environmental disturbance to cause extinction and thereby promote speciation" are required for such evolution.[25]

From the point of view of the fine-tuned universe that the astrophysicists reveal for us, the picture that we get from evolutionary history leaves us puzzled about the mixture of necessity and contingency through which life has survived over the millennia, developing into the advanced forms. Physics is full of laws, and laws are important in natural systems, but natural law is not the complete explanatory category for natural history, any more than is openness or chance. So what are we to say when the laws of science pass over into the epic of natural history? Sometimes these vicissitudes seem more than we can comprehend. Sometimes they recall the old theological paradox that God writes straight with crooked lines.

One response is to see in nature, beyond any laws, a kind of grace. Grace, some will think, belongs in the theological tradition that posits the appearance of a goodness that one has no cause to expect, a salvation that one has not merited, a favor that one does not deserve. Here too there is surprising goodness, something given that has no justification in law or logic, even if there does seem some destiny filling up the world with these wonders. There is creativity by which this more emerges from less. Science prefers lawlike explanations without surprises. One predicts, and the prediction comes true; but biology is full of unpredictable surprises. Our account of natural history cannot be by way of implication, whether deductive or inductive.

There is no covering law (such as natural selection), plus initial conditions (such as trilobites), from which one can deduce primates. Nor is there any induction (expecting the future to be like the past) by which one can expect trilobites later from procaryotes earlier, or dinosaurs still later by extrapolating along a regression line (a progression line!) drawn from procaryotes to trilobites. There are no humans invisibly present (as an acorn secretly contains an oak) in the primitive eucaryotes, to unfold in a lawlike way. All we can do is tell the epic story — eucaryotes, trilobites, dinosaurs, primates, persons who are scientists, ethicists, conservation biologists, and saints — and the drama may prove enough to justify it.

Indeed, the drama may evoke a sense of marvelous natural given, the experience of grace. If we define a miracle as a wondrous event without sufficient natural causes, so far as is known, then there remains miracle here, and we hardly yet find that, under bioscience, the secret of life stands explained, certainly not explained away. Man and woman arising via all the intermediate steps (trilobites, dinosaurs, primates) from the maternal Earth is not less impressive, rather more so, than Aphrodite arising from the formless seas.

Loren Eiseley, with whom we began, surveying evolutionary history, exclaims: "Nature is one vast miracle transcending the reality of night and nothingness."[26] Ernst Mayr, troubled by those higher forms arising, finding the creativity in natural history undeniable, says: "Virtually all biologists are religious, in the deeper sense of this word, even though it may be a religion without revelation.... The unknown and maybe unknowable instills in us a sense of humility and awe."[27] We sense something sublime in the awe-inspiring sense because there is something sublime that takes us to the limits of our understanding, and mysteriously beyond.

Ecological Spirituality

Natural history is the story of what has been taking place over past evolutionary epochs, at levels from the biomolecular incubating, coding, conserving, and elaborating of life to the marine and continental ecosystems that are the womb of life. This natural history brings us, in the end, to the present, to the drama of life continuing around us, a scene on which we humans have, especially in the twentieth century, been having so dramatic an impact. Here we reach, in closing, what we can call an ecological spirituality, rising from the human response to a nature now threatened by our human choices. (This theme is continued in chapter 17, below.) The end of this century, passing into the beginning of twenty-first century, may well be the era of the end of nature.

Science brings us just that possibility. The late-coming, moral species, *Homo sapiens,* has still more lately gained startling powers for the rebuilding and modification, including the degradation, of this home planet. We have been recalling how the two great marvels of our planet are life and mind, both among the rarest things in the universe, so far unknown elsewhere. Life is the product of evolutionary natural history, the toil and achievement of three and a half billion years. For perhaps two hundred thousand years, the human mind has produced cultures superposed on natural systems. Diverse combinations of nature and culture worked well enough over many millennia, but no more. Our recent modern cultures threaten the stability, beauty, and integrity of Earth, and thereby of the cultures superposed on Earth.

Perhaps the four most critical issues that humans currently face are peace, population, development, and environment. Human desires for maximum development drive population increases, escalate exploitation of the environment, and fuel the forces of war. Those who are not at peace with one another find it difficult to be at peace with nature, and vice versa. Those who exploit persons will typically exploit nature as readily. All this has produced, in the century when science has flourished as never before, a crisis of the human spirit. In other centuries, critics might have complained that humans were alienated from God. In this century, critics complain that humans are alienated from their planet. This secular crisis proves to demand, at depth, a spiritual quest. To the questions about who we are and where we are we must add another question: What ought we to do? Perhaps we can set aside cosmological questions, but we cannot set aside global issues, except at our peril. We humans face an identity crisis in our own home territory, trying to get the human spirit put in its place.

The late twentieth century has been a time of seeing Earth ecosystemically, as a whole, the home planet. Viewing Earthrise from the Moon, the astronaut Edgar Mitchell was entranced:

> Suddenly from behind the rim of the moon, in long, slow-motion moments of immense majesty, there emerges a sparkling blue and white jewel, a light, delicate sky-blue sphere laced with slowly swirling veils of white, rising gradually like a small pearl in a thick sea of black mystery. It takes more than a moment to fully realize this is Earth . . . home.

Mitchell continued, "My view of our planet was a glimpse of divinity."[28] Mitchell enjoys an overview of the material Earth, a marvelous view of a marvelous place, and believes that he is seeing God.

A first response of both scientists and theologians may be that the astronaut is going to extremes. Earth is not divinity. A frequent fear of creation spirituality is that it slips over into vague pantheism and uncritical naturalism; we begin romantically and naively to worship Nature and not intelligently and diligently to worship God. A frequent complaint by hard-nosed scientists is that we must stick to the facts and not get carried away in mystical interpretation.

Earth is, after all, just earth. Earth is, in a way, a big rock pile like the Moon, only one on which the rocks are watered and illuminated in such a way that they support life. No doubt Earth is valuable, but that is because humans are able to value it. It is really human life that we value and not the Earth, except as instrumental to life. We do not have responsibilities to rocks, air, ocean, dirt, or Earth; we have responsibilities to people, or living things. We must not confuse duties to the home with duties to the inhabitants. We must get clear about what it is that is deserving of such respect.

Yet is it so amiss to see this home biosphere as the sphere of divinity? Consider all the complexity and diversity, integrity, richness, natural history, and cultural history — the whole storied natural and cultural history of our planet. Say, if you like, that Earth is only a big rock pile, mere matter, but, as Eiseley insisted, when we consider the story these rocks spin, it must indeed be plain to the materialist that matter contains dreadful powers. Really, the story is little short of a series of "miracles," wondrous, fortuitous events, unfolding of potential; and when Earth's most complex product, *Homo sapiens,* becomes intelligent enough to reflect over this cosmic wonderland, everyone is left stuttering about the mixtures of accident and necessity out of which we have evolved. Nobody, though, has much doubt that this is a precious place, a pearl in a sea of black mystery. Earth could be the ultimate object of duty, short of God; and if one cannot get clear about God, there is ample and urgent call to reverence the Earth.

Earth is dirt, all dirt, but here we find revealed what dirt can do when it is self-organizing under suitable conditions with water and solar illumination. That is pretty spectacular dirt. We can, if we insist on being anthropocentric, say that it is all valueless except as our human resource, though quite valuable in that respect; but we will not be valuing Earth objectively until we appreciate this marvelous natural history. This really is a superb planet. Earth is the only planet, so far as we know, that is a home. This is the biosphere, the planet known to have an ecology (etymologically, "the logic of a home").

The astronaut Michael Collins recalled being Earthstruck:

> The more we see of other planets, the better this one looks. When I traveled to the Moon, it wasn't my proximity to that battered rock pile I remember so vividly, but rather what I saw when I looked back at my fragile home — a glistening, inviting beacon, delicate blue and white, a tiny outpost suspended in the black infinity. Earth is to be treasured and nurtured, something precious that *must* endure.[29]

Ernst Mayr's thoughtful biologist not only has a sense of religious humility but also a sense of respect for nature: "And if one is a truly thinking biologist, one has a feeling of responsibility for nature, as reflected by much of the conservation movement."[30]

Edward O. Wilson, a biologist who has been repeatedly, sometimes intensely, critical of the classical religions with their hope for transcendence, is, interestingly, as a secular humanist, the biologist who most demonstrates a virtually religious respect for the life he finds on Earth. He preaches its conservation with evangelical intensity: "What event likely to happen during the next few years will our descendants most regret?" His answer: "The one process now going on that will take millions of years to correct is the loss of genetic and species diversity by the destruction of natural habitats. This is the folly our descendants are least likely to forgive us."[31] In another place he writes: "Of all the evils of the twentieth century, the loss of genetic diversity ranks as the most serious in the long run."[32]

Why is it an almost unforgivable sin to destroy thousands of other species? Because in so doing we harm other people, but that is not Wilson's deepest reason. He urges forming a human bond with other species, loving not only human diversity but biodiversity throughout the fauna and flora. He wants to stretch the self over to a "nobility . . . defined as reasoned generosity beyond expedience," to "the ultimate ennobling act."[33] We ought to respect life, to value other forms of life as we do our own. This is in our enlightened self-interest, but for those humans who can move outside their own pragmatic utilities and learn to appreciate the "mysterious and little known organisms" with which we coinhabit this planet, "splendor awaits in minute proportions."[34] Wilson marvels and rejoices at his prolific home planet with its teeming life, exuberantly projected up from the primeval ooze and mud, an emergent vitality expressed in millions of species.

The planet loves life, and so ought we, Wilson urges. In this biophilia, innate within us, "the more the mind is fathomed in its own right, as an organ of survival, the greater will be the reverence for life for purely rational reasons."[35] In this love we are the evolutionary epic become conscious of itself. We are, Wilson holds, innately inclined to act in our self-interest; this is the law of the survival of the fittest; but, unique among the species, we humans find that our own survival, and flourishing, requires a loving concern for the nature, the biodiversity, with which we have an entwined destiny. "Natural philosophy has brought into clear relief the . . . paradox of human existence. . . . We need the most delicate, knowing stewardship of the living world that can be devised. . . . The paradox can be resolved by changing its premises into forms more suited to ultimate survival, by which I mean protection of the human spirit."[36]

The sermon continues: "The green prehuman earth is the mystery we were chosen to solve, a guide to the birthplace of our spirit, but it is slipping away. . . . If there is danger in the human trajectory, it is not so much in the survival of our own species as in the fulfillment of the ultimate irony of organic evolution: that in the instant of achieving self-understanding through the mind of man, life has doomed its most beautiful creations."[37] We hardly yet understand that evolution and ecology because we take it all for granted:

> The flower in the crannied wall — it *is* a miracle. . . . Pull out the flower from its crannied retreat, shake the soil from the roots into the cupped hand, magnify it for close examination. . . . The handful may be only a tiny fragment of one ecosystem, but because of the genetic codes of its residents it holds more order than can be found on the surfaces of all the planets combined. It is a sample of the living force that runs the earth — and will continue to do so with or without us.[38]

That living force runs through the preacher himself, and we can hear Wilson's own spirituality embodied in what he urges:

> Humanity coevolved with the rest of life on this particular planet; other worlds are not in our genes.... Humanity is part of nature, a species that evolved among other species. The more closely we identify ourselves with the rest of life, the more quickly we will be able to discover the sources of human sensibility and acquire the knowledge on which an enduring ethic, a sense of preferred direction, can be built.... We do not understand ourselves yet and descend further from heaven's air if we forget how much the natural world means to us. Signals abound that the loss of life's diversity endangers not just the body but the spirit.[39]

Perhaps the noumenal world lies beyond our kin, but the world of phenomena, revealed by science and seen at hand, is phenomenal enough to ennoble our spirits.

Biology and religion are not always easy disciplines to join, as illustrated by Wilson's misgivings about any transcendence to be detected as immanent in world history or his efforts to join selfish genes and reverence for life. One place they have increasingly joined in recent years is in admiration for this marvelous planet that we inhabit. That respect sooner or later passes over to a reverence. No other species can be either responsible for or religious toward this planet, but *Homo sapiens* reaches a responsibility that assumes spiritual dimensions: "There can be no purpose more inspiriting."[40] In a planetary, environmental age, spirituality requires combining nature and grace at new levels of insight and intensity. Nature is grace, whatever more grace may also be. The geophysical and biological laws, the evolutionary and ecological history, the creativity within the natural system we inherit, and the values these generate are the ground of our being, not just the ground under our feet.

Life persists because it is provided for in the ecological Earth system. Earth is a kind of providing ground, where the life epic is lived on in the midst of its perpetual perishing, life arriving and struggling through to something higher. Ultimately, there is a kind of creativity in nature demanding either that we spell nature with a capital *N* or pass beyond nature to nature's God. Biology produces many doubts. Here are two more. I doubt whether one can take biology seriously, the long epic of life on Earth, the prolific fecundity that surrounds us as human spirits on this planet, without a respect for life, and the line between respect for life and reverence for life is one that I doubt that you can always recognize.

When J. B. S. Haldane found himself in conversation with some theologians and was asked whether he had concluded anything about the character of God from his long studies in biology, he replied that God had an inordinate fondness for beetles. God must have loved beetles, since he made so many of them. Species counts, however, are only one indication of diversity, and perhaps the fuller response is that God must have loved life, since God animated such a prolific Earth. Haldane went on to say that the marks of biological nature were its "beauty," "tragedy," and "inexhaustible queerness."[41]

This beauty approaches the sublime; the tragedy is perpetually redeemed with the renewal of life, and the inexhaustible queerness recomposes as the numinous. If anything at all on Earth is sacred, it must be this enthralling creativity that characterizes our home planet. If anywhere, here is the brooding Spirit of God. So the secular — this present, empirical epoch, this phenomenal world, studied by science — does not eliminate the sacred after all; to the contrary, it urges us on a spiritual quest. If there is any holy ground, any land of promise, this promising Earth is it.

Notes

1. Loren Eiseley, *The Immense Journey* (New York: Vintage, 1957), 210.
2. John A. Wheeler, "The Universe as Home for Man," in *The Nature of Scientific Discovery*, ed. Owen Gingerich (Washington, D.C.: Smithsonian Books, 1975).
3. John D. Barrow and Joseph Silk, "The Structure of the Early Universe," *Scientific American* 242:4 (April 1980): 128.
4. Marek Demianski, quoted in Dietrick E. Thomsen, "In the Beginning Was Quantum Gravity," *Science News* 124:10 (3 September 1983): 152.
5. P. C. W. Davies, *The Accidental Universe* (New York: Cambridge University Press, 1982), 90, 110.
6. Bernard Lovell, "Whence?" *New York Times Magazine*, 16 November 1975, 88, 95. See also Bernard Lovell, *In the Center of Immensities* (New York: Harper and Row, 1978), 123–26.
7. B. J. Carr and M. J. Rees, "The Anthropic Principle and the Structure of the Physical World," *Nature* 278 (12 April 1979): 605, 609.
8. Fred Hoyle, "The Universe: Past and Present Reflections," *Engineering and Science* 45:2 (November 1981): 12.
9. Cited in John Boslough, *Stephen Hawking's Universe* (New York: Morrow, 1985), 121.
10. Mike Corwin, "From Chaos to Consciousness," *Astronomy* 11:2 (February 1983): 16–17, 19.
11. Albert Einstein, *The World as I See It* (New York: Philosophical Library, 1949), 28.
12. Freeman J. Dyson, "Energy in the Universe," *Scientific American* 225:3 (September 1971): 59.
13. John D. Barrow, "Anthropic Definitions," *Quarterly Journal of the Royal Astronomical Society* 24 (1983): 151.
14. C. W. Misner, "Cosmology and Theology," in *Cosmology, History, and Theology*, ed. Wolfgang Yourgrau and Allen D. Breck (New York: Plenum, 1977), 95.
15. Melvin Calvin, "Chemical Evolution," *American Scientist* 63 (1975): 176.
16. Ibid., 169.
17. George Wald, "Fitness in the Universe: Choices and Necessities," in *Cosmochemical Evolution and the Origins of Life*, ed. J. Oró et al. (Dordrecht, Netherlands: Reidel, 1974), 9.

18. Manfred Eigen, "Self-Organization of Matter and the Evolution of Biological Macromolecules," *Die Naturwissenschaften* 58 (1971): 519.

19. Michael Polanyi, *Personal Knowledge* (New York: Harper and Row, 1964), 382–87.

20. John Maynard Smith, *On Evolution* (Edinburgh: University of Edinburgh Press, 1972), 89, 98.

21. Ernst Mayr, *Toward a New Philosophy of Biology* (Cambridge, Mass.: Harvard University Press, 1988), 251–52.

22. Edward O. Wilson, *The Diversity of Life* (Cambridge, Mass.: Harvard University Press, 1992), 187, 194.

23. Niles Eldredge, "Mass Extinction and Human Responsibility," in *Biology, Ethics, and the Origins of Life,* ed. Holmes Rolston (Boston: Jones and Bartlett, 1994), 79.

24. David M. Raup, *Extinction: Bad Genes or Bad Luck?* (New York: Norton, 1991), 187.

25. Ibid., 188–89.

26. Loren Eiseley, *The Firmament of Time* (New York: Atheneum, 1972), 171.

27. Ernst Mayr, *The Growth of Biological Thought* (Cambridge, Mass.: Harvard University Press, 1982), 81.

28. Edgar Mitchell, quoted in Kevin W. Kelley, ed., *The Home Planet* (Reading, Mass.: Addison-Wesley, 1988), at photographs 42–45.

29. Michael Collins, foreword to Roy A. Gallant, *Our Universe* (Washington, D.C.: National Geographic Society, 1980), 6.

30. Ernst Mayr, "How Biology Differs from the Physical Sciences," in *Evolution at a Crossroads,* ed. David J. Depew and Bruce H. Weber (Cambridge, Mass.: MIT Press, 1985), 60.

31. Edward O. Wilson, *Biophilia* (Cambridge, Mass.: Harvard University Press, 1984), 121.

32. Edward O. Wilson, "Comparative Social Theory," in *The Tanner Lectures on Human Values, 1980,* ed. Sterling M. McMurrin (Cambridge: Cambridge University Press; Salt Lake City: University of Utah Press, 1980), 1:61.

33. Wilson, *Biophilia,* 131.

34. Ibid., 139.

35. Ibid., 140.

36. Ibid.

37. Wilson, *Diversity of Life,* 344.

38. Ibid., 345.

39. Ibid., 347–48, 351.

40. Ibid., 351.

41. J. B. S. Haldane, *The Causes of Evolution* (Ithaca, N.Y.: Cornell University Press, 1966 [1932]), 167–69.

Bibliography

Barbour, Ian. *Religion in an Age of Science.* San Francisco: Harper and Row, 1990.

Barrow, John D., and Frank J. Tipler. *The Anthropic Cosmological Principle.* New York: Oxford University Press, 1986.

Davies, Paul. *God and the New Physics.* New York: Simon and Schuster, 1983.

Drees, Willem B. *Beyond the Big Bang: Quantum Cosmologies and God.* La Salle, Ill.: Open Court, 1990.
Granberg-Michaelson, Wesley. *A Worldly Spirituality: The Call to Take Care of the Earth.* San Francisco: Harper and Row, 1984.
Leslie, John. *Universes.* London: Routledge, 1989.
Margenau, Henry, and Roy Abraham Varghese. *Cosmos, Bios, Theos: Scientists Reflect on Science, God, and the Origins of the Universe, Life, and Homo Sapiens.* La Salle, Ill.: Open Court, 1992.
Midgley, Mary. *Science as Salvation: A Modern Myth and Its Meaning.* London: Routledge, 1992.
Peacocke, Arthur. *Theology for a Scientific Age.* Oxford: Blackwell, 1990.
Rockefeller, Steven E., and John C. Elder, eds. *Spirit and Nature: Why the Environment Is a Religious Issue.* Boston: Beacon, 1992.
Rolston, Holmes, III. *Environmental Ethics: Duties to and Values in the Natural World.* Philadelphia: Temple University Press, 1988.
———. *Science and Religion: A Critical Survey.* New York: Random House, 1987.
Wilson, Edward O. *Biophilia.* Cambridge: Mass.: Harvard University Press, 1984.

16

Naturalistic Recreations

JOSEPH L. PRICE

AFTER SWIMMING through the chilling waters of the swimming hole below the natural water slide in the Big Sur River, my teenage son and I climbed the August-sun-warmed rocks of the river bed. We then waded through ankle-deep eddies in the stream and swam again, through clear channels and deep pools, beneath the steep rock walls of the river banks. The day-long trek was difficult but did not require special training or equipment. We continued on, making our way through a canyon, a narrowing stream, and the ever-easing current. At one bend in the river bed, my son stood atop a midstream boulder and bellowed, "Yes," pumping and punching his pitching arm in exultation and conquest. Concerned and curious, I asked him what the yelled "Yes" was for. "This is what life is all about," he replied.

With that simple testimony, he expressed the heart of the spirituality of naturalistic forms of recreation. As an urban adolescent comfortable with numerous high-tech entertainment media, he was not the most likely candidate to celebrate nature in a wilderness encounter. However, in his annual trek up the Big Sur River, he, like so many other persons from largely secular cultures of North America, seemed to find a restorative, refreshing sense of well-being in wilderness recreational pursuits.

The spiritual encounter with nature is increasingly considered a secondary effect of recreational activities, especially in Western cultures. To suggest that a genuine sense of spirituality might come from a recreational pursuit in and of nature runs counter to several dominant strains of traditional Christian theology. For recreation has often been perceived as a leisure activity, and leisure was particularly distrusted by Puritans; or it has been deemed mere entertainment, something that diverts people from the kinds of moral demands and acts that Christians have often been urged to pursue. Although the Christian religious tradition has routinely expressed concern about recreational activities detracting from one's mission to do God's will, other religious traditions have had more positive views toward recreation. Various Taoist and Buddhist traditions have resonated with an understanding of spirituality as something realized in and through nature, even as it is encountered and experienced in what Americans consider recreational activities.

Some people claim the experience of finding oneself in and through naturalistic recreations is very much like the practice of t'ai chi, a martial arts discipline that embodies and teaches a Chinese philosophy of organic relationships. For Delores LaChapelle, a Native American author and naturalist, t'ai chi became a way of experiencing the ritual harmony and bliss that she had previously experienced when powder skiing, a recreational and spiritual pursuit that she had to give up because of a back injury. After learning t'ai chi from a master teacher, LaChapelle hiked through portions of the Olympic range, ascending Blue Glacier, which peers down a mile at the Pacific Ocean at its foot. She writes:

> When you do Tai Chi, you enter a real wilderness within that joins with the wilderness without. There's no ego, only awareness and a kind of bonding quality. It's infinitely satisfying and wholly what you need. You only know you've reached that level when you come out of it, when you become conscious of it. At that point you know you were there and that you're not there anymore. That's what real wilderness is. You can't control it, you can't push it around, and you can't make it happen. It happens when it's right. We only get a chance to feel this once in a while, and that's the sorrow — the longing to experience our original nature.[1]

In a variety of natural venues many secular persons experience a kind of spiritual joy or renewal while pursuing recreational pleasures and activities in nature: hiking the Appalachian Trail, soaring from cliffs on a hang glider, scaling the sheer face of Half Dome in Yosemite, diving deep in the caves of Huautla, snorkeling with sea turtles near Sipidan Island off the Malaysian coast, surfing huge hollow barrels off Ocean Beach or the "cloud breaks" along Waikiki, or fly-fishing in the catch-and-release streams of the Sierras. Each of these recreational activities offers an experience in nature that often provides the participants with a sense of wonder, awe, wholeness, harmony, ecstasy, transcendence, and solitude. Each of these nature-focused activities affords the possibility of a kind of recreational spirituality. Each can transfix and transform. Each takes place in a natural arena where the trials of the heart and the tribulations of the soul can be overcome.

The variety of recreational and sporting activities in nature that facilitate, evoke, or generate a spiritual experience is not restricted to primitive pursuits in wilderness contexts; for forms of play in nature that germinate and cultivate spiritual awareness also include technologically oriented or facilitated activities. Somewhat ironically, in fact, a number of technological devices and materials that have been developed to address secular and scientific concerns in urban settings have expanded the possibilities for naturalistic recreations and their attendant possibilities for increasing or intensifying spiritual awareness. Some years ago, for instance, the development of air tanks for medical purposes made scuba diving possible in ways that could not have been foreseen a century ago. The discovery of parachute fabrics such as 1.1 ounce ripstop nylon and lightweight frames of aircraft aluminum or titanium alloy have made hang gliding — and its experience of the incredible, unbearable lightness of being — possible. More commonly, the development of lightweight fibrefills for sleekly designed sleeping bags has expanded the recreational opportunities for wilderness hiking and camping to many who would not have been able to undertake the burdens of the adventure years ago.

With such technological advances have often come the impetus for recording competitive performance. In the wake of developing statistical records to measure degrees of excellence in performance, professional competition and attendant organizations have begun to dominate the activities that began as recreational. For instance, the Southern California Ultra Circuit is an organization that calculates course difficulty, records race times, and rates competitors who participate in competitive wilderness trail events. As the professionalism in certain natural, recreational activities increases, the emphasis often shifts from the recreational contact with nature itself to a focus on speed and power and style of performance. Rather than seeking to enjoy the contact with and the invigoration by wind and water simply for the sake of those experiences, competitors in windsurfing, for example, frequently focus on exceeding the point total of another athlete. In these cases, nature or environment becomes the forum for competition rather than the focus for recreation or retreat. Although the professionalization of a recreational activity does not annul its possibilities for evoking spiritual enrichment, the emphasis on competition and standards reduces the likelihood that one might engage the activity for its own sake.

Although a range of recreational activities and sporting adventures in nature can enhance, generate, or facilitate a spiritual experience, it is the simpler, naturally focused activities that encounter nature as wilderness — with a focus on nature as Other — that have provided the foundation and lure for other forms of naturalistic recreations in the history of American leisure. In this regard, then, I will turn attention first to the spiritual dimensions of nature and wilderness experiences and then to the varieties of relevant recreational pursuits in secular America. In these contexts, I will examine more closely the kinds of spiritual encounters and sensitivities that might emerge from several specific recreational and sporting activities. As a way of prefacing the recreational sections, I should point out that these expressions of spirituality often come in the form of testimonies from the participants themselves. As is often the case for passionate testimony, the language used in describing experiences of nature and play frequently becomes poetic and invokes religious metaphors. Naturalistic recreations offer symbols and orientations by which secular Americans have begun to organize their conceptions of the physical world and to render them meaningful.

Nature and Wilderness

Although nature is regarded by many monotheists as a manifestation of the sacred — as God's handiwork — it also can be perceived by secular persons as an arena for spiritual encounter and rejuvenation. In and through nature, humans beings can wondrously perceive modes and manners of life that differ quite markedly from their own. In so doing, humans have, at times, considered nature as a manifestation of Otherness, revering it as sacred. "The worship of nature thus highlights both the freedom of the sacred to appear in any form, and the capacity of the human being to recognize it for what it is in any expression," notes historian of religion Lawrence E. Sullivan. "[For] nature transcends its brute physicality."[2]

Although what we now call nature itself has been revered regularly in diverse cultures and epochs, the recreational attention to nature conjoined to a kind of reverential respect has emerged as a modern phenomenon. For the objectification of nature — the conceptualization of nature as an "object" for study and an arena for exploration — is a modern idea that has emerged with the process of secularization since the Renaissance. In his essay "Good, Wild, Sacred," Gary Snyder similarly observes that in monotheistic traditions, the Christians completed the act of cutting down the sacred groves, which had begun with the Israelite kings. "The idea that 'wild' might also be 'sacred' returned to the Occident only with the Romantic movement," he remarks. "This nineteenth-century rediscovery of wild nature is a complex European phenomenon — a reaction against formalistic rationalism and enlightened despotism that invoked feeling, instinct, new nationalisms, and a sentimentalized folk culture."[3] Certainly, the natural world has existed and natural laws have been operative and observed throughout prehistory and human history, but the natural wonders that we now identify as constitutive of nature were previously conceived in different, primarily theological, terms.

A new experience of nature gained charter expression in the American mind with the publication of *Walden* by Henry David Thoreau (1817–62) and with the issue of the essay "Nature" by Ralph Waldo Emerson (1803–82). Both of these expressions arose in a period in which transcendentalism was a major philosophical current, and both works express a perception and articulation of the mysterious and cosmic experience of nature. Both Emerson and Thoreau lived in New England during the emergent industrialism of the mid-nineteenth century, and they sounded a warning about the possible destruction of nature while also recommending its spiritual importance and its recreational prospects. Although neither Emerson nor Thoreau celebrated recreational pursuits in these foundational texts, Thoreau did write rhapsodically about nature in works more oriented toward recreational activities. His essay on trout fishing, "Katahdin," and his treatise *A Week on the Concord and Merrimack Rivers* focus on the lure of fishing, canoeing, camping, wilderness encounter, and the search for solitude.

Despite its emergence in modernity, the *concept* of "nature" itself has become particularly elusive or ambiguous at the onset of the postmodern period. Elizabeth Raymond muses:

> Long an influential touchstone of value, its import and even its precise location have become increasingly difficult to specify. Is nature our mother, or a remote but scientific system of ecological niches? Is it "red in tooth and claw," or filled with friendly species like dolphins, who are trying to communicate with us? Do we find it outside the back door or in officially designated wilderness preserves? Is the proper human stance toward nature use or protection, observation or worship? Is nature dead? Is nature even out there?[4]

Not only is the concept of nature itself elusive, so are many of its constituent components or arenas, such as mountain, sea, forest, desert, and cave. Each terrain or expanse offers and prompts association with different sets of spiritual sensibilities and with religious myths dealing with notions such as transcendence, depth, wholeness, and harmony.

For many persons, Raymond goes on to argue, "*wilderness* has come to replace *nature* as the foundational concept," and the "deification of wilderness" has begun to occur "at a historical moment when wilderness is vanishing in the United States, and when a slackening economy threatens to undermine the political will necessary to strengthen existing environmental protections. Because nature is particularly vulnerable, environmental activism is understood to be a moral imperative."[5] Although we should avoid considering Otherness — alterity — and wilderness as being coincidental, we should note that throughout religious traditions and their history, the idea of wilderness and its encounter have been formative in the development of spirituality, often because wilderness has served as a spatial symbol for the existential trials that provoke or accompany personal transformation.

The lure and challenge of the American wilderness have exerted a formative influence on the American experience since the earliest decades of the continent's exploration, colonization, and conquest by the European settlers. In 1670, Samuel Danforth delivered his election sermon, "A Brief Recognition of New England's Errand into the Wilderness," a title and theme that have been made prominent in recent years by Perry Miller. Early Puritans felt that they had been sent into the wilderness of the New World in order to convert the heathen and to establish a pure form of civil order under divine guidance. As Miller puts it:

> A society dispatched upon an errand that is its own reward would want no other rewards: it could go forth to possess a land without ever becoming possessed by it; social gradations would remain eternally what God had originally appointed; there would be no internal contention among groups or interests, and though there would be hard work for everybody, prosperity would be bestowed not as a consequence of labor but as a sign of approval upon the mission itself.[6]

The wilderness did not always prove to be a fertile field, and hardship confronted the Puritan settlers. New non-Puritan immigration and unplanned economic development also thwarted the Puritans' achievement of their errand, and, consequently, several New England preachers proclaimed the mission a failure by the 1660s. Yet the wilderness remained as a challenge, unknown and uncivilized.

Three centuries later, the lure of wilderness has shifted from the early Puritan emphases on Christian mission to a civil affirmation of its wholesomeness. At about the time of the birthing of 1960s environmental awareness, former Supreme Court Justice William O. Douglas, himself an avid mountain climber, noted that "a wilderness trip is about as cheap a vacation as a family or youth group or couple of buddies can take. Certainly it is physically the most refreshing and mentally and spiritually the most satisfying."[7] So strongly did he hold that wilderness would provide the combination of family recreation and spiritual refreshment that he drew up a creed, some of whose affirmations specifically address the convergence of recreation, nature, and spirituality:

> We believe in the right of children to an understanding of their place in nature's community, of which they are a part.

> We believe in their right to acquire skills for living in the out-of-doors as part of their heritage as descendants of pioneers, to swim, to fish, to manage a canoe, to climb, to hike, to worship.

"Wilderness," Douglas concludes, "helps us preserve our capacity for wonder — the power to feel, if not to see, the miracles of life, of beauty, and of harmony around us. All humans have that capacity; children are the most sensitive to their environment."[8]

For much of the twentieth century, various religious denominations have recognized the recreational and healing potential associated with a degree of natural wilderness, especially for urban and suburban dwellers. Consequently, they have established state and national retreat centers in remote areas that feature natural environs, if not wilderness: Ridgecrest and Crestridge in the Smoky Mountains of North Carolina; Green Lake, Wisconsin; Eagle Eyrie, near the Blue Ridge Parkway; Jonathan Creek, Kentucky; and Gulfshores, Mississippi — to name only a few. In each of these instances the natural landscape is named or implied in the retreat's name, thus capitalizing on the lure of nature and wilderness for recreation that is designed within a religious community.

Obviously, wilderness need not be associated exclusively with forested plains, as did the early New England Puritans, nor with mountains, as several East Asian languages suggest.[9] In fact, Jonathan White identifies an aqueous wilderness as another venue of the natural world in which the encounter with Otherness and its mystery can take place. Having conceived and now directing the Resource Institute, a kind of naturalistic/aesthetic study program in life aboard a sixty-five-foot schooner named the *Crusader,* White considers *all* of the program's activities — from writing to playing, including kayaking with whales — as guided by images and conceptions of wilderness: "No matter what we did, it was always the wilderness, both on and off the water, that served as our primary guide." He further notes that "as long as we insist on thinking of ourselves as separate from . . . the rest of nature, we will always be hungry for something 'out there' " — whether in desert, in forest, or in open sea.[10]

Wilderness can also be enjoyed as a means to relieve everyday stresses. Edward O. Wilson, the Harvard sociobiologist, has noted that "wilderness settles peace on the soul because it needs no help. It is beyond human contrivance."[11] On a more personal note, Wilson adds that he goes to the wilderness, as he puts it, to "unwind and chase the demons from my head." The spiritual wisdom of Native American traditions is renowned for its recognition of the value of the wilderness. In its promotional literature, the educational organization Outward Bound attributes to Black Elk the saying that "peace comes within the soul of people when they realize their relationship, their oneness, with the universe and all its power." In this spiritual vein, David Douglas, reflecting on his sojourn in desert wilderness, specifically correlates the geography of wilderness with the personal threat of alienation. "For me," he writes, "wilderness depends not only upon the terrain and wildlife but upon one other quality: my vulnerability. Is this the setting where I feel less sufficient, more conscious of my reliance upon God?"[12]

Although Douglas poignantly identifies the existential character of wilderness, and certainly a great deal of its biblical meaning, a more formal definition of wilderness, in terms of its natural association, is appropriate. In this regard, some of the language that the U.S. Congress used in the Wilderness Act is both particular and poetic:

> A wilderness, in contrast with those areas where man and his own works dominate the landscape, is hereby recognized as an area where the earth and its community of life are untrammeled by man, where man himself is a visitor who does not remain. An area of wilderness is . . . an area of undeveloped . . . land retaining its primeval character and influence, without permanent improvements or human habitation, which is protected and managed so as to preserve its natural conditions and which generally appears to have been affected primarily by the forces of nature, with the imprint of man's work substantially unnoticeable, . . . [and which] has outstanding opportunities for solitude or a primitive and unconfined type of recreation.[13]

One of the cultural impulses that has brought about the widespread appreciation for wilderness spaces and the surge in the development of wilderness societies in the United States is that, according to Catherine Albanese, "many Americans feared that without wild nature to invigorate them, they would become like the rest of the world. They would lose their innocence and strength, like people out of touch with the saving power of sacred story and ritual."[14] In previous generations, the religious perception of nature often resulted from or was confirmed by the ritual encounter with nature; but with secularization, religious rituals have become unmeaningful for many people, and in their place, recreational pursuits have often assumed a form of secular, ritualistic contact with nature and wilderness.

Recreational Activities

The etymology of the word *recreation* suggests that it is an activity that refreshes or restores. It is an activity that is pursued or entertained for its own sake. It is usually thought to be voluntary, immediately and intrinsically rewarding, as opposed to offering delayed gratification and reward by virtue of extrinsic means such as money or recognition. Although recreation often occurs in conjunction with, or as an expression of, leisure, it is not inherently connected to the availability of unprogrammed time. Recreation is, above all, an activity whose experience as pleasurable often depends upon the spirit in which it is undertaken; it is a frame of mind. This understanding permits even some contracted exercises to be considered recreational.

At issue, obviously, is the definition of recreation. Most definitions of recreation classify it as a process or a condition. Process definitions focus on the activity as it is pursued in leisure, and they characterize the activity as being voluntary, pleasurable, and immediately appealing. Definitions that identify recreation as a condition focus on the emotional state of the recreator as being directly pleased by an experience. Common to all definitions of recreation, however, are several features: its voluntary character, usually undertaken in leisure time; its immediate gratifications, as opposed to monetary compensation for work; its wholesome influence on individuals and society.[15]

The different forms of recreational activities that one might pursue in natural environments can be classified according to the ways in which one experiences the refreshment and renewal of recreation. The classification employed here will emphasize the contrast between adventurous and observational recreations and will stress the educational benefit of such activities. It is hoped that such an approach will offer insight into the various kinds of spiritual experiences that recreational activities make possible. It directs attention to several crucial questions: How do growth and self-transformation occur? Through contestation and struggle? Through acquisition of knowledge and contemplation? Through experience and practice? Or through a unique combination of these?

Adventurous Recreations

One of the spiritual dimensions of naturalistic recreations stems from the adventuresome elements that take place in liminal experiences — those that depart from an ordinary sequence of events, dulling consciousness of time, heightening awareness of the concrete, taking persons to the edge of understanding, and often providing intense or transformative encounters with transcendence.[16] In adventurous forms of recreation, sometimes referred to as thrill-seeking activities, one confronts the *risk* of physical injury and real *threat* of death. In so doing one encounters a liminal experience at its extreme. Analyzing the excessive exercise of physical power that can produce the thrill of personal conquest in adventurous recreational activities, Michael Murphy concludes, "Where capacities are stretched to their limits, metanormalities tend to appear, despite the expectations or desires of their recipients."[17]

According to Murphy, the world of physical adventure dramatizes and focuses the human "capacity for self-exceeding," especially as the demand for high-level physical performance creates risk, demands, and sacrifice and generates pain. In other words, human striving for contact with transcendence can be known in the liminal occasions of physical exertion in recreational activities. Indeed, it is this convergence of conditions of extreme physical demand and a mental orientation of recreational play that interests Murphy in his analysis of adventure. In adventure, one often experiences a sense of ecstasy, an altered state of consciousness that might be described as mystical. "That such experience comes unbidden into the lives of many sportspeople, affecting them deeply and challenging their beliefs about themselves," Murphy contends, "dramatizes the fact that flesh and consciousness tend to converge during the practice of strenuous disciplines. The fact that spiritual moods occur spontaneously in many athletes indicates that disciplines for the body sometimes catalyze depths of the mind, even in people who have little or no understanding of such experience."[18]

Mountaineering One of the most spiritually oriented naturalistic recreations is mountaineering. Throughout the world and throughout history, mountains have been considered sacred places, and mountain climbers have quested for self-perfection and self-transcendence by conquering mountains and their own fears and inadequacies. In his essay "The Spiritual Dimensions of Mountaineering," Edwin Bernbaum notes: "Climbing the mountain has become a symbol of the value that Western civilization has put on the conquest of nature, a conquest that glorifies the spirit of man and establishes his dominion over the things of this world."[19] Although few mountain climbers articulate their motivation for climbing in religious terms, a spiritual urge often underlies the desire to escape from quotidian comforts and routines, to transcend everyday events and worries, and to experience the grandeur and purity of being on a high peak in an open sky.

At times, the intensity of a spiritual experience is correlated with the degree of difficulty in a climb: the greater the challenge and physical exertion, the greater is the personal achievement; the more rugged the ascent and the more liminal the experience, the more transformative is the power of the experience. The experience of achieving transcendence by standing atop one of the world's highest mountain peaks is most dramatic. Consider British climber Frank Smythe's liminal experience as he recalls a presence that permeated Mt. Everest: "It was cold. Space, the air we breathed, the yellow rocks were deadly cold. There was something ultimate, passionless, and eternal in this cold. It came to us as a single constant note from the depths of space; we stood on the very boundary between life and death." In a similar way, Guido Rey, an expert climber in the Alps, shares the excitement — the ecstasy — of reaching the summit: "I tasted the fresh, ineffable joy of reaching the highest point — the summit; the spot where the mountain ceases to rise and man's soul to yearn. It is an almost perfect form of spiritual satisfaction, such as is perhaps attained by the philosopher who has at last discovered a truth that contents and rests his mind."[20] Quite simply, atop the world, mountain climbers often experience — like Abraham, Moses, Jesus, Muhammad, and gods and heroes throughout numerous religious traditions and periods — an intimation of transcendence.

The final ascent and full conquest of majestic peaks sometimes enable climbers to find fulfillment in their lives, attaining something that is absent from the customary places and common problems of their day-to-day experiences. Bernbaum remarks: "The ascent of a peak provides them with a natural symbol of the transcendence they seek."[21] It is possible that even mountain climbers who think of their recreation in terms of conquest and dominion can experience an unanticipated cosmic centrality when they reach the top of the mountain. As Bernbaum himself recalls of his perception atop a peak near Everest: "I had the distinct impression of standing at the center of a universe far vaster than anything I had ever known or imagined." Like other conquerors of majestic peaks, he perceived the mountain as the omphalos, the cosmic center, for the mountain's "height represents an ultimate value that endows the mountain with a kind of sacred significance for the modern world to which mountaineers belong."[22]

Despite the accomplishment that comes when the most difficult challenge has been met, when the highest mountain has been scaled, the feeling of bliss or cosmic connectedness can engulf a climber on a simple ascent that is not a heroic conquest. Such was the situation for Delores LaChapelle in her springtime ascent to the peak of Colorado's thirteen-thousand-foot Mt. Snowden, half the height of Mt. Everest. Although she and her companion did not need to rope up the fourth-class mountain, they enjoyed the activity. "Then," she remarks, "the bliss took over — a state of total relaxation, total alertness, total joy and thankfulness that the mountain is allowing you to do this. It's being at home — completely at home, like nowhere else." LaChapelle's friends had accused her of merely being an adrenaline junkie, but she distinguishes her experience from the physiological rush of an adrenaline surge: her bliss, she says, not only was one of total alertness and joy but was also "so safe, so good, so flowing."[23] Her description calls to mind Mihaly Csikszentmihalyi's work on the psychology of optimal experience that utilizes the concept of flow. Csikszentmihalyi defines "flow" as "the state in which people are so involved in an activity that nothing else seems to matter; the experience itself is so enjoyable that people will do it even at great cost, for the sheer sake of doing it."[24] Like LaChapelle, Edwin Bernbaum reports the feeling of safety rather than fear while he was on a steep, difficult face en route to a Himalayan peak he had not climbed before:

> Poised on a wall of green ice two thousand feet above a glacier, I found myself moving with uncanny precision and certainty — so different from the hesitant way I usually groped myself from hold to hold. It seemed absolutely impossible to fall. I felt connected to the face. If my foot should slip, I knew I could simply reach out a hand and grab an icicle to stay on. I crossed the section in no time at all, and when my companion struggled up and commented on the difficulty of my lead, I felt puzzled: it had seemed so incredibly easy.
>
> In such experiences, when everything becomes clear and simple, a climber momentarily becomes one with himself and the world around him.[25]

Amid the experience of conquering mountains, vanquishing personal fears, and sensing release from their normal pains and concerns, climbers also often undergo a concomitant spiritual experience that increases their wonder and rekindles their reverence for the simpler outcroppings of nature. In his meditation on going to Mt. Ranier, Belden Lane notes that the Native American name for the mountain, Tahoma, is translated as "The Mountain That Was God." The mountain itself, its majestic peak rising to fourteen thousand feet in the Cascade range, provided a lure like a pilgrimage center, toward which progress increasingly slows as one nears the site. "As the trees got larger, we stopped more and more often — to study waterfalls trickling down distant slopes, to listen to melted snow rushing over rocks, to breathe the air made almost palpable by its clarity. . . . The simple act of being present assumes a sense of gathered immediacy."[26] Almost a century ago, John Muir, a passionate mountaineer and founder of the Sierra Club, advocated the expansive blessing that one can experience when climbing. "Climb the mountains and get their good tidings," he urged. "Nature's peace will flow into you as sunshine flows into trees. The winds will blow their own freshness into you, and the storms their energy, while cares will drop off like autumn leaves."[27]

Skiing and Snowboarding The kind of spiritual bliss that LaChapelle experienced in mountain climbing, she had initially experienced as a deep-powder skier when she interacted with snow and friends in what she later came to understand as ritual. Her realization of the social spirituality in skiing occurred initially in an unusual skiing condition known as graupel, a kind of snow that combines the best of powder and corn snow. On the memorable graupel day, all of the skiers were in the lodge except for the few in LaChapelle's party. Her expression of feeling one with the mountain, of the mountain virtually skiing her rather than her exerting effort to make the run, recalls again the spiritual character of flow that Csikszentmihalyi identified. "When I'm letting the mountain and the snow do the turning, I can ski in two to three feet of powder all day without being tired," she muses. "This is where I first learned about this feeling" of bliss and the experience of the sacred.[28]

Similar in landscape and orientation to downhill skiing, the recreation of snowboarding provides adventures in winter wilderness that thrive in new snow and unmarked routes. Certainly, one of the lures of snowboarding is the prospect of travel to exotic locations and remote ranges throughout the Rockies and Andes. Although the lure of the Other (in terms of location and terrain) provides incentive for some snowboarders, the spiritual possibilities of the recreation can be identified with the creative energy and experience that characterize the rapid descent. As one snowboarder expressed it: "I don't think of snowboarding as a sport . . . but [as] the spiritual experience of gliding down [an] 85–degree incline on top of two feet of fresh powder." The enthusiast concludes: "Snowboarding is being original, losing the world behind you, and entering your own reality, where no matter what you do . . . it was fun, 'cause it was you."[29] Comparing snowboarding to several other mountain adventures that she had tried, Kathleen Gasperini remarks that "only snowboarding can give the feeling of floating, uninhibitedly. And riding on new terrain, with my board an extension of my body," she recollects, "it was a rush so powerful, so feminine, I felt like a creature of nature." The spiritual wonder that is evoked by snowboarding also manifests itself in the kind of social bonding that Gasperini and four other women experienced as they relaxed their inhibitions with each other and discovered what they could do on their own. In the end, they found that they had tested their skills by conquering the mountain but that the primary conquest had been of their own fears and anxieties. In their recreational descents in the winter wilderness, the women discovered, as Gasperini puts it, "camaraderie without pretenses or unrealistic expectations of our abilities."[30]

The spiritual character of the snowboarding experience, however, is not confined either to the adrenaline surge associated with the downhill rush or to the communal bonding that takes place among the snowboarders. An experience of awe and serenity during the preparation for snowboarding derives from the appreciation for nature, as Schnoa Miller vividly recalls of her excursion to Chile's winter during California's summer. "I arrived at a steep plateau with untracked trails where it appeared no one had ever been," she remembers of her trekking to the back side of the La Parva Ski Resort. She continues:

> The valley and peaks surrounding me had such an intense surrealistic energy that I felt permission was needed before heading downward. I asked for protection from Mother Earth as I looked toward the sun and rising moon, which seemed to be awakening to my stunt. I gathered faith, stood up, pushed off, and separated my spirit from my soul like a possessed warlock flying through the sky.[31]

One of the attractions of snowboarding is the challenge of the descent — the threat posed by chasms and precipices; another is the lure toward liminal spaces — high, cold, remote, exotic, almost primeval. These orientations increase the prospect for experiencing a snowboarding descent in a spiritual way.

Surfing Although "wilderness" and its threats are frequently associated with desert spaces, glacial fields, mountain ranges, or densely forested areas, the ocean and its power can also be experienced as wilderness. As rugged surfers in San Francisco know, "Ocean Beach in winter is a wilderness, as raw and red-clawed as any place in the Rocky Mountains."[32] The waves become more than shifting shapes; they are a fluid terrain, an aqueous wilderness. "For most surfers waves have a spooky duality," William Finnegan notes in a portrait essay about San Francisco's legendary surfer Mark Reneker. "When you are absorbed in surfing them, they seem alive, each with a distinct, intricate personality and quickly changing moods, to which you must react in the most intuitive, almost intimate way — too many surfers have likened riding waves to making love — and yet waves are not alive, not sentient, and the lover you reach to embrace can turn murderous without warning."[33]

Surfing, however, is more than merely "riding waves." It is a spiritual experience for many who enjoy the recreation. As skiers revel in becoming one with the mountain, surfers similarly seek to become "one with the wave." Surfing is, as some enthusiasts have suggested, a path that calls forth more and more dedication from the surfer but gives back even in excess of its increasing lure and demands. For big-wave surfers, the experience is intensified by "the purer, more elemental challenge of giant waves," which occasionally exceed the height of a four-story building. As former big-wave surfer Mark Foo puts it: "If you want to ride the ultimate wave, you have to be willing to pay the ultimate price."[34] His words proved prophetic, for a forty-foot-high "barrel" at a place called Maverick's along the Big Sur coast claimed his life in 1994 when he and other champion surfers sought and challenged the ultimate wave. Although the challenge afforded by Maverick's gigantic waves is not common, the desire for the perfect ride motivates all surfers, regardless of their level of expertise. "To me," one of the world's five million surfing enthusiasts writes to the leading surfing magazine, "surfing's a spiritual quest to gain... happiness and that adrenaline rush that's kept me blissful."[35]

In addition to their Zenlike quest to move beyond an experience of cosmic harmony to one of particular unity with the natural world, and in addition to their pursuit of the optimal experience of bliss that at times accompanies a great ride, surfers also experience a different aspect of spirituality as they seek to be creative, original, pioneering — "to surf previously unattempted conditions, in previously unimagined ways."[36] A lot of what surfing is about, Mark Reneker insists, is for a surfer to make a wave his or her own — to establish order over the chaos of water. In this sense, then, it is also a spiritual activity since the act of settling and ordering wilderness is, as Mircea Eliade reminds us, an act of consecration.[37]

The premise of Eliade's work is that the process of secularization involves the profanization of sacred rituals. Originally dramatizing and generating a sacred cosmology, many rituals have become disconnected from their sacred mythic substructures; yet they continue to be practiced and enjoyed with a kind of visceral or subconscious remembrance of their initial importance. An example of the religious origin of a ritual activity that has become disconnected from its sacred context is the recreation of surfing, which originated in relation to various religious rituals and impulses among the indigenous peoples of the Pacific islands. After making prayers and offerings, ancient Hawaiian artisans would craft boards from the wiliwili or koa trees, whose wood was thought to be sacred. Perhaps because of its connections to the sacred cosmology of the native peoples, surfing was seen as a challenge or threat to early Christian missionaries to the islands. After three decades of work among the islanders, the leader of the initial mission group to Hawaii, Hiram Bingham, expressed approval of the decrease in surfing that he had observed: "The decline and discontinuance of the use of the surfboard, as civilization advances, may be accounted for by the increase in modesty, industry or religion."[38]

In light of the loss of the sacred origins of surfing, surfing enthusiasts have often remarked on the difficulty in explaining the experience. Seeking nevertheless to offer some description of the sense of wonder and connectedness that surfers experience amid the bliss of riding a huge, cresting, and curling wave, Finnegan turns to musical and religious metaphors, appealing to aesthetic and spiritual sensibilities: "Is this swell one of God's jazz solos, whose structure is beyond our understanding?" he ponders. "When the surf is very big, or in some other way humbling, such questions tend to fall away. The heightened sense of a vast, unknowable design silences the effort to understand."[39]

In his essay "Adventure and Sport," Michael Murphy concludes that "athletic feats can mirror contemplative graces,"[40] and this reflection of spiritual enrichment in physical accomplishment is manifest in the way that athletes often invoke religious terminology to describe their recreational experiences. This sense of spirituality is professed by Finnegan, who describes his own surfing exploits: "The places I've surfed sometimes seem like so many beads on a memory string, a rosary of hundreds of small stereopticons, wherein multicolored waves break in amber. More often, they seem like stations on some looping, ragged pilgrimage, my wave hound's *Wanderjahre* — a long search through a fallen world for shards of a lost bliss."[41]

Rafting Combining some of the sensations and adventure of skiing and surfing, white-water rafting presents a different orientation for spiritual experience. For the most part, the oceanic adventures of surfing provide spiritual encounters that emerge out of solitary pursuit. By contrast, the sense of spirituality that often accompanies white-water rafting comes from a dependence that one develops on and for one's companions in running the rapids and, literally, going with the flow.

So potentially powerful and transformative are the experiences of bonding that take place in white-water rafting that some recreational adventure companies orient a number of their trips to women who desire to face the threat and challenge of river travel with other women. On one such trip the women rafters took river names, paid homage to the river as priestess, and knew that they would travel "into other realities" on their white-water rafting trip on a soigné float down the Colorado. At the outset of their journey, they recognized and celebrated the fusion of the recreational and spiritual dimensions of their venture. They smudged each other with soot from a pile of grass burned in a seashell, expecting that the power of the residue from the fire and smoke would increase their spiritual sensitivity. Their perception became so keen, in fact, that several of them began to appreciate the beauty of their bodies for the first time. "The further we retreat from Madison Avenue, the International Slaughterhouse of the Female Image," one of the rafters reflected, "the deeper we travel down the river, the higher we climb in the canyons, the more beautiful the bodies of the women become."[42] Much like the movement of the child in the birthing process, the violent descent of the raft through river rapids restored a primal sense of identity and vitality to the women.

As rafters confront crises together and experience common vulnerability, they begin to forge a sense of sacred community that anthropologist Victor Turner calls *communitas.* Unlike the spatially oriented concepts of community and unlike the established relationships of society, *communitas* derives from and reinforces sacred aspects of life. It creates new levels of personal awareness and interaction that are not dependent on prior social structures such as class, ethnicity, or gender. It engenders immediate, existential, I-Thou relationships. "*Communitas,*" Turner concludes, "does not merge identities; it liberates them from conformity to general norms."[43]

The communal bonding through cooperative achievement is not the only — or even necessarily the primary — spiritual dimension of the recreational adventure generated in white-water rafting. E. Jean Carroll recalls, for instance, the experience of seemingly unending threat — a paradigmatic, liminal event — and subsequent jubilation that took place in the act of encountering and overcoming the rapids. Riding the swell, rising so high that the rise did not seem to peak, she remembers that her heart felt like it too had swelled to its maximum size and beat. "You are riding so far on The Edge," she reasons, "your fear turns into ecstasy."[44] Describing the feeling of simultaneous terror and delight, she also manifests the complex sensations that Rudolf Otto describes as encountering the *mysterium tremendum et fascinans* — the terrifying, fascinating, and "aweful" experience of the Wholly Other in all its power.[45] A canoer similarly recalls her own discovery of knowing wildness again — remembering her Minnesota boundary-waters excursion as taking her again and again to the edge. During her adventure, she concluded: "I have felt so alive on this trip. But now I feel so close to death, so cold, so tired, so numb."[46] As these river runners realize, fear of the Other can be confronted and overcome in the liminal experiences of recreational pursuits.

Observational Recreations

Adventure-oriented activities are not the only recreational pursuits in nature that evoke a sense of spirituality. Sometimes, forms of recreation that demand less physical activity induce a sense of harmony through their evocation of simplicity and patience. We might call these leisure activities observational recreations, wherein the purpose is to be in nature, observing natural inhabitants and their behavior and identifying oneself as a participant observer connected with nature itself. Among observational recreations, we might identify such obvious activities as bird-watching, whale-watching, and photographic safaris. We also might include the more active recreations of hiking, backpacking, and snowshoeing. One of the primary purposes of observational sorts of recreation is to enjoy nature and, while doing so, to refine one's ability to perceive and seek harmony.

Annie Dillard's *Pilgrim at Tinker Creek* and Sue Hubbell's *A Country Year: Living the Questions* explore the wonder of life manifest in the simple and routine processes of nature — in the creek behind Dillard's house and in the Hubbell's farm surrounded by government land.[47] For Dillard and Hubbell, a sense of cosmic mystery seems manifest in common animals and their patterns of behavior, in ordinary plants and their seasons of growth and decay. For each, the observation of mundane elements, routine growth, and daily decay offers opportunities for discovering beauty, simplicity, and harmony. The uncommon spiritual possibilities afforded by the commonplace in nature form the theme of these books.

The orientation that Dillard and Hubbell identify is one reminiscent of Henry David Thoreau. In his essay "Walking" he provides the charter statement for a romantic, recreational respect for nature because in the essay Thoreau advocates learning how to walk so that one might properly observe and appreciate the mysteries of nature. Repeatedly celebrating the beneficent character of nature wild and free, Thoreau begins his essay with the simple assertion: "I wish to speak a word for Nature, for absolute freedom and wildness."[48]

Somewhat similarly, Scott Russell Sanders, president of the Sierra Club, recalls the way in which his father encouraged him to wonder while wandering: "Will you look at this?" he would say time and again in an effort to increase the appreciation for the newness of nature. Before taking his own daughter for a canoe trip to the boundary waters of northern Minnesota — the first such trip since his father's death — Sanders wrote this meditation about excursions that he had enjoyed with his father:

> These outings were never trials of endurance, with a quota of miles to cover and hazards to overcome, but always musing saunters. "Will you look at this," he would say, and time and again we paused to look. Paddling through rapids, portaging between moosey lakes, hunting for arrowheads in a plowed field, or picking beans in the yard, he moved with the same deliberation and delight. The point was to be in contact with dirt and water and wood and sky, in the presence of animals, wide awake. Whatever his indoor faults, and he certainly had them, when he was outdoors my father radiated a steady, savoring attentiveness, and that was a great gift. He was so mindful of the Creation that in his company I forgot clocks and calendars, let go of words, and became mindful as well.[49]

Sanders's tribute not only recognizes the energy that can be derived from a kind of intimate interaction with and observation of nature but also celebrates the memory of family as a part of nature.

Because observational recreational activities do not require excessive physical exertion or specialized equipment, they often become the focus for family experiences of the wonder of nature, whether watching hummingbirds flit to stems of English lavender, or seeing a flock of Morganser ducks alight on a small pond at dawn, or glimpsing the smooth flight of a red-tailed hawk surveying possible prey before sundown. Even going to zoos and wild animal parks can produce of a sense of spiritual connectedness with and respect for other living creatures. When people criticize zoos and aquariums for confining animals, they often forget that most people live in cities and suburbs where they mostly encounter cats, dogs, mice, pigeons, and cockroaches. These are not species that inspire awe or instill a great passion for preserving endangered species. Zoos and aquariums do both these things, while also re-creating as best they can the natural habitats of the creatures they display.

Whale-watching Roger Payne, director of the Whale Conservation Institute in Massachusetts, notes: "Seeing a whale close-at-hand in the wild ... is something you never forget. Seeing whales at close quarters is a very important experience for people to have in terms of positioning their attitudes in favor of the wild world."[50] Like many similar recreations, whale-watching performs a valuable social function of raising awareness about other creatures and helping to direct resources to them. What is so compelling about whale-watching is the combination of the elements of chance (on a given day there might be no whales to be seen), the openness of the sea (as opposed to the controlled nature of museums or preserves), and the presence of creatures of such magnitude and intelligence (in contrast to viewing landscape). "When you encounter a large species like a redwood or a whale, it introduces awe into your life. And awe," Payne avers, "is ... what started the major religions. Experiencing awe in the hands of the wild can cause you to feel the same essential ecstasy."[51] Although he knows that human language is incomprehensible to nature, he acknowledges that our experience of awe allows nature to speak to us.

Size, however, is not the only factor that can evoke a spiritual response while animal-watching. Payne also recalls that once a chickadee perched on his finger to take a seed from his hand, an image that calls to mind garden statuary of St. Francis. The powerful experience of contacting and feeding the wee bird was one that he will also not forget: "never," he underscores. "Any situation where you allow an animal to trust you, and you trust it, builds a faith in your ability and the truth of what that represents. I think nothing could be a greater gift."[52] The process of getting close to animals, Payne believes, enhances and solidifies one's self-identity, especially as one acknowledges loving an animal.

Sightseeing At the heart of observational recreations lies the pleasure derived from sightseeing. In America the desire to see and experience natural wonders has been institutionalized by the establishment of national parks and national wilderness areas. Founded by Congress in 1872 with Yellowstone identified as the first national park, the national park system, along with its sibling system of National Wilderness Areas, has helped to define the American spirit and identity. Initially, the national parks were promoted as America's natural counterpart to the great cathedrals and castles in western Europe. Now they are often experienced as places manifesting a sort of natural mystery, and they present a space in which it is often possible to imagine reliving natural history.[53] Consider the spiritual connotations evoked by several visual images of national park landmarks: the grandeur and radiance of the Grand Canyon at sunset; the power and ethereal shroud of mist at Niagara Falls; the majesty and strength of the sheer face of Half Dome in Yosemite; the inverted absence suggested by the depth and spread of volcanic ash at Mt. St. Helens; the predictability, yet ever-newness, of the spouting of Old Faithful. And the list could go on.

Among the observational recreations in nature, some persons focus on landscape rather than plant and animal life. In so doing these observers at times experience the wonder of nature's immensity and the grace of its intricacy. Painters and photographers have long sought to capture these aspects of nature. John James Audubon's paintings collected in *The Birds of America* (1827–38) provide a stunning artistic and scientific celebration of American wildlife. In this century Ansel Adams used the new medium of photography to similarly celebrate the landscapes of the American West. Thousands of American painters each year travel to wilderness spots to capture some of America's natural beauty, and the number of amateur photographers who snap shots of mountain peaks and grizzly bears probably runs into the millions.

The deserts of the American Southwest have a special appeal for spiritually inclined sightseers. Their different beauty and expanse — their Otherness — evoke intimations of transcendence. The desert's "particular beauty is *the unfamiliar*," as one Sierra Club naturalist describes: "rumpled chocolate-brown mountain ridges; monumental, wind-rippled sand dunes; splashes of green lichen adorning vermilion rocks; and everywhere the interactions of light and shadow as an omnipotent sun moves across the sky." The landscape is perceived and described explicitly as "otherworldly," and one of the distinct impressions it gives is that of "a two-lane blacktop leading off into incomprehensible infinity."[54]

Hiking and Backpacking Recognizing the restorative power and rejuvenating spirit of his sojourn at Walden, his week spent on the Concord and Merrimack Rivers, his exploration of the Maine woods, and his trout-fishing expedition to Katahdin, Thoreau concluded that walking itself is the activity of a *free* person, one who has paid debts in full, one who is loosed from the obligations of family, one who is able to revel in the minutiae of the ordinary without feeling limited by time expectations. Certainly, one of the motivations of campers, hikers, and backpackers is to experience the freshness of clean air, to retreat from the pressures of the city and the routines of daily life, and to walk and sleep in touch with the ground, Mother Earth. Hikers revere their contact with the earth.

One of the aspirations of campers who flock to Yosemite and other natural recreational areas is to hike — to follow, like pilgrims, paths toward destinations that promise solitude, beauty, or merely difference and variety. Occasionally in the process of hiking, one might experience a spiritual connectedness that comes through observing the freshness of the surrounding natural world or experiencing its remoteness from ordinary contacts. An example of the kind of spirituality that hikers might sense is that of Chris McEntee, a fairly typical young urban dweller. The youngest son of staunch, churchgoing Christians, he is the only one of his siblings who quit attending church, even though religion remains a significant part of his family's life. Instead of attending church, he regularly does a derivative of Zen meditation, writes reflections in a journal, rides a mountain bike, and enjoys bird-watching. "For me," he says, "God is a walk in the woods. That's hard for my parents to understand."[55] He savors leisure and his private search for a kind of spiritual presence and peace, even if the combination of leisure and solitude, recreation and meditation perplexes his churchgoing parents and other mainstream Christians.

In winter the experiences of refreshment and contact with nature are intensified by encountering the purity and simplicity of new-fallen snow. As one snowshoeing enthusiast puts it: "There's nothing that refreshes the spirit like slipping on lightweight snowshoes and heading out on a sunny day for a trek (or a workout) in the invigorating winter air."[56] Others note the pristine experience — one with greater solitude — afforded by backpacking the trail during winter. "Winter on the Appalachian Trail brings its own magic," notes one hiker. "The feeling of space and solitude offers stark contrast to the jumble of summer hikers. . . . There is something special about camping in the snow. Everything is clearer, more defined. . . . You'll come home with a new-found sense of freedom."[57] Winter hikers report that quietly observing falling snow has a centering effect similar to the more traditional experience of meditating on lit candles or geometrical designs.

In addition to the spiritual experiences associated with the search for solitude, the discovery of purity, and the celebration of freedom, snow trekkers also find that their encounter with surviving animals and plants in winter intensifies their experience of harmony. In this regard Thomas S. Kirkland remarks on his increased wonder in winter backpacking, particularly "the harmony of trekking, in tandem, with a red fox." After moving with the fox and waiting for the natural light to turn before photographing the animal, Kirkland writes: "Tears of joy poured from my eyes, for I had felt the true meaning of the words *patience* and *faith*. . . . I left . . . with a feeling of harmony and confidence."[58]

Blended Recreations

Obviously, recreational activities and pursuits do not conform completely to the general classifications and orientations that I have identified as adventurous and observational recreations. Although the adventurous recreations include times for appreciating nature and feeling a part of it and although the observational recreations involve some degree of physical exercise (as in hiking), other recreations more evenly blend the two sorts of orientations, thus generating a sense of spirituality both from the physical responses to the activity itself (typified by a surge of adrenaline) and from the perceptual frames of reference (characterized by an interpretation that stresses cosmic connections and harmony). Examples of such blended forms of recreation include fly-fishing and scuba diving. Each of these recreational pursuits demands active participation that aerobically energizes the fishers and swimmers; it is also fair to say that much of the spiritual meaning in these activities derives from the keen interpretations offered by their practitioners.

Fly-Fishing Although fly-fishing is a sporting activity, it can be done alone, with little equipment, and for recreational purposes. It must be done in nature, often by wading in a river or the shallows of a small lake. The catch-and-release program in the sport, initiated to reinforce an appreciation for ecological balance, now emphasizes its recreational orientation. The purpose is to cast, catch, and enjoy the wilds, rather than to secure fish for consumption. As one fly-fisher puts it succinctly: "To achieve mastery is to rise above the need to catch fish."[59] The physical action of fishing is for many fly-fishers secondary to their being in retreat, in flowing water, working with and for a fish, enjoying the natural world. Fly-fishers who enjoy this spiritual regeneration do not focus only on the act of catching fish; instead, they enjoy also the preparations for catching fish — tying flies, studying currents and eddies, casting the fly.

Robert Traver, author of the angling classic *Trout Madness,* concedes that, although the fish are one of the main ingredients in the event of fly-fishing, they are certainly not everything. In contrast, he confesses:

> I fish mainly because I love the environs where trout are found: the woods; and further because I happen to dislike the environs where crowds of men are found: large cities; but if, heaven forbid, there were no trout and men were everywhere few, I would still doubtless prowl the woods and streams because it is there and only there that I really feel at home.[60]

The pastoral and pacific feelings associated with the natural environs of trout make the pursuit of the fish seem secondary to the pursuit of solitude.

In his recent meditation entitled *Fly Fishing through the Midlife Crisis,* however, Howard Raines specifies some of the spiritual aspects of trout-fishing: "Like many Southerners, I was ruined for church by early exposure to preachers," he admits. He continues:

> So when I need to hear the sign of the Eternal, I find myself drawn to a deep hollow between Fork Mountain and Double Top Mountain on the eastern flank of the Blue Ridge. This is where the Rapidan River plunges through a hemlock forest and through gray boulders that jut from the ferny earth like the aboriginal bones of old Virginia. This is a place of enlightenment for me, the spot where I received the blessing of my middle years. Here, after three decades of catching fish, I began learning *to fish.*[61]

The great reward of fly-fishing, he realizes, is not the catching of fish but experiencing the wonder of nature — of river and remoteness, or fish and their evasiveness — in all of its immediacy.

Fishing storytellers from Thoreau and Hemingway to Norman Maclean and Richard Brautigan tell the same story, not about the proverbial "big one" that got away but about the fisher's "search for wholeness, if not holiness."[62] In recent years Maclean and David James Duncan have written about how fly-fishing is a mystical experience of the wonder, purity, and alterity of wilderness itself. Maclean has remarked that the coordination required for casting seems to defy conscious discipline and depend instead on divine grace.[63]

American presidents throughout the twentieth century have turned to fly-fishing as a retreat from the pressures of their high office, finding restoration and refreshment in the wilderness simplicity and solitude. In fact, two twentieth-century presidents have written about the spiritual significance and recreational lure of the sport. In his book *Fishing for Fun — and to Wash Your Soul,* Herbert Hoover expresses a strong spiritual sense, especially with his well-known comment that "Presidents have only two moments of personal seclusion. One is prayer; the other is fishing — and they cannot pray all the time!" He elaborates:

> Next to prayer, fishing is the most personal relationship of man; and of more importance, everyone concedes that the fish will not bite in the presence of the public, including newspapermen.
>
> Fishing seems to be one of the few avenues left to Presidents through which they may escape to their own thoughts, may live in their own imaginings, find relief from the pneumatic hammer of constant personal contacts, and refreshment of mind in rippling waters.[64]

With a similar fusion of poignancy and humor, Jimmy Carter has exhibited a collection of his flies under the title "The Tie That Binds." Also, Carter recalls that, on the day following his defeat in 1980, he turned his attention to tying flies as he searched for solace and healing of his wounded spirit. This testimony succinctly shows how fly-fishing in the variety of its aspects affords a contemplative form of spiritual experience.

Scuba Diving At times a sense of pilgrimage seems to characterize the project of traveling to remote sites in quest of ideal scuba diving and snorkeling. Pursuing isolation, adventure, and beauty, Randy Wayne White set his sights on scuba diving at Sipidan Island, Sabah, Malaysia. In reaching the island, which is thirteen thousand miles from his home, he endured tribulations from lost luggage to sea-sickness. The exploration of the sea, however, held incredible beauty and evoked a sense of flow akin to that described by the mountain climbers cited above. At Sipidan, White recalls:

> There were clow triggerfish, gold anthius, velvet unicorn tangs, and hundreds of other species I didn't recognize. The coral walls could have been a Disney garden; the fish could have been wildflowers or butterflies. If you dive, you know the protoplasmic gush and flow of activity. You know the streaming colors. Individual elements blur into a glittering pointillist image.... The effect is overwhelming.[65]

Much of the awesome beauty of color and intimate harmony with animals emerged from the unprogrammed encounter with the wilderness of underwater life. The wild wonder seemed to have no bounds, as reflected in his notebook entries:

> Then a whole shoal of barracuda, thousands of them, like a curtain of saber blades. Put myself in the middle of them and drifted through. Maybe two dozen white-tip

> sharks cruised the perimeter. Current so strong that it was similar to being swept along by a mountain river. There were moments when I was out of control, had no hope of stopping myself. Not that I minded.[66]

Radical Otherness encountered in nature — here, the remote location, the aquatic environs, the exotic animal life, and the pervasiveness of beauty — often evokes a sense of awe, creating a numinous experience and generating an experience of, as Rudolf Otto put it, the *mysterium tremendum et fascinans.*

Educational Recreations

In continuity with the original nautical use of the phrase *outward bound,* which means the moment when a ship slips its mooring and departs for open sea, the program called Outward Bound is a wilderness education "school." Its primary purpose is educational rather than recreational. Nonetheless, the nature-oriented adventures of the program are designed to be fun and to generate a sense of discovery — of oneself and of one's relations to the environment. Such a radical voyage of self and natural exploration, however, involves commitment and sacrifice, both terms being used repeatedly in the promotional literature about the program. The program is often referred to as providing a "rite of passage" not only for adolescents who seek to move into the confidence and experience of adulthood but also for adults who are seeking transition from one phase of their lives to another. All participants seek to become more informed, more experienced, and more confident. The Outward Bound program seeks to "teach *through* the wilderness, not for it."[67]

The Outward Bound courses — oriented toward mountaineering, seafaring, and river-rafting, to name only three forms of wilderness activities — are about the exploration of terrain and temperament, about searching through the wilderness in nature and in one's own being: the hollow spaces of boredom and anxiety, the dark crevices of fear and anger. In 1941 the founder of Outward Bound, Kurt Hahn, declared: "Without the instinct for adventure, any civilization, however enlightened, any state, however well ordered, will wilt and wither."[68] The idea behind the program is that adventure and challenge in wilderness settings can become restorative and rejuvenative. What participants often discover within themselves is a reservoir of hope:

> In the midst of winter
> I finally learned
> That there was in me
> An invincible summer.

Citing these lines from Albert Camus, Kris Worrell identifies the kind of personal transformation that she and many other participants have experienced in the encounter with the challenge and threat of the Otherness of wilderness.

One of the reasons for the success of the confrontational courses is, as the promotional literature for the program explains, the radical Otherness of the mountains that the mountaineering expeditions encounter and the awesome power that the rafting expeditions confront. The courses seek to balance physical exercise and mental reflection, with most of the courses including a transformative "solo" period—a stretch of twenty-four to seventy-two hours during which one plunges into the inner depths of self to explore the nature of being itself as nature itself has been encountered and traversed. Another reason for the courses' success is that the groups often are made up of like-minded persons. An example of this is the women's river-rafting excursion. On one such Outward Bound expedition, Kris Worrell reports that her group of nine women overcame "fears and learned about wilderness survival and ourselves while hiking, whitewater canoeing, camping and rappelling in the mountains near Asheville. All of us took an incredible inner journey, too, and discovered some part of ourselves that was unknown, missing or buried in everyday life." Worrell concludes: "I found that I have great resources of patience I never suspected, and that I'm not as afraid of heights as I thought."[69]

Recognizing the possibility for naturalistic recreations engendering a sense of community, even among diverse strangers, Outward Bound designed one expedition to promote peace. As the Cold War was beginning to thaw, American veterans from the Vietnam War joined Russian veterans from the Afghanistan War to undertake an Outward Bound venture on neutral territory. They discovered that a joint encounter with nature and the mutual responsibility for one another it necessitated proved to be a stimulus to peacemaking.[70]

Conclusion

Commenting on the need for contact with the natural world in our secular and industrialized world, Roger Payne, the director of the Whale Conservation Institute, insists that "everybody could gain something from having more contact with the natural world. It brings rewards unequaled by anything else they could find in the human world." His reasoning resonates with that of Walt Whitman, who a century earlier urged a return to nature amid the increasing industrialization and urbanization of the Northeast. "Now I see the secret of making the best persons," Whitman proffered. "It is to grow in the open air and eat and sleep with the earth."[71] Although Payne does not specify the nature of the desired contact with the natural world, he does promote various ecological and recreational encounters, including several of the ones featured here. At its deepest level the need to escape the clutches of the human world — to return to nature — is driven not primarily by ecological or recreational interests. The reason for returning to nature, whether in recreational pursuits or in ecological commitments, is finally to regain touch with the divine.

In addition to the natural recreations heretofore mentioned, numerous others (such as bicycling, hang gliding, horseback riding, sea-kayaking, and scores more oriented toward mountain, sea, and desert) foster contact with the Otherness of nature and the unknown dimensions of oneself. Wilderness running, for instance, has occasionally been compared in its rhythmic patterns to spiritual awareness that one might gain through chanting. Consistently, however, the spiritual experiences generated within adventurous recreations and germinated within observational recreations emerge from the liminal character of the activity — that it moves the participant to the edge of understanding and self-awareness, providing clarity of insight and imagination of possibilities, of hope. The spiritual revivification that one experiences in naturalistic recreations emerges from the convergence of the beauty or remoteness of the natural setting and the kind of activity that takes one beyond the routines of day-to-day life.

The spirituality of natural recreations is also signaled by the terminology that designates certain areas as "wildlife sanctuaries" or "marine wildlife refuges." The language designating a space as a sanctuary or refuge orients hikers in a wildlife sanctuary or snorkelers in a marine wildlife refuge toward a spiritual kind of experience. In each case, expectations are raised about encountering that which is rare, other, living, and somehow in need of protection by human beings from other members of the human species.

At various times, in various ways, and for various persons, naturalistic recreations spawn a sense of spiritual renewal. The perception of the experience as spiritual, however, is not shared by all participants. For even as Christians, Muslims, Buddhists, and Native Americans, for example, experience spiritual refreshment in different ways, they recognize that others have spiritual (even if not saving, according to them) experiences that differ from their own. Naturalistic recreations that generate a spiritual experience do not depend upon the duration of their engagement, the popularity of their practice, the inaccessibility of their venues, the prominence of their participants, the simplicity of their style, or the expense of their adventure. For the experience of the spiritual dimension in recreational pursuits has been correlated with the various participants' orientation toward a transformative encounter with that which is *totaliter aliter,* totally other, that which removes them from the routines of everyday life and thereby offers escape, entertainment, and refreshment. Replenished spiritually by the experience, the participants hope to retain its joy, its serenity, its freedom, its harmony.

Although a number of naturalistic recreations often reflect an origin in or a connection to a specific sacred cosmology, the primary lure for secular participants in the modern era lies in their recreational promise. Touching the Otherness of nature through recreational activities or meeting the challenges afforded by natural barriers, persons pursue a journey outward and a journey inward. They often experience a sense of transcendent presence, and, simultaneously, they explore hidden depths of their own well-being. In recreation, then, persons can find and enjoy the nurture of nature.

Notes

1. Delores LaChapelle, "Mountains Constantly Walking," in Jonathan White, *Talking on the Water: Conversations about Nature and Creativity* (San Francisco: Sierra Club, 1994), 176.
2. Lawrence E. Sullivan, "Nature: Worship of Nature," in *Macmillan Encyclopedia of Religion,* ed. Mircea Eliade, 33 vols., 13:324–25.
3. Gary Snyder, "Good, Wild, Sacred," in *The Practice of the Wild* (New York: North Point, 1990), 80. See also M. H. Abrams, *Natural Supernaturalism: Tradition and Revolution in Romantic Literature* (New York: Norton, 1971), 11–17, 373–462.
4. C. Elizabeth Raymond, "Alternative Narratives of Nature: Middle Western Sense of Place" (paper read at the annual meeting of the American Studies Association, Boston, 7 November 1993).
5. Ibid.; emphasis added.
6. Perry Miller, *Errand into the Wilderness* (New York: Harper, 1956), 6.
7. William O. Douglas, *A Wilderness Bill of Rights* (Boston: Little, Brown and Co., 1965), 19.
8. Ibid., 27, 34.
9. Gary Snyder, "Blue Mountains Constantly Walking," in *Practice of the Wild,* 100.
10. White, *Talking on the Water,* xiii–xiv.
11. Quoted in Buck Tilton, "Wilderness as Tranquilizer," *Backpacker* 22:7 (September 1994): 24.
12. David Douglas, *Wilderness Sojourn: Notes in the Desert Silence* (San Francisco: Harper and Row, 1987), 10.
13. Quoted in Douglas, *Wilderness Bill of Rights,* 28.
14. Catherine Albanese, *America: Religion and Religions,* 2d ed. (Belmont, Calif.: Wadsworth, 1992), 492.
15. For a succinct survey of definitions and characteristics of *recreation,* see Clayne R.

Jensen, *Leisure and Recreation: Introduction and Overview* (Philadelphia: Lea and Febiger, 1977), 9–10.

16. See Mark Taylor, "Liminality," in *A New Handbook of Christian Theology*, ed. Donald W. Musser and Joseph L. Price (Nashville: Abingdon, 1992), 293–95.

17. Michael Murphy, *The Future of the Body: Explorations into the Further Evolution of Human Nature* (Los Angeles: Tarcher, 1992), 443.

18. Ibid., 415.

19. Edwin Bernbaum, *Sacred Mountains of the World* (San Francisco: Sierra Club, 1990), 236.

20. Quoted in ibid., 239, 247.

21. Ibid., 244.

22. Ibid., 241.

23. LaChapelle, "Mountains Constantly Walking," 165.

24. Mihaly Csikszentmihalyi, *Flow: The Psychology of Optimal Experience* (San Francisco: Harper and Row, 1990), 4. See also the editor's introduction to the present volume.

25. Bernbaum, *Sacred Mountains*, 244.

26. Belden C. Lane, *Landscapes of the Sacred: Geography and Narrative in American Spirituality* (New York: Paulist, 1988), 66.

27. Quoted in Bernbaum, *Sacred Mountains*, 243.

28. LaChapelle, "Mountains Constantly Walking," 165.

29. John "TroLL" Wuerfel, "Letters," *Transworld SNOWboarding* (April 1995): 34.

30. Kathleen Gasperini, "The Bedouins of Nevada: Five Women Snowboard the First Descent of Wheeler Park," in *Another Wilderness: New Outdoor Writing by Women*, ed. Susan Fox Rogers (Seattle: Seal, 1994), 108.

31. Schnoa Horizon Miller, "Storytime," *Transworld SNOWboarding* (April 1995): 50.

32. William Finnegan, "The Sporting Scene: Playing Doc's Games, I," *New Yorker*, 24 August 1992, 46.

33. Ibid., 35.

34. Jon Krakauer, "Mark Foo's Last Ride," *Outside* (May 1995): 68.

35. "Letters," *Surfing* (January 1993): 14–16.

36. Finnegan, "Sporting Scene," 41.

37. Ibid. See also Mircea Eliade, *The Sacred and the Profane: The Nature of Religion*, trans. Willard R. Trask (New York: Harcourt, Brace, 1959), 34.

38. Quoted in Finnegan, "Sporting Scene," 42.

39. Ibid., 59.

40. Murphy, *Future of the Body*, 444.

41. Finnegan, "Sporting Scene," 58.

42. E. Jean Carroll, "Women Who Run with No Clothes On," *Outside* (November 1993): 130.

43. Victor Turner and Edith Turner, *Image and Pilgrimage in Christian Culture* (New York: Columbia University Press, 1978), 250; see also Victor Turner, *The Ritual Process: Structure and Anti-Structure* (Ithaca, N.Y.: Cornell University Press, 1969), 96–97.

44. Carroll, "Women Who Run," 132.

45. Rudolf Otto, *The Idea of the Holy*, 2d ed., trans. J. W. Harvey (New York: Oxford University Press, 1950), 12–30.

46. Alice Evans, "In the Canoe Endlessly Paddling," in *Another Wilderness*, 127.

47. Annie Dillard, *Pilgrim at Tinker Creek* (New York: Harper's Magazine Press, 1974); and Sue Hubbell, *A Country Year: Living the Questions* (New York: Harper and Row, 1986).

48. Henry David Thoreau, "Walking," in *Walden and Other Writings* (New York: Modern Library, 1937), 627.

49. Scott Russell Sanders, "News of the Wild," Sierra Club Wilderness Calendar, 1995.

50. Roger Payne, "Voices from the Sea," in *Talking on the Water,* 29.

51. Ibid., 31–32.

52. Ibid., 35.

53. Alston Chase, introduction to Alston Chase and Debra Shore, *Outside's Guide to Our National Parks* (Chicago: Mariah, 1992), 1.

54. Reed McManus, "The Enduring Desert," *Sierra* (November/December 1994): 104–5; emphasis added.

55. Patti Puckett, "The Lost Generation: Alternative Paths to Spiritual Enlightenment," *Atlanta Constitution,* 4 June 1994, E6.

56. Bob Darby, "An Intro to Snowshoeing," *Running Wild* (early winter 1995): 43.

57. Sue Smith-Heavenrich, "Savor the Magic of Winter Backpacking," *Appalachian Trailway News* (November/December 1993).

58. Thomas S. Kirkland, "A Christmas Gift," *Appalachian Trailway News* (September/October 1993): 7.

59. Howard Raines, *Fly Fishing through the Midlife Crisis* (New York: Doubleday, 1993), 19.

60. Robert Traver, *Trout Madness: Being a Dissertation on the Symptoms and Pathology of This Incurable Disease by One of Its Victims* (Santa Barbara: Peregrine Smith, 1979), x.

61. Raines, *Fly Fishing,* 17.

62. Ibid., 32. See also Richard Brautigan, *Trout Fishing in America* (New York: Dell, 1967).

63. David James Duncan, *The River Why* (San Francisco: Sierra Club, 1983); and Norman Maclean, *A River Runs through It and Other Stories* (Chicago: University of Chicago Press, 1976), 1–3.

64. Quoted in Raines, *Fly Fishing,* 303–4.

65. Randy Wayne White, "Into the Wild Biru Yonder," *Outside* (January 1994): 59.

66. Ibid., 61.

67. *Outward Bound* (promotional brochure; Portland, Oreg.: Pacific Crest Outward Bound School [0110 SW Bancroft St., Portland], 1995), 8.

68. Ibid., 7.

69. Kris Worrell, "Outward Bound — a Journey of Discovery," *Atlanta Constitution,* 29 May 1994, K1, 4.

70. Elizabeth Anderson, "Veterans of Unpopular Wars Form Bonds," *New York Times* 5 November 1989, 12:1, 11.

71. Quoted in *Outward Bound,* 24.

Bibliography

Albanese, Catherine. *Nature Religion in America: From the Algonkian Indians to the New Age.* Chicago: University of Chicago Press, 1990.

Birnbaum, Edwin. *Sacred Mountains of the World.* San Francisco: Sierra Club, 1990.

Douglas, William O. *A Wilderness Bill of Rights.* Boston: Little, Brown and Co., 1965.

Lane, Belden C. *Landscapes of the Sacred: Geography and Narrative in American Spirituality.* New York: Paulist, 1988.

Murphy, Michael. *The Future of the Body: Exploration into the Further Evolution of Human Nature.* Los Angeles: Tarcher, 1992.

Raines, Howard. *Fly Fishing through the Midlife Crisis.* New York: Doubleday, 1993.

Rogers, Susan Fox, ed. *Another Wilderness: New Outdoor Writing by Women.* Seattle: Seal, 1994.

Snyder, Gary. *The Practice of the Wild.* New York: North Point, 1990.

White, Jonathan. *Talking on the Water: Conversations about Nature and Creativity.* San Francisco: Sierra Club, 1994.

Zelinski, Mark. *Outward Bound, the Inward Odyssey.* Hillsboro, Oreg.: Beyond Words, 1991.

17

Ecological Activism

LOIS K. DALY

THE NOTION of secular spirituality provides a useful way of understanding the growth and development of contemporary environmental activism.[1] In the last forty years, there has been a virtual explosion of public interest and concern about the effects of human life and activity on the planet. This is not to say that no one considered these questions prior to the 1950s; indeed, there have been significant voices raised on these issues in other historical periods. What is different is the number of individuals who now indicate that the consequences of their actions for the environment are important in their everyday decisions.[2] This issue has clearly taken on moral relevance for increasing numbers of people.

It is important to begin with a fairly clear sense of the phrase *secular spirituality.* Spirituality is often a vague or ambiguous term or simply a synonym for a particular religious commitment. It can, however, be given more specificity as well as be differentiated from identification with a religious tradition. In the introduction to the present volume, Peter H. Van Ness seeks to do this, saying that life is spiritual to the extent that it "engages reality as a maximally inclusive whole and makes the cosmos an intentional object of thought and feeling." He adds that spiritual life has an inner complexion when it "is apprehended as a project of people's most enduring and vital selves, and is structured by experiences of sudden self-transformation and subsequent gradual development."[3] This is not the only way in which spirituality can be specified. Louis Bouyer suggests that the spiritual life is attained when the " 'interior life' develops, not in isolation, but in the awareness of a spiritual reality, however this be understood, a reality that goes beyond the consciousness of the individual."[4] Dominic George calls this a "depth encounter" with the "depth dimension of Reality.... Human spirituality is a mode of human contact or encounter with Reality by which man/woman gets 'humanized'; that is, becomes more and more of a human being."[5] Especially this last perspective shows that spirituality has an ethical dimension; it encourages activities that further the encounter with reality. Put in another way, spirituality provides a system of meaning and an orientation for one's life activity.

As should be obvious, such a notion of spirituality and its attendant activity may have either a religious or a secular denotation. In a religious spirituality, the "reality that goes beyond the consciousness of the individual" is identified and construed according to traditional religious discourse, such as Christian God-talk. Secular spirituality, in contrast, develops without this discourse yet not necessarily in opposition to it. That is, the secular orientation emerges without any specific religious reference, but it may spur the same sort of attitudes and concrete activities in the world as an identifiable religious spirituality.

Analysis of the modern ecological movement and its roots provides a clear view of this phenomenon; furthermore, taking seriously the spiritual dimension of secular environmental movements helps explain their vigor despite the overwhelming opposition to them found in the dominant economic, political, social, and perhaps even religious paradigms operative in the late twentieth century. As will be described below, there is no doubt that these dominant paradigms and contemporary ecological organizations share very few assumptions about the world and human beings' place in it. Because their worldviews are radically opposed to each other, adherents of the dominant paradigms have had very little access to understanding environmentalists, except perhaps those whose ecological orientation has a clear religious affiliation. Recognizing the secular spirituality beneath the ecological activism provides this access; it helps to explain what otherwise may seem inexplicable to those who embrace the dominant paradigms.

One of the simplest ways to define the difference between the worldviews of the dominant paradigms and the ecological paradigm is to distinguish between anthropocentrism and biocentrism. Anthropocentrism, as the components of the term suggest, is a viewpoint that centers on human beings. According to this view, human beings are fundamentally different from all other creatures, over whom they have control. Furthermore, human beings, unlike others, can choose their own goals and learn to do what it takes to achieve them. The world, this view maintains, provides the unlimited resources for human beings to pursue their goals. Finally, "the history of humanity is one of progress; for every problem there is a solution, and thus progress need never cease."[6]

A biocentric paradigm does not begin with the distinctiveness or centrality of human life. Rather, it calls attention to the connections and interdependencies among all forms of life and, indeed, with the so-called nonliving world. It sees the entire planet as something to be cherished in itself, for its intrinsic value and not merely for its utility. Progress toward the goal of material wealth does not have a singular place of honor in a biocentric worldview. Rather, environmental protection and a "generalized compassion" for nature and its parts are developed. Biocentrism values a holistic approach to life. In this case, human beings are recognized as a part of nature and not set apart from it.[7]

A biocentric view of life and the environmental paradigm that follows from it call for a recentering of values. Human beings are called upon to remove themselves from the top of the hierarchy of creatures and take a place among the rest. As such, biocentrism poses a direct challenge to the dominant anthropocentric view that enthrones human beings and removes them from responsible interrelationship with the world. However, its very distance from the dominant view makes it difficult for open confrontation between the two to take place. As long as the challenger is "so far out," it is easy to keep it at bay, to keep it marginalized. This happens most effectively by naming the environmentalists "misguided," "crazy," or "terrorists." When these labels stick, those ensconced in the dominant paradigms need not worry about losing their position. Despite some sympathy that individuals may have for some of the claims of the environmentalists, who would be crazy enough to give up the "good life" of economic wealth to follow them? Seeing environmental activism as an instance of secular spirituality opens up new possibilities for challenging the dominant paradigms. It does this because it explains the "sense" of the movement. It gives reasons for altering one's life that go much deeper than material gain. It speaks to the spiritual depth and dimension of human life and activity. Moreover, given the distinctively secular character of the dominant social paradigms, the notion of environmentalists as engaged in a secular spirituality is much more threatening than religiously inspired environmental movements, although these too have been growing thanks to Lynn White's 1967 indictment of Christianity's conception of the natural world.[8] Such religious movements are less threatening because they are more easily marginalized and controlled by the dominant paradigms. An alternative secular view poses a different sort of threat.

In this chapter I will trace strands of ecological activism that develop from secular spirituality. I will look at John Muir and the origins of the Sierra Club, Rachel Carson and the impact of her book *Silent Spring*, and Dave Foreman and the rise of so-called radical environmentalism. In each of these cases, I will describe the meaning system within which the person or group operates and the sort of ecological activism that follows. This will explain the "sense" of their activities in spite of the dominant social and political paradigms.

Three Examples

John Muir is clearly one of the most important leaders in the early conservation movement. Born in Scotland in 1838, Muir emigrated with his father and two siblings to Wisconsin in 1849.[9] There he spent his time working on his father's farm while the elder Muir pursued his religious goals. Muir's father was convinced that the only book worth reading was the Bible. While John grew up with the same belief, gradually he began to recognize other sources of truth, in particular science and experience. His experiences in the wild were the most significant.

In June 1864, while wandering in the Canadian woods around the Great Lakes, Muir had an experience that marked the beginning of a new way of looking at the world for him. He saw a rare orchid, a *Calypso borealis,* growing by the side of a swamp. He wrote: "I never before saw a plant so full of life; so perfectly spiritual, it seemed pure enough for the throne of its Creator. I felt as if I were in the presence of superior beings who loved me and beckoned me to come. I sat down beside them and wept for joy."[10] Its beauty, although hidden from the sight of most human beings, suggested to Muir that nature did not exist solely for human use or pleasure. The flower, in other words, was beautiful and valuable in itself even if no human being ever saw it.[11] With this realization, Muir began moving away from the Christian anthropocentrism of his day and toward a biocentric view of the world.

During the next several years, Muir continued his travels by exploring parts of the American South. As he walked, his insight into the intrinsic value of nature continued to gather strength. He wrote:

> Nature's object in making animals and plants might possibly be first of all the happiness of each one of them, not the creation of all for the happiness of one. Why ought man to value himself as more than an infinitely small composing unit of the one great unit of creation? And what creature of all that the Lord has taken the pains to make is not essential to the completeness of that unit — the cosmos? The universe would be incomplete without man; but it would also be incomplete without the smallest transmicroscopic creature that dwells beyond our conceitful eyes and knowledge.[12]

As Stephen Fox has stated, Muir's central insight was that "the world did not spin at man's whim — despite the teachings of orthodox Christians. Creation belonged not to a manlike Christian God, but to the impartial force of Nature."[13]

Muir first ventured into the Yosemite Valley when he was thirty years old. His four-year stay cemented his biocentric views. The wilderness of Yosemite and the Sierras provided Muir with a spiritual replenishing he could find nowhere else.[14] Its spiritual resources were evident in the many experiences Muir had of "unity" with nature. Time after time, Muir found himself in dangerous situations, for example, going too far into the mountains in one day to turn back. Each time Muir found himself in such a situation, he experienced another "self," nature, taking over and steering him to safety. One of these experiences occurred while he was climbing Mt. Ritter:

> At length, after attaining an elevation of about 12,800 feet, I found myself at the foot of a sheer drop in the bed of the avalanche channel I was tracing.... After scanning its face again and again, I began to scale it, picking my holds with intense caution. After gaining a point about half-way to the top, I was suddenly brought to a dead stop, with arms outspread, clinging close to the face of the rock, unable to move hand or foot either up or down. My doom appeared fixed. I *must* fall.... When this final danger flashed upon me, I became nerve-shaken for the first time since setting foot on the mountains, and my mind seemed to fill with a stifling smoke. But this terrible eclipse lasted only a moment, when life blazed forth again with preternatural clearness. I seemed suddenly to become possessed of a new sense. The other self, bygone experiences, Instinct, or Guardian Angel, — call it what you will, — came forward and assumed control. Then my trembling muscles became firm again, every rift and flaw in the rock was seen as through a microscope, and my limbs moved with a positiveness and precision with which I seemed to have nothing at all to do. Had I been borne aloft upon wings, my deliverance could not have been more complete.... But the strange influx of strength I had received seemed inexhaustible. I found a way without effort, and soon stood upon the topmost crag in the blessed light.... In my first hour of freedom from that terrible shadow, the sunlight in which I was laving seemed all in all.[15]

Muir did not reserve such experiences to himself. His essay "Twenty Hill Hollow" ends with this paragraph:

> It may be asked, What have mountains fifty or a hundred miles away to do with Twenty Hill Hollow? To lovers of the wild, these mountains are not a hundred miles away. Their spiritual power and the goodness of the sky make them near, as a circle of friends. They rise as a portion of the hilled walls of the Hollow. You cannot feel yourself out of doors; plain, sky, and mountains ray beauty which you feel. You bathe in the spirit-beams, turning round and round, as if warming at a camp-fire. Presently you lose consciousness of your own separate existence: you blend with the landscape, and become part and parcel of nature.[16]

Although he often used language that suggests Christian affiliation, Muir clearly saw himself in opposition to what he saw as Christianity's focus on human beings as the purpose of creation. His spirituality was clearly secular, given the terms of his day, and shaped in contrast to a spirituality directed toward the Christian God as personal and distinct from the world. For Muir, the wilderness became a place for spiritual pilgrimage, something he recommended for everyone. The wilderness was home.

Muir's devotion to the wilderness led to preservation activity on its behalf. The pen became his most powerful tool. Muir's descriptions of the wonders of nature were very popular. Unlike many contemporary literary adventures in the wild that depicted human struggle against nature, Muir's descriptions stressed the "essential kindliness" of nature.[17] His writings likely contributed to the increasing number of visitors to places like Yosemite. Although Muir did not relish the presence of these "lowlanders," he knew that their support was necessary to preserve the wild. "If people knew about a special place, they would want to protect it. Muir ... managed, by word and sketch, to let them know."[18] The following paragraphs describing the "winter beauty of the valley" convey the "kindliness" of Yosemite:

> When the first heavy storms stopped work on the high mountains, I made haste down to my Yosemite den, not to "hole up" and sleep the white months away; I was out every day, and often all night, sleeping but little, studying the so-called wonders and common things ever on show, wading, climbing, sauntering among the blessed storms and calms, rejoicing in almost everything alike that I could see or hear: the glorious brightness of frosty mornings; the sunbeams pouring over the white domes and crags into the groves and waterfalls, kindling marvelous iris fires in the hoarfrost and spray; the great forests and mountains in their deep noon sleep; the good-night alpenglow; the stars; the solemn gazing moon, drawing the huge domes and headlands one by one glowing white out of the shadows hushed and breathless like an audience in awful enthusiasm, while the meadows at their feet sparkle with frost-stars like the sky; the sublime darkness of storm-nights, when all the lights are out; the clouds in whose depths the frail snowflowers grow; the behavior and many voices of the different kinds of storms, trees, birds, waterfalls, and snow-avalanches in the ever-changing weather.
>
> Every clear, frosty morning loud sounds are heard booming and reverberating from side to side of the Valley at intervals of a few minutes, beginning soon after sunrise and continuing an hour or two like a thunder-storm. In my first winter in the Valley I could not make out the source of this noise. I thought of falling boulders, rock-blasting, etc. Not till I saw what looked like hoarfrost dropping from the side of the Fall was the problem explained. The strange thunder is made by the fall of sections of ice formed of spray that is frozen on the face of the cliff along the sides of the Upper Yosemite Fall — a sort of crystal plaster, a foot or two thick, cracked off by the sunbeams, awakening all the Valley like cock-crowing, announcing the finest weather, shouting aloud Nature's infinite industry and love of hard work in creating beauty.[19]

In addition, he knew that exposure to the mountains, even for tourists, meant spiritual renewal: "Thousands of tired, nerve-shaken, over-civilized people are beginning to find out that going to the mountains is going home; that wildness is a necessity; and that mountain parks and reservations are useful not only as fountains of timber and irrigating rivers, but as fountains of life."[20] It is important to note that Muir did not refrain from using "practical" arguments in defense of the mountains. He was well aware of nature's utility, but that was clearly not his primary focus.

Between 1881 and 1888 Muir spent no significant amount of time in the wilderness. Upon his return the fact of widespread forest destruction was blatantly obvious. In Yosemite, Muir found the land full of cattle and sheep as well as entrepreneurs catering to the tourists. This led him to write for *Century Magazine* and to enlist the support of its editors to save his beloved wilderness from the likes of the Yosemite Stage and Turnpike Company, the Southern Pacific Railroad, and cattlemen and sheep herders.[21] The struggle eventually led to the founding of the Sierra Club.

At the first meeting of the Sierra Club, in 1892, John Muir was elected president for life. A supper guest in his home is quoted as saying: "I had never seen Mr. Muir so animated and happy before. Hitherto, his back to the wall, he had carried on his fight to save the wilderness. In the Sierra Club he saw the crystallization of the dreams and labor of a lifetime."[22] Within weeks, the club was fighting a bill to reduce the size of Yosemite. Despite the club's contribution to the establishment of Yosemite National Park, in 1895 Muir told the Sierrans: "The battle we have fought and are still fighting for the forests is a part of the eternal conflict between right and wrong, and we cannot expect to see the end of it."[23]

The primary strategy used by Muir in these battles was personal. He invited presidents, their cabinet members, and others to camp with him in Yosemite. In doing so he hoped to persuade them of the spiritual resources to be found there. For example, in 1903 Muir guided President Theodore Roosevelt for four days in the Yosemite wilderness. The result was significant: "One day after leaving Muir and the valley Roosevelt asked Secretary Hitchcock to extend the Sierra reserve northward all the way to Mount Shasta."[24]

In those cases where personal influence was not so successful, Muir and the Sierra Club attempted to use public opinion to wage political battles. The proposal to make Hetch Hetchy into a water reservoir for San Francisco provides an illustration. Muir and the Sierra Club wrote letters to recruit women's clubs and mountaineering groups, and they published articles hoping to sway the public to the defense of the valley. He wrote: "Dam Hetch Hetchy! As well dam for water-tanks the people's cathedrals and churches, for no holier temple has ever been consecrated by the heart of man."[25] Although in this case they failed and the dam was built, the Sierra Club along with other preservation societies continued to press for protective legislation during the next half century.[26]

Although there was concern about national park and wilderness areas prior to the 1960s due to the efforts of the Sierra Club, the National Audubon Society, and others, the publication of Rachel Carson's *Silent Spring* in 1962 launched the modern environmental or ecological movement. Carson's book reached a mass audience, despite attempts to discredit it and her.[27] As Al Gore has noted, "*Silent Spring* planted the seeds of a new activism that has grown into one of the great popular forces of all time."[28] Carson's interest in pollution and its effects stemmed from her firmly held love of nature. In that love is a strand of secular spirituality much like John Muir's.

Born in 1907, Rachel Carson grew up near Pittsburgh. "Carson's childhood was one that fostered a sense of herself and a sense of respect for the natural world."[29] Writing nurtured the former. Her first story was published when she was ten. Her respect for nature grew from the many hours she spent on her own in the woods and orchards in and around her family's property. In college she studied biology; she earned a master's degree in marine zoology. She went to work for the U.S. government and "became only the second woman hired by the U.S. Bureau of Fisheries for a nonsecretarial post." In 1936, she was a junior aquatic biologist. She was promoted three times during the next ten years.[30]

During her time at the bureau, Carson wrote regularly, publishing many articles and two books. These writings give a solid indication of the spirituality that led to the activism contained within *Silent Spring*. She developed an important concept she called "material immortality." Her first description of it came in the final paragraph of her first article, "Undersea":

> Thus we see the parts of the plan fall into place: the water receiving from earth and air the simple materials, storing them up until the gathering energy of the spring sun wakens the sleeping plants to a burst of dynamic activity, hungry swarms of planktonic animals growing and multiplying upon the abundant plants, and themselves falling prey to the shoals of fish; all, in the end, to be redissolved into their component substances when the inexorable laws of the sea demand it. Individual elements are lost to view, only to reappear again and again in different incarnations in a kind of material immortality.... Against this cosmic background the life span of a particular plant or animal appears, not as a

drama complete in itself, but only as a brief interlude in a panorama of endless change.[31]

According to the foreword to the original edition of *Under the Sea-Wind,* the book that she developed from "Undersea," Carson's reason for writing the book follows in the same vein:

> It was written, moreover, out of the deep conviction that the life of the sea is worth knowing. To stand at the edge of the sea, to sense the ebb and the flow of the tides, to feel the breath of a mist moving over a great salt marsh, to watch the flight of shore birds..., to see the running of the old eels and the young shad to the sea, is to have knowledge of things that are as nearly eternal as any earthly life can be. These things were before ever man stood on the shore of the ocean and looked out upon it with wonder; they continue year in, year out, through the centuries and the ages, while man's kingdoms rise and fall.[32]

Near the end of her life, in a letter to her friend Dorothy Freeman, Carson reaffirmed this notion: "Of two things I am certain. One is the kind of 'material immortality' of which I wrote in...'Undersea.'...Barney's comparison of the life-death relationship to rivers flowing into the sea is to me not only beautiful but somehow a source of great comfort and strength."[33]

Carson clearly believed that all material things are interrelated: they emerge from and then dissolve back into an ever-changing whole. Moreover, being aware of that wholeness of nature, of its beauty, is spiritually necessary for human life and development. In the early 1950s, Carson included "a statement of something I believe in very deeply" in a talk she gave. In it she referred to the following lines from Richard Jefferies: "The exceeding beauty of the earth, in her splendor of life, yields a new thought with every petal. The hours when the mind is absorbed by beauty are the only hours when we really live." Those lines, Carson wrote, "are, in a way, a statement of the creed I have lived by."[34] She explains:

> I am not afraid of being thought a sentimentalist when I say that I believe natural beauty has a necessary place in the spiritual development of any individual or any society. I believe that whenever we destroy beauty, or whenever we substitute something man-made and artificial for a natural feature of the earth, we have retarded some part of man's spiritual growth....For there is symbolic as well as actual beauty in the migration of birds; in the ebb and flow of the tides; in the folded bud ready for the spring. There is something infinitely healing in these repeated refrains of nature — the assurance that dawn comes after night, and spring after the winter....I believe that the more clearly we can focus our attention on the wonders and realities of the universe about us, the less taste we shall have for destruction.[35]

That these writings provide the background for locating *Silent Spring* as the outcome of Carson's spiritual commitments is reaffirmed in the book itself. At the end of the book, she writes: "The 'control of nature' is a phrase conceived in arrogance, born of the Neanderthal age of biology and philosophy, when it was supposed that nature exists for the convenience of man. The concepts and practices of applied entomology for the most part date from that Stone Age of science." Moreover: "The chemical barrage has been hurled against the fabric of life — a fabric on the one hand delicate and destructible, on the other miraculously tough and resilient, and capable of striking back in unexpected ways. . . . Practitioners of chemical control . . . have . . . no humility before the vast forces with which they tamper."[36]

Two other factors need explanation before the response the book received, from both its critics and its supporters, becomes clear. First, Carson challenges the prevailing view of science and technology in her day. One of her staunchest critics, Robert White-Stevens, characterized the controversy in this way: "The crux, the fulcrum over which the argument chiefly rests, is that Miss Carson maintains that the balance of nature is a major force in the survival of man, whereas the modern chemist, the modern biologist and scientist, believes that man is steadily controlling nature."[37]

Second, Carson herself knew that she was challenging the dominant economic paradigm of American society. At the conclusion of the first chapter, she notes that "[this] is an era dominated by industry, in which the right to make a dollar at whatever cost is seldom challenged." The intertwining of the scientific and economic ideas is epitomized in White-Stevens, who worked for the American Cyanamid Company, one of the largest manufacturers of the pesticides Carson attacked. Her warnings about the effects of chemicals in the environment directly challenged the assumptions of an industry dependent on scientists for new products and of scientists dependent on industry for research money and facilities.

The connection between Carson's spiritual source in nature and the response sparked by her book is underscored in the comments she made in a letter to Dorothy Freeman shortly after completing the manuscript:

> And suddenly the tension of four years was broken and I let the tears come. I think I let you see last summer what my deeper feelings are about this when I said I could never again listen happily to a thrush song if I had not done all I could. And last night the thoughts of all the birds and other creatures and all the loveliness that is in nature came to me with such a surge of deep happiness, that now I had done what I could — I had been able to complete it — now it had its own life.[38]

Carson wrote *Silent Spring* in order to make a difference. Her sense of the wholeness of nature and of the deleterious effects of unregulated use of chemicals led her to advocate government action and to educate the public. Carson gathered and synthesized evidence of wildlife fatalities due to pollution in both her publications and her correspondence with specialists.[39]

She called on her readers to "pay attention":

> Who has decided — who has the *right* to decide — for the countless legions of people who were not consulted that the supreme value is a world without insects, even though it be also a sterile world ungraced by the curving wing of a bird in flight? The decision is that of the authoritarian temporarily entrusted with power; he has made it during a moment of inattention by millions to whom beauty and the ordered world of nature still have a meaning that is deep and imperative.[40]

The result of Carson's call was dramatic. Despite the concerted efforts of her critics, Carson's position was accepted by many who would take up political arms against the pollution industry and insist that government perform its protective function.

In the wake of *Silent Spring*, the environmental movement broadened beyond its earlier concern to preserve wilderness areas to include all forms of pollution as an equal concern. New groups such as the Environmental Defense Fund were founded. The old strategy of legislation was supplemented by efforts at environmental litigation although the majority of this was to wait for the National Environmental Policy Act of 1969.[41] Another new strategy focused on mobilizing individuals. This culminated in the national "teach-in" known as Earth Day, 22 April 1970. On that day, twenty million people participated in activities aimed at raising awareness of environmental issues; even Congress suspended session so that members could take part.[42]

Mass mobilization was furthered through the education of individuals about the effects of their actions on the environment. Books such as the Sierra Club's *Ecotactics* began to appear. Following an introduction by Ralph Nader, this book includes specific suggestions for actions and stories about individual activists. It also includes calls for new curricula for schools and provides information about taking legal action against polluters. The book's appendices include "The Activist's Checklist," "The Activist's Bookshelf," "Congressional Directory" (listing key federal agencies), as well as a listing of local Sierra Clubs, including the names and addresses of contact persons.[43]

The results of these sorts of activities were phenomenal. Between 1970 and 1985, the major environmental organizations enjoyed monumental growth. The National Audubon Society grew from 120,000 to 450,000; the Sierra Club grew from 113,000 to 350,000; and the Wilderness Society increased from 54,000 to 100,000. The biggest of them all, the National Wildlife Federation, went from 271,000 in 1970 to 825,000 in 1985.[44] By 1991, the membership numbers were even more impressive: National Audubon Society, 600,000; Sierra Club, 650,000; Wilderness Society, 350,000; and National Wildlife Federation, 5,600,000.[45] In addition to these staggering increases, new groups also formed, groups that have come to be known as the radical environmentalists.

These radical groups include Earth First!, The Sea Shepherd Conservation Society, Greenpeace, and the U.S. Greens. Their members continue the same themes evidenced in Muir and Carson; all of them embrace the same brand of secular spirituality. What is added is direct action on behalf of the earth. Rather than relying on legislation, court action, and high-powered negotiation, these groups learned a lesson from the civil rights era: they made their activities visible and public. Dave Foreman and Earth First! provide a good example.

In 1979, Dave Foreman resigned his position with the Wilderness Society in Washington. He had witnessed firsthand the transformation of environmental organizers from grassroots activists to professional administrators. He was tired of the compromises of negotiation. While on a camping trip with four friends, he realized "exactly where the environmental movement had failed."[46] He saw that the opposition to environmental proposals was winning compromise after compromise precisely because "there was nobody out on the environmental edge, demanding it all, nobody pushing the rest of the environmental groups away from their concessions. Nobody who could make the most strident environmentalists look downright reasonable." The five friends agreed that a new organization was needed, "one that would make no compromise in defense of Mother Earth." Its governing principle and the principle that ought to dictate any public policy decisions: "Earth First!"[47]

The new organization's first activity was a protest at the Glen Canyon Dam. The dam was the result of an earlier environmental battle, a battle in which David Brower of the Sierra Club and other environmentalists during the 1950s had won protection for the wilderness up and downstream in exchange for their going along with the building of the dam. It was precisely this sort of compromise that the members of Earth First! were committed to challenging. Foreman and company arrived at the dam on 21 March 1981, ready to demand the dam be removed. Their demonstration involved unfurling a large plastic sheet over the face of the dam that depicted a large crack. After it was cut down, the FBI took the banner as evidence of possible terrorist activity.[48]

In addition to direct action, Earth First! has also pursued other avenues. It has provided "wilderness inventories" and made suggestions for preserving biodiversity. Neither of these violates its refusal to compromise. Still, Earth First! is probably best known for its trademark "monkey-wrenching." Taking cues from Edward Albee's *The Monkeywrench Gang*, members stop environmentally degrading activities by "interfering" with them. They spike trees, "decommission" vehicles, and remove surveyor stakes. According to Foreman, the principles of monkey-wrenching include that actions are nonviolent, not organized, individual, targeted, timely, dispersed, diverse, fun, not revolutionary, simple, deliberate, and ethical.[49] Spiking trees has been the most controversial. It involves driving metal spikes into old-growth trees targeted for clear-cutting. In particular the trees are spiked in order to prevent a sale that would result in clear-cutting. The idea is to take the profit out of cutting the trees. As explained by Foreman: "A monkeywrench thrown into the gears of the machine may not stop it. But it might delay it, make it cost more. And it feels good to put it there."[50]

Foreman's *Confessions of an Eco-Warrior* provides insight into the ideas and the spirituality behind this activism. Like Muir, Foreman is devoted first and foremost to the wilderness. When asked why, Foreman replies: "Because it *is*.... Because it is the real world, the flow of life, the process of evolution, the repository of that 3.5 billion years of shared travel." The preservation of the wilderness, he explains, is "an ethical and moral matter. A religious mandate. Human beings have stepped beyond the bounds; we are destroying the very process of life."[51] Beneath this explanation is the same kind of experience of oneness or unity evident in Muir and in Carson:

> Our passion comes from our connection to the Earth and it is only through direct interaction with the wilderness that we can unite our minds and our bodies with the land, realizing there is no separation.... It is through becoming part of the wild that we find courage far greater than ourselves, a union that gives us boldness to stand against hostile humanism, against the machine, against the dollar, against jail, against extinction for what is sacred and right: the Great Dance of Life.[52]

What Foreman describes coheres with "deep ecology" and the "green perspective." The origins of deep ecology lie in the thought of Norwegian philosopher Arne Naess, who distinguished between "deep" and "shallow" ecology. The objective of the latter type is human health and wealth. There are two key points in deep ecology: ecocentric identification and biocentrism. Both are clearly illustrated in Foreman's position. First, eco-centric identification refers to a feeling of identification or solidarity with nature. Foreman describes a unity with the land, just as Muir experienced unity in the mountains. Naess himself found evidence of such identification in Rachel Carson's writings. The second key point is biocentrism, which, as we have already seen, is the recognition that human beings are part of the web of life and not set apart from it.[53] Like Muir and Carson before him, Foreman clearly challenges an anthropocentric valuation of nature.

Radical environmentalism, deep ecology, and the "green perspective" are interrelated. Jonathon Porritt describes the primary concern of the greens as reminding "people of the inseparable links between ourselves and the planet on which we depend." He contrasts the green perspective with the alienation that characterizes most of modern life. Following Fritz Schumacher, he explains that most Americans are "daily bludgeoned with economic necessities and seduced by the delights of materialism." In direct opposition, greens advocate the need to "rediscover our links with the Earth, and to work in sympathy with rather than against the organic harmonies that make life possible."[54]

Radical environmentalists, deep ecologists, and the greens share common ground. All three are "discouraged by the compromising attitude of mainstream groups, by the bureaucratization of the groups, by the professionalization of leaders and their detachment from the emerging concerns of grassroots supporters, and by the lack of success . . . in countering the . . . anti-environmental agenda."[55] In other words, as a result of their vision of how individuals are related to the world as a whole, they call for a different way of living in that world. Although some of the strategies are different, the spiritual resources they find in nature nourish an activism that harks back to Muir and Carson. Their commitments signal a clear challenge to the dominant social, political, and economic paradigms.

Conclusion

Secular spirituality is not the only spiritual understanding of the world that celebrates nature as something inherently valuable – valuable apart from its ability to yield human health and wealth. For instance, ancient Chinese and Native American spiritual traditions have understandings of the natural world that are quite different from that of Western biblical religions. In the U.S. context, the resources of Native American cultures are increasingly being used to articulate and effectuate lifestyles that are more ecologically sound. The Native American scholar Vine Deloria in his book *God Is Red: A Native View of Religion* gives ample attention to issues regarding the sacredness of natural spaces and the moral responsibility of preserving them. A new generation of Native American scholars is beginning to give more specific development to these central themes. Jace Weaver's *Defending Mother Earth: Native American Perspectives on Environmental Justice* is an excellent example of these new efforts.[56]

It remains true, however, that most Americans gain what knowledge they have of ecological issues through schooling and media that are primarily secular. Even the influences of non-Western religious traditions regarding nature are filtered through a largely secular sensibility. Therefore, the notion of secular spirituality probably provides the major means of insight into the worldviews of the ecological activists. It opens a window into their value systems and commitments that results in their looking and sounding a little less "crazy." As a form of spirituality, ecological activism can now be understood as a meaningful human endeavor despite the fact that it does not fit comfortably into the dominant paradigms. That environmentalists can be seen as meaningful suggests that they may become more and more influential and attractive. Indeed, it may be precisely their alternative way of understanding human beings in the natural world that explains the rapid growth of ecological concern, if not activism, among the public. The more attractive this view becomes, the more serious a challenge it will be to the reigning anthropocentric view of the world.

Notes

1. Throughout this chapter I will use *environmental* and *ecological* as synonyms; the differences between them are not significant for the argument.

2. See, for example, the opinion polls discussed in Riley E. Dunlap, "Trends in Public Opinion toward Environmental Issues: 1965–1990," in *American Environmentalism: The U.S. Environmental Movement, 1970–1990,* ed. Riley E. Dunlap and Angela G. Mertig (Philadelphia: Taylor and Francis, 1992), 106–14.

3. See the introduction to the present volume.

4. Louis Bouyer, *Introduction to Spirituality,* trans. Mary Perkins Ryan (New York: Desclée, 1963), 4.

5. Dominic George, "Secular Spirituality as an Antidote to Religious Fundamentalism," *Journal of Dharma* 15 (April–June 1990): 172–73.

6. Lester W. Milbrath, *Environmentalists: Vanguard for a New Society* (Albany: State University of New York Press, 1984), 8.

7. Ibid., 26–28; Jonathon Porritt, *Seeing Green: The Politics of Ecology Explained* (Cambridge, Mass.: Blackwell, 1984), 106.

8. Lynn White Jr., "The Historical Roots of Our Ecologic Crisis," *Science* 155, 10 March 1967, 1203–7.

9. Frank E. Buske, introduction to *Wilderness Essays: John Muir,* ed. Frank Buske (Salt Lake City: Gibbs-Smith, 1980), viii.

10. Cited in Stephen Fox, *John Muir and His Legacy: The American Conservation Movement* (Boston: Little, Brown and Co., 1981), 43.

11. Ibid., 43–44.

12. John Muir, "Anthropocentrism and Predation," in *Reflecting on Nature: Readings in Environmental Philosophy,* ed. Lori Gruen and Dale Jamieson (New York: Oxford University Press, 1994), 24.

13. Fox, *John Muir and His Legacy,* 53.

14. Robert Gottlieb, *Forcing the Spring: The Transformation of the American Environmental Movement* (Washington, D.C.: Island, 1993), 30.

15. John Muir, *The Mountains of California* (New York: Century, 1894), 64–65; Catherine L. Albanese, *Nature Religion in America: From the Algonkian Indians to the New Age* (Chicago: University of Chicago Press, 1990), 97–99.

16. John Muir, "Twenty Hill Hollow," in *Wilderness Essays,* 88.

17. Fox, *John Muir and His Legacy,* 56.

18. David Brower, foreword to *The Yosemite,* by John Muir (San Francisco: Sierra Club, 1988), xv.

19. Muir, *Yosemite,* 32–33.

20. Quoted in Fox, *John Muir and His Legacy,* 116.

21. Ibid., 86, 103.

22. Quoted in ibid., 107.

23. Quoted in ibid.

24. Ibid., 126–27.

25. Quoted in ibid., 144.

26. Ibid., 139–45.

27. See H. Patricia Hynes, *The Recurring Silent Spring* (New York: Pergamon, 1989), chap. 3.

28. Al Gore, introduction to *Silent Spring,* by Rachel Carson (Boston: Houghton Mifflin, 1994), xviii.

29. Mary A. McCay, *Rachel Carson* (New York: Twayne, 1993), 3.

30. Ibid., 12.

31. Quoted in Paul Brooks, *The House of Life: Rachel Carson at Work* (Boston: Houghton Mifflin, 1972), 29.

32. Quoted in ibid., 32.

33. *Always Rachel: The Letters of Rachel Carson and Dorothy Freeman, 1952–1964,* ed. Martha Freeman (Boston: Beacon, 1995), 446–47. The reference in the quote is to Dr. George ("Barney") Crile Jr., Carson's oncologist and the author of *Cancer and Common Sense* (1955) and some books on breast cancer.

34. Quoted in Brooks, *House of Life,* 325.

35. Quoted in ibid., 325–26.

36. Rachel Carson, *Silent Spring* (Boston: Houghton Mifflin, 1962), 297.

37. Quoted in Gore, introduction, xvii.

38. Quoted in Brooks, *House of Life,* 272.

39. Hynes, *Recurring Silent Spring,* 32.

40. Carson, *Silent Spring,* 126.

41. See Marc Mowrey and Tim Redmond, *Not in Our Backyard: The People and Events That Shaped America's Modern Environmental Movement* (New York: Morrow, 1993), 54–56.
42. Cited in *American Environmentalism,* 2.
43. John G. Mitchell with Constance L. Stallings, eds., *Ecotactics: The Sierra Club Handbook for Environment Activists* (New York: Pocket, 1970).
44. Kirkpatrick Sale, *The Green Revolution: American Environmental Movement 1962–1992* (New York: Hill and Wang, 1993), 23, 33, 53.
45. Ibid., 80.
46. Mowrey and Redmond, *Not in Our Backyard,* 250.
47. Ibid.
48. Ibid., 247–51.
49. Dave Foreman, *Confessions of an Eco-Warrior* (New York: Crown, 1991), 113–16.
50. Ibid., 23.
51. Ibid., 3, 4.
52. Ibid., 6,9.
53. Bill Devall, "Deep Ecology and Radical Environmentalism," in *American Environmentalism,* 52.
54. Porritt, *Seeing Green,* 19, 93, 199.
55. Devall, "Deep Ecology," 55.
56. Vine Deloria Jr., *God Is Red: A Native View of Religion,* 2d ed. (Golden, Colo.: Fulcrum, 1994); and Jace Weaver, *Defending Mother Earth: Native American Perspectives on Environmental Justice* (Maryknoll, N.Y.: Orbis, 1996).

Bibliography

Brooks, Paul. *The House of Life: Rachel Carson at Work.* Boston: Houghton Mifflin, 1972.

Buske, Frank E., ed. *Wilderness Essays: John Muir.* Salt Lake City: Gibbs-Smith, 1980.

Carson, Rachel. *Silent Spring.* Boston: Houghton Mifflin, 1962.

Dunlap, Riley E., and Angela G. Mertig, eds. *American Environmentalism: The U.S. Environmental Movement, 1970–1990.* Philadelphia: Taylor and Francis, 1992.

Foreman, Dave. *Confessions of an Eco-Warrior.* New York: Crown, 1991.

Fox, Stephen. *John Muir and His Legacy: The American Conservation Movement.* Boston: Little, Brown, and Co., 1981.

McCay, Mary A. *Rachel Carson.* New York: Twayne, 1993.

Milbrath, Lester W. *Environmentalists: Vanguard for a New Society.* Albany: State University of New York Press, 1984.

Mowrey, Marc, and Tim Redmond, eds. *Not in Our Backyard: The People and Events That Shaped America's Modern Environmental Movement.* New York: Morrow, 1993.

Muir, John. *The Mountains of California.* New York: Century, 1894.

———. *The Yosemite.* Foreword by David Brower. San Francisco: Sierra Club, 1988.

Naess, Arne. *Ecology, Community and Lifestyle: Outline of an Ecosophy.* Edited and translated by David Rothenberg. Cambridge: Cambridge University Press, 1989.

Porritt, Jonathon. *Seeing Green: The Politics of Ecology Explained.* Cambridge, Mass.: Blackwell, 1984.

Weaver, Jace. *Defending Mother Earth: Native American Perspectives on Environmental Justice.* Maryknoll, N.Y.: Orbis, 1996).

White, Lynn, Jr. "The Historical Roots of Our Ecologic Crisis." *Science* 155, 10 March 1967, 1203–7.

H. Culture

18

Arts

STEPHEN HAPPEL

The Arts as a Matrix of Spiritual Experience

I want to show you how the
clumsiest love
Transfigures if you let it, if you dare.
—James Merrill, "In Nine Sleep Valley"

DAVID FREEDBERG writes: "All we can do is remain alert to the pull of the image."[1] In *The Power of Images,* Freedberg argues that human experience contains a transcultural lure that makes us identify with or smash the images that surround us. Not only was this a fact for confessional and traditional doctrinal images "before the era of art,"[2] but it remains true of secular icons in the present. "Once our eyes are arrested by an image, so the argument more or less runs from Plato onward, we can no longer resist the engagement of emotion and feeling."[3] An object's power to entice us permits idolatry, on the one hand; on the other, its seductive energy beyond our controlling reason sometimes invites violent iconoclasm.

The notion of image used here describes the significant forms that operate as basic units in *all* the arts.[4] Image, then, is an answer to the question: *What* does the artist create? or a response to the question: *How* do artists communicate to an audience what they *mean*? Images involve both formal, structural aspects and dimensions of meaning; they are a dynamic, embodied discourse, at once utterly material and absolutely filled with ideas. Hence they "contain" (sometimes in differentiated, at others in undifferentiated, ways) sensual experiences, interpretive grids through which the world can be known, judgments about the way the world is or ought to be, and an invitation to decisions about how to live. Images accomplish this through a primarily sensual pattern — touch, smell, sight, taste, and hearing — often combined in a synesthetic experience. Such images need not represent objects in the world; they may simply be material units of meaning (stone, paint, sounds) in an artwork.

Part of an artwork's power is that once the artist produces it (whether it be a dance, a melody, a painting, a sculpture, or some other work), it maintains a certain ecstatic independence of both its author and the audience. It is precisely this relative autonomy that bewilders, entices, and repels us. Other dimensions of its power include its evocation of intense feeling, the affect from which attachments and repulsions flow, and/or the crucial ideas they awaken. The artwork becomes the medium of human interaction — and often an invitation or a provocation to build or rebuild societies and cultures.

Images subvert our presumptive ability to author ourselves, to be the norm of our own history, and to order our own lives without the aid of an other. Hence the Enlightenment suspected images, especially religious artworks, as manipulative priestcraft, and the eighteenth-century philosophes extended the Reformation's rejection of figural representations. The postmodern context, however, has recognized that images, stories, and symbols not only cannot be excised but continue to influence thoughts and actions. We cannot narrate our lives without referring to the images of others — whether the community of others whose lives we share or the unconscious other within our own subjectivity. Images accomplish this by inviting us into alternative worlds and by liberating us from the exigencies of convention. The wonder images evoke makes them an appropriate vehicle for the difference that counts as a spiritual encounter with an ultimate other.

The artistic world of postmodernism ranges from the most figural, hyperreal creations through highly abstract conceptual art to installations of the ready-made and the found object. Self-expressive performance artists jostle against stylized historical dramas by Shakespeare and Racine. Generalizing about such a radical pluralism requires a philosophical attitude; maintaining that some of these postmodern artifacts embody or evoke a spiritual dimension transgresses the boundaries of philosophy and religious studies. It would be difficult for anyone to maintain that even the most secular images have had no traditionally religious historical origins or analogues. The theosophical influence alone on the emergence of modern abstract art during the last one hundred years has been profound.[5] However, the explicitly secular dimension of most postmodern artworks makes any generalized claims highly suspect. The complexities of maintaining that the arts could generate a spiritual experience require analyses of specific artworks and their contexts.

In what follows, I shall offer a controversial figural work (Frederick Hart's *Three Soldiers*) as an example of postmodern spiritual expression. The political arguments about the sculpture and its placement in a public space make its secularity clear. Moreover, the fact that the sculpture remembers a *war*, and a highly polarizing conflict, is even more useful for this discussion. The goal of the discussion will be to determine what kind of spiritual realm the grouping could evoke and how that evocation might occur. To situate Hart's work (and any such representational artwork), however, requires that the sculpture be mapped on a contemporary geography of aesthetics and be related to the production of twentieth-century arts. As Arthur Danto has pointed out, we do not have a common narrative of the present; every claim for the truth, let alone the spirituality of the secular, demands a statement of context.[6] In an art world in which pluralism reigns, why or how could a representational work appear as spiritual? Would it not be politically reactionary and/or religiously nostalgic?

The first portion of the essay will discuss the modernist story about the musical, literary, and dramatic arts that has fueled European and American creativity since the end of the nineteenth century.[7] The second will map the current narratives about the relationship of the visual arts, spirituality, modernism, and postmodernism to locate the meaning of Hart's artwork. The final section will examine the power of Hart's image and its role in reshaping the politics and ethics of secular spiritual discourse.

Abstraction as a Spiritual Event: The Traditional Narrative

Modernism, which emerged at the end of the nineteenth century, rejected the rationalist and romanticist resolutions of institutional religious problems.[8] However, literature, painting, dance, architecture, and sculpture, at various stages and in different ways, developed an artistic vocabulary that, first, strove for a secular spiritual embodiment, and, second, substituted for institutionalized religions within Western public discourse.[9] In this way, the arts aimed for an expression of the whole predicated upon a cosmic connection between humanity or nature and the universe; they expressed the intense personal authenticity of the artists and their strategic ability to contact the formal essence of things through their genial consciousness. Modernity and its spirituality extended the program of the romantic hero/ine who could discover the truth only by entering a sensually enhanced, intellectually challenging world. The artists of the last one hundred years often identified their meanings by manipulating, rejecting, and ignoring explicitly confessional religions; but at the same time, they evoked the spiritual dimensions of humanness by recovering that archaic Other, the Silence from which images emerge. It is little wonder, therefore, that the institutionalized religions often rejected the contemporary arts and even explicitly loathed them as competitors. In this section, I will provide a context for some artists whose work gives evidence of these themes in the development of modernity.

The Musical Modern

The story told about "high" musical evolution has patterned itself on the development of the visual arts, although in many ways its innovations preceded modernism in painting and sculpture. As it was often told, the narrative began with the nineteenth-century romantics like Ludwig van Beethoven (1770–1827), Franz Peter Schubert (1797–1828), and Robert Schumann (1810–56), with their highly resonant melodies; the middle of the story struggled with the complications between Johannes Brahms (1833–97), Richard Wagner (1813–83), and Gustav Mahler (1860–1911) at the end of the century over classical romanticism and music as dramatic content; it ended with the abstract "new music" of Arnold Schoenberg (1874–1951), Igor Stravinsky (1882–1971), Alban Berg (1885–1935), and Anton Webern (1883–1945). This evolution in Germany paralleled movements in France with the musical impressionism of Claude Debussy (1862–1918) and the surrealism of Erik Satie (1866–1925), although until Pierre Boulez (especially *Le Marteau sans maître*, 1954; rev. 1957), the French movement toward musical abstraction was (in some important ways) less obvious. In the United States, the emphasis upon new sounds and a-thematic nonharmonies began with Charles Ives (1874–1954), who in isolation developed some of the most important elements of twentieth-century music, such as dissonance, polytonality, polyrhythm, and experimental form. At the end of the story is the highly abstract work of John Cage (1912–92). He used musical tones and sounds from life that were "prepared," distorted, and reshaped into different patterns, often using electronic resources. Study of Asian philosophy led him to chance and silence as principles of musical meanings.

The spiritual meaning in this story of developing musical modernism, sometimes argued explicitly by the participants, involved a more and more refined sense of hearing, a distance from the material, a pure tonal form, and an authentic sound. Twentieth-century atonality or serialism refused the academic niceties of the last century's music to embrace the cacophony, complexity, and diversity of this century. Figures like Paul

Hindemith (1895–1963) and Olivier Messiaen (1908–92) explicitly appealed to sound as symbolic of a spiritual sense, a link to the cosmic tones of the universal harmonies. In his unfinished three-act opera *Moses und Aaron* (1931–32), Schoenberg embodied in the work itself the conflict between sensual image and abstract concept, lush sounds and silence as expressions of the spiritual conflict of the twentieth century. How does humanity see and speak the presence of a spiritual reality that appears radically invisible and silent?

Some recent music has reacted against the austerity of modernism by expanding the overtones in electronic sounds. The Windham Hill label, originally designed to make available the free-form piano work of George Winston, has provided expansive neoromantic sounds for meditation. The recovery of medieval plainsong (sometimes called "Gregorian chant") in itself or in the pop music of the group Dead Don't Dance or in the symphonic poems of Arvo Part returns to the modal music of the premodern period that had been earlier exploited by the Beatles in the 1960s and 1970s. The drift away from the chromatic scales of twelve equidistant semitones in the space of an octave (used almost exclusively since the eighteenth century) has allowed the inclusion of non-Western motifs into Western music and a certain indeterminacy of vocal and sound patterns in figures like Peter Maxwell-Davies, Karlheinz Stockhausen, Philip Glass, and Krzysztof Penderecki.

The complex development of modern music has bifurcated between popular and high culture as in all the other arts during the industrial period of Western development. High art has told itself as a story of the progressive modernity of the avant-garde, a shift toward ever-greater, self-absorbed abstraction, accomplished by the pure integrity of the isolated genius.[10] Musicians reacted against the academic kitsch of the nineteenth century; they broke open new ground for original musical edifices, while leaving behind the popular (and supposedly lower-class) music around them.[11]

Postmodern musicology questions these suppositions about the noncontextual nature of modernist music. With Cage or even Messiaen, the distinction between what is noise, melody, dissonance, bird songs, traffic or instrumental music is no longer so clear. The modernist quest for the essence of music has collapsed in upon itself, making it difficult to discern text and context, music from nonmusic. The return to melody, whether synthesized by machines or expressed by individuals like Winston, asks whether it is possible to overcome the modernist musical story and portray another kind of artistic endeavor. Can the melodic line survive modernist abstraction, dissonance, and silence?

Literary Modernism

Nineteenth-century literature was dominated by the lengthy realist novels of Walter Scott (1771–1832), William Makepeace Thackeray (1811–63), Charles Dickens (1812–70), George Eliot (Mary Ann Evans, 1819–80), and Fyodor Dostoyevsky (1821–81). The explicitly spiritual dimension of those works focused upon a growing doubt in Victorian life about the effectiveness of institutional religion and the stresses wrought by a burgeoning industrial economy upon traditional agricultural class distinctions and local community values. The lengthy form of these novels was itself important: they required academic and bourgeois leisure to read them.

Mario Praz has argued for the emerging "democratization of the heroic" in these novels. In Dickens, he saw the "exaltation of the domestic hearth," in which the Victorian novel became a drama for the masses. Just as Biedermeier painting transformed grand historical themes on canvases into genre painting, into the picturesque, so novels turned their characters into the psychological portraits of middle-class readers. The characters of Anthony Trollope (1815–82) did not take readers outside their ordinary lives. "Every individual can be his hero, his own Messiah."[12] Georg Lukács made a similar argument for the realist historical novel, such as Scott's *Ivanhoe:*

> The hero of the Scott novel is always a more or less mediocre, average English gentleman. He generally possesses a certain, though never outstanding, degree of practical intelligence, a certain moral fortitude and decency which even rises to a capacity for self-sacrifice, but which never grows into a sweeping human passion, is never the enraptured devotion to a great cause.[13]

By focusing upon the characters' particular interactions with the times, Scott provided his readers with believable figures with whom they could identify and whose successes supported their own. This was a "historical faithfulness" through which readers saw their own inner motives and behavior.[14]

Modernism in literature aimed to overturn this supposed bourgeois realism by appealing explicitly to transcultural symbolism in lyric poetry and by rewriting the form of the novel. William Wordsworth (1770–1850) and Samuel Taylor Coleridge (1772–1834) attempted to bridge the linguistic gap between the narrative ballads of popular culture and the lyric language of high art. Later nineteenth-century poets, such as Robert Browning (1812–89) and Alfred Tennyson (1809–92), expressed the complex attitudes of the new middle class toward wealth and religious faith.

The symbolists at the end of the century rejected any wedding of middle-class language and art. Stéphane Mallarmé (1842–98), Arthur Rimbaud (1854–91), and Paul Verlaine (1844–96) focused their poetry upon its musical sound and its emotionally evocative impressions. The highly idiosyncratic language often made the supposedly cross-cultural images obscure; but the bohemian style of life these men espoused became a spiritual icon for the struggling artist. Resistance to middle-class pieties and personal suffering marked authentic artists. As Rimbaud stated: "The same bourgeois magic wherever the mailtrain sets you down. Even the most elementary physicist feels that it is no longer possible to submit to this personal atmosphere, fog of physical remorse, which to acknowledge is already an affliction."[15]

By the end of the twentieth century, Allen Ginsberg (1926–) and James Merrill (1926–95) had developed a mystical sense of the poetic subject that had some ancestry in traditional religious imagery, but more often extended a spiritual sense of the self based upon Enlightenment autonomy. Ginsberg's self-proclaimed vision of William Blake in 1948 in East Harlem saw the sky as the blue hand of God and the old tenements as a disclosure of divine creativity. Ginsberg believed that he had become a seraphic prophet to announce profound truths to the world. Although he has reinterpreted his vision over the years, his commitment to overturning injustice and his loudly registered laments for the outrages perpetrated by oppressive governments have continued with a biblical ferocity.[16] Merrill's extensive trilogy, *The Changing Light at Sandover* (1976–83), recorded his experiences communicating with another world through a Ouija board. In the poems, the narrator and his companion, David Jackson, make a pilgrimage into a new cosmic dimension, while gathering their personal and political friends into communion. Merrill stated:

> Earlier we'd been admiring an inch-high
> Prism set in noon light on the sill.
> Outflung, slowshifting gouts of color stain
> Ceiling, walls, us. DJ: It's really how
> His lessons flow through us. JM: And will
> Forever be deflected by the grain
> Of imperfection in that quartz capstone,
> The human mind — Aknaton's or our own.[17]

Consciousness for Merrill was a multilayered event that reached into the ancient past as well as toward all prospective futures of humanity.

The novel underwent a similar transformation during the modernist period. The grand realism of the nineteenth century ceded to novels of inwardness, such as those of Virginia Woolf (1882–1941) and James Joyce (1882–1941). Focused upon the inner consciousness of sometimes undetermined narrators, such writing destroyed the omniscient authors of stories in realist novels. Joyce's *Finnegan's Wake* (1939) played with English vocabulary as well as novelistic form, making the whimsical lyricism of the language as important as the dreamlike unconscious recorded in the text. Later authors, such as Alain Robbe-Grillet (1922–) or Jorge Luis Borges (1899–1986), have reimagined narrative structures completely, making it difficult for readers to discern what has occurred or will happen in a plot, who is speaking, and what is "real" and what is "fictive." The language of allusive metaphor guides the text rather than characters, plots, or sharply defined events.

The modernist struggle to find the essence of language, to reveal the underlying transcultural structures of consciousness, and, consequently, to reject the social justifications of bourgeois life in storytelling has deeply affected the spiritual quest of postmodern literature. By emphasizing the autonomous, even isolated or solipsistic, subject, modernist authors focused upon rational or emotional consciousness as a medium for entry into deeper realities. The *mysterium tremendum* that was disclosed here appeared at once frightening and seductive; it could both startle by its demonic expressions and release readers into a rapturous transcendence.

The modernist story in literature, as it began, searched for the features of writing that are sonically, symbolically, and formally universal. As it ended, it became difficult to discern the differences between life anecdotes, fragments of emotional expression, and luminous moments of insight from life as lived. Text and context became coimplicated in such a way that expression in art and expression in life could often not be distinguished. Is it fiction or history, a diary or a fictive autobiography? In the postmodern context, one of the questions that emerges is whether it is possible to tell stories that do not always or inherently oppress individuals or communities, or, more hopefully, that can genuinely and benignly, however incrementally, transform people.

The Modern Drama

Nineteenth-century drama, in its performance as well as in its construction, mirrored the growing naturalist realism of the novel. It was not simply empty spectacle and melodrama. Acting assumed a psychological realism as the century progressed, eventually emerging in the United States in the twentieth-century "naturalist realism" of the acting methods of Konstantin Stanislavski (1863–1938). Characters became less types of moral virtue or vice and more believable, ambiguous, rounded figures.[18] It is possible to watch this same evolution from exaggerated moral types to "natural" realism in a compressed fashion in the way actors have worked in films during the past seventy-five years. No longer about grand historical (usually aristocratic) figures, the "problem plays" of Arthur Pinero (1855–1934) and Henrik Ibsen (1828–1906) focused issues of social reform through individual and familial crises. However, by the end of World War I, these playwrights themselves had become antiquated to the modern mind.

The explicitly modernist story of theater in England begins with George Bernard Shaw (1856–1950). His strident rejection of past British dramatists, his claim to have set a conscientious standard for future plays, and his commitment to theater as an agent of social change mark the modernist era. "The theatre is not there to amuse people. Its object should be to make them think."[19] In Germany, staging by Bertold Brecht (1898–1956) rejected narrative unities and envisioned drama as a series of loosely connected scenes.[20] His highly stylized acting refused to create an illusion of reality, alienating the audience from any easy identification with characters or plot. He exposed the mechanics of performance by using clinically bright and nonatmospheric lighting on bare stages. The objective was satiric criticism of the reigning political regimes.

Aggressive alienation and gritty naturalism — two contrary impulses of modernist theater — have continued throughout the century. Each in its own way rejected nineteenth-century melodrama and searched for a purity of form focused upon essential human traits. Both used drama as a medium of social critique, exposed dystopian societies, and proposed models for personal and societal transformation.

Eugene Ionesco (1912–94) and the theater of the absurd emphasized the unfollowability of ordinary dialogue; and *Waiting for Godot*, by Samuel Beckett (1906–95), stressed the incommensurability of human communication and quickly undercut any teleological pretensions to unity of plot, character, or tone. Luigi Pirandello (1867–1936) deliberately disoriented his audiences by mixing history and fiction, past and present, madness and sanity. What appeared to be true was as significant for him as what seemed factually evident. The self was no longer coincident with its own history or psychology. As one of his characters states in *Henry IV:* "Has it never happened to you, my Lady, to find a different self in yourself? Have you always been the same?"[21]

At once satire about the "normal" world, philosophical critique of ordinary rhetorical clichés, and social tracts against the economic and political status quo, these plays reflected the deeply disturbing work of Antonin Artaud (1896–1948). Artaud destabilized dramatic genres just as surely as did the musicians, novelists, poets, and painters who transformed their subject matter. For these modernists, "art becomes a statement of self-awareness—an awareness that presupposes a disharmony between the self of the artist and the community."[22] This alienation of the artist from the self and from the community at once made artists into victims and at the same time called them to violate the distance between the reader and the artwork. For Artaud, all the arts were dramatic action, and to be authentic, they must prove brutal. Artaud wanted actors to train viscerally and physically as though they were dancers or athletes. He hoped for a pure theater, determined by the "physics of the absolute gesture, which is itself idea."[23] Dispensing with a previously written script, the actor must become the author, like a surgeon operating upon a patient. Such explicit cruelty, without an anesthetic, was meant to excise cultural nightmares from the body politic.

At the end of the modernist story, Peter Brook, Jerzy Grotowski, Judith Malina, Herbert Blau, and their followers have learned from Artaud a new mode of theater that blends the differences between audience and actors, between life and art. Deeply interdisciplinary in practice, improvisation, and methods, each has chosen to reassert the intimate relationship between theater-work and life-work. Artaud himself had been influenced by a trip to Bali; Brook has explored improvisatory acting techniques in Africa; Grotowski sought Indian yoga and Kathakali as guides for his actors. Each transgressed the traditional boundaries between actor and agent in the "real" world, between the play and the audience's "real" life, between theatrical conventions, training, and ritual performances. Grotowski's "poor theater" lasted about ten years (1959–69), probably because the heightened consciousness required of actors (and audiences) could not be sustained except through his rigorous system of training. Brook's International Center for Theater Research is directed from Paris, but it includes performers from Asia, Africa, Europe, and the Americas. Its field trips travel to these continents, exchanging dramatic techniques and research materials. The objective is not only to re-create a dialogue between culturally similar artifacts but to reinsert dramatic events within the rituals of life from which they emerged.

These dramatic tendencies promote an examination of Western theater's inner connections with daily rituals, religious sacraments, and mythic retellings in dance and choreographic folk movements. For Brook and others, the quest for the essential structures, for the underlying foundations of human expression, originates within the human body: "Our work is based on the fact that some of the deepest aspects of human experience can reveal themselves through sounds and movement of the human body in a way that strikes an identical chord in any observer, whatever his cultural conditioning."[24] Each of these movements is guided by an individual whose work appears highly original in often striking contrast to the conventions of traditional theater.

The spiritual themes of this modernist movement in theater are similar to those in music, literature, and the visual arts. They emphasize the growth of the individual within community, an existential holism in union with the forces of the cosmos, and the political and personal transformation of the actors and audiences. By focusing upon the formal integrity of the work, modernist artists believe they offer an embodied cipher that discloses the microcosm of the inner self and the macrocosm of the universe. Disciplined artistic practice, akin to ritual preparation, leads beyond the self into an uncontrollable other, often encountered in an ecstatic, even trancelike, state.

The modernist story of artistic production, performance, and artifacts in music, literature, and drama has dominated Western theory about art until relatively recently. In each case, the values espoused center upon the genial individual whose originality has rejected the bourgeois conventions of an artwork separated from life. In the case of contemporary theater, the self-expression of performance artists, such as Tim Miller or the Living Theater, deliberately subverts any distinction between the personal life of the actors, the text being performed, and the audience's individual or group identity. Modernist art looks for the essence of things — across cultures, within a collective unconscious, and between different individuals. However, once it becomes difficult to see the difference between "art" and "life," then the philosophical issue of "What counts as art?" appears. Can one differentiate the unique contribution that art makes to life? Can one return to the straightforward telling of stories, conventional drama, or melodic harmonies without falling into oversimplified and culpable support of a social status quo? Are there values intrinsic to premodern and modern art that can survive in a postmodern environment? In what follows, the visual arts will be the exploratory vehicle for responding to these questions.

Art and Modernity: The Search for Full and Immediate Presence?

The Catholic theologian Karl Rahner argued that the most spiritual artwork in the late twentieth century occurred outside organized religion. He wrote about the "anonymous reverence" of an impressionist painting and recognized that much institutionalized religious art was kitsch.[25] Genuine religious art awakens the depths of experience, the place where the limits constantly invite to a transgression of the boundaries. As a result, what is genuinely spiritual in the contemporary arts might be no longer intelligible to people raised in traditional pieties. A painting by Rembrandt, for example, without thematic "religious" content could evoke a more radical spiritual response than an explicitly biblical theme. For Rahner, "Our endless questioning becomes the one place where the question itself becomes the answer," and surrendering to such a mystery, especially in the arts, is a path toward what is at once most human and most transcendent.[26] True holiness may reside in one who has simply developed all the dimensions of human existence in as open-ended a fashion as possible.

What Rahner notes as the end of *religious art*, the philosopher Arthur Danto has called in 1984 (and again in his 1995 Mellon Lectures) the end of *art itself*.[27] In reflecting upon *Brillo Box* (1964), a work by Andy Warhol (1928–87), Danto argued that the painterly project that began with the emergence of modern art at the end of the nineteenth century has ended. What has come to an end, of course, is not the making of artworks, but a particular narrative that Western art has been telling its culture. With Warhol's work, one cannot tell the difference between art and life simply by looking at it, since now there is no particular way art *must* look.

Finally the object of art could no longer be distinguished materially from the commercial product that it imitated. The Canadian customs office insisted that Warhol's work, destined for a museum exhibition, required a business tax upon entry into the country since it was clearly not a work of art. James Harvey, the commercial artist who designed the industrial graphics for the Brillo product, would have distinguished sharply between art and advertising. By collapsing high and low art, by transgressing the limits, Warhol had transformed *means* (industrial artifacts) into *meanings* (artwork). High art and the commonplace had been reunited by the avant-garde, deliberately undermining itself. The reflective attitude of the philosopher must be included in art criticism, since the intellectual, affective, and contextual *meanings* of a work, as well as its *formal structures and materials*, now define what makes an object or action art.

The reconnection of formal art with other aspects of life meant the end of the modernist aesthetic, which presumed that art and the genial artist were entities separated and alienated from their other contexts of meaning. In the modernist story of art, the fundamental function of the artwork was to be found in its own formalized appreciation by admiring audiences in museums. Artists like Paul Gauguin (1848–1903) and Vincent van Gogh (1853–90) began this process, according to Danto, in the 1880s when Japanese prints no longer became curiosities but something for western European artists to emulate. This aesthetic narrative rejected the representational academicism of the nineteenth century (such as that of Adolphe William Bouguereau [1825–1905] or Lawrence Alma-Tadema [1836–1912]), espoused an ahistorical formalism supported philosophically by Kant's *Critique of Judgment,* and sought material purity and clarity. Artists believed that they participated in a narrative of progress that advanced by a continual revolutionizing in the ways of painting. They were Shelley's "unacknowledged legislators of the world." Where the Renaissance was a story about the recovery of antiquity and the Enlightenment a narrative about the coming of age of the West, modernist aesthetics and its consequent artifacts rejected the past and constantly strove for the new. But with the emergence of pop art, that narrative ceased. It is impossible to "see" what the difference is between the new art and the reproduced, fabricated commonplace.

The differences between art and life, therefore, cannot be perceptual; the discrimination requires philosophical reflection. Indeed, with the end of modernism, artists can give up the pretense to a philosophical articulation in paint and simply be painters or sculptors in a pluralistic world. Danto maintains that philosophy now explicates the artful meanings that emerge; however, it does not dictate them. This ending to the modernist aesthetic also means that nothing can any longer be excluded from the realm of art; pluralism of expression is the "norm." Not only can individual artists rifle the styles of the centuries and cultures; but at any given moment in time, a jumble of artistic modes is available. Art need no longer have a reigning manifesto. An African can paint French impressionism; a German artist can draw Chinese calligraphy; any given artist can shift styles from year to year. To pursue a consistently progressive history in contemporary artistic style is the hobgoblin of small minds. There are only the margins or a polyfocal sensibility — no longer a central, governing paradigmatic narrative for art to follow.

Mark C. Taylor has scored this narrative melody decisively. For Taylor the project of modernity itself was a *religious* aesthetics that reached back to the Renaissance. Danto notes, for example, that the historical development of the Napoleonic museum for the masses supplanted prerevolutionary religious devotions. The hush of museums replaced the silence of churches. Taylor argues that the artistic projects of modernity, which began with the Renaissance, had as their underlying theme a thirst for the reified Total Presence, a dream of envisioned immediacy.[28] Modernity is institutional religion in disguise. Danto maintains that it was an irresistible thought that art should reveal "a higher reality to which we would become greater and more spiritual in consequence of adapting to it."[29] Taylor has proposed to unmask the carnival.

Without doubt this underlying religious narrative is operative in the influence of theosophy upon early modernist painters.[30] The turn to a variety of antimaterialist philosophies was evident; an emphasis upon the mystical and occult gave artists direct access to the source — away from organized religions. Piet Mondrian (1872–1944) joined Amsterdam's Theosophical Society in 1909. In the modernist manifesto *On the Spiritual in Art* (1912), Wassily Kandinsky (1866–1944) praised the paths of inner consciousness to be found in the theosophy of Rudolf Steiner (1861–1925). Meditation and spiritual training were ways of learning how to paint, while rejecting the positivist impulse of the age. As Kandinsky said: the artist "must learn to produce images, even where there is no object to arouse [the] senses."[31]

Theosophy was a widespread spiritual movement at the end of the nineteenth century. Helena Blavatsky (1831–91), who founded the Theosophical Society in 1875, included an eclectic mixture of ancient Neoplatonist ideas, Western mysticism, Jewish cabala, and Buddhism in her spiritual proposals. Her successor, Annie Besant (1847–1933), shifted the society even more toward the East. Astral auras of rainbow hues enveloped the initiate who could "see." The spiritual was formless — a new realm of color and shape unlike the world in which humans now live — yet it could be awakened in consciousness by careful rituals, heightened modes of awareness, and spiritual techniques.

Whereas Kandinsky seems to have believed that the inner vision of color could be reproduced on canvas and that abstraction could be dematerialization, Mondrian believed that art grew slowly toward the spiritual, even when artists themselves were unaware of it. Should the artist reach a stage in which he or she had conscious, direct interaction with the spiritual, then one would have attained the ideal art.[32] Dualism and monism share a common principle within the whole that will be revealed only in the end of things. Mondrian saw theosophy as a doctrine of evolution in which change is the primary operator. The exterior and the interior, male and female, spirit and matter will be overcome. And when this recovery of primal union occurs, there will no longer be any need for art, since all human activity will be artful. Adherents to this utopian modernism believed that the day would come when "the individual will be capable of governing himself. The new art demonstrates all this."[33]

Kasimir Malevich (1878–1935) decided in 1915 to abandon the depiction of objects and representational forms. His work explored geometry, color, and open-ended space. In Petrograd, he displayed *Black Square*, a black square on a white border. As Malevich wrote: "The black square on the white field was the first form in which non-objective feeling came to be expressed. The square = feeling, the white field = the void beyond this feeling."[34] By focusing upon the subject, one could go beyond reason and elevate oneself into a deity, "saying that I am all and that besides me there is nothing and all that I see, I see myself, so multi-faceted and polyhedral is my being.... I search for God, I search within myself for myself." Malevich wanted to produce in his artwork an "empty place where nothing is perceived but sensation."[35]

The explicit modernist emphases of Kandinsky, Mondrian, and Malevich, among others, were inherently theological according to Taylor; but their discoveries in painting were preceded by the romantic unification of the natural landscape and religious sensibility. *Monk by the Sea,* by Caspar David Friedrich (1774–1840), is Taylor's fundamental example, but there are many others. Friedrich hoped to revitalize religious affections by divinizing landscape.[36]

The romantic affinity for religion was supported philosophically by Kant's *Critique of Judgment.* The philosopher attributed to nature the kind of inner teleology that one can ascribe to the work of beauty, but in nature the dynamic sublime exceeded every form and escaped any ability to formulate concepts to analyze it. Kant used the examples of bold, overhanging rocks; clouds piled high in the sky; lightning and thunder flashes; volcanoes and hurricanes; the boundless ocean and lofty waterfalls. The sublime has *might* but no superior dominion over us, thus exciting fear. Fear means that we can form no conceptual judgments about the sublime in nature. When our uneasiness is overcome, then there emerges a state of joy. Threatening landscapes, if witnessed from a position of security, "raise the energies of the soul above their accustomed height and discover in us a faculty of resistance... which gives us courage to measure ourselves against the apparent almightiness of nature."[37]

Basing the status of artwork on these principles, romantic painters like Friedrich combined landscape and religious sensibility into a therapy that was meant to cure the fragmentation of the times, overturning the ills of industry and applied science. Healing nature could overturn the ugliness of the emerging urban, industrial environment. The goal of painting was to re-present the immediacy of divine creativity in nature — a complete presence of God.

For Taylor, the artistic iconoclasm at the beginning of this century was simply the dialectical reverse of the pursuit of total immediate presence. The shift toward abstraction, while rejecting the artistic language of academicism and romantic nostalgia, nonetheless marked a thirst for an autotelic, self-referential presence in the artwork. Now the goal of Mondrian's gridlike paintings in primary colors, Malevich's monochrome squares, and Kandinsky's cosmic swirls of color was to achieve the sublime — but by negation. As Ad Reinhardt (1913–67) stated about his entirely black paintings: the *telos* of the mystical quest is perfect oneness with the "divine dark." The religious mystification of nature had been replaced by a mystification of culture. Instead of getting lost in the landscape, one was enraptured in meditation before fields of color painted by Mark Rothko (1903–70).

Abstract expressionists after World War II, like Barnett Newman (1905–71) and Jackson Pollack (1912–56), painted canvases that exceeded the usual easel space, making them almost certainly destined for galleries and museums. The deliberate excess without clear figural content translated Kant's dynamic sublime from nature to cultural objects. Pollack's drip paintings became ritual studies, layered with their own internal patterns determined "only" by the conscious and unconscious will of the artist. Newman's zip paintings, with their biblical names (*Lema Sabachtani*, *Adam*), stripped away any superfluous ornament so that viewers were confronted by what they could neither control nor conceptualize. In that sense, form and content were united in a pure abstract negation.

Taylor's narrative aesthetics, however, concludes with a further sublation in a postmodern art that "disfigures" neither by absolutizing figures nor by erasing them. This nondialectical third element articulates the ineffable, an other with which reconciliation is impossible. Hence, Taylor continues the story as though it has a goal or teleology beyond Danto's *end of art* and the consequent pluralism. Sensing a force that has "no reference to human beings," Anselm Kiefer paints artwork in which the negativity neither of figure nor of ground can be posited. Michael Pistoletto's broken mirrors and multiple frames fracture the totalizing image and articulate the fault in experience. Negativity and irony are here not indirect means of affirmation but an endless, "impossible mourning" for an unreconcilable other. Taylor hopes to recover the spiritual dimensions of postmodern art, but within the "progress" beyond modernist stories of art and religion.

Taylor's narrative about postmodern art and theology is also a political narrative. It involves an "ethics of resistance," a refusal in which irreconcilable differences are repeatedly negotiated. The modernism of the romantics with their figural representations, the iconoclastic abstractions of the moderns, and postmodern reuse of figures are irretrievably utopian, with the alternate underside of a dominating uniformity. Both the fascist enthusiasm for *Volkskunst* in genre paintings of hearth and home and the totalitarian interest in function-defined architecture lead to the crematoria of the Third Reich, the complete exclusion of otherness in social life. Only an art and an a/theology that insist upon the impossibility of reconciliation, the persistent hiddenness of the Other's difference, can permit a genuine spiritual stage in human experience. "Though never present, the unrepresentable is unavoidable. It is the unsaid in all our saying that undoes all we do."[38] There is no synthesis, only the dynamism between polarities. Such art rejects both the domestic genres that comfort the middle class as well as the abstractions of the modern avant-gardes that dialectically replaced them. The Other cannot be located within form; any presence is always already absent. What is available in Kiefer is a dialectic of form and disruption, an incompleteness.

Sketching these stories about art and religion raises serious questions about some forms of postmodern art. If the narrative of Taylor is to be believed, figures or representations can appear in current artworks only as something to be rejected or as something to be integrated as fractured and ironic. The same would need to be said about musical melody, narrative drama and novels, decorative and iconic architecture, or lyric poetry; each would be a return to comfortable and oppressive bourgeois values. To figure is to bathe in nostalgia, to request the past to be totally present. Such work can only be kitsch for Taylor; and by its very nature, artwork that echoes past traditions without dissonance will be idolatrous, never dangerous or challenging, or rather dangerous *because* it will support the comfort of the political, institutionalized status quo. For Taylor, such work refuses to face the hiddenness of transcendence. Rahner would have seen such art as avoiding the ever-receding horizon of mystery. The fragments of German culture in Kiefer's monumental vacant rooms speak the terrifying Silence for Taylor, precisely because they dis-figure the embodiment.

Taylor's attempts to differentiate the unattainable, uncontrollable and hidden Other beyond the neoorthodoxy of Karl Barth are laudable and subtle. One of his goals is to recover in the contemporary context what religious believers have maintained is the Other's ability to originate world-shattering as well as (perhaps) world-comforting discourse. For him, this can only be accomplished in a contemporary art that constantly exceeds the limits and refuses to name, and therefore reify, the ground from which figures emerge.

But is it possible to articulate a nonnostalgic notion of figure as spiritual? Can postmodern arts that revive traditional, even beaux-arts, particularities of nineteenth-century form speak (be)for(e) the Silence in their own way? Here I will argue that Frederick Hart's *Three Soldiers*, a sculpture at the Vietnam Veterans Memorial (VVM), can stand for all the

Figure 1
Three Soldiers (1984). Artist: Frederick Hart
Bronze Sculpture at Vietnam Veterans Memorial, Washington, D.C.
Photo © Sculpture Group Ltd., Wheeling, Ill.

postmodern arts that risk a specifically shaped hope for the future of the planet. This hope need be neither nostalgic nor dominating; hope need not be fantastic and utopian. An artwork can articulate the conditions of the emergence of its acceptance as true or good. The archaic Other that precedes and succeeds all form may yet be available as Other within figured artwork. If this might be so, it will help answer a question Taylor asks: "The question that remains is whether this is the space of resurrection or of crucifixion."[39] In what follows, I will use Hart's sculpture *Three Soldiers* to question whether a public work of art can evoke the sense of the spiritual in a nonconfessional manner – an invitation that is both seductive and fearful. This will also provoke questions about the story of art and religion that Danto and Taylor have told.

Three Soldiers and the Vietnam Veterans' Memorial

The Setting and the Wall

Significant public art almost always creates controversy. Art about the Vietnam War stirs the passions.[40] Which public would be in control of the memory of the war? The veterans looked for vindication; politicians hoped to allay local pressures; artists wanted to make a stylistic statement; war resisters looked for validation of the defeat in Southeast Asia. In the United States, art about the Vietnam War invariably raised the issue of consensus about the common good. Who or what values are held "in common"? The war itself and the antiwar movement it awakened signaled a resurgence of fissiparous politics in which competing interest groups claimed control over culture and government. Any genuinely public art in this context found it necessary to address all these groups; it could not avoid being political, even partisan. The original requirements of the governmental commission were plain. The artwork was to be reflective and contemplative, harmonious with the two-acre site near the Lincoln Memorial, inclusive of the names of the fifty-eight thousand men and women who died during the war, and nonpartisan about the conduct of the war. Competitors submitted their plans for the memorial by November 1980, and in May 1981 the committee chose Maya Lin's black-granite wall with the names of the dead. There was some modification of the design in January 1982, with ground breaking shortly thereafter. The dedication took place in November 1982. After the choice of the wall structure, Vietnam veterans, believing that a black-granite wall indented in the earth was insufficient, chose Frederick Hart to add a figural artwork to the Maya Lin design (see fig. 1). The sculpture was located near the wall in March 1983 and dedicated in November 1984.

The architectural monument participates in the larger scheme of memorials that surround the Mall, stretching from the Capitol to the Lincoln Memorial on an east to west axis and from the Jefferson Memorial to the White House from north to south (see fig. 2). The minimalist, polished, black-granite wall is chevron-shaped and is located at a strategic spot near the north side of the Lincoln Memorial. One wing of the V-shaped sculpture of 125 degrees points toward the Lincoln Memorial, the other toward the Washington Monument. Horizontal rather than vertical in its orientation, the wall is quite different from the monuments toward which it points and with which it is related. It is situated below ground with the deepest point at the meeting of the two arms, which taper at their ends. It marks a progress of monuments in which the dome fresco of the Capitol enshrines the "apotheosis of George Washington" through

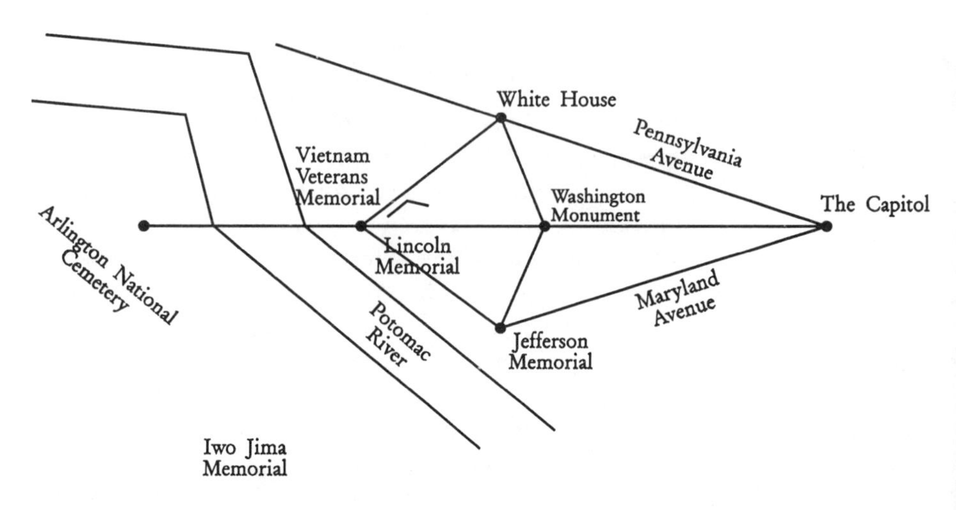

Figure 2 Schema: Mall Area
Washington, D.C.

the obelisk-monument to rationality for Washington and the brooding memory of the Civil War in Lincoln's Gettysburg Address and Second Inaugural Address. Of the other two points of the schema, one focuses Jefferson's Enlightenment ideals for the national identity and the other simply constitutes the president's home and office.

The VVM by Maya Lin is a charged place of pilgrimage. It is marked as a special ritual space (no eating, jogging, dog-walking, smoking, and so on), and the passage downward over the cobblestones beside the black-granite, polished masses — bearing the fifty-eight thousand engraved names — immerses the pilgrim in a sea of death. The artist-architect has said that death is a personal and private matter that every individual must resolve alone. The chevron gives no orientation; the pilgrim can enter from either side. At each entrance, there are sheltered lecterns with books of the names in readily discernible alphabetical order. Because it is underground, the structure is only visible when entering the space. (The above-ground ridge was added at the Park Service's insistence for the protection of park-wanderers.) Like a catacomb open to the sky, the wall reflects those who pass by as well as inscribes those who have passed from life into stone. The living and the dead mingle together, even if the dead are represented only by name and the living by mirrored identity. Since the two planes of the granite reflect each other in certain lights, the virtual space becomes an open-ended crossing. The yearly death inscriptions begin (1959) at the crease in the chevron and conclude (1975) there as well. In one sense, there is even a historical iconographic reference, since the memorial represents "the course of the Vietnam War from its secret beginnings to its final, unspectacular end, growing and growing and then dwindling away again."[41] The names are chiseled in the succession of their bearers' deaths, and those who enter and those who leave the site are wrapped in the dead. In a very important sense, the pilgrim never leaves the ambiance evoked by the wall. The grassy space that leads away from the chevron, although almost always unoccupied by Park Service custom, faces the wall like an amphitheater in which the pilgrims become the actors against the stage set of the granite. Their reactions are the rhetorical drama of the artwork.

Stressing purity of form, honesty of materials, and an autonomy of self-presentation, the architectural style of the wall, abstract and unoriented, reflects the ambiguous stylistic ideals of modernity. As a result, its ambivalence has been interpreted alternately as an embracing profundity or as vacuous nihilism. Most read the abstract minimalist style as a physical gash or scar in the earth, antiheroic, a trace of violence suffered. It is read by some as therapeutic, but not comforting.[42] This is a wound that will never heal. Like modernist works of art, it refuses to be "about things in the world" and wants to be a thing in the world.[43] It clings to its own implacability, its existence as an autotelic, self-directed world. In these senses, it fulfills many of the values that Taylor claims for a modern work of art.

The immediate intellectual and political history of the United States (the dead — comrades, parents, children, sons, lovers, relatives — are "present") gives the wall an event-character for those who visit it. Participants in the pilgrimage are vocal in their attitudes toward the wall. Shame, honor without glory, reconciliation, and pride are projected onto the space. Even though it supposedly makes no overt partisan statement about the war in Vietnam, it consistently functions in the interrogative. It provokes responses by its sheer blankness. The wall is nonnarrative. It records "only the mind-numbing and undifferentiated chronology of violence and death."[44]

Although it is often compared to the Wailing Wall, it has no continuing living tradition of worship to sustain it (other than the one individuals and families are now making). There are no confessional affiliations marked, as there would be at a national cemetery. There are no ranks given, no local geography: place of death or birth. Each is an individual substantive without connection other than its relation to the other names around it. There is only the sequence of dying. Each name can suggest the absolute dignity of the individual or the anonymous loneliness of death among the thousands.

The questions that veterans asked about the design involved concerns

Figure 3
Iwo Jima Memorial (1950–54). Artist: Felix de Weldon
Bronze Sculpture, Washington, D.C.
Photo © Sculpture Group Ltd., Wheeling, Ill.

about the historical specificity of the war (issues of identity), anticipated monumentality (questions of scale and grandeur), and contemporary relevance (vindication of their service to country). They were all about the relationship of art to life. Maya Lin stated that she did not know anything about the war and refused to read about U.S. involvement in Southeast Asia. "It didn't enter my world. . . . I don't read the papers. I just ignore the world." Such modernist artistic nonchalance about the contextual role of art fueled the antagonisms. The veterans' questions might be rephrased: Is the artwork sufficiently challenging so that fifty or two hundred years from now it will still be a place of pilgrimage for those seeking the meanings of *this* war? Or does it simply appear as a monument against any war?

Current existential investment makes the granite walls an authentic pilgrimage site, a memorial for leaving food, flowers, and mementoes for the dead (carefully collected by the Smithsonian shrine-keepers each night). If the divisive politics of the post-Vietnam era continue to affect life in the United States, perhaps the wall will be validated as a space of public debate. But does the VVM set up the aesthetic conditions for its own recurring power? Or will it become in the future an "object of aesthetic consciousness, a merely shadowy reality, living a distorted life only in the degenerate form of an object of interest to tourists or a subject for photography"?[45] William Hubbard remarks that since the public no longer imagines modern art as providing "guidance in human dilemmas," it may not sense the lack of this dimension of public art in the VVM.[46] The sheer emotional impact of the current situation hides the flaws in the monument. Will the memorial eventually become a visitors' passageway to the Lincoln Memorial? The addition of the figural sculpture by Hart ensures that it will not.

The Bronze Sculpture

In a sense, *Three Soldiers* concludes the visual project of Felix de Weldon's Iwo Jima Memorial. The World War II memorial to U.S. Marines who have died in war lies across the Potomac River at the edge of Arlington Cemetery (see fig. 3). It is several times larger than life; a unified group of soldiers mounted on a huge pedestal raises a civil flag in triumph. Hart's sculpture is about a distinctly different kind of nontriumphal heroism, but its placement links it to the one across the river near the cemetery.

Placed in a copse of trees, at the leading edge of the chevron closest to the Lincoln Memorial, Hart's *Three Soldiers* ushers pilgrims into the arena of death. Only slightly larger than human size, the soldiers stand among the living at the same level, recalling the ambiguities of comradeship in combat. They are a very particularized representation of the Vietnam veteran, with a mixture of military uniforms, towels for the tropical heat, and suntan lotion stashed in belts and helmets (see fig. 4). One has dog tags entwined in his shoelaces so that if his feet are blown off by a land mine, they can be recovered by the medics (see fig. 5). The three men, of different racial origins, are enfolded in military gear, utterly accurate and crafted with absolute attention to details. The inclusion of the harsh, extensive hardware contrasts with their youth and seeming innocence. Each man lightly touches the other and emphasizes the intimate bonding that Vietnam buddies felt for one another. "I entered the war for political reasons; I ended up being there to save my friends," said many veterans. Hart has said that the true heroism of the sculpture lies in the "bonds of loyalty in the face of their aloneness and their vulnerability."

Vulnerability The guiding metaphor of vulnerability is important since it locates the power of *this* war in the psyche of the United States. The three soldiers are always calling attention to the wall, so that the loss

Figure 4
Three Soldiers (1984, detail). Artist: Frederick Hart
Bronze Sculpture at Vietnam Veterans Memorial, Washington, D.C.
Photo © Sculpture Group Ltd., Wheeling, Ill.

will not be forgotten. The men are eternally alert — perhaps looking for their own names or those of their friends on the wall (see fig. 6). They are peering toward a home that is unknown; they also survive despite incredible human destruction. As survivors, though, they embody the mourning and the guilt of those who remain, challenging pilgrims to identify with the dead.

Despite some statements to the contrary, Hart's sculpture has an intimate relationship to Maya Lin's wall.[47] This embodies a dimension of his original design for the memorial competition. It was to include a curved wall with two groups of soldiers reaching toward one another — across a wide gap, permanently fixed in a disabled encounter. The three soldiers have become the first pilgrims, guiding encounters with the wall and its record of death. In effect, the wall now has a narrative structure, either a beginning or an ending. To be open to the death of others who died as a

Figure 5
Three Soldiers (detail of maquette). Artist: Frederick Hart
Photo © Mr. Darrell Acree, Washington, D.C.

result of one's own political choices, partisan votes, and economic support will remain an excoriating invitation and confrontation.

Attentiveness At the same time, the three soldiers do not deny angrily nor reject their own or their viewers' futures; they are waiting expectantly. They do not memorialize stoic endurance or a frowning recognition of error. They are not Wordsworthian epitaphs for feelings that have died. They focus an affective and cognitive direction for the future. The rhetoric of the two sculptures seen together is fundamentally hopeful; the wall and the soldiers remain in tensive dialogue. Around them is the constant stream of the pilgrims.

The waiting is not furtive, nor is it presumed. It is taut, intense; it anticipates self-sacrifice for the sake of the other. This wait is not the slack boredom of bureaucratic or industrial delay; no one here is slowly making a way through a supermarket line. The attentiveness required here is existentially critical to the details of the future. It includes an antecedent willingness without an absolutely clear and definite sense of what that future might entail. Some of the conditions for the waiting are present;

Figure 6
Three Soldiers (1984). Artist: Frederick Hart
Bronze Sculpture at Vietnam Veterans Memorial, Washington, D.C.
Photo © Sculpture Group Ltd., Wheeling, Ill.

many are not. Without attending to the details, there will be no future — only death.

Friendship The commitment to bonds of loyalty, a friendship that envisages the unknown, is a figural presence that is also incomplete. It announces tentative possibilities but does not presume the three soldiers' security in the present or the future. Friendship equals waiting, tending to the living — and to the dead. The soldiers do not trumpet their connection; they establish a comradeship that leaves them individuals. The sculpture articulates the power of community, power as cooperation. "In the measure that the community becomes a community of love and so capable of making real and great sacrifices, in that measure it can wipe out the grievances and correct the objective absurdities that its inauthenticity has brought about."[48] The announcement of such solidarity in the face of a future over which control is impossible makes a figural art subversive. Resistance against death, in the face of death, can cooperate for the achievement of the mutual good.

It is this irony — that cooperation exists in the context of a memorial about conflict — by which the sculpture makes an important contribution to the memory of *this particular war*. Everyone — including the former secretary of defense Robert McNamara, who prosecuted the war assiduously — now finds it difficult to be clear about the purposes of the Vietnam War. An element internal to conflict situations has been embodied by Hart in the figures — their interaction as friends who supported one another in the context of the end of things. The solidarity is not taken lightly nor easily, but it indicates that survival need not invite the Hobbesian response to human experience. For Hobbes, "The Right of Nature ... is the liberty each man hath, to use his own power, as he will himself, for the preservation of his own nature; that is to say, of his own life; and consequently, of doing any thing, which in his own judgment, and reason, he shall conceive to be the aptest means thereunto."[49] This will for oneself, enshrined in the individualist ideals of Enlightenment politics, created a war — but it also had to be overcome to conduct it and to conclude it. Without that cooperation, we have only the struggle for commonly claimed property. People must "become enemies; and in the way to their end, which is principally their own conservation and sometimes their delectation only, endeavor to destroy, or subdue one another." Here Hart's work confronts Hobbes's anthropology without apology.

The relationship among the soldiers is also their tentative, though not halfhearted, relationship to the wall on which their brothers and sisters are fixed in death. They, both in their contrasting artistic style and in their demeanor, claim to approach death without regret, anger, or stoic resignation. It is as though they believe it is possible to cooperate with death to achieve their own identities. "Befriending death" is a frightening possibility since distinguishing it from masochism, self-victimization, and perverse self-destructive fanaticism is difficult. The imagined status of cooperative comrades requires participants in the memorial to attend to the conditions under which such friendship might escape these results. The realistic sculpture maintains that this is possible before a wall of death.

Friendship is an intermediate public infrastructure between the politics of nations and personal intimate commitments such as marriage or domestic partnerships. The survival of these soldiers is not simply based upon utility. They are not acquaintances who have joined to fight a war; they evince some common feeling as well as reciprocal goodwill. Here their mutual regard involves not just hoping for the good of the other but an attentiveness to well-being in the presence of death itself. The tension inherent in the sculpture and its dialogical placement near the wall of names escalates rather than diminishes the power of the two artworks. Attentive friendship can support the polis, if we allow it.[50]

The establishment of friendship as a hope for the future is emphatically *not* a nostalgic yearning for fusion with total presence. Mutual, cooperative hope need not be seen as an illusory wish; indeed, hope cannot be accomplished alone. The figures promise and anticipate a tentative reconciliation, but not a completion. This is a dangerous memory for the sake of the future; they propel pilgrims through a passage toward something new that includes solidarity with the veterans and the victims of the war. By combining the almost hyperreal intensity of the soldiers with the black-granite wall, the site refuses easy comfort. Here figure and ground, human beings and their deadly end, combine both to seduce and to challenge the visitors.

The conditions under which this hope may be exercised are embodied in their youth (simultaneously sad and strong) as well as in the touching protectiveness and compassion of the figures. The tentative and fragile bonds of their lives become the possibility of a future. Their friendship is situated within the specific world of the war in Vietnam; their comradeship permits other possibilities but does not authenticate particular conditions. The VVM therefore demands of its visitors a complex meeting: a ritual burial with the dead through the mausoleum of the wall, silent and simple, as well as an identification with the soldiers whose particular lives are attending to the future. There are the inscription of the people and the embodiment of the names. The combination refuses simple fusion, pure positive presence. The constant, necessary struggle and responsibility speak in the face of unspeakable events. Here possibility survives, also renewal — within limits. Hope is chastened, but not dead.

The Spirituality of Figure and Ground Hart's work has always been about the relationship of the emergence from, the confrontation between, and cooperation between figure and chaotic ground.[51] His earlier monumental work for the façade of the Washington National Cathedral involved three tympana and three portal figures. In each, the figures are caught at the moment of transformation. Paul, lifted up into the third heaven, is dropping his sword, blinded by the mystical night; Peter, the builder of the church, is captured when he lays down his nets to follow the Sun of Justice. Respectively, they are located below the creation of the Moon and the stars and the fiat that produces the Sun and day. The central tympanum, *ex nihilo,* creates a dialogue in stone between the primeval, archaic chaos and the choric dance that we call humanity. An invisible other pulls Adam, the portal figure, out of formless blindness toward becoming a fully formed body. Simultaneously, the emergent nude aggressively pushes himself away from the stone. Again, Hart emphasizes the reality of the possible — and that the possible future is a matter of cooperation with the Other.

The language of hope applied to *Three Soldiers* is not inappropriate. The soldiers move beyond the dialectical confrontation of opposites to evidence a partial but real resolution of our common future. In this sense, figure steps between the academic nostalgia for the past and the negation of figure in the wall itself to announce a possible advent. In vulnerability, friendship, and attentiveness, the sculpture gives the conditions under which a meeting with death, even the unwarranted death of the young, must be met.

The spirituality that this secular sculpture registers is neither Whiggish progressive idealism, enshrined in the self-confident monuments of the nineteenth century, nor a simple negation of that ideal in a modernist confrontation. It mediates imaginative possibilities that, under certain conditions, can become true. The postmodern figural imagination criticizes both the spiritual nostalgia of traditional religious art and the silence of the wall. *Three Soldiers* makes statements about cultural possibilities, those that can and must be realized.[52] The figures witness to the dead on the wall; they take the risk of figuring an attitude toward death and the ultimate limits of human idealism. They do so in cooperative attention, vulnerability to one another, and mutual respect. Though I cannot literally die in the place of those inscribed on the wall, I can commit myself responsibly to living my own life and death in solidarity with others who have and will die. In this sense, the pilgrims who mingle between the dead on the wall and the attentive soldiers beside the wall are challenged to be responsible for what lies ahead, without knowing that future, only knowing that the commitment to cooperate and to be attentive will be the conditions under which such a future can occur. Though every decision appears unique, it nonetheless bears some analogy to the decisions made before. Figural public art, such as *Three Soldiers*, belongs to a tradition of risks in the face of the otherness of death. It is willing to commit itself to resist amnesia and to announce a prospective future, however tentative. Such a promise is not undertaken casually; instead of the resignation of constant mourning, it offers humanity a spiritual advent.

Notes

1. David Freedberg, *The Power of Images: Studies in the History and Theory of Response* (Chicago: University of Chicago Press, 1989), 27.

2. See Hans Belting's magisterial study, *Likeness and Presence: A History of the Image*

before the Era of Art, trans. Edmund Jephcott (Chicago: University of Chicago Press, 1994); for information prior to 300 C.E., see Paul Corbey Finney, *The Invisible God: The Earliest Christians on Art* (New York: Oxford University Press, 1994).

3. Freedberg, *Power of Images,* 358.

4. Suzanne K. Langer, *Feeling and Form: A Theory of Art* (London: Routledge and Kegan Paul, 1967), 46–52; and idem, "The Dynamic Image: Some Philosophical Reflections on Dance," in *Problems of Art* (New York: Scribner's, 1957), 1–11.

5. See the 1986–87 exhibition catalogue by Maurice Tuchman et al., *The Spiritual in Art: Abstract Painting, 1890–1985* (New York: Abbeville, 1986); Roger Lipsey, *An Art of Our Own: The Spiritual in Twentieth Century Art* (Boston: Shambhala, 1988); and for background, Antoine Faivre and Jacob Needleman, eds., *Modern Esoteric Spirituality* (New York: Crossroad, 1992).

6. Arthur C. Danto, *Beyond the Brillo Box: The Visual Arts in Post-historical Perspective* (New York: Farrar, Straus and Giroux, 1993), 10.

7. It is not realistic to portray a comprehensive development in literature, music, dance, drama, and the visual arts in this essay. Certain figures will be isolated for their contextual importance and their contribution to the development of a sense of the spiritual in modernity.

8. I am deeply indebted to the analysis and categories of Mark Wedig, "The Hermeneutics of Religious Visual Art in *L'Art Sacré,* 1945–1954, in the Context of Aesthetic Modernity" (Ph.D. diss., Catholic University of America, 1995), esp. 19–84.

9. This story has been told in many places, but more recent versions can be found in Tuchman et al., *Spiritual in Art;* Lipsey, *An Art of Our Own;* and Yve-Alain Bois, "The Iconoclast," in *Piet Mondrian, 1872–1944* (Washington, D.C.: National Gallery of Art, 1995), esp. 327–40.

10. See Rose Rosengard Subotnik, *Developing Variations: Style and Ideology in Western Music* (Minneapolis: University of Minnesota Press, 1990), esp. 165–93.

11. There are significant exceptions to this generalization, such as Béla Bartók (1881–1945), Gabriel Fauré (1845–1924), Leos Janácek (1854–1928), and Antonin Dvorák (1841–1904). They used folk melodies and integrated them into often highly complex musical compositions.

12. Mario Praz, *The Hero in Eclipse in Victorian Fiction,* trans. Angus Davidson (London: Oxford University Press, 1956), 49, 137, 153, 187, 332–33; see also Geraldine Norman, *Biedermeier Painting, 1815–1848* (New York: Thames and Hudson, 1987), 7–25

13. Georg Lukács, *The Historical Novel,* trans. Hannah and Stanley Mitchell (Lincoln: University of Nebraska Press, 1983), 33; parallel remarks are made about love in the novel in Peter Gay, *The Tender Passion,* vol. 2 of *The Bourgeois Experience: Victoria to Freud* (New York: Oxford University Press, 1986), 135–97. For social background, see F. M. L. Thompson, *The Rise of Respectable Society: A Social History of Victorian Britain, 1830–1900* (Cambridge, Mass.: Harvard University Press, 1988); and Michelle Perrot, ed., *A History of Private Life: From the Fires of Revolution to the Great War,* trans. Arthur Goldhammer (Cambridge, Mass.: Harvard University Press, 1990), esp. 4:216–337.

14. Lukács, *Historical Novel,* 60.

15. Arthur Rimbaud, "Soir historique," in *Illuminations and Other Prose Poems,* trans. Louise Varèse (New York: New Directions, 1957), 115.

16. Paul Berman, "Intimations of Mortality," in *On the Poetry of Allen Ginsberg,* ed. Lewis Hyde (Ann Arbor: University of Michigan Press, 1984), 342–53.

17. James Merrill, *Mirabell: Books of Numbers,* book 7.2, in *The Changing Light at Sandover* (New York: Atheneum, 1983), 227.
18. Clarence C. Green, *The Neo-classic Theory of Tragedy in England during the Eighteenth Century* (New York: Blom, 1966 [1934]).
19. Cited in Christopher Innes, *Modern British Drama, 1890–1990* (Cambridge: Cambridge University Press, 1992), 53.
20. Johannes Birringer, *Theatre, Theory, Postmodernism* (Bloomington: Indiana University Press, 1993), 29.
21. Luigi Pirandello, *Henry IV,* act 1, in *Naked Masks: Five Plays by Luigi Pirandello,* ed. Eric Bentley (New York: Dutton, 1952), 169.
22. Susan Sontag, "Antonin Artaud," in *Antonin Artaud: Selected Writings,* ed. Susan Sontag, trans. Helen Weaver (New York: Farrar, Straus and Giroux, 1976), xix.
23. Ibid., xxxii.
24. Peter Brook, "On Africa (an Interview)," *Drama Review* 17:3 (1973): 50; cited in Richard Schechner, *Between Theater and Anthropology* (Philadelphia: University of Pennsylvania Press, 1985), 27.
25. Citations in this paragraph are taken from Karl Rahner, "Theology and the Arts," *Thought* 57 (March 1982): 27, 29.
26. These notions are explored in a popular and practical fashion by Julia Cameron and Mark Bryan in *The Artist's Way: A Spiritual Path to Higher Creativity* (New York: Putnam's, 1992).
27. For a convenient collection of essays on what follows, see Arthur C. Danto, *Beyond the Brillo Box;* and Danto's earlier collection, *The Philosophical Disenfranchisement of Art* (New York: Columbia University Press, 1986).
28. Mark C. Taylor, *Disfiguring: Art, Architecture, Religion* (Chicago: University of Chicago Press, 1992).
29. Danto, *Philosophical Disenfranchisement,* 208.
30. For the interpretation that follows, see Tuchman et al., *The Spiritual in Art.*
31. Sixten Ringbom, "Transcending the Visible: The Generation of the Abstract Pioneers," in Tuchman et al., *The Spiritual in Art,* 132.
32. Bois, "The Iconoclast," 327–30.
33. Cited in Lipsey, *An Art of Our Own,* 77.
34. Ibid., 136.
35. Charlotte Douglas, "Beyond Reason: Malevich, Matiushin, and Their Circles," in Tuchman et al., *The Spiritual in Art,* 189–90.
36. Robert Rosenblum, *Modern Painting and the Northern Romantic Tradition: Friedrich to Rothko* (New York: Harper and Row, 1975), 10–40.
37. Immanuel Kant, *Critique of Judgment,* trans. J. H. Bernard (New York: Hafner, 1968), 99–106.
38. Taylor, *Disfiguring,* 319; then see p. 302.
39. Ibid., 88.
40. Much literature on politics and art has been published on this installation. For an overview, see Charles L. Griswold, "The Vietnam Veterans Memorial and the Washington Mall: Philosophical Thoughts on Political Iconography," *Critical Inquiry* 12:4 (summer 1986): 688–719; William Hubbard, "A Meaning for Monuments," *The Public Interest* 74 (1984): 17–30; and Karal Ann Marling and Robert Silberman, "The Statue Near the Mall: The Vietnam Veterans Memorial and the Art of Remembering," *Smithsonian Studies in American Art* 1:1 (spring 1987): 5–29.

41. Michael North, "The Public as Sculpture: From Heavenly City to Mass Ornament," *Critical Inquiry* 16 (summer 1990): 876, 877.

42. W. J. T. Mitchell, "The Violence of Public Art," *Critical Inquiry* 16 (summer 1990): 888.

43. Hubbard, "A Meaning for Monuments," 26.

44. Mitchell, "Violence of Public Art," 888.

45. Hans-Georg Gadamer, *Truth and Method,* trans. Joel Weinsheimer and Donald Marshall, rev. ed. (New York: Crossroad, 1989), 156.

46. Hubbard, "A Meaning for Monuments," 27.

47. North, "The Public as Sculpture," 878.

48. B. J. F. Lonergan, "Dialectic of Authority," in *A Third Collection: Papers by Bernard J. F. Lonergan, S.J.,* ed. Frederick E. Crowe (New York: Paulist, 1985), 5–12, quotation on 10.

49. Thomas Hobbes, *Leviathan, or the Matter, Forme and Power of a Commonwealth: Ecclesiasticall and Civil,* ed. Michael Oakeshott (New York: Collier, 1962), 98–99; then see p. 103.

50. Friendship as a secular, spiritual virtue that supports the polis or *civitas* is reflected upon in Aristotle *Nicomachean Ethics* 8–9 and in Cicero *Laelius: On Friendship* 1–27.

51. Homan Potterton, "Metamorphosis: Stone Carver to Artist," in *Frederick Hart: Sculptor,* ed. Marshall Lee (New York: Hudson Hills, 1994), 19–39.

52. The argument in Danto, Taylor, and the present essay is a not so surreptitious discussion of the legacy of Clement Greenberg in art history. See T. J. Clark, "Clement Greenberg's Theory of Art," *Critical Inquiry* 9 (September 1982): 139–56; and Michael Fried's response, "How Modernism Works: A Response to T. J. Clark," *Critical Inquiry* 9 (September 1982): 217–34.

Bibliography

Apostolos-Cappadona, Diane, ed. *Art, Creativity, and the Sacred.* New York: Crossroad, 1984.

Belting, Hans. *Likeness and Presence: A History of the Image before the Era of Art.* Translated by Edmund Jephcott. Chicago: University of Chicago Press, 1989.

Cameron, Julia, and Mark Bryan. *The Artist's Way: A Spiritual Path to Higher Creativity.* New York: Putnam's, 1992.

Danto, Arthur C. *Beyond the Brillo Box: The Visual Arts in Post-historical Perspective.* New York: Farrar, Straus and Giroux, 1992.

Freedberg, David. *The Power of Images: Studies in the History and Theory of Response.* Chicago: University of Chicago Press, 1989.

Krauss, Rosalind E., ed. *The Originality of the Avant-Garde and Other Modernist Myths.* Cambridge, Mass.: MIT Press, 1993.

Lipsey, Roger. *An Art of Our Own: The Spiritual in Twentieth Century Art.* Boston: Shambhala, 1988.

May, Rollo. *The Courage to Create.* New York: Bantam, 1976.

Neumann, Erich. *Art and the Creative Unconscious.* Translated by Ralph Manheim. Princeton, N.J.: Princeton University Press, 1959.

Schechner, Richard. *Between Theater and Anthropology.* Philadelphia: University of Pennsylvania Press, 1985.

Storr, Anthony. *The Dynamics of Creation.* New York: Atheneum, 1972.

Taylor, Mark C. *Disfiguring: Art, Architecture, Religion.* Chicago: University of Chicago Press, 1992.

Tuchman, Maurice, et al. *The Spiritual in Art: Abstract Painting, 1890–1985.* New York: Abbeville, 1986.

19

Sports

CAROLYN E. THOMAS

What is play indeed if not an activity of which man is the first origin, for which man himself sets the rules, and which has no consequences except according to rules posited? . . . He himself sets the values and the rules for his acts. . . . It might appear that when man is playing, bent on discovering himself as free in his every action, he certainly could not be concerned with *possessing* a being in the world. His goal, which he aims at through sports and games, is to attain himself as a certain being, precisely the being, which is in question to his being.

—Jean-Paul Sartre, *Being and Nothingness*

Whether as athletes we liked it or not, the four minute mile had become like an Everest — a challenge to the human spirit.

—Roger Bannister, *The Four Minute Mile*

SPORT in its many manifestations is a popular and dominant feature of most Western cultures. The leisure player who seeks diversion and health benefits often finds moments of joy and self-fulfillment. The professional player who represents the commercial packaging of an increasing number of sporting activities sometimes finds fame and wealth. Neither of these manifestations, per se, can be considered as evidence of the spiritual dimension of human existence. However, within the sport context there are the serious participants, usually but not necessarily amateur, who seek more than diversion and superiority from the sport experience. Such participation requires skill, or at least a consistent command of the activity, as well as commitment, discipline, and perseverance.

For the many people who commit to sport for the sake of values that go beyond diversion, winning, or the extrinsic or financial rewards of achievement, a spiritual potential exists. Sport is a lived experience that, despite teammates or fans, is ultimately a solitary quest that reflects highly individual, personal, and subjective intents. Whether the engagement is test or contest, the athlete — alone — faces the realities of self in the context of a voluntary and structured quest. Serious athletes are not engaged in the lived experience of sport merely to exercise, to achieve fitness benefits, or to pursue recreative fulfillment. Often unknowingly, they enter the world of sports in search of self, in search of the reality of a given moment, in search of truth. What happens in the quest for excellence and truth is usually not sought intentionally. Athletes find not only a sense of personal identity, or of reality's limits, but a new way of understanding the world and how one relates to the world. New meanings not deliberately sought and new understandings not necessarily expected evolve from the playing out of a particular quest at a particular point in time. The result may not yield cognitive or even reflective ideas of moral or religious significance but rather an existential transformation that makes individuals available to themselves for their own understanding. Such experiences reveal our broader engagements and connections with others, with the physical world and the broader cosmos. This essay will examine what I call the "world-for-the-moment" experience in sport, a moment in which the serious, solitary participant voluntarily brings "who I am" at a given moment in time to an artificial project to evaluate two questions: Who can I become? and Why?

Early Origins

Some of the first organized sporting competitions that we have records of occurred in the context of religious festivals in Greek antiquity. For many centuries, organized sports and games were under the control of religious authorities and were permitted only on holidays or in association with the celebration of religious rites or festivals. The great competitions in archaic cultures frequently formed part of the sacred festivals and were seen as indispensable activities promoting health and happiness. David Sansone in his *Greek Athletics and the Genesis of Sport* examines the seriousness with which the Greeks treated sport and concludes that the numerous associations between sport and sacrificial ritual in Greece suggest that sport was itself a form of sacrificial ritual.[1] In the ancient Olympics and other religious festivals, the central activity was ritual sacrifice for the purpose of maintaining the continuity of life. The most articulate chronicler of the sport of the time was Pindar, whose critics bemoaned the triviality of his subject matter but not his seriousness of expression. However, such a genre of poetry and art could not have arisen and flourished if the Greeks had not felt it appropriate to praise athletic victors.[2]

Pindar's thought suggests that there was a belief that all values by their very essence are of one and the same nature and that human value, or *arete,* is a unitary whole:

> It is only in this way that we can understand the high value that Pindar and his world set upon victories in the games. They thought not in terms of a specialized technical ability, but in terms of the demonstration, in this particular way, of the worth of an individual. If a man throws all that he has to give into pursuing a wholly ideal end: if he gives up his time and money, if he takes the risk of defeat and disgrace, if he undergoes the long and severe discipline of training with all its pains and privations and efforts, and puts out every ounce of his strength in the event itself; and if then the grace of the gods, without which no achievement is possible, chooses him as victor from all his competitors, then in Pindar's eyes he has given convincing proof of his *arete.*[3]

Claims that contests were religious seem borne out by the fact that athletic events were staged in sacred places and at times sacred to the Greeks (two or three full moons after the summer solstice). As ritualistic attempts to please the gods with the best of human effort, music, dance, poetry, drama, and athletic performances focused on the performers and gave victors simple rewards. The contests were intended to please the gods and not festival spectators. Such participant practices are the cornerstone of contemporary amateur sport.

Thus, the ancient Panhellenic Games embodied the spiritual relationship the Greeks saw between the athlete and the gods. It is prudent to note that participation was limited to males who performed naked before their gods in a context where females were prohibited even as spectators. Victory was important in pleasing the gods and as a representation of good sacrifice:

> The god must be given a worthy gift; he will feel slighted if he is not given the best. The athletic contest performs two functions at the same time. In the first place, it is, in itself, the means whereby the sacrifice of human energy takes place. Among the Timbira Indians, and in many other societies, this is its primary, or even sole, function: everyone who participates in the contest is felt to have sacrificed; winning or losing is not, as they say, as important as having taken part. But for the Greeks the contest performed a second function as well. By testing to see who could run the fastest or throw the farthest, it determined who was considered to be worthy of sacrificing to the god. For the losers were embarrassed and ashamed, cowering in back alleys, hiding from their enemies, smitten with disgrace. Only the victor was dedicated to the god.[4]

While the Greeks seriously involved sport in their worship and in their cultural expressions of art and literature, the Romans saw sport as war training. The Greek principles of the harmonious development of the body and striving for physical beauty and grace were effeminate affectivities to the Romans. Richard Mandell in his *Sport: A Cultural History* suggests that Greek sport became an increasingly prominent and negative social activity within Roman culture and eventually contributed to the decline of Rome. He also notes that Christianity, in general, became increasingly hostile to all but utilitarian acts of the body.[5]

Puritan Influences and Commercial Interests

The association of sport with paganism and the emphasis on competitive outcomes rather than excellent efforts steadily eroded the relationship of sport and religion in Christian Europe. The shift to spectator events, in Rome and later in other parts of Europe, brought with it gambling, corruption, and paid professional participants. Christian disgust with pagan festivals eventually brought about abolishment of the public sacrifice of gladiators and a great deal of social criticism against the idleness and frenzies of spectators. The eventual discontinuance of the ancient Olympic Games in 393 C.E. remains the benchmark for the separation of sport and religion. With the Christian dominance of Europe and then, over time, the "New World," this separation was solidified. Sports, after all, like many areas of human creativity, reflect the time and place in which they are acted out. Thus, as European sports were transported to new lands, they were transformed. In the new American colonies, the Puritan religious temperament saw sport and recreation as frivolous — antithetical to more serious religious and industrial pursuits. Governmental intervention to suppress recreation and merriment at least on the Sabbath reflected the strong undercurrent of thought that sport was a spectator distraction and a participant frivolity.

Despite the increasing number of participants in sport and the increasing variety of sporting activities, contemporary sport remains peripheral to the mainstream of significant social activities. A love-hate relationship exists. On the one hand, adulation of athletes is evident in the volume of media coverage, in the record spectator attendance each year, and in the economic impact of sales of tickets, advertising, licensed merchandise, equipment, and lessons. On the other hand, many people believe that sport is not really a "suitable" career to which one might aspire, that it represents the worst in terms of public moral behavior, and that it leads to a distortion of priorities among social values.

While sport has been revered historically as a reflection of physical ideals and as an attempt at attaining the greatest skill and trained perfection that humans can achieve, it has also been condemned as a frivolous, nonutilitarian activity interfering with productive secular and religious quests. Such judgments usually stem from a view of sport taken by the *nonparticipant*. Whether that outside perspective has been one of avid fans or negative critics, it fails to reflect the lived experience of sport as one of the many possible sites for humans' existential quests. Nonparticipants can, of course, appreciate the technical skill and theatrical drama of any serious sporting activity and can enjoy vicarious involvement in it. They can also justifiably criticize the off-the-field policies and antics, the displays of poor sportsmanship, and the seemingly distorted priority sport holds in the social structure of industrialized countries. All this points away from any connection between modern sport and religion, and indeed the casual observer would be hard-pressed to describe modern sport, particularly professional and Division I intercollegiate athletics, as having a religious or spiritual dimension. Often portrayed in terms of greed, egocentricity, and immorality, these forms of sport — that is, athletics that focus on competitive ends — seem a far cry from a historic dependence on religion. Conversely, to advocate sport as the functional equivalent of religion, inculcating discipline, a taste for perfection, and the experience of beautiful and graceful acts, seems ill-founded. These appreciations and appraisals, however, do not reflect the experiential nature of sport, the fascination it holds for those who *play*, nor do they reflect the meanings derived from the moments of glory and angst that endure far beyond a particular event and that can provide the kind of self-understanding often attributed to other cultural forums of human life.

The Sport World

The search to fulfill elementary needs is arduous, even to civilized peoples, but the search for personal meaning or a purpose in life is even more difficult. Yet it is this search for personal identity or for the meaning of existence that has produced some of our most creative endeavors: our myths, religions, works of art, philosophical systems, scientific theories, and sports. Because human cultural evolution is in good measure haphazard, one must admire the inventiveness expressed in the creation of the many artificial frames of orientation that have provided meaning or, at least, the illusion of meaning in our lives. One such frame of orientation is constituted of those movement forms that have come to be called sport, dance, exercise, play, and games. The sport form, like many of the other nonutilitarian modes created by humans to examine and/or experience their own sense of being, has been described in sport literature as a kind of "world."

For the purpose of this discussion, *world,* as used in the above sense, will be defined as a medium through which a human being is actively involved in and committed to a specific activity and in which he or she discovers and constructs meanings while encountering and choosing among possibilities. The French philosopher Jean-Paul Sartre, among others, suggests that a world, in this sense, defines itself by the ends that the individual pursues. In addition, he implies that this "world" is more than the empirical data or the perceptions of the individual. It is the integration of both: "Without the world there is no selfness, no person; without selfness, without the person, there is no world."[6] In effect, there is no single "real" world for every individual, but many worlds that each person structures and understands by choice and action. "What then, is the world? — All things whatsoever, seen in their relation to an ultimate or final project of man. Such projects are open to free and creative choice. Your world is the way you order things and processes in relation to your final purpose."[7] Any one individual may exist in several worlds. These worlds may be as broad as national or religious worlds or as specific as family, teaching, music, and/or sport-worlds.

Eleanor Metheny has examined the nature of sport as a nonutilitarian mode, or world, fashioned after the task of Sisyphus. Her 1968 work, *Movement and Meaning,* has withstood more than two decades of sophisticated and critical thought to become a classic description of sport.[8] Metheny maintains that sport provides a world in which the freedom to act is guaranteed because the rules eliminate the demands of necessity by defining an unnecessary and futile task that produces nothing of material value. All sport forms are governed by an elaborate code of rules in which every Sisyphean task is described, defined, and denoted in explicit terms. The only question left unanswered, she says, is this: "How well can the performer do what is prescribed by these rules?" The task, activity, or occupation to be carried out is voluntarily conducted according to rules that are freely accepted but absolutely binding; it is autotelic and separate from ordinary life.

Similarly, Paul Weiss speaks both to the nonutilitarian nature of the sport-world as well as to the commitment of the athlete to this world:

> The athlete's world is set over against the every day world. Economic demands and the satisfaction of appetites are for the moment put aside. . . . Artists and historians similarly bracket off their distinctive, dynamic spatiotemporal worlds. What he (artist or athlete) is and what he does is, for the moment, thereby severed from the rest of the world.[9]

There is substantial support suggesting that the sport experience is separate and apart from the everyday world in conduct and intent and in its nonutilitarian and absurd functions. It becomes a world apart for the participant. Of course, certain conditions must be met in order for this to occur, and it is possible that not all players are capable or desirous of what might be called a sporting "world-for-the-moment." However, some persons' commitment to the pursuit of individual excellence allows them to transcend the external world and to enter, be it for the duration of the one-hundred-meter dash or the climbing of Mt. Rainier, a separate world that they themselves create and fashion with skill, desire, and intensity — a world created after their own unique images. As Martin Buber has noted, there is nothing in "man" (the I) nor in the world (the Thou) except the relation between them.[10] Sport, like a book, a script, a score, or a canvas, is inert until defined or interpreted by the *acts* of a participant. Sport is not unlimited; individuals bring their own limitations and thereby structure sport in their own image. Sport is, essentially, amoral and does not generate values; we each bring our values to sport and make it as worthy as we are. Hence, the athlete becomes largely responsible for defining his or her own "world-for-the-moment."

A number of major factors simultaneously define a sport-world and promote the achievement of meaning and self-understanding there. The first of these factors can be very broadly described as commitment: it includes the willingness to prepare optimally for the encounter through training; the development of required expertise; and the sacrifice of time and other activities to become all one is capable of becoming. It is the "getting ready" stage that few see or care to see. It is the hours of training, of pain, of fatigue, and of trial and error that are often discouraging, physically stressful, and psychologically dissonant. It is a requirement if the performance (which can last less than ten seconds) is to carry its full meaning. It is difficult to enter the experience wholly or to create a gestalt of actor and act without such a commitment. For the contest to take on potentially meaningful dimensions, the athlete must be fully prepared; the athlete's technique and training become the background in front of which he or she is free to move.

A second factor has to do with a conscious intent to pursue individual excellence and to measure oneself against goals set by oneself and represented by the achievements of other athletes. Intent may stem from the concrete motivation to demonstrate superiority or from the more tacit need to identify personal uniqueness. Metheny maintains that a person is "drawn or driven [to sport] by his own need to test the limits of human ability."[11] Existential philosophy, literature, and psychoanalysis are replete with similar concepts and problems of commitment, choice, and freedom. The comparisons are instructive as we consider the sport-world as a separate, nonutilitarian stage for the inevitable human search for commitment to a cause, fulfillment of a potential, acceptance by others, and a sense of purpose or even immortality. While it may be possible to explain these motives in the context of some hierarchy of psychological needs, it, nonetheless, remains that sport can be one medium for the playing out of the human search for selfhood, for the fulfillment of goals, or for a life purpose.

Sartre emphasized the moral necessity for individuals to make commitments by choosing a project and assuming the responsibilities for choices, successes, and failures.[12] Living under the bondage of self-imposed tasks and imperatives and devoting oneself to higher ideals is, he insists, the only way to give meaning to one's existence. When athletes enter a sport-world, they can know the self symbolically as a powerful agent in being since, in that particular world, they literally use externally controlling necessities to serve their purposes. Regardless of the individual motive for commitment to the sport-world, the sport contest, like the script or the choice of any secular life project, provides one medium to play out a variety of searches for self-knowledge, self-assessment, self-actualization, or life purpose.

Sport and Meaning

In the context of the sport-world, the search for meaning can be seen in two distinct ways. First, in subtle and overt ways, individuals seek to identify their own uniqueness — their selfhood — and to measure themselves against other persons and against the world in the hope of coming to know who they are. In the context of participating in sport, we can, upon reflection, become our own audience. This influences future choices we eventually make relative to our participation in the sport-world or any of our many other worlds. As individuals we take action in ways that are consistent with who we think we are. The quest for self-understanding or for the meanings that help explain who we are requires a certain degree of introspection. To experience the deepest truth concerning oneself and others, it is necessary to retreat within — to introspect and to engage in a process of open inquiry, dissent, and meditation that reveals oneself to oneself. Dialogue with oneself is a prerequisite to a clarity of awareness, a sense of direction and action. It is this aspect of sport that cannot be available to either the fan or the critic.

A second search for meaning involves finding a purpose to life or a rationale for death. It involves, in short, answering the question Why? We seek out "projects," as Sartre calls them, in which we try to find both purpose and justification for life. Why am I here? and What for? are very complex questions for every individual. Many living creatures seek both pleasure and power, but only humans care about or seek personal meaning or spiritual satisfaction. Human "projects," including sport, give some indication that we have not only recognized but organized our quests for self-understanding, self-actualization, and purpose.

Sport, in its spectatorial and participatory forms, permeates our technological society to the extent that few are left untouched by it. Despite its pervasiveness, dualistic attitudes persist that place the value of sport participation a distant second to work, religious quests, intellectual activities, and artistic accomplishment. Despite these societal tendencies to discount sport or related physical activities, people persist in seeking out participation. Philosophers and social scientists have pointed to varying degrees of alienation Americans face in their attempts to find and give meaning to their lives. They also note with increasing degrees of certainty that people seek out participation in activities that are meaningful, self-enhancing, and positively complementary to their daily, routine, and utilitarian activities. This voluntary search has led people to religion, to a variety of art forms, and to sport. The key notion here is that the involvement is *voluntary*. By nature, people do not engage in activities voluntarily if those activities are meaningless or if there is no return on the time and energy invested. From these premises, then, let us examine the potential of sport to provide meaning in response to the human needs for self-understanding and purpose in life.

We look for the "I" of our fundamental nature and for clarity about who we are in many endeavors. The nonutilitarian nature of sport sets it apart from the "real world." Some have said sport is *absurd*. Pointless. Useless. Of little value as a functional activity. After all the effort exerted in the sport endeavor, nothing is lasting or ever really accomplished. Nothing has been changed by the performer's attempt. Like Sisyphus, whom the Greek gods condemned to roll a rock up a hill in full knowledge that it would always roll back down to the valley, the athlete leaves no physical trace of his or her efforts. The athlete's javelin flies through space and falls to the ground; the distance is measured; and the javelin is brought back to the starting point or stored away unchanged. The basketball is tossed into a bottomless basket, only to fall to the ground. The putt is holed only to be removed. Some claim that the absurd and useless character of sport is precisely what makes it the possible site for meaningful experience.

The athlete is removed from external factors upon entering sport, and sport becomes a world of personal creation within the rules. Left behind are pressures of school, work, family, finance, and interpersonal relationships, which often impact on actions in other life projects. In sport, if there is sufficient commitment to the sport task, albeit a futile and absurd one, these pressures are set aside to focus on the accomplishment of the goals of sport:

> Within the complex conditions of life, we are seldom, if ever, free to focus all our attention on one well-defined task and bring all our energies to bear on one wholehearted attempt to perform the task effectively.... In contrast the rules of sport provide us with a man-made world in which this freedom is fully guaranteed. These rules eliminate the demands of necessity by defining an unnecessary task.[13]

The structure of sport and the freedom to act within its framework, combined with the fact that the involvement is voluntary, provide performers with a unique opportunity to achieve some understanding about themselves. These boundaries of sport provide a fundamental source of personal meaning and allow for an encounter with others. People playing together create a paradigm of interpersonal freedom that generates its own meaning and its own forms of communication. It has also been argued that sport allows a freedom to act authentically because despite the involvement of others, the individual is alone in sport:

> Whether he is hurling a javelin, soaring off a ski-jump, performing a double back flip off a diving board or screaming toward earth in a free fall dive, man is alone. He is beyond the world of public determinations; of official identities; of functions; of self-deceptions and everydayness. And in the solitary state of oneness, man can meet himself. Sooner or later in sport, the serious striver after excellence will meet a situation that is almost too big for him to master. Such situations occur in ordinary life and can often be dodged. We can play hide and seek with reality, avoiding facing the truth about ourselves but in sport we can't do this.... As a result, sport leads to the most remarkable self-discovery, of limitations as well as abilities. The discovery is partly physical... but mainly the discovery is mental. In time we learn how far from being self-sufficient we are, we realize the value of cooperation and assistance from others. But unless we start out alone, we never learn the answers others can best answer and those we must answer for ourselves.[14]

Sport provides an opportunity for an individual not only to leave a mark at least for the moment but also to assume control over a personal destiny. Despite the absurdity of sport, players enter into it often believing their performance is unique and will somehow be remembered. There are any number of risks involved in sport, including social defeat, loss of status, damaged ego, physical injury, or even death. By placing oneself in a risky situation where one must assume complete responsibility for the outcome, it may be possible to overcome the social conditions that lead to feelings of purposelessness, helplessness, and alienation. Intentional and planned risk demands all the qualities most valuable in life: intelligence, skill, intuition, subtlety, and control. Sport provides a place where people can dominate fear and passion; a place where adventure and purpose and commitment can remove a sense of dread that may otherwise prevail. The element of risk can turn a weekend hobby into a small-scale model for living, a life within a life. The moments of glory, of recognition, of taking part — however fleeting they may be — provide the athlete with the knowledge that achievement, control, and worth are possible ways of being-in-the-world. The athlete finds that he or she is of some use in this world.

The Body Subject

Sartre has described three dimensions of the body that are revealed during the involvement of the player in the sport experience.[15] Briefly stated, the first dimension is the body as it is given to an embodied self; the second is the body as it is encountered and known by other people; and the third combines elements of the first two — it is one's own body experienced as something known by others. J. H. Van DenBerg comments:

> The second and third dimensions of the body delineated by Sartre are akin to Buber's I-It relationship from the standpoint that the body is treated as an object. However, rather than the performer treating the body like an object in preparation for the event, an audience sees "it" (the body) as it performs and treats it as another thing among things capable or incapable of completing a successful sport task. The second dimension of the body comes into being under the eyes of his fellowman.... His situation is watched by another who remains unperceived.[16]

Unknown to the performer, the spectator sees what the performer has forgotten, that is, those parts of the preparation stage that the performer is no longer conscious of. The audience focuses on the nuances of technique, equipment, strategy, and injury and visually/cognitively treats the body as a thing. "This dissectible thing-body is a derivative of the second dimension."[17] It is, also, possible that the player can "constitute his body in the second dimension," that is, become his own audience. "This happens, for instance, when he tends the wound in his leg. The wounded place is examined and touched *in order to* cure it, or: *in order to* be able continue on his way."[18] The player temporarily takes him/herself out of any commitment to the totality of the experience to examine the body, considering it a piece of equipment that may have temporarily broken down. It is not uncommon to hear athletes refer to the injured body or body part with statements like, "*It* let me down." Somehow the body in the second dimension is seen as outside, or separate from, the self.

The third dimension comes into play later in the involvement stage, when the performer realizes that there is an audience. Many athletes' concern with "the look" prevents them from making a total commitment to sport. They become too concerned about what others think and are never free to play or to be themselves in a contest. Using a mountain climbing experience, Seymour Kleinman explains "the look":

> For Sartre, this dimension of being is always destructive. It destroys the "passing beyond." The climber becomes annoyed, uncomfortable. He feels vulnerable and defense-less. He miscalculates, he stumbles, he becomes ashamed. For Sartre, the look of the other always results in alienation. Van DenBerg disagrees. There is [on the other hand] the look of understanding, of sympathy, of friendship, of love.[19]

The look, then, may be one of alienation where the player is inhibited by coaches, fans, or critics and is made nervous or anxious enough to make a mistake.

Without commitment, an athlete's involvement is a playing *at* sport rather than a playing *of* it. The belief that commitment yields meaning rests on the premise expressed by Helmut Plessner: "It is only the behavior, the act, the movement that explains the body."[20] The body as subject, as an integrated and embodied entity, is not separate from the experience but becomes the experience. Sartre's first dimension of the body involved in sport calls for going beyond the body-object stage. Van DenBerg writes:

> He no longer thinks of his shoes to which an hour ago he gave such great attention, he "forgets" the stick that supports him, ... he "ignores his body" which he trained. For only by forgetting, in a certain sense, his plans and his body, will he be able to devote himself to the laborious task that has to be performed. What there still is, psychologically speaking, is only the mountain: he is absorbed in its structure, his thoughts are completely given to it.[21]

This first dimension approaches Buber's I-Thou, the relationship of mutuality. Unlike Sartre, Buber believed that people are not doomed to live alone and alienated and can find themselves in relation to a Thou, to a Being who is Other. Similarly, Sartre's first dimension is a coming together of the athlete and the sport experience, a union that allows performers the opportunity fully to experience what sport can be and what they can be in sport. When performers voluntarily enter sport and commit their whole beings to the sport experience, they transcend, or go beyond, outside distractions to a fusion of subject and object that allows them to know both the sport and self in an authentic, profound, special, and very individual way. It is this kind of "knowing" that has the potential to provide a source of meaning, a sense of purpose, and a basis for self-understanding.

The fusion of the performer with the experience represents one kind of commitment. An attendant phenomenon involves the "body-as-subject" experience. Rather than treating the body as an object, or as an "it," as is done in the preparation and training stage, the athlete becomes one with the body. In the phenomenological sense, the athlete not only *has* a body but *is* her or his body. In this regard, the body becomes the athlete's access to the world — the source of subjective knowledge and meaning. In the first dimension, the performers pass over the landscape, so to speak. On one level, they do not know if it is cold or if people are hollering at them, but at the body level they do know these things:

> My body is already a meaning-giving existence, even if I am not yet conscious of this meaning-giving activity. My body invests my world with meaning even before I think about this meaning.... My body makes the world and the other available to me.... My behaving body-which-I-am is the locus for the appropriation of sense and meaning.[22]

Although body subjectivity is a relatively recent concept in Western philosophy, the concept of an integrated mind, body, and spirit, or at least the desire for this integration, reaches back to ancient Greece. The Delphic spirit, which embraces both the objective and subjective dimensions of existence, represents the striving and struggling to reach perfection and conceives of a human being as a unity. Because each individual can come to know his or her personal uniqueness as a result of "being" in a sport situation, there are an infinite number of modes of such self-understanding. Each person comes to sport with a different history of experiences, different intents and motivations, and varying degrees of commitment. As a result the kinds, degree, and quality of self-understanding are highly individualistic. Perhaps the easiest aspect of self-understanding to examine is that of physical prowess, or the sensations that one is made aware of first on a prereflective level and later on a reflective and/or evaluative level:

> Perhaps a contestant may find a particular sport particularly meaningful because it does formulate a conception of a man who performs certain kinds of work,... because it formulates the patterns of his own personality structure,... because his own physical being is so admirably designed for the performance of that action. ...Perhaps he chooses to ski because he likes the feeling of the cold air as it stings his face, or because he likes the whiteness of the snow and the blueness of the sky. Perhaps he chooses to swim because he likes the sensation of being supported by the water.[23]

The physicalness of football, the communion with nature in hiking, the skinny-dipping sensation of skydiving, the open air and green grass of the golf course — these factors not only provide motives to participate but also become physical sensations that the player becomes aware of in the process of knowing self and the physical world. One can watch a thousand golfers and a thousand swings, but when *you* personally hold the club in *your* hand and swing, you are a uniqueness among commonality. A shot is *your* shot. You may ski down a mountain that thousands have skied previously, yet *you* come to know speed, balance, grace, and timing as unique aspects of who you are or what you are not. An individual in situations like this comes to an awareness of a unique, personal identity and a shared, archetypical humanity. The experience of the body as self is crucial to the individual's self-identification. In sport the athlete experiences self as a strong or weak, skilled or unskilled person — one who is or is not able to accomplish certain physical tasks with a high degree of excellence. Before anyone tells you or before you think about it, you, as your body, experience yourself as a moving being and as all the physical components that comprise movement. There is no way one can know static balance, or whether one is capable of static balance, unless one experiences a situation that demands it. The body tells the performer what it is to achieve or not achieve. It is not an experience that requires reflection or evaluation beyond the evaluation as it occurs in the ongoing experience.

Altered States and Mystical Unions

The athlete fuses body and action in a phenomenon that entails a voluntary commitment to a nonutilitarian, even absurd, act, yet one that is also grounded in purpose and in the search for new possibilities. Often those possibilities involve a dominance achieved by meeting a challenge of skill, fear, or passion; reflection in those circumstances sometimes yields only base or mundane understandings. On occasion, though, in this artificial world-for-the-moment, our reflections are less rational and concrete, and our feelings tell us we have achieved a special moment. Such moments reflect a sense of completeness, harmony, achievement, sensuousness, personal insight, or spiritual joy. Abraham Maslow has pointed out that they occur in experiences of love and sex, in bursts of creativity, in flashes of insight and discovery, and in certain athletic experiences. They are occasions when the "sacred is in the ordinary."[24] They cannot be arranged or guaranteed by virtue of merely participating. The prerequisites for such moments to occur ultimately defy analysis, yet they seem prominent in a wide variety of athletic experiences from mountain climbing to track events to basketball and swimming. They engender feelings of a closeness to God and a cosmic sense of self. There is no waiting, no goal, no doing, yet nothing is left undone. In these delightful moments, the thrower is not separate from that which is thrown but blended in a single motion.

A great deal has been written over the past two decades about what has been broadly termed "altered states of consciousness." Theorists have called such moments "flow," "peak-experiences," "oneness," "inner games," and "perfect moments." Athletes have described such experiences as "highs." While these kinds of experiences or "moments" are not commonplace, they do indeed occur, and when they do, they are highly significant for those who experience them. In experiences of such mystical union, the dualistic state disappears and one emerges from the experience knowing something one did not know previously. Such experiences are often attributed to individual activities — running, tennis, skiing — yet in many ways even a team player acts alone while a part of the group. For as Seymour Kleinman points out: "Although all participants . . . may be performing exactly the same movements, the individual, if he is truly engaged in the act, knows nothing of the others. He is completely absorbed in his landscape. He is acting only as *he* can act. He is deriving meaning and significance only in the way [in which] *he* is capable."[25] When an authentic I-Thou relationship takes place, the subject and object, while in a dualistic state at the outset, come together to achieve a "oneness" of experience. Runners claim, "I become the running." The literature has provided many accounts of athletes' feelings about being in union and harmony, not only with the activity but with something transcending and transforming the ordinary self. In such accounts athletes say things like: "I am at one with everything. There is no distinction between myself, the bicycle, speed, or anything. It is effortless. I am everything at this time and everything is me. It was no longer the hill and I, but both of us; it was perfect."

Maslow's original concept of the "peak-experience" was grounded in his study of motivation and personality, but the characteristics of the phenomenon are found in all experiences that are called "altered states" or "transcending" experiences in sport. These peak-experiences are characterized by a disorientation in space and time during which the sport participant becomes oblivious to surroundings and the passage of time. There is an intense sense of wholeness and completeness as if one small part of the world is perceived for the moment as everything. There is a sense of nowness, a freedom from past and future, and a here-and-now character that makes the experience very immediate. Individuals, more integrated with themselves and their total environment, feel at the peak of their powers.

Mihaly Csikszentmihalyi in writing about the concept of "flow" sums up many of the ideas embodied in the literature about altered states of consciousness. He suggests that flow may occur in many life situations but that "games are obvious flow activities and in play the flow experience is par excellence."[26] He also writes:

> We shall refer to this particular dynamic state — the holistic sensation that people feel when they act with total involvement — as "flow." In the flow state, action follows upon action according to an internal logic that seems to need no conscious intervention by the actor. He experiences it as a unified flowing from one moment to the next, in which he is in control of his actions, and in which there is little distinction between self and environment, between stimulus and response, or between past, present, and future.[27]

Too frequently the phrase "altered state of consciousness" has come to imply an association with mind-altering agents — alcohol, drugs, hypnosis. In some respects, flow or a peak-experience is mind-altering. The "highs" reported by athletes rival the "highs" reported in other mind-altering experiences. One of the keys to an altered state of consciousness in sport is that frequently it leads to a "higher state of consciousness," to a keen awareness of self and world. Such awareness is consciousness combined with a realization of what is happening in the activity and of what is going on within oneself. While awareness in these situations is not a cognitive thinking *about* movement to the point of disrupting it, prereflectively the athlete becomes audience to his or her own act at the moment of performing it. A statement about skiing powder snow in the film *Ski the Outer Limits* captures this completeness: "It is not often given to man to create poetry let alone recognize its beauty at the moment of its creation." Such awareness can allow participants to more fully understand the meaning and limits of their being not only in sport but in life.

In Western culture emphasis has been given to achieving end results in sport, and little importance has been given to attaining body awareness. Timothy Gallwey argues that body awareness is directly related to body achievement, and he points to Eastern philosophies and approaches to movement for their advocacy of awareness. Achievement, he says, is an inevitable and natural by-product of awareness. He advocates a balance between the desire to achieve, with its goal-directed emphasis, and attention to the awareness achieved in "altered-state" sport experiences. "Pure awareness with little will to achieve lacks direction, but the will to achieve with too little awareness is strained and lacks the requisite refinement to achieve the highest levels of excellence."[28] The coming together of running and the runner and the jump shot and the shooter facilitates an increased bodily awareness. Once the crowds, the coaches, the criticism, and the environment are "passed over" and the athletes' cognitive considerations of technique and strategy are minimized or eliminated, it is possible for flow, oneness, or the peak-experience to occur.

The true mystical union becomes a meditative state where thought and action become inseparable whether in sport or in some other activity. Such a state may be difficult to achieve in sport, since any activity involving the use of the external "target" (object of concentration) is *not* conducive to attaining a mystical union. Many Eastern philosophies, Taoism and Zen Buddhism in particular, have for thousands of years believed in the integration of mind and body, in the reality of "the unmoved movement," of "unity in polarity." These beliefs are grounded in an entire lifestyle. The skepticism of Westerners stems in large part from an analytic rather than an experiential approach to philosophy, science, sport, and life in general. The experience of satori — of enlightenment, involving the mystical union of mind and body, and sport and player — is difficult to communicate and, to most Westerners, has suspect validity. To be understood, these Zenlike experiences must be experienced in the sense of letting things happen, giving up the self, and suspending judgments. The process must start and develop within each person. Striving to achieve inner wholeness, inner peace and unity, and inner freedom replaces Western goals of superiority, status, fame, and material acquisitions. However, it is easier and often more acceptable to talk about the practical and quantifiable aspects of a phenomenon than to talk of the spiritual and affective dimensions of that same phenomenon.

Athletes who have transcended the need to focus cognitively on technique have freed themselves to move into what Gallwey calls the "inner game"; they thereby prepare themselves for the possibility of a perfect moment or a flow-experience. Eugen Herrigel in his *Zen in the Art of Archery* directs us to become unconscious and self-forgetful in order to move to the state of oneness, for "as soon as we reflect, deliberate, and conceptualize, thought interferes with the ability to move into a higher state of consciousness."[29] Such states of consciousness have been described by Sue Durrant as "fused" or "transcended":

> The fused state is the state of pure experiencing. There is a merging of awareness and action; one's identity has blended into activity. Everything is operating smoothly, automatically, harmoniously. The transcended state is characterized by a high level of affect. It may be experienced as extremely blissful, "oceanic," as cosmic love.... Everything feels ideal.[30]

Durrant tells us that self-knowledge is increased through awareness of the range of experiences that are possible in human existence. We are all the same, and yet we are each different and unique. Descriptions of fused and transcended states of consciousness by athletes and sports enthusiasts have been in both trade and professional literature for decades. These descriptions have too often been ignored as emotive, and the moments themselves have frequently been seen as not really being part of the game, yet for those who participate, these moments *are* the game — the essence of what it is to train, to sacrifice, and to take one's turn at bat. At any one of these moments the "rush" or the "high" can serve as the basis for reflection on the fundamental existential question, Who am I? They can also evoke the more cosmic mystery question, What is my place in the world?

Conclusion

Perhaps the spiritual aspects of the sport experience can be somehow shared with teammates, coaches, or perhaps even fans. However, in the "world-for-the-moment" elaborated in this essay, the communion of the individual athlete with the broader cosmos goes beyond camaraderie, teamwork, shared victory, and even beyond the well-executed technique that involves others. Mountain climbers are often considered the ultimate team members because the kinship of the rope is such an indelible and unspoken part of the experience. Maurice Herzog defines both the camaraderie and the individuality of achieving an ultimate goal:

> On reaching the top of Annapurna: Our mission was accomplished. But at the same time we had accomplished something infinitely greater. How wonderful life would now become! What an inconceivable experience it is to attain one's ideal and, at the very same moment, to fulfill oneself. I was stirred to the depths of my being. Never had I felt happiness like this — so intense and so pure. We knew we were there now — that nothing could stop us. No need to exchange looks — each of us would have read the same determination in the other's eyes. A slight detour to the left, a few more steps — the summit ridge came gradually nearer — a few rocks to avoid. We dragged ourselves up. Could we possibly be there? Yes! A fierce and savage wind tore at us. We were on top of Annapurna! 8,075 meters, 26,493 feet. Our hearts overflowed with an unspeakable happiness. If only the others could know. If only everyone could know.[31]

The others on the climbing team could not know just this joy, nor could anyone who had not been there. Both the *I* and the *We* are exclaimed, perhaps because of the interdependent nature of the achievement's technical demands, perhaps because of the singularity of the shared goal; yet each individual climber at the end is given over to the happiness, the thanksgiving, and the introspection that constitute a separate and unique set of understandings about self and a way of being-in-the-world. Similarly, no-hit pitching and goalie shutouts contribute to team victories; field goals kickers, running backs, quarterbacks, and receivers score the points, but only the football team wins the games. These collective achievements are noted. However, it remains for the individual to put the achievement in perspective. Here are two testimonials to the solitary character of sport experiences:

> In surfing the challenge is wholly individual. There is no team nor any human competitor. Surfing is just you and the ocean, you against the waves or with the waves. You call the signals. You lay the strategy. You execute the maneuvers. You make on-the-spot improvisations and adjustments to suit the situation of the moment. Add to these things the fact that no two waves are the same....
>
> A solitary person, an individual, meeting unique challenge after unique challenge.[32]

> There are no phonies in body surfing. There is no glory in carrying a pair of fins. It's a basic, primitive thing. It's just you and the ocean.[33]

Some athletes are never sensitive to what it feels like beyond the simple achievement of the task. Others know with clarity that the moment is precious, special, and may never come again. At such moments explanations seem simplistic. Becoming audience to their own art, finding finally, and perhaps once only, the fusion of intent, act, and outcome, their reaction is mistaken for egocentricity when, perhaps, it is a failing of the symbolism of a language to capture the spirit and sensitivity of what they have come to know and feel. Winning can be exhilarating. After running the first sub-four-minute mile, Roger Bannister exclaimed: "No words could be invented for such supreme happiness, eclipsing all other feelings. I thought at that moment I could never again reach such a climax of single-mindedness. I felt bewildered and over-powered."[34] About winning a gold medal at the 1960 Olympics, Herb Elliot recollects: "I had won! The gold medal was mine. And for the first time since the first lap I could hear the crowd's roar. How can I describe the jubilation that I felt in my heart at this moment? It is indescribable and something I'm quite resigned never to experience to the same degree again."[35]

Golfers, sky divers, surfers, sailors, skiers, swimmers, and others often seem eloquent in their descriptions of their relationship with the natural world in which they seek their achievements. It becomes a communion with nature that is as much a part of the sport as the defined task. The weather, the course, the mountain, the ocean, the river — they treat all comers to a common frontier. Respect for what we cannot control is coupled with a knowledge that one never really conquers but achieves only a temporary mastery of the elements. Injury and death are serious possibilities in some sports where calculations of risk are coupled with a belief in a guardian angel. Racing cars, climbing mountains, or skiing icy courses becomes a flirtation with death: a living on the edge and a sensitivity to the finite quality of existence: "Free fall is free being, man diving is man alive, . . . the exhilaration of sinking to the world of nothingness, or at least to stillness, and thereby creating the self as ALL."[36]

The umbilical cord is cut at birth. We are alone: to find a purpose, a way of being, a sense of self, a sense of relationships. We choose life projects to bring ourselves into a clearer focus. For some these projects are called sport. For those athletes fortunate to achieve the fusion of act and actor and the "flow" of a perfect moment, the lived-experience of sport is also the opportunity to know the cathedral without stained glass. It represents one forum in which to stand voluntarily alone, to test, to strive, and to be. Simply, it is a place to say, "I am." One runner has stated:

> In the last half mile something happened which may have occurred only one or two times before or since. Furiously I ran; time lost all semblance of meaning. Distance, time, motion were all one. There were myself, the cement, a vague feeling of legs, and the coming dusk. I tore on. . . . My running was a pouring feeling. Perhaps I had experienced a physiological change, but whatever, it was magic. I came to the side of the road and gazed, with a sort of bewilderment, at my friends. I sat on the side of the road and cried tears of joy and sorrow. Joy at being alive; sorrow for a vague feeling of temporalness, and a knowledge of the impossibility of giving this experience to anyone.[37]

Notes

1. David Sansone, *Greek Athletics and the Genesis of Sport* (Berkeley: University of California Press, 1988), 130.
2. Ibid., 78.
3. H. Frankel, *Early Greek Poetry and Philosophy* (Oxford: Oxford University Press, 1975), 487.
4. Sansone, *Greek Athletics,* 75.
5. Richard Mandell, *Sport as a Cultural History* (New York: Columbia University Press, 1984), 75.
6. Jean-Paul Sartre, *Being and Nothingness,* trans. Hazel Barnes (New York: Washington Square, 1953), 712.
7. Ibid., 157.
8. Eleanor Metheny, *Movement and Meaning* (New York: McGraw-Hill, 1968).
9. Paul Weiss, *Sport: A Philosophic Inquiry* (Carbondale: Southern Illinois University Press, 1969), 243, 245.
10. Martin Buber, *I and Thou,* trans. W. Kaufmann (New York: Scribner's, 1970).
11. Metheny, *Movement and Meaning,* 74.

12. Sartre, *Being and Nothingness,* 96.
13. Metheny, *Movement and Meaning,* 59.
14. William Harper, "Man Alone," *Quest* 12, (1969): 127, 128.
15. Sartre, *Being and Nothingness,* 368–431.
16. J. H. Van DenBerg, "The Human Body and the Significance of Human Movement," in *Psychoanalysis and Existential Philosophy,* ed. H. M. Ruitenbeck (New York: Dutton, 1962), 112.
17. Ibid., 113.
18. Ibid.
19. Seymour Kleinman, "The Significance of Human Movement: A Phenomenological Approach," in *Sport and the Body,* ed. E. W. Gerber (Philadelphia: Lea and Febiger, 1972), 178.
20. Helmut Plessner, *Laughing and Crying,* trans. J. S. Churchill (Evanston, Ill.: Northwestern University Press, 1970), 6.
21. Van DenBerg, "The Human Body," 107.
22. Adrian Van Kaam, "Sex and Existence," in *Readings in Existential Phenomenology,* ed. J. Lawrence and L. O'Connor (Englewood Cliffs, N.J.: Prentice Hall, 1967), 229.
23. Eleanor Metheny, *Moving and Knowing* (Mt. View, Calif.: Peek, 1975), 235.
24. Abraham Maslow, *Religions, Values, and Peak-Experiences* (New York: Viking, 1964).
25. Kleinman, "The Significance of Human Movement," 178.
26. Mihaly Csikszentmihalyi, *Beyond Boredom and Anxiety: The Experience of Play in Work and Games* (San Francisco: Jossey-Bass, 1975), 36–37.
27. Ibid., 36.
28. Timothy Gallwey, "You've Got to Increase Your Awareness to Improve Your Play," *Tennis Magazine* 9 (1977): 89.
29. Eugene Herrigel, *Zen in the Art of Archery* (New York: Vintage, 1971), 11.
30. Sue M. Durrant, "States of Consciousness Experienced in Sport," in *Persons, Minds, and Bodies,* ed. S. Ross and L. Charette (North York: University Press of Canada, 1988), 68.
31. Maurice Herzog, *Annapurna,* trans. Nea Morin and Janet Adam Smith (New York: Dutton, 1952), 168.
32. Jim Allen, *Locked in: Surfing for Life* (New York: Barnes and Noble, 1970), 17.
33. Curry Kirkpatrick, "The Closest Thing to Being Born," *Sports Illustrated,* 22 February 1971, 63.
34. Roger Bannister, *The Four Minute Mile* (New York: Dodd, Mead and Co., 1963), 215–16.
35. Herb Elliot, *The Herb Elliot Story* (New York: Thomas Nelson, 1961), 176.
36. Joseph Kittenger, *The Long Lonely Leap* (New York: Dutton, 1961), 174.
37. Mike Spino, "Running as a Spiritual Experience," in *The Athletic Revolution,* ed. Jack Scott (New York: Free Press, 1971), 224–25.

Bibliography

Gerber, E. W., and W. J. Morgan, eds. *Sport and the Body.* 2d ed. Philadelphia: Lea and Febiger, 1979.

Herrigel, Eugene. *Zen in the Art of Archery.* New York: Vintage, 1971.

Hoffman, Shirl J. "The Athletae Dei: Missing the Meaning of Sport." *Journal of the Philosophy of Sport* 3 (1976): 42–51.

Kleinman, Seymour, ed. *Mind and Body: East Meets West.* Champaign, Ill.: Human Kinetics, 1988.

Metheny, Eleanor. *Movement and Meaning.* New York: McGraw-Hill, 1968.

Morgan, William J., and Klaus V. Meier, eds. *Philosophic Inquiry in Sport.* Champaign, Ill.: Human Kinetics, 1988.

Murphy, Michael E. *Golf in the Kingdom.* New York: Viking, 1972.

Sansone, David. *Greek Athletics and the Genesis of Sport.* Berkeley: University of California Press, 1988.

Stone, Roselyn. "Of Zen and the Experience of Moving." *Quest* 33 (1981): 96–107.

Thomas, Carolyn E. *Sport in a Philosophic Context.* Philadelphia: Lea and Febiger, 1983.

Weiss, Paul. *Sport: A Philosophic Inquiry.* Carbondale: Southern Illinois University Press, 1969.

20

Games

PETER H. VAN NESS

GAMES FIGURE PROMINENTLY in many areas of contemporary American culture. Televised sports competitions are one of the most popular of today's public spectacles; video games are among the fastest growing segments of the electronic entertainment industry; and lotteries and casino gambling have become a leading source of new government revenues. Even eminently practical and serious activities have taken on the trappings of gamelike contests. For instance, the news media report the course of the U.S. presidential "race"; the business press follows the stocks of corporate takeover targets that are "in play"; and expert commentators assess the fortunes of legal "teams" in daily coverage of celebrated trials. "All the world's a stage/and all the men and women merely players," wrote William Shakespeare (*As You Like It* 2.7.139–40). In contemporary America all of society appears to be a game show in which most citizens are merely contestants. Despite the crassness of much contemporary cultural life, some old and new varieties of game playing retain elements of the spiritual character of their religious origins. Religious institutions, though, have lost integral ties to games and their players, church sponsored bingo and raffles, for instance, being more pecuniary than pious in their origins. Thus to the extent that game playing retains some spiritual character it does so primarily as a secular spiritual practice.

The Cultural Contexts of Game Playing

Most games occur within prescribed boundaries of time and space. The hourly revolution of a chess clock and the fine reticulation of a Go board establish finite domains suggestive of a macrocosmic whole. Part of the meaning of games is that they are potential bearers of larger meanings. In particular, they can be ways of apprehending the world as a maximally inclusive whole of the sort associated in the introduction to this volume with spiritual activities. Most games involve quests for completion or victory amid opposition or risk. The crossword puzzle is perhaps the purest example of a game of skill motivated by an urge for completion; the dice game of craps attracts players interested in winning other people's money; backgammon uniquely combines all of the elements of completion and victory, and opposition and risk. Game playing can become more than a pastime — it can become a practice in which people experience a progressive sense of mastery and vitality, even to a point of self-transformation. In presenting his influential definition of a practice, Alasdair MacIntyre offers examples of game playing and so does Mihaly Csikszentmihalyi in his development of the concept of "flow."[1] In this chapter I shall argue that game playing is provocatively suggestive of important cultural developments, both good and bad, both spiritual and otherwise.

The contemporary cultural impact of game playing is not restricted to popular pastimes and public media. Evidence for both its ubiquity and ambiguity is the surprising prominence that game playing has attained in the intellectual productions of philosophers and social scientists. The Austrian philosopher Ludwig Wittgenstein made games a staple item of epistemological inquiry. In his *Philosophical Investigations* he compared using a language to playing a game, and he used the notion of a game as an example of concept without rigid boundaries.[2] Language-games are correlated with the "forms of life" in which they are used and of which they are constitutive. Wittgenstein gave language-games a certain autonomy by tying them to forms of life in ways that denied legitimacy to any single standard of meaning and truth. So, for instance, he resisted efforts to hold religious idioms of discourse accountable to scientific strictures of rationality.[3] Religious philosophers have found this appealing and have celebrated religious language-games as sanctuaries from the purview of powerfully institutionalized ways of thinking.

The notion of games has been employed in theoretical projects of a precisely opposite type — ones that seek to describe the behavior of powerful agents in very public aspects of human life, such as economic activity. John von Neumann and Oscar Morgenstern introduced the idea of games to social scientific reflection in their classic study, *Theory of Games and Economic Behavior.*[4] Their interest in games was related to the ability of certain games to exemplify a mathematical theory dealing with strategies for maximizing gains and minimizing losses in precisely circumscribed decision-making contexts. Games of chance and competition are clearly the examples to which von Neumann and Morgenstern appeal. Such games provide contexts in which risks can be taken but losses limited — one places limits on bets by consensual fiat or by individual strategy. Thinking about economic behavior in terms of games encourages economic agents to make decisions in ways that limit their risks. At the same time, though, it also helps to conceal the human impact of gains and losses for others who are not active players yet who are affected by the game's outcome. The game metaphor is attractive to powerful economic agents because it allows them to act in abstraction from troubling economic consequences.

Finally, Claude Shannon's treatise on how to program a computer to play chess contributed basic ideas to the areas of computer science and cognitive psychology concerned with problem solving. It also gave impetus to the development of myriad computer games other than chess.[5] Shannon's work symbolizes the conjunction of games and technology that has become so great in recent years that young people usually read the word *game* as synonymous with *computer game.*[6] Many computer games have science fiction themes; for instance, the currently popular *Dark Forces* game is the most recent in a series of computer games based upon the popular *Star Wars* film trilogy. Thus games in this context acquire a connotation of imaginative prospect. (That the future according to many creators of computer games is rife with the ancient evils of war and sexism will be discussed subsequently.)

Games have figured in many more intellectual projects than the few described above. Those mentioned are sufficient to show that such theoretical projects are related to the wider cultural appropriation of games, for good or ill, as vehicles for sanctuary, abstraction, and imagination as well as amusement. The inclination to use game metaphors in the description of human behavior is not without dangers. Developing accounts of human behavior, or understanding oneself, using the premise that social life is a game runs the risk of trivializing real human sorrows and joys.[7] Why then has reflection on games continued to be such an attractive model for human behavior? In seeking to answer this question the anthropologist Clifford Geertz has helpfully proposed that "gamelike conceptions of social life" share "the view that human beings are less driven by forces than submissive to rules, that the rules are such as to suggest strategies, the strategies are such as to inspire actions, and the actions are such as to be self-rewarding."[8] The social history and function of game playing, including games' probable religious origins and professed spiritual satisfactions, provide support for Geertz's appraisal of games as disciplined strategies yielding intrinsic rewards.

A related question deserves attention. Is the prominence of games and the gaming mentality especially characteristic of contemporary American society? Probably not, says a point of view indebted to Johan Huizinga, the Dutch author of the classic text *Homo Ludens: A Study of the Play Element in Culture.* Huizinga contends that play is prominent in cultures throughout the world, accomplishing the important functions of expressing, mediating, and changing societal values. "It is through playing that society expresses its interpretation of life and the world. By this we do not mean that play turns into culture, rather that in its earliest phases culture has the play-character, that it proceeds in the shape and mood of play."[9] Huizinga proceeds to say that the play-element does not always maintain its prominence, receding, for instance, in archaic contexts, into the sphere of religion. This point will be of subsequent interest, but relevant now is Huizinga's comment that the play-element at various times and places reasserts itself. "But at any moment, even in a highly developed civilization, the play 'instinct' may reassert itself in full force, drowning the individual and the mass in the intoxication of an immense game."[10] This description closely resembles the portrayal of American society given above, rendering it one of the periodic, but by no means unique, examples of the reappearance of the play-element in a specific culture.

A more radical response to the question is offered by Jean Baudrillard, a social theorist of postmodernism. Building on the insight of Freud and others that play and games originate in children's impulse to repeat impressive experiences, and especially the behavior of adults, Baudrillard has characterized postmodern society as one in which there occurs a "precession of the simulacra."[11] By this phrase he means that techniques of representation and communication have become so technologically sophisticated and culturally ubiquitous that simulated realities have become more primary to people than the reality originally simulated. "The play of simulation" has proceeded to such an extent that original realities have been eclipsed — simulacra preceding them in postmodern experience.[12] The computer game *SimCity* (and now *SimCity 2000*) effectively illustrates Baudrillard's point. In this game the player is a city planner and architect who constructs very detailed — and orderly — cities. The precession occurs as players begin to feel themselves more comfortable as the inhabitants of the orderly world of their simulated city than of the flawed actual world. I suspect that this phenomenon is also one of the game's most alluring features.

Baudrillard himself identifies Disneyland, with its simulated worlds from the past, the future, and the imagination, as a cultural paradigm. He sees it as no mere recreational diversion. Instead he sees it as genuinely constitutive of contemporary reality. Its self-presentation as a place of play is disingenuous, serving the ideological function of trying to convince the public that the world outside its borders is really "real." Clearly Baudrillard is unconvinced.[13] A point of view indebted to his thinking characteristically understands that games precede the political, commercial, and legal matters they model, and the gaming mentality precedes utilitarian reckoning as the central dynamic of late capitalist society. The United States, in this analysis, is in the forefront of the movement toward postmodernism. In this context it is interesting to note that Marshall McLuhan, a social theorist to whom Baudrillard occasionally refers approvingly, has also cited the example of Disneyland as a cultural paradigm of play. He gives it, though, a quite different connotation. In *Understanding Media,* he stressed the imaginative power of game playing: "Games are a sort of artificial paradise like Disneyland, or some Utopian vision by which we interpret and complete the meaning of our daily lives."[14] Games as cultural metaphors have acquired more ambiguous, and even menacing, meanings among postmodernist critics.

Despite their many differences, the views of Huizinga and Baudrillard share a common fault: they detect game playing in so many places that the notion loses concrete meaning, and the analysis of the practice yields only vague generalities. For the purposes of this chapter, games will initially be considered to be contests of skill and or chance involving players who follow a set of rules for the amusement of themselves and possibly spectators. Among other things the rules of the game specify permissible actions ("the moves"), delimit the time and space of action ("the field of play"), and identify the goal of action ("winning the game"). People play games most often because they find them enjoyable. Game playing at its best is intrinsically satisfying and, like happiness in any form, does not require practical motivation or rational justification. It is potentially autotelic. It is not important whether games take place with or without great physical exertion; athletic competitions fit the definition given above but are not emphasized in this chapter. (The preceding chapter on sports covers this material.)

A Classification of Games

Roger Caillois, a French social anthropologist, has made a famous classification of games.[15] The scheme is not entirely satisfactory, but aspects of it are helpful because they highlight the social functions — and the potential social pathologies — of various types of games. He subsumes games under four rubrics: *agon,* or competition; *alea,* or chance; *mimicry,* or simulation; and *ilinx,* or vertigo. Examples of the first category are athletic contests like foot races or board games like chess; examples of the second are gambling activities like dice games or lotteries; magical displays and theatrical spectacles are instances of the third category, while carnival activities like ecstatic dancing and thrill-seeking pastimes like skydiving are examples from the fourth category.

Caillois's categories highlight features of games that suggest their ability to engender practices that are at once secular and spiritual. With at least the first two of these four categories Caillois associates a serious, secular realm of activity. Competitive games warrant comparison with economic competition in a market economy. Games of chance have analogy with speculative investment activities. In these cases games preceded and influenced the development of their more serious correlates. For instance, Blaise Pascal and Pierre de Fermat formulated the basic principles of probability theory by reflecting on games of chance; in turn, probability theory is among the set of mathematical tools that professional investors use in "playing" the markets. If such economic activities are undertaken too avidly, with an unconstrained fierceness and abandon, they succumb to the obvious dangers of greed and fatalism. The economically ambitious are not allowed by legal statute, nor are they encouraged by moral sentiment, to aspire to monopolistic profit making. Habitual gamblers are often inveterate losers who, contrary to their expressly stated hopes, are convinced that they deserve to lose and will lose eventually. A central theme of this chapter is that to the extent that games approximate commercial activities and their corruptions, they are unlikely candidates for spiritual practices.

The other two categories, *mimicry* and *ilinx,* are not as clearly associated with serious, secular activities, but they do bear obvious comparisons with the phenomenon of religious ritual and mystical experience. Caillois listed theatrical performances as primary examples of games as *mimicry.* Luigi Pirandello's *The Rules of the Game* is a striking example of how the game motif has been used to explore dramatically issues about illusion, reality, and meaningful human life. The preoccupation of the play's main character is arguably spiritual as he professes mastery of the rules to "the whole game — of life."[16] Related to this use of the game motif is the major movement in twentieth-century theater to reclaim the ritual origins of dramatic performance. Peter Brook's staging of the Indian classic the *Mahabbharata* suggestively begins with the scene of Śiva playing a cosmogonic game of dice.[17] A danger associated with absurdist readings of life as a game and aesthetic retrievals of religious classics is that the rational criticism one might apply to straightforward metaphysical or religious claims will be muted when these claims are suggested by artistic projects. Obscurantism and supernaturalism can seem more acceptable in aesthetic dress.

The contemporary cultivation of vertigo may take blatant forms like high-speed boating or bungee jumping. The generic rubric of *extreme sports* is increasingly being used for these sorts of activities. The cultivation of vertigo also receives more self-consciously aesthetic expressions. Sixties rock concerts celebrated loud music and frenzied dancing as a sort of pagan spirituality: Jim Morrison of the Doors proclaimed himself a shamanistic "Lizard King" and notoriously encouraged Dionysian excess in concert performances.[18] The fact that Morrison died from alcohol and drug abuse shows the real dangers involved with the pursuit of vertigo as a cultural ideal. Examples from the arts are not casually offered but emphasize a second theme of this chapter: games become plausible vehicles of spiritual significance in contemporary society when they are invested with aesthetic meaning.

The two themes may be stated more forcefully. Games lose both their playful and spiritual character when they become dominated by the commercial culture of contemporary society. The fate of baseball since its most recent labor conflict makes this point. The scramble for money on the part of owners and players has alienated the fans, who now attend and view fewer games. It is harder to imagine baseball as a metaphor for American life in it higher aspirations when the memory of bitter and venal negotiations are still fresh in the fans' minds. The plight of professional chess is equally lamentable. Professional chess players have squabbled with FIDE (Fédération Internationale des Échecs) officials, resulting in separate tournaments making claims to establish the world champion. Complicating the malaise in this case is the specter of computer competitors. Computer manufacturers and software teams are competing to build computers that can beat one another at chess and that may even beat all human players in the near future. (As of this writing only a small group of top players can consistently defeat the best chess computers.) Tournament officials are so aware of the prospect of computer dominance in the mere winning of chess games that they are giving increasing importance to "brilliancy prizes" — acknowledgments of style in winning, such as winning by means of an intricate combination or an innovation in established openings. When the style in which a chess game is played is emphasized, then the game's aesthetic and creative aspects are likewise accentuated.

The advent of brilliancy prizes in chess supports the second thesis: games take on a spiritual significance by their investment with aesthetic meaning. Game playing in Chinese and Japanese culture, like religious ritual, has generally been more aesthetic than in European traditions. A comparison of the Chinese tangram with Western jigsaw puzzles illustrates this point. A jigsaw puzzle is basically a picture cut into pieces that the player must reassemble into the original picture. From one set of pieces only one picture can be made, each piece having only one place in the puzzle. Tangram, or in Chinese *ch'i ch'ae pan,* meaning loosely "board of wisdom," is a game that includes what jigsaw puzzles do, but also much more.[19] The seven shapes cut from a square can be used as puzzle pieces to make preestablished geometric patterns and naturalistic images. Here the comparison with a jigsaw puzzle is strong. A difference occurs because one of the great fascinations of tangram is the creative task of making new patterns and images as an artist might from the constitutive elements of an art form. The comparison here is with a child's set of blocks — or more recent Lego sets — which can make both new and predetermined constructions. In China, and now elsewhere, old and new tangram creations are gathered in increasingly comprehensive book collections. A second fascination of tangram is the satisfaction that comes from making many diverse patterns and images from only seven pieces hewn from a single square. The experience of doing this makes possible a perception of an underlying unity amid a diversity of shapes, and as one's skill at the game increases, this unifying perception is sharpened. This satisfaction, in my view, is potentially spiritual.

Understanding games as bearers of aesthetic meaning does not guarantee their enduring spiritual character. This point is evident in Yasunari Kawabata's novelistic commentary on the ancient Chinese game of *wei ch'i,* more widely known in the West by its Japanese name of Igo or Go. Kawabata's book, *The Master of Go* (1941), is an elaboration of his newspaper reportage of a 1938 Japanese Go match. In the book, Kawabata uses the narrative of the defeat of an old master by a younger player as a parable of the decline of traditional Japanese society at the hands of Western culture and, more immediately, the postwar American occupation. "Modern rationalism" is Kawabata's phrase for this corrosive influence:

> It may be said that the Master was plagued in his last match by modern rationalism, to which fussy rules were everything, from which all the grace and elegance of Go as an art had disappeared, which quite dispensed with respect for elders and attached no importance to mutual respect for human beings. From the way of Go the beauty of Japan and the Orient had fled. Everything had become science and regulation. The road to advancement in rank, which controlled the life of a player, had become a meticulous point system. One conducted the battle only to win, and there was no margin for remembering the dignity and the fragrance of Go as an art.[20]

Kawabata argues that the deleterious influence of modernity not only was evident in the circumstances pertaining to Go — its rules, its rankings, its emphasis on winning — but pervaded even the play of the game. Of a decisive move by the young challenger, Kawabata writes:

> The Master had put the match together as a work of art. It was as if the work, likened to a painting, were smeared black at the moment of highest tension. That play of black upon white, white upon black, has the intent and takes the forms of creative art. It has in it a flow of the spirit and a harmony as of music. Everything is lost when suddenly a false note is struck, or one party in a duet suddenly launches forth on an eccentric flight of his own. A masterpiece of a game can be ruined by insensitivity to the feelings of an adversary.[21]

The mutual respect of players, the grace and elegance of an art, and the flow of the spirit — these are elements of Go that the Master and Kawabata prized. They are shared, says Kawabata, with the Noh drama, the tea ceremony, and other quintessentially Japanese cultural forms that are deeply spiritual yet secular at least in the sense of not being exclusively clerical prerogatives or salvific gestures. The game of Go as described by Kawabata is a paradigm of game playing as a spiritual practice, and its spiritual meaning is inextricably related to its aesthetic character.

The Aesthetics of Play

Since its inception Western philosophy has acknowledged the kinship of game, ritual, and art: Plato's recommendation in the *Laws* (803d) that people should live their lives in playing games (παίζοντά . . . παιδιάς) of sacrifice, song, and dance is illustrative. Philosophers, however, have also been made wary of aesthetic play by the eminently serious examples of the natural and formal sciences. Perhaps more than any other recent Western philosopher Hans-Georg Gadamer has retrieved play as a crucial element in aesthetic experience. Although Gadamer refuses to locate play in the subjective consciousness of the artist or aesthete, as, for instance, Friedrich Schiller did in his famous letters on aesthetic education, there is a sense in which he says that game playing introduces a transcendent quality to experience. Early in *Truth and Method,* Gadamer writes about the role of play in "the ontology of the work of art":

> If we examine how the word "play" is used and concentrate on its so-called metaphorical senses we find talk of the play of light, the play of the waves, the play of gears or parts of machinery, the interplay of limbs, the play of forces, the play of gnats, even a play on words. In each case what is intended is the to-and-fro movement that is not tied to any goal that would bring it to an end. Correlatively, the word "Spiel" originally meant "dance," and is still found in many word forms (for example, in "Spielmann," "jongleur"). The movement of playing has no goal

> that brings it to an end; rather it renews itself in constant repetition. The movement backward and forward is obviously so central to the definition of play that it makes no difference who or what performs this movement. The movement of play as such has, as it were, no substrate. It is the game that is played — it is irrelevant whether or not there is a subject who plays it. The play is the occurrence of the movement as such. Thus we speak of the play of colors and do not mean only that one color plays against another, but that there is one process or sight displaying a changing variety of colors.[22]

According to Gadamer, human players experience a certain selflessness in aesthetic play by yielding to the larger whole of a to-and-fro movement in which they participate but do not dominate. There is no conscious sense of vertigo, but there is a sort of spiritual union with the impersonal and inclusive phenomenon of the game. Gadamer quotes with approval the expressly mystical sentiment of Friedrich von Schlegel: "All the sacred games of art are only remote imitations of the infinite play of the world, the eternally self-creating work of art."[23] Here there is an explicit statement that art understood as play, or games aesthetically conceived, can provide an apprehension of the world as a maximally inclusive whole. Gadamer uses this insight in the interpretation of art and other cultural works. Interest here is more in how people experience this sort of game experience as a means of self-transformation in the direction of greater vitality and well-being.

Gadamer appeals to a primordial sense of play that is not formalized by rules or oriented toward winning. He stresses its autotelic character. Play that does not have this quality he almost regards as fallen from its purest state. The French philosopher Jacques Derrida, from a very different vantage point, provocatively makes a similar point: "Play is always lost when it seeks salvation in games."[24] He is speaking about play as an ingredient in the experience of reading and writing texts. This theme is taken quite seriously in France. Georges Perec wrote *La Disparition,* a three-hundred-page novel, as a lipogram, a verbal construction in which one letter (here *e*) of the alphabet is suppressed.[25] For Derrida play connotes sensitivity to textual contradictions, ironies, and disseminations that are uncovered by deconstructionist readings of texts. Games as rule-governed and goal-oriented instances of play tend to enforce univocal meanings and determinate outcomes, and by so doing, they tend to preserve what Derrida rejects as an untenable metaphysics. I think the situation is more various than Derrida allows. Certainly games lend themselves to co-optation by powerful interests, both metaphysical and political; yet they also socialize the play element in human experience and generalize the philosophical element in human thinking. If one thinks that human well-being is attainable for most people only in the context of a vital community that acts with some measure of concurrence regarding important beliefs, then the movement from play to games is not a predestined fall from grace but a prudent wager on larger meanings and communal flourishing. The spiritual appreciation of games need not be captive to a nostalgia for the innocence of childhood games. The role of games in children's experience does, however, merit serious reflection.

As conceived according to the definition preferred here, games occur in diverse contexts of contemporary culture. Two have been mentioned thus far. Games function as products and services in a multi-billion-dollar entertainment industry. In intellectual life they have served as objects of disciplined reflection yielding a considerable theoretical bounty. In educational contexts they are amusements that also serve significant pedagogical purposes, especially for children. Games have long been associated with childhood; standard commentaries stress the child's need for the skill development and group socialization that games can provide. Others have emphasized the child's propensity to relax by dispersing superfluous energy in game activities.[26] Each point of view has merit and relevance to the theme of games as a species of secular spirituality. First to be explored will be the role of games in development and socialization.

The role of games in the lives of children has suggested to psychologists that game playing serves a transitional function in their development. From different vantage points, Jean Piaget and D. W. Winnicott make this point about infant development. In his major work on this topic, *Play, Dreams, and Imitation in Childhood,* Piaget is especially concerned to describe the child's development in play behavior lacking formal opponents, explicit rules, and conscious pretense. He describes such play as "egocentric thought in its pure form."[27] Here he finds that the "assimilating processes characteristic of the beginnings of individual representation are most clearly evident."[28] In other words, games serve as improvisatory conceptual maps that simplify the larger world and enable the child to journey more satisfactorily through it. Piaget contends that when the child comes to play games with opponents, rules, and pretense (that is, more intellectual and social games), then this impetus toward social reciprocity becomes an accommodative process that balances the egocentric assimilative process. There arises in such games the equilibrium and reversibility characteristic of the rational behavior that civil societies presuppose and encourage.

It is not surprising that the psychoanalyst Winnicott understands children's play in less strictly cognitive terms. Certainly he retains the Freudian insight that games, like other cultural preoccupations, often serve as means for sublimating sexual energies that are not allowed to receive direct expression. More distinctively, Winnicott builds upon his influential contribution to object-relations theory in which he described "transitional phenomena" as behaviors related to the use of objects "that are not part of the infant's body yet are not fully recognized as belonging to external reality."[29] In *Playing and Reality,* he is concerned with the "development from transitional phenomena to play, and from playing to shared playing, and from this to cultural experiences."[30] More so than Piaget, Winnicott believes that play behavior continues in adolescent and adult life to be a means for creatively making important psychological transitions. He even goes so far as to say that psychotherapy itself is a project of cooperative play, taking place in the "overlap" of the play activity of the patient and therapist.[31] Play is therapeutic and therapy playful.

Reference to the playing behavior of very young children makes evident that there is a difference between playing and game playing. Piaget details the difference, and Winnicott implies it when he extends play to "cultural experiences." It is a crucial point. The word *play* can occur in English as an intransitive or a transitive verb. In its intransitive usage, such as in the sentence, "The children went outside and played," it is not stated that a formal game such as baseball is played. The children may have simply moved freely from one playful activity to another: chasing a cat, piling up leaves, throwing stones at trees, and so forth. Of course, there must be elements of levity, rhythm, and contest in order for such behavior to count as play. When the word 'play' takes a direct object, as in the sentence, "The children played ball," that direct object is a putative game — a more discretely identifiable and socially stipulated process. Piaget sees it becoming a more rational, and Winnicott a more cultural, experience. Sentences like "The children play together" and "The children played intently" lack a gamelike direct object but nevertheless suggest social cooperation and task concentration; they are intermediary instances. Some commentators see the development from playing to game playing as implying a loss of spontaneity and creativity. I see it as a movement toward making play a bearer of larger meanings and an instrument for social as opposed to merely individual transitions. I see it as raising the possibility of play taking on spiritual meaning similar to the meaning of traditional religious practices.

Games and Religion

Anthropologists and sociologists have likewise noted that games occur as a spectrum of activities, some more improvisatory and others more regulated. Trickster figures in Native American cultures well represent how the more improvisatory sort of game playing is related to religious life. The early history of games seems intimately connected with ritualistic, and so rather regulated, religious practices. Whether this is so because games gave rise to ritual behavior or because religion appropriated game playing in early cultural history, as Huizinga implies, is irresoluble by available evidence. Still, scholars have especially linked archaic games to the casting of lots as a practice of divination. For instance, the boards on which backgammon and chess are played have been supposed to derive from divinatory cosmograms—images of the entire universe upon which prognosticating implements were thrown. The evolution from casting lots as a means of divination to rolling dice as a part of race games to purely strategic moves in war games seems to be a reasonable reconstruction. Scholars say that chess probably originated in this way in ancient India (perhaps in the sixth century of the Christian era) and made its way to the West via Persia and the Arab world.[32]

The connection between game playing and religious prognostication is not a simple one in which religious origins yield secular pastimes. Cards as a medium of game playing arrived in fourteenth-century Europe as secular artifacts, probably from Mameluke Egyptians and, before them, medieval Persians. Some of the earliest textual references to cards occur in prohibitions on gambling promulgated by civil authorities or counseled by Christian clerics.[33] At this time cards were not used as means for occult fortune-telling as, for instance, Tarot cards have been used since the late eighteenth century. Tarot cards, like the more standard Western playing cards, were originally used for game playing. Only subsequently were they appropriated for practices claiming insight into players' characters and futures. Among certain people today Tarot cards are used to play an occult parlor game in which one person deals a hand to another and then reads the cards in the sense of interpreting them as augurs of health, romance, and success. Such readings of Tarot cards provide an example of a secularized activity becoming respiritualized—again oriented toward the most comprehensive context of one's world and well-being.

Games that involve elements of both skill and chance are attractive metaphors of people's lives. When card playing became initially popular in fourteenth-century Europe, it was quickly interpreted as an allegory of sinfulness: the fifty-two cards were said by one commentator to represent the fifty-two weeks of the year, and the four suits and thirteen ranks to symbolize the variety of sins committed during that time.[34] More positive interpretations are possible. A game that combines skill and chance can be interpreted as analogous to how people's lives are both partially within and beyond their personal control. How well one does at such games is revelatory of how well one's life is going or will go. Interpreted in this way a person's occasional trip to the gaming tables of Las Vegas or Atlantic City is analogous to a nineteenth-century European's visit to the proverbial "Gypsy fortune-teller" or, more remotely, to ancient Greek's journey to consult the oracle at Delphi. The chance verdict of the role of the dice or the fall of the cards gives a sign of how the whole of one's life is faring. One's increasing knowledge of the game, relevant or not to how skillful one is at playing it, gives a sense of mastery. The confluence of good luck and perceived skill gives people a sense of intense well-being that extends beyond monetary gain. It provides a psychological satisfaction that bears comparison with a spiritually enlivening experience.

It can be plausibly argued that the satisfactions obtained from a trip to Las Vegas are more deluding and deadening than genuinely life-affirming. A second way in which games were originally related to religion offers more contemporary promise. The meaning of contestation in games of several players was probably originally related to rites of invigoration in which the new year, and the world it brings, overcame the exhausted world of natural infertility and human hardship. Athletic races were elements of the Greek Eleusinian mysteries celebrated in honor of Demeter, the Greek corn-goddess. The Olympic Games probably emerged from the separation of athletic contests from cultic ritual. One commentator remarks on the social transitions with which games are primordially associated:

> Games transform ambiguous, perturbed, or displaced potentials and conditions into certain outcomes, and this is one reason for their widespread association, in myth or in practice, with such ritualized natural and social transitions as seasonal cycles, birth, initiation, marriage, funerals, and warfare. Furthermore, games necessarily incorporate a dialectic between hierarchy and equality, two central organizing principles of human social arrangements and cognitive functioning. From an (at least asserted or presumed) equality before the rules of the game results a ranked hierarchy of outcomes.[35]

The cosmic expanse and the mediating function of archaic games lend their contemporary descendants to appropriation on behalf of projects of theoretical generality and practices of psychological and social mediation. Victor Turner's supplementation of his notion of the liminal, which figures prominently in his theory of ritual, by the idea of the liminoid, is designed to describe just how this aspect of game playing in more contemporary cultures can serve similar functions as ritual did in archaic societies.[36]

In his influential book *The Ritual Process,* Turner defines liminality (related etymologically to *limin,* meaning "threshold" in Latin) as the condition of something or someone outside of society's traditional scheme of social classification.[37] Persons are liminal in this sense when they undertake a rite of passage that first separates them from a customary social status. The liminal separation is not designed to achieve alienation or even individuation, but rather to achieve new and more vital social bonds. The major rituals of the Ndembu people of northwestern Zambia that Turner describes in *The Ritual Process* concern women who have either experienced infertility or given birth to twins. Both the absence and abundance of children generate social tensions. Although the rituals described do not address the biological realities involved in these circumstances, they do, through their character as communal activities, draw the women's larger social group into a sort of shared responsibility for the tensions. Even more, they engender social creativity because the liminal experience in which traditional standings and rules are relaxed allows for a playful reconsideration of cultural possibilities. In his more recent writings Turner has generalized this scenario by saying that where a playful reconsideration of cultural possibilities occurs, or even where there is a socially significant occurrence of what Csikszentmihalyi calls a flow-experience, there is potentially a "liminoid" condition — one similar to the liminality phenomenon of explicitly religious rituals.

In this context consider the experience of the serious, but amateur, chess player or golfer. They take periodic lessons from professionals; they practice their game with regularity; and they participate in occasional local tournaments. They are part of a club, and their game playing is predominantly social. In a weekend of tournament play the amateur chess player will predictably open each game with five to ten theoretically sound moves — "book moves" — and then, amid the complexity of play, will vary from the book into demonstrably inferior lines of play that against a master will result in a losing position. So begins the player's descent down the hierarchy of chess players — first theoretically, by the quality of moves, then actually, by result of game losses. The weekend golfer experiences something similar. After not too many holes the amateur player starts to take more strokes per hole than is required for "par" play. He or she falls short of the expert standard and may suffer tournament losses as a result. Before the equality of the rules of the game, these players eventually become allocated their less than preeminent status.

In the course of play, however, the amateur chess player or golfer can have moments of excellence. A subtle combination of moves wins a piece, or a sacrificial gambit pays off with positional advantage; a distant green is hit, or a long putt drops. These inspired moments are what the players consciously seek but most often attain by means they cannot regularly repeat. They are the moments of the game that players remember and relive.

They symbolize the transition gracefully accomplished, the obstacle agilely surmounted, the opponent aggressively bested. That they take place in the course of a game or tournament the player will probably lose is, however, equally important. They are redemptive moments, giving meaning and value to larger experiences that do not have optimal results. As the game redeems the work week, the excellent move redeems a tournament of inexpert play. Each speaks eloquently to the life story of the players — to the largest context of their serious and playful undertakings. They allow the drive for personal excellence to coexist with modest expectations; they allow an estimate of individual worth to endure in the apprehension of the larger and more splendid wholes in which individuals participate.

Turner formulates his conception of the liminoid character of play experiences with conscious awareness of the Piagetian and Freudian traditions of interpreting children's play as a transitional phenomenon. He speaks respectfully of their insights; however, his account of play has a distinctive difference. He does not see the movement from spontaneous, individualistic play to socially regulated rituals and games as a resigned accommodation to sober rationality. Rather he sees the liminal playfulness of ritual and the liminoid playfulness of games and art as engines of a social creativity that enables human flourishing to achieve completion in communal forms. In the final section of this chapter I will reflect upon the recent advent of video and computer games as means with which adolescents manage the transitions of puberty and with which adults undertake more diverse changes. A relevant question will be whether game playing in this modality involves an ersatz sociality — the playing partner sometimes being a machine rather than a human being — or an inchoate sociality in which game players traverse computer networks in order to establish novel personal relationships.

Video and Computer Games

The first video games, which appeared in the late 1970s, were unpretentious and almost innocent. Atari's *Pong* was a video simulation of traditional Ping-Pong. *Pac-Man* was a variant on the theme of overcoming obstacles in a labyrinthine environment. A third early game, *Space Invaders*, introduced the high-tech war theme in a fairly innocuous way because the invading spaceships players sought to destroy were only blurry geometrical images. Each of these early games initiated genres of video games that have been elaborated with the introduction of more sophisticated game hardware and software.

Simulated sports games, adventurous quest games, and high-tech war games were given added potential and popularity by the introduction to the United States of the Nintendo system in the mid-1980s. *Super Mario Brothers* gave a winsome but addictive variation on the quest theme that attained huge popularity in several editions. *The Legend of Zelda* gave a more mythic turn to the quest theme, transporting the players to the world of Hyrule, where they sought to assemble the pieces of the Triforce of Wisdom, a cosmic source of goodness, and thereby to protect Princess Zelda from the machinations of the evil Gannon. The obstacles players face in the *Zelda* games are more ominous and violent than in *Pac-Man* and *Super Mario* contexts; however, the spiritual meanings are also more evident. Many subsequent video games have had narrative themes of quest, discovery, and restoration that self-consciously draw upon mythic and legendary sources.

The increasing popularity of these games among young people has attracted notice from psychologists. Alarm is a consistent component of their assessments, a fact indicated by the title *Endangered Minds,* a treatise that includes a discussion of video games by educational psychologist Jane Healy. Healy challenges the rationalizing bromide that video games are better for children than television because they are more interactive, developing hand-eye coordination and introducing computer concepts and sensibilities. She questions the extent to which skills learned playing video games are translatable to other, more productive, activities.[38] Other studies adopt a more appreciative posture.[39] They take note of the obviously worrisome attributes of video games, especially the violent and sexist content of many games and the addictive quality of the playing they induce. The *Mortal Kombat* series of video games is among the most violent and most popular of recent games. These observers note that the popularity of video games suggests that they serve some purpose, especially for boys in early adolescence who make up the vast majority of players.

Playing video games seems to ease the difficult transitions of adolescence with its fast and large doses of technological excitation and calibrated competition. Clearly there is some dispersal of excess adolescent energy in the playing of video games. More deeply attractive to young people is the thrill of something new, something suggestive of the future they are coming to think about in more serious ways. In video games they greet this future in the medium of a game that is designed to reward rather than frustrate their efforts. Playing tournament chess or bridge presents the possibility of being a rather consistent loser, or of making significant progress, then faltering. Video games calibrate competition to an individual's level of play; they are designed to allow players to progress from lower levels to higher levels and from games to their sequels. Certain qualities that are shared by excellent game players generally also promote success at video games — the capacity for concentration, the imagination of alternatives, and the cultivation of levity.

Imaginative creativity is especially valued. A mark of high achievement in playing video games is the ability of players to modify existing games and to create their own. Id Software of Mesquite, Texas, the maker of the *Doom* series of games, provides players with the resources for elaborating and extending elements of the game environment and action. New maps, music, and graphics are favorite additions. Another company, Maxis, Inc., of Orinda, California, has even released a software program called *Klik and Play* that allows players to create their own games. Finally, one of the highest forms of creativity occurs in new role-playing or fantasy games. These are the most popular type of games available on the Internet via services like American Online, Compuserve, and the Imagination Network — the last being an Internet access service entirely devoted to computer games. Influenced by the popular 1980s video game *Dungeons and Dragons,* these fantasy games are multiplayer, real-time games set in medieval or mythic locales in which players adopt fantasy personas in order to search for treasure, battle monsters, and compete with other players. Increasingly the players are being given more freedom to create their own game identities. Unchanging icons in current games are being updated with video puppets with changeable features; virtual reality versions of game figures are designated by the originally religious term *avatars.*[40] Playing games in an electronic network with invented identities may be a mark of creativity; it may also be a simulation that provides a shallow sense of community and an ersatz taste of spirituality.

Unfortunately, a frequent measure of progress in video games like *Doom* and many fantasy games is the player's dexterity at simulated violence and adversarial domination. This has an all too ready correlation with strategies for success in social and economic life. Of course, other measures of performance have been present in video games from their origin. A game like *Tetris* puts pattern recognition and hand-eye coordination to more constructive uses — to score points players must orient falling shapes to fit into a seamless wall at the bottom of the video screen. Word games and strategy games have likewise been adapted to video and computer screens. A second major technological transformation of video games is allowing a new standard of game playing excellence to emerge.

The conjunction of CD-ROM technology with the personal computer is transforming video games into more and more complex computer games. The most advanced electronic games now appear on compact discs capable of storing and communicating to personal computers the vast amount of information required to present attractive images and stereo music to game players. Not surprisingly, the quality of games and the quality of game players are beginning to be evaluated according to aesthetic criteria. One new game entitled *Myst* has been described as "a work of art" in an annual review of the best games of 1995;[41] and "*Wired* magazine, the bible of the new technology, even thinks that it [*Myst*] has defined a new art form."[42]

The creators of *Myst* claim that it offers players "the most depth, detail and reality that you've ever experienced in a game." Their motivation in presenting this vivid experience is not purely aesthetic. Game materials that come with the game presume that players are questers and that *Myst* "will offer up the answers you seek, if only you have eyes to see, ears to hear." The allusion to New Testament sayings of Jesus is evident here (Mark 4:9 par.). The spiritual language becomes more explicit when the material specifies that one of the things that players seek to know is "the identity of that betrayer of ages past, that destroyer of cultures, that defiler of sacred traditions." To be forewarned is to be forearmed — knowing the defiler allows one to protect and affirm what is sacred.[43]

As its creators claim, *Myst* represents a significant advance in commercially available simulation games operable on personal computers. It anticipates the more complete, or immersive, mode of simulation popularly called "virtual reality." Virtual reality is the electronic simulation of natural realities and the creation of artificial realities in which there is a significant degree of interaction with the virtual environment and with other active agents therein. More than a computer screen and a mouse are required for immersions of this sort. At a minimum, virtual reality equipment combines a computer with some form of head-mounted display (HMD), either goggles or helmet, that both eliminates real-world sensations and provides stereoscopic imaging, and a dataglove that transmits hand movements to the virtual environment. Although this technology is highly complex and still expensive, and was originally the preserve of government agencies like NASA and the U.S. Air Force, the production of virtual reality hardware for arcade game playing has begun. Also underway is speculation about the spiritual meaning of this technology.

Virtual reality is not simply a new media for games of contestation and chance, but, given Caillois's criteria of classification, it is almost intrinsically gamelike. It is all about simulation; in fact, it provides such an intense experience of alternative reality that it has been described as vertiginous. The comparison to mind-altering drugs like LSD has been made by sources as diverse as psychological researchers, reporters for the *Wall Street Journal,* and the late Jerry Garcia of the Grateful Dead.[44] Michael Heim, writing in his book *The Metaphysics of Virtual Reality,* thinks the comparison too tame: "The profundity of the VR experience calls for something of grander stature, something philosophical or religious." Later in the same book he describes the fascination engendered by such computer phenomenon as "more spiritual than utilitarian." "The ultimate promise of VR may be to transform, to redeem our awareness of reality — something that the highest art has attempted to do."[45]

Heim is not alone in seeing spiritual significance in virtual reality experiences. Howard Rheingold, editor of the *Whole Earth Review,* thinks similarly; he compares the advent of virtual reality technology to the origin of art and ritual in the Paleolithic caves of Lascaux, France. The painted walls and carved passages, Rheingold suggests, provided initiates access to an alternative reality that helped effect the cultural transitions of late Paleolithic society, especially the increasing mastery of tools, the proliferation of symbols, and the development of new social relations. Rheingold and the sensibility he articulates are not naive. They recognize that virtual reality may, like television, become a new media of commerce, diversion, and addiction; yet he hopes that virtual reality as experienced in play and work might become "a new laboratory of the spirit."[46]

A Question of Irony

A vision of playing virtual reality games over computer networks as a source for aesthetically playful satisfaction and technologically elite sociality is not unrealistic, yet it is difficult to interpret specifically. When this new form of game playing is given spiritual interpretation, what meaning will it have? Will such game players of the future be bearers of an elite ideal of aesthetically nuanced contestation — something like Hermann Hesse's *Magister Ludi* transposed into cyberspace?[47] Or will they form a technological cult in the computer heartland — their game playing being a variation on E-meter auditing in the contemporary Church of Scientology?

A historian of American religion, Martin Marty, named the first volume of his history of modern American religion *The Irony of It All.* In explaining his choice of titles he distinguished between literary and historical varieties of irony. The former type is the familiar figure of speech in which an intended meaning is the opposite of what the words literally say. Marty says that this form has little application to American religious history.[48] For perhaps different reasons, this sort of irony has similarly little relevance to the postmodern situation of contemporary secular spirituality. Deconstructionist expressions of secular spirituality are apt to see all spiritual professions and vocations as ultimately ironic, turning into their opposites if too sincerely embraced. New Age eclecticism, however, is apt to allow so many things to be spiritual paths and instruments that it approaches a naïveté to which irony is effectively foreign. From these different perspectives irony is everywhere and nowhere; consequently, in this context literary irony is not very apt.

Other expressions of secular spirituality avoid the language of post-modernism altogether and seek to combine straightforward expression with critical evaluation. They criticize aspects of traditional religious spiritualities, and they seek to provide better alternatives. They promote spiritual lives that accent personal health, social comity, cultural creativity, and a respect for the natural world. Many examples of this sort of secular spirituality have been surveyed in this volume. To these projects Marty's variety of historical irony is potentially relevant. Historical irony applies to circumstances in which the actions of historical agents have consequences contrary to what they intended. Will such spiritual beliefs and practices actually have the intended effects in the historical lives of the individuals and communities in which they inhere? Or will they engender only simulacra, or worse? Unlike in Marty's history of American religion from 1893 to 1919, no judgment is offered that historical irony applies to the material discussed here. It is surmised, though, that consideration of its relevance raises a worthy question.

Notes

1. Alasdair MacIntyre, *After Virtue* (Notre Dame, Ind.: Univ. of Notre Dame Press, 1981); Mihaly Csikszentmihalyi, *Flow: The Psychology of Optimal Experience* (New York: HarperCollins, 1991), 72–73.

2. Ludwig Wittgenstein, *Philosophical Investigations,* trans. G. E. M. Anscombe (New York: Macmillan, 1953), esp. nos. 68–75.

3. Ludwig Wittgenstein, *Lectures and Conversations on Aesthetics, Psychology and Religious Belief,* ed. Cyril Barrett (London: Blackwell, 1978).

4. John von Neumann and Oscar Morgenstern, *Theory of Games and Economic Behavior,* 3d ed. (New York: Wiley, 1964).

5. Claude E. Shannon, "On Programming a Computer for Playing Chess," in *Claude Elwood Shannon: Collected Papers* (New York: IEEE, 1993).

6. If one consults popular magazines with *game* in the title, one finds that almost all of them feature computer games most prominently if not exclusively: *Games Magazine,* published by the B. and P. Publishing Company is a relevant example.

7. Erving Goffman's writings provide a prominent example of this approach to social behavior, and although Goffman is aware of its dangers, he is not immune to criticism on this point. See, for example, his reference to checkers in the presentation of his notion of "primary frameworks" (*Frame Analysis: An Essay on the Organization of Experience* [New York: Harper and Row, 1974], 23–25).

8. Clifford Geertz, "Blurred Genres: The Refiguration of Social Thought," in *Local Knowledge: Further Essays in Interpretive Anthropology* (New York: Basic Books, 1983), 25.

9. Johan Huizinga, *Homo Ludens: A Study of the Play Element in Culture* (Boston: Beacon, 1955), 46.

10. Ibid., 47.

11. Jean Baudrillard, *Simulacra and Simulation,* trans. Sheila Faria Glaser (Ann Arbor: University of Michigan Press, 1994), 1–42. For Freud on this topic, see his famous comments on the child's game of *fort-da* in *Beyond the Pleasure Principle,* trans. James Strachey (New York: Norton, 1989), 12–17.

12. Baudrillard, *Simulacra,* 22. In later writings Baudrillard makes even more use of the notions of play and games, but seduction rather than simulation becomes the paradigm of play; see Jean Baudrillard, *Seduction,* trans. Brian Singer (New York: St. Martin's, 1990).

13. Baudrillard, *Simulacra,* 12–14.

14. Marshall McLuhan, *Understanding Media: The Extensions of Man,* 2d ed. (New York: New American Library, 1964), 210.

15. Roger Caillois, *Man, Play, and Games,* trans. Meyer Barash (New York: Free Press of Glencoe, 1961), 36–37.

16. Luigi Pirandello, *The Rules of the Game,* trans. Robert Rietty and Noel Cregeen, in *Collected Plays,* 3 vols. (New York: Riverun, 1992), 3:13.

17. Jean Claude Carrière, *The Mahabharata: A Play Based upon the Indian Classic Epic* (New York: Harper and Row, 1987).

18. Morrison's poem "Celebration of the Lizard" contains his famous proclamation, "I am the Lizard King," and also includes an invitation to play "the game called 'go insane'"; see the liner notes to the Doors's third album, *Waiting for the Sun* (1968), or the text in *The American Night: The Writings of Jim Morrison* (New York: Random House, 1990), 37–47.

19. A brief history of the game and a small catalog of shapes can be found in Joost Elfers, *Tangram: The Ancient Chinese Shapes Game,* trans. R. J. Hollingdale (New York: Penguin, 1978).

20. Yasunari Kawabata, *The Master of Go,* trans. Edward G. Seidensticker (New York: Putnam's, 1972), 52.

21. Ibid., 164.

22. Hans-Georg Gadamer, *Truth and Method,* rev. ed., trans. rev. Joel Weinsheimer and Donald G. Marshall (New York: Crossroad, 1989), 103.

23. Ibid., 105.

24. Jacques Derrida, *Dissemination,* trans. Barbara Johnson (Chicago: University of Chicago Press, 1981), 158.

25. Perec's novel has recently been translated into English as *A Void,* trans. Gilbert Adair (New York: Harvill/HarperCollins, 1995).

26. For standard theories of children and play, see Édouard Claparède, *Experimental Psychology and the Psychology of the Child,* trans. M. Louch and H. Holman (London: Edward Arnold, 1911).

27. Jean Piaget, *Play, Dreams, and Imitation in Childhood,* trans. C. Gattegno and F. M. Hodgson (New York: Norton, 1962), 166. For the place of Piaget's work in the context of other social scientific work on this topic, see Jerome S. Bruner, Alison Jolly, and Kathy Sylva, *Play — its Role in Development and Evolution* (New York: Basic Books, 1976).

28. Piaget, *Play,* 2.

29. D. W. Winnicott, *Playing and Reality* (New York: Basic Books, 1971), 2.

30. Ibid., 51.

31. Ibid., 38.

32. Richard Eales, *Chess: The History of the Game* (New York: Facts On File, 1985), 31–35; the classic chess history is H. J. R. Murray's *A History of Chess* (Oxford: Oxford University Press, 1913).

33. David Parlett, *A History of Card Games* (Oxford: Oxford University Press, 1991), 35–46. See also: Michael Dummett, *The Game of Tarot* (London, 1980).

34. Parlett, *A History of Card Games,* 51.

35. John J. MacAloon, "Games," in *The Encyclopedia of Religion,* ed. Mircea Eliade, 16 vols (New York: Macmillan, 1987), 5:476–77.

36. Victor Turner, *From Ritual to Theatre: The Human Seriousness of Play* (New York: Performing Arts Journal Publications, 1982), 20–60.

37. Victor Turner, *The Ritual Process: Structure and Anti-structure* (Ithaca, N.Y.: Cornell University Press, 1969), 95–96. For a description of Turner's influence on the development of "performance studies," a discipline involving a deliberate imbrication of the categories of religious ritual and artistic performance, see Catherine Bell, *Ritual Theory, Ritual Practice* (New York: Oxford University Press, 1992), 37–46.

38. Jane Healy, *Endangered Minds: Why Our Children Don't Think and What We Can Do about It* (New York: Simon and Schuster, 1991.)

39. Eugene F. Provenzo Jr., *Video Kids: Making Sense of Nintendo* (Cambridge, Mass.: Harvard University Press, 1991); Patricia Greenfield, *Mind and Media: The Effects of Television, Video Games, and Computers* (Cambridge, Mass.: Harvard University Press, 1984); and Geoffrey and Elizabeth Loftus, *Mind at Play: The Psychology of Video Games* (New York: Basic Books, 1983).

40. See Will Moss and Joe Pantuso, *Online Games* (Indianapolis: Brady, 1995), 372; and Hillary McLellan, "Beam Me Up to My Avatar," *Virtual Reality: The Magazine for Virtual Reality Development and Utilization* (March/April 1994): 33.

41. *1995 Buyer's Guide to Games,* editorial staff of *Games Magazine* (Boston: B. and P., 1995), 59.

42. Edward Rothstein, "A New Art Form May Arise from the 'Myst,'" *New York Times,* 4 December 1994, arts and leisure section.

43. Quotations are from the user's manual and journal that comes with the 1994 *Myst* software, a product of Broderbund Software, Inc., and Cyan, Inc.

44. Howard Rheingold, *Virtual Reality* (New York: Simon and Schuster, 1992), 353–57.

45. Michael Heim, *The Metaphysics of Virtual Reality* (New York: Oxford University Press, 1993), xvii, 85, 124.

46. Rheingold, *Virtual Reality,* 378–86, 391.

47. Hermann Hesse, *Magister Ludi,* trans. Richard and Clara Winston (New York: Bantam, 1969).

48. Martin Marty, *The Irony of It All,* vol. 1 of *Modern American Religion* (Chicago: University of Chicago Press, 1986), 1–14.

Bibliography

Caillois, Roger. *Man, Play, and Games.* Translated by Meyer Barash. New York: Free Press of Glencoe, 1961.
Csikszentmihalyi, Mihaly. *Beyond Boredom and Anxiety: The Experience of Play in Work and Games.* San Francisco: Jossey-Bass, 1975.
Hesse, Hermann. *Magister Ludi.* Translated by Richard and Clara Winston. New York: Bantam, 1969.
Huizinga, Johan. *Homo Ludens: A Study of the Play Element in Culture.* Boston: Beacon, 1955.
Kawabata, Yasunari. *The Master of Go.* Translated by Edward G. Seidensticker. New York: Putnam's, 1972.
Moss, Will, and Joe Pantuso. *Online Games.* Indianapolis: Brady, 1995.
Murray, H. J. R. *A History of Board Games Other Than Chess.* Oxford: Oxford University Press, 1952.
———. *A History of Chess.* Oxford: Oxford University Press, 1913.
Parlett, David. *A History of Card Games.* Oxford: Oxford University Press, 1991.
Piaget, Jean. *Play, Dreams, and Imitation in Childhood.* Translated by C. Gattegno and F. M. Hodgson. New York: Norton, 1962.
Provenzo, Eugene F., Jr. *Video Kids: Making Sense of Nintendo.* Cambridge, Mass.: Harvard University Press, 1991.
Turner, Victor. *From Ritual to Theatre: The Human Seriousness of Play.* New York: Performing Arts Journal Publications, 1982.

Contributors

PETER H. VAN NESS, editor of this volume, is Associate Professor of the Philosophy of Religion at Union Theological Seminary in New York City. He is the author of *Spirituality, Diversion, and Decadence: The Contemporary Predicament* (1992).

DAVID E. AUNE is Professor of New Testament and Christian Origins at Loyola University in Chicago. He is the author of *The New Testament in Its Literary Environment* (1987) and *Greco-Roman Literature and the New Testament: Selected Forms and Genres* (1988).

LUCY BREGMAN is Associate Professor of Religion at Temple University in Philadelphia. She is the author of *Death in the Midst of Life* (1992) and coauthor (with Sara Thiermann) of *First Person Mortal: Personal Narratives of Illness, Dying, and Grief* (1995).

J. MICHAEL CLARK teaches at Emory University and Georgia State University in Atlanta. He is the author of *Gay Being, Divine Presence: Essays in Gay Spirituality* (1987) and *Beyond Our Ghettos: Gay Theology in Ecological Perspective* (1993).

LOIS K. DALY is Professor of Religious Studies and Dean of Arts at Siena College in Loudonville, New York. She is the editor of *Feminist Theological Ethics: A Reader* (1994).

CHARLOTTE DORMANDY is an independent scholar who received her doctorate from Oxford University for her 1992 dissertation "George Eliot's Religious Life" and now resides in Kingston-on-Thames, Surrey, England.

NANCY FRANKENBERRY is Professor of Religion at Dartmouth College in Hanover, New Hampshire. She is the author of *Religion and Radical Empiricism* (1987).

ROBERT C. FULLER is Professor of Religious Studies at Bradley University in Peoria, Illinois. He is the author of *Alternative Medicine and American Religious Life* (1989) and *Naming the Antichrist: The History of an American Obsession* (1995).

STEPHEN HAPPEL is Associate Professor and Chair of the Department of Religion and Religious Education in the School of Religious Studies at the Catholic University of America in Washington, D.C. He is the author of *Coleridge's Religious Imagination* (1983).

DWIGHT N. HOPKINS is Associate Professor of Theology at the University of Chicago Divinity School. He is the author of *Black Theology USA and South Africa: Politics, Culture, and Liberation* (1989) and *Shoes That Fit Our Feet: Sources for a Constructive Black Theology* (1993).

JUNG HA KIM is Assistant Professor of Sociology at Georgia State University in Atlanta. She is the author of *The Bridge-Makers and Cross-Bearers: Korean-American Women and the Church* (1995).

ERNEST KURTZ is an independent scholar affiliated with the Center for Self-Help Research at the University of Michigan in Ann Arbor. He is the author of *Not-God: A History of Alcoholics Anonymous* (1991) and coauthor (with Katherine Ketcham) of *The Spirituality of Imperfection: Modern Wisdom from Classic Sources* (1992).

LAURA LEVITT is Assistant Professor of Religion at Temple University in Philadelphia. She is the coauthor (with Miriam Peskowitz) of *Feminist Critical Study and Judaism* (1996).

ROBERT CUMMINGS NEVILLE is Professor of Philosophy, Religion, and Theology and Dean of the School of Theology at Boston University. He is the author of *The Tao and the Daimon: Segments of a Religious Inquiry* (1982) and *Normative Cultures* (1995).

JOSEPH L. PRICE is Associate Professor of Religion at Whittier College in Whittier, California. He is the coeditor (with Donald W. Musser) of *A New Handbook of Christian Theology* (1992).

CARL A. RASCHKE is Professor of Religious Studies at the University of Denver. He is the author of *The Interruption of Eternity: Modern Gnosticism and the Origins of the New Religious Consciousness* (1980) and *Lacan and Theological Discourse* (1989).

HOLMES ROLSTON, III is University Distinguished Professor of Philosophy at Colorado State University in Fort Collins. He is the author of *Religion and Science: A Critical Survey* (1987) and *Conserving Natural Value* (1994).

CAROLYN E. THOMAS is Associate Professor of Physical Therapy and Exercise Science at the State University of New York at Buffalo. She is the author of *Sport in a Philosophic Context* (1983).

MARK I. WALLACE is Co-Chair and Associate Professor of Religion at Swarthmore College in Swarthmore, Pennsylvania. He is the editor of *Figuring the Sacred: Religion, Narrative, and Imagination* (1995) and the author of *Fragments of the Spirit: Nature, Violence, Renewal* (1996).

CHARLES E. WINQUIST is Thomas J. Watson Professor of Religion at Syracuse University. He is the author of *Epiphanies of Darkness: Deconstruction in Theology* (1986) and *Desiring Theology* (1995).

Indexes

Page numbers in parentheses are contextual citations for notes whose context is not already listed. Bold page numbers refer to figures.

Subjects

Names

A TITANIC MYTH

Contents

List of Illustrations

ILLUSTRATIONS IN THE TEXT

Acknowledgments

Although I first became involved in Captain Lord's case in my official capacity as General Secretary of the Mercantile Marine Service Association, it is my duty to point out that I have written this book as a purely personal enterprise. It follows that, unless otherwise stated, the opinions and conclusions expressed in it should not be taken as necessarily reflecting the official policy of the MMSA or the views of past or present members of the Executive Council of the association. At the same time, I must acknowledge my indebtedness to the late Captain R.W. Roberts, OBE DSC, a past president of the MMSA, for his consistent encouragement and active support of my efforts to clear Captain Lord's name. Before his death Captain Roberts was able to read and to approve what was to become the final draft of this book.

First among the many other friends and correspondents to whom I owe a similar debt of gratitude is Edward S. Kamuda of Indian Orchard, USA, founder and currently Secretary of the flourishing Titanic Historical Society. Since he first wrote to me in June 1962 he has supplied me with a steady flow of invaluable information and material; above all, for ten years he permitted me to retain his personal copy of the proceedings of the United States Congressional inquiry into the loss of the *Titanic*. Without unrestricted access to that extraordinarily detailed record of the experiences of survivors, my analysis of the evidence relating to the *Californian* incident would have been immeasurably more difficult. When the time came for that volume to be returned, it was quite unexpectedly replaced through the unselfish generosity of the late Miss Teresa M. Beddoes, SRN, of Buxton, Derbyshire, whose compelling interest in every detail of the *Titanic* disaster is shared by so many others throughout the world.

I must also acknowledge my indebtedness to Harry Milsom, the only professional journalist to meet Captain Lord in the closing years of the latter's life, not only for the most helpful interest he has taken in the case, but in particular for his detailed appraisal of the wholly inadequate first draft of this book which alone enabled a less deficient typescript to be prepared.

My detailed research work has been greatly facilitated by the assistance extended to me by those responsible for the administration of the Public Record Office, the General Register of Shipping and Seamen, and the British Library's newspaper branch at Colindale, London. The co-operation I have received from those staffing these departments has on occasion gone far beyond that which an intending author could reasonably expect.

I have also received greatly appreciated help from the editorial staff of the *Sunday Express*, the Information Officer of Canadian Pacific Limited, Mr P. Connell, of Sewill's, Liverpool, and Mr William Dutton, of Ellesmere Port. Keith Medley, of Wallasey, from the outset of my involvement in Captain Lord's case has given me every assistance in resolving photographic problems.

Permission to reproduce copyright material is gratefully acknowledged to the *Boston Globe*; *Boston Herald American*; G.T. Foulis & Company Ltd. (*Spunyarn* by Commander H.B. Boothby, DSO); George G. Harrap & Company Ltd. (*A History of Fireworks* by A.H. Brock); William Heinemann and the Houghton Mifflin Company (*The Loss of the ss. Titanic* by Lawrence Beesley); Hodder & Stoughton Ltd. (*The Titanic and the Californian* by Peter Padfield); William Hodge & Company Ltd. (*The Seddons*, edited by Filson Young); Mrs Margaret Howman (Captain Arthur Rostron's letters); *Journal of Commerce & Shipping Telegraph*; *Liverpool Daily Post & Echo* Ltd.; John Long Ltd. (*Advocates of the Golden Age* by Lewis Broad); Mercantile Marine Service Association; *Nautical Magazine*; Oxford University Press (*From the Dreadnought to Scapa Flow* by A.H. Marder); Hilary and Michael Rubinstein; *Sea Breezes*; and the *Sunday Times* (*Re-inventing Hitler* by H.R. Trevor Roper).

Transcripts of Crown-copyright material in the Public Record Office appear by permission of the Controller of HM Stationery Office.

LESLIE HARRISON

Preface

In April 1912 the White Star liner *Titanic* struck an iceberg and sank in the Atlantic on her maiden voyage. Subsequent courts of inquiry in the United States and Great Britain held that, while the *Titanic* lay sinking, another British ship, the *Californian*, also lay stopped not more than eight to ten miles away, and that if only Captain Stanley Lord, master of that other ship, had acted immediately on receiving reports that a nearby vessel was sending up rockets, he could have gone to the *Titanic*'s rescue and saved many, if not all, of the 1,500 lives that were lost.

Captain Lord appeared at these inquiries only as a witness. He was not warned in advance of the charge that was later held to have been proved against him, nor was he given any opportunity to prepare and to present a proper defence – a defence which could have included evidence then available proving that the *Californian* was at least twenty miles from the sinking *Titanic*. As a witness, however cruelly censured, he had no statutory right of appeal (a disqualification removed in 1970 in a new Merchant Shipping Act as a direct result of Captain Lord's tragic case), and all his efforts to have the British inquiry re-opened were frustrated by the Board of Trade.

Captain Lord was forced to resign by the Leyland Line, the *Californian*'s owners, whose directors accepted the view of an influential member of the board that public opinion would be against them if they did not do so. Fortunately, within a few months, he was offered a command in another shipping company. He served at sea throughout the First World War, and subsequently saw no necessity to renew his challenge of the 1912 inquiry findings, for in no way were they then affecting his personal or professional interests. He retired from the sea in 1927.

In July 1958, however, when over eighty years of age, he was horrified to discover that he was being inaccurately portrayed in a film based on a best-selling book about the *Titanic* disaster. In spite of his age and indifferent health, he immediately went to the

Mercantile Marine Service Association, the British shipmasters' representative organisation of which he had been a member since 1897, to ask that his case be re-opened.

In the first part of this book, I have done my best to tell Captain Lord's personal story just as I consider that it must have appeared to him, without benefit of hindsight and so far as possible in his own words, up to that morning in July 1958 when he decided to call on me. I was then General Secretary of the Mercantile Marine Service Association, and subsequently, as described in Part Two, it became my official responsibility to do everything possible to demolish the by then firmly established legend that by his apathy, negligence or cowardice – or even because of his drunkenness – Captain Lord had allowed up to 1,500* people to perish in particularly dreadful circumstances.

Such a monstrous charge, aggravated by the knowledge that there was no way in which it could be officially challenged, might have destroyed a lesser man. Captain Lord's unique strength of character enabled him to live with it, however, but he always bitterly resented the slur on his otherwise outstanding professional reputation. He was a man of absolute integrity, and he relied on the knowledge that those who really knew him, and whose judgement he respected, never believed for one moment that he could have been guilty of the alleged misconduct. Incredibly, he also bore no malice towards those who, wittingly or unwittingly, had placed him in such an appalling predicament.

Captain Lord died in January 1962, shortly before the fiftieth anniversary of the *Titanic* disaster, confident to the last that one day his name would be officially cleared.

LESLIE HARRISON
Heswall 1986

* There is no exact figure. The US Inquiry stated there were 1,517 deaths out of a complement of 2,223; the UK Inquiry stated 1,490 out of 2,201.

Technical Terms

The question as to whether or not the *Titanic* could have been the ship seen from the *Californian* and *vice versa* can be determined only on the basis of evidence given subsequently by professional seamen from both vessels. Inevitably this evidence contains technical terms familiar enough to seamen, but perhaps requiring explanation for some readers of this book.

The most significant of this evidence establishes the direction by compass in which another ship could be seen, and by the direction in which the observer's own ship was pointing. The diagrams facing page 16 show firstly the outline of a ship and the sectors from which the general direction of another ship can be reported; secondly, a typical compass card as used in 1912. The shipboard terms are self-explanatory; the compass card is more technical. From it, the direction, or bearing, of another ship, and a heading (if stationary) or course (if moving, that is, under way) can be given either in degrees, from 0° to 89°, measuring from the north (N) or south (S) points; north-east, for example, can be given as N45E. In addition, each 90° quadrant of the card is sub-divided into eight 'points' of $11\frac{1}{4}$°. The large black diamond shapes indicate north-north-east (NNE), ENE, ESE and so on; the intermediate points, marked by smaller triangles, are named north-by-east (NxE), NExN, NExE, ExN, and so on. Each point of $11\frac{1}{4}$° is divided again into four quarters, enabling a more precise course or bearing to be selected. An example of this, SW$\frac{1}{2}$W, appears in the written report submitted to Captain Lord by the *Californian*'s second officer, Herbert Stone (pages 46-47).

An essential point to bear in mind – and one which confused Lord Mersey at one stage of the British inquiry – is that the *bearing* of Ship A from Ship B remains the same regardless of any change in either vessel's *heading*.

To complicate matters further, a magnetic compass unfortunately does not indicate the true or geographical north, because the earth's magnetic north pole, to which a magnetic needle points in the northern hemisphere, does not coincide with the true north pole. In fact, in 1912, in the area in which the *Titanic* sank, the north-seeking point of a magnetic compass would be pointing about 24° to the westward of true north. In addition, the metal components of a ship's structure can also deflect a compass needle, an effect known as deviation. The combined effects of variation and deviation are known as compass error, allowance for which must be made when converting magnetic compass readings into *true* courses or bearings before these are laid off on a chart.

Out of sight of land a ship's position is conventionally given in latitude and longitude. Latitude is the angular distance, measured from 0° (the equator) to 90° (the poles); longitude is the angular distance, measured from 0° (the Greenwich meridian) to 180° east or west. The position in which the *Titanic* sank was approximately 42° North (N) latitude, 50° West (W) longitude.

One minute of arc of latitude can conveniently be assumed to be equal to one nautical mile, that is, 6,080 feet. A seaman's expression for a speed of one nautical mile covered in one hour is one knot, a term literally derived from the knots marked on a line paid out astern from a ship in earlier days as a primitive but relatively effective speed measuring device. As a nautical mile of 6,080 feet is longer than a statute mile of 5,280 feet, a speed measured in knots must be converted to obtain the equivalent in miles per hour. The *Titanic*'s speed of just over 22 knots when she collided with an iceberg was consequently a little over 25 miles per hour.

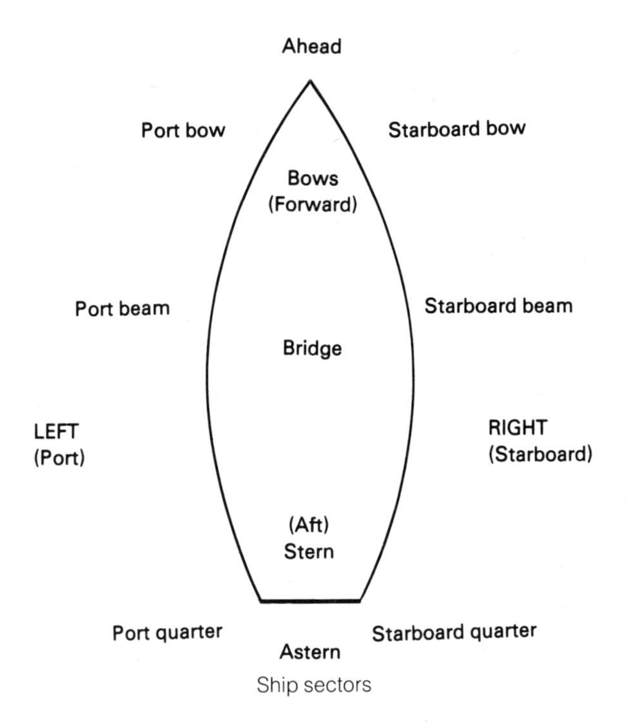

Ship sectors

A typical compass card as used in 1912

Captain Stanley Lord

PART I – THE FACT

History is what men did, not what armchair theorists afterwards think that they ought to have done.

– Professor H.R. Trevor-Roper

CHAPTER ONE

A Very Deceiving Night

From the open bridge of the *Californian*, Captain Lord and his young third officer had frequently been misled. The sea was flat calm, it was hard to distinguish where the sky ended and the water commenced, and sometimes they thought that stars low down on the horizon were other steamers' lights at the full range of their visibility.

It was the night of Sunday, 14 April 1912, and the *Californian* was on the final stage of her trans-Atlantic voyage from London to Boston, Massachusetts, heading due west at about eleven knots. Wireless messages received from other ships had reported ice ahead; indeed, at 6.30 p.m. the *Californian* herself had passed five miles to the northward of three distinctive icebergs reported earlier in the day by an Allan liner, the *Parisian*, also bound towards Boston. These messages prompted Lord to take what he considered to be the normal precautions required of any efficient shipmaster in such circumstances. He doubled the lookout, posting a man on the fo'c'sle head in addition to one already stationed in the crows nest, and at 8 p.m., meeting George F. Stewart, the chief officer and his second-in-command, as he came off watch, Lord told him that he intended to go to the bridge and stay up there himself until Stewart came on duty again at four the following morning.

Normally the eight to twelve forenoon and evening watches were the responsibility of the ship's third officer. On this particular voyage, however, they were being kept by Charles V. Groves, an ambitious 24-year-old eager to complete the qualifying watchkeeping service required before he could obtain his master's certificate of competency. He already held a certificate entitling him to serve as the only officer in addition to the master in a restricted class of ship, and the Leyland Line management had been prepared to allow him to sign on the ship's articles of agreement as second officer. Herbert Stone, the holder of a first mate's certificate and technically serving as second officer, consequently became the *Californian*'s nominal first officer, with Stewart as chief officer.

All three had sailed with Lord before. He got along very well with Stewart, a slight, heavily-moustached man looking older than his 34 years; Stone, 24, quiet, short, thickset, also with a moustache, was assessed by Lord as honest and responsible, if rather stolid; while Groves, taller, clean-shaven, with an assertive chin, was undoubtedly a very able young officer. Nevertheless, relatively experienced and well qualified as his third officer might be, Lord considered it his duty as master that night to be up there on the bridge so long as there was the possibility of encountering ice. Shortly after 8 p.m., therefore, he took over on the starboard side of the open flying bridge, the quartermaster at the wheel to his left and Groves on duty over on the port side.

Five feet ten inches in height, well built, with spare, aquiline features, Lord was wholly dedicated to his profession as a shipmaster. He expected all those who sailed with him to try to match his high standards of efficiency, and veiled an inner sensitivity behind a reserved manner which to some appeared to border on the autocratic. At the same time, he never resented the expression by a junior officer of an opinion at variance with his own; all else apart, to discourage such an approach was potentially dangerous when the safety of a ship and her complement could well hang on a split-second decision. His exchanges with Groves that night were accordingly limited strictly to matters concerning the navigation of the ship.

It was a bitterly cold night, but remarkably calm and clear. Apart from the confusion occasionally created by stars setting low down on the horizon, the watch was uneventful until 10.15 p.m., when Lord detected an unusual brightening of the horizon ahead. He watched this carefully for a few moments, then his suspicions were confirmed. It was 'ice blink', and there, close ahead of them and right across their track, lay field ice. Before the two lookouts had time to report their own sighting of the obstruction, Lord jammed the engine room telegraph at his side to full astern and ordered the quartermaster to put the helm hard-aport.* Under the combined effects of the reversed

* Before 1931, an order in a British ship to put the 'helm' to port meant that the steering wheel was put to *starboard*. This archaic practice was changed in 1931 and British custom brought into line with that followed in the majority of other maritime nations, in which steering orders were directly related to the direction in which the wheel, rudder and ship's head were required to go.

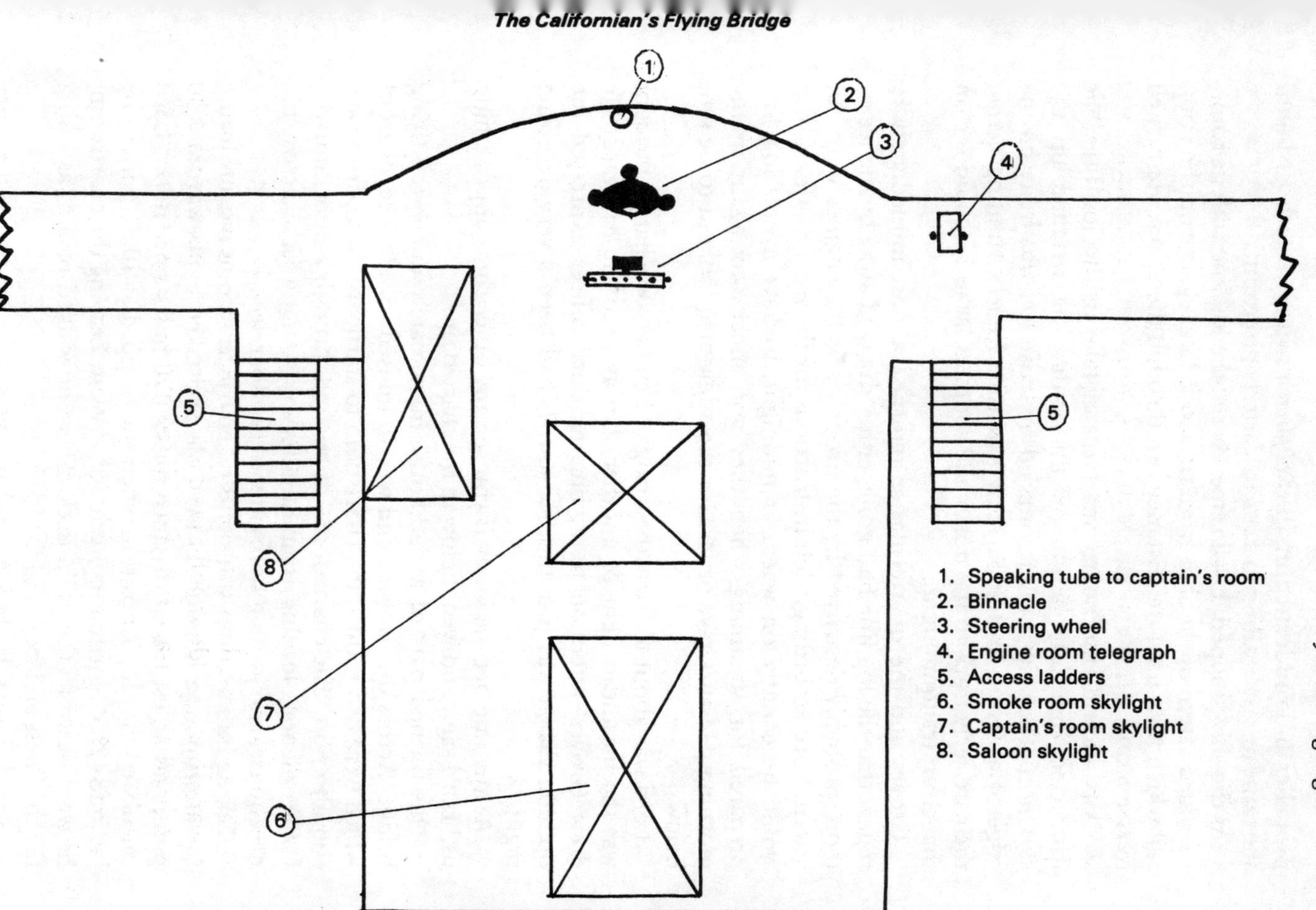
The Californian's Flying Bridge
1. Speaking tube to captain's room
2. Binnacle
3. Steering wheel
4. Engine room telegraph
5. Access ladders
6. Smoke room skylight
7. Captain's room skylight
8. Saloon skylight

propeller and rudder action, the *Californian* swung to starboard until she came to rest heading in a north-easterly direction.

As the ship stopped, Lord remembered the log line with its rotor, streamed astern of the ship from the clock-like register on the poop rail which measured the distance run through the water. He turned to Groves.

'Skip aft with the quartermaster and take in the log line,' he instructed him. Left alone on the bridge, he weighed up the situation. The ship was surrounded by loose ice, which lay on the edge of a denser and apparently extensive icefield running across their westerly track to the north and south as far as he could see on that clear, tranquil night.

Groves and the quartermaster returned almost immediately to report that the log line had gone, either dragged away by the ice or more probably destroyed by the propeller as the engines were put astern. Lord accordingly left instructions for the second officer, who would be coming on watch at midnight, to have a new log line prepared for streaming when they got under way again in the morning. He also gave orders for the additional lookout to be sent below.

Lord was about to leave the bridge when he saw what he thought was the masthead light of another ship away to the eastward. He drew Groves' attention to it, but the third officer expressed the opinion that it was just another star. It had been a very deceiving night.

'At any rate, let me know if you see any other ships approaching us,' Lord said, and went below to the chartroom.

This formed part of a deckhouse immediately under the flying bridge. Across the forward end was an unused wheelhouse, abaft of which were two rooms, the chartroom to starboard and Lord's own room to port. The chartroom was entered through a door, louvred for ventilation, leading from an alleyway running right across the deckhouse, and joining both sides of the boat deck.

Taking into account sun sights taken by the second officer during the afternoon, a latitude by the Pole Star taken by Stewart at 7.30 p.m., and an estimated distance run of 120 miles since noon, Lord calculated the ship's position when she stopped at 10.21 p.m. to be latitude 42° 5′ North, longitude 50° 7′ West. Leaving the chartroom, he went down to the main deck. There he walked round, assessing the thickness and extent of the ice.

He was joined by H.S.A. Mahan, the chief engineer, and as they

Captain/Chartrooms layout, ss Californian

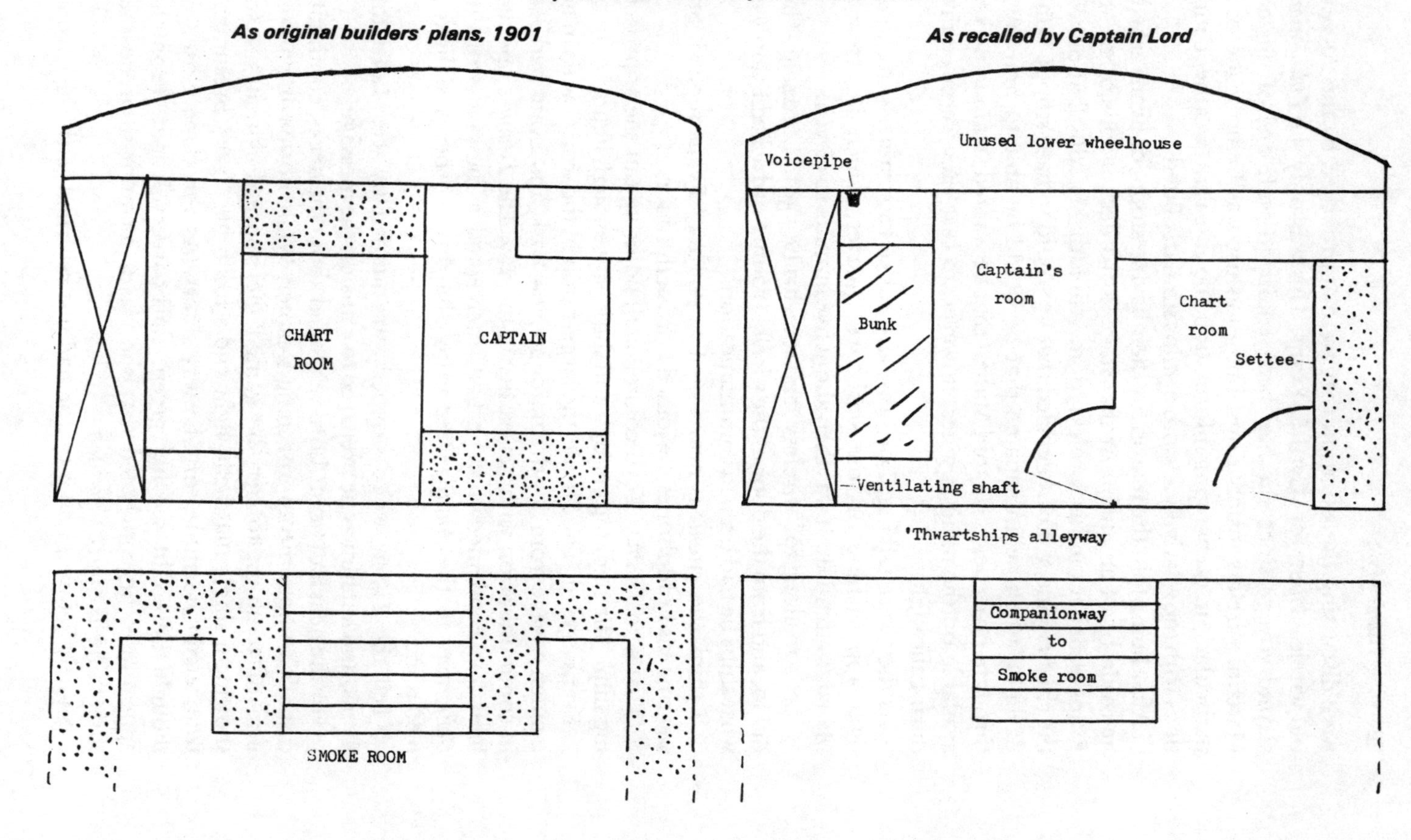

were discussing the situation they were approached by the 20-year-old wireless operator, Cyril F. Evans. This was only the *Californian*'s second voyage since she had been equipped with one of the new Marconi wireless installations, but good use was being made of it, particularly in exchanging information about sea and weather conditions with the relatively few other ships similarly fitted.

After being told the reason for their having stopped, Evans asked if he could be of any help. At that stage, Lord declined his offer, and Evans went back to his wireless room. After further consultation with the chief engineer, Lord decided that he would remain stopped until daylight, when he anticipated that he would be able to find a way through the icefield. He told Mahan that he wanted steam to be kept available on the main engines, however, in case they were required during the night.

As they were talking, Lord casually noticed a steamer's masthead light approaching on the starboard quarter, which he drew to Mahan's attention. It was then about five minutes to eleven.

'Let's go along to "wireless" and see what he's got,' Lord said. They did so, and from the door of the wireless room Lord asked Evans with what ships he had been in communication.

'I think the *Titanic* is near us – I've got her,' Evans replied. Still wearing his headphones, he joined Lord at the door.

'That's no *Titanic*,' Lord commented, pointing out the approaching ship. 'She's not big enough and she hasn't enough lights.'

Evans agreed. The *Titanic*, the largest ship in the world, was on her maiden voyage from Southampton to New York, and Evans had been in communication with her earlier in the day. The *Titanic*'s operator had then confirmed that he had intercepted a message from the *Californian* to the *Antillian* reporting the three icebergs sighted at 6.30 p.m.

'Tell the *Titanic* we're stopped, surrounded by ice,' Lord told Evans, and left him as he prepared to transmit the message.

For the next half hour, Lord remained about the decks, continuing casually to note the approaching steamer. While not paying a great deal of attention to her, he gained the impression that she was showing a single masthead light and a few other lights, presumably from cabin portholes or alleyway doors. As she came closer, he thought he could see her green, starboard, sidelight. From her appearance, he concluded that she was a medium-sized steamer, something like the *Californian*.

Shortly before 11.30 p.m., he had just returned to the chartroom when Groves knocked on the door. He had come down from the bridge to report the steamer approaching them on the starboard side.

'Call her up on the Morse lamp,' Lord instructed him. 'Let me know if you can get any reply.'

Shortly afterwards he went out on deck again. The powerful Morse lamp on the post above the bridge was blinking out the calling up signal and Lord went up to join Groves as he operated the key. The other ship was now lying stopped, about four or five miles away, on a south-easterly bearing broad on the *Californian*'s starboard bow. She was well within range of their signal lamp, which in Lord's opinion would have been visible for up to ten miles on such an unusually clear, calm night.

'She's answering you,' Lord commented, but he had been misled by the flickering of the other ship's masthead light. She was probably using oil lamps, he concluded; not every ship was fitted with a dynamo to power electric lights or wireless equipment. Otherwise there was no indication of any response to their attempt to communicate, and Lord required only a couple of minutes to confirm his earlier judgement that she was an ordinary cargo steamer, certainly no bigger than the *Californian*, and he left the bridge.

It was now 11.45 p.m. Walking past the wireless room, Lord noted that no light was showing. Evidently Evans had gone off watch and turned in.

Shortly after midnight Lord was out on deck again, standing at the foot of the bridge ladder, when Stone approached on his way to relieve Groves. Lord stopped him. The night was still remarkably fine and peaceful, the sea smooth, and Lord pointed out the ice which surrounded them. He also drew Stone's attention to the nearby ship, and told him to report any alteration in her bearing or if she were to drift towards the *Californian*.

As Stone went up on to the bridge, Lord returned to the chartroom. It was furnished with a short settee, and he sat down to read and smoke for a while; but the steam-heated atmosphere, contrasted with the crisp, cold air outside, soon made him feel drowsy.

He got up and walked across through an inter-connecting door into his own room. It was a poky little place, in his estimation the worst master's accommodation he had ever known. The room had no porthole; from forward, it was shut in by the unused wheelhouse, from aft by the bulkhead separating it from the transverse alleyway, and, on the port side, by a large ventilating shaft leading up from the saloon on the deck below to a skylight opening on to the flying bridge above. The only ventilation, apart from the louvred door to the chartroom, came from a smaller skylight, also opening on to the bridge above, a skylight which on occasion provided a useful direct means of communication with the officer of the watch, but at the expense of privacy. Tonight it was closed, however, and Lord called up Stone by removing the brass whistle inserted at the end of a speaking tube at the head of his bunk and blowing up the pipe. At the other end was a similar whistle, which Stone removed and acknowledged the captain's call.

Lord asked him if the other ship was any nearer.

'No, sir,' Stone replied. 'She's still the same. I've called her up again by Morse lamp, but she hasn't replied and isn't taking any notice of us.'

'Everything seems very peaceful,' Lord commented. 'I think I'll have a nap – we may have fog tomorrow.'

'Everything's quiet, sir,' Stone agreed. 'I think that's a good idea.'

'If that steamer starts moving around, or comes any closer, let me know,' Lord directed, then replugged the speaking tube and returned to the chartroom, where he lay down on the settee. It was too short to accommodate his near six-foot length, so that he was unable to stretch out his legs, and his discomfort was aggravated by his decision to remain fully dressed, despite the heat from the radiators. He even retained his cap, the peak pulled well down over his eyes to shield them from the electric light which he left switched on.

Despite the awkwardness of his situation, the warmth and his tiredness after a long day spent mainly in the open air ensured that he dropped off almost immediately into a sound sleep. He had no major worries. He had safeguarded the *Californian* and her crew by stopping when the ship ran into ice; a responsible and fully-qualified officer was on the bridge; there was nothing he could do until daylight, when the chief officer would call him; and he was fully dressed, immediately available if called out to cope with an emergency.

Barely half-an-hour later, at about 1.15 a.m., he was roused from his sleep by the sound of the whistle blowing in the speaking tube at the head of his bunk. He got up, walked across into his room, and acknowledged the call. Stone was speaking, and Lord understood him to say that the other ship was steaming away, altering her bearing towards the south-west, and had fired a white rocket.

'Was it a company signal?'* Lord enquired.

'I don't know, sir,' Stone replied. 'She didn't answer the Morse lamp, and has begun to go away from us.'

'Call her up again,' Lord instructed him. 'Let me know at once by the apprentice what her name is.'

He heard Stone replace the whistle in the speaking tube, and as he lay down again on the settee he could clearly hear the clicking of the Morse lamp key on the bridge above. Once more he fell into a sound sleep.

Some time later he was disturbed for a second time, when he thought he saw Gibson, the young apprentice, open the chartroom door.

'What is it?' he asked.

But there seemed to be no acknowledgment, and, as the door closed, he fell asleep again.

* See page 170.

CHAPTER TWO

Stanley Lord

What events had helped to shape the character of the man who lay sleeping on the chartroom settee in the *Californian* on that April night in 1912?

Stanley Lord was born on 13 September 1877 in Bolton, Lancashire. He was the youngest of the six sons of James and Charlotte Lord, and grew up in a disciplined, church-going environment. Of Stanley's five brothers, one died at the age of seven; another, after service in the army, emigrated to America, where he qualified as a doctor and settled in San Francisco; the remaining three all went into the firm of Dobson and Barlow, at that time pre-eminent in the manufacture and export of textile machinery. They travelled widely, supervising the erection of their firm's machinery in Germany, Russia and Japan: at an early age, Stanley decided that he, too, would travel the world, but in the Mercantile Marine. There were no family precedents for such an ambition; indeed, the only – and very tenuous – link with the sea which Stanley possessed was through an elder brother, one of whose fellow pupils at the local High School, Arthur Rostron, had joined HMS *Conway*, the Liverpool-based school ship, to be trained for a career as a ship's officer.

Both Stanley's parents were opposed to the idea of his going to sea, but his will-power and determination prevailed. On 7 May 1891, his father took him to Liverpool, where they jointly signed a standard form of indenture, binding Stanley to serve for six years with J.B. Walmsley & Company, owners of a fleet of thirteen sailing ships.

For their part, the company undertook to teach Stanley the business of a seaman; to provide him with sufficient meat, drink, lodging, washing, medicine and medical assistance; and to pay him £4 in each of the first and second years of his service, rising to £6 in the third, fourth and fifth years, and to £10 in the sixth and final year.

For his part, Stanley undertook faithfully to serve his new masters, by obeying their lawful commands, keeping their secrets and refraining from embezzling or wasting their goods. He also pledged himself not to be absent from their service without leave, or to frequent taverns or alehouses except upon their business, or to play at unlawful games. Failure on his part to carry out the agreement would expose his father, as surety, to the forfeiture of the sum of £20.

That same day, and still four months short of his fourteenth birthday, Stanley joined his first ship, the Liverpool-built iron barque *Naiad*, 205 feet long and of 1,039 tons net. She was commanded by Captain Davies, a shipmaster who had joined Walmsley's in 1886 and been appointed to command in the following year.

The *Naiad*'s four apprentices – Gibb, Lord, Walsh and Watson – shared a bare room, the 'half-deck', furnished only with their sea chests and a bunk apiece. Conditions were always spartan, and in anything approaching heavy weather their room could be awash. Stanley's powers of endurance were soon to be tested to the full, for the apprentices were expected to serve on deck and to handle sail aloft just as any other seaman in the barque's crew of twenty or so. His transition from schoolboy to deckhand was necessarily a rapid one.

Despite the hard life and primitive conditions, Stanley steadfastly applied himself to the business of turning himself into an efficient seaman and navigator, studying and working towards the time when he would be entitled to sit for his first professional qualification, a second mate's certificate of competency.

The *Naiad* was one of a large number of sailing ships engaged in carrying coal, cement and general cargo to the west coast of South America, returning to European ports with bulk cargoes of nitrate of soda or guano. In the *Naiad*'s case, sailing as she did from a European port in the spring meant her arrival off the southern tip of South America in the mid-winter of that region and an inevitable hard beat to windward before rounding Cape Horn. What this could mean in practice was soon demonstrated. After the *Naiad*'s long haul down the Atlantic, Staten Island, to the south and east of the Horn, was sighted. A month later, the ship was back in exactly the same position off Staten Island. She had made no progress whatsoever in her unremitting struggle to round the Cape against the relentless westerly gales.

Cape Horn offered the supreme test of a sailing shipmaster's skill and the endurance of his crew. Some ships might spend more than two months in the region before winning sufficient distance to the westward to enable them to bear up for their destinations on the Chilean or Peruvian coasts. Others, damaged or with their crews exhausted, might be forced to turn back for rest or refitting in the Falkland Isles or River Plate before returning to the struggle. Many were never seen again.

Once arrived on the west coast of South America, there was little relief for a sailing ship's crew. Antofagasta, Corrizal Bajo, Chilo Island, Coquimbo, Coronel, Corral, Caleta Buena, Huasco, Lota, Mejillones, Talcahuano, Taltal, Valparaiso – the names of the individual ports might sound romantic enough, but the reality was harsh.

Sailing ships lay moored or anchored off shore, discharging into lighters, the work being carried out by hand by the crews themselves. Loading, it was the same backbreaking routine. Nitrate was hoisted inboard by hand in 2-cwt bags from lighters in desolate and barren bays, offering nothing to visiting crews but hard work and boredom.

For the apprentices, there was an occasional break from cargo routine when the captain would detail them to row him over to another ship for a social call. While waiting for him, the *Naiad*'s boys would yarn with other apprentices, and the name of one whom Stanley met on such an occasion, while lying off Talcahuano, was to be recalled later. It was Ernest Shackleton.

Cargo work in an open roadstead could be disrupted by what were known as 'surf days', when sea conditions made it too difficult for lighters to come out. Given a run of unfavourable circumstances, loading a full cargo of nitrate by hand could take as long as three months, and the relief felt by the crews of ships ready for sea at last was reflected in a time-honoured ceremony, when any other ships which might be in the same port cheered the homeward-bounder.

Each of the *Naiad*'s voyages took about a year to complete, so that Stanley had endured five winter passages around Cape Horn by the time he had completed the sea service required before he could sit for his first professional examination. The *Naiad* sailed from Talcahuano on 18 February 1896 on what was to be Stanley's last homeward voyage as an apprentice. After what he had come to regard as a fairly average passage of 110 days, the barque docked at Swansea on 6 June, and three weeks later she was in her home port of Liverpool. Here Stanley was free to complete his studies, and the following month he sat for the Board of Trade's examination for a second mate's certificate of competency. He passed without undue difficulty.

Being still indentured to Walmsley's, Stanley had no option but to remain with the company. His next appointment, however, carried with it promotion, for he was sent as second officer to another of the barques in the fleet. She was the *Lurlei*, 185 feet long and of 835 tons gross, built by Royden's of Liverpool in 1875 and, since 1893, under the command of Captain S. Gunn. Young as he was, Stanley coped well with his new duties, and the youth became Stanley Lord the man as he learned to accept the burden of responsibilities borne by an officer in his handling of ship and crew.

The *Lurlei* sailed for Valparaiso on 3 September 1896, and Lord had served in her for just twelve months when, on arrival in Philadelphia on 27 August 1897, news reached him that his father was seriously ill. He was accordingly allowed to leave the ship and to return home by passenger steamer. Accustomed as he was to the primitive conditions in a sailing ship, he was fascinated by the relative luxury of steamboat life, with electric lighting and other, to him, novel amenities.

By this time, Lord's indentures had expired, and on 23 September 1897 they were returned to him endorsed by Walmsley's to the effect that they had been completed to the company's entire satisfaction. The document also bore a simple statement of account covering his six years' service. All in all, Walmsley's had done quite well out of the agreement. Over the six year period they had paid Lord just £37, including £1 in lieu of washing. In return, they had benefited from his services as a deckhand, able seaman, and latterly as an officer.

From Lord's point of view, on the credit side was the fact that his watchkeeping service as an officer in the *Lurlei* now qualified him to sit for a first mate's certificate of competency. His family home was now in Blackpool; it was consequently necessary for him to go to Liverpool to attend a navigation school. He lodged at 35 Bedford Street North, and after a brief period of study he passed the examination at his first attempt. He was just twenty years old, and having a first mate's certificate put him ahead of most of his contemporaries, a position he was determined to maintain.

One of Lord's fellow students was Henry T. Wilde, a slightly older officer with whom he became friendly, and at whose suggestion he applied for an appointment in the White Star Line. At that time, however, the company could only place his name on their long waiting list. Another acquaintance of Lord's who had gone into the White Star Line as an officer was William M. Murdoch. They had first met in Rotterdam: Murdoch was then serving as an apprentice in the barque *Iquique*, and he came on board the *Naiad* on a social visit to the half-deck.

Christmas 1897 was approaching, and at first Lord was influenced by his mother's wish for him to stay at home over the holiday period. On reflection, however, he concluded that this was the best possible time to apply for a job as a junior officer in some reputable steamship company in which he could settle down and establish himself. So he returned to Liverpool, where he heard that the West India & Pacific Steam Navigation Company had a vacancy for a junior officer. He managed to secure an interview with the company's marine superintendent, Captain J.M. Bridgewater, to whom he outlined his past career and future intentions.

Bridgewater weighed him up, then commented that, at twenty, he was perhaps a little young to hope for an appointment in their company.

There was only one reply.

'But that is a defect I am remedying day by day,' Lord quite reasonably pointed out.

Bridgewater laughed, and turned to one of the shore staff who was sitting with him.

'Well, I suppose we'll have to take him,' he said. 'We can't get anybody else at this time of the year.'

So Lord's decision was justified, and on 29 December 1897 he joined the ss *Barbadian* as third officer. He also enrolled in the Mercantile Marine Service Association, an old-established, Liverpool-based organisation representing shipmasters and officers.

The *Barbadian*, 4,504 tons gross, built in 1892, was one of a fleet of fifteen ships, inaugurated some forty years previously to trade to ports in the West Indies, Caribbean Sea and Mexican Gulf. Lord's introduction to his new company was inauspicious. While boarding the *Barbadian*, he had the mortification of seeing his cabin trunk, containing all his personal possessions, dropped between the ship's side and the quay. Fortunately it jammed before reaching the water and was safely recovered.

Then came his first encounter with Captain A.H. Highton, master of the *Barbadian*, who approached him malevolently chewing his whiskers. He eyed his new third officer up and down, then turned and walked away without saying a word. He then approached Lord a second time.

'Have you ever been in steam before?'

'No, sir,' Lord replied.

Captain Highton walked away. A third time he approached him, still chewing his whiskers, and delivered his verdict.

'I've no time for officers who have only been in sail,' he observed. 'They're a dirty, lazy, slovenly bunch of buggers.'

He then retired, leaving behind him a very thoughtful new third officer. There was only one thing to be done, he decided. He must do his very best to prove to Captain Highton that, in whatever category he otherwise placed him, he was neither dirty, lazy, nor slovenly.

With that aim, he got on with his job as efficiently as he knew how, and his relationship with Captain Highton eventually became quite cordial. It came as no surprise to Lord, however, to learn that the captain's nickname in the company was 'Mad Jack'.

Lord stayed in the *Barbadian* as third officer for nearly two years, serving mainly under Captain A.S. Campbell. The general pattern of voyages involved approximately six weeks away from Liverpool, followed by an interlude in port of from four to fourteen days.

His service in the *Barbadian* was interrupted in September 1899 and followed by promotion to the rank of second officer in the *Jamaican*, a 2,947-ton steamer under the command of Captain J.N. Pickthall.* The ship had been taken up under a special government charter as Transport No 37, for service in support of the army engaged in the Boer War, and she sailed from Queenstown on 23 October 1899 carrying the Inniskillen Dragoons with their horses. She disembarked them in Capetown, where she then took on board a detachment of the newly formed South African Light Horse and sailed for Durban.

* Lord's official record in the Board of Trade's files is endorsed: 'Did not join *Barbadian* 7.8.1899. Satisfactory letter from owners produced 2.3.1901'. In 1959, Captain Lord casually mentioned to the author that the only interruption he ever experienced during his sea career was caused when he accidentally broke his leg. His promotion to second officer six weeks after 'failing to join' the *Barbadian* and the company's 'satisfactory letter' covering what was otherwise the most serious of offences makes it reasonable to assume that Lord's service in the *Barbadian* was in fact terminated by that accident.

The unit's commanding officer was 37-year-old Major the Hon Julian Byng,* who regularly used to join Lord during his watch on the bridge and talk with him. Lord took an immediate liking to the man, and formed the opinion that, quiet though his manner might be, he was obviously an exceptionally capable officer. He was certainly in complete control of the varied personalities to be found in his regiment, which he had raised himself.

For the rest of her stay in South African waters the *Jamaican* was engaged in carrying military stores and personnel between Durban and East London. One particularly urgent task, about the time of the relief of Ladysmith, was the transfer of a battery of artillery. These novel operations provided Lord with an exceptionally valuable opportunity to extend his professional experience. In particular, he carefully noted the practical steps required to ensure the well-being of horses when carried in a ship.

The *Jamaican* returned to London in June 1900, resuming her normal sailings to the West Indies and New Orleans a month later. In January 1901, Lord completed the necessary watchkeeping service required before he could sit for his master's certificate of competency. After only a brief spell at a navigation school, he took the examination successfully in February. Encouraged by this achievement, he decided to stay ashore a little longer and to study for an extra master's certificate, the highest voluntary professional qualification it was possible for him to obtain. He passed the examination on 3 May.

While in Liverpool, Lord stayed at 56 Grey Road, Walton. Just around the corner, in Highfield Road, lived a retired master mariner, William Tutton, with whose family Lord became very friendly.

In 1900, the West India & Pacific Steam Navigation Company, in which Lord had now served for three years, was taken over by the Leyland Line, the combined fleet totalling over thirty ships. In turn, within the year the Leyland Line itself became part of the International Mercantile Marine shipping combine. These changes had little direct impact on the sea staff, however, other than to widen the field of their trading operations, and Lord was particularly pleased that Captain Bridgewater remained as a marine superintendent, for the two had established a very happy relationship based on mutual confidence. Nevertheless, even the

* Later created Viscount Byng of Vimy.

ss *Californian*

The *Californian*'s captain and officers, April 1912. (The caption to this illustration in the first edition of *A Night to Remember* by Walter Lord commented: 'The spyglass in Captain Lord's lap is somewhat ironical, considering she lay within 10 miles of the *Titanic* all during the sinking'.)

(Above) The *Californian*'s captain and officers, April 1912. *(L to R)* (back): H. St (second officer); C.V. Grov (third officer). (Front): Capt Lord, G.F. Stewart (chief officer)

(Left) Benjamin Kirk

distinction of having obtained an extra master's certificate failed to earn Lord more than another second officer's berth, this time in the relatively small *Bernard Hall* of 1,706 tons, under Captain Richard Griffiths. His expected promotion followed their return to Liverpool on 11 July 1901, however, and a fortnight later he sailed on his first voyage as chief officer in the *Darien*, 2,178 tons, with Captain J. Myles.

They were away for three months on a voyage to West Indian and Gulf ports, during which an incident occurred which Lord was never to forget. While the *Darien* was lying in the quarantine anchorage in the Mississippi, the river pilot informed Captain Myles that another of the company's ships, the *Atlantian*, would shortly be passing, outward bound for the Cape with horses.

In the West India Company's fleet an informal custom had become established by which passing ships saluted each other by firing distress signals, for they had as yet no special night recognition signals such as were used in many other shipping companies. It came as no surprise to Lord, therefore, when Captain Myles told him to call the second officer, as he proposed to salute the *Atlantian* as she passed, for while serving as second officer himself it had often been Lord's duty to fire a distress signal on such an occasion. The second officer had gone below, however, so he decided to do the job himself. Taking a detonator from its stowage, he fitted it into the socket on the bridge from which it was to be discharged. As the *Atlantian* approached, he jerked the firing lanyard, and the signal soared upwards, to burst high overhead with a report loud enough to be heard up to ten miles away.

The *Atlantian* responded with a similar signal, and, as she closed, her master, Captain W.S. Wallace, could be seen standing in the wing of the bridge. He was holding a megaphone, through which he hailed the *Darien*.

'Is that you, Myles?' he called.

Captain Myles' acknowledgment reflected the fact that, not so long ago, he had been serving under Captain Wallace as chief officer.

'Yes, sir,' he replied. 'How are you?'

A brief exchange of conventional good wishes closed the incident. For Lord, it was to be the last occasion on which he personally fired a distress signal, and every detail remained imprinted on his mind.

After a single voyage in the *Darien*, Lord received a very unusual appointment for a relatively junior chief officer, when he was sent to join the *Colonian*, of 4,142 tons, a new ship then fitting out in North Shields. He was greatly impressed by this significant demonstration of the management's confidence in his ability, for the post was a particularly responsible one. Careful attention to structural maintenance during the first year or so of a ship's life is essential if she is to give efficient service for the optimum length of her operational employment, and it is the chief officer who is primarily responsible for this.

The *Colonian*'s maiden voyage took her to New Orleans, following which she made a voyage to Capetown via Fiume.

As she was about to sail from the Alexandra Dock in Liverpool, it was found that one of her seamen was missing. Standing on the quay side was a young man called Davies, whose ambition it was to get to South Africa so that he could enlist in the British army there. Although he had nothing other than the clothes he was wearing, and had never been to sea before, he volunteered to sail in the ship, explaining his inability to produce a discharge book by claiming that he had sent for it, but it had not as yet been delivered. He was duly signed on, but it was not long before it became clear that he was a first tripper. He did his best, however, and his shipmates put up with him, but after three weeks' hard work his clothes began to wear out. Lord noticed this and became concerned.

'Haven't you any more clothes, lad?' he asked him one day.

Davies could only admit to his sorry situation, so Lord took him along to his own room. There he searched among his personal belongings and produced a new brown shirt, which he gave to Davies to replace his own tattered one. Davies rewarded him by deserting the ship on her arrival in South Africa.

Lord stayed in the *Colonian* for nearly three years, the whole of that time with Captain W.N. Bullock: on leaving her, he received two references. The first was from the Atlantic Transport Company, managers of the ship from April 1903 to June 1904. It recorded that they had always found Lord to be 'energetic in the discharge of his duties, keeping his ship in excellent condition in every respect'.

The second was a more personal testimonial from Captain Bridgewater, handwritten. It covered the whole of Lord's time in the company, from his first appointment in 1897, and referred particularly to his service as second officer of the *Jamaican* while she was employed as Transport No. 37. The reference concluded:

> During the whole time Mr Lord has been in this service and the whole time under my supervision, he has *always* been reported favourably by the various masters he has sailed with as being sober, industrious, and a good seaman and navigator. From my own observations I have always found him most attentive to his duties and at all times gentlemanly and courteous.

Bridgewater's underlining of the word 'always' particularly pleased Lord, for it distinguished the reference from the standard form in which these were normally given to officers.

Lord's next appointment was as chief officer of the *Antillian*, 5,608 tons, with accommodation for 38 passengers, under Captain William H. Howell's command. He joined her at Antwerp on 4 August 1904, signing on for a routine voyage to New Orleans. Once again, however, he found himself appointed to a ship selected for special duties. After calling at London, the *Antillian* sailed for Southampton, where she joined nine other British ships chartered to carry an army force under Lieutenant-General Sir John French engaged in a seaborne invasion exercise.

On Monday, 5 September, the transports went alongside to pick up their allotted troops, the *Antillian* embarking over 1,000 men of the Irish Guards and 1st Royal Berkshire Regiment. After anchoring off Spithead, the ten transports, in two divisions and escorted by cruisers, sailed at 9 a.m. the following day. By 7.30 a.m. on the 7th, they had anchored about a mile off Clacton-on-Sea and began to send the troops ashore in ships' boats towed by Royal Naval steam launches and picket boats. All went well, and the operation was completed by mid-afternoon.

After just under a week on manoeuvres in Essex the troops returned, and re-embarkation began on Tuesday, 13 September. The recovery of the men and their equipment proved to be much more difficult than the original landing, however, and the operation had to be continued all night with the help of searchlights. After a break from 7 to 10 a.m. on Wednesday, re-embarkation was resumed, although the beach parties were becoming exhausted. The task was approaching completion by midnight, and the laden transports weighed anchor and sailed on Thursday. They returned to Southampton the following day and, led by the *Atlantian*, which had been acting as headquarters and signals ship, they berthed at twenty minute intervals to land their weary passengers.

It had been a unique experience for Lord: as chief officer, he had been primarily responsible for solving the many technical problems involved in taking one thousand tired men aboard from lifeboats and providing accommodation for them within the ship.

During the exercise, the ship had been visited by HRH the Duke of Connaught, accompanied by his son, Prince Arthur. The strain imposed on Captain Howell by this additional social burden was reflected when he was later asked what the Duke had said to him. He had to confess that he had no recollection whatsoever, for he had been so overwhelmed by the occasion that his mind had become a complete blank.

In October 1905, Howell was succeeded in command of the *Antillian* by Captain William Japha, with whom Lord had previously sailed for one voyage in the *Jamaican*. Japha became unwell, however, and during a voyage from Hull to New Orleans he was forced to delegate almost all his duties to Lord, who completed the trip virtually in command of the ship. On arriving in Liverpool in February 1906, Japha had to be taken out of the *Antillian*, and the Leyland Line management had no hesitation in displaying their full confidence in Lord's abilities by allowing him to remain in command of her.

Lord was only 28 years old, and it delighted him to recall Bridgewater's initial reluctance, nine years earlier, to engage him as a junior officer because he was then considered to be too young.

As a master in the Leyland Line, it became Lord's duty loyally to implement the company's operational policies. So far as safety was concerned, the following instructions applied:

> Commanders must run no risk which might by any possibility result in accident to their ships. It is to be hoped that they will ever bear in mind that the safety of the lives and property entrusted to their care is the ruling principle that should govern them in the navigation of their vessels, and that no supposed gain in expedition or saving of time on the voyage is to be purchased at the risk of accident. The company desires to maintain for its vessels a reputation for safety, and only looks for such speed on the various voyages as is consistent with safe and prudent navigation.
>
> Commanders are reminded that the steamers are to a great extent uninsured, and that their own livelihood as well as the company's success depends on immunity from accident; no precaution which ensures safe navigation is to be considered excessive.

In July 1906, Japha had recovered and was able to resume command of the *Antillian*, Lord transferring to the *Louisianian*, of 3,643 tons and carrying up to 30 passengers.

Once promotion to command had been firmly established and his professional advancement completely fulfilled, Captain Lord was enabled to bring to fruition a more personal but vitally important enterprise. On the afternoon of Sunday, 17 March 1907, he docked the *Louisianian* in Liverpool: two days later, in Walton-on-the-Hill parish church, he was married to Miss Mabel Tutton.

Almost immediately the new Mrs Lord had to face up to the realities of life as the wife of a shipmaster, for only four days later Lord went back to sea, outward-bound for Tampico. He returned from that voyage to join his wife in their first home together, at 10 Ormonde Street, Liscard, on the Cheshire side of the River Mersey.

Lord carried his responsibilities as captain of a ship with ease, for he was thoroughly experienced in the company's trade and had formed a wide circle of professional contacts in the West Indies and America. As master, he had greater freedom to develop these relationships, and one man in particular he got to know very well indeed. He was Frank Strachan, of Scottish descent, who operated a successful agency in Savannah which handled Leyland Line ships. Lord always looked forward to his visits to Savannah and Brunswick, where the Strachan family used to entertain him in their home.

In November 1909, Lord took over the *William Cliff*, of 3,352 tons, with up to 30 passengers; from her, in March 1911, he went to the largest ship of all those he had commanded, the *Californian*, of 6,223 tons, carrying up to 47 passengers.

In general his voyages were uneventful, but there were outstanding incidents which impressed themselves on his memory. On one occasion he visited San Juan de Ulua, the Mexican port close to Vera Cruz, famous for the naval engagement in 1568 in which the Elizabethan sea captain John Hawkins was heavily defeated by a Spanish force. Here Lord was shown over the island fortress, used as a place of detention, where he was greatly distressed to witness the inhuman conditions under which the prisoners, dressed in little more than rags, were kept. He tried to help by buying some of the pathetic carvings which they were allowed to sell to visitors, but never forgot the hopeless look of despair on their faces as they were hustled back into their primitive cells.

Also memorable were the eccentricities of individual passengers. Travelling to the West Indies with his wife on a fishing holiday, the Hon Heber Percy approached Lord one day, when the ship was in mid-Atlantic, and asked that the vessel be stopped so that he could take a swim. Lord's tactful rejection of this unusual and impractical request was obviously made without offending its proposer, for later on, as the ship was steaming out of the port at which the Heber Percys had disembarked, he was amused to see the couple energetically waving to him from their fishing launch, an exercise which they continued until left far astern.

Another problem involving a passenger arose early in 1912. The *Californian* was outward-bound for the West Indies, and among the passengers was a little girl who was reported to Lord by her mother as suffering from constipation. No doctor was carried on the ship, and it was consequently the captain's responsibility to handle any medical cases. Lord visited the child in her cabin where, after due consideration, he prescribed the standard shipborne remedy, 'black draught'. She flatly refused to swallow it. Eventually, however, she compromised, agreeing to do so on one condition – that the captain also took a dose. Lord solemnly obliged, comforting himself with the thought that by his action he was successfully maintaining that delicate balance between the preservation of his authority as captain and his duty to retain the goodwill of a passenger, however young.

During the voyage, a group of passengers asked if they might photograph the *Californian*'s captain and his three navigating officers. Lord invited them on to the bridge, and as he and the others took their places before the camera, Lord was asked to hold the ship's telescope.

'We want you to look like a *real* skipper,' one of the passengers helpfully explained.

A second photograph was taken with Lord's small patient sitting on his knee and his chief officer nursing a somewhat older child, who had taken charge of the ceremonial telescope.

It was on the following voyage, with the same complement of officers and a number of the crew who had elected to remain in the ship, but carrying no passengers, that the *Californian* sailed from London on Good Friday, 5 April 1912, a passage interrupted when the ship encountered field ice on that Sunday night, 14 April.

CHAPTER THREE

'There is a Ship Sunk!'

At half past four on the morning of Monday, 15 April, Captain Lord was roused from his cramped position on the chartroom settee by the chief officer. Stewart reported that it was breaking day, and Lord gathered that the steamer that had fired the rocket was in sight to the southward.

'Yes, the second officer said something about a rocket,' he commented. He got up, and after a walk round the boat deck to study the loose ice by which the ship was surrounded, he joined Stewart on the bridge.

They were about a quarter of a mile from the edge of the main icefield. This seemed to be about one or two miles wide and free from icebergs. They discussed the possibility of pushing through the ice towards the westward, and for some little time Lord was undecided whether to attempt this or to turn and look for a clearer passage down to the south and east. Eventually he decided that he would go on, and told the chief officer to put the engines on stand by. As Stewart did so, he said: 'Will you go down and look at this steamer to the southward?'

He pointed to a ship lying about eight miles away, in the direction of but beyond where they had seen another ship the previous evening.

'Why? What's the matter with him?' Lord asked.

'He might have lost his rudder,' Stewart suggested.

'Why? He hasn't any signals up.'

'No,' Stewart admitted. 'But the second officer in his watch said he fired several rockets.'

Lord took another look at the steamer. He decided that it could not be the same one as that with which they had been trying to communicate the night before, for that one had been showing only one masthead light, whereas this, a yellow-funnelled steamer, had four masts, from which, in the semi-darkness of early dawn, two lights could be clearly seen. Nevertheless he decided that he would follow up Stewart's suggestion.

'Yes, they certainly told me something about a rocket,' he recalled. 'Go and call "Wireless" and see what ship it was.'

Stewart left the bridge. It was now about five o'clock, and at 5.15 Lord put the engines ahead. They had been turning for only a few moments when Stewart came running back with startling news.

'There is a ship sunk!' he called.

Lord rang the engine-room telegraph to stop.

'Go back and wait until you find out what it is,' he ordered. 'Get some news about it.'

Stewart was away for about ten minutes. He returned with a shattering report.

'The *Titanic* is sunk – she hit an iceberg!' he told Lord.

'Go back again. Find the position as quickly as possible.'

Stewart was soon back with a position, 41° 46′ N., 50° 14′ W., but it was unofficial. It had come from a German ship, the *Frankfurt*, and Evans thought that it seemed a bit doubtful.

'You must get a better position,' Lord commented. 'We don't want to go on a wild goose chase.'

Once again Stewart left the bridge for the wireless room, while Lord pricked off on the chart the position he had been given. It lay S16W (true), distant 19½ miles, from where they had stopped the previous night.

After a quick visit to the wireless room to check for himself what Evans had to report, Lord got the *Californian* under way, heading down at slow speed through the ice, making the best course he could towards the position he had been given.

It was now shortly after 6 a.m., and Stewart rejoined Lord on the bridge to report that at last they had an official position. The *Virginian* had intercepted their exchange with the *Frankfurt*, and her master had addressed the following official message to the *Californian*:

> 4.10 a.m. New York Time: *Titanic* struck berg. Wants assistance. Urgent. Ship sinking, passengers in boats. His position 41.46 50.14.

This confirmation of the position initially received from the *Frankfurt* enabled Lord to proceed with confidence, pushing through the ice and making the best possible course between south and south-west. The ice was so thick, however, that at first their progress was very slow. As they pushed on, Lord instructed Stewart

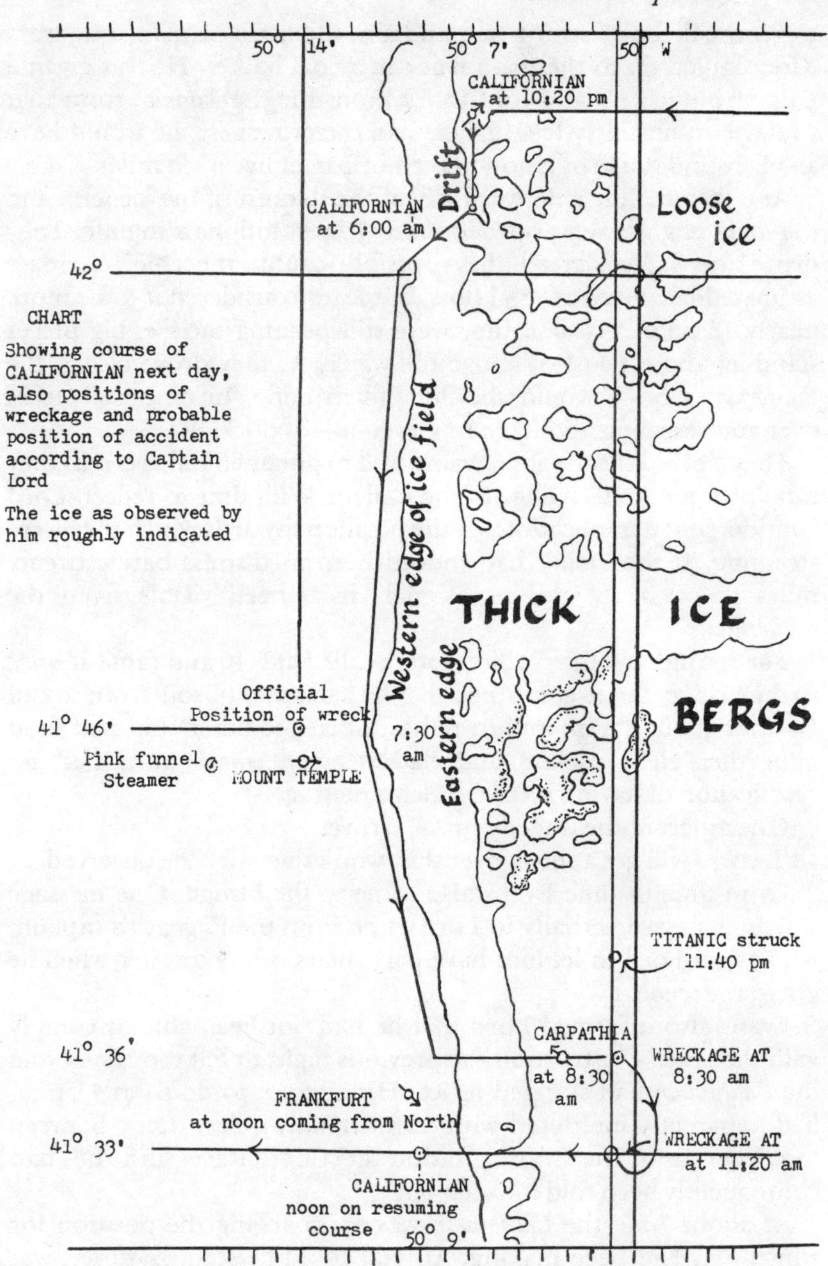

Mr A.M. Foweraker's sketch of the area in which the TITANIC was lost

to get the lifeboats swung out, and also to have a seaman, Benjamin Kirk, hauled up to the main truck in a coal basket. He was given a pair of binoculars and told to look out for the *Titanic*: from that vantage point, thirty feet higher than the crowsnest, he would have an all-round range of vision to the horizon of up to ten miles.

At 6.20 a.m., the ship was clear of the thickest of the icefield, and the main engines were opened up to 70 revolutions a minute. They drove the *Californian* all they possibly could: the chief engineer estimated her speed at 13½ knots, but Lord considered it to be more nearly 13 knots. At first, they were still pushing the ice, big pieces standing about two feet above the water. As they drove along, the *Californian*'s bows would shoulder them aside, turning the pieces over and revealing about ten or eleven feet of thickness.

They cleared the ice at 6.30 a.m. and maintained full speed as they ran down the western edge of the icefield. With time to reflect, Lord considered the implications of the position towards which they were steaming. If the *Titanic* had indeed been in distress barely twenty miles away, might not her signals have been visible from the *Californian*?

The second and third officers were called at 6.40 and came at once to the bridge. Stone confirmed that he had sent Gibson down to call Lord at about 2 a.m. and to tell him that the other ship had fired altogether eight rockets and had steamed away. Lord had no recollection of having received such a message.

One aspect of the tragedy struck Groves.

'Lloyd's will get a shock over this, won't they, sir?' he observed.

From time to time Evans also came to the bridge. One message which he passed verbally to Lord came from the *Virginian*'s captain, who asked Lord to let him have particulars of the disaster when he got to the scene.

Evans also informed Lord that he had not been able to comply with the latter's instruction the previous night to tell the *Titanic* that the *Californian* had stopped in ice. His attempt to do so at 11 p.m. had apparently interfered with commercial wireless traffic between the liner and the shore station at Cape Race and he had consequently been told to 'keep out'.

At about 7.30, the *Californian* was approaching the position for which they had been making. All that could be seen, however, was one of the Canadian Pacific Railway Company's fleet, the *Mount Temple*, lying stopped, and an unidentified steamer, having two masts and a pink funnel with a black top, similar to their own, heading between north and north-west.

Passing the *Mount Temple*, the *Californian* continued at full speed on her southerly course. Another verbal message from Evans gave the impression that the Cunard liner *Carpathia* was standing by the *Titanic* and recommended that boats and lifebelts be made ready. By now, in fact, the *Carpathia* could be seen, lying stopped on the eastern edge of the icefield, with her forward derricks raised. Lord held on until she was abeam, bearing north-east, then swung to port towards her, cutting through the ice at full speed.

The wireless messages received from the *Carpathia* were signed 'Rostron'. What a curious way in which to encounter his brother's old schoolmate, Lord reflected.

The *Californian* closed the *Carpathia* at about 8.30, in time to see the last of the survivors being taken aboard from the *Titanic*'s lifeboats. The Cunarder was flying the two-flag signal from the International Code indicating that she wished to communicate by semaphore. Lord ordered a similar signal to be hoisted in the *Californian* and, as they stopped close alongside the *Carpathia*, messages by hand flag signals were exchanged between the two ships.

The *Carpathia*'s first enquiry was whether the *Californian* had any survivors on board. Lord could only reply that they had none. He was then informed that the *Titanic* had struck an iceberg at midnight, sinking at 3 a.m., and that the *Carpathia* had taken on board between 700 and 800 survivors, including the chairman of the White Star Line, Bruce Ismay.

Rostron declined an offer of assistance from Lord, but accepted his suggestion that the *Californian* should carry out a search to the eastward of the icefield. The *Carpathia* then got under way, heading towards New York, and, as she turned on to her westerly course, those in the *Californian* clearly heard the two strokes on her bell indicating that it was nine o'clock.

The area in which they had stopped was practically surrounded by icebergs. Those in the south-east, up to 150 feet in height, were much larger than those to the westward, which were not so high and lying in the field ice.

Posting the second officer and a seaman in the crowsnest as additional lookouts, Lord took the *Californian* at full speed in circles, searching over an area and then returning to the abandoned lifeboats from the *Titanic*. There were about six of them, the remainder having been picked up by the *Carpathia*. One was capsized, and there were two smaller boats with collapsible canvas sides. In one of these Lord noted objects which looked like luggage.* Otherwise, there was surprisingly little wreckage considering the scale of the disaster: some floating planks, a few deckchairs, cushions and lifebelts, but no bodies. To Lord, it seemed as though nothing more than a fishing boat had gone down.

On one of the sweeps, Groves drew Lord's attention to what seemed to be two or three dark forms on an ice floe. Lord studied them through his binoculars.

'Seals,' he decided.

They continued their search for over two hours, concentrating latterly on a sort of gully running for some ten miles to the southward, but there was nothing else to be seen. At about 11.20, Lord turned to Stewart, standing by his side on the bridge.

'Well, it's no use stopping here any longer,' he commented, and turned the *Californian* to the westward. At slow speed, he took the ship into the icefield for the third time that morning, clearing it at about 11.50 a.m.

During the day they had seen the smoke of several steamers on the horizon in different directions, and as they came out of the icefield they sighted the *Frankfurt*, heading south. She seemed to be looking for a way through the ice, for as the *Californian* pulled clear and increased to full speed on a due westerly course, they saw the *Frankfurt* apparently heading for the place through which they had just pushed. The *Mount Temple* could also be seen, a considerable distance to the south-west, steering a westerly course.

Lord left it to Stewart and the other two officers to fix the noon position. They had good sights, taken under the most favourable conditions and confirmed later that afternoon: they placed the ship in a position 41° 33′ N., 50° 9′ W. Working back, Lord calculated that the position in which they must have left the abandoned lifeboats and wreckage at 11.20 must have been 41° 33′ N., 50° 1′ W., that is, bearing about S5E, distant 33 miles, from the position in which the *Californian* had stopped at 10.20 the previous night.

As soon as normal routine had been re-established, Lord questioned Stone about what he had seen during the night.

'Were the rockets you saw distress signals?' he asked him.

'I'm confident they were *not* distress signals,' the second officer

* This 'luggage' may well have been three corpses deliberately abandoned in collapsible lifeboat 'A', subsequently sighted and investigated by the *Oceanic* on 13 May.

asserted. 'They didn't go any higher than the masthead light and I didn't hear any report. If they had been – if there'd been any emergency I would have come down myself and *pulled* you out.'

Lord accepted his word. He was quite sure that Stone was an honest man, who wouldn't tell him any lies.

His second enquiry was about the movements of the other ship. Stone confirmed that her original bearing, on which she at first lay stopped, was SSE by compass, and that he last saw her at about 2.10 a.m. bearing SW½W. In between she had been steaming slowly away, and Lord estimated that to have changed her bearing by such a large amount she must have covered at least five miles, more probably eight, depending on her speed.

Stone also repeated his earlier statement, that he had sent Gibson down at about 2 a.m. with instructions that he should tell the captain that the ship had fired several rockets and was steaming away. On his return to the bridge, Gibson had told him that the captain was awake and had replied: 'All right, let me know if anything is wanted.'

Stone assured Lord that he had not been surprised when he did not come up on to the bridge, for he himself did not consider that there was any emergency. He surprised Lord, however, by telling him that they had spoken together by voice pipe at about 2.40 a.m., for he had no recollection whatsoever of such a conversation. Stone's account was that he had blown down to tell Lord that the other steamer had disappeared bearing SW½W; that Lord had asked him if he was sure that there were no colours in the lights he had seen; and that when Stone had confirmed that they were white lights, Lord had simply commented: 'All right'.

So far as Gibson was concerned, the apprentice told Lord that when he spoke to him from the doorway of the chartroom, he opened his eyes and said: 'What is it?' On being given Stone's message – that the other ship had fired several rockets and was steaming away – Lord had asked him what time it was, and whether the rockets were all white.

Lord himself could remember only Gibson's opening and closing of the chartroom door: as with Stone, however, he did not doubt for one moment that the apprentice was telling the truth.

On reflection, Lord decided that he would ask both Gibson and Stone to let him have in writing statements recording what they had seen and done, for they were the only people on board able to describe what had happened between midnight and 4 a.m.

Stone submitted this account:

At your request I make the following report of the incidents witnessed by me during my watch on the bridge of this steamer from midnight 14 April to 4 a.m. of the 15th.

On going up to the bridge I was stopped by yourself at the wheelhouse door, and you gave me verbal orders for the watch. You showed me a steamer a little abaft of our starboard beam and informed me she was stopped. You also showed me the loose field ice all around the ship and a dense icefield to the southward. You told me to watch the other steamer and report if she came any nearer and that you were going to lie down on the chartroom settee.

I went on the bridge about eight minutes past twelve, and took over the watch from the third officer, Mr Groves, who also pointed out ice and steamer and said our head was ENE and we were swinging. On looking at the compass I saw this was correct and observed the other steamer SSE dead abeam and showing one masthead light, her red sidelight, and one or two small indistinct lights around the deck which looked like portholes or open doors. I judged her to be a small tramp steamer and about five miles distant. The third officer informed me he had called him up on our Morse lamp but had got no reply. The third officer then left the bridge, and I at once called the steamer up but got no reply. Gibson, the apprentice, then came up with the coffee at about 12.15. I told him I had called the steamer up and the result. He then went to the tapper with the same result. Gibson thought at first he was answering, but it was only his masthead lamp flickering a little.

I then sent Gibson by your orders to get the gear all ready for streaming a new log line when we got under way again. At 12.35 you whistled up the speaking tube and asked if the other steamer had moved. I replied no and that she was on the same bearing and also reported I had called him up and the result.

At about 12.45 I observed a flash of light in the sky just above that steamer. I thought nothing of it as there were several shooting stars about, the night being fine and clear with light airs and calms. Shortly after, I observed another distinctly over the steamer which I made out to be a white rocket, though observed no flash on the deck or any indication that it had come from the steamer, in fact it appeared to come from a good distance beyond her. Between then and about 1.15 I observed three more the same as before, and all white in colour. I at once whistled down the speaking tube and you came from the chartroom into your own room and answered. I reported seeing these lights in the sky in the direction of the other steamer which appeared to me to be white rockets. You then gave me orders to call her up with the Morse lamp and try to get some information from her. You also asked me if they were private signals and I replied I did not know, but they were all white. You then said: 'When you get an answer let me know by Gibson.'

Gibson and I observed three more at intervals and kept calling them up on our Morse lamp but go no reply whatsoever.

The other steamer meanwhile had shut in* her red sidelight and showed us her stern light and her masthead's glow was just visible. I observed the steamer to be steaming away to the SW and altering her bearing fast. We were also swinging slowly all the time through south and at 1.50 were heading about WSW and the other steamer bearing SWxW. At 2 a.m. the vessel was steaming away fast and only just her stern light was visible and bearing SW½W.

I sent Gibson down to you and told him to wake you and tell you we had seen altogether eight white rockets and that the steamer had gone out of sight to the SW, also that we were heading WSW. When he came back he reported he had told you we had called him up repeatedly and got no answer, and you replied: 'All right. Are you sure there were no colours in them?' and Gibson replied: 'No, they were all white.' At 2.45 I again whistled down and told you we had seen no more lights and that the steamer had steamed away to the south-west and was now out of sight, also that the rockets were all white and had no colours whatever.

We saw nothing further until about 3.20 when we thought we observed two faint lights in the sky about SSW and a little distance apart. At 3.40 I sent Gibson down to see all was ready for me to prepare the new log at eight bells. The chief officer, Mr Stewart, came on the bridge at 4 a.m. and I gave him a full report of what I had seen and my reports and replies from you, and pointed out where I thought I had observed these faint lights at 3.20. He picked up the binoculars and said after a few moments: 'There she is then, she's all right, she is a four-master.' I said: 'Then that isn't the steamer I saw first,' took up the glasses and just made out a four-masted steamer with two masthead lights a little abaft our port beam, and bearing about south; we were heading about WNW. Mr Stewart then took over the watch and I went off the bridge.

Gibson's statement, dated 18 April, read:

In compliance with your wishes, I hereby make the following statement as to what I saw on the morning of 15 April 1912:

It being my watch on deck from 12 o'clock until 4 o'clock, I went on the bridge at about 15 minutes after twelve and saw that the ship was stopped and that she was surrounded with light field ice and thick field ice to the southward. While the second officer and I were having coffee a few minutes later, I asked him if there were any more ships around us. He said that there was one on the starboard beam, and

* A ship's sidelights were screened so as to prevent their being seen other than from directly ahead to two points (22½°) abaft the beam. A sidelight was said to be 'shut in' when a screen came into effect and the light appeared to be switched off. Masthead lights showed ahead, covering an arc extending from two points abaft the beam on either side.

looking over the weather cloth I saw a white light flickering, which I took to be a Morse light calling us up. I then went over to the keyboard and gave one long flash in answer, and still seeing this light flickering, I gave her the calling up sign. The light on the other ship, however, was still the same, so I looked at her through the binoculars and found that it was her masthead light flickering. I also observed her port sidelight and a faint glare of lights on her afterdeck. I then went over to the second officer and I remarked that she looked like a tramp steamer. He said that most probably she was, and was burning oil lights. This ship was then right abeam.

At about 25 minutes after twelve I went down off the bridge to get a new log out and not being able to find it, I went on the bridge again to see if the second officer knew anything about it. I then noticed that this other ship was about one point and a half before the beam. I then went down again and was down until about five minutes to one. Arriving on the bridge again at that time, the second officer told me that the other ship, which was about 3½ points on the starboard beam, had fired five rockets and he also remarked that after seeing the second one to make sure that he was not mistaken he had told the captain, through the speaking tube, and that the captain had told him to watch her and keep calling her up on the Morse light. I then watched her for some time and then went over to the keyboard and called her up continuously for about three minutes. I then got the binoculars and had just got them focussed on the vessel when I observed a white flash apparently on her deck, followed by a faint streak towards the sky which then burst into white stars. Nothing then happened until the other ship was about two points on the starboard bow when she fired another rocket. Shortly after that I observed that her sidelight had disappeared but her masthead light was just visible, and the second officer remarked after taking another bearing of her, that she was slowly steering away towards the south-west. Between one point on the starboard bow and one point on the port bow I called her up on the Morse lamp but received no answer. When about one point on the port bow she fired another rocket which like the others burst into white stars.

Just after two o'clock, she was then about two points on the port bow, she disappeared from sight and nothing was seen of her again. The second officer then said: 'Call the captain and tell him that the ship has disappeared in the south-west, that we are heading west-south-west, and that altogether she has fired eight rockets.' I then went down below to the chartroom and called the captain and told him, and he asked me if there were any colours in the rockets. I told him that they were all white. He then asked me what time it was and I went on the bridge and told the second officer what the captain had said.

At about 2.45 he whistled down to the captain again but I did not hear what was said. At about 3.20, looking over the weather cloth, I observed a rocket about two points before the port beam, which I reported to the second officer. About three minutes later I saw another

> rocket right abeam which was followed later by another one about two points before the beam. I saw nothing else and when one bell went, I went below to get the log gear ready for the second officer at eight bells.

Lord also discussed with Groves what they could recall seeing of the nearby ship. They were unable to reconcile their impressions of the number of masthead lights she was displaying, however, Groves maintaining that there had been two, while Lord shared the view of Stone and Gibson that she had been showing only one.

Lord exchanged his last wireless messages with the *Carpathia* on 16 April. He learned that the *Titanic*'s surviving officers had confirmed that all the lifeboats had been accounted for, while so far as weather conditions were concerned, Rostron reported that he had experienced haze for two hours that morning. This had cleared, however, and a strong south-westerly breeze was then blowing. The *Californian* encountered the fog which Lord had been expecting, followed by strong winds, but these created no navigational problems.

On Thursday, 18 April, Evans handed Lord several wireless messages which he had received from various American newspapers, asking for information about the *Titanic* disaster, and particularly whether or not the *Californian* had any survivors or bodies on board.

A typical appeal was that received from the *Boston Post*: 'Send collect any news even if slight and survivors aboard relieve world's anxiety.'

From the Leyland Line management came a request for a report on what had been happening. The company also told Lord that, in view of the press interest which had been aroused, they would leave it to his judgement whether or not to allow journalists to board the ship.

The *Californian* arrived off Boston without further incident and berthed at the Clyde Pier at 4 a.m. on Friday, 19 April.

CHAPTER FOUR

Gill the Donkeyman

Reporters boarded the *Californian* as soon as she arrived in Boston. Lord did his best to answer their many questions and to give a factual account of what had happened after he had been informed of the *Titanic* disaster. His story was obviously too factual for editorial taste, however, and later he was interested to read what he was supposed to have said, improved for the benefit of the general public. In the *Boston Globe* of Friday, 19 April, he was reported as having stated:

> We set about reaching the scene of the accident as quickly as possible. At best, however, it was slow going. At times, nervous and anxious as we were, we hardly seemed to be moving. We had to dodge the big bergs, skirt the mass field ice, and plow through the line of least resistance. For three full hours we turned, twisted, doubled on our course – in short, manoeuvred one way or another through the winding channels of ice. The hour of eight-thirty found us within sighting distance of the scene of the disaster. Of course the waters were pretty well littered with wreckage, but we were really a bit surprised, considering the size of the wreck, that there wasn't more. We seamen would describe the amount of floating material as 'scant wreckage', but I suppose a landsman would have thought that the waters teemed with floating stuff. The wreckage consisted of cushions, chairs and similar things.

The report also conveyed the inaccurate impression that three of the *Titanic*'s lifeboats were missing, contrary to Rostron's confirmation that all had been accounted for.

A less demanding visitor to the *Californian* identified himself as Endicott, a wholesale boot manufacturer in Boston. He explained to Lord that he had received a cable from an acquaintance, the son of a married couple from the West Coast who had been passengers in the *Titanic*, who was most anxious to learn whether or not any news about his missing parents could be obtained from the *Californian*. Despite Lord's inability to help, the meeting led to his being invited to visit the Endicott family in their home. They gave him a most pleasant welcome, and one evening he went with them to a theatre.

On Thursday, 25 April, however, the *Californian*'s normal harbour routine was quite unexpectedly disrupted. On that day, a local newspaper, the *Boston American*, came out with most serious allegations against Lord. He was accused of having refused to risk the *Californian* on the night the *Titanic* was lost, despite three calls from the bridge, and of having ignored distress signals from a ship only ten miles away. He was further charged with having forced Stone to sign a statement denying that he had seen distress signals and with having persuaded the quartermaster on duty that night to similar effect.

The report appeared under startling headlines:

> ADMITS HE SAW ROCKET SIGNALS – *Captain Lord of 'Californian' Saw Ship Within Five Miles of Him Sending up Rockets – Made no Attempt to go to Her – Seaman Gill Tells Damaging Story – Says Crew Wanted to Protest Captain's Act in not Answering.*
>
> 'The *Californian* of the Leyland Line was the ship which was sighted by the *Titanic*, but which refused to respond to her signals of distress. Captain Lord of the *Californian* thought it was some small vessel and refused to risk his ship by sending her through the ice at night to the rescue.'
>
> These charges are made in affidavits by Ernest Gill, second donkeyman on board, who is on his way to Washington to testify before the Senate Investigating Committee. They were repeated in the presence of four members of the crew and a notary public, and by an officer of the ship, who affirmed them in a confidential communication to the *Boston American.*
>
> Captain Lord is alleged to have forced the second officer, Mr Stone, to sign a statement in which he denied having seen any signals of distress. He is also charged with having persuaded the quartermaster on duty between midnight and 4 a.m. Monday, 15 April, to deny having seen signals.
>
> According to the officer, whose name the *American* is withholding, Captain Lord was called from his bunk three times by the officers of the watch, Mr Stone, or the apprentice officer, Mr Gibson, and notified that some vessel in distress was discharging rockets ten miles away.
>
> The wireless operator, Mr Evans, turned in at 11.20. When the chief officer, Mr Stewart, came on deck at 4 a.m. he was told that the skipper had been notified of a ship in distress, but had not permitted the *Californian*, which was drifting, to start her engines.
>
> The chief officer immediately rushed into the wireless man's room, tore him from his bunk and exclaimed: 'For God's sake, get to your key. Some ship has been sending rockets all night and we have done nothing.'

The wireless operator caught a message from the *Virginian* that the *Titanic* had gone down. As soon as Captain Lord knew that it was the *Titanic* of his own line which had sunk he rushed the *Californian* full speed to the rescue.

Captain Lord, when the *Californian* reached Boston last Friday, stated that his ship was about thirty miles from the scene of the disaster, that she had drifted all night and he had heard and seen nothing. Chief Officer Stewart yesterday declared that the *Californian* was only twenty miles away. The *American*'s informant says he worked out the position and it was seventeen miles when the wireless operator was called at 4 a.m.

Donkeyman Gill says it was about ten miles at midnight. The drift of the *Californian* during the four hours would account for the difference between ten and seventeen miles. Captain Lord's ship was in the ice and he had stopped his engines. He feared to proceed through the ice, even on such a night, because of the ever present danger that a berg might strike his own ship.

When once he learned of the *Titanic* trouble, however, according to Gill, he forced his vessel to do her best.

Gill's affidavit follows:

'I, the undersigned, Ernest Gill, being employed as second donkeyman on the steamer *Californian*, Capt. Lloyd (*sic*), give the following statement of the incidents of the night of Sunday, 14 April:

'I am 29 years of age; native of Yorkshire; single. I was making my first voyage on the *Californian*.

'On the night of 14 April I was on duty from 8 p.m. until 12 in the engine room. At 11.56 I came on deck. The stars were shining brightly. It was very clear and I could see for a long distance. The ship's engines had been stopped since 10.30, and she was drifting amid floe ice. I looked over the rail on the starboard side and saw the lights of a very large steamer about 10 miles away. I could see her broadside lights. I watched her for fully a minute. They could not have helped but see her from the bridge and lookout.

'It was now 12 o'clock and I went to my cabin. I woke my mate, William Thomas. He heard the ice crunching alongside the ship and asked: "Are we in the ice?" I replied: "Yes; but it must be clear off the starboard, for I saw a big vessel going along full speed. She looked as if she might be a big German."

'I turned in, but could not sleep. In half an hour I turned out, thinking to smoke a cigarette. Because of the cargo I could not smoke 'tween decks, so I went on deck again.

'I had been on deck about 10 minutes when I saw a white rocket about 10 miles away on the starboard side. I thought it must be a shooting star. In seven or eight minutes I saw distinctly a second rocket in the same place, and I said to myself: "That must be a vessel in distress."

'It was not my business to notify the bridge or the lookouts; but they could not have helped but see them.

'I turned in immediately after, supposing that the ship would pay attention to the rockets.

'I knew no more until I was awakened at 5.40 by the chief engineer, who said: "Turn out to render assistance. The *Titanic* has gone down."

'I exclaimed and leaped from my bunk. I went on deck and found the vessel under way and proceeding full speed. She was clear of the field ice but there were plenty of bergs about.

'I went down on watch and heard the second and fourth engineers in conversation. Mr J.C. Evans is the second and Mr F.R. Hooton is the fourth. The second was telling the fourth that the third (*sic*) officer had reported rockets had gone up in his watch. I knew then that it must have been the *Titanic* I had seen.

'The second engineer added that the captain had been notified by the apprentice officer, whose name, I think, is Gibson, of the rockets. The skipper had told him to Morse to the vessel in distress. Mr Stone, the second navigating officer, was on the bridge at the time, said Mr Evans.

'I overheard Mr Evans say that more lights had been shown and more rockets went up. Then, according to Mr Evans, Mr Gibson went to the captain again and reported more rockets. The skipper told him to continue to Morse until he got a reply. No reply was received.

'The next remark I heard the second pass was: "Why in the devil didn't they wake the wireless man up?" The entire crew of the steamer have been talking among themselves about the disregard of the rockets. I personally urged several to join me in protesting against the conduct of the captain, but they refused, because they feared to lose their jobs.

'A day or two before the ship reached port the skipper called the quartermaster, who was on duty at the time the rockets were discharged, into his cabin. They were in conversation about three-quarters of an hour. The quartermaster declared that he did not see the rockets.

'I am quite sure that the *Californian* was less than 20 miles from the *Titanic*, which the officers report to have been our position.

'I could not have seen her if she had been more than 10 miles distant, and I saw her very plainly.

'I have no ill will toward the captain or any officer of the ship, and I am losing a profitable berth by making this statement. I am actuated by the desire that no captain who refuses or neglects to give aid to a vessel in distress should be able to hush up the men.'

ERNEST GILL

Sworn and subscribed to before me this 24th day of April, 1912

SAMUEL PUTNAM
Notary Public

Lord dismissed Gill's statement as pure imagination. For one thing, how could one of the engine-room crew decide that a ship ten miles away, hull down over the horizon, was 'going along full speed' after watching her for only a minute? The change of bearing would be imperceptible. The only ship Gill could have been watching must have been the relatively small ship which at midnight had been lying completely stopped for about twenty minutes only four or five miles away. When Gill turned out again half-an-hour later to smoke a cigarette, the *Californian*'s slow swing to starboard could easily have given the impression that the other ship had steamed away, whereas in fact she was merely screened from Gill's view by the *Californian*'s intervening superstructure.

As for the rockets which Gill claimed to have seen at twelve-thirty, they could not possibly have come from the nearby ship, which Stone was closely watching; the first rockets the second officer saw were not until close upon one o'clock. The allegations that Lord had 'forced' Stone to sign a false statement, and had by implication influenced the quartermaster to keep quiet about what he had seen, were so ridiculous that they were not worth bothering about. Nevertheless a public accusation had been made that Lord had deliberately ignored the *Titanic*'s distress signals, and in view of the sensational press interest in the disaster, Lord could only assume that some form of inquiry would follow. He accordingly prepared a rough sketch showing where the *Titanic* and the *Californian* must have been on the night of the disaster, the ice areas, and the course followed on the way down to the lifeboats on the following morning. He also drafted in pencil a detailed statement summarising the *Californian*'s movements, the reports he had received, and the action he had taken.

There was prompt official reaction to Gill's charges. At about 7.30 that same evening, a United States marshal boarded the *Californian* and served Lord with a subpoena requiring him and the wireless operator to appear forthwith before the Senate's sub-committee on commerce which was hearing evidence in Washington relating to the *Titanic* disaster.

After a short delay while Lord obtained the local management's permission for him to leave the ship, he was able to make the necessary arrangements and go ashore with Evans. They were accompanied to the station and seen off on the midnight train by a companionable newspaper reporter who had come on board that evening to question Lord about the turn events had taken.

Lord settled down in the sleeper with which he had been provided confident as to the eventual outcome of the inquiry which faced him. He had been wholly satisfied by Stone that the steamer which they had been watching could not have been in distress, for she had steamed away, altering her bearing by over six points before going out of sight. Surely that would satisfy anyone that there could have been no emergency?

CHAPTER FIVE

Senator Smith

Lord and Evans arrived in Washington shortly after midday. They were met by an official who escorted them to the United States Senate office building where the *Titanic* investigation was being carried out. The chairman of the committee was Senator William Alden Smith, and before Lord gave evidence he was taken into Smith's private room for a brief introductory interview. While there, Lord had a glimpse of Harold G. Lowe, one of the surviving officers from the *Titanic*, who called in to enquire about some expenses. Two officers who had not survived were Lord's one-time acquaintances William Murdoch, the *Titanic*'s first officer, and Henry Wilde, chief officer.

From Smith's office Lord was ushered into a waiting room and to a chair next to someone who appeared to be expecting him.

'Hello. Are you Lord?' was the greeting he received. The other man introduced himself as they shook hands.

'I'm Franklin, manager of the White Star in New York. How are you?'

In addition to his White Star Line appointment, Franklin was vice-president in the United States of the International Mercantile Marine Company, the combine which, through its British interests, owned the majority of the stock in the Leyland Line. Nevertheless, Lord was immediately put at his ease by Franklin's friendly approach, and they chatted together very pleasantly for the next ten or fifteen minutes.

Beyond Franklin sat another man, whom Lord recognised as J. Bruce Ismay, chairman of the White Star Line. He remained completely silent, however, and to Lord he appeared to be a man keeping very much to himself.

When called to give evidence, Lord was placed in a chair close to Senator Smith. Sitting nearby was a woman who appeared to be sketching him. Although naturally interested, Lord was disappointed that he was not able to see what sort of a likeness she was producing.

After being sworn, Lord was asked about his sea career, following which Smith turned to the *Californian*'s movements on the night of 14/15 April. These Lord was able to confirm from the ship's official log book, which he had brought with him. It was soon made clear that Smith was not a technical man.

'Where were you in your ship on the 14th day of April last ... at 9.40 a.m.?' Smith enquired.

'42, 47,' Lord replied.

'A little more specifically, please.'

'42 north and 47 west.'

Smith questioned him about the day's progress, up to the time of Evans' attempt to communicate with the *Titanic*.

'What was that communication?'

'We told them that we were stopped and surrounded by ice.'

'Did the *Titanic* acknowledge that message?'

'Yes, sir. I believe he told the operator he had read it, and told him to shut up, or stand by, or something – that he was busy.'

'Did you have further communication with the *Titanic*?'

'Not at all, sir.'

'Did the *Titanic* have further communication with you?'

'No, sir.'

'Do you know the *Titanic*'s position on the sea when she sank?'

'I know the position given to me by the *Virginian* as the position where she struck an iceberg: 41.46 and 50.14.'

'Figuring from the *Titanic*'s position at the time she went down and your position at the time you sent this warning to the *Titanic*, how far were these vessels from one another?'

'From the position we stopped in to the position at which the *Titanic* was supposed to have hit the iceberg nineteen and a half to nineteen and three-quarter miles; Sl6W, sir, was the course.'

Smith wanted to know what the *Californian*'s average speed would be under fair conditions.

'It would depend on the consumption of coal,' Lord replied. 'On our present consumption we average eleven in fine weather.'

'In case of distress, I suppose it would be possible for you to exceed that considerably.'

'Oh, we made thirteen and thirteen and a half the day we were going down to the *Titanic*.'

'Were you under full speed then?'

'We were driving all we could.'

Some questions on the prevailing ice conditions followed, after which Smith asked Lord what was his purpose in notifying the *Titanic* of those conditions.

'It was just a matter of courtesy,' Lord told him. 'I thought he would be a long way from where we were. I did not think he was anywhere near the ice. By rights, he ought to have been eighteen or nineteen miles to the southward of where I was. I never thought the ice was stretching that far down.'

Lord went on to say that, in his opinion, the *Titanic* was beyond their range of vision, nineteen and a half or twenty miles away, and from the log book confirmed that it took them two and a half hours to reach the scene of the wreck the following morning.

Reverting to the night of 14 April, Smith questioned Lord about his reasons for taking extra precautions before encountering the ice. Lord explained that he had received reports about it three or four days before, and quoted from the wireless messages he had received. He described the weather conditions on the Sunday night, and expressed his preference for reliance on natural eyesight for picking up ice rather than binoculars.

'If you had received the CQD* call of distress from the *Titanic* Sunday evening after your communication with the *Titanic*, how long, under the conditions which surrounded you, would it have taken you to have reached the scene of the catastrophe?' Smith enquired.

'At the very least, two hours ... the way the ice was packed around us, and it being night time.'

'Do you know how long it took for the *Carpathia* to reach the scene of the accident from the time the CQD call was received by Captain Rostron?'

'Only from what I have read in the paper.'

'Captain Rostron told you nothing?'

'Oh, no. I asked him the particulars of the accident, that was all.'

'It took the *Carpathia* about four hours to reach the scene of the *Titanic*'s accident, after they received word,' Smith told him, continuing:

* The original radio morse preamble to a distress signal. The signal SOS was used for the first occasion in the later stages of the *Titanic*'s distress traffic.

'You were about twenty miles away?'

'Nineteen and a half to twenty miles from the position given me.'

'And the *Carpathia* was fifty-three miles away?'

'Yes, sir.'

'How long after the *Carpathia* reached the scene of this accident did you reach the scene?'

'Well, I don't know what time he got there.'

'Had the lifeboats, with their passengers, been picked up and taken aboard the *Carpathia*?'

'I think he was taking the last boat up when I got there.'

'Did you see any of the wreckage when you got there?'

'I saw several empty boats, some floating planks, a few deck chairs and cushions; but considering the size of the disaster, there was very little wreckage. It seemed more like an old fishing boat that had sunk.'

'Did you see any life preservers?'

'A few lifebelts floating around.'

'Did you see any persons, dead or alive?'

'No, sir.'

After enquiring about the size and characteristics of the icebergs in the area of the disaster, Smith switched to another topic.

'I do not want to seem to be impertinent, captain, and hope you will not so regard it, but the question arose this morning as to whether there had been any attempt on the part of anyone to prevent you from responding to the Senate's request.'

'I do not think so. I applied for permission as soon as the marshal served me with the notice. I applied to the local manager for permission, or rather the assistant local manager. I could not get the manager. He said he would enquire from the manager. That is all I know about it.'

'The *Californian*, of which you are commander, belongs to what line?'

'The Leyland Line.'

'The Leyland Line is a member, or part of, the International Mercantile Marine Company, is it not, and is represented in this country by Mr Franklin?'

'So I understand. Yes.'

'And in England by Mr Ismay?'

'Yes, sir.'

Lord was then questioned about his practice in respect of the way in which wireless operators were expected to carry out their duties, and Smith went on to ask what his opinion was as to watchkeeping at night.

'Would it not be well to have your wireless operator at his post on duty at night, when other eyes are closed, in order that any possible signal of distress might not escape your attention?'

'We have the officer on the bridge, who can see as far at night as in the daytime.'

'But the officer on the bridge could not see the *Titanic* even with glasses, you said, that night.'

'No.'

'The wireless operator could have heard the call from the *Titanic* if he had been at his post of duty?'

'Yes, he would have heard that,' Lord agreed.

After some general questions from Smith's fellow committee members, Senators Bourne and Perkins, Senator Fletcher took up the point raised earlier.

'You were asked by Senator Smith a moment ago whether, if the wireless operator on the *Californian* had been on duty, he would have picked up this message from the *Titanic* giving the alarm?'

'Yes.'

'Could you have gone to the relief of the *Titanic* at that time?'

'Most certainly ... The engines were ready. I gave instructions to the chief engineer, and told him I had decided to stay there all night. I did not think it safe to go ahead. I said: "We will keep handy in case some of these big fellows come crunching along and get into it".'

Smith joined in.

'Captain, did you see any distress signals on Sunday night, either rockets or the Morse signals?'

'No, sir, *I* did not. The officer on watch saw some signals, but he said they were not distress signals.'

'They were not distress signals?'

'Not distress signals.'

'But he reported them?'

'To me. I think you had better let me tell you that story.'

'I wish you would.'

'When I came off the bridge, at half past ten, I pointed out to the officer that I thought I saw a light coming along, and it was a most peculiar night, and we had been making mistakes all along with the stars, thinking they were signals. We could not distinguish where the sky ended and where the water commenced. You understand, it was a flat calm. He said he thought it was a star, and I did not say anything more. I went down below. I was talking with the engineer about keeping the steam ready, and we saw these signals coming along, and I said: "There is a steamer coming. Let us go to the wireless and see what the news is.' But on our way down I met the operator coming, and I said: "Do you know anything?" He said: "The *Titanic*." So then I gave him instructions to let the *Titanic* know. I said: "This is not the *Titanic*. There is no doubt about it." She came and lay, at half past eleven, alongside of us until, I suppose, a quarter past one, within four miles of us. We could see everything on her quite distinctly – see her lights. We signalled her at half past eleven with the Morse lamp. She did not take the slightest notice of it. That was between half past eleven and twenty minutes to twelve. We signalled her again at ten minutes past twelve, half past twelve, a quarter to one, and one o'clock. We have a very powerful Morse lamp. I suppose that you can see it about ten miles, and she was about four miles off, and she did not take the slightest notice of it. When the second officer came on the bridge, at twelve o'clock or ten minutes past twelve, I told him to watch that steamer that we did not get any closer to her. At twenty minutes to one I whistled up the speaking tube and asked him if she was getting any nearer. He said: "No; she is not taking any notice of us." So I said: "I will go and lie down a bit." At a quarter past one he said: "I think she has fired a rocket." He said: "She did not answer the Morse lamp and has commenced to go away from us." I said: "Call her up and let me know at once what her name is." So he put the whistle back and apparently he was calling. I could hear him ticking over my head. Then I went to sleep.'

'You heard nothing more about it?'

'Nothing more until about something between then and half past four I have a faint recollection of the apprentice opening my room door – opening it and shutting it. I said: "What is it?" He did not answer and I went to sleep again. I believe the boy came down to deliver me the message that this steamer had steamed away from us to the south-west, showing several of these flashes or white rockets – steamed away to the south-west.'

'Captain, these Morse signals are a sort of language or method by which ships speak to one another?'

'Yes, sir, at night.'

'The rockets that are used are for the same purpose and are understood, are they not, among mariners?'

'As being distress rockets?'

'Yes.'

'Oh, yes. You never mistake a distress rocket.'

Smith pressed his point.

'Suppose the Morse signals and the rockets were displayed and exploded on the *Titanic* continuously for a half to three-quarters of an hour after she struck ice, would you, from the position of your ship on a night like Sunday night, have been able to see those signals?'

'From the position she was supposed to have been in?'

'Yes.'

'We could not have seen her Morse code. That is an utter impossibility.'

'Could you have seen rockets?'

'I do not think so. Nineteen and a half miles is a long way. It would have been way down on the horizon. It might have been mistaken for a shooting star or anything at all.'

Smith left it at that, and turned to the movements of other ships in the vicinity, especially the *Frankfurt*, and messages exchanged with them.

Fletcher asked about the ship seen from the *Californian*, and Lord confirmed that to him, to the second officer and to the apprentice it appeared to be an ordinary cargo steamer which, according to the second officer, must have travelled seven or seven and a half miles to have changed her bearing from SSE to WSW as she steamed away.

After Bourne had checked some practical points about the *Californian*, Smith asked a final question.

'From the log which you hold in your hand, and from your own knowledge, is there anything you can say further which will assist the committee in its inquiry as to the cause of this catastrophe?'

'No, sir,' Lord replied. 'There is nothing, only that it was a very deceiving night. That is all I can say about that. I only saw the ice a mile and a half off.'

As Lord left the witness chair, he thought to himself that Smith's approach to him had seemed to be very straightforward, very polite, and with nothing very formal about it. Certainly his replies to the questions which he had been asked seemed to have been accepted factually, without comment or criticism.

Evans took Lord's place. Questioned, he stated that he was twenty years of age and that, after ten months' training, he had gone to sea as a wireless operator six months previously in the White Star liner *Cedric*, moving from her to the *Californian*. He was employed by the

Marconi Company at £4 a month.

The committee's examination followed no set pattern, members jumping from one topic to another. The greater part of it, however, was directed towards the technical aspects of the *Californian*'s wireless equipment and the messages sent and received by Evans. He was asked about his attempt to communicate with the *Titanic* at 11 p.m. on 14 April.

'I went outside of my room just before that,' Evans explained. 'We were stopped, and I went to the captain and I asked him if there was anything the matter. The captain told me he was going to stop because of the ice and asked me if I had any boats. I said the *Titanic* and he said: "Better advise him we are surrounded by ice and stopped." So I went to my cabin and at 9.05 New York time I called him up. I said: "Say, old man, we are stopped and surrounded by ice." He turned around and said: "Shut up, shut up, I am busy; I am working Cape Race," and at that I jammed him ... I was stronger than Cape Race, therefore my signals came in with a bang and he could read me and he could not read Cape Race ... At 11.25 I still had the phones on my ears and heard him still working Cape Race, and at 11.35 I put the phones down and took off my clothes and turned in.'

Fletcher wanted to know if Evans had had any conversation with Gill about the ship seen that night to be throwing up rockets.

'I think so,' Evans admitted. 'Practically everybody on the ship – it has been common talk on the ship.'

Although questioned at length on this point, Evans proved unwilling or unable to comment further, other than to add that Gibson had told him the captain had been notified three times that a vessel was sending up rockets. Senator Burton then raised an issue which particularly interested Lord.

'Has anyone told you that he was to receive five hundred dollars for a story in regard to these rockets – anyone on your boat?' he asked.

'I think the donkeyman, Gill, mentioned it,' Evans admitted.

'What did he say?'

'He said: "I think I will make about five hundred dollars on this".'

'Did he say that to you?'

'Yes, sir.'

'When was that said?'

'The night before last.'

'Where were you then?'

'I had gone ashore, and I was outside the station, I think ... He asked if I was not going back any more. He said he had been up and told the newspaper about the accident.'

'And he said that he would make about five hundred dollars out of it?'

'He said: "I think we will make about five hundred dollars out of it".'

Five hundred dollars to a man earning only £7 a month was a lot of money and a great temptation, Lord reflected. It was more than a year's salary to a man like Gill, and it was not surprising if it induced in him a great stretch of imagination.

After further questions about the circumstances under which he had been roused by the chief officer, and an assertion that personally he would refuse to accept money for any information which he might have picked up about the *Titanic* disaster, Evans' testimony was concluded, and both he and Lord were released by the committee.

They were provided with transport to the railway station and an escort in the form of a clerk who kept up a non-stop barrage of questions about the *Californian* and her involvement in the *Titanic* affair. The clerk also mentioned that, during the morning, Gill had appeared before the committee and had confirmed what he had stated in his affidavit.

Once aboard the train, Lord could relax, and the return journey to Boston was uneventful. Back on board the *Californian*, he was kept fully occupied with catching up on official business which had built up during his absence, and with the many formalities which had to be completed before the ship could sail. He was so busy, in fact, that he was unable to obtain any newspapers, and consequently never had a chance to read a report of his appearance before Senator Smith's committee.

Not surprisingly, perhaps, having regard to all the circumstances, Gill was missing, and Lord was left with no alternative but to enter against his name in the ship's articles of agreement the endorsement: 'Deserted'.

Just as the *Californian* was about to cast off, a man came hurrying along the wharf. He had an armful of flowers and some parcels, and just as Lord was wondering who he might be, the man called up to him.

'Say, cap,' he shouted. 'I've got something for you.'

'All right, bring it aboard,' Lord replied. He sent a quartermaster down from the bridge, and he returned with gifts from Endicott's mother, flowers and boxes of chocolates which Lord took home to his wife.

The *Californian* sailed for Liverpool on Saturday, 27 April, and having regard to the fascination which the *Titanic* disaster seemed to be exerting over everybody, it came as no surprise to Lord to find himself engaged in an animated discussion about the affair with the local pilot who took the ship out of the port as far as the fairway buoy.

CHAPTER SIX

Lord Mersey's Inquiry

The *Californian*'s trans-Atlantic passage to Liverpool was uneventful, and arrangements were made for her crew to pay off on Friday, 10 May. Shortly after the ship docked, Lord and his three navigating officers were called into the chief marine superintendent's office.

Captain Fry, a thickset, bearded man, questioned them about what had happened on the night the *Titanic* was lost. Lord and Stone confirmed their opinion that the ship which had stopped close by was not a passenger ship: on the other hand, Groves not only asserted that she was, but also expressed his opinion that the rockets seen coming from her had been distress signals. Lord was surprised to hear this, and commented to Fry that it was the first time that he had heard Groves make such a statement.

With a few other members of the *Californian*'s crew, Lord and his officers went to the local Board of Trade office to make formal statements covering their recollection of events on the night of the *Titanic* disaster. The Board's official investigation into the circumstances attending her foundering had opened in London on Thursday, 2 May, and the authorities wasted no time in arranging for nine witnesses from the *Californian* to travel down to London to appear before the court.

On Tuesday morning, 14 May, Lord arrived outside the London Scottish Drill Hall in Buckingham Gate, where the inquiry was being held. Here he joined William Roberts, general manager of the Leyland Line, and was briefly introduced to C. Robertson Dunlop, KC, who, Roberts told him, was watching the proceedings on behalf of the company.

Lord also spoke to Leonard S. Holmes, whom he had met before. Holmes was the senior partner in the Liverpool firm of Miller, Taylor & Holmes, solicitors representing the Imperial Merchant Service Guild, to which five of the *Titanic*'s officers belonged. Before they parted, Holmes told Lord to let him know if there was anything he could do for him.

Shortly before 10.30, Lord and Roberts went into the large hall. Across one end, on a raised platform, tables had been placed for the President and his assessors, to the right of which, also raised above floor level, stood a table and stool for witnesses. Behind was a large model of the *Titanic*; further down on that side of the hall was displayed a chart of the Atlantic. The extensive floor space was covered with rows of tables and chairs, those in front reserved for counsel and their advisers, those behind for the general public. On this occasion there was a large attendance, predominantly brightly dressed women, attracted by the anticipated appearance of Bruce Ismay and the *Titanic*'s surviving officers.

The President of the court took his place, flanked by his five assessors. He was 72-year-old Lord Mersey,* whose successful career as a lawyer, before being made a judge, had been in the commercial field; for a year, however, prior to his retirement in 1910, he had served as President of the Admiralty, Probate and Divorce Division of the High Court. He had been specially appointed as Wreck Commissioner to inquire into the loss of the *Titanic*.

Lord Mersey was assisted by five nautical advisers. Rear-Admiral the Hon. Somerset Gough-Calthorpe, CVO, was 42 years of age; in 1909/10 he had served as Captain of the Fleet in the Home Fleet. Commander F.C. Lyon, RNR, had been for a number of years in command in the P. & O. Company, in which Groves, the *Californian*'s third officer, had also served before joining the Leyland Line. Lyon had had considerable experience of marine inquiries. Commander A.W. Clarke, an Elder Brother of Trinity House, had been retired for a number of years from an active life at sea. Mr E.C. Chaston had been an engineer officer and was currently serving as head engineer superintendent in a shipping company operating fifteen steamers; he also held a commission in the Royal Naval Reserve. The fifth assessor was Professor J.H. Biles, a distinguished naval architect who had started his career with the Royal Navy.

Principal counsel for the Board of Trade, the government department responsible for convening the inquiry, was Sir Rufus

* *The Dictionary of National Biography* was later to record of Lord Mersey: 'As a judge, he showed the ability that was expected of him, though he was inclined to the failings of those whose minds work quickly. Disliking tedious arguments, and full of robust common sense, he often took a short cut.'

Isaacs,* the Attorney-General, an influential politician and one of the outstanding advocates of his day.

The proceedings opened with an application from Dunlop for permission to appear on behalf of the owners, master and officers of the *Californian*. Responding, the Attorney-General explained that the question at issue appeared to be between the *Californian*'s master and the donkeyman, who claimed to have seen the *Titanic*'s distress signals. He stated that he did not propose to go into the matter at any length, although he intended to ask the *Californian*'s witnesses those questions essential for Lord Mersey to be able to say whether or not what the donkeyman said was right.

Lord Mersey consequently refused Dunlop's application, but promised to let him know if anything was said requiring explanation from his clients.

Lord was then called on to the witness stand and sworn. At first he stood erect, answering the Attorney-General's questions crisply and pitching his voice to ensure that his replies were plainly audible. Later, as the examination gathered weight, he eased his position by resting his hands on the table before him.

The Attorney-General took Lord through the *Californian*'s movements on the afternoon and evening of 14 April up to the time they stopped at 10.20 p.m. He was asked what he recalled seeing of the lights of the steamer which had approached them, and how far away he estimated her to have been.

'Can you tell us at all how this ship was heading?' the Attorney-General enquired.

'She was heading to the westward, that is all I can tell you.'

'Could you tell her bearing at all?'

'Well, I have heard it since. I heard what it was at midnight – SSE from us by compass.'

Lord Mersey intervened.

'Was the compass correct?'

'No,' Lord replied.

'What variation?' asked the Attorney-General.

'The variation that day at noon was 24 and three-quarters. It was about 24 when we were stopped; the deviation would be about 2 East, making an error of 22W.'

* Of Sir Rufus Isaacs (later to become Lord Reading) *The Dictionary of National Biography* states: '(His) greatest asset at the Bar was not eloquence but a penetrating power of judgement which enabled him to see the point on which the case would ultimately turn (and) the main difficulty of fact to be surmounted.'

'Are these minute particulars of importance?' demanded Lord Mersey.

'No, I do not think they are, my lord,' the Attorney-General assured him.

In reply to further questions, Lord gave an account of his actions up to the time he lay down in the chartroom at 12.40 a.m., to be roused shortly afterwards by Stone's message through the speaking tube that the other ship was altering her bearing to the south-west and had fired a white rocket.

Lord Mersey intervened again.

'Is it right, Mr Attorney,' he asked, 'that at this time the *Titanic* would be bearing to the south-west of where the *Californian* was?'

The Attorney-General agreed that this was so.

'Is it also true, as this witness is telling us, that the vessel of which we do not know the name was also bearing to the south-west?'

'I understand him to say so.'

Lord Mersey turned to Lord.

'Is that so? Do you hear him?'

'I did, my lord. The steamer was heading SSE by compass till ten minutes to one.'*

'Yes, I know it was, but at the particular time we were talking about it was heading south-west.'

'*Towards* the south-west,' Lord corrected him.

Lord Mersey reacted sharply.

'I do not know what that means,' he rebuked him. 'Does it mean *not* south-west? What does "towards south-west" mean? Does it mean south-west or does it not?'

'It does not mean exactly south-west – she was heading *towards* the south-west.'

'Well, near enough. Is it the fact – am I right in supposing that this vessel, the name of which you apparently do not know, from which a rocket appeared, was at the time that the rocket was sent up in the position in which probably the *Titanic* was?'

'No.'

'Well, then, you have conveyed to me an erroneous impression. How did this rocket bear to you?'

'I have never heard the exact bearing of it.'

'Dear me! Your second officer is alive, isn't he?'

'Yes.'

* Lord meant '*bearing* SSE', an error repeated by Lord Mersey.

'Have you never asked him what the bearing of that rocket was?'

'He told me that it was heading towards the south-west. Between the bearings SSE and south-west would be a distance of at least five miles and she was going slowly between those two bearings.'

Lord Mersey addressed the Attorney-General.

'Mr Attorney, again I want to know this: apparently the *Titanic* would be at this time fourteen or fifteen miles away from this vessel?'

After some discussion as to the probable distance, in which Lord Mersey and the Attorney-General were assisted by Sir Robert Finlay, counsel for the White Star Line, Lord Mersey returned to the point that he was trying to make.

'Let us assume it was something between fourteen and nineteen miles. This mysterious vessel would be between the *Californian* and the *Titanic*, and must have been well within sight of the *Titanic*. We have heard about the mysterious light that was seen – the imaginary light, as it was called – that was seen from the *Titanic*, but, dismissing that light, was there any light or any vessel seen by any witness from the *Titanic* at this time?'

'There is some evidence of a light having been seen,' the Attorney-General responded.

'I know. I say, dismissing that imaginary light, is there any evidence of any ship having been seen at this time, or about this time, by the *Titanic*?'

'No, I do not think so.'

'What is in my brain at the present time is this – that what they saw was the *Titanic* ... That is in my brain, and I want to see whether I am right or not ... Clear it up if you can.'

'I think it will clear up as we go on – at least, as far as it can be cleared up,' the Attorney-General submitted. 'It is a point your Lordship will probably have to determine on the evidence.'

'Yes, and therefore I want the evidence put before me as clearly as possible.'

The Attorney-General turned to Lord.

'Can you tell us whether you saw one or two masthead lights?'

'I only saw one.'

'You only saw one?'

Lord thought he might be able to help the court.

'The third officer said he saw two,' he volunteered.

'Now that is important,' the Attorney-General commented.

'That is *very* important, because the *Titanic* would have two,' Lord

Mersey agreed.

Both he and the Attorney-General pressed Lord heavily on this point, wanting to know when and where the third officer had made this remark to him. He explained that it was on the following day.

'Why did you ask him how many there were?' Lord Mersey enquired.

'Well, I was curious about this *Titanic* accident. I was trying to locate the ship that was supposed to be between us and the *Titanic*.'

'Were you in doubt as to whether you had seen one or two lights?'

'I had not myself.'

'Then I cannot understand why you should ask him how many lights he had seen if you yourself had no doubt whatever about it,' Lord Mersey observed.

The Attorney-General followed up this point.

'If he did see two lights, it must have been the *Titanic*, must it not?'

Lord disagreed.

'It does not follow.'

'Do you know any other vessel it could have been?'

'Any amount.'

'Which? I mean at this particular time, you know, and at this particular spot. Can you suggest any other vessel it could have been?'

'Well, I do not know.'

'Carrying two lights?'

'That particular spot? The spot mentioned here as nineteen miles away is not, in my opinion, where the *Titanic* hit the berg.'

'Within a radius of twenty miles of you?'

'No, thirty miles ... She was thirty-two miles from where I left the wreckage.'

Lord was questioned intensively about his conversation with the third officer at 11.45 p.m. He firmly denied that Groves had said to him that the nearby ship 'was evidently a passenger steamer' or that he had ever expressed the opinion to Lord that it was the *Titanic* he saw. The Attorney-General pressed him about this.

'Did you say to him: "The only passenger steamer near us is the *Titanic*"?'

'I might have said that with regard to the steamer, but he did not say the steamer was a passenger steamer.'

'You might have said what?'

'The *Titanic*.'

'What about the *Titanic*?'

'The *Titanic* we were in communication with.'

'That is not what I put, you know.'

'No,' Lord Mersey commented. 'And it is not what he said.'

'That is a very different thing,' the Attorney-General emphasised.

'You said, according to your statement: "The *Titanic* is the only passenger steamer near us",' Lord Mersey insisted. 'You said that to him?'

'She was.'

'But you said it to him?'

'I do not recollect saying it.'

'You have just told me you *did* say it,' Lord Mersey complained. 'Do collect your mind. Did you say it?'

'I do not recollect saying it.'

The Attorney-General resumed his interrogation.

'Did you know of any other passenger steamer near you except the *Titanic*?'

'I did not.'

'But you knew the *Titanic* was not far from you?'

'I had no idea where the *Titanic* was.'

'But you had been in communication with it?'

'Yes, but I never had its position.'

'Do you know whether the steamer was pointed out by Groves to Mr Stone?'

'He told me afterwards that she was.'

'And that it was a passenger steamer?'

'I never heard that.'

'That he had said that it was a passenger steamer?'

'I never heard that.'

The atmosphere became even more hostile.

'You do not give answers that please me at present,' Lord Mersey warned Lord. 'You said just now as plainly as possible that you answered the third officer, I think it was, and said: "The only passenger steamer near us is the *Titanic*". You now suggest that you do not remember whether you said that or not.'

'I do not recollect saying anything to him about it, my Lord.'

'Could you have forgotten such a thing?'

'Well, I have heard so many stories about the *Titanic* since that I really do not know what I heard that night.'

'But that would be rather an important matter, would it not, if you thought the steamer that was approaching you was the *Titanic*?' the Attorney-General asked.

'I never thought it. I saw a steamer.'

'That is exactly what you said: "I might have said that the only passenger steamer likely to be near us is the *Titanic*",' Lord Mersey insisted.

'You *might* have said that,' the Attorney-General suggested. 'That is what you said before. That is right, is it not?'

'I *might* have said it; I do not recollect it.'

Lord confirmed his account of events after he lay down at 12.40 a.m. up to his being called by the chief officer at 4.30. He became confused, however, on being asked when he first understood that several rockets had been seen rather than the single rocket he initially thought Stone had reported.

'Who told you?' the Attorney-General asked him.

'The second officer first ... He said she had fired several rockets in his watch – no, the chief officer told me, about five o'clock, that she had fired several rockets.'

The Attorney-General addressed Lord Mersey.

'My lord,' he said. 'I think it very desirable that the other witnesses from the *Californian* should be out of court whilst this witness is giving evidence.'

'By all means,' Lord Mersey agreed, and the group accordingly left the court room. In addition to Stewart, Stone, Groves, Gibson and Evans, it included a seaman, W. Ross, and two firemen, G. Glenn and W. Thomas, the latter being Gill's cabinmate.

The Attorney-General returned to the question of the number of rockets reported to Lord and the message sent down with the apprentice.

'Gibson, the apprentice, had been told by the second officer to go to the chartroom to tell you that the vessel had fired altogether eight rockets, or, as you say, several rockets, and that the vessel had disappeared?'

'Had steamed away. That was the message that I understand was given.'

'I am putting to you, you know, that what was said was the vessel had disappeared.'

'No, it was never mentioned, "disappeared", to me.'

A series of questions followed probing Lord's reason for staying in the chartroom although not satisfied that the rocket reported to him was a company's signal.

'If it was not a company's signal, must it not have been a distress signal?' the Attorney-General enquired.

'If it had been a distress signal, the officer on watch would have told me.'

'I say, if it was not a company's signal, must it not have been a distress signal?'

'Well, I do not know of any other signals but distress signals that are used at sea.'

'You do not expect at sea, where you were, to see a rocket unless it is a distress signal, do you?'

'We sometimes get these company's signals which resemble rockets; they do not shoot as high and they do not explode ... I asked the officer: "Was it a company's signal?" '

'And he did not know?' Lord Mersey enquired.

'He did not know.'

'Very well,' the Attorney-General continued. 'That did not satisfy you?'

'It did not satisfy me.'

'Then if it was not that, it might have been a distress signal?'

Not knowing why the signals reported by Stone had been sent up, Lord could only agree.

'It *might* have been.'

'And you remained in the chartroom?'

'I remained in the chartroom.'

'Expecting Gibson, the apprentice, to come down and report to you?'

'Yes.'

'Gibson did come down?'

'So I understand.'

'But you know perfectly well that he came.'

'I know now.'

'Did you know then?'

'I did not.'

'I think you told us you heard Gibson open and close the door?'

'Yes.'

'And you said: "What is it?" '

'Yes.'

'And he said nothing?'

'He did not say anything.'

'And you were expecting him to come down and tell you what the meaning of the rocket was?'

'But in the meantime I was asleep.'

'Yes, but you were not asleep – at least, I suppose not – when you said to the boy: "What is it?" ' Lord Mersey commented.

'I was wakened by the opening of the door – the banging of the door.'

Lord Mersey turned to the question of when the first Morse lamp signals were used.

'Half past eleven at night,' Lord told him.

'And no reply was ever obtained?' the Attorney-General asked.

'No reply.'

'So it would follow from what you have said, would it not, that if your man Gill says he did see a distress signal he was right?'

'No. At the distance we were away from that steamer, if it had been a distress signal we would have heard the report ... We were close enough – about four or five miles – to hear the report of any distress signal.'

Lord was urged to say why, after he had been called by the chief officer, he did not discuss with him what had been seen of rockets or the possibility of the other ship having been the *Titanic*. He agreed that, at nineteen miles, he thought that they ought to have seen the *Titanic*'s signals. It was the only thing that was worrying him after he had heard that the *Titanic* had sunk.

The Attorney-General followed this up.

'Does it not strike you now that the steamer you saw sending up rockets must have been the *Titanic*?'

'No, I am positive that it was not the *Titanic*.'

'Why are you positive it was not?'

'Because a ship like the *Titanic* at sea – it is an utter impossibility for anyone to mistake.'

'That must depend on the distance you are from her.'

'Well, my distance, according to my estimate, is four to five miles.'

Lord agreed, however, that he could not suggest any other steamer that might have been sending up rockets between 1 and 2 a.m. on 15 April.

After asking Lord about the *Californian*'s movements after she set course for the position which they had been given, the Attorney-General gave way to Thomas Scanlan, MP, appearing for the *Titanic*'s crew.

'When you were in doubt as to the name of this ship, and as to the meaning of her sending up a rocket, could you not have ascertained definitely by calling in the assistance of your Marconi operator?' Scanlan asked.

'When? At one o'clock in the morning?'

'Yes.'

'This steamer had been in sight, the one that fired the rocket, when we sent the last message to the *Titanic*, and I was certain that the steamer was *not* the *Titanic*, and the operator said he had not any other steamers, so I drew my conclusion that she had not got any wireless.'

'What reason have you for thinking that this steamer, a steamer which you say was, at all events, as big as your own, had not got wireless?'

'At eleven o'clock, when I saw her, the operator told me he had not got anything, only the *Titanic*. I remarked then: "That is not the *Titanic*", judging from its size and the number of lights about it, and if he only had one ship, then it was not the *Titanic*. I do not see how he could still have that ship.'

'Suppose the *Titanic* was seven or eight miles from you between 11.30 and twelve o'clock, would those on her bridge have been able to see your lights?'

'Easily.'

Adair Roche, appearing on behalf of the *Titanic*'s engineers, suggested that Lord was not anxious, if he could help it, to move his engines because he was treating the ice with great respect. Lord assured him that, while he did not want to move them, they were ready for use at a moment's notice.

'Was that the reason, perhaps, why you were not so inquisitive as to these signals as you might otherwise have been?'

'No, that had not anything to do with it,' Lord affirmed.

Examined by Mr W.D. Harbinson, representing the *Titanic*'s third class passengers, Lord was unable to help him by speculating how he considered a 21-knot steamer should be handled when in proximity to ice. He also disagreed with Harbinson's suggestion that a ship's crowsnest should be manned with a junior officer in addition to an able seaman: in Lord's opinion, an officer on the bridge was quite sufficient.

Clement Edwards, MP, of the General Workers' Union, questioned Lord unproductively on the basis of what appeared to be a quite inaccurate account of the evidence he had given at the United States inquiry.

Edwards was followed by Thomas Lewis, appearing for the British

Seafarers' Union. Lord confirmed that he considered it reasonable in the circumstances for him to retire to the chartroom and to allow the wireless operator to go off watch without the latter's first telling him what acknowledgment had been made by the *Titanic*'s operator to their communication about being stopped in ice.

Sir Robert Finlay rose to put a few concise questions, asking for Lord's opinion on the best siting of lookouts; the relative positions of the *Mount Temple*, at the position of the disaster as reported by wireless, and the actual wreckage, and the *Californian*'s courses between the two points.

After that brief examination, Dunlop requested permission to ask Lord some questions, but the Attorney-General resumed his own interrogation. He questioned Lord intensively on the discrepancy between the formal statements made to the Board of Trade by Gibson and Stone, as to the reports they had passed to Lord at 2 a.m. and 2.40 respectively, and his own account.

Lord could only repeat that he had no recollection of any such conversations. Noticing that Lord had with him the ship's official log book, Lord Mersey asked that it be handed over to him: he then enquired as to why there were no references in it to the rockets which had been seen.

'If we had realised they were distress rockets, we would have entered them,' Lord told him. 'The second officer, the man in charge of the watch, stated most emphatically they were *not* distress rockets.'

Dunlop was then allowed to examine Lord. He took him through his statement of events, twice being halted by the Attorney-General and once by Lord Mersey for allegedly putting words into the witness's mouth. Lord confirmed his account of what had happened. He also described what he had seen of the ice, and at this stage the rough sketch and draft statement he had prepared in Boston were disclosed, and, at Lord Mersey's request, handed over to him.

Reverting to the *Titanic*'s sinking, Dunlop asked Lord if, having known about it at 1.15 a.m., he could have reached her before, say, 3 a.m.?

'No, most certainly not,' Lord replied.

'Could you have navigated with any degree of safety to your vessel at night through the ice that you in fact encountered?'

'It would have been most dangerous.'

Lord Mersey intervened.

'Am I to understand that this is what you mean to say, that if he had known that the vessel was the *Titanic* he would have made no attempt whatever to reach it?'

'No, my lord,' Dunlop replied. 'I do not suggest that.'

Turning to Lord, he said: 'What would you have done? No doubt you would have made an attempt?'

'Most certainly I would have made every attempt to go down to her,' Lord confirmed.

'Would the attempt from what you now know in fact have suceeded?'

'I do not think we would have got there before the *Carpathia* did, if we would have got there as soon.'

With that, Lord's ordeal was concluded.

Gibson, the apprentice, followed him on to the witness stand. First to question him was Sir John Simon, KC, MP, the Solicitor General, and Lord was immediately impressed by his polite, gentlemanly approach when contrasted with the hostile attitude adopted by the Attorney-General.

Gibson's evidence was generally on the lines of the personal statement he had written out for Lord. There were differences, however, and two very significant additions.

A relatively minor detail was Gibson's twice repeated error in describing the *Californian* as swinging to the northward, whereas throughout the night she had been slowly swinging to starboard, through south. As to the ship they had been watching, Gibson confirmed his impression that, despite a faint glare of light from her afterdeck, she was not a passenger vessel. He told the court that he had seen nearly all the large passenger ships at sea, and there was nothing at all about her to resemble a passenger vessel: in fact, he had told the second officer that he thought she was a tramp steamer.

Gibson's evidence was interrupted by a short adjournment for lunch. Leaving the court, Lord noticed that he was the object of attention from photographers, presumably from the press.

On the resumption of the inquiry, the first detail about the night's events entirely new to Lord was Gibson's revelation that, between 1 and 1.20 a.m., Stone had passed the binoculars to him with the comment: 'Have a look at her now, Gibson – she seems to look queer.'

Looking at her through the glasses, Gibson thought that her red sidelight seemed higher out of the water, and that the lights on her afterdeck, although in the same position, seemed somehow to look different. He was unable to describe just what that difference was, however, although he expressed the opinion that it seemed as if she had a heavy list to starboard.

Secondly, Lord was surprised by Gibson's statement that Stone had remarked to him that a ship was not going to fire rockets at sea for nothing. Gibson explained that, at the time, this did not convey to him the impression that the second officer thought that the other ship was in distress. It was rather that everything was not all right with her, and Gibson said he felt the same way.

He confirmed the terms of the message given to him by the second officer at 2 a.m. He had been told to call the captain, and to tell him that the ship had disappeared in the south-west; that the *Californian* was heading WSW; and that the other ship had fired altogether eight rockets. On the bridge, however, Stone had spoken of the other ship as 'steaming away', and Gibson understood the term 'disappeared' to mean that she had gone out of sight.

In answer to Dunlop, Gibson confirmed that over the period from 12.15 to five past two, using glasses, he saw only one masthead light; that he could not have missed a second masthead light if it had been there; and that the second officer had said that the cause of the white masthead light's flickering was probably because the other ship was burning oil lights.

Gibson's place on the witness stand was taken by Stone, and, as in the apprentice's case, his evidence was generally on the lines of the statement he had written out for Lord. Examined by Butler Aspinall, KC, for the Board of Trade, he confirmed that when he went on watch he could see one masthead light, a red sidelight, and two or three small indistinct lights on the other steamer, which was bearing SSE by the standard compass, about five miles away.

Asked what he thought the five rockets seen between 12.50 and 1.10 a.m. meant, Stone suggested that perhaps the ship was in communication with some other ship a greater distance away, or possibly she was signalling to the *Californian* to tell them that she had big icebergs around her.

'*What* was she communicating?' Lord Mersey asked.

'I do not know.'

'Is that the way in which steamers communicate with each other?'

'No, not usually.'

'Then you cannot have thought that,' Lord Mersey declared. 'Just attend to the question.'

Aspinall repeated his enquiry.

'I did not know at the time,' Stone replied.

Lord Mersey intervened again.

'Now try to be frank.'

'I am,' Stone protested.

'If you try, you will succeed. What did you think these rockets were going up at intervals of three or four minutes for?'

'I just took them as white rockets, and informed the master, and left him to judge.'

'Do you mean to say you did not think for yourself? I thought you told us just now that you *did* think.'

Stone made no reply, and Aspinall took up the questioning again.

'You know they were not being sent up for fun, were they?'

'No.'

Lord Mersey looked hard at him.

'You know, you do not make a good impression upon me at present.'

Stone maintained that he did not think that the rockets were distress signals. While he agreed with the comment that he did not think they were being sent up for fun, it did not occur to him that the other ship was in trouble.

Lord Mersey pressed Stone on this point.

'What did you think they were being sent up for?'

'Naturally, the first thought that crossed my mind was that the ship might be in trouble, but subsequent events showed that the ship steamed away from us. There was nothing to confirm that the rockets came from that ship, in the direction of that ship.'

'Where did you think they came from, if they did not come from that ship?'

'Possibly from a greater distance past the ship.'

'Did you tell that to the captain?'

'Yes, afterwards ... the next day.'

'Have you ever said it to anybody else?'

'Yes. I think I have said it both to the chief officer and to the third officer in conversation ... I have remarked at different times that these rockets did not appear to go very high; they were very low-lying; they were only about half the height of the steamer's masthead light and I thought rockets would go higher than that ... But I could not understand why, if the rockets came from a steamer beyond this one, when the steamer altered her bearing the rockets should also alter their bearings.'

Stone went on to describe how he had kept the other ship under

An artist's impression of the *Titanic* at night

One of the *Titanic*'s inadequately manned lifeboats (probably No 2, under J.G. Boxhall, fourth officer) approaching the *Carpathia*

The *Californian* seen from the *Carpathia*, 15 April 1912. The coal basket in which Benjamin Kirk was hoisted to the mainmasthead can be clearly seen

The *Mount Temple* ashore off Nova Scotia 1908

observation until she went out of sight, a happening which, he said, was a gradual disappearing of all her lights, which would be perfectly natural with a ship steaming away from them. By 'all her lights' he explained that he meant the deck lights which were in view; the masthead light, which would be shut in except for a slight flickering, the glare of it; and the red side light, which would be shut in altogether. The lights he saw would be the lights at the end of the alleyway or engine-room skylight, and the stern light, which gradually faded as if the steamer were steaming away from them.

'Did it have the appearance of being a light on a ship which had suddenly foundered?' Aspinall enquired.

'Not by any means,' Stone affirmed.

He was asked why, if he thought nothing had happened to the other ship, he had reported her disappearance to the captain at 2.40 a.m.

'Simply because I had had the steamer under observation all the watch, and that I had made reports to the captain concerning her, and I thought it my duty, when the ship went away from us altogether, to tell him.'

'But why could not you have told him in the morning?' Lord Mersey asked. 'Why wake up the poor man?'

'Because it was my duty to do so, and it was his duty to listen to it.'

'Were you anxious about her?'

'No.'

'Was he anxious about her?'

'No, as far as I could judge from his answers and instructions.'

Questioned further by Lord Mersey about his conversation with Gibson, and whether or not either of them expressed an opinion that there was something wrong with the other ship, Stone said that they were concerned merely with the change in her lights; he had remarked that the *lights* looked queer, not the ship.

'The lights are what I call part of the ship – the whole thing, lights and all, make up the ship,' Lord Mersey pointed out, adding sceptically: 'You want me to believe, do you, that notwithstanding these rockets, neither you nor Gibson thought there was anything wrong on board that ship? You want me to understand that?'

'Yes, sir,' came Stone's unhesitating reply.

Aspinall concluded his examination by pressing Stone as to why the chief officer, at 4 a.m., should have said that the four-masted steamer then in sight to the southward was 'all right'.

'Why should he have said it, in view of the evidence you have given us here today, you know? Do not you think you told the chief officer that you were fearful the steamer you had seen had gone down?'

'No,' Stone replied. 'I told him the steamer had steamed away from us in a south-westerly direction.'

Questioned by Scanlan, Stone agreed that the proper method of signalling distress at night was the firing of 'rockets or shells, throwing stars of any colour or description, fired one at a time at short intervals'.

Lord Mersey took him up on that admission.

'And is not that exactly what was happening ... The very thing was happening that you knew indicated distress?'

'If that steamer had stayed on the same bearing after showing these rockets ... ' Stone began, but Lord Mersey interrupted him.

'No, do not give a long answer of that kind. Is it not the fact that the very thing was happening which you had been taught indicated distress?'

'Yes,' Stone had to accept. 'I knew that rockets shown at short intervals, one at a time, meant distress signals; yes.'

'Do not speak generally,' Scanlan admonished him. 'On that very night, when you saw those rockets being sent up, you knew, did you not, that those rockets were signals of distress?'

'No,' Stone steadfastly maintained.

'Now do think about what you are saying,' Lord Mersey cautioned him. 'You have just told me that what you saw from that steamer was exactly what you had been taught to understand were signals of distress. You told me so.'

'Yes.'

'Well, is it true?'

'It is true that similar lights are distress signals; yes.'

'Then you had seen them from this steamer.'

'A steamer that is in distress does not steam away from you, my lord.'

Sympathetically watching Stone's ordeal, Lord was confident that this reply answered absolutely everything. To his amazement, it seemed to have no effect whatsoever on Lord Mersey or his colleagues, nor on their sustained efforts to force Stone to express the opinion that the ship he had been watching was the *Titanic*.

Stone was asked at what time he sent word to the captain that he first noticed the other ship was steaming away.

'At ten minutes past one. I reported to the master that she was altering her bearings, which was the same thing.'

Aspinall intervened.

'Altering her bearings does not mean steaming away.'

'I do not see how two ships can alter their bearings when stopped.'

Lord Mersey put an end to this exchange.

'You need not press this any further,' he said.

There followed what, to Lord, seemed to be a very curious interlude during which Mr F. Laing, KC, one of the counsel appearing for the White Star Line, supported by Lord Mersey, tried unsuccessfully to persuade Stone that in some way the *Californian*'s swinging to starboard during his watch could have influenced the appearance of the other ship's navigation lights as seen from the *Californian*. Stone could only maintain that he never saw the other ship's green sidelight, just her stern light being visible for about an hour after she started to steam away.

Questioned by the Solicitor-General about this stern light, Stone was asked whether he knew any means on a dark night at sea by which one could tell whether or not a light was a very powerful light some way off, or a less powerful light not so far off.

'Yes,' he replied. 'A powerful light generally throws a glow round it into the surrounding atmosphere. The more moisture there is in the air, the greater the glow you will see around this light.'

'How much glow was there round these lights?'

'Very little.'

With this remark, Stone's evidence was completed, and with it the day's proceedings. Dunlop rose to ask for permission for Lord to return to Liverpool, but Lord Mersey intimated that he would rather that he did not leave that night, but remain until the following day, when the court should have finished with the witnesses from the *Californian*.

Lord walked away with an overwhelming impression that Lord Mersey and the Attorney-General between them had made up their minds that it was the *Titanic* which had been seen from the *Californian*, and that they were not prepared to consider any evidence proving otherwise. That he was not alone in carrying away such an impression was confirmed by what appeared in the popular press the following morning.

The *Daily Mirror*, which described Lord as 'a tall, typical-looking merchant skipper, with sea-reddened, clean-shaven face, wrinkled brow, spare features and high forehead, bald to the crown of his head', carried the following account of Gibson's appearance on the witness stand:

> DRAMATIC MOMENT AT DISASTER INQUIRY – *Ship with List to Starboard Seen from 'Californian' – Was It the 'Titanic'?*
>
> ... [Sir John Simon, the Solicitor-General] examined Gibson in the gentle, understanding way which coaxes so much out of witnesses ... It seemed the apprentice was describing the going down of the *Titanic* as viewed from a vessel only five miles away, that he had unconsciously been a witness of the dread catastrophe that has wrung the emotions of a world of men and women. His language was technical but understandable enough. The second officer and he were on the bridge of the *Californian* observing a vessel believed to be a tramp steamer. They had seen rockets fired into the air from her direction, they had sent up Morse signals by lamp to which no answer came, they had wondered what the rockets meant.
>
> At 1.20 a.m., the officer said to him: 'Look at her now. She looks very queer out of the water. The lights look queer.'
>
> 'She seemed as if she had a heavy list to starboard.' He was certain of this. Her port light, her red light, was higher in the water than it had been when he first looked at the ship. Moreover, the white glaring lights aft seemed different somehow, he could not explain how.
>
> The luncheon interval brought a welcome relief to the strain of examination to which the youth had been subjected, and the laymen in the audience went out convinced that they had heard the story of one who had seen from a distance the last hours of the *Titanic*.

CHAPTER SEVEN

The Third Officer's Opinion

Groves was the first witness to be called when the court resumed on Wednesday morning. As his examination proceeded, Lord found himself increasingly forming the impression that the third officer was enjoying himself and his situation as the central figure on such an important occasion.

Questioned by Mr S.A.T. Rowlatt, appearing for the Board of Trade, Groves described events as he recalled them up to 10.26 p.m., when, he said, the *Californian* stopped. He first sighted an approaching ship at 11.10, about ten to twelve miles away. About five minutes later he began to pay particular attention to her, and at 11.25 considered that he could see two white masthead lights. At about 11.30, he left the bridge and went down to the chartroom to report to Captain Lord that what he considered to be a passenger ship was coming up obliquely on the starboard quarter. The *Californian* was then heading north-east, with the other ship bearing about three points abaft the beam, in a direction slightly to the west of due south.

The captain told him to call her up by Morse lamp, Groves told the court, and he did so. At first he thought she was replying, and the captain, who had joined him on the bridge, commented: 'She is answering you.' On checking through binoculars, however, Groves came to the conclusion that they had been misled by a flickering light, not a Morse lamp, and he was satisfied that there was no reply whatsoever.

'Did you have any more conversation with the captain about the steamer?' Rowlatt enquired.

'When he came up on the bridge, he said to me: "That does not look like a passenger steamer." I said: "It is, sir – when she stopped, her lights seemed to go out, and I suppose they have been put out for the night ... She put her lights out at 11.40".'

'Then had she put her lights out before the captain came on the bridge?' Lord Mersey asked.

'Yes, my lord ... at 11.40.'

'What did he say to that? Did he say anything?'

'Yes. He said: "The only passenger steamer anywhere near us is the *Titanic*".'

'He said that, did he?' Lord Mersey remarked, with eyebrows raised.

'Yes, my lord.'

'What makes you fix the time 11.40 for her lights going out?' Rowlatt wanted to know.

'Because that is the time we struck one bell to call the middle watch.'

'Do you remember that bell was struck at that time?'

'Most certainly ... She stopped ... That was at the time that her lights appeared to go out.'

'Were the lights you saw on her port side or starboard side?'

'Port side.'

'Supposing the steamer whose lights you saw turned two points to port at 11.40, would that account to you for her lights ceasing to be visible to you?'

'I quite think it would.'

'Mr Rowlatt,' Lord Mersey interrupted. 'At 11.40 the engines were stopped on the *Titanic*.'

There then followed what seemed to Lord to be a quite extraordinary discussion involving Rowlatt and Laing, who between them shared the difficult task of explaining to Lord Mersey that the stopping of the *Titanic*'s main engines at 11.40 would not automatically plunge the liner into darkness. This point having been cleared up, Lord Mersey and Rowlatt went on to recall evidence from the *Titanic* about a two-point change of course to port at the time of the collision with the iceberg, following which Groves confirmed his private opinion that a similar alteration of course on the part of the ship he was watching would have concealed her lights. Amplifying his impressions, he explained that initially he had considered that the approaching steamer had put her decklights out, as had been the custom at that time of night in his previous company. On reflection, however, he had come to the conclusion that she had altered course to avoid some ice.

Lord Mersey seized on this point.

'Would a change of course such as we know took place on the

Titanic cause the two white masthead lights to alter their relative positions?'

'Yes, it would,' Groves agreed. 'But I do not think at that distance the difference would be perceptible.'

'It would bring them a little nearer together?' Rowlatt suggested.

'Yes, a little nearer together.'

'Did you notice anything of that sort?'

'No, I did not.'

Groves went on to explain that, after he had tried to Morse the other ship without obtaining any response, he did not pay any particular attention to her. On being relieved by Stone, he went to the wireless operator's room. He woke Evans up and asked him what ships he had got. 'Only the *Titanic*,' Evans replied. Groves picked up the headphones, but could hear nothing at all, and from there he went to his own cabin and turned in.

At 6.40 a.m., he was called by the chief officer, who told him to go to the bridge as the *Titanic* had sunk and the passengers were in the lifeboats ahead. He jumped from his bunk and went across to Stone's room. He found the second officer getting dressed, and asked him: 'Is this right, Mr Stone, about the *Titanic*?' Stone replied: 'Yes, that is right. Hurry up and get dressed – we shall be wanted in the boats. I saw rockets in my watch.'

'That conveys to me the notion that when he said he saw rockets in his watch he was referring to the rockets which he believed had come from the *Titanic*,' Lord Mersey commented deliberately. 'Did he give you that impression?'

'Well, it is rather difficult for me to say what impression I got then, because I was rather excited,' Groves explained. 'But I have told you what he said to me and what I said to him.'

Groves then described what he saw when he reached the bridge at about 6.50. The boats were being swung out and the ship had a good speed on her. They passed the *Mount Temple*, and he saw another, smaller, vessel with a black funnel coming down almost end on, a little on their port bow. They reached the *Carpathia* about 7.45, he thought, and exchanged signals by semaphore. She left almost exactly at 9, when he heard her bell strike, following which they searched the area, finding nothing but boats and wreckage. They resumed their course at exactly 10.40, he said.

Answering Scanlan, Groves stated that he thought that the other ship stopped about five to seven miles away. From that ship, he considered that a person would be able to see the *Californian*'s white masthead lights and green sidelight, but was rather doubtful as to whether they would be seen from a boat lower down.

Some brief questions from Harbinson, Laing, Holmes and Edwards followed. In reply to the latter's question, Groves assured him that they got perfectly good sights that day.

Dunlop took up the question of the *Californian*'s navigation, and Groves repeated that their sights were perfectly good. He agreed that if the *Titanic*'s wreckage were in latitude 41° 33′ N. and the latitude in which the *Californian* had stopped was 42° 5′ N. then there would be about thirty miles between them, and no navigation lights whatsoever would be seen.

'If this vessel which you did see was only some four to five miles to the southward of you, do you think she could have been the *Titanic*?' Dunlop asked him.

'That is a question I want this witness to answer,' Lord Mersey commented. He turned to Groves.

'Speaking as an experienced seaman, and knowing what you do know now, do you think that steamer that you know was throwing up rockets, and that you say was a passenger steamer, was the *Titanic*?'

'Do I think it?'

'Yes.'

'From what I have heard subsequently?'

'Yes.'

'Most decidedly I do, sir,' Groves replied firmly, adding in the same breath: 'But I do not profess to be a very experienced seaman.'

'But that is your opinion as far as your experience goes?'

'Yes, it is, my lord.'

'That would indicate,' Dunlop pointed out, 'that the *Titanic* was only four to five miles to the southward of the position in which you were when stopped.'

Lord Mersey replied for Groves.

'If this judgement on the matter is true, it shows that those figures, latitudes and longitudes that you are referring to are not accurate. That is all it shows.'

'The accuracy we will deal with, my lord.'

'I mean to say, if what he says is right, it follows that the figures must be wrong.'

Groves agreed with Dunlop's submission that if the latitudes were right, then of course his opinion was wrong, but went on to maintain that, although the other steamer approached the

Californian obliquely, he was still sure that the glare of lights from her indicated that she was a large passenger steamer.

He became involved in a confused argument with Dunlop about the red sidelight he had seen, and what course a ship displaying it must have been following.

'She is south of you,' Dunlop repeated, 'and apparently proceeding to the westward.'

'Yes, some course to the westward.'

'Does it not follow from that that the side which she was showing to you at that time must have been her starboard side?'

'No, it does not follow at all. If she is steering a direct west course, yes.'

'Did you see her green light at all?'

'Never.'

To Lord, listening intently, this was essentially as significant an answer as Stone's had been, when he stated that a ship which is in distress does not steam away from you. Groves' point was inescapably met by the fact that, at the time of which he had been speaking, the *Titanic* must have been steering a course for New York of practically due west. But once again the court allowed what seemed to Lord to be a vital point to pass without comment, although Dunlop elicited from Groves a final statement that nothing in the appearance of the lights he had seen, and their apparent going out, led him to think that the vessel was in any way in distress.

The Solicitor-General questioned Groves about the log books kept in the *Californian*, and in particular the custom of destroying the pages of the scrap log book. The third officer stated that he had made no attempt to look back in the scrap log book to check if the rockets seen by Stone had been recorded. He assured Lord Mersey that, had he seen them during his watch, then most decidedly he would have recorded the fact.

Stewart followed him on the witness stand. If Lord had felt sympathy for Stone when he was being questioned, he was even more sorry for Stewart. Of all the *Californian*'s officers, the chief officer was least involved in the night's happenings: indeed, for much of the time he was quite legitimately asleep in his bunk. Yet between them Lord Mersey and the Solicitor-General hounded him quite relentlessly, his offence apparently being that, unlike Groves, he was not prepared to express the opinion that the ship seen nearby was the *Titanic*, or to admit that the rockets seen by Stone must have been distress rockets.

His inquisitors were particularly critical of Stewart's theory that the nearby ship might have been replying to rockets fired by another ship further to the south, and that the vessel seen to the southward at 4 a.m. might have been the one Stone had watched steaming away which had later returned.

Stewart was pressed by the Solicitor-General about the practice of destroying scrap log books page by page, but unexpectedly Laing came to his assistance.

'I can tell your lordship what the practice is,' he explained. 'The practice, so far as the White Star vessels are concerned, is that the scrap logs are not to be kept. They are torn off a block or pad day by day. What is called the chief officer's log is kept and handed in as soon as completed to the owners, but the scrap logs are not kept.'

Lord Mersey addressed the Solicitor-General.

'Do your questions suggest the log has been doctored?'

'What I want to know is how they arrived at the latitude which is put down, I presume, by dead reckoning at 10.20,' he replied, then resumed his interrogation of Stewart. 'I am right – it would be by dead reckoning you would get it?'

'Not only that,' Stewart pointed out. 'I had the Pole Star at half-past-seven.'

The Solicitor-General was still very suspicious, however, of the fact that the *Californian*'s latitudes on 14 April as entered in the log book apparently indicated a cessation of her progress towards the southward, that is, in the direction of the position officially accepted as being that in which the *Titanic* struck the iceberg. Supported by Dunlop, Stewart pointed out that in fact this was precisely what *had* happened, for the course of the *Californian* had been altered to due west at 9.40 a.m.

The Solicitor-General returned to the general question of log entries.

'Supposing you were keeping the scrap log on a watch when you were in ice, and supposing you saw a few miles to the southward a ship sending up what appeared to be distress signals, would you not enter that in the log?'

'Yes,' replied Stewart, then added hesitantly: 'I do not know.'

'Oh yes, you do,' Lord Mersey admonished him.

'Yes, I dare say I should have entered it, but it was not in our scrap log book.'

'That is not what I asked you,' the Solicitor-General pointed out. 'What I asked you – apply your mind to it – supposing you had been keeping the scrap log in those circumstances, and you saw distress signals being sent up by a ship a few miles from you, is that, or is not that, a thing you would enter in the log?'

'Yes.'

'How do you account for it not being there?' Lord Mersey enquired.

'I do not know, my lord.'

'It was careless not to put it in, was it not?'

'Or forgetful.'

'Forgetful? Do you think that a careful man is likely to forget the fact that distress signals have been going on from a neighbouring steamer?'

'No, my lord.'

'Then do not talk to me about forgetfulness.'

Dunlop rose, and brought out details of the *Californian*'s navigation up to 10.20 p.m. Stewart confirmed that the latitude by Pole Star which he took at 7.30 p.m. was an accurate one, and expressed the opinion that the rockets seen by Stone could not have been the *Titanic*'s if she had been in latitude 41° 46′ N. as reported by the *Virginian*.

'All this does not impress my mind much,' Lord Mersey remarked. 'It all proceeds upon the assumption that all these figures are right. The other evidence to my mind is of vastly more importance. However, I do not want to shut you out from it, you know.'

'You have heard my lord's observation,' Dunlop remarked to Stewart. 'Have you any reason to doubt the accuracy of these latitudes?'

'No, sir.'

Lord Mersey intervened again.

'The previous officer told me, in answer to a question that I think you yourself suggested, that he was satisfied that it was the *Titanic*, and at present I do not mind telling you that is my attitude of mind. You may perhaps change it.'

'I hope to succeed, my lord,' Dunlop replied.

'What do you think?'

'I submit, my lord – ' Dunlop began, but Lord Mersey cut him short.

'Oh, no, I am not asking you. I am asking the witness.'

Dunlop turned to Stewart.

'What do you think?'

'I do not know, sir.'

'That is a very safe answer,' Lord Mersey commented sternly. 'You think it may have been?'

'I think if it had been the *Titanic* there would have been no doubt about it.'

'Do you think it may have been the *Titanic*?'

'No, sir.'

Mr Cotter, representing the National Union of Stewards, suggested to Stewart that the ship he had seen at 4 a.m. was the *Carpathia*, but he denied this, saying that he thought she had a yellow funnel, unlike the Cunarder. He agreed with Cotter, however, that he now thought that, assuming no definite reply could be obtained from a ship from which rockets were going up, it would have been best to call the wireless operator.

Evans was the next witness. In comparison with the experiences of the other officers from the *Californian*, he had a very much easier time, although on the witness stand for almost as long. The questions which he was asked related mainly to the messages he had sent and received, the general practice of wireless operators when at sea, and the events of the night of 14 April and the following morning. He stated that he could give no estimate of how far off the *Titanic* was when he last communicated with her at 11 p.m., but the liner had very good and clear signals and a good power. He regarded her as the senior ship and did not take the request to 'keep out' as being in any way an insult.

Shortly after a brief adjournment for lunch, Evans concluded his evidence. The Solicitor-General told the court that, with the exception of Gill, he had three or four other witnesses from the *Californian* standing by, but it did not appear to him that they would add anything to what they had already been told. Dunlop pointed out that the *Californian* was due to sail from Liverpool on the coming Saturday, and Lord Mersey accordingly consented to the request that her people might be allowed to leave the court.

Once again the popular press reflected Lord's overwhelming impression of the hostility of the court towards him. The following morning the report in the *Daily Mirror* opened:

> MYSTERY OF *CALIFORNIAN'S* LOG BOOK – *No Mention of Rockets Seen on Night of Titanic Wreck – Lord Mersey's View – President of Opinion that Signals were Those of Sinking Liner – Witnesses Differ* ...
>
> No one paid closer attention to the evidence at the *Titanic* disaster inquiry in London yesterday than Captain Lord, of the Leyland liner

Californian. The court is at present attempting to establish for certain:

(1) whether the *Californian* is the ship whose mysterious lights were seen by many of the passengers and crew of the *Titanic.*

(2) whether a ship which sent up rockets a few miles away in the same icefield in which the *Californian* spent the night of 14/15 April was the *Titanic.*

The captain, the second officer and the apprentice on Tuesday, the third officer, chief officer and wireless operator yesterday, have all given evidence – some of it conflicting.

As a result of the evidence he had heard, Lord Mersey, the President of the court, made it clear yesterday that he was of the opinion that the ship whose rockets were clearly discerned from the *Californian* only about five miles distant was the *Titanic.*

The caption to a photograph of Lord and Stewart reproduced in the *Daily Sketch* noted equally bluntly: 'Lord Mersey said he believed the rockets seen from the *Californian* were those of the *Titanic.*'

In Lord's opinion, the atmosphere from beginning to end seemed to indicate that Lord Mersey had made up his mind before he started the inquiry, and was disinclined to listen to any further evidence – he'd had it all.

CHAPTER EIGHT

The Noose Tightens

Despite Lord's disquieting experiences at the inquiry, he returned to Liverpool confidently expecting that he would be taking the *Californian* to sea on Saturday, 18 May. To his great surprise, however, the management instructed him to remove his gear from the ship. Anticipating a relatively early re-appointment, he arranged for it to be stored on a temporary basis in the marine superintendent's dock office, and he also continued to report daily at noon at the company's head office in James Street, as was the custom among unattached masters in the Leyland Line.

For eighteen pence a copy, he was able to buy the official daily record of the verbatim proceedings at the *Titanic* inquiry. Reading the full transcript of his own appearance as a witness, he experienced once again the emotion at having been exposed to the hostile approach adopted towards him by Lord Mersey and the Attorney-General. Their later unquestioning acceptance of Groves' opinion that the ship they had been watching was the *Titanic* was so marked that it caused him the gravest possible concern.

He still could not see what grounds the court could possibly have for criticising him. A responsible officer had been on the bridge who would have insisted on his turning out had there been any emergency: in fact, Lord had remained fully dressed throughout the night, immediately available for any such call. None had been received. The second officer had been confident that the rocket-like flares which he had seen came from a ship that was steaming away from them, and that they were not distress signals. Both he and Lord were equally confident that the other ship could not have been the *Titanic*. Nevertheless, Lord decided that it would be as well if he were to consolidate the pencilled notes he had previously made, and on Wednesday, 21 May, he typed them out as a full statement of what had happened in the *Californian* on the night of 14/15 April. He summed up in these words:

> The second officer has since informed me that the rockets he saw were not distress rockets as they did not go any higher than the steamer's masthead light, he couldn't hear any report, which would have been possible under conditions prevailing at that time, also that she altered her bearing from SSE at 0.50 a.m. to SW½W at 2.10 a.m. Presuming the steamer was five miles off the *Californian* when she stopped at 11.30 p.m., the distance she must have steamed between these two bearings was at least eight miles.
>
> I should like to point out that the steamer mentioned above was well in sight of the *Californian* at 11 p.m. 14 April, but from the evidence given in Washington by the lookout man of the *Titanic* who was on duty from 10 p.m. to midnight he didn't see anything only ice until after he was in the lifeboat. The *Californian*'s engines were not moved from 10.21 p.m. until 5.15 a.m. next morning and from 11 p.m. to midnight she was heading to east, having both masthead lights and green light open to the ship we had plainly in view.

Three days later, he read in the newspapers that the United States committee had found against the *Californian*, their report stating:

> The committee is forced to the inevitable conclusion that the *Californian*, controlled by the same company, was nearer the *Titanic* than the nineteen miles reported by her captain, and that her officers and crew saw the distress signals of the *Titanic* and failed to respond to them in accordance with the dictates of humanity, international usage, and the requirements of law. The only reply to the distress signals was a counter signal from a large white light which was flashed for nearly two hours from the mast of the *Californian*.
>
> In our opinion such conduct, whether arisng from indifference or gross carelessness, is most reprehensible, and places upon the commander of the *Californian* a grave responsibility. The wireless operator of the *Californian* was not aroused until 3.30 a.m. New York Time, on the morning of the 15th, after considerable conversation between officers and members of the crew had taken place aboard that ship regarding these distress signals or rockets, and was directed by the chief officer to see if there was anything the matter, as a ship had been firing rockets during the night.
>
> The inquiry thus set on foot immediately disclosed the fact that the *Titanic* had sunk. Had assistance been promptly proffered, or had the wireless operator of the *Californian* remained a few minutes longer at his post on Sunday evening, that ship might have had the proud distinction of rescuing the lives of the passengers and crew of the *Titanic*.

Lord never received any official communication whatsoever relating to the United States committee's finding, but following so closely upon the hostile reception he had encountered at the British inquiry, it inevitably increased his concern, which reports of Gill's reception at the British inquiry on 4 June did nothing to allay.

Introducing Gill, the Attorney-General said: 'Your lordship will remember that this was the assistant donkeyman of the *Californian*, with regard to whom some statement was made by the other witnesses of the *Californian*. The only point was that he was referred to as a deserter at Boston. The suggestion at one time was that he had made a statement which was not true in America about the distress signals having been sent up, and there was a suggestion at one time made that in consequence of a story which he had put forward, which would not bear examination, he had deserted the vessel at Boston. It is no longer necessary to clear that up, because Mr Gill's story, as told in America, has – and I do not want to say more than this – been very much confirmed by the evidence which we have put before the court of the various officers (your lordship will remember we called a number of them) and also of Gibson, the apprentice, so that it is not necessary now to go into his story, whatever it may be, as your lordship will see the substance of it is no longer in dispute, and he was fully justified in what he said in America. The officers have now borne out the substance of his statement.'

Examined by Rowlatt for the Board of Trade, Gill affirmed what he had originally claimed in his affidavit. He went on to describe the ship he had seen at midnight as 'a large steamer'.

'It could not have been anything but a passenger boat – she was too large,' he continued. 'I could see two rows of lights which I took to be porthole lights, and several groups of lights which I took to be saloon and deck lights. I knew it was a passenger boat. That was all I saw of the ship.'

Of events half-an-hour later, after he had gone up on deck, he said: 'I could not see anything of the steamer at all. She had disappeared. She had either steamed away, or I do not know what she had done. She was not there ... I had nearly finished my smoke and was looking around, and I saw what I took to be a falling star. It descended and then disappeared. That is how a star does fall. I did not pay any attention to that. A few minutes after, probably five minutes, I threw my cigarette away and looked over, and I could see from the water's edge – what appeared to be the water's edge – a great distance away, well, it was unmistakably a rocket. You could make no mistake about it. Whether it was a distress signal or a signal rocket I could not say, but it was a rocket. It was slightly astern of where I had seen the steamer.'

Lord Mersey

Sir Rufus Isaacs

Dunlop suggested to Gill that neither he nor anyone else who saw the signals attached any importance to them at the time.

'I do not know whether anyone else did who saw them, but I did not,' he replied.

'What he said was: "It was nothing to do with me",' the Attorney-General pointed out, and Lord Mersey added the comment that he was a donkeyman, working in the engine-room.

In reply to further questions, Gill admitted that he was unable to say whether or not the other ship was moving, or in what direction she was heading. Finally, he claimed that he had not intended to desert the *Californian*; after giving evidence in Washington he had returned to England by the next Leyland Line steamer, the *Cestrian*.

Winding up, the Attorney-General told Gill: 'You are perfectly right. You are justified in what you said in America by what has transpired since. I am not going to ask questions, my lord, in detail about it, because your lordship has the evidence from the *Californian* before you, but I want to say this, so that my friend Mr Dunlop may understand the contention, that I disagree entirely with his observation that, according to the evidence, nobody paid any attention to these rockets. I have the evidence.'

'It is not in accordance with my recollection,' Lord Mersey agreed.

Earlier that same day, another witness had given evidence which both Lord Mersey and the Attorney-General evidently considered to be of significance so far as the case against the *Californian* was concerned. It was given by Alfred Crawford, a first-class bedroom steward in the *Titanic*, with thirty years' seagoing experience. He described how he was sent away from the sinking liner in No. 8 lifeboat at about 1 a.m., with three other members of the crew – two sailors and a kitchen hand – and thirty-five women passengers. He was questioned by Butler Aspinall.

'Before you left the ship's side did Captain Smith give you any directions with regard to a light?'

'Yes,' Crawford replied. 'He pointed to a light on the port side, the two masthead lights of a vessel, and told us to pull for there and land the people and return to the ship.'

'Is there anyone here representing the *Californian*?' Lord Mersey enquired.

'Somebody will be here, because we are calling somebody from the *Californian* today, and we have given them notice of it,' the Attorney-General assured him.

Aspinall resumed his examination of Crawford.

'I do not know whether you are a judge of distance of lights at sea, but what would you say?'

'I should say she was five to seven miles away from us.'

'The captain gave the directions?'

'Yes, he pointed the ship out.'

'Having got down to the water's edge, did you obey that direction as well as you could?'

'We did ... we pulled all night in the direction of the steamer.'

Lord Mersey intervened.

'Does five to seven miles agree with the information from the *Californian* as to the position she took up when she anchored?'*

'It is widely different, my lord,' Aspinall replied.

'That is what I was thinking,' Lord Mersey commented. 'The distance would be about twenty miles, would it not?'

'The point your lordship is upon is one which wants a little clearing up,' the Attorney-General explained. 'Our attention has been directed to the same point.'

'Very well,' said Lord Mersey. 'I will not say anything more about it now.'

Crawford went on to tell the court how, after rowing all night, they sighted a second steamer as day broke.

'We left that one – we could not seem to make it,' he told them. 'It seemed as if the vessel was turning round and leaving us.' They lost sight of the first vessel just as it got daylight; from the lifeboat he had earlier seen both her red and green sidelights. Previously, Captain Smith had personally helped to lower No 8 lifeboat and instructed them to make for the steamer and return to the *Titanic*.

'And return to the *Titanic*?' repeated counsel.

'What were you told to do?' questioned Lord Mersey. 'To make for the light?'

'To make for the light, land the passengers, and return to the ship.'

'Who gave you that order?'

'Captain Smith.'

'The gentleman who gave you that order must have thought, I suppose, that the lights that were visible were close to. Did Captain Smith say to you: "Make for those lights"?'

'He did.'

* The *Californian* was not anchored but lying with engines stopped in mid-Atlantic.

' "Put your passengers on board that ship with those lights and then come back here"?'

'Yes, my lord.'

'Then I presume – I do not know – that he must have thought those lights were close to. I do not at present think he is right about that. He may very well have been told to keep away, to go out a bit and be ready to go back.'

'I will ask him to give the exact order he got, my lord,' counsel said, then, turning to Crawford, asked: 'Will you tell my lord exactly what the captain said to you as to what you were to do when your boat was lowered? What order did you get?'

'He pointed in the direction of the two lights, and said: "Pull for that vessel, land your people and return to the ship." Those were Captain Smith's words.'

'And did you think you would go to that ship and land your passengers, and go back to the *Titanic* and pick up more?'

'We did at the time.'

'This was about one o'clock in the morning?' Lord Mersey questioned.

'About one, yes.'

Replying to questions from Harbinson, appearing for the third class passengers, Crawford stated that he saw about a dozen rockets sent up from the *Titanic*.

'Should those lights have been seen by the steamer towards which you were pulling?'

'Yes, I think they ought to have been seen.'

'Well, we know they were,' Lord Mersey commented.

Questioned by Dunlop, Crawford repeated that he had the other vessel under observation nearly all night.

'What happened to her afterwards? Did she come nearer to you, or did she disappear?'

'I could not say. We saw the *Carpathia* coming up, and we turned round and made for that one.'

'Your interest in the *Californian, if it was the Californian*,* ceased as soon as you saw the *Carpathia*?' Lord Mersey enquired.

'Yes, my lord.'

'Very naturally,' Lord Mersey commented.

While Crawford was being questioned by Thomas Lewis, counsel

* Author's italics. These qualifying words appear in the official record but not in contemporary press reports.

for the seamen's union, Lord Mersey took exception to his approach.

'Do you ask these questions at random, or have you some instructions upon which you put them?' he asked.

Lewis disclosed that his 'instructions' were in writing, whereupon Lord Mersey insisted that counsel's notes be handed up to him. After studying them, he personally questioned Crawford on the basis of Lewis's paper. It related to a disputed statement alleged to have been made by Thomas Jones, one of the two sailors in Crawford's lifeboat, to the effect that at one stage a suggestion had been made that the boat should abandon the attempt to reach the other ship and return to the *Titanic* as she went down. At the American inquiry, Jones had stated that Captain Smith had told him 'to row for the light and land the passengers and return to the ship'.

Lord Mersey's questions resulted in no conclusive answers, and he accordingly returned the paper to Lewis. Counsel's acknowledgement was studiedly courteous.

'I am obliged to your lordship ... I should like to ask whether I have to submit documents in future to your lordship, or whether I am entitled to ask the witnesses questions.'

'You are quite entitled to ask the questions.'

'Thank you, my lord.'

Further questioned, Crawford said that he considered his lifeboat to have covered between three and four miles in the direction of the other ship, which seemed to be drifting away from them. They were certainly furthest away from the *Carpathia* in the morning, the Cunarder appearing on their quarter.

The Attorney-General submitted that the *Carpathia*'s bearing from the life-boat would be almost exactly south-east, and went on to remind Lord Mersey of the significance of part of Crawford's evidence. This seemed to imply that Captain Smith had condemned an inadequately manned lifeboat, mustering only four relatively inexpert oarsmen, to row a distance of at least fourteen miles in the time it would take the *Titanic* to sink, that is, in little more than one hour.

'There was one question your lordship put to the witness,' he said. 'I think it is the first time we have heard of the order from Captain Smith to which he deposed. He said something to the effect – I am not giving his exact words – that the orders of Captain Smith were that they were to row the boat to the light, that is, to the ship of which he had seen the lights, and to put the women on board and then come back, no doubt with the object of fetching more. It is right to say with regard to this witness that there are two other witnesses who were in this boat who deposed to the same thing. We have not got them.'

'The proof that Mr Lewis has of Jones says the same thing,' Lord Mersey agreed.

'Jones has been examined in America, and I have his evidence before me, but I am speaking of something apart from Jones.'

'What occurs to me – I do not know whether it is right – as to what the captain probably meant is this,' Lord Mersey suggested. 'This is one o'clock in the morning, and my opinion is the captain knew that she was a doomed ship at that time, and what he meant was: "Go to the light, put your passengers off, and come back to this *place*".'

'Yes, quite.'

'It is different from saying: "Come back to this *ship*".'

'Yes.'

'Perhaps he would not say it in words, but it would mean to come back to pick people up.'

'According to one lady who has given evidence in America, what he said was: "Put these women in safety and come back for others".'

Sir Robert Finlay contributed to the exchange of views: 'Of course, it is possible the captain might have thought that ship would make for them.'

'Yes,' said the Attorney-General.

'Of course it is, and very natural,' Lord Mersey agreed. 'That may, to a large extent, explain it.'

And so Lord Mersey and the Attorney-General left the matter, having done their best to satisfy themselves that two witnesses, testifying on oath, had not meant what in fact they had categorically and repeatedly stated.

Any residual doubt which Lord Mersey and the Attorney-General might have had as to the precise wording of Captain Smith's order could have been finally dispelled had they called as a witness the Countess of Rothes, a passenger sent away in No 8 boat. In an interview published in the Paris edition of the *New York Herald*, reprinted in the *Journal of Commerce* on 24 April, the Countess was reported as having said: 'Captain Smith stood next to me as we got in and told Tom Jones, a seaman who acted nobly, to row "straight for those ship lights over there, leave the passengers aboard, and return as soon as possible". The captain thought an unknown vessel whose lights we could plainly see would pick us up ... For three hours we pulled steadily for the lights seen three miles away; then we saw a port light vanish and the masthead lights grow dimmer until they disappeared.'

Evidence given at the United States inquiry was also on record to the effect that a similar 'row, land and return' order had been given to those setting off in No 6 boat.

As to whether or not the vessel seen from the *Titanic* had been moving (the *Californian* was lying stopped from 10.20 p.m. until 5.15 a.m.), very significant evidence had been given before the British inquiry on 22 May by Joseph Boxhall, the *Titanic*'s fourth officer.* He described how, after having a light reported to him, he had first gone to the chartroom to work out the liner's position. Having given this to the wireless operator, he then went on to the bridge. There, with the aid of binoculars, he could see the two masthead lights of a vessel about half-a-point on the port bow. It was then about 12.30 a.m.

'I was paying most of my attention to this steamer then,' he continued. 'She was approaching us, and then I saw her sidelights. I saw her green light and the red. She was end on to us. Later I saw her red light. This is all with the aid of a pair of glasses up to now. Afterwards I saw the ship's red light with my naked eye, and the two masthead lights ... I judged her to be between five and six miles away when I Morsed to her, and then she turned round – she was turning very, very slowly – until at last I only saw her stern light.'

The anti-*Californian* attitude adopted by Lord Mersey and the Attorney-General, and particularly the way in which they had accepted Gill's story, compelled Lord to consider taking some sort of action to protect himself. Initially he thought of writing to the newspapers, but before doing so he decided to seek the advice of someone he had known for over fifteen years, and on whose judgement he was prepared to place implicit reliance. Now 73 years old, Captain J. Macnab had been principal examiner of masters and mates in Liverpool from 1886 until 1905, when, on his retirement from public office, he became a member of the Executive Council of

* At the United States inquiry, Boxhall had stated: 'I saw the masthead lights first, the two steaming lights; then, as she drew up closer, I saw her side-lights through my glasses, and eventually I saw the red light. I had seen the green, but I saw the red most of the time. I saw the red light with my naked eye ... I do not know when she turned ... I do not think she was doing much steaming, but by the time I saw the red light with my naked eye she was not steaming very much. So she had probably gotten into the ice and turned around.'

the Mercantile Marine Service Association. Lord sent him a copy of his statement and supporting documents; on 7 June, Macnab wrote to him to confirm that he had studied them carefully, but the conclusion to which he had come was that it were better to wait for Lord Mersey's report before writing to the papers. It would not be long before it would be published, he forecast, and concluded:

> What I can write will be more valuable then. One thing I am certain of – if there was laxity in your ship it was *not on the part of the captain*. Your life history would give the lie to such a charge, so let your innocence cheer you up under the sore trial, and no matter what 'Inquiries' may say, I for one will never believe you guilty.'

Lord accepted Macnab's advice, but it was to be a long wait.

CHAPTER NINE

An Unenviable Position

Lord Mersey's public inquiry was not closed until 3 July, and it was to be another four weeks after that before his report was published. In the meantime, Lord continued to read reports of the case with the closest attention. He noted with interest the appearance as a witness of 18 June of that chance acquaintance of his sailing ship days, Ernest Shackleton, last met in Talcahuano. Now Sir Ernest – he had been honoured for his achievements in polar exploration – he was called before the inquiry to give his views on the handling of ships in ice.

An earlier witness was Edward Wilding, a naval architect and one of the design team responsible for the construction of the *Titanic*. He had analysed the progressive flooding of the liner and the time taken to sink, as described by survivors. On that basis, he put forward his technical conclusions as to the nature of the damage sustained by the vessel. In his opinion, it consisted of a sort of 'wound', an intermittent gash extending in 'a series of steps' over a total length of 500 feet. It was not 'a continuous rip' but 'punctures ... in places ... equivalent to a hole three-quarters of an inch wide and 200 feet long ... The total area through which water was entering the ship was somewhere about twelve square feet.'

Although no one in court specifically drew attention to the fact, it was obvious that, if Wilding's expert opinion were correct, then the *Titanic* must have been essentially intact from a structural point of view immediately after her collision with the iceberg. Her engines were certainly undamaged, for evidence had been given that they were put slow ahead for a few moments just after the impact. Initially, then, the *Titanic* was fully capable of being steamed in any direction for some considerable time. If so, and had there been another ship within sight, as Lord Mersey considered the *Californian* to have been, why had not Captain Smith taken the liner towards that potential rescuer while the *Titanic* was still manoeuvrable, instead of immobilising her, as he had done, by starting to send the passengers away in lifeboats?

If this question ever presented itself to Lord Mersey, or to anyone else concerned with the inquiry, no public mention was made of it.

Of more direct concern to Lord were those occasions when specific reference was made to him or to the *Californian*. On 14 June, the Attorney-General warned Lord Mersey that he might have to ask for permission to add to the questions already formally submitted to the court, and that one such question might refer to the *Californian*.

'I do not see Mr Dunlop here, who represented the *Californian*,' Lord Mersey observed.

'May I say this with reference to that,' the Attorney-General replied. 'That brings us to another point which I was going to raise at the end of the evidence, but I might raise it now, because it is convenient. There are questions, and at the end of the evidence, according to the practice, it would be my duty to submit to your lordship any further questions which ought to be put in addition to those I placed before the court at the beginning of the inquiry. According to my view at present – and I do not think anything is likely to occur which will alter it – the only question which should be added is one relating to what I may call compendiously the *Californian* incident. There is no question in the twenty-six before you which would cover that. It does occur to me and to my friend the Solicitor-General associated with me in it, that it is important that the question should be specifically put and that your lordship should take it into account, and that it ought not to be passed over merely as a matter throwing some general light upon the inquiry. It had been already examined into, and my friend Mr Dunlop has been here representing the *Californian*, and therefore we ought to put the question and ask your lordship to answer it.'

'Quite so. I do not suppose I have any jurisdiction to direct that the captain's certificate should be interfered with?'

'No. I think that only arises in a collision between two vessels. Then there is jurisdiction.'

'Assume that I take a view adverse to the conduct of the captain of the *Californian*, all I can do is to express an opinion about it?'

'Yes. What we were going to ask your lordship to do was to express your view upon the evidence which you have heard, and to give us the benefit of your lordship's conclusions of fact.'

'Quite.'

'And then we shall be able to consider it.'

'I think that disposes of that,' Lord Mersey concluded.

Five days later the Attorney-General returned to the matter of a formal question affecting the *Californian*, requesting that Question 24 be amended. Originally it read: 'What was the cause of the loss of the *Titanic* and of the loss of life which thereby ensued or occurred?' To this the Attorney-General asked that the following be added: 'What vessel had the opportunity of rendering assistance to the *Titanic* and, if any, how was it that assistance did not reach the *Titanic* before the *Carpathia* arrived?'

'Will that involve my dealing with the *Frankfurt*?' Lord Mersey enquired.

'Well, only a reference,' the Attorney-General said. 'It is quite simple, I think. The only one that gives any difficulty with regard to this – any examination – is the *Californian*. As to the *Mount Temple*, you have the evidence about that. That question will cover the *Californian*.'

Lord Mersey granted the Attorney-General's request. Dunlop was not reported as having been in court, and consequently a very grave development from Lord's point of view went completely unchallenged.

On 21 June, Captain Rostron was called as a witness, the opportunity being taken for him to be publicly congratulated and acclaimed for his handling of the *Carpathia* during the rescue operations.

Among those who subsequently questioned him was Alfred Bucknill, who, on behalf of Dunlop, asked him formally to confirm the facts given in an affidavit which Rostron had sworn in New York on 4 June. It read:

> I approached the position of the *Titanic*, 41.46 N.L., 50.14 W.L., on a course substantially N.52 W. (true), reaching the first boat shortly after 4 a.m. It was daylight at about 4.20 a.m. At five o'clock it was light enough to see all round the horizon. We then saw two steamships to the northwards, perhaps seven or eight miles distant. Neither of them was the *Californian*. One of them was a four-masted steamer with one funnel, and the other a two-masted steamer with one funnel. I never saw the *Mount Temple* to identify her. The first time I saw the *Californian* was at about eight o'clock on the morning of 15 April. She was then about five to six miles distant, bearing WSW (true) and steaming towards the *Carpathia*. The *Carpathia* was then in substantially the position of the *Titanic* at the time of the disaster as given to us by wireless. I considered the position of the *Titanic* as given to us by her officers to be correct.

Rostron formally confirmed that his affidavit was a true account of events as he had seen them.

Closing addresses by counsel representing those involved in the inquiry began on 21 June. Clement Edwards, for the Dock, Wharf, Riverside and General Workers Union of Great Britain and Ireland, said that from the evidence there was no doubt whatever that the lights that had been seen from the *Californian* were those of the *Titanic*. The statement of the captain that he thought they were private signals was the merest excuse.

'What I think the *Californian* attempts to say is that, having regard to the bearings, those lights cannot be the lights of the *Titanic*,' Lord Mersey pointed out.

'His conduct is equally reprehensible, whether they were the lights of the *Titanic* or of any other vessel,' Edwards asserted.

'The captain of the *Californian* is going to say that these were not distress signals at all necessarily – that they were ship's signals.'

'But the officer Groves admitted to you that in the light of the facts he thought the lights were those of the *Titanic*.'

'I think you may take it that I think the onus of proof in this matter is on the *Californian*. It will be for the master to satisfy us that these were not the *Titanic*'s signals. Whether he will succeed I cannot say, but I think you may leave that point.'

From Lord's point of view, the crucial date was 28 June. He bought a copy of that day's proceedings, a verbatim transcript from which he was able to follow Dunlop's attempt, in his final submissions to the court, to present a case for Lord and the *Californian*.

Dunlop opened by referring to his attendance record, commenting: 'I wish to say a word on behalf of myself, because although I have been present very rarely during the course of this inquiry, some of my friends who have been present have told me that my position as an advocate for the *Californian* is not altogether an enviable one.'

Just how unenviable that position was had been clearly indicated by Lord Mersey a few moments earlier.

'Now, Mr Dunlop,' he had said. 'How long do you think you will take to convince us that the *Californian* did not see the *Titanic*'s lights?'

'I think, my lord, I will take about two hours,' Dunlop replied.

From the official record, it was clear that he must have taken much longer. His address filled fifteen pages of the transcript; it began before lunch and occupied the whole of the afternoon's proceedings.

Twelve of those pages recorded an almost constant barrage of interruptions from Lord Mersey, actively supported by the Attorney-General, as in the following passage:

> *Mr Dunlop*: ... It was not suggested to the master or officers of the *Californian*, nor are there any grounds for the suggestion, that the log before your lordship has been 'cooked'. The log on the face of it appears to be a perfectly genuine log.
> *The Attorney-General*: I think you are putting that too high – you say there is no suggestion.
> *Mr Dunlop*: No question was put, my lord, to the master.
> *Lord Mersey*: Just a moment, please. The scrap log is gone.
> *Mr Dunlop*: The scrap log is gone, and the explanation of that was given by the witnesses when they were asked about it.
> *Lord Mersey*: And as far as I remember it was given in a way that satisfied me that it had gone.
> *Mr Dunlop*: Yes, your lordship was satisfied at the time.
> *Lord Mersey*: Yes, I thought so. The log places the latitude when the bergs were passed two miles further north, and therefore two miles further away from the *Titanic* than the message places them.
> *Mr Dunlop*: That is so, and the explanation of that is this ...
> *Lord Mersey*: Why should you make your log show a position two miles further north?
> *Mr Dunlop*: The explanation, my lord, of that is this, that the bergs were passed at 6.30. At 7.30 the observation was taken which enabled them to check their latitude. At 7.30 they found their latitude to be 42° 5′ North.
> *Lord Mersey*: That was the Pole Star observation.
> *Mr Dunlop*: That was the Pole Star observation at 7.30. An hour before, 6.30, was the time when they passed the icebergs, and when they communicated the position of those icebergs to the *Titanic* and the *Antillian* they communicated 42° 3′ North.
> *Lord Mersey*: They did.
> *Mr Dunlop*: The explanation of the chief officer was that his 7.30 observation enabled him to ascertain that the 6.30 position was wrong by two miles.
> *Lord Mersey*: So that you say he entered up the log later on and entered it up as he thought correctly.
> *Mr Dunlop*: Yes, he entered it up correctly ... My lord, I submit that the master of the *Californian*, if he is to be judged at all, must get the benefit of his log book, which, after all, is not his log. It is the log kept by the chief officer, a person whose conduct is not in any way the object of this inquiry and who is not concerned in the result of what your lordship's views may be.

A full page of the transcript was taken up with a querulous request from Lord Mersey for the production of the *Californian*'s compass deviation book, without which, he claimed, the accuracy of the courses steered could not be depended upon. This approach contrasted sharply with that he had adopted earlier in the proceedings, while Lord was giving evidence. Lord had stated that the nearby ship was bearing SSE by compass. Lord Mersey asked whether the compass was correct, whereupon Lord responded to a specific question from the Attorney-General by giving details of the magnetic variation and deviation which together made up the compass error.

'Are these minute particulars of importance?' Lord Mersey complained.

It appeared that 'minute particulars' on 14 May had become matters of major importance by 28 June, so far as the *Californian*'s navigation was concerned, and Dunlop's attempt to present a coherent and reasoned case for the *Californian* was obviously gravely impeded, to say the least, by the obstructive tactics employed by Lord Mersey and the Attorney-General. Nevertheless, at one stage, Dunlop succeeded in uninterruptedly presenting a succinct and conclusive dismissal of the opinions expressed by Groves and Gill, that the ship they had seen from the *Californian* was the *Titanic*.

He recalled Gill's conclusion that what he had seen at midnight was a passenger ship: 'He thought so because of her row of deck lights and porthole lights, and it is important to remember that he says he saw her shortly after twelve o'clock, which was the end of his watch, as he was going forward to call his mate. According to Groves, whose evidence was the more dramatic of the two, he said he saw the deck lights and this glare of lights go out at 11.40. That is when they disappeared, according to him. Groves says the lights disappeared at 11.40. Gill, nevertheless, sees them all ablaze a few minutes after twelve. If Groves is right, Gill must be wrong, and if Gill is right, Groves cannot be right. So much for Gill ... Groves attached no importance at the time to the vessel which he had seen, and he attached no importance at all to any of the incidents which he described when here in the witness box. I submit that his evidence was largely the result of imagination stimulated by vanity.'

Quite suddenly, however, all interruptions by Lord Mersey and the Attorney-General ceased, and the last three pages of the transcript were completely free from any questions or comment by the court. It was impossible not to conclude that Dunlop finished his address in a coldly hostile atmosphere. This would also explain why, at the last, his approach changed from an attempt to present a factual case to an almost desperate appeal for clemency.

'It was not until the fourteenth of June, a month after Captain Lord has left the witness box,' Dunlop pointed out, 'that an intimation is given that the Board of Trade propose to formulate a question relating to the *Californian*, which would give the court an opportunity of censuring Captain Lord. It is not my province nor my purpose to criticise the procedure which has been adopted with relation to the *Californian*, but it is manifest from the statement of facts, as I have stated them, that Captain Lord has been treated here in a way which is absolutely contrary to the principles on which justice is usually administered, or on which these inquiries are generally conducted.

'I respectfully urge the Attorney-General to consider whether this question ought really to be put at all. The object of it was explained by the Attorney-General on 14 June. There it was stated that the object of this question is that the Law Officers of the Crown should get from your lordship a finding of the facts relating to the *Californian* incident in order to enable them to make up their minds whether, in the public interest, they ought to institute criminal proceedings which may be instituted under Section 6 of the Maritime Convention Act. If that is the object of the question, I submit it is a wholly unfair object. If this man may be prosecuted hereafter, he ought to have had notice of this question before he entered the witness box; he ought to have known precisely what the charge made against him was; and he ought to have had an opportunity of hearing the evidence given by the other witnesses before he himself had to give his own evidence.

'If you deal with this question, my lord, and find the facts against Captain Lord, what chance would he have of a fair and impartial trial before a jury which had read your lordship's report? If that is the object, my lord, of this question, this invitation to your lordship to find the facts with regard to the *Californian* incident, if the object is with a view to future proceedings, I respectfully and strongly urge that it is a most unfair object. If that is not the object, then I do not know what the object of the question is. If it is not in the public interest that Captain Lord should be charged with a failure to render assistance, then the question ought not to be raised so publicly here in the form of the question which has been submitted to you.

'Captain Lord has already been sorely and severely punished for his apparent inactivity during these fatal midnight hours. That inactivity, whichever view your lordship may take of the facts, is, I venture to submit, an inactivity due to mere thoughtlessness or error of judgement and not to any wilful disregard of duty. He may have relied too much on his second officer and Gibson, the apprentice; he may have erroneously drawn a wrong inference from the reports which they made to him. Whatever his conduct was, it was conduct due to a want of appreciation of what the real circumstances at that time were, and not to any wilful disregard of duty.

'The ordeal of public criticism and public censure through which he has already passed will, without further censure, be a sufficient warning to him and to other masters of the strict duty that lies upon those who go down to the sea in ships of rendering assistance if they can to other vessels in distress. It requires no further rebuke to impress upon master mariners the importance of that duty. That counsel should have to appear here to vindicate his reputation and defend his honour is not the least humiliation this man has had to undergo.

'For all the reasons I have urged,' Dunlop concluded, 'I do ask your lordship not to pass any censure upon this man, and I venture to think that if your lordship does not censure him, then truth and justice and mercy will meet together in your lordship's report.'

As soon as Dunlop had concluded his address, the court adjourned for the day. When the proceedings were resumed the following morning, the Attorney-General opened an address which was to take the better part of three days. In the course of this, Lord Mersey commented on a reference the Attorney-General had made to Captain Smith, master of the *Titanic*.

'I said a long time ago that I doubted whether I ought to find a dead man, or a man who is not represented, guilty of negligence.'

'Your lordship will decide upon that when you come to your judgement,' the Attorney-General observed.

'Taking the *Californian*, that man is not represented. He came here merely as a witness.'

'Who?'

'Captain Lord.'

'Oh yes, my lord, he was represented.'

'Yes, he is here in the sense that somebody sent by his owners did speak for him.'

'Then, my lord, I would sooner deal with that separately, if I may; I know what your lordship has in your mind.'

'What I mean is that he has not been cited here to defend himself against the charge made against him of negligence.'

'Your lordship is speaking now of the captain of the *Californian*?'

'Yes, Captain Lord.'

'But that is quite a different thing.'

'I am not sure. You are talking at present about Captain Smith. What I am pointing out is this, that Captain Smith could not be here; he is dead. He could not have been cited. But the captain of the *Californian* is here really merely as a witness. He has not been cited to answer a charge of negligence, and I have great reluctance to find people guilty of negligence when they are not cited and charged with it, and have not had a proper opportunity of answering the charge.'

'I will deal with Captain Lord's case, my lord.'

'Later on. I am only suggesting that there is an analogy between the two cases. I may be wrong, you know, but that is what I am suggesting.'

The Attorney-General left the *Californian* issue until the very end of his address. As he opened, he was immediately interrupted by Lord Mersey, who asked that he be told what his (Lord Mersey's) position was with regard to the matter.

'Yes, my lord,' the Attorney-General responded. 'First of all, the view which I take of it is that so far from being desirous of bringing home to the captain of the *Californian*, or to any of the officers of the *Californian*, that they saw distress signals and that they took no step after they had seen them, I am most anxious, and have been throughout, to find some possible excuse for the inaction on the part of the *Californian*. It is not a case of desiring to bring home to them that they did not do their duty; our anxiety, and your lordship's anxiety, would be, if possible, to find some reason to explain the failure by them to take any steps when they had seen distress signals. I can only say that to me it is a matter of extreme regret that I have come to the conclusion that the submission I must make to you is that there is no excuse. Whether I am right or wrong in that is, of course, for your lordship's consideration.'

The Attorney-General went on to submit that Dunlop had appeared throughout not for the Leyland Line, who were unaffected by the proceedings, but for Lord, a man who had been an unsatisfactory witness and to whom Dunlop had put leading questions on the most vital points in the case. By such actions, the Attorney-General claimed, Lord had become a party to the proceedings. Nevertheless, all the Attorney-General was proposing that Lord Mersey should deal with the conflict of fact that arose upon the evidence, and nothing more. There was no conflict, he said, as to the fact that the *Californian* saw distress signals.

'To be quite accurate with regard to it,' the Attorney-General added, 'I think one might say that the captain does not admit that they were distress signals, but he admits that they might have been ... The comment I make upon it is that for the master of a British vessel to see distress signals, whether they came from a passenger steamer or not, and whether from a passenger steamer of the size of the *Titanic* or not, is a very serious matter; and because it is a serious matter we have enquired into it very carefully during the course of this investigation; but, having regard to the inquiry, I think all that your lordship is asked to do, certainly all that I am asking you to do, is to give the view of the facts which you have formed after hearing all the evidence ...

'I do not ask you to do anything more. In point of fact Captain Lord is not summoned before you to answer some attack upon his certificate. That is not the position of matters. What has happened here is that in the course of the inquiry facts which are relevant to this inquiry have been brought before your lordship, that there is a conflict of evidence as to these facts, that on one view of the facts they have a bearing undoubtedly upon the conduct of one or more persons upon the *Californian*, but they are also relevant to the inquiry, and if they are relevant to the inquiry the fact that your lordship may in arriving at your conclusion find a state of things to have existed which reflects upon some person who is not actually on trial and cited to appear before you as on trial is no reason, I submit, why your lordship should not express your opinion on the facts.'

'Finding the facts and expressing an opinion on them are two different things,' Lord Mersey pointed out.

'I agree,' the Attorney-General concurred. 'That is why I said expressing your opinion on the facts, and ask you to say on the somewhat conflicting evidence which is the correct one.'

'Let me put it quite plainly,' Lord Mersey observed. 'If Captain Lord saw these distress signals and neglected a reasonable opportunity, which he had of going to the relief of the vessel in distress, it may very well be that he is guilty of a misdemeanour. That is so, is it not?'

'Yes, under the Merchant Shipping Act, 1906.'

'Am I to try that question?'

'Certainly not.'

'I think not.'

'Certainly not, my lord. I never asked, and could not ask, your lordship to try that question, but nevertheless the facts which you are asked to find, whether they reflect upon him or not, are material to the inquiry.'

'The facts I can find, but I do not want, unless I am obliged to do it, to find a man guilty of a crime.'

'No, my lord.'

'I do not think I have tried him for any such purpose.'

'I agree.'

'And, moreover, as you know perfectly well, he might, if he had had any idea that he was going to be tried for a crime, have said when he was in the witness box: "I refuse to answer these questions because they may incriminate me".'

'Yes.'

'But he did not do that, you know.'

'Different considerations apply, I think, when you are determining whether a crime has been committed, and your lordship would have to go into questions which certainly, it appears to me, it is unnecessary to find in this case, and which I am not asking you to find in order to determine whether a crime was committed ... What I am asking you to find is the fact that they did see on the *Californian* distress signals, that they were distress signals from the *Titanic*, and that the distance of the *Titanic* from the *Californian* was only a few miles.'

'How many?'

'I should put it at something like seven or eight. It is very difficult to say. I do not profess to be able to say with precision.'

'That is a very difficult question on the evidence.'

'I agree that it is very difficult to say. I think it was put by him in America and also here at nineteen and a half miles; and then by a later explanation he says he had to steam just on thirty miles to get there.'

'Because he could not go the direct way.'

'Yes, that is as far as I ask the court to go. It is as far as it is necessary to go for the questions I am putting to you. For one thing, I should be very sorry to do an injustice to Captain Lord, and I am very anxious that in any event nothing should be said as a conclusion by your lordship which would suggest that he had committed a misdemeanour. Of course, as your lordship says, no such question is put to you and no such question is made by me. But still we must get to some conclusion upon this state of the evidence ... Now the evidence, which is voluminous, is undoubtedly to some extent very conflicting on some points. I am not sure that it is possible to reconcile some of these statements that are made, from whatever aspect you look at them. But upon the material points, I submit there is not any real difficulty. The material points are first of all whether the *Californian* saw distress signals. One answer of the captain, it seems to me, quite disposes of that.'

At one stroke, Lord Mersey cut through to the heart of the matter.

'I do not know whether it will relieve you at all in the trouble you are taking,' he remarked, 'but I think we are all of the opinion that the distress rockets that were seen from the *Californian* were the distress signals of the *Titanic*.'

'That relieves me of a great deal of evidence, my lord,' the Attorney-General commented. 'That is the material fact of this case.'

Having the court with him, the Attorney-General was now able to proceed virtually unchallenged with his aim of establishing beyond all possible doubt that Lord was indeed to blame. He began by reviewing in detail the questions and answers leading up to Lord's admission that the other ship's rocket 'might have been a distress signal'.

'Now, my lord,' he continued, 'that establishes quite clearly this, that he thought it might have been, and the moment a man thinks it might have been a distress signal and does not know what else it could be, I should have thought it really means that he knew – I will not say he was quite certain – but he knew at any rate this, that there was a serious possibility of some vessel being in urgent need of assistance close by. It is very difficult to understand. I find it very difficult to understand, in reading through all this evidence, why it was that in those circumstances he remained in the chartroom and took no step ... He says he remained there expecting Gibson, the apprentice, to come down and report. I want to make this comment upon that evidence. It is very unfortunate, to say the least of it, that there is no entry made in the log of these distress signals. The shifting of time, according to the evidence that is given, has some bearing upon it. It is said, for example, in this case that this white rocket, the first distress signal, was not seen till a quarter-past one. It is very difficult to explain that, in view of the evidence of the *Titanic*, which is that they were sending up these rockets from 12.45. I should have thought upon this evidence, and upon the evidence which follows it, that the estimate of time must be quite wrong.'

'There might be some difference in the clocks of the two vessels,' Lord Mersey suggested.

'Yes, certainly, there might be.'

'That might partly account for it.'

'Yes, it might; but having regard to the news they got in the early morning of the loss of the *Titanic*, I cannot help thinking it is very striking that you find no entry of any sort or description of the distress signals which had undoubtedly been seen during that night.'

The Attorney-General went on to remind the court of the conflicting accounts given by Lord and Gibson of the latter's visit to the chartroom at 2 a.m., and asserted that he found it impossible to accept Lord's statement that he had been asleep.

'When you have got as far as that, I submit it is really as far as one need go in this case,' he said. 'The important fact is this, having regard to what your lordship has said you are satisfied about: it means this, that that establishes that the signals were sent, that they were seen by the *Californian*, that they came from the *Titanic*, that the captain knew that these signals had been sent up, and that the captain remained in the chartroom and did nothing. Those are the facts which are relevant for the purpose of this inquiry ... I do not profess to say – I doubt very much whether anyone can say – exactly the distance which the *Titanic* was from the *Californian* at the time of sending up the rockets. But according to the testimony – and this is not unimportant – of all those on the *Titanic* who saw the lights, the vessels they saw was, according to them, at a distance of something like five or six miles.'

'Who were the witnesses on the *Titanic* who saw the Morse light?' Lord Mersey enquired.

'My Lord, I think it is only Boxhall,' the Attorney-General replied.

'Captain Lord says this with reference to the green light that he saw and the distance. He was asked: 'What distance do you think she was from you when you could see the lights?' He replied: "About five miles".'

'That is about what is said by the *Titanic* witnesses.'

'And that agrees with the *Titanic* witnesses.'

'Yes.'

The Attorney-General then embarked on a confused attempt to make out that the *Californian*'s swing to starboard during the night somehow could have accounted for Lord's having seen the *Titanic*'s green sidelight between 11 p.m. and 11.30. He selected Lord's reference to a casually observed light which he thought was a green one as providing positive proof that the ship seen to the southward was the *Titanic*, on a westerly heading; he made no reference to the specific statement of Groves, then officer of the watch, that the light *he* was watching at that time, as later confirmed by both Stone and Gibson, was a red light, that is, displayed from a ship on an easterly heading.

The Attorney-General went on to select the opinion of Rowe, one of the *Titanic*'s quartermasters, as proof that the liner's head swung to the northward after the collision with the iceberg; he made no reference to the opinion of Boxhall and other witnesses from the *Titanic* that she settled down after the impact on a westerly heading.

The Attorney-General selected Gibson's description of 'a blaze of light' on the deck of the other vessel as incontrovertible proof that he must have been watching a passenger vessel; he made no reference to Gibson's further statements that, in spite of what he later called 'a faint glare of light' from the other ship's afterdeck, he considered that 'there was nothing at all about (her) to resemble a passenger boat'.

'Once we have got as far as having established that these distress signals came from the *Titanic*,' the Attorney-General continued, 'and that the captain knew of them and did not proceed either to the rescue of the vessel in distress or take what I should have thought was the step which was dictated at once when there was any doubt about it, that is, to call up the wireless operator and let him get into communication with the vessel, one gets really a state of things which is quite inexplicable ... the more extraordinary inasmuch as I have certainly understood as the rule which everybody who goes to sea would never fail to observe, that if you see a vessel in distress you must do your utmost to get to it. I have always understood, certainly amongst sailors, not only in this country but elsewhere, that that is a rule of honour from which they do not depart, although they may commit other errors. In this particular case I am unable to find any possible explanation of what happened, except it may be that the captain of the vessel was in ice for the first time, and would not take the risk of going to the rescue of another vessel which might have got into trouble, as he thought, from proceeding through the ice when he himself had stopped. But even that does not explain why they did not call up the wireless operator to ascertain what the condition of things was.* We have heard no explanation of it. I think your lordship is left absolutely in the dark with reference to it.

* See answer to Scanlan's questions, pp. 75-76.

One can only conjecture, and I do not know that it is perhaps quite safe to speculate upon the reasons that made Captain Lord neither come out of his chartroom to see what was happening, nor to take any step to communicate with the vessel in distress, even such a very slight effort as to have the wireless operator called up ...

'We know, fortunately, in one way the times at which the various things happened on board the *Titanic* with some exactness, partly by reason of the wireless messages which enable us to tell accurately what was happening within a few moments right up to the time when the *Titanic* was no longer able to send wireless messages; and if you put those times together, and compare them with the times of the *Californian*, it is quite plain that at a quarter to one they were sending up rockets, and it is equally plain that the *Californian* must have seen the first, or among the first, of the rockets that were sent up by the *Titanic*; and it, therefore, must place the time, if you are comparing it with the *Titanic* time, at a quarter to one or thereabouts, and not a quarter past one.

'In point of fact the *Titanic* did not go down for an hour and a half after that, and that gave an hour and a half for this vessel, which could steam as much as thirteen knots, but was certainly able to steam eleven knots; and putting it even further than the five to seven miles, it still gave her ample time to get there. Of course, the captain says he was nineteen and a half miles away. That evidence, I submit, is quite unsatisfactory. One understands, of course, why he should be anxious to put himself as far as he can from the *Titanic*. Apart altogether from the fact that he wants to make out that it is not the *Titanic*, he is naturally desirous of showing that he could not have got there, or at any rate, that there was a doubt as to whether he could have got there if he had gone at once. But if you bear in mind what I submit are the salient features of this evidence, that is, that the sidelights were seen of the *Titanic*, you get rid altogether of this distance of nineteen and a half miles. No human being would suggest that the *Californian* could have seen the sidelights of the *Titanic*, either her red light or her green light, at a distance of nineteen and a half miles. She must have been within an easy distance in order that her masthead lights and her sidelights were seen, as they were, by the *Californian*.

'And, my lord, I would add to that that the *Californian* is shown to have been seen by the *Titanic*; that in any event the light that was seen, so far as we know, according to all enquiries made and according to all the evidence put before you, was the light of the

Californian. I will not say that all the evidence points irresistibly to that, but I do say this, that if you compare the *Titanic* evidence with the *Californian* it is abundantly plain that the distance between them must have been comparatively small, that is to say certainly within five to seven miles, and could not have been nineteen to twenty miles, as the captain of the *Californian* suggests.

'Now, I do not propose to go further into this evidence of the *Californian* unless your lordship desires it, because it seems to me that when you have got those facts, really there is sufficient to establish quite clearly that these distress signals which were seen, were seen at a distance which would have enabled the *Californian* to get to the *Titanic*. That is no doubt a material point, in view of the question which is put to your lordship.'

With that, the Attorney-General concluded the case against Lord and the *Californian*. With a few remarks of a more general nature, he also concluded the case for the Board of Trade, the conveners of the inquiry, and the court then adjourned until such time as Lord Mersey was ready to present his report.

CHAPTER TEN

Sacrificed

Forewarned as Lord was by events, it was still a bitter blow when Lord Mersey's report, published on 31 July, condemned him in the eyes of the world as the man who could have saved all those lost with the *Titanic*, but who had failed to do so.

The main charge against him was summed up in Lord Mersey's reply to the question added on 14 June. This stated quite unequivocally: 'The *Californian* had the opportunity of rendering assistance to the *Titanic* and could have reached her if she had made the attempt when she saw the first rocket. She made no attempt'.

A section of the report was headed: 'The circumstances in connection with the s.s *Californian*'. In this, the evidence given by the witnesses from Lord's ship was reviewed in great detail. In a reference to the *Californian*'s position at 10.20 p.m on 14 April, recorded in the log book and 'said to have been fixed by dead reckoning and verified by observations', Lord Mersey commented: 'I am satisfied that this position is not accurate.' He gave no reason for this conclusion.

On four occasions, the report drew attention to the fact that Lord was not on the bridge at crucial moments, particularly when the approaching vessel was first sighted. Yet this sighting had been by Lord himself, from the main deck, at 10.55 p.m.; it was not until a quarter of an hour later, at 11.10, that Groves, the officer of the watch, had first noted the other ship, which he had not formally reported to Lord until 11.30. That delay in no way implied that he had been negligent in his watchkeeping; probably his lookout would have been concentrated ahead of the *Californian*, to the northward and eastward, whereas the other ship was coming up obliquely from behind him, on the starboard quarter.

The report emphasised the fact that Lord did not join Groves on the bridge until after the other vessel had stopped, implying that it was for this reason that Lord had failed to identify her as a passenger steamer, for Groves had claimed that by then she had put out her lights for the night. Quite illogically, however, the report instanced Gill's opinion that the ship he had seen had been a passenger vessel, yet he, too, did not see her until after she had stopped.

The report went on to record that Lord 'only remained upon the bridge for a few minutes', and that, at midnight, he 'was also up (but apparently not on the bridge)' when he pointed out the other steamer to Stone, with instructions to report 'if her bearing altered or if she got any closer'. What possible difference could there be, Lord reflected, between a conversation at the foot of the starboard bridge ladder and one on the open flying bridge, just eight feet higher up? Lord Mersey made no attempt to explain why he considered that it told against Lord for him not to have been on the bridge of a ship lying stopped in mid Atlantic.

The report embodied, but made no attempt to clarify, Groves' 'admission' that a turn to port by the approaching vessel could explain both a diminution of her lights and the coming into view of her port sidelight.

There was a surprising and very significant misquotation from Gill's evidence. The report stated as a fact that 'some time after 12.30 a.m., Gill, the donkeyman, said that he saw two rockets fired from the ship which he had been observing'. This was the precise opposite of what Gill had actually stated, however, for in his evidence he had categorically affirmed that when he saw the rockets he 'could not see anything of the steamer at all. She had disappeared'.

Reference was made to the fact that if the *Californian*'s positions (based on sights taken by all the officers which agreed) were correct, then she was nineteen miles away from the *Titanic*'s given position at 11.40 p.m., and thirty miles away from where the wreckage was left at 11.30 a.m. the following day. The report concluded, however:

> There are contradictions and inconsistencies in the story as told by the different witnesses. But the truth of the matter is plain. The *Titanic* collided with the berg at 11.40. The vessel seen by the *Californian* stopped at this time. The rockets sent up from the *Titanic* were distress signals. The *Californian* saw distress signals. The number sent up by the *Titanic* was about eight. The *Californian* saw eight. The time over which the rockets from the *Titanic* were sent up was from about 12.45 to 1.45 o'clock. It was about this time that the *Californian* saw the rockets. At 2.40 Mr Stone called to the master that the ship from which he had seen

> the rockets had disappeared. At 2.20 a.m. the *Titanic* had foundered. It was suggested that the rockets seen by the *Californian* were from some other ship not the *Titanic*. But no other ship to fit this theory has ever been heard of.
>
> These circumstances convince me that the ship seen by the *Californian* was the *Titanic* and if so, according to Captain Lord, the two vessels were about five miles apart at the time of the disaster. The evidence from the *Titanic* corroborates this estimate but I am advised that the distance was probably greater though not more than eight to ten miles. The ice by which the *Californian* was surrounded was loose ice extending for a distance of not more than two or three miles in the direction of the *Titanic*. The night was clear and the sea was smooth. When she first saw the rockets the *Californian* could have pushed through the ice to the open water without any serious risk and so have come to the assistance of the *Titanic*. Had she done so she might have saved many if not all of the lives that were lost.

Lord's initial bitter and angry reaction was that, so far as he was concerned, it was all a damned shame. Whatever Lord Mersey might think, the *real* truth of the matter was indeed plain enough to anyone who cared to examine the actual evidence. The *Californian* had stopped at 10.20 p.m., with nothing in sight. The *Titanic* had stopped at 11.40, with nothing in sight. Nearly an hour later, a ship had appeared approaching the *Titanic*, to turn and steam away again. How the devil could that be the *Californian*, when all the evidence proved that she never moved all night?

It was all so simple that Lord felt strongly that surely matters must soon be put right. Yet the national press appeared to accept Lord Mersey's report without question. Commenting on the findings, the *Liverpool Daily Post & Liverpool Mercury*'s editor wrote:

> With reference to a painful incident, the court points out that under the existing law it is a misdemeanour not to go to the relief of a vessel in distress when possible to do so. Lord Mersey suggests that the attention of masters should be drawn by the Board of Trade to the fact. May we point out that a way of arresting the attention of sea captains much more striking than anything the Board of Trade could say or do would be to put the existing law into operation whenever a case occurs to which it seems to apply? The Maritime Convention Act of 1911 may be everything that could be desired, but so long as it is obvious that when gross and undesired infractions of it take place it remains a dead letter, very little good would be done by directing attention to the existence of the measure.

A more technical shipping paper, the *Liverpool Journal of Commerce*, remarked in its leader column:

> The praise to Captain Rostron of the *Carpathia* stands out in strong contrast to the simple narration of the facts in regard to the action of the *Californian*, but we think that Lord Mersey has wisely confined himself to the statement of the circumstances, the suffering which Captain Lord must necessarily already have experienced being quite enough punishment for the unfortunate error of judgement which he undoubtedly committed.

The Times of London, without doubt the most influential of British newspapers, had this to say:

> The severest blame is implied rather than expressed, and it concerns the *Californian*. The proofs that the *Californian* saw the distress signals of the *Titanic* and could have come to her, with the probable result of saving 'many if not all of the lives that were lost', are set out with a deadly conciseness and merciless logic.

The *Daily Telegraph* was harsher in its judgement:

> [Lord Mersey's findings against the *Californian*] is an indictment which is held to have been proved against a British shipmaster. It stands on record for all time; it calls for no comment, for the condemnation is as unmitigated in its simple consequences of this fatal lapse from the high standard of conduct on the sea, accepted by sailors everywhere as a commonplace duty which none would dare to escape even at personal peril. This portion of the report stands out as a thing apart – a horror which in the days to come will wound the human instinct of the race whenever the story of the *Titanic* is recounted.

Against this background, however, Lord received some encouragement from a comment made by Professor W.S. Abell of the Liverpool University in his introduction to the *Journal of Commerce*'s edited report of the proceedings of the British inquiry:

> It also appears from the evidence that the *Californian* observed the signals of distress which were sent up by the *Titanic*; but whether this was the actual vessel whose lights were seen from the sinking ship the evidence does not show.

On 2 August, the promised letter from Captain Macnab appeared in the *Journal of Commerce*, being reprinted the following day in the *Daily Post*. It read:

> Now that the memorable *Titanic* disaster is no longer *sub judice*, I beg space for a word in favour of one who has been, and still is, a deep sufferer from the happenings of that fateful April night in the Atlantic. I

> mean Captain Stanley Lord of the *Californian*. I am not out to defend Captain Lord's inaction, but to ask for sympathy in his terrible misfortune of failing to realise that the signals seen by his officers indicated distress. His past life and character go to prove that, had he realised this, he would have braved the ice dangers which beset his own ship, and gone to the rescue. But seamen are only mortals, and, especially when wearied with long watching, liable like other people to temporary dullness of apprehension of matters happening outside the limits of their own charge.
>
> Captain Lord passed all his Board of Trade examinations most brilliantly before me, his testimonials for good conduct and ability at sea being invariably of the highest order. Since then I have ever heard him spoken of as a humane and clever officer and commander, as well as a kind husband, a loving father, and a high-principled gentleman. His mental punishment, however, may be assuaged by the reflection that his sin was of omission, not of commission, and certainly in no sense intentional.

While Lord appreciated Macnab's tribute to his character, he was not at all happy about his acceptance of the allegation that the *Californian* had seen, and ignored, distress signals. For the moment, however, he took no action to rebut this reference, for events were overtaken by a completely unexpected and initially quite overwhelming development.

Reporting at the Leyland Line's head office as usual, Lord was taken on one side by Captain Fry.

'Mr Roper says he can't give you another ship,' Fry gravely informed him.

This was a thunderbolt.

'That's not right, sir,' Lord protested when he had recovered from the shock of Fry's announcement. 'I'd been given to understand I would have the *Californian* again. Can I see Mr Roper?'

Roper was managing director of the Leyland Line, and in normal circumstances inaccessible at short notice to a master. After a brief absence, however, Fry returned and ushered Lord into the managing director's office. Roper got up from his chair and greeted Lord sympathetically.

'Captain Fry tells me you can't give me another ship,' Lord said. 'But I'd been told I would be given the *Californian* again.'

'Yes, that's what you were told,' Roper replied. 'It's none of our doing – it's been taken out of our hands altogether. It's strongly against my wishes. Our intention was to put you back in the ship, but the directors in London have decided that public opinion is against you and you must resign. We now have no say in the matter.'

There was nothing left for Lord to do but express his grief at this shattering news. William Roberts, the general manager, confirmed that so far as the Liverpool management were concerned, as distinct from the board of directors in London, Lord retained their full confidence. Indeed, Roberts told him that Roper had expressed the opinion that if he were the sole owner of a ship, he would gladly and willingly give command of her to Lord.

If the London director's decision was final, the sympathetic attitude of the Liverpool management was reflected in the actions of Gordon, Roper's private secretary. Exceptionally, he began to take every opportunity which presented itself to talk to Lord, apparently casually. During these conversations, however, he would drop hints and convey information which Lord was confident he would never have divulged except on Roper's direct authority. For instance, it transpired that, in June, the company had been approached by the Board of Trade and asked to confirm which of their ships might have been in the vicinity of the *Titanic* on the night of 14/15 April. They replied that only the *Californian* and the *Antillian* were involved, and that the *Antillian* had been outside the affected region, seeing no ice and having clear weather. Later, at the Board's request, they sent them the *Antillian*'s log books: in doing so, they took the opportunity of drawing attention to the fact that in one of them were recorded the *Californian*'s wireless messages giving in particular her position at 6.30 p.m. on 14 April.

The Board of Trade had also asked for, and been supplied with, a copy of the Leyland Line's standing instructions to masters relating to the safe navigation of their ships.

Perhaps the most interesting piece of information Lord was given was that only one man had been opposed to him on the Leyland Line's board of directors. He was Sir Miles Walker Mattinson, KC, however, unquestionably one of the most influential figures in British shipping of the day, who had threatened to resign unless Lord were dismissed.

It was no good trying to fight such powerful opposition. On 13 August Lord formally resigned from the company. Up to that time, he was given full sea pay and associated bonus, quite contrary to the company's normal practice of placing masters on half-pay when standing by awaiting appointment to a ship. But it was the saddest of ends to a career in a company in which he had earned such rapid promotion.

In reply to a personal letter which Lord sent to Captain Bridgewater, the latter wrote:

> My dear Stanley: I received yours of the 13th inst., and quite agree that you were sacrificed to public opinion. I also showed your letter to Captain Bartlett* and Captain Fry. The former wished me to tell you that he believed in you and only felt that you might have gone on deck, but that in his report to the Leyland Line he recommended you to be given another command in the West Indian trade until you have lived it down. However, keep a good heart, you have a lot of friends – and they outnumber the others. Don't hesitate to refer anyone to me if you hear of anything. I asked a shipowner friend of mine (sail) if he should hear of anything to let me know. I would look for a good solid tramp and go in for making money, Eastern Trade.
>
> At any time you wish to see me I am at your service. Hoping you will soon hear of something to your advantage, and assuring you of my good wishes,
>
> Believe me,
> Yours very sincerely,
> M.A. Bridgewater

So Lord's service with the Leyland Line ended, as it had begun, with Captain Bridgewater, the man who had done so much to further his career.

* Captain Charles Bartlett: marine superintendent of the White Star Line and senior marine superintendent in the United Kingdom of the International Mercantile Marine combine, majority shareholders in the Leyland Line.

CHAPTER ELEVEN

An Unavailing Struggle

As soon as it became evident that the Leyland Line's decision to sacrifice him was irrevocable, Lord decided that it was up to him to do what he could to get the British inquiry findings reversed. Accordingly, on 10 August, three days before his resignation came into effect, he posted a hand-written letter addressed to the Assistant Secretary of the Board of Trade's Marine Department:

> Dear Sir: With reference to Lord Mersey's report on the *Titanic* disaster, he states the *Californian* was eight to ten miles from the scene of the disaster.
>
> I respectfully request you will allow me as master of the *Californian* to give you a few facts which proves she was the distance away that I gave of seventeen to nineteen miles.* 14 April 6.30 p.m. I sent my position to the *Antillian* and *Titanic*; this gives me seventeen miles away, and you will see it was sent some hours before the disaster. 15 April about 6.30 a.m. I gave my position to ss *Virginian* before I heard where the *Titanic* sunk; that also gave me seventeen miles away. I understand the original Marconigrams were in court.
>
> The evidence of Mr Boxhall of the *Titanic* who was watching the steamer they had in view states she *approached* them between one and two a.m.; the *Californian* was stopped from 10.30 p.m. to 5.15 a.m. next day.
>
> The steamer seen from the *Californian* was plainly in view from 11.30 p.m.; the one seen by the *Titanic* was not, according to her lookout men, seen until 0.30 a.m.
>
> Captain Rostron of the *Carpathia* states when at the scene of the disaster: 'It was daylight at 4.30 a.m. I could see all around the horizon; about eight miles north of me (this was the direction the *Californian* was) there were two steamers. Neither of these was the *Californian*.' Had the *Californian* been within ten miles from the *Titanic* she would have been in sight at this time from the *Carpathia*, as she was in the same position as when stopped at 10.30 p.m. the previous evening.

* The dead reckoning positions of the *Californian* and the *Titanic* were 19 miles apart (see chart on p. 176).

With regard to my own conduct on the night in question I should like to add a little more. I had taken every precaution for the safety of my own ship, and left her in charge of a responsible officer at 0.40 a.m., with instructions to call me if he wanted anything, and I lay down fully dressed. At 1.15 a.m. (twenty-five minutes after he had seen the first signal) the officer on watch reported the steamer we had in sight was altering her bearing, in other words was steaming away, and had fired a rocket. I did not anticipate any disaster to a vessel that had been stopped nearly for an hour, and had ignored my Morse signals, and was then steaming away. I asked him was it a company's signal, and to signal her and let me know the result. It is a matter of great regret to me that I did not go on deck myself at this time, but I didn't think it possible for any seaman to mistake a company's signal for a distress signal, so I relied on the officer on watch.

Although further signals were seen between 1.15 a.m. and two a.m. I was not notified until two a.m., and then I had fallen into a sound sleep, and whatever message was sent to me then, I was not sufficiently awake to understand, and it was sufficient indication to anyone that I had not realised the message by the fact that I still remained below; curiosity to see a vessel pushing through the ice would have taken me on deck. The message sent to me at two a.m. was, I heard later, to the effect that the steamer we had in sight at 11.30 p.m. had altered her bearing from SSE to SW½W (to do this she must have steamed at least eight miles; the *Titanic* did not move after midnight) and had fired eight rockets, and was then out of sight.

The question of 'drink' has been raised as the reason I could not be roused. I don't drink, and never have done.

Further signals were seen after two a.m., but the officer was so little concerned about them that he did not think it necessary to notify me. I was called by the chief officer at 4.30 a.m., and in conversation he referred to the rockets seen by the second officer. I immediately had the wireless operator called, heard of the disaster, and proceeded at once, pushing through field ice to the scene, and I would have done the same earlier had I understood, as I had everything to gain and nothing to lose.

There is the conversation between the second officer and the apprentice whilst watching the vessel, that they thought she was a tramp steamer; this is their opinion at the time, which is most likely the correct one.

My employers, the Leyland Line, although their nautical advisers are convinced we did not see the *Titanic*, or the *Titanic* see the *Californian*, say they have the utmost confidence in me, and do not blame me in any way, but owing to Lord Mersey's decision and public opinion caused by this report, they are reluctantly compelled to ask for my resignation, after fourteen and a half years' service without a hitch of any description, and if I could clear myself of this charge, would willingly reconsider their decision.

(Right) Captain Lord, 14 May 1912

(Below) Outside Lord Mersey's courtroom, 14 May 1912. *(L to R)*: G. Glenn, W. Thomas, C.F. Evans, J. Gibson, H. Stone, W. Ross, C.V. Groves and G.F. Stewart

Lord Mersey's inquiry in session, 4 June 1912,
with J. Bruce Ismay on the witness stand

If you consider there was any laxity aboard the *Californian* the night in question, I respectfully draw your attention to the information given here, which was given in evidence, which also proved was not on my part.

I am told that at the inquiry I was a very poor witness. This I don't dispute, but I fail to see why I should have to put up with all this public odium, through no fault or neglect on my part, and I respectfully request you will be able to do something to put my conduct on the night in question in a more favourable light, to my employers and the general public.

I am, Sir,
Your obedient servant,
Stanley Lord

As an example of the 'public odium' which so deeply wounded him, Lord could have quoted from an open letter, addressed to him by name and published in the notorious magazine *John Bull*. It appeared on 25 May, the day after the United States inquiry findings were made public but while the British inquiry was still in progress. It read:

Sir: Perhaps by this time you are heartily ashamed of yourself. Although you were called by the officer of the watch, by your apprentice, Gibson, and through the speaking tube, and informed that a vessel was firing rockets of distress, you took no heed of the signal.

No doubt it was a cold night, and it was not pleasant to turn out of a warm bed, to go on to the bridge, and drive through the ice, but surely you might have taken the trouble to instruct somebody to call up your Marconi operator, and get him to try and find out what was the matter, yet on your own evidence you slept on, and largely through your action 1,500 fellow creatures have perished.

There is no doubt that your officers saw the *Titanic* (it is quite evident that your vessel was within a few miles of her), and had you acted like a man, turned out at the first call, and driven your ship with all possible speed, you would have been able to save every soul on board.

I fear you are a remnant of an old type of skipper, and it strikes me that your officers were somewhat too timid in expressing their views to you. They should have insisted on your going to the assistance of the distressed vessel. They should have chanced your displeasure, and pulled you out of bed.

Another matter I don't like is the utter absence of any reference to these distress signals in your log book. Was the idea to say nothing about it, had the donkeyman not split?

Your whole action is, to say the least of it, reprehensible and un-British, and if the Board of Trade were a real live business body, I rather think they would take stringent action without waiting for the

> findings of the court. You have brought discredit on the fair name of the British marine service. I rather fancy some of my American friends will give you a warm reception when next you reach New York.
>
> *John Bull*

It was of no consolation to Lord to know that, as the object of such an attack, he was in good and varied company. Of far greater concern was the knowledge that the periodical's slogan was: 'If you read it in *John Bull* – it is so', a slogan accepted without question by the mass of the general public.

Such hurtful remarks were to some extent counter-balanced by Lord's having every reason to believe that the seafaring community in Liverpool were on his side. From the beginning, the MMSA's monthly *Reporter*, reflecting the views of seagoing shipmasters and officers, had shown extreme moderation in its references to the part which the *Californian* might have played in the *Titanic* disaster. A sixteen-page article on the loss of the liner featured in the September 1912 issue contained only three references to the *Californian*. J. Bruce Ismay was quoted as having said that, while he did not think that the *Californian* was the ship seen from the *Titanic*, he had no doubt from the evidence that distress signals were seen from her. Secondly, the article itself went on to state:

> The *Californian*, which had seen the rockets but had erroneously assigned them to another vessel (which had passed out of sight to the south-west while she lay stopped on account of ice) also steamed at daylight to the locality indicated by wireless signals for assistance, lat. 41° 46′ N., long. 50° 14′ W. She arrived too late to be of service.

Finally, in a reference to Lord Mersey's findings, the article simply stated that the inactivity of the *Californian* was censured.

The September issue of the *Reporter* also featured a long letter from Lord himself, originally published in the *Journal of Commerce* on 17 August, opening:

> The issue of the report of the court, presided over by Lord Mersey, to inquire into the loss of the *Titanic*, ends a compulsory silence on my part on points raised in the course of the proceedings which affect me as the late master of the steamer *Californian*, and it is a duty I owe to myself and my reputation as a British shipmaster to do what I have hitherto been prevented from doing, for obvious reasons, in giving publicity to circumstances which the inquiry failed to elicit, and at the same time to show that the deductions which have been drawn, reflecting upon my personal character as a seaman, are entirely unfounded.

Lord's letter went on to re-state the facts of the case as he saw them, and continued:

> The evidence is conclusive that none of the responsible officers of the *Californian* were aware of the serious calamity which had taken place. That any seaman would wilfully neglect signals of distress is preposterous and unthinkable – there was everything to gain and nothing to lose. The failure to adopt energetic means of making me aware of the gravity of the signals is conclusive of the fact that my officers did not attach any significance to their appearance …
>
> When I asked the second officer the next day why he had not used more energy in calling me, and insisted on my coming on deck at once, he replied: 'If the signals had been distress signals he would have done so, but as the steamer was steaming away, he concluded there was not much wrong with her'. He was the man on the spot – the only officer who saw the signals, so I think I was justified in relying upon his judgement, which ought to carry some weight …
>
> My position at the inquiry was that of a witness only, and a nautical man rarely makes a good witness …
>
> I trust this lengthy explanation, which I ought to have made earlier but for various reasons could not, will be the means of removing the undeserved stigma which rests upon me, and, through me, upon an honourable profession.

The MMSA's *Reporter* also reprinted an item published on 14 September in the *Journal of Commerce* in a weekly feature, *Chartroom Gossip*:

> One of the features of the *Titanic* inquiry which has caused no little comment among nautical men was the incident of the *Californian* and the manner in which her commander was singled out for censure when so many other vessels were in the vicinity of the disaster. The mysterious moving vessel whose lights were seen from the *Titanic* and by the survivors in the boats has never been identified. There are many who believe it could not have been the *Californian*, which did not move her engines on that night, and which, according to Lord Mersey's report, was not more than eight or ten miles away, but according to the master's and officers' recorded observations was nineteen and a half miles distant. The exhaustive inquiry has failed to clear up this important point in the evidence, and leaves us still in doubt as to the vessel nearest to the scene of the disaster.

A more personal note of encouragement came in the form of a barely legible letter in pencil from 66 Hopwood Street, Spring Bank, Hull. Signed by Sid Cass, it read:

> I am a seafaring man, too, and you have my best wishes and respect. No British seaman would ignore a signal of distress. But armchair critics I have no use for. Nil Desperandum!

Lord was also encouraged by the attitude adopted by the widely read monthly *Nautical Magazine*, 'a technical and critical journal for the officers of the Mercantile Marine, Royal Naval Reserve and yachtsmen'. In an editorial comment on the British inquiry in the August 1912 issue, before Lord Mersey's report was available to the publishers, it was stated:

> As to the *Californian* incident, the sea lawyers have done their very best to blacken the commander's character, in our opinion without success. *An experienced seaman* can alone understand what happened. It is very seldom that a master in the Atlantic trade can get a peaceful sleep, undisturbed by anxiety, yet here was a chance! As to the *Titanic* foundering, such a wild idea never entered the heads of any one on board the *Californian*. Captain Lord's ship was stopped. It was clear and smooth. His ship was in ice, so that danger of collision was absent. He turned in, and naturally slept heavily. The officer of the watch, who confessed to his limited experience, saw rockets; did not appreciate the fact that they were distress rockets, but thought the captain had better be told; the small amount of importance which in his mind the matter held is plainly seen by his sending an apprentice below to call him. This youth, with bated breath, called the autocrat; he was easily satisfied with the answers of a half-awakened man – hence disaster. The court *thought* that the rockets seen by the *Californian* were the distress rockets of the *Titanic*, and in view of this *thought* did their best to ruin the career of Captain Lord. We can only trust that his owners will take no notice of this dry, legal, wretched stuff. Does any seaman suppose for an instant that if Captain Lord had been satisfied that he saw distress rockets he would not have made some attempt to reply? Possibly he did not show well in the witness box. What man would, with such an insinuation hurled at him?

Although Lord disagreed with some of the assumptions made in the article, he approved of its general tone. He received assistance of a more practical kind when he was shown a report from the British steamer *Almerian*, which identified her as the ship they had seen close to the *Mount Temple* on the morning after the *Titanic* was lost.

The *Almerian* had been bound to the eastward, from Mobile, when at 3 a.m. on 15 April her master was called and told that there was ice alongside. He at once stopped his ship. Another steamer was in sight on the port quarter, with which the second officer tried to communicate by Morse lamp: all he could make out of her reply, however, was the sequence of letters '... ount ...'. At daybreak, about 4 a.m., field ice and icebergs became visible, extending to the north-east and southward as far as they could see.

The *Almerian* was taken at various speeds in a northerly direction on the western extremity of the ice field as they searched for a way towards the clear water in the east. The ship first seen at 3 a.m., then lying stopped, was now also seen to be under way, apparently looking for a passage through the ice field, on the other side of which a third ship was observed. She was a large four-masted steamer, whose funnel markings could not be distinguished, but having her derricks rigged over her foremost hatch. Shortly afterwards, smoke was sighted ahead which on nearer approach was seen to be coming from a Leyland liner. Before they got up to her, however, she altered course to the eastward and steamed through the ice in the direction of the other four-master lying on the far side of the ice.

The *Almerian*, which was not equipped with wireless, continued to steam in a northerly direction without attempting to communicate with any of the other three ships. The first of these, after remaining in sight throughout the morning, headed towards the east. They came sufficiently close to her to be able to read her name, *Mount Temple*, and then saw her turn again on to a north-westerly course. The *Almerian* maintained her northerly progress until about 10 a.m., when the ice field thinned sufficiently for her to be able to steam slowly through it. She cleared the last floes on the eastern edge about half an hour later and continued on her passage towards Europe.

Lord made a copy of the *Almerian*'s report: from this, it was clear that the Leyland liner she had seen must have been the *Californian* on her way down to the *Titanic*'s lifeboats.

The *Mount Temple* cropped up again early in August, in a most surprising context. Lord received a letter from a complete stranger, W.H. Baker, writing from on board the Canadian Pacific liner *Empress of Britain*, at Quebec. The letter opened with a reference which showed that the writer was mistaken about one aspect of Lord's nautical background:

> You will be surprised to get a letter from me after all these years, but when I mention the old *Conway* you will then remember me. My wife had heard that you were living quite close to us in Liscard, and sent me your address, so I am writing to tell you how deeply sorry I am for you with regard to the *Titanic* affair, for I know how you must have suffered.

I came home in the *Mount Temple* from Halifax that voyage, having been taken out of the *Empress* at ten minutes notice to fill up a vacancy, as one of her officers had been given a shore billet on her arrival in Halifax, homeward bound. The officers and others told me what they had seen on the eventful night when the *Titanic* went down, and from what they said, they were from ten to fourteen miles from her when they saw her signals. I gather from what was told me that the captain seemed afraid to go through the ice, although it was not so very thick. They told me that they not only saw her decklights but several green lights between them and what they thought was the *Titanic*. There were two loud reports heard, which they said must have been the 'finale' of the *Titanic*; this was sometime after sighting her, I gathered. The captain said at the inquiry in Washington that he was 49 miles away – but the officers state he was not more than *fourteen* miles off. I must tell you these men were fearfully indignant that they were not then called upon to give evidence at the time, for they were *greatly* incensed at the captain's behaviour in the matter. The doctor had made all preparations and rooms were turned into hospitals, etc., and the crew were standing by ready to help, on deck, watching her lights and what they said were the green lights burnt in the boats. On our arrival at Gravesend the captain and Marconi operator were sent for, also the two log books, scrap and chief officer's. What they wanted with the scrap log I cannot understand, for there was only about a line and a half within of what occurred during the four hours, and quite half a page in the chief's book! I saw this myself. These fellows must feel sorry for you, knowing that you could not, in the face of this, have been the mystery ship!

I have been residing in South Africa for some years with my wife and family and have only within the last five years returned to England, and have taken up the sea again, and have once more had to begin at the beginning, but I live in hopes of getting promotion sometimes! You will of course have heard about our collision.

I hope to see you when I get back. By the way, Rostron was also on the *Conway* with us, as you will of course remember.

Well, no more now. All news when we meet.

Wishing you a happy issue out of all your troubles …

Lord was initially at a loss as to what he should do with this quite staggering information. He eventually decided to refer the matter to the MMSA, whose secretary, C.P. Grylls, suggested that he should write to the Board of Trade about it. Grylls did so on 27 August, sealing his letter under 'private and confidential' cover: after referring to Lord Mersey's remarks concerning the *Californian* after the British inquiry, Grylls' letter went on to submit that there appeared to be 'strong grounds' for concluding that the steamer's lights seen from the *Titanic* were those of the *Mount Temple*. He went on to suggest that sworn statements be taken from her officers on her imminent arrival in London.

An immediate consequence of the MMSA's approach was apparently to remind the Board of Trade that they had not as yet replied to Lord's own letter of 10 August, for Sir Walter Howell, Assistant Secretary, wrote on 29 August regretting that, 'through an oversight', Lord's communication was not earlier acknowledged. The letter continued:

> ... I fear all I can say is that as all the circumstances attending the casualty have formed the subject of a searching investigation by a court of inquiry, the Board of Trade would not feel justified in taking any steps with regard to your present statement.

The Board's reply to the MMSA's letter, dated 4 September, was equally unhelpful. It opened with the statement that, in so grave a matter, the department could scarcely take action on information given in strict confidence and contained in a letter marked 'private and confidential'. The reply concluded:

> If any persons considered themselves in a position to throw light on the circumstances attending the unfortunate disaster, it was their obvious duty to communicate with the Board of Trade before the conclusion of the inquiry. If anything is to be done by the Board of Trade it can only be after such persons have put themselves directly into communication with the Board, as it is open to them to do even now, and perhaps you would suggest this to them.

Subsequently Lord met Baker in Wallasey, being introduced by him to A.H. Notley, the *Mount Temple*'s fourth officer who had been relieved by Baker in Halifax. Interestingly enough, Notley – who also held an extra master's certificate – had taken the very accurate sights on the morning of 15 April which conclusively demonstrated that, at that time, the *Titanic*'s wreckage and lifeboats were some eleven miles to the south-east of the position of the disaster as sent out by wireless, and as Lord had maintained at the inquiries.

Over lunch one day, Lord and Notley had a long but inconclusive discussion about the whole affair. While Notley assured Lord that he would willingly give him any information he asked for, he was not prepared to volunteer a statement to the Board of Trade in case it prejudiced his prospects within the Canadian Pacific Railway Company. In the light of his own tragic experience, Lord could only confirm Notley's fears, and he accepted his decision without question. At the same time, he considered that the matter was one which must be followed up. Both he and Baker accordingly wrote to Dr W.A. Bailey, who had been serving in the *Mount Temple* on the voyage in question, asking for his help. Dr Bailey had subsequently transferred to the P & O Company, and it was from their ss *Persia*, in Marseilles, that he replied.

In their letters, dated 15 September, Lord and Baker stressed their opinion that now Bailey was in a different company, he might feel more free to act. He replied promptly, four days later: to Baker he wrote:

> As your letter is practically full of appeal on behalf of Captain Lord, what value would an unprofessional and worthless expression of details as to what occurred on the *Mount Temple* be in the face of what has been found? It is clearly Captain Lord's best plan to seek his evidence from Notley at Montreal and the officers who were on the ship at the time who saw certain things and freely discussed matters together; why come to ask me, who doesn't know the blunt from the sharp end of a ship?

His reply to Lord's letter was equally discouraging:

> Not being a navigating officer, no information I could give would, in the circumstances, be of the slightest use to you, when all the evidence as to what occurred on the *Mount Temple* on the morning of the *Titanic* catastrophe are close to you in the officers of that ship and now in the service of the CPR. These might, if obtained, be valuable to your cause.

Others to whom Lord turned in his efforts to obtain evidence which might help him in his attempt to obtain a re-hearing of that part of the *Titanic* inquiry which had led to his being censured included Rostron of the *Carpathia* and Charles H. Lightoller, the senior surviving officer from the *Titanic*. Both were sympathetic, but could add nothing to the evidence they had given at the two inquiries.

Asked about the two ships he had seen in the vicinity of the wreckage, Rostron could only reply:

> All I know – one, a four-masted one funnel steamer dodging about, I suppose, amongst the ice to the northward; the other, two masts and one funnel coming from west to east straight on his course. I did not see the colour of funnels or notice anything which might distinguish either. You can imagine I was quite busy enough. Anyway, Lord, you have my sympathies. I understand more than I can say, especially about the calling business. I may state *for your private* information I have had quite long talks with Captain Bartlett about you.

In a subsequent letter, Rostron commented: 'Lord – I certainly think Mersey was both unkind and unfair in his treatment of you, and his remarks were anything but proper from a judge.'

In response to specific written enquiries from Lord, Lightoller proved unable to confirm the direction in which the *Titanic* was heading as the boats were lowered, nor could he say whether a light he had casually observed on the port bow was one or two mastheadlights or a sternlight.

Of all those who extended a helping hand to Lord in his distressing predicament, the most valuable advocate turned out to be a man with whom he corresponded but never met.

It all began with a letter from A.M. Foweraker, a solicitor living in Carbis Bay, Cornwall. He had apparently been struck by some of the obvious discrepancies between evidence as given at the British and American inquiries and Lord Mersey's finding that only two ships, the *Californian* and the *Titanic*, had been involved. Although Foweraker's practical sea experience was limited to what he had acquired as an amateur yachtsman, he found the essential facts of the case to be so simple that he went on to make an extraordinarily detailed analysis of it. At his request, Lord sent him copies of the statements written out by Stone and Gibson, the report he had copied giving the *Almerian*'s movements, and all the other information for which he was asked and was able to provide.

Despite the encouragement Lord received from his more helpful correspondents and his many professional acquaintances, he was no closer to resolving his two basic problems, that is, of securing a reversal of the inquiry findings and obtaining another seagoing appointment. Frustrated, he was put in touch by one of his brothers with A.H. Gill, member of Parliament for his birthplace, Bolton. Through him, Baker's letter and supporting documents were re-submitted to the Board of Trade through the department's Parliamentary Secretary, J.M. Robertson. Writing to Gill on 17 October, Lord commented:

> My brother forwarded your letter on 16 instant to me; in reply to the question you ask I wish to say that Mr Baker's address is Carlton Villa, Aughton, near Ormskirk, He is now in England at the above address, but he expects to leave on another voyage about the 24th instant. I took the liberty of showing your letter to Mr Baker. He says he is quite willing to give evidence at any time.
>
> A copy of Mr Baker's letter was sent to Sir Walter Howell last week, so it will be quite in order for you to show your copy to anyone you wish.

> As I mentioned to you in Bolton some time ago, I admit there was a certain amount of 'slackness' aboard the *Californian* the night in question, but I strongly maintain that the position I gave at the inquiry was correct, and there hasn't been any evidence produced to prove the contrary, and until such evidence is produced, or proof of my log book being 'cooked', I am entitled to the benefit of that document.
>
> Thank you for the interest you are taking in this matter.

The Board of Trade took six weeks to consider their reply. When it reached Lord, it merely confirmed the previously expressed opinion that Baker's letter did not throw any real doubt on Lord Mersey's findings, although the Board undertook to give the most careful consideration to any signed statements which Lord might be able to obtain from witnesses who had served in the *Mount Temple*.

On 14 December, Lord made a last desperate attempt to re-establish contact with Dr Bailey, whom he considered to be the only witness from the *Mount Temple* able to act independently. He called on Bailey's brother, also a doctor and practising in Liverpool, but he was out. In a subsequent letter, Dr Mathias Bailey expressed regret that, because of family differences, he was unable to help Lord by putting him in touch with his brother. The final sentence of his letter read:

> I can say this: I have been told by an officer on the *Mount Temple* that distress signals were observed and preparations made, etc. I may be mistaken, they were ten to fourteen miles away, you were twenty-five.

The year 1912 had been a disastrous one for Lord. Through no fault of his own, it closed with his professional career in ruins as a result of Lord Mersey's report, with no avenues of redress open to him, and no apparent hope of any future employment.

It seemed to be a quite hopeless situation.

CHAPTER TWELVE

Lawther Latta

If 1912 closed on the gloomiest of notes, the New Year opened with a completely unexpected development which at first sight seemed almost too good to be true. On 19 January, Lord received a letter from a London firm, Lawther Latta, managers of the Nitrate Producers Steam Ship Company, whose fleet of steamers traded primarily to South American ports:

> Our Mr Latta has just returned from Switzerland, and is in receipt of a letter from Mr Frank Strachan of Brunswick, speaking strongly in your favour, and asking us, if we had an opening, whether we would be disposed to give you an appointment, as he apparently considers that you have been subjected in the recent well-known conflict to unfair treatment.
>
> Mr Strachan is a very old friend of ours, and we do not think would write so strongly unless he really knew you well, and was absolutely satisfied of your unquestioned ability and undoubted reputation.
>
> We have not at the moment an appointment, but may possibly have one within the next month or so. In that regard, however, the steamer we have is somewhat smaller than that to which you have been accustomed, and our trade also somewhat different, as our masters must be thorough business men, inasmuch as frequently the cargoes themselves belong to us, so that an all-round business man as well as a seaman is necessary.
>
> If you think you could fill our bill, we shall be quite pleased to have an interview with you when you first happen to be in London.

Lord's bitter experiences in 1912 made him look very carefully at any new development, however, no matter how initially promising it might appear to be. Two considerations influenced his immediate reaction. His first concern was to ensure that Lawther Latta's knew exactly why he had had to resign from the Leyland Line; additionally, he now had very little money left and preferred not to incur the cost of a fruitless journey to London. His acknowledgment of the approach was accordingly very carefully worded, and ended with the simple statement that he had no immediate plans for a visit to London.

Lawther Latta's reply came by return of post.

> We have to acknowledge receipt of your straightforward and frank letter of yesterday, the tone of which we appreciate, and naturally we observe it is possible that you may not have had a proper opportunity of setting out your case. So far as our recollection of the examination goes, the chief point against you was not so much as to whether it was your command that was nearest the *Titanic*, but the alleged fact that rockets were seen by your officers, that you were called, but remained callous to the call. Be that so or not, the circumstances were altogether exceptional, and not such as it appears to us sufficiently serious to condemn the reputation of any man.

The final paragraph of the letter made it clear that the company had accurately interpreted his reference to any future visit to London, for it read: 'We need not say if you care to come to London by appointment with us, we shall be pleased to pay your expenses in event of an engagement not resulting.'

Lord wasted no time in making an appointment. He was interviewed by John Latta, an energetic Scotsman now chairman of a company he had built up into one having an excellent reputation in shipping circles. In the course of an hour's conversation, the two men found themselves in complete sympathy with each other, and Lord left the office knowing that an appointment as master of one of the company's vessels would be offered to him subject to the Leyland Line's providing him with a favourable reference.

On 30 January he heard from the company again:

> We have today had a satisfactory reference from Mr Roper, and are agreeable to offer you command of our ss *Anglo Saxon* on the basis of £20 per month, with a bonus of £5 per month if everything proves satisfactory, as it no doubt will, and your further advancement would depend on circumstances. On hearing from you that you are agreeable to accept this position we will further give you the necessary particulars governing the requirements of our company. In any event you will be good enough to keep this communication private.

Lord accepted the offer, and the confidentiality of his new appointment was ended on 7 March 1913, when he took over the *Anglo Saxon* as master. Built by Short's of Sunderland in 1902, she was a single screw, triple-expansion engined steamer of 4,263 tons gross.

Among those who wrote to wish him well was Roper: the Leyland Line also provided him with a reference covering his service with them from 1897 to 1912. This concluded: 'We have always found Captain Lord a sober, industrious and careful officer, good navigator and disciplinarian, and whilst he has been in command of our steamers, they have run free from accident.'

From Captain Bartlett came a letter expressing his pleasure at the news and commenting: 'I still believe that you were unjustly treated, and would gladly help you at any time, if it is in my power to prove it'.

Lord experienced no difficulty in adapting himself to Lawther Latta's pattern of trading; indeed, in many ways he found it to be more interesting and rewarding than the Leyland Line's.

He returned to home waters from his first voyage in the *Anglo Saxon* in August 1913. As was the custom in the company, he went down to London to discuss the voyage and future plans for the ship with John Latta himself. He was received very cordially, and after the interview released to return to his home in Wallasey for a spell of leave.

He found that in his absence considerable publicity had been given to his case. A long and detailed review of points in the *Californian*'s favour had been published in the January issue of the MMSA's monthly *Reporter* under the heading: '*Pushed under the Wheels of Juggernaut*'. The article was attributed to 'JDM', initials barely concealing the identity of 69-year-old Captain John d'Arcy Morton, nautical adviser to the MMSA since 1893. Captain Morton was a most unusual character, distinctive both in appearance, with his long, white, straggly beard, and in his scholarly accomplishments: he was not only a linguist fluent in French, Spanish, Latin and Greek, but also an unrivalled mathematician and a frequent contributor to the *Reporter* and other nautical publications.

In his article, Morton suggested that the most probable solution of the mystery of the *Californian*'s alleged involvement in the *Titanic* disaster was that the ship seen from her lay on the line of bearing between her and the distant *Titanic*, whose rockets confused Stone by consequently appearing to be associated with the intervening stranger. The article concluded:

> The details we have given in this article represent absolute facts and show that the blame and obloquy which have been cast upon the unfortunate shipmaster were entirely undeserved. Public indignation

> influenced his employers, who called for the resignation of his command, at the same time informing him that they believed in his account of the casualty and explanations of delay, but were unable to withstand 'public opinion', which had condemned him unheard, and to which they were obliged to bow, as affecting their own commercial interests.
>
> Our object is to lay the truth underlying *absolute* facts before 'public opinion', who is appealed to as such a powerful and remorseless castigator, but appears to us to be greatly maligned.

Morton's article was illustrated by two charts supplied by 'an anonymous friend', signing himself as 'Sea Lawyer'. He turned out to be Lord's correspondent from Carbis Bay, the solicitor Foweraker, who commented on the feature in a long letter published in the subsequent issue of the *Reporter*. In this, he suggested that in fact there must have been *two* 'mystery' ships, one seen from the *Californian* and the other from the *Titanic*. He quoted from the statements written by Stone and Gibson, and also drew attention to the serious error in Lord Mersey's report which attributed to Gill the statement that he had seen two rockets fired from the steamer which he had first seen at midnight. In Foweraker's opinion, this error by Lord Mersey technically annulled that portion of his report applying to the *Californian*.

Continuing his energetic efforts to publicise Lord's case, Foweraker also contributed four illustrated articles to the *Nautical Magazine*. These were published in the April, May, June and July issues under the heading: '*A Miscarriage of Justice*'.

In the first article, Foweraker explained that his analysis of the case was based on 'a careful study of the minutes of evidence'. He submitted that Lord Mersey's opinion rested on 'a belief in certain appearances which were in part undoubtedly suggestive of the idea that the *Californian* must have seen the *Titanic* sink ... On the strength of these appearances he discredited the evidence attesting the accuracy of the *Californian*'s position but on the other hand accepted the *Titanic*'s position in the face of a conflict of opinion.'

Reviewing the 'strange resemblance between what was seen from the *Californian* and certain features of the disaster', Foweraker repeated his theory that there had actually been two unidentified steamers, 'X' seen by the *Californian*, which fired low-lying rockets and which Lord Mersey said was the *Titanic*, and 'Z', seen by the *Titanic* to approach the liner and which Lord Mersey said was the *Californian*.

Foweraker went on to criticise Lord Mersey's acceptance of the *Titanic*'s position as communicated by wireless, which put her to the westward of the barrier of thick field ice, and his dismissal of the postions of the *Californian* given by witnesses from her which fixed the overnight location of their ship and the place in which the *Titanic*'s lifeboats and wreckage were found the following morning. He also stressed the fact that the *Titanic*'s wireless message confirmed that her first distress rocket was fired half an hour before any signals were seen from the *Californian*.

Of the two 'hostile' witnesses from Lord's ship, Groves, 'who had firmly got it into his head that they had seen the *Titanic*', had flatly contradicted that opinion by equally firmly maintaining that he had seen a red light on a steamer approaching obliquely and bearing due south, at a time when the *Titanic*'s course was almost due west; Gill had never seen 'two rockets fired from the ship he had been observing', as Lord Mersey claimed.

Foweraker tabulated seven important differences proving that 'X', seen from the *Californian*, could not have been the *Titanic* and four proving that 'Z', seen from the *Titanic*, could not have been the *Californian*.

Finally Foweraker stated that Lord, whom the author had never met, although they had corresponded, was a shipmaster who had sent out three wireless warnings of ice, two directly to the *Titanic*; furthermore, when he heard of the accident, he pushed his ship twice through an icefield that other shipmasters preferred to go round. Yet in the eyes of the general public, he was a man too apathetic to lift a finger to save about 1,500 lives.

Foweraker's second article drew attention to the conflict of interest which must have adversely affected Dunlop. He had been appointed by the Leyland Line as counsel with instructions to watch the proceedings on the behalf of the company and the *Californian*'s master and officers. He had then been confronted by a situation in which one of those officers expressed an opinion contrary to that held by the master and the other two.

His third article summed up those arguments which showed that Lord Mersey's findings in relation to the *Californian* were wrong, and he appealed to the press to help in putting Lord 'right with the public on this side of the Atlantic'. He drew attention to a reference in the *Daily Mail* to the earlier articles and to comment in Lord's favour by a leading journalist, Filson Young, in the periodical the *Pall Mall Gazette*.

A special point was made of Groves' momentary 'lapse of mind' in the witness box when he maintained his opinion that a ship bearing south and heading to the westward could be showing him a red sidelight. The relevant section of the inquiry proceedings was quoted in full.

Finally, the third article listed those points which should have been followed up at the inquiry if the alleged involvement of the *Californian* were to have been properly investigated. Stone should have been asked how many rockets he reported to Lord at 1.15 a.m.; Gibson should have been asked for further details of what happened and what Lord had said before he closed the door of the chartroom after giving his report; other *Californian* witnesses, such as the lookouts and the quartermaster on duty during the night, should have been called; an attempt should have been made to establish from the evidence how the *Titanic* was heading after the impact; Marconi Company records might have confirmed the actual time at which the *Titanic*'s distress rockets commenced; Rostron should have been asked to verify the position in which he left the wreckage; and the Board of Trade should have made an attempt to obtain a list of vessels in the vicinity.

Foweraker's fourth article dealt briefly with the ice reports transmitted by ships in the area in which the *Titanic* was lost.

In Lord's absence at sea, his wife had taken out a subscription to a press cuttings agency and had been able to collect for him clippings relating to Foweraker's articles. He also obtained translations of other articles in his defence, notably from the Antwerp *Metropole* and Hamburg *Neptune*, based on those published in the *Nautical Magazine*. Apart from a relatively brief reference in the *Daily Mail* of 5 May, however, the national press had not taken up the case, although provincial newspapers doing so included the *Manchester Evening Chronicle*, the *Liverpool Express*, the *South Wales Daily News*, the *Western Mail* and the *Exeter Express & Echo*, this last being followed up by a letter from the indefatigable Foweraker.

The majority of these references were in connection with a long article contributed to the *Saturday Review* by Filson Young, published on 24 May. This wholly accepted the case put forward by Foweraker on Lord's behalf, and under the heading 'Things that Matter' in the *Pall Mall Gazette*, Filson Young also wrote: 'It is because I was among those who did Captain Lord what I now believe to have been an injustice that I wish to call what attention I can to this convincing vindication of his honour as a sailor and a

In the Wreck Commissioner's Court.

Scottish Hall,
Buckingham Gate,
Friday, 28th June, 1912.

PROCEEDINGS

BEFORE

The Right Hon. LORD MERSEY,
Wreck Commissioner of the United Kingdom,

WITH

Rear Admiral the Hon. S. A. GOUGH-CALTHORPE, C.V.O., R.N.,
Captain A. W. CLARKE,
Commander F. C. A. LYON, R.N.R.,
Professor J. H. BILES, LL.D., D.Sc.,
Mr. E. C. CHASTON, R.N.R.,
Acting as Assessors.

ON A FORMAL INVESTIGATION

Ordered by the Board of Trade into the

LOSS OF THE S.S. "TITANIC."

THIRTY-THIRD DAY.

THE RIGHT HON. SIR RUFUS ISAACS, K.C., M.P. (Attorney-General), SIR JOHN SIMON, K.C., M.P. (Solicitor-General), MR. BUTLER ASPINALL, K.C., MR. S. A. T. ROWLATT and MR. RAYMOND ASQUITH (instructed by Sir R. Ellis Cunliffe, Solicitor to the Board of Trade) appeared as Counsel on behalf of the Board of Trade.

THE RIGHT HON. SIR ROBERT FINLAY, K.C., M.P., MR. F. LAING, K.C., MR. MAURICE HILL, K.C., and MR. NORMAN RAEBURN (instructed by Messrs. Hill, Dickinson and Co.) appeared as Counsel on behalf of the White Star Line.

MR. THOMAS SCANLAN, M.P. (instructed by Mr. Smith, Solicitor), appeared as Counsel on behalf of the National Sailors' and Firemen's Union of Great Britain and Ireland, and of the personal representatives of several deceased members of the crew and of survivors who were members of the Union. (Admitted on application.)

MR. BOTTERELL (instructed by Messrs. Botterell and Roche) appeared on behalf of the Chamber of Shipping of the United Kingdom. (Admitted on application.)

MR. THOMAS LEWIS appeared on behalf of the British Seafarers' Union. (Admitted on application.)

MR. L. S. HOLMES (of Messrs. Miller, Taylor and Holmes, of Liverpool) appeared on behalf of the Imperial Merchant Service Guild. (Admitted on application.)

MR. COTTER appeared on behalf of the National Union of Stewards. (Admitted on application.)

MR. HAMAR GREENWOOD, M.P. (instructed by Messrs. Pritchard and Sons), watched proceedings on behalf of the Allan Line Steamship Company; and (instructed by Messrs. William A. Crump and Son) also on behalf of the Canadian Pacific Railway Company.

MR. ROCHE (instructed by Messrs. Charles G. Bradshaw and Waterson) appeared on behalf of the Marine Engineers' Association. (Admitted on application.)

MR. A. CLEMENT EDWARDS, M.P. (instructed by Messrs Helder Roberts and Co.), appeared as Counsel on behalf of the Dock, Wharf, Riverside and General Workers' Union of Great Britain and Ireland. (Admitted on application.)

MR. W. D. HARBINSON (instructed by Mr. Farrell) appeared on behalf of the third class passengers. (Admitted on application.)

MR. C. ROBERTSON DUNLOP watched the proceedings on behalf of the owners and officers of the s.s. "Californian." (Leyland Line). (Admitted on application.)

MR. H. E. DUKE, K.C., M.P., and MR. VAUGHAN WILLIAMS (instructed by Messrs. A. F. and R. W. Tweedie) appeared as Counsel on behalf of Sir Cosmo and Lady Duff Gordon. (Admitted on application.)

MR. F. LAING, K.C., and MR. ALFRED BUCKNILL appeared on behalf of Messrs. Harland and Wolff. (Admitted on application.)

LONDON:
PUBLISHED BY HIS MAJESTY'S STATIONERY OFFICE.
To be purchased, either directly or through any Bookseller, from
WYMAN & SONS, Ltd., Fetter Lane, E.C.; or
OLIVER & BOYD, Tweeddale Court, Edinburgh; or
E. PONSONBY, Ltd., 116, Grafton Street, Dublin.

PRINTED BY
JAS. TRUSCOTT and SON, Limited, Suffolk Lane, Cannon Street, E.C.
1912.

Price One Shilling and Sixpence.

(9552.) Wt. 4193—292. 500. 6/12. J. T. & S.

The cover of the printed proceedings of Lord Mersey's inquiry. (There is no reference to any instructing solicitors for C. Robertson Dunlop, without whom Captain Lord would have had no means of influencing his actions.)

(Right) The small starboard sidelight on the *Titanic*, which Captain Knapp claimed could have been seen at a range of 16 miles

(Below) Captain John J. Knapp, USN

man.' His article in the *Saturday Review* concluded:

> Those who believe that a grave injustice was done to Captain Lord do not ask anything for him; there is nothing, of course, that the public who misjudged him can do. All they can do, and all presumably that he would wish, is to correct that judgement and realise that he was condemned on opinion rather than evidence. The career of a merchant captain is unlike other careers in this: there are no great chances of reward in it; no fortuitous circumstances can suddenly and enormously improve it. But there are chances of great disaster, and fortuitous circumstances may suddenly and completely destroy it. There is no chance of honour, because the qualities that in other walks of life would bring honour to a man are at sea taken as a matter of course; but there is the chance of disgrace if the slightest mistake is made, or if the strictest vigilance is for a moment relaxed. And I do not think that anyone can read the analysis of this evidence in the *Nautical Magazine* without being convinced that Captain Lord suffered an injustice, that he did nothing disgraceful, and that he should not be disgraced.

Lord was particularly heartened by a favourable reference to the articles appearing in the July issue of the *Review of Reviews*, for the late editor of that magazine, William T. Stead, a respected publicist, was in fact one of those who had perished in the *Titanic* disaster. The case was summed up in these words:

> That a witness giving evidence before a court of inquiry may have imputed to him what may be regarded as a crime, this by innuendo and not by direct assertion; that he may suffer injury in consequence and then be refused a fair trial; this seems to have happened to a man who risked his ship in rendering assistance as soon as he knew that assistance was required, and who lost his employment in consequence, and has been refused an inquiry into his conduct.

A copy of the April issue of the *Nautical Magazine* had been forwarded to Lord. As soon as he had read Foweraker's first article, he wrote to the editor:

> I have just received the April issue of your magazine and have read with much interest the article under the heading: '*A Miscarriage of Justice*'. The writer states the case very clearly, and bears out the statement I made at the inquiry – that the *Californian* could not have been the steamer seen from the *Titanic*. I hope the publicity your magazine will have given to this article will be the means of clearing the matter up to the general public, who were certainly given an erroneous idea of the *Californian* case at the time.

If more time had been devoted at the inquiry to investigating the movements of other steamers known to be in the vicinity of the disaster that night I am convinced that the moving steamer really seen from the *Titanic* would have been discovered.

Lord's letter appeared in the August issue of the magazine and was accompanied by two others. The first was from Foweraker himself, reiterating the general principle as summed up in the *Review of Reviews*. The second came from 'Master Mariner (Retired)', who held a novel viewpoint on the controversy:

I have read the articles which have appeared in your last three numbers *re* the *Californian* and the *Titanic*. It has always appeared to me, and to many others with whom I have discussed the subject, to be a mere matter of detail whether those on board the *Californian* saw the *Titanic* or they did not. They evidently saw a vessel of some sort firing rockets, a signal of distress. It was the duty of the *Californian* to have gone to her assistance. They did nothing! Whose fault it was is only known to Captain Lord and his officers. They might not have been able to get near her on account of the ice, but they might have tried. There is no dispute, I think, about their having seen a vessel firing distress signals.

The point raised in 'Master Mariner's' letter was taken up by a correspondent using the pen name 'Blue Light', a possible indication that he was serving in the Cunard Line, who used a company signal of this colour. His letter appeared in the September issue of the *Nautical Magazine*:

I do not think that 'Master Mariner (Retired)' has studied the case in all its details. He says: 'They evidently saw a vessel of some sort firing rockets, a signal of distress'. Here is where he trips up. Many of the private signals of Atlantic steamship companies are so like rockets that it is impossible, at any distance, to discriminate. The words of the regulations are: 'Rockets or shells throwing stars of any colour or description, fired one at a time at short intervals'. Anyone acquainted with private signals will see how necessary an alteration of this is. Now 'a vessel of some sort' has nothing to do with the matter. Captain Lord was penalised in quite an unlawful way, for not attempting to go to the rescue of the *Titanic*, which foundered nineteen miles from him. It *may* be possible, on a very clear night and by the use of extremely powerful glasses, to see rockets nineteen miles away, but it would be impossible at such a distance (which distance would be unknown to the observer) to say whether they were private signals or distress rockets. A certain number of persons are aware that the *Titanic*'s signals *were* seen and noted from another steamer, on which preparations were made to receive rescued persons, but that steamer was not the *Californian*. We may yet find a member of the crew of that vessel who will 'split'. Even now it is not too late.

Foweraker himself also contributed yet another detailed letter to the September issue, amplifying an earlier reference to the accuracy of the *Californian*'s positions as given by her master and officers. He also commented on 'Master Mariner's' letter, agreeing with his point that *if* the vessel seen from the *Californian* had been firing distress rockets, then the *Californian* should indeed have tried to get to her; subsequent considerations tended to confirm that, in fact, they were *not* distress signals.

Yet another letter from Foweraker was published in the November issue. It drew attention to an apparently unsolved mystery of the sea, similar to that in which the *Californian* had become involved, as described in the following extract from *Lloyd's Weekly Index* of 9 May 1912:

> *New York*, 27 April: Norwegian steamer *Romsdal* reports 26 March, position 45° 50′ N, 57° 10′ W, in the afternoon, saw an immense field of ice, with a steamer of about 8,000 tons fast in it. After dark the steamer commenced signalling for aid by rockets. Endeavoured to assist her and ran into the ice, but was compelled to stop, as the ice had injured the vessel in several places. After midnight the signalling ceased and all lights disappeared. After daylight nothing was seen of the steamer. She had probably sunk. Remained fast in the ice for three days. Finally forced a passage through the ice, breaking the ends of the propeller blades and cracking and bending the bow plates.

Foweraker's articles and the generally sympathetic way in which they had been received filled Lord with new hope and impelled him to appeal for a second time to the Board of Trade. On 8 August he wrote:

> During my absence from England, from March to August 1913, I find the press have been drawing public attention to the injustice of Lord Mersey's decision at the *Titanic* inquiry as far as the *Californian* was concerned, also to myself.
>
> I appealed to your department last August for a further hearing, pointing out that I had been asked to resign from the Leyland Line purely on Lord Mersey's decision. The management were convinced through this inquiry a great injustice had been done to me, and if I could get the Board of Trade to give me a further hearing and I could, as they believed, clear myself, they would willingly reinstate me. Your

department declined to give me a further hearing.

I wish to draw your attention to the articles on the *Californian* incident that have appeared in the *Nautical Magazine* of Glasgow for April, May, June and July (these were written by a person with whom I was not acquainted), also the replies to these articles by British shipmasters in the same magazine. I also wish to draw your attention to Lord Mersey's remarks during the inquiry, when he frequently expressed his opinion that the *Californian* was the so-called mystery ship before he had heard the whole of the evidence.

By the general public the *Titanic* inquiry is forgotten, but to me the undeserved stigma of the *Californian* which I have to bear will always remain, unless your department by opening an inquiry will give me an opportunity of clearing myself. A further hearing by an independent court, on the evidence already submitted at the former inquiry, is all I ask for.

While he was waiting for the Board to reply, Lord was further encouraged by an additional expression of support and confidence in his case coming from a man whose judgement and ability he had come to respect. John Latta was writing from an hotel in Bude, and in suggesting how Lord should deal with a chartering problem which might arise during the coming voyage, he enquired:

When on the coast last voyage, did anyone say anything to you about the *Titanic?* Friends there have had the presumption to say they are surprised under the circumstances we gave you command and that you should have again gone to sea and that your ship is likely to suffer. I made short work of them, and as I did not even mention the matter to you in London it serves to shew it has not weighed with me and only mention the matter in case something was said and so that you may know. I look at the matter the other way about, viz., that when the truth is known the ship will benefit.

But Lord's optimism was destroyed a fortnight later. Dated 4 September, the Board of Trade's reply to his appeal, signed by Ernest J. Moggridge, read simply:

With reference to your letter of 8 August and to previous correspondence respecting the report of the official inquiry held in London into the loss of the s.s. *Titanic*, I am directed by the Board of Trade to state that they have carefully considered the statements to which you refer, but, as you were informed in August last year, they are unable to re-open the matter.

CHAPTER THIRTEEN

Making a Living

Lord went back to sea bitterly disappointed at the Board of Trade's rejection of his appeal. For the time being, however, there was nothing left for him to do but to concentrate on re-establishing himself and making a living. Fortunately, in Lawther Latta's he found this to be the easiest of tasks, for the relationship he formed with the management professionally and with John Latta personally could not have been better.

Only once did anything in the nature of criticism come from his new employers. Arriving off Dover for orders, he obeyed the port's by-laws and engaged a pilot. Berthing later in Hamburg, he received a letter from the company informing him that they had been sent an account charging for the services of the Dover pilot, and pointing out that it was their policy for masters to do their own piloting in that area. Before Lord had time to reply, he received another letter, apologising for the first and confirming that the management now fully appreciated the fact that he had simply been complying with regulations.

Lord Mersey's apparently unchallengeable findings still left Lord with a deep sense of injustice, but he was sustained by the knowledge that a good many people didn't accept the charge made against him. A man like John Latta would never have given him command of one of his ships if he had thought for one moment that it was true. The Leyland Line management certainly didn't believe it, and from the Endicott family in Boston came a letter congratulating him on his new appointment and confirming that they had always said they would never believe that his was the ship seen from the *Titanic*.

Endicott's letter also reported a curious incident. Apparently Groves, on his return to Boston in the *Californian* in June 1912, called at the offices of the *Boston Herald*, but the editorial staff refused to see him. While no one but Groves knew the reason for his call, Lord could only presume that he wanted publicity. He recalled

Dunlop's comment in his closing address at the inquiry that Groves' evidence was 'largely the result of imagination stimulated by vanity'.

As for Frank Strachan, he certainly didn't think that Lord was guilty, and in March 1914 a visit by the *Anglo Saxon* to Brunswick gave Lord a most welcome opportunity to thank him personally for recommending him to John Latta.

'They wanted a bloody goat, Lord, and they got you,' was Strachan's summing up of the situation. They were sitting in Strachan's office and he went on: 'You've got to write something about it for the local newspapers. A reporter will be coming down soon to interview you.'

'I'm not going to write a damn thing,' Lord replied. 'I'm sick of it.'

But a reporter did arrive, and was introduced to him.

'Well, here you are,' Strachan said. 'Here's Lord, and he'll tell you all about it.'

'I can't tell you anything more,' was Lord's unhelpful reply.

Strachan obviously knew the reporter well and wasn't going to disappoint him.

'Now look here,' he said. 'I'll write an article tonight, and I'll let you have it tomorrow, and Lord will agree to it all right.'

The reporter accepted Strachan's offer. As he was leaving, he held out his hand to Lord, but he refused to take it.

'I'm not going to shake hands with you, a fellow who'd believe I'd do a thing like that.'

'Don't be a damn fool, Lord,' Strachan reproved him. 'He's only here earning his living, like you're doing.'

So Lord shook hands with the reporter, and he left them. The following morning Strachan showed Lord the typescript of a ten-page article, a detailed description of events as Lord might have seen them. It was so accurate that Lord had no hesitation in approving it: indeed, the only amendments required were the insertion of certain times and navigational positions.

Strachan's article was published in the *Brunswick Evening Banner* on Wednesday, 25 March, under the headlines:

HOW CAPTAIN LORD WASN'T A HERO
His Own Story of the *Californian*'s Conduct
Says Decision was Unjust

The *Anglo Saxon* was about to sail for Savannah. Before she left,

Strachan spoke about the article to Lord.

'I'm posting a copy to meet you in Savannah,' he told him. 'It's a bigger port, and they're more particular than here. You have something ready for them.'

As expected, another reporter came on board on arrival, and Lord gave him a copy of the article. It was reprinted in full in the *Savannah Evening News* on Sunday, 29 March.

Lord sent a copy to Foweraker, with whom he was still corresponding, and was not surprised to receive in return a copy of a long letter Foweraker had addressed to the editor of the *Brunswick Evening Banner*, summing up the discrepancies between Lord Mersey's findings and the evidence given at the inquiry.

Nowhere in his voyages to the ports in North and South America which Lord had previously visited while in the Leyland Line did he experience the slightest hostility or receive any critical comment about his alleged involvement in the *Titanic* disaster. In New Orleans, for instance, a port in which he was particularly well known, he was always received cordially by everyone.

'Hello, cap, glad to see you back again,' was the greeting he was accustomed to receive from the shore gangs waiting on the wharf. Nevertheless it was impossible for him to shake off the deep sense of grievance at the treatment he had received.

In August 1914, however, he became involved in a disaster immeasurably greater than the loss of the *Titanic*, with the outbreak of the war that was soon to involve all the great nations of the world. Lord saw it as his duty as much to his country as to his employers to keep his ship running as safely and efficiently as possible in the face of the many difficulties and dangers created by the war at sea, and this overrode any of his personal problems.

The early months of the war found him mainly engaged in the transport of horses from America to France, a specialised trade in which the experience he had gained during the Boer War proved invaluable. The United States Department of Agriculture in Norfolk, Virginia, and the French authorities in Bordeaux wrote formally to congratulate him on the way in which horses were cared for while being carried in his ship and their condition on arrival in port. To Lord, however, the problem was a simple practical one. Treat a horse like a human being, with plenty of water and a balanced diet, and it would respond appropriately.

What Lawther Latta's thought about his achievements was illustrated in a letter dated 29 July 1915 which he received on arrival in La Pallice from Newport News. He was now in command of the *Anglo Patagonian*, a steamer of 5,017 tons gross built in 1910. He had transferred directly to her from the *Anglo Saxon* at the shortest of notice to help the company to resolve a temporary staffing difficulty. To do so meant foregoing any visit to his home after the voyage he had just completed, for the *Anglo Patagonian* had to be taken to sea immediately he joined her in Blyth. To Lord, it was a simple matter of putting his duty to his employers before his personal interests; for their part, the company subsequently made it abundantly clear just how much they appreciated his loyal services.

It was wartime, yet in the company's letter they even went so far as to suggest that, if he wanted to take some leave, it was up to him to decide whether or not to bring his ship to a British port for that purpose. Displaying as it did what seemed to Lord to be a quite remarkable trust in his judgement, the letter gave him so much satisfaction that from the mass of official correspondence coming his way as a shipmaster, he selected it for retention among his personal papers.

The company wrote:

> We were very glad to hear of your having got away from Newport News, everything apparently being in all respects satisfactory, and trust that you will reach La Pallice safely and be able to show a good return, although as so often mentioned before, we have found in your case if there is not a good return it is because the horses were shipped in bad condition.
>
> We wrote you last trip that we appreciated, and felt deeply disappointed, how long it has been since you have had an opportunity of getting home and that we proposed to provide another captain to let you have at least one voyage ashore, but it would look as if you had not received that letter as we never got any reply. Now, we can only repeat that we appreciate your consistent work and don't think it fair that this should be continued, even if you are willing that it should. Unfortunately, the arrangement we had in view when we last wrote has been upset by the unfortunate death of Captain Parslow, necessitating our immediately employing Captain Davies to fill his place, which was further accentuated by a necessity that arose for Captain Westacott to remain ashore, and now Captain Richardson of the *Brazilian* says owning to home business of urgency, he would like a trip off. We propose therefore that if you urgently want an immediate holiday, you should come with the steamer to Cardiff, when if we have not another master available, we feel disposed, provided you approve of it as being sensible, to let your chief officer take the steamer for a trip, but will

place much importance on your recommendation in that respect. On the other hand, should it so happen that next trip will suit you equally well, it would fit in with our arrangements best, but we don't ask you to consider our arrangements in this sense, therefore come to Cardiff if you so feel disposed. If, however, as we have said it does not make much difference, then presumably we will ask you to return straight to Newport News to fulfil another charter which we hope to make, not with your present charterers but with the original firm, Messrs. Dunn, for whom you previously have made six voyages and with so much satisfaction to them. Immediately therefore you receive this letter, don't fail to telegraph your wishes in regard to yourself. We have not referred to our last letter, but we think we did not mention that we think your holiday the more necessary as the new steamer has been indefinitely delayed owing to Short's yard having been taken over entirely by the government, and work therefore on the new boat brought to a standstill. They still think, under certain circumstances, that they may be able to arrange with the government to let them so work as will allow of her being completed in the early months of next year, but it seems to us that, too, is doubtful. In any event, over and above the month's holiday, this or next trip, as you may decide, we propose that you shall also have a considerable holiday before you take command of the new steamer if you should elect to command her.

As you have been to La Pallice before and know precisely what has there to be done, we have no special instructions to give, but leave you to handle affairs as these arise and as you have so competently done in the past.

We are writing this letter rather early as Mr Latta, who has been very much overworked, hopes to go off for a week's holiday in two days time, but of course will always be in touch with the office and only mention the matter to account for writing thus early.

(*Later*): Since writing above we have definitely fixed your steamer for another trip to Messrs Dunn's so wire early whether you go straight back or have decided to have a holiday this trip, therefore coming to Cardiff.

Lord relinquished command of the *Anglo Patagonian* in August 1916: sadly she was lost by enemy action shortly afterwards, four of her crew losing their lives. After a spell of leave, he moved to the Grand Hotel, Sunderland, to stand by the company's new ship, the *Anglo Chilean*, and to supervise her completion. Unfortunately her commissioning was seriously delayed, major faults being discovered on her trial trip, and this led to his being sent home for a further three months.

While Lord appreciated this unexpected opportunity to enjoy family life with his wife and young son, there was one considerable disadvantage. As was the practice, like other masters standing by awaiting an appointment he was on half-pay. He had already been ashore for quite a long time, and this additional period put a strain on his financial resources which he felt he should draw to the management's attention. He did so through Hudson, the company's 'outside man', and John Latta gave immediate instructions that his full pay should be reinstated. No master, he commented, should be out of pocket when, through no fault of his own, a ship was held up.

While at home waiting for the *Anglo Chilean*, Lord ran into Stewart one day while he was over in Liverpool.

'Good Lord, fancy meeting you!' he greeted his one-time chief officer. They were just outside the Kardomah café, and over a coffee they had much news to exchange, for Stewart himself was now in command. Inevitably the conversation turned to the *Californian*.

'What ship do you think the *Titanic* saw?' Lord asked.

'I don't know,' Stewart replied. 'I don't think there's any question it wasn't us. But what the devil did Stone see? I've never been able to gather together what he *did* see.'

The pair of them found so much to talk about that Lord was very late returning home, a disruption of normal domestic routine which drew a pointed comment from Mrs Lord.

As the time for the *Anglo Chilean*'s maiden voyage approached, Latta addressed a personal letter to Lord in which he reviewed the wartime problems of minefields and the importance of complying with Admiralty instructions, particularly the courses recommended for the ships to follow. In concluding his letter, Latta commented: 'You are my trusted representative, and I leave you, on examining the facts, to come to whatever decision you would have done if the steamer had been your own.'

Lord commissioned the *Anglo Chilean* in March 1917. She was the largest and most up-to-date of Lawther Latta's fleet, 6,900 tons gross, 470 feet long, and propelled by quadruple expansion engines. Lord's remaining wartime voyages in her were completed without major incident, although he had an isolated encounter with an enemy submarine. The ship was in the Mediterranean, bound for Alexandria, when at 9.30 a.m. on 13 May 1917, midway between Cape Matapan and Benghazi, the officer of the watch called Lord to report that he could see another steamer, just off the starboard bow about five miles away, which appeared to be sinking. She actually foundered as he was completing his report.

Lord immediately ordered the helm to be put hard-aport, and as they began to swing they sighted a submarine on the port bow. She appeared to have a sail up, possibly a ruse in the hope that she might be mistaken for a small sailing ship, but was emitting smoke.

As Lord steadied the *Anglo Chilean* on a due westerly course and called on the engineers for the highest possible speed, the submarine opened fire from two guns on her foredeck. In the ensuing two-hour engagement, Lord noted that she fired altogether 67 shots, all of which fell short. The *Anglo Chilean*'s gun, mounted on the poop as defensive armament, had been manned, and at 11.20 Lord considered that the pursuing submarine had come within range. He gave the order to open fire, and the second shot was seen to drop very close to the submarine; in fact, it was the general opinion that it had struck her. Whether or not this was so, the submarine swung to starboard, exposing her full broadside for about a minute, and appeared to take a list to port. She then abandoned the chase, and five more shots fired from the *Anglo Chilean* as the range opened had no effect.

Early on, Lord had sent out an SOS by wireless, reporting that his ship was under attack, and at 12.30 they closed HM Trawler No 302. Lord passed a message to her commanding officer, giving the position in which they had seen the other ship sink. As the trawler carried on to search for survivors, Lord turned the *Anglo Chilean* towards the east and resumed his voyage to Alexandria, leaving the prescribed Admiralty route so as to avoid what had now obviously become a danger area. On arrival, he submitted an official report to the naval authorities covering the incident.

Eighteen months previously, another ship had been sunk by a submarine not so very far away. On 11 November 1915, the *Californian* had been steaming at twelve knots off Cape Matapan when at 7.45 a.m. a torpedo struck her. She was being escorted by a French patrol boat which took her in tow, but shortly after 1 p.m. the hawser parted. While efforts were being made to re-connect the tow, a second torpedo hit the *Californian* as she lay stopped in the water. Within an hour she had gone to the bottom, taking one member of the crew with her.

Another wartime casualty was the *Naiad*, sunk by a German U-boat on 16 December 1916, 25 miles to the south-eastward of the Bishop's Rock.

In November 1917 the *Anglo Chilean* was detailed to act as leader of a convoy bound from New York to the United Kingdom. Captain W.H. Owen, RNR, boarded her as commodore of the convoy, and after his arrival in England sent Lord a copy of a report he had submitted to Lawther Latta's. In this, he expressed his keen appreciation of the whole attitude and great help afforded him by Lord, and continued:

> I feel greatly indebted to Captain Lord for all his help, which must have added very considerably to his work. Third Officer Johnson and Apprentice Goodchild were also most willing helpers and of great assistance with the necessary signalling. May I be allowed as a simple sailor to congratulate you on owning such a very completely equipped cargo steamer; as marine superintendent in the West Indies for the Royal Mail Steam Packet Company for the last twenty years, one has had some experience, and one hopes you will not consider it presumption on my part to express my appreciation of this splendidly equipped ship, and still more of the loyal and able man in command ... Pray forgive my writing to you, my only desire is to express admiration of a well appointed ship and her able and courteous commander.

Lord's final practical involvement in the war at sea came when he attended an Admiralty's 'Submarine Menace' course, held on board ss *Accrington* in Portsmouth early in October 1918. Within a few weeks, the Armistice put an end to hostilities.

CHAPTER FOURTEEN

The *Titanic* Again

With peace came a return to normal commercial trading for Lord and the *Anglo Chilean*, the ship in which he was to remain for the rest of his service with Lawther Latta's. No one he now met, either socially or professionally, ever referred critically to his alleged involvement in the *Titanic* affair, with a single possible exception. At the end of one voyage, Lord was left with no alternative but to endorse the discharge book of a member of the crew with the prejudicial letters 'DR' in the 'Conduct' column, because of the man's continued misbehaviour. Abbreviated from the words 'Decline to report', this 'bad discharge' carried a clear message for any potential employer in the future.

Lord could not be sure, but he was left with a very strong impression that, as the man turned to leave the pay-off table, he looked down at the critical entry, and muttered: 'That's all you'd expect, from a bugger who'd let a thousand people drown!'

Lord was also involved in another curious encounter which he never forgot. Early in 1925, he took the *Anglo Chilean* in ballast from the Tyne to Australia by way of the Cape of Good Hope, a voyage lasting 46 days. The ship arrived in Sydney on 22 February to join a number of other cargo vessels lying at anchor in Rose Bay, waiting for loading instructions.

The delay extended into five weeks. Each day the agent's launch would tour the anchorage, collecting individual masters and taking them ashore. One morning Lord was in the launch as it pulled alongside a British north-east coast tramp steamer, the *Sheaf Mount*. She was in ballast, her side high out of the water, and as her captain climbed down to board the launch, he accidentally dropped some letters he was carrying. They fell into the water, but Lord was able to fish them out and to restore them to the other man when he sat down beside him.

As the launch carried them ashore, they chatted sociably, and slowly Lord came to realise that the man to whom he was speaking must be Groves, his third officer on that eventful voyage thirteen years earlier. Neither of them mentioned the *Californian*, but a day or so later, as Lord was walking along the quay after disembarking from the launch, Groves, accompanied by another man, came towards him. Groves' companion addressed him.

'Are you Lord, of the *Californian*,' he enquired.

Lord's reaction was instinctive.

'What of it?' he snapped.

'Oh, nothing,' the other replied, and the pair of them walked away. On reflection, Lord rather regretted his negative response, for it occurred to him that he and Groves might have had a very interesting discussion.

The *Sheaf Mount* had gone from the anchorage on 2 March to load wheat for the United Kingdom and the Continent. The *Anglo Chilean* followed her to the grain elevator a fortnight later, and after ten days' loading sailed for home on 27 March, calling at Port Natal and Las Palmas.

During the voyage, Lord was faced with an emergency which caused him extreme concern. The ship's cook, 40-year-old F. Peterson, fell seriously ill, but fortunately one of the P & O Company's 'Branch' Line ships, the *Barradine*, outward-bound for Australia, was not far away. On 5 May, 400 miles north of Capetown, the sick man was safely transferred by lifeboat into the care of the other ship's surgeon.

What had been an eventful voyage concluded on 19 June at Cardiff with a demonstration on the part of the crew which greatly pleased Lord: without exception, every man signed on with him again for another voyage.

The incident involving the cook worried Lord. It showed the vulnerability of a merchant seaman falling ill out of the reach of skilled medical attention. Although he had always considered his own health to be reasonably good, he occasionally suffered from inexplicable stomach pains, while his eyesight was also giving him cause for concern.

During an extended leave beginning in March 1927 he was able to take stock of his financial and domestic situation. His final conclusion, reinforced by the medical advice which he received, was that he could, and should, retire from the sea. On 12 July 1928, he formally advised Lawther Latta's of his intention.

Characteristically his decision was received with cordial sympathy.

On behalf of Sir John Latta (he had been created a baronet in 1920), E.A. Agate, of the company's head office staff, signed the chairman's interim acknowledgment:

> I have to acknowledge receipt of your kind letter for which very many thanks. I am very sorry indeed to hear that your eyes are giving you trouble, but if it does not go beyond wearing spectacles, you should be all right. I have been condemned to these for over forty years. As I am dictating this letter from the country to my secretary at the office, please excuse it not bearing my signature. On my return to London, it will give me the very greatest pleasure to express in the form of a reference the very high appreciation we all had of your invaluable services when with the Nitrate Producers Steamship Company.

Sir John's personal letter followed shortly:

> I have been out of town, so have only just received your letter, and am sorry that you are not altogether well, but trust that with the care you are taking, and the good advice you are receiving, that your sound constitution will prove sufficiently strong to overcome your trouble. I have very great pleasure in sending the reference to which you refer, and if it not worded as you would like it, I shall be glad if you will alter it according to your own ideas, when I am quite sure I will be able to subscribe to all you want.

But Lord had no need to consider altering Sir John's reference by so much as a comma. He read it with the keenest pleasure and satisfaction, and it became one of his most treasured possessions:

> It gives us very great pleasure to state that Captain Stanley Lord held command in this company from February 1913 until March 1927, during the whole of which period he had our entire confidence, and we regard him as one of the most capable commanders we have ever had. It was a matter of much regret to us that he felt compelled to retire owing to indisposition. He carries with him our grateful appreciation of his excellent services, and we earnestly hope that he will soon recover his wonted health.

Lord settled happily into retirement in Wallasey. He had little need for outside activities or social contacts beyond his immediate family circle, although for several years he was a member of the Wallasey Golf Club, starting each day with a round on which he would be accompanied by whoever might be available in the clubhouse. He had no specially close companions among his fellow members. Freedom from any form of business commitments enabled him to occupy himself with whatever leisure activities he fancied, particularly reading and touring by car with his wife and son.

He regarded the *Californian* incident as completely closed. If in the local library close to his home he picked up a book about the *Titanic*, he immediately put it down again. There was nothing anyone else could tell him about what the *Californian* might have done and what she saw: he knew all about it, and he knew they hadn't seen the *Titanic*.

In March 1940, however, there came a grim reminder of that voyage. In a newspaper he read an account of the death of a 62-year-old retired shipmaster who had temporarily returned to sea as a third officer to oblige a friend, captain of the ss *Barnhill*. Off the Isle of Wight, German aircraft had bombed and sunk the ship. Lost with her was the third officer: his name was G.F. Stewart, his home was in Sale, Cheshire, and Lord had little doubt but that he must have been the ex-chief officer of the *Californian*.

Two years later came another unusual reminder of 1912. Out of the blue, Lord heard from a firm of solicitors in Swanage that Foweraker had died. His will bequeathed to the British Museum 'annotated minutes of evidence and notes dealing with the American and London inquiries into the loss of the ss *Titanic* and correspondence in reference to the publication of same, as the existing reports and records are in part suppressions of the truth in regard to matters of importance'. The solicitors' letter stated that the documents, contained in two iron boxes and a sealed parcel, had been rejected by the British Museum as not being of national interest; they were consequently available if Lord cared to accept them. At the time, however, the Lord family were temporarily living at 29 Salisbury Avenue, West Kirby, their own house having been damaged during the intensive bombing to which Wallasey had been subjected. Although Lord had no idea just how big the two iron boxes and accompanying parcel might be, he saw no immediate prospect of being able to find sufficient space to accommodate them. Above all, however, the papers related to an event which, so far as he was concerned, was over and done with. He accordingly declined the offer.

The family returned to Wallasey, and life continued uneventfully until 1957. In that year, Mrs Lord fell mortally ill, and her death profoundly affected Lord. He was now eighty years of age, his eyesight deteriorating with the onset of cataracts, and with the inevitable physical problems of old age he faced the future with extreme concern.

On 6 July 1958, however, there was a completely unexpected development which for the time being compelled him to put aside such handicaps. His Sunday routine was based on the leisurely reading of three newspapers, the *Sunday Times, Observer*, and *Sunday Express*. On that day, his attention was caught by prominent headlines: 'Remembering the *Titanic*'; 'The Cruel Sea'; 'The *Titanic* Still Sends out her Chilling Message'. And the chilling message that Lord received was that in a new film, *A Night to Remember*, not only was the old legend revived, that the *Californian* stood passively by in sight of the sinking liner, but also that her officers – and presumably Lord himself – were portrayed by actors wondering why 'the great *Titanic*' should be sending up rockets.

The film was said to be based on a book of the same name which Lord recalled had been serialised in a local evening newspaper. He had not been greatly impressed by what he had seen as he scanned those extracts, however, nor could he remember noticing any references to the *Californian*.

The film's purpose was set out in the *Observer* as being 'to assemble the ascertainable facts about the life and death of the *Titanic* and to present them with fidelity and without prejudice as dramatically and economically as possible'. How that purpose had been achieved so far as the *Californian* was concerned was described by the film critic of the *Sunday Express*:

> Only ten miles away the lights of another ship, the *Californian*, winked as she rode at anchor. Her only radio operator was in bed. Her officers watched the *Titanic*'s desperate flares going up and wondered why a big ship was firing rockets so persistently into the middle of the night. They did nothing. As Captain Smith realised that to all intents and purposes a ship which could save them all was watching and ignoring he murmured: 'God help them'.

This was too much. Something must be done about it. Lord made no mention of his intention to his son: this was a matter for his professional judgement alone. The following morning he took the ferry over to Liverpool. From the Landing Stage he walked the short distance up to Rumford Place, where the head office of the Mercantile Marine Service Association was situated. He had remained a member since first enrolling in 1897: he now intended to ask that the file relating to the association's support of his case in 1912 be looked out, as a first step towards its re-opening.

The MMSA's general office was on the ground floor, and Lord was left standing for a few moments at a small reception counter while a telephonist relayed his request for an immediate meeting with the General Secretary. A young clerk then took him up a flight of stairs to the first floor and into a narrow room, the Council Chamber, almost entirely filled with two long polished tables, arranged in the form of a 'T'. At the other end, a door led into a tiny anteroom, barely large enough to accommodate a secretary, her desk, and some filing cabinets. Beyond was yet another door, and through this Lord was shown into the General Secretary's room.

PART 2 – THE LEGEND

Regrettably, as so often happens in history, the legend was far more important than the fact.

Professor Arthur J. Marder

CHAPTER 15

The Case for the *Californian*

As General Secretary of the Mercantile Marine Service Association, I was expected to be able to speak with authority on any topic relating to the professional interests of British shipmasters, for whose representation the MMSA bore particular responsibility.* On my appointment in 1956, I realised that I would have to do my best to meet as many members as possible, so that I could personally discuss with them their individual approach to common problems. Relatively few shipmasters visited Liverpool regularly, however, and even when in port could rarely spare the time to visit the MMSA's head office. This meant that I had to make myself immediately available to anyone calling unexpectedly, despite any consequent disruption of normal routine. Accordingly, when on that Monday morning in July 1958 I was told that a Captain Lord wished to see me, I immediately asked for him to be brought up to my office.

A tall, spare man was shown in. He introduced himself briefly and authoritatively.

'I'm Lord, of the *Californian*.'

As I invited him to sit down, I was momentarily puzzled. Although he was obviously elderly, I thought it possible that he might still be serving at sea, and I couldn't place the name *Californian* in any shipping company then known to me. To my surprise, he told me that he was over eighty; I was even more surprised to learn why he was calling on me.

In 1912, Captain Lord explained, his ship, the *Californian*, had

* This specialist representation, accepted in 1944 by agreement with the other Merchant Navy officers' organisations, was relinquished in June 1985, when the MMSA amalgamated with the newly formed National Union of Marine, Aviation & Shipping Transport Officers.

been blamed by the official court of inquiry into the *Titanic* disaster for failing to save the lives of the 1,500 people who had died when she went down. He had always firmly maintained that the *Californian* was at least twenty miles away at that time, but he had no statutory right of appeal against the court's finding. In any event, he claimed, the Board of Trade had rejected his appeals on the grounds that it was the *ship* which had been censured, and not her captain.

Now, nearly fifty years afterwards, he had just read in the newspapers that, in a new film called *A Night to Remember*, the old charge had been raked up, and he wanted something done about it. The MMSA had supported him in 1912: could he see the original file, and would the association re-open his case?

As General Secretary, my authority to act on behalf of any member came directly from the MMSA's Executive Council, some 40 serving or retired British shipmasters, whose formal approval was necessary before I could commit the association to a member's defence. My first duty, therefore, was to try to establish the facts of Captain Lord's case and to report them to the Council. I tackled the job with a completely open mind, having long forgotten anything I might once have read about the *Titanic* and the *Californian*.

Captain Lord's own summing up of the situation was concise: *Californian* stopped, nothing in sight; *Titanic* stopped, nothing in sight; half an hour later a ship approached the *Titanic*, turned, and steamed away again. How could that ship have been the *Californian*, when all the evidence proved she never moved?

But the case against the *Californian* and Captain Lord had been established by an official court of inquiry, under the formidable direction of Lord Mersey and Sir Rufus Isaacs, Attorney-General, and the court's findings, in the words of *The Times*, had been 'set out with a deadly conciseness and merciless logic'. It was consequently essential to examine that case in an equally logical way, and to try to find out how the simple and superficially unanswerable argument put forward by Captain Lord might be wrong.

Lord Mersey's rejection of Captain Lord's case was based on five apparent coincidences. To become established as facts, apparent coincidences must 'occupy the same portion of space and occur at and occupy the same time'. Space and time were consequently the essential elements of any coincidences strong enough to convict a man of causing the deaths of up to 1,500 people, as Captain Lord had been convicted.

In his report Lord Mersey rejected the 'spatial', in the sense of the navigational, evidence from the *Californian* supporting the claim that she had been at least twenty miles away from the officially accepted position in which the *Titanic* sank. He put forward no reasons for that rejection and consequently freed himself from any subsequent detailed criticsm of his decision. The 'time' element of the apparent coincidences was quite a different matter, however. It was never properly investigated by Lord Mersey's court, yet there was ample – and in part fascinating – evidence before them establishing beyond all possible doubt the precise timing of significant events very relevant to the case for the *Californian*.

The time kept in ships in 1912 was determined by the sun. By its rotation the earth creates an impression that the sun is circling it once a day covering 360° of longitude in twenty-four hours, that is, 15° in one hour or 1° in four minutes. Just as in London a clock time was being kept generally five hours ahead of that being kept in New York, so in the *Titanic*, to the eastward of New York, a clock time was being kept 2 hours 2 minutes fast on New York time at the time of the disaster. This clock time was based on the *Titanic*'s noon longitude on 14 April of approximately 44½° W.; as the liner steamed to the westward, her clocks were being put back daily by an amount sufficient to ensure that they would be showing approximately the correct apparent time at noon on each successive day, when the sun would again be on the meridian. On the night of 14/15 April it had been intended to put the clocks back 47 minutes (23 minutes before midnight, 24 minutes after), but this was never done; as Herbert Pitman, the *Titanic*'s third officer, remarked at the United States inquiry: 'We had something else to think of'.

Similarly in the *Californian*, her clocks showed a time ahead of that being kept in New York. Her noon longitude on 14 April was about 47½° W., that is, 3° further west than the *Titanic*, so that her clocks were set 1 hr 50 mins fast on New York time, or twelve minutes slow in relation to the *Titanic*'s clock time. Here is a comparison of the contrasting clock settings at four crucial moments during 14 April:

New York	*Californian*	*Titanic*
9.58 a.m.	11.48 a.m.	Noon (44½°W.)
10.10 a.m.	Noon (47½°W.)	12.12 p.m.
9.38 p.m.	11.28 p.m.	11.40 p.m.
9.50 p.m.	11.40 p.m.	11.52 p.m.

Adopting an 'off the cuff' estimate of Lightoller's, the United States inquiry accepted a time difference between New York and the *Titanic* of 1 hr 33 mins, a difference only applicable had the *Titanic*'s noon position on 14 April been in longitude 51¾° W., that is, 33 miles further to the westward than the position of 41° 46′ N., 50° 14′ W. in which she was officially regarded as having collided with the iceberg at 11.40 p.m. (*Titanic* time).

Lord Mersey's complete failure to establish the correct time factors is emphasised by the inclusion in his report of a long and detailed list of wireless messages transmitted and received on 14/15 April. In this list, a factor of 1 hr 50 mins (actually the *Californian*'s time difference) is used throughout to convert *Titanic* times into New York times and *vice versa*. Whether accidental or deliberate, this action obviously damaged Captain Lord's case by accentuating the time element in the apparent coincidences used against him, particularly in the case of what was held to be a most significant event occurring at 11.40 p.m. (*Californian* time). This was the precise moment the timing of which was so confidently stated by Groves, when the stopping of the approaching ship he was watching coincided with the striking of one bell, to call the watchkeepers in the *Californian*. Yet at 11.40 by the *Californian*'s clock, the *Titanic* had already been stopped for twelve minutes, a very appreciable length of time in a ship steaming at over 22 knots, or when standing exposed on an open bridge on a very cold night in mid-Atlantic.

In his report, Lord Mersey stated: 'The *Titanic* collided with the berg at 11.40 (*Titanic* time). The vessel seen by the *Californian* stopped at this time.' Lord Mersey was wrong: his report should have read; 'The *Titanic* collided with the berg at 11.28 (*Californian* time). The vessel seen by the *Californian* did not stop until 11.40.' Consequently the first of the five apparent coincidences held against the *Californian* is not what initially it seemed to be. In fairness to Captain Lord, surely the very exactitude of Groves' timing should be counted in his favour rather than against him.

Lord Mersey's list of wireless messages has an even greater significance for Captain Lord, however. From these messages and related evidence it is possible to state with absolute certainty the time by which three of the *Titanic*'s lifeboats had been sent away, an approaching ship initially sighted, and the first detonator fired.

Unless otherwise stated, in the discussion which follows all times will be given as they would have registered on the *Californian*'s clock. Additionally, for convenience a ten minute time difference will be assumed as having existed between those times and the *Titanic*'s instead of the more precise twelve minutes.

The first of the *Titanic*'s wireless distress calls was picked up at 12.15 a.m. on 15 April by the shore station at Cape Race, by the British liner *Mount Temple*, and by the French liner *La Provence*; it was logged three minutes later by the German liner *Ypiranga*. Quite independently, the four wireless operators concerned recorded the first position as sent out by the *Titanic* as 41° 44′ N., 50° 24′ W. At 12.25, however, the position being transmitted from the *Titanic* was amended to 41° 46′ N., 50° 14′ W: Cape Race, the *Carpathia*, and several other ships received and logged it in this new form at that time.

The man responsible for amending that position was Joseph Boxhall, the liner's fourth officer. In evidence at the British inquiry, he described in detail how the sighting of another ship's lights was first reported to him while he was helping to clear away the lifeboats. Before going to the bridge to look at those lights for himself, he went to the chartroom, reworked the *Titanic*'s position, and gave it in an amended form to the wireless operator. He then went on to the bridge; having confirmed that another ship was in fact in sight and approaching them, he began to fire distress signals.

Up to that time, 32-year-old George Rowe, one of the *Titanic*'s six quartermasters, had been standing a routine watch on the liner's stern. His duties were to be immediately available to release a lifebuoy should anyone fall overboard, and to read the ship's log at two-hourly intervals – in fact, as the *Titanic* collided with the iceberg, Rowe noted the time, 11.40, and the fact that the log registered 260 nautical miles covered since it had been re-set to zero at noon.

He was due to be relieved at midnight, but no one came. Naturally concerned at apparently having been overlooked in what was obviously an emergency, at 12.25 he seized an opportunity to communicate with the bridge, telephoning to report that he had seen two lifeboats launched from the starboard side. Rowe's evidence was confirmed by Boxhall: 'I knew one of the boats had gone away, because I happened to be putting the firing lanyard inside the wheelhouse after sending off a rocket and the telephone bell rang. Somebody telephoned to say that one of the starboard boats had left the ship and I was rather surprised.'

Incidentally, by then Rowe's relief, Arthur Bright, had joined him on the poop. At about the same time, on the ship's bridge, Bright's watchmate, Walter Perkis, was relieving Robert Hitchens, who had been standing by the steering wheel ever since the collision.

Hitchens' evident resentment of Perkis' late arrival was made all too clear during his evidence given before the United States Congressional committee of inquiry: 'I stood to the wheel until 23 minutes past 12 ... I do not know whether they put the clock back or not.* The clock was to go back that night 47 minutes, 23 minutes in one watch and 24 in the other ... I left the wheel at 23 minutes past 12. I was relieved by Quartermaster Perkis. He relieved me at 23 minutes past 12.'

This repetitive and precise pinpointing of the time Hitchens was relieved leads to the inevitable conclusion that Bright and Perkis at least among the *Titanic*'s crew appear to have put back their watches to conform to the first part of the intended clock adjustments.

Boxhall instructed Rowe to report to the bridge, taking with him the spare detonators or distress signals from their stowage on the poop. There he helped Boxhall in his attempts to attract the attention of the approaching ship by detonator and Morse Lamp.

Pitman, the *Titanic*'s third officer, told the United States inquiry that No 7 lifeboat was the first to go, two or three minutes before No 5, with No 3 next. He saw the first distress signal 'shortly after' No 5 boat left, and at the British inquiry said that he thought 'it would be about 12.30 (*Titanic* time) when No 5 boat reached the water'.

At the United States inquiry, Harold G. Lowe, the fifth officer, said: 'I pursued the same course in filling No 3 boat as in No 5 ... [Mr Ismay] assisted ... I distinctly remember seeing him alongside of me when the first detonator went off. I will tell you how I happen to remember it so distinctly. It was because the flash of the detonator lit up the whole deck. I did not know who Mr Ismay was then, but I learned afterwards who he was, and he was standing alongside of me.'

Sir Cosmo Duff Gordon, at the British inquiry, confirmed that the firing of rockets began 'while they were lowering No 3 lifeboat'.

The completely independent times recorded by Cape Race and those ships which picked up the *Titanic*'s first distress calls, supported by subsequent inter-related accounts by survivors of what they had observed on board the liner, prove conclusively that the first distress rocket was sent up from her at, or very shortly after, 12.25 a.m. From the *Californian*, Stone, the officer of the watch, did not see any signal from the nearby ship until at least twenty minutes later, at about 12.45 a.m. During the intervening period, he – and

* See Pitman's remark, page 165.

Gibson for part of the time – were watching her closely, studying her through binoculars and trying to get in touch with her by Morse lamp. At 12.40, in fact, Stone was able to respond to Captain Lord's enquiry by voice pipe that she had neither moved nor responded to any attempts to communicate with her.

Unfortunately there is no similarly conclusive evidence from the *Titanic* to show how frequently the detonators were being fired: estimates vary from 'every minute or so' to every five minutes. It is also impossible to say exactly how many detonators were actually fired, although Boxhall, the man most closely concerned, later described how 'some' were still left in a box originally holding twelve when firing was abandoned. Lord Mersey decided that the number sent up was 'about eight. The *Californian* saw eight.'

The time at which the first detonator was fired was about 12.25 a.m.; the time at which the last was sent up may have been less than thirty minutes after the first, or as much as one hour later. Stone described how he saw five signals between 12.45 and 1.15, the remaining three being observed between 1.15 and 1.40 approximately. Despite this uncertainty, one clear fact emerges: a series of 'about eight' rockets starting at 12.25 or thereabouts cannot possibly be the same series of eight rockets starting twenty minutes later. If the interval between the firing of the *Titanic*'s detonators was as much as five minutes, then four of them had already been sent up before Stone saw the first of the eight which he later described.

In his report, Lord Mersey stated: 'The number (of detonators) sent up by the *Titanic* was about eight. The *Californian* saw eight. The time over which the rockets from the *Titanic* were sent up was from about 12.45 to 1.45 o'clock. It was about this time that the *Californian* saw the rockets.' Here Lord Mersey is clearly appropriating into the *Titanic* sequence of events the times given in evidence by Stone, using them against the *Californian*. It was wrong of him to do so, and, if the correct times are taken, then two more of the apparent coincidences condemning Captain Lord are suspect, to say the least.

When brought together, the major events as they occurred in the *Californian* and the *Titanic* can be set out as in the accompanying Schedule of Events,* in which 'X' denotes the ship seen from the *Californian*, and 'Z' that seen from the *Titanic*. From the schedule, a striking fact is immediately apparent: there is only 55 minutes

* Page 171

between Stone's first reporting of 'rockets' and the sinking of the *Titanic*, a hopelessly inadequate period of time in which to take the Californian up to ten miles through the ice and to embark 1,500 men, women and children from the sinking *Titanic*.

But those rockets ... The *Titanic* fired rockets; the *Californian* saw rockets; therefore they must have been the *Titanic*'s rockets. So Lord Mersey pronounced, and his judgement has subsequently been widely accepted. But how were rockets used at sea in 1912? Here is an extract from A.H. Brock's *A History of Fireworks*, published in 1949:

> Wireless has rendered practically obsolete the elaborate, not to say picturesque, systems of identification formerly used by vessels of all nations to make themselves known when passing Lloyd's stations at night and on similar occasions. Each line had its characteristic pyrotechnic display, consisting of Roman candles, rockets, hand and Coston lights. The last-mentioned are cases charged with fire of various colours in layers, so that any required combination of colour may be burned in succession from one unit. These were more frequently in use by foreign shipping. A glance at the *Universal Guide*, setting out the signals employed, makes one realise that their passing has taken something from the colour of night-life at sea. The following are a few examples taken at random: the Zud-Amerika Lyn of Amsterdam employed a white light at stern, green at bridge, and blue at bow; the White Star Line a green light at bow and green at stern; W. Johnston & Co., a green light followed by a Roman candle throwing red, white and blue stars three times successively shown from aft; J.L. Burnham & Co., a blue light changing to white, then to red, followed by a red star; a vessel of the Cunard Line when off the coast of Ireland fired a blue light followed by two golden star-rockets; the Ulster Steamship Co. Ltd., three lights, yellow, blue, and red above one another, followed by two Roman candles fired together, each throwing two yellow, two blue and two red stars. As suffixes to the identification signal, a red light indicated 'all's well', a green light signified 'wish to communicate'. Elders & Fyffe's banana boats employed a code of their own, designed to advise the quantity and condition of their cargoes; the number of bunches carried 'ripe', 'green', or 'turning'.

To those examples could be added the Leyland Line (as distinct from the old West India and Pacific Steam Navigation Company), using three red lights in succession, and the Cunard Line, showing a blue light and two Roman candles throwing up six blue balls each.

Against this colourful background, the *Titanic* carried no distress 'rockets' as such. Lord Mersey's own report records that she actually had on board '36 socket signals in lieu of guns'.

SCHEDULE OF EVENTS 14/15 APRIL 1912

New York Time		*Californian Time*		*Titanic Time*
9.58 am	—	11.48 am	Clocks set 2 hrs 2 mins fast on New York Time (longitude 44½° West).	Noon
10.10	Clocks set 1 hr 50 mins fast on New York Time (longitude 47½° West).	Noon	—	12.12 pm
8.30 pm	Stopped in ice.	10.20 pm	Course S86W(true), speed 22¼ knots.	10.30
9.05	Ship 'X', approaching slowly from the southwest, seen by Captain Lord, the chief engineer and radio officer.	10.55	Nothing in sight.	11.05
9.10	Radio message sent to Titanic: 'Am stopped in ice'.	11.00	From *Titanic* to *Californian*: 'Keep out'.	11.10
9.40	Third officer reports 'X' to Captain Lord.	11.30	*Titanic* strikes iceberg and stops.	11.40
9.50	'X' stops bearing SE'ly, 4 to 5 miles away. Morse lamp signals flashed but ignored by 'X'.	11.40	Nothing in sight.	11.50
9.55	Captain Lord joins the third officer on the bridge briefly. Morse lamp signals continued.	11.45	Nothing in sight.	11.55
10.20	'X' under observation by Captain Lord, the second officer, and the third officer.	12.10 am	Nos 5 and 7 lifeboats lowered.	12.20 am
10.25	'X' under observation by the second officer and apprentice; Morse lamp signals still ignored.	12.15	First radio distress calls transmitted, giving position 41° 44′N, 40° 24′W.	12.25
10.30?	—	12.20?	Ship 'Z's' lights sighted on port bow.	12.30?
10.35	'X' lying quietly, closely observed by second officer.	12.25	Amended position 41° 46′N, 50° 14′W, sent out. First detonator fired.	12.35
10.50	Second officer tells captain that 'X' is still lying quietly, ignoring Morse lamp signals.	12.40	Detonators being fired and Morse lamp signals flashed.	12.50
10.55	Rocket, apparently fired from 'X', seen by second officer.	12.45	'Z' turning away, about 4 to 5 miles off.	12.55
11.25	Second officer tells captain that he has seen five rockets from 'X', which is now steaming away.	1.15	'Z' steaming away, showing stern light.	1.25
12.10 am	Apprentice reports to captain in the chartroom.	2.00	Last lifeboats being launched.	2.10
12.20	'X's' sternlight receding.	2.10	*Titanic* sinks.	2.20
12.30	'X's' sternlight disappears.	2.20	—	
12.50	Second officer reports to captain that 'X' has gone out of sight.	2.40	—	

Incidentally, of those 36 socket signals only 'about eight' were fired. Why only about eight? Surely every available detonator would have been sent up to attract the attention of a *stationary* ship, had one been in sight. The only conclusion must be that the firing of detonators was abandoned when it was realised that the ship first seen approaching at about 12.30 a.m. – a sighting which led to the firing of distress signals – had turned and was steaming away.

'Socket signals' were described by Lightoller as 'timed shells', fired from a tube near the bridge, and intended to attract attention by an explosion as they reached a height of some 150 to 200 feet. What Stone and Gibson saw from the *Californian* were not 'timed shells' four or five miles away, but ordinary rockets or flares rising to no more than half the masthead height of the nearby vessel, and having no explosive content whatsoever. Had there been the slightest indication of a report or an explosion, Stone would have gone down to the chartroom himself. As he later told Captain Lord, if there had been any sign of an emergency, he would have *pulled* him out. In any case, 'a ship that is in distress does not steam away from you'.

In 1912, distress signals for use at sea were included as Article 31 in the *International Regulations for the Prevention of Collisions at Sea*, which every candidate for an officer's certificate of competency had to learn by heart. Those for use at night were:

1. A gun or other explosive signal fired at intervals of about a minute.
2. Flames on the vessel.
3. Rockets or shells, throwing stars of any colour or description, fired one at a time, at short intervals.
4. A continuous sounding with any fog signal apparatus.

Not surprisingly in the circumstances, the potentially very dangerous confusion inevitably resulting from the similarity between 'private' company signals and distress rockets at a distance, as revealed by the *Titanic* disaster, formed the subject of very critical comment in both technical journals and the newspapers generally in 1912 and 1913.

Could there have been some atmospheric abnormality that night, damping out any explosion at four to five, or even ten, miles' range? If there were, then it must have been extraordinarily local in its effect. The *Carpathia* was firing detonators as she steamed to the rescue, although not in distress herself, and the explosions were heard (and mistaken for gunfire) by the survivors in the *Titanic*'s lifeboats a considerable time before the vessel's masthead lights came into view.

Incidentally, while steaming towards the *Titanic*'s lifeboats, the *Carpathia* passed another subsequently unidentified ship. From that steamer, the Cunarder would be seen at full speed, fully lit, firing explosive signals and sending up blue Cunard flares. What must the watchkeepers in that vessel have thought, and, what is more interesting to contemplate, what were they supposed to do? Should they have altered course and steamed after the *Carpathia*, and, assuming that they had sufficient speed, overhaul her and enquire by Morse lamp or by megaphone as to why she was firing detonators and displaying flares? Evidently they applied common sense to the problem, shrugged their shoulders, and made no attempt to do anything about it. Lord Mersey found no reason for criticism of this technically improper use of distress signals or of its possible consequence of creating confusion in another ship: he did condemn the *Californian*, however, for *her* inactivity when faced with a comparable situation.

Tragically, as events proved, much of Captain Lord's service as an officer had been in a company in which distress signals had been habitually employed for saluting purposes in a very careless manner. Undoubtedly it was that experience which influenced his drowsy enquiries as to whether or not the signals reported to him had any colours in them. There were no colours; at the same time, there were no detonations. It is only by the extreme application of hindsight that Stone can be faulted for deciding that low-lying, non-explosive signals from a ship only four to five miles away were not distress rockets, the more so when she was altering her bearing and obviously steaming away.

In his report, however, Lord Mersey stated categorically that 'the *Californian* saw distress signals'. If Stone's judgement as a qualified watchkeeping officer on the spot is accepted against the subsequent views of a shore-based court of inquiry committed from the first to a theory that the *Californian* saw the *Titanic* and vice versa, then the fourth of the apparent coincidences held against Captain Lord is invalid.

The fifth apparent coincidence is summarised in Lord Mersey's comment that 'at 2.40 Mr Stone called to the master that the ship from which he had seen the rockets had disappeared. At 2.20 a.m. the *Titanic* had foundered'.

When the time of 2.20 a.m. at which the *Titanic* is known to have gone down is adjusted to *Californian* time it becomes 2.10 a.m. Stone was most emphatic in his evidence at the British inquiry that the sternlight of the ship he was watching was still in sight up to at least ten minutes later. He described the going out of sight of that vessel as 'a gradual disappearing of all her lights, which would be perfectly natural with a ship steaming away', the sternlight itself 'gradually fading as if the steamer was steaming away'. What a striking contrast Stone's description makes with the following eye-witness account of the *Titanic*'s end, given by Lawrence Beesley, a surviving passenger: '[The *Titanic*'s] lights, which had shone without a flicker all night, went out suddenly, came on again for a single flash, then went out altogether'.

If the ship Stone was watching was still in sight – and consequently afloat – up to ten minutes after the *Titanic* sank, then she was not the *Titanic*. In Stone's own words: 'At two o'clock [the other ship] was disappearing in the south-west ... I could still see her sternlight. I saw this light for twenty minutes after that [and did not make any report to Captain Lord] until about twenty minutes after that again.'

Turning to the related elements of space and time in the apparent coincidences held against the *Californian*, Lord Mersey dismissed the navigational evidence recorded in her official log book. He joined with the Attorney-General in obliquely indicating an impression that the entries were false, but shrank from pressing this point to its logical conclusion. If Captain Lord and Stewart were indeed guilty of falsifying entries in what was a legal document, normally accepted in a court of law as allowable evidence, then it was Lord Mersey's clear duty to pass on that information to the appropriate authority for punitive action. He did not do so, but simply rejected the evidence contained in the log book, despite its being unanimously confirmed by Captain Lord and his three officers and based on good astronomical sights taken under perfect conditions. Lord Mersey also rejected the obvious implication of the fact that, on the basis of that navigation, the *Californian* was successfully taken from the position in which she had been stopped all night to the reported position of the *Titanic*'s sinking; from there, a position marked by the *Mount Temple*, to where the *Carpathia* lay; and thence, despite fog and strong winds encountered on the way, to Boston.

But Lord Mersey refused to accept that navigational evidence. If his judgement were correct, and the *Californian* in fact lying stopped within ten miles of the *Titanic* up to the time she went down and of her lifeboats thereafter, then there are certain inescapable conclusions which follow, as illustrated in the accompanying sketch (page 176) which shows the general features of the locality in which the disaster occurred. The most prominent of these is the broad belt of field ice, approximately six to eight miles wide, lying north and south in the vicinity of longitude 50° West.

Position A indicates the approximate position of a group of three icebergs. This distinctive trio was sighted five miles to the southward of the *Californian* at 6.30 p.m. on 14 April when she was in a position estimated by dead reckoning to be 42° 3′ N., 49° 9′ W. This information was broadcast by wireless at 7.30 to the *Antillian*, the message also being received and acknowledged by the *Titanic*. There is no reason to doubt that the *Californian* was reporting the same three icebergs also referred to in a wireless message sent out earlier in the day by the *Parisian* in an estimated position within four miles of the *Californian*'s.

Consequently the fact emerges that the *Californian*, with no foreknowledge of the searching investigation into her movement which was to follow, was publicly stating that at about 7 p.m. she was to the northward of latitude 42° N., a claim substantiated by the *Parisian*'s message. At 7.30 under perfect conditions, the *Californian*'s chief officer took a latitude by the Pole Star which established her as being in 42° 5′ N.

The *Californian* maintained a due westerly course, Captain Lord taking over on the bridge at 8.10. He remained there until the ice which he was expecting was encountered at 10.21, when he stopped his ship in a position which he estimated by dead reckoning was 42° 5′ N., 50° 7′ W. (Position B).

Lord Mersey accepted the position of the *Titanic*'s collision, based on Boxhall's calculations, as 41° 46′ N., 50° 14′ W. (Position C). The ship seen to stop at 11.40 from the *Californian* bore south-east (true). Had that ship been the *Titanic*, then the *Californian* must have been on a reciprocal bearing ten miles to the north-west of the position accepted by Lord Mersey (Position D). To have reached this position from the vicinity of the group of three icebergs encountered at 6.30 p.m. it would have been necessary for the *Californian* to have steered in error at least ten degrees to port of her anticipated course; to have averaged a speed of at least 14.7 knots, over three knots in excess of the speed at which she was cruising; and to have passed completely through the icefield which ran north and south across her track.

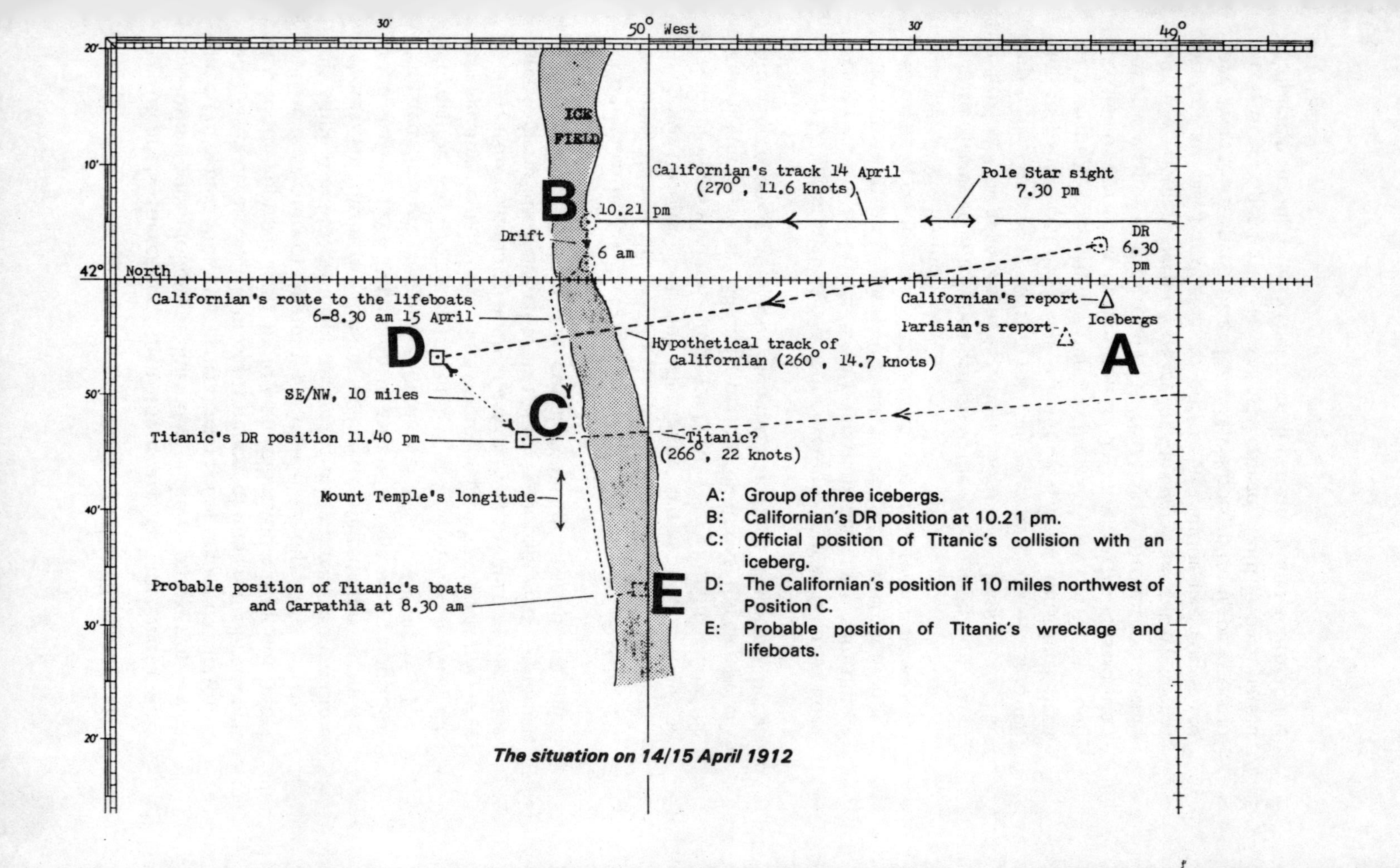

The situation on 14/15 April 1912

It is most unlikely that any one of those hypothetical errors could have passed unnoticed, and inconceivable that a combination of all three could have occurred.

The *Californian* steamed nearly thirty miles between 6 and 8.30 a.m. on 15 April, for half-an-hour at slow speed pushing through ice, and for the next two hours at her full speed of thirteen knots. Gill's mates in the stokehold, shovelling into the furnaces the extra coal required to produce that speed, would have been able to confirm the distance run had there ever been any real doubt about it. In any event there was readily available the positive and irrevocable evidence provided by the revolution counter incorporated in the main engines. If the *Californian* had been required only to cover a mere ten miles, as Lord Mersey subsequently decreed, then Gill certainly, and Groves most probably, would have been the first to draw attention to the discrepancy between that relatively short distance and the thirty miles actually claimed by Captain Lord.

Coldly and logically examined, none of the evidence given before the two inquiries is sufficient to support the conclusions which might otherwise be drawn from the apparent coincidences upon which Lord Mersey relied to justify his finding that upon Captain Lord rested entire responsibility for the tragic loss of life in the *Titanic* disaster. Captain Lord's own succinct and common sense analysis of the reasons why the ship seen from the *Titanic* could not have been the *Californian* has already been quoted. Here is another purely practical point proving that the *Titanic* could not have been the ship seen from the *Californian*.

At 10.55 p.m. on 14 April, Captain Lord casually sighted the lights of another ship, approaching obliquely from the south and west. He was then standing on the main deck of the *Californian*, less than thirty feet above sea level. To be visible to him, that ship must have been no more than five or six miles away, as shown in the accompanying illustration. There is no possible doubt as to the existence of that ship at that time. Captain Lord drew her to the attention of the chief engineer and the wireless operator, and because she was so obviously *not* the *Titanic*, the only other ship then apparently within wireless range, he instructed Evans to tell the *Titanic* that the *Californian* was stopped in ice. Evans duly tried to send that message at 11 p.m., but it was rejected by the *Titanic*'s operator because it interfered with his commercial traffic with Cape Race. At that time, the *Titanic* still had at least eleven miles to run at

Hypothetical situation at 10.55 pm, 14 April 1912

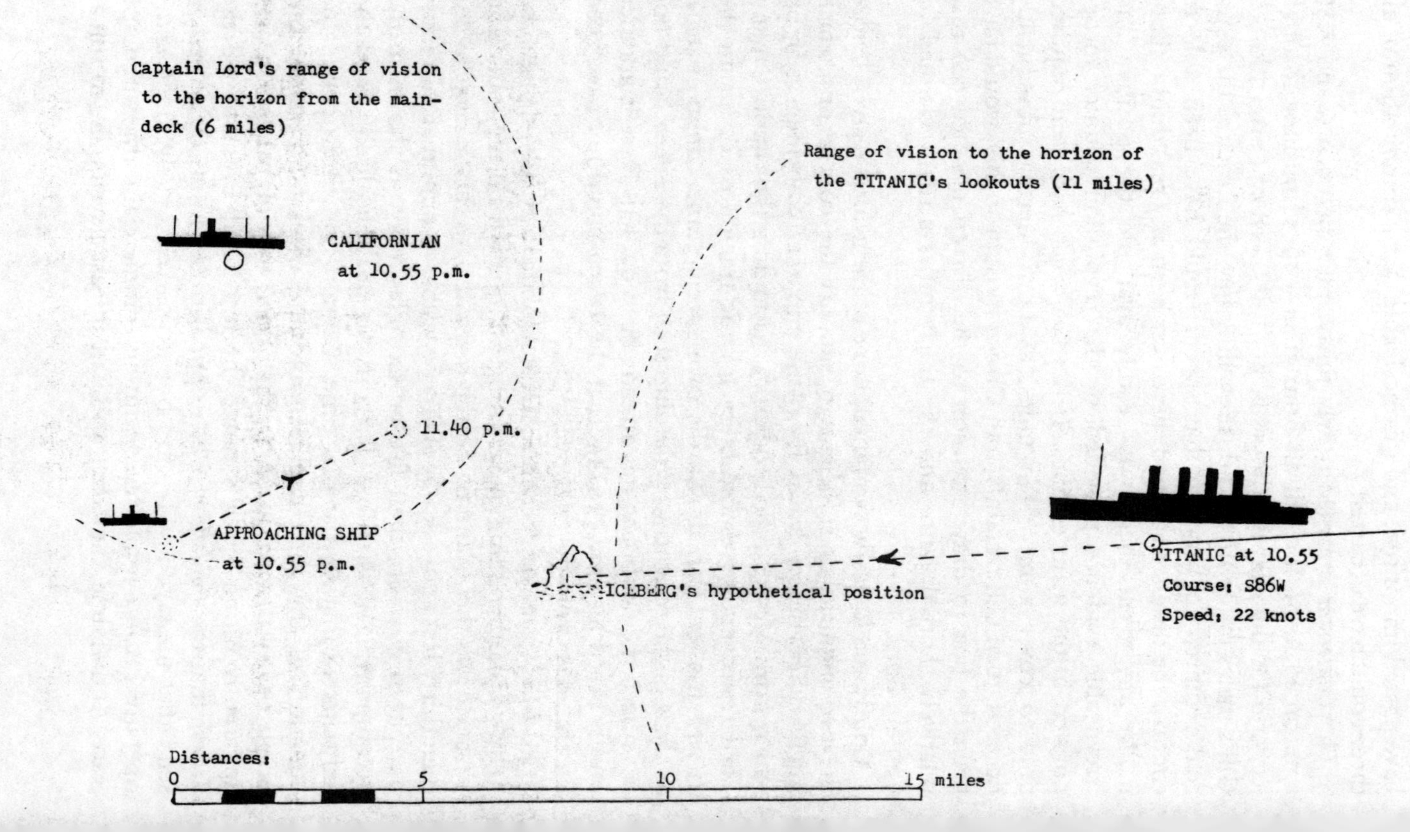

over 22 knots on almost a due westerly course before her collision with the iceberg. If that iceberg had been within eight to ten miles of the *Californian*, as Lord Mersey was later to claim, then the *Titanic* herself at 11 p.m. must have been at least eighteen miles away, out of sight over the horizon, at a time when another ship could clearly be seen from the *Californian* no more than six miles away. That ship could never have been the *Titanic* and if she were not, then Lord Mersey's main 'finding of fact' against the *Californian* was completely wrong.

Above all, however, there is in Captain Lord's favour the single incontestable fact that at 1 a.m. on 15 April Captain Smith of the *Titanic* gave the order for two inadequately manned lifeboats to be rowed to an approaching ship; for her passengers to be transferred to her; and for the two boats then to return to the *Titanic*. The potential closest approach of a ship motivating Captain Smith to consider giving such an order – an order accepted without question by those to whom it was issued – must have been measurable in yards rather than miles. How could such a ship have been the *Californian*, lying motionless and – as Lord Mersey later asserted – as much as eight to ten miles away?

CHAPTER SIXTEEN

Sighting Shots

Satisfied that the case for the *Californian* was valid, the MMSA Council on 22 July 1958 formally approved action to defend Captain Lord's professional reputation.

The campaign opened on three fronts. Of primary concern was the film *A Night to Remember*, then being widely shown and receiving critical acclaim. Then came the book, by now a best-seller, on which the film was based. In the background loomed the Ministry of Transport & Civil Aviation, carrying residual responsibility for the official mishandling of Captain Lord's case in 1912 and 1913, who still had the power to order a re-hearing of that part of the original inquiry which had censured him.

Immediately effective action to counter the adverse publicity created by the film was crippled, however, by none other than Captain Lord himself. Because of the relatively poor state of his health and his age, he declared himself adamantly opposed to personal involvement in any legal proceedings, nor would he approve of steps being taken which might have the effect of attracting unwelcome publicity to himself. In consequence, it was of academic interest only to consider the potentially very interesting possibilities of taking out an injunction against the Rank Organisation, producers of the film, to prevent its further screening, or of initiating a libel action on Captain Lord's behalf against the author and publishers of the book. Such steps had been immediately suggested by Herbert M. Allen, senior partner in the firm of Whitley & Company, of Liverpool, for many years the MMSA's legal advisers, to whom the case had been referred.

A less formal approach was made to the Rank Organisation, however. In a preliminary letter, concern was expressed on behalf of Captain Lord at the way the *Californian* incident was apparently covered in the film, and at the failure of the author of the book to get in touch with him before writing it. Unfortunately, it had to be emphasised in the letter that, as Captain Lord was now over eighty years of age, no risks had to be run likely to cause him serious concern or to place too great a strain on his health.

The film itself proved to be impressive both for its technical quality and, surprisingly, for the relatively restrained way in which the *Californian* incident was handled. Factually, so far as Captain Lord was concerned, it could be faulted only on the way in which it showed him asleep in his bunk, a blanket pulled up to his chin, instead of lying fully dressed on an inadequate chartroom settee.

On the crucial issue as to whether or not the *Californian* could have been the ship seen from the *Titanic*, there was one very puzzling point. After over half an hour had been spent vainly trying to summon help from distance ships by the then relatively unproved means of wireless, the actor playing the part of Captain Smith was shown as making a very remarkable discovery. After passing an almost casual comment to his wireless operator in reference to a ship whose lights can be clearly seen 'about ten miles away' ('Isn't she replying?'), he suddenly remembers the quite elementary fact that the *Titanic* carries distress signals expressly intended to attract the attention of nearby ships, which in those days were very likely not to be fitted with wireless. He immediately orders those signals to be used.

This incident poses a simple but essential question. If another stationary ship, such as the *Californian*, had actually been in sight of the *Titanic* only ten miles away, ever since the crippling impact with the iceberg, why was it that not one of the liner's very experienced and highly qualified officers – or, come to that, any other intelligent person among the 2,000 or more passengers and crew – thought to urge upon the captain the use of those visual distress signals a long, long time before he himself thought of it? The only reasonable – and obvious – answer to that question is that there was no such ship, nor was one in sight before about 12.30 a.m. This is the only logical explanation of why a ship apparently invisible at 11.40 p.m. should suddenly spring clearly into sight at 12.30 a.m. She was then steaming towards the sinking and immobilised *Titanic*, just as Joseph Boxhall, the liner's fourth officer, clearly described at the 1912 inquiries. If she was under way, then she was not the *Californian*, whose alleged fault was that she lay stopped all night.

At this point, it is appropriate to refer to another vital factor confirming that the ship seen from the *Titanic*, the sighting of which led to the firing of detonators, was under way and in view for only a relatively short period of time. Lord Mersey's report established that the *Titanic* carried '36 socket signals in lieu of guns'. Only about eight of these detonators were actually fired. Common sense decrees that *all* of these signals would have been used if the ship whose attention the *Titanic* was trying to attract had remained in sight, as a stationary *Californian* would have done. But common sense appears to have played little part in the proceedings and final reports of both the British and United States inquiries insofar as they affected the *Californian*.

The Rank Organisation's reaction to the pointing out of such a technical point was predictable. They obviously knew that they had nothing to fear by way of legal action from an eighty-year-old in poor health, so that they could simply claim, as they did, that the film was based on the book, which in turn was based on the findings of the official 1912 inquiry.

Quite correctly, they were also able to point out that, before the film was made, appeals had been widely published in the national press for survivors or any others who had authentic information about the disaster to come forward. It was 'a pity', they commented, that those appeals had not come to the attention of Captain Lord. It was indeed a pity.

Correspondence with the solicitors acting for the author and publishers of *A Night to Remember* was slightly more productive. One passage in the book attributed to Captain Lord the specific statement in respect of the ship they were watching from the *Californian*: 'That will be the *Titanic* on her maiden voyage.' The source of such a damaging and quite erroneous statement lies in an obvious typographical error in the official verbatim transcript of the proceedings of the British inquiry – an error typical of the misfortunes which dogged Captain Lord through the whole affair. The official record has this account of a question put to Groves by Lord Mersey, arising out of the third officer's reference to a remark he claimed to have made to Captain Lord:

> 8215. What did he say to that; did he say anything? – When I remarked about the passenger steamer near us is the 'Titanic.' "

The two sets of inverted commas which end that passage clearly indicate a line of type has inadvertently been omitted from the transcript. This is confirmed by contemporary press reports, which record Groves' actual reply as: 'When I remarked about the passenger *steamer's lights, he said: "The only passenger* steamer near us is the "Titanic".'

A second inaccurate reference to Captain Lord, which possibly explains why he was shown as lying in his bunk in the film, described him as having 'pulled on some clothes' when called by the chief officer in the morning. In fact, he had remained fully dressed all night.

Later in the book he was said to have been 'uneasily' examining the *Carpathia*'s flag half-masted for death, the obvious innuendo being that he must have felt a sense of guilt for the lives that had been lost. This was a reference deeply wounding in its baseless reflection on Captain Lord's character.

These three factual errors were put to the publishers' solicitors, Rubinstein Nash & Company (now Rubinstein Callingham). After an exchange of views, an offer was received from them that, 'out of compassion' for Captain Lord, the passages might be amended in future editions of the book. In accepting the offer, it was emphatically pointed out that Captain Lord wanted no compassion but simply the correction of what were manifestly inaccurate statements.

As in the case of the Rank Organisation, attempts to raise basic practical and technical issues failed. The inquiry findings were quoted as providing a final and authoritative basis for any critical references to Captain Lord and his alleged culpability.

There was a quite unexpected development arising out of that correspondence, however, when an unusual ally surprisingly revealed himself. The solicitor handling the correspondence concluded one of his letters with these words: 'Having read the documents, the writer would like to express his personal appreciation of the motives that have actuated you in seeking to rehabilitate Captain Lord's reputation'.

'The writer' was Harold F. Rubinstein, a distinguished figure in artistic and literary circles in London. Our subsequent correspondence became quite informal, although neither of us found any real difficulty in keeping the personal and professional aspects of our lives completely separate. This curious relationship survived some difficult moments, not least when individual publishers of new editions of *A Night to Remember* omitted to carry out the changes which it had earlier been agreed would be made to the first edition of the book.

A personal letter from Harold Rubinstein came to me after the first broadcast of a BBC sound radio feature, *The Other Ship*:

> You will undoubtedly regard me as the Devil's Advocate, but I must stick my neck out and congratulate you on the most impressive vindication of Captain Lord broadcast last night, which must have come as an eye-opener to many besides myself. What a fine man he must have been.

Support such as this, coming above all from the solicitor responsible for the protection of the interests of the author and publishers of the book which had done so much harm to Captain Lord was most encouraging. Subsequently I was greatly to regret the fact that tentative arrangements made from time to time for us to meet proved unsuccessful, for when Harold Rubinstein died in 1974 I learned for the first time from obituary notices how individualistic and intriguing a character he must have been.

Far less amenable adversaries confronted us in the Marine Division of the Ministry of Transport & Civil Aviation, the lineal heirs of the Marine Department of the Board of Trade of 1912. With Captain Lord's approval, a formal approach was made to the Ministry, asking for their official help in combating these new attacks on his professional reputation. They were also asked whether or not they would be prepared to examine the practical points supporting Captain Lord's claim that the *Californian* must have been at least twenty miles from the *Titanic*; what would be the Minister's probable reply to a formal request from a re-hearing of the 1912 inquiry; and whether or not they would be prepared, without prejudice, to permit a technical observer from the Ministry to attend any discussions which might be arranged between the MMSA and the author and publishers of *A Night to Remember*.

Initially, it is true, the Ministry proved helpful; over a lengthy period they enabled us to complete the file of correspondence exchanged between Captain Lord and the MMSA and the Board of Trade in 1912 and 1913, for the MMSA's own records of that period had disappeared during the intervening years. Continuity had not been helped by the MMSA's forced evacuation from its long-established head office in Tower Building, Liverpool, following bomb damage during the Second World War.

A very full and frank discussion was also held with Sir Gilmour Jenkins, Permanent Secretary, and D.C. Haselgrove, the Assistant Secretary responsible for the Marine Division. They could only confirm, however, that officially unless 'new and important evidence' could be brought forward, the original inquiry could not be re-opened.

By a sad coincidence, I had to report the Ministry's final decision to Captain Lord on his 81st birthday. He found the official attitude incomprehensible. To him, the basic facts of the case were so elementary.

'*Californian* stopped,' he would repeat time and again. '*Californian* stopped, nothing in sight. An hour later, the *Titanic* hit the berg, nothing in sight. Half an hour later, they saw a ship approaching. How the devil could that ship be the *Californian*, when all the evidence proved she never moved?'

All we could do to help Captain Lord was to follow up any published accounts of the *Titanic* disaster which appeared to ignore the incontrovertible facts in the *Californian*'s favour, and approach any authors known to be writing books in which there might be references to Captain Lord and his ship. Otherwise his case was necessarily at a standstill: looking towards the future, however, it was clear that sadly, but inevitably, his life was approaching its end. The MMSA's endeavours would presumably continue to be directed towards securing a reversal of the 1912 inquiry findings, particularly if 'new and important evidence' came to light. Such action would involve court proceedings; if Captain Lord himself were no longer there to participate in them, all his original papers would still be on hand, and early in 1959 Herbert Allen suggested that Captain Lord should swear an affidavit, giving his story as he recalled it, and annexing to it the more important of the contemporary documents he had retained. In this way, his evidence would be recorded in a form in which it could play a practical part if ever the inquiry were to be re-opened.

Captain Lord accepted the suggestion, and we started to draft his statement. Inevitably I had to do most of the work, for his eyes were giving him increasing trouble as cataracts developed and hampered his ability to read. By now he could only do so with the aid of a large magnifying glass, his 'telescope' as he wryly called it. I visited him frequently for sessions during which he did his best to remember what had happened in 1912 and 1913.

The necessity for completing the affidavit as soon as possible became ever more evident as the days passed, for Captain Lord's health was giving him increasing cause for concern. After a brief spell in hospital for an internal examination, he suddenly expressed his extreme reluctance to sign any document requiring the presence of a solicitor, maintaining that he preferred a simple form of statement that he could sign without formality. This problem was still unresolved when there was a most disturbing development.

In the May issue of the *Nautical Magazine* an account was published of an address by Commander Joseph G. Boxhall, the *Titanic*'s ex-fourth officer, in which he was reported as having said:

> The ship on the *Titanic*'s port side was now clearly visible, with portholes brightly shining, and contrary to the master's later given evidence was still moving slowly. And when this ship, the *Californian*, arrived in port, the master decided not to make any report on the night's happenings, and if it had not been for a donkeyman who left her upon arrival, it is doubtful if she would ever have been identified.

Boxhall's specific allegation that Captain Lord had committed perjury at the 1912 inquiries was clearly defamatory. It had to be contradicted immediately, for it was inaccurate and damaging statements such as this, made with all the authority of a technically qualified person who had actually been closely involved in the disaster, which was doing so much to foster the *Californian* legend.

I had to break the news to Captain Lord. I also had to ask him if he would permit me to approach the editor of the *Nautical Magazine* and to point out to him the defamatory nature of the report.

On the strict understanding that no threat of legal action were to be made, Captain Lord approved the suggested approach. Fortunately, following a brief exchange of letters and a timely telephone conversation, the editor undertook to publish a generously worded correction and an apology unreservedly withdrawing any 'unfounded reflections' on Captain Lord's character.

Towards the end of May, Captain Lord finally agreed to complete his statement in the form of an affidavit, but it was not until 23 June that the last of his many afterthoughts and amendments was received and it became possible for Allen to have a final copy prepared. Two days later, the two of us called on Captain Lord, and, to my infinite relief, the document and its accompanying papers were formally attested.

At long last, Captain Lord's personal account of events was on record in a legally acceptable form, and for the moment we could relax.

CHAPTER SEVENTEEN

The Closing Years

'Well, young man, have you forgotten the *Californian*?'

From time to time, Captain Lord's distinctive voice on the telephone would remind me of the MMSA's duty to maintain our efforts to protect his reputation. In 1960, it seemed that he was a little less concerned about the possible consequences should it become more widely known that he was still alive. In fact, on 16 March he agreed to be interviewed by Harry Milsom, an ex-radio officer who had become a staff reporter on the Liverpool *Journal of Commerce*. The meeting was a confidential one, arranged so that there would be at least one completely independent witness as to Captain Lord's character and personality at the time of the signing of the affidavit. Later Milsom expressed himself as being greatly impressed by Captain Lord's evident integrity and objectivity. In general, however, it seemed advisable to maintain a protective screen around Captain Lord for as long as possible, the more so as his heart was causing some concern and early in 1960 he was seen by a specialist.

I reported any developments in the case to Captain Lord at his home in Wallasey, generally in an evening. There, sitting at a large table in a dark, heavily furnished dining-room, with a grandfather clock tunefully chiming off the quarter-hours behind me, I used to enjoy the company of a charming octogenarian whose fluency and remarkable memory belied his years.

Captain Lord had a distinctive voice style, a measured, courteous delivery with a resonant clarity I had become so used to over the telephone. At first his accent had completely misled me; it seemed to have a 'burr' indicating a West Country origin, so that it came as a surprise to me to learn that in fact he was a Lancastrian from Bolton.

Certain words he pronounced in a manner uniquely his own. 'Californian' became '*Carl*-ifornian'; 'Titanic' was 'TITT-annic', instead of the more usual 'Tie-tannic'; the 'berg' of iceberg sounded as 'burrg'; and 'Latta' came out as 'Larter'.

He was always studiedly polite in his conversation, and one of my ineradicable memories of him, happily preserved in one of the two long conversations I recorded on tape, is of an occasion when, following some slight confusion which left us both speaking at once, he yielded graciously to me by inclining his head and saying: 'Proceed'.

One question I put to him was: what facts would he put to critics to convince them that the *Californian* was not to blame?

Captain Lord's response illustrates both his fluency in conversation and his approach to the basic problem:

'Well, there are two things I've always stressed. The *Californian* stopped in the ice at 10.20 and her engines never moved. The *Titanic* came up, stopped. There was nothing in sight when she hit the berg. Nothing, by two lookout men and two expert officers on the bridge. They saw nothing. Now how could it possibly have been the *Californian* that they saw? *Californian* never moved. This steamer approached them. You don't want any techncial adviser to point it out – it's all bunk, isn't it? Those two things would prove to me – and prove to any nautical examiner – that the *Californian* couldn't have been the ship. They proved that she never moved after 10.20, and they proved that the *Titanic* never saw anything after she hit the berg until the steamer they saw steamed towards them. Dammit, that clears everything, doesn't it? Clears everything.

'And if Mersey and his advisers – I don't think he wanted any advisers, anyhow; he advised himself – if they'd only looked at those questions ...

'They wanted a goat, that was my opinion. That's what Strachan said: "They wanted a bloody goat, Lord, and they got you!"

'I do not understand where men like Mersey and Isaacs – they were not nautical men, but they had nautical advisers – they'd four men on that bench with them, all naval men, I think, unfortunately ...

'All the trouble is, why did the captain of the *Californian* not come on deck and look at those lights? For the simple reason a responsible officer was on the bridge, who told me they were *not* distress rockets. And he was asked: were they company's signals, which would lead him to know what I was thinking, and if he'd been in any doubt he would have called me. But he was not in any doubt. He was quite satisfied they were not distress signals. He heard no distress signals, which he would have done if they were seven to ten miles off, as Mersey said – the explosion leaving the deck and the explosion up in the air, he would have heard them. Never a mention of them. And he was a quiet young follow, and he wouldn't tell me lies, I'm quite sure of that. And he wouldn't exaggerate. The other fellow might, but he wouldn't.

'A responsible officer was on the bridge, and if he'd thought there was any danger or risk, or any other ship in trouble, he could quite easily have got me out by coming down and, as he said: "I'd have *pulled* you out if there'd been any trouble". That was his words. I said: "Did you think there was any distress rockets about?" He said: "If there had been I would have *pulled* you out". The very words he used.

'Gibson you've never heard of since. I don't know what became of him. Nice boy, he called me all right. I'm not denying that. He called me, and I told him: "All right, tell the second officer to let me know if he wants anything", or something like that, and dozed off again. A damn cold night and I was in a steam-heated room fully dressed – no wonder I went to sleep.

'No, I think I've had a dirty deal. It all turned out, as it happened, very well, but there's always this stigma – was Lord to blame, or was he not to blame?'

A very much briefer but equally revealing conversation took place between us in 1959 during our joint work on the affidavit. A complete draft had just about been pieced together when, on the evening of Saturday, 4 April, Captain Lord greeted me with what was almost an off-hand enquiry.

'Will this be of any use to you?'

'This' turned out to be a typed aide-memoire dated 21 May 1912. It contained all the *Californian*'s basic log book entries for the night of 14/15 April 1912 with amplifying notes, and as such it was invaluable, providing as it did a unique check on the work we had been doing so laboriously together. On examination, it also proved how reliable Captain Lord's recollection of events had been.

I restrained my natural emotions, however: past experience as General Secretary of the MMSA warned me that I must be prepared to meet any future criticism of our jointly prepared narrative and its sources. I had to be absolutely sure of my facts.

'Who typed this?' I asked, perhaps a little too casually, for Captain Lord drew himself up. There was an awkward pause, then ...

'I did,' he replied frigidly. 'I typed it on my Corona portable. I gave that typewriter to Bertram Samuel Day, one of my chief officers in the *Anglo Chilean* when he was promoted to command in Lawther Latta's. I bought another similar machine, which is upstairs now. Do you wish to see it?'

I courteously declined the offer. Captain Lord's immediate reaction to my enquiry provided perhaps the most striking example in my experience of his mental acuity and phenomenal memory. Never again did I directly challenge him as to the accuracy of any statement he might make.

The year 1961 proved to be a very difficult one for Captain Lord from the point of view of his health. In March, he underwent an operation for cataract which restored the sight of his right eye, but he developed pneumonia and his stay in hospital was protracted. In June, he had to have an emergency operation for a strangulated hernia, and when I next saw him I was shocked to observe how frail he had become. My call on that occasion was made at his special request, when I accepted from him for safe keeping the affidavit of 1959 and all his original papers relating to the *Californian* incident, together with others bearing on his career at sea.

We also discussed a very tentative suggestion that I should write a book about his case, the first part of which would be his own story, so far as possible as he might have told it, the second part being an account of what the MMSA had attempted to do after he had come to see me in 1958. I mentioned the impending fiftieth anniversary of the *Titanic* disaster.

'Well, it will be interesting to see if I'm still here in April,' he reflected. 'I'm sometimes feeling very down and dozey.'

'I shall miss you very much if you're not,' was my inadequate reply. 'But you can rest assured that I'll keep plugging away at the case.'

On my next visit, a fortnight later, I was accompanied by my father, Ernest Harrison, who happened to be staying with me. Both he and Captain Lord obviously enjoyed their meeting, during which they were amused to discover that they had one thing in common. Each had encountered, however briefly, C. Robertson Dunlop, KC, the man who had appeared at the 1912 inquiry as counsel for the Leyland Line. About that time, my father was in the Customs service in Grimsby, a flourishing fishing port in which, as official Receiver of Wrecks, he was inevitably kept very busy. In that capacity, he was called as a witness in a case heard in the Admiralty court, where he was cross-examined by Dunlop. In one of his replies, my father described a certain incident as having been unique in his experience. He was under thirty years of age and looked considerably younger. Understandably Dunlop concluded that he could score an easy point.

'Perhaps you would be kind enough to tell the court just how extensive that experience might be,' he requested in a patronising manner.

My father obliged, and when he had come to the end of what had been a quite detailed account the presiding judge beamed paternally on him.

'A very proper answer, Mr Harrison,' he observed. 'Pray continue, Mr Dunlop.'

Within a few weeks of that meeting with Captain Lord, my father died. Clearing up his papers, I came across another curious link with the events of 1912, in the form of printed details of 'Harrison's Marine Liferooms'. Patented in June 1913, these were to be selected public rooms in passenger liners, constructed as quite independent miniature ships, separately equipped and ballasted. In an emergency, they would be launched through otherwise watertight 'gangway doors'. It was claimed that had these liferooms been fitted in the *Titanic* they would have enabled every life to be saved.

As a master mariner, I could appreciate the impracticability of such an invention. Quite apart from the engineering problems involved, there was the physical risk to its occupants as a 'liferoom' was precipitated into the sea. Nevertheless encouraging comments had been received from shipping companies such as the White Star and Hamburg Amerika lines, and from individuals such as Sir Archibald Denny, shipbuilder, and John Stead, editor of *The Review of Reviews*, whose father, William T. Stead, the previous editor of that publication, had lost his life in the *Titanic*.

As I read those papers, I began to appreciate for the very first time the significance of what had been one of my first childhood toys. This was a wooden box, fitted with hinged flaps on opposing sides, down which a little rectangular ship on wheels could be induced to trundle. It was obviously the prototype model of 'Harrison's Marine Liferooms', and if nothing else the incident illustrated just how far reaching in its emotional impact the *Titanic* disaster had been.

Family commitments following my father's death and my heavy responsibilities as General Secretary of the MMSA combined to reduce the number of occasions on which I was able to call on Captain Lord in the autumn and winter of 1961. In any event, I had now become involved in a chain of circumstances which rendered it quite impossible for me to report regularly to him, for a very determined effort was being made within the Executive Council of the MMSA to withdraw the association's support from Captain Lord.

While the MMSA had had some success in influencing authors to modify their critical references to Captain Lord and the *Californian*, one who had slipped through the net was Captain Sir James Bisset. In April 1912 he had been serving as second officer of the *Carpathia* when she picked up the *Titanic*'s survivors, and his contemporary notes had been used in his autobiographical *Tramps and Ladies*, published early in 1960. In this book, the culpability of Captain Lord was taken for granted, and the *Californian* incident embellished with a wealth of imaginative detail. An Australian friend of Sir James, P.R. Stephensen, had helped him to write his book, which may have accounted for some of the more curious technical errors, but the total effect was seriously damaging to Captain Lord.

I had been warned of Sir James's anti-*Californian* attitude by Captain Sir Ivan Thompson, since 1942 one of the MMSA Council's most distinguished members. Sir Ivan was now 66, a man of forceful character accustomed to the unquestioning acceptance of his personal assessment of any particular situation. Knighted in 1955 for his services while in command of the great Cunard 'Queens', he had retired two years later, and now had time to play an increasingly prominent part in MMSA affairs.

In the same month that *Tramps and Ladies* was published in the United Kingdom, Sir Ivan wrote to me from Australia, which he was visiting while on a post-retirement cruise. He told me that he had called on Sir James Bisset while in Sydney and that they had discussed the *Californian* case, on which Sir James held decidedly critical views. Subsequently Sir Ivan made it very clear that he shared those views: indeed, on one occasion he bluntly told me that, in his opinion, the *Californian*'s watchkeepers were at fault in failing to warn the *Titanic* that she was running into an iceberg; that they had kept a defective 12-4 a.m. watch; and that all the lives that were lost could have been saved if only prompt and efficient action had been taken by Captain Lord.

Despite Sir James Bisset's personal attitude, his publishers responded most sympathetically to an approach made on behalf of Captain Lord, and gave an undertaking that no new edition of the

Leslie Harrison *(right)* with Arthur C. Notley, 1937

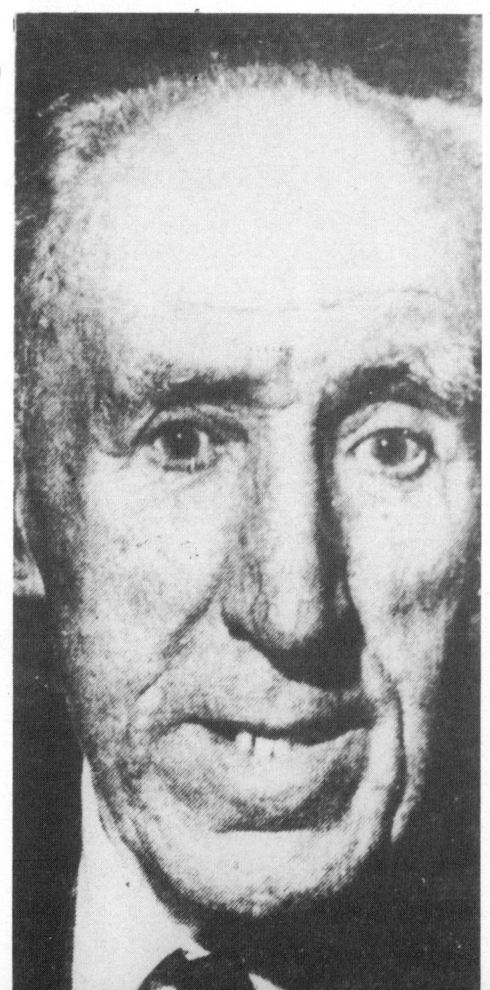

(Above) The *Anglo Chilean*, renamed *Heraclides* when sold to the Houston Line in 1930. She became Vichy-French property in 1939, and as the *Alcamo* under the Italian flag was bombed and sunk by Allied aircraft north-east of Bizerta in February 1943

(Right) Benjamin Kirk, 1969

book would be published without the MMSA's being given a prior opportunity to comment on the critical references to the *Californian*. The success of the MMSA in challenging old colleagues of Sir Ivan such as Commander Boxhall and Sir James Bisset placed him in an intolerable position when, in May 1961, he was elected President of the association. Matters came to a head when I asked for the Council's approval for the publication in the March 1962 issue of the *Merchant Navy Journal*, on the eve of the fiftieth anniversary of the *Titanic* disaster, of an article setting out all the facts in support of the case for Captain Lord and the *Californian*. The *Merchant Navy Journal* was a quarterly magazine, published jointly by the MMSA and the Merchant Navy & Airline Officers Association. Captain Lord had approved of my suggestion, subject to no personal references being made in it to him, and I was able to let him have a copy of the first draft on 13 January. Interestingly enough, this was a day or so after he had paid his 64th consecutive annual subscription as a member of the MMSA. I could tell him nothing of Sir Ivan's attitude, of course, fearing what the effect might be, nor was it possible for me to let him know that on 30 January there was to be a crucial meeting of the MMSA Council at which their future policy in relation to his case was to be decided.

On 25 January, I spent the afternoon visiting an MMSA member in hospital, where he was slowly recovering from severe injuries sustained in a collision in which his ship had been involved, and for whose representation at the subsequent formal investigation the MMSA was responsible. On my return to the office I was told that, in my absence, Captain Lord's son had telephoned to report that his father had died. He wished no public reference to be made to this sad event until after the funeral, which was to take place the day before the crucial Council meeting.

I attended the funeral, and subsequently, as General Secretary of the MMSA, issued this press notice:

> Captain Stanley Lord, who died on 24 January at the age of 84, gained unenviable notoriety in 1912 when the British court of inquiry which investigated the loss of the White Star liner *Titanic* found that his own ship, the Leyland liner *Californian*, was within ten miles of the scene of the disaster and could have saved many, if not all, of the 1,500 lives which were lost if only he had appreciated the nature of certain rocket signals which had been reported to him. Captain Lord always emphatically rejected these findings, although his sustained efforts to obtain a re-hearing of that part of the inquiry which related to him were

> unsuccessful. His closing years were overshadowed by a revival of public interest in the disaster, particularly the publicity afforded to the book *A Night to Remember* and the widely shown film of that name. Unhappily, Captain Lord's failing health handicapped him in his efforts to combat the effects of such adverse publicity, but he was able to co-operate in the preparation of a detailed article setting out considered reasons why the 1912 inquiry findings are open to the strongest criticism. It is hoped that this article, a draft of which he approved shortly before his death, will be published in mid-March, on the eve of the fiftieth anniversary of the *Titanic* disaster, and it is also hoped that a final judgement on a tragic event in the life of a most capable shipmaster and a man of absolute integrity will be postponed until that date.

At the Council meeting on 30 January, it was agreed that a final decision on Captain Lord's case should be deferred until the February meeting, by which time all members would have had time to consider the draft article. In the event, an overwhelming majority supported the proposition that there had been a miscarriage of justice in Captain Lord's case and that the article should be published.

Its publication was followed by Sir Ivan's resignation as President. He was succeeded by Captain C.P. Vaughan, who on 9 April 1962 was able to sign a press statement, issued in the name of the MMSA, drawing attention to the fact that, following the circulation of the article internationally, no attempt had been made by anyone to answer the detailed questions it posed, or to challenge the reasons given in support of the claim that there had been a gross miscarriage of justice in Captain Lord's case. The statement went on to ask that, on the occasion of the fiftieth anniversary of the *Titanic* disaster, a thought be spared for Captain Lord, who for fifty years had borne with patience and fortitude the burden of a monstrous charge against which he had not been able properly to defend himself, and of which in his heart he knew that he was innocent.

CHAPTER EIGHTEEN

The Battle Joined

As a feature linked with the fiftieth anniversary of the *Titanic* disaster, the Norwegian Television Authority revived a story claiming that a sealing vessel, the *Samson*, had seen the *Titanic*'s lights and distress signals, but had turned away from them. This report was based on statements made in later years by Captain Henrik Naess, who in 1912 was serving as chief officer of the *Samson* engaged on what he claimed were 'unlicensed' sealing operations.

An earlier reference to the *Samson* story had been published in the Trondhjem *Arbeideravisa* on 9 June 1928:

> Captain Naess comes from the town of Tromsø and started his Arctic career in 1877 under his foster-father, Captain Nils Johansen, Tromsø. Later, ever since 1913, he has for many years ploughed the Arctic Sea both as whaler and pilot. His name is known from a number of famous expeditions to the Arctic regions. In 1896 he acted as pilot and interpreter with Sir Baden Powell's expedition on the yacht *Otoria* for studies of the total solar eclipse in the Arctic. It was on the return trip from this expedition that *Otoria* in August of the same year took on board Fridtjof Nansen in Vardø after Nansen's and Hjalmar Johansen's famous voyage to Frans Josef Land. In 1912, Naess was engaged as harpoon gunner and mate on the well-known Arctic vessel *Samson*. It was during this expedition that he experienced an event which was far more eerie even than the many days and nights in the Arctic.
>
> 'We were engaged in sealing operations on prohibited territory,' Naess explains. 'One night while the skipper and I were sitting in his cabin, the helmsman reported lights ahead. This was about half-an-hour before midnight and the weather was clear. I ran up on deck. In fact, we did not feel quite safe from the Americans. On the horizon, a few miles to the west, we saw a faint light. "Use your telescope", I said to the helmsman. "I see lots of lights," answered the helmsman; we finally became aware that rockets were being fired, and this continued until half-an-hour after midnight. Then the light disappeared. About a month later our ship arrived at Iceland. There we were told that the great steamer *Titanic* had been lost after colliding with

> an iceberg about a month ago, which was exactly the night when we saw the lights out at sea. The hour and place corresponded precisely to our observations.'
>
> Visibly moved, Captain Naess explains how the report affected him and the others: 'Had we had the slightest idea of what was happening out there, or had our vessel been equipped with radio, we would probably have been able with our twelve dories to save most of the lives.'

If Naess' statement was accurate, and could be verified in a legally acceptable form, it seemed that the MMSA might be able to call on the Board of Trade to re-open the 1912 inquiry, invoking Section 475 (i) of the Merchant Shipping Act 1894:

> The Board of Trade may, in any case where under this part of the Act a formal investigation as aforesaid into a shipping casualty ... has been held, order the case to be re-heard either generally or as to any part thereof, and shall do so –
>
> (a) if new and important evidence which could not be produced at the inquiry has been discovered; or
>
> (b) if for any other reason there has in their opinion been ground for suspecting that a miscarriage of justice has occurred.

Enquiries in Norway revealed that in 1939 Captain Naess was engaged in writing his memoirs, in which he gave further details of the alleged *Titanic* incident. Through the kindness of his son, the section of the unpublished manuscript describing what his father recalled of the incident was made available to the MMSA.

Further research established that there was indeed a wooden barque of 506 tons named *Samson* in 1912, trading under the command of Captain Ring, as stated in the manuscript. She had an auxiliary steam engine, and most certainly visited the Icelandic port of Isafjordjur in May 1912, for as late as 1965 there were still inhabitants of that town who recalled the occasion: there had been what was described as 'a big riot between the crew of the *Samson* and the local men', the crew having bought up all the spirits they could get hold of and having to be returned to their ship by force. The *Samson* was later to have a more distinguished career when bought by the American polar explorer Commander Richard E. Byrd, who re-named her *City of New York*.

None of the evidence relating to the *Samson*'s alleged involvement in the *Titanic* disaster could be obtained in a legally admissible form, however, and so, for the time being, it had to be regarded as a tantalising glimpse of the possible solution of the riddle of the identity of the ship seen from the *Titanic*.

In the Norwegian television documentary, a rather different picture was painted of the reason why the *Samson* did not intervene. A report prepared by Naess in 1912 was said to contain the following passage:

> We feared that we might be taken for violating the territorial borders and the lights out there meant that there were Americans in the neighbourhood. When the lights went out, this probably meant that we had been observed, the rockets being, maybe, signals to other ships. We therefore changed course and hurried northwards.

If the *Samson* had indeed turned away, if unwittingly, from the *Titanic*, a vessel in distress, was it an incident unique in maritime history? In the April 1973 issue of *Sea Breezes*, Captain P. Walsh described a voyage he made in the 71-ton *Camborne*, built in 1948 as a herring carrier. She stranded off Mine Head, Co Waterford, and Captain Walsh recalled his unsuccessful attempt to attract attention:

> Climbing to the top of the wheelhouse, I scanned the horizon and saw not very far away the navigation lights of a vessel approaching us head on. She was not more than a mile away when I sent up two parachute distress rockets, lighting up the sky and the whole area around us, and giving us a boost of confidence after all our bad luck.
>
> I kept the vessel under close observation and had my glasses on him when I saw him make a complete turn around and head away out to sea in the opposite direction. Such an action in response to a distress signal is unheard of on any ocean; I was completely bewildered and disappointed and could only think that the vessel must have been a foreign trawler intent on some illegal fishing and had mistaken our distress signals for star shells fired by a fishery protection vessel. Hence his hasty departure.

If the *Samson* was the ship seen from the *Titanic*, what was the vessel seen from the *Californian*? All that can be deduced from the evidence given by the witnesses from the *Californian* is that she was of medium size, probably burning oil lamps (which might explain why she ignored Morse lamp signals) and was being navigated by officers well accustomed to handling their ship in the dark in ice. She was certainly not bound to the eastward, towards Europe, for otherwise she would have continued on her way after clearing the icefield and reaching open water.

Lawrence Beesley had a theory which he considered might have accounted for her signals:

> An engineer who has served in the trans-Atlantic service tells me that it is a common practice for small boats to leave the fishing smacks to which they belong and row away for miles; sometimes even being lost and wandering about among icebergs, and even not being found again. In these circumstances, rockets are part of a fishing smack's equipment, and are sent up to indicate to the small boats how to return.

The ship being watched from the *Californian* was to the southward of her, some seven miles closer to the *Titanic*. Is it possible that her watchkeepers saw the traces of the liner's distress signals, low down on the horizon but out of sight of Stone and Gibson, and decided to go down and investigate, notifying their intention – just as Rostron in the *Carpathia* was doing – by sending up rockets?

If so, where was she in the morning? Only Groves from the *Californian* and Captain Moore of the *Mount Temple* mentioned another unidentified steamer in the area where the wreckage was lying. She was described as a small steamer with a black funnel, having on it a white device. Although both the British and American governments originated attempts to identify that ship, they were not pressed; there was insufficient time to complete them before the United States and British inquiries opened, and afterwards the findings that the *Californian* was to blame were so positive that there was no reason for anyone formally to conclude such enquiries.

Today, over fifty years after the event, it is still not unreasonable to hope, and to believe, that somewhere there are records – old log books, voyage reports, diaries, contemporary letters – which could lead to a positive identification of the two mystery ships. After all, Captain Lord himself never considered that the original statements written for him by Stone and Gibson had any relevance to his case, and left them undisturbed for nearly fifty years after 1912 and 1913. Somewhere, possibly in a port on the eastern seaboard of the United States or Canada, evidence is available but lying undisturbed which could resolve what must otherwise remain a mystery.

Inconclusive as the *Samson* development might have been, it provided a stimulating boost to the MMSA's efforts in 1962 to sustain the interest created in the world press by the article published in the *Merchant Navy Journal*.

Much more positive were the consequences of an approach we received from an ex-Merchant Navy officer, Peter Padfield. Initially he sought advice from the MMSA in connection with a book he was writing about collisions at sea. Reading the transcript of the *Titanic* inquiry proceedings caused him to change course, however, and instead he began to write *The Titanic and the Californian*. He explained his reasons for doing so in the introduction to that book:

> I came to the transcript with an open mind and my purpose was merely to collect material for one, or at the most two chapters of a book about collisions at sea. This idea was soon shelved. The *Titanic* became all engrossing. Besides the remarkable drama of that unfinished maiden voyage – drama which comes more clearly through the old pages of the transcript than through most of the subsequent books about her – besides this there were the question marks, the unprobed basic facts, the crazy deductions, the distortions, the prejudice, the occasional bone-headed obstinacy of both witnesses and the court refusing to accept facts which are so obvious outside and fifty years away from the court room. The gaps in the evidence were tantalising; I began to suspect that however much historical detection work anyone put in, the whole truth of the *Titanic*'s one voyage would never be known.
>
> But more than this, my astonishment that Captain Lord was censured on the half-cock evidence I was reading grew with each day – and with it anger, not manufactured, literary anger, but the real blood-bubbling bile. This book was begun in anger.

So said Peter Padfield. Parallel with the help we were able to give him an increasingly acrimonious correspondence was being exchanged with the Ministry of Transport.

It began innocuously enough in May 1963, with the MMSA addressing a friendly enquiry to Ernest Marples, then Minister of Transport (and oddly enough also the Member of Parliament for Wallasey, Captain Lord's constituency, and the recipient of his vote at the previous election). The MMSA notified Marples that the association intended to make a formal submission on the late Captain Lord's behalf based not so much on new evidence but rather on his situation in 1912 when he had been prevented from producing evidence then available in his defence. The Minister was accordingly asked for an assurance that the MMSA's approach might be broadly based, and include evidence that not only could have been produced at the original inquiry, but in some cases actually was.

Replying on behalf of the Minister, Sir Thomas Padmore, the Permanent Secretary, told us that the submission could be made in any form we liked, but the Minister could not be expected in advance to restrict his freedom of judgement on what might be, or might not be, relevant to the issue of whether or not, after over fifty years, the original formal investigation should be re-opened.

After the MMSA Council had considered that reply, I was

authorised to ask Sir Thomas for a personal meeting, so that he could be fully informed of the MMSA's attitude to what the Council considered to be an extremely important case, and what they thought might be done to bring it to a successful conclusion.

Sir Thomas replied that he was already fully informed on the MMSA's attitude through reports he had received from his colleagues. His letter continued:

> Unless you have something new to say, which you have not previously stated in these interviews, I cannot but doubt whether a personal interview with me would serve any useful purpose. If in fact you wish to state something new, I should be grateful to have it in writing at any rate in the first instance.

In acknowledgment, I pointed out that it had been hoped that a personal meeting would provide a generally more convenient opportunity for me to explain to him why the MMSA Council, and indeed other members of the association, were beginning to form the opinion that the Minister was more zealous in invoking the penal clauses of the Merchant Shipping Acts against British shipmasters than he was in applying the more protective provisions in their defence, as we considered should be done in Captain Lord's case. At such a meeting, I would also have hoped to be able to stress our sincere desire to avert the possible development of any damaging public controversy over what we considered to be a very simple case. Finally, I enquired whether or not the Ministry's technical advisers might be authorised to meet me and to concede any practical or navigational points about which we might be in agreement. This would reduce the balance of such points, if any, on which the Minister might wish to receive more detailed written submissions.

The Ministry was unyielding, however, and in his reply Sir Thomas merely repeated what had been said in his earlier letters. He appeared to resent the statement about the Minister's attitude towards the penalising of shipmasters, however, commenting: 'You will hardly expect me to accept what you say in your first paragraph, either as to its substance or as to the language in which it is couched.'

Obviously the official Juggernaut of 1912 was still rolling, for the letter confirmed that no help was to be expected from the only government department having the power to rectify the miscarriage of justice of that year. The MMSA was accordingly left with no alternative but to concentrate on publishing the facts about Captain Lord and the *Californian* in the hope that eventually public opinion would be aroused and pressure brought to bear on the government through Parliament. After all, we reasoned, in theory a government department, through Parliament, is a servant of the people.

Throughout this period, correspondence was being maintained with the host of authors, journalists and editors who catered for the general public's insatiable interest in the *Titanic*. Some who were approached were prepared to take a fresh look at the facts of the case; others were not.

We did our best to maintain Parliamentary pressure on the Ministry of Transport, but found our representatives at Westminster to be curiously vulnerable. Two members who had given us most useful assistance lost their seats at a general election. Another – initially the most promising of our advocates, for he had himself served in the Merchant Navy – disappeared from view after telling us that he had arranged a special appointment at which he was to discuss Captain Lord's case with the Minister then responsible for shipping affairs. What happened at that interview we were never told officially: all we know is that subsequently the member of Parliament concerned failed to reply to eight letters from us, nor did he return a stamped addressed postcard we enclosed with our last letter for his convenience in acknowledging that it had actually reached him.

A distinguished member of the House of Lords with a legal background who initially expressed a very keen interest in the case also sank without trace. Our final letter to him was returned from his last known address in England marked simply: 'Gone abroad'.

By mid-1963 it was becoming clear that there was insufficient Parliamentary pressure and strength of public opinion to modify the Ministry's hostile attitude. Against the background of his extensive knowledge of shipping inquiries, our specialist legal adviser in London, supported by counsel's opinion, suggested that the MMSA should formally petition the Board of Trade to re-open the inquiry, on the basis that there had been a miscarriage of justice in 1912. The MMSA Council formally approved of such action at a meeting in September 1963.

By this time, Peter Padfield was making good progress with his book, and it seemed sensible for us so to arrange matters that the presentation of the petition and the publication of the book should coincide. This meant that there was no immediate pressure on the drafting of the petition, and in fact the necessary work did not begin until November 1964.

There was one rather curious development while the petition was being put together. The MMSA's legal adviser in London notified us that he had formed a very clear impression that any criticism of Lord Mersey would meet with 'strong opposition' in official quarters. For this reason, it was agreed that the emphasis in the petition should be slanted towards the world-wide stigma which, through Captain Lord and the *Californian*, rested on the British Merchant Navy as a whole.

The petition was produced as a self-contained booklet, in which relevant technical points were discussed in detail, particularly the timing of events. It also covered the personal opinions expressed by Groves and Gill; 'contradictions and inconsistencies'; and the evidence proving that four ships must have been involved, not just the *Titanic* and the *Californian*. The booklet also contained a comprehensive set of appendices, including all the supporting documents to which an interested reader might wish to refer, such as Lord Mersey's findings in relation to the *Californian*; a selection of critical references to Captain Lord taken from newspapers, magazines, films, and other sources; the correspondence with the Board of Trade in 1912 and 1913; and full extracts from evidence given at both the United States and British inquiries supporting the points made in Captain Lord's defence.

The petition was signed by Captain W.W.P. Lucas, President of the MMSA, and by Stanley T. Lord, Captain Lord's son, and its purpose was summed up in the following passage:

> The findings of both the British and United States inquiries in respect of the *Californian* were openly based on an acceptance of apparent coincidences and personal opinions which were not properly checked at the time. They led to Captain Lord being blamed for the loss of over 1,500 lives, yet he had become involved in the *Titanic* disaster quite unwittingly. He could have done no more to stop it than he did, which was to try to warn the liner by radio that there was ice ahead of her; and he could have done nothing afterwards to save the lives which were lost, for his ship was too far away to have reached the liner before she sank.
>
> It is not only British authors who use the findings of the 1912 inquiry to pillory Captain Lord in their often imaginative accounts of the *Titanic* disaster, and the MMSA accordingly calls on the Board of Trade to act now so that these findings can be officially amended and such authors deprived once and for all of the present basis for continued attacks on the conduct of a British shipmaster. The Merchant Shipping Acts were

> framed as much for the protection of seamen as for their regulation, and the death of Captain Lord has not removed the need for the righting of the wrong which was done to him in 1912. Indeed, the renewal of active interest in the *Titanic* disaster in recent years makes it even more essential that the truth about the *Californian* incident should be officially established.
>
> In 1912 the Board of Trade, a government department acting in the name of the people of Great Britain, condemned Captain Lord without affording him those rights of defence and appeal which are fundamental to the concepts of justice and liberty as normally applied in the United Kingdom. Today the Board of Trade, in the name of the people of Great Britain, has the power and, it is submitted, the moral duty to make amends by frankly admitting and expunging a past mistake.

The petition was formally presented to the Board of Trade on 5 February 1965, and they took seven months to consider it. In the meantime, Peter Padfield's book was published and met with a considerable success. Two impressions were printed in the United Kingdom and one in the United States, with further editions in Braille and large print. It was also published in a Book Club edition.

Padfield had been hampered when preparing his book by an unhelpful action on the part of the Ministry of Transport. In January 1964 they refused his request for access to the *Titanic* files and he completed his book without the assistance which reference to those files would have afforded him. Six months later, however, the files were released to the Public Record Office at the instance of a member of Parliament acting for another author not so well disposed towards Captain Lord as Padfield was.

Nevertheless publication of Padfield's book was a most promising and helpful development. For one thing, it led directly to Professor K.C. Barnaby dedicating his own book, *Some Ship Disasters and their Causes*, to 'two much maligned master mariners', one of whom was Captain Lord.

In his book, Padfield concluded that the British inquiry was rigged so as to saddle Captain Lord with responsibility for the heavy loss of life, and to divert attention from the Board of Trade themselves, whose inadequate regulations had allowed the *Titanic* to go to sea with lifeboats for only 1,178 people as against the 2,566 she could actually carry.

I could not share Padfield's opinion. For one thing, I am confident that had the Board of Trade actually decided to frame the inquiry and to condemn the *Californian*, then they would most certainly have set at least one technically qualified official on to the task of investigating the practical points involved. Such a concentrated study of the case must inevitably have revealed the obvious flaws in the superficial case against the *Californian* and brought to the Board's attention the fact that there must have been more than two ships involved. Those of the Board's files released to the Public Record Office reveal that, so far from there being a systematic attempt to frame Captain Lord, a very confused state of affairs appears to have existed. Captain Lord was condemned simply because of Lord Mersey's conviction, formed at a very early stage in the proceedings – a conviction shared by others in a position of authority who considered it unnecessary to look any further – that the *Californian* was the guilty ship. Thereafter, as one official actually minuted: 'The Board cannot well undertake to consider the matter after Lord Mersey has pronounced upon it.'

Lord Mersey had indeed pronounced upon it, with such tragic consequences for the unfortunate Captain Lord, and his influence was apparently still very much in evidence in September 1965, when Roy Mason, the then Minister of State (Shipping), rejected the petition. No reasons were given for the decision, nor was any attempt made to answer any of the practical points so carefully put forward.

Roy Mason also rejected the MMSA's request for a meeting with his technical advisers at which we could be advised of those reasons, commenting:

> We recognise that there was conflicting evidence on certain points but the thorough investigation which we have carried out, both from the legal and from the technical point of view, has satisfied us that there was evidence to justify the court coming to the conclusion that it reached. The Board consider that after all these years it would not be in the public interest to re-open this matter.

So, for the time being at least, the Board of Trade's interpretation of what was 'the public interest' had to prevail over Captain Lord's private interest.

CHAPTER NINETEEN

Lawrence Beesley

As Captain Lord's advocate, my job was to prove that he was never personally involved in what happened to the *Titanic*. As pointed out in the MMSA's petition, initially he could have done no more for her than he did, which was to try to warn her by wireless that she might be running into ice. After the collision, he was too far away to have been able to rescue anyone before she sank. Yet the more I looked into his case, the more I found myself becoming very interested in the details of what actually went on in the *Titanic* herself.

I naturally read every book I could trace in which there might be a reference to the *Californian*. Undoubtedly the most impressive was *The Loss of the s.s. 'Titanic' – Its Story and Its Lessons*, by Lawrence Beesley. In April 1912, he was a young science master, a passenger in the *Titanic*, on his way to the United States for a brief holiday. Invited to jump into a partly-filled lifeboat as it was about to be lowered, he did so. After being picked up by the *Carpathia*, he decided 'to prepare as accurate an account as possible ... The first impression is often the most permanent, and in a disaster of this magnitude, where exact and accurate information is so necessary, preparation of a report was essential'.

The notes he made and on which his book was based were 'written in odd corners of the deck and saloon of the *Carpathia*', and his book records some vivid visual impressions. Here is how he saw the *Titanic* from his lifeboat:

> We gazed broadside on the *Titanic* from a short distance ... The mere bulk alone of the ship viewed from the sea below was an awe-inspiring sight. Imagine a ship nearly a sixth of a mile long, 75 feet high to the top decks, with four enormous funnels above the decks, and masts again high above the funnels; with her hundreds of portholes, all her saloons and other rooms brilliant with light, and all round her little boats filled with those who until a few hours before had trod her decks ...

> I had often wanted to see her from some distance away, and only a few hours before, in conversation at lunch with a fellow-passenger, had registered a vow to get a proper view of her lines and dimensions when we landed at New York ... Little did I think that the opportunity was to be found so quickly and so dramatically. The background, too, was a different one from what I had planned for her: the black outline of her profile against the sky was bordered all round by stars studded in the sky, and all her funnels and masts were picked out in the same way: her bulk was seen where the stars were blotted out. And one other thing was different from expectation: the thing that ripped away from us instantly, as we saw it, all sense of beauty of the night, the beauty of the ship's lines, and the beauty of her lights – and all these taken in themselves were intensely beautiful – that thing was the awful angle made by the level of the sea with the rows of porthole lights along her side in dotted lines, row above row. The sea level and the rows of lights should have been parallel – should never have met – and now they met at an angle inside the black hull of the ship. There was nothing else to indicate she was injured; nothing but this apparent violation of a simple geometrical law – that parallel lines should 'never meet even if produced ever so far both ways'; but it meant the *Titanic* had sunk by the head until the lowest portholes in the bows were under the sea, and the portholes in the stern were lifted above the normal height.

How could the ship Beesley described so minutely have been the same ship which Stone and Gibson studied for over two hours, much of that time through binoculars? Stone described her at the British inquiry as being about five miles away, showing 'one masthead light and a red sidelight, and two or three small indistinct lights around the deck, which looked like portholes or open doors'. Gibson thought she was 'a tramp steamer, five to seven miles away, with nothing at all about her to resemble a passenger boat'.

And there was one extremely significant omission from this graphic passage. Beesley said nothing at all about rockets. This could only mean that the last of the distress signals from the *Titanic* had been fired before Beesley's lifeboat cleared the sinking liner, and in his book he gave an indication of what that time might have been:

> At about 2.15 a.m., I think we were any distance from a mile to two miles away. It is difficult for a landsman to calculate distance at sea but we had been afloat an hour and a half.

Even if Beesley were as much as half an hour out in his estimate, this meant that the last distress signals must have been fired from the *Titanic* before 1.15 a.m. If his estimate were in any way accurate, then it confirmed that the last of the distress signals fired from the *Titanic* had been sent up by 1 a.m. *Californian* time, that is, at least ten minutes before Stone decided to make his first report to Captain Lord, telling him that he had seen five rockets, with three more still to come.

Beesley's account also confirmed that, contrary to Lord Mersey's opinion, on that night, and in that area, there must have been two entirely different series of rockets, and hence two separate ships firing them. The *Titanic* used explosive signals, 'in lieu of guns', sent up to a height of up to two hundred feet; the ship Stone and Gibson were watching fired rockets having no explosive content and rising only to half masthead height.

Beesley was also quite confident that the *Titanic* was heading in a westerly direction as she lay sinking:

> We rowed slowly forward – or what we thought was forward, for it was in the direction the *Titanic*'s bows were pointing before she sank. I see now that we must have been pointing north-west, for we presently saw the Northern Lights on the starboard, and again, when the *Carpathia* came up from the south, we saw her from behind us on the south-east, and turned our boat around to get to her. I imagine the boats must have spread themselves over the ocean fanwise as they escaped from the *Titanic*: those on the starboard and port sides forward being almost dead ahead of her and her stern boats being broadside from her; this explains why the port boats were so much longer in reaching the *Carpathia* – as late as 8.30 a.m. – while some of the starboard boats came up as early as 4.10 a.m. Some of the port boats had to row across the place where the *Titanic* sank to get to the *Carpathia*, through the debris of chairs and wreckage of all kinds.

Approaching the wreckage, the *Carpathia* headed for Boxhall's boat, which had been showing green White Star Line recognition flares. His boat was lying off what had been the *Titanic*'s starboard quarter, 'to the north-east', as Boxhall stated in evidence. At the American inquiry, he also expressed the opinion that the ship he had been watching, two points on the *Titanic*'s port bow, went away in a westerly direction, 'in the direction in which she had come'.

This 'fanwise' distribution of the lifeboats fixed and confirmed the *Titanic*'s westerly heading as she lay sinking. It also confirmed that the ship seen to approach the liner, turn, and then steam away again must have been bearing west-south-west. All that time, the *Californian* must unquestionably have been bearing to the northward.

The completely independent evidence provided in Beesley's book relating to the time by which the last of the *Titanic*'s detonators had been fired and her heading after the collision with the iceberg was of such significance to the *Californian*'s case that I used it in the article I was writing for the *Merchant Navy Journal* in January 1962. I knew that Beesley was still alive, for one of the authors to whom I had supplied information about Captain Lord's case had met him, and suggested that I do the same.

At first I was most reluctant to trouble him: as the time approached for the publication of the article, however, I decided that, in fairness to him, I ought to let him see what I had written, and provide him with an opportunity to comment on the conclusions which I had drawn.

Beesley's response could not have been more cordial and encouraging. I was particularly impressed by the way in which, in layman's terms, he explained how distances can be approximately estimated at sea at night. Describing the approaching ship he had seen from the *Titanic*, he wrote of her as being 'much nearer than the horizon', which on that night appeared to him to be 'so sharp that it seemed to cut rising stars in two'.

The distance from an observer of the visible horizon depends on his height of eye: from the *Titanic*'s boat deck, 75 feet above sea level, the horizon would be ten miles distant. A ship 'much nearer than the horizon' must have been within eight or nine miles at the most to be seen so clearly from the *Titanic*. At such close range, any observer on that other ship must have seen the *Titanic* exactly as she was, the largest passenger liner in the world, fully illuminated up to the last.

On the MMSA's intimidating task in challenging the *Californian* legend, Beesley commented that a false idea once implanted is difficult to eradicate. As an example, he instanced his own unsuccessful efforts over the years to correct the widely believed report that the *Titanic*'s orchestra played 'Nearer my God to Thee' at the last. He told me that he had been asked to see the film of *A Night to Remember* only in its closing stages of preparation; his plea for the makers not to use that fiction had been without success.

Beesley also held decided views on Sir Ivan Thompson's opposition to what was being done to clear Captain Lord's name, writing that he had been disgusted to read of his demand: 'Let the thing drop; it is no use bringing it up again.' Sir Ivan would not be so keen to do that, Beesley commented, if his father had been in

(Right) Leslie Harrison, 1958

(Below) (L to R): Captain A. Penrice (President of the Mercantile Marine Service Association) and Stanley T. Lord, co-signatories of the MMSA's second petition, with Leslie Harrison (General Secretary of the MMSA), March 1968

Captain Lord, 1961

Captain Lord's position: how astonishing it was to think that a fellow seaman would refuse to consider the standpoint of justice for someone now dead. Surely posthumous justification, he added, was just as important as when a person was still alive.

In a very early letter, Beesley suggested that we should meet and 'get better acquainted' than we were doing by correspondence. I was all too often in London on official MMSA business, in fact, but while greatly appreciating his invitation, I was concerned not to worry him too much. For one thing, he had made it clear just how busy he was kept in running his coaching school in Northwood. Towards the end of 1962, however, an unexpected development brought us together.

In October of that year, I received a letter from Stanley Williamson, a features producer in the BBC's North Region, telling me that he was working on a programme for sound radio based on the transcript of the British court of inquiry into the loss of the *Titanic*. The idea was to show how a man's career and reputation can be damaged as much by proceedings of this kind as by a criminal trial. He thought that the *Merchant Navy Journal* article had a very direct bearing on the subject of the programme, and asked me to meet him to discuss it.

From that meeting stemmed a collaboration during which I was able to help him with the preparation of two BBC feature programmes based on the *Californian* incident, the first for sound radio and the second for television. Incidentally, during a rehearsal for the sound radio feature, Felix Felton, the actor cast to play the part of Lord Mersey, startled Williamson by flatly refusing to believe that a judge of the High Court could possibly have spoken some of the lines included in the script. Only when it was proved to him that the dialogue was taken word for word from the official transcript of the 1912 inquiry would he carry on with his part: he then played it superbly.

At a very early stage in his preliminary research work, Williamson arranged to call on Lawrence Beesley, and it was agreed between the three of us that this provided an ideal opportunity for me to meet him as well. At 4 p.m. on Thursday, 13 December, I joined Williamson at Baker Street station: from there, we went by train to Northwood, where we were met by one of Beesley's daughters, Mrs Laurien Wade, and driven to his home.

Beesley, a slight, very alert octogenarian, welcomed us most hospitably. Over tea, he answered our various enquiries: for my part, I had only two vital questions to put to him.

The first – and, as I asked it, I crossed my fingers instinctively – was whether or not he could recall seeing any distress signals after his lifeboat left the *Titanic*. Unhesitatingly he confirmed the account given in his book – the striking visual impression he had received and retained of the brightly lit *Titanic* was uncomplicated by distress signals. He reminded me of how he had described these in his book:

> Suddenly a rush of light from the forward deck, a hissing roar that made us all turn from watching the boats, and a rocket leapt upwards to where the stars blinked and twinkled above us. Up it went, higher and higher, with a sea of faces upturned to watch it, and then an explosion that seemed to split the silent night in two, and a shower of stars sank slowly down and went out one by one ... And presently another, and then a third.

'An explosion that seemed to split the silent night in two': yet Stone and Gibson heard nothing.

My second question was prompted by the action taken to preserve Captain Lord's documents for possible use in a court of law. Would Beesley be prepared, I asked, to swear an affidavit confirming the point about the distress signals, and declaring that the facts as recorded in his book were those he would have given in evidence had he been called as a witness at the inquiries in 1912?

Again he unhesitatingly confirmed that he was willing to do so, and two months later his solicitor sent us a statutory declaration he had made, for use in our campaign to clear Captain Lord's name. It read simply:

> I was born on the thirty-first day of December 1877. I was a passenger on the R.M.S. *Titanic* when on the fourteenth day of April 1912 the ship struck an iceberg in the Atlantic. I am the author of the book *The Loss of the R.M.S. 'Titanic' – Its Story and Its Lessons* ... The account of my experiences contained in this book is the same as that which I would have given had I been called to appear as a witness at any of the subsequent official inquiries. While still on board the *Titanic* I saw about eight distress rockets fired from her. I left the ship in Number Thirteen lifeboat and I am quite confident that the last of these rockets had been fired *before* this lifeboat cleared the *Titanic*'s side after being lowered into the water. And I make this solemn declaration conscientiously believing the same to be true and by virtue of the provisions of the Statutory Declarations Act 1835.

Lawrence Beesley was now 86 years old, and he told me quite frankly that his family were understandably anxious to protect him from any undue emotional stress or physical strain. In consequence, our correspondence came to an end in April 1963, at which time he was about to go into hospital for attention to his eyes.

In his final letter, he told me that he had been able to listen 'with great interest' to Stanley Williamson's radio feature, broadcast under the title *The Other Ship*. This was the last direct communication I was to have with Lawrence Beesley.

Four years later, in February 1967, I left my Liverpool office for ten days for official meetings in London and the West Country, following which I took a brief holiday in Cornwall. During this period of relaxation, completely free from official worries, I found myself increasingly preoccupied with thoughts of Lawrence Beesley. These became so obsessive that when I got back to my office on Monday, 20 February, I ignored the heavy accumulation of mail and business papers which had built up on my desk: instead, as a priority task, I began to dictate a letter to Beesley's solicitors, asking for news of him.

Before I could complete it, my secretary, Brenda Gilley, put down her pencil and looked up at me.

'I was going to tell you as soon as I had an opportunity,' she said. 'Mr Beesley died last week.'

Press cuttings she had kept for me confirmed her report. He had died in a nursing home in Lincoln at the age of 89 on Tuesday, 14 April, the day on which my Cornish holiday had started. As I read the cuttings, I recalled a comment in a very early letter from him. In May 1962, referring to Captain Lord's death, he had written: 'To die without knowing that his name was clear must have been the last straw.'

Was it simply coincidence, or, at the last, had some way been found of reminding me of Lawrence Beesley's great kindness, and the encouragement so generously given towards the task of restoring Captain Lord's good name?

In the four years which had passed since Beesley and I had last corresponded with each other, the major development in Captain Lord's case had, of course, been the submission and rejection of the 1965 petition. The controversy over the *Californian* continued, however, as did the screening both in cinemas and on television of the film *A Night to Remember*. It was now even included in the catalogue of films available for showing in schools; indeed, I estimated that hardly a day could pass without the film being shown somewhere in the world, propagating its misleading impression that the ship seen from the *Titanic* was the guilty *Californian*.

As always, it was the Board of Trade which had the power to put an end to the commercial exploitation of Captain Lord's misfortune. The 1965 petition had relied on that part of the Merchant Shipping Act which required the Board to form an 'opinion' that there was 'ground for suspecting that a miscarriage of justice had occurred'. In law, we were advised, there is no way in which a ministerial 'opinion' can be challenged in the courts. That same act of Parliament, however, specified that the Board were *compelled* to re-open an inquiry if 'new and important evidence which could not be produced at the inquiry has been discovered'. Our legal adviser on maritime affairs in London confirmed that, in his opinion, the facts recorded in Beesley's book, attested to by the statutory declaration, constituted 'new and important evidence' within the meaning of the act – evidence which, so far as Captain Lord was concerned, it was impossible for him to have been able to produce in his defence at the 1912 inquiry.

Beesley's death had freed us from the restriction previously imposed upon us not to do anything which might cause him emotional stress or physical strain, and in November 1967 the MMSA Council formally approved the preparation and submission of a second petition, putting forward Beesley's book as new and important evidence. Before taking any action in the matter, we naturally made every effort to get in touch with his family so that our intentions might be discussed with them, but our approaches were not acknowledged.

The petition was drawn up generally in much the same form as that of 1965, forming a self-contained 39-page booklet. A foreword gave Captain Lord's background, the effect on him of the 1912 inquiry findings, and the reasons why he then wished for it to be re-opened. The significance of the timing of the first and last distress signals fired from the *Titanic* and of her heading was then discussed, with special reference to Beesley's confirmation of these points. Finally, the booklet contained as appendices full supporting additional evidence, including the original written statements of Stone and Gibson.

In the petition, it was emphasised that, in the MMSA Council's opinion, Beesley's evidence contained in his book was 'new', in that it had not been given before the British court in 1912; it was important', in that it confirmed the time of the firing of the last distress signal and the *Titanic*'s heading after she stopped; it 'could not be produced' at the original inquiry because Beesley was not only in the United States at the time, but also had not then decided to publish his book; and, finally, the evidence had been 'discovered' in that its significance was not confirmed until the meeting at Beesley's home on 13 December 1962.

The petition was formally submitted to the President of the Board of Trade, the late Anthony Crosland, in March 1968. Four months later, his decision was given to Parliament in a way which clearly indicated the Board of Trade's intention to do everything possible to sweep the whole *Californian* business under the carpet.

Crosland's statement was made in the form of a written reply to a question, on which a minister cannot be pressed to comment in the House of Commons. That question had been tabled by Hugh D. Brown, member of Parliament for Glasgow, Provan, who could not be traced then – or afterwards – as ever having displayed the slightest interest in the *Californian* case. The reply was issued on a Friday afternoon, on the very last day of a session, just as Parliament rose for the long summer recess. As a final dismissive gesture, the Board of Trade's official confirmation of the reply, first noted in press reports, was sent by the way of the normal postal service, which meant that it was not received in the MMSA's head office until the following Monday, that is, three days later.

All too obviously the Board of Trade hoped that the lapse of time before Parliament re-assembled, and pressure of business as the new session began, would ensure that little, if anything, more would be heard of that petition in the House of Commons. It was a measure of the importance attached by the Board of Captain Lord's case that they should feel compelled to employ a Parliamentary tactic rarely used and only in cases where a government department is extremely apprehensive – and usually with good reason – of public reaction to a minister's decision.

Crosland in his reply referred initially to the 1965 petition, recalling that the Board's opinion at that time was that there had been no miscarriage of justice, and that, having regard to the time which had elapsed, and the death of majority of the persons concerned, it was considered that their discretionary power to order a re-hearing should not be exercised. The Board's views on these two aspects of the matter remained unchanged.

Crosland went on to say that the new question posed by the 1968 petition was whether the evidence raised was such as to require him to order a re-hearing under the appropriate provisions of the Merchant Shipping Act. He continued:

> I am advised that the provisions of the Act do not impose upon me an obligation to order a re-hearing, primarily because the evidence submitted is not evidence which could not have been produced at the inquiry but also because that evidence is not 'important' within the meaning of the section. In these circumstances I see no reason to depart from my predecessor's view that a re-opening of the inquiry would serve no useful purpose.

Removing some double negatives from that reply, the Board's conclusion, more simply stated, would seem to be that Beesley's evidence *could* have been produced at the 1912 inquiry, but in any event was not significant.

As to its importance, the MMSA's views remained unchanged. So far as its production at the original inquiry was concerned, it was impossible to follow the Board's reasoning. Captain Lord appeared at the British inquiry on 14 May 1912; it was not until the end of that month that the decision was taken in the United States to publish Beesley's book, which appeared in July. How Captain Lord was expected to have located and produced this evidence at the inquiry the Board did not attempt to explain.

I wrote to William Rodgers, the Minister of State (Shipping), to tell him that while we were sorry that the petition had been rejected, we were pleased to learn that both it and the one submitted in 1965 had been very carefully considered. In such circumstances, we assumed that the Board were now in a position to answer those practical points which, in the MMSA's view, conclusively demonstrated that there had been a grave miscarriage of justice in Captain Lord's case. We therefore renewed our suggestion that representatives of the Board and of the MMSA Council should meet, when the former would be able to explain their reasons for rejecting the petition. If the MMSA Council were to accept those reasons as conclusive, then they would naturally be under a duty formally to withdraw both petitions.

At a somewhat higher level, Captain R.W. Roberts, OBE, DSC, President of the MMSA, was similarly corresponding with the President of the Board of Trade. No other shipmaster in the world was better qualified than Captain Roberts to identify himself with the case. He had been awarded the OBE for his outstanding services in October 1942, when the Orient liner *Oronsay* had been torpedoed at four o'clock in the morning.

It was a dark, moonless night, and the liner at once developed a heavy starboard list. Nevertheless, within an hour 750 people had been sent away in the lifeboats. All on board were saved, with the exception of four of the crew killed in the original explosion.

As Staff Captain of the *Oronsay*, Captain Roberts had been responsible for the organisation and training which had enabled a desperately critical situation to be handled so efficiently and effectively. No living man had better knowledge of the type of emergency which, in the *Titanic*, had led to such a heavy loss of life, and in his final letter to Crosland he wrote:

> Your decision is in effect a re-affirmation of the 1912 court's appalling charge that Captain Lord was responsible for the deaths of up to 1,500 people. As such, it provides a justification for the continued world-wide showing of the film *A Night to Remember* both on television and in cinemas, and for its author, Walter Lord, to continue his critical campaign against Captain Lord in his lectures and writings. We also know that another author, Geoffrey Marcus, has completed a book which is shortly to be published critical of Captain Lord.
>
> We do not wish to embark on any pointless discussion of *conflicting* evidence, but rather to give your advisers an opportunity to explain to us how their interpretation of the basic *incontrovertible* facts is diametrically opposed to our own. So long as your advisers refuse to meet us for this purpose, you must forgive us if we naturally conclude that considerations other than purely technical ones are being allowed to influence your decisions. The MMSA's inescapable duty towards our members requires us to do everything possible to ensure that the protective provisions of the Merchant Shipping Acts are invariably applied in their favour. Consequently we greatly regret that we are left with no alternative but to continue to press Captain Lord's case by all available means, in circumstances under which, with the best will in the world, public criticism of your Marine Division's attitude cannot be avoided.

Anthony Crosland's reply ended the correspondence:

> I am afraid that I cannot accept your interpretation of the meaning of my decision nor can I agree that discussions with officials of the Board would serve any useful purpose. My views remain unaltered by your modified basis for such discussions. I hoped that I had made it clear both to the House of Commons and to your association that my decision was taken after careful consideration, in consultation with the Attorney-General, of all aspects of this matter. I am sorry about this.

We of the MMSA were perhaps even sorrier. There was still one line of action open to us, however, and that was to apply for a writ of *mandamus*. This is a judicial order from a higher court instructing a lower one to carry out a particular function, and would have enabled our dispute about the relative significance of what we claimed to be new evidence to be fought out in public. We were advised, however, that in the light of the Board of Trade's rigid attitude, such an action could well be protracted, legalistic, most probably unsuccessful, and certainly extremely costly. It was consequently an unjustifiable risk: so, for the time being, formal action to try to reverse the 1912 inquiry findings had to stop.

It was 56 years before the Board of Trade's internal minutes relating to Captain Lord's case were released to the Public Record Office. What will some future historian discover when – if ever – the Board's minutes covering their consideration of the 1965 and 1968 petitions are made public? Early in 1984, the increasing pressure being exerted to secure greater freedom of information about official decisions led to an approach being made to three people who might possibly have been able to throw some light on the reasons for the Board of Trade's odd reticence. Mrs Susan Crosland, Anthony Crosland's widow, had no recollection of his discussing Captain Lord's case with her, however, nor could she find any reference to it in his commonplace book of that period. William Rodgers could recall no details of his involvement in the matter as Minister of State (Shipping) in 1968; and Roy Mason had no comment to make.

The Board of Trade have consistently refused to discuss what are purely practical points. Only one conclusion is possible: the Board cannot refute those points. In such circumstances, an inevitable question is posed: were those practical points arbitrarily dismissed by Lord Mersey (if, indeed, he ever troubled to consider them)? If so, it is all too easy to understand why the law officers of the Crown appear subsequently to have done their utmost to protect Lord Mersey's handling of the case from inescapably embarrassing public scrutiny. Such an inference would explain not only Crosland's reference to consultation with the Attorney-General but also that earlier curious verbal warning received by the MMSA in 1965, to the effect that any criticism of Lord Mersey in the petition then being prepared would meet with 'strong opposition' in official quarters.

Are there any grounds for such criticism? Quite apart from Lord Mersey's unconcealed hostility towards Captain Lord – a defenceless witness – there were many other instances demonstrating his uncompromising way with anyone presuming to express an opinion contrary to his own. An outstanding occasion was when Sir Walter Howell, head of the Marine Department of the Board of Trade, was giving evidence. He was being questioned by Harbinson, appearing on behalf of the *Titanic*'s third class passengers (from among the survivors of whom, incidentally, not one was called as a witness).

'Have the Board of Trade any regulations enjoining upon shipowners the necessity of having printed notices put up in, say, the third class accommodation to indicate which way third class passengers should go – which staircase they should use – in cases of emergency?' Harbinson asked.

'No,' Sir Walter replied, whereupon Lord Mersey immediately intervened.

'Exercise your own common sense. Do you think, Mr Harbinson, that if such notices were stuck up anybody would ever read them? Judging for myself, I do not believe anyone would ever read them. I never should. Perhaps I ought to. The question is what *would* happen, not what ought to happen. Have you ever been on board a ship?'

'I have never been to America,' Harbinson admitted, 'but if I may relate my personal experience, every time I go across the Channel, one of the first things I do is to read the notices.'

'You are one of the most extraordinary men I have ever come across,' Lord Mersey commented. 'The first thing I do, if it is about the middle of the day, when I get on a cross-Channel steamer, is to get some lunch, and the notion that I should go about the decks, or about the ship, reading all the notices that are stuck up never occurred to me.'

The Attorney-General backed him up.

'This is not the class of literature your Lordship chooses,' he suggested.

The last word lay with Harbinson, and in concluding what by any standards had been a quite extraordinary exchange, he spoke for generations of travellers who, over the ages, have embarked on a ship with less than enthusiasm: 'I regret that luncheon is an occupation I am never able to take part in at sea,' he confessed.

So an eminently practicable suggestion, subsequently universally adopted and lying at the heart of any problem involving crowd control, was derisively dismissed by the very man charged with the public duty of extracting from the evidence the lessons to be learned from the disaster.

Lord Mersey's condemnation of Captain Lord in 1912 surely represents the grossest miscarriage of justice in the history of British marine inquiries. In his conduct as president of a court of inquiry investigating one of the greatest tragedies of the sea, it may justifiably be considered that he staged an extraordinary performance – and the word 'performance' is used in its dictionary sense of 'the execution of tricks at a public show, expressly intended to amuse and entertain an audience'. How else can one interpret Lord Mersey's frequent would-be humorous comments and interjections?

Surely the refusal of successive British governments to allow Captain Lord's case to be re-opened can only indicate a reluctance to risk the exposure of a judicial performance, and subsequent official protective measures, both morally and technically indefensible.

There was a sequel to my correspondence and meeting with Lawrence Beesley. A new edition of his book, published in 1979, contained a preface by his daughter, Mrs Laurien Wade, in which she said:

> The only detail of the whole book on which my father subsequently wavered concerned the timing of the collision – 'about a quarter to twelve' he says at the start of Chapter Three. The question of timing became more than a matter of simple historical interest: at courts of inquiry in both Britain and the United States evidence was brought that a merchant ship, the *Californian*, was standing off some ten miles from the site of the disaster, that its crew observed the *Titanic*'s distress rockets, and that its captain, Stanley Lord, remained in his cabin and ordered no action to be taken. The *Californian* had the capacity to take on board every one of the passengers and crew lost on the *Titanic*.
>
> After Lord's death a campaign was begun to clear his name; and my father's statement about the timing of the collision became a crucial piece of corroboratory evidence in deciding the relative position of the two ships. My father, then in his eighties, was subjected to some considerable pressure, and eventually signed an affidavit to the effect that he could no longer be so certain about the time of the collision. Subsequently, however, he insisted to me that in this matter – as in every other detail – he stood by every word of what he had written in 1912.

The following points should be noted:

1. The exact time, 11.40 p.m., at which the *Titanic* collided with an iceberg is well established and has never been in dispute.

2. No evidence as to a distance of 'some ten miles' was brought before either the United States or British courts of inquiry, at which

all technically qualified witnesses from both the *Titanic* and the *Californian* agreed that the closest approach of another ship as seen from each of those two vessels was about four to five miles. A distance of 'not more than eight to ten miles' was introduced into the findings of the British court by Lord Mersey's assessors as being the closest approach of another vessel which could be reasonably accepted if the *Californian* were in fact, as Lord Mersey maintained, a vessel from which the *Titanic*'s distress signals were observed but not acted upon.

3. Two only of the *Californian*'s crew, one of whom in fact 'observed' no rockets of any description, later expressed the personal *opinion* that the ship they had seen was the *Titanic*.

4. Captain Lord was *not* in his cabin at the time rockets were seen, but in the chartroom, fully dressed and immediately available if called upon to cope with any emergency. So far from ordering 'no action' to be taken when the sighting of rockets was first reported to him by his second officer, he gave immediate instructions for the renewal of previously unsuccessful attempts to establish contact by Morse lamp with a ship which, the second officer told him, was now 'steaming away' from the position only four to five miles away in which she had been lying stopped for over an hour.

5. Had the *Californian* in fact been the ship seen from the *Titanic* and ten miles away at the time the second officer first reported to Captain Lord that he had seen rockets, then barely an hour remained in which to get under way, to cover the intervening distance at her maximum speed of thirteen knots, and 'to take on board every one' of the 1,500 men, women and children left in the *Titanic*, a manifestly impossible task in that short time.

6. The 'campaign' to clear Captain Lord's name was officially inaugurated at his specific request some three and a half years *before* his death in 1962.

7. The 'timing of the collision' with the iceberg has relatively little bearing on the question of whether or not the *Californian* could have been the ship seen from the *Titanic*.

8. The only statutory declaration so far publicly known to have been signed by Lawrence Beesley (used as the basis for the unsuccessful petition addressed to the Board of Trade on Captain Lord's behalf in 1968) states categorically that the account of his experience contained in the book is the same as that which he would have given had he been called upon to appear as a witness at either of the two subsequent inquiries.

In an interview on the BBC's PM programme on 9 August 1979, Mrs Wade amplified the reference in her preface to her father's having been subjected to 'some considerable pressure' to sign an affidavit to the effect that 'he could no longer be so certain about the time of the collision':

> *Interviewer*: Did your father ever subsequently feel that he wanted to change some of the facts he had included in the book he wrote in 1912?
>
> *Mrs Wade*: Never. Never. But very much towards the end of his life – I think he was between 87 and 88 – there was someone, a fanatical person, who wanted to clear Captain Lord's name, of the *Californian* ...
>
> *Interviewer*: That was the ship in proximity – they saw the rockets being fired by the *Titanic* and did nothing about it ...
>
> *Mrs Wade*: They did nothing about it, no, and this man was fanatically keen to clear Captain Lord's name – in fact, he wanted the whole *Titanic* situation reviewed by the government on a commission, and my father was, I am afraid, tired out by this man, and in the end he did sign an affidavit to say he wasn't quite sure when the actual collision occurred, but he told me after he had done this – and I tried very hard to persuade him not to – he did say a week or two after he signed it he knew it wasn't true, and he would like to stick completely to his original story.

If Mrs Wade's statements are to be relied upon, then Lawrence Beesley must have signed *two* legal documents relating to the *Titanic* in 1962/63. The first was the statutory declaration given to me confirming the accuracy of his original account; the second, an affidavit given to 'a fanatical person', casting doubt on one aspect of that account. Through the Solicitor's Department of the BBC it was ascertained that Mrs Wade is unable to recall the name of the 'fanatical person' who, she claims, visited her father in 1962 or 1963 accompanied by 'at least two other men'.

Should that 'fanatical person' chance to read this book, I ask him to accept my assurance that he was quite wrong to try to influence Lawrence Beesley to cast doubt upon the accuracy of his book, for to do so would damage rather than promote Captain Lord's case. I also suggest that he should return the affidavit (if it is still in existence) to Mrs Wade so that she can destroy it, thus concluding, as satisfactorily as possible, a most unhappy incident causing such needless distress to Lawrence Beesley and his family.

CHAPTER TWENTY

Critics

> SHOCKING SCANDAL OF THE 'TITANIC' – 1,500 MEN, WOMEN & CHILDREN MURDERED! – *A Night to Remember* reveals only some of the *minor* blunders relating to the tragedy, while brazenly omitting or kissing off the most shocking scandals of all! These scandals, never exposed before, are four-fold ... (and include) (3) the captain of a nearby ship who could have saved everybody aboard the *Titanic* (but who) lay stinking drunk in his cabin while 1,500 died in agony ... Add to the list of seaborne murderers the name of Captain John [sic] Lord, master of the steamship *Californian*. This ship was only ten short miles away from the *Titanic* – close enough to see its lights – yet didn't show up at the disaster scene until it was too late.
>
> John Lord said he was asleep when the collision occurred, and that his radio operator had gone off duty ten minutes before the SOS was flashed from the luxury liner. Members of his crew saw a spectacular display of rockets fired as signals of distress from the *Titanic*, but according to Lord they didn't realize what the signals meant.
>
> Lord's testimony was completely disproved by a statement from Second Officer Stone – a statement that *never* got into print. He had gone to the captain's cabin to report on the distress rockets and to get orders to rush to the *Titanic*'s help. The captain never gave such orders and for a good reason – he was too drunk to realize what his officer was telling him. Instead he ordered Stone in his best whiskey voice to 'Forget thish whole thing and lemme sleep.'

The above extract from an article by John Gregory, featured in the United States magazine *Inside Story*, is an extreme example of the vulnerability of Captain Lord's reputation so long as Lord Mersey's adverse findings remain on record. A variation on this theme of drunkenness was played by Robert Prechtl in his fantasy-novel *Titanensturz*:

> [Captain Lord] saw no reason to display great courage for the sake of his cargo of sweaters and felt hats, and steam through ice drifts at night ... The aversion of a captain to a nocturnal trip through the ice was quite

justified. He gave the order to stop ...

At eleven o'clock Evans sat in the messroom with the captain and the first officer. They were playing a persistent rubber, and were indulging in various stimulants to which only a small quantity of water had been added. The third officer, Grove, had the watch. The second officer was asleep; he would have to turn out for the dog watch. Just then Grove called down through the speaking tube that he had sighted the lights of a steamer which was coming from the east.

'What ship could that be?' asked the captain. His interest was slight; he held six trumps in his hand.

'It must be the *Titanic*; I've just been in touch with her,' said Evans.

The captain said: 'It might be of interest to them to know we've struck ice. Send the message: "Are surrounded by ice; stopping".

This recurrent question of possible drunkenness on Captain Lord's part undoubtedly stems from a comment by Sir Rufus Isaacs during his closing address, as Attorney-General, at the British inquiry: 'I do not know that it is perhaps quite safe to speculate upon the reasons that made Captain Lord neither come out of his chartroom to see what was happening, nor to take any step to communicate with the vessel in distress, even such a very slight effort to have the wireless operator called up.'

The obvious inference to be drawn from this comment is that Captain Lord was under the influence of alcohol, an inference that he bitterly resented. We discussed this point during a tape-recorded conversation we held in August 1961.

'The only drink I ever took at sea was at Christmas,' he told me. 'If I happened to be at sea on Christmas Day, we would open a bottle of port wine in the saloon. Well, you know what Christmas is, and one bottle of port wine wouldn't go very far among half-a-dozen. I would only have one glass – that's the only drink I ever took at sea, Christmas.'

In addition to Groves' testimony as to Captain Lord's sobriety,* I can add my own. I had been visiting him at his home, usually during the evening, for several months, when quite unexpectedly he asked me if I would like a drink. I declined, for as usual I was my own chauffeur.

'It's just as well,' he commented. Indicating a sideboard cupboard, he added: 'There might be a bottle of sherry in there, but if so it hasn't been touched for three or four years.'

Of the many critical comments which have been published since

* See page 239.

Lord Mersey gave his judgement in 1912 – and they have proliferated since 1958 – it would be quite impossible to deal analytically with each separate one. For the purpose of this chapter, therefore, detailed reference will be made to three only of the better known books about the *Titanic* disaster. Incidentally, Lawrence Beesley in his book wrote:

> There is undoubted evidence that some of the crew on the *Californian* saw our rockets; but it seems impossible to believe that the captain and officers knew of our distress and deliberately ignored it. Judgement on the matter had better be suspended until further information is forthcoming.

Another survivor from the *Titanic* who published a book about his experiences was Colonel Archibald Gracie. He was more forthright in his condemnation of Captain Lord, and in *The Truth about the Titanic* bluntly stated:

> The fate of thousands of lives hung in the balance many times that ill-omened night, but [the British inquiry findings] furnish the evidence corroborating that of the American investigation, viz., that it was not chance, but the grossest negligence alone which sealed the fate of all the noble lives, men and women, that were lost ...
>
> The captain of the *Californian* and his crew were watching our lights from the deck of their ship, which remained approximately stationary until 5.15 a.m. on the following morning. During this interval it is shown that they were never distant more than six or seven miles. In fact, at 12 o'clock, the *Californian* was only four or five miles off.

Amazingly, however, Gracie elsewhere records a diametrically-opposed impression of events at twelve o'clock:

> [Shortly before midnight] we strained our eyes to discover what had struck us. From vantage points where the view was not obstructed ... I sought the object, but in vain, though I swept the horizon near and far and discovered nothing. It was a beautiful night, cloudless, and the stars shining brightly ... If another ship had struck us, there was no trace of it ... I made a complete tour of the deck, searching every point of the compass with my eyes.

Gracie's unequivocal statement that no other ship was in sight at midnight was substantiated by Frederick Fleet, one of the two lookouts on duty in the crowsnest, stationed 95 feet above the waterline and having a completely unrestricted view all round the horizon. From that position, in the darkness, an iceberg was sighted at a range of about three-quarters of a mile. At the United States inquiry, Senator Smith demanded of him: 'I want to know whether you saw ahead, while you were on the watch, on the lookout, Sunday night, after the collision occurred, or before, any lights of any other ship?' Fleet replied: 'No, sir.' At the British inquiry, he was asked: 'Did you see this light on the port bow before you left the crowsnest?' 'No,' he replied. 'It must have been about one o'clock.'

A few pages later, Gracie writes about 'a bright white light of what I took to be a ship about five miles off and which I felt sure was coming to our rescue ... but instead of growing brighter the light grew dim and less and less distinct and passed away altogether.'

A ship not in sight at midnight; a ship later as close as 'four or five miles off'; a ship passing out of sight – how could such a ship be the *Californian*, as Gracie asserted, a ship actually blamed for lying stopped all that night?

Unquestionably the most widely read of all books about the *Titanic* is Walter Lord's *A Night to Remember*. Incidentally, the author was not related to Captain Lord.

The acid test of any account of the *Titanic*'s sinking which attempts to incriminate the *Californian* is the way in which it covers the point made so devastatingly, if unwittingly, by Gracie: how does another ship suddenly become visible to the 2,150 people whose lives depend on such a vessel coming to their rescue?

In the first edition of his book, Walter Lord simply brings her in as 'a promising contact ... the light that winked ten miles off the *Titanic*'s port bow'. He makes no attempt to explain how the liner's watchkeepers have apparently failed until now to pick up the lights of another steamer which later become clearly visible to all from the *Titanic*'s boat deck.

Once that ship is mentioned, Walter Lord records events in the *Titanic* and the *Californian* as though they are occurring simultaneously, using an amalgam of the times later given by witnesses from both ships and ignoring the twelve minute time difference which actually existed.

From the *Californian*, Groves is described as noticing 'at about 11.10 ... the lights of another ship racing up from the east on the starboard side, rapidly overhauling the motionless *Californian*'. He knocks on the chartroom door 'around 11.30' and tells Captain Lord about it. The impression created by this account is that this is the first Captain Lord knows about any other ship: in fact, Groves is reporting the vessel noted casually by Captain Lord himself half an hour earlier from the main deck – a sighting which prompted him to instruct Evans to tell the *Titanic* that the *Californian* was stopped in ice. Curiously enough, Walter Lord actually records elsewhere in his book the rejection of that message at 11 p.m. by Phillips, the overworked wireless operator in the *Titanic*; he does not mention that it originated with Captain Lord, however, a crucial omission in the circumstances.

As for 'another ship racing up from the east', nowhere in the evidence given by Groves at the British inquiry is there to be found any basis for such a statement. It is indeed what Groves *would* have seen had the approaching ship been the *Titanic*, as Walter Lord assumes; but a ship 'racing up from the east' at twenty-two knots and stopping ten miles away on a south-easterly bearing would never have been in sight from the *Californian* for over half-an-hour, as can be seen from the sketch reproduced on page 178.

In the book, Stone is described as seeing the last of the *Titanic* when he considers that she has 'definitely gone' at 2.20 a.m. From the point of view of the *Titanic*'s people, no mention at all is made of the ship that they have been watching once Rowe has been ordered by his captain to stop Morsing her and to take charge of one of the last boats to leave.

Thereafter, nothing: until at about 6 a.m., still only 'ten miles away', Captain Lord learns of the disaster and immediately 'does just what a good skipper should do'. He starts the engines and heads for the *Titanic*'s given position, arriving alongside the *Carpathia* at about 8.30. Walter Lord is apparently completely unaware of the implications of the undisputed fact that it has taken the *Californian* a full two and a half hours to cover only ten miles.

A revised illustrated edition of *A Night to Remember* was published in 1976. One revision the late Captain Lord would undoubtedly have welcomed is a change in the caption to an illustration reproduced in both editions. It shows Captain Lord and his three navigating officers on the bridge of the *Californian*, and in the first edition the caption reads:

> Officers of the Leyland liner *Californian*. The spyglass in Captain Lord's lap is somewhat ironical, considering she lay within ten miles of the *Titanic* all during the sinking.

The true irony of this wounding reference to Captain Lord lies in the fact that he was holding the telescope only because of the insistence of the passenger for whom he was posing that he should do so to look 'like a real skipper'. There is no reference to 'the spyglass' in the caption to that illustration reproduced in the later revised edition.

In his preface to the 1976 edition, Walter Lord writes:

> The text, except for minor corrections, has been left as it was. This is because, even after twenty-one more years of contemplation, I still think this is the way it happened. On the *Californian*, for instance, I've examined the petitions and arguments put forth by those seeking to clear her, and I've re-examined my original sources – the testimony and findings of the British and US inquiries, recollections given me by her third officer, articles strongly defending her at the time – and I still feel the overwhelming weight of evidence puts her on the scene.
>
> So there it is, although an observation made in the original edition remains as true as ever: 'It is a rash man indeed who would set himself up as a final arbiter on all that happened the incredible night the *Titanic* went down.'

Walter Lord has the potential to add to that 'overwhelming weight of evidence' if he chose to accept the challenge to try to answer some of the points made in 'the petitions and arguments put forth' by those seeking to clear Captain Lord, and to attempt to explain in simple terms how he reconciles the discrepancies between what was seen from each of the two ships.

An author who appears to be setting himself up as 'final arbiter' on certain aspects of that 'incredible night' is Geoffrey Marcus. In his book *The Maiden Voyage*, he argues that it is immaterial whether or not the *Titanic* was the ship seen from the *Californian*, for, while Captain Lord might have 'positively denied that the unknown vessel was or possibly could be the *Titanic*', it did not alter the fact that he had failed to take proper action in response to signals of distress. Marcus takes no account of the fact that no distress signals as such were ever reported to Captain Lord, and dismisses Stone's insistence that the signals he had seen could not have been distress rockets as a vain and embarrassed attempt 'to temporize ... this line of argument ... the only possible defence ... reasoning [which] failed to impress the court.' Marcus does not suggest the name of any other ship which, on that night and in that vicinity, was in distress, for there was no such ship.

In an attempt to cast doubt on Stone's evidence, Marcus comments parenthetically: 'Incidentally, what Stone would sometimes say in private was very different from what Stone had said in public.' He gives no source for this information, however, nor does he comment on the fact that what Stone said 'in public' on this point, as a witness at the British inquiry, tallied exactly with what he had written down in his statement for Captain Lord long before there was any indication that there would be a searching investigation into what had happened during his watch.

If Stone did indeed commit perjury at the British inquiry, as Marcus implies, then he put up a staggering performance by holding on to his original story in the teeth of relentless questioning by highly experienced lawyers.

On the acid test of how the ship seen from the *Titanic* first becomes visible, Marcus writes:

> While he was preparing the lifeboats for lowering, Boxhall heard the clang of the lookout bell once again. Returning to the bridge, he saw through his telescope that it was another steamship, bearing about half a point on the port bow.

There never was any such 'clang of the lookout bell'. The two lookouts detailed for the 12 – 2 a.m. watch were Frank Evans and Alfred Hogg. They relieved Fleet and his companion Lee on time at midnight, but stayed in the crowsnest for less than half an hour. As Hogg explained at the United States inquiry:

> I dressed myself, and relieved the lookout at twelve o'clock, me and my mate Evans. We stopped about twenty minutes, and lifted up the back cover of the nest, the weather cover, and I saw people running about with lifebelts on. I went to the telephone then, to try to ring up on the bridge and ask whether I was wanted in the nest, when I saw this. I could get no answer on the telephone ... I went straight to the boat deck. I assisted in starting to uncover the boats.

Having so simply produced another ship, Marcus calls her the *Californian*, events on which start with 'a steamer's light ... seen approaching from the eastward'. In fact, Groves' evidence was to the effect that the ship he was watching came up on the starboard quarter, from west of south. As in Walter Lord's case, Marcus must have this ship steaming towards the *Californian* from the east, as the *Titanic* would have done.

Discrepancies are also evident when Marcus comes to describe events outside the courtroom after Stone completed his evidence:

> In court, his officers had done their best for Captain Lord. Outside, in the luncheon interval, however, they were a good deal less reticent about the commander's responsibility for what had happened; and presently in response to the angry reproaches of the wife of one of the *Titanic*'s officers, they frankly admitted that distress signals had been seen that

> night from the *Californian*: but they said they had been unable to get Captain Lord to bestir himself; in fact, they were unmistakably afraid of him.

In a subsequent letter to the editor of the *Nautical Magazine*, Marcus expanded on this touching scene:

> As they stood around chatting, the wife of one of the *Titanic*'s officers was unwilling even to shake hands with the master of the *Californian*; but her husband, putting his arm round the indignant lady, gently remonstrated with her – 'Look here, dear! You don't want to kick a man when he is down'.

Three points stand out. Firstly, Stone's evidence was given *after* lunch on 14 May; Groves, Stewart and Evans appeared the following day. Secondly, how did Captain Lord manage to keep his officers 'unmistakably afraid of him' and yet retain a loyalty which made them 'do their best for him'? Groves, for one, was so little in awe of his captain that he was prepared to disagree with him over the question of whether or not the approaching ship was a passenger vessel. Thirdly, the fact is that Captain Lord never met Lightoller, although he corresponded with him at the time.

The episode of the indignant lady can be easily explained. In September 1965, Mrs Sylvia Lightoller, widow of the ex-second officer of the *Titanic*, became indignant once again when she learned that the MMSA had presented a petition to the Board of Trade asking for a reopening of the inquiry. She at once approached her local Member of Parliament, R. Gresham-Cooke, and told him that she was prepared to swear an affidavit to the effect that 'several' of the *Californian*'s officers had told her that they had to go down to Captain Lord's 'bunk' to wake him up and to tell him of the rockets; that he would not go to the bridge, maintaining 'that they must be having high jinks on the *Titanic* because of its first voyage'; and that the ship her husband saw ten miles away was 'of considerable size – all lit up and clearly visible and had three masts'. It is one of the lesser tragedies of the *Titanic* disaster that, over the years, fact should have become clouded with fantasy for some of those directly concerned. And so the legends breed on themselves and multiply.

In his book, Marcus finally dismisses Captain Lord, on the basis of a poorly reproduced photograph, as 'a self-assured, autocratic, overbearing character', who 'suffered something of a sea-change' after the 1912 inquiry, and 'went softly, so to speak, throughout the rest of his time afloat'.

For Marcus, the *Californian* incident resolves itself into a single issue: rockets. The MMSA's efforts to widen the discussion is, in his opinion, 'a case of not seeing the wood for the trees, of failing to draw the inescapable conclusions from the evidence, of rejecting the essential from the inessential'.

Predictably, such a narrow approach had its effect, if the comments of two reviewers of *The Maiden Voyage* are any guide. Cyril Connolly in the *Sunday Times* wrote: 'It is clear that [the *Californian*'s] captain did not want to endanger his ship in the icefields and so ignored the rockets and cooked his log.'

Captain A.G. Course, one of the most respected of Britain's sailor-authors, commented in *The Mariner's Mirror*: 'While it is true that other accounts of this unhappy affair have been written, this seems to be the most likely one.'

Finally, an unattributed review in *The Times Literary Supplement* included this passage: 'Captain Lord may have been guilty of cowardice, a fear of endangering his company's ship, or both. There is also the possibility not considered even by Mr Marcus, that he was drunk.'

Another comment on Captain Lord made by Geoffrey Marcus in his book is this:

> According to the master of the *Californian*, no bodies could be found and after an hour or so he resumed his voyage. It is to be observed that he could not have searched very effectively; for there were in fact hundreds of corpses, drifting to and fro on the face of the waters.

In making this statement about 'hundreds of bodies' it would seem that Marcus has relied on Sir James Bisset's statement in his *Tramps and Ladies* that 'A cable-laying ship, the SS *Mackay-Bennett*, went out from Halifax two weeks afterwards, and picked up 205 bodies, which were given religious burial.'

That bodies were to be found two weeks later, however, is no evidence that they were visible when the *Californian* arrived in the area. Sir James himself is witness of that. He, from the *Carpathia*, saw only one body (though he remarks that some people later said, perhaps mistakenly, that they had seen many bodies).

Quite apart from Captain Lord, other eye-witnesses who testified that no bodies could be seen at the scene of the disaster at 8.30 on that April morning were Boxhall, Groves, Lightoller and Pitman; Captain Rostron, at both the British and United States inquiries, spoke of seeing but one body.

Major Arthur G. Peuchen, a surviving passenger from the *Titanic*, went into considerable detail when giving evidence at the United States inquiry as to what, in this context, he did *not* see:

> Something that astonished me very much – I was surprised, when we steamed through this wreckage very slowly after we left the scene of the disaster – we left the ground as soon as this other boat, the *Californian*, I understand, came along – that we did not see any bodies in the water. I understood the *Californian* was going to cruise around, and when she came we started off, and we went right by the wreckage. It was something like two islands, and was strewn along, and I was interested to see if I could see any bodies, and I was surprised to think that with all these deaths that had taken place we could not see one body; I was very much surprised. I understand a life preserver is supposed to keep up a person, whether dead or alive ... I was standing forward, looking to see if I could see any dead bodies, or any of my friends, and to my surprise I saw the barber's pole floating ... There were a great many chairs in the water; all the steamer chairs were floating, and pieces of wreckage.

Captain Lord can scarcely be blamed for not finding any bodies when the sworn testimony of seven witnesses actually present at the scene of the disaster supports him.

Another instant pundit for whom the emotive word 'rockets' completely removes all uncertainty from the *Californian* incident was the columnist Bernard Levin. Writing in the *Daily Mail* of 8 March 1968, he criticised the MMSA for supporting Captain Lord and attempting to re-open the *Titanic* inquiry. His technical limitations when commenting on the practical issues involved were exposed when he claimed that when Captain Lord was told of 'the first six rockets at 1.10 ... the *Californian* would still have been in time'.

In time for what? If in fact Lord Mersey had been right, and the *Californian* only eight to ten miles from the *Titanic*, Levin is claiming that, in barely an hour, she could have covered the intervening distance at night, through ice, *and* taken on board 1,500 people. Yet later that same morning, in daylight, it took the *Carpathia* over four hours to pick up 703 survivors from the *Titanic*'s lifeboats. My attempt to point out to Levin some of the purely practical issues arriving from the incontestable evidence given at the original inquiries failed. It provoked from him the comment: 'I find distasteful your air of dogmatic certainty about matters which happened nearly sixty years ago'.

Ignoring the fact that Levin's own 'dogmatic certainty' as to Captain Lord's culpability is apparently beyond criticism, a purely technical point remains a technical point regardless of the passage of time – for example, Pythagoras' theorem. On the basic question as to whether or not the *Californian* could ever have been 'in time', Lightoller made a curious suggestion. Although sympathetically disposed towards Captain Lord in 1912, if his letters are to be taken as meaning what they say, he later came to accept the legend of his culpability, and, in 1935, in his autobiographical *The Titanic and Other Ships*, he wrote: 'Nothing could have been easier than [for Captain Lord] to have laid his ship actually alongside the *Titanic* and taken every soul on board.'

Captain R.W. Roberts, for one, disagreed, and commented:

> The *Californian* could never have gone alongside the sinking ship. All she could have done was to lower her own boats to pick up such people as were in the water or prepared to jump for it, and get those people in boats already on board. In any case, the *Titanic* would not have had ladders for each boat position, and the *Californian*, even if only ten miles away, could not have rescued those people still on board and for whom there were no boats. The non-seaman has queer ideas about rescuing people from sinking ships, and while wooden ships in days gone by used to go alongside, to do so with modern steel ships of this kind of tonnage would be nearly impossible.

But what if circumstances had permitted of there being such a shipmaster handy, prepared 'to lay his ship alongside'? Securing her reasonably firmly in place would have been the first major problem, and would only have been the beginning of a hazardous operation. As the *Titanic*'s bows sank lower and lower in the water, there would have been only a single point of useful contact, restricting access to virtually single file. Inevitably pressure and panic would build up as over a thousand people began to realise that their chances of survival were diminishing minute by minute, and an appalling situation would have developed.

The closest approximation to the hypothetical 'single file' transfer of such a large crowd is perhaps that offered by the entry of spectators into a sports stadium. The secretaries of both the Everton and Liverpool football clubs have confirmed that the maximum number of people passing through turnstiles without being delayed by having to pay is of the order of 1,000 an hour – and generally speaking this involves an orderly and good-humoured assembly already mustered in long queues. Can there be any clinging to the theory that a hypothetical *Californian* could have rescued 1,500 people in a matter of minutes who have ever thought the problem through to its logical conclusion? One of the most baffling aspects of the *Californian* incident is the obstinate refusal of Captain Lord's critics to face up to such facts and to offer some reasonable explanation of how the *Californian* could have been the ship seen from the *Titanic* and vice versa. In 1968, however, there was a development which for the first time led to a memorandum being prepared in which an attempt was made to explain what is really the inexplicable.

From 1958 to 1970, the MMSA was guided on what might be called the 'maritime' aspects of Captain Lord's case – particularly in connection with a possible re-hearing of 1912 evidence before a marine court of inquiry – by the association's legal adviser in London. A master mariner with unrivalled experience of arranging for the representation of shipmasters and officers at formal investigations, he was a lawyer who, we hoped, would be better able than most to appreciate the practical points arising out of the *Californian* incident, and to help us to hack a path through the legalistic jungle which had grown up around it.

In all fairness, it must be stated that he never left the MMSA in any doubt as to the extreme difficulties facing the association in our attempt to overturn a legal ruling of half a century earlier. In particular, at the last he was rightly concerned to ensure that the MMSA did not find itself committed to an attempt to compel the Board of Trade to re-open the inquiry only to discover that opposition on strictly legalistic grounds, as the Board had indicated would be the case, had led to catastrophic and costly failure.

Nevertheless, this very proper advice was increasingly accompanied by indications that, as an individual, he had no real personal conviction as to the merits of Captain Lord's case. As this divergence between our basic points of view grew more evident, it became obvious that everything possible must be done to resolve it. Despite a very full and protracted correspondence, however, and some detailed personal discussions, we came no nearer to reaching agreement on those practical issues which I was convinced proved that the findings against Captain Lord were untenable.

In a final effort to pin down the issues which divided us, I drafted a memorandum in which I tried to piece together what I understood to be his views on the inconsistencies in the case against the *Californian*. When completed, I submitted it to him for comment and amendment.

In its finally mutually agreed form, the memorandum contains almost all the arguments I have heard put forward by those very few critics who have attempted to justify Lord Mersey's findings. As such, here it is, in full:

The whole of the evidence from the *Californian*'s witnesses, with the possible exception of part of that given by the third officer, is so manifestly unreliable as to render it impossible to determine what actually happened. The captain and second officer were particularly evasive, and the unanimity of evidence that the ship seen from the *Californian* was only four to five miles distant is suggestive of an agreed distance after discussion and tends to support the court of inquiry rejecting this evidence and coming to their own conclusion.

A possible sequence of events was as follows:

In the *Titanic*, the two lookouts in the crowsnest and the two watchkeeping officers on the bridge were so intent on their watch for ice that they all overlooked the steaming and decklights of the stationary *Californian* as she came into visual range to northward.

After striking the iceberg, the *Titanic* continued swinging to port under full starboard (old style) helm, creating an impression on the *Californian*'s third officer that her cabin and deck lights had been extinguished. She continued to swing through south and east until stopping on a northerly heading, displaying masthead lights and her port sidelight towards the *Californian*.

The captain, officers and everyone else on board the *Titanic* were so convinced that she was unsinkable that they did not consider that the help of any other vessel was immediately required. It was only when they realised that the liner was certain to founder that the order was given to abandon ship and to lower the lifeboats. For the first time, an interest was then taken in adjacent waters and the *Californian* initially detected, lying stopped eight to ten miles away. Distress rockets were immediately fired and Morse lamp signals flashed to attract her attention.

There is no fully acceptable explanation for the action of the *Titanic*'s fourth officer in volunteering detailed evidence at both the British and American inquiries to the effect that the ship seen for the *Titanic* seemed to approach from hull down, to close to a distance of about five miles, to turn and to steam away. He can only have been mistaken, in common with other witnesses from the *Titanic* who testified to similar effect. However, the *Californian* did swing clockwise and could have created the effect of a vessel approaching and turning away.

At about the time the *Titanic* sank, a screen of icebergs may have drifted between her and the *Californian*, which explains why the latter was not in sight of the survivors at daybreak and was delayed in closing the *Carpathia*.

Any court of inquiry convened fifty years after the original formal investigation would find difficulty in not upholding Lord Mersey's rejection of the evidence given by the *Californian*'s witnesses, as he had the opportunity of observing their demeanour under cross-examination. In these circumstances, little useful purpose would be served by a further examination of certain points of detail in apparent support of Captain Lord's case, no matter how persuasively such arguments might be presented, as against the broad effect of such evidence as the court accepted.

It may be considered that certain difficulties were created by the failure of the 1912 court of inquiry to probe such points of detail, for example by requiring the engine-room log book to be produced with a view to checking the distance steamed while proceeding to the scene of the disaster. It must be borne in mind, however, that a detailed examination of such points was omitted only after the court had apparently formed the conclusion at an early stage in the proceedings that the case against the *Californian* was irrefutable. It is incredible that Captain Lord's counsel did not himself insist on such logs being examined. So far as Captain Lord was personally concerned, he was undoubtedly guilty of the grossest neglect of duty in failing to go up to the bridge on being informed that rockets which could only have been distress rockets had been seen. This failure could not, and would not, be excused by any British court of inquiry. Had Captain Lord gone to the bridge, he could have steered his ship directly towards the rockets and investigated. The court's finding that he might then have saved 'all' of the lives that were lost is clearly unjustified. In practical terms, however, this is a matter of degree only, and the *Californian*'s participation in the rescue operations would have been fully justified had she been instrumental in saving but one life.

Captain Lord was probably fortunate in *not* being made a party to the inquiry, for the evidence given against him would most probably have led to the cancellation of his certificate or alternatively a prosecution under the Maritime Convention Act 1911 Section 6 (1). As it was, he was subsequently fortunate in being able to resume a successful career at sea. In this respect, the fact that both before and after the *Titanic* incident his professional competency and conduct was of the highest order is quite irrelevant in the context of the inquiry, for no individual is free from the consequences of making an isolated mistake.

In the event, Captain Lord appears to have accepted the findings or come to terms with himself, and any subsequent concern which he experienced on discovering that his involvement in the *Titanic* disaster was being commercially exploited in the publication of such a book as *A Night to Remember* came only towards the end of his life and was consequently experienced for only a limited period, virtually a double penalty.

Summing up, the circumstances as revealed in the transcript of the proceedings of the 1912 court of inquiry are such as to make it probable that the findings against Captain Lord were legally justified and that little useful purpose would be served by seeking to disturb them, the *crucial factor* being the undisputed position in which Captain Lord did not go on the bridge after rockets which were probably distress signals were reported to him.

An opinion has been requested upon an incident in which the *Carpathia* was involved while steaming towards the scene of the disaster.

> Although not herself in distress, she was then firing a distress rocket every fifteen minutes, interspersed with Cunard Company roman candle recognition signals. She passed a small steamer on the way, and the question is what duty, if any, lay on the master of that ship.
>
> In the special circumstances of the case, the *Carpathia* was fully justified in using distress signals in this way, for they could have given comfort to the *Titanic*'s survivors. Similarly, no real criticism should be directed against the other steamer's captain for his inaction in not subsequently reporting what he saw or in not altering course to follow the *Carpathia* as she proceeded on her way still firing distress rockets and recognition signals.

It is difficult to read that memorandum without feelings of incredulity and despair.

The proposition that a recurrence of an earlier emotional penalty, revived in Captain Lord's old age, can be regarded as mitigated because he lived to experience it 'for only a limited period' is totally abhorrent to anyone who was close to him over those few years.

The suggestion that, despite the evidence from the *Californian*'s witnesses being 'manifestly unreliable', those points can be selected from it, and relied upon, which confirm the allegations levelled against Captain Lord's conduct, is a surprising one.

The contention that Boxhall and a number of other experienced witnesses from the *Titanic* should mistake a stationary, swinging ship for one approaching from over a clearly defined horizon, turning, and steaming away again until out of sight, is hard to accept.

The theory that a screen of icebergs should suddenly become mobile and interpose themselves between the two ships at the precise moment that the *Titanic* sank seems debatable, to say the least.

But the most extraordinary suggestion of all is that it was not until it was realised that the *Titanic* was certain to founder that those on board began to take an interest in adjacent waters. In other words, it is seriously proposed that 2,150 people (excluding Colonel Gracie, who carried out his own personal search at midnight, and Fleet, high in the crowsnest), under the command of a highly qualified and experienced shipmaster, supported by six hand-picked navigating officers, participated for nearly an hour in a collective 'eyes down' before the discovery that another ship, on which their lives could depend, had been there all the time, only eight to ten miles away.

In my opinion, this last suggestion does not merit serious discussion and there, perhaps, it is better to leave it.

CHAPTER TWENTY-ONE

Survivors

In the 1960s, half a century had passed since the *Titanic* disaster: nevertheless Captain Lord was not the only survivor of those concerned in the *Californian* incident. There were still direct links to be uncovered with others personally involved in those events of 1912, and one link which was unfortunately broken – those boxes containing the priceless *Titanic* inquiry papers bequeathed by Foweraker but rejected both by the British Museum and by Captain Lord were apparently lost for ever. It was discovered that Mrs M.C. Simpkins of West Brow, Western Avenue, Bournemouth, Foweraker's executrix, had gone to live in the United States in the early 1950's after the death of her husband. Before leaving, she had what her representative in the West Country described as 'wonderful bonfire of papers'. It consequently seemed highly unlikely that any of Foweraker's detailed analyses of the case could have survived, apart from two foolscap notebooks he had given to Captain Lord and which were still preserved among the latter's *Californian* papers.

The Leyland Line was no longer in existence, having been absorbed in the 1930's by another Liverpool-based shipping company, the Harrison Line. However, Sir Leslie Roberts, CBE, chairman of the Manchester Ship Canal Company from 1950 to 1970, not only proved to be the son of William Roberts, general manager of the Leyland Line in 1912, but had also himself been appointed to that post in 1929. Although only a schoolboy at the time of the loss of the *Titanic*, he clearly remembered his father's conviction that Captain Lord was blameless, and his distress at the way things turned out.

Cuthbert Bridgewater, author of a number of articles on ships and the sea, was the son of the Captain Bridgewater who had first engaged Stanley Lord as an officer in a steamship company. Writing in March 1962, Bridgewater commented:

> I was seventeen when the *Titanic* was lost, and even today the horror of the disaster remains vividly in my mind, as also does my father's distress at the awful position in which it placed poor Stanley Lord. He was a grand chap and a fine seaman, besides being a first class shipmaster. I met him several times when he was master of the *Californian*, and like my father, marine superintendent of the Leyland Line in his day, never believed him negligent, slackness being so foreign to his nature. Captain Lord was a fine character who, as my father believed, was the unhappy victim of extremely cruel circumstances.

Frank Duncan Macpherson Strachan, President of the Strachan Shipping Company of Savannah, Georgia, and son of Frank Garden Strachan, Captain Lord's benefactor and the Scotsman who in 1886 was co-founder of that company, was another who remembered his father's high regard for Captain Lord and the latter's visits to their home. Curiously, he had been unaware of the part his father played in securing Captain Lord's appointment in Lawther Latta's until one evening in the early 1920's, when Sir John Latta himself told him of it. At the same time, Sir John expressed his satisfaction at what he and Frank Strachan had been able to do for Captain Lord and spoke of him in the highest terms.

One who got to know Captain Lord very well in his Lawther Latta days was G.E. Pearce. I met him quite by chance on 20 December 1961 at an official luncheon on board the Palm Line's *Ikeja Palm*, of which company he was then a director. He was keenly interested to learn that Captain Lord was still alive, recalling how he first met him in 1921. He was then in his teens, a junior clerk sent down to help Captain Lord with the signing off of the *Anglo Chilean*'s crew at the Mill Dam, South Shields. Over the next six years, he met Captain Lord on a number of occasions and formed the opinion that he was an outstandingly able shipmaster, very strict and insisting on a high degree of efficiency on the part of his officers, but respecting those with ability and treating them accordingly.

So far from finding Captain Lord arrogant or overbearing, Pearce's experience was that he always behaved like the perfect gentleman he was. He assessed him as essentially a shy and retiring man, exceedingly thoughtful and kind, and held in high esteem by his employers. There were occasions when he sensed that Captain Lord was embittered about something, but at that time he had no idea what the cause might be. In the light of his subsequent knowledge, he wondered whether or not it might be the aftermath of the *Californian* episode.

Pearce told me that he had nothing but the happiest recollections of Captain Lord's sincere friendship, extended to him when he was what he termed 'a humble junior' in a Tyneside shipping office. During the luncheon he scribbled a few notes on the back of a menu card, recalling some personalities of those days, such as Hudson, the company's 'outside man', which I took along to show to Captain Lord. Although the message, and particularly the thought that lay behind it, cheered him, he was in failing health and very low spirits: in fact, it proved to be almost the last occasion on which I visited him before his death.

Of those who had served at sea with Captain Lord there was at least one who dissented from the general opinion as to his capabilities as a shipmaster. A semi-anonymous correspondent, 'J.B.', writing from Sandown, Isle of Wight, recorded:

> I served for many years in the Leyland Line as an officer and master, and sailed with Captain Lord for two voyages. I found him to be a very disagreeable man, a martinet and a bully to anyone that feared him. At the end of my second voyage I saw the marine superintendent and got a transfer along with the second and third officers who also refused to sail with him ... Captain Lord was dismissed from the Leyland Line and went to Lawther Latta's and was greatly disliked by all who had the misfortune to sail with him in that firm too.

An entirely different assessment of Captain Lord's standing as a master in Lawther Latta's came from C.R. Allen, a seaman who had sailed with him in the *Anglo Chilean*, notably on that eventful voyage to Australia when the ship's cook fell ill, and during which Captain Lord had his brief encounters with Captain Groves. Perhaps Allen's letter provides a clue as to why 'J.B.' found it so difficult to get along with Captain Lord:

> I sailed with Captain Lord as A.B. for two voyages in the *Anglo Chilean*, and found him the most fairest, conscientious captain I was ever with during my thirty years at sea. The first voyage I paid off and signed on right away, which I have done quite a few times in other ships, but his was the only one when every one of the crew did the same thing. Having been with Captain Lord was a passport into any other of the same company's ships, a fact I proved twice in the *Anglo Canadian* and the *Anglo Egyptian*. In those days you got a job on your discharge book. When I went aboard these two ships, I only had to mention I had been with Captain Lord and the first thing the mate did was to look through the book, verify it, and you were in right away. Captain Lord was very

> strict in all things but he worked on the principle he was there to do a job and expected everyone else to do theirs.

Of those who had actually sailed in the *Californian* in April 1912, Stewart died tragically in 1940, as already related. I made no attempt to trace Stone. By 1963, he would have been in his 70's; having regard to the demonstrably false allegation reliably attributed to him, that Captain Lord was under the influence of drink on the night of the *Titanic* disaster, I had no wish to become involved in any sort of controversy with him.

Whatever motivated Stone to make such a deplorable charge, it was effectively countered by what Groves, the *Californian*'s one-time third officer, wrote in 1959:

> The question of the sobriety of Captain Lord – although I was with him for only some three months, it is quite long enough to know whether or not a man is of temperate habits. I never saw him take a drink or heard of him desiring one, and he was thoroughly abstemious always.

Groves had a distinguished career in the Merchant Navy. After service in the Royal Naval Reserve in the First World War, he went into W.A Souter's, shipowners based in Newcastle, where he attained command. After eleven years as a shipmaster, he was appointed marine superintendent, also serving on the marine superintendents' committee of the Chamber of Shipping. He was elected a Younger Brother of Trinity House and, by an interesting turn of fortune, in 1931 was appointed as a nautical assessor to serve on marine inquiries. In that capacity he had a reputation for being always a considerate and humane man. In the 1939-45 war, he returned to service in the Royal Navy Reserve.

I wrote to Captain Groves in April 1959 suggesting that I might meet him to discuss Captain Lord's case. I also considered that his comments on the affidavit we were engaged in drafting might be very useful.

Captain Groves was then 71 and living in retirement in Ipswich. As the man whose opinion that the ship seen from the *Californian* was the *Titanic* had been preferred by Lord Mersey to the factual evidence proving that she was not, Captain Groves could have been forgiven for finding my approach to be most unwelcome, resurrecting as it did such a controversial incident. If so, he certainly never showed it, either in his letters to me or during a most interesting personal meeting at his home – a meeting he later described as having been 'more enjoyable' than he had previously thought possible. In retrospect, his reaction was that of a truly Christian gentleman. Although he would not debate the navigational aspects of the case, nor give any indication as to whether or not he had changed his original opinion, he was most helpful and encouraging in other ways. In particular, he lent me his irreplaceable copy of the transcript of the proceedings of the eighth day of the British inquiry. This covered not only the evidence he, Stewart and Evans had given, but included as a most valuable bonus the evidence given by the captain and wireless operator of the *Mount Temple*.

Although from the purely navigational point of view it appeared that the *Mount Temple* could not have been the ship seen from the *Titanic*, certain evidence had been given by her captain which was significant. It proved that at daybreak the lifeboats and wreckage from the *Titanic* were well to the south and east of the accepted position of the collision with the iceberg, as Captain Lord had maintained; it also confirmed that the *Californian* was first seen that morning coming down from the north, on the western edge of the icefield, through which she had to steam for a second time in order to reach the *Carpathia*.

It was Notley, the *Mount Temple*'s fourth officer, who had triggered off the MMSA's action calling for an investigation into the possibility of the *Mount Temple*'s having been the ship seen from the *Titanic*. The Canadian Pacific Steamship Company confirmed that Captain Notley, as he then was, had died in 1956, eleven years after retiring from a senior shore appointment which he had held in the company. My enquiries also revealed that, for over a year, in 1937 and 1938, I had sailed in the same ship as Captain Notley's son. He was then second officer in the Nourse Line's steamer *Jumna*, in which I was serving as third officer. There had been an unusual amount of off-watch leisure during that voyage, which had taken us all round the world, with long sea passages, and Arthur C. Notley, who was connected through his family with literary circles in London, played a considerable part in encouraging me in my first commercially successful efforts at writing.

I now recalled that I had actually met Captain Notley himself, when he and his wife came on board the *Jumna* to visit their son while the ship was docked in Liverpool, but have no recollection of ever discussing the *Titanic* disaster with either.

Tragically the younger Notley was also dead. He had been killed on Christmas Day 1940, when the *Jumna*, in which he was serving as chief officer, had been sunk with no survivors by the German heavy cruiser *Admiral Hipper*, fleeing towards Brest after an unsuccessful brush with the escort of a British troop convoy.

James Gibson, the youngest of the *Californian* group, would have been just over 70 in 1963. He came from Southport, close to Liverpool, and it was the simplest of matters to trace his family, who were still living there. My enquiries were originated in August 1963; sadly, they were six months too late, for Gibson had died in the February of that year. Before then, I was told, he had seen the press references to the March 1962 article, and in fact was in hospital when told of Captain Lord's death, news of which had greatly affected him.

I drove out to Southport, where I was received in a most friendly manner by Mrs Pattie Gibson, his widow, and their daughter. Of the events of 1912 the only memento was a small exercise book, into which had been pasted press cuttings covering the day on which Gibson had appeared as a witness at Lord Mersey's inquiry. There were also copies of photographs taken outside the court room, showing him dressed in a high-buttoned, double breasted reefer jacket, wearing a bowler hat and smoking a cigarette. I was allowed to borrow the book for photo-copying; it also provided me with the first opportunity to read more personal accounts of the inquiry proceedings than the factual official record.

Whether or not the ordeal to which Stone and Gibson were subjected following their jointly shared early morning watch on 15 April 1912 had any adverse effect on their subsequent careers can only be a matter for conjecture. It was certainly the cruellest of luck for both of them that what should have been a perfectly uneventful and routine four hour spell of duty, carried out on the bridge of a ship lying quietly in mid Atlantic in perfect weather conditions, should subsequently become the focus of an international controversy unresolved during their respective lifetimes.

Captain Lord, Stewart, Stone, Groves and Gibson: that, for me, seemed to complete the list of those from the *Californian* who might have anything to contribute towards retrospectively filling in the picture of what had actually happened on that April night so relatively long ago.

I was wrong, however.

In Mariners Park, Wallasey, on the banks of the River Mersey, the MMSA administered a large Victorian building, Cliff House, providing residential accommodation for elderly retired seafarers.

In December 1966, the association's head office was transferred from Liverpool to a new building, Nautilus House, erected in a corner of the grounds, and it was there, one morning in February 1968, that the matron of Cliff House told me that a new entrant, Benjamin Kirk, was not only very interested in any books about the *Titanic* disaster which we might be able to lend him, but also claimed to have been one of the crew of the *Californian* on that memorable voyage in 1912.

I checked the signature on Kirk's application form against that of an AB of the same name who had signed the April 1912 articles of agreement of the *Californian*, a copy of which I had acquired; they were identical.

A day or so later, I walked over to Cliff House to meet Kirk, an active if now somewhat bowed figure of a man, his features dominated by a beak of a nose. I took with me my file of *Californian* documents, and he showed an immediate and amused interest in the photograph of the ship, taken by a passenger in the *Carpathia*. In this print, an object can clearly be seen suspended from the mainmast, and Kirk confirmed that not only had he been on lookout on the night the *Californian* stopped in the ice, but, when he came on duty again the following morning, he had also been selected by the chief officer to be given a pair of binoculars, put into a coal basket, and hoisted to the main truck with instructions to look for the *Titanic*.

While his recollection of the main events of that voyage and of the impression Captain Lord had made on him were still clear, he was understandably somewhat hazy as to any other aspects of the voyage or the layout of the *Californian*'s decks and superstructure. In fact, he seemed much more interested in accounts of what had been happening on board the *Titanic*. It was obviously going to be difficult, if not impossible, to get anything of a coherent story out of him without running the risk of unduly influencing him as a result of the detailed knowledge of events which I had acquired through reading and re-reading the contemporary evidence given at the two inquiries. Apart from passing on to him any books or articles about the *Titanic* which came my way, I consequently made no special effort to follow up Kirk's link with the *Californian*. I invited him to attend a press conference held at Nautilus House at which the 1968 petition was introduced, but he failed to turn up. It also proved impossible to obtain his co-operation in having a tape recording of his voice made for the BBC's archives.

Against this background, I was rather surprised when one day in

December 1968 Kirk came up to me while we were both travelling across to Liverpool on the Mersey ferry to ask if I would help him to put his story on record. In fact, he had very little to tell, but I met him again a few days later at Cliff House, where I jotted down the main points about which he seemed to be quite clear. I had these typed out and returned the draft to him for amendment. The statement he finally signed was simple enough;

> I was born in Liverpool on 30 September 1890. I made my first trip to sea as a deck boy on the *Runic*, a White Star boat, in 1905. I did a trip in the *Californian* to New Orleans in March 1912, and came back to London. She was a Leyland liner. I stayed by the ship and went on the next voyage from London to Boston and back to Liverpool. I was on lookout 10 to 12 on the night she stopped, surrounded by field ice. I was on the fo'c'sle head. There was a glare of light from another ship on the starboard beam. I cannot remember when I first saw it but I did not report it as an approaching ship so think it must have come up from astern. It was still there when I went off watch at twelve o'clock.
>
> I came on watch again at four in the morning. There were no icebergs in sight. Later the chief officer asked me to go up in a coal basket shackled to a mainmast stay and hoisted by a gantline to look for survivors or wreckage or boats from the *Titanic*. I could see nothing. I remember very plainly first seeing the *Mount Temple* on the port bow and then the *Carpathia*. There were no boats or wreckage in the water, which was calm, but the *Carpathia* had boats on her foredeck. She steamed away and I came down.
>
> When the *Californian* docked in Liverpool no one questioned me about what had happened. I did not go down to the inquiry.
>
> This statement is made of my own free will and to the best of my recollection.

Among the books which I lent to Kirk was *The Maiden Voyage*. He disagreed with the author's assessment of Captain Lord as a shipmaster, and in a letter to the editor of the *Nautical Magazine*, published in November 1969, he recorded his own first-hand impression, that of 'having always found Captain Lord very understanding and a good master to serve under'.

Subsequently Kirk led the normal life of a retired seafarer domiciled in Mariners Park. On the chance occasions when we met, we used to chat about the progress of the MMSA's efforts to protect Captain Lord's reputation. Kirk also had some fascinating stories to tell about his 35 years at sea, and of the two occasions during the First World War when he had to swim for his life after being torpedoed while serving in the Royal Navy Reserve. He had kept his discharge books, with their official record of the individual voyages he had made in British ships from 1905 to 1940: in these books, I was intrigued to find the signatures of five shipmasters who, in 1912, had been closely involved in the aftermath of the *Titanic* disaster. These signatures confirmed that, at one time or another, Kirk had sailed in the *Baltic* with Captain E.J. Smith (who went down with the *Titanic*); in the *Cymric* with Captain Charles A. Bartlett; in the *Oceanic* with Captain H.J. Haddock (who in April 1912 was in command of the *Titanic*'s sister ship *Olympic*); in the *Lancastria* and *Scythia* with Captain James Bisset; and, of course, in the *Californian* with Captain Lord.

Latterly, as Kirk's health began to fail and his eyesight to deteriorate – an affliction he found hard to bear, for he was a great reader – he spent more and more time in the small infirmary provided for residents in Mariners Park. Coincidentally, one of his fellow patients there also had a direct link with the *Titanic* disaster. J.J. Kirkpatrick had been a quartermaster in the *Carpathia* when she picked up the *Titanic*'s survivors; as a memento, he had kept one of the nameplates taken from a salvaged lifeboat. He insisted on presenting this to the MMSA; in turn, we presented it in his name on permanent loan to the Liverpool Maritime Museum. Kirkpatrick died on 13 March 1978, at the age of 86.

I last met Benjamin Kirk just before I retired from the MMSA in July 1975. He was then in a local hospital after falling and breaking his thigh, and I was permitted to visit him outside normal hours. I found him virtually blind, very deaf, and sedated, all of which combined to make it very difficult for me to establish any sort of contact with him. Our conversation, such as it was, inevitably hinged on the *Californian* incident. If it had relatively little significance for poor Kirk, it seemed to create a great deal of interest in the wider audience of patients and nursing staff on what otherwise would have been a very quiet afternoon in the ward.

Benjamin Kirk died on 17 April 1977 at the age of 87. At 22, he was not the youngest of the *Californian*'s crew in 1912: as none of the others has come forward since the incident was revived in 1962, however, he was most likely to have been the last surviving member of that controversial ship's company.

This chapter would be incomplete without a reference to an incident reported to me by Olwen Dennis, a Wallasey resident who knew Captain Lord slightly. On 22 September 1969 she attended a 'transfiguration' seance at nearby Moreton: the medium was someone she had never met before. During the seance, the medium asked whether there was anyone present to whom the year 1912 and the ship *Titanic* meant anything. At first, there was no response; then, somewhat hesitantly, but motivated by her knowledge of Captain Lord's alleged involvement, Mrs Dennis volunteered to accept any communication.

Through the medium, she was asked to pass on to 'the right person' the following message, said to be from Captain Smith of the *Titanic*:

> When the *Titanic* was sinking, I blamed the captain of the nearest ship for not helping to save many more lives. After I had passed over, I found out that Captain Lord was being blamed. It was not his fault; my old comrade and I have now met up again and I have told him so. However, in the future, everything will be straightened out and the truth will be unfolded.

I record this incident simply as it was reported to me. As to its significance, I have a completely open mind.

CHAPTER TWENTY-TWO

What Went Wrong?

If the evidence in Captain Lord's favour is so overwhelming, how was it that two official courts of inquiry found him guilty in 1912?

It all started on the night of Sunday, 14 April 1912. Had Captain Lord been clairvoyant, and realised as soon as Stone reported that he had seen 'a rocket' that, unless he did something about it, he would later be blamed for failing to save the lives of up to 1,500 people then in peril somewhere close at hand, he would at once have left the chartroom and joined Stone on the bridge. There the second officer would have pointed out to him a ship that was altering her bearing, steaming away in the direction from which she had come, and firing occasional rocket-like signals rising only to half the height of her masthead light.

What could Captain Lord have done? Two courses were open to him which might have satisfied subsequent potential critics.

Firstly, Captain Lord could have called out his wireless operator, despite their conviction that a medium-sized steamer which did not respond to Morse lamp signals and appeared to be burning oil navigation lights was not fitted with wireless. Had Evans been called, he would have established at about 1.20 a.m. that the *Titanic* was in distress in 41° 46′ N., 50° 14′ W. From Captain Lord's position by dead reckoning, the liner would thus be bearing S16W, 19½ miles distant, from the *Californian*. It was night time; the following morning, in daylight, it took him half an hour to work his ship through field ice towards the clear water to the westward, and a further two hours at full speed to reach the lifeboats. A direct course towards the *Titanic*'s reported position would have kept the *Californian* in that icefield all the way, ending up in an area infested with icebergs – an area in which the *Carpathia* found it necessary to navigate with extreme caution.

To attempt to proceed at full speed would certainly have resulted in damage to the *Californian*, perhaps lost her, and she could not have reached the *Titanic* before the liner sank. Perhaps few would have blamed Captain Lord for risking such heavy odds, having regard to the extraordinary circumstances, but it would not have helped anyone.

The second course open to him was to get under way and to try to overtake the other ship, with the intention of closing her and enquiring by megaphone why she was behaving in such a curious way. There were no other means of communicating with a ship which did not respond to Morse lamp signals and was apparently not fitted with wireless. If that ship were steaming away at only three knots, and Captain Lord was prepared to risk his own at her maximum speed of thirteen knots, it would have taken him about three-quarters of an hour to catch up. No shipmaster in the prevailing conditons would have embarked on such a risky and irresponsible venture.

As it was, lying on the chartroom settee fully dressed and ready for any emergency which might be reported to him, Captain Lord relied on the judgement of his second officer, 24 years old and the holder of a certificate issued by the Board of Trade certifying after an examination that he was competent to serve in any British steamship as first mate, second in command to the master. But Stone never reported distress signals as such, remaining adamant at the British inquiry that the rockets he saw rose to only half masthead height, had no explosive content, and came from a ship that was steaming away from the *Californian*.

In those circumstances, it is difficult enough to fault Stone for his conclusion that the other ship was *not* in distress, and manifestly unfair to blame Captain Lord for his inactivity after receiving purely negative reports from a fully qualified watchkeeping officer. If the Board of Trade subsequently sought to blame anyone for the *Californian*'s alleged failure to respond to what might have been distress signals, then surely any such blame should have been attached to the man certified by them as competent to carry out the duties of a first mate.

But could Stone have been wrong all the time? Was the ship he was watching so intently *not* a ship steaming away from a position only four or five miles off, altering her bearing by nearly eight points, but the *Titanic*, lying stopped on a steady bearing some eight to ten miles distant?

It seems highly unlikely that anyone could have mistaken that change of bearing, which Stone was constantly checking: as Gibson testified, he was 'taking bearings of her all the time'. Gibson, too, unconsciously checked her bearing, when he noted that, from a position on the starboard bow, when the *Californian* was heading north-easterly, that other ship, just before she went out of sight, was on the *Californian*'s port bow as she lay heading in a south-westerly direction after swinging to starboard.

But assuming that Lord Mersey was correct in his conviction that it *was* the *Titanic* they were watching, Stone confirmed that what he was seeing were rockets, and not shooting stars, at 1.15 a.m. The *Californian*'s engines were ready for almost immediate use, and the ship could have been under way by 1.20. It was completely dark, although clear, and she was surrounded by ice of a then unknown density and potential menace – only a few miles away another, much larger, ship was sinking because of damage from ice. At what speed should Captain Lord have taken his ship towards that hypothetical *Titanic*, about nine miles away?

At three knots, it would have taken the *Californian* three hours to cover nine miles. She would have arrived at 4.20, two hours after the liner had foundered.

At six knots, it would have taken the *Californian* one and a half hours, and she could not have got to the scene until nearly thirty minutes after the *Titanic* had gone down.

At nine knots, she would have reached the *Titanic* just as the liner disappeared.

In such circumstances, how could Lord Mersey possibly have justified his finding that the *Californian* could have 'saved many, if not all, of those who were lost'?

The time it would have taken the Californian to cover nine miles poses a simple arithmetical problem that a child of average intelligence could have solved mentally. One of the most mystifying aspects of the *Titanic* inquiry is that, so far as is known, not one of Lord Mersey's five nautical advisers ever paused to consider the practical implications of his judgement. On the two retired shipmasters rested a particularly heavy burden of responsibility for the protection of Captain Lord's professional interests. If either of them ever realised the true nature of the situation in which Captain Lord was being placed, and had doubts about the practicability of the conclusion reached by Lord Mersey, then it was his clear duty to voice his opinion, if necessary to the point of dissenting from the final report.

'All naval men, unfortunately', Captain Lord was later to remark, and it may well be that, against their naval background, they found themselves unable to comprehend what, to them, must have been an inexplicable and inexcusable failure on the part of two merchant ships, only a few miles apart, to communicate with each other, for the Royal Navy in 1912 had reached the peak of perfection in exchanging signals by visual means, particularly by Morse code. Wireless telegraphy had as yet a more limited application.

If the assessors' seamanlike judgement *was* in fact overruled by what must have seemed to them to be an incomprehensible inability on the part of two ships so close together, and with so much at stake in one of them, to communicate with each other, it is, perhaps, a little easier to understand, if not to excuse, why they were so ready to go along with Lord Mersey and support his conclusion, from a very early stage in the inquiry, that the *Californian* saw the *Titanic*, and the *Titanic* saw the *Californian*.

The only occasion upon which the assessors unquestionably and successfully pressed their views on Lord Mersey was when the final report was being drawn up. Incredibly, by so doing they rejected evidence given by all the technically qualified witnesses from both the *Titanic* and the *Californian* to the effect that the closest approach of the other ships was from four to five miles. At such a close range, the *Titanic*, the world's largest passenger liner, would have been unmistakable, and she remained fully illuminated up to the last. As practical seamen, the assessors realised this, but to equate such a situation with the evidence before them was impossible. So, to make Lord Mersey's opinion credible, they had to do what he, as a lawyer, should not have permitted, which was to reject completely the evidence given before them, evidence which confirmed a closest approach of well within the clearly defined horizon, and to replace it with a distance no witness had given and which was *over* the horizon, from eight to ten miles – nearly twice the distance given in evidence.

Writing later about his involvement in the inquiry, Captain Lord spoke of himself as being 'a very poor witness'. In one respect, he handicapped himself, and that was by his transparently honest approach to the business in hand. A striking illustration of his almost naive attitude was his firm adherence to his impression that, from the *Californian*, he saw a green sidelight on the approaching vessel he first noticed at 11 p.m. This is what he *would* have seen had that ship been the *Titanic*, bound to the westward and bearing to the south of him. Yet he was observing her only casually; Groves, the officer of the watch, and using binoculars, was confident that she

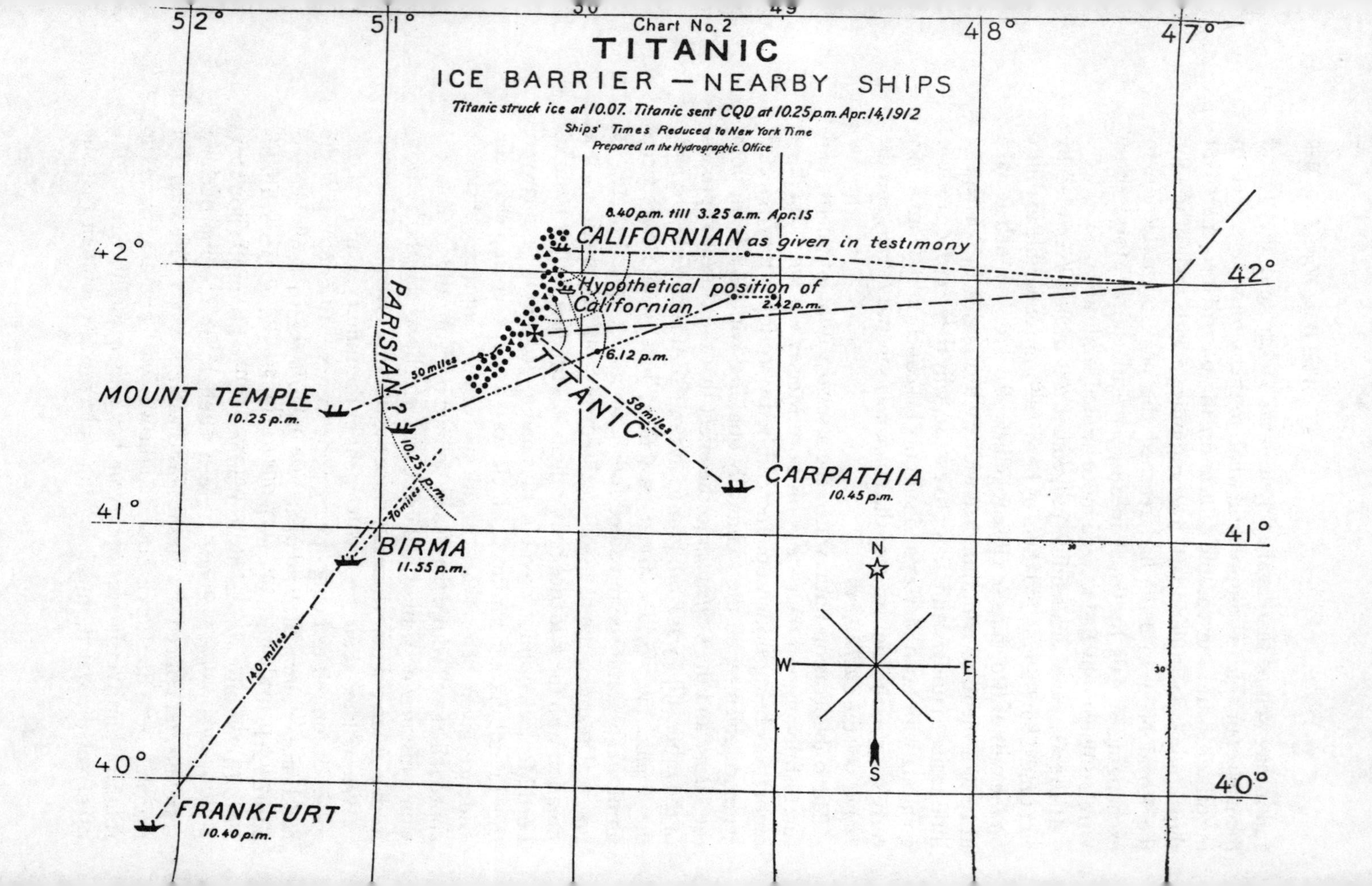
Chart No. 2
TITANIC
ICE BARRIER — NEARBY SHIPS
Titanic struck ice at 10.07. Titanic sent CQD at 10.25 p.m. Apr. 14, 1912
Ships' Times Reduced to New York Time
Prepared in the Hydrographic Office
52°
51°
50
49
48°
47°
42°
41°
40°
8.40 p.m. till 3.25 a.m. Apr. 15
CALIFORNIAN as given in testimony
Hypothetical position of Californian
2.42 p.m.
6.12 p.m.
TITANIC
58 miles
50 miles
PARISIAN ?
10.25 p.m.
70 miles
MOUNT TEMPLE
10.25 p.m.
CARPATHIA
10.45 p.m.
BIRMA
11.55 p.m.
140 miles
FRANKFURT
10.40 p.m.
N
S
E
W

never displayed a green light, always showing a red one. It would have been so very easy for Captain Lord to keep back this obviously damaging impression from his evidence: the fact that he did not hold it back confirms not only his rigid adherence to the truth but also his tragically misplaced belief that the court could be relied upon to protect him and to judge his case solely on the facts so clearly put before them.

To revert to the question of whether or not the *Californian* could have reached another ship eight to ten miles away, with little more than an hour in hand, in time to rescue up to 1,500 people, surely the truth of the matter is that it was not the *Titanic* that could be seen. Subsequent suppositions are consequently purely academic: for the unfortunate Captain Lord, however, the consequences were anything but academic.

The first real warning of what lay ahead of him came in the newspaper reports published in Boston, featuring Gill's allegations. In response to this threat, Captain Lord was content to rest on the simple facts of the case as he saw them, and to which he testified when appearing before the United States inquiry in Washington. It simply never occurred to him to initiate legal proceedings for libel against Gill, whose story he dismissed as imaginative nonsense. But, completely without his knowledge, the United States inquiry was to call before it a witness far more highly qualified than Gill, a witness whose testimony and theories were to prove as deadly as any.

The first nail officially to be driven into Captain Lord's metaphorical *Californian* coffin was manufactured and hammered home by Captain John J. Knapp, United States Navy, the Hydrographer of the Bureau of Navigation, Navy Department, Washington. He appeared before Senator Smith, who was unattended by any other members of his committee, on Saturday, 18 May, and he began by describing the ice conditions in the area in which the *Titanic* was lost.

He submitted three charts. The first showed the ice reported near the *Titanic*, the northern limits of which, beyond 42° N., he based on evidence provided by the *Californian*. The second chart (opposite) showed what he called 'the ice barrier', running mainly north and south, and the positions of nearby ships. One of these was the *Californian*: ominously, two positions were given for her, one marked 'as given in testimony', the other, further south, being identified as 'the hypothetical position of the *Californian*'.

On the third chart, the positions and movements of the *Baltic*,

Birma, Californian, Carpathia, Frankfurt, Mount Temple and *Titanic* were shown, based on information derived from their wireless messages.

Knapp supported the third chart with an explanatory memorandum, and, at the conclusion of his statement, he was asked a question by Senator Smith leading to the direct involvement of the *Californian*.

'Captain,' Smith said. 'Can you think of anything else that you desire to say that will tend to throw any light upon the inquiry being made by the committee into the causes leading up to this wreck, and subsequent events, including any memorandum or data bearing upon the position of the steamship *Californian* on the night of this accident?'

As it so happened, Knapp had just such a memorandum to hand, which he desired to submit. It read:

> The chart ... shows the ice barrier into which the *Titanic* undoubtedly steamed ... A further inspection of this chart shows the *Californian* as located by the master thereof.
>
> A still further inspection of the chart will show certain arcs of circles, shown in dotted lines drawn from the following centers: the position of the *Californian*, the position of the *Titanic*, the 'hypothetical' position of the *Californian*. These arcs are drawn to represent the following: the radii of the arcs drawn about the *Titanic* as a center and the *Californian* as a center are identical, the larger radius being sixteen miles and the smaller radius being seven miles. Sixteen miles represents the distance at which the sidelights of the *Titanic* could be seen from one standing on the *Californian* at the height of the latter ship's sidelights, or the reverse, the seven miles radius being the distance at which the sidelights of the *Californian* would cease to be seen by a person from a boat in the water. A further reference to the chart will show, midway between the plotted positions of the *Californian* and *Titanic*, a plotted 'hypothetical position of the *Californian*'. With the hypothesis that the *Californian* was in this plotted position, a dotted line is drawn on a bearing SSE given by the master of the *Californian* as the bearing in which he sighted a large steamer. This dotted line is drawn to intersect the track of the *Titanic*. A line parallel thereto is drawn to also intersect the track of the *Titanic* at a point at which the *Titanic* appears to have been at 10.06 p.m. New York time, April 14 – at 11.56 p.m. of that date by the *Californian*'s time at which time the large steamer is testified to have been seen by Ernest Gill, of the *Californian*. It thus appears that the bearings of the steamer given by the master of the *Californian* and the testimony of Ernest Gill of that ship will fix the *Californian*'s position near or about the hypothetical position shown on the chart, if the lights seen on that ship were those of the *Titanic*.
>
> A still further inspection of the chart will show that the *Californian*, if

> located in the position given by the master thereof, could have reached the scene of the disaster in about two hours, and, if located in the hypothetical position shown on the chart, the *Californian* certainly could have reached the *Titanic* in a little over an hour after she struck. The evidence taken in the hearings shows that the *Titanic* floated for two and a half hours after she struck the barrier.

So Knapp proved to his own complete satisfaction that, if the *Californian* was not where Captain Lord's evidence showed she was, then she must have been somewhere else. He also appeared to believe that sidelights, by international agreement required to show at least two miles, on this particular occasion could be seen with the naked eye at sixteen miles range. Whether his calculations and hypotheses were all his own work, or whether he was assisted in making them by technically qualified assistants within the Hydrographic Department, his evidence did not show. One can only hope that, for the sake of the safety of United States naval ships of that day, Captain Knapp's theoretical methods of navigation were unique to himself.

But Knapp was an expert witness, technically qualified to pronounce upon such matters, with no one available to challenge the conclusions he drew from his hypothetical reasonings, and inevitably Senator Smith's findings reflected Knapp's views and condemned the *Californian*:

> The committee is forced to the inevitable conclusion that the *Californian*, controlled by the same company, was nearer the *Titanic* than the nineteen miles reported by her captain ... Had assistance been promptly proffered, or had the wireless operator of the *Californian* remained a few minutes longer at his post, that ship might have had the proud distinction of rescuing the lives of the passengers and crew of the *Titanic*.

These findings were published in the United Kingdom on 24 May, and in the light of his previously expressed opinion that the *Titanic* was the ship seen from the *Californian*, it is understandable if Lord Mersey thereupon concluded that the major part of his inquiry into the *Californian*'s inexplicable conduct had been completed for him.

Gill was called as a witness on 4 June. Up in Liverpool, Captain Lord reacted to press reports of Lord Mersey's acceptance of his evidence by turning for advice to a man for whom he had the utmost respect, Captain John Macnab. He had been in Board of Trade service as an examiner – indeed, he had passed Lord in the four examinations for certificates of competency which he had taken. He was also a senior and greatly respected member of the Executive Council of the MMSA, and to him Captain Lord formally put the facts of his case. Equally formally in writing Macnab advised him to do nothing until the inquiry findings were published.

In retrospect, it is blindingly obvious that this was the worst possible advice that could have been given. Lord Mersey and the Attorney-General were openly proclaiming their firm conviction that Captain Lord was the guilty man, and the situation cried out for him to be provided with immediate, effective and completely independent legal representation at the inquiry.

So far, his representation, such as it was, was wholly unsatisfactory. Dunlop, nominally his advocate, in fact was in a hopeless situation. He had been appointed by the Leyland Line with express instructions to do nothing which might lead to the identification of any other ships involved. At one and the same time, Dunlop was also supposed to be protecting the interests of Groves, who had expressed the opinion that the ship seen from the *Californian* was the *Titanic*, and the interests of Captain Lord and Stone, who were confident that she was not. Above all, as he was later to confess to the court in his closing address, Dunlop had been present 'very rarely' during the course of the proceedings.

Once the *Californian*'s witnesses had been heard, it would obviously have required a very powerful push to get things going on Captain Lord's behalf. Nevertheless, the Board of Trade would surely have found it very hard to resist such a move, especially if it had been backed by the MMSA, for there was a point at issue of the utmost concern to all British shipmasters and officers. If, as a result of evidence given as witnesses, Captain Lord and Stone were exposed to prosecution for the offence of failing to proceed to the assistance of a vessel in distress, then they became liable to the penalty on conviction of being fined or facing up to two years' imprisonment, with or without hard labour. In fact, some of Captain Lord's critics have expressed the view that he was fortunate in that he did not push his luck too far in his opposition to Lord Mersey's findings, when his punishment might have been far, far worse than mere public opprobrium and dismissal from the Leyland Line. As to that, Captain Lord was the one who knew best as to whether or not his case was good enough to stand up in court, and so far as he was concerned there was no risk involved in his search for justice.

In such circumstances, even Lord Mersey, convinced as he was of

Captain Lord's culpability, and the Board of Trade – caught up as they were in an inquiry as much into their own shortcomings as into those of anybody's else's – could not have resisted a determined effort to put things back on the rails and ensure proper representation for Captain Lord. This would have led to the fullest possible investigation of the allegations being made against him, and, in particular, would have enabled the evidence given before the United States inquiry being used in his defence, just as the Attorney-General was quoting from it when it suited him to do so in his attack on the *Californian*.

Fatally, however, Captain Lord accepted Macnab's advice, and on 19 June the official trap was finally set for him. On that day, at the Attorney-General's request, the terms of reference of Lord Mersey's formal investigation were amended so as to permit of the *Californian*'s direct involvement in the proceedings, and a potentially incriminating question added to those already before the court.

In considering the Attorney-General's subsequent presentation of the case against Captain Lord, and in particular his treatment of the *Californian* incident in his closing address, it is impossible to avoid comparison with an earlier case in which he was involved. Sir Rufus Isaacs first appeared as a prosecuting counsel in a murder trial against the alleged poisoner, Seddon. Writing about that affair in *Advocates of the Golden Age*, the author Lewis Broad had this to say:

> By his presentation of the case [Rufus Isaacs] induced judge and jury into the belief that Seddon's guilt was established by a chain of circumstances. In fact, the chain was incomplete; there were missing links ... The gap between suspicion and proof never was bridged by evidence, but judge and jury were satisfied of Seddon's guilt beyond the law's reasonable doubt. That is the measure of the achievement of Rufus Isaacs ... Reviewing the evidence, one is very conscious of its limitations.

To Filson Young, an eminent journalist present in court throughout the trial, it appeared 'as if, in fact, Seddon was convicted not because the Crown succeeded in proving his guilt, but because he failed to prove his innocence'. Coincidentally, it was the same Filson Young who, in the *Saturday Review* of 24 May 1913, recorded his conviction that Captain Lord had suffered an injustice at the hands of another tribunal before which Sir Rufus had appeared as 'prosecutor'.

Incidentally, the *Titanic* inquiry was not the first occasion on which Lord Mersey and Sir Rufus Isaacs had met as judge and prosecuting counsel. In January 1904 they had both been involved in the private prosecution of Whitaker Wright, charged with fraudulent dealings in connection with company finance. *The Dictionary of National Biography* records that Lord Mersey's 'firm handling of the case helped to secure the conviction of the defendant; but counsel for the defence resented what they regarded as unjudicial hostility to their client'.

It was Captain Lord's misfortune to become the victim on an occasion when history appeared to be repeating itself. Lord Mersey accepted the Attorney-General's arguments; Captain Lord was duly found guilty and formally condemned in the eyes of the world on the charge of having caused the deaths of up to 1,500 people.

The management of the Leyland Line in Liverpool did not believe that he had done so, but one of the directors did. He was Sir Miles Walker Mattinson, KC, one of the most influential men in British shipping at that time, and his threat to resign from the board unless Captain Lord was dismissed was sufficient to ensure that it was Captain Lord who went.

Only one avenue of possible redress remained open, an appeal to the Board of Trade, with their discretionary powers to re-open the inquiry. There is one unexpected advantage in reviewing a case which occurred as long ago as fifty years, for the contemporary and previously confidential Board of Trade files are now available for scrutiny in the Public Record Office. These files are contained in haphazard disorder in six cardboard boxes and cover the widest possible range of topics, from resolutions submitted by various local trades councils, condemning the lack of adequate lifesaving facilities in the *Titanic*, to disputed travel and subsistence allowances for disgruntled witnesses.

The files relating to the *Californian* open chronologically with a letter addressed to the President of the Board of Trade, Sydney Buxton, MP, written by Gerard Jensen a fortnight after the disaster:

> I think I am discharging a public duty in bringing the following matter to your notice and to suggest that at the forthcoming inquiry witnesses should be called and closely examined from the Leyland Company's s.s. *Californian*. My information is from a letter written by the carpenter of the *Californian* to a friend of his, but I should be obliged if you would consider the source of your information as confidential.
>
> Briefly stated the facts are:
>
> 1. That while the *Californian* was lying in the ice with engines stopped, the *Titanic*'s signals of distress were seen by various members of the crew.

2. That the matter was reported to the captain of the *Californian* on at least three occasions.
3. That the *Californian*'s captain took no notice of the matter.
4. That the signals were reported to the first officer when he relieved the captain in the ordinary course (of duty).
5. That the first officer then set his Marconi operator to work and got in touch with the *Titanic* – but that it was then too late to be of service.
6. That the *Californian* was within ten miles of the *Titanic* and could have saved every soul, had her captain responded to the call for help.
7. That Newfoundland fishing boats are occasionally run down by the *Californian* and other liners and no attempt is made to save the lives of the fishermen in the endeavour to keep time in crossing the Atlantic.

Jensen was writing from his office at 14 Victoria Street, London: his letter-head announced that he was a specialist in drainage, water supply, and sewage disposal, with the telegraphic address: 'Cloacalis, London'.

The *Californian*'s carpenter on that voyage was H. McGregor, aged 41, of Edge Lane, Liverpool, but apart from a formal acknowledgment of Jensen's letter there is no record in the files of any 'follow up' by the Board of Trade; they certainly did not bring McGregor down to the inquiry with the other members of the crew concerned.

A typical Board of Trade file in the collection contains the original letters and documents relating to its subject, prefaced by foolscap sheets on which individual officials have noted their comments and opinions as the file passed from one to the other. Minuted comments in the *Titanic* files are normally verified simply by the initials of those making them. At that time, in addition to Buxton as President, these included his Parliamentary Secretary, J.M. Robertson, MP; Sir Hubert Llewellyn Smith, Permanent Secretary; and, in the Marine Department, Sir Walter Howell, Assistant Secretary; Charles Hipwood; G.E. Baker; A. Donald; and Captain A.H. Young, Principal Professional Officer and nautical adviser. The Board's solicitor, who was very closely concerned in the case, was R. Ellis Cunliffe, assisted by G. Vaux and G.E. Potter.

On 1 August, Buxton asked for consideration to be paid to the institution of proceedings against Captain Lord, on the basis of the inquiry findings, for failing to proceed to the assistance of persons in distress, under Section 6 of the Maritime Convention Act 1911. The solicitor minuted:

> Captain Lord gave his version of what happened in the witness box here and in America. He might have taken the objection that he declined to reply lest he should incriminate himself; he did not do so and though the Wreck Commissioner [Lord Mersey] did not accept his crew's explanations or excuses I would not advise a prosecution of Captain Lord under Section 6 of the above Act under the circumstances. I need hardly add that his punishment is already very great. Moreover he was in ice and stopped by the ice to a certain extent for, I believe, the first time.

Baker commented that, in view of the solicitor's minute, he presumed that no action should be taken against Captain Lord. So far as it was desired to call attention to the obligation upon masters to render assistance to persons in distress at sea, he suggested that this might be done by issuing an official notice calling attention to the Maritime Convention Act, as had been recommended by Lord Mersey.

Sir Walter confirmed that Buxton's concern was from the point of view of giving full publicity to the matter, and added: 'As regards Captain Lord, his punishment already is very bad and very heavy'.

Events were overtaken by the arrival of Captain Lord's letter appealing for a re-opening of that part of the inquiry which had censured him. On this request, Baker minuted: 'The Board cannot well undertake to consider the matter after Lord Mersey has pronounced upon it.'

Captain Young, the one man above all upon whom Captain Lord depended for the protection of his professional interests, most unfortunately not only held the strongest possible views on his culpability (had not distress rockets been seen and ignored?) but also was now suffering from an imagined slight because he had not been consulted before the decision was taken not to prosecute Captain Lord. He commented:

> In view of the fact that signals of distress were reported to Captain Lord and no action was taken by him with a view to rendering assistance at the time these signals were made it appears to me that as the President has decided that he is not to be proceeded against for misdemeanour he has been treated with very great consideration and, I think, any further action is unnecessary.

Writing to Buxton from Llangollen, where he was having 'a delightful time' on holiday, Sir Walter advised against Captain Lord's appeal being referred to Lord Mersey; to do so, he suggested, 'might be misunderstood and create a bad precedent'.

On 20 August, Captain Lord was accordingly formally notified of the Board's rejection of his appeal, but their internal debate continued, for on that same day Sir Walter suggested that action might be taken against Captain Lord under Sections 470 and 471 of the Merchant Shipping Act 1894. His proposal was demolished by Donald, however, who pointed out that those sections did not appear to be applicable to the case, as Captain Lord could scarcely be regarded as guilty of a gross act of misconduct, drunkenness or tyranny, and his failure to render assistance was not 'in a case of collision' involving his own ship. He drew attention to Section 422 of the Act.

Sir Walter replied to Donald's points nine days later:

> Section 422 refers only to collisions between vessels and is clearly not applicable to this case, but I am not so sure that there has not been 'misconduct' under Section 471 or 'gross misconduct' under Section 470. A point is that Lord Mersey's court could have dealt with Captain Lord's certificate and did not do so. In any case we shall be attacked for acting in far less clear cases than this and in letting Captain Lord hold his certificate. Captain Young should see. I am not in the least saying that we ought to do anything more in this case but we must consider it in all its bearings and be ready for criticism.

Captain Young, however, was still obviously harbouring a sense of resentment at his exclusion from the previous consultations:

> I was not aware until the 13th *ultimo* that it had been decided not to proceed against Captain Lord but I have had the opinion from the first that a special inquiry should have been ordered not only as to his neglect to answer to distress signals but also as a consequence of such almost inexplicable neglect into his competency to continue to act as master of a British ship. It appears also to me on reading the observations of the Attorney-General at the *Titanic* inquiry that he was already of this opinion. From the point of view of 'gross misconduct' I think an inquiry should have been held but, as I gather from this paper that it has been decided by the President not to do so I cannot well offer any further observations.

In defence of the system, Baker pointed out that, although Captain Young had been away when the decision not to prosecute was taken, he had been informed very soon after, and Sir Walter, agreeing that there had been some confusion about the matter, asked Captain Young to re-consider the case. He did so:

> In response to your minute of 5th (September), I have given this matter further consideration and note that the solicitor has advised against proceedings under Section 6 of the Maritime Convention Act 1911. While agreeing generally with the opinions expressed that Captain Lord's fault carries its own punishment, I also agree with your view that we must be in a position to justify, if need be, our inaction. It appears to me that if the Board consider it desirable to carry the matter further the case must fall into Section 470 (b) of the Merchant Shipping Act 1894 re 'gross act of misconduct' but I think this point is for the solicitor. On the other hand, should the Board consider it desirable to drop the matter, it would perhaps be a sufficient answer to any eventual criticism that the case had been really or already dealt with by the *Titanic* court of inquiry, when Lord Mersey's strictures on Captain Lord's evidence amounted to a tacit condemnation. All things considered, I am inclined to the opinion that the latter course would be the best one to adopt.

Sir Walter was disposed to agree with Captain Young, but Sir Hubert Llewellyn Smith decided that the matter must first go to the solicitor before he was prepared to report to Buxton. The solicitor's considered comments, countersigned by Potter and Vaux, were submitted on 17 September.

> Captain Lord was summoned to appear at the inquiry as a witness but was not made a party to the proceedings. On the seventh day of the hearing Mr Robertson Dunlop asked the Commissioner (Lord Mersey) for leave to appear under Rule 5 of the Shipping Casualties, etc., rules on behalf of the owners, master and officers of the *Californian* but the Commissioner declined to deal with the application at that time and said that if anything required explanation he would let Mr Dunlop know.
>
> In fact, however, thereafter Mr Dunlop cross-examined the witnesses and at the close of the inquiry addressed the Commissioner on behalf of his clients so that for practical purposes, though possibly not technically, it may be said that Captain Lord became a party to the proceedings under Rule 5. But the most that the court could find was that lives might have been saved if the *Californian* had gone to the rescue earlier. They could not find as a certainty that lives would have been saved. The inquiry was into the loss of the *Titanic* and loss of life from her. The court could not find that the loss of the *Titanic* and the loss of life from her was caused by 'the wrongful act or default' of Captain Lord (Section 470 (i) (a)) and there was therefore in my opinion no power to deal with his certificate.
>
> It seems to me to be very doubtful whether the conduct of Captain Lord comes within the contemplated meaning of the words 'misconduct rendering him unfit to discharge his duties' in Section 471 (i) which is the section giving the Board power to order a Local Marine Board

inquiry. But apart from that, to prove that Captain Lord had been guilty of 'a gross act of misconduct' it would be necessary to show that he had knowledge of the events, was a free agent, and notwithstanding this, acted or refrained from acting deliberately, and I do not think this could be done on the evidence given at the inquiry before the Wreck Commissioner.

Sir Hubert minuted: 'I think that with this advice you will probably decide not to take any further step in this matter.' Buxton, Sir Walter Howell, Baker and Donald concurred, and Vaux noted the decision on behalf of the solicitor.

The whole matter was re-opened later in the year, however, when Robertson, as Buxton's Parliamentary Secretary, was approached on behalf of Captain Lord by A.H. Gill, member of Parliament for his home town, Bolton. This influential approach led Ellis Cunliffe to draft a thirteen-page review of the case. In general, his attitude was that Captain Lord's new approach threw no real doubt, on Lord Mersey's findings. His memorandum contained two gross errors of fact, however, which must have influenced him in his approach to the case. He erroneously recorded that 'Captain Lord was told *before* [author's italics] he went to his cabin to lie down that the vessel in question had sent up a rocket, though he did not see it himself'; he also stated that the ship seen from the Californian 'was heading west'.

Much of the memorandum dealt with the renewed allegation that the *Mount Temple* was the ship seen from the *Titanic*. It contained a curious reference to her tending to support the inference that special consideration was being paid by the authorities to ensure that no criticism of her movements or alleged inaction was to be made, for the solicitor commented:

> Whatever may be said against the captain of the *Mount Temple* by those on board – and there are rumours that people on board seemed to think that at some time she saw lights (probably the flares from the boats in the water) and that she did not do all she could to get to the *Titanic* – as I am not able to agree that the vessel that the *Titanic* saw was the *Mount Temple*, whether the captain of the *Mount Temple* did or omitted to do something that he ought not to have done or should have done (and according to his evidence and that of the Marconi operator he did everything he could) may be a matter for further inquiry, but so far as I can see does not help Captain Lord.

If the captain and others in the *Mount Temple* actually saw 'flares from the boats in the water' and did nothing at all about it, then they were manifestly as culpable as anyone could be of failing to proceed to the assistance of persons in distress; yet the solicitor accepted such a possible situation without comment.

Another inference he failed to draw from the fact that flares were displayed from some of the *Titanic*'s lifeboats (notably Boxhall's) was this: if, as Lord Mersey maintained, the *Californian* was only eight to ten miles from the *Titanic* and her lifeboats, why did no one from her see those distinctive green flares, flares which were sighted at extreme range from the *Carpathia*?

The solicitor concluded his memorandum by suggesting that Gill be informed that it appeared to the Board that Captain Lord's most recent submission did not throw any real doubt on the findings of the court insofar as they related to the *Californian*, although they would very carefully consider any signed statements that Captain Lord might obtain from witnesses on board the *Mount Temple*. The Board accepted this suggestion, and on 2 December wrote to Gill accordingly.

Captain Lord's second appeal in August 1913 was ill-timed, for, as the Board's solicitor minuted:

> If these articles from the *Nautical Magazine* have to be compared with the evidence given at the inquiry, it is not a matter I can undertake to do satisfactorily while on my holiday. I do not see with or in these magazines the replies of the British shipmasters referred to by Captain Lord in his letter of 8 August 1913. No *new evidence* has been produced, the articles are apparently directed to showing that the court came to a wrong conclusion on the evidence before it. If the Leyland Line management are convinced that Captain Lord has been subjected to an injustice I am surprised that they have not taken up his case or that his solicitors and counsel do not support him.

Six days later, Ernest J. Moggridge, who also appears to have been on holiday, was instructed on his return to inform Captain Lord that the Board were unable to reopen the case. His letter conveying this information recorded that the statements referred to in Captain Lord's appeal had been 'carefully considered'; the minutes do not reveal who, if anyone, had 'carefully considered' them in the intervening three days.

The final position taken up by the Board of Trade in relation to Captain Lord's case appears to be as stated as 1918 by Charles Hipwood. He had now become head of the Marine Department, in which capacity he was approached on a semi-personal basis by Sir

Willoughby Maycock KCMG writing from the St James Club, Piccadilly, London, to enquire whether or not Captain Lord had been punished in any way following the *Californian*'s involvement in the *Titanic* disaster.

Before replying, Hipwood asked the Registrar General to let him have the official papers relating to the *Titanic* inquiry of 1912. These were delivered under cover of the following note:

> Mr Stanley Lord is the holder of an OC certificate No. 030740. He failed to join the *Barbadian* ON.102072 on 7/9/99 and was censured by the President of the court of inquiry into the loss of the *Titanic*.

In a letter to Sir Willoughby dated 13 December, Hipwood wrote:

> I have now had our papers looked up to ascertain what occurred in the case of Captain Lord of the s.s. *Californian* at the time of the sinking of the *Titanic*. Lord Mersey in his report on the investigation which was held gave what amounts to a censure of Captain Lord, but he does not state that lives would certainly have been saved if the *Californian* had gone earlier to the rescue; the furthest that Lord Mersey and the assessors would go was to say that those lives *might* have been saved.
>
> The court could not find that the loss of the *Titanic*, and the loss of lives from her, was caused by 'the wrongful act or default' of Captain Lord (see Section 470, Merchant Shipping Act 1894), and the view appears to have been taken that there was no case for dealing with his certificate.
>
> As I said in my letter of 6 December, Captain Lord protested very strongly against the report of the court and asked for a further hearing which, however, we did not see our way to grant him. He had no further punishment than the censure of the court.

And that was the last in a series of unfortunate events leaving Captain Lord officially branded as the man who could have converted the *Titanic* sinking from a dreadful tragedy into an exciting and unusual nocturnal escapade involving no loss of life.

Against the background of those events, the simple answer to the question of what went wrong for Captain Lord is: 'Everything.' It was as though Fate had decided that here was a man against whom every malign influence must be unleashed. One can only marvel at the strength of character which enabled him to resist that attack with such indomitable resolution.

CHAPTER TWENTY-THREE

Summing Up

This book was written for two reasons. The first was to place on record the facts about Captain Lord's life, as accurately as they could be pieced together. The second is, quite unashamedly, to try to interest the general public in a matter which constitutionally involves them all, for it was 'in the public interest' that the Board of Trade decided in 1965 that Captain Lord's case should not be reopened.

Against the tragedy of the *Titanic* disaster as a whole, Captain Lord's misfortune must rank as a comparatively minor incident: yet is there any other individual who, in time of peace, is known to have been left defenceless against an officially recorded charge of having negligently caused the deaths of up to 1,500 people?

Over seventy years after the event, with Captain Lord himself now dead, it is sometimes asked whether anything can be done, or needs to be done, to clear up any doubts about the *Californian* incident.

The facts are clear enough. In the United Kingdom, Captain Lord was censured by a tribunal set up under British law, under an Act of Parliament administered by a government department. A minister of the Crown is responsible to Parliament for the efficient running of that department. Through Parliament, the British people as a whole are responsible for what is done in their name, and must bear collective responsibility for any miscarriage of justice which might occur.

In the United States a broadly similar situation exists. In both cases, Captain Lord appeared before the respective tribunals as a witness only, having no effective legal representation or advice, and with no right of appeal. He was left with his reputation exposed to attack, both during his lifetime and since his death, because those official tribunals failed to protect him as they should have done.

The passage of time seems to stimulate interest in the *Titanic* disaster rather than to diminish it. So long as that interest remains, authors, publishers and film producers can exploit the *Californian* incident, concentrating on the superficial aspects of the apparent mystery of her inactivity rather than the illogicalities and inconsistencies of the case.

When Parliament revised the Merchant Shipping Acts in 1970, an express provision was incorporated which would permit of the reopening of Captain Lord's case and the restoration of his professional reputation. Before that can be done, perhaps the greatest obstacle to be overcome is that massive inertia and evident expert ability to close ranks in defence of their own demonstrated by the Board of Trade and associated national institutions so far as Captain Lord's case is concerned.

It is a formidable alliance. The resistance of the government's legal advisers to accept a procedure involving the inevitable exposure of Lord Mersey and his colleagues to some measure of criticism is understandable; but why should their reputations be of greater concern and more sacred than that of Captain Lord?

If sufficient people consider that there is a need to right the wrong done to Captain Lord through the inadequate investigation of his case in 1912, and the damage still being done to his reputation through the activities of authors and others exploiting the *Titanic* disaster for commercial gain, then pressure of public opinion, exerted through individual members of Parliament, is strong enough to achieve this. After all, it was fear of adverse public opinion in 1912 which caused the directors of the Leyland Line to dismiss Captain Lord from their employ; public opinion today, if sufficiently motivated and exercised, has similar power to influence events, this time in Captain Lord's favour.

Two principles are involved in Captain Lord's case. The first has already been discussed, that is, the responsibility of the nation as a whole to protect and defend the rights of an individual. There is also the professional aspect, a principle rising out of the Board of Trade's sustained refusal to use the protective provisions of the Merchant Shipping Acts for the benefit of a British shipmaster. The only conclusion to be drawn from the Board's refusal to discuss the practical merits of the case is that they are either covering up some so far undisclosed departmental error, or are unwilling for 'political' reasons to reveal the true facts about the original inquiry.

Such an attitude on the part of a government department is not in the national interest. Unless it is successfully challenged, there is always the risk that another professional reputation might be sacrificed in the same way as Captain Lord's.

If the case were to be reopened on the basis of mutually agreed facts, acknowledging the navigational and technical points which are incontestably on record in the proceedings of the United States and British inquiries and in Lawrence Beesley's book, the subsequent legal proceedings could be very brief. They would only be protracted, and correspondingly costly, if the submissions made on behalf of Captain Lord were to be opposed. If an agreed case, on a narrow issue, were to be presented, then surely that case would have to be accepted.

Perhaps the United States leads the way when it comes to correcting past mistakes leading to posthumous attacks on personal and professional reputations. In 1967, the United States Army formally cleared the name of Major Marcus Reno, dismissed the service in 1880, amending official records to show an honourable discharge. This action followed the successful contention of Major Reno's great-grand-nephew that his ancestor had been unfairly convicted because of prejudice following allegations that, four years earlier, he had failed in his duty as one of General Custer's aides at the famous 'last stand' battle of the Little Big Horn.

Then there was Lieutenant William S. Cox, found guilty in 1813 of neglect of duty and unofficerlike conduct while serving in the United States frigate *Chesapeake*, defeated in her engagement with the British frigate *Shannon*. He was sentenced to be cashiered, with perpetual incapacity to serve in the United States Navy, but the sentence was officially quashed over a century later. So there are precedents for any posthumous rehabilitation of Captain Lord.

Perhaps the closest parallel in British history is that provided by the case of General Sir Hubert Gough. Deliberately made the scapegoat for the inadequacies of the Fifth Army, overwhelmed on the Western Front in the initially successful German offensive in March 1918, Sir Hubert had to wait eighteen years before his name was officially cleared.

'A further hearing, by an independent court, on the evidence already submitted at the former inquiry, is all I ask for.' That was that Captain Lord wanted in 1913, and in this book, so far as possible, conclusions have been based on such evidence and on contemporary factual statements.

How unreliable memory can be is all too evident from what those concerned have said about the disaster in later years. Sometimes it is possible to trace the source of a particular misconception. Here is

Miss Edith Russell, a *Titanic* survivor, interviewed by Sheridan Morley in a BBC television interview on 10 May 1970:

> I remember looking over the rail and seeing a fully lighted ship very close by. I've always said that I saw a man walking on the deck, and I did. They claim I didn't, but I was extremely far-sighted. As a matter of fact, I had defective eyesight, but I was too far-sighted. Now that ship, we were told, was the *Californian*, and it *was* the *Californian*. With all the denials that have been made since, it *was* the Californian ... It was the only other ship. The officers on the *Titanic* told us all: 'Don't worry, the *Californian* will pick up everybody in case you don't come back for breakfast.' No danger whatsoever – we would all be back for breakfast.

The truth is that only one of the *Titanic*'s officers – Phillips, one of the two wireless operators – knew that the *Californian* was anywhere near, and he was too fully occupied with transmitting passengers' messages to Cape Race to tell anyone else at the time. The key to Miss Russell's illusion is to be found in the following passage in Lawrence Beesley's book, describing an event during the *Carpathia*'s return passage to New York:

> There is no doubt that a good many (survivors) felt the waiting period of four days very trying ... with, in many cases, the knowledge that other friends were left behind and would not return home again ... We encouraged them to hope that the *Californian* and the *Birma* had picked some up; stranger things have happened, and we had all been through strange experiences.

So what Miss Russell was told in the *Carpathia*, from which she had seen the *Californian* standing by at 8.30 in the morning, appears to have become fused in her mind with what she remembered of events in the *Titanic* during the night. It is all perfectly explicable; what is so sad is that such illusions, repeated often enough and with such authority, should become accepted as facts.

This summing up would be incomplete without a final reference to the main points held against Captain Lord. First, those emotive rockets – and what a pity it is that the emotion aroused by their mere mention does not lead to further investigation rather than the complete blanking off of mental processes which usually ensues.

Stone held a professional qualification establishing him as competent to serve as the first mate in a foreign-going steamship. He had sailed with Captain Lord before, on that earlier voyage to New Orleans, and, from what he had observed of Stone's watchkeeping performance, Captain Lord had no reason whatsoever to consider that he was not fully justified in leaving him in charge of the watch on that night of 14/15 April. He relied on Stone to act as his eyes and ears while he was resting in the chartroom.

For the reasons repeated earlier in this book, Stone decided that the signals he saw were *not* distress signals. He also established that the ship he was watching was moving by taking repeated compass bearings. What are you supposed to do when a ship displaying confusing signals steams away from you?

What it is like to stand a 12–4 a.m. watch on the bridge of a steamer lying stopped in mid-Atlantic may be outside the personal experience of the majority of readers of this book. The nearest landsman's analogy to the situation which confronted Stone is possibly this:

You are a motorist driving along a quiet country road at night in mid-winter when you find that is becoming increasingly covered with ice. Conditions become so hazardous that you decide to stop and wait for daybreak.

There is a convenient lay-by on the other side of the road; as you brake, your car skids half-way round, so that it is convenient for you to complete the turn and park facing in the direction from which you have come.

At about 11.30, another car comes up from behind you and pulls into the lay-by ahead. You get out of your car and walk along to the stranger. You tap on the window; your approach is ignored, and so you return to your own car. You repeat your visit on half-a-dozen occasions, with the same negative response.

At 12.50 a.m., the other car's hazard warning lights are suddenly switched on and, with horn intermittently blaring, it starts up, turns round, and is driven away in the direction from which it has come.

What do you do? If you are worried about the safety of the other driver, there is only one thing you *can* do: you must also start up, turn around, and drive after that car. But it is now well ahead of you, and, if you are to catch it up, you will have to drive much faster than you consider to be really safe. Consequently, unless you are very, very public-spirited and prepared to take risks which the average motorist would rather avoid, you will presumably do just what Stone did, in comparable circumstances but a vastly different environment. You will come to the conclusion that, inexplicable as the other driver's actions appear to be, he or she is a free agent, and perfectly entitled to behave as he chooses.

So Stone metaphorically shrugged his shoulders, reported the simple facts to his captain, and left it at that.

To complete the analogy, a car-to-car radio telephone link must be introduced, the only other contact you have that night being the chairman of your company, travelling somewhere in the locality in his Rolls-Royce. The car which stopped in front of you was very definitely *not* a Rolls-Royce, however.

And there the analogy has to stop. To complete it would require the Rolls-Royce – and the chairman – to be found later crashed at the side of the road within sight of you; but roads have firmly established distinguishing features, and positions can be immediately and accurately located. In mid-Atlantic, the equivalents of milestones are rare, although not unknown – such a one, the significance of which was ignored by Lord Mersey and his assessors, was provided by the group of three icebergs seen from and reported by both the *Parisian* and the *Californian* of 14 April, well to the northward of the *Titanic*'s track. Otherwise the accuracy of positions and distances depends entirely upon the standard of navigation being applied in each ship, and, as in the case of the *Californian* and the *Titanic*, can lead to controversy.

The essence of the case against Captain Lord is to be found in some quite extraordinary coincidences: indeed, an alternative title for this book might well be *Condemned by Coincidence*.

It was a critical coincidence, influencing Captain Lord's sleepy reaction to Stone's report about 'a rocket', that so much of his sea service as an officer should have been spent in a company in which it was customary to use distress signals for inter-ship saluting purposes.

It was a crucial coincidence that sent to the *Californian* on that voyage three such disparate figures as Stone, Groves and Gill. Stone, honest but stolid and unimaginative, would have served Captain Lord better had he shown a little more urgency in informing him of his bewilderment at the odd conduct of the ship he was watching. Groves, with a lot more imagination and unfortunately prone to jump to conclusions at that stage in his career, would have helped everyone if only he had sat back for a moment and, quietly and logically, looked at the facts of the case, and reflected on the inevitable consequences of the expression of any opinions he had formed. As for Gill, whatever his motives or however sincerely held his views, he 'did for' Captain Lord as effectively as a Merchant Navy rating has ever 'done for' a British shipmaster.

It was a superficially convincing coincidence, more apparent than real, that the times at which the ship seen from the *Californian* stopped and later went out of sight seemed to agree with the times at which the *Titanic* stopped and later sank.

It was a potential, but in the event unfulfilled, coincidence that had the *Californian* actually been able to take part in the rescue operations on the night of the *Titanic* disaster, she would have been commanded by a man who, in September 1904, off an Essex beach, had gained practical experience of the problems involved in embarking over a thousand tired men from lifeboats.

It was an infinitely depressing coincidence that the United States inquiry should be conducted by a man such as Senator Smith, who was to be described by James Bryce, the British ambassador in Washington, as 'one of the most unsuitable persons who could have been charged with an investigation of this nature'. It was an equally depressing coincidence that Senator Smith should accept as technically definitive the opinions of someone like Captain Knapp – a man who could assert that the relatively small green and red sidelights of a ship could be seen at a distance of sixteen miles. Incidentally, it was an ironic coincidence that later, at the British inquiry, with the intention of proving Captain Lord guilty, the Attorney-General should assert that no human being would suggest that the *Californian* could have seen the sidelights of the *Titanic* at the relatively slightly greater distance of nineteen miles. Any stick, it appeared, would do with which to beat poor Captain Lord.

It was a deadly coincidence that reunited two lawyers such as Lord Mersey and Sir Rufus Isaacs to control the British inquiry. It will be recalled that of the former it was said that 'he was inclined to the failings of those whose minds work quickly', and how, 'disliking tedious arguments, and full of robust common sense, he often took a short cut'. Of Sir Rufus Isaacs, the same source commented on his 'penetrating power of judgement which enabled him to see the point on which the case would ultimately turn and the main difficulty of fact to be surmounted'. For Captain Lord to receive justice at the inquiry, there was much 'tedious argument' to be endured, and 'difficulties of fact' to be accepted.

It was a decisive coincidence that Captain John Macnab, the one man above all others on whom Captain Lord was prepared to depend for advice, should have completely failed to appreciate that there could be no official appeal against Lord Mersey's findings once they had been delivered.

It was a fatal coincidence that the only member of the Leyland Line's board of directors to demand that Captain Lord should be dismissed was one of the most influential men in British shipping at that time.

It was an unavoidable coincidence in the circumstances that Captain Lord's appeals to the Board of Trade in 1912 and 1913 should have to be submitted in midsummer, at a time when senior government officials are accustomed to take their holidays undisturbed by departmental business.

Finally, there was the minor coincidence that, although unrelated, Walter Lord the author should bear the same surname as Stanley Lord the man he condemned.

After taking up Captain Lord's case, I too found myself involved in a number of curious personal coincidences.

It was a remote coincidence that I should have two links with the *Mount Temple* of 1912. Commander Hubert Boothby, DSO, RNR, was a near neighbour and a close family friend during my childhood. In 1908, he was captain of the *Mount Temple* on a trans-Atlantic voyage, bound for St John, New Brunswick. The ship ran ashore on the Nova Scotian coast in direct consequence of the officer of the watch's failure to obey underlined written instructions to call the captain at once 'if it turned thick'. With the very best of intentions – the captain had been up most of the previous night and would most certainly be up all the following one – the officer decided to let him sleep, despite running into intermittent thick snow squalls. During one of these squalls, the officer missed sighting the Sambro light, a sighting which would have warned them that, due to abnormal tidal conditions, the ship was well ahead of her dead reckoning position.

No lives were lost; the ship was salved, largely due to Captain Boothby's own exertions; and the subsequent court of inquiry in Halifax not only exonerated him, but also complimented him on the way he had handled things after the stranding. Nevertheless, the Canadian Pacific Railway Company dismissed him.

Coincidences again: the court of inquiry also sought to suspend the officer of the watch's certificate of competency for two years, having found him completely to blame. Having failed to warn him that he should be represented at the inquiry, however, their sentence was invalid.

Not surprisingly, Captain Boothby laboured under a deep sense of injustice for the rest of his life: as he subsequently described the incident in his autobiography *Spunyarn*, it was 'a fair sample of the fate which overhangs anyone in command of a ship in the British Merchant Navy; he goes about with a rope round his neck all the time'. So discouraging an event, often discussed in my presence in my younger days, nearly led to my abandoning my own ambition to go to sea and qualify as a master mariner.

Despite the warning, I did go to sea, later to find myself serving for over a year with the son of the man who, as fourth officer of the *Mount Temple* in 1912, had triggered off the MMSA's misguided approach to the Board of Trade. It was the younger Notley, on that protracted voyage over 25 years later, who did much to foster my literary interests and so helped to make this book possible.

It proved to be a very valuable coincidence that I should be the first General Secretary of the MMSA in nearly a hundred years to be qualified as a master mariner. Had Captain Lord come to the association immediately prior to March 1956, he would have found no one on the head office staff technically capable of assessing his case.

It was an unexpected coincidence to discover that the major part of the substantial financial resources of the pension funds administered through the MMSA's Welfare Branch had accrued from gifts originally made by members of the Ismay family, and that, parallel with my efforts on behalf of Captain Lord, I was able to play a small part in countering some of the wilder allegations made against J. Bruce Ismay and his conduct both during the *Titanic* disaster and afterwards.

It was the unhappiest of coincidences that the MMSA's President, in the crucial years 1961 to 1962, should have been one-time Commodore of the Cunard White Star fleet, and a man prepared to go to extreme lengths to stop what was being done to clear Captain Lord's name.

It was an unlikely coincidence that 29 Salisbury Avenue should be the only house in West Kirby I came to know well as an occasional visitor, for it is the house in which Captain Lord was temporarily living during the Second World War when Foweraker's unexpected bequest was declined.

It was a doubly interesting coincidence that both Benjamin Kirk of the *Californian* and J.J. Kirkpatrick of the *Carpathia* should come to live in their retirement in an establishment for the administration of which I was responsible.

It was a most helpful coincidence that C.R. Allen, the only correspondent to approach me who had sailed in Lawther Latta's with Captain Lord, should voluntarily describe, in detail, the background to that particular voyage to Australia in 1925 during which there was the chance meeting with Groves and the mid-ocean transfer of a sick member of the *Anglo Chilean*'s crew which influenced Captain Lord's relatively early retirement.

It was a moving and thought-provoking coincidence that I should be obsessed with thoughts of Lawrence Beesley at the time of his death.

Undoubtedly the weirdest personal coincidence happened four years after my retirement. My house overlooks the estuary of the River Dee, now silted up and no longer navigable by even the smallest commercial coaster. Nevertheless in 1979 the 4,500 ton ex-Irish Sea cross channel packet *Duke of Lancaster* was brought in on the top of a spring tide and beached on the opposite shore. Re-named the *Duke of Llanerch-y-mor*, she was intended for conversion into a conference and shopping centre; painted white overall, she now stands out as the most prominent single feature on the Welsh coast line, exactly five miles from my home – that is, the same distance as that to which those two hitherto unidentified ships approached the *Titanic* and the *Californian* on the night of 14/15 April 1912. She is consequently a constant reminder of my professional involvement in the tragic case of Captain Stanley Lord. And that is not all. In the 1961 edition of *The Observer's Book of Ships*, the *Duke of Lancaster* is featured as a typical cross-channel packet; on the facing page, the profile of a similar vessel is superimposed on the silhouette of a large trans-Atlantic passenger liner as a graphic demonstration of the impossibility of mistaking the one for the other ...

Considered individually, it may be that each of the above coincidences, except perhaps the last two, is unremarkable. Nevertheless, considered collectively I find it impossible not to speculate as to the odds against each one happening by itself, and the astronomical odds against their happening all together.

Of all my personal *Californian* coincidences, however, that which I consider to be the most singular is this: the findings of Lord Mersey's court of inquiry, which dealt a near-fatal blow to Captain Lord's reputation, and which, many years later, it became my task to try to reverse, were published on 31 July 1912.

I was born on 31 July 1912.

Publications Consulted

BOOKS

BARNABY, K.C., *Some Ship Disasters & their Causes* (Hutchinson, 1968).

BEESLEY, Lawrence, *The Loss of the s.s. Titanic* (William Heinemann, 1912. New edition, Star Books, 1979).

BISSET, Sir James, *Sail Ho!* (Rupert Hart-Davis, 1961).

—, with P.R. Stephensen, *Tramps & Ladies* (Angus & Robertson, 1959).

BOOTHBY, Commander Hubert B., *Spunyarn* (Foulis, 1936).

FARRAR-HOCKLEY, Anthony, '*Goughie*' (Hart-Davis, MacGibbon, 1975).

GRACIE, Colonel Archibald, *The Truth about the 'Titanic'* (from *The Story of the 'Titanic' as told by its Survivors*, edited by Jack Winocour, Dover publications, 1960).

HURD, Sir Archibald, *The Official History of the Merchant Navy in the First World War*.

LARGE, Captain Vincent, with Desmond Jackson, *Windjammer 'Prentice* (Jarrolds Publishers, London, 1971).

LIGHTOLLER, Commander C.H., *'Titanic' and Other Ships* (Ivor Nicholson & Watson, 1935).

LORD, Walter, *A Night to Remember*:
(Longmans Green, 1956).
(Allen Lane, 1976).

MARCUS, Geoffrey, *The Maiden Voyage* (Manor Books, 1974).

NORIE'S NAUTICAL TABLES (Imray, Laurie, Norie & Wilson, 1907).

PADFIELD, Peter: *The 'Titanic' & the 'Californian'* (Hodder & Stoughton, 1965). *Broke & the 'Shannon'* (Hodder & Stoughton, 1968).

PRECHTL, Robert, *Titanensturtz* (published in the United Kingdom as *'Titanic' – a Novel*, Richards Press, 1938).

OFFICIAL DOCUMENTS

Proceedings on a Formal Investigation into the Loss of the ss 'Titanic'.

— *Report of a Formal Investigation into the Foundering of the British Steamship 'Titanic'* (HM Stationery Office, 1912).

'Titanic' Disaster: Hearings before a Sub-committee on Commerce, United States Senate (Document No 726).

— *Report* of the above Committee (Report no. 806), Government Printing Office, Washington, USA, 1912).

PERIODICALS

Daily Mail

Daily Mirror

Daily News & Leader

Daily Sketch

Daily Telegraph

Journal of Commerce (including *Report of the 'Titanic' Inquiry reprinted from the Journal of Commerce*, July 1912).

Liverpool Daily Post & Liverpool Mercury

Liverpool Echo

MMSA Reporter

Nautical Magazine

The Times

Index